Dictionary
of the
Middle Ages

AMERICAN COUNCIL OF LEARNED SOCIETIES

The American Council of Learned Societies, organized in 1919 for the purpose of advancing the study of the humanities and of the humanistic aspects of the social sciences, is a nonprofit federation comprising forty-six national scholarly groups. The Council represents the humanities in the United States in the International Union of Academies, provides fellowships and grants-in-aid, supports research-and-planning conferences and symposia, and sponsors special projects and scholarly publications.

Röttgen Pietà. Gothic sculpture in wood, early 14th century. BONN, RHEINISCHES LANDESMUSEUM

Dictionary of the Middle Ages

JOSEPH R. STRAYER, *EDITOR IN CHIEF*

Volume 3

CABALA—CRIMEA

CHARLES SCRIBNER'S SONS • NEW YORK

Copyright © 1983 American Council of Learned Societies

Library of Congress Cataloging in Publication Data
Main entry under title:

Dictionary of the Middle Ages.

Includes bibliographies and index.
1. Middle Ages—Dictionaries.   I. Strayer,
Joseph Reese, 1904–1987

D114.D5   1982   909.07   82-5904
ISBN 0-684-16760-3 (v. 1)   ISBN 0-684-18169-X (v. 7)
ISBN 0-684-17022-1 (v. 2)   ISBN 0-684-18274-2 (v. 8)
ISBN 0-684-17023-X (v. 3)   ISBN 0-684-18275-0 (v. 9)
ISBN 0-684-17024-8 (v. 4)   ISBN 0-684-18276-9 (v. 10)
ISBN 0-684-18161-4 (v. 5)   ISBN 0-684-18277-7 (v. 11)
ISBN 0-684-18168-1 (v. 6)   ISBN 0-684-18278-5 (v. 12)

3 5 7 9 11 13 15 17 19   B/C   20 18 16 14 12 10 8 6 4 2

PRINTED IN THE UNITED STATES OF AMERICA.

The *Dictionary of the Middle Ages* has been produced with
support from the National Endowment for the Humanities.

The paper in this book meets the guidelines for
permanence and durability of the Committee on
Production Guidelines for Book Longevity of the
Council on Library Resources.

Maps prepared by Joseph Stonehill and Sylvia Lehrman.

Editorial Board

Advisory Committee

Editorial Staff

Contributors to Volume 3

DOROTHY AFRICA
Clonard (Cluain-Iraird)

GORDON A. ANDERSON
University of New England
Clausula

AVERY ANDREWS
George Washington University
Caffa

ANI P. ATAMIAN
Columbia University
Cilician Kingdom; Cilician-Roman Church Union

AZIZ S. ATIYA
University of Utah
Copts and Coptic Church

LORRAINE C. ATTREED
Cade, Jack/Cade's Rebellion

SUSAN M. BABBITT
Institute for Advanced Study, Princeton
Catalan Company

JOHN W. BARKER
University of Wisconsin, Madison
Constantine XI Palaiologos

CARL F. BARNES, JR.
Cathedral; Chartres Cathedral; Cluny, Abbey Church; Collar Beam

ROBERT BARRINGER
University of Toronto
Confession; Confessor, Royal

WILLIAM W. BASSETT
University of San Francisco
Consulate of the Sea; Corporation

ROLAND BECHMANN
Castles and Fortifications; Construction: Building Materials

SILVIO A. BEDINI
Smithsonian Institution
Clocks and Reckoning of Time; Compass, Magnetic

JOHN BEELER
Cannon

JEANETTE M. A. BEER
Purdue University
Chronicles, French

BETH S. BENNETT
University of Alabama
Cassiodorus Senator, Flavius Magnus Aurelius

ALEXANDRE BENNIGSEN
University of Chicago
Crimea, Khanate of

THOMAS N. BISSON
University of California, Berkeley
Catalonia (800–1137)

N. F. BLAKE
University of Sheffield
Caxton, William; Chronicles

HERBERT BLOCH
Harvard University
Constantine the African

ROGER BOASE
University of Fez
Courtly Love

DIANE BORNSTEIN
Queens College
Courtesy Books; Courtly Love

C. E. BOSWORTH
University of Manchester
Commander of the Faithful

G. W. BOWERSOCK
Institute for Advanced Study, Princeton
Consistorium

EDMUND A. BOWLES
Chansonnier

MICHAEL BRETT
University of London
Cavalry, Islamic

CYNTHIA J. BROWN
University of California, Santa Barbara
Chartier, Alain; Complainte

LESLIE BRUBAKER
Wheaton College, Norton, Massachusetts
Campanile; Canon Table; Capital; Carpet Page; Carver, William (Bromflet); Castrum; Catacombs; Cathedra; Centering; Chairete; Chalice; Chancel; Chapel; Cherub; Chevet; Choir; Chrismon; Christogram; Church, Types of; Ciborium; Clerestory; Clipeus (Clipeatus); Cloister; Codex Aureus; Colobium (Colobion); Column Figure; Constantine (Kostandin) the Armenian; Cook (Coke), Humphrey; Corbel; Corbel Table; Cosmati Work

JAMES A. BRUNDAGE
University of Wisconsin, Madison
Casuistry

ix

CONTRIBUTORS TO VOLUME 3

ROBERT G. CALKINS
Cornell University
CATHERINE OF CLEVES, MASTER OF;
COENE, JAQUES; COLOMBE, JEAN;
COLOMBE, MICHEL

DANIEL CALLAM
St. Thomas More College
CELIBACY

ANNEMARIE WEYL CARR
Southern Methodist University
COSTUME, BYZANTINE

EDMUND DE CHASCA
CID, THE, HISTORY AND LEGEND OF

COLIN CHASE
University of Toronto, Centre for Medieval Studies
CAROLINGIAN LATIN POETRY

FREDRIC L. CHEYETTE
Amherst College
CATHARS; CHÂTELET

MASSIMO CIAVOLELLA
Carleton University
CAVALCANTI, GUIDO; CECCO
ANGIOLIERI; CINO DA PISTOIA

WANDA CIŻEWSKI
Pontifical Institute of Mediaeval Studies, Toronto
CLEMENS SCOTUS; COSMAS OF
PRAGUE

DOROTHY CLOTELLE CLARKE
University of California, Berkeley
COPLA

ALAN B. COBBAN
University of Liverpool
CAMBRIDGE, UNIVERSITY OF

MARK R. COHEN
Princeton University
CAIRO GENIZAH

LAWRENCE I. CONRAD
American University of Beirut
CALIPHATE

MADELEINE PELNER COSMAN
City College of New York
COOKERY, EUROPEAN; COSTUME,
WESTERN EUROPEAN

F. EDWARD CRANZ
Connecticut College
CLASSICAL LITERARY STUDIES

GILBERT DAGRON
CONSTANTINOPLE

DON DENNY
University of Maryland
CHARONTON (QUARTON),
ENGUERRAND

WALTER B. DENNY
University of Massachusetts, Amherst
CAFTAN

E. TALBOT DONALDSON
CHAUCER, GEOFFREY

A. A. M. DUNCAN
University of Glasgow
CLANS, SCOTTISH

ANN WHARTON EPSTEIN
Duke University
CAPPADOCIA

MARCY J. EPSTEIN
Pontifical Institute of Mediaeval Studies, Toronto
CACCIA

ROGER EVANS
Loyola Pastoral Institute
CANTOR

THEODORE EVERGATES
Western Maryland College
CHAMPAGNE, COUNTY; COLONUS

ROBERT FALCK
University of Toronto
CONDUCTUS; CONSONANCE/
DISSONANCE; CONTRAFACTUM

ANN E. FARKAS
CHIN

S. C. FERRUOLO
Stanford University
COURSON, ROBERT OF

CLIVE FOSS
University of Massachusetts, Boston
CAESAREA

JOHN B. FREED
Illinois State University
CANOSSA; CONSTITUTIO DE FEUDIS

MICHELLE A. FREEMAN
Vanderbilt University
CHRÉTIEN DE TROYES

STEPHEN GARDNER
Columbia University
CANTERBURY CATHEDRAL; CONRAD,
PRIOR

NINA G. GARSOÏAN
Columbia University
CAVALRY, ARMENIAN

ADELHEID M. GEALT
Indiana University
CAVALLINI, PIETRO; CENNINI,
CENNINO; CIMABUE, CENNI DI PEPI;
CIUFFAGNI, BERNARDO; CONTE DEL
LELLO ORLANDI; COPPO DI
MARCOVALDO

PATRICK GEARY
University of Florida
CANONIZATION; CAPITULARY;
CAROLINGIANS AND THE
CAROLINGIAN EMPIRE;
CHARLEMAGNE; COUNTY

STEPHEN GERSH
University of Notre Dame
CONCEPTUALISM

C. M. GILLMOR
United States Naval Academy
CAVALRY, EUROPEAN

STEPHEN GILMAN
Harvard University
CELESTINA, LA

ROBERT S. GOTTFRIED
Institute for Advanced Study, Princeton
CLIMATOLOGY

ARYEH GRABOIS
University of Haifa
CHRISTIAN HEBRAISTS

JAMES A. GRAHAM-CAMPBELL
University College, London
CELTIC ART

RICHARD LEIGHTON GREENE
CAROLS, MIDDLE ENGLISH

TIMOTHY E. GREGORY
Ohio State University
CONSTANTINE I, THE GREAT

CONTRIBUTORS TO VOLUME 3

JOHN L. GRIGSBY
Washington University, St. Louis
CHÂTELAIN DE COUCY; COUTUMES
DE BEAUVAISIS

ARTHUR GROOS
Cornell University
CARMINA BURANA

M. GRUNMANN-GAUDET
University of Western Ontario
CANTILÈNE

J. GULSOY
University of Toronto
CATALAN LANGUAGE

PIERRE-MARIE GY, O.P.
Couvent St. Jacques, Paris
COLLECTARIUM

R. F. GYUG
CONSECRATION OF CEMETERIES

NATHALIE HANLET
Columbia University
CATO'S DISTICHS (LATIN)

EDWARD A. HEINEMANN
University of Toronto
CHANSONS DE GESTE

R. H. HELMHOLZ
Washington University, St. Louis
CONCUBINAGE, WESTERN;
CONSANGUINITY

JOHN BELL HENNEMAN
University of Iowa
CABOCHIEN RIOTS; CHARLES V OF
FRANCE; CHARLES VII OF FRANCE

MICHAEL HERREN
York University
COLMAN, BISHOP OF LINDISFARNE;
COLUMBA, ST.; COLUMBANUS, ST.

JUDITH HERRIN
University of London
CONSTANTINE V

ROBERT HEWSEN
Glassboro State College
CAUCASIA; CAUCASUS MOUNTAINS;
CILICIAN GATES

BENNETT D. HILL
University of Illinois
CAMALDOLESE, ORDER OF;
CARTHUSIANS; CELESTINES;
CISTERCIAN ORDER

JOHN H. HILL
CLERMONT, COUNCIL OF

ROBERT HILLENBRAND
University of Edinburgh
CÓRDOBA

MICHAEL J. HODDER
Sotheby Parke Bernet, Inc.
CANVAS; COTTON

ANDREW HUGHES
University of Toronto
CADENCE; CANTATORIUM;
CANTICLE; CAUDA; CLEF;
CONTRATENOR

LUCY-ANNE HUNT
University of Birmingham
COPTIC ART

SYLVIA HUOT
University of Chicago
CHANSON DE LA CROISADE CONTRE
LES ALBIGEOIS; CHRISTINE DE PIZAN;
CONON DE BÉTHUNE

MOSHE IDEL
Hebrew University of Jerusalem
CABALA

OLGA TUDORICA IMPEY
Indiana University
CALILA E DIGNA

ALFRED L. IVRY
Brandeis University
CRESCAS, ḤASDAI

W. T. H. JACKSON
Columbia University
CAPELLANUS, ANDREAS

JAMES J. JOHN
Cornell University
CARTULARY; CHANCERY; CHARTER;
COMPUTUS

D. W. JOHNSON
Catholic University of America
CHRISTIAN CHURCH IN PERSIA;
CHRISTIANITY, NUBIAN

WILLIAM CHESTER JORDAN
Princeton University
CHAMBERLAIN; CONSTABLE OF THE
REALM; CORVÉE

BERNICE M. KACZYNSKI
McMaster University
CREEDS, LITURGICAL USE OF

WALTER EMIL KAEGI, JR.
University of Chicago
CAVALRY, BYZANTINE; CONSTANS
II, EMPEROR; CONSTANTINE IV

RICHARD W. KAEUPER
University of Rochester
CONSTABLE, LOCAL; COPYHOLD;
COURT LEET

ALEXANDER P. KAZHDAN
Dumbarton Oaks Research Center
CONSTANTINE VII PORPHYROGENITOS

THOMAS E. KELLY
Purdue University
CHANSON; CHANSONS DE FEMME;
CHANSONS DE MALMARIÉE;
CHANSONS DE TOILE; CHANT ROYAL

ERIC KEMP
CONVOCATIONS OF CANTERBURY AND
YORK

MARILYN KAY KENNEY
*University of Toronto, Centre for
Medieval Studies*
CADOC, ST.; CASNODYN; CHESTER,
TREATY OF; CONWAY, PEACE OF

G. L. KEYES
University of Toronto
CHURCH FATHERS

JOHN M. KLASSEN
Trinity Western College
COMMUNION UNDER BOTH KINDS

ALAN E. KNIGHT
Pennsylvania State University
CONFRÉRIE; CONGÉ; COURTOIS
D'ARRAS

ANGELIKI LAIOU
Harvard University
CHARISTIKION

IRA M. LAPIDUS
University of California, Berkeley
CAIRO

ANDREW W. LEWIS
*Southwest Missouri State
University*
CAPETIAN FAMILY ORIGINS

ARCHIBALD R. LEWIS
*University of Massachusetts,
Amherst*
CONSULS, CONSULATE

CONTRIBUTORS TO VOLUME 3

DONALD P. LITTLE
McGill University
CIRCASSIANS

LESTER K. LITTLE
Smith College
CHURCH, LATIN: 1054 TO 1305

MICHAEL P. LONG
University of Wisconsin, Madison
COUNTERPOINT

NIELS LUND
University of Copenhagen
CNUT THE GREAT

BRYCE LYON
Brown University
CLARENDON, ASSIZE OF;
CLARENDON, CONSTITUTIONS OF;
COMMUNE

MICHAEL McCORMICK
*Dumbarton Oaks Research
Center*
CHAINED BOOKS; CODEX;
COLOPHON

JOHN M. McCULLOH
Kansas State University
CATACOMBS

DAVID R. McLINTOCK
University of London
CHARMS, OLD HIGH GERMAN;
CHRISTUS UND DIE SAMARITERIN

GEORGE P. MAJESKA
University of Maryland
CHASOVNYA

KRIKOR H. MAKSOUDIAN
Columbia University
CALENDARS, ARMENIAN

IVAN G. MARCUS
*The Jewish Theological Seminary
of America*
CIRCUMCISION, JEWISH

ROBERT MARK
Princeton University
CONSTRUCTION: ENGINEERING

S. E. MARMON
Princeton University
CONCUBINAGE, ISLAMIC

JOHN MARTIN
Harvard University
CONDOTTIERI

GUY MERMIER
University of Michigan
CENT NOUVELLES NOUVELLES;
CHASTELAINE DE VERGI, LA;
COMINES (COMMYNES), PHILIPPE DE

BRIAN MERRILEES
University of Toronto
CAMBRIDGE PSALTER; CATO'S
DISTICHS (OLD FRENCH); CHARDRI;
CHRONIQUES DE LONDRES

UTA C. MERZBACH
Smithsonian Institution
CALDENDARS AND RECKONING OF
TIME

RENÉ METZ
Université de Strasbourg
CLERGY

JOHN MEYENDORFF
Fordham University
CLERGY, BYZANTINE; COUNCILS
(ECUMENICAL, 325–787); COUNCILS,
BYZANTINE (859–1368)

DAVID MILLS
University of Liverpool
CHESTER PLAYS

LEONEL L. MITCHELL
*Seabury-Western Theological
Seminary*
CONFIRMATION

B. F. MUSALLAM
CONTRACEPTION, ISLAMIC

ALAN H. NELSON
University of California, Berkeley
CASTLE OF PERSEVERANCE

HELMUT NICKEL
Metropolitan Museum of Art
CATAPULTS; CHIVALRY, ORDERS OF

JOHN D. NILES
University of California, Berkeley
CÆDMON

JOHN T. NOONAN, JR.
University of California, Berkeley
CONTRACEPTION, EUROPEAN

FRANCIS OAKLEY
Williams College
CHURCH, LATIN: 1305 TO 1500;
CONCILIAR THEORY; COUNCILS,
WESTERN (1311–1449)

JOSEPH F. O'CALLAGHAN
Fordham University
CALATRAVA, ORDER OF; CORTES

TOMÁS Ó CATHASAIGH
University College, Dublin
CORMAC MAC AIRT

DONNCHADH Ó CORRÁIN
University College, Cork
CASHEL; CONNACHT

NICOLAS OIKONOMIDES
Université de Montréal
CAESAR

PADRAIG P. Ó NÉILL
University of North Carolina
CELTIC CHURCH; CINÉAL EÓGHAIN;
CORMAC MAC CUILENNÁIN

ARSENIO PACHECO-RANSANZ
University of British Columbia
CATALAN NARRATIVE IN VERSE

PETER D. PARTNER
Winchester College
COLA DI RIENZO

OLAF PEDERSEN
University of Aarhus
CLOCKWORK, PLANETARY

CLAUDE J. PEIFER, O.S.B.
St. Bede Abbey
CAESARIUS OF ARLES, ST.; CELESTINE
I, POPE

KENNETH PENNINGTON
Syracuse University
CODEX THEODOSIANUS; CORPUS
IURIS CIVILIS

PAUL B. PIXTON
Brigham Young University
COUNCILS, WESTERN (1215–1274)

ELIZABETH WILSON POE
Tulane University
CANSO; CERCAMON; CHANSON
D'ANTIOCHE

NORMAN J. G. POUNDS
Indiana University
CHARCOAL; COAL, MINING AND
USE OF

WALTER H. PRINCIPE
*Pontifical Institute of Mediaeval
Studies, Toronto*
CHRISTOLOGY

CONTRIBUTORS TO VOLUME 3

CHARLES RADDING
Loyola University
COMPURGATION

FRITZ RECKOW
Christian-Albrechts-Universität zu Kiel
COPULA

WILLIAM T. REEDY
State University of New York, Albany
COMMENDATION; COMMON PLEAS, COURT OF

THOMAS RENNA
Saginaw Valley State College, Michigan
CHURCH, LATIN: ORGANIZATION; CLUNY, ORDER OF

ROGER E. REYNOLDS
Pontifical Institute of Mediaeval Studies, Toronto
CARTHUSIAN RITE; CHRISTMAS; CHURCHING OF WOMEN; CLUNIAC RITE; COLORS, LITURGICAL

A. G. RIGG
University of Toronto, Centre for Medieval Studies
COMMONPLACE BOOKS

MAXIME RODINSON
Université du Sorbonne
COOKERY, ISLAMIC

H. ROE
University of Toronto, Centre for Medieval Studies
CELTIC LANGUAGES

PAUL ROREM
CANONICAL HOURS; CARNIVAL; CORPUS CHRISTI, FEAST OF

LINDA ROSE
CATAPHRACTI; CHRYSOBULLON; COSMAS INDICOPLEUSTES; CRETE

RHIMAN A. ROTZ
Indiana University Northwest
CLASS STRUCTURE, WESTERN (1000–1300); CLASS STRUCTURE, WESTERN (1300–1500)

M. A. ROUSE
University of California, Los Angeles
CODICOLOGY, WESTERN EUROPEAN

R. H. ROUSE
University of California, Los Angeles
CODICOLOGY, WESTERN EUROPEAN

TEOFILO F. RUIZ
Brooklyn College
CASTILE; CASTILIAN LANGUAGE; CONVERSO

JEFFREY B. RUSSELL
University of California, Santa Barbara
CHURCH, EARLY; CHURCH, LATIN: TO 1054

MICHAEL SARGENT
CAPGRAVE, JOHN

BARBARA NELSON SARGENT-BAUR
University of Pittsburgh
COLIN MUSET

V. J. SCATTERGOOD
Trinity College, Dublin
CLANVOWE, SIR JOHN

BERNHARD SCHIMMELPFENNIG
Universität Augsburg
CORONATION, PAPAL

COLIN SMITH
St. Catherine's College, Cambridge
CANTAR DE MÍO CID

ROBERT J. SNOW
University of Texas at Austin
CANTIGA

JAMES SNYDER
Bryn Mawr College
CAMPIN, ROBERT; CHRISTUS, PETRUS

JOSEP M. SOLA-SOLÉ
Catholic University of America
CANTIGAS DE AMOR, AMIGO, AND ESCARNIO

ROBERT SOMERVILLE
Columbia University
COUNCILS, WESTERN (869–1179)

RUTH STEINER
Catholic University of America
COMMUNION CHANT

YEDIDA K. STILLMAN
State University of New York, Binghamton
COSTUME, ISLAMIC; COSTUME, JEWISH

ALAIN STOCLET
University of Toronto, Centre for Medieval Studies
CARMEN DE BELLO SAXONICO

PAUL W. STRAIT
Florida State University
COLOGNE

JOSEPH R. STRAYER
Princeton University
CAEN; CAESARIUS OF HEISTERBACH; CAESAROPAPISM; CARROCCIO; CASTELLAN; CHARLES MARTEL; CLERK; CLOVIS; COMMENDAM; CONFESSOR: SAINT; CONGÉ D'ÉLIRE; CONRAD OF MEGENBERG

RONALD GRIGOR SUNY
University of Michigan
CHOSROIDS (MIHRANIDS)

DONALD W. SUTHERLAND
University of Iowa
CORONER

R. N. SWANSON
University of Birmingham
CONCLAVE, PAPAL; CONCORDAT

JAMES ROSS SWEENEY
Pennsylvania State University
CHIVALRY

EDWARD A. SYNAN
Pontifical Institute of Mediaeval Studies, Toronto
CASSIAN, JOHN; CLEMENT V, POPE

JOSEPH SZÖVÉRFFY
Wissenschaftskolleg zu Berlin
CAMBRIDGE SONGS

EMILY ZACK TABUTEAU
Michigan State University
CHAMPION IN JUDICIAL COMBAT

ROBERT TAYLOR
Victoria College
COMTESSA DE DIA

PAUL R. THIBAULT
Franklin and Marshall College
CLEMENT VI, POPE

xiii

CONTRIBUTORS TO VOLUME 3

WARREN T. TREADGOLD
Stanford University
CONSTANTINE IX MONOMACHOS

LEO TREITLER
State University of New York, Stony Brook
CENTONIZATION

DAVID H. TRIPP
CATHAR LITURGY

A. L. UDOVITCH
Princeton University
CASBAH; COMMENDA

KRISTINE T. UTTERBACK
University of Toronto, Centre for Medieval Studies
CANDIDUS OF FULDA (BRUUN); CHRISTIAN OF STABLO

M. F. VAUGHAN
University of Washington
CHARLES OF ORLÉANS

PHILIPPE VERDIER
CERAMICS, EUROPEAN; CHIP CARVING

CHARLES VERLINDEN
Commission Internationale d'Histoire Maritime
CANARY ISLANDS AND BÉTHENCOURT

CHRYSOGONOUS WADDELL, O.C.S.O.
Abbey of Gethsemani
CARMELITE RITE; CARMELITES; CISTERCIAN CHANT; CISTERCIAN RITE

JEANETTE WAKIN
Columbia University
CIRCUMCISION, ISLAMIC

ROGER M. WALKER
University of London
CAVALLERO ZIFAR, LIBRO DEL

ANN K. WARREN
Case Western Reserve University
CHAPLAIN; CHAPTER; CHAPTER HOUSE

ANTHONY WELCH
University of Victoria
CALLIGRAPHY, ISLAMIC

BONNIE WHEELER
Southern Methodist University
CANTERBURY

KEITH WHINNOM
University of Exeter
CANCIONERO GENERAL

MARINA D. WHITMAN
CERAMICS, ISLAMIC

JOHN WILLIAMS
University of Pittsburgh
CAPILLA MAYOR

CURT WITTLIN
University of Saskatchewan
CATALAN LITERATURE

CHARLES T. WOOD
Dartmouth College
CELESTINE V, POPE; CLERICIS LAICOS

ABIGAIL YOUNG
University of Toronto, Centre for Medieval Studies
CALBULUS

NORMAN ZACOUR
University of Toronto, Centre for Medieval Studies
CARDINALS, COLLEGE OF

MARK A. ZIER
Pontifical Institute of Mediaeval Studies, Toronto
CLAUDIUS OF TURIN; CORIPPUS

RONALD EDWARD ZUPKO
Marquette University
CHALDER; CLOVE

Dictionary
of the
Middle Ages

Dictionary of the Middle Ages

CABALA. Three main features characterize the cabala as an authentic Jewish phenomenon. First, it adds to all the previous Jewish religious movements a symbolic view of the Scriptures, Commandments, man, history, and nature. All together are seen as a symbolic reflection of the divine configurations and processes. The understanding of this nature of the extradivine world, and of the actions intended to imitate the Deity and to establish harmony within the Deity are the main purposes of the cabala.

Second, two aspects of the Deity are central to cabalistic theosophy: the hidden one is named *Ein-Sof* (Godhead) and is mostly described in negative terms; the revealed aspect is composed of ten *Sefirot* (potencies or emanations) and reflects the influence of the Gnostic pleroma (divine fullness). The term *Sefira* appears for the first time in the *Sefer Yetzirah* (Book of Creation), a cosmological treatise that was composed between the third and the eighth centuries. Here the significance of "sefira" is "number." In the cabalistic interpretations of this term it means either "divine power," a component of the dynamic system that forms the revealed aspect of the Deity, or instruments used by the divine power in order to create the world and govern it. There are ten *Sefirot*, arranged in the form of a tree or in human shape:

	Keter–Crown
Binah–Intelligence	*Hokhmah*–Wisdom
Gevurah–Power	*Hesed*–Love
or *Din*–Stern Judgment	
	Tiferet–Beauty
	or *Rahamin*–Compassion
Hod–Majesty	*Nezah*–Eternity
	Yesod–Foundation
	Malkhut–Kingdom

From its beginning in the twelfth century until the expulsion of the Jews from Spain in 1492, the cabala was an esoteric movement. The majority of the cabalistic literature was written and read only in closed circles, and its esoteric nature was emphasized by its major exponents.

The earliest cabalistic document extant is the *Sefer Bahir* (Book of clarity) attributed to Rabbi Nehunyah ben Ha-Kanah, an ancient author; the surviving version, however, was compiled in the second half of the twelfth century. For the first time a theosophical view of the *Sefirot* emerges together with other ancient Gnostic elements in a book written in Hebrew. Despite its fragmentary and obscure nature it became a cabalistic classic, and its influence was dominant until the appearance of the *Zohar* in the thirteenth century.

The first cabalists known as historical persons lived in Provence in the second half of the twelfth century. Rabbi Abraham ben David of Posquières and his contemporaries clearly alluded to cabalistic ideas, but no written cabalistic treatise by them has survived. Rabbi Isaac Saggi Nehor (Isaac the Blind), the son of Abraham ben David, wrote a commentary on *Sefer Yetzira*, the first cabalistic work whose author is known. An analysis of this work, of scattered fragments written by Rabbi Isaac on various subjects, and of the writings of Rabbi Isaac's pupils and followers shows that the Gnostic tradition of *Sefer Bahir* has been combined with Neoplatonic thought. The synthesis between them is the most important achievement of the cabala in this period. The pupils of Rabbi Isaac were Rabbi Asher ben David (Rabbi Isaac's nephew), Rabbi Ezra, and Rabbi Azriel of Gerona. In their writings are the first detailed exposition of the cabala.

From Provence the cabala reached Spain, mainly Gerona, Burgos, and Toledo, where cabalists in the first half of the thirteenth century included Rabbi Barzillai and Rabbi Jacob ben Sheshet. Between 1230 and 1270 Rabbi Moses ben Nahman (Nahmanides) continued the Geronese cabalistic school, and orally transmitted cabalistic secrets to his pupils Rabbi Solomon ben Adret (*d.* 1310) and Rabbi Isaac ben Todros. Their pupils, the last representatives of the Geronese cabalistic school, wrote a number of commentaries on Nachmanides' cabalistic allusions, scattered in his commentary on the Pentateuch.

A number of different cabalistic schools developed during the second half of the thirteenth century and combined at the beginning of the fourteenth century. The cabalistic circle around the Book of Speculation produced a number of short treatises, some anonymous, some attributed to ancient Jewish authorities, that deal with cosmological issues and with the various divine names. The unknown cabalists belonging to this school employed a rich light imagery that had a deep influence upon later cabala and made extensive use of terms and quotations from the *Merkabah* (divine chariot) literature; the discussion on the nature of the *Sefirot* and the mystical interpretaton of the Commandments is only secondary.

The circle of the Gnostic cabala, a group of Castilian cabalists including Rabbi Jacob ben Jacob Ha-Cohen, his brother Rabbi Isaac, their pupil Rabbi Moses ben Simon of Burgos, and Rabbi Todros ben Joseph Abulafia, gave in their writings the first detailed description of the "evil side"—the realm of evil, which is arranged in a form parallel to the ten *Sefirot*. Formerly almost completely neglected, the problem of evil became, under the impact of this circle, a central issue in the later cabala.

The works of Rabbi Isaac ibn Latif (*fl. ca.* 1238–1280) contain Neoplatonic interpretations of the Scriptures of highly speculative interest, but few allusions to cabalistic tenets.

The most important cabalistic circle is that around the *Sefer ha-Zohar* (Book of splendor) and includes Rabbi Moses de Leon, Rabbi Joseph Gikatilla, Rabbi Joseph of Hamadan, and the anonymous author of the last stratum of the *Zohar*. The *Zohar*, the most important cabalistic work, is composed of three main strata. The earliest, philosophical stratum is called *Midrash ha-Ne'lam* (Hidden Midrash) and was written by Moses de Leon between 1275 and 1280.

The same author wrote, between 1280 and 1286, the bulk of the *Zohar* in a new cabalistic vein characterized by sexual and anthropomorphic imagery conveying a mythical and dynamic theosophy; the language is an artificial Aramaic influenced by medieval terminology but of a high literary quality. The central figure is Rabbi Simeon ben Yohai, to whom Rabbi Moses de Leon attributed the book.

The last stratum contains two main treatises,

Raaya Mehemana (The faithful shepherd) and *Tikkunei ha-Zohar* (Adornments to the *Zohar*), composed by an anonymous cabalist at the beginning of the fourteenth century; written in a poor Aramaic, this part continues the pseudepigraphic frame of the *Zohar,* but in important theosophical matters it diverges from the Zoharic system.

The first two strata of the *Zohar* immediately influenced a number of books that later became classics of the cabalistic literature—for instance, the *Sha*are Orah* (Gates of light) of Rabbi Joseph Gikatilla (1248–*ca.* 1305), the most important guide to cabalistic symbolism. Rabbi Joseph of Hamadan wrote both Hebrew and Aramaic books in which the sexual imagery of the *Zohar* reached its peak. A wide influence of the *Zohar* is discernible in the important cabalistic commentaries on the Pentateuch written in that period: those of Rabbi Bachya ben Asher (1291), Rabbi Menahem Recanati (*ca.* 1305), Rabbi Joseph Angelino's *Kupat ha-Rochlim* (1311), and Rabbi David ben Judah He-Hasid's *Marot ha-Zoveot*. The last author is also the first translator of large parts of the *Zohar;* he and Joseph Angelino wrote the first commentaries on various parts of the *Zohar*.

In the second half of the thirteenth century there appeared a different branch of the cabala, the "prophetic" or "ecstatic" cabala. Its main exponent was Rabbi Abraham ben Samuel Abulafia, who propagated his teachings in Spain, Greece, and particularly Italy. The aim of this branch of the cabala is the achievement of ecstatic experiences by means of an elaborate technique that includes combinations of the letters of the divine names, music, breathing exercises, and movements of the head and hands. This technique was developed by Abulafia within the framework of Maimonides' metaphysics and psychology, but in the writings of his pupils the penetration of the Sefirotic system may be clearly discerned.

Sufic influence seems to have appeared when the prophetic cabala reached Palestine and later was transmitted to the Spanish cabalists. This influence could be the result of previous penetration by Sufism of Jewish circles in the Orient, as early as the beginning of the thirteenth century. Under the influence of Ashkenazi Hasidism the prophetic cabala made use of hermeneutic techniques such as gematria and notarikon, which were also taken over by other cabalistic circles.

The first cabalist to write in Italy was Abraham Abulafia. At the beginning of the fourteenth century a great corpus of Spanish cabalistic works was known to Rabbi Menahem Recanati, one of the most important Italian cabalists. Although he wrote under the influence of the *Zohar,* he combated its anthropomorphic trend by attributing the anthropomorphic expressions found in the Jewish tradition to the *Sefirot,* which are, in his system, instruments of the divine work and not a part of the divine nature. A younger contemporary, Rabbi Reuben Tzarfatti, reached the same goal by a nominalistic interpretation of the *Sefirot.*

In the Byzantine Empire the cabala flourished from the middle of the fourteenth century; no major innovations occur in the majority of the works written there between 1300 and 1500. Rabbi Elnatan ben Moses Kalkis' voluminous encyclopedia, *Even ha-Sappir* (1362–1368), and the anonymous books *Peliah* and *Kanah* are mainly large collections of previous cabalistic works written in Spain and Italy. The only original contribution to cabalistic doctrines is the anonymous *Sefer Temunah* (Book of the image), which elaborated upon the *Shemittah* (each period of world history) and gave them a peculiar turn.

Our knowledge of the Spanish cabala in the pre-Expulsion period is scanty; though various pieces of information show that cabala was studied in several circles, only a few cabalistic treatises have survived. *Sefer ha-Emunot* (The book of beliefs, *ca.* 1400), written by Rabbi Shem Tov ibn Shem Tov, contains the first major cabalist attack on philosophy. More important is the voluminous treatise *The Answering Angel,* written as God's answer to questions put by an unknown cabalist on redemption, alchemy, magical operations, and astrology. Related to this book are the practices of Rabbi Joseph della Reina (*fl. ca.* 1470), a cabalist who was reported to have tried to bring redemption by magical means.

Cabalistic literature flourished immediately after the Expulsion. That dramatic event seems to have been the main stimulus for such cabalists as Rabbi Juda Hayyat and Rabbi Abraham ben Eliezer, who wrote their books, which reveal clear messianic tendencies, in Italy and in the East. In this period some cabalists settled in Palestine, which in the middle of the sixteenth century became a cabalistic center of major importance. Jewish apostates used cabalistic doctrines and methods for Christian purposes; the first seems to have been Abner of Burgos.

More substantial influences of cabalistic views appear in Paulus of Heredia's works, written in Spain during the second half of the fifteenth century. How-ever, it was not until the Renaissance that the cabala became a discipline per se. Latin translations of many cabalistic works by the apostate Flavius Mithridates influenced Pico della Mirandola's view of the cabala as an ancient Jewish theology containing allusions to Christian tenets. These allusions are the result of the translator's biased rendering of genuine cabalistic passages.

Thereby the cabala, together with the new translations of the Platonic, Neoplatonic, and Hermetic corpora, became part of the *prisca theologia* ("ancient theology"), which nourished the occult philosophies of Europe from the Renaissance on. Owing to the importance given by Pico della Mirandola, such outstanding scholars as Egidio da Viterbo, Cornelius Agrippa von Nettesheim, and Francesco Giorgi of Venice studied the cabala and used it extensively in their works.

BIBLIOGRAPHY
Alexander Altmann, "The Motif of the Shell in Azriel of Gerona," in *Journal of Jewish Studies,* **9** (1958); Efraim Gottlieb, *Studies in the Literature of the Kabbalah* (1976), in Hebrew; Gershom G. Scholem, *Major Trends in Jewish Mysticism,* 3rd. rev. ed. (1955), with detailed bibliography; *Von der mystichem Gestalt der Gottheit* (1962); *On the Kabbalah and Its Symbolism* (1969); *The Messianic Idea in Judaism* (1971); *Kabbalah* (1974); and *Bibliographia kabbalistica* (1976), in Hebrew; François Secret, *Les kabbalistes chrétiens de la Renaissance* (1964); Isaiah Tishby, *The Wisdom of the Zohar,* 2 vols. (1957–1961), in Hebrew; Georges Vajda, "Les origines et le développement de la Kabbale juive d'après quelques travaux récents," in *Revue d'histoire des religions,* **134** (1948); "Recherches récentes sur l'ésotérisme juif (1947–1962)," ibid., **147** (1955) and **164** (1963); and *Recherches sur la philosophie et la kabale* (1962).

MOSHE IDEL

[See also **Abraham ben David of Posquières; Abulafia, Abraham ben Samuel; Moses ben Shem Tov de Leon.**]

CABOCHIEN RIOTS. The Cabochien riots, which occurred in Paris in the spring of 1413, took their name from Simon le Coustellier (called Caboche), a leader of the city's turbulent butchers' guild. The riots occurred after the French government failed to effect reforms demanded at the Estates-General early in February. Divided into hostile factions under the deranged Charles VI, the government had become the prey of interest groups. A large part of the royal revenues were being diverted to the princes and their clients. The administration was considered to be overstaffed and corrupt, but moderate reformers failed to present a united front and fiscal abuses seemed to mount after the Estates disbanded without action. Encouraged by John the Fearless, duke of Burgundy, the artisans took to the streets late in April and forced the Crown to produce an ordinance of 259 articles that repeated, in greater detail, earlier efforts to enact reforms. The riots did not abate, and the death toll mounted, discrediting Burgundy sufficiently to enable his opponents to gain the upper hand with support from conservative bourgeois. By September order was restored and the ordinance cancelled.

BIBLIOGRAPHY

The basic work remains Alfred Corville, *Les Cabochiens et l'ordonnance de 1413* (1888).

JOHN BELL HENNEMAN

[See also **France: 1314–1494.**]

CACCIA, an Italian lyric song form of the fourteenth and fifteenth centuries. The text is composed of five- or seven-syllable lines and typically deals with the theme of hunting (often an amatory metaphor). The poetry may incorporate hunting cries and calling of hounds by name; a few examples represent market scenes with the cries of vendors. The text may end, like that of the madrigal, with a ritornello.

The musical form is often canonic—usually written for two voices, sometimes for three—with an instrumental countermelody. The texted voices are florid and agile; the texture generally includes passages of hocket between them, as well as parlando declamation of descriptive text. Noncanonic cacce are written for two contrapuntal texted voices, also with an instrumental part. Cacce can be found among the works of the trecento composers Gherardello da Firenze, Lorenzo da Firenze, Andreas of Fleury, Donato da Cascia, Giovanni da Cascia, Jacopo da Bologna, Vincenzo da Rimini, Niccolò da Perugia, Francesco Landini, Magister Piero, and Zacharias.

There is some controversy among scholars about what, precisely, distinguishes the form of a caccia from that of a trecento madrigal. A number of extant trecento cacce are properly canonic madrigals; those that are not are difficult to classify with respect to meter and versification. It seems reasonable to assume that the caccia was conceived as a subgenre of the madrigal, distinguishable less by poetic form than by thematic content of the text and characteristic "programmatic" devices in the music. The canonic caccia was limited to the trecento, and probably had some relation to the French *chace* (canon) of the ars nova. A few examples of the noncanonic type are known from the fifteenth century, and the hunting theme with incorporated cries persisted into the sixteenth century among the Florentine carnival songs.

BIBLIOGRAPHY

Giuseppe Corsi, *Poesie musicali del trecento* (1971); Thomas W. Marrocco, ed., *Fourteenth-century Italian Caccie* (1942, 2d ed. 1961); Nino Pirrotta, "Per l'origine e la storia della 'caccia' e del 'madrigale' trecentesco," in *Rivista musicale italiana*, 48 (1946) and 49 (1947).

MARCY J. EPSTEIN

[See also **Madrigal; Music, Western European.**]

CADE, JACK/CADE'S REBELLION. Jack Cade's origins are unknown, although the English government called him an Irishman and he himself claimed kinship with the duke of York through the Mortimers. The rebellion that he organized in the summer of 1450 expressed dissatisfaction with the royal government felt by craftsmen and gentlemen in southeast England. Throughout the 1440's resentment grew over the costly war with France, the loss of Normandy, and French raids on the coast of Kent. Many believed Henry VI an ineffectual king, misguided by his counselors.

At the end of May 1450, thousands of men from Kent and Sussex armed themselves and chose a captain named Jack Cade, who also used the pseudonym John Mortimer. They marched toward London and camped at Blackheath, south of the capital, on 1 June. Henry raised about 10,000 men and sent delegates to the camp to learn the rebels' demands. Cade pledged his support to Henry and gave the deputation a charter of complaints. The rebels demanded the removal of the king's traitorous counselors, "the false progeny and affinity of the duke of Suffolk," whose influence was blamed for the loss of many French territories. The "commons of Kent" also complained about taxes and corrupt judges, and pleaded that Henry replace Suffolk's relations with true counselors such as Richard, duke of York.

After presenting the charter, Cade and his forces retreated on 16 June to Sevenoaks, and when Sir Humphrey Stafford and his brother rode after them, the two men were slain by Cade's forces. By the end of June the king had fled to Kenilworth, leaving London unprotected against Cade's new advances. To pacify their enemies, the civic officials committed to the Tower of London Lord Say, the treasurer and chamberlain hated by the rebels for his conduct in the French campaign. By 1 July the insurgents had reached Southwark. Cade entered London the next day without resistance, dressed in the Stafford armor and declaring, "Now is Mortimer lord of this city."

The order he promised to maintain that day was shattered the following morning, when Cade's men beheaded Say and William Crowmer, his son-in-law, the sheriff of Kent, then burned and looted parts of London. On Sunday, 5 July, Cade remained south of the Thames and the citizens prepared to resist his reentry. They occupied and defended London Bridge, but Cade drove them back and set the bridge on fire. The next day Cade conferred with the lord chancellor and accepted the order to disband. He demanded and received pardons for his men and for himself, although his own pardon was in the name of John Mortimer and was therefore invalid. Within three days Cade fled eastward, followed by a proclamation that offered 1,000 marks for his capture. He escaped to Sussex, where on 12 July, at Heathfield, he was mortally wounded by Alexander Iden, sheriff-elect of Kent. Cade's body was taken by cart to London, where it was later beheaded and quartered.

The uprising had mixed results. Many of Cade's followers were condemned to death as risings continued in the south throughout the summer. A judicial commission in Kent acted on a few of Cade's complaints against local administration by indicting offending sheriffs and gaolers. In August, upon hearing of the rebellion, the duke of York returned from Ireland to bid for a place on the royal council. His involvement in the rising is doubtful. The November 1450 parliament passed an act of attainder against Cade, an indication that the commons feared rebellion more than false counselors.

BIBLIOGRAPHY

Henry Ellis, ed., *New Chronicles of England and France by Robert Fabyan* (1811), 622–625; James Gairdner, ed., "Gregory's Chronicle," in *Historical Collections of a Citizen of London* (1876); Ralph A. Griffiths, *The Reign of Henry VI* (1981), 610–665; Charles L. Kingsford, *Prejudice and Promise in Fifteenth Century England* (1925, repr. 1962); George Kriehn, *The English Rising of 1450* (1892); Helen M. Lyle, *The Rebellion of Jack Cade, 1450* (1950); Eric N. Simons, *Lord of London* (1963); Robert L. Storey, *The End of the House of Lancaster* (1966); Roger Virgoe, "Some Ancient Indictments in the King's Bench Referring to Kent, 1450–1452," in F. R. H. DuBoulay, ed., *Kent Records: Documents Illustrative of Mediaeval Kentish Society* (1964).

LORRAINE C. ATTREED

[See also **England: 1272–1485; Henry VI of England; Hundred Years War.**]

CADENCE (from the Latin *cadere*, to fall), is a stereotyped formula for ending a piece of music or a phrase, and very important for marking changes in style. It is generally thought to affirm the tonal center of the piece by emphasizing a pitch to which others are related. There is usually some relationship to the text, especially if the latter is poetic.

In Gregorian plainsong the standard cadence falls by step to the cadence note, although in some melodies the fall is by a small leap. In plainsongs and other unharmonized music of the later Middle Ages, the cadence usually rises by a whole-tone step to a repeated note. The rise by a semitone, familiar from more recent music, almost never occurs.

In harmonized music, written down since the ninth century, cadences are perhaps the most striking aural feature for the modern listener because their forms are so different from the modern cadence. Medieval cadences change significantly and lead up to forms anticipating those of classical tonal music. In the ninth to eleventh centuries, consonances are emphasized, and the fifth expanding to an octave (example A) remains the nucleus of most later forms. The cadence passing from a consonance through dissonances to a unison was also common: in example B, the third and second are both dissonant in medieval terms.

By the thirteenth century the standard cadence falling by step was accompanied not with a fifth above, but with a sixth expanding to the octave: in a

CADENCE

three-voice piece the middle voice would move from a third to a fifth. By theoretical convention both sixth and third ought to be major, rising by a semitone (in these "ornamental" parts) to the perfect consonances (example C). Such forms are called "double leading-note cadences."

In the fourteenth century the sixth was ornamented with the intervening fifth (example D); sometimes misleadingly called the Landini cadence, it is more accurately referred to as the "under-third" cadence. Fourteenth-century composers introduced cadences using a minor third closing to the unison (example E). In pieces with two sections, cadences on different degrees of the scale, usually a step away from each other, were called *ouvert* and *clos* (or *aperto* and *chiuso*). This contrast increases the cadence's importance as a means of articulating tonal areas.

Important from the fourteenth century on was a form with a new, lower voice part (the contratenor), which added to the standard "falling step with sixth-octave" formula a part leaping up an octave (example F). Called the "octave-leap" cadence, this form completely changed the sound of the medieval cadence because the ear hears the lowest sounding notes as an upward leap of a fourth; this "bass" movement laid the foundation for the later tonal cadence. Not until the fifteenth century did the third become a regular note in the cadence chord, but from then on, the cadence as a chordal progression

determining tonality became more firmly established.

BIBLIOGRAPHY

"Kadenz und Klausel," in Friedrich Blume, ed., *Die Musik in Geschichte und Gegenwart,* VII (1958).

ANDREW HUGHES

[See also **Consonance/Dissonance; Gregorian Chant.**]

CADI. See **Qadi.**

CADOC, ST. (*b. ca.* 497). After St. David, Cadoc is probably the best known of the early Welsh saints. Accounts of his career are Lifris' *Vita Cadoci* (composed *ca.* 1081–1104) and the *Vita* written by Caradoc of Llancarfan (*ca.* 1120–1150); also valuable as sources are accounts of events found in the *Cartulary of Llancarfan* (*ca.* 1100), the closely related *Life of St. Gwynllyw,* and the Irish and Latin Lives of St. Finnian. Unfortunately, the historicity of these tales is not easily verified.

According to the stories, Cadoc's father was Gwynllyw; he and his father, Glywys, were eponyms for Gwynlliog and Glywysing (modern Morgannwg). Gwladus, Cadoc's mother, was the daughter of Bychan, eponymous founder of Brycheiniog (Brecknockshire in Powys). Since it was fashionable to ascribe royal parentage to saints, Cadoc's origins are doubtful. Cadoc was baptized and educated by an Irish hermit named Meuthi or Tatheus. Little is known of Meuthi, but his cult was centered in Caerwent and his name is preserved in the place-name Llanfeuthin (close to Llancarfan).

Upon completion of his education in the classics and in religion, Cadoc (or Cathmail, as he was baptized) retired to the territory of his uncle, Paul Penychen. There, with a grant of land from his uncle, he founded his first monastery, Nantcarfan (later known as Llancarfan). An alternative tradition concerning the monastery names Cadoc as the third abbot rather than its founder. Garmon (Germanus of Armorica) is the founder, with St. Dyfrig (Dubricius) his first successor and Cadoc his second. Nevertheless, it is Cadoc who became most strongly associated with Llancarfan.

St. Cadoc's lives paint him as a great scholar and an even greater traveler. He supposedly visited Ireland on several occasions, traveled to Scotland and Brittany, and went on pilgrimages to Rome and to Jerusalem. In what is by far the most fabulous of tales told by Lifris, Cadoc is transported on a white cloud to Benevento, Italy. There he is consecrated bishop under the name of Sophias, and at his own request is martyred. His body is interred there, which is why Llancarfan does not possess his relics. Caradoc of Llancarfan's version of the event is a little more realistic. He says that Cadoc died in Benevento while en route to Jerusalem. It was a natural death, and Cadoc was not made a bishop.

In spite of the fantastical elements, archaeological evidence suggests that either Cadoc or members of his cult traveled as far south as Brittany and as far north as Anglesey.

Although Rhygyfarch, whom Lifris apparently used as a source for his own hagiographical writing, does not mention Cadoc in his *Life of St. David*, Lifris makes David a rival to Cadoc. While Cadoc is away, St. David conducts the synod of Llanddewi Brefi without receiving prior permission from Cadoc. In the Latin and Irish lives of St. Finnian, Finnian acts as arbitrator among David, Cathmael (Cadoc), and Gildas, naming David as primate over the other two.

King Arthur also enters Cadoc's life on two occasions, as recorded in Lifris' *Vita Cadoci*. The first time he is the abettor of Gwynllyw's abduction of Gwladus. Later Arthur is forced to confirm Cadoc's power of sanctuary.

St. Cadoc's cult flourished mainly in south Wales and parts of Brittany. Because of the similarity of names he is often confused with another Breton saint, Cadou or Catfodw, whose cult is centered on the Île Cadou.

BIBLIOGRAPHY

Sabine Baring-Gould and John Fisher summarize Cadoc's (Catwg's) life in *Lives of the British Saints,* II (1908). See Christopher Brooke's excellent chapter "St. Peter of Gloucester and St. Cadog of Llancarfan," in Nora Kershaw Chadwick, ed., *Celt and Saxon: Studies in the Early British Border* (1963). For the medieval lives, see Arthur Wade-Evans, ed., *Vitae sanctorum Britanniae* (1944), 24–141; Père Jean Grosjean, ed., "Vita Cadoci by Caradoc of Llancarfan," in *Analecta Bollandiana,* **60** (1942).

MARILYN KAY KENNEY

[See also **Gildas; Wales: History.**]

CÆDMON (*fl. ca. 675*). According to Bede (*Historia ecclesiastica,* IV, 24), Cædmon was an unlettered cowherd who worked at the monastery now known as Whitby during the time that Hilda was abbess (657–680). One night, when the brethren were feasting and singing to the harp, he left the company early to sleep in the cowshed, for he knew no songs. While he slept, a man appeared to him and commanded him to sing of the Creation. He sang the following verses (here quoted in their original Northumbrian dialect):

Nu scylun hergan   hefaenricaes uard,
Metudæs maecti   end his modgidanc,
uerc uuldulfadur,   sue he uundra gihuaes,
eci dryctin,   or astelidæ.
He aerist scop   aelda barnum
heben til hrofe,   haleg scepen;
tha middungeard   moncynnæs uard,
eci dryctin,   æfter tiadæ,
firum foldu,   frea allmectig.

Now it is our duty to praise the Guardian of the heavenly kingdom, the Maker's might and purpose, the acts of the Glory-Father, just as He, the eternal Lord, established the origin of everything wondrous. He, the holy Creator, first created heaven as a roof for the children of men; then the Guardian of mankind, the eternal

Lord, the almighty God, later fashioned the land, middle earth, for men. [Author's translation]

The next morning, when Cædmon sang the hymn to Hilda and the learned brethren, they agreed that it was a gift from God. From this time until his holy death, which like other gifted persons he foresaw, he composed songs on many religious subjects. Literate brethren would teach him sacred history, and after a night of rumination he would return with the subject matter transformed into songs of compelling sweetness.

Other Old English poems that were once thought to be Cædmon's are now no longer attributed to him, with the possible exception of *Genesis A*. Still, "Cædmon's Hymn" is important as the first complete English poem that has survived, and perhaps the earliest poem recorded in any European vernacular.

Bede's account is of great interest for its description of how an unlettered singer and lettered scribes collaborated in the recording of vernacular poetry. Analogs to Bede's story of divine inspiration have been cited from many lands, from Iceland to India, but the story is not therefore to be dismissed as a mere legend.

Some scholars have viewed Cædmon as a traditional oral singer who unconsciously assimilated a knowledge of Anglo-Saxon formulaic diction from native poetry in praise of chiefs and kings. Others have seen his chief source as the Psalms, have interpreted his hymn as Trinitarian, or have traced his debt to Christian exegetical authors. Probably both approaches are partly justified: the unlettered Cædmon composed in a traditional Germanic verse medium and also, for the first time, used this medium to express basic Christian doctrine and sentiment.

BIBLIOGRAPHY

E. V. K. Dobbie, ed., *The Anglo-Saxon Minor Poems* (1942), xciv–c, clxx–clxxi, 105–106, 198–199; Donald K. Fry, "Caedmon as a Formulaic Poet," in Joseph J. Duggan, ed., *Oral Literature: Seven Essays* (1975); Bernard F. Huppé, *Doctrine and Poetry: Augustine's Influence on Old English Poetry* (1959), 99–130; G. A. Lester, "The Cædmon Story and Its Analogues," in *Neophilologus*, 58 (1974); Francis P. Magoun, Jr., "Bede's Story of Cædman: The Case History of an Anglo-Saxon Oral Singer," in *Speculum*, 30 (1955); and C. L. Wrenn, "The Poetry of Cædmon," in *Proceedings of the British Academy*, 32 (1946).

JOHN D. NILES

[See also **Anglo-Saxon Literature; Bede.**]

CAEN, a Norman town on the river Orne, became prominent only under William the Conqueror. He fortified the center of the town and founded two influential abbeys in the suburbs, St. Étienne for men and La Trinité for women. Under William and his successors Caen became the administrative center of Normandy. It had a good location in the middle of the duchy, could easily be reached from England, and unlike Rouen with its archbishop and restless bourgeoisie, was completely controlled by the duke. The Norman treasury was at Caen and the law court (called the Exchequer) met there, as did the financial Exchequer that audited accounts.

After the conquest of Normandy by Philip Augustus of France in 1204, Caen slowly lost its prominence. Rouen, on the Seine, was easier to reach from Paris and was less closely identified with the old Norman dynasty. The judicial Exchequer was held for a while at Falaise, then alternated during most of the thirteenth century between Caen and Rouen. The financial Exchequer was moved to Rouen certainly by the time of St. Louis (1226–1270), and probably earlier. After 1300 the judicial Exchequer met only at Rouen, and Caen had lost most of its importance.

Caen revived somewhat during the English occupation of Normandy during the Hundred Years War, and for somewhat the same reasons that had made it important in the twelfth century. It was remote from Paris, accessible from England, and more easily controlled than Rouen, a much larger city. Thus Henry V established the Chambre des Comités in the town. Later the English, trying to counter the influence in Normandy of the University of Paris, founded the University of Caen in 1432. The university survived, but with the French reconquest Caen fell back to its position as the second city of Normandy.

BIBLIOGRAPHY

Charles Homer Haskins, *Norman Institutions* (1918); Joseph R. Strayer, *The Administration of Normandy Under St. Louis* (1932, repr. 1972).

JOSEPH R. STRAYER

[See also **Exchequer; Exchequer, Court of; Normans and Normandy; Rouen; William the Conqueror.**]

CAESAR, Roman imperial title distinguished from, and second to, *augustus*. From the reign of Diocletian until the eleventh century, it was bestowed on one or more members of the imperial family in a ceremony resembling the elevation to the throne. The main insignium was a crown different from the imperial one. The caesar, addressed as *eutychestatos (felicissimus)*, had vast prerogatives (this title is the origin of the Slavic czar) and was often seen as a potential successor to the emperor. He held the first position in the Byzantine imperial hierarchy until the reign of Alexios I Komnenos (1081–1118), when he was superseded by the *sebastokrator*. With the creation of the dignity of despot in the twelfth century, the caesar was relegated to the third rank, where he remained until the end of the empire.

BIBLIOGRAPHY

R. Guilland, "Le césar," in *Orientalia Christiana Periodica*, **13** (1947), repr. in his *Recherches sur les institutions byzantines*, II (1967); A. N. Oikonomides, *Les listes de préséance byzantines des IXe et Xe siècles* (1972), 293; B. Ferjančić, "Sevastokratori i kesari u Srpskom carstvu," in *Zbornik filozofskog fakulteta* (Belgrade), **11**, no. 1 (1970), in Serbo-Croatian with French summary.

NICOLAS OIKONOMIDES

[See also **Despot; Sebastokrator**.]

CAESAREA (Kayseri). Caesarea, a city on the southeastern side of the Anatolian plateau in the middle of modern Turkey, has always owed its importance to its strategic location at the junction of roads that connect Anatolia with the Near East. It was the capital of the Roman province of Cappadocia and, as the home of St. Basil, gained the ecclesiastical rank of first metropolis after Constantinople. After enjoying considerable prosperity in late antiquity, the city received a new but reduced circuit of walls under Justinian. It was captured and plundered by the Persians in 611 and by the Arabs in 646 and 724, but remained one of the great Byzantine military bases and a gathering point for the imperial army on the great military highway across Anatolia. In the eleventh century Caesarea was the goal of extensive Armenian immigration. Sacked by the Turks in 1067, it fell to their rule in the confused years after Manzikert and was in ruins when the First Crusade passed it in 1097. Subsequently it fell to the Danishmendids, who restored it, and in 1163 to the Seljuks of Konya (Rum), for whom it was frequently the capital.

The Seljuks adorned Kayseri, which became a great center of trade and learning. The city was sacked by the Mongols in 1243 and the Mamluks in 1277. From 1343 to 1381 it was ruled by the Ertanid emirs, who made it their capital. Ibn Baṭṭūṭa, visiting it during this period, described Kayseri as one of the chief cities of Anatolia, governed by the head of the local *akhis*. In 1398 it fell briefly to the Ottomans, but four years later Tamerlane defeated the Ottomans and turned it over to the Karamans, who disputed its rule with the emirs of Dulgadir until it definitively became Ottoman around 1515.

Late antique and Byzantine Caesarea left no substantial traces, but subsequent periods, especially that of the Seljuks, have left many fine monuments, including city walls, mosques, and tombs.

BIBLIOGRAPHY

Claude Cahen, *Pre-Ottoman Turkey* (1968); Albert Gabriel, *Monuments turques d'Anatolie*, I (1931); Friedrich Hild and M. Restle, *Tabula imperii byzantini*, vol. 2: *Kappadokien* (1981).

CLIVE FOSS

[See also **Anatolia; Baṭṭūṭa, Ibn; Danishmendids; Karamania; Seljuks of Rum**.]

CAESARIUS OF ARLES, ST. (*ca.* 470–542). Born near Chalon-sur-Saône, Caesarius became a monk of Lérins at age twenty. Sent to Arles for his health, he there became deacon, priest, abbot of a nearby monastery, and finally archbishop (502–542). In 514 he was named primate of Gaul and Spain, in which capacity he held six reforming synods that were important for doctrine and discipline. Though not an original theologian, Caesarius was a model of pastoral care, and his sermons offer valuable insight into church life of the time. A promoter of monasticism, he wrote a rule for a convent governed by his sister Caesaria, and a briefer rule for monks. His feast day is 27 August.

BIBLIOGRAPHY

Mary M. Mueller, *St. Caesarius of Arles: Sermons*, 3 vols. (1956–1973); Henry G. J. Beck, *The Pastoral Care of Souls in South-east France During the Sixth Century* (1950); W. M. Daly, "Caesarius of Arles, a Precursor of Medieval Christendom," in *Traditio*, **26** (1970).

CLAUDE J. PEIFER, O.S.B.

CAESARIUS OF HEISTERBACH (*ca.* 1180–*ca.* 1240) was educated at the cathedral school of Cologne, became a Cistercian monk, and spent the rest of his life in the convent of Heisterbach. He wrote sermons, saints' lives, and a very useful account of the archbishops of Cologne.

His most important work is *Dialogue on Miracles*. His examples of miracles were carefully selected to illustrate points of Christian doctrine and morality. The work was widely used by preachers and writers on problems of faith and Christian behavior.

BIBLIOGRAPHY

The Dialogue on Miracles of Caesarius of Heisterbach, H. von E. Scott and C. C. S. Bland, trans. (1929).

JOSEPH R. STRAYER

[See also **Cologne; Hagiography, Western European; Historiography, Western European.**]

CAESAROPAPISM is not a word that was used in the Middle Ages. It was coined by modern scholars to describe a situation in which the emperor (of Rome, of Byzantium, and later of Russia) acted as if he were also head of the church. It was a natural result of the circumstances in which Christianity became the official religion of the late Roman Empire. The conversion of Constantine was the decisive step in this change, for, as emperor, he was also *pontifex maximus*, the chief priest of the old pagan religion. It was natural to assume that he would play the same role in the Christian church, since the authority of the pope was not yet fully established, especially in the eastern part of the empire. Moreover, there were serious doctrinal problems concerning the nature of Christ that had not been resolved, and that tended to pit provinces against provinces, cities against cities, and factions in cities against each other. These religious quarrels threatened the unity of the empire.

Also, Constantine was creating a new capital, named for himself, in the East. What would be the status of the bishop in this new imperial city? Obviously he would have to rank high in the church; would the bishop of New Rome (Constantinople) be the equal of the bishop of Old Rome (the pope)? And since the bishop or patriarch of Constantinople (as he was soon to be called) was very much under the control of the emperor, of whom the pope was much more independent, who would prevail if the two dis-

agreed? And what if the patriarch of Constantinople tried to discipline the patriarchs of Alexandria and Antioch, both of whom (like the pope) could claim that their churches were founded by an apostle and not by an emperor?

Constantine, who wanted to strengthen a weakened empire, saw that religious controversy was a divisive force and tried to restore unity by calling the First General Council of the church at Nicaea in 325. There the bishops accepted a creed that, with slight later modifications, became the official creed of orthodox Christians. Constantine certainly put pressure on the bishops to agree, but he did not dictate the terms of the agreement.

Later emperors were less forbearing. They not only called councils; they tried to reconcile factions in the church by defining orthodox doctrine in imperial edicts. For example, in 482 Zeno issued the *Henotikon* in an attempt to settle disputes over the nature of Christ. Justinian, in an attempt to reconcile the Monophysites (the Christians who emphasized the divine nature of Christ and denied that he was also human), in 543 condemned the writings of three bishops whose works had been approved by the Council of Chalcedon in 451. When Pope Vigilius protested, Justinian had him brought to Constantinople and forced him, under heavy pressure, to agree to support the condemnation. The emperor nailed down his victory by calling a council at Constantinople in 553 that accepted the emperor's condemnation. Vigilius reluctantly accepted this decision in 554. Later examples were the *Ekthesis* (638) and the *Typos* (648), dealing with the question of whether Christ had one or two wills (human and divine). When Pope Martin I (649–655) denounced these documents, he was arrested (the Eastern emperor still had control of Rome) and sent to the Crimea, where he died in exile.

One of the most striking examples of imperial control of the Eastern church was the Iconoclastic Controversy. The churches of the empire were beautifully adorned with images of saints, and some theologians felt that veneration of these images was verging on idolatry. The Muslims, who were pushing hard against the Christians in the Asian provinces, taunted them as image worshipers. Emperor Leo III, III, who came from Asia Minor, became concerned that the images were dangerous to the faith. He issued an edict against them and deposed the patriarch when he objected to the order. Images were destroyed, and others who objected to the policy also lost their positions. Persecution became more severe under Leo's son, Constantine V. In 753 he called a church council that condemned the images, and by the 760's he had fully determined to wipe out all opposition. He spared no one; in 767 he executed the deposed patriarch of Constantinople. Iconoclasm ended, as it began, with an imperial order. Empress Irene, regent for her son Constantine VI, who was a minor, called another council that in 787 condemned iconoclasm.

As these examples show, there was no doubt that the Byzantine emperor controlled the Greek church. But as time went on, it also became clear that there were limits to what the emperor could ask of the church. He had purged it of heterodox beliefs so that it was a united force; he had also made it a symbol of Greek independence from the West. The emperor could make and break patriarchs at will, but he could not bring about a lasting union or even an accommodation with Rome. The emperors were not responsible for the final break with the pope in 1054; and as Byzantium weakened, they strove desperately to reunite the churches in order to gain Western aid. Even when the Turks were at the gates of Constantinople, there were those who said that they preferred the turban of the Turk to the tiara of the pope. The emperors disappeared; the church that they helped to create endured.

Caesaropapism was less of a problem in the West, partly because the caesars, such as they were, were usually far away from Rome, partly because the pope had an older claim to authority than the patriarchs of Constantinople. The Byzantine emperors interfered in Rome as long as they held some Italian territory, but their position weakened steadily as Lombards, then Franks and Normans, took over all of the peninsula except Venice. Moreover, the popes were more aware of the danger of caesaropapism than were the patriarchs. As early as the reign of Zeno, Pope Felix II told the emperor that in matters of religion he was subordinate to the church. Gelasius I repeated this statement and later wrote a letter that became the official statement in the West of proper relations between state and church:

> There are indeed, Your Majesty, two agencies by which this world is mainly ruled—the sacred authority of the prelates and the power of the king. The burden on the priests is the heavier, for they will have to give account in the Last Judgment even for kings. . . . Thus you should submit to them and their judgment in religious matters. . . . The bishops obey your laws on matters of government . . . you should obey them who can proclaim the meaning of the divine mysteries.

Some Western rulers forgot these injunctions at times, but on the whole they were observed.

The closest approach to caesaropapism in the West came in the period when the Western empire had been revived and the papacy had fallen into the hands of the Roman aristocracy. Charlemagne felt responsible for the welfare of the church in his domains; he called local councils, sponsored tracts on doctrines, legislated on the training and behavior of the clergy, and intervened in Rome to save Pope Leo III from his enemies. In return he received the imperial crown from the pope in 800. Charlemagne's son, Louis the Pious, was also active in the affairs of the church. In the end, however, the descendants of Charlemagne lost power and Rome came under the control of local noble families. The German line of emperors rescued and dominated the papacy for almost a century. On the whole they selected able and upright men as popes and did not meddle with doctrine. The Investiture Controversy (1075–1122) put an end to imperial control of the papacy, and for the rest of the Middle Ages, while Western kings influenced, and often controlled, appointments to bishoprics and abbeys, they did not control the central government of the church.

Curiously, the end of the Middle Ages saw a revival of caesaropapism. The Reformation left the Protestant churches under the control of their kings and princes. Henry VIII of England put it in terms that would have satisfied Justinian or Zeno: "This realm of England is an empire"; therefore he could choose bishops, use church property for his own purposes, and determine doctrine. He was, officially, head of the church.

At the other extremity of Europe, the same thing was taking place. The grand princes of Moscow were now czars (from *Caesar*), and they controlled the Russian church just as the Byzantine emperors (who helped convert Russia to the Greek form of Christianity) had controlled theirs. The conclusion seems to be that when you have both an emperor and a pope (or patriarch), it is difficult, and at times impossible, to keep the lay rulers from interfering in religious affairs.

BIBLIOGRAPHY

In the East. Charles Diehl, *Byzantium: Greatness and Decline* (1957); George Every, *The Byzantine Patriarchate* (1947); E. J. Martin, *A History of the Iconoclastic Controversy* (1930); R. V. Sellers, *The Council of Chalcedon* (1953); Alexander A. Vasiliev, *History of the Byzantine Empire,* 2 vols. (1952).

In the West. R. W. Carlyle and J. A. Carlyle, *History of Medieval Political Theory in the West* (1930), I, chs. 13 and 15, and II, chs. 11 and 12; Walter Ullman, *The Carolingian Renaissance and the Idea of Kingship* (1960); and *The Growth of Papal Government* (1970).

JOSEPH R. STRAYER

[See also **Byzantine Church; Charlemagne; Councils (Ecumenical, 325–787); Councils, Byzantine (787–1368); Ekthesis; Gelasius I, Pope; Henotikon; Hieria, Council of; Iconoclasm, Christian; Investiture and Investiture Controversy; Justinian I; Leo III, Pope; Monophysitism; Nicaea, Councils of; Vigilius, Pope; Zeno the Isaurian.**]

CAFFA (modern Feodosiya), the principal Genoese colony in the Crimea, appears to have been organized as an individual proprietor's enterprise at Theodosia, a minor Byzantine port, about 1266 and to have possessed autonomous institutions by the 1280's if not sooner. It prospered as a vassal commune tolerated by the Mongols of the Golden Horde and a terminus of their safe overland route to China. The mendicant orders, making Caffa their base for missions into much of Asia, dominated religious life there. In 1307 Khan Tokhta turned against the colonists, who abandoned the town after eight months of resistance behind their cemented wooden palisade. Özbeg allowed it to be refounded, and the city was revived by 1316, though stone fortifications were finished only in 1352 with aid from Pope Clement VI. From 1314 the Officium Gazarie (Khazariae) at Genoa, under a succession of statutes, supervised the consuls, whose authority extended over satellite towns in the Crimea and elsewhere on the Black Sea coast. As at Pera, the two local representative assemblies had seats for non-Genoese.

The Mongol collapse in the mid fourteenth century cut the trans-Asian trade route and began the second phase of Caffa's history. New trading connections with Russia and eastern Europe, as well as with the Turco-Mongol ("Tartar") successor states, drew advantage from rapidly developing cultures, exchanging European and Far Eastern goods (the latter by way of Egypt) for products of the northern forest zone. Long-established local exports, such as dried fish and grain, predominated, along with the notorious slave trade. It was still prudent to recognize the suzerainty of the nearest Tartar prince, and because of the Tartar princes' rivalries, hostilities with some of them could not always be avoided. One attacker, Janibeg, is said to have had his siege engines fling plague-infected corpses over the walls, thereby introducing the Black Death into Europe.

But Caffa was never richer than in the late fourteenth and early fifteenth centuries. The polyglot population, proud of preserving the amenities of a great city in a dangerous part of the world, may have approached 100,000, with strong Greek, Armenian, Jewish, and Tartar elements. Several major religious bodies lived there side by side. Contemporary writings describe busy, colorful streets, well-frequented public baths and games, horse and boat races, and rich *feste* presided over by the consuls, international figures entertaining with commingled Renaissance and Eastern pomp a stream of visiting prelates, envoys, and Tartar princes.

In 1453 the Commune of Genoa made over its Black Sea colonies to the Bank of St. George, which worked to strengthen Caffa's finances and fortifications against the Ottoman Turks. Sultan Mehmed II defeated his last strong rival, Uzun Ḥasan, the Turkoman ruler of Persia, in 1473 and was then free for the attack, which was occasioned by an uprising of the Tartar population. A large Turkish fleet landed an army with artillery, and Caffa surrendered after a six-day siege (6 June 1475). The inhabitants became slaves or were exiled, some settling in Constantinople and a few returning to Genoa. The port never recovered any substantial life until the late nineteenth century.

BIBLIOGRAPHY

A. A. Vasiliev, *The Goths in the Crimea* (1936), is the most thorough modern study of the medieval Crimea. Also see Wilhelm von Heyd, *Histoire du commerce du Levant au moyen-âge*, rev. ed., F. Raynaud, trans., 2 vols. (1885–1886, repr. 1967); Raymond J. Loenertz, *La Société des Frères Pérégrinantes: Étude sur l'Orient dominicane* (1937); Ştefan Pascu, ed., *Colocviul Romano-Italian: Genovezii la Marea Neagră in secolele XIII–XIV* (1977), in French and Italian. The Archivio di Stato and other collections in Genoa are rich in materials on the Black Sea colonies, many published, along with monographs, in the continuing *Atti della Società Ligure di Storia Patria* (Genoa, from 1859; title varies).

AVERY ANDREWS

[See also **Crimea, Khanate of; Genoa; Golden Horde; Mongol Empire; Trade, European; Uzun Ḥasan.**]

CAFTAN (or kaftan; French *cafetan;* from Ottoman Turkish *qaftān*) is a term used in Europe to denote a

Traditional caftan from the Levant.
FROM R. TURNER WILCOX, THE DIC-
TIONARY OF COSTUME

long-skirted robe that can be worn by either sex. Its Turkish etymology accounts for its long association with the Orient in European sources; Russian boyars adopted the caftan as a ceremonial costume, from either Byzantine or Mongol usage, and literary sources in Europe associate the caftan with Jewish costume.

The Turkish term originally denoted a robe of honor, loose, long, and with voluminous sleeves, that was made of fine fabric and could be worn over regular costume. "Caftan" is also used in Europe, especially with respect to women's clothing, to denote a gown closely fitted above the waist and closed up the front with frogs and buttons or toggles. In Turkish such a garment is called an *entar*.

BIBLIOGRAPHY

Robert Halsband, ed., *Complete Letters of Lady Mary Wortley Montagu*, I (1965), 326, 350, 381.

WALTER B. DENNY

[See also **Costume**.]

CAIRO. Today the largest city of the Arab world, Cairo has been since the seventh century a capital of Arabic and Islamic culture and politics.

The area around modern Cairo, including ancient Memphis and Heliopolis, and Roman Babylon, had been the site of various capitals of Egypt, but the first major city to be founded in the region was the Arab capital of Al-Fusṭāṭ (the entrenchment). Al-Fusṭāṭ (later Cairo) was an entirely new city without trace of its ancient predecessors. The city was founded in

641 by the Arab Muslim conquerors of Egypt in order to garrison the conquering armies, administer the country, and provide a base for further Muslim conquests in North Africa. The Muslim armies established a tent city on the east bank of the Nile, slightly north of the Byzantine fortress and capital of Babylon. Although the new capital, centered at the mosque of ᶜAmr ibn al-ᶜĀṣ, was founded as an Arab Muslim garrison, it soon attracted a large Coptic population of administrators, merchants, and artisans who came to make their fortunes. The settlers developed textile, glass, pottery, and ship-construction industries, and made Al-Fusṭāṭ in its first century a mixed Arab-Muslim and Coptic society.

The further development of Al-Fusṭāṭ and eventually of Cairo was conditioned by political history. Successive regimes developed new garrison centers in the vicinity of Al-Fusṭāṭ. By the creation of new palaces, mosques, and military cantonments, they stimulated the physical expansion of the urbanized district. The Abbasid dynasty, which took control of Egypt in 750, built a new palace, mosque, and garrison settlement in the area north of Al-Fusṭāṭ, called Al-ᶜAskar. Al-ᶜAskar soon attracted its own markets, civilian population, and, especially, a Muslim learned elite.

The process of constructing new government centers and expanding the size of the urban area was repeated in the late ninth century. Aḥmad ibn Ṭūlūn, who was appointed governor of Egypt in 868 but soon made himself an independent ruler, developed Al-Qaṭāᵓiᶜ, to the northeast of Al-ᶜAskar, in order to settle his newly recruited slave army. The mosque of Ibn Ṭūlūn was completed in 879 along with palaces, *mayādīn* for sports, markets, gardens, and houses, and the district was divided into separate quarters for each of the slave regiments. Al-Qaṭāᵓiᶜ was demolished by the Abbasids when they again took control of Egypt in 905 and returned the capital to Al-ᶜAskar. In the meantime Al-Fusṭāṭ remained the commercial center of the urban region.

In 969 the Fatimid dynasty (969–1171) added Egypt to its North African empire. The Fatimids continued the urban expansion by building a new palace and garrison center some two miles to the north of Al-Fusṭāṭ and a mile north of Al-Qaṭāᵓiᶜ. This was Al-Manṣūrīya, renamed Al-Qāhira (City of Victory), which gave its name to the whole of the urban agglomeration. Though committed to the Fatimid Ismaili version of Islam, the Fatimids were supported by Berber armies and Jewish and Christian administrators ruling the mass of the Egyptians, who remained Sunni Muslims and Copts. Under the Fatimids Cairo was a walled court city half a mile square. Cairo was expanded between 1087 and 1091 by the constructions of the great Fatimid walls and gates of Bāb al-Naṣr, Bāb al-Futūḥ, and Bāb Zuwayla, which are still among its most impressive monuments. The interior of the city was provided with two great palaces, the east palace and the west palace, separated by a large parade ground called Bayn al-Qaṣrayn. The mosque of Al-Azhar was built as a center of Fatimid Ismaili law and religious teaching. Berber and other ethnic regiments were settled in separate quarters.

With the construction of the new city center, Al-ᶜAskar fell into decay, but Al-Fusṭāṭ (also called Miṣr) remained the center of commercial life. However, the political anarchy of the mid eleventh century and the struggle between the Fatimids and the Crusaders for control of Egypt in the twelfth century did extensive damage to the urban fabric, culminating in the total burning of Al-Fusṭāṭ in 1168 to keep it from falling into the hands of the Crusaders. By the end of the Fatimid era, Cairo was a faint shadow of its former brilliance.

The conquest of Egypt by Saladin in 1171 and the establishment of the Ayyubid dynasty (1171–1249) marked a new era in the redevelopment and expansion of Cairo. As had every previous regime, Saladin symbolized the founding of the new political order by constructing a government center and citadel south and east of Al-Qāhira along the edge of the Muqaṭṭam hills. He built new walls to include Al-Qāhira proper, the territory west of the city to the Nile, and that south to the citadel. New quarters and gardens developed to the south and west of Al-Qāhira between the city and the river. As the city's palaces were replaced by schools and markets, the new city absorbed the once-flourishing commercial life of Al-Fusṭāṭ, and under Saladin's patronage became a center of the Sunni Muslim religious revival. Judges and scholars from Iran, Iraq, and Mesopotamia were attracted to the new city, provided with salaries and endowments, and housed in newly built mosques and schools. Under Sunni auspices Cairo again became a major capital of Muslim scholarship, commercial life, and political empire.

In 1250 the Mamluk slave regiments employed by the Ayyubid dynasty took control of the state and established a military regime that lasted in Egypt and Syria until 1517. The new regime was dominated by an exploitative slave elite who appointed the sultan, or head of government, and also gave strong support to Sunni Muslim religious activities. The Mamluks and the Muslim religious leaders, the ulama, jointly governed the society. Mamluk patronage provided support for religious life and endowed schools, mosques, and tombs. Under Mamluk rule both scholarship and Sufi devotional life flourished.

The first part of the Mamluk era, from the middle of the thirteenth to the middle of the fourteenth century, continued the political stability, cultural sponsorship, and economic prosperity, based partly on a flourishing international trade, of the era of Saladin and the Ayyubids. Cairo expanded considerably in population, size, and facilities. The construction of hospitals, caravansaries, colleges, and mosques endowed by the sultans and the leading military officers helped expand both the population—which reached some 250,000 to 500,000 persons—and the physical size of Cairo. The Mamluks redeveloped the interior of the old city by the construction of the mosque, a hospital, and the college of Qalāʾūn (1284) and by the construction of other colleges and bazaars.

Outside the center of old Cairo, the city grew rapidly, filling in the area between Cairo and Al-Fusṭāṭ, and between the Muqaṭṭam hills and the Nile. Bulaq developed as a port on the Nile in the late thirteenth and early fourteenth centuries. Construction of a long canal consolidated the development of the northwestern sector of Cairo by 1325. South of the city the cemeteries became new centers of Muslim religious life as a result of the construction of tombs with attached colleges, endowed with funds for scholars and Sufis. The tomb of Al-Shāfiᶜī became a cult center for Sunni Muslims. Several districts were favored by the construction of aristocratic residences for the Mamluk emirs. The area from the citadel to Bāb Zuwayla, the Birkat al-Fīl, and the citadel region became the center of Mamluk residences.

This extraordinary urban development was set back in the late fourteenth and fifteenth centuries by a number of interrelated factors. The Black Death of 1348 and frequently renewed plagues of the late fourteenth and fifteenth centuries, Mamluk factionalism and civil wars leading to economic exploitation, the decline of international trade and of sugar and textile production, and the imposition of government monopolies of spices and other valuable products compromised the political security and the economic prosperity that had been the basis of Cairo's growth. There was a temporary revival under the Circassian Mamluk sultan Barqūq (1382–1399). The suqs were rebuilt. But defeat of the Mamluks at the hands of Tamerlane and the economic depression that followed completed the decline. By 1403 the northern suburb of Al-Ḥusaynīya was desolate and the western suburbs were reduced. Only the cemetery cities south and east of the city continued to grow. In the fifteenth century population further declined. In 1517 Syria and Egypt were absorbed into the Ottoman Empire, and Cairo, once an independent capital, became subordinate to Istanbul.

BIBLIOGRAPHY

Janet Abu-Lughod, *Cairo: 1001 Years the City Victorious* (1971); Marcel Clerget, *Le Caire: Étude de géographie urbaine et d'histoire économique,* 2 vols. (1934); K. A. C. Creswell, *The Muslim Architecture of Egypt,* 2 vols. (1952–1959); Ira M. Lapidus, *Muslim Cities in the Later Middle Ages* (1967); Susan J. Stoffa, *Conquest and Fusion: The Social Evolution of Cairo 642–1850* (1977).

IRA M. LAPIDUS

[See also Azhar, Al-; Crusades and Crusader States; Egypt, Islamic; Fatimids; Mamluk Dynasty; Mosque; Saladin.]

CAIRO GENIZAH. A Hebrew word derived from Persian, *genizah* means "hiding or burial place." Medieval Jews employed it to designate a repository for discarded sacred writings, which, since they were presumed to contain the name of God (hence the nickname *shemot,* "names," for such items), it was forbidden to destroy. Periodically these worn-out fragments of Bible codices, Torah scrolls, prayer books, and other religious writings were transferred from the synagogue building to a grave in the Jewish cemetery. The Cairo genizah differed in an important respect: its contents were left for centuries in the storeroom set aside for them in a synagogue in Old Cairo (Al-Fusṭāṭ).

The reason for this remains something of a mystery. S. D. Goitein hypothesizes that the idea of a permanent genizah was born at the time of the persecution of Christians and Jews by the Fatimid caliph al-Ḥākim. On 31 December 1011, during the height of interfaith tensions accompanying that oppression, a Muslim mob attacked a Jewish funeral procession and captured two dozen Jews (the incident is described in a genizah document). When, sometime thereafter, the Jews set about restoring a Fusṭāṭ synagogue destroyed by the caliph, they decided, Goitein surmises, to construct a genizah large enough that it would not be necessary in the future to hold funeral corteges for inanimate objects.

The Cairo genizah became known to European

travelers and scholars in the latter part of the nineteenth century. Quite unsystematically over a period of many years, the manuscripts were acquired, through purchase and other means, and transferred to European and American libraries and private collections. Solomon Schechter, reader in rabbinics at Cambridge, is credited with making the Cairo genizah famous. In 1896, after identifying a fragment of the lost Hebrew original of the apocryphal Book of Ecclesiasticus (Ben Sira) among some pages acquired in Cairo by two Scottish ladies, Schechter, backed by Cambridge colleagues (most notably the wealthy master of St. John's College, Charles Taylor), launched a personal mission to the presumed source of the exciting find.

The mass of papers that he brought back from Cairo to his university—estimated by him at 100,000 but now known to number three times that amount—as well as his scholarly publications based on them, brought worldwide attention to the genizah. Other major caches at the Bodleian Library in Oxford, the British Museum, the State Public Library in Leningrad, the Jewish Theological Seminary in New York, as well as such smaller accumulations as those housed in the Hungarian Academy of Sciences in Budapest, the library of the Alliance Israélite Universelle in Paris, and Dropsie University in Philadelphia, joined Cambridge's Taylor-Schechter collection as an important source for Jewish historical and literary research.

Sensational discoveries in a variety of areas have punctuated twentieth-century genizah scholarship. The material preserved in the Cairo genizah covers every facet of Jewish intellectual, communal, and material life, and even includes pieces of non-Jewish literature. Specimens of biblical text with systems of vocalization different from the received Masoretic version were found. From these fragments Paul Kahle made startling revelations about the history and pronunciation of the Hebrew text of the Bible. Vast quantities of Hebrew poetry were unearthed among the genizah papers. These led to the discovery of new poems by old authors and even of new poets. The material has added much to knowledge of the history and literary nature of medieval Hebrew poetry.

In 1910 Schechter published fragments describing the praxis and beliefs of a previously unknown Jewish sect (*Documents of Jewish Sectaries,* vol. 1: *Fragments of a Zadokite Work*), which the subsequent discovery of the Dead Sea Scrolls showed to have substantial affinity with the antirabbinic religious communities of late antiquity that withdrew to the Judaean desert. The genizah materials have revealed much about the medieval Middle Eastern sect of the Karaites, who in some ways continued the antirabbinic opposition voiced by those earlier sectarians and who likely were responsible for preserving their ancient writings in the Middle Ages. Correspondence relating to the Jewish Khazars has shed important new light on that fascinating but obscure chapter of the Jewish past. Tremendous advances in the linguistic study of Judeo-Arabic, the vernacular of the genizah Jews, have been made possible by the masses of genizah documents written in that dialect.

The field of Jewish history has probably benefited more than any other realm of Jewish knowledge from the discovery of the Cairo genizah. Personalities from the lower ranks of Jewish society have been rescued from oblivion. These merchants and communal leaders played important roles in Jewish life, even though they did not write books. One example is the merchant-scholar Nahray ben Nissim, whose family evidently discarded batches of letters and business accounts from his archive into the genizah. More than 300 items relating to this individual have thus far been identified. As expected, too, hitherto unknown biographical details about great Jewish intellectuals like Maimonides and Judah Halevi have been recovered from routine genizah letters.

So much information about Jewish life in the medieval Middle East has been gleaned by studying the genizah that entirely new chapters of Jewish history have come to be written. Genizah documents tell about the inner workings of the great institutions of Jewish learning and self-government in Iraq (the yeshivas and the exilarchate). Letters and polemical treatises relate intricate aspects of communal and religious controversies that rocked the Jewish community in the Islamic world during the Middle Ages. Genizah manuscripts have divulged the existence of vital Jewish communities and institutions in medieval Palestine, generally unknown to history owing to the ascendancy of Iraqi (Babylonian) Judaism in the early Middle Ages. The communities of Egypt and North Africa have emerged from genizah documents as important areas of Jewish life and culture.

S. D. Goitein, continuing and expanding the genizah research of Jacob Mann and others, has described in fine detail the economic structure, communal life, and family ambience of this Mediterranean Jewish society of the Arab world. In addition, he has demonstrated the genizah's value for general history. Facts about Islamic political figures and events, both known and unknown, have been found imbedded in genizah documents. Furthermore, the genizah materials contain much information indirectly pertinent to general history, since in their economic activities and many of their social habits Jews did not differ markedly from their Muslim and Christian neighbors. In addition, hundreds of genizah documents have been found that relate to the medieval India trade, in which Jews participated during the High Middle Ages. This subject promises to be an important new chapter in medieval economic history.

BIBLIOGRAPHY

S. D. Goitein, *A Mediterranean Society: The Jewish Communities of the Arab World as Portrayed in the Documents of the Cairo Genizah*, 3 vols. (1967–1978); and "Urban Housing in Fatimid and Ayyubid Times (as Illustrated by the Cairo Geniza Documents)," in *Studia Islamica*, **47** (1978); Norman Golb, "Sixty Years of Genizah Research," in *Judaism*, **6** (1957); Abraham M. Habermann, *Ha-genizah veha-genizot* (1971); Paul Kahle, *The Cairo Geniza*, 2nd ed. (1959); Alexander Marx, "The Importance of the Geniza for Jewish History," in *Proceedings of the American Academy for Jewish Research*, **16** (1946–1947).

MARK R. COHEN

[See also **Jews in the Middle East; Khazars, Jewish.**]

CALATRAVA, ORDER OF. The Military Order of Calatrava was founded in 1158 by Abbot Raymond of Fitero, who received the fortress of Calatrava, on the Guadiana River, from King Sancho III of Castile. Raymond's monks assumed the defense of Calatrava, and in a few years the order took on a military character under the command of a master. In 1164 it was affiliated with the Cistercians and approved by the pope. The abbot of Morimond in 1187 was given the duty of visiting the order annually and of appointing the prior of the conventual brothers who resided at Calatrava. The knights, whose function was primarily military, were garrisoned in commanderies at strategic points in the Guadiana Valley, guarding the approaches to Toledo. An Aragonese branch was established at Alcañiz, and the orders of Alcántara, Avis, Christ, and Montesa were affiliated with Calatrava.

Calatrava fell to the Almohads in 1195, forcing the knights to move to Salvatierra until it fell in 1211. The Castilian victory at Las Navas de Tolosa in 1212 enabled the knights to recover their losses, but they moved their headquarters to Calatrava *la nueva,* some miles south of the original fortress. The order collaborated in the reconquest of Andalusia in the thirteenth century, but as the Reconquest slowed in the fourteenth and fifteenth centuries, the knights became embroiled in Castilian politics. Ferdinand and Isabella, therefore, with papal authorization, took over the administration of the order and its resources in 1489. By that time the order's monastic character had already been greatly modified, and it became an honorary association of nobles.

BIBLIOGRAPHY

Joseph F. O'Callaghan, *The Spanish Military Order of Calatrava and Its Affiliates* (1975).

JOSEPH F. O'CALLAGHAN

[See also **Chivalry, Orders of.**]

CALBULUS. Little is known of Calbulus, a North African poet who flourished in the early sixth century. We can deduce that he lived under the Vandals, was a Christian, and that his profession was that of a *grammaticus.* His only two known poems, preserved in the *Anthologia latina,* seem to have been intended as decoration upon a baptismal font and for a cross. The latter was often engraved in medieval times on crosses.

BIBLIOGRAPHY

Texts. Emil Baehrens, ed., *Poetae latini minores,* IV (1882), 428–430.

Criticism. Max Manitius, *Geschichte der christlich-lateinischen Poesie bis zur Mitte des 8. Jahrhunderts* (1891), 340; Frederic J. E. Raby, *A History of Christian-Latin Poetry,* 2nd ed. (1953), 96.

ABIGAIL YOUNG

CALENDAR OF OENGUS. See **Martyrology, Irish.**

CALENDARS AND RECKONING OF TIME

INTRODUCTION

Time reckoning is based on both natural and social phenomena. The occurrences in nature that have served as bases for calendrical computations are re-

current ones, such as the earth's completing its orbit around the sun, observed through the changes of the seasons; the phases of the moon, observed through the changes in its shape; and the rotation of the earth about its axis, observed through the change from daylight to darkness. These have served to define the length of the calendrical units: the year, the month, and the day. Among religious and historical concepts and events that have determined calendrical measures are the birth date or reign of major leaders, the names of gods, and the observation of holy days. These have served to define the length of the week and the hour, the duration of eras, the names and beginning dates of all calendrical subdivisions, and the determination of holidays.

Joining calendrical units based on such a wide variety of occurrences into unified systems has been a troublesome task throughout history. The difficulty has been compounded by the fact that the natural phenomena chosen for basic definitions often lead to incompatible situations. For example, most calendrical systems of antiquity had been based either on the solar year, which equals the time interval between two crossings by the sun of the celestial equator, or the lunar year, obtained by multiplying by twelve the length of time it takes the moon to pass once through all its phases. We now take the length of a solar year to be 365 days, 5 hours, 48 minutes, and 46 seconds (365.2422 days). This is known as the mean length of a tropical year. The length of a lunar month is approximately 29.5 days (29 days, 12 hours, 44 minutes, 3 seconds), so that the length of a lunar year amounts to a period slightly exceeding 354 days, 8 hours, and 48 minutes.

Although the accepted values for the solar and lunar year in antiquity differed somewhat from ours, they were sufficiently accurate to make clear the discrepancy between the two modes of calculating the length of a year. As a result, methods of reconciling the two—or, rather, of rationalizing systems based on one or the other or a combination of both—became the chief task of chronologists and calendar reformers.

An additional problem plaguing calendar computers in the Middle Ages was that of the precession of the equinoxes. It particularly complicated the reconciliation of a solar calendar with lunar religious observations. For example, it affected the determination of dates such as that of Easter, defined in terms of the relationship between a lunar phase and the vernal equinox. The sun's apparent annual path on the celestial sphere is called the ecliptic. The ecliptic is inclined 23°27′ to the celestial equator, which it intersects in two points called the equinoxes. These points of intersection move westward along the ecliptic at a rate of 50.27 seconds of arc per year. Since these points define the seasons—the vernal equinox marks the first day of spring; the autumnal equinox, the first day of fall—the year of the seasons, the "tropical year," is shorter than the period of the earth's revolution about the sun. This latter period, the sidereal year, has a length of 365 days, 6 hours, 9 minutes, 9.54 seconds.

Religion played a dominant role in time reckoning, as attested by the fact that the major medieval calendars used are commonly referred to as the Christian, the Islamic, and the Jewish calendars. They all considered a day as being determined by the changes between darkness and daylight, and a month as being determined by the phases of the moon—the period from new moon to new moon, for example. They differed in the definition of the year, however.

THE CHRISTIAN CALENDAR

The calendar prevailing in the Latin West at the beginning of the Middle Ages was the Julian calendar. This was the result of reformations of the Roman calendar, which, like its Egyptian predecessor, was based on a solar year; according to Julius Caesar's reform the length of this year was fixed at 365 days and 6 hours.

Eras. There was considerable variation in the eras used to group and count the years of the Julian calendar. The Roman calendar under the Consulate had used the reign of the chief consul to define its official eras. This custom prevailed in the early Middle Ages, although the last consuls had reigned in the sixth century. They were Decius Paulinus Iunior in the West and Flavius Basilius Iunior in the East; their names appear in chronologies for a considerable period after their deaths. When, starting with Justin II (565–578), emperors reestablished the consular title for themselves, the consular year was listed along with that of the imperial reign.

Dating official records by imperial reign had been introduced by Justin's predecessor, Justinian I, in 537. Using years of a ruler's reign was a custom from earlier times; during the Middle Ages it found favor in royal as well as imperial courts, and eventually with the papacy.

A third means of grouping years also had its origin in the Roman calendar. This was use of the "indiction," which was based on a continuous sequence of fifteen-year cycles, beginning in 3 B.C. The indiction gave the number of the year in this cycle. Occasionally the number of the indiction cycle was also recorded. Indictions were differentiated depending on the day taken as beginning of the year. There was a Greek indiction (1 September), a Caesarean or "Bedan" indiction (24 September), a Roman indiction (25 December or 1 January), and a Sienese indiction (8 September).

An era of particular importance in Byzantium was the Alexandrian, which was based on two chronographies. One is that of the Alexandrian monk Panodoros, who flourished about A.D. 400. This era let the birth of Christ fall in the year 5493; it begins with 29 August 5493 B.C. The other is based on the work of Anianos, whose era begins with 25 March 5492 B.C. Anianos placed the birth of Christ eight years later than Panodoros, however. Subsequent discussions led to the emergence of the Byzantine era. This took its starting point as 1 September 5509 B.C. It began to be used officially in the seventh century but coexisted with the Alexandrian in Byzantium until the tenth century.

Another era of some importance in the early Middle Ages was that of Diocletian. Its epoch, or starting date, was 29 August A.D. 284. Used primarily in Egypt, the era commemorates the inauguration of Emperor Diocletian in 284. Among Coptic Christians it was called the Era of Martyrs.

A regional era that demonstrated strong persistence was the Spanish era; its epoch was 38 B.C. It appeared in the fifth century, became widespread on the Iberian Peninsula in the sixth, and was the dominant era there until the end of the fourteenth. It was also used in neighboring areas of southern France and northern Africa. Twelfth-century efforts to replace it with the Christian era had only limited success, but various decrees passed in the fourteenth century led to its demise. Peter IV caused it to be replaced by the Christian era in Aragon in 1349; the Christian era took its place in Valencia in 1358; in Castile and León in 1383; and in Navarre early in the fifteenth century.

The Christian era is generally credited with having been established in the sixth century by the Roman abbot Dionysius Exiguus. He was the author of an influential set of Easter tables in which important dates were listed in terms of *anni domini nostri Jesu Christi.* The era gained acceptance rather slowly, however. Cassiodorus, a contemporary of

Girdle book, folding computus-type calendar. Made by Father Mamert Fichet, France, 1440. THE PIERPONT MORGAN LIBRARY

Dionysius Exiguus, used years *ab incarnatione* in an Easter tract, and Julianus of Toledo referred to it a century later; but these were scattered references. The first group apparently using the Christian era in official records was the Anglo-Saxons; indeed, the attention paid to it in the writings of Bede did much to assist its dissemination. Nevertheless, the era made its way slowly, appearing in private documents in French regions in the eighth century and in German in the ninth. It has been used in papal records since the tenth century but did not become official until the fifteenth.

Divisions of the year. The Julian year was divided into twelve months. These, in turn, were divided into 31, 28, 31, 30, 31, 30, 31, 31, 30, 31, 30, and 31 days. Their names were Januarius, Februarius, Martius, Aprilis, Maius, Junius, Julius, Augustus, September, October, November, and December. Every fourth year an extra day was inserted (intercalated) after 24 February. In practice, for most of the Middle Ages the insertion took place between 23 and 24 February, the latter being regarded as the extra day.

The beginning of the year varied between different eras and within given eras. For the Roman civil year according to the Julian calendar it was 1 January, although the Roman military still utilized the older 1 March. This style was also used in Russia until the middle of the thirteenth century. When, toward the end of the third century, the fiscal indiction cycle became accepted in the Roman empire, 1 September was used—obtained by slightly modifying the Egyptian starting date of 29 August for the cycle—as the beginning of the year. As a result the Byzantine year began on 1 September.

The Christian church calendar gave rise to three more styles: those using Christmas, 25 March, and Easter as the beginning of the year.

Bede records the year's beginning at Christmas, and this style continued to be used by the major Benedictine houses of England until the beginning of the seventeenth century. The custom appears to have passed to the Continent from England. The Frankish emperors used it at least by the last quarter of the ninth century, and it was retained in French royal records until the twelfth century. It was used in imperial records and began to be used by the popes, after the coronation of Otto the Great in 936. It is found in official papal records from John XIII (965–972) to 1098, after which time it was retained in papal correspondence but was replaced by the Annunciation style (25 March) in dating the *privilegia*.

Except for a period of sole use lasting more than two decades in the early thirteenth century, until the seventeenth century the Christmas style either alternated, or was used concurrently, with the two Annunciation styles in papal records. In general the Christmas style dominated in all of western Europe except for the Iberian peninsula until the twelfth century.

The "Annunciation" style, which let the year begin on 25 March, took two forms. The first begins its count nine months before Christmas; the second begins on 25 March after Christmas. The style's origins are not quite clear. There is a ninth-century example of its use in Arles. It may have spread from Burgundy to northern Italy in the early tenth century, after Hugh of Arles had become king of Lombardy. The version of the style that begins its count before the birth of Christ appeared in papal records in the first half of the twelfth century but disappeared after that. It is called the Pisan style because of its unusual persistence (into the eighteenth century) in Pisa. The second version of the style, the Florentine, spread in the eleventh century. It appeared sporadically in official French and Italian records during the next two centuries and is associated with the spread of the Cistercian order. It was generally overtaken by the "Circumcision" (1 January) style in French regions, however. It gained widest acceptance in England, where it was apparently promoted by the Normans, and was generally used by the end of the twelfth century. Known as the "Lady Day" style in the British Isles, it continued in use until 1752.

Another Christian style that had some currency was that with Easter as the initial point of the year. There is evidence of such usage in the eighth century among the monks of Jarrow. In general it seems to have been employed only in conjunction with the 25 March style until the thirteenth century. In 1215 the Easter style was mandated in the chancery of Philip Augustus; it remained the French court style for the rest of the century but became confused with the 25 March style in subsequent French records, until 1 January was established in 1564.

Although the church had steadily opposed the use of 1 January as the prevailing style, several factors merged to lead to its eventual dominance over Christmas and 25 March; perhaps chief among these was its use in Roman law. An increasing number of almanacs using 1 January appeared toward the end of the Middle Ages, and the church itself had paved the way toward turning it from a pagan to a Chris-tian day of note by establishing it as the Feast of the Circumcision in the sixth century.

In northern Europe, use of the Roman calendar was less prevalent during the Middle Ages than in other parts of western Europe. At the beginning of the medieval period, northern calendars still showed traces of the ancient Germanic calendar, under which the primary division of the year was into two parts, corresponding to summer and winter. Winter was the dominant form: rather than referring to someone's age or length of service in number of years, the reference was frequently to "number of winters." The year began with the onset of winter. Gradually this division expanded. Three seasons—spring, winter, and summer—are recognized in the accounts by Tacitus of Germanic customs; and at some time, perhaps preceding his, these were expanded to four. Eventually there was further subdivision of the year into months, which were counted from new moon to new moon. At least in early medieval times, the Germanic names of the months reflected natural phenomena and activities associated with them, such as "freezing month," "egg month," "harvest month," and "autumn month." Further subdivisions into fortnights and, somewhat later, into weeks were established before the Christianization of northern Europe. For example, the seven-day week appears to have been introduced in Scandinavian countries as the result of seventh- and eighth-century accounts concerning the Julian calendar.

By the beginning of the Middle Ages, northern calendars indicate efforts to reconcile the length of the lunar year with the seasonal solar year. Bede noted the use by the Anglo-Saxons of a leap month. In the Icelandic calendar each month was subdivided into 30 days, except for the ninth, which had 34 days. This made a year of 364 days, or 52 7-day weeks. This system also used a 28-year cycle.

Divisions of months. Under the Roman system three days in each month served as dating markers. These were the first day of the month, known as the Kalend; the Nones, which fell on the fifth day in January, February, April, June, August, September, November, and December, and on the seventh in March, May, July, and October; and the Ides, which fell on the fifteenth day in March, May, July, and October, and on the thirteenth in January, February, April, June, August, September, November, and December. Days were designated according to the count by which they preceded the nearest marker. Thus 9 November was the fifth Ide of November or the fifth day before the Ides of November, and 24 February was the sixth Kalend of March, the "sextile" (for that reason leap years were called bissextiles).

The traditional Roman manner of specifying the days of the month prevailed in official documents of western Europe until about 1300. There are, however, French documents of the sixteenth century that still use it, while it disappeared from some German regions as early as the twelfth century.

Generally, throughout Europe the chief alternative to the Roman method of dating was that of numbering the days of the month in consecutive order. In many regions the two methods supplanted one another with changes in administration. Consecutive numbering came to predominate by the fifteenth century.

Official dating methods less widespread than the preceding two included the *Consuetudo Bononiensis* and the *Cisiojanus*.

Under the *Consuetudo Bononiensis* each month is divided into two parts. The first, *mensis intrans,* includes the first sixteen days for months of thirty-one days, and the first fifteen for those of thirty days, and the first fourteen and fifteen days of February in an ordinary year and a leap year, respectively. These days are designated by a simple forward count: 1, 2, 3, . . . 14, 15, or 16. In the second part of the month, *mensis exiens,* days are counted in reverse order. Thus, 25 September would be *dies vi. exeunte mensis.* The next-to-last day of the month was called *penultimus dies;* the last, *ultimus.* This dating method was used primarily in Italy. It first appeared in northern Italy—there are documents dating from the eighth–tenth centuries in that region; there are also examples of its use in France and, between the twelfth and fifteenth centuries, in German lands.

Another dating method primarily of regional interest is the *Cisiojanus,* which was a mnemonic device. For each month there were two-line verses having as many syllables as there are days in the corresponding month. It derived its name from the verse commonly used for January:

> Cisio Janus Epi sibi vendicat Oc Feli Mar An
> Prisca Fab Ag Vincen Ti Pau Po nobile lumen.

Here *ci* refers to the first, *sio* to the second, and *ja* to the third of January. Occasionally the syllables were abbreviations for names assigned to the days, as in one verse for January that begins *cir ste jog.* . . . Here the syllables are the initial syllables of the feasts and saints' days corresponding to the days of the

month: specifically, *cir* is short for *circumcisio domini, ste* stands for Stephanus, and *jog* for Johann-Genovefa. There were numerous variants of the *Cisiojanus.* Besides the Latin versions there are examples of French and German verses. *Cisiojanus* was most prevalent in central Europe: Poland, Bohemia, Silesia, and Prussia. It occurred elsewhere, however; for example, the verse fragment above is taken from a manuscript of a thirteenth-century Cistercian abbey in Alsace.

Whereas the preceding dating techniques were used for official documents, everyday usage was based most often on the seven-day week and on the names of feast days, the number of which grew substantially during the Middle Ages. Traditional Christian feast days at the beginning of the Middle Ages included fixed days such as Sunday, Epiphany, and Christmas, and movable feasts such as Easter, Pentecost, and Ascension Day. Despite the growing number of saints' days, these major feast days were those primarily used for dating purposes. Thus the six Sundays of Lent, the six Sundays between Easter and Pentecost, and the Sundays following Pentecost served as special markers in diocesan calendars, particularly in the later Middle Ages.

A seven-day week was in use throughout the Latin West. The chief differences concerning the week pertain to the naming of the days and the beginning of the seven-day cycle. The Roman calendar inherited in the Latin West used the planetary names for the days of the week: *dies Saturni, dies soli, dies lunae, dies Martis, dies Mercurii, dies Jovis, dies Veneris.* Under pressure from the church, the first two names were replaced by the Sabbath *(sabbata)* and the Lord's day *(domenicus). Domenicus* became the first day of the week in the Christian calendar.

Feast days. In popular usage days were frequently established by combining the name of the weekday with the name of the feast or saint associated with that day. Certain saints' days were established by the fourth century; a calendar of 448 lists Christian feast days. One of the first major calendars listing a substantial number of saints' and feast days is that of Charlemagne.

During the first several centuries of its celebration, the date of Easter created considerable discussion and uncertainty among Christians. The resulting differences in the celebration of Easter caused concern for the church; various councils stressed the need for celebrating Easter on the same day in all Christian communities. Among various efforts to establish the date of Easter, it was the rule developed

21

by Dionysius Exiguus that eventually gained widespread acceptance.

According to Dionysius, Easter is to be celebrated on the first Sunday after the full moon following the vernal equinox. If that full moon fell on a Sunday, Easter was to be celebrated on the following Sunday. The vernal equinox was assumed to fall on 21 March. The time of full moon was computed by using a 19-year cycle, based on the ancient observation that 19 tropical solar years are approximately equal to 235 (synodic) lunar months, so that a full moon occurs on approximately the same day of the month every 19 years. Since the length of the Julian year was 365 days and 6 hours, the total cycle had a length of 6,939 days, 18 hours. The lunar months consisted of 29 and 30 days alternately, and contained 7 years having a 30-day leap month (*mensis embolismalis*).

Since these made for a lunar cycle of 6,940 days, 18 hours—a day more than 19 Julian years—one day in each cycle was omitted. The point at which this occurred was usually referred to as the "lunar jump"

(*saltus lunae*). Whereas the leap months were inserted at fixed points in the cycle—the third, sixth, eighth, eleventh, fourteenth, seventeenth, and nineteenth years within the cycle—there was no uniform rule establishing the point at which the "lunar jump" was to occur; it was most commonly taken from the last year in the cycle. The determination of a year within the cycle was given by the "golden number" (*numerus aureus*). In the early years there were competing Easter cycles. Notable among these was the eighty-four-year cycle of the Roman church, which for approximately two centuries was used in contrast with the nineteen-year cycle adopted by the Alexandrian church. The latter was generally adopted after the sixth century.

Calendar reform. The discrepancies between the computed dates of the Easter moon and the actual full moon were recognized throughout the Middle Ages. Early in the period the reason was not generally understood, although the phenomenon of precession had been noted by Hipparchus and discussed by Ptolemy, who used Hipparchus' figures. As time

Calendar for September with occupation of the month on one page, and sign of zodiac on opposite page. From Jean Pucelle, *Hours of Jeanne d'Evreaux*, 1325–1328. THE METROPOLITAN MUSEUM OF ART, CLOISTERS COLLECTION, 1954

passed, the discrepancies became larger and knowledge of the astronomical phenomena underlying the problem became more widespread.

In the thirteenth century Roger Bacon examined the problem and suggested that Pope Clement IV institute a reform of the calendar. Bacon recommended calling upon astronomers to aid in this endeavor and replacing the nineteen-year cycle with the thirty-year cycle of the Islamic world. Clement IV took no such action.

In the following century Pope Clement VI solicited a study of calendar improvements. The resulting tract, by the Parisian mathematicians Jehan des Murs and Firmin de Belleval, appeared after Clement's death in 1352. They recommended setting the equinox at 21 March and decreeing the omission, in a year to be specified, of a number of days equal to the number by which the equinoctial points had been moved from the originally assigned date. Alternatively this omission could be accomplished by skipping the extra day in as many forthcoming leap years. They were highly critical of the use of the nineteen-year cycle, proposing four alternatives, one of which was use of the Alfonsine Tables to compute mean motions and attaching the resulting table to subsequent calendars.

The Alfonsine Tables, created at the court of Alfonso X and based on Arabic sources, were issued in Spanish at Toledo between 1263 and 1272. A Latin revised version was prepared at Paris in the 1320's. They gave the length of the tropical year as 365 days, 5 hours, 49 minutes, 24 seconds.

Another tract that gained some attention by being presented at two church councils of the early fifteenth century was that of Pierre d'Ailly. He noted that the Alfonsine value of the tropical year still led to a discrepancy of 1 day in 134 years, and that the lunar calendar led to an "anticipation" of 1 day in 304 years. He recommended leaving the equinoxes on the date they fell at the time and keeping them from sliding further back by omitting the extra day of leap years as necessary either after 134 years, resulting in correction of the solar year, or after 304 years, resulting in correction of the lunar cycle. He also recommended giving up the cycle—urging, however, that if it were to be retained, the golden number should be corrected in 1473, when it differed by exactly five days. His preferred solution was that of Roger Bacon: to give up the nineteen-year cycle, replacing it with the Arabic thirty-year period.

Despite efforts such as these, reform proposals gained ground rather slowly. Thus the Council of Basel, after discussions concerning calendar reform in the 1430's, formulated a planned decree that was never carried out because of fear of new schisms in the church. It included provisions for setting Easter as the first Sunday after the equinoctial full moon by omitting seven days in 1440, reducing the lunar cycle by 3 days, and subsequently omitting a leap day every 300 years. This council's efforts concerning calendar reform are remembered particularly because of the participation by Nicholas of Cusa. Yet another century was to pass before a major reform was formalized by Pope Gregory XIII in 1582.

Determination of days of the week. To determine the weekday on which a given date falls, use was made of the concepts of the "solar cycle" and the "dominical letter." The solar cycle was a twenty-eight-year cycle. Its length was based on the fact that it takes twenty-eight years for a given day of the year to fall twice on the same weekday. The epoch of the solar cycle was 9 B.C. Thus, in order to compute the cycle for a given year, it is necessary only to add 9 to the number of the year and divide the result by 28. The remainder gives the number of the cycle; if the remainder is zero, the number is taken to be 28. To determine the dominical letter of a year, one assigns the letters A–G to the days of the year, starting with 1 January. These are called the *litterae calendarum*. The letter that falls on the first Sunday after the New Year is the "dominical letter" for that year.

Divisions of the day. During early medieval times there were three major ways of dividing the day: by shadow measurement, by unequal hours, and by equal hours. Measurement by shadow length was inherited from classical antiquity; numerous medieval calendrical manuscripts contain tables or "calendars" listing shadow lengths for different hours in each month of the year. The tables tended to take the following form:

	Ian. / Dec.	Feb. / Nov.	Mar. / Oct.	Apr. / Sep.	Mai. / Aug.	Iun. / Iul.
1 and 11	$x+14k$	$x+13k$	$x+12k$	$x+11k$	$x+10k$	$x+9k$
2 and 10	$x+9k$	$x+8k$	$x+7k$	$x+6k$	$x+5k$	$x+4k$
3 and 9	$x+8k$	$x+7k$	$x+6k$	$x+5k$	$x+4k$	$x+3k$
4 and 8	$x+7k$	$x+6k$	$x+5k$	$x+4k$	$x+3k$	$x+2k$
5 and 7	$x+6k$	$x+5k$	$x+4k$	$x+3k$	$x+2k$	$x+k$
6	$x+5k$	$x+4k$	$x+3k$	$x+2k$	$x+k$	x

The size of x and k varied with latitude and, on a more subjective level, from calendarmaker to calendarmaker.

The major official form of dividing the day made use of the unequal hours. It, too, was derived from earlier Greek and Roman time-reckoning procedures. Each day and night was divided into twelve equal parts; this caused summer daylight hours to be longer than winter daylight hours. Under the original Roman terminology, *hora prima* referred to the hour at sunrise, *hora tertia* to midmorning, *hora sexta* to the noon hour, and so on. In addition, informal designations for various parts of the day existed, some of which preceded establishment of the numbered hours, some of which were added subsequently. Among these terms were *ante lucem* or *matutina* for the predawn period, *mane* for early morning, *ad meridiem* for morning, *meridies* for noon, *de meridie* for early afternoon, *vespera* for the onset of twilight, *crepusculum* for twilight, *media nox* for midnight, and *gallicinum* for the time of the cock's crow.

Since the Christian church specified the time for certain prayers, some of these hours took on special importance in the Latin West. The times associated with mandatory prayer came to be known as the canonical hours; they varied in number and period over the years. By the sixth century it was common to distinguish seven: *matutina, hora prima, hora tertia, hora sexta, hora nona, vespera,* and *completorium*. Initially their meanings coincided with those of the original Roman terms; as time passed, however, their prayer function came to take precedence. For example, the *hora nona* initially referred to the midafternoon hour—the ninth hour after sunrise, designating the time three-quarters of the way between sunrise and sunset. Since St. Benedict in the sixth century had established the *hora nona* as mealtime, this led to abolition of the *hora sexta* as a canonical hour and caused the *hora nona* to become midday, or noon. While the canonical hours dominated the division of the day in the Latin West, many regional variations governing further subdivisions or additional hours carried special secular significance. Examples of these are market hours, curfew hours, and the simple divisions of morning and afternoon customary in France.

Until about the fourteenth century, equal hours were used almost exclusively by astronomers, as they had been since antiquity. (As we shall see in the discussion on timekeeping devices below, their introduction into everyday life was closely tied to the spreading use of mechanical timekeepers.) The division of the day into equal hours took two forms: in one the day was divided into twenty-four hours counted continuously; in the other it was grouped into two sets of twelve hours each. There were two primary versions of the twenty-four-hour day. The Italian or Bohemian hours began half an hour after sunset; the astronomical hours began at midnight. It should be noted, however, that Italian clocks struck twelve hours twice. They were adjusted whenever the change in the hour of sunset amounted to fifteen minutes from the last setting. The double-twelve-hour day took noon and midnight as the starting points of the hours' count. With the exceptions noted, the twenty-four-hour day prevailed in Italy; the double-twelve-hour day, in the rest of western Europe.

A variant of the twenty-four-hour day, constituting a transitional form from the unequal hours, was the Nuremberg hours, which also was used in several nearby towns, beginning in the fourteenth century. Here daytime hours could vary from eight to sixteen in number. Sunrise and sunset were marked by the ringing of a bell (the *Garaus*), and hours were counted with respect to this. Beginning of day and night varied from 4 to 8 o'clock, changing at half-hour intervals approximately every twenty-four or twenty-five days.

Divisions of the hour. Most medieval subdivisions of the hour did not go beyond the half or quarter hour. The chief exception to this is found in traditional scientific usage with its division of the hour into sixty minutes and, less frequently, of the minute into sixty seconds, or even the second into sixty "thirds" *(tertia)*. Other subdivisions found among ecclesiastical authors were the point *(punctum)*, moment *(momentum)*, ounce *(uncia)*, and atom *(atomus)*. Their definitions varied; the "point" most commonly represented a quarter hour; the other units were usually defined in terms of further decimal or duodecimal divisions.

The Jewish calendar used in the Middle Ages was the result of a reform that took place in the second and third centuries and is associated with the fourth-century nasi, Hillel II. It utilizes a lunisolar year of 354 days, divided into months of 29 or 30 days. A day consists of 24 hours, each of which is divided into 1,080 *ḥalakim;* each of these, in turn, is divided into 76 *regaim*.

Eras. Although several other eras were used in earlier times, Hillel II introduced the world era, the epoch of which falls on 7 October 3761 B.C. (in

Christian terms). More precisely, it begins on the morning of 7 October, at 5 hours, 204 *halakim,* which corresponds to 11.33 minutes past 11 P.M. of 6 October according to the Christian calendar.

The use of Hillel's world era spread gradually during the Middle Ages, although it did not become the exclusively used era until after 1500. Its chief competitors in earlier centuries were the era of Adam, beginning on 1 Tishri 3760 B.C., and the Seleucid era, beginning in 312 B.C.

Divisions of the year. The reformed calendar is based on a lunisolar year consisting of twelve lunar months. Since the mean length of the synodic month is 29 days, 12 hours, and 793 *halakim* (29 days, 12 hours, 44 minutes, 3.33 seconds), the months are alternately assigned lengths of 29 and 30 days. The names of the months are Tishri, Marheshvan, Kislev, Tebet, Shebat (Sebat), Adar, Nisan, Iyar, Sivan, Tammuz, Ab, and Elul. Tishri has 30 days, Marheshvan and Kislev either 29 or 30, Tebet 29, Shebat 30, Adar 29, Nisan 30, Iyar 29, Sivan 30, Tamuz 29, Ab 30, and Elul 29. In a common regular year the total is 354 days. The first day of the month is *Rosh Ḥodesh,* the day of the new moon. For months having thirty days the same name is given to the thirtieth day.

The reformed calendar utilizes the traditional approximation that sets 19 solar years equal to 235 lunar months. Since the mean lunar year is 10 days, 21 hours, and 204 *halakim* shorter than the Julian year, 7 months are intercalated in a period of 19 years. Considering the 19-year period as one cycle, the intercalations take place in the 3rd, 6th, 8th, 11th, 14th, 17th, and 19th years. This rule is known as *Guḥadset;* the name is an anagram derived from the fact that the Hebrew letters corresponding to this term are those representing the numbers 3 (*gimmel*), 6 (*waw*), 8 (*ḥet*), 11 (*alef*), 14 (*dalet*), 17 (*zayin*), and 19 (*tet*). It should be noted that in the early Middle Ages there was a variation to this rule. Al-Bīrūnī lists the fifth instead of the sixth, and the sixteenth instead of the seventeenth, as leap years in the nineteen-year cycle. It has been suggested that the reason for this divergence from the later, generally accepted rule lies in the fact that Hillel II's reform was not adopted until the sixth century A.D. by Jews living in areas such as Syria.

Thirty days are added to each leap year. To accomplish this, an extra month is inserted between Adar and Nisan. This results in a month called First Adar, having twenty-nine days, and a month called Second Adar, or Weadar, having thirty days. The month following Second Adar is Nisan with its usual thirty days.

Although in earlier antiquity Nisan was the first month of the year, since the time of the Babylonian exile the Jewish civil year has begun near the autumnal equinox. Hence, Tishri was the first month of the year in the Middle Ages, as it is now.

The week consists of seven days, which are assigned numbers rather than names—only the seventh day is given the name of Sabbath. Specific Sabbaths are frequently referred to by the name designating the section of the Torah that is read on that particular day. The sixth day of the week is occasionally called *ereb shabbat,* the day preceding the Sabbath. The week begins at 6 P.M. on Sabbath eve; the twenty-four-hour day begins at 6 P.M.

The determination of the day of the week for a specific date is undertaken by means of the *molad* (birth) computations. To compute the day for a *molad,* the conjunction of sun and moon, one uses as epoch the Molad-Tishri of the first year of the Jewish era; this is taken to be the second day at 5 hours, 204 *halakim,* or Monday evening at 11.33 minutes past 11 P.M., of 3761 B.C. This is known as the *molad Beharad.* Several residues are obtained by dividing calendrical units by the number of weeks they contain: one computes the "character" of a month by subtracting the number of full weeks from the mean length of the month; this results in 1 day, 12 hours, 793 *halakim.* The character of a year is obtained by subtracting 50 weeks from 12 mean lunar months, giving 4 days, 8 hours, and 876 *halakim.* The character of a leap year is obtained by subtracting 54 weeks from 13 mean lunar months, giving 5 days, 21 hours, and 589 *halakim.* The character of a 19-year cycle is obtained by noting that the remainder of dividing 6,939 days, 16 hours, and 595 *halakim* (235 × 29 days, 12 hours, and 797 *halakim*) by 7 is 2 days, 16 hours, and 595 *halakim.*

It is now possible to determine the day of the week for a given date by successive divisions and use of residues. There are, however, five special cases governing computation for the date of the New Year, the first conjunction of sun and moon (*molad tishri*), that must be taken into account. These exceptional cases, known as *deḥiyyot,* are the following:

If *molad tishri* takes place at 18 hours (noon by Christian reckoning) or later in the day, the New Year starts the next day. This exceptional case is called *molad yaḥ* or *molad saken.*

25

Hebrew calendar, after 1540. THE JEWISH THEOLOGICAL SEMINARY

If *molad tishri* falls on the first, fourth, or sixth day, then New Year starts on the following day. In other words, New Year cannot fall on Sunday, Wednesday, or Friday. This case is known as *molad adu*.

If both of the preceding occur—if moving the New Year because it begins after 18 hours causes it to fall on a Sunday, Wednesday, or Friday—then New Year's Day is moved an additional day. This case is known as *molad yaḥ-adu*.

If in a regular year following another regular year *molad tishri* falls on a Tuesday at or after 9 hours, 204 ḥalakim (3 hours, 11.33 minutes), the New Year falls on the following Thursday.

If in a regular year following a leap year *molad tishri* falls on a Monday at 15 hours, 589 ḥalakim (9 hours, 32.72 minutes), then New Year falls on Tuesday. This is known as *molad betuthakpat*.

Since these exceptional cases bring about a change in the beginning of the New Year that adds a day to certain years but subtracts it from the following, regular years may vary in length from 353 to 355 days; the 353-day-year is called "defective"; the 355-day-year, "perfect." Similarly, leap years may be "defective" and consist of 383 days, or "perfect" and consist of 385 days. The necessary adjustments are made by changing the length of the months Marheshvan and Kislev. In a regular year Marheshvan has twenty-nine days and Kislev has thirty. In deficient years both months have twenty-nine days; in "perfect" years both have thirty.

These five cases, although appearing somewhat complicated, are rather straightforward results of adjusting the calendar to retain certain customs. The first ensures keeping the beginning of the month close to the first observation of the new moon's crescent. The second ensures that preparation for the High Holy Days of Rosh Hashanah (1 Tishri), the Jewish New Year, and Yom Kippur (10 Tishri) will not fall on a Sabbath. The third case involves a combination of the preceding two. The fourth avoids having to postpone the New Year according to the preceding case, which would result in a year of 356 days. The final, rather rare case similarly avoids obtaining a leap year of 382 days.

The computation of the beginnings of the seasons is known as *tekufot*. Four seasons are recognized, of which spring is associated with the month of Nisan, summer with Tammuz, fall with Tishri, and winter with Tebet. There are two modes of computing *tekufot*: one, devised by the third-century Rabbi Samuel, is based on the Julian year; the other, traditionally attributed to Samuel's contemporary, Rabbi Adda bar Ahaba, although probably of a later period, is based on the tropical year. To determine the *tekufa* according to Samuel, the solar year of 365 days, 6 hours is divided into four equal parts; this gives *tekufa* of 91 days, 7.5 hours. To determine *tekufa* according to the other method, the year having 365 days, 5 hours, 997 *halakim*, and 48 *regaim* is divided by 4, giving *tekufa* of 91 days, 7 hours, 519 *halakim*, and 31 *regaim*.

Feast days. Aside from Rosh Hashanah and Yom Kippur, the chief Jewish feast days and fast days observed in the Middle Ages were Sukkot, lasting from 15 to 22 Tishri, with 15, 16, and 22 Tishri as holidays; Simhat Torah on 23 Tishri; Passover, lasting from 15 to 22 Nisan, with 15, 16, 21, and 22 Nisan as holidays; and Shavuot on 6 and 7 Sivan. Other celebrations included Hoshana Rabba (21 Tishri); Hanukkah (eight days starting 25 Kislev); Tu B'Shevat (15 Shebat); Purim (14, or 14 and 15, Adar); and Lag B'Omer (18 Iyar).

THE ISLAMIC CALENDAR

The Islamic calendar, established by Muḥammad and in effect from A.H. 10, is based on a pure lunar year having 354 or 355 days that is divided into twelve months: Muharram, Safar, First Rabia, Second Rabia, First Jumada, Second Jumada, Rajab, Shaban, Ramadan, Shawwal, Dhu-l-Qada, and Dhu-l-Hijja. These months are alternately thirty and twenty-nine days long, Muharram having thirty days. Dhu-l-Hijja may have either twenty-nine or thirty days.

Eras. The Islamic era has the hegira as its epoch—more precisely, 1 Muharram of the year of the hegira. This began at sunset on Wednesday, 14 July 622 (by Christian reckoning). It was traditionally set at Thursday, 15 July 622, and many inscriptions use 15 July as the beginning of the era. However, it became customary to start counting the era at sunset of Thursday, 15 July, so that the epoch came to be Friday, 16 July. This is the date used in most tables for conversion between the Islamic and Christian calendars. The era appears to have been introduced as official under Caliph ᶜUmar I, although there is some uncertainty as to the precise year of its first use. In particular, it is unclear to what extent Muḥammad used it himself. It appears to have become official between A.H. 16 and 18 (A.D. 637 and 639). An extant coin, minted at Damascus in 638, is marked with the year 17. It should be noted that the era is variously referred to as the "Arabic" or the "Saracen" era.

Other eras used in Islamic calendars along with that of the hegira were those of the Roman indiction and the Diocletian era.

Divisions of the year, months, days, and hours. The week had seven days and began on Sunday. The days were assigned numbers in Arabic, and names in Turkish, Hindu, and other languages used in Islam. The day was divided into twenty-four hours. Initially these were temporal—unequal—hours, twelve falling during the period of daylight, twelve during nighttime. They were eventually replaced by the equal hours of the astronomer, as they were in the Latin West. The day began at sunset.

Five prayer hours had special designations; they fell at daybreak, noon, in midafternoon, at dusk, and after it has become dark.

Feast days. The major feast days of Islam fall on the first three days of Shawwal and on the tenth through thirteenth days of Dhu-l-Hijja. The first of these marks the end of Ramadan, the month of fasting. The second marks the end of the hajj, the pilgrimage to Mecca, which should be undertaken on 10–12 Dhu-l-Hijja. These two holiday periods are known as the large and the small Bairam, respectively.

Other Islamic feast days of special note in medieval times include the first ten days of Muharram, devoted to celebration of the New Year (especially 10 Muharram, called Yom Ashoora); 12 and 13 First Rabia, commemorating the birth and death, respectively, of Muḥammad; 26 (or 29) Rajab, marking the ascension of Muḥammad; and 5 Dhu-l-Hijja, the sending of the Kaaba.

AIDS TO RECORDING AND COMPUTING TIME

Aids to reckoning time in the Middle Ages consisted of written forms, such as tables and calendars, and other devices, such as sundials, astrolabes, and various types of clocks. Among the written forms the most prevalent were Easter tables, designed to indicate the date of movable feasts, and the computi, which led to the later forms of calendars and almanacs.

Among traditional time-recording devices in the early Middle Ages were sundials; water, sand, and oil clocks; and candles. Of these, sundials became the most diversified and complex. Water clocks were the most elaborate aids to time keeping during the early Middle Ages, and for that reason their ownership was a sign of prestige.

Water clocks. Water clocks of antiquity had reached a sufficient degree of sophistication by the time of Vitruvius to permit their use in marking both the equal and the unequal hours. Extant bowls from ancient Egypt usable for measuring equal time periods are estimated to represent the state of the art about 1400 B.C. Vitruvius reports on the improvements attributed to Ctesibius: obtaining constant flow by using an overflow pipe to ensure a constant head, using a nonerosive material around the drain hole, and measuring the water flowing out of the jar, usually by having it flow into a container, such as a cylinder, that allows measurement of the amount received by simply noting the height. This provided the basic means of operating the reliable time-measuring devices still used in the Middle Ages.

In order to make these devices usable for unequal hours, the scales marking the height of the water column were suitably modified. One method, also going back to Vitruvius' account of Ctesibius' improvements, was that of the parastatic clock. This involved placing the hour marks on a cylinder, the *parastatica;* to reflect the change in the hour length during different parts of the year, these marks took the form of curved hour lines, each of which represented a specific hour. The lines were arranged so that the hours of a given day in the year were aligned vertically. This allowed their being "read" either by noting when the water level reached the hour points along that vertical or, on more elegant devices, by placing a pointer on a float and noting when it reached the hour points in question.

More elaborate water clocks were combined with automata; for instance, a different door opened at each hour on a sixth-century Italian clock that featured a light source on the pointer at night; various figures moved and Hercules appeared under an eagle that crowned him with a laurel wreath. A similarly extravagant clock was presented to Charlemagne from the realm of Hārūn al-Rashīd in 807. Water clocks made in Islamic regions showed the same variety as the clocks known since antiquity. There are tenth-century accounts of relatively simple clocks that denoted only the hours for prayer. Thirteenth-century accounts describe clocks for noting both equal and unequal hours, as well as clocks with automata that provided action on the half hour and the full hour. Still other water clocks denoted not only hours but also astronomical phenomena, such as the motion of the planets.

Sundials. Whereas medieval water clocks maintained and elaborated upon rather elegant concepts inherited from antiquity, the far more numerous early medieval sundials were considerably more primitive than their ancient predecessors. The simplest form, found on churches of the Latin West, consisted of a semicircle on the south wall of the building with equidistant hour lines and a gnomon extending at a right angle to the wall. The earliest extant Anglo-Saxon dials, such as one found on a seventh-century stone in Bewcastle, have only four divisions: for 3, 6, 9, and 12 o'clock. Another form of which numerous examples are extant is the south dial with eight divisions; an early example at Fulda dates from the ninth century. Most of the later medieval south dials had twelve divisions. Although these dials were common until the fourteenth century, other, more accurate devices were in use for time reckoning by then.

Numerous varieties of sundials were in use by the fourteenth century. In many cases their underlying theory had been established for centuries. In the ninth century Thābit ibn Qurra taught design of sundials on an arbitrary plane with the gnomon perpendicular to that plane. The old-style quadrant was known by the end of the same century. Hermann of Reichenau is credited with the invention of the cylinder dial in the eleventh century, at the end of which the "Bamberg-style" portable vertical dial appeared. The new-style quadrant became known in the thirteenth century. There are fourteenth-century examples of south dials with horizontal and with equatorial gnomon, and of the "ship of Venice." By the end of the fifteenth century there were orientable (compass) dials, declining dials, equatorial dials, block dials, ring dials, chalice dials, diptych dials, and compendia. The writings of Regiomontanus in the second half of that century laid a particularly important foundation for the work of the better-known dialists of succeeding centuries.

Bells. In the early seventh century Pope Sabinianus decreed that the canonical hours be made public by bell ringing. For centuries this was the primary public means of recording the hours. Bells were used not only to announce the times of prayer but also to mark the beginning or end of such activities as work, public entertainment, market, and official meetings.

Astrolabes. A device of particular importance for timekeeping in the Islamic world was the astrolabe. A complex instrument designed to measure the altitude and relative angular positions of celestial bodies, an astrolabe consists of several parts. Attached to the top of the circular body is a suspensory device, usually consisting of a triangular "throne" with a handle, attached at the top vertex, through which a ring passes at right angles, thereby allowing the astrolabe to move without constraint when suspended by a cord passing through the ring. The front of the body consists of a central surface, the "mother," and a protruding outer rim. In Islamic astrolabes a set of disks lies within the rim; usually with one exception, each of these represents a stereographic projection of the heavens for a specified latitude. A small protrusion on each disk fits into a hole at the side of the body to keep the disks from rotating; occasionally hole and protrusion are reversed. An alidade rests on the back of the body; a cut-out stereographic projection of certain fixed stars, known as the rete (or "spider" or "net"), lies on the front. These two components rotate. The body, alidade, rete, and each disk have a hole in the center; this allows the passage through them of a pin that is attached to a wedge and keeps all components together.

The hole in the center represents the celestial pole; turning the rete or disks thus corresponds to the apparent motion of the stars about the pole. In addition to the projections of certain fixed stars, the rete contains a circle representing the ecliptic, and segments of circles representing the Tropic of Cancer, the Tropic of Capricorn, and the celestial equator. Among the curves drawn on the disks are a line representing the user's horizon, concentric circles representing the Tropics of Cancer and Capricorn and the celestial equator, circles of constant altitude known as almucantars, and lines of equal or unequal hours. To tell time, the altitude of the sun is measured. Then the rete is set so that the degree of the ecliptic for the current day coincides with the almucantar of that altitude. The time is then read by noting where the nadir point intersects the equal or unequal hour line.

Although dating from antiquity, and in widespread use in Islam throughout the medieval period, the astrolabe did not come to be generally known in the Latin West until after 1200. Numerous early Arabic treatises exist, some dating from the ninth century; the eleventh-century scholarly Western treatment by Hermann of Reichenau added to that author's fame. Yet it is probably Geoffrey Chaucer's treatise on the astrolabe, written in the English vernacular, that marks the period of popular adoption of this device in western Europe.

Clocks. The earliest known records describing weight-driven clocks date from the thirteenth century. The 1271 course of lectures by Robertus Angli-

cus on the *Sphere* of Sacrobosco provides evidence of efforts to construct weight-driven clocks. By the 1280's monumental weight-driven clocks could be found in English cathedrals. Exeter Cathedral had a clock in 1284; St. Paul's in London is said to have had one in 1286; Canterbury Cathedral had one by 1291. An astronomical clock was designed by Richard of Wallingford, abbot of St. Albans, prior to 1330. The use of clocks spread early in the fourteenth century; records of that period allude to clocks in Paris, Rouen, Nevers, Caen, Avignon, Milan, and Modena. Although it is not known exactly when the first escapement was invented, it is assumed that clocks with verge escapement existed before 1300.

While the clocks mentioned above tended to be monastic clocks, designed to enable a sexton to round up the worshipers for prayer, in the early half of the fourteenth century public clocks appeared in Italy. Some of these had astronomical faces as well as regular hour dials. In 1344 the Palazzo del Capitano in Padua was enriched with a public astronomical clock showing the course of sun and moon along with the hours. It was built by Jacopo de'Dondi, whose son, Giovanni, completed an astronomical clock in 1364. Among other early public clocks are those of Milan (1336), Bruges (1345), Strasbourg (1352, 1354), Genoa (1353), and Bologna (1356). Other fourteenth-century clocks are known in Regensburg, Brussels, Freiburg im Breisgau, Wrocław, Zurich, Mainz, and Paris. The earliest extant mechanical clocks are those at Salisbury and Rouen; the latter struck the quarter hour. Public striking clocks are credited with helping to spread the use of equal hours.

By the fifteenth century smaller weight-driven clocks began to be found in homes. Late in the fifteenth century portable sundials also appeared. The notion of replacing weights by a spring drive also dates to the fifteenth century. This became practicable with the invention of the fusee, which appears to have occurred by 1450. The earliest extant example of a fusee clock is the "Burgundian" table clock in the Germanisches Nationalmuseum in Nürnberg; constructed for Philip the Good of Burgundy, it dates from about 1430.

BIBLIOGRAPHY

General. Joachim W. Ekrutt, *Der Kalender im Wandel der Zeiten* (1972); J. K. Fotheringham, "The Calendar," in *Nautical Almanac for 1929* (1931); Friedrich Karl Ginzel, *Handbuch der mathematischen und technologischen*

Chronologie, I–III (1906–1914), a standard reference that should be consulted for source material published prior to 1910; Wilhelm Kubitschek, *Grundriss der antiken Zeitrechnung* (1928); Paul Victor Neugebauer, *Astronomische Chronologie,* 2 vols. (1929); William M. O'Neil, *Time and the Calendars* (1975); Alexander Philip, *The Calendar: Its History, Structure, and Improvement* (1921); Broughton Richmond, *Time Measurement and Calendar Construction* (1956); Philip W. Wilson, *The Romance of the Calendar* (1937); Ernst Zinner, "Kalender," in Paul Merker and Wolfgang Stammler, eds., *Reallexikon der deutschen Literaturgeschichte,* 2nd ed., I (1958).

Christian calendar. P. Aufgebauer, "Die Gregorianische Kalenderreform im Urteil zeitgenössischer Astronomen," in *Die Sterne,* 45 (1969); Adolphe-F. Chauve-Bertrand, "Le debut de l'année à travers les siècles et chez divers peuples," in *Annales françaises de chronométrie,* 27 (1957); Robert Fruin, *Handboek der Chronologie, voornamelijk van Nederland* (1934); Hermann Grotefend, *Taschenbuch der Zeitrechnung des deutschen Mittelalters und der Neuzeit,* 10th enl. ed., Theodor Ulrich, ed. (1960); Kenneth Harrison, "The Primitive Anglo-Saxon Calendar," in *Antiquity,* 47 (1973); Cyril Hart, "The Ramsey Computus," in *English Historical Review,* 85 (1970); Henry R. Huttenbach, "Muscovy's Calendar Controversy of 1491–1492," in *Science and History. Studies in Honor of Edward Rosen* (1978); Charles W. Jones, ed., *Bedae opera de temporibus* (1943); Bruno Krusch, *Studien zur christlich-mittelalterlichen Chronologie. Die Entstehung unserer heutigen Zeitrechnung. I. Victorius. . . .* (1938); Polska Akademia Nauk, Instytut Historii, *Chronologia polska,* Bronisław Włodarski, ed. (1957); Reginald L. Poole, *Studies in Chronology and History* (1934); August Strobel, *Ursprung und Geschichte des frühchristlichen Osterkalenders* (1977); A. Van de Vyver, "Hucbold et le nombre d'or," in *Mélanges Auguste Pelzer* (1947); Henryk Wasowicz, "Elementy chronologiczne kalendarzy Krakowskich od XIII do połowy XVI wieku," in *Roczniki humanistyczne,* 23, no. 2 (1975); Cérès Wissa Wassef, "Le calendrier copte, de l'antiquité à nos jours," in *Journal of Near Eastern Studies,* 30 (1971); Walter Emile van Wijk, *Le nombre d'or* (1936); and *Origine et développement de la computistique médiévale* (1954).

Jewish calendar. Azriel Eisenberg, *The Story of the Jewish Calendar* (1958); E. S. Kennedy, "Al-Khwārizmi on the Jewish Calendar," in *Scripta mathematica,* 27 (1964); Eduard Mahler, *Handbuch der jüdischen Chronologie* (1916); Moïse Sibony, "Le calendrier juif et ses problèmes," in *Revue des études juives,* 136 (1977).

Islamic calendar. Reinhart Dozy, ed., *Le calendrier de Cordoue,* annotated French trans. by Charles Pellat, new ed. (1961); Adolf Grohmann, Joachim Mayr, and Walter C. Till, *Arabische Chronologie* (1966); Henri Paul Joseph Renaud, *Le calendrier d'Ibn al-Bannâ de Marrakech (1256–1321 J. C.)* (1948).

Aids to reckoning and computing time. Pierre d'Ailly, *Imago mundi,* E. Buron, ed., 3 vols. (1930–1931); Samuel John Crawford, *Byrhtferth's Manual* (A.D. 1011) (1929, repr. 1966); Olga Koseleff, *Die Monatsdarstellungen der französischen Plastik des 12. Jahrhunderts* (1934); Henri Michel, *Traité de l'astrolabe* (1947); Otto Pächt, "Early Italian Nature Studies and the Early Calendar Landscape," in *Journal of the Warburg and Courtauld Institutes,* 13 (1950); Ferdinand Piper, *Karls des Grossen Kalendarium und Ostertafel* (1858, repr. 1974); Joseph Prinz, "Der karolingische Kalender der Handschrift Ambros," in *Festschrift für Hermann Heimpel,* III (1972); Regiomontanus, *Der deutsche Kalender des Johannes Regiomontanus, Nürnberg, um 1474,* with intro. by Ernst Zinner (1937); Reinherus de Paderborn, *Le comput émendé de Reinherus de Paderborn (1171)* (1951); Emil Schnippel, *Die englischen Kalenderstabe* (1926); David Eugene Smith, *Le comput manuel de magister Anianus* (1928); Ernst Zinner, *Deutsche und niederländische astronomische Instrumente des 11.–18. Jahrhunderts* (1956).

UTA C. MERZBACH

[See also **Ailly, Pierre d'**; **Alfonsine Tables**; **Astronomy**; **Canonical Hours**; **Clement VI, Pope**; **Clocks and Reckoning of Time**; **Computus**; **Dionysius Exiguus**; **Feasts and Festivals, Islamic**; **Jehan des Murs.**]

CALENDARS, ARMENIAN. The antiquity of the Armenian calendar is not known; the etymologies of the names of months and days indicate a pre-Christian origin. It was a solar calendar that had twelve months of thirty days' duration and five epagomenal days; it lacked a leap year. As a result, every four years the Armenian year fell short one day and, every 1,460 years, an entire year. The beginning of the Armenian era is traditionally calculated from the year 2492 B.C., the date of the legendary victory of Hayk^c, the eponymous ancestor of the Armenian people, over the Babylonian giant Bel.

Because the New Year's Day changed every four years, such a mobile system could not be used for the liturgical year of the Christian church, which depended on the date of Easter and required a fixed calendar.

For this reason, the Armenians adopted the Era of Andreas of Byzantium, which indicated the paschal cycle for the years 353 to 552. This era, of non-Armenian origin, is considered the successor of the Anatolian and the predecessor of the Proto-Byzantine and the Greater Armenian Era. Our knowledge about it derives mainly from excerpts in Armenian sources. Nevertheless, there are no known instances where the Era of Andreas has been used for dating events. Its major importance lies in its role as the predecessor of the Greater Armenian Era which picks up where the Era of Andreas ends in 552.

The sources testify that the completion in 552 of the 200-year cycle of the Era of Andreas created a great deal of confusion. Errors in the correct calculation of the date of Easter from 552 to 560/561 forced the Armenians to abandon the Era of Andreas and resort to a new system. They adopted the reforms of Aeas, which were presumably proposed in a conference of scientists that met at Alexandria in 562; the date of Easter 552 was set on 25 March. The Armenians also adopted the cycle of 532 years (the number of years in a solar cycle [28] times the number in a lunar cycle [19]). Theoretically, this cycle could be repeated forever; it is still the basis of the Armenian church calendar.

With the newly adopted system began a new era called the Greater Armenian Era; the New Year's Day of its first year fell on 11 July 552. Unlike the paschal cycle of 532 years, which was based on the Julian calendar, the Greater Armenian Era still lacked an intercalary day. Nevertheless, medieval scholars did not have any difficulty in making the correspondence between the mobile Armenian and the fixed Julian years. In the seventh century a serious attempt was made to introduce the concept of the leap year into the Armenian calendar. The astronomer Anania Širakacᶜi made all the necessary calculations, but circumstances did not permit its official adoption.

The leap year was not actually introduced until 1116 by Yovhannēs Sarkawag Vardapet of Ani. The latter made his calculations from the year 1084, which marked the end of the first cycle of 532 years from 552. Yovhannēs set the New Year's Day on 11 August, which according to him marked the legendary beginning date of the mobile Armenian calendrical system. The reformed calendar of Yovhannēs is known as the Lesser Armenian Era, and its first year begins on 11 August 1084. The intercalary day is appended to the end as the sixth epagomenal day. Although frequently used, the Lesser Era was never officially accepted, and the older system prevailed until the eighteenth century. Major reforms other than the ones discussed above were not introduced until the seventeenth and eighteenth centuries.

BIBLIOGRAPHY

H. S. Badalyan, *Hayocᶜ tomari patmutᶜyun* (1976); V. Grumel, *Traité d'études byzantines, I, La chronologie* (1958); B. E. Tᶜumanyan, *Ařjeřn tomaracᶜuycᶜ* (1965); and *Tomari patmutᶜyun* (1972); E. Dulaurier, *Recherches sur la chronologie arménienne, I, Chronologie technique* (1859).

KRIKOR H. MAKSOUDIAN

[See also **Easter**.]

CALILA E DIGNA (*ca.* 1251) is the first vivid and cohesive manifestation of Castilian prose and an important link in the transmission of the *Panchatantra*, a Sanskrit book of fables from about the third century. The Spanish version, commissioned by Alfonso X before he became king, and based on Ibn al-Muqaffaᶜ's *Kalīla wa-Dimna* (the descendant of a Persian translation of the *Panchatantra*), was instrumental in formulating the style and techniques of one of the most prolific literary products of medieval Spain, the collection of tales and exempla presented within a unitary narrative framework.

The title is furnished by two jackals whose story covers almost one-third of the book. The purpose is mainly didactic: to probe and expand human wisdom so that man may lead a prudent life—quite unlike that of the scheming Digna or Dimna, who in his thirst for power causes his own disgrace and death by destroying the friendship of the lion and the bull. Numerous fables and tales—which generate other tales so that certain characters take on the role of narrator—are interwoven in the fabric of Digna's story. At the same time, in accordance with a well-known Oriental narrative technique, Digna's story and the tales embedded in it are contained in an even ampler frame, the dialogue between a king and a philosopher. *Calila*'s interlace technique, which gives a novellalike structure to heterogeneous contents, as well as its verbal spontaneity and stylistic smoothness—so unusual for Spanish prose of the thirteenth century—prepared the rich literary soil in which the *Libro de Patronio*, the *Corbacho*, the episodic picaresque novel, and other genres were to flourish. The Castilian version was translated into Latin in 1313 by Raymond de Béziers, thus ensuring *Calila e Digna* a wide circulation in Europe.

BIBLIOGRAPHY

Editions. Pascual De Gayangos, "Calila e Dymna," in *Escritores en prosa anteriores al siglo XV*, Biblioteca de autores españoles, LI (1860); Clifford G. Allen, *L'ancienne version espagnole de Kalila e Digna* (1906); José Alemany y Bolufer, *La antigua versión castellana del Calila y Dimna, cotejada con el original árabe de la misma* (1915); John E. Keller and Robert W. Linker, *El libro de Calila e Digna* (1967).

Studies. Alvaro Galmés de Fuentes, "Influencias sintácticas y estilísticas del árabe en la prosa medieval castellana," in *Boletín de la Real Academia Española,* 35 (1955), and 36 (1956); María del Pilar Palomo, "De cómo Calila dio exenplo del arte de narrar," in *Prohemio,* 4 (1974).

OLGA TUDORICA IMPEY

[See also **Alfonso X; Muqaffa^c, Ibn al-; Spanish Literature.**]

CALIPHATE (from the Arabic *khilāfa*), the primary institution of rulership in medieval Islam, at the head of which stood the caliph *(khalīfa).* The terms *khilāfa* and *khalīfa* do not in themselves signify any specific form of government but, rather, bear general connotations of appointment, delegation, succession, accession, and authority. The role within Islamic society of the caliphal institution—in its practical functions, powers, and responsibilities—was always subject to evolution, elaboration, and rearticulation. Far from being an immutable institution fixed from earliest Islamic times, the caliphate can be studied and understood only in relation to the historical factors and developments that did so much to shape it.

ORIGINS: THE COMMUNITY AND THE LAW

The institution originated in 632, when Abū Bakr, an eminent and loyal companion of Muḥammad, was elected *khalīfat rasūl Allāh,* "khalīfa of the Apostle of God," after the Prophet's death in Medina. This event was one of the most momentous in Islamic history. Neither the Koran nor the precedent *(sunna)* set by the Prophet's own words, deeds, and tacit approvals had provided for any kind of succession, nor was it acknowledged throughout Arabia that revelation from God could not continue through other religious figures. Thus Muḥammad's death could easily have sparked a movement of defection from Islam to other Arabian personalities (the famous Maslama, for example) advancing claims of special access to the divine. A general reversion to the Arabian tribal order was also conceivable. Indeed, such a resurgence of tribalism did occur in the form of the *ridda,* or "apostasy" of many of the Arabian tribes after Muḥammad's death.

Any such defection would have precluded the continuation of Islam as an integral religious and social system. It was thus by no means inevitable that the transition from prophethood to caliphate should have proceeded with as little disruption and fragmentation as it in fact did, or even that it should have occurred at all. That the Prophet's followers were able to reach agreement on some type of succession, and that they opted for a unified leadership under one of his most trusted associates, marked a decisive victory for the concept of the universal community of believers, or *umma,* reflecting the Muslim consensus that the faith revealed to Muḥammad should continue as a unitary religious system according to which society would continue to be reshaped. And that the Islamic ideal emerged victorious at this critical moment demonstrates the enormous impact of the faith on the nascent community in Medina and Mecca, and reveals much about how the institution of the caliphate was conceived. The community could continue and have meaning after the death of the Prophet, for the head of the *umma* was God, not the person of Muḥammad, whose sole source of prophetic inspiration, and hence of authority, was divine revelation. The goal of the *umma* was thus to adhere to and promote the faith expounded in the Koran and to make divine revelation the basis for all law, government, and personal conduct.

All Islamic conceptions of rulership begin with this concept of the *umma;* the caliphate was its logical consequence. As the law handed down in the Koran was intended to guide the *umma,* there was clearly a need for some form of authority to enforce the law. But in this interplay between ruler and law, the latter was paramount. God, not man, comprises the sole source of law, revealed through the Koran, and exemplified in prophetic *sunna.* The law is therefore of an incomparably higher order than government and is independent of the ruler and his will. Furthermore, government exists not to make law but only to execute and enforce it; rulers do not embody the law as such but in fact are, like other men, subject to its authority.

This conception of law as an overarching divine code also meant that, theoretically, there could be no distinction between its spiritual and temporal domains: social law was an integral element in the fabric of the comprehensive religious law. Extremely high standards were thus set in the field of political institutions. The early *umma* clearly believed that the entire raison d'être of the caliphate should be the protection and promotion of Islam, and that the holder of the office should ensure the comprehensive application and execution of the law, and thereby maintain the spiritual and material integrity of the *umma*. But while recognizing differences among individuals with regard to their proper roles in society, this view at the same time upheld the intrinsic equality and individual accountability of all men before God, and did not concede to the ruler more right or ability than any other Muslim to interpret the law. Thus the caliphate, though expected to uphold and promote the law of the *umma*, lacked any explicit constitutional authority for imposing its will either on individual Muslims (except for clearly specified offenses) or on the community in general.

EMERGENCE OF THE CALIPHAL INSTITUTION

The effort to express these ideals in practical form is a primary theme in the history of the caliphate, which began as a rudimentary governing institution of a conquering military society. The first four caliphs were, in a sense, patriarchal figures; and in the Arabic sources they are known as the *rāshidūn*, "those who follow the right path." But this attitude toward them, which did not gain general acceptance until the eighth century, must not be allowed to obscure the fact that Islam had arisen in a sociopolitical environment which, although dominated by settled folk and centered in the towns, was essentially a tribal order not possessed of stable governing institutions. And since the Koran and *sunna* had provided only general guidelines indicating how the *umma*, and the law established as its code of conduct, should be maintained after Muḥammad's death, it was entirely natural that the caliphate, though inspired and infused by a thoroughly religious ideal of communal leadership, should adopt and absorb much from the tribal ideal of leadership familiar to the Arabs and accepted by them as legitimate.

This interplay is evident from the very first. Abū Bakr was chosen to lead a spiritual community that transcended tribal lines; but the procedure followed—convocation of a council of notables *(majlis)*, followed by a general consensus and confirming oaths of loyalty *(bayᶜa)* from those in attendance—was fully in keeping with prevailing Arabian custom. Similarly, the refusal of many tribes to offer their *bayᶜa* signaled their rejection of both Islam and the Medinan hegemony that it represented. In

the ensuing *ridda* wars, Abū Bakr was a caliph defending the integrity and future of the *umma;* but it is doubtful that he ever formally assumed the title of *khalīfa,* and he surely won as much support and obedience by acting as an archetypal tribal leader or *sayyid*—a "first among equals" who could claim general obedience only by virtue of his role as military commander in a time of crisis. The *umma* expected its first caliph to govern solely on the basis of his personal prestige within the community, as a *sayyid* would; the possibility that the office might develop into a more autocratic institution was never considered. Abū Bakr exercised the authority to dispatch military expeditions, collect taxes, and deal with the tribes on behalf of the *umma*, but he made no effort to extend these powers. A small circle of scribes and advisers assisted him, but there was as yet no real administrative structure. He was the leader of the *umma* in prayer services, but beyond the deference shown to a *sayyid*, no special formalities surrounded the caliph.

Abū Bakr died in 634 after less than two years as caliph, but in his reign one can already discern the advance of the Islamic element in the institution. In the name of the faith he launched a series of campaigns to spread Islamic hegemony throughout Arabia. The caliphate, as an emerging institution based on principles of unity transcending those of tribalism, had a critical interest in reducing the divisive influence of clan loyalties and rivalries. The suppression of the other Arabian prophets, especially the dangerous Maslama (henceforth called Musaylima al-Kadhdhāb, "Little Maslama the Liar"), was of particular importance to the ideal of Islamic unity. The failure of these figures contrasted sharply with the success of Islam and became a further sign of divine favor. Similarly the victories of a unified *umma* reflected highly on the caliph and the new office he represented. This symbiosis of spiritual and temporal factors endowed the institution with tremendous prestige, which in fact comprised the fundamental basis for the legitimacy of the *rāshidūn* caliphate.

Abū Bakr's reign was largely dominated by the figure of ᶜUmar ibn al-Khaṭṭāb (634–644), who enjoyed such enormous prestige in the *umma* that Abū Bakr simply named him as his successor, the notables being willing to give their *bayᶜa* without detailed discussion. Like his predecessor, ᶜUmar ruled through personal appeal and prestige. But whereas Abū Bakr's task had been to preserve Islam as a community, ᶜUmar's was to consolidate the expanding *umma*'s gains into a unitary empire. By 636 the raids and expeditions of Abū Bakr's time had burgeoned into a vast campaign of permanent conquest, creating a pressing need for stable institutions of government. These had to be established and supervised with very little coercive authority and applied in new provinces conquered by fiercely independent tribesmen led by their clan notables (the *ashrāf*). That ᶜUmar achieved the success he did is an enormous tribute to his diplomatic skill and forceful personality and, more generally, to the prestige that the caliphate had already won as the victorious ruling institution of Islam.

One of ᶜUmar's greatest achievements was his judicious imposition of the caliphate's authority over the tribes engaged in the conquests. He induced them to settle in new garrison towns founded especially for them in the provinces and to give the caliphate direct control of abandoned and forfeited lands in these regions, as well as indirect control of all conquered lands; in return the caliphate paid them stipends in cash and kind. Troops and others entitled to support were enrolled according to tribe in a new registry system (the *dīwān*), first in Medina, then in the garrison towns and other urban centers of the empire. Land taxes, tribute, and a fifth of the movable booty from conquests were turned over to a central treasury (*bayt al-māl*, also newly founded) from which payments were made for the various *dīwān*s. This was a decisive victory for order and unity, for the natural inclination of the tribes would have been simply to seize the conquered territories outright and to scatter across the countryside, with disastrous consequences for agriculture and the military posture of the *umma*.

The caliphate's nascent system of provincial administration was very loosely organized, an inevitable consequence of extremely rapid conquest and the need to accommodate an enormous variety of social, economic, and political conditions in different regions. Governors were appointed to administer the provinces, but their activities were restricted more by the sensitivities of the tribes than by orders from Medina. Disruption of existing arrangements, however, was minimal. The conquered non-Muslim peoples, except for polytheists, were regarded as *ahl al-dhimma* (people under protection) and *ahl al-kitāb* (people of the book), and their civilian and religious affairs were left to function as before. Local customs and laws remained; Byzantine and Persian coinage continued to be used and even minted (with slight modifications); many bureaucrats of the defeated empires were maintained in office; and Greek, Coptic, and Persian prevailed as the provincial languages of administration. Although it meant that there would never be uniform administration in the Islamic empire, this flexibility and readiness to assimilate probably account for the ease with which the transition to Arab rule and the formation of local administrations under the auspices of the caliphate were carried out.

The continued success of such efforts to maintain unity and order, however, was completely dependent on the prestige of both caliph and the caliphate. ᶜUmar's task was thus to establish the faith as the unifying principle for a vast empire, and hence to promote the Islamic character of the caliphate. In this regard, one of his most illustrative measures was his assumption of the title *amīr al-muᵓminīn* (commander of the faithful), which was to remain standard usage in Islamic protocol throughout the history of the caliphate. An *amīr* (emir) was essentially a military leader. The new title, however, stressed the caliph's special role as head of a community based on religious faith encompassing far more than a tribe, and in far more than military affairs.

It was a clear and decisive twist of terminology, and its implications were borne out by the extent to which ᶜUmar made Islam the criterion for reshaping Arab society. Muslims took precedence under the principle of Islamic priority, or *sābiqa*, and positions of responsibility went to the closest associates of Muḥammad and to the earliest converts. ᶜUmar's establishment of a new dating system, a lunar calendar beginning with the *hijra* of 622, especially reflects the caliph's conception of his office as a permanent one with a major role to play in history. ᶜUmar was the true founder of the Arab-Islamic empire.

Yet despite his successes, the caliphate of ᶜUmar was not without weaknesses. There was a lack of centralization and of any compelling sanction for imposing the caliph's will. The principle of *sābiqa* inevitably generated friction even among Muslims, since early converts took priority over later ones. And as ᶜUmar's reign drew to a close, the authority and accountability of the caliph were becoming significant issues. ᶜUmar's diplomatic skill, his compelling personality, and the success of the early conquests made it possible to forestall the conflict. But in 644 the caliph was struck down by a non-Muslim assassin, and tensions soon began to escalate.

CRISIS AND CIVIL WAR

ᶜUmar lived just long enough to make arrangements for selection of a new caliph, and appointed a deliberative committee (shūrā) of six prominent Meccans who were to choose one of their number as caliph. This was yet a third method, in as many caliphates, for the transfer of power. Ultimately, this body narrowed its choice to ᶜAlī ibn Abī Ṭālib, cousin and son-in-law of the Prophet, and ᶜUthmān ibn ᶜAffān, also a son-in-law as well as a very pious early convert to Islam, but very old and a member of the Umayyad clan, which had been bitterly opposed to the Prophet until his conquest of Mecca. ᶜAlī was offered the caliphate on condition that he adhere to the precedent of Abū Bakr and ᶜUmar, that is, that he do nothing to arouse further opposition to his office. Resisting the drift toward a caliphate that he saw as being too closely identified with the ashrāf, ᶜAlī refused and insisted that he, like his predecessors, would use his own judgment to deal with new conditions. The shūrā then made the same offer to ᶜUthmān, who accepted.

It soon became apparent, however, that if the unity of the empire was to be maintained, the caliph would have to check the growing power of provincial forces. As the situation was still too fluid for a consensus of the umma to be reached, ᶜUthmān embarked on a bold series of initiatives to establish the caliphate as a strong central ruling institution. He began to appoint his Umayyad kinsmen to key posts throughout the empire, using his position as clan leader to strengthen his position as caliph, and also gave posts to several recent converts to Islam, including some ridda leaders. In economic affairs, he asserted the duty and right of the caliph, as the representative of the interests of the umma, to protect these interests, if necessary at the expense of provincial and factional priorities. He revised taxation and landholding regulations, enforced them more vigorously, and in so doing undermined the position of the ashrāf and their tribesmen. In Medina itself, ᶜUthmān used provincial revenues for whatever purpose he saw fit, including payments to his Umayyad relatives at the expense of the Meccan and Medinan dignitaries accustomed to receiving generous stipends. The concern for unity within the umma was illustrated by his establishment of a definitive text of the Koran, minor variant readings in which had already begun to emerge.

There were charges of arrogance, of nepotism, and of harsh treatment of the companions of the Prophet. Tensions finally reached such proportions that even ᶜUthmān's allies and sympathizers could no longer afford to support him. The caliph quickly found himself besieged in his own house by unruly mobs. Negotiations and bitter arguments failed to resolve the conflict and finally touched off a riot. The rāshidūn caliphs had no palaces or bodyguards, and in this disturbance irate tribesmen broke into ᶜUthmān's house and killed him.

The impact of the deed was catastrophic, for the umma had for the first time murdered its own leader. The rāshidūn caliphate lost the inviolable aura of religious and moral authority that had legitimized it and served as a critically important principle of communal unity. The collapse of this ideal thus ushered in a period of great turmoil, the fitna (trials), referred to by Western historians as the First Civil War (656–661).

In the crisis atmosphere prevailing in Medina, the only viable candidate for the caliphate was ᶜAlī ibn Abī Ṭālib, who had in fact been a candidate since 632. As Muḥammad's closest male relative, ᶜAlī enjoyed the support of a significant faction known as the Shīᶜa. He had quickly risen to prominence as a figure of opposition, criticizing some of ᶜUmar's policies and even more vociferously opposing ᶜUthmān. This made ᶜAlī an ideal spokesman for the broad range of grievances against ᶜUthmān, and after the latter's murder he was acclaimed as caliph by the opposition forces in control of Medina. In other quarters, however, he was suspected of complicity in the crime. Just as the caliphate of ᶜUthmān had been brought to ruin by strife over the powers of the caliph, ᶜAlī's reign would be plagued by the additional question of whether the killing of a caliph had been a licit act and hence whether his own accession had been legitimate.

The First Civil War had three main foci of conflict, each of which had important effects on the caliphate. The first of these arose almost immediately, in the form of an uprising in Mecca by ᶜĀᵓisha, once Muḥammad's favorite wife, and Ṭalḥa ibn ᶜUbayd Allāh and al-Zubayr ibn al-ᶜAwwām, two members of the old shūrā. The rebellion was crushed in the "Battle of the Camel," near Basra (656), but the episode vividly demonstrated that for ordering the affairs of a great empire, Arabia could not serve as a viable base of operations. ᶜAlī maintained his headquarters in Al-Kufa in Iraq, and the caliphate was never again to return to Arabia. The fact that the institution would henceforth have to resort to military means to maintain the unity of Islam was in no small part due to this inevitable move from the relatively neutral isolation of Medina directly into the main theaters of factional strife and regional rivalry.

The second focus of the conflict was ᶜAlī's struggle with Muᶜāwiya ibn Abī Sufyān, ᶜUthmān's cousin. Governor of Syria for eighteen years, Muᶜāwiya had established a strong power base there founded on traditional patterns of clan leadership and cooperation among the *ashrāf*. By contrast, ᶜAlī in Iraq was trying to find a formula, based on the tenets of Islam, for achieving the justice demanded by the heterogeneous groups that had opposed ᶜUthmān and now supported him. Thus, when Muᶜāwiya took up the call for vengeance for ᶜUthmān, nothing less than supreme power and the future character and orientation of the caliphate was at stake in the struggle that was to follow.

The final focus of the conflict was the internal one among ᶜAlī's followers. Shortly after the battle of Ṣiffīn (657), the inconclusive outcome of which had led ᶜAlī and Muᶜāwiya to agree to a plan for formal arbitration of their differences, some of ᶜAlī's own followers objected that as the legitimate caliph he had erred in agreeing to arbitration of his right to rule. Taking up the slogan "The decision is God's alone," they insisted that the Koran clearly condemned rebellion by one believer (Muᶜāwiya) against the legitimate rule of another (ᶜAlī), making the struggle against the former a religious obligation not subject to modification by human arbitrators. When ᶜAlī refused to accept their views, they disowned him, proclaimed his sin and betrayal of God's trust, and elected their own caliph, thus initiating a movement known as that of the Kharijites (*khawārij*, rebels, or seceders). Although these initial Kharijites were defeated by ᶜAlī at Al-Nahrawān (658), the massacre cost the caliph further defections, and Kharijism long remained a potent and destructive force in the eastern provinces.

According to the Kharijite view of communal leadership, a blend of religious fundamentalism and tribal egalitarianism, the caliph should be essentially powerless. True authority is vested in the *umma* of righteous believers, from which the iniquitous are excluded. The community selects its best member as caliph but follows him only as long as he remains the best; it judges his every deed as a test of his righteousness and judgment, and defies or deposes him if he errs. Such a strict sociopolitical ideal was easily perceived as an invitation to anarchy and so found con-

siderable support among refractory Iraqi tribesmen. The persistent trouble that the Kharijites gave ᶜAlī, and later the Umayyads, did, however, focus attention on such questions as the importance of the caliph's deeds, the extent of his accountability to the *umma*, and the legality of rebellion against his rule.

THE UMAYYADS: MUᶜĀWIYA AND THE ARAB KINGDOM

The First Civil War ended in 661 with ᶜAlī's death at the hands of a Kharijite assassin and the accession of Muᶜāwiya to the caliphate, leaving unresolved many of the issues that had precipitated the conflict. Feelings of grievance and resentment still ran high and were to find violent expression in years to come. With his strong military command, Muᶜāwiya could keep Syria free of the factional strife that beset his rivals. Of all the contending parties, only he was able to maintain firm central authority in his domains and hence cohesion and order. Although many continued to oppose him in principle, all but the Kharijites eventually reconciled themselves to his rule precisely because the alternative was chaos. His victory was also that of order and thus led not to the dissolution of the caliphate but, rather, to its reestablishment in Syria, where Muᶜāwiya's branch of the Umayyad clan, the Sufyanids, controlled and reshaped it for the next two decades.

With the caliphate already removed from Arabia and robbed of its previous aura of sanctity, a return to the ideal of the *rāshidūn* patriarch was now clearly impossible. Finding a new basis for the Umayyad reassertion of central authority was thus Muᶜāwiya's primary task; and his solution was to rule the empire as caliph in much the same way he had ruled Syria as governor, establishing himself as head of what Julius Wellhausen aptly described as an "Arab kingdom." In this arrangement, the caliph's main internal concern was to coordinate the diverse systems of rule that had arisen in the provinces, and to do so in such a way that the affairs of the Arab ruling sector could be coherently planned and managed.

Because tribalism remained the dominant social force among the Arabs generally, the avoidance of confrontation and violence among the tribes became a matter of utmost importance. Muᶜāwiya thus presented himself as an Arab *sayyid* and was always anxious to maintain the support and loyalty of the *ashrāf* as the key to controlling the tribesmen who followed them.

Mu^cāwiya accordingly took care to confer with the *ashrāf* of Syria in periodic meetings of his *shūrā*, a consultative body not unlike the pre-Islamic tribal *majlis*. Delegations of tribal *ashrāf* from the provinces also made their way to Mu^cāwiya's court in Damascus, where the caliph received and consulted them. Similarly, the *ashrāf* of the provinces were consulted and cultivated in the *majlis* of the Umayyad governor and then sent back to their clans, where the process was repeated between the *ashrāf* and their tribesmen. In this way the caliph sought to enhance the power of the caliphate by solidifying the allegiance of the *ashrāf* and, at the same time, to make these chieftains dependent on the caliphate through a system in which their power rested not only on their standing within the tribe, but also on their ability to gain benefits and concessions from the governor and caliph, and hence on the willingness of the Umayyads to deal with them.

A skillful diplomat, Mu^cāwiya nevertheless presided over the development of the caliphate into a more authoritarian institution, a trend that followed logically from the fate of ^cUthmān. Unlike a tribal *sayyid*, Mu^cāwiya exercised absolute command of a well-trained army and was prepared to use it as a last resort; thus his efforts to persuade ultimately met with general success. The caliph was determined to tolerate no active opposition to his rule; and the principle of personal responsibility to clan and *umma*, which had been the justification for his call of vengeance for ^cUthmān in the First Civil War, was not disallowed. This shift was vividly demonstrated in 676 when Mu^cāwiya nominated his own son, Yazīd (680–683), to succeed him. This was not in itself a marked departure from Arab tradition, and there was a great deal of consultation with the provinces. But there was also a great deal of intimidating pressure. In fact a principle of dynastic succession was established.

It was at this time that the ceremony and symbolism of the authoritarian ideal began to surround the caliph. In contrast to the simple lives of the *rāshidūn*, the Umayyads, beginning with Mu^cāwiya, increasingly tended to set themselves apart from the rest of the *umma*. The first caliphal palace, Al-Khaḍrā^ɔ (the Green [Dome]), was built in Damascus by Mu^cāwiya and became the focus for an emerging Umayyad court. Access to the caliph was restricted, and a new official, the *ḥājib* (chamberlain), was entrusted with organizing palace ceremonies, admitting visitors, and introducing them to the caliph. Al-

ways on prominent display were a number of important symbols: the staff *(qaḍīb)*, the signet ring *(khātam)*, and the *burda*, a cloak once owned by Muḥammad. During audiences and receptions, the caliph usually sat on a low throne *(sarīr)*, surrounded by retainers and protected by bodyguards. He was addressed by his formal title, *Amīr al-mu^ɔ-minīn*, and in the third person; in response he often invoked the majesty of the royal "we." Umayyad ceremonies were not, however, the magnificent spectacles that were to develop in later times. There was no ritual for approaching or withdrawing from the caliph's presence, and the visitors were mostly tribal representatives, individual plaintiffs, or poets seeking patronage.

The development of a palace court was paralleled by the rapid expansion of the *dīwān* into an imperial bureaucracy. A *dīwān al-kharāj* (revenue department) became the most important agency of Umayyad government. The *dīwān al-jund* regulated the affairs of the military. In the *dīwān al-rasā^ɔil* Mu^cāwiya personally reviewed all communications while scribes noted his comments and decisions and saw to the preparation of the appropriate replies or official documents. These then went to the *dīwān al-khātam*, where final drafts of documents were made, stamped with a seal, and passed on for dispatch. To preclude forgery, this *dīwān* made copies of all documents it prepared and deposited them in what amount to the archives. Other *dīwān*s kept records of government expenditures, assessed the canonical taxes payable by Muslims, administered government lands in the cities, and supervised the production of ceremonial equipment, such as robes, official costumes, banners, and flags.

To ensure the maintenance of his authority in the rest of the empire, Mu^cāwiya entrusted governorships to a limited number of loyal emirs, military commanders who also exercised full administrative and financial powers to their provinces. Provincial *dīwān*s supervised military affairs generally, assessed taxes, collected revenues, and handled correspondence with Damascus. Communications were sent through the *dīwān al-barīd*, an official courier system that also maintained and marked the main routes in the empire and provided the caliph with the latest news and confidential information concerning provincial affairs and the conduct of his governors.

Mu^cāwiya and the Umayyads had a definite policy toward the lands beyond their control. The

Koran had enjoined believers to "fight those who believe not in God and the Last Day . . . until they pay the tribute (jizya) out of hand and have been humbled." This and other similar passages came to be viewed as a summons to military expansion, which in turn brought revenues and new taxable lands to the caliphate. By Umayyad times, it had thus become an explicit and indispensable function of the caliph to sponsor campaigns of conquest. Under the Umayyads, these campaigns spread Islamic rule across North Africa and into southwestern Europe, and far into central Asia. The main target, however, was the Byzantine Empire. The Sasanians had been destroyed completely, and their religion thereby discredited; but Byzantium, the greatest empire of early medieval Christendom, still survived and disputed the claims of Islam to universal authority. Beginning with Muᶜāwiya, and lasting until the early eighth century, the caliphate's foreign policy was preoccupied with the destruction of Byzantium as the necessary precondition for the Umayyads' assumption of their proper place as undisputed imperial masters of the eastern Mediterranean world. Aspects of Byzantine administration, ceremonial, imperial architecture, and ideas of rulership were assimilated by the caliphate with this end in mind. But more important, Muᶜāwiya and his successors launched continual raids from Syria across the Taurus Mountains into Anatolia, and on three occasions (669, 674–680, and 716–718) they besieged Constantinople itself.

With the responsibility for maintaining tribal order and Arab unity throughout the empire, the caliphal institution became a clearinghouse for compromise. Yet master of ḥlim that Muᶜāwiya was, his caliphate already began to display long-term weaknesses. Syrian hegemony rankled many Arab elements. Clan rivalries increased. Newly converted Muslim "clients" (mawālī) came to resent their second-class status. And the Kharijites and the Shīᶜa continued to uphold an Islamic ideal that severely disapproved of turning the caliphate into a mere kingship serving the interests of the Umayyad family and the Syrian tribes. Through all this, Muᶜāwiya and his successors continued to regard the caliphate as an expression of faith, the religious message of Islam being its constitutional basis and guardianship of the umma its primary role. But as no distinction yet existed between the spheres of religion and political affairs, the caliph regarded any active opposition to his rule as both unbelief and treason and dealt with it harshly. Stern measures of course solved nothing and simply intensified and broadened the opposition.

THE MARWANIDS: THE STRUGGLE FOR UNITY AND LEGITIMACY

After Muᶜāwiya's death in 680 conflicts quickly escalated to a new outbreak of chaos and factional violence in which the Umayyad caliphate was very nearly destroyed. The caliphate after the death of Muᶜāwiya was thus heavily influenced by this period of extreme crisis, in which the Umayyads were challenged on all sides to defend and justify their interpretation of the institution and its role in Islamic society.

The Second Civil War was not a monolithic uprising against Umayyad rule but, rather, a general collapse of order in which a broad range of Arab factions, Shiite and Kharijite groups, and even some of the mawālī participated, fighting the Umayyads and each other. The primary opponent of the regime, ᶜAbd Allāh ibn al-Zubayr (d. 692), did establish an "anticaliphate" at Mecca, and for a time his rule was acknowledged everywhere except in central Syria; but he never had enduring control of any region beyond the Hejaz, and his rebellion rapidly degenerated into anarchy as Arab factions in Egypt, Syria, and Iraq merely used his name to legitimize their own efforts to throw off Umayyad suzerainty. The conflict thus proved once again that the caliphate could never return to Arabia and that the Umayyads were still the only group capable of maintaining unity and order in the empire. At the same time, however, it discredited the Sufyanid system of rule through delicate cultivation and manipulation of tribal kinship patterns: the ashrāf, the keystone of the whole system, proved to be completely unreliable, quickly plunging into the general melee against the Umayyads, and changing sides as it suited their interests. The same problem was highlighted again by the great provincial revolt of Ibn al-Ashᶜath in 700.

Measures gradually taken by the caliphate in response to this situation were intended to concentrate power in the hands of its staunchest supporters and to extend this authority into the provinces. One of the most outstanding developments was the elaboration of generally acknowledged guidelines to govern the succession. The dynastic principle introduced by Muᶜāwiya was unpopular in many quarters, and in 684 it had to be set aside of necessity when the pro-Umayyad ashrāf met in a last great majlis to select a successor to Muᶜāwiya (II) ibn

Yazīd (683–684) and, in so doing, replaced the defunct Sufyanid of Muᶜāwiya with that of Marwān (I) ibn al-Ḥakam (684–685), the progenitor of the Marwanid branch of the Umayyad caliphate. But henceforth it was seen that dynastic succession was the only means of guaranteeing an orderly transfer of power, and the rest of the Umayyad caliphs were all either sons, brothers, or cousins of their predecessors.

The establishment of a dynasty allowed for agreement within the Umayyad family on certain conditions for accession to the caliphate. It was acknowledged that the caliph must be male, and an adult, as defined by the attainment of sexual maturity (ḥulum, iḥtilām). The prevailing feeling of Arab superiority also dictated that the caliph should not be the son of a non-Arab concubine. Immediate political realities also had to be considered, but as long as these criteria were met there were no other limitations on the succession. Yazīd I was able to nominate his son Muᶜāwiya, despite the latter's very poor health; the youth succeeded his father in 683 and died within months.

The bayᶜa, which in principle involved allegiance freely given, was soon relegated by the Umayyads to secondary importance; beginning with ᶜAbd al-Malik (685–705), the caliph designated his successor by leaving a written testamentary deposition (ᶜahd) signed and acknowledged by witnesses capable of ensuring its enforcement. The enormous authority of the ᶜahd was demonstrated in the procedure adopted by Sulaymān ibn ᶜAbd al-Malik (715–717), who sealed his ᶜahd and gained the bayᶜa for an heir whose identity was unknown to most of the Umayyad notables. Thus, once an heir apparent had been named and acknowledged, it was extremely difficult to displace him. This raised serious problems, for beginning with Marwān I the Umayyad caliphs displayed a tendency for nominating their next two successors, leading inevitably to jealousies and attempts to bypass unpopular senior heirs.

There was also no procedure for removing a caliph; as we might well imagine, such a possibility was out of the question as far as the reigning caliphs were concerned. The Kharijites upheld the principle of deposition by the community, and their revolts repeatedly proclaimed the unworthiness of the Umayyads to rule; but aside from their propaganda value, such calls had little effect. Whenever the issue of removal was raised, it always had to be resolved by military means. As in most medieval regimes, opposition to the ruler or his designated heir amounted to a general call to arms.

The Umayyad effort to consolidate the authority of the caliphate also required measures to ensure order in the provinces. As a tribal family themselves, the Umayyads could not afford to undermine the role of the Syrian ashrāf; but they did abandon their efforts to rule the provinces through such intermediaries. Instead, the provinces were governed by extremely powerful generals who ruled vast areas by force of arms. Most immediately affected was Iraq, the focus of anti-Umayyad sentiment, where al-Ḥajjāj ibn Yūsuf (d. 714) was appointed governor and came eventually to rule Iraq as an occupied enemy territory from his base at Wāsiṭ, a new provincial capital founded in 702. The regional emirs continued to enjoy great power, but the caliphate sought to place limits on their authority. Judicial jurisdiction was gradually shifted to the qadi (judge), who was to settle disputes between Muslims according to Islamic guidelines. A similar trend was to transfer financial power to the ᶜāmil, a provincial director of financial affairs who reported to the caliph. The dīwān al-barīd, already a rudimentary intelligence network, was reorganized and expanded by ᶜAbd al-Malik at about this time. These measures made it more difficult for the emir to abuse his power, but excesses continued to occur. In any case, however, officials could be discharged by the caliph without notice; and against those suspected of embezzlement the ruler could employ, from ᶜAbd al-Malik's time on, the institution of the muṣādara, in which such officials were arrested, investigated, and sometimes tortured to force them to reveal how the funds in question could be recovered.

The early Marwanid era also witnessed a vigorous Umayyad effort to legitimize the caliphate in Islamic terms. The Second Civil War saw the entire empire, except for central Syria, repudiate the Umayyads in favor of the caliphate of Ibn al-Zubayr. A succession of extremely violent Kharijite revolts and growing tensions with new and radically messianic forms of Shiism put enormous pressure on the Umayyads, leading them to stress the Islamic character of the caliphate. Such an emphasis became a matter of particular urgency as opposition movements became stronger and more violent and assumed a more decidedly Islamic theological character.

The Umayyad response is indicative of their own conception of the caliphate: stress on their descent from ^cUthmān, elected by a duly constituted *shūrā;* and denial that the charisma of leadership was restricted to the Quraysh clan of Hāshim, to which Muḥammad and ^cAlī had belonged. In theology the Umayyads turned increasingly to the doctines of the Murji^ɔa, which stressed faith over works. Since the latter were to be judged only by God on Resurrection Day, it was implied that the ^cAlī-^cUthmān question should be "postponed" until that time, with the Umayyads continuing to reign in the here and now. The regime also benefited from the emerging concept of *ijmā^c* (consensus), according to which any collective decision of the *umma,* such as the caliph's accession, was in itself a sign of divine approval. Hence the increasingly frequent title *khalīfat Allāh,* caliph of [appointed by] God; defiance of the Umayyad caliph was tantamount to defiance of God. After one revolt in Iraq, all prisoners were executed who would not confess that rebellion against the Umayyads had made them unbelievers.

The foreign policy of the Umayyads also had a definite Islamic tone, particularly as regarding the Byzantine Empire, for their attacks on Byzantine lands emphasized the role of the Umayyad caliph as a conqueror, like the *rāshidūn,* of the lands of the adherents of religions now abrogated by Islam. At the same time, however, it should be noted that the greatest of these campaigns, the three expeditions against Constantinople, were unsuccessful. Umayyad court poetry probably reflects a more general attitude in placing little stress on the *jihād,* or war (literally, struggle) for the cause of God.

This effort at Islamic legitimation was not mere propaganda. Koranic exegesis, prophetic tradition, law, theology, and history all gained the interest and support of the Umayyad caliphs. Although the poetry and lore of the Arab tribal legacy remained very much in vogue, men of Islamic learning, the ^c*ulamā^ɔ,* now began to gain considerable influence. ^cAbd al-Malik also initiated a program of Arabization, which due to the Umayyad view of Islam as an Arab faith, was also one of Islamization. In the government itself, Arabic was adopted as the language of administration, replacing the Greek, Coptic, and Pahlavi of the pre-Islamic systems. This was not only a measure centralizing the bureaucracy along Arab lines but also an Islamic reform, since it henceforth became easier for Arab Muslims to gain government positions. In like manner, new gold and silver coinage struck under ^cAbd al-Malik replaced Byzantine iconophile motifs with Arabic inscriptions, mainly Koranic phrases stressing the power of the faith and refusing the Christian veneration of Jesus as the Son of God. This new coinage also carried the reigning caliph's name, thus drawing attention to the Islamic character of the caliphate. This particular symbol's importance can be gauged from the fact that inclusion of the caliph's name on the coinage quickly became one of the two actions (along with including his name in the Friday prayers) by which a province or region acknowledged his rule.

In this era too the Umayyad caliphate began to sponsor building and public works projects on a large scale, a sponsorship that included not only palaces, works, and residences but also such magnificent Islamic monuments as the Dome of the Rock (691) in Jerusalem and the Umayyad Mosque (*ca.* 711) in Damascus. These activities reached their peak under ^cAbd al-Malik's sons al-Walīd I and Hishām, and were a vivid expression of the Umayyad caliphate's self-image of its majesty, imperial power, and central role in the promotion of both the spiritual and the material welfare of the *umma.*

THE COLLAPSE OF THE UMAYYAD CALIPHATE

Thanks to a period of peace and internal consolidation, the Umayyad caliphate still seemed secure at the death of al-Walīd in 715. But the Syrian, Arabic, and tribal perspective was becoming increasingly archaic in the eighth century as many Arabs were settling in the towns and living, as landowners, merchants, and craftsmen, in harmony with the non-Arab *mawālī,* whose own ranks of conversion to Islam continued to swell. The resultant society increasingly perceived Islam as a universal faith without the old limiting ties to Arabism—or to a conception of the caliphate that favored Arab warriors and military expansion, yet ignored the abuses and inequalities in personal status, taxation, and land tenure endured by what was rapidly becoming the majority of the *umma.* A crisis gradually developed as Islam evolved into a more fully articulated system of religious belief capable of upholding its own specific social ideology, and achieved the means to give that ideology practical social expression. Ideals of Islamic identity and Muslim equality were gaining currency within the *umma* yet sharply contradicted the conceptions of ethnicity and privilege that had long comprised essential principles of Umayyad rule.

The institution of the Umayyad caliphate was incapable of resolving this dilemma. On the one hand, it was itself becoming increasingly involved in disruptive Arab factionalism. The process of Islamic assimilation tended to set Arabs who remained military men, particularly the Syrians, against those who did not, particularly the Iraqis. This trend was all the more pronounced since lucrative stipends and privileges were at stake, and since the Umayyad army was evolving into a force of full-time soldiers led by professional officers and used to maintain control by Syria over the rest of the empire's population, both Arab and non-Arab. The Umayyad caliphs found it no less difficult to control their extremely powerful generals and armies than it had been to control the provincial *ashrāf;* and in the wake of the Second Civil War there began to form Syrian factions, on the lines of the old tribal confederacies, competing for power and influence. The caliphs found it increasingly difficult to contain such rivalries and rather often used them to their own advantage. This contention, with its attendant strife and instability, was thus carried to the provinces by governors and troops, and made Umayyad rule even more distasteful.

At the same time, the caliphate was unable to draw the emerging social vision of Islam closer to its own view—or even to compete with it effectively. The promulgation and interpretation of law had never been considered the special domain of the caliphate. The sources of law, the Koran and *sunna,* were entrusted to the community at large, some members of which, the *ᶜulamāᵓ,* devoted themselves to the study of these subjects. Their authority on such matters sprang not from an official sanction but from their personal reputations in the *umma* for piety, integrity, and sound scholarship; their judgments and pronouncements carried weight when and to the extent that they gained the consensus, or *ijmāᶜ,* of the other *ᶜulamāᵓ* and hence of the community in general.

The Umayyad caliphs, though their efforts toward Islamization further enhanced the influence of the *ᶜulamāᵓ,* had no similar authority. Thus the Umayyad espousal of the Murjiᵓite position of political quietism had little deterrent effect on their opponents but, rather, caused them to place similar stress on the opposing doctrines of the Qadarīya, an appellation loosely applied to individuals and groups stressing personal accountability before God and the *umma* for wrongdoing, and hence favoring the right of the community to judge the actions of the caliph. In like manner, the caliphate had no particular right to pass judgment on religious matters; though the Umayyads considered themselves the champions of Islam when they crushed Shiite and Kharijite rebellions and executed Qadarite "heretics," such actions

actually served to inflame the general sense of grievance against them.

Several caliphs did recognize the gravity of these problems and tried to resolve them. ᶜUmar II (717–720) withdrew from the disastrous siege of Constantinople in 718, pulled back from frontier posts in certain areas, and in general strictly limited the caliphate's interest in military adventures.

Sweeping fiscal measures regularized stipends, established a normative policy for land tenure and taxation, and abolished all measures discriminating against the *mawālī.* In sum, the caliphate was to treat all Muslims on a basis of equality, which included putting a stop to the cursing of ᶜAlī, ending the persecution of the Qadarīya, and seeking to come to terms with the Kharijites. The profound effect of this program may be gauged from the fact that for the first time since Muᶜāwiya, an Umayyad caliph governed by general consent.

Although the importance of this was not lost on the other members of the ruling house, ᶜUmar's measures may have precipitated a decline in revenue and certainly alienated some factional elements. The caliph died before he was able to consolidate the gains of his new policies; and almost all of his work was undone by his successor Yazīd II (720–724). The next caliph, Hishām, enjoyed a peaceful reign, but his death plunged Syria and the rest of the empire into a third civil war in 744.

In the final analysis, the institution of the Umayyad caliphate had served to maintain the unity of Islam through its first tumultuous century, and this was its redeeming virtue. It was supported by many groups that were very dissatisfied with it but that rallied around it because the alternative seemed to be anarchy and the dissolution of the empire—hence the Umayyad victories in the First and Second Civil Wars. But in the midst of the renewed communal violence in the 740's, a new revolutionary Arab movement revealed itself in Khorāsān. Based on the propaganda and messianic ideas of the extremist Shīᶜa, the Abbasid movement called for sweeping social reform along Islamic lines and proclaimed a new era of justice under the leadership of an as yet unnamed ruler of the Prophet's line. The last Umayyad caliph, the able Marwān II (744–750), was too preoccupied with factional strife elsewhere to give this revolt his serious attention until it was too late. Once the uprising demonstrated its commitment to order and unity, it swelled into a general revolution. The Umayyads were abandoned on all sides, and their caliphate collapsed in 749–750.

THE EARLY ABBASID CALIPHATE

The Abbasid revolution quickly brought about two significant developments affecting the institution of the caliphate. The center of the empire shifted to Iraq, where, after Abbasid experiments with several other sites proved unsatisfactory, the caliph al-Manṣūr (754–775) built a new capital, Baghdad. Except for brief interludes, the caliphate was to remain there until 1258. The second development had much to do with the shift in geographical focus. At Baghdad, only thirty kilometers (eighteen miles) north of the old Sasanian capital of Ctesiphon, the caliphate was exposed to the rich legacy of the Persian imperial tradition. In administration, ceremonial, and self-image, the Abbasid caliphate was to borrow much from the Sasanian heritage.

But there was no radical change in the caliphate, nor was it transformed into a Persian institution. Iraq had already been the economic heartland of the Islamic world under the Umayyads (as also of the Sasanian Empire); and when Islamic culture began to develop in the provinces after the conquests, it flourished in Iraq to an extent unrivaled elsewhere. By the early eighth century, for example, Basra enjoyed a far higher level of population, prosperity, and culture than even Damascus, the Umayyad capital.

Despite the marked Persian influence on the caliphate, the institution remained essentially Arab. The office of caliph itself was still reserved to Arabs, and Arabic remained the language of court and culture. The feeling of Arab superiority remained prevalent enough to induce Persians both to assume Arab patronymics and to fabricate their genealogies so as to claim Arab ancestry. The early Abbasid caliphs borrowed from the Sasanian imperial tradition not out of fascination with things Persian but simply because they found the kind of structures and images provided by the Sasanian model to be extremely useful. The Abbasid revolution had been an essentially Arab movement, directed not against the idea of Arab rule but, rather, against the narrow principles of Arab privilege upheld by the Umayyads and their Syrian supporters. Many Umayyad bureaucrats and administrators stayed on and served the new regime. Thus the Abbasid caliphate did not break with the past; it built upon it and gradually broadened into an institution to which Arab and non-Arab influences had equal access, and under which privilege and power depended not on ethnicity but on the favor of the Abbasid sovereign and his powerful lieutenants. This era, from the mid eighth to the mid ninth century, marked the apogee of the caliphate's power and prestige.

Critical though they had been of the Umayyad family's monopolization of power, the Abbasids applied the same dynastic principle of succession once they came to control the caliphate. Shortly before his death, Abū 'l-ʿAbbās al-Saffāḥ (749–754), the first Abbasid caliph, nominated his elder brother al-Manṣūr to succeed him. This dynastic principle, in the face of continued resistance, was henceforth rigorously defended. Within this framework the Abbasid caliph nominated his own successor, taking care to consult groups or individuals whose support the new ruler would need. Testaments of succession continued to carry great authority, and on two occasions (802, for the sons of Hārūn al-Rashīd; 874, for al-Muʿtaḍid) they were solemnly executed in Mecca and displayed in the Kaaba. Though by now of definitely secondary importance to the ʿahd, the bayʿa for the heir apparent was sometimes called for more than once, in order to preclude any later pretext for opposition to his succession. Strictures against rule by a minor were eventually violated when al-Muqtadir, then a thirteen-year-old boy, was raised to the throne in 908. Candidates were no longer considered ineligible because of a non-Arab mother; in fact, all but two of the Abbasid caliphs fell into this category.

Elevation to the caliphate continued to follow Umayyad precedent, although with far greater pomp and ceremony, and to stress the universal acknowledgment of the new caliph's accession. Magnificent ceremonies marked the occasion in Baghdad, where the ruler accepted the traditional caliphal emblems of the staff and signet ring, donned the cloak of the Prophet, and received the bayʿa from the inner circles of the court. The news was then announced to the people of Baghdad, who proclaimed their loyalty by acclamation as presents were lavishly distributed among them. In the provinces, the caliph's accession was acknowledged, as before, by including his name on the coinage and invoking God's blessing upon him in the Friday prayers. New Abbasid caliphs also tended to appoint new governors, who would receive the bayʿa for their master when they assumed their posts.

Very frequently, however, the transfer of power could not be made smoothly. The Umayyad system had left many important questions unresolved, and under the Abbasids there was still no generally acknowledged provision for choosing a new ruler when a caliph died without naming a successor. Power struggles among the most important officials often resulted in the selection of a caliph unlikely to threaten the interests of his electors. Similarly, there was still no provision for disqualifying an heir apparent once the testament of succession had been executed for him, or for deposing a caliph deemed unfit to rule. As under the Umayyads, challenges to an heir's right to succeed, and pronouncements of deposition against a reigning caliph, invariably had to be backed up by force; thus the constitutional difficulty was repeatedly resolved—or, rather, avoided—by the coercion or military defeat of all but one of the contending parties. Particularly dangerous was the continuing tendency of the Abbasid caliph to nominate his next two successors; the first heir, upon his accession, usually sought to disqualify the second in favor of a candidate (such as his son) of his own choosing. Hārūn al-Rashīd was particularly innovative in arranging a dual succession, dividing the lands and powers of his realm between his sons al-Amīn and al-Maʾmūn, in addition to providing that the latter should succeed his brother. This resulted in a conflict in which the two heirs exchanged curses, accusations of misconduct, and pronouncements of deposition until the issue was settled in a civil war (810–819) that gravely weakened the unity of the empire and left much of Baghdad in ruins.

The institution of the Abbasid caliphate was associated with powers and responsibilities in several fields of activity. The caliph was, first, an emir in the old military sense, commander of a standing army led by professional officers and based at Baghdad. He was also the guardian of the internal security and well-being of the empire, supervising the conduct of his officials, suppressing internal rebellions and other disorders, and managing taxes and other revenues. The caliphate did not, however, hold or seek authority over institutions of public welfare, such as mosques, schools, hospitals, rest houses, and caravansaries; these were usually supported by privately endowed foundations. Individual caliphs took an interest in specific establishments, but as wealthy Muslims, not as caliphs. Most of these institutions were founded and managed beyond the sphere of government, and certainly their character and goals did not depend on the caliph's initiative or will. The only truly civic institution maintained by the caliphate was that of the *muhtasib*, a market inspector similar to the Umayyad *ṣāḥib al-sūq* but now, in Abbasid times, more an official guarantor of public integrity, morality, and fair business practices.

As the well-being of the empire involved a definite spiritual dimension, the caliph was also considered to have an important role in the protection of the integrity of the Islamic faith. Suppression of heresy fell in his domain and, under certain caliphs, was pursued with great vigor, as in the campaign against crypto-Manichaeanism under al-Mahdī (775–785). The *ahl al-dhimma*, on the other hand, continued to fare well, though their role in official capacities was steadily eroded as government assumed a more specifically Islamic orientation. At certain times they were subjected to detailed social and economic regulations, as under al-Mutawakkil (847–861); but for the most part these restrictions were ignored. Christians and Jews were expected to adhere to their own legal canons in their internal affairs. The caliphate maintained its influence by requiring that the *ahl al-dhimma*, on electing new heads for their communities, submit the candidate's credentials to the caliph for approval and obtain a formal diploma investing the man in office. The caliph's role in such religious affairs was unquestioned as long as it involved non-Muslims or fringe minority views. But the caliph's right to impose his will was vigorously disputed when it came to fundamental points of dogma under dispute within the main body of the community.

The caliph supervised the administration of justice, overseeing the activities of his judicial officials and reserving for himself the final authority in all judicial proceedings. Under the Abbasids there developed a system of courts, known as the *maẓālim*, in which grievances against the government or powerful men were heard; the caliph often conducted these proceedings himself, thereby enhancing his personal reputation for justice and integrity. He could, like the Umayyad caliph before him, legislate by rescript and decree on fiscal matters, as well as deliver judgments on individual cases that came before the courts, but he was not empowered to make or interpret religious law.

The early Abbasid period was one of great political tension and of enormous economic growth and social development; and as these trends rendered the task of government increasingly complex and difficult, the caliphate had to develop more sophisticated and efficient methods for dealing with an immense range of problems and needs. The institution thus rapidly expanded and attached to itself a vast hierarchy of specialized departments and officials, a process that had started under the later Umayyads, who had already begun to turn for inspiration to the same Sasanian system now adopted as the administrative model by the Abbasids.

The earliest and most important of the new officials was the vizier *(wazīr),* believed by some modern scholars to be a recreation of the Sasanian *vuzurg-framādhār.* It became a regular government post to which the caliphs soon came to entrust great power and responsibility. The vizier managed the Abbasid administration, advised the caliph on matters of policy, and played a major role in caliphal relations with the army, provincial governors, and foreign governments. Though always subject to the approval of the caliph, the vizier enjoyed a considerable range of authority that was rarely contravened except by the appointment of a new vizier.

Under the authority of the vizier came the vast Abbasid bureaucracy. From the simple military registry system of ⁽Umar ibn al-Khaṭṭāb, Islamic administration evolved under the Abbasids into a complex hierarchy of *dīwān*s administered by secretaries so numerous and important that they came to form a social class unto themselves. The *mawālī* entered the administration in large numbers under the Abbasids, and it was in this domain that Persian influence on the caliphate was strongest. Though here, as elsewhere, there was a strong element of continuity from Umayyad times, the structure and scope of Abbasid bureaucracy was largely the work of the viziers of the Barmakid family, who rose to power under al-Manṣūr and managed Abbasid affairs of state for almost half a century. *Dīwān*s became highly specialized departments, and new ones were created to handle such matters as petitions, special taxes, confiscations from criminals and enemies of the government, inventory and warehousing, maintenance of palace servants, slaves, and attendants, and pious endowments. *Dīwān*s were established simply to maintain coordination among the *dīwān*s and communications with the vizier; the *dīwān al-rasā⁾il* evolved into an elaborate state chancery; and the imperial archives became a depository for receiving, classifying, and storing the vast quantities of documents generated by the process of government. By the ninth century, the Abbasid bureaucracy was keeping thousands of secretaries, clerks, scribes, servants, and slaves fully occupied in managing the affairs of state.

Caliphal authority was also delegated to other individuals. Hārūn al-Rashīd was very active in the frontier campaigns against Byzantium, and al-Manṣūr himself led the Iraqi pilgrimage caravan to Mecca five times during his caliphate. But by the middle of the ninth century it increasingly became the custom for the caliph to appoint others to perform such functions. In the judicial system, the ca-

liphs reserved the right to overrule any decision by the qadis, but beginning with Hārūn they delegated the task of judicial supervision and review to a supreme judge, the *qāḍī al-quḍāt,* a position inspired by a similar Sasanian office, that of *mōbedān-mōbed.* This official, like the vizier, often played a very powerful and influential role in the determination of government policy; the spectacular career of Aḥmad ibn Abī Du⁾ād (d. 854), *qāḍī al-quḍāt* under three successive caliphs, demonstrated how powerful this official could become.

In the provinces, it was usually the task of the Abbasid governor (emir) to oversee the civilian administration in his province, maintain the armed forces, and make appointments to the positions of qadi and *muḥtasib.* He also supervised the government mint and often shared in the caliph's sovereignty by including his own name on the coinage, as well as in the *khuṭba* at Friday prayers. The Abbasids continued the Umayyad trend to separate administrative and fiscal responsibilities. The emir eventually lost his fiscal powers to the ⁽*āmil,* who was appointed to the provincial capital and was responsible for the assessment and collection of taxes and for the general management of provincial financial affairs.

The maintenance of such an immense system of government posed special problems for the caliphate. The administration was too large for the ruler personally to ensure the loyalty of all those who served him. The vast size of the empire and the enormous variety of economic, social, and political conditions in the provinces made uniform administration impossible. Numerous characteristics of the Abbasid caliphate should be viewed in relation to the effort to address such problems. Although the duties of official positions were defined in theory, in practice they had to be left vague and flexible. Similarly, administrators served not for any fixed term of office but for as long as the caliph deemed their performance satisfactory. As the precipitous fall of the Barmakid viziers in 803 demonstrated, they were at every moment held accountable for their activities and were subject to summary dismissal, disgrace, punishment, torture, and even execution on the caliph's command. The character and will of the caliph could thus have a dramatic and immediate impact on the character of government in general.

Ensuring the loyalty of these officials was another problem, which the Abbasids dealt with through the use of presents, patronage, cultivation of complex patterns of social and ethical obligation, and in general binding the welfare and fate of the official to that of the caliph himself. As a dynasty born of a provincial revolt, the Abbasids were well aware of the need to maintain firm rule in the provinces and yet to prevent the governors from becoming powerful enough to challenge the authority of the caliph. Governors were selected for their loyalty and lack of connections and influence among provincial power groups, and were shifted frequently from one province to another. Members of the ruling house often received posts but were assigned where they could pose no threat to their kinsmen, and almost never to such critical positions as emir of Khorāsān. The separation of political and fiscal authority in the provinces was at least partially motivated by similar security concerns. And as a further check, the caliph had the *barīd,* now an elaborate intelligence as well as courier system whose representatives reported directly to him.

The aspirations and anxieties of the caliphs all found quintessential expression in the Abbasid court. Although the caliphs did on occasion make appearances in majestic processions, they only rarely exposed themselves to public view; having delegated much of their authority to the administration, they instead withdrew into the inner precincts of their palace and court. This continued the caliphate's tendency to follow the Sasanian example of the sovereign raised above his subjects and isolated in a surreal world, in which imperial image was used to buttress imperial function, as both were integrated into magnificent displays of power and wealth. Poets and scholars presented works dedicated to the caliph or his officials (many of whom were great patrons of culture), and scholars at the Bayt al-Ḥikma (House of Wisdom), founded in 830, translated Greek and Indian works of science, philosophy, and theology. Magnificent fetes regaled imperial guests, and the *ḥarīm* (harem) became a prominent part of the scene at the court. Rich presents were bestowed on those who gained the caliph's favor, while the executioner and his leather mat, always present at the side of the throne, awaited those who provoked his rage.

All this took place in surroundings of awesome splendor, ostentatious ceremonial, and fantastic wealth, all carefully orchestrated and adapted to the status of the viewer and the significance of the occasion. In the palace complexes, the maintenance of which required staffs numbering in tens of thousands, an important visitor would be conducted through elaborate rituals confronting him, in stages, with indications of the caliph's majesty and power: rank upon rank of lavishly appointed guards, pages,

servants, slaves, and other retainers, lush parks of exotic wild beasts, staggering arrays of gold and silver objects, gems, ornamented furniture, precious carpets and tapestries, pools of mercury, and ingenious mechanical devices, most famous of which was a gold and silver tree with leaves that rustled, branches that swayed, and mechanical birds that sang as the breeze blew through the device. These displays culminated in the presence of the caliph, concealed behind a curtain at first, then revealed reclining in magnificent splendor on his throne. The supplicant kissed the carpet before the sovereign, often several times, or if very important, kissed his hand, his foot, or the hem of his robe; only then could he present his petition or request. The desired effect of such ritual and ceremony was to inspire in the caliph's subjects a sense of awe and servile impotence, and hence, obedience and loyal service.

The caliph was not, however, a true despot; that is, he did not exercise absolute arbitrary power, free from checks and limitations. Numerous elements, particularly in the capital, wielded considerable power and influence in their own right: the Abbasid family, the army, the ᶜulamāʾ, and the secretarial class generally. Officials in the government usually sought and gained, to varying degrees and in different ways, the support of such elements, and also at times tried to ingratiate themselves to the people of Baghdad. In practice, then, the power of the caliph was limited by the ability of powerful officials to muster the levels of support necessary to resist his will and, in the long term, to discourage the blatant abuse of imperial power. In fact, the measures taken by the Abbasids to preserve their central authority did not prevent provincial power from finally concentrating in the hands of great local families; and even in Baghdad, high officials were often able to monopolize administrative authority in their families for decades.

ISLAM AND THE ABBASID CALIPHATE

The effort of the Abbasids to maintain the caliphate as an effective governing institution leads to a question that requires special consideration: that of the changing relationship between Islam and the institution of the caliphate in Abbasid times. The Abbasid revolution had temporarily united in armed opposition to the Umayyads a multitude of heterogeneous groups. Each of them was attracted to the movement's propaganda, generally, by prospects for a new era of justice under the auspices of Islam and, more particularly, by expectations that this new order would necessarily satisfy that group's own grievances and demands. The Abbasids were of course well aware that the faith was the only positive element uniting support behind them; and once the Umayyads had been destroyed, they did seek to make Islam the unifying principle of their domain. But in order to restore stability after the revolution, the Abbasids had to gain the support of the critically important and largely conservative urban Muslim population, which, much as it had been willing to see Umayyad authority overturned, was not prepared to accept an Islamic brand of esoteric messianism in its place. Thus, as the new rulers gradually abandoned their extremist ideals, disposed of their most radical and powerful lieutenants, and moved to establish their own narrow family dynasty, many groups felt betrayed and rose against them. There were frequent Shiite rebellions, and the serious rifts even in the Abbasid family were highlighted in 754 when ʿAbd Allāh ibn ʿAlī, al-Manṣūr's uncle, rejected the latter's right to succeed, revolted, and proclaimed himself caliph. The Kharijites also continued to give trouble; and in Syria, Arab rebellions were raised in the name of the Sufyānī, a messianic figure associated with the fallen Umayyads.

The Abbasids, like the Umayyads before them, combated these ideological challenges, while trying to give meaning and legitimacy to their rule, by using the caliphate as the vehicle for promotion of their own values, thus leading to important new developments in the institution. Against Alid claims that a revolution should have brought a descendant of ʿAlī to the throne, the Abbasids argued for a broader legitimacy among the Hashimites, the kinsmen of the Prophet. The claim to primacy in preserving the legacy of the Prophet was most clearly reflected in the Abbasid caliphate's ceremonial use of relics, especially the Prophet's cloak, or burda, which he wore at all important ceremonies, particularly that of his accession. The caliph's Koran was claimed to be that of ʿUthmān; and in processions the caliph was preceded by the chief of police carrying his lance (ḥarba), which evoked memories of the umma's early leaders in Medina planting their lances in the ground as a signal for the warriors to gather. Such claims to precedence were buttressed by repeated allusion to the importance of the Abbasid victory over the Umayyads, whose memory was now regularly cursed.

While advancing the claim to merit based on past deeds, the Abbasids laid further stress on the Umayyad principle of divine right. Claims that the caliph was the shadow or power of God on earth reportedly began with al-Manṣūr, and toward such a sovereign the only acceptable attitude was one of unqualified submission and obedience. In an innovation of their own, all of the Abbasids assumed regnal titles of marked spiritual significance. At first these were of eschatological tenor: al-Manṣūr, he whom God has made victorious, or the positively messianic title of his son al-Mahdī, he whom God has rightly guided. As the extremist doctrine of the revolution was repudiated, this concept was deemphasized in favor of stress on the ruler's piety: al-Maʾmūn, he in whom is God's confidence; al-Wāthiq, he who trusts in God. The implications of this divine connection were promoted by Abbasid ceremonial, which surrounded the caliph in an aura of otherworldly splendor beyond the means or comprehension of his subjects. Displays of the ʿahd of succession in Mecca evoked a similar dual responsibility to God and the caliph who ruled in his name.

This ideology also found expression in the administration. The office of vizier, though a purely political post inspired by a Sasanian prototype, was so entitled after references in the Koran to the divine appointment of Moses as a prophet with his brother Aaron to assist him as vizier thus illustrating the office's religious connections with a caliph reigning by divine right and approval. Much the same can be said of the office of muḥtasib, whose holder, in enforcing fair business practices and public morality, was acting on behalf of God's appointed agent on earth.

The principle of "enjoining the good and forbidding the evil" became a particular preoccupation of the Abbasid caliphs, who inscribed this Koranic slogan on their caliphal banners and rapidly came to conceive of their office in the more precise sense of imams, implying responsibility for leading the umma in correct religious conduct. Although the title of imam, abandoned in later Umayyad times because of its Shiite associations, was not openly readopted until the reign of al-Maʾmūn (when it begins to appear on coins and inscriptions), the functions associated with it were a part of the Abbasid image of the caliph from the very beginning. Leadership of the hajj, jihad, and Friday prayers in Baghdad were prerogatives of the imam; and even when these tasks were delegated to others, they were still performed on the caliph's behalf. By assuming this title, the Abbasids also seem to have been laying claim to divine inspiration similar to that which gave the legal reasoning of the Shiite imams religious authority.

This last observation leads us to a complex and critical problem encountered by the Abbasids. Although they managed to endow their rule with legitimacy and meaning for a considerable time, during which their claims gained general assent, their efforts ultimately failed. The groups that they had repudiated and suppressed after the revolution continued to give trouble, in some cases of an increasingly serious order; but even within the main body of the *umma* the attitude toward them was generally ambivalent. The ideals of political organization emerging in Islamic circles, differ as they might on specifics, all agreed that to be truly Islamic a governing order must place ruler and ruled in a relationship of mutual rights and duties based on Koranic revelation. In other words, the caliphate, in order to win effective acceptance as an Islamic governing institution, had to do more than simply uphold and defend Islam; it had itself to become an Islamic institution, by entrusting ultimate authority to the holy law. But under the Abbasids this did not happen.

One reason was that it was manifestly impossible for the ruler to concede the superior authority of a divine law, the formulation and interpretation of which was not beyond dispute, without also undermining his own position. It was precisely this principle of the primacy of the law, major points of which were hotly contested within the *umma,* that enabled such movements as the Kharijites and the Shīᶜa to raise violent opposition to the *umma*'s governing head and yet continue to be, in their own estimation and that of others, believing members of the community. This was also what made these uprisings so dangerous: they highlighted the possibility of faithful Muslims opposing the reigning caliph and separating themselves from his leadership in the name of the faith. As the Abbasids discovered after the success of their own uprising, the transformation from revolutionaries to caliphs made it, paradoxically enough, impossible for them to realize the mandate that had brought them to power. They were hardly in a position to promulgate a politicoreligious program limiting their own power and recognizing the rights of individual Muslims against the government, at a time when uncertainty over the definition of these limitations and rights would have played into the hands of the increasing ranks of their powerful enemies.

Desperately seeking to consolidate their rule, they engaged in endless compromise and buttressed their position by building up a vast bureaucracy and a standing army. Thus transformed, the caliphate was able to maintain unity and order, but it was not itself particularly Islamic in its conduct of the affairs of state. The idea of a dynasty was no more palatable after the revolution than before, and it was obvious that the Abbasids were becoming more royal and autocratic than the Umayyads had ever been. The servility and unquestioning obedience demanded by a caliph raised in august isolation above his subjects came very close to blasphemy in the estimation of many Muslims, who noted that worship was reserved to God alone. Only slightly less offensive were such abuses of Islamic legal procedure as the elimination of "enemies of Islam" who in fact were simply opposed to imperial policy.

The problem could have been solved, had the caliphate been able to seize the initiative and to codify the law in a standard form to which all Muslims would adhere. But in this regard there arose the second and more decisive factor underlying the caliphate's failure to become a genuinely Islamic institution in Abbasid times: the efflorescence of religious activity and culture beyond the control of the caliphate. As related above, the *umma* had never granted or conceded to the caliphate the authority to interpret or promulgate law. This task was entrusted, like the sources of the law themselves, to the community at large and was carried out by the ᶜulamāʾ, which from the foundations laid in Umayyad times, had risen to become the moving force behind almost every aspect of the social and religious development of Islam. In the course of this long process, which was actually that of the development of Islamic society itself, Muslims gradually came to accept the ᶜulamāʾ as the true exponents of Islamic identity and to esteem them—not the caliphs—as the authoritative sources of legal counsel, moral guidance, and religious instruction.

These two factors, then, tended to separate Islam from the institution of the caliphate and thus to erode the latter's religious authority and prestige. Indeed, most of the schools of law specifically rejected the personal judgment *(raʾy)* of the caliphs (except for the *rāshidūn* and ᶜUmar II) as a valid basis for the elaboration of law. And by the mid eighth century, the old Kharijite slogan of "No obedience to the creature [caliph] in disobedience of the Creator" began to gain wider currency in the community.

The caliphs were caught in a dilemma, for to redeem the situation they had either to compel the *umma* to acknowledge their religious authority or to make the caliphal institution itself conform to an absolute legal code developing in various channels, none of which they controlled. The Abbasid caliphs attempted a compromise by trying to draw the ᶜulamāᵓ closer to the caliphate. Beginning with al-Manṣūr, they surrounded themselves with theologians, favored and supported their work, encouraged religious discussions at the court (where the caliph even engaged in debate with the Nestorian patriarch), and made a point of providing their sons with religious training. Their organization of religious courts and their efforts to persuade influential ᶜulamāᵓ to accept posts as qadis were in part a concession to the primacy of the law; the creation of the office of qāḍī al-quḍāt, however, served as the caliph's check on their activities. Desire to conciliate the ᶜulamāᵓ was also a factor behind al-Mahdī's persecution of crypto-Manichaeanism, a campaign that leveled widespread accusations of blasphemy against the court and bureaucracy, both of which the ᶜulamāᵓ distrusted; and it may have partly motivated Hārūn's purge of the Barmakids in 803.

This compromise effort failed, for the ᶜulamāᵓ remained suspicious of the caliphs' motives and other activities, and in any case were little interested in matters of public law and administration that were so important to the rulers. The crisis finally erupted after the civil war between al-Amīn and al-Maᵓmūn, when the latter resolved to assert the primacy of his office by promulgating a series of measures calculated to extend caliphal authority to dogma and ritual. This direct challenge to the ᶜulamāᵓ culminated in 833 with the miḥna, an investigation in which government officials and religious figures were required to acknowledge the caliph's new doctrines and his religious authority to impose them. Refusal to do so could mean loss of office, imprisonment, physical abuse, and in some cases death. The campaign met with great popular opposition and stubborn resistance among the ᶜulamāᵓ, many of whom preferred to suffer the consequences rather than submit. Such resolve dramatized even further the contrast between Islamic ideals and the method and structure of the caliphate. Though pursued with varying degrees of vigor over the next decade, the miḥna ultimately proved so futile and counterproductive that it was completely abandoned shortly after 847.

The weathering of this storm was a decisive triumph for the ᶜulamāᵓ. It not only vindicated their role as the guardians and elaborators of the law and as the motivating force behind the development of Islamic society, but also reaffirmed the principle of the responsibility of individual Muslims, regard-less of the caliph's character or deeds, to uphold the ideals of Islam and hence—and most important—reiterated the freedom of the umma to pursue its universalist aims as a community of faith, irrespective of the political order under which this activity would take place. From this time on, it is possible to speak of a separation of the development of Islam from the fortunes of the caliphate.

This leads us, in sum, to three important conclusions that must be borne in mind in viewing the later Abbasid caliphate. First, it remained an important symbol of the ultimate unity of Islam, as was frequently demonstrated by the efforts of later dynasts and provincial powers to obtain at least titular Islamic legitimation of their rule from the reigning caliph. But the only practical meaning left to the institution was its role in maintaining order. The Abbasids were supported and esteemed as long as they guaranteed this essential precondition for normal settled life; but when they could not, there was no longer any ideological or religious impediment to the establishment of a new regime that could. The apparently paradoxical readiness of Islamic society to accept governing institutions that often stood in sharp contrast to prevailing Islamic values and norms in fact stems from the simple fact that the preservation and realization of these ideals no longer depended on government, any form of which was acceptable as long as it maintained order and remained unhostile to the faith.

Second, and closely related to this point, the decline of the caliphate as an institution did not involve the decline of Islam as well. Islamic culture, separated from the fortunes of the governing institution, continued to flourish and in many fields pushed on to new heights of brilliance, even as political affairs became increasingly chaotic.

Finally, the various military and political "revivals" of the later Abbasid caliphate were more apparent than real. They did not represent the revival of the institution but, rather, only the skill or good fortune of a particular caliph in efforts to reassert or extend his own personal authority. The institution of the caliphate, once rendered superfluous, remained so, as indicated by the failure of the periods of "revival" to survive the passage from the scene of the personalities responsible for them.

THE POLITICAL DECLINE OF THE CALIPHATE
One of the caliphate's primary responsibilities was to control the forces of local particularism in the empire, and in this respect the institution encoun-

tered difficulty very soon after the Abbasid revolution. At first the problem was simply one of enormous distance from the center of imperial authority. An Umayyad prince who escaped the massacres of his kinsmen made his way to Spain and there established an independent Umayyad emirate in 756; this was followed by the appearance of independent principalities in North Africa: the Kharijite Rustamids in 761, the Shiite Idrisids in 789, and the Aghlabids in 800. The Abbasids, never again to rule west of Egypt, did try to undermine such principalities but made no positive effort to repossess them. In fact, the loss of Tunisia resulted directly from Hārūn's sale to the Aghlabids of the hereditary right to govern a province too remote to be controlled effectively from Iraq.

Far more serious was the alienation of important provinces by governors who, despite the obstacles set in their path, became powerful enough to defy the caliphate's authority. First Khorāsān, then other eastern provinces became virtually independent in this fashion. In 868 a hereditary governorship was established in Egypt and Syria. Although many of these principalities acknowledged the suzerainty of the Abbasids and even sent them tribute, the caliphate's authority hardly extended beyond Iraq by the mid ninth century.

The deterioration of the caliphate's power to maintain central control of the empire was directly linked to problems of the institution at the center. The extravagant Abbasid court was a tremendous financial burden. The bureaucracy, the key to orderly administration, became inefficient and corrupt. And as its members became so numerous as to form a distinct social grouping with a definite self-serving view of how government should function, it aroused the suspicion of the ᶜulamāʾ and the caliphs, leading to a series of demoralizing purges that further reduced its administrative effectiveness. Such conditions, particularly serious in the unsettled atmosphere of early Abbasid times, led to revolts, many of which were expressed in messianic terms, in Syria, Arabia, and particularly Persia. The northern frontier was repeatedly threatened by Byzantium and the Khazars, and from 868 to 883 the great slave rebellion of the Zanj devastated lower Iraq. Such disturbances incurred great expense, led to agricultural disorder and a corresponding decline in tax revenues, increased the caliphs' reliance on their military commanders, and diverted attention from grave structural problems that seemed to pose less immediate danger, such as the alienation of lands in the provinces.

Out of sheer necessity, the caliphate began to decentralize, resorting to tax farming and placing the collection of provincial revenues directly in the hands of provincial figures. Such a system not only allowed for great fiscal and social abuses but also, since many of the tax farmers were governors, marked a retreat from the important principle of separation of financial and administrative authority in the provinces. And as military commanders were becoming stronger contenders for regional hegemony in any case, the ultimate result was the concentration of power in the hands of extremely powerful emirs. By the mid ninth century, these generals were able to make and unmake caliphs almost at will.

The caliph al-Muᶜtaṣim (833–842) attempted to reverse this trend by expanding his own military guard into a large corps of slave troops, mostly Turks from central Asia, who were personally loyal to him alone. To ensure their isolation from the prevailing controversies and rivalries in Iraq, al-Muᶜtaṣim in 836 moved 100 kilometers (sixty-two miles) up the Tigris and built a new city, Samarra, which remained the capital until 892. But the Turkish guard soon came to realize that the caliph was as dependent on them as they were on him, and so began to vie for influence and power. The Abbasids tried to play factions off against one another; but once one party gained the advantage over the others, the caliphs found it increasingly difficult to resist its demands and encroachments. A Turkish element in Abbasid politics thus came to the fore, and it is at this time that one can speak of an end to the Arab domination of the caliphate.

As the competition for power by the military became more formidable, the caliphs could muster little effective resistance. The religious developments described above had already limited the spiritual authority of the institution, and responsibility for the excesses of the military tended to be laid at the door of the caliphate as well; the move to Samarra only aggravated its isolation from the broader concerns of the community. Also, the caliphate had done little to attract the support of landed or mercantile interests that were beginning to play important roles in society and the economy. Insofar as the caliphate had anything to do with them at all, it was to hinder them (though unintentionally) through heavy taxation and obstructive regulations. With the murder of al-Mutawakkil by the Turkish troops in 861 the caliphate was reduced to almost complete subservience. The efforts of a few capable and energetic caliphs and princes in the late ninth and early tenth centuries arrested the process of decline temporarily, but in 936, the governor of Wāsiṭ, Ibn Rāʾiq, forced the caliph al-Rāḍī to grant him the title *amīr al-umarāʾ* (literally emir of emirs). This gave Ibn Rāʾiq precedence over the other military commanders in Iraq; but far more important, it also amounted to an implicit relegation of the caliphate to a merely titular office symbolizing the spiritual unity of Islam.

When the Shiite Buyids (Buwayhids) of Persia occupied Baghdad in 945, the title of *amīr al-umarāʾ* passed to the Buyid emir Muʿizz al-Dawla and the caliphate was subjected to new humiliations. The Abbasid vizierate was abolished; the caliphs had to condone the celebration of Shiite festivals, though they and most of the people of Iraq were of the mainstream Sunni branch of Islam; and the Buyids frequently forced the caliphs to grant them special privileges and honors. The caliphs were occasionally able to play on partisan rivalries and so to resist the will of the emirs, but failure to cooperate could provoke retaliation. In 946 al-Mustakfī, suspected of plotting against his new overlords, was pulled from his throne, dragged on the ground to the palace of Muʿizz al-Dawla, blinded, and deposed as caliph. Blinding, adopted from the Byzantines as a means of rendering the sovereign incapable of carrying out his duties, was not uncommon for a time: in 946 there were three blinded ex-caliphs living in Baghdad.

How was the caliphate preserved for another 300 years? The answer lies in its symbolic importance. Even in its feeblest days, the caliphate's diplomas were sought by local rulers seeking to legitimize their authority; on a practical level, such diplomas did in fact lend greater authority to legal and civil proceedings. The Shiite Buyids also made use of their immediate control of the caliphate to promote their image in Sunni Iraq, to assert their preeminence over other local dynasties, and to impress visiting dignitaries with the awesome ceremonial of the renowned Abbasid court, where they made obsequious pretensions of loyalty and service to the caliph.

Of even greater importance was the symbolic importance of the caliphate in combating Ismailism. This extremist form of Shīʿa Islam had already given much trouble and near the end of the ninth century gave rise to violent rebellions by the Qarmatians. In 909 the more systematic Ismaili movement of the Fatimids established a principality in North Africa and proclaimed themselves the true caliphate led by the divinely guided *mahdī*. The exclusive right of the

Abbasid caliph to the title of *amīr al-muʾminīn* had been usurped before (for example, by the Qarmatians) and in fact was sometimes delegated by the caliphs to local dynasts. But here for the first time, a powerful principality not only denied the Abbasids titular suzerainty but actually founded a rival caliphate. That this claim was serious was demonstrated in 969 when Fatimid forces conquered Egypt, then invaded Syria and took control of Mecca and Medina in the Hejaz. For more than a hundred years they posed a grave threat to Iraq, and in 1058 a Turkish general briefly seized Baghdad and pronounced the name of the Fatimid caliph in the Friday prayers. And meanwhile, the rise of the Fatimids prompted the Umayyads in nearby Spain to assume the titles of *khalīfa* and *amīr al-muʾminīn* and to declare their own caliphate at Córdoba in 928.

The emergence of two rival caliphates and the Ismaili menace in general gave the symbolic potential of the caliphate great political importance. The Buyids, though Shiite themselves, were violently opposed to Ismailism and made full use of the propaganda value of their control of the caliphate. When the Seljuks occupied Baghdad in 1055, they too found the institution a valuable Islamic symbol. In fact, they justified their occupation of Baghdad as a measure to defend the Sunni caliphate. But though Sunni themselves, they accorded no power to the Abbasids, and the caliphs' relations with the Seljuk sultans were hardly less strained than they had been with the Buyid emirs.

It was in this period of decline that there arose the voluminous and exceedingly rich literature on the political theory of the caliphate and imamate. This literature is beyond the scope of discussion here, except to note that it was heavily influenced by the course of events at the time. Thus al-Bāqillānī (*d.* 1013) was preoccupied with defending the Sunni caliph against the claims of the Shīʿa; and such eminent theorists as al-Māwardī (*d.* 1058) and al-Ghazālī (*d.* 1111) conceded that faced with the alternative of rejecting government altogether, Muslims are compelled by practical necessity to accept and obey regimes that are less than ideal.

The last years of the Abbasid caliphate produced further resurgences under al-Muqtafī (1136–1160) and al-Nāṣir (1180–1225), who actually tried to formulate a new basis for rebuilding the institution by gaining the support of the *ʿulamāʾ* on their own terms. But final disaster overwhelmed the caliphate in 1258, when the Mongols swept into Iraq. Baghdad was sacked with frightful slaughter, and al-Mustaᶜṣim, the last Abbasid caliph, was brutally executed.

The violent extinction of a venerable institution was an enormous shock to the Islamic world, but its real effects were quite limited. Effective political power continued to be exercised as before; and Islamic culture and values, long since freed to follow their own independent course, were hardly affected. The institution of the caliphate had long performed the task of protecting and nurturing a new world order, and even in its latter centuries it was still considered valuable enough to finance and preserve. But as Ibn Taymīya (d. 1328) was later to point out, Islamic society could now function smoothly as long as there was accord between the ᶜulamāʔ and those exercising military and political power. Within this framework a caliphate was no longer necessary. The Mamluks of Egypt maintained a line of Abbasid princes as powerless figureheads from 1261 until 1517, but with rare exceptions they were not taken seriously elsewhere. The jurists dismissed or ignored them, and in general, the Mongol catastrophe had definitively impressed on Muslims the fact that the institution itself had come to an end.

BIBLIOGRAPHY

The history and development of the caliphate as a living institution have yet to be subject to full monographic treatment. Thomas W. Arnold, *The Caliphate* (1924), is outdated but still of interest; Émile Tyan, *Institutions du droit public musulman,* 2 vols. (1954–1957), is far more useful but highly theoretical. See also Gustave E. von Grunebaum, *Medieval Islam* (1946), 153–159; Maurice Gaudefroy-Demombynes, *Muslim Institutions,* John P. MacGregor, trans. (1950), 108–126; Claude Cahen, "The Body Politic," in Gustave E. von Grunebaum, ed., *Unity and Variety in Muslim Civilization* (1955), 132–163; Reuben Levy, *The Social Structure of Islam* (1957), 271–354; Anwar Chejne, *Succession to the Rule in Islam* (1960); W. Montgomery Watt, *Islamic Political Thought* (1968), and *The Formative Period of Islamic Thought* (1973); Patricia Crone, *Slaves on Horses: The Evolution of the Islamic Polity* (1980); Ann K. S. Lambton, *State and Government in Medieval Islam* (1981).

For discussions of particular topics and issues, see Ignaz Goldziher, "Du sens propre des expressions Ombre de Dieu, Khalife de Dieu pour désigner les chefs dans l'Islam," in *Revue de l'histoire des religions,* 35 (1897); D. S. Margoliouth, "The Sense of the Title Khalīfah," in *A Volume of Oriental Studies Presented to Edward G. Browne,* Thomas Walker Arnold and Reynold A. Nicholson, eds. (1922), 322–328; Adam Mez, *The Renaissance of Islam,* Sa-

lahuddin Khuda Bukhsh and D. S. Margoliouth, trans. (1937), 8–14; H. A. R. Gibb, "The Caliphate and the Arab States," in Kenneth M. Setton, ed., *A History of the Crusades,* I (1955), 81–98; "Constitutional Organization," in Majid Khadduri and Herbert J. Liebesny, eds., *Law in the Middle East,* (1955), 3–27; "The Evolution of Government in Early Islam," in *Studia islamica,* 4 (1955), and "The Fiscal Rescript of ᶜUmar II," in *Arabica,* 2 (1955); Dominique Sourdel, "Questions de cérémonial ᶜabbāside," in *Revue des études islamiques,* 28 (1960); H. A. R. Gibb, "Government and Islam Under the Early ᶜAbbāsids: The Political Collapse of Islam," in *L'élaboration de l'Islam* (1961), 115–127; S. D. Goitein, *Studies in Islamic History and Institutions* (1966); Bernard Lewis, "The Regnal Titles of the First ᶜAbbāsid Caliphs," in *Dr. Zakir Husain Presentation Volume* (1968); Heribert Busse, *Chalif und Grosskönig: Die Buyiden im Iraq, 945–1055* (1969); Amir H. Siddiqi, *Caliphate and Sultanate in Medieval Persia* (1969); Rudi Paret, "Signification coranique de ḫalīfa et d'autres dérivés de la racine ḫalafa," in *Studia islamica,* 31 (1970); W. Montgomery Watt, "God's Caliph: Qurʔānic Interpretations and Umayyad Claims," in C. E. Bosworth, ed., *Iran and Islam: In Memory of the Late Vladimir Minorsky* (1971), 565–574; Rudi Paret, "Ḫalīfat Allāh-Vicarius Dei," in *Mélanges d'Islamologie* (1974), 224–232; Ira M. Lapidus, "The Separation of State and Religion in the Development of Early Islamic Society," and George Maqdisi, "Les rapports entre calife et sulṭān à l'époque saljûqide," in *International Journal of Middle East Studies,* 6 (1975); Oleg Graber, "Notes sur les cérémonies umayyades," in *Studies in Memory of Gaston Wiet* (1977), 51–60; Tilman Nagel, "Some Considerations Concerning the Pre-Islamic and the Islamic Foundations of the Authority of the Caliphate," in G. H. A. Juynboll, ed., *Studies on the First Century of Islamic Society* (1982), 177–197.

LAWRENCE I. CONRAD

[See also **Abbasids; Abū Bakr; ᶜAlī ibn Abī Ṭālib; Alids; Baghdad; Barmakids; Buyids; Emir; Hārūn al-Rashīd; Hishām ibn ᶜAbd al-Malik; Imam; Islamic Administration; Maʔmūn, al-; Manṣūr, al-; Medina; Muᶜāwiya; Sasanians; Shīᶜa; ᶜUlamāʔ; ᶜUmar I ibn al-Khaṭṭāb; ᶜUmar II ibn ᶜAbd al-Azīz; Umayyads; Vizier.**]

CALLIGRAPHY, ISLAMIC. The Arabic term *khatt* does not mean "fine writing" (calligraphy). Instead, it is best translated by the unmodified word "writing" and includes renderings of script that have both high and low aesthetic merit.

Arabic script is a Semitic script with origins in the early centuries of the Christian era. Its twenty-eight letters are formed from seventeen different characters; sublinear or supralinear dots distinguish a number of otherwise identical characters, and diacritics indicate short vowels. In any of its many styles the script is a combination of horizontals, verticals, diagonals, dots, and curves that at its best is a rhythmic continuum moving from right to left with carefully modulated grace.

Initially centered on a small part of the Near East encompassing southwestern Arabia, the script spread with Muslim power in the great expansion of Islam after 622. The key figure in the establishment of the Arabic language and script was the Umayyad caliph ᶜAbd al-Malik (685–705), who decreed that Arabic should be the language of administration both in the capital of Damascus and in provincial centers throughout the empire, and that Muslim coinage should eschew figural images in favor of epigraphs. It was also during his reign that the first monumental uses of Arabic script occurred: in the Dome of the Rock in Jerusalem and on milestones. In these cases finely written, stately, angular styles of script (loosely called *kūfī*) were employed; having acquired status from these early uses, *kūfī* styles continued to be the aesthetically dominant forms until the eleventh century. While ᶜAbd al-Malik's decrees were probably the formal crystallization of two generations of development in Islam, his role was seminal in establishing state patronage for script and in advancing script as the foremost visual expression of the state and faith.

Without the revelation of the Koran, Arabic script could not have achieved this preeminence. Regarded by Muslims as the literal Word of God, the holy book was the focus of Muslim society. While the oral recitation of the Koran provided a model of Arabic usage for a people who had long prided themselves on verbal brilliance, the visible forms of the language brought a major new element into a society in which the visual arts had hitherto played a relatively minor role. The scripture had divine foundation, and the Koran endowed Arabic script with a sacrosanct quality it had never enjoyed before. Thus, centrality of scripture led to centrality of script, and the written word became the "sacred symbol" of Islam.

As the visible sign of Allah's revelation, script also functioned as an expression of political and religious power. The presence of Arabic script, particularly in monumental form, in new lands asserted the transformation of the non-Muslim *dār al-ḥarb* (abode of war) into the *dār al-Islām*. Arabic script also denoted unity, not simply because Arabic and Allah's Koran were written in it, but also because it was

adopted as the script for languages (such as Turkish and Persian) newly brought within the Muslim world.

Certain religious inscriptions were extremely common and repeated throughout Islam. Not only the words "Allah" and "Muḥammad" but also the initial words of the Koran (the *basmala:* "In the name of Allah, the merciful, the compassionate") and the creed (the *shahāda:* "There is no god but Allah, and Muḥammad is his Prophet") could be seen on buildings and objects from Spain to Indonesia, and they constituted the basic symbols of the faith. Much of Islamic religious life concentrated on the written word, for the contemplation of these and other pious epigraphs (such as the *asmāʾ al-ḥusnā,* the ninety-nine beautiful divine names) was one of the major vehicles for spiritual experience. Like the icon in Christian usage or the godly image on a Hindu temple, the written word functioned as Islam's manifestation of the intangible divine.

The interweaving of political and religious life that is characteristic of medieval Muslim culture is evident in the use of script. By the end of the seventh century the *shahāda* had become the fundamental visual symbol of Muslim power; written on coins, banners, standards, and state documents, its predominantly vertical forms were ubiquitous within Islam. Their ascending pattern served as a model for royal and official inscriptions that sought to associate temporal with divine power, and in similar fashion many of the *asmāʾ al-ḥusnā* were used as rulers' titles. Complexly interlocked epigraphs, visually rendering the repetitions of prayer, may have served as the inspiration for royal signatures, such as the Ottoman *tughra.*

The revelation of the Koran also created a division between the *Jāhiliyya* (Days of Ignorance before Islam) and the Muslim era. Islam's calendar recognized the fact by starting its first year in 622—the date of the prophet Muḥammad's establishment of the first Muslim state in Medina. This distinction in time between the past and the new age needed visual demarcation, and script was the most important means for doing so. Thus the presence of Arabic script on buildings, metal objects, textiles, ceramics, and objects in wood and glass, stone and ivory, served not only to decorate them and often to convey significant content, but also to make them visibly Muslim, distinct from the days before Islam.

Culturally and religiously Arabic script made other distinctions. Islam's most serious rival in its early centuries was Christian Byzantium, and much

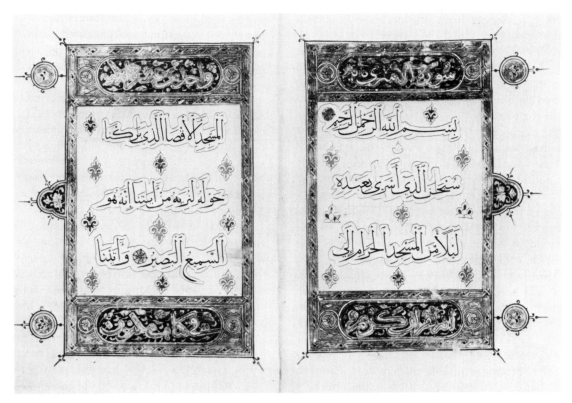

Initial pages, section 15 of the Koran. Egypt, late 14th century. COLLECTION OF PRINCE SADRUDDIN AGA KHAN

of the territory absorbed by the new Muslim state had been Byzantine. It became vitally important to the new state to create a visual language that would separate it and its acquired lands from Christendom with its powerful and highly developed tradition of figural arts. Thus the artistic and architectural use of Arabic script seems to have developed synchronously with Islam's official disavowal of the figural arts. This aversion to the figural arts in a sacred context differentiated Islam's visual culture from those of Byzantium and of other neighbors such as India and China, and the omnipresent use of script served the same purpose. Whether Arabic script rendered the Koran or other religious and nonreligious epigraphs, it stated the Muslim presence in a unique, immediately recognizable way and functioned as a "symbolic affirmation" of Islam.

Calligraphic script was vitally important on many levels and transcended narrow definitions of art. Documents, petitions, letters, and other archival instruments were often the work of master scribes; a good hand was fundamentally important to an administrative official, and a badly written document was sometimes considered evidence of the writer's insincerity, incompetence, or bad intention. Aesthet-

ics thus were closely allied with expressions of power, and rulers vied with each other to obtain the services of impressive calligraphers, just as they competed to collect the writings of illustrious past masters. Displays of connoisseurship were a major means of demonstrating princely culture. Script was essential to the value and acceptability of Muslim coinage, and both sacred and secular buildings were frequently adorned with monumental inscriptions designed by leading calligraphers. Objects in all materials could be provided with epigraphs suitable for either religious or mundane purposes; that these inscriptions were often misspelled or even illegible indicates that the visible presence of script was more important than specific content. And for the literate elite, scribes produced individual pages of calligraphy as well as whole manuscripts of works of literature, often illustrated with paintings executed to complement the aesthetics of script and text.

Such diverse products meant that scribes necessarily had multiple roles within Muslim society. They were, in fact, among the best-educated and most honored professionals, and the art of fine writing always ranked as the highest art form in Islam. Because of their necessary role in the administration of the state, scribes frequently occupied important governmental posts, and their careers could be affected by the vicissitudes of political life. While many held such salaried positions, others earned their living by teaching their skills, working as copyists and booksellers, or selling individual samples of their art.

The ninth-century introduction of paper into the Near East was as significant an event on a technical level as ᶜAbd al-Malik's decrees had been socially and politically. Largely replacing parchment and other expensive surfaces, paper was a cheap material; its availability led to the expansion of the scribal profession and to the proliferation of works of calligraphic art. Medieval Islam abounded in texts dealing with calligraphy and its practice. The Ṣubḥ al-aᶜshā (published 1913–1920) of al-Qalqashandī (d. 1418) was an Egyptian administrative manual that included a substantial chapter on calligraphic styles, techniques, and traditions, and the implements that a scribe needed; in the late sixteenth or early seventeenth century the Iranian official Qadi Aḥmad wrote a memoir (in *Calligraphers and Painters*, 1959) that devoted most of its pages to the careers of leading scribes; the great Iranian calligrapher Sultan ᶜAli Mashhadi (d. 1520) composed a poetical treatise on the techniques, training, and moral virtue essential to an aspiring scribe (*ibid.*, 106–125). The process and act of writing formed an integral part of the wider intellectual life of medieval Islam.

More than 100 distinct styles of Arabic script were in use in the sixteenth century. They ranged from the formal, angular *kūfī* to flowing, cursive forms like *thuluth* and *nastaᶜlīq*, and the choice of style depended on several factors. Foremost among them was the function a style served: slow-moving styles like *kūfī* and *thuluth* were favored for monumental inscriptions and for Koran chapter headings, while stately but less ponderous styles like *naskhī* and *rayhānī* were used for whole Korans and histories; from the fifteenth century on, *nastaᶜlīq* was

widely used in works of literature, *dīwānī* was used largely for governmental documents, and *shikasta* was a favorite letter-writing style of the seventeenth and eighteenth centuries. While most styles prevailed throughout Islam, some were geographically restricted. *Maghrebi* was used only in northwest Africa and Spain, while *shikasta* was limited largely to eastern Islam. Naturally, individual masters developed distinctive hands: despite adherence to the same canon of proportion and form, *nastaᶜlīq* by Mīr ᶜAlī al-Haravī (sixteenth century) could be distinguished from that of his contemporary Shāh Maḥmūd Nīshāpūrī.

Aesthetic canons for script styles are still far from clear, particularly for the first centuries of Islam, when *kūfī* styles were dominant. The period from the ninth through the thirteenth centuries is traditionally regarded by Muslim chroniclers as the great age of codification. Ibn Muqla (886–940), an official at the Abbasid court in Baghdad, is credited with the establishment of formal rules for writing *kūfī* and for developing the *sitta*, six widely accepted styles of script. His follower Ibn al-Bawwāb (d. 1022 or 1031/1032) refined and beautified Ibn Muqla's rules, while the thirteenth-century scribe Yaqūt al-Mustaᶜṣimī, who survived the Mongol conquest of Baghdad, made the *sitta* more elegant by cutting the nib of his reed pen at an angle appropriate to each style. The lives of these men and their dedication to their art were held up as models for later generations of scribes.

Writing supplied a metaphorical vocabulary that enriched Muslim languages. Allah was the supreme calligrapher, and human beings were likened to pens in Allah's hand. The reed pen was among his first creations. The features of the mystical beloved in poetry were compared to specific letters, and poems were composed by and for calligraphers, the words being selected for their calligraphic potential as much as for their content. A human being bowing in prayer was seen in the form of the word "Muḥam-

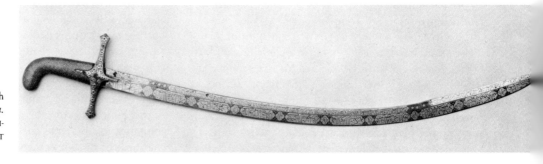

Steel saber inscribed with calligraphy. Turkey, *ca.* 1520–1566. THE METROPOLITAN MUSEUM OF ART, BEQUEST OF GEORGE C. STONE, 1936

mad," while the slender vertical letter alif was not only the first letter of Allah's name but also the first letter of the alphabet and the equivalent of the number 1; hence it expressed the fundamental unity of Allah and his creation. In the elaborate *abjad* system each letter of the alphabet had a fixed numerical value, and those devoted to the ᶜ*Ilm al-Ḥurūf* (science of letters) examined words in a search for esoteric knowledge in their values and meanings.

One of the most widely used Koranic passages was the celebrated *āyāt al-kursī* (2:255), a fundamental statement of divine omnipotence. It was inscribed on nearly every kind of object and on a vast number of buildings, particularly tombs and sarcophagi. Its wide visual use reflects its highly significant role in Muslim life, for it is usually recited after each of the five daily prayers and is credited with ensuring entrance to paradise for those who repeat it frequently. The verse was often recited as a defense against fear. Its artistic use then bespoke two purposes: the first was directed toward salvation; the second was a talisman to protect the reciter during his life. The fact that it was frequently inscribed on amulets, medicine bowls, and weapons, as well as on tombstones, indicates its dual function.

The preceding discussion indicates how inexact the translation "calligraphy" is for the Arabic *khaṭṭ*, for the latter encompasses far more than just "fine writing." The written word in Muslim culture can be metaphor, talisman, and expression of power as well as statement of content and aesthetic delight, and its component letters can have individual meanings of their own. Inscriptions too had substance that mattered, whether they were the constantly recurring epigraphs that shaped a Muslim environment or were statements with highly specific content directed at a definite political or social situation. The significance of the written word extended far beyond its formal beauty. Islam's devotion to the Arabic script stems from and nearly matches its devotion to its scripture; the written word is a testimony of cultural belonging and adherence to the faith.

BIBLIOGRAPHY

Nabia Abbott, *The Rise of the North Arabic Script* (1939); Adolf Grohmann, *Arabische Paläographie*, 2 vols. (1967–1971); Martin Lings, *The Quranic Art of Calligraphy and Illumination* (1976); Martin Lings and Yasin H. Safadi, *The Qurʾan*, catalog of an exhibition at the British Library (1976); Yasin H. Safadi, *Islamic Calligraphy* (1978); Annemarie Schimmel, *Islamic Calligraphy* (1970); Janine Sourdel-Thomine, Ali Alparslan, and M. Abdullah Chagh-
atai, "Khaṭṭ," article in the *Encyclopaedia of Islam*, IV (1978), 1113–1128; Anthony Welch, *Calligraphy in the Arts of the Muslim World* (1979).

ANTHONY WELCH

[See also **Dome of the Rock; Koran; Kūfi; Naskhi; Nastaᶜliq; Thuluth; Tughra; Writing Materials, Islamic.**]

CALPURNIUS SICULUS TITUS (*fl.* A.D. 50–60), was a Latin pastoral poet. The cognomen "Siculus" may denote a Sicilian origin, or be an acknowledgment of his literary debt to Theocritus, who was Sicilian. His seven surviving eclogues owe much to Vergil. Three of them (1, 4, and 7) are concerned with the praise of Nero and his reign, a new Golden Age; the remaining four are more traditionally pastoral in character.

His verse is generally considered conventional and uninspired, though by no means poor. It was popular in Carolingian times, being excerpted for schools, and was read by Paul the Deacon, Hrabanus Maurus, and others, whose own pastoral work was deeply influenced by him. Only in the nineteenth century was his corpus clearly distinguished from four other poems shown to be by the later writer Nemesianus.

BIBLIOGRAPHY

Texts. Charles Haines Keene, ed., *The Eclogues of Calpurnius Siculus and M. Aurelius Olympius Nemesianus*, 2nd ed. (1969). *Criticism.* Frederic J. E. Raby, *A History of Secular Latin Poetry in the Middle Ages*, 2nd ed. (1957), 1.37.

ABIGAIL YOUNG

[See also **Latin Literature.**]

CAMALDOLESE, ORDER OF, one of the earliest expressions of the eleventh-century monastic reform movement that stressed a return to the primitive eremitism of early Christian Egypt, total separation from lay society, and greater austerity. The Italian cities, because of their Byzantine connections and Eastern influences, seem to have been the source for eremitical interests in southern Europe.

About 1012 St. Romuald of Ravenna (ca. 952–1027), having attracted individuals and wandering groups in northern Italy who were united only in their wish for a more ascetic life, founded a monastery in the Tuscan-Romagnese Apennines near Arezzo, on land granted him by the count of Maldi (*campus* Maldi, hence Camaldoli). Romuald imposed the Rule of St. Benedict, as adapted to the eremitical life, on the new community, with the goal of infusing a more contemplative spirit than that common in contemporary Benedictine houses. Some of the monks led the communal life within the monastery, while the more spiritually advanced lived in nearby hermitages; the monastery existed to prepare the monk for the hermitage.

Romuald intended that life in the hermitages should be characterized by fasting, silence, and solitude. The approximately thirty monasteries in central Italy that he established or reformed had the distinctive feature of some of the monks living as cenobites, others as hermits; Camaldolese monks wore a habit composed of a white (rather than the Benedictine black) tunic, scapular, and hood. Romuald saw his monasteries as reformed Benedictine monasteries; he did not mean to begin a new order. The customs of the Sacro Eremo di Camaldoli, as the new monastery was called, were first written down by the fourth prior, Rudolph (1074–1089), and circulated as *Eremiticae regulae*. In 1072 Alexander II's approval of the existing Camaldolese houses amounted to official recognition of the new order. Gregory VII took the order under papal protection, and in 1113 Paschal II confirmed the actions of his predecessors. The first general chapter of priors of all houses met in 1239.

The two houses of the order that became most famous, Camaldoli and Fonte Avellana, served as centers of spiritual vitality and attracted the attention of the papacy, which appointed many Camaldolese monks as bishops in Umbria and Ancona. The most eminent member of the order was Peter Damian (1007–1072), later cardinal bishop of Ostia and distinguished reformer and scholar.

In the fourteenth and fifteenth centuries, the observance of the eremitical life declined and many monks became active in clerical ministries. Tensions between the cenobitic and eremitical objectives, together with the widespread practice of commendatory priors, provoked strong calls for reform. Ambrose (Ambrogio) Traversari (1386–1439), who had a reputation as a distinguished humanist and who in 1431 was elected general of the order, preached the reform of the order. Blessed Paul Giustiniani (1476–1528) sought a return to a more eremitical life through the Congregation of Monte Corona, which he established, and in his voluminous writings he tried to provide a doctrinal foundation for the eremitical life.

BIBLIOGRAPHY

Sources. Gian Benedetto Mittarelli, *Annales Camaldulenses ordinis Sancti Benedicti*, 9 vols. (1755–1773); Giovanni Tabacco, ed., "Petri Damiani Vita Beati Romualdi i–viii," in *Fonti storia d'Italia*, **94** (1957).

Studies. M. Elena Magheri Cataluccio and A. Ugo Fossa, *Biblioteca e cultura a Camaldoli: Dal medioevo all'umanesimo* (1979); Jean Leclercq, "St. Romuald et la monachisme missionaire," in *Revue bénédictine*, **72** (1962), and "L'eremitisme en Occident jusqu'à l'an mil," in *L'eremitismo in Occidente nei secoli XI e XII* (1965); Jean Leclercq, François Vandenbroucke, and Louis Bouyer, *The Spirituality of the Middle Ages* (1968), 110–115; Giovanni Tabacco, "La data di fondazione di Camaldoli," in *Rivista di storia della chiesa in Italia*, **16** (1962).

BENNETT D. HILL

[See also **Benedictine Rule; Monasticism; Peter Damian; Romuald of Ravenna; Traversari, Ambrogio.**]

Eadwine, scribe of the Cambridge Psalter. Canterbury Psalter, mid 12th century. BY PERMISSION OF THE MASTER AND FELLOWS OF TRINITY COLLEGE, CAMBRIDGE

CAMBRIDGE PSALTER, an Anglo-Norman interlinear translation, dating from around 1115, of the Hebrew version of the Psalms. It is in Trinity College, Cambridge (MS R.17.i), a manuscript copied at Christ Church, Canterbury, around the middle of the twelfth century by a scribe named Eadwine. The Canterbury Psalter also contains the Roman version of the Psalms with an interlinear version in Anglo-Saxon.

BIBLIOGRAPHY

An edition is Francisque X. Michel, *Le livre des Psaumes ... d'après les manuscrits de Cambridge et de Paris* (1876), facs. ed. by Montague R. James, *The Canterbury Psalter* (1935). See also Montague R. James, *The Western Manuscripts in the Library of Trinity College, Cambridge,* II (1901), 402–410.

BRIAN MERRILEES

[See also **Anglo-Norman Literature.**]

CAMBRIDGE SONGS (*Carmina Cantabrigiensia*), the Latin songs and poems in one of the most important poetic anthologies of the Middle Ages (Cambridge, University Library, Gg. 5. 35 [formerly 1567]), not to be confused with the songs of the "younger" Cambridge Song Book described by Schumann. The *Carmina Cantabrigiensia* occupy only a portion (fols. 432–441) of the manuscript, which was written in England in the eleventh century. Between the twelfth and seventeenth centuries the entire manuscript was kept in St. Augustine's Abbey at Canterbury, before coming to Cambridge. Opinions on the origin and purpose of this collection are divided. Some place it in the same category as the early-thirteenth-century manuscript of the *Carmina burana*, written for a patron of poetry; others point to the possibility of its having been a "repertory" of an entertainer. The pieces in the collection are heterogeneous: religious and secular songs and poems appear side by side. Undoubtedly the original was compiled in Germany, possibly in the Rhineland. Strecker believed that numbers 2–15 of the present collection belonged to a sequence collection. Some pieces are found in other manuscripts as well.

Many of the forty-nine pieces in the collection are from Germany; others were written in France and Italy as early as the tenth century. The age and the occasions for which some of these songs were composed can be determined on the basis of allusions to contemporary events. Other songs, however, are much older than the collection itself. Merovingian and Carolingian compositions are found among them, and nos. 31, 32, 34, and 46 are extracts from poems by Statius, Vergil, and Horace.

Eight groups can be distinguished in this collection. First, Merovingian and Carolingian rhythms and hymns: an old Christmas hymn, "Gratuletur omnis caro" (represented by one stanza); and the moral admonition "Audax es, vir iuvenis" (nos. 1 and 18).

Second, religious songs and prayers. They begin with a short extract from the poem *Ad Felicem episcopum* by Venantius Fortunatus (including: "Tempora florigero"), centos of which are often used in the liturgy as a processional hymn (no. 22). There are also a Marian prayer (no. 36) and praises of the Resurrection (no. 44) and of the church (no. 47).

Third, religious sequences (nos. 4, 5, 8, and 13) and a narrative borrowed from the St. Basil legend in sequence form (no. 30a).

Fourth, secular songs in sequence form such as the friendship story of Lantfrid and Cobbo (no. 6) and the sequence of Pythagoras (no. 12).

Fifth, songs belonging to the literary form of the *ridiculum* (humorous tale) in sequence form: the story of the "Snow Child" (no. 14), the "lying tale" about the Swabian who wins the hand of the princess in a lying contest (no. 15), the "Priest and Wolf" (no. 35), the tale of Abbot John from the *Vitas patrum* (no. 42), and perhaps even "Heriger of Mainz and the Pseudo-Prophet" (no. 24) and the fable of the donkey of Alfrad and the sisters from Homburg (no. 20), the last two not in sequence form.

Sixth, historical songs, laments, and royal poems in the form of sequences or of stanzaic poems: on the coronation of Conrad II (no. 3), on the death of Henry II (no. 9), on Ottonian emperors (no. 11), on the coronation of Henry III (no. 16), on the death of Henry II (no. 17), on the death of Conrad II (no. 33). To these may be added, perhaps, a poem congratulating an unidentified queen on her recovery (no. 41), and praises of Archbishop Heribert of Cologne (no. 7) and of William I of Poitiers (no. 43). A unique poem deals with Archbishop Poppo and his church in Trier (no. 25), the church addressing the archbishop as his mystical "bride." "De Henrico," a macaronic poem in Latin and German, speaks of affairs of the future Emperor Henry II and his Ottonian predecessor, around 996 (no. 19). Two other poems (nos. 26 and 38) belong in this group only marginally.

Seventh, love and nature lyrics appear in large numbers for the first time in this collection. Both heterosexual and homosexual love are represented. Number 40 is the spring complaint of a young girl or nun ("Levis exurgit zephirus"); number 27 is the famous *Invitatio amicae,* which incorporates material reminiscent of the Song of Songs ("Iam dulcis amica venito") and occasionally appears as a Marian hymn in liturgical manuscripts. There also are a fragmentary macaronic text, ingeniously reconstructed by Dronke ("Suavissima nunna," no. 28), and the homosexual love poem "O admirabile Veneris idolum" (no. 48), from northern Italy (Verona, perhaps tenth century).

The *Tierstimmendichtung,* in which the voices of animals or birds are "cataloged" and characterized, are represented by an enticing sapphic, "Vestiunt silvae" (no. 23), set in the framework of a pleasant summer scene. The song, like most medieval "nature poetry," ends on a religious note. "Aurea personet lira" (no. 10), a poem generally attributed to Bishop Fulbert of Chartres, represents the widespread "Nightingale song," known in variations from the poetry of Eugenius II of Toledo to later stages of medieval literature, in both Latin and the vernacular.

There are also poems (such as no. 26) that do not fit into any of the above categories. Of number 37 ("Ad mensam philosophiae") only one stanza appears in the Cambridge manuscript. The presence of neumes, various passages in the songs, and a few items, such as number 45 *(De musica),* indicate interest in and association with music. Some texts are illegible fragments.

Several of the forty-nine pieces are specifically attributed to various authors or at least assumed to be their compositions. Several were written by Wipo of Burgundy (nos. 16, 17, and 33). The story of Abbot John and the "Nightingale song" (no. 10) are among the poems of Bishop Fulbert. The song titled *Modus liebinc* ("Snow child") has been ascribed to Heribert of Rothenburg; the author of number 2 (among the historical songs) probably came from the royal chapel.

The relatively large number of songs dealing with German rulers and ecclesiastical princes from Germany not only supports the theory of a German and Rhineland origin of the collection but also rules out the assumption that the collection is a selection of "migrating" popular songs. Instead, one must assume that the compilation was made by an entertainer or singer and specialized for the higher classes, the songs and poems being selected for the entertainment of imperial court circles. The coexistence of secular and religious poetry and songs in the collection reflects a typical medieval attitude that saw no real gap between the two spheres of life.

The historical songs express loyalty by celebrating the coronation of rulers and formulating the feeling of grief at their death. These poems also serve as propaganda for the political leaders in both secular and religious terms. The poem (sequence) on Lantfrid and Cobbo propagates the idea of friendship. The narratives described as *ridiculum* bear witness to the medieval sense of humor and give some idea of the types of narratives considered both humorous and profitable in the Middle Ages. The use of the sequence form indicates the popularity of that relatively recent poetic invention.

Application of the term *modus* to both secular and religious songs in sequence form shows the influence of certain established melody types that were imitated by poets dealing with varied subjects. The larger concentration of love poetry in this collection heralds the advent of love songs, both Latin and vernacular, characteristic of both the goliardic and the courtly poetry of the twelfth century and afterward.

BIBLIOGRAPHY

Fr. J. Worstbrock, "Cambridger Lieder (Carmina Cantabrigiensia)," in *Verfasserlexikon,* 2nd ed., I (1979); Karl Strecker, ed., *Die Cambridger Lieder,* 2nd ed. (1955); Walther Bulst, ed., *Carmina Cantabrigiensia* (1950); "Zur Vorgeschichte der Cambridger und anderer Sammlungen," in *Historische Vierteljahrschrift,* **27** (1932), and "Zu Wipo's *Versus pro obitu Chuonradi imperatoris,"* in *Festschrift Percy Ernst Schramm,* Peter Classen, ed., I (1964); Hans Spanke, *Studien zu Sequenz, Lai and Leich* (1977); Peter Dronke, *Medieval Latin and the Rise of European Love-Lyric,* 2nd ed., 2 vols. (1968), I: 271ff., 277ff., and II: 353–356. F. J. E. Raby, "Philomena praevia temporis amoeni," in *Mélanges Joseph de Ghellinck, S.J.,* II (1951); St. Ebbesen, "Zum Carmen Cantabrigiense VI," in *Mittelateinisches Jahrbuch,* **3** (1966); V. Schupp, "Der Dichter des 'Modus Liebinc,'" in *Mittelateinisches Jahrbuch,* 5 (1968); M. H. Hengstl, *Totenklage und Nachruf in der mittellateinische Literatur* (1936).

JOSEPH SZÖVÉRFFY

[See also **Latin Literature; Sequence.**]

CAMBRIDGE, UNIVERSITY OF. The evidence for the origins of Cambridge University is of the most fragmentary kind. The thesis that the university was an outgrowth of the town's twelfth-century grammar schools, augmented by the academic activities of the monks of Ely, Croyland, and Barnwell, is too speculative to carry conviction. By 1200 there are no clear signs of an embryonic center of higher learning in Cambridge. It appears that the university crystallized only as a result of the impetus given by a migration of Oxford masters and scholars to Cambridge in 1209. In essence, therefore, the university would seem to owe its foundation primarily to an exodus from Oxford.

By 1225 a chancellor is recorded; and in 1233 what seems to be the first papal recognition of Cambridge University was conferred. The earliest extant enactment of the chancellor and regent masters dates from 1246, and the earliest dated statute was promulgated on 17 March 1276. In organizational terms Cambridge was no mere derivative of Oxford but, in the course of the thirteenth century, exhibited many features of indigenous growth. In 1318 Pope John XXII officially confirmed Cambridge's legal status as a *studium generale,* a university of the first rank. But throughout at least part of the thirteenth and early fourteenth centuries Cambridge had already been recognized as a *studium generale* by custom (*ex consuetudine*), and as such is to be classed with those universities such as Paris, Bologna, Oxford, and Padua which had attained the status of *studium generale* by custom and not by formal papal act.

It is probable that even toward the end of the fourteenth century Cambridge University had a population of only between 400 and 700, at which time the number of scholars at Oxford may have been about 1,500. By the mid fifteenth century, however, Cambridge seems to have numbered some 1,300 students, compared with an Oxford population of perhaps 1,700.

One of the factors that promoted the near equalization of the two university populations was the differing positions of Cambridge and Oxford with regard to the heresies of John Wycliffe and of the Lollards. Although the most stringent efforts had been made to purge Oxford University of its Wycliffite and Lollard associations, the stigma of heresy lingered there throughout the fifteenth century. Its murky reputation as the "university of heresies" seems to have redounded to the profit of Cambridge, which, because of its orthodoxy, came to be regarded as a sound investment for patrons of learning and a safe haven for undergraduate students. The

founders of the Cambridge secular colleges in the fifteenth century—King's College (founded by Henry VI), Queens', St. Catharine's, and Jesus—shared in this objective of reinforcing the university as a bastion of orthodoxy in the community.

The secular collegiate movement at Cambridge was inaugurated with the establishment of Peterhouse in 1284. Seven colleges were founded in the fourteenth century and five in the fifteenth, making a total of thirteen by 1500. Of these the most celebrated, the most unusual, and, until the mid fifteenth century, the largest was the royal college of the King's Hall, which had its genesis in a detachment from Edward II's chapel royal planted in the University of Cambridge. This brought into being the first royal colony of clerks to be domiciled in an English university.

Ten secular colleges were established at Oxford in the same period, and seven had ecclesiastical founders. By contrast, the Cambridge colleges were far less exposed to ecclesiastical influences and were strongly insistent on their independent status. This collegiate dissimilarity is an indicator of the differing intensities with which the struggle for university autonomy from episcopal authority was fought at Oxford and Cambridge. The slowness of the movement at Cambridge may have resulted from the fact that the ecclesiastical jurisdiction of the bishop of Ely, in whose diocese the university lay, was more a matter of troublesome theoretical definition than one affecting the daily round of university life to any significant degree. Whereas Oxford acquired a complete exemption from an interventionist ecclesiastical authority in 1395, Cambridge did not obtain legal exemption from a distant and quiescent ecclesiastical power until 1432.

In the Middle Ages Cambridge was a rather insular institution geographically, recruitment of scholars being mainly from the British Isles, in particular from the eastern and northern English counties (the dioceses of Lincoln, Norwich, and York). Only about 1 percent of students was drawn from Wales, Scotland, and Ireland, and a similarly low percentage from continental Europe. Italy seems to have been the main venue for the minority of Cambridge scholars who sought foreign study; they were attracted especially to the law courses of the Italian universities. Although Cambridge was the smaller and, until the fifteenth century, the less prominent of the two English universities, several eminent scholars, including Thomas of York, John Duns Scotus,

CAMELOT

John Bromyard, Robert of Holcot, Roger Marston, and Thomas of Cobham, are known to have studied and taught there. Like Oxford, Cambridge was slow in coming to terms with European humanism, a palpable impact being made only in the last quarter of the fifteenth century.

By the early sixteenth century much of the teaching at Cambridge had come to be decentralized in the colleges, which, through their developing tutorial and lecturing facilities, could now cater to basic undergraduate needs. The attempts by Cambridge to revive the system of university teaching proved ineffective, and in Elizabeth's reign the colleges had recognizably emerged as the principal teaching units. This decentralized system remained fairly constant until the early twentieth century, when once again university teaching facilities began to retrieve some of the prominence lost for almost 400 years.

BIBLIOGRAPHY

Bibliographies. The main classes of manuscript sources in the Cambridge University Archives and publications relating to the University of Cambridge are listed by Heather E. Peek and Catherine P. Hall, *The Archives of the University of Cambridge* (1962), 72–86, and A. B. Emden, *A Biographical Register of the University of Cambridge to 1500* (1963), xiii–xxvi. General bibliographies are found in A. B. Cobban, *The King's Hall Within the University of Cambridge in the Later Middle Ages* (1969), 321–330, and in M. B. Hackett, *The Original Statutes of Cambridge University: The Text and Its History* (1970), 344–370.

Studies. A. B. Cobban, *The Medieval Universities: Their Development and Organization* (1975), 110–115; M. B. Hackett, *op. cit.;* T. H. Aston, G. D. Duncan, and T. A. R. Evans, "The Medieval Alumni of the University of Cambridge," in *Past and Present,* **86** (1980); A. B. Cobban, "The Medieval Cambridge Colleges: A Quantitative Study of Higher Degrees to *c.* 1500," in *History of Education,* **9** (1980).

ALAN B. COBBAN

[See also **Oxford, University of; Universities.**]

CAMELOT. See **Arthurian Literature.**

CAMPANILE, Italian for bell tower, usually a structure separate from the main building. The earliest known example was attached to St. Peter's in Rome during the middle of the eighth century, and

CAMPIN, ROBERT

Cathedral and campanile. Florence, mid 14th century. FROM SIR BANISTER FLETCHER'S A HISTORY OF ARCHITECTURE

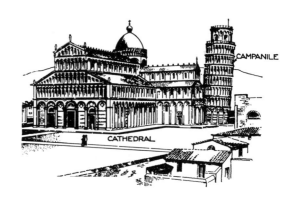

Cathedral and campanile. Pisa, late 12th and early 13th centuries. FROM SIR BANISTER FLETCHER'S A HISTORY OF ARCHITECTURE

campaniles from the ninth century are preserved in Ravenna. Campaniles may be round (as in Pisa) or square (as in Florence); they often contained arched openings at several levels.

LESLIE BRUBAKER

CAMPIN, ROBERT (*ca.* 1378–1444). A pioneer in late Gothic painting in the Low Countries, Robert Campin is first mentioned in the archives of Tournai in 1406. He was elected deacon of the painter's guild in 1423, and his name is recorded frequently until his death. Campin had a number of illustrious apprentices, including Rogier van der Weyden and Jaques Daret. He left no signed works, but it is almost certain that his oeuvre is that of an artist previously identified as the Master of Flémalle after three panels (one painted on both sides, today in the Städelisches Kunst Institut, Frankfurt-am-Main) allegedly executed for an abbey of that name near Liège that display unmistakable relationships to the early works of van der Weyden and Daret.

Campin's earliest work, the *Altarpiece of the Deposition* (Count Antoine Seilern Collection, London), can be dated to about 1415–1420 and displays characteristics of the late Gothic International Style: the archaic use of gold backgrounds, elaborate drapery patterns, and compositions derived from French miniatures and Sienese painting. The *Nativity* (Musée des Beaux-Arts, Dijon, *ca.* 1420–1425) exhibits Campin's earthy realism with the birth of the child on the ground, in a ramshackle hut placed in a charming country landscape. The subject matter also reveals Campin's departure from traditional themes. The unusual appearance of the midwives, one with a withered hand, is derived from early apocryphal gospels; and the candle held by Joseph, together with the humble position of the Virgin, kneeling on the ground before her child, who radiates light, depend on the *Revelationes* of St. Brigid of Sweden, a popular mystical treatise in the fifteenth century.

Campin's best-known work is the *Mérode Altar-piece* (Metropolitan Museum, Cloisters Collection, New York), dating from about 1425–1430. The Annunciation takes place, perhaps for the first time, in a domestic interior, with the Virgin seated on the floor in a pose of humility. The right panel depicts Joseph at work as a carpenter in a typical Flemish shop interior. He has made mousetraps, alluding to his presence as "bait for the devil." Campin's figures are stocky and boldly modeled, with colorful, cumbersome drapery wrapped about them, and his interests in light and space are exaggerated with deep perspective plunges and stark double shadows cast against the walls.

The last work by Campin, the *Werl Altarpiece* wings of 1438 (Prado Museum, Madrid), shows the influence of his illustrious apprentice, Rogier van der Weyden, on his style. In recent scholarship Campin has been regarded as a precursor of the traditional founder of the *ars nova* in Flemish painting, Jan van Eyck. His art was grounded in the more vigorous climate of bourgeois patronage of the Netherlands, while van Eyck's reflects the richer tastes of the aristocratic Burgundian court.

BIBLIOGRAPHY

Max J. Friedländer, *Early Netherlandish Painting,* vol. 2: *Rogier van der Weyden and the Master of Flémalle,* Heinz Norden, trans. (1967); Erwin Panofsky, *Early Netherlandish Painting* (1953).

JAMES SNYDER

[See also **Gothic Art: Painting and Manuscript Illumination; Weyden, Rogier van der.**]

Annunciation. Central panel of Mérode Altarpiece, *ca.* 1425–1430. THE METROPOLITAN MUSEUM OF ART, NEW YORK: THE CLOISTERS COLLECTION

CANARY ISLANDS AND BÉTHENCOURT. The Canary Islands were vaguely known to the ancient world as the Fortunate Islands. They were not really explored, however, until two Genoese in the service of Portugal (Lanzarotto Malocello and Nicoloso da Recco) visited them in 1336 and 1341, respectively. After 1370 the island of Lanzarote (named for its discoverer) was occupied by the Portuguese as a fief of the crown, but a revolt of the natives wiped out this settlement in 1385. Even before this date a Castilian expedition under Martin Ruiz de Avendaño had landed on Lanzarote in the name of their king, and Gonzalo Perez de Martel of Seville, authorized to conquer the island by Henry III of Castile, made another landing in 1393. In neither case was there a lasting occupation. It was only in July 1402

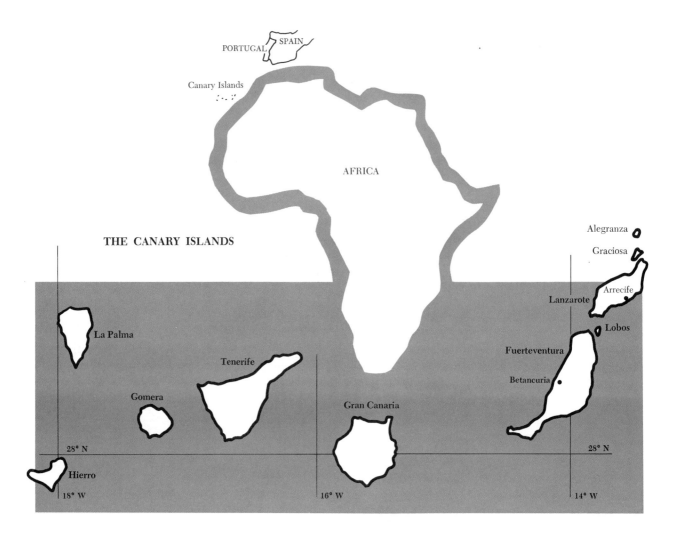

THE CANARY ISLANDS

that the Norman Jean de Béthencourt and the Poitevin Gadifer de La Salle undertook a permanent conquest and settlement. They were acting by virtue of a concession of the Canaries as a fief of the Castilian crown to Admiral Robert de Braquemont, a relative of Béthencourt.

For more than a year, Béthencourt and La Salle hesitated about the attitude they should take toward Castile. At first they seem to have considered acting independently, but by 1403 growing problems persuaded Béthencourt to recognize Castilian sovereignty. Since Béthencourt had not consulted his colleague on this move, La Salle felt injured, and returned to France in 1404. Nevertheless, it was the sixty or so Poitevins and Gascons of La Salle who conquered the islands of Lanzarote and Fuerteventura while Béthencourt was intriguing in the court of Castile. Béthencourt returned to France in 1405 to recruit new settlers, especially farmers and artisans.

On his return Béthencourt toured the islands with his nephew and heir Maciot, but only the islands of Lanzarote, Fuerteventura, and Hierro were brought partially under cultivation. The sale of archil, a vegetable coloring used in clothmaking, was made a monopoly. Gadifer de La Salle had already given the natives the choice between surrender, with conversion to Christianity, and war, followed by slavery for the survivors. Béthencourt continued this brutal policy, but he also tried to gain the support of the tribal chiefs. This did not keep them from losing part of their lands, which were divided, like those of their subjects, among the French settlers. These settlers in turn were subjected to a seigneurial regime not unlike that of their native land. Their labor force was made up partly of native slaves and partly of Moorish and black slaves imported from Africa.

It seems clear that Béthencourt left the Canaries for good before 1415. Maciot stayed behind and founded a family, but he lost his land little by little because no new settlers came from France and money was soon lacking. Prince Henry the Navigator then tried to revive Portugal's claim to the islands by virtue of the discoveries of the preceding century and by actual settlement for fifteen years (1370–1385). Maciot, however, finally sold his fief to the count of Niebla, in southern Spain. Several other Spanish nobles exercised feudal rights in the name of Castile over other islands in the group, until the Treaty of Alcaovas between Castile and Portugal (1479) definitely recognized the rights of the Castilian crown. From that time on, the Castilian element in the population grew steadily. The conquest of the islands was completed in 1496.

BIBLIOGRAPHY

Michel Mollat, "La place de la conquête normande des Canaries (XVᵉ siècle) dans l'histoire coloniale française," in his *Études d'histoire maritime* (1977), 141–157; Antonio Pérez Voituriez, *Problemas jurídicos internacionales de la conquista de Canarias* (1958); E. Serra Rafols and A. Cioranescu, "Le Canarien: Cronicas francesas de la conquista de Canarias," in *Fontes rerum Canariarum*, **8, 9, 10** (1959–1965); Charles Verlinden, "La découverte des archipels de la 'Méditerranée atlantique' (Canaries, Madères, Açores) et la navigation astronomique primitive," in *Revista portuguesa de historia*, **16** (1978).

CHARLES VERLINDEN

[See also **Castile; Exploration by Western Europeans; Portugal.**]

CANCIONERO GENERAL, an anthology of late medieval Spanish verse, first published at Valencia in 1511 in an edition of 1,000 copies printed by Christofal Kofman. It was compiled over a period of twenty years, apparently solely from manuscript sources, by Hernando del Castillo, a Castilian living in Valencia and serving the count of Oliva. It consists of 8 + 234 folios (484 pages) printed mainly in three columns, and contains more than 1,000 poems representing some 200 named poets and sundry anonymous contributors, mostly from the late fifteenth century. A thematic and metrical classification of the material in ten sections, proposed by the

compiler in his prologue, is only loosely adhered to and breaks down in the middle, where poems are grouped by author.

There is enormous disparity in the quality of the material; some major poets scarcely figure, while some negligible writers are abundantly represented; and the texts are often unreliable or corrupt. Nevertheless, the Cancionero is of unique importance—in that it rescued from oblivion a huge quantity of material for which manuscript sources are no longer extant, in that its unselectivity provides an unrivaled breadth of perspective, and in that it ensured the persistence of traditional verse throughout the Italianizing period, until the revival of the use of literary conceits *(conceptismo)* in the seventeenth century. It was reprinted in a revised version in 1514 with 190 additions (but also numerous suppressions not advertised by the compiler), and with a few of the original poems in superior texts; it appeared again, usually with modifications, in 1517, 1520, 1527, 1535, 1540, 1557, and 1573. The final section was reprinted separately with additions as the *Cancionero de obras de burlas provocantes a risa* (1519). The *Cancionero general* was plundered by other anthologizers, such as Juan Fernández de Constantina *(Guirlanda esmaltada de galanes)*, and it was imitated in Portuguese by Garcia de Resende *(Cancioneiro geral, 1516).*

BIBLIOGRAPHY

Hernando del Castillo, *Cancionero general de muchos y diversos autores* (1511), also facsimile with introduction by Antonio Rodríguez-Moñino (1958); Antonio Rodríguez-Moñino, *Suplemento al Cancionero general* (1959); Keith Whinnom, "Hacia una interpretación y apreciación de las canciones del *Cancionero general*," in *Filología*, **13** (1968–1969), and *La poesía amatoria de la época de los Reyes Católicos* (1981); J. M. Aguirre, *Cancionero general: Antología temática del amor cortés* (1971).

KEITH WHINNOM

[See also **Spanish Literature.**]

CANCUN D'ANTIOCHE. See **Chanson d'Antioche.**

CANDIDUS OF FULDA (BRUUN) (*d.* 845), hagiographer and theologian. He entered the monastery

CANDLES

of Fulda sometime between 779 and 802, and studied under Einhard from 802 until 817. Although he was a teacher at Fulda, it is not certain that he became head of the school after Hrabanus Maurus became abbot (822–842).

His chief literary work is the Life of St. Eigil (*ca.* 840), in both a prose and a poetic form, which provides information about the internal history of Fulda. Other works long attributed to Candidus may not actually be by him. *De imagine Dei* of the *Dicta Candidi* was almost certainly written by Candidus Wizo, a disciple of Alcuin. Two other works—a series of homilies titled *Opusculum de passione Domini*, and a letter, *Num Christus Corporeis oculis Deum videre pocuerit* (Whether Christ could see God with his bodily eyes), both have the same author, but it is uncertain which Candidus wrote them.

BIBLIOGRAPHY

"Vita Eigilis," in *Monumenta Germaniae historica: Scriptores*, XV, 1 (1963), 221–233; Max Manitius, *Geschichte der lateinischen Literatur im Mittelalter*, I (1911), 660–663.

KRISTINE T. UTTERBACK

[See also **Benedictines; Fulda; Hagiography, Western European.**]

CANDLES. See **Lighting Devices.**

CANNON. The first recorded use of artillery in Europe can be dated to the siege of Metz in 1324; cannon and cannonballs are mentioned in a Florentine document of 1326. The first pictorial representation of a gun is in the Milemete manuscript, an English dedicatory address presented to King Edward III at his accession in 1327. It is a strange device, looking very much like a vase laid on its side, from which a large arrow is being propelled toward a town or castle gate. It is laid on a sort of trestle table, with no apparent means of holding it in position. The gunner, a man-at-arms holding a lighted linstock, would surely have been caught by the recoil of his insecurely mounted weapon.

After 1325 documentary evidence testifies to the existence of cannon all over western Europe. By 1331 German troops were using them at the siege of

CANNON

Cividale, in northeastern Italy. In the same year the Moors were using guns in a campaign against Aragon. A French squadron that raided Southampton in 1338 seems to have been provided with one cannon and a modest supply of projectiles. A year later the Scots are recorded as having employed artillery at the siege of Stirling; Edward III expended considerable sums on artillery and ammunition for his siege of Calais in 1346–1347. By the middle of the fourteenth century there is solid evidence for the use of artillery in England, Scotland, France, Flanders, Germany, Italy, and the Iberian peninsula.

These guns were clearly experimental, and no one at mid century could have foreseen their eventual revolutionary impact on the art of war. The experimentation continued through the rest of the century and tended in two directions. The first consisted of small-caliber weapons, firing bolts or pellets, obviously antipersonnel in purpose. They were often mounted on beams, with several tubes clamped together so that the gunner could, with one sweep of his linstock, discharge them almost simultaneously. These precursors of rapid-fire weapons were suitable only for defending a prepared site or gate, or to command a breach. And since they were muzzle-loaded

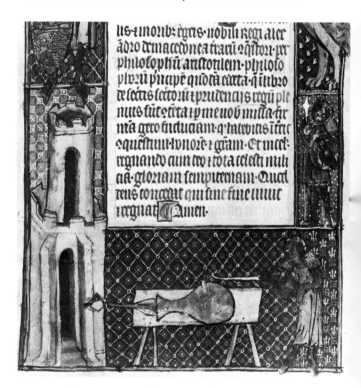

First pictorial representation of a cannon. Milemete MS, 1327. BY KIND PERMISSION OF THE GOVERNING BODY OF CHRIST CHURCH, OXFORD

64

guns, they would be unable to get off a second round before the enemy closed.

Other experiments led to the development of cannon of increasingly larger bore, which in turn led to additional problems. The casting techniques of the time were so imperfect that flaws and local weaknesses often produced fatal explosions. No more satisfactory was the process of making wrought-iron guns. Iron rods were welded around a wooden core, then beaten into a solid tube while red-hot. To strengthen the barrel further, iron hoops were clamped about the outside, but this was no more effective in preventing accidents than the casting process had been. However, by the end of the fifteenth century, the casting process had been so improved that welded and hooped guns had been supplanted by bronze pieces of Renaissance workmanship. Experiments were also made with breech-loading weapons, but these were not overly successful and apparently were abandoned by the end of the century.

As cannon grew heavier, other problems emerged. That of mobility was partially solved by putting guns on wheeled carriages, but until the invention of the trunnion in the late fifteenth century, the recoil of a gun merely strapped to its carriage must have shaken it to pieces after a few discharges. The muzzle could be elevated or depressed by various clumsy expedients, but even after wheels were attached to the carriage in the fifteenth century, any change of position must have been a slow and laborious process.

By the end of the fourteenth century, siege artillery had been developed with barrels weighing as much as 600 pounds. The fifteenth century saw the production of even larger pieces that cast projectiles weighing several hundred pounds. This led to the introduction of stone cannonballs; metal was too scarce and too expensive to be used in this manner. This development in turn produced the skilled artisan who cut cannonballs, and whose pay in England eventually equaled that of a man-at-arms.

By the middle decades of the fifteenth century, siege trains, not only in western Europe but also in the Islamic lands, were rapidly reversing the centuries-old dominance of the defense over the offense. In France the royal siege train of Charles VII had, by 1453, reduced Henry VI's "kingdom of France" to the bridgehead of Calais.

The most celebrated victory of siege artillery over conventional fortifications was the reduction of Constantinople by Mehmed II the Conqueror in

German cannon, *ca.* 1405. FROM KONRAD KYESER'S BELLIFORTIS, GÖTTINGEN UNIV. MS 63 phil.

1453. His seventy-piece siege train, some of its weapons firing balls weighing as much as 800 pounds, succeeded in opening breaches in the land walls that had withstood attack for over a thousand years.

Moreover, the defenders of Constantinople discovered, as had garrisons elsewhere, that use of the new artillery on ramparts soon had to be discontinued because the recoil threatened the fabric of the walls. This fact, coupled with the vulnerability of medieval walls and towers to artillery fire, set fifteenth-century engineers to devising defenses that would offer a minimal target to the highly improved weapons developed in the last half of the century. This led to a virtual revolution in fixed defenses that continued for the next two and a half centuries. The new Renaissance fortifications had a low profile, with designs to provide flanking fire along the base of the walls. These were built with sloping sides to minimize the effect of artillery fire, and were usually backed by earthen revetments.

By the end of the Middle Ages artillery not only had proved its superiority in siege warfare but also had indicated that it could be a factor in tactical situations. During the Hussite wars in Bohemia (1419–1434) the Czechs devised a defensive tactic, apparently borrowed from the Russians, in which artillery played a key role. The Hussite armies moved with numerous carts and wagons; when the enemy appeared, the vehicles were chained together in a circle. Artillery covered them, while the infantry (positioned inside the carts and wagons), usually armed with handguns, kept up as steady a fire as was possible with the crude weapons of the day. In like manner, the French at Castillon (1453) used artillery in entrenched lines of contravallation to halt an English assault in its tracks.

Field artillery of a sort appeared during the fifteenth century. The first engagement in which cannon may be said to have played a decisive role was the French victory over a small English army at Formigny (1450). Thereafter artillery was a normal component of field armies, although it was not always utilized to maximum advantage.

BIBLIOGRAPHY

Useful summaries of the early use of artillery are in W. Y. Carman, *A History of Firearms from the Earliest Times to 1914* (1955); and O. F. G. Hogg, *Artillery: Its Origin, Heyday, and Decline* (1970). An excellent survey is in Charles Oman, "Gunpowder and Cannon 1250–1450," in his *A History of the Art of War in the Middle Ages*, II (1924). The most detailed description of the early use of gunpowder and cannon is J. R. Partington, *A History of Greek Fire and Gunpowder* (1960). The effect of the increasing effectiveness of artillery is developed in B. H. St. J. O'Neil, *Castles and Cannon: A Study of Early Artillery Fortifications in England* (1960).

JOHN BEELER

[See also **Castles and Fortifications; Hundred Years War; Metalworking; Technology; Warfare.**]

CANON, CATHEDRAL. See **Clergy.**

CANON TABLE, a concordance of passages narrated in the four Gospels, compiled by Eusebius of Caesarea around 330, that normally preceded the Gospel text and enabled a reader to locate parallel texts in the Gospels. Following antique practice, the tables were normally arranged in columns under arches; they seem to have been decorated from the start with ornamental floral, animal, and/or architectural motifs. The number of tables and the decorative forms vary; generally a seven- or eight-page sequence was favored in the East, and a twelve-page series attributed to St. Jerome was most common in the Latin West. Notable decorative schemes include marginal scenes of Christ's life, found in early Syriac books such as the Rabula Gospels; medallion portraits of the twelve apostles in the arches above the tables; and, also in the arches, images of the symbols

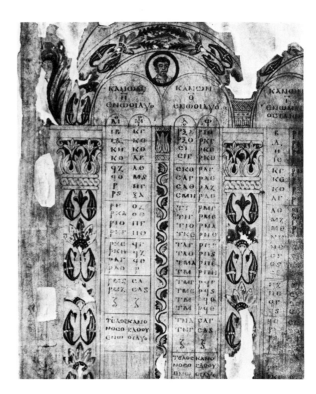

Canon table from a Gospelbook. Late 6th century, possibly Constantinople. THE BRITISH LIBRARY, MS Add. 5111, fol. 11

of the evangelists. The latter scheme, called a beast canon table, apparently originated in the seventh century, possibly in Spain, and remained popular in the West.

BIBLIOGRAPHY

Carl Nordenfalk, *Die spätantiken Kanontafeln*, 2 vols. (1938); and "The Apostolic Canon Tables," in *Gazette des beaux-arts*, 6th ser., **62** (1963).

LESLIE BRUBAKER

[See also **Bible; Manuscript Illumination.**]

CANONES HIBERNENSES. See **Law, Canon: Before Gratian.**

CANONICAL HOURS, the times of day devoted to formal services of prayer. The first Christians remembered Jesus' command "to pray always" (Luke 18:1), but they also followed some Jewish customs of communal prayer at specific hours, especially morning and evening. Other hours of prayer were gradually added. In the fourth and fifth centuries Ambrose, Augustine, and others endorsed the zeal of the Psalmist: "At midnight I rise to praise thee" (Psalm 119:62) and "Seven times a day I praise thee" (Psalm 119:164). While many parishes and cathedrals had their own hours of daily prayer, it was St. Benedict's sixth-century adaptation of the schedule at the basilicas of Rome that proved decisive. The number and order of canonical hours in the Benedictine rule (chapters 8–19) spread to all Europe through the influence of Benedict's order and Charlemagne's empire.

The major features of this daily schedule were the two services of morning and evening prayer, and the use of psalms throughout the day. Originally the first service was the single night office at 2 A.M., then called vigils or nocturns, but later delayed to daybreak and called matins. The seven original day hours were *laudes matutinales* at daybreak, later called lauds and attached to matins; the four "little hours" (prime at 6 A.M., terce at 9 A.M., sext at noon, and nones at 3 P.M.); vespers as the evening prayer (also called *lucernarium* from the opening ceremony of lamplighting); and compline before retiring. The little hours come from ancient Roman timekeeping, marking the first, third, sixth, and ninth hours of the day; but they also marked the hours of Jesus' condemnation (terce), crucifixion (sext), and death (nones). In Byzantium the overall pattern was similar; the *Horologion* contained services for midnight, dawn (*orthros*), the third, sixth, and ninth hours, evening, and nightfall (*apodeipnon*).

The services themselves, known collectively in the West as the Divine Office, consisted principally of psalms, other Scripture readings, and prayers. Eventually some hymns were added, as well as readings from the lives of the saints and from the scriptural interpretations of the church fathers. The weekly cycle included all 150 psalms; the annual cycle originally included most of the Bible. From the ninth to the eleventh century, these services were observed as corporate hours of worship by monks and clergy. Some read from the Bible, some sang the responses from the antiphonal, others read from the other books or recited the psalms from memory.

In the eleventh century a few communities combined some of these components into a single volume. When the responsibility for praying the Divine Office shifted from the community to the individual, especially with the thirteenth-century increase of Franciscan and Dominican brothers who traveled

and lived alone, the contents of these several books were systematically abbreviated and arranged in one portable volume, the breviary. In the later Middle Ages these services became increasingly complicated and obscured by the relentless accumulation of saints' days and readings (200 separate days by 1300), until the reform of Pope Pius V in 1568. A book of hours for lay devotion was modeled on the breviary and included the office of the Virgin, seven penitential psalms, the office of the dead, and (eventually) lavish and exquisite illustrations.

BIBLIOGRAPHY
Andrew Hughes, *Medieval Manuscripts for Mass and Office* (1982); Pierre Salmon, *The Breviary Through the Ages*, Sister David Mary, S.N.J.M., trans. (1962).

PAUL ROREM

[See also **Blessed Virgin Mary, Little Office of; Book of Hours; Breviary; Dead, Office of the; Divine Office.**]

CANONIZATION. From antiquity to the end of the first millennium, the recognition of sanctity rested essentially on the public cult rendered an individual. Popular recognition of a "saint," translated into pilgrimages, offerings, and rituals at the tomb, could and did take place without official hierarchical approval or even, at times, in spite of its disapproval. Increasingly, however, the episcopal hierarchy claimed the exclusive right to inscribe the feast of a saint in the local calendar of feasts or, in effect, to "canonize" the saint. Between the tenth and thirteenth centuries, as part of the general centralization of papal prerogatives, canonization became increasingly a papal right and, in the early thirteenth century, an exclusive papal right.

In the early church, when saint and martyr were essentially synonymous, recognition of sanctity was unambiguous. The anniversary of the execution of a member of the community was commemorated at the tomb of the martyr, and no examination of the individual's case was necessary. Already in the African church of the fourth century, however, bishops faced with rival Donatist and orthodox factions and cults began to insist on the exclusive right to grant the title of martyr only after an examination of particular cases and to term others so venerated as false martyrs. The culmination of this process was the canon *Item placuit* of the Fifth Council of Carthage held in 401, which ordered that altars dedicated to martyrs established in fields or along roads be destroyed if it was proved that they contained neither relics nor the bodies of martyrs. This canon in time became the basis for ecclesiastical legislation on canonization.

In western Europe, initiative for identification of saints continued for centuries to lie with the populace, although the hierarchy was involved in attempting to direct popular devotion toward certain saints by manipulating their physical remains and the memory of their lives and deaths, their *vitae* and *passiones*. The bodies of saints were exhumed and placed in new sepulchers, this taking place in ritual elevations that amounted to episcopal approval of the cult. The feasts of these saints' deaths or elevations were entered in the calendar of local feasts, and accounts of their lives and deaths were read on these days. Such ritual elevations constituted what might be called the canonization process of the early Middle Ages.

As in many other areas, Carolingian ecclesiastical reform, without introducing any substantive innovations, codified and reconfirmed the traditions of previous centuries. In 789 the African prohibition of the veneration of "false names of martyrs and uncertain *memoria* of saints," and in 801 the customary right of bishops to approve new cults were made explicit. Frequently, this approval was made within the context of a local synod involving clergy and important laity of the diocese.

The recognition of a saint by the Ordinary of a diocese, which was the early medieval form of "canonization," resulted in the saint's inclusion only in local calendars. While throughout the Middle Ages transferrals of relics among dioceses affected the diffusion of saints' cults, from the tenth century bishops began to request that the pope recognize and promulgate the cult of their local saints. These pronouncements, which were preceded by the submission of an account of the life and miracles of the saint and which were pronounced in papal synods, did not replace episcopal elevations and were not always directed to the universal church. However, during the twelfth century, papal canonizations increased in frequency and solemnity. Publication came to be made by papal bull and to be directed to the entire church. Instead of consultation with a papal synod, Eugenius III and Alexander III consulted the College of Cardinals. Likewise, investigations into the life and miracles of the prospective saint were increasingly made by a local commission established by the bishop but with the approval of the pope. Significantly, the term "canonize" (*canonizare corpus*) began to appear in the second half of the twelfth century.

In his bull canonizing Saint Kunigunde in 1200, Innocent III introduced the argument that the cult of the new saint should be judged by all the faithful and that only the pope was competent to proclaim such a judgment. Although this text spoke only of universal canonization and did not claim exclusive competence in canonization, it was apparently seen as a reservation of authority to canonize by the pope, for the following year the process by which Gilbert of Sempringham was canonized marked a change in the traditional process of papal ratification of a local examination: the Ordinary acted only in virtue of a papal mandate.

This exclusivity of papal competence was solidified and elaborated by the canon 62 of the Fourth Lateran Council of 1215 and in the decretal *Audivimus* of Gregory IX in 1234. The sense of this text, taken from a letter of Pope Alexander III to King Cnut of Sweden written between 1170 and 1180, was henceforth understood by canonists and commentators as a declaration of papal prerogative: "Only the pope is able to canonize saints."

From the thirteenth century, the process leading to canonization began, as it had since the primitive church, with popular devotion to the individual indicated by miracles, usually at the tomb. When the "popular" enthusiasm was sufficiently organized and politically powerful to influence Rome, a papal commission was organized to examine the life and miracles of the person in question. This commission, composed of papal commissioners and procurators representing the pressure group supporting the candidate, initially operated in a somewhat unstructured way and tended to examine the miracles more than the life of the individual. In the course of the later Middle Ages, the procedure became increasingly stabilized, organized, and complex. Testimony, both written and ocular, was taken concerning the life and miracles, and these witnesses became more probing, increasing specificity was required, and emphasis shifted from miracles to proof of virtuous life. From the end of the thirteenth century, the commission reported to a college of three cardinals. Their recommendation was the basis for the pope's ultimate decision.

BIBLIOGRAPHY
Pierre Delooz, *Sociologie et canonisations* (1969); Michael Goodich, *Vita perfecta* (1981); Nicole Herrmann-

Mascard, *Les reliques des saints: Formation coutumière d'un droit* (1975), 74–105; Stephan Kuttner, "La réserve papale du droit de canonisation," in *Revue historique de droit français et étranger*, 4th ser., 17 (1938); André Vauchez, *La sainteté en occident aux derniers siècles du moyen âge d'après les procès de canonisation et les documents hagiographiques* (1981); Donald Weinstein and Rudolph M. Bell, *Saints and Society: The Two Worlds of Western Christendom, 1000–1700* (1982).

PATRICK GEARY

[See also **Beatification; Donatism; Hagiography; Innocent III, Pope.**]

CANONS. See **Law, Canon.**

CANOSSA. Bismarck declared during the Kulturkampf, "We will not go to Canossa." As his words indicate, this ruined castle twelve miles southwest of Reggio had become a symbol of German humiliation eight centuries earlier. Henry IV's submission to Gregory VII at Canossa had been the most dramatic incident in the Investiture Conflict, the king's and pope's dispute over their respective positions in Christendom.

After Henry and a synod of German bishops had deposed Gregory in Worms on 24 January 1076, the pope excommunicated the king on 15 February, suspended him from office, and released his subjects from their oaths of fealty. The pope's actions rekindled the recently suppressed rebellion in Saxony, and the southern German dukes joined the revolt in the summer. No longer sure of the support of the bishops, Henry was forced to negotiate with his princely opponents at Tribur in October. They abandoned their plans to elect a new king, but he agreed to dismiss his advisers, to release his remaining Saxon prisoners, to return Worms to its bishop (who had been expelled from his see by townspeople loyal to Henry), and to apologize to the pope. Before leaving Tribur, the princes invited Gregory to judge their dispute with the king at a diet to be held in Augsburg on 2 February and decided to elect a new king if Henry did not procure absolution within a year of his excommunication.

When Gregory rejected Henry's written promise to obey and to do penance, since it contained a reference to the accusations that had been levied against the pope, the king crossed the Alps to intercept Gregory on his journey to Augsburg. Since the princes had failed to provide the pope with the armed escort they had promised, Gregory took refuge in Canossa, which belonged to his chief Italian supporter, Countess Matilda of Tuscany. Seeking absolution, Henry went to Canossa on 25 January 1077 and stood for three days before the gate of the castle as a penitent, allegedly barefoot in the snow. His godfather, Abbot Hugh of Cluny, and Matilda interceded on his behalf. It was a direct appeal to the pope's duty as a priest to forgive a sinner. Gregory lifted the excommunication but did not reinstate Henry as king. Henry swore on 28 January to settle his quarrel with the princes in accordance with the pope's advice and not to hinder Gregory in continuing his journey.

Canossa was a tactical victory for Henry since Gregory never resumed his trip. Henry's followers quickly renewed their allegiance once he had procured absolution, while Gregory's German allies were angered by what they perceived as the pope's betrayal of their united opposition to the king. They elected Duke Rudolf of Swabia king on 15 March in Forchheim, but the pope did not decide in Rudolf's favor until 1080, after three years of civil war. Canossa was, nevertheless, an ideological defeat for the German monarchy. Henry had recognized the pope's superiority in spiritual matters and had acknowledged that he, rather than the German king, was the head of Christendom.

BIBLIOGRAPHY

Karl F. Morrison, "Canossa: A Revision," in *Traditio*, 18 (1962); *Canossa als Wende: Ausgewählte Aufsätze zur neueren Forschung*, Hellmut Kämpf, ed. (1963); Brian Tierney, ed., *The Crisis of Church & State, 1050–1300* (1964), 53–73.

JOHN B. FREED

[See also **Gregory VII, Pope; Henry IV of Germany; Investiture and Investiture Controversy.**]

CANSO, the standard designation for the troubadour love song. Until the late twelfth century there seems to have been little or no systematic distinction made between the *canso* and the *vers;* but by the early thirteenth century, as evidenced by certain of the "biographies" (*vidas*) of the troubadours and by the *Doctrina de compondre dictats* (a thirteenth-century document describing various Old Provençal lyric genres), the *canso* had become a rigidly defined genre. It was, according to Jeanroy's description, a lyric piece accompanied by a melody composed especially for it. Its stanzas, numbering five or six, were of identical structure. Generally the stanza consisted of eight or nine verses of seven or eight syllables each. Because uniqueness of form was the common goal of the troubadours, the number and length of the stanzas varied somewhat from one *canso* to another, and the number of syllables per verse likewise fluctuated.

Unquestionably, though, the troubadours found the greatest range of possibilities in the choice and arrangement of rhymes. Sometimes a single set of rhymes is used to structure a whole *canso* (in Old Provençal, *coblas unissonans*); in other *cansos* stanzas are paired on the basis of their common rhymes (*coblas doblas*); in many *cansos* the rhymes change with every stanza (*coblas singulars*). The troubadours experimented with masculine and feminine rhymes and with other sophisticated techniques of prosody such as grammatical rhyme and word refrains.

The link between stanzas (*coblas*) is often accomplished by formal rather than logical means. Devices by which a poet might bind together *coblas* include *coblas capfinidas*, the repetition of a word from the last verse of one stanza in the first verse of the following one, and the even more specific artifice known as *coblas capaudadas*, the repetition of the end-rhyme word from the final verse of one stanza as the end-rhyme in the first verse of the succeeding stanza. Frequently, however, the connection between stanzas is loose enough that the order in which they occur may vary considerably among the manuscripts. The typical *canso* begins with an evocation of springtime and ends with one or more *tornadas* (short stanzas) in which the poet addresses his lady or his patron or both.

Without exception the *canso* treats of *fin' amors*, a highly conventionalized phenomenon that seems to bear little resemblance to classical or other traditional conceptions of love. *Fin' amors* is a love predicated on free choice, not determined by fate. The poet selects as the object of his affection that lady whom he knows, either from his own observation or from the reports of others, to be without equal. Humbled by her surpassing merit, he strives to perfect himself in order to appear worthier in her eyes. In the typical *canso* the poet is separated from his lady; he suffers but finds joy in the hope of some sort of recompense: whether a friendly glance, a smile, an encouraging word, a kiss, or the ultimate prize of sexual union. However, should the troubadour have the good fortune to receive a reward, he must refrain from boasting of his success, for secrecy is essential to the perpetuation of *fin' amors*.

The three characters of the *canso* are always the same: the lady, exalted by virtue of her noble birth, exceeding beauty, and impeccable moral qualities; the adoring poet-lover, who patiently endures her apparent indifference while doing everything in his power to make himself worthy of her; and the *lauzengiers* (jealous ones), comprising the lady's husband and all rival lovers who together personify the obstacles that beset this clandestine love.

BIBLIOGRAPHY

István Frank, *Répertoire métrique de la poésie des troubadours*, I (1953), introduction; Alfred Jeanroy, *La poésie lyrique des troubadours*, II (1934), 62–135; Erich Köhler, "Observations historiques et sociologiques sur la poésie des troubadours," in *Cahiers de civilisation médiévale*, 7 (1964); J. H. Marshall, "Le *vers* au XII siècle: genre poétique?" in *Actes et mémoires du IIIe Congrès international de langue et littérature du Midi de la France* (1965); S. Nichols, "Toward an Aesthetic of the Provençal *Canso*," in Peter Demetz *et al.*, eds., *The Disciplines of Criticism* (1968).

ELIZABETH WILSON POE

[See also **Courtly Love; Troubadour, Trouvère, Trovadores.**]

CANTACUZENI. See **Kantakouzenoi.**

CANTAR DE MÍO CID

THE MANUSCRIPT AND THE TEXT

The *Cantar* (or *Poema*) survives in a unique parchment quarto manuscript copied in the mid fourteenth century from (or via copies derived from) an original of Spanish Era 1245 (A.D. 1207, a date retained in the explicit). The manuscript is first heard of in 1596, when Juan Ruiz de Ulibarri copied it in the Consejo of Vivar, near Burgos. It was then in its present state. It passed to the Convent of Santa Clara in Vivar, but was taken from there so that Tomás Antonio Sánchez could publish it in the first volume of his *Colección de poesías castellanas anteriores al siglo XV* (1779). The manuscript was not returned,

CANTAR DE MÍO CID

CANTAR DE MÍO CID

but passed through private hands until it was bought in 1960 for the Spanish state. It is now in the Biblioteca Nacional, Madrid.

The manuscript is modest and clearly written but, in some spellings and errors, and especially in its failure to record line divisions correctly, a less than perfect representation of the assumed original (for a description, see Menéndez Pidal [1908], 1:1–18, and Michael [1976], 53–56). It has seventy-four folios, each with some fifty lines of verse. Three folios are missing. It is likely that the first folio bore the poet's introduction, perhaps a title, and a few lines of verse that led up to the surviving first line, "De los sos ojos   tan fuerte mientre lorando," the subject of which is unexpressed. The two folios lost within the text were removed with scissors; it is usually assumed that their removal produced lacunae, but this is not wholly certain, since the lacunae—which are certainly observable—could have been caused at a very early stage in the original manuscript.

In its present state the poem has 3,730 lines, plus 3 containing the explicit copied from the original of 1207, all in the same hand. There are several more lines in a different hand, the final address of a performer to his public; but with its often defective line divisions, the manuscript cannot have been used for an oral delivery of the work. It was probably made for a noble family or religious house, or as a matter of local pride, or in order to preserve an already poor manuscript from further deterioration. The surviving copy was conscientiously made; the copyist corrected his work, and it was reviewed by another corrector having the model manuscript before him. There are some who hold that the manuscript is a "dictated text," one dictated by a minstrel who had memorized the poem or was improvising it. It could equally have resulted from the dictation of one reading aloud from the model manuscript. There is no absolutely unmistakable proof of either process.

It is certain that other texts of the poem existed, but none is known to have survived the end of the Middle Ages. The original, probably composed in or near Burgos, evidently remained in that area; the extant manuscript was copied or derived from it. A copy of the latter was made about 1260–1270 and transmitted to the chroniclers of King Alfonso X of Castile-León; from this a prose version was made and included in the *Crónica de veinte reyes* shortly before 1300. This is the only chronicle to give a version that follows the verse original fairly closely, though it omits some poetic episodes and features.

Perhaps also early in the thirteenth century a new poetic version was made in which what was, in historical terms, an error of the original was adjusted: in the original, the Cid kills King Búcar, but in the revised version Búcar escapes in a boat. This revised version was known to the monks of San Pedro de Cardeña, the monastery near Burgos where the Cid was buried and where a considerable cult of him developed. The monks incorporated the poem into their *Estoria del Cid (Leyenda de Cardeña)*, a vernacular prose account in which lengthy pious legends about the Cid's death, burial, and miraculous posthumous actions are recounted. This now lost *Estoria del Cid* was handed to the royal chroniclers, probably in 1272, and incorporated into their main *Estoria de España*, which is known to us in the partly post-Alfonsine compilation called the *Primera crónica general*. It can be assumed that other manuscripts of the poem, in either of its two early recensions, circulated among poets of the thirteenth century; other epics imitated it, and the so-called *mester de clerecía* poets took much from the epic style. In an increasingly tenuous tradition the poem was probably known also to the poet of the lost *Gesta de las mocedades de Rodrigo* in about 1300, and to the ballad poets of the fourteenth century.

At one time it was thought that the prose versions of the *Cantar* in the chronicles could be used to adjust and supplement the unique poetic manuscript. It is likely that a few lines missing from the poem are indeed preserved in the *Crónica de veinte reyes* and others, but it is now recognized that the chroniclers were given to making their own adjustments and rationalizations, and that their testimony is of doubtful use in textual restoration.

The language of the *Cantar* is that of Old Castile about 1200, and (although Menéndez Pidal and others have thought that it corresponds more closely to that of Medinaceli about 1140) there is no linguistic reason why the text should not have been composed in or near Burgos, the capital of Old Castile and the city with which, by birth, the Cid was most closely connected. However, several points should be noted. Spanish epic, like that of other countries, cultivated a certain dignity of diction, with some archaism. There are obvious poetic features, such as formulas of reverence and respect, narrative clichés, and inversion of verb forms. There is a certain amount of technical language, not only (as is natural) about clothing and weapons, but also that drawn from the domain of the law, which is a principal theme of the poem. Most of the vocabulary is solidly Castilian, with a proportion of words drawn from Arabic and now not current, and a few significant borrowings from French and Provençal. This vocabulary appears in the assumed original of 1207; in the fourteenth-century copy some modernization of the language has occurred, and some poetic phraseology has been reordered.

POETIC FORM AND METRICAL STRUCTURES

The poem is divided into three sections, each called a *cantar,* a division plainly indicated by lines 1,085 and 2,276. For these the titles *Cantar del destierro, Cantar de las bodas,* and *Cantar de Corpes* were devised by Menéndez Pidal and have been widely adopted. The purpose of such division was presumably to mark off the amount of verse to be delivered by a performer in one of a series of sessions. There are natural breaks in the narrative at the points indicated. The poet may have borrowed the idea of such a division from one of the French chansons de geste, such as the *Chevalerie d'Ogier,* which he certainly knew, even though in French it was devised for poems very much longer than the Spanish work.

The poem is organized in 152 verse paragraphs, for which the French term *laisse* or Spanish *tirada* or *serie* is used. Within each the assonance is more or less unified. The system corresponds exactly to that of French epic and is likely to have been adopted from that source. The 152 *laisses* are of uneven length, the shortest having 3 lines and the longest 190 (with an average of 13). A few *laisses,* perhaps imitating French *laisses similaires* (Spanish, *series gemelas*), echo the content of a preceding section in a way that summarizes or gives a more lyrical tone to the earlier narration (for instance, *laisse* 129). As in French, certain practices can be discerned in the starting and ending of *laisses,* such as a change of speaker or a change from narrative to direct speech (Michael [1976], 27–38, analyzes these structural aspects).

Assonance—rhyme of vowels only—unites the line endings within each *laisse.* Assonance need not be an imitation of French, since there are early examples in Mozarabic (eleventh century) and in Galician from about 1190, and of course it was widely used in medieval Latin verse. Epic assonance in Spanish may consist of two vowels, as in *laisses* 1 (*á-o*) and 2 (*ié-a*), or a single vowel, as in *laisses* 3 (*ó*) and 13 (*á*), but these "single" rhymes should probably be considered "double," since in *laisse* 68, for instance, *más-delánt-avrá* are mingled with *Fáñez-*

pláze-Yágue. This leads to the supposition that to the seemingly single assonances in *á* there should be added in all cases an *-e* ("paragogic") making all the rhymes double and equal. There are written indications of this *-e* in the epic fragment of *Cantar de Roncesvalles* and some ballad texts. (For an analysis of the assonances, see Menéndez Pidal [1908], 1:103–124.)

It has been generally assumed that within each *laisse* the assonances must be uniform. Editors, believing that the numerous imperfect rhymes in the manuscript resulted from scribal corruption, have adjusted all of them to achieve regularity. Recent editors, reverting to the belief of some nineteenth-century editors, have been disposed to accept aberrant readings of the manuscript, thinking that occasional "approximate" rhymes, and an occasional assonating couplet not in accord with the rhyme of the *laisse,* together with "transitional" rhymes at the start and end of some *laisses,* were tolerable within the poet's system. It could also be argued that if the *Cantar* were the first poem of its kind, its metrical system might be in some degree experimental, and that imperfections would have been removed in a more polished version.

The most debated aspect of the metrics concerns length of line. After allowing for the fact that the copyist often deformed the line structures (by writing two as one, or by dividing one into two), what is left seems to obey no known or visible system. At one time it was assumed that irregularity of line resulted from scribal error, and attempts were made to restore the text to an assumed regularity—for instance, on the basis of the Spanish double octosyllable (8 + 8 syllables), the basis of the Spanish *romance* (ballad), which derived, in the fourteenth and fifteenth centuries, from epic meter. But it has long been recognized that the lines of the *Cantar* are basically and essentially variable, ranging from as few as ten syllables (perhaps even fewer) to as many as twenty. Other texts and fragments confirm this essential variability, though poems later than the *Cantar* tend to vary their line lengths over a lesser range. One universally recognized fact is that the line has a marked caesura, the first hemistich often being slightly shorter than the second.

It now seems increasingly likely that analysis of the line by syllable count, natural in a Romance language, is inapplicable, and that instead some sort of stress system should be discerned. We know on the whole how Old Spanish was stressed, but cannot be sure whether in performing epic a presenter placed stresses in somewhat artificial (though hardly anti-etymological) ways. If the performance was accompanied on an instrument, stresses would have been marked by the music, perhaps with special emphasis on the final stressed (and main assonating) vowel, perhaps also with a crescendo at the end of each *laisse*. Strong rhythmic effects can often be noted in the verse, and are a major part of its power. If Spanish epic verse did have this accentual basis, it contrasted with French, which had and retained its syllabic basis (in epic mostly decasyllabic, 4 + 6 or occasionally 6 + 4, and the alexandrine, 6 + 6).

But for all this, the comparison remains relevant. Since many lines of the *Cantar* can be juxtaposed with their French models or analogues, the Spanish poet may have been adapting the French syllabic system to Spanish speech habits. A line such as "Grándes fuéron los duélos   a la dèpartiçión" (2,631) clearly echoes the decasyllable "Grans fut li deus a celle departie" (*Prise de Cordres*, 647), and "mántos e piélles   e buénos çendáles d'Ándria" (1,971) echoes the alexandrine "De pennes et de drais, de riches cendaus d'Andre" (*Florence de Rome*, 451). Possibly, then, a stress system of 2 + 2 or 2 + 3 was the norm, but hemistichs having one stress or four stresses were by no means excluded.

If Spanish epic verse did indeed have this accentual basis, there is no need to relate it to an entirely hypothetical survival of Germanic (in Iberia, Gothic) accentual verse, for such verse could hardly have survived the demise of the Gothic language (about 600 in Spain). The readiness to accept such a system would be best related to much medieval Latin verse (hymns and songs) and to a knowledge of it in Spain in the twelfth and thirteenth centuries.

SYNOPSIS

In *cantar* I, Ruy (Rodrigo) Díaz de Vivar, the Cid, is unjustly banished by King Alfonso VI, for a reason probably stated on the missing first folio. He is coldly received in Burgos owing to the king's prohibition of aid to him, but enlists a few followers and, by a ruse involving two chests filled with sand, secures a loan of 600 marks from two moneylenders. He leaves his wife Jimena and two daughters in the care of the abbot of S. Pedro de Cardeña. With vassals and recruits he crosses the frontier south of Burgos and enters Moorish lands. By ruses he takes two small fortified towns, Castejón and Alcócer, defeating a relieving army sent up from Valencia. Further east the Cid encroaches on lands tributary to the count of Barcelona, defeats him at Tévar, and, when the count refuses food for three days, humiliates and mocks him before releasing him unransomed.

In *cantar* II, with new recruits and a now sizable army, the Cid subdues parts of the Muslim Levant region of Spain and eventually besieges and takes Valencia, winning immense booty. Bishop Jerónimo is appointed to the see, and the Cid's emissaries, with presents selected from the booty, gain the king's permission for Jimena and their daughters to join the hero in Valencia. At Valencia there is a splendid and emotional reunion in lands now considered the family's *heredad* (estate). Yúçef, "rey de Marruecos," brings a huge army across the sea to recover the city, but is defeated. When the Cid's emissaries appear before the king with further rich presents, the king offers to pardon the Cid, and the two infantes (young princes) of Carrión, of noble Leonese family, attracted by the Cid's power and new wealth, seek to marry his daughters. At a meeting on the Tagus, the king receives the Cid back into favor, and the marriages are agreed to, with great reluctance on Cid's part. The *cantar* closes with the celebration of the weddings in Valencia.

In *cantar* III the Cid's lion escapes from its cage; the infantes disgrace themselves when they hide, and are mocked for it. "King Búcar" of Morocco attacks the city and is defeated; one of the infantes shows cowardice; Búcar is chased and killed by the Cid. The infantes, conscious of their shame, resolve to avenge their loss of face by action against their wives. The Cid grants them permission to leave for Carrión and loads them with gifts. On the journey the infantes, lodging overnight with the Cid's Moorish ally Avengalvón, plot to kill their host but are overheard. Next night the infantes pitch camp in the *robleda* (oak grove) of Corpes and make love to their wives (the poet possibly intending this to be the consummation of the marriages, the Cid's daughters having been said earlier to be still very young). Next day they send their retainers ahead and mercilessly beat their wives "for the matter of the lion," leaving them "for dead." A knight of the Cid's who had traveled with the party, fearing trouble, returns and finds the girls; he revives them and takes them to safety in the nearest town.

News of the outrage reaches the Cid, who sends an emissary to demand justice from the king. A court is called in Toledo, at which the Cid's claim is upheld by independent judges: the infantes are forced to return to the Cid his two swords and 3,000 marks (the girls' dowry), and they with their brother are challenged to duels by three of the Cid's men to avenge the dishonor suffered by the hero's daughters. Ambassadors from the princes of Navarre and Aragón arrive to ask the Cid for his daughters' hands on behalf of their masters (divorce following automatically, it seems, upon the Corpes outrage). The Cid's men win the duels at Carrión: the Cid's honor is restored, and his line is assured of regal continuation in the new marriages. The poem closes with the Cid's death at Valencia.

ASPECTS, THEMES, AND STRUCTURE

The outline does little justice to the qualities of the poet's conception and execution. He creates a rich texture of narrative and incident, with a keen eye for the selection of telling and evocative details. His descriptive powers, used with marked economy, are considerable: notable passages are those of the Cid's arrival at Cardeña (242–245), the plight of the besieged inside Valencia (1,170–1,180), the viewing of Valencia by the women (1,610–1,617), and the journey to Corpes (2,689–2,700). Accounts of battles, journeys, and meetings are partly conventional but are well handled. The presence of a large number of named lesser personages, many having some individuality, helps to convey the impression of a fully peopled continuum.

The poet is also a master in the creation of direct speech in a wide variety of settings and tones: for example Jimena's prayer (330–365) and all the speeches in the court scene (3,146–3,462). Entirely relevant to the progress of the action are the almost self-contained dramatic cameos of the moneylenders (100–200), Ramón Berenguer and the Cid in their clash of wills (1,017–1,076), and Avengalvón as he lectures the treacherous infantes (2,671–2,685). At all points the wealth of realistic detail and the ordinary credibility of the geographical locations, social settings, and especially the sentiments of the personages enhance the conviction of the whole.

The chief theme is simple. From a situation of poverty, powerlessness, legal disabilities, and social disgrace consequent upon his banishment, separated from his family, estranged from his feudal lord the king, and suffering the psychological prostration resulting from the loss of his estates, the Cid rises progressively to final vindication and triumph. This triumph consists not only in the restoration of royal favor and the cleansing of his honor, not only in the recovery of possessions and achievement of great wealth, but also—perhaps more—in self-justification by the hero's steadfastness and legal rightfulness. His success in battle and conquest is that of a brave fighter and great general, but the Moors are not his real enemies: his foes are envy at court (that of the king, at first, and of conniving courtiers such as García Ordóñez, instrumental in securing his banishment) and the evil nature of the infantes and their powerful family.

The infantes marry the Cid's daughters because they seek to inherit his wealth, but their immaturity, cowardice, hurt pride, and possibly sexual inadequacy prove their undoing. The Cid agrees to the unions because it is the king's wish; his reluctance stems not from personal distaste, but from the unequal social standing of the families (this inequality was the defense offered by the infantes in court, in seeking to justify their abandonment of their wives).

Moral worth—that of the Cid and of all his men, who share a collective honor—has triumphed over obstacles and adverse factors. The Cid—steadfastly honorable, both trustworthy and trusting, loyal to his king even when unjustly exiled by him, generous to his men, devout to his God (who is constantly thanked for victories and booty), devoted to his family—is at the end rewarded for his goodness. The triumph is not only that of the Cid in this life, for the royal second marriages will continue his worthy blood, nor is it his alone; rather, it is a triumph for uprightness and the rule of justice.

The rule of law constitutes another central theme. The king as ultimate arbiter acts hastily when following bad advice, he banishes the Cid. On realizing his error, he lifts the penalties imposed on the Cid's vassals and on others who had joined him, and after due time (and the receipt of rich presents and loyal messages) he receives the Cid back into favor. The Cid at all times behaves like a model vassal; he gives an example of conduct to his king. Throughout the poem a good deal of legal detail is given, in proper terminology, and in the Toledo court scene the author's legal expertise is given ample scope in the preliminaries, the staging of the confrontations, the judgments, and various procedural matters. The closing duels are perhaps a concession to epic tradition (including the French one); the true climax to the poem has come in the court scene that precedes them, in the hearing of pleas before impartial judges, an entirely modern and forward-looking process.

The military theme is a natural one: the Cid harangues his men, charges at their head, and strikes great blows, all in fairly formulaic terms. Tactics and even strategy are discussed. But the Cid is firmly portrayed as a good Christian soldier, aware that he is fighting God's battles. He remembers his duty to Cardeña and to the cathedral of Burgos, and immediately after his capture of Valencia establishes a bishop there (both a pious act and a sign of intended permanence) with rich endowments. He is kindly, even generous, to conquered Moors. The notion of crusade was not native to the Iberian Peninsula (though one was proclaimed for the campaign that led to Las Navas in 1212), but it is possible that the military theme of the poem, and the portrayal of the Cid as a Christian commander, are related to the situation of the years around 1200. Emphasis is placed on the way in which recruits join the Cid, on the benefits of serving such a commander, on the richness of the booty, and on its fair division ("los que fueron de pie   cavalleros se fazen," 1,213). This theme, strongly contemporary and even mundane, contrasts with the corresponding aspect of French epic.

There is some sense of Castilian predominance—in qualities of character and in military force—over other peninsular states, but this is not unduly emphasized. The Catalans are in some ways figures of fun, but if the Leonese family of the counts of Carrión is portrayed in dark hues, it has to be remembered that King Alfonso VI ruled Castile and León jointly (as emphasized in the poem) and that the Cid's enemy at court, García Ordóñez, was Castilian. There is a stronger sense of the way in which the talented *infanzón* (nobleman), the Cid, with right on his side, overcomes opposition among the decadent higher nobility, both Castilian and Leonese.

In keeping with the civic virtues portrayed, the Cid is shown as domestic exemplar, especially in the presence of his wife and daughters, and in connection with the marriages of the girls and the outrage they suffer. These scenes of tenderness, even intimacy, add much to the human qualities of the poem, and parallel the portrayal of the Cid as father of his *mesnada* (which is both household and fighting band).

The poem responds well to an analysis of its structures, for the author built carefully and economically, and had a clear sense of what would retain the interest of his public. There is a steady progression in the Cid's rise to power and wealth (capture of Valencia) and restoration of honor (reconciliation with the king), a rise that seemingly culminates in the marriage of his daughters to the infantes; but these marriages have in them the seed of the disaster at Corpes, which requires a further struggle—a judicial one—to restore lost honor. Within this general structure both major and minor climaxes are effectively placed. In both narrative and direct speech the poet constantly depicts the action as a continuum and looks backward and forward, a strong feature of his art. There are no irrelevancies and no longueurs.

For a "structuralist" analysis of a part of the poem, see Orduna (1974); an analysis of numerological aspects is given by De Chasca (1972), chapter 12.

MATERIALS OF THE POEM

The poem has a more historical basis than most epics, partly because it was composed within about a century of its protagonist's death, partly because the poet's conception of his art demanded a *verista* (true-to-life) representation of history and geography. The historical Rodrigo Díaz lived from about 1040 until 1099 and was arguably, after royalty, the most imposing figure of his time. The action of the poem corresponds to the years from 1081 to 1099, though with large gaps (since the poet was in no sense writing a chronicle); the poet does not mention dates, but occasionally states the duration of a campaign or alludes to a season. The poem uses the following facts about the Cid: that he was married to Jimena; that he was banished (1081); that he defeated the count of Barcelona and captured him; that he subdued a large part of the Levant region of Spain (from 1089); that he took Valencia (1094) and established Bishop Jerónimo there; that his daughters married princes of the eastern states (perhaps in 1097 or 1098); and that he died in Valencia.

But the poet has made adjustments for the purposes of his drama. In history the Cid was banished in 1081, reconciled with the king in 1086 or 1087, and banished anew in 1089. In history the Cid defeated the count of Barcelona twice (1082, 1090). The poet also omits reference to the Cid's years in the service of Moorish Saragossa (from 1081). Further, to the historical record the poet adds a good deal of fiction of a plausible kind. The main action of the second half of the poem—the marriages of the Cid's daughters to the infantes, and hence what flows from them: the Corpes outrage, the trial, the duels—are literary invention. It was natural for the poet to invent such episodes as those of the moneylenders and of the lion, but he also created the Cid's campaign after his exile (Castejón, Alcocer, the victory over the Valencian army). In some instances the poet has naturally adjusted what he learned from history: he recounts Búcar's expedition against Valencia twice, the Moorish general figuring as himself and as the emperor Yúçef (Yusuf); he makes Jerónimo a fighting bishop on the model of the Frankish archbishop Turpin; and for some reason he tells only in abbreviated form the story of the siege of Valencia.

Most of the personages named existed in history. The Cid's daughters were Cristina and María (they are called Elvira and Sol in the poem); they married, respectively, Prince Ramiro of Navarre and Ramón Berenguer III, count of Barcelona. The Cid's poetic lieutenants can mostly be shown from diplomas to have existed at the right time, but there is no certainty that they had any connection with the Cid, and it is sure in several instances (the most important being Álvar Fáñez) that they did not act as the poem says. King Alfonso VI of León (1065–1072) and of Castile-León jointly (1072–1109) is eminently historical, as are three of the four judges named in the court scene. The villains of the poem, the infantes and their relatives, existed in history but were there blameless; their ally, the powerful courtier García Ordóñez, is known in the historical record as an enemy of the Cid. Among the Moors, Yúçef ruled the Almoravid empire from 1059 to 1106, and "King" Búcar is probably the general Sīr ibn Abī Bakr; Avengalvón ruled at Molina, where the poem places him, in the Cid's day.

Both titles repeatedly used of the poetic Cid have ample justification in history. *Cid,* borne by others also, represents the Arabic *sayyid* (lord); *Campeador* (an honorific, not the name of an office) is "battler" or "master of the field."

The relation of the Cid to the monastery of S. Pedro de Cardeña is controversial. On the abandonment of Valencia in 1102, the Cid was buried at Cardeña, as was Jimena later. In the thirteenth century the monastery developed a considerable tomb cult of the hero, and composed its *Estoria del Cid* as justification and expression of it. The important scenes in the *Cantar* that involve Cardeña may have no historical basis, and it is curious that the name of the abbot in the Cid's day (to 1086), the famous Sisebuto, is given as "Sancho" in the poem.

The geography and topography of the *Cantar* are in many respects exact. The itineraries of the Cid and his emissaries, and of the infantes to Corpes, can be traced on the map in ways first plotted by Menéndez Pidal and since modified by Manuel Criado de Val and by Ian Michael. The location of Corpes is problematical, and Alcocer (*cantar* I) is a fictional lo-

cation. The poet mentions the stages of journeys by days and resting places, and sometimes briefly describes a landscape. This geographical verisimilitude is an important feature of the poem: even fictional events must be seen to happen in real locations.

We do not know in any detail from what sources the poet derived his historical knowledge about the Cid. The "traditionalist" and "oralist" schools believe that the surviving text is a late version of a poem that originated in or shortly after the Cid's lifetime, a hypothesis that would explain some historical features of the poem (up to the capture of Valencia) while failing to account for the major fiction of the poem, the very core of the drama, after that point; moreover, no historically minded early poem could have contained the scenes involving Cardeña or the numerous historical minor personages in their nonhistorical roles. The surviving twelfth-century Latin text about the Cid, the *Carmen Campidoctoris* poem of the monastery of Ripoll (dated by some as early as 1093–1094), and the Navarrese *Linaje,* are in no way sources for the poem, though they do testify to the growing power of the Cid legend.

In a different category is the *Historia Roderici,* composed in one of the eastern states (perhaps Catalonia or Navarre), dated by Menéndez Pidal to about 1110 but by A. Ubieto Arteta and others to 1144–1147. Though largely historical, it includes legendary features (notably a long genealogy of the hero) and makes much of the discomfiture of the count of Barcelona at the Cid's hands, though the *Historia* was not a source for the poem. It is certain that the poet took names and details of his minor personages from diplomas, and there may have survived in his day, in Burgos or Cardeña, items from the Cid's personal archive (about estates, campaigns and conquests, division of booty, legal affairs, relatives) that provided further details. Cardeña tradition may have offered more. Whether for some aspects he had a further source, perhaps one common to the *Historia Roderici* and the poem and perhaps in Latin, is open to question.

It is likely that about 1200 the poet combined aspects of the historical Cid with themes of his own day. The possibility that the poem partakes of the atmosphere of the campaign that led up to Las Navas (1212) has been mentioned above. For his major fiction the poet may have had events at the 1188 cortes of Carrión in mind (and may have been a youth at that time). At these cortes Alfonso VIII betrothed two of his daughters in a double ceremony. Berenguela did not thereafter proceed to marry as pledged; in 1197 she married Alfonso IX of León, but this union was annulled by the pope in 1204 amid much and continuing litigation about the dowry and other matters. Moreover, Alfonso IX, having been knighted by the king of Castile and done homage to him, later fought against him. The legal aspects of these events would have interested, and may have professionally concerned, any Castilian civil and canon lawyer; a man of this class could well (on the internal evidence) have composed the *Cantar*. Family rivalries involving descendants of the Cid and their enemies in history could also explain some features of the poem. The choice of the Carrión family as villains may have to do with such rivalries, or may stem from intermonastic hostilities.

The relative exactness of the poem's itineraries may be explained by direct acquaintance on the part of a lawyer-poet with the routes he traveled on business. It is noteworthy that little is said about the stages of journeys near Valencia (in 1200 again in Moorish hands) and in certain parts of Castile-León.

In addition to history, the poet drew significantly upon literary material. Much of his distinctive epic style was very successfully adopted from French epic. The long prayer of Jimena echoes similar prayers in French epic. The episodes of Castejón and Alcocer are adapted from Sallust (*Bellum Iugurthinum*) and Frontinus (*Strategemata*) respectively. Some aspects of the Corpes outrage are adapted from the French poem *Florence de Rome*. Other, less prominent features and individual motifs were derived from other French texts and from Carolingian annals. Not all scholars assent to such identification of sources and analogs, the question being one that pertains to debate on the nature and origin of the *Cantar;* the work in this field is very recent and has hardly been subjected to critical scrutiny. A further field of ongoing study is that of the folkloric motifs and patterns of Spanish epic (see for example Deyermond [1972] and Gifford [1977]). Whatever the truth about the poem's literary sources and incorporation of folkloric motifs, all agree on the skill with which the author blended his materials into the narrative and endowed them with characteristic *verismo*.

LITERARY QUALITIES

Whether viewed as a new and experimental work or as part of a possibly lengthy tradition, the *Cantar* is a good, and in some respects a masterly, literary artifact. In its parts and as a whole it amply convinces with regard to its narrative line, its exemplary and moral intention, and its presentation of convincing characters. The poem's place at or near the start of histories of Spanish literature is natural, but it is only in relatively recent decades that the work has been recognized as a masterpiece.

The poet's essential *verismo* has been mentioned; certainly it is an aspect of personal temperament, perhaps a characteristic of the race. Critics rightly contrast the sobriety of the *Cantar* with the imaginative excesses of some (very far from all) French epics; in the *Cantar* one can point to only one miraculous occurrence, the visitation of the archangel to the Cid (405–412), surely imitated from French tradition, and to the exaggeration of the Moorish forces, as nonrealistic aspects.

The extreme economy of the narration is a further facet of the poet's temperament, and hence of his artistic conception: the poem is much shorter than the breadth of its action in time, space, and complexity might justify. Descriptions of places and settings are very brief, of personages (other than the hero) nearly absent; when details are given—for example, of the Cid's patriarchal beard—there is sound dramatic reason for them, and descriptions of the Cid arming and dressing (such as 3,084–3,100) have good precedents in epic tradition, notably that of France. In accounts of battles, journeys, and meetings, the poet selects his details admirably and shows the same careful economy. At times he is too brief, leading editors to identify probably nonexistent lacunae when abrupt transitions are made, or to doubt the attribution of words to speakers in a dialogue; but this is of little account.

Some critics have not hesitated to write of the poem in terms of drama—and rightly so, because it is easy to imagine the poet writing for the stage. His ability to present personal confrontations and to create the direct speech of credible personages produces this strong impression. The proportion of direct speech is very high, and no chance is lost to introduce it—for instance, when the "niña de nuef años" (40) addresses the Cid, or when the hero and his agent Martín Antolínez deal, in terms often richly humorous or ironical, with the moneylenders of Burgos (78–200). This direct speech succeeds at once in having the ring of heroic verse and the naturalness of real discourse.

The multifaceted character of the Cid has features to be expected in the portrayal of any hero, but many less obvious ones as well: his great tenderness toward his wife and daughters (shown in some of the finest scenes and lines of the poem), his elegant courtliness (as in 1,749), his staid pride and cheerful confidence tempered by realistic assessments (for instance, 1,633–1,643), his capacity for humor—sardonic (1,068–1,073), grim (2,411), jocular and courtly (1,650), even punning (1,068; 3,302). His most notable quality, perhaps a civic and exemplary rather than an epic one, is his *mesura,* compounded of gravity, good sense, even tact, which are features constantly illustrated in word and deed.

The subtlety of the dealings of the Cid with the infantes is great, since together with private feelings, questions of diplomacy, military discipline and morale, and public "face" are involved. The Cid is not above certain necessary deceits, as in his duping of the moneylenders (who are never repaid, despite their plea: 1,431–1,438) and in his instruction that his men are to accompany him to the court with concealed weapons (3,076). The portrayal of the infantes, characterized in ways designed to contrast at all points with the hero, is a bold and subtle one also.

Lesser personages, such as Bishop Jerónimo, Ramón Berenguer, Avengalvón, and even the infantes' brother in a very brief appearance, are well drawn too, and there is some neat differentiation among leading members of the Cid's *mesnada.* It has long been noted that the poet's genius led him to effect characterization by direct speech rather than by formal narrative presentation.

The style of the *Cantar* maintains a consistent level of nobility and dignity, without undue artificiality; the language has "flow" and is on the whole simple, as befits a poem to be offered viva voce to listeners. Much of the language is conventional and formulaic, closely paralleling in this respect that of contemporary French epic, from which much was borrowed. The formulaic aspects have been analyzed in recent years on the basis of "oralist" theory.

Traditional epic motifs are also constantly present—for instance, in battle descriptions, meetings, journeys, and prayers; it is notable that the poet, though he had probably traveled some of the routes he describes (so that these have an entirely real basis), recounts journeys with many formulas borrowed from, or analogous to, those of French epic. A few stylistic features and motifs appear to be adapted from Latin, either that of twelfth-century histories written in Spain or that of the Vulgate. A few words are adopted from church Latin, others from the language of the law. An elaborate range of epic epithets is applied to the hero, and to a slight extent to others; there are notable reverential (perhaps astrological) formulas applied to the Cid.

Even if many of the stylistic features were imitated from French and Latin, the poet made an entirely personal and successful assimilation of them to the needs of his art. He has occasional weak lines, even a few dull sections, but more often impresses by the power of his verse: the most notable passages, among many that might be cited, are (within *cantar* I only) lines 40–48, 235–245, 274–292, 636–642, 960–984.

ORIGINS AND NATURE OF THE POEM

The origins and nature of the *Cantar* have been and are the subject of much debate. The poem is in many respects not to be considered in isolation but as an item, albeit the major item, in the Old Spanish epic genre; and what is believed about other national epics—Homeric, Germanic, French—is obviously to be taken into account. Theory about the *Cantar* has evolved just as it has in the general fields mentioned. However, there have been factors peculiar to Spain and to Hispanic studies. The firm establishment of "traditionalist" belief (and later, as modified, of "neotraditionalist" belief) in Spain in the late nineteenth and early twentieth centuries was the work principally of Menéndez Pidal, who followed in part the teachings of Manuel Milá y Fontanals and Gaston Paris.

The traditionalist view derived substantially from the ideas of the great Romantic theorists concerning *Volkspoesie.* Pidal, long the doyen of Hispanic medievalists (in philology and history as well as in literature), constantly refined his work in a long series of fundamental publications from 1908 to 1966 that are, even for those who disagree with his ideas, indispensable. His traditionalist view became the established truth in histories and manuals of Spanish literature and among most Hispanicists. Its persistence in Spain and elsewhere, most notably in the United States, can be attributed to the excellence of Pidal's writings, to his continuing personal authority, and to his exceptionally long working life.

The positivist or "individualist" view of Joseph Bédier, published from 1908 to 1913, immediately revolutionized the study of French epic, but hardly penetrated Spanish studies for many years. The first critical voices raised were those of P. E. Russell and Ubieto in the 1950's. The publication of Albert B. Lord's *The Singer of Tales* in 1960 stimulated the sudden growth of "oralist" theory and analysis of the Romance epic, and there are now major studies of the *Cantar* and other epic texts of Spain from this perspective.

In a way it could be said that oralist theory and analysis came to the rescue of neotraditionalist thought, even though Menéndez Pidal, in his last publication (1965–1966), had reservations of some weight, and even though De Chasca was forced eventually to disagree with him. Both schools of thought believe that the *Cantar* was composed very early, perhaps within the Cid's lifetime in some primitive form, and that its relative fidelity to history (which they exaggerate) is to be explained in this way. Traditionalists hold that the poem thereafter developed in a series of versions, in each of which a minstrel might introduce variants and which occasionally amounted to major reworkings *(refundiciones)*, presumably made orally, though Menéndez Pidal and others have not excluded the use of writing at times. The sole extant text "of 1207" thus represents a stage, no more, in a continuing evolution. Oralists would reject the notion that writing intervened (except, of course, when the surviving version was recorded); and whereas the traditionalists envisage a text largely memorized by the performer and subject only to variants, the oralists insist on the new and more or less total improvisation of the poem at each performance, the performer using for the purpose his stock of time-honored formulas and motifs.

Both points of view can readily be defended from the text of the *Cantar* and from what we know about it in an external way. Other aspects of traditionalist views, which would presumably be supported by oralists, may be added to the above: that epic has a fundamentally historical conscience *(apetencia historial)* on behalf of a people; that the *Cantar* is of popular inspiration (and hence free of learned influences); that the author, being an *autor-legión* (collective or serial) is not only anonymous but also unknowable and, for the oralists at least, unlettered. Oralist expositions have been mentioned above; among recent good exponents of the traditionalist view are Jules Horrent and Samuel Armistead.

In the 1970's a new positivist approach was attempted, chiefly by British scholars, following in some details the lead given by Russell in the 1950's but also taking up the approach that had long been made to French epic. Whereas nearly all printings and translations of the poem in the twentieth century have followed the critical text established by Menéndez Pidal in 1911, two British scholars, Colin Smith (1972) and Ian Michael (1976), produced radically new editions that tend on the whole to respect the manuscript readings, including some imperfection of rhyme and some freedom of line length, and that are accompanied by introductory materials in no way beholden to (though respectful toward) the nearly canonical views of Menéndez Pidal.

Other critical work has been in this spirit: demonstrations of sources in French epic and in classical and medieval Latin, both for some episodes and in many stylistic aspects; demonstrations of the links of the *Cantar* with the realm of the law (in spirit, in notable scenes, in much technical parlance); suggestion of the likelihood that the poem, whatever its historical materials, corresponds closely to the ambience and to certain events of the reign of Alfonso VIII (for instance, the 1188 cortes).

The traditionalist and oralist cases can be demonstrated too, but they demand a good deal of faith and rest on a number of assumptions (about the early date of the epic in Spain, about unknowable lost texts, about the autonomy of the Spanish epic vis-à-vis the French). The positivist view dispenses with these considerations. It takes the date of 1207 in the explicit of the poem as truly that of its composition (or of its writing, if composed a few years before that) and, in view of the learned written sources in foreign languages now identified, postulates composition by a relatively learned and certainly individual author, perhaps (the view is hardly extreme) by that Per Abbat who says he *escrivio* the text (line 3,732; he is usually taken as a copyist only). There have been recent attempts to identify this man as an individual alive about 1207. Moreover, in view of factors mentioned above, it has been held that he was some sort of legal practitioner.

The poem need not have been preceded by a long (or any) tradition of epic verse in Spanish, but could be the first of its kind and the originator of the epic genre of the thirteenth century, a possibility that is enhanced by the absence of clear references to vernacular epic in twelfth-century Spain and by the relative poverty of Hispanic literary culture in that period. Finally, it seems certain that a close association between the author (perhaps from Burgos) and the monastery of Cardeña is to be postulated. It is perhaps significant that it is foreign scholars, free of any need to defend the autonomy and early date of Spanish literary culture, who have begun to suggest the dependence of the *Cantar* in many respects on the French example—a logical thesis in view of the dominance of the latter in Europe at the time. But these same scholars have strongly emphasized at the same time the power of the poet's conception and the success with which he assimilated elements of foreign origin.

BIBLIOGRAPHY

A good facsimile of the manuscript, with Menéndez Pidal's paleographic text in a companion volume, was published in 1961. A concordance to the poem was published by Franklin M. Waltman (1973). The best English prose translation is that of Rita Hamilton and Janet Perry in Ian Michael, ed., *The Poem of the Cid* (1975).

K. Adams, "The Metrical Irregularity of the *Cantar de mio Cid,*" in *Bulletin of Hispanic Studies,* 49 (1972); Dámaso Alonso, "Estilo y creación en el *Poema del Cid,*" in *Ensayos sobre poesía española* (1944); Samuel G. Armistead, "The *Mocedades de Rodrigo* and Neo-Individualist Theory," in *Hispanic Review,* 46 (1978); Louis Chalon, *L'histoire et l'épopée castillane du Moyen-Âge* (1976); M. Criado de Val, "Geografía, toponimia, e itinerarios del *Cantar de mio Cid,*" in *Zeitschrift für romanische Philologie,* 86 (1970); Edmund de Chasca, *El arte juglaresco en el "Cantar de mio Cid,"* 2nd ed. (1972); and *The Poem of the Cid* (1976); A. D. Deyermond, ed., *"Mio Cid" Studies* (1977), which includes his "Tendencies in *Mio Cid* Scholarship, 1943–73"; A. D. Deyermond and Margaret Chaplin, "Folk-motifs in the Medieval Spanish Epic," in *Philological Quarterly,* 51 (1972); Joseph J. Duggan, "Formulaic Diction in the *Cantar de mio Cid* and the French Epic," in *Forum for Modern Language Studies,* 10 (1974); Peter N. Dunn, "Theme and Myth in the *Poema de mio Cid,*" in *Romania,* 83 (1962).

Charles Faulhaber, "Neo-traditionalism, Formulism, Individualism, and Recent Studies on the Spanish Epic," in *Romance Philology,* 30 (1976–1977); José Fradejas Lebrero, *Estudios épicos: El Cid* (1962); Miguel Garci-Gómez, *"Mio Cid": Estudios de endocrítica* (1975); D. J. Gifford, "European Folk-tradition and the *Afrenta de Corpes,*" in A. D. Deyermond, ed., *"Mio Cid" Studies* (1977); Robert A. Hall, "Old Spanish Stress-timed Verse and Germanic Substratum," in *Romance Philology,* 19 (1965–1966); Thomas R. Hart, "The Rhetoric of (Epic) Fiction: Narrative Technique in the *Cantar de mio Cid,*" in *Philological Quarterly,* 51 (1972); L. P. Harvey, "The Metrical Irregularity of the *Cantar de mio Cid,*" in *Bulletin of Hispanic Studies,* 40 (1963); Michael Herslund, "Le *Cantar de mio Cid* et la chanson de geste," in *Revue romane,* 9 (1974); E. C. Hills, "Irregular Epic Meters: A Comparative Study of the Meter of the *Poema de mio Cid* and of Certain Anglo-Norman, Franco-Italian and Venetian Epic Poems," in *Homenaje a Menéndez Pidal,* I (1925); Jules Horrent, *Historia y poesía en torno al "Cantar del Cid"* (1973).

Miguel Magnotta, *Historia y bibliografía de la crítica sobre el "Poema de mio Cid" (1750–1971)* (1976); Francisco Maldonado de Guevara, "'Knittelvers,' 'Verso nu-doso,'" in *Revista de filología española,* 48 (1965); Ramón Menéndez Pidal, *Cantar de mio Cid,* 3 vols. (1908–1911, 3rd ed. 1956); *La España del Cid,* 2 vols. (1929, 7th ed. 1964); *En torno al "Poema del Cid"* (1963); and "Los cantores épicos yugoeslavos y los occidentales: El *Mio Cid* y dos refundidores primitivos," in *Boletín de la Real Academia de Buenas Letras de Barcelona,* 31 (1965–1966); Ian Michael, "Geographical Problems in the *Poema de mio Cid:* I. The Exile Route," in A. D. Deyermond, ed., *Medieval Studies Presented to Rita Hamilton* (1976); "Geographical Problems in the *Poema de mio Cid:* II. The Corpes Route," in A. D. Deyermond, ed., *"Mio Cid" Studies* (1977); and Ian Michael, ed., *Poema de mio Cid* (1976); S. G. Morley, "Recent Theories About the Meter of the *Poema de mio Cid,*" in *PMLA,* 48 (1933).

Germán Orduna, "El *Cantar de las bodas:* Las técnicas de estructura y la intervención de los dos juglares en el *Poema de mio Cid,*" in *Studia . . . Lapesa,* II (1974); P. E. Russell, *Temas de "La Celestina" y otros estudios (del "Cid" al "Quijote")* (1978), including Spanish versions of his 1952 and 1958 studies; Colin Smith, "The Choice of the Infantes de Carrión as Villains in the *Poema de mio Cid,*" in *Journal of Hispanic Philology,* 4 (1980); "The Diffusion of the Cid Cult," in *Journal of Medieval History,* 6 (1980); *Estudios cidianos* (1977); *The Making of the 'Poema de mio Cid'* (1983); and Colin Smith, ed., *Poema de mio Cid* (1972; Spanish version, 1976); M. J. Strausser, "Alliteration in the *Poema de mio Cid,*" in *Romance Notes,* 11 (1969); Antonio Ubieto Arteta, *El "Cantar de mio Cid" y algunos problemas históricos* (1973); R. M. Walker, "A Possible Source for the *Afrenta de Corpes* Episode in the *Poema de mio Cid,*" in *Modern Language Review,* 72 (1977); Anthony Zahareas, "The Cid's Legal Action at the Court of Toledo," in *Romanic Review,* 55 (1964).

COLIN SMITH

[See also **Cid, The, History and Legend of; Spanish Epic Poetry; Spanish Versification and Prosody.**]

CANTATORIUM, a term used in the seventh- or eighth-century Ordo Romanus I (which describes the papal Mass at Rome), refers to the book containing the chants sung between the readings. These chants—the gradual, alleluia, and tract—are characterized by elaborate music sung by a soloist. Such famous books as the so-called Gradual of Monza (eighth century), which gives only the texts of the chants, and the St. Gall MS 359 (ninth century) are cantatoria in the strict sense. They contain only the solo sections (the St. Gall manuscript refers to other items by incipits without music) and are practical as to arrangement and size (St. Gall is 28 cm. × 12 cm.).

Unfortunately, the term has sometimes come to be used by modern scholars to refer to compendia that include a cantatorium proper; many of the manuscripts referred to by Stäblein are of this type. They frequently contain sections of tropes, offertory verses, and other solo chants. Since they are like separate *libelli* bound together, their organization is by item rather than by Mass; they are thus not books for practical use.

BIBLIOGRAPHY

Cantatorium, No 359 de la Bibliothèque de St-Gall (ix siècle), Paléographie Musicale, 2nd ser., II (1924), is a complete facsimile; René-Jean Hesbert, ed., *Antiphonale missarum sextuplex* (1935, repr. 1967); Bruno Stäblein, "Cantatorium," in Friedrich Blume, ed., *Die Musik in Geschichte und Gegenwart*, II (1952).

ANDREW HUGHES

CANTEFABLE. See **Aucassin et Nicolette.**

CANTERBURY. The principal metropolitan see of England, and a significant pilgrimage site of the later Middle Ages, Canterbury enjoyed a position of major ecclesiastical and political influence on medieval England. Originally a settlement fording the ancient mouth of the river Stour, Canterbury has long been an important location on the main road to the British interior.

There is archaeological evidence of settlement before 200 B.C. Known to the Romans as Durovernum (possibly from the Celtic *dur,* water), Canterbury is mentioned as a town by Ptolemy, around A.D. 150. Medieval writers fancifully ascribe its origins to even earlier times; Nennius claims Canterbury was a *caer ceint* (fortified city) of the ancient British. Geoffrey of Monmouth credits a mythic British king, Lud-Hudibras, with founding Canterbury in 900 B.C. After the successful conquest of Claudius (from A.D. 43) Canterbury assumed a fairly typical Roman pattern of walls, buildings, and theater; excavated areas show some continued use until the end of the fourth century. Saxon settlement can be dated to around 450: within a single insula several Saxon huts and distinctive Anglo-Frisian pottery have been discovered.

The medieval life of Canterbury gained importance with the reign of Ethelbert, the fifth Jutish king of Kent and the *Bretwalda,* the paramount king of the heptarchy. The name Canterbury or Cantwaraburh (town of the Kentishmen) may indicate that the conquering Jutes did not seriously disturb the natives, who had been called *Cantii* since pre-Roman times. Bede refers to Canterbury as Ethelbert's metropolis, a center of authority for all Britain. Ethelbert married the Frankish Christian Bertha, great-granddaughter of Clovis. With her came Bishop Liuthard, who established himself in the existing church of St. Martin at Canterbury.

The potential conversion of England fired the imagination of Pope Gregory I. The Roman monk Augustine arrived in 597 with forty companions to evangelize the Anglo-Saxons. Although Gregory mandated that Augustine establish his see in London, with another at York, Augustine instead chose Canterbury, capital of the most civilized Anglo-Saxon kingdom. Sixth-century Frankish and Jutish grave sites testify to the wealth and power accrued in Kent; glass and jewelry of high skill were produced locally. Ethelbert was hospitable to Augustine's mission; the king himself converted to Christianity. In Canterbury, Augustine was responsible for founding the Benedictine abbey of Sts. Peter and Paul, and after his installation as bishop of the British, he established the cathedral of Christ Church in a building reputedly used by Romano-British Christians.

Although Christianity was not securely established by the time of Augustine's death (*ca.* 604), the forms of English Christendom were recognizable, for Canterbury seemed a small Rome, with standard ecclesiastical organization, small stone missionary churches patterned on the Roman basilica, and relics. Bede tells of Augustine's relics in the abbey; in later times, parceling of relics to the abbey or the cathedral was deeply disputed. In the early ecclesiastical foundation are incipient the controversies that gave impetus to Canterbury's struggles in later periods: the murkiness of Canterbury's claim to metropolitan and primatial jurisdiction, the competition between the monks of Sts. Peter and Paul and those of the cathedral priory, and the ambiguity of Canterbury's reliance on royal power.

Prelates after Augustine were hampered by Britain's uncertain Christianity, Kent's diminishing political power, and the increased influence of Irish missionaries, who observed a liturgical calendar varying from Rome's. The Synod of Whitby (664) settled the calendrical dispute in favor of Roman usage, thus asserting Anglo-Saxon ecclesiastical conformity, of which Canterbury was a prime beneficiary. Canterbury's claim to exercise primatial jurisdiction over all Britain, presumably implied in Gregory's mandate, was resisted by the Welsh church for centuries, but a second metropolitan see was established at York in 735.

Canterbury's ecclesiastical dignity was strongly reinforced under the episcopate of Theodore of Tarsus (668–690), who perambulated England, calling many councils and synods. Theodore imposed order on the regular and secular clergy of the Anglo-Saxon kingdoms; he extended Canterbury's control over Irish missionary centers as well. Under Theodore, Canterbury gained a reputation as an intellectual center; with the aid of Abbot Hadrian, Theodore endowed the Canterbury school. He also created a stable diocesan structure, extending the authority of Canterbury over areas larger than those ruled by any king.

Canterbury was the seat of at least six meetings of a general witenagemot between 764 and 1003. The first such assembly of ecclesiastical and lay magnates of all England was summoned in 764 by King Offa of Mercia. Later kings of Wessex and of unified England convened meetings of the witan, attesting to Canterbury's secular as well as ecclesiastical importance.

Canterbury was relatively untouched during the first period of intense Viking activity in England, even though from 855 Viking raiders regularly wintered on the Isle of Thanet, ten miles to the northeast, and the Great Army frequently operated in the area. In the second phase of Viking activity (990's to 1016), however, Canterbury was repeatedly the object of pillage, and in one raid Archbishop Elfheah (St. Alphege) was grotesquely murdered. The subsequent outcry convinced the Danish king Sweyn to reach a rapid settlement with the English leadership to secure peace for his son Cnut.

From Anglo-Saxon times on, Canterbury was an important center of coinage; sceats were minted from the 690's, and from the 780's, King Offa's coins were issued mostly at Canterbury. Widely circulated in Europe, these silver pennies were the common coin of the realm until Tudor times. Canterbury was a natural center of minting activity: cross-channel trade required monetary exchanges near ports of entry.

Archbishop Dunstan acted as practically the prime minister for several less forceful monarchs of the united English kingdom. A Benedictine monk who was made abbot of Glastonbury in 940, Dunstan carried on the Wessex dynasty's long-standing policy of fusion between the Anglo-Saxon and native British traditions of that composite kingdom. He appointed talented men educated in the monasteries of the southwest to be abbots and bishops in the northeast. Through them he encouraged educational programs designed to convert the Danelaw to the English language as well as to regular Christianity. Exiled to the Continent in 955, Dunstan became involved in the monastic reform movement; he later composed the *Regularis concordia,* which served as a model for monastic reorganization. Dunstan played a decisive role in shaping the ideology of Anglo-Saxon sacred monarchy, composing in 973 a coronation ritual for Edgar the Peaceable.

In 1053 the see of Canterbury became the focus of serious conflict between the Norman-influenced King Edward the Confessor and the ethnic patriotism of Earl Godwin's faction. Godwin's candidate, Stigand, was elevated to the metropolitan dignity, much to the outrage of the nascent papal reform movement; Stigand was excommunicated by Rome in 1059. William the Conqueror took advantage of this contretemps to gain a papal banner and made the isolation of Stigand one of his prime tactical goals. Canterbury fell to William's forces on 29 October 1066, fifteen days after the Battle of Hastings. The city surrendered without resistance, although Abbot Ethelsige of St. Augustine's Abbey (as the Abbey of Sts. Peter and Paul was then most commonly called) organized subsequent English resistance to William in Kent. When Stigand was deposed in 1070, William hastened to secure the election of his adviser and favorite, Lanfranc, the first Norman archbishop, whose espicopacy was one of the most precedent-setting in the history of the achdiocese.

Lanfranc was followed as archbishop by two other monks of Bec, Anselm (1093–1109) and Theobald (1138–1161). Anselm had studied with Lanfranc at Bec, and like Lanfranc became abbot of Bec, from which position he defended traditional orthodoxy. He was also a master of the new piety, writing emotional prayers and letters that considerably influenced the literary sensibilities of the twelfth century. Under Lanfranc and Anselm, Canterbury became a center of literary activity; typical is the biography of Anselm by Eadmer, a cultivated practitioner of the art of eyewitness hagiography. Exiled several times during the conflict over lay investiture, Anselm maintained a tradition of stubborn resistance based on principle that was later imitated by Thomas Becket.

The other major Canterbury style, that of adroit conciliation, was exemplified by Archbishop Theobald, who amassed an uncommonly large library and built up a learned household that trained four archbishops and six bishops. Two of his most outstanding secretaries were Becket and John of Salisbury.

Thomas Becket, the fortieth archbishop, found in Anselm and Theobald his models of episcopal deportment. An Anglo-Norman from London, Thomas received his legal and political education in Theobald's household. In 1155, Henry II appointed Becket chancellor of England, in which post his political cunning and propensity for splendid display were exhibited. Henry maneuvered Becket's election as archbishop in 1161, also arranging a papal dispensation in order to maintain him as chancellor. Becket resigned the latter post; the complete rupture of relations between king and archbishop occurred in 1163, with a dispute over the jurisdiction of cases involving criminous clerks addressed in the Constitutions of Clarendon. Attempted reconciliations failed, and after Becket excommunicated the archbishop of York and others for usurping Canterbury's right to crown Henry's heir, four knights of Henry's household felt themselves propelled to action. On 29 December 1170, they murdered Becket in Christ Church Cathedral.

Almost immediately there were reports of miracles at Becket's tomb, and Canterbury swiftly became a prime site of pilgrimage devotion. In 1174, Henry II performed a penitential pilgrimage to Becket's tomb; Louis VII of France made a pious visit in 1179.

The popularity of Canterbury pilgrimage endures in stones and stories. Canterbury responded to pilgrim fervor with bursts of building activity; hospitals and inns (of which the Chequers is the most famous) were available to the throngs. Canterbury had long been a place of trade, and by the time of Domesday Book (1086) it was a thriving center of population. Geoffrey Chaucer himself was elected a knight of the shire from Kent in 1386, during the period in which he was composing the *Canterbury Tales.*

Christ Church Cathedral, which held Becket's relics, was reconstructed several times during the Middle Ages. Augustine's cathedral burned in 1067, and Lanfranc and Anselm rebuilt it on a much larger scale, with a nave of nine bays but a small choir.

Prior Conrad directed the construction of the "glorious choir"; elaborately dedicated in 1130, it also burned in 1174; the reconstruction was completed in 1184. From 1379 the nave was reconstructed in Perpendicular style by Henry Yevele, and additional chapels were added. The Perpendicular central tower ("Bell Harry") was constructed between 1495 and 1503. The cathedral is characterized by the separation of the choir from the nave by a wide set of stairs; the floor from the choir eastward is also raised. The extraordinary stained glass was executed according to a coherent program before 1220, when Becket's relics were translated to Trinity Chapel; the glass depicting the miracles of Becket is especially vivid.

The late twelfth century witnessed continued struggles between the archbishops and the monks of St. Augustine's Abbey. Stephen Langton took the archiepiscopacy in 1207 after a much-disputed election. Another combative intellectual, Langton (author of the Pentecost sequence *Veni, Sancte Spiritus* and largely responsible for the now traditional separation of the Bible by chapters and verses) was forced on King John. An active ally of the baronial resistance of 1214, and probable author of those articles of Magna Carta that guaranteed the liberties of the church, Langton shied from direct confrontation with the king and appeared on his side at Runnymede.

The see of Canterbury was distinguished for the next century and a quarter by several other intellectual archbishops, including the theologians Edmund Rich and John Peckham, and the Dominican logicians Robert Kilwardby and Thomas Bradwardine. From the mid fourteenth century to the Reformation, the archbishops were typically political. Simon of Sudbury was beheaded by the mob during the Peasant's Revolt of 1381 as a representative of the reactionary heads of the realm. In 1256, Canterbury purchased from Henry III the right to elect bailiffs; under Henry VI, the city was incorporated.

Archbishop Henry Chichele (1414–1443), alumnus of New College and founder of All Souls, Oxford, was one of the several archbishops dedicated to suppressing the Lollards. He embodied the style of merit-conscious, institution-building prelacy that reached a climax under Archbishop John Morton (1486–1500); Morton's cultivated, disciplined household welcomed the humanist John Colet and trained the young Thomas More, who set his *Utopia* around Morton's table.

BIBLIOGRAPHY
Bede, *Ecclesiastical History,* I, 25–33, II, 5–8, and IV, 1–2; Richard W. Southern, *Saint Anselm and His Biographer* (1963); Frank M. Stenton, *Anglo-Saxon England,* 3rd ed. (1971); William Urry, *Canterbury Under the Angevin Kings* (1967).

BONNIE WHEELER

[See also **Anselm of Canterbury; Augustine of Canterbury; Becket, Thomas, St.; Dunstan, Life of; England, Anglo-Saxon; Henry II of England; Lanfranc; Pilgrimages, Western European; Theodore of Canterbury, St.**]

CANTERBURY CATHEDRAL. Established in 602 by St. Augustine of Canterbury as the archiepiscopal seat of the primate of England, Canterbury Cathedral remains the spiritual symbol of Anglican Christianity. Site of the murder of Archbishop Thomas Becket in 1170, the cathedral soon became the object of the nation's most important pilgrimage. It was rebuilt several times, especially in the eleventh, twelfth, and fourteenth centuries.

Of special architectural interest is the chevet. Rebuilt after a fire in 1174, it was the first fully Gothic structure in England, and the account by Gervase of its burning and reconstruction stands as the most complete medieval treatise of its kind.

BIBLIOGRAPHY
Madeline Harrison Caviness, *The Early Stained Glass of Canterbury Cathedral, Circa 1175–1220* (1977); Gervase

Canterbury Cathedral, 11th–15th centuries. FROM SIR BANISTER FLETCHER'S A HISTORY OF ARCHITECTURE

of Canterbury, "Tractatus de combustione et reparatione Cantuariensis ecclesiae," in William Stubbs, ed., *The Historical Works of Gervase of Canterbury,* I (1879), with English translation in Robert Willis, *The Architectural History of Canterbury Cathedral* (1845); Francis Woodman, *The Architectural History of Canterbury Cathedral* (1982); Charles Everleigh Woodruff and William Danks, *Memorials of the Cathedral and Priory of Christ in Canterbury* (1912).

STEPHEN GARDNER

[See also **Augustine of Canterbury; Becket, Thomas, St.; Gervase of Canterbury.**]

CANTICLE, a poetic passage from Scripture (apart from the Book of Psalms). The Song of Moses and the Hymn of the Three Boys are Old Testament examples; from the New Testament come the canticle of Zacharias (the Benedictus), the canticle of the Virgin (the Magnificat), and the canticle of Simeon (the Nunc Dimittis). In the Eastern church, canticles were expanded and arranged in odes; they were performed at the offices and came to be known as *akolouthia* or canons. Around 540, St. Benedict prescribed canticles for the Western offices: the Magnificat, Nunc Dimittis, and Benedictus are important canticles sung daily in vespers, compline, and lauds respectively. Lauds also has an Old Testament text for each day of the week; other texts are used at Mass on Ember Saturdays and Holy Saturday. The third nocturn at monastic matins begins with an antiphon and nonscriptural canticles chosen by the abbot. In the context of the offices, their manner of performance is identical to that of psalms but with more elaborate music.

BIBLIOGRAPHY
Andrew Hughes, *Medieval Manuscripts for Mass and Office* (1982), 24, *passim.*

ANDREW HUGHES

[See also **Kanōn.**]

CANTIGA is a medieval Spanish and Portuguese word used throughout the Iberian peninsula until the middle of the fifteenth century to designate a monophonic song in Galician, a language closely related to Portuguese and thought to be eminently suited for lyric poetry. The largest collection of such songs is that known as *Las Cantigas de Santa María*. Consisting of slightly more than 400 works, it was assembled under the direction of King Alfonso X el Sabio between about 1260 and 1280 and has been preserved in four manuscripts dating from the late thirteenth and early fourteenth century.

One of these manuscripts, Madrid, Biblioteca Nacional, MS 10,069, contains the text and music of only 128 items and thus represents an early stage of the collection. El Escorial, Biblioteca del Real Monasterio, MS T.j.1, has come down in an incomplete state and now contains only 200 of the *Cantigas*. Florence, Biblioteca Nazionale Centrale, MS II.1.213, is closely related to the El Escorial manuscript but contains only the texts of the songs; the melodies were never copied into it even though the five-lined music staves needed for these were. El Escorial, MS J.b.2, the most complete of all, contains not only all 402 of the *Cantigas* collected by Alfonso and the prologue to these but also 12 additional songs (also preceded by a prologue) intended for use on one or another of the five feasts of the Virgin then celebrated during the liturgical year. In this source all of the texts except four are provided with their melodies.

Each of the four manuscripts is lavishly decorated, but the miniatures found in them differ in subject matter except for those portraying Alfonso, who is depicted in each as supervising various scribes engaged in compiling the collection. The other miniatures usually depict performing musicians with their instruments, and consequently these manuscripts also are of great importance for the history of musical instruments, more than forty of which are shown in the four sources.

Most of the *Cantigas de Santa María* can best be described as balladlike accounts of miracles performed by the Virgin, but every tenth one is a hymn in her praise. In the manuscripts these two kinds of songs are designated respectively as *cantigas de miragres* and *cantigas de loor*. The *cantigas de miragres* are short narratives that recount the more popular medieval legends and anecdotes dealing with the many miracles attributed to Mary. It was undoubtedly this narrative content that was responsible for much of the *Cantigas'* appeal in both sacred and secular circles.

Although the texts vary considerably in length of line and in the number of lines per stanza, they all have refrains and almost 90 percent have the form of the *zajal*. The music, however, is, with few excep-

tions, cast in the form of the virelai, and consequently musical patterns such as AB (refrain) CCAB (stanza) AB (refrain) or ABCD (refrain) EFEFABCD (stanza) ABCD (refrain), or variants thereof, predominate. This wedding of the poetic form of the *zajal* to the musical scheme of the virelai resulted in a kind of asymmetrical *villancico* that remained popular until the early sixteenth century, as can be seen from a number of works in the *Cancionero musical de palacio*, a collection of polyphonic songs dating from about 1500.

The melodies are cast in one or another of the eight modes constituting the medieval modal system, with the majority being in either the first mode (Dorian) or in the seventh (Mixolydian). The notational system used to record the melodies was, however, one in which the relative temporal length of notes could not always be set forth unambiguously. Consequently, there still are serious problems of transcription in the area of both meter and durational values, and the transcriber or performer of the *Cantigas* must frequently rely on musical sensitivity when trying to resurrect them.

On the basis of the contents of those miniatures in the *Cantigas* manuscripts which depict performing musicians, and from evidence drawn from other thirteenth-century sources, it seems that the *Cantigas* were performed either by one singer or by several singing in unison and/or in octaves, and that they could have been accompanied in the same manner by one or more instrumentalists. The only instrumental part that would not have been at the unison or the octave with the melody line would have been a modestly ornamented drone sounding below the melody, and most likely such a drone was present in the vast majority of performances. On occasion, variety may well have been achieved by using a solo singer for the stanzas and a larger performing group for the refrain. Also, the *Cantigas* may sometimes have been danced to, since the virelai was one of those medieval *formes fixes* with a history of serving as sung dance music.

There has been much disagreement as to whether Alfonso X limited himself to supervising the compilation of this collection or whether he also wrote some of the texts and melodies included in it. It is possible—even probable—that he did write some of the works, and others may well have been created by noble members of his immediate court. Most of the melodies, however, undoubtedly were well-known troubadour- or trouvère-like tunes of the time, which had originally been composed for use with secular texts and to which Alfonso's scribes fitted their own newly written sacred texts, thereby producing *contrafacta*. In any case, the collection, along with the manuscripts preserving it, stands as one of the greatest artistic achievements of medieval Spain.

A substantial number of secular *cantigas* also have been preserved. They include *cantigas de amor* (love songs), *cantigas de amigo* (love songs sung by a girl), *cantigas de gesta* (narrative and epic texts), and *cantigas de escarnio* (satirical or scurrilous texts), as well as others that do not always lend themselves to categorization. All survive without music except for six of a group of seven *cantigas de amigo* by the thirteenth-century poet-musician Martín Códax. These were found in Madrid in 1914 on a parchment folio that had escaped destruction by having been cut up and incorporated into the binding of a copy of Cicero's *De officiis*. This folio was acquired by the Spanish musicologist Rafael Mitjana shortly after it was removed from its protecting volume. It disappeared soon after Mitjana's death in 1921, but its contents have been preserved in facsimile in various publications. A comparison of the music of these six secular *cantigas de amigo* with that of the sacred *Cantigas de Santa María* reveals no significant stylistic differences; neither does a comparison of the texts of the secular repertory as a whole with those of the sacred.

BIBLIOGRAPHY

Higinio Angles, *La música de las Cantigas de Santa María del Rey Alfonso el Sabio*, 3 vols. (1943–1958, vol. I repr. 1964), a comprehensive study, is a facsimile edition of El Escorial, MS J.b.2 with a transcription of its 402 *cantigas,* and includes a study of the texts and music, as well as several facsimiles of folios from the other *cantigas* MSS and of the folio containing the *cantigas de amigo* by Martín Códax, together with an exhaustive bibliography; Albert I. Bagby, Jr., "The Moslem in the *Cantigas* of Alfonso X, El Sabio," in *Kentucky Romance Quarterly,* **20** (1973), a study of the character of the Spanish Muslim as he is presented in the *Cantigas;* John G. Cummins, "The Practical Implications of Alfonso el Sabio's Peculiar Use of the Zéjel," in *Bulletin of Hispanic Studies,* **47** (1970), a reexamination of certain assumptions about the mode of presentation of some of the *Cantigas* and other medieval material in similar form; José Guerrero Lovillo, *Las Cantigas: estudio arqueológico de sus miniaturas* (1949), contains reproductions of most of the miniatures; José J. Nunes, *Cantigas d'amigo dos trovadores galego-portugueses,* 3 vols. (1926–1928), contains an introduction to the study of the

repertory, a critical edition of the preserved texts, and a commentary and glossary; and *Cantigas d'amor dos trovadores galego-portugueses* (1932, repr. 1972), a critical edition of the preserved texts; Isabel Pope, "Mediaeval Latin Background of the Thirteenth-Century Galician Lyric," in *Speculum,* 9 (1934), a poetico-musical study of the *cantigas de amigo* by Martín Códax in light of the medieval Latin poetic types that form their background, includes facsimiles of four portions of the original folio containing these *cantigas.*

ROBERT J. SNOW

[See also **Alfonso X; Galician-Portuguese Poetry; Music, Western European; Virelai.**]

CANTIGAS DE AMOR, AMIGO, AND ESCARNIO,

lyric compositions (*cantigas de amor/amigo*) and satiric poems (*cantigas de escarnio*) in the Galician-Portuguese, preserved in three famous *cancioneiros* (song books): *Ajuda, Colocci-Brancuti,* and *Vaticana.* This poetry flourished from the end of the twelfth century (the earliest poet known is João Soares de Paiva, born in 1141) until the mid fourteenth century (the latest poet, Count Pedro of Barcelos, died in 1354). With the appearance of the Galician-Castilian school, it entered a period of decadence represented in the *Cancionero de Baena* (1445) and continued in the Castilian-Portuguese schools of the first part of the sixteenth century.

The *cantigas de amigo,* probably the oldest and most indigenous form, are spoken by ladies lamenting the absence of a lover. Simple compositions, with a great feeling for nature and repeated references to rustic life, they possess strong rhythm and great musicality, based in the parallelism of the verses. Rhythmic unity is achieved not in the strophe but in a pair of strophes that say the same thing; the pair of verses or lines differs only in one word in the rhyme, which alternates on the basis of *a/A, i/I, e/E.* Frequently, also, the last verse of each strophe is the first verse of the following strophe (*lexa-pren:* literally, "leave and retake"); each strophe is followed by a refrain.

By their popular character, ample use of parallelism, and expression of the search for a lover who is never described or defined, the *cantigas de amigo* resemble certain types of religious poetry that could very possibly have been centered around Santiago de Compostela. They are also related to the Mozarabic *kharjas,* in which the lady is much more sensual and aggressive. Outstanding among the poets who produced this type of poetry are Nuno Fernandez Torneol, João Zorro, Airas Núñes, Pero Moego, King Diniz, and above all the great seafaring poets: Martín Codax and Payo Gomez Charrino y Meendinno.

The *cantigas de amor* are much more elaborate compositions that develop an amorous sentiment centering on the concept of *mal d'amor* (lovesickness) and, especially, *morrer d'amor* (dying of love). The poems are expressions of love for a woman, which can never be mentioned to the woman (often because of the illicit nature of the love). They were evidently influenced by the lyric of the troubadours of Provence, to whose works they bear both thematic and strophic resemblance. Instead of the parallelistic device, the strophes are predominantly divided into two large groups, according to whether or not they have a refrain. The latter are called *de maestria.* Common to some is the concluding *finda* or refrain. Important poets of the *cantigas de amor* are Pero Barroso, Men Rodriquez Tenorio, Fernán Gonçalves, and Alfonso X of Castile and León, all of whom are well represented in the *Cancioneiro da Ajuda.*

The *cantigas de escarnio* and *cantigas de maldizer* develop individual or collective critique and satire—and not always in a refined way: commonly, they attack and censure the physical and moral defects of friends and enemies alike; they discredit poets who demonstrate a lack of originality; they ridicule jongleurs who sing badly. From a social and historical point of view, they are valuable documents not only from the Galician-Portuguese society but also from the Castilian society. A considerable number of poets were at the Castilian court of Ferdinand III and Alfonso X, for Galician-Portuguese was by the early thirteenth century, and for several centuries afterward, the poetic lingua franca of the western Iberian peninsula.

BIBLIOGRAPHY

José Joaquim Nunes, *Cantigas d'amigo dos trovadores galego-portugueses,* 3 vols. (1926–1928), and *Cantigas d'amor dos trovadores galego-portugueses* (1932); Manuel Rodrigues Lapa, *Cantigas d'escarnho e de mal dizer* (1965); Silvio Pellegrini, *Studi su trove e trovatori della prima lirica ispano-portoghese,* 2nd ed. (1959).

JOSEP M. SOLA-SOLÉ

[See also **Alfonso X; Cantiga; Galician-Portuguese Poetry; Portuguese Literature, History of.**]

CANTIGAS DE S. MARIA. See **Cantiga.**

CANTILÈNE. Although *cantilène* and "chanson de geste" were synonymous in the Middle Ages, the former term was used in the nineteenth century to explain the origins of the chanson de geste. First conceived by Friedrich Wolf, Johann Herder, and the Grimm brothers, the Romantic theory of the *cantilène* was introduced into France by Claude Fauriel and developed by Gaston Paris, who claimed that memorable historical events dating from the Merovingian and Carolingian periods were recorded by spontaneous epic chants (*cantilènes*). As these short, anonymous poems describing Germanic folklore and tradition were transmitted orally over centuries, they were gradually combined and amplified around a central theme, becoming by the end of the eleventh century what is commonly known as the chanson de geste. Partly for want of evidence and partly because of the conflicting viewpoints of Pio Rajna, Joseph Bédier, and other critics, the theory lost prestige in the early 1900's.

BIBLIOGRAPHY

Léon Gautier, *Les épopées françaises,* I (1865); Gaston Paris, *Histoire poétique de Charlemagne* (1865, repr. 1974); Italo Siciliano, *Les origines des chansons de geste* (1951).

M. GRUNMANN-GAUDET

[See also **Chansons de Geste; French Literature.**]

CANTOR. While, in medieval Latin, the word *cantor* may mean simply "one who sings," the English word normally refers to the precentor or other solo singer in the Western liturgy. The idea that the cantoral office in the patristic and medieval church is a continuation of a Hebrew cantoral ministry is as unfounded as it is widely held. The development of the specialized ministry occurs somewhat earlier in the Christian community than in the Jewish. The first canonical recognition of the cantor was accorded in the fourth century by the Council of Laodicea. In both communities, the emergence of the role came with increased complexity of liturgy. Since the medieval church normally sang all its public utterances, and since some of those sung texts became very elaborate, a specialized caste of cantors developed. Some medieval reckonings of the number of clerical orders include cantors among ordained ministers.

By the time of Amalarius of Metz (ninth century), the cantoral function was well established and held in high honor. In most ecclesiastical centers, the cantor found his primary employment in the round of the Daily Office, which was sometimes called the *officio cantorum.* Some of this prestige was undoubtedly connected with the cantor's role as custodian of the repertory and, when applicable, as initiate into the mysteries of musical notation.

By the late Middle Ages, the relatively immutable repertory, the ironing-out of regional and expressive peculiarities into an established convention, and increased professionalism in other ecclesiastical offices contributed to make the dignity of the cantor less overwhelming. This was witnessed to, in England, by the fact that cathedrals of the Old Foundation place the precentor second in precedence to the dean, while those of the New Foundation put him among the minor canons. Standardization was gradually attached to the behavior, dress, and number of cantors for any given day or place, and as the role became of less musical importance it also became of less clerical importance.

BIBLIOGRAPHY

Amalarii episcopi opera liturgica omnia, Jean Michel Hanssens, S.J., ed., 3 vols. (1948–1950); Ismar Elbogen, *Der jüdische Gottesdienst in seiner geschichtlichen Entwicklung* (1913); Edward Foley, Capuchin, "The Cantor in Historical Perspective," in *Worship,* 56 (1982), with bibliography.

Roger Evans

[See also **Amalarius of Metz; Liturgy, Jewish; Music, Jewish.**]

CANUTE. See **Cnut the Great.**

CANVAS, a coarse fabric derived from the hemp plant (*cannabis,* hence the name) used in the Middle Ages chiefly in the maritime trades for sails, rigging, rope, and sacking. Interwoven with fibers from the flax plant, canvas provided strength and durability to textiles meant for clothing, and herein lay its second use during medieval times. One center of production

after the twelfth century in France was Cahors, which supplied sailors' needs in the Mediterranean trades.

Cultivation of the hemp plant resembled that of flax, but required less intensive labor. Manufacture of hempen fibers into thread ready for weaving also resembled the processes used for flaxen fibers, and consequently both plants were often grown together in the same cottage plots.

Canvas might be natural in color, or it could be bleached or dyed. The best grades of canvas rivaled, in texture and dye retention, the lower grades of linen; and since the cultivation, manufacture, and uses of canvas so closely resembled those of flax these two textiles may be considered virtually interchangeable.

Hemp production followed the same historical path as noted for flax, remaining essentially a cottage industry. Its manufacture into finished cloth became concentrated in urban centers under various guild monopolies. While not a luxury textile in itself, its clothing applications mentioned above lent added incentives to small producers. Its primary purpose remained, however, linked with the maritime trades.

BIBLIOGRAPHY

Georges Duby, *Rural Economy and Country Life in the Medieval West,* Cynthia Postan, trans. (1968); James Westfall Thompson, *Economic and Social History of the Middle Ages,* 2 vols. (1966).

Michael J. Hodder

[See also **Flax; Textiles.**]

CAPELLA, MARTIANUS. See **Martianus Capella.**

CAPELLANUS, ANDREAS (André le Chapelain, Andrew the Chaplain, *fl. ca.* 1170–1190), is described in manuscripts as "chaplain to the king of France," but nothing is known of his life. In his only known work, *De amore libri tres* (Three books about love), also known as *De arte honeste amandi* (The art of loving honorably), he mentions Queen Eleanor of England (Eleanor of Aquitaine), her daughter Marie, countess of Champagne, and other female notables. From this it has been assumed that Andreas was active at the court of Champagne. The work is ostensibly written for a certain Walter, who has asked for advice on love. The first, and by far the longest, book defines the nature and goals of love and then offers a series of dialogues between men of the upper nobility, gentry, and the bourgeoisie and their female counterparts. These are essentially an exercise in rhetoric, for they detail suitable approaches for men of each class to use when asking for the love of a woman of each of the three social ranks. The book closes with a brief glance at love among clerics, nuns, and prostitutes.

The second book deals with the retention and loss of love. It includes a cautionary tale for those who reject love and a series of judgments on questions on the behavior of lovers that was allegedly given at the courts of love organized by Marie of Champagne. The third book retracts all the advice given to Walter and repeats all the clichés of medieval antifeminism. A few critics consider this book the most important part of the work.

De amore is a witty, mock-serious treatise about the game of love-dialectic as played at a few sophisticated courts, but it owes its reputation to the mistaken belief (fostered by the unjustified title of the English translation) that it is the key to the understanding of "courtly love," as found in the twelfth-century lyric and romance. It does, however, throw some light on the audience for those literary works.

BIBLIOGRAPHY

De amore libri tres, E. Trojel, ed., 2nd ed. (1964); *The Art of Courtly Love*, John Jay Parry, trans. (1941, repr. 1969); John F. Benton, "The Court of Champagne as a Literary Center," in *Speculum*, 36 (1961); Felix Schlösser, *Andreas Capellanus: seine Minnelehre und das christliche Weltbild um 1200* (1960).

W. T. H. JACKSON

[See also **Antifeminism; Courtly Love; French Literature: To 1200; Rhetoric, Western European.**]

CAPETIAN FAMILY ORIGINS. In tracing Capetian family origins, matters of status are as important as the genealogy. The ancestry and family connections prior to the tenth century are poorly known. What is essential is the outline of the kin group and the rank of the persons. Three elements are most instructive: the emergence of the Capetians—or Robertinians, as the early generations are usually called—as a noble lineage; their appearance as members of a powerful extended clan in the West Frankish kingdom; and the evolution of the family into a princely dynasty.

The Robertinians appear among the high nobility at least as early as the first half of the eighth century. They may have originated in the Rhine-Meuse region, where one of their members was duke of Haspengau in 733. By the middle of that century, some of them were established in the Rhine-Main region, where in 764 the widow and a son of Count Robert I founded the abbey of Lorsch, with which the family was long associated. The royal favor shown to the family during the rule of Pepin the Short may have been due in part to their kinship with Chrodegang of Metz. Four generations of the descendants of Robert I were counts of Upper Lorraine or of Worms. The last count of that series, Robert IV, because of his support for Louis the Pious and Charles the Bald against Charles's brothers, abandoned or lost his family holdings in the Rhineland. From the 840's on, this Robert, known subsequently as Robert the Strong, lived in the western kingdom.

In Charles's kingdom Robert the Strong was active in a faction of the high nobility composed largely of extended, interrelated clans. He was allied to Odo, count of Châteaudun, later also count of Angers and then of Troyes; some evidence suggests that Robert and Odo were brothers-in-law. Odo's family connections linked Robert to royal patronage, for Odo appears to have been a close cousin of Ermentrude, first wife of Charles the Bald. Robert was also related by marriage to Adelhelm, a count in the region of Laon, and perhaps to Donatus, count of Melun. With the support of such allies, Robert was raised to high rank. In or by 852, he was count of Angers and lay abbot of Marmoutier. In the 860's he became count of Blois and abbot of St. Martin at Tours. At Robert's death his holdings passed to another noble, Hugh the Abbot. They were later recovered by Robert's son Odo.

The Robertinian family assumed dynastic form during the first half of the tenth century. The change in familial organization was linked to the hereditary transmission of the family *honores* as a patrimony from Odo to his brother Robert, from him to his son Hugh the Great, and from him to his eldest son, Hugh Capet. By the death of Hugh the Great, in 956, the new family system had been established. It governed the organization of the Capetians as a kin group for the next several centuries.

BIBLIOGRAPHY

Jean Dufour, ed., *Recueil des actes de Robert Ier et de Raoul, rois de France (922–936)* (1978); Karl Glöckner, "Lorsch und Lothringen, Robertiner und Capetinger," in

Zeitschrift für die Geschichte des Oberrheins, 89 (1936–1937); Walther Kienast, *Der Herzogstitel in Frankreich und Deutschland (9. bis 12. Jahrhundert)* (1968), 55–77; Karl Ferdinand Werner, "Untersuchungen zur Frühzeit des französischen Fürstentums, 9. bis 10. Jahrhundert," in *Die Welt als Geschichte*, 19 (1959); and "Important Noble Families in the Kingdom of Charlemagne ...," in Timothy Reuter, ed. and trans., *The Medieval Nobility* (1978).

ANDREW W. LEWIS

[See also **Carolingians and the Carolingian Empire; France: To 987; Germany: 843–1137.**]

CAPGRAVE, JOHN (1393–1464), Augustinian friar, prior of the house at Lynn in Norfolk, prior provincial, theologian, and historian. His *De illustribus Henricis* was occasioned by the visit of Henry VI to Lynn priory. He wrote an English *Chronicle of England;* Lives of Sts. Catherine of Alexandria, Augustine, Gilbert of Sempringham, and Norbert; Latin commentaries on the Bible; sermons; and other theological works. Several manuscripts of his works are said to be autographs.

BIBLIOGRAPHY

John Capgrave, *The Chronicle of England,* Francis Charles Hingeston, ed. (1858, repr. 1964), *Liber de illustribus Henricis,* Francis Charles Hingeston, ed. (1858, repr. 1964), and *The Life of St. Norbert,* Cyril L. Smetana, ed. (1977); Edmund Colledge, "The Capgrave 'Autographs,'" in *Transactions of the Cambridge Bibliographical Society,* **6,** pt. 3 (1974).

MICHAEL SARGENT

[See also **Augustinian Friars; Middle English Literature.**]

CAPILLA MAYOR, in Hispanic architecture, the chapel of the high altar, that dedicated to the titular saint of the church. It faced the choir and was entered from the crossing of nave and transept. With the development of Gothic architecture it was bounded on its other three sides by an ambulatory.

JOHN WILLIAMS

CAPITAL, the head or crown of a column, pier, shaft, or pilaster that forms the transition between the column and the arch or architrave above. At the base of the capital there is usually a narrow molding

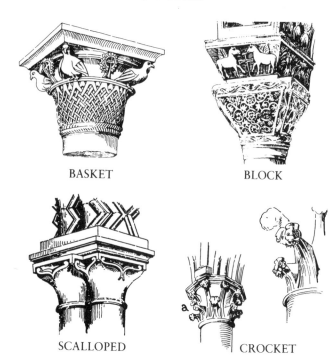

BASKET   BLOCK

SCALLOPED   CROCKET

Four main types of medieval capitals. FROM SIR BANISTER FLETCHER'S A HISTORY OF ARCHITECTURE

(the necking), and above the capital there is frequently an abacus, usually rectangular. During the early Christian and medieval periods an impost block was often placed between the capital and the arch or architrave. Capitals usually were decorated. The basket capital, developed in Byzantium during the sixth century, was nearly hemispherical in shape and was decorated with deeply cut designs, often foliate, that sometimes resembled a wicker basket.

Early medieval capitals generally imitated Roman or Byzantine types, but during the Romanesque and Gothic periods several new forms appeared. The Romanesque block capital (cubic capital, cushion capital) was cut from a cube of stone with its lower parts rounded off to conform to the shape of the column (as at Canterbury Cathedral). The junction between the curved and flat surfaces was often sharp and usually described a semicircle; the flat surfaces were either left plain or sculpted in low relief. On the scalloped capital, developed from the block capital in England (as at Durham), the flat surface on each face of the cube ended in several semicircular forms rather than one. During the Romanesque period capitals were often carved with figural decoration (as at Autun), but this was rare in the Gothic period, when foliate decoration was more popular.

From the middle of the twelfth century on, a chalice shape was most commonly used for capitals. The crocket capital, with stylized foliage springing upward from the neck, usually along the diagonals, and curving outward below the abacus, was introduced in early Gothic churches in France (for example, Chartres Cathedral) and spread throughout the Continent. In High Gothic churches, capitals were sometimes omitted in order to preserve the continuity of line between the column and the arch, as in the transept facades of Notre Dame, Paris.

BIBLIOGRAPHY
Rudolf Kautzsch, *Kapitellstudien* (1936).

LESLIE BRUBAKER

CAPITULARY, an administrative and legislative order of certain Carolingian kings and emperors divided into articles *(capitula)*. These diverse instruments included ecclesiastical and lay capitularies, and among the latter one distinguishes articles designed to be joined to one or more of the national laws of the Carolingian Empire, collections of ad hoc articles *(capitula per se scribenda),* and instructions for royal *missi.* Further, capitularies destined for the kingdom of the Lombards are distinguished from those intended for the kingdom of the Franks.

The authority of the capitularies was based on the royal power of the ban *(bannum):* the right of the sovereign to command, forbid, and punish. Frequently the consensus of an assembly was noted in a capitulary, but under the early Carolingians this consensus was merely the recognition by lay and ecclesiastical leaders of the royal prerogative of the ban and was designed to assure the efficacy of the capitulary. It was not itself a necessary condition for validity. Under the later Carolingians, as factional disputes eroded royal authority, the consensus became increasingly necessary for validity of the capitulary.

In the world of restricted literacy that was the Frankish empire, the essential element of the promulgation of royal instruments was the *verbum regis* or *verbum imperatoris,* a solemn oral statement addressed to an assembly by the king or emperor. Thus, the written form in which capitularies are preserved is often cursory and frequently seems limited to the order to observe the dispositions of the verbal order. Moreover there was never a uniformity in the language, style, or structure of the capitularies. Some resemble diplomas and were prepared by the royal chancery; others were prepared outside the chancery by an ad hoc secretary or by a notary who accompanied royal *missi.*

Capitularies were normally published through *missi dominici,* who read them before local and regional assemblies, which then gave their consensus. Counts and bishops were occasionally charged with publishing capitularies in their own counties or dioceses, without passing through the intermediary of the *missi.*

The most important capitularies were the Capitulary of Herstal (779), the General Admonition (789), the Frankfurt Capitulary (794), the Programmatic Capitulary of 802, and the Capitulary of Thionville (805). The Capitulary of Herstal, publication of which followed a period of crisis (failure of the Spanish expedition in 778, Saxon attacks, troubles in the Midi), sought to reform and reorganize secular and ecclesiastical administration and justice in Francia. The General Admonition, along with two lesser capitularies for *missi* prepared in 789, dealt primarily with ecclesiastical matters. The General Admonition expressed the fundamental principle of Carolingian administration: peace and concord, that is, cooperation and collaboration between ecclesiastical and lay authorities in administration of the kingdom.

The capitulary published at Frankfurt likewise dealt with ecclesiastical matters and followed the revolt of Pepin the Hunchback, a new revolt of the Saxons, and famine caused by poor harvests. The capitulary sought to regulate prices on grain, establish legal jurisdiction over clergy, and regulate weights, measures, and coinage. The so-called Programmatic Capitulary presented a program of imperial government, ecclesiastical and civil, elaborated after Charlemagne's imperial coronation in 800. The last important capitulary of Charlemagne, that of Thionville, sought to deal with the many growing problems in the governance of the empire: bribery of officials, a breakdown in the administration of justice, and concern over the problem of succession.

Many of the capitularies issued by Charlemagne's son Louis the Pious presented a more elaborate and thoughtful structure and wording than those of the early Carolingians, evidence of the sophisticated conception of the empire held by Louis and his advisers. After his death in 840, Charles the Bald was the last Carolingian to continue the capitulary tradition, which had ended in the eastern parts of Francia and disappeared in the west as well after his death.

BIBLIOGRAPHY

Monumenta Germaniae historica, Legum sectio II: Capitularia regum Francorum, Alfred Boretius and Victor Krause, eds., 2 vols. (1883–1897, repr. 1960), contains more than 300 documents. See also H. R. Loyn and John Percival, *The Reign of Charlemagne: Documents on Carolingian Government and Administration* (1975); Rudolf Buchner, *Die Rechtsquellen* (1953), 44–49, supp. to Wilhelm Wattenbach, *Deutschlands Geschichtsquellen im Mittelalter: Vorzeit und Karolinger;* and François L. Ganshof, *Recherches sur les capitulaires* (1958), and *The Carolingians and the Frankish Monarchy,* Janet Sondheimer, trans. (1971).

PATRICK GEARY

[See also **Ban, Banalité; Carolingians and the Carolingian Empire; Law, French; Missi Dominici.**]

CAPPADOCIA is located on the high plateau of central Anatolia, in the heart of present-day Turkey. From this province of the Roman Empire came the fourth-century synthesizers of Christian thought, the Cappadocian fathers: St. Basil the Great, St. Gregory of Nyssa, and St. Gregory Nazianzus. By the beginning of the tenth century Cappadocia was one of the border themes of Byzantium. After the iconoclast emperors' military successes had pacified the eastern frontier and their theological defeat had facilitated the growth of monasticism, the Cappadocian valleys of Göreme, Soğanlı, and Peristrema became popular sites for eremitic and cenobitic settlement. The monks carved their cells and chapels into the soft volcanic tuff of this moonlike terrain. Scores of these rock-cut churches were then painted. The historical importance of these monuments is derived from their density, their relatively good state of preservation, and the number of dated inscriptions in them. These inscriptions allow the clear documentation of the stylistic changes that took place in the province between *ca.* 900 and the third quarter of the eleventh century, when Cappadocia fell to Seljuk rule.

This artistic development may be summarized as follows: The late-ninth–early-tenth-century (inappropriately referred to as the "Archaic Group") works, centering on Ayvalı Kilise (913–920), include the Old Church of Tokalı Kilise, Tavşanlı Kilise (913–920), and Kılıçlar Kilise, which are stylistically related to such contemporary works as those in Hagia Sophia in Constantinople and Hagia Sophia in Thessaloniki. The only high-quality monumental

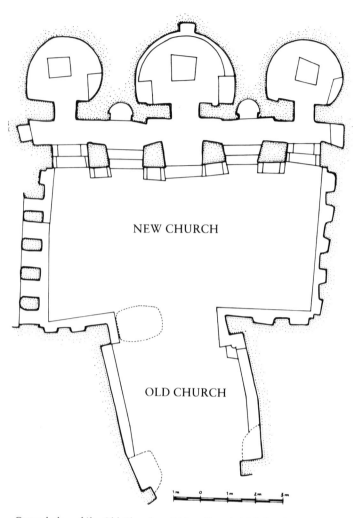

Ground plan of the Old Church and New Church. Tokalı Kilise, Cappadocia, early to mid 10th century. DRAWING COURTESY OF ANN WHARTON EPSTEIN

decoration to survive from the so-called Macedonian renaissance of the mid tenth century is found in the New Church of Tokalı Kilise and its cognate, the Great Pigeon House of Çavuşin. Eleventh-century churches include St. Barbara (1006 or 1021) and Karabaş Kilise (1060–1061) in the Soğanlı Valley, the Column Church group, and Eski Gümüş.

These monuments are sensitive reflectors of the artistic developments in Constantinople. However, their programs are distinguished by a strong narrative bias, and their style tends toward abstraction. Further, alien architectural types, such as the transverse-nave plan from Mesopotamia, were rapidly assimilated into the local architectural dialect. Thus, the small, rock-cut chapels of Cappadocia express a considerable degree of provincial autonomy.

North side of the nave, New Church. Tokalı Kilise, Cappadocia, mid 10th century. PHOTOGRAPH COURTESY OF ANN WHARTON EPSTEIN

BIBLIOGRAPHY

Guillaume de Jerphanion, *Une nouvelle province de l'art byzantine: Les églises rupestres de Cappadoce*, 4 vols. (1925–1942); Marcell Restle, *Die byzantinische Wandmalerei in Kleinasien* (1967); Nicole and Michel Thierry, *Nouvelles églises rupestres de Cappadoce, région du Hasan daği* (1963).

ANN WHARTON EPSTEIN

[See also **Early Christian and Byzantine Architecture; Macedonian Renaissance**.]

CARPINI, JOHN OF PLANO. See **John of Plano Carpini.**

CARAVANS. See **Han; Trade, Islamic; Travel and Transport, Islamic.**

CARAVANSARY, CARAVANSERAI. See **Han.**

CARDINALS, COLLEGE OF. The college of cardinals took shape in the eleventh century from the coalescence of groups of clerics (priests, bishops, deacons) in Rome. The cardinal-priests were rectors of the twenty-eight *tituli,* which had originated as private houses owned by Roman Christians who donated them for the needs of the faithful. Long known by the "title" of the original owners (for example, *titulus Vestinae*), in time they developed into real churches with names reflecting their dedication (such as San Vitale). Since there was no cathedral as such in Rome, the *tituli* exercised quasi-diocesan functions. Each had several priests, all of whom may have been called "cardinals" at one time. As internal hierarchies developed in each, though, one priest became the superior of the others and appropriated the term. The seven cardinal-bishops, on the other hand, held small, unimportant sees in the vicinity of Rome, but were prominent because of their close association with the pope through their liturgical functions in St. John Lateran.

It was not until near the end of the eleventh century that the deacons of the Roman church also began to be called "cardinals," and were thus assimilated to the others. By this time the term "cardinal" implied superior rank and association with the pope in the management of the Roman church. Significantly, about the same time there arose a new institution, the consistory—the regular meeting of pope, cardinals, and lesser advisers that soon replaced the infrequent synod as the chief organ of church government.

It took some time for these clerical elements to form a coherent body. One impetus came from their role as papal electors. In the Roman Synod of 1059 Pope Nicholas II promulgated an electoral decree giving the cardinal-bishops the right to initiate the selection of a new pope. The specific terms of the decree soon fell into abeyance, but the reservation of papal elections to cardinals alone contributed much to their prestige. So did the tendency of reforming popes of the eleventh century, starting with Leo IX, to appoint like-minded reformers to ecclesiastical posts. This quickly led to a gathering around the pope of a group of close friends and advisers, many of whom were cardinals.

It was some time before the cardinals developed

an esprit de corps. The cardinal-priests resented the growing importance of the cardinal-bishops. Some of the priests even insisted that papal power exercised without their concurrence was illegitimate. Also, the divisive influence of powerful Roman families became institutionalized by the inclusion of their representatives in the college. The rivalry of the Frangipani and Pierleoni factions was instrumental in exacerbating the tensions surrounding the disputed papal election that led to the schism of 1130–1139.

As the role of the pope in church governance grew, so did the influence of those around him. There soon developed a mythology of the apostolic foundation of the college, making it a divine rather than a human institution. This was accompanied by an inflated language of metaphor and symbol: the cardinals were the successors of the apostles; part of the pope's body; the columns supporting the church; the *cardines*—hinges—upon which the great door of the church swings; senators of the church, recalling the senators of a Roman Empire now become Christian. Physical symbols followed: the miter, mark of episcopal rank, worn by all cardinals; the red hat, the color symbolic of imperial rule taken over by the papacy; the white horse or mule, once reserved to the pope alone.

Special financial arrangements underlined the cardinals' status. By the thirteenth century they had their own camera, a joint treasury giving them an income over and above that provided by their churches. Various popes of the thirteenth century occasionally granted the cardinals shares of the tribute from England and Sicily, and in 1289 Pope Nicholas IV confirmed their right to half the income from all territories from which the Roman church drew revenues.

The college was never a large body. In theory there might be six bishops, twenty-eight priests, and eighteen deacons (the last based on the number of deaconries in Rome in the eleventh century), but in fact their actual number was usually much smaller. This may have been dictated by financial considerations, but it certainly enhanced the influence of individual cardinals. By the thirteenth century, Gregory IX and Innocent IV clearly aimed at maintaining something like eighteen or nineteen cardinals as a maximum. The pattern changed markedly in the Avignon period, with as many as thirty-one cardinals under John XXII.

Churchmen abroad, especially in the twelfth century, often looked on the college as a body of up-

starts whose ambitions undermined the tradition that the church should be governed by its bishops, the true successors of the apostles. Bernard of Clairvaux was particularly scathing about the pretensions of cardinal-deacons who claimed superiority over bishops because they represented the pope, and there was always resentment over the arrogant claim that cardinals could pass judgment on all bishops. There was a notable clash of cardinals and bishops at the Synod of Rheims (1148), where the cardinals insisted that the matter of Gilbert de la Porrée's orthodoxy was not a question for the synod, a mere gathering of local French bishops, but for the consistory—that is, for the pope and cardinals. In effect, this was a claim that the primacy of the Roman see embraced themselves as well as the pope.

The tension over status was not helped by the fact that few bishops became cardinals. Those who did so became cardinal-bishops; but it was rare to find a bishop made cardinal-priest. However, the occasional election of a cardinal-priest to some see or other, as in the case of Stephen Langton to the see of Canterbury in 1207, suggests that bishops were still thought of as superior to cardinal-priests and deacons. But this was slowly changing; within a century Clement V was appointing bishops as cardinal-priests and having them renounce their sees in the process. This marked the culmination of a long process whereby the dignity of cardinal gradually came to precede that of bishop.

The responsibilities of cardinals were manifold. Three stand out. First, they had the occasional duty of choosing a pope. The vagueness of procedure surrounding elections was finally settled at the Third Lateran Council of 1179 when Pope Alexander III promulgated the constitution *Licet de vitanda*, introducing the principle that the candidate who received two-thirds of the votes of the cardinals was to be recognized as pope. He made no distinction between bishops, priests, and deacons, an indication that such distinctions were now dead, and he made no mention of the right of confirmation by "clergy and people," a traditional right of formal acclamation that had allowed too much outside interference.

Gregory X's constitution *Ubi periculum*, promulgated at the Second Council of Lyons in 1274, gave legal force to the "conclave," the practice, which had appeared in some thirteenth-century papal elections, of locking up the cardinals and making life increasingly miserable for them until they chose a pope. The constitution denied the cardinals any right to exercise papal authority during a vacancy, subjected them to the supervision of local lay authorities, required that they be cut off from the outside world, and reduced their diet to a bare minimum if they were not prompt in doing their duty. The cardinals opposed the constitution, but could not stop its promulgation, and eventual enshrinement in canon law.

As a second major responsibility, the cardinals served as papal assistants, acting as legates, nuncios, arbitrators, judges, administrators, and the like. Since the development of the papacy after the eleventh century was marked by a large growth in the legal business of the curia, the consistory was soon overwhelmed with legal matters. It increasingly became a matter of practice to assign cases to cardinals or to lesser members of the curia, depending on the importance of the case or the ranks of the parties involved. Soon virtually all but the most important cases came to the consistory only for a pro forma confirmation of the hearing already held and a sentence already promulgated. Thus were born the tribunals of the cardinals, each of whom soon surrounded himself with a staff of legal advisers.

Third, as a group in consistory the cardinals were consulted about and expressed their opinions on a wide range of ecclesiastical and political matters. References to such consultation are frequent in papal letters of the twelfth century, and the more or less standard formula de fratrum nostrorum consilio (with the counsel of our brethren) soon appeared in all those papal acts decided upon with the advice of the cardinals. Such consultation was usual in important or particularly difficult cases: the transfer of bishops; the appointment of legates, vicars, nuncios, and rectors of the papal patrimony; the regulation of curial offices; and all matters touching on the finances of the Roman church or the administration of its territories. Cardinals also counseled on relations with secular states in matters of war, peace, and succession, and on grave questions of religious and theological importance.

It was not legally binding on the pope either to consult the cardinals or to follow their advice, but long tradition, the weight of venerable opinion, and the practical value of acting in concord with the cardinals, especially those with great influence, meant that popes rarely acted in important matters without seeking their advice. For a pope not to do so was to run the risk of having his acts declared invalid by his successor. It was from this long-standing practice of consultation that the cardinals developed a claim to a share in the governance of the church.

Such a claim never received general acceptance, but it was given powerful expression by the cardinals Pietro and Giacomo Colonna, who were deposed by Boniface VIII. It continued to influence the college throughout the fourteenth century, to judge from the famous capitulatio of 1352, an agreement struck by the conclave that elected Innocent VI, that conferred broad legal rights upon the college. What the college had hitherto enjoyed in the form of papal concessions was now to be given legal force: the cardinals might henceforth control and limit their own membership, exercise effective supervision over the papal estates and curia, and establish an effective control over the instruments of diplomacy with secular governments.

Innocent almost immediately declared the agreement void, as prejudicial to the pope's "plenitude of power," but this did not blunt the oligarchical ambitions of the college. In 1378, disturbed by the erratic actions of Urban VI, whom they had just elected, they declared his election invalid and proceeded to another, that of Clement VII. It was a bold step, inconceivable except by a group now convinced of its superior role in ecclesiastical affairs. The ensuing schism and the conciliar period that followed saw two, and later three, curias and colleges of cardinals, as well as the swift development of a theory of conciliar government of the church that swept aside the pretensions of the cardinals. These events, together with the growing custom in the fifteenth century of recruiting cardinals among the advisers of European royalty who did not join the Roman curia, mark the end of the medieval period in the history of the college.

BIBLIOGRAPHY

See Giuseppe Alberigo, Cardinalato e collegialità: studi sull' ecclesiologia tra l'xi e il xiv secolo (1969); M. Andrieu, "L'origine du titre de cardinal dans l'église romaine," in Miscellanea Giovanni Mercati, V (1946); A. Paravicini Bagliani, Cardinali di curia e familie cardinalizie dal 1227 al 1254, 2 vols. (1972); Paul Maria Baumgarten, Untersuchungen und Urkunden über die Camera collegii cardinalium für die Zeit von 1295 bis 1437 (1898); Mario Fois, "Papa e cardinali nel secolo XI," in Archivum historiae pontificiae, 14 (1976); Carl G. Fürst, Cardinalis: Prolegomena zu einer Rechtsgeschichte des römischen Kardinalskollegiums (1967); Hans Walter Klewitz, Reformpapsttum und Kardinalkolleg (1957), 9–134. S. Kuttner, "Cardinalis: The History of a Canonical Concept," in Traditio, 3 (1945); J. B. Sägmüller, Die Thätigkeit und Stellung der Cardinäle bis auf Papst Bonifaz VIII (1896).

NORMAN ZACOUR

[See also **Clergy; Curia, Papal; Papacy, Origins and Development of.**]

CARMATIENS. See **Karamans.**

CARMEL, USE OF. See **Carmelite Rite.**

CARMELITE RITE. The move of the early Carmelites from Palestine to Europe in the thirteenth century, and their subsequent transition from an eremitical to a mendicant order, resulted in their partial abandoning of the Franco-Roman liturgy brought to Jerusalem by the early Crusaders and practiced at the basilica of the Holy Sepulcher. Borrowing from Dominican liturgical sources while retaining elements of the earlier Jerusalem usages, and tending to conform to Roman practice while being much influenced by local customs, this eclectic liturgy was slow to achieve that ideal of order-wide uniformity officially called for in the constitutions of 1281 and 1294, and preconized by the normative Ordinal composed by Sibert of Beka in 1312. On the basis of the relatively few extant Carmelite chant manuscripts, it would seem that there was no one particular form of chant proper to the whole Order.

The origins of the Carmelites in the Holy Land, and a spirituality in which devotion to the Virgin Mary features large, are evident in the calendar of the Order, in numerous proper formularies of Mass and Office, and in devotional practices that, although varying considerably according to region and periods of history, have always been characteristic of Carmelite piety.

BIBLIOGRAPHY

Archdale A. King, "Carmelite Rite," in *Liturgies of the Religious Orders* (1955), 235–324; *Ordinaire de l'Ordre de N.-D. du Mont Carmel (Sibert de Beka)*, B. Zimmermann, ed., Bibliothèque liturgique, XIII (1910); Margaret Rickert, *The Reconstructed Carmelite Missal* (1952).

CHRYSOGONUS WADDELL, O.C.S.O.

CARMELITES. Founded according to legend in the milieu of the Old Testament prophet Elijah, but dating historically from the semieremitical community established on Mount Carmel around 1155 by St. Berthold and his European companions, the first Carmelites combined a predominantly contemplative orientation with preaching and active works of charity. At the request of Berthold's successor Brocard, the Latin patriarch of Jerusalem, St. Albert of Vercelli, wrote the primitive Carmelite rule around 1209, drawing largely from monastic practices described by St. Basil and Cassian. New foundations multiplied, and in 1226 Pope Honorius III approved the primitive rule. The decline and fall of the Crusader States resulted, soon after 1238, in the gradual migration of Carmelite communities to Cyprus and western Europe. Despite this mass exodus, the original association of Mount Carmel with the prophet Elijah and, according to popular belief, with the Virgin Mary, remained determining influences in the desert spirituality and Marian devotion characteristic of the order.

Under St. Simon Stock, sixth prior-general, the primitive rule was modified in 1247; urban foundations were permitted, and the order of solitaries quickly evolved into a mendicant order engaged, like the Franciscans and Dominicans, in pastoral work and university teaching.

By the fourteenth century the rapidly expanding order numbered more than 300 houses divided into twenty-one provinces; and in the following century there were further foundations in Scandinavia, Portugal, and Slavic territory. But the Black Death, the effect of continual wars between European nations, and the divided loyalties brought about by the Western Schism (1378–1417) all contributed to the progressive decline of Carmelite observance.

Whatever the evolution of Carmelite institutions during the medieval period, the distinctive notes of the primitive Rule remained normative. Brief (some 2,000 words divided into sixteen chapters or paragraphs) and biblical both in inspiration and literary expression, St. Albert's fundamental Rule of 1209 was characterized by its emphasis on obedience, continual prayer, asceticism, simplicity, silence, manual work, and solitude. Still, by the end of the Middle Ages, the practical assimilation of the Carmelites into the Friars Preachers had resulted both in the mitigation of the original Rule and in the diminution of the prophetic spirit characteristic of early Carmel. Reaction to abuses took the form of sporadic but uncoordinated reform movements. These pointed to the need of, and prepared the way for, the far-reaching reform effected in the sixteenth century, when the spirit and institutions of early Carmel were to be revived with renewed vigor.

BIBLIOGRAPHY

T. Brandsma, "Carmes," in *Dictionnaire de spiritualité,* 'I (1953); François de Sainte-Marie, O.C.D., ed. and trans., *Les plus vieux textes du Carmel* (1945); Patrick R. Mc-Caffrey, *The White Friars* (1926); Melchior de Sainte-Ma¬ie, "Carmel," in *Dictionnaire d'histoire et de géogra-phie ecclésiastiques,* XI (1949); Peter-Thomas Rohrbach, O.C.D., *Journey to Carith: The Story of the Carmelite Order* (1966); "Jean le Solitaire," in *Aux sources de la tra-diti du Carmel* (1953); Lancelot C. Sheppard, *The English Carmelites* (1943).

CHRYSOGONOUS WADDELL, O.C.S.O.

[See also **Mendicant Orders; Monasticism, Origins.**]

CARMEN DE BELLO LEWENSI. See Lewes, Song of.

CARMEN DE BELLO SAXONICO, poem in three books written in hexameter, composed shortly after Henry IV's victory over the Saxons in 1075. Following oral tradition, it tells of the troubles in Saxony during the minority of the king, the siege of Harzburg, the taking of the fortresses of Goslar, the alleged success of the king in the fall of 1073, the destruction of the fortresses and in particular of Harzburg by the Saxons, and the final victory of Henry. Far from being an objective account of these events, the *Carmen* reads like a panegyric for the king.

The date of this work and the identity of its author have long been the subject of heated argument. Georg Waitz has clearly shown that the *Carmen* dates from the eleventh century, in contrast to G. H. Pertz, who took it for a fifteenth–early sixteenth-century work. The work has been attributed to Godescalc of Aix, Lambert of Hersfeld, and Meinhard of Bamberg. The continuers of August Potthast's *Bibliotheca historica medii aevi* have shown themselves more cautious ("the author may have been a cleric of the royal court"), but F.-J. Schmale unhesitatingly ascribes the work to Erlung von Würzburg.

BIBLIOGRAPHY

Manuscripts, editions, and critical studies are catalogued in the *Repertorium fontium historiae medii aevi,* III (1970), 137–138. Also see F.-J. Schmale, "Erlung von Würzburg," in *Die deutsche Literatur des Mittelalters, Verfasserlexikon,* II (1980) (in the second line of this article, read 1045/50 for 1145/50).

ALAIN STOCLET

[See also **Henry IV of Germany; Middle High German Literature; Saxony.**]

CARMINA BURANA, the largest and most important collection of secular medieval Latin song. The name of the early-thirteenth-century anthology ("Songs of Beuren") derives from the monastery of Benediktbeuren, where it was discovered after the dissolution of Bavarian monasteries in 1803 and transferred to what is now the Bayerische Staatsbibliothek. The manuscript (Clm 4660) lacks the beginning and concluding leaves, and has suffered some internal losses and rearrangement of gatherings because of a later rebinding. Several portions of the missing text have been recovered (*Fragmenta burana,* Clm 4660a, I–VII).

The manuscript, written by several scribes in an early Gothic hand, also contains musical notation for a number of songs and eight colored miniatures. Recent studies conclude that the codex does not date from around 1300 but is earlier than 1250, possibly by several decades. A stanza from a crusading song by Neidhart von Reuenthal (168a), which refers to events of 1217–1219, establishes a terminus post quem and narrows the probable date of the anthology to around 1225–1230. Further paleographical and textual details revealed by Bernhard Bischoff suggest that the manuscript originated in southern Austria (Styria) rather than in Bavaria, possibly at the court of a bishop of Seckau, either Karl (1218–1231) or Heinrich (1232–1243).

The anthology contained in the *Carmina burana* comprises about 300 pieces (including some fifty-six in Middle High German, mostly single stanzas) and is arranged into four main groups. The first (1–55) consists of moral and satirical poems dealing with avarice and simony, the instability of fortune, the decline and improvement of morals, conditions at Rome, the Crusades, particular events of political significance, and several exorcisms. Introductory rubrics and concluding metrical *versus* indicate further subdivisions based primarily upon thematic similarity, but these occur with decreasing frequency in later sections of the manuscript.

Wine drinkers *(Potatores)*. Carmina burana, *ca.* 1200. BAYERISCHE STAATSBIBLIOTHEK, MUNICH, MS CLM 4660, fol. 89v

The second and largest group of poems (56–186) contains mostly love songs and laments. The love songs present a broad spectrum of viewpoints ranging from haunting delicacy to unbridled obscenity, with a predominant tone of sensuality that has ensured their popularity. Two prominent features are the use of a nature introduction *(Natureingang)* set in spring and a sophisticated manipulation of school subjects, particularly classical mythology and allegory. Most of the Middle High German songs appear among the love poems, where they provide the melody and stanzaic form around which the Latin poems have been composed, or—less often—translate a Latin stanza or have been included because of their similarity to the adjacent Latin poem. The large group of laments frequently deals with love but also addresses other themes ranging from classical and political to personal and parodic topics.

The third main group of songs (187–226) is devoted to drinking and gambling, as well as to satires on life at court, begging poems, vagrancy, and parodies, all of which have frequently been overly romanticized in portrayals of "the goliardic life" and "the wandering scholars."

The fourth part (227–228) contains two liturgical plays, the Benediktbeuren Christmas Play and a fragmentary play on the king of Egypt that incorporates sections from the Tegernsee *Ludus de Antichristo* as well as several love songs.

Later additions to the manuscript (1*–26*), ranging from nearly contemporary to fourteenth-century entries, include four additional plays, two *planctus Mariae*, four Latin poems by the Marner, and five hymns to St. Catherine.

The great majority of poems in the *Carmina burana,* some three-fifths of the total, have survived only in this collection and remain for the most part anonymous. Since the authors are indicated only in three instances in the manuscript, identification of the poems in the collection depends upon the parallel transmission of texts in other manuscripts. Among the authors who have been identified are several from classical antiquity (Horace, Ovid, Juvenal, Ausonius), Otloh of St. Emmeram, and a large group of poets from the great renaissance of Latin lyric in the twelfth and early thirteenth centuries: Marbod of Rennes, Geoffrey of Winchester, Hilarius, Hugh (Primas) of Orléans, the Archpoet, Walter of Châtillon, Geoffrey of St. Victor, Peter of Blois, and Philip the Chancellor. The identifiable Middle High German authors include Otto von Botenlauben, Dietmar von Aist, Walther von der Vogelweide, Reinmar der Alte, Heinrich von Morungen, Neidhart von Reuental, Freidank, and the author of the *Eckenlied.*

The broad spectrum of subject matter and authors is also reflected by a wide variety of poetic and metrical forms. Modes of presentation and genres include dialogue, debate, narrative, satire and parody, pastourelles, dancing songs, songs of praise, and the *planctus*. Metrical poems and *versus* occur both in unrhymed and rhymed formats. The rhythmical poems that constitute the majority of the collection employ the variable forms of lays and sequences, as well as regular forms such as the "goliardic" and "Stabat Mater" stanza and more complicated strophic types. Some poems contain a mixture of metrical and rhythmical lines, others a mixture of Latin and Middle High German, Latin and Old French, or—in one instance—Latin and Greek, a reflection of the international nature of the collection.

Some texts in the *Carmina burana,* including most of the plays, have been provided with sporadic and irregular musical notation in staffless neumes, from which the melodies cannot be accurately determined. In some cases there is a parallel transmission of texts with legible notes, generally relating to the repertoires of St. Martial (Limoges) and Notre Dame (Paris), and about forty melodies have been reconstructed with varying degrees of certainty. The *Carmina burana* of Carl Orff, a modern musical setting of poems from the Benediktbeuren manuscript first performed in 1937, has done much to establish the reputation of the medieval anthology among the general public.

BIBLIOGRAPHY

Bernhard Bischoff, *Carmina Burana,* 2 vols. (1967), is a facsimile reproduction of MSS Clm 4660 and Clm 4660a; Alfons Hilka and Otto Schumann, eds., *"Carmina Burana," mit Benutzung der Vorarbeiten Wilhelm Meyers,* 2 vols. (1930–1970), is a critical edition. See also Günter Bernt, "Carmina Burana," in Kurt Ruh *et al.,* eds., *Die deutsche Literatur des Mittelalters: Verfasserlexikon,* I (1978).

ARTHUR GROOS

[See also **Goliards; Latin Literature.**]

CARMINA CANTABRIGIENSIA. See Cambridge Songs.

CARNIVAL. In the Middle Ages the term "carnival" designated the season of entertainment and feasting immediately before the somber fast of Lent. The exclusion of meat from the Christian diet for the forty days of fasting between Ash Wednesday and Easter produced the "carnival," perhaps meaning "meat-farewell" but more likely derived from *carne levare* (to remove meat). Depending upon local custom, the festivities could begin on or just before Epiphany (6 January) and last several weeks, or on Quinquagesima Sunday (the Sunday before Ash Wednesday) and last three days. The climax was always the Tuesday before Lent began, now called Shrove Tuesday or Mardi Gras (fat Tuesday). Although a medieval carnival was thus defined by its relationship to the Christian calendar, the origins of its customs probably go back to the pagan Saturnalia feast of ancient Rome.

Carnival was celebrated in Spain, France, Germany, and, most flamboyantly, in Italy, especially in Rome and Venice. This medieval merrymaking was often tolerated and even promoted by church officials, such as Pope Paul II (1464–1471), who staged elaborate races in Rome. Not until Sixtus V (1585–1590) did a pope systematically curb the often riotous feasts. The medieval tradition of annual carnivals is credited with a great influence on costume, popular theater, vernacular songs, and folk dances.

BIBLIOGRAPHY

Edward T. Horn, IV, *The Christian Year* (1957), 96–97.

PAUL ROREM

[See also **Fasting, Christian; Feasts and Festivals; Lent.**]

CAROLINGIAN ARCHITECTURE. See Pre-Romanesque Architecture.

CAROLINGIAN ART. See Pre-Romanesque Art.

CAROLINGIAN LATIN POETRY is the tradition of verse composition practiced at the court of Charlemagne and his successors until the end of the ninth century. In the course of the seventh century, the great rhetorical schools that had shaped education in civilized Europe disappeared. The resulting widespread illiteracy characteristic of the Merovingian period marked a definite break with the tradition of composition practiced by such sixth-century poets as Boethius, Avitus of Vienne, and Venantius Fortunatus. Modern scholars therefore sometimes refer to the period including the final quarter of the eighth century and the first quarter of the ninth as the "Carolingian renaissance." The term is accurate enough, since these years did witness a renaissance of learning in grammar, dialectic, rhetoric, and calligraphy, but an implied comparison with the much deeper intellectual and aesthetic ferment beginning in fourteenth-century Italy would be misleading.

The beginning of the Carolingian Latin poetic tradition can be dated to a chance meeting between Charlemagne and Alcuin at Parma in 781. The Frankish king convinced the English deacon to leave his library and school at York in order to take on a leading pedagogical role at the court school. From at least as early as Pericles' Athens, the reading and composition of poetry had been a primary means and an essential aim of education in Europe. With the end of the Roman Republic and the consequent deemphasis of practical oratory, poetry had come to be seen as the chief accomplishment of any educated person. Most of the scholars invited to Charlemagne's palace school were practicing poets who would continue and increase their production at Aachen and elsewhere in Charlemagne's empire. Initially, they were for the most part from the British Isles and from Italy, though in a short time men of Frankish birth began to rival and replace their teachers.

Indicative of the central role that poetry assumed in the ideals and aims of the palace circle was the members' practice of addressing one another with pseudonyms, often referring to an important classical poet. Thus, Alcuin was called Flaccus (Horace); Theodulf, Pindar; Angilbert, Homer; Modoin, Naso (Ovid); and the otherwise unknown Drances, Maro (Vergil). Other names were biblical, such as that of Charlemagne himself, who was called David, and of Paulinus of Aquileia, who was known as Timothy.

Such an affectation suggests something of the character of the poetry written at Charlemagne's court, a poetry written largely for the appreciation and entertainment of the group itself, habitually interpersonal, rarely introspective, and never lyric in the sense of modern lyric poetry. On occasion the members could adopt a public tone, as in Alcuin's numerous church dedications—"Haec porta est caeli, aeternae haec est ianua vitae, / Ista viatorem ducit ad astra suum" (This is the gate of heaven, this is the door to eternal life, / This leads its visitor to

the stars; *MGH* I, 306; all quotations from this edition). Similarly ceremonial and public is Theodulf's famous rhythmic hymn welcoming the newly crowned Louis the Pious to Orléans:

> En adest Caesar pius et benignus,
> Orbe qui toto rutilat coruscus,
> Atque prae cunctis bonitate pollet munere Christi.

> Behold, Caesar is here, faithful and kind, / Who shines brilliantly over the whole world, / And excels all in goodness, by the grace of Christ. (I, 529)

More typical of the general output of the court circle and illustrative of its frequently interpersonal character are the many verse epistles addressed to individuals. In this kind of verse Alcuin pleads with one of Charlemagne's daughters to intercede on behalf of a mutual friend, and Peter of Pisa poses a verse conundrum to Paul the Deacon.

Many kinds of poetry were contained in such verse epistles—riddles, fables, acrostics, eclogues, begging poems, and poems of praise or advice, among others—but there were also important genres of a less individual, personal kind: versified saints' lives, such as Alcuin's *Life of Willibrord,* and historical poems, such as the versified account attributed to Angilbert of the attack on Pope Leo in 799 (I, 366–379). There were formal, public laments or *planctūs,* as at the death of Charlemagne (I, 435–436) or the violent destruction of a monastery (I, 229–235; II, 148–149). There were also poems written to celebrate great public events, such as the victory of Charlemagne's son Pepin over the Avars in 796 (I, 116–117) and the coronation of Louis the Pious.

Throughout the period verses were composed in both quantitative and accentual meters. Although there are interesting exceptions, such as Sedulius Scotus, who composed lyrics in everything from anapestic to trochaic tetrameter, most of the surviving quantitative verse is in hexameters or elegiac couplets. Aside from a general tendency to shorten final -*o* where it would not have been shortened in classical times, the verse is in general metrically accurate.

If sheer quantity of surviving work is a reliable indicator of influence, then Alcuin was the most influential Carolingian poet, for his verse occupies nearly 200 pages in Dümmler's collective edition, which omits the rhythmical poetry. The overall impression when reading through these works is of a sustained technical mastery characteristic of the careful, dedicated pedagogue that Alcuin was. Although the "Farewell to His Cell" ("O mea cella, mihi habitatio dulcis amata"; I, 243–244) and the "Lament for a Nightingale" ("Quae te dextra mihi rapuit, luscinia, ruscis"; I, 274–275) are well known today and frequently anthologized, the solitary, lyric note found there is much less characteristic of Alcuin than more social verse, in which he is paying a compliment, asking a favor, or simply exhorting a student to apply himself:

> Surge, precor, iuvenis, vigeas dum corpore sano,
> Et tibi pande viam precibus ad regna polorum:
> Nec dederis sensus tota, rogo, nocte sopore.
> Assiduus gelidae somnus est mortis imago.

Son, get up, I beg you, as long as you are young and healthy, / And with your prayers open up a path to the kingdom of heaven: / Please, do not surrender your mind to sleep all night. / Unbroken sleep is the image of icy death. (I, 318)

Alcuin's pedagogical verses and his metrical epistles addressed to students and friends reflect the nature of the man and his work more accurately than the brief elegies, the numerous dedicatory verses, or even the longer historical poems such as *The Life of Willibrord* or the important history of the church at York. Some are directly concerned with study:

> O vos, est aetas, iuvenes, quibus apta legendo,
> Discite: eunt anni more fluentis aquae.
> Atque dies dociles vacuis ne perdite rebus:
> Nec redit unda fluens, nec redit hora ruens.

O youth, whose years are ripe for learning, / Study hard: time passes like a flowing river. / Don't waste this time for learning in idle games. / The flowing wave does not come back, the fleeting hour does not return. (I, 299–300)

Others have to do with Alcuin's more restricted interests in scriptural studies, in books, and in the reform of writing:

> Est opus egregium sacros iam scribere libros:
> Nec mercede sua scriptor et ipse caret.
> Fodere quam vites melius est scribere libros.
> Ille suo ventri serviet, iste animae.

It is an excellent work to copy out sacred books, / And the scribe will not lack his reward. / Copying out books is better than planting vines. / The one serves the belly, the other the soul. (I, 320)

And yet, while Alcuin was characteristically more concerned with books, study, grammar, and calligraphy, there is even in such poetry a haunting sense of the mutability of human aspiration, well exemplified in his repeated use of the Ovidian water image quoted above: "Instruat in studiis iuvenum bona tempora doctor, / Nam fugiunt anni more fluentis aquae" (May a teacher instruct the good season of youth in studies, / For the years flee like flowing water; I, 319) and "Omnia fluxa fluunt saeclorum gaudia longe / Nec redeunt iterum more fluentis aquae" (All the fleeting joys of the world flow far away / And like flowing water do not come back again; I, 297. Compare Ovid, *Ars amatoria*, 3.62–64.) This note is sounded for the last time in his epitaph, in which Alcuin addresses the person standing at his grave:

> Quod nunc es fueram, famosus in orbe, viator,
> Et quod nunc ego sum, tuque futurus eris.
> Delicias mundi casso sectabar amore,
> Nunc cinis et pulvis, vermibus atque cibus.

What you are now, I was, pilgrim: well known in the world, / And what I am now you will be one day. / With vain desire I used to follow the world's delights, / Who am now dust and ashes and food for worms. (I, 350)

Much less verse survives that can be safely ascribed to other poets closely associated with Charlemagne's court: Paul the Deacon, Peter of Pisa, Angilbert, Paulinus of Aquileia, and Einhard. Paul the Deacon, for example—better known for his *History of the Lombards*—composed a thirty-six-line summary of the traditional ages of the world, two poems in praise of St. Benedict, a description of Lake Como, a series of poems exchanged with Peter of Pisa solving the paradox "Dat genitor genito quod se non sentit habere" (The father gives his son what he knows he does not possess; I, 53), half a dozen epitaphs, a sixty-line episcopal history, and possibly a set of three beast fables.

Although the lines on Lake Como are often quoted ("Cinctus oliviferis utroque es margine silvis; / Numquam fronde cares cinctus oliviferis" [You are bounded by olive groves on either shore; / You never lack leaves, bounded by olive groves]; I, 43), at least as interesting are some verses apparently written in response to Charlemagne, who had praised him for his gifts of poetry and languages. But the praise seems ridiculous to Paul—"Totum hoc in meam cerno prolatum miseriam; / totum hoc in meum caput dictum per hyroniam" (I see that all of this is intended for my misery; / That it was said ironically against my [poor] wit; I, 49). He would wholly reject comparison with Homer, Horace, Vergil, and other pagan authors—"potius sed istos conparabo canibus" (I will, rather, compare them to dogs)—and denies any knowledge of Greek beyond a few letters: "Si non amplius in illa regione clerici / Graece proferunt loquellae, quam a me didicerint, / Vestri, mutis similati deridentur statuis" (If your clerics don't speak more Greek / In that area [the Eastern Empire] than they learned from me, / They will be laughed at for being as mute as statues; I, 49–50).

Although Paul's verses begging Charlemagne to free his brother are often quoted for the touching picture drawn ("Illius in patria coniunx miseranda per omnes / Mendicat plateas ore tremente cibos" [His wretched wife at home begs her food in the streets with trembling lip]; I, 47), more successful poetically is the brief epitaph for the baby Hildegard, who died forty days after her mother of the same name: "Parvula, non parvum, linquis, virguncula, luctum, / Confodiens iaculo regia corda patris" (Tiny little girl, you leave no little sorrow, / Piercing with a dart your father's royal heart; I, 60).

Although Alcuin was more prolific, Theodulf is generally considered the better poet. As he said to his friends when they inquired why he no longer answered the verses they sent him with compositions of his own:

> Sunt mihi lacrimis potius deflenda piacla
>   Carmina quam lyrica nempe boanda pede.
> Non amor ipse meus Christus mea carmina quaeret,
>   Sed mage commissi grandi lucra gregis.

> I must shed tears for my sins / Rather than bawl out songs in lyric measure. / My Christ, who is love itself, will not be looking for poems / But rather for great increase in the flock he has entrusted to me. (I, 542)

Clearly his duties as bishop of Orléans had cut him off from many of the pleasures he once enjoyed at Charlemagne's court, including frequent poetic composition.

Among Theodulf's most interesting poems are those that help us to understand the Carolingian imagination. For instance, in one he describes how classical poetic fables should be understood mystically, and speaks of the twin gates of sleep described in the sixth book of the *Aeneid* (893–896), one of horn (*cornea*), one of ivory (*eburnea*); one telling truth, the other lies. This is interpreted by Theodulf to refer to man, for "Est portis istis virtus non una duabus, / Os fert falsa, oculus nil nisi vera videt" (These two gates do not have the same power, / The mouth tells lies, the eye sees nothing but truth; I, 544). In another, Theodulf interprets the rewards in

the parable of the sower (Matt. 13:8): "Terdena in nuptu, in viduis sexdena coruscat, / Ista duo superat tertius ordo boni" (Thirtyfold shines out in marriage, sixty among widows, / But the third order of good surpasses both; I, 471). This *tertius ordo* is that of virgins and martyrs, whose reward is a hundredfold.

Theodulf's official responsibilities and his love of poetry come together in a work of 956 lines reflecting his experience as one of Charlemagne's *missi dominici* and today inaptly titled *Contra iudices* (Against judges). While the poem contains some satire against judicial venality and laziness, and much practical advice about such things as how to distinguish kindness from bribery, the poet's overwhelming concern is for justice and for the defense of the poor and weak against the wealthy and powerful: "Pauperibus quicumque praees, mitissimus esto, / Teque his natura noveris esse parem" (Whoever has authority over the poor be very gentle, / For you know you are the same as them in nature; I, 516). The rich grow richer at the expense of the poor, and men treat one another like wild beasts: "O genus, exemplum fugito, mortale, ferarum, / Nec homo sit homini quod fera torva ferae" (O mortal race, flee the example of the wild / And let man not be to man as beast is to cruel beast; I, 516).

At the same time, Theodulf had a satiric wit that he sometimes enjoyed exercising. His portrait of life at Charlemagne's court, addressed to the king, is an enthusiastic exercise in rhetorical praise and blame. Alcuin's appetite, Einhard's size, Angilbert's absence, and Cadac's Irish accent all come in for comment. Perhaps the conclusion contains the only lines not written with tongue in cheek, for there he speaks of his poem as a joke and hopes no one is offended: "Qui ne quem offendat, placeat dilectio Christi, / Omnia quae suffert, cui bona cuncta placent" (May the love of Christ—that bears all things, that delights in all good things—be pleased that this offend no one; I, 489).

The last years of Theodulf's life were spent in disgrace and exile. Among his final poems is one written to Modoin of Autun asking for advice and intercession with the king, lamenting his exile, and suggesting that the times were dangerous for everyone. Saddest of all is Modoin's answer to his old friend that it would be better to confess his guilt: "Nam prodesse tibi confessio pura valebit, / Si te voce probas criminis esse reum" (For a clean confession can profit you, / If you attest that you are guilty of the crime; I, 572). What happened afterward is not clear, but Theodulf may have been released from exile in 821, just before his death.

The literary influence of Irishmen at the Carolingian court grew as the ninth century progressed, culminating in the great figures of Sedulius Scottus and the philosopher John Scottus Eriugena. Even in Alcuin's day, however, an Irish student named Joseph followed his master to the Continent, where he eventually became an abbot. Poetically, his predilection seems to have been for the construction of acrostic poems, thirty-five lines long, each line of thirty-five letters, and the whole poem written so as to interweave four or five lines of verse in a shape consistent with the poem's theme. For instance, Joseph's poem on the cross as the sure road to heaven, "Inclyta si cupias sancti sub culmina templi . . ." (If you want [to enter] under the glorious roof of the sacred temple . . . ; I, 158), weaves a quatrain on the cross into the poem in the form of a temple enclosing three crosses.

Hrabanus Maurus composed at least one acrostic poem on the same principles as those used by Joseph, but for the most part his poetic production is of a more occasional and social character, including dedications, inscriptions, hymns, and epistolary verse. Perhaps reflecting a suspicion of pictorial art following the iconoclastic controversy are some lines written to urge his friend and successor at Fulda, Bonosus, to occupy himself more with writing than painting: "Plus quia gramma valet quam vana in imagine forma" (Because the letter has more value than the vain shape of an image; II, 196). Ermoldus Nigellus is responsible for a historical poem in honor of Louis the Pious extending to four books and more than 2,500 lines. It contains much Carolingian royal history done in medieval Vergilian epic style.

Walafrid Strabo became a student of Hrabanus Maurus at Fulda, but only after he had spent nine years at court as tutor to the young Charles the Bald. The best-known of his verses—which also include saints' lives, an eclogue, hymns, epitaphs, and epistolary poems—are the account of a vision experienced by a Suebian monk named Wetti in November 824, and a delightful poem on gardening. The *Visio* was composed when Walafrid was eighteen years old, and is intended to communicate to others the lesson Wetti learned when an angel showed him the punishments reserved for us in the next life. One section describes Charlemagne, who, though destined for eternal life, suffers an excruciating punishment for his sins of the flesh (II, 318). The poem on gardening gives some practical advice but, for the most part, simply describes the different plants one might want to raise, such as sage, rue, gourds, gladiolas, and lilies. For instance, the brief section on rue begins, "This shady grove is colored with a little living forest of sky-blue rue, whose tiny little leaves make small umbrellas and transmit the wind's breath and the sun's rays to the stalks below and at a light touch give off a strong scent," describing at the close the plant's medicinal and antitoxic properties.

The final poet to be discussed is Abbo, a deacon and monk of St. Germain in Paris, whose major work, describing the Viking attack on the city in 885–887, may be taken as emblematic of the close of the Carolingian era. The poet's concern is not just with the violence and bloodshed he has witnessed: "Coniugis ante oculos caedem tribuere marito, / Coniugis ante oculos strages gustat mulierem" (Before the eyes of his wife, they slaughtered the husband, / Before the eyes of her husband, murder takes the woman; IV, 106–107), but also with the social chaos attending it: "Efficitur servus liber, liber quoque servus; / Vernaque fit dominus, contra dominus quoque verna" (The slave is set free, and the free man is made a slave; / The slave becomes master and master slave). But while Carolingian power was to end shortly, the culture and learning it had promoted was to provide a solid base for several centuries of European civilization.

BIBLIOGRAPHY

A standard collective edition is *Monumenta Germaniae historica: Poetae latini aevi carolini,* E. Dümmler, L. Traube, P. Winterfeld, and K. Strecker, eds., 4 vols. (1880–1923). Commentaries include Ernst R. Curtius, *European Literature and the Latin Middle Ages,* Willard Trask, trans. (1953), 36–61, esp. 45–48; M. L. W. Laistner, *Thought and Letters in Western Europe: A.D. 500 to 900* (1930, rev. ed. 1955), 330–361; Max Manitius, *Geschichte der lateinischen Literatur des Mittelalters* (1911), I, 537–636; F. J. E. Raby, *A History of Christian-Latin Poetry from the Beginnings to the Close of the Middle Ages* (1927, rev. ed. 1953), 154–201, and *A History of Secular Latin Poetry in the Middle Ages* (1934, rev. ed. 1957), 178–251.

COLIN CHASE

[See also **Alcuin of York; Angilbert, St.; Einhard; Hrabanus Maurus; Latin Meter; Paul the Deacon; Paulinus of Aquileia; Peter of Pisa; Theodulf of Orléans; Walafrid Strabo.**]

CAROLINGIANS AND THE CAROLINGIAN EMPIRE. The ancestors of the Carolingians first appear in the early seventh century, during a period of crisis in the kingdom of the Franks. This kingdom was founded by the Merovingian Clovis, who had united disparate Frankish tribes and had destroyed the last Roman presence in Gaul at the battle of Soissons in 486 or 487. During the early sixth century it subjugated the Visigothic kingdom of Aquitaine, the kingdom of the Burgundians, the Alamanni, the Thuringians, the Bavarians, and Provence. The Merovingians and their Frankish warriors, enormously enriched by these victories, treated their more distant conquests as sources of booty and were content to allow government there to follow indigenous traditions and structures, except that they appointed the duke who headed the regions in their name. The Merovingians treated the center of the kingdom, which included the old Roman "kingdom" of Soissons and the former kingdom of the Burgundians, as their personal property, dividing it in each generation among all males, each of whom was considered royal. By the mid sixth century the major divisions of Merovingian Francia, each with its own Merovingian king, were Austrasia (the "east land" between the Rhine and Meuse), Neustria (the "new west land" including the central and northwest portions of modern France), and Burgundy (modern Burgundy plus eastern France to around Troyes and western Switzerland). In addition, each kingdom controlled a portion of Aquitaine and Provence.

These subkingdoms were, in the sixth century, less governed than exploited by the Merovingians and their Frankish warriors, who left the pre-Frankish economic and fiscal mechanisms largely intact and contented themselves with appropriating what wealth they could. Toward the end of the century, however, under the influence of Roman and Visigothic traditions that had survived in the South, the Merovingians began to introduce into their kingdoms Roman concepts and institutions of central government with which to control their Frankish followers. The result throughout Francia was revolt and resistance by the aristocracy. In Austrasia, where Brunhilde, the Visigoth wife of Sigebert I, led the reform, the opposition leaders were the ancestors of the Carolingians, Arnulf of Metz and Pepin the Elder (of Landen).

These two men, whose power was drawn from their followers in, respectively, the areas of Metz-Verdun and of Malmédy (Herstal and Stablo in modern Belgium) sealed their alliance with the marriage of their children: Ansegisel, son of Arnulf, and Begga, daughter of Pepin. This alliance is seen as the foundation of the family frequently referred to as the Arnulfingians or the Pepinids.

The success of the anti-Brunhilde party established the importance of this family, whose origins, while noble, were not from the highest segments of the Frankish aristocracy. The defeat and death of the queen (613) marked the rise of the Austrasian aristocracy's power at the expense of royal authority, and Arnulf and Pepin benefited most from this change. Arnulf became bishop of Metz in 614 and Pepin the *maior domus* (mayor of the palace)—in theory, principal administrative and judicial officer of the Austrasian palace; in fact, the most powerful person in Austrasia. Both men became close advisers of the Austrasian king Dagobert I, who after the death of his father Chothar II of Neustria in 629, ruled over a united Frankish kingdom.

The spectacular rise of Arnulf and Pepin at first continued, and then was temporarily checked during the career of Pepin's son Grimoald, who managed to eliminate rivals and succeed his father as *maior domus* in Austrasia. His attempt to secure the Austrasian royal succession for his descendants by forcing the Merovingian king Sigebert III to adopt his own son, to whom he had given the Merovingian name Childebert, ended in failure. Neustrian opposition to the presumption of a family that had risen too far too fast resulted in Grimoald's capture and death by torture at Paris in 661/662.

This setback removed the family from the center of power for two decades, but its power base in the Austrasian aristocracy was such that it could not be destroyed. The factional disputes in the 670's, in particular the efforts of the Neustrian *maior domus* to dominate Austrasia and Neustria-Burgundy, gave the family its chance. Pepin II, the son of Ansegisel and Begga, emerged as one of the leaders of the Austrasian opposition to the Neustrians. The centrifugal forces that had allowed Pepin to take the lead in an anti-Merovingian noble faction had also allowed the rise of other autonomous duces in the Frankish kingdoms, notably Ebroin in Burgundy-Neustria, Rodulfus in Thuringia, Eudo in Aquitaine, Antenor in Provence, and Theodo in Bavaria. As the power of Pepin grew, these other factions found a convenient rallying point in the Merovingian dynasty, in particular Theuderich III, the last Merovingian to pursue an anti-Arnulfingian course. Thus the life of Pepin was dominated by his largely successful struggle to destroy these other Frankish duces and to win over

CAROLINGIANS

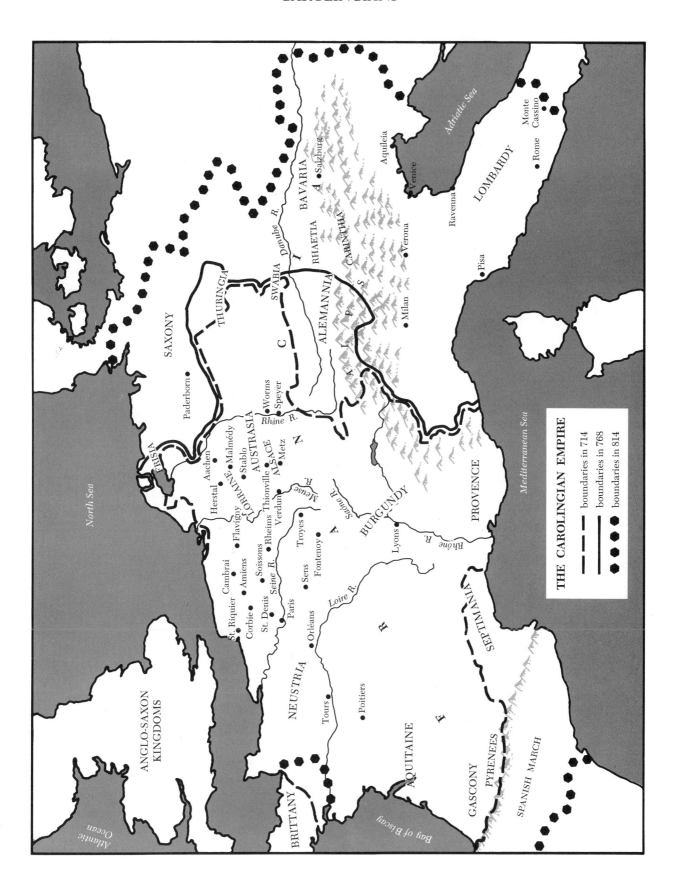

THE CAROLINGIAN EMPIRE

- - - boundaries in 714
—— boundaries in 768
⬡⬡⬡ boundaries in 814

Adriatic Sea

Monte Cassino
Rome
Aquileia
Venice
Ravenna
LOMBARDY
Verona
Pisa
Milan

Salzburg
BAVARIA
RHAETIA
CARINTHIA
A L P S

SWABIA
Danube R.
ALEMANNIA
THURINGIA
SAXONY
Paderborn

Worms
Speyer
Rhine R.

Mediterranean Sea

FRISIA
Aachen
Malmédy
Herstal
Stablo
LORRAINE
AUSTRASIA
ALSACE
Metz
Thionville
Verdun
Meuse R.
Saône R.
PROVENCE
BURGUNDY
Lyons
Rhône R.

Flavigny
Rheims
Soissons
Troyes
Fontenoy
Sens

St. Riquier
Cambrai
Amiens
Corbie
St. Denis
Seine R.
Paris
Orléans
Loire R.

North Sea

ANGLO-SAXON
KINGDOMS

Atlantic Ocean

NEUSTRIA
Tours
Poitiers
AQUITAINE
GASCONY
PYRENEES
SEPTIMANIA
SPANISH MARCH

BRITTANY
Bay of Biscay

their supporters. His victory over Theuderich III and his Neustrian *maior domus* Bertharius at Tertry in 687 assured Austrasian, and hence Arnulfingian, dominance over Neustria.

Pepin wisely avoided the temptation to follow his uncle's example and attempt to usurp the Frankish kingship, contenting himself with the titles of *maior domus* and dux, and thus remaining within his own aristocratic faction. At his death in 714, however, he left no legitimate sons, and his illegitimate son Charles Martel had to fight his stepmother Plectrude, the Frisian dux Radbod, and the anti-Arnulfingian Neustrian, Aquitanian, and Burgundo-Provençal Franks to regain the position his father and his Austrasian faction had enjoyed. This he accomplished through constant wars, financed by massive confiscation of ecclesiastical lands and wealth, and characterized by ruthless scorched-earth warfare in Aquitaine and the Viennois.

Charles Martel consolidated his victories by imposing his Austrasian comites (counts) in positions of authority throughout the kingdom and by using missionaries such as Boniface, Permin, and Willibrord, who worked to replace the locally controlled, decentralized church structure with a hierarchical, centralized episcopal structure controlled by the Carolingians. In this effort he was supported by the papacy, which looked to the Frankish dux as a support against the often hostile Lombard kingdom in Italy. Charles's image as defender of Christendom was further enhanced by his victories near Poitiers in 732, and in the Rhône Valley a few years later, over Arab expeditionary forces that had expanded from Spain and Muslim Septimania with the apparent encouragement of Charles's enemies.

At his death in 741, Charles left to his son Carloman the regions of Austrasia, Alemannia, and Thuringia, and to his son Pepin III (the Younger or the Short) Neustria, Burgundy, and Provence. Of the semi-independent regna only Bavaria remained outside the family's domination. The two brothers worked in relative harmony, first to consolidate their position against other family members, and then to reduce, through ecclesiastical reform, some of the gains their supporters had made at the expense of ecclesiastical and fiscal power and lands. In 747 Carloman abdicated in favor of his brother and entered the monastery of Monte Cassino.

EARLY CAROLINGIAN KINGS

Pepin, who now effectively ruled the entire Frankish kingdom, determined that he could finally dispense with the Merovingian dynasty, and looked to the papacy for legitimization of his royal usurpation. In 750 he sent as emissaries to Pope Zacharias two important ecclesiastics, Fulrad, abbot of St. Denis, and Burchard, bishop of Würzburg, to ask whether it was proper for the king in Francia to be without royal power. Zacharias, abandoned by the Byzantines and pressed by the Lombards, naturally responded as Pepin wished: "It is better for him to be called king who has the power than him who is without royal power." Further, so that "divine right should not be perverted," the pope ordered by apostolic authority that Pepin be made king. Shortly after, in 751, Pepin was proclaimed king and anointed in Soissons.

The bonds between the new king and the papacy were strengthened in 754 when Pope Stephen II, increasingly threatened by Lombard expansion and abandoned by a Byzantine Empire too involved with Muslim wars, iconoclasm, and fiscal difficulties to concern itself with Italy, traveled to Francia. There, in return for the double promise of intervention against the Lombards and the return to the papacy of the exarchate of Ravenna, which they had conquered, he apparently showed marked deference to Pepin, and later, at St. Denis, anointed him and his sons and gave them the title of *patricius Romanorum*, a title formerly held by the imperial (East Roman) exarch of Ravenna. Pepin's reliance on papal authority for the legitimization of his coronation established the pattern for his own and his successors' policy: although brought to power by, and ultimately dependent on, the support of an alliance of Austrasians and other powerful families who, in the words of Karl Ferdinand Werner, "held a monopoly of government and administration," the Carolingians looked to the Roman church as a second source of power that could be played against that of the magnates. This dual alliance of the Carolingians was the source of both their remarkable power and their greatest difficulties in the next two centuries.

The kingdom of Pepin, which passed in 768 to his sons Charles (Charles the Great or Charlemagne) and Carloman, and then, after the elimination of the latter in 771, to Charles alone, had been created and could be maintained only by continuous military conquest. The family had received the support of other families because it had been able to provide them with land and booty. The social structure uniting such a military leader and his followers demanded a constant flow of gifts and a style of life that emphasized free spending and squandering of wealth. In the seventh and early eighth centuries these conquests had been largely of other Frankish factions and had resulted in the reunification of the Frankish kingdoms. Under Charles the conquests were largely external: the Lombards in 773–774, Saxony from 772 to 802, Bavaria in 787, the Avars in 791, and the Spanish march beginning in 778.

The result of these conquests was the augmentation of Carolingian power, but simultaneously the augmentation of the power of the noble families to which the conquered wealth, in the form of land, ecclesiastical office, and precious objects, passed. These aristocrats threatened at every moment to join with local nobility in the regions of their responsibilities to attempt the development of semiautonomous principalities of the sort from which the Carolingians themselves had emerged. This constant threat could be held in check only through the discipline of annual military expeditions against external enemies and through the distribution by the king of still more booty. Given the enormous physical, cultural, and ethnic diversity of the empire thus created, the only long-term hope for stability was an internal consolidation and structuring of the imperial government and of ecclesiastical institutions and culture. Although probably doomed to fail from the start by the enormousness of the difficulties, Charles and his advisers were able to accomplish much in both spheres.

CAROLINGIAN ADMINISTRATION

The diversity of legal and institutional traditions throughout the empire was continued and even strengthened by Charles, who, like his father and grandfather, guaranteed and continued the particular laws of the Saxons, Bavarians, Goths, Lombards, and Romans as well as the laws of the Franks. Moreover, from his victory in 774 over the Lombards he ruled under the combined title of "Charles by the grace of God king of the Franks and of the Lombards and *patricius* of the Romans," an indication that he saw his authority as a collection of individual powers rather than as a real unity. However, he did try to introduce some unity into the empire through the development of centralized institutions, which, if far from the elements of a real bureaucracy, were still able, at the height of his power, to help him exert some control over the nobility who filled the higher positions in the government.

Administration of the smallest divisions of the empire was entrusted to comites (counts), who were important aristocrats drawn in large part from the Austrasian families that had risen with the Carolingians, but also from those other Frankish and Gallo-Roman families that had allied themselves with the Carolingians. These counts administered a comitatus that corresponded, in the Romanized areas of the empire, to late imperial divisions of civitates or *pagi* and, in Germanic regions, to preexisting local divisions (*gaue*). At the height of Charles's reign these counts numbered around 400 and were, at least in theory, appointed and removed at the will of the king. Their primary responsibilities were to exercise, in the king's stead, his royal rights of *bannum* (the power to command, prohibit, and punish) and to maintain the public peace.

Modern scholarship is finding that the relationship between these comites and the king was not that of officials and their sovereign, but a function of the alliance between the king and such great aristocratic families as the Unrochs, Nibelungen, and Lambertiners, without whose consent the Carolingians would have been unable to govern. These kin groups, more clans than noble houses in the later medieval sense, were rewarded for their support with countships, positions that often passed from one member to another, although not usually in patrilinear succession or necessarily in the same comitatus. Royal prerogative to control or replace these local administrators was severely limited by the necessity of keeping them and their kin faithful to the king, and out of secret alliances with the numerous opposition groups that appeared sporadically throughout the Carolingian period and continued the tradition of opposition to royalty from which the Carolingians themselves had risen.

The king had more direct control over his entourage, loosely referred to as the *palatium* or palace, which was composed of his domestics as well as his most important advisers and officers. These men, closest to the king and drawn from trusted, powerful families with whom the royal power was intertwined, included the seneschal, butler, constable, chamberlain, and count palatine. The Carolingians had abolished the position of *maior domus,* no doubt wishing to eliminate the possibility of another family's repeating their rise through this office.

Since the time of Pepin the Younger ecclesiastics at court had formed a group around the oratory of the palace, where they guarded the most important sacred relics of the household, particularly the *capa* (cloak) of St. Martin of Tours, the patron of the Frankish kings. In time this group of clerics came to be known collectively as the *capellani* (chaplains).

The most important of these, the *capellanus* (later *archicapellanus* under Louis the Pious), was one of the most influential people in the empire. He and his clerics were responsible for the continuous religious cult considered an essential spiritual support of the monarchy. They were also responsible for the preparation of royal and imperial documents, since, perhaps because of declining literacy among the laity or the lower level of literacy among the Arnulfingians' Austrasian followers relative to that of older Merovingian supporters, these clerics had replaced, under Pepin, the *referendarii* and the *scriniarii,* laymen who had had charge of royal documents under the Merovingians. In addition to these loose groups of clergy and officials, there was in the palace an even more amorphous body of *vassi dominici* (royal vassals), who were free men bound to the king by an oath of fidelity and maintained by him in his household.

Contact between the royal palace (which, like all early medieval palaces, was never entirely fixed at one place but moved about with the king) and the provinces of the empire was maintained through the annual assembly of the most important elements of the aristocracy, held in close conjunction with the mustering of the army in the spring, and through the regular use of *missi dominici* (agents of the king). The assembly, which included the royal entourage, counts, bishops, abbots, and other important royal vassals, was the chief means by which advice and consent were elicited from the major figures in the empire. During Charles's years of strength these assemblies were advisory; in his decline and under his successors, they were used increasingly by the magnates to bind the king to their will.

The *missi dominici* made the royal personality felt in the provinces. They were given oral directives by the king, sometimes summarized in a capitulary, and brought the words of the king to the places where they were sent. *Missi* might perform specific missions, such as investigations of alleged abuses by local administrators, or could be used as judicial officers to look into injustice and corruption of local courts, to collect revenues, or to prepare for military mobilization. In the later years of Charles's reign these ordinary *missi* were sent out every year. In general the *missi* were drawn from the aristocracy, primarily from among the counts and higher ecclesiastics. This was increasingly true after 802, perhaps a sign of the weakening of royal power. *Missi* were effective increasingly because of who they were in

their own right, and not merely because they represented the king.

The most important instrument Charles used to transmit his authority, direct his *missi,* and promulgate the decisions he made with his assemblies was the capitulary. These documents, which vary widely in form, content, and purpose, were designed in general to correct abuses of traditional rules and to apply these rules to specific circumstances. They include memorandums established to review various questions at forthcoming assemblies, responses to *missi* asking for directions from the king, additions to the national laws, and directives destined for specific areas of the empire. The content of the capitularies includes a mixture of ecclesiastical and lay material. Among the most important capitularies were those of Herstal (779), the first substantial reform document of Charles's reign; the General Admonition (*Admonitio generalis,* 789), which states the fundamental program of peace and concord between secular and ecclesiastical powers that characterized the Carolingian system; the Programmatic Capitulary (802), which deals with the new situation brought about by the imperial coronation of 800; and the Capitulary of the *Missi* (Capitulary of Thionville, 805), which attempts to deal with the problems arising from the disintegration of royal power toward the end of Charles's life.

THE CAROLINGIAN CHURCH

Ecclesiastical reform and reorganization were the second element of Charles's program, and included both institutional and cultural reform movements. Charles Martel had already laid the foundations of ecclesiastical reform through his support of missionaries and reformers in the Roman tradition, a practice that was particularly useful to Charles's own political consolidation. Other than those already mentioned, the most important was Chrodegang, former referendar of Charles, who became bishop of Metz in 742. Chrodegang was particularly involved in the moral and liturgical reform of canons, for whom he prepared a rule modeled on that of Benedict that obligated them to a common life, poverty, and faithful performance of the Roman liturgy.

Charles Martel's son Pepin the Younger continued and expanded this support and encouragement of intellectual and reform ideology in the Frankish church, and in turn used this reformed and educated clergy in his administration. He used monks from St. Denis to restructure the royal administration and was responsible for the clericalization of its personnel. He also encouraged and supported foreign ecclesiastics and intellectuals such as the Irishman Virgilius, later bishop of Salzburg, and, because of the growing importance of papal influence at his court, Italians such as Wilthair of Nomentana and George of Ostia, later (respectively) bishops of Sens and of Amiens.

An integral part of this reform was the replacement of the Gallican liturgy by the Roman, a change inspired by the desire to unify the church through a unified rite, to demonstrate the importance of the papacy, and to solidify and publicize, throughout the empire, the alliance between the new dynasty and the papacy.

This tradition of Roman-style reform was continued and expanded by Charles the Great, whose ecclesiastical reform had three central purposes: to establish peace and concord throughout the empire by means of standardized, properly performed services that would win divine favor; to create an educated clergy capable of undertaking missionary and pastoral work throughout Europe; and to create a body of clerics in his administration capable of reestablishing literacy as a tool of government, as it had been under Roman and early Merovingian rule. These goals implied both a greatly elevated status of the church in the life of the empire and unprecedented royal control over every aspect of that church.

A major step toward the accomplishment of these goals was the Capitulary of Herstal (779), which provided for secular assistance to the clergy in enforcing payment of the traditional donation of one-tenth of one's revenues to the church. This payment was to be made to the local church at which one received the sacraments, and while in time it often came to be appropriated by bishops, monasteries, and even lay magnates, it nevertheless assisted the expansion of a parish system into rural areas throughout the empire. These parish churches brought regular, supervised services into many regions for the first time, and contributed to the Christianization of the countryside. Charles also strengthened the episcopal structure of the church through the establishment of new bishoprics in recently converted areas and the restoration of ancient ones. Ultimately the empire was divided into twenty-one ecclesiastical provinces, a division that largely restored the late Roman provincial structure.

Concerned not just with financial and institutional reform, Charles sought also to require proper discharge of duties by bishops, abbots, and their subordinates. His goal in these reforms was never the creation of an independent church but, rather, of one subordinated in every essential aspect to the king as the divinely appointed head of Christendom. Thus Charles bypassed the provincial system he had created, dealing directly with bishops rather than with the twenty-one archbishops; he continued his grandfather's practice of rewarding his followers with church lands and offices; and he appointed bishops and abbots as part of his political system of securing loyal supporters. The result was a greatly enriched and strengthened church, but a church more closely bound to the state than at any time since the fourth century.

The moral and cultural reform of the clergy could be accomplished only with outside assistance. To these ends Charles collected scholars from the intellectual centers of Europe, primarily Italy (Peter of Pisa, Paulinus of Aquileia, Paul the Deacon) and England (Alcuin, Fredegisus). In his *Admonitio generalis* (789) he ordered the establishment of schools for teaching basic literacy and the collection in monasteries and dioceses of libraries of those texts essential for the liturgy. In 794 he ordered bishops and abbots to improve the level of literacy of their clerics and monks.

As in his political reform, the results that Charles achieved in the area of education and culture were modest. The most important success was at court, where his foreign scholars, members of the *capella*, and young aristocrats developed a highly artificial court literature. Nevertheless, under the influence of the Goth Theodulf, bishop of Orléans, and various Irish or Scots (Dungal, Dicuil, Clement) the court became a center for the study of the liberal arts of the trivium and quadrivium, and the copying and preserving of classical authors. Outside of the court the principal centers of study during Charles's lifetime were primarily north of the Loire, in the area of Burgundy-Lyons, and Italy.

Scriptoria for copying manuscripts were more important than schools for studying texts; the most important among the latter were those of Corbie, St. Riquier, St. Denis, St. Wandrille, St. Martin de Tours, Flavigny, Lyons, Metz, Verona, and Lucca. In these centers little creative intellectual activity took place during this first phase of Carolingian educational reform, but creativity was not its purpose. This generation of scholars accomplished three essential tasks that made possible later scholarly advances. First, they expanded literacy not only among the clergy but also in some lay aristocratic circles. Second, they introduced a reformed, clarified script, Caroline minuscule, which formed the basis for the later medieval book hand as well as for modern typefaces. Third, and most important, they copied, and thus preserved, an immense number of classical, patristic, and early medieval texts that otherwise would surely have been lost to future generations. These basic accomplishments made possible the activities of a second, more stimulating generation of Carolingian intellectuals.

THE IMPERIAL TITLE

The realities of Charles's political dominance of most of the former western territories of the Roman Empire, the continued development of his family's relations with the papacy, and the influence of his cultural advisers, particularly Alcuin of York, led to his coronation as emperor on Christmas Day, 800. This step was considerably facilitated by the particular circumstances of political and religious turmoil in the Byzantine Empire during the reign of Empress Irene (780–790, 792–802). Charles had opposed the Council of Nicaea (787), at which she had ended the iconoclastic controversy, in his *Libri Carolini*, written presumably by Theodulf of Orléans but in Charles's name as "king of the Franks ruling the Gauls, Germany, and Italy." In his relations with the Abbasid caliphate of Baghdad and with the patriarch of Jerusalem, Charles acted as leader of the West. His choice of symbolism, the construction of his palace and chapel at Aachen, and his modifications to the liturgy all pointed toward a claim of parity with the Byzantine emperors. This parity was encouraged and increased by Alcuin's presentation of Charles as the universal leader of the *imperium christianum.*

The specific circumstances that led to Charles's coronation were the difficulties experienced by Pope Leo III (795–816) in his traditional relationships both with the emperor and with local Roman political factions. In the reign of Adrian (771–795) the names of the Byzantine emperor and empress had been removed from papal documents and coins in favor of the pope's own. Adrian attempted to maintain himself in an independent position based on the Donation of Constantine. His successor, Leo III, was unable to maintain his position in the face of Roman aristocratic opposition and for support depended increasingly on Charles, to whom he was forced to flee at Paderborn in 799. When Charles came to Rome

in 800, he was treated by the pope with the respect due only the emperor. Two days after Leo had been allowed by Charles to clear himself of charges brought by his opponents on December 23, he crowned Charles at the beginning of Mass. The Romans acclaimed Charles as emperor, and the pope performed the traditional *proskynesis* (obeisance) due the emperor.

If, as Einhard related, Charles was displeased, his irritation may have been at the active role of the pope in the coronation—a role that presented him in a much more powerful position vis-à-vis the emperor than the patriarch of Constantinople ever assumed. Certainly when he associated his son Louis as emperor, Charlemagne bestowed the crown himself and had the new emperor acclaimed not by the Romans but by the Franks.

After some initial hesitation in the Frankish chancery, the new *nomen imperatoris* became an integral part of Charles's title (*serenissimus augustus a Deo coronatus magnus pacificus imperator, Romanum gubernans imperius qui et per misericordiam Dei rex Francorum et Langobardum:* "the most serene, august, pacific great emperor crowned by God governing the Roman Empire who is by the mercy of God king of the Franks and the Lombards"). Although his old and politically more meaningful royal titles were retained, Charles made the new imperial dignity the guiding concept of his last years. The image that he and his advisers formed was not, however, a copy of the Eastern emperor's, but a return to the biblical image of David, and to the combined images of Theodoric the Great and Constantine. It was specifically a Christian empire, and the imperial motto *Renovatio romani imperii* implied a revival of the Western Empire in the image of Augustinian political philosophy as interpreted for Charles by Alcuin.

The years that followed the coronation failed to fulfill its promise. By 804 the great period of political expansion was over, and immediately the tremendous power and relative independence that Charles had enjoyed began to be eroded in the interests of the Frankish noble factions that had served him and governed for him over the previous decades. The power of these old aristocratic groups continued to grow during the remaining decade of Charles's life, both throughout the vast empire and at court, which in Charles's declining years remained generally at Aachen.

For these aristocratic families the imperial dignity and title were meaningless. While they conferred certain political advantages in Italy, in the rest of the empire, despite Charlemagne's attempts to reestablish the allegiance of all free men to himself through a new oath of fidelity to him as emperor, to his Frankish supporters he remained a Frankish king responsible for cooperating with them in their domination of the rest of society in the empire. With the cessation of wars of conquest, these *potentes* turned increasingly to the exploitation of the powerless (*impotentes* or *pauperes*), who gradually lost their status of free men to merge with the unfree layers of European society. Counts increasingly perverted justice and their local powers as military leaders to their own ends, and attempted to transform royal benefices (grants of land intended to be held only during the period of a vassal's service) into alodial property.

Charles attempted to deal with these problems through increasing attention to members of aristocratic factions such as Wala, Adalhard, and Einhard, at the expense of his imperial and ecclesiastical theorists such as Alcuin. The extent to which this return to an older, less ambitious, and less Romanized form of constitutional arrangement had progressed by 806 was shown by the *Divisio regnorum,* Charles's disposition of his succession made at Thionville. The kingdoms were to be divided after his death among his three sons: Charles, Pepin, and Louis. The text of this settlement, devoid of any mention of the disposition of the imperial title or even discussion of the empire except in a geographical sense, indicates the extent to which, toward the end of his life, Charles fell back upon the strengths of the Frankish traditions that had brought him so far.

To judge from the witness list Einhard records in his (probably apocryphal) testament of Charles, by his death in 814 the emperor's closest advisers were a cross section of East Frankish aristocrats who displayed no interest in the reform ideas of the clerical advisers of the 780's and 790's but, rather, held the traditional values of their class. Under their management the innovative machinery of government introduced by Charles at the height of his power, never very effective, was in serious if not fatal disarray. Since Charles's sons Pepin and Charles had predeceased him, his sole surviving son, Louis, whom he had himself crowned emperor in 813, inherited an empire in crisis.

SUCCESSORS OF CHARLES THE GREAT

Louis was clearly the most intelligent of the Carolingians, the best prepared for rule through his long period as king of the Aquitanians (781–814), and the man most closely in touch with the proponents of the ecclesiastical-imperial ideology that had characterized his father's first years as emperor. These characteristics made possible the considerable progress toward a reform of the disastrous situation he inherited, and also made almost inevitable his ultimate disastrous failure. Under the influence of his ecclesiastical advisers, particularly Benedict of Aniane, Louis had absorbed the ideology of political Augustinianism and his role as emperor, to the detriment of traditional royal Frankish and Lombard constitutional principles. He abandoned not only his own royal title but also those of his father, and termed himself simply *Hludowicus divina ordinante providentia imperator augustus.* The empire he ruled was seen as synonymous with the church, the temporal embodiment of the kingdom of God. His attempts to reform and correct the abuses and dangers to the empire's stability were consistent with this image.

At court Louis began by largely replacing those advisers from the old Frankish aristocracy who had been closest to Charles with his own, more radical reformers. Wala was exiled, and Louis's sisters, who under his father had formed centers for factional quarreling and opposition groups, were sent to convents. In place of this loose group of notables he introduced a number of new dignitaries, *magistri,* who were to control more formally the various groups of servants, suppliers, and petitioners at court. In order to counter the new military threats posed by increasing border problems with Danes, Bretons, Arabs, and Slavs, as well as internal revolts in the no longer expanding empire, Louis introduced or expanded a system of speedy mobilization of army contingents for localized, defensive operations.

More fundamentally, Louis attempted to separate the traditional role of the annual assembly, the Placitum Generale, from the army. No longer was the assembly held only at the beginning of the annual military campaign, the May Field, as it had been under his father, but several times a year, when Louis called together the aristocracy in administrative and civil assemblies so that he could be better informed about the state of the empire and could maintain closer control. This effort to systematize and standardize the empire was also carried to specifically ecclesiastical matters. In the first years of his rule Louis apparently ordered all previous royal and imperial grants to ecclesiastical institutions resubmitted to him for his confirmation. In 818–819 he issued a series of four reform capitularies that presented a clear, well-prepared program for the reform of monastic and regular religious life as well as of secular matters.

All of these reforms were possible because of the maturing of the educational and cultural reforms begun by Louis's father. The first Carolingian renaissance was beginning to yield its fruits in the form of literate, educated men capable of expanded use of written materials in administration, of clear, logical thinking, and of serious intellectual and literary activity. This was true not only of the so-called radical reformers like Benedict of Aniane, Agobard of Lyons, Florus of Lyons, and Jonas of Orléans, but also of members of the old aristocratic tradition like Einhard and Wala. These and others, such as Walafrid Strabo, Paschasius Radbertus, Amalarius of Metz, and Lupus of Ferrières, were in contact with Louis and contributed to both the intellectual and the cultural climates of his reign and to the subsequent intellectual history of the Middle Ages.

The first fourteen years of Louis's reign were marked by considerable apparent success in all these reform programs, but the ultimate disintegration of the fragile empire put together by his father's conquests, inevitable in any case, was hastened by his ecclesiastical reforms, which increasingly opposed aristocratic interests, and by the difficulties of his succession. In 817, consistent with his sense of the necessary unity of the empire, he had acted in sharp contrast with the arrangements made by his father and previous Frankish rulers. Rather than a simple division of the empire as a personal possession, as Charles had done in 806, Louis provided that the entire empire should remain united under himself and his eldest son, Lothar, whom he associated in the imperial authority. His younger sons, Pepin and Louis, would rule the subkingdoms of Aquitaine and Bavaria, respectively, and would be strictly subordinate to their older brother. This ultimate statement of imperial unity, which was successfully defended in 817 against the revolt of Louis's nephew Bernard, king of Italy, was clearly distasteful to a considerable segment of the aristocracy, and particularly to Pepin and Louis.

Resentment also grew against Louis's ecclesiastical reforms, which aimed to remove church institutions from the control of local aristocrats and counts. This resentment was natural in a period characterized by defensive rather than offensive warfare, when local authorities, particularly those with responsibilities for protection of border areas, felt that they needed authority to mobilize ecclesiastical wealth to maintain their military security. Increasingly, radical ecclesiastical reformers such as Agobard of Lyons urged an ecclesiastical and political program that could only further alienate large segments of the aristocracy in cooperation with whom the Carolingians had traditionally ruled, men who understood little of political Augustinianism or ecclesiology, and cared less.

Tensions reached the breaking point with the marriage of Emperor Louis to Judith, the daughter of the Welf duke of Bavaria, and the birth of their son Charles (the Bald) in 823. The marriage was apparently an attempt by Louis to gain the support of this powerful family that had never before been closely allied with the Carolingians. His subsequent attempts to please the Welf party and carve out an inheritance for Charles from his half brothers' territories (he was given Swabia, Alsace, Rhaetia, and part of Burgundy) marked a retreat from his earlier ideal of unity and pitted Louis against not only the reformers led by Wala, Agobard, and Archbishop Ebo of Rheims, but against his older sons as well. The result was bitter internal strife and constantly shifting alliances that tore the empire apart and wrecked the reform efforts of Louis's first fourteen years.

Louis's death in 840 cleared the way for open civil war among Charles, Louis (the German), and Lothar, which culminated in the disastrous Battle of Fontenoy in 841, a battle that decimated the ranks of the Frankish nobility. The warfare was ended (and then only temporarily) with the Treaty of Verdun in 843, by which Lothar surrendered all pretensions to the ideal of a unified empire. The treaty divided the territory on the basis of *affinitas, congruentia,* and *equa portio,* but the exact meaning of these terms (and hence the principles behind the division) remains uncertain. Whatever the principles, the result was that Louis received the Germanic areas north of the Alps and east of the Rhine, the three counties of Speyer, Worms and Metz, and Alemannia and Raetia. Charles received the lands west of the Schelde, then the area south of Cambrai as far east as Sedan, the Argonne, the upper Marne Valley, the Langres Plateau, the west bank of the Saône, then east of the Lyonnais and Vivarais and the Uzège, and finally down the Petit-Rhône to the Mediterranean. Lothar received the remaining portion: the central band between East and West Francia from Frisia to Campania and including Aachen and the heartland of the old Carolingian family possessions, Lotharingia, Alsace, Burgundy, Provence, and Lombardy.

The middle kingdom, divided on the death of Lo-

Division of the Empire in 843

Division of the Empire in 870

thar in 855 among his sons, was ultimately fragmented by the absorption of major portions of the kingdom into East and West Francia by Charles the Bald and Louis the German, as well as by the establishment of the non-Carolingian kingdoms of Burgundy and Provence. His son Louis received the imperial crown and the kingdom of Italy. Lothar II was given the area from Frisia to Langres and Alsace, the heart of which included what is today Lotharingia or Lorraine. Charles, the youngest brother, received the remaining portions. Charles and Louis II died without male heirs; Lothar II's son by his mistress, Waldrada, was declared illegitimate, thus ending the succession of Lothar in the middle kingdom.

THE EASTERN CAROLINGIANS

In the east, Louis the German's kingdom developed increasingly in the direction of a particularist, Germanic kingdom as Louis looked to the aristocracy of his kingdom, itself increasingly regional in its power base, for his support. He strengthened these local ties through marriages of his sons to daughters of leading aristocrats of Saxony, Bavaria, and Swabia. These ties, disputes with Charles the Bald over Lorraine, and the disputes among Louis's sons accelerated the decline of Carolingian power in the east.

Following Louis's death in 876 his kingdom was divided among his three sons, each with one of the great duchies. The two elder sons, Louis III (the Younger), who had received Saxony, and Karlmann, who had received Bavaria, soon died without legitimate male issue, leaving the entire kingdom united under the youngest son Charles the Fat (884–887, d. 888). During the latter's short and incompetent reign the great duchies increased their particularist tendencies. Following his deposition in 887, the East Frankish magnates chose as king the illegitimate son of Karlmann, Duke Arnulf of Carinthia. Arnulf (887–899) proved a capable and successful king, able to contain the Slavs on the eastern border of the kingdom and to defeat an important Viking army before Louvain in 891. His successes encouraged Pope Formosus (891–896) to appeal to him for assistance against Italian factions and in 894 and again in 895 Arnulf made expeditions into Italy. Even though he was never able to assert real authority in Italy, his second expedition culminated in his imperial coronation in 896.

Arnulf had relied for support on a number of important noble families within each of the duchies of his kingdom, in particular on the Salomons in Swabia, the Liudolfings in Saxony and in Lorraine (where he had established his illegitimate son Zwentibold as king in 895), the Konradins in Franconia, and the Liutpoldings in Bavaria. After his death he was succeeded by his six-year-old son Louis the Child (899–911).

During Louis's reign the aristocracy fought constantly among itself, uniting only rarely to oppose the Magyars who, beginning in 894, conducted periodic raids deep into Germany and Italy. Local resistance to the Magyars was organized most effectively by the dukes of the duchies, thus increasing their political autonomy. After Louis's death, the aristocracy passed over the Carolingian king of the West Franks, Charles the Simple, to elect as king the Franconian duke Conrad.

THE WESTERN CAROLINGIANS

In the kingdom of the West Franks, the tradition of Carolingian universalism was similarly eroded by the increasing power of aristocratic factions and by the inability of Charles the Bald and his successors to provide internal security against the incursions of Scandinavian and Islamic raiders. Charles looked to the ecclesiastical hierarchy for the necessary support for his reign and received this assistance from such churchmen as Hincmar of Rheims in return for a greatly increased role of the church in the affairs of the kingdom. Charles was also diverted from the increasing problems of disintegration in his kingdom by imperial politics involving the papacy and Italy. He succeeded in receiving imperial coronation in 875 but he died the following year.

The aristocracy took advantage of the weakness of Charles to dismantle the central government structures established by the early Carolingians. In order to win supporters, the sons of Louis the Pious had given out vast amounts of royal lands as well as various immunities and privileges which weakened central government. The *missi dominici* ceased to supervise local administration. In the Capitulary of Quierzy in 877, on the eve of leading his last expedition to Italy, Charles guaranteed to those accompanying him the hereditability of their offices and benefices.

The brief reigns of Charles's sons, Louis II the Stammerer (877–879) and Carloman (877–884) did nothing to halt either the decline of central power or to check the destructive force of Viking raids. Successful resistance to the latter was organized only rarely, and then by local magnates such as the counts of Paris who withstood sieges by Vikings in 861, 885–887, and 889.

Following the death of Carloman, the West Frankish aristocracy elected the East Frankish king Charles the Fat, thus reuniting for the last time virtually all of the empire of Charles the Great. Charles the Fat, however, reigned merely by the good will of the various regional aristocracies rather than as a powerful ruler, and after his deposition in 887 the West Frankish aristocracy passed over the legitimate Carolingian heir, the future Charles the Simple, and chose as king Count Odo (French, Eudes), the leader of the successful defense of Paris in 885–887.

Odo was unsuccessful in ending Viking raids in the kingdom and was opposed by supporters of the Carolingian family. In order to reestablish harmony he supported Charles as his successor, and the latter reigned from 898 to 923 (d. 929). Although ultimately defeated, deposed, and imprisoned by his enemies, in part because of East Frankish leanings, Charles the Simple managed to establish the outlines of a political program that was later adopted and pursued successfully by the next dynasty. In effect, while emphasizing a program of Carolingian restoration modeled on his ancestors Charles the Great and Charles the Bald, he recognized the limitations of his political situation and opted for compromise with both the Norse to the west and the new non-Carolingian kings to the east, so that he could concentrate on the reabsorption of Lorraine and the consolidation of his kingdom. In 911 in the Treaty of St. Clair-sur-Epte, a few weeks after his conquest of Lorraine, Charles granted the Norse leader Rollo the Duchy of Normandy (which he already held de facto) as a fief on the condition that the Viking chief become a Christian and a royal vassal. Likewise, in 921 he met the East Frankish king Henry I on a barge at midstream in the Rhine at Bonn and recognized the legitimacy of this non-Carolingian ruler.

After the defeat and imprisonment of Charles the family of Count Odo (known as Robertinians and later as Capetians) returned to the throne with Robert I of Neustria (922–923) and Rudolf of Burgundy (923–936). Both faced serious opposition from supporters of the Carolingian tradition and after the death of Rudolf the leader of the Robertinian family Duke Hugh the Great cooperated in recalling from exile the son of Charles the Simple, Louis IV d'Outremer (936–954), whom the duke hoped to use as his puppet. However, Louis and his son and successor

Lothar (954–986), supported by the opponents of the Robertinians, attempted to pursue an independent course of action, and continued in the kingdom.

The last ruler of the Carolingian dynasty was Louis V (986–987), the son of Lothar, who was killed in an accidental fall from his horse. Following the death of the young king, the magnates passed over Duke Charles of Lorraine, brother of the late King Lothar, and elected instead the Robertinian Hugh Capet.

BIBLIOGRAPHY

There is no outstanding study of the Carolingian era in English, and much of the otherwise extensive bibliography concentrates on Charlemagne. The following are the most important references in English and the major Continental studies and collections that will provide the specialist with a more complete bibliography.

Wolfgang Braunfels, ed., *Karl der Grosse, Lebenswerk und Nachleben,* vol. 1: *Persönlichkeit und Geschichte* (1965); Karl Brunner, *Oppositionelle Gruppen im Karolingerreich* (1979); Donald Bullough, *The Age of Charlemagne* (1965); Joseph Calmette, *Karl der Grosse* (1948); Heinrich Fichtenau, *Das karolingische Imperium: Soziale und geistige Problematik eines Grossreiches* (1949), partial trans. by Peter Munz as *The Carolingian Empire* (1957, repr. 1964); F. L. Ganshof, *The Carolingians and the Frankish Monarchy,* Janet Sondheimer, trans. (1971); Bruno Gebhardt, *Handbuch der deutschen Geschichte,* 9th ed., Herbert Grundmann, ed., vol. 1: *Frühzeit und Mittelalter* (1970); Louis Halphen, *Charlemagne et l'empire carolingien* (1947); trans. without notes by Giselle de Nie, *Charlemagne and the Carolingian Empire* (1977); Friedrich Heer, *Charlemagne and His World* (1975).

Arthur Kleinclausz, *Charlemagne* (1934); *Nascita dell'Europa carolingia: Un'equazione da verificare,* Settimane di studio del Centro italiano di studi sull'alto medioevo, XXVII (in press); Edouard Perroy, *Le monde carolingien* (1974); Pierre Riché, *La vie quotidienne dans l'empire carolingien* (1973), trans. Jo Ann McNamara as *Daily Life in the World of Charlemagne* (1978); Heinz Thomas, "Die Namenliste des Diptycon Barberini und der Sturz des Hausmeiers Grimoald," in *Deutsches Archiv,* 25 (1969); Wilhelm Wattenbach and Wilhelm Levison, *Deutschlands Geschichtsquellen im Mittelalter,* I–V (1952–1973); Herwig Wolfram, ed., *Intitulatio II: Lateinische Herrscher- und Fürstentitel in neunten und zehnten Jahrhundert* (1973).

Patrick Geary

[See also **Aachen; Alcuin of York; Arnulf; Benedict of Aniane; Capitulary; Charlemagne; Charles Martel; Einhard; France: To 987; Germany: 843–1137; Merovingians; Missi Dominici; Pepin.**]

CAROLS, MIDDLE ENGLISH. In England during the later Middle Ages the term "carol" was consistently applied to a poem suitable for singing and made up of uniform stanzas with a burden, or chorus, that precedes the first stanza and is repeated after each stanza. The carol corresponds in form to the French *chanson à carole,* the Italian *ballata,* the German *Reigenlied,* and one type of the medieval Latin *cantilena.* The structure of initial burden and uniform stanzas derives from the music sung in the round dance called in France and England the *carole.* Typically the *carole* was directed by a leader (*coryphée* or *Vorsänger*) who sang the stanzas as soloist, the dancers in chorus singing the burden after every stanza. While singing the burden, the dancers moved in their circle; they stood still or marked time during the singing of the stanzas.

The medieval English carol may treat any subject, secular or religious, and is not restricted, like the French *noël,* to celebration of the Nativity or the Christmas season. Its form, and not its content, distinguishes it from other songs. Many carols have one or more variant versions, which appear in general to be the products of written transmission, though there are passages that indicate oral transmission and imperfect memory.

The carols are popular by destination rather than by origin. Most are certainly the work of churchmen, although authors' names are known for only a minority. One group of more than 100 was written by James Ryman (*fl.* 1492), a Franciscan friar of the Canterbury house; and another collection, specifically marked for use at Christmas, is signed by John Audelay (*fl.* 1426), a blind and deaf chaplain at Haughmond Abbey in Shropshire. Some 400 of the almost 500 pieces are explicitly religious, and many are macaronic English and Latin. The most frequent subjects are the Nativity, the Annunciation, and direct praise of the Virgin. There are many didactic or moralizing carols, and a small but significant number of a convivial, humorous, or amorous kind that bespeak the existence and circulation of earlier popular songs now lost. Although there is good reason to believe that vernacular songs in the carol form were in use before 1300, the extant pieces were written down after that date and for the most part before the middle of the sixteenth century. The form appears occasionally after 1550, but it gives way rather suddenly to new and more sophisticated poetic and musical fashions. Only now and then is it possible to fix a precise date of composition for a particular text; many carols had certainly been in circulation for some time before they were recorded in the manuscripts and early prints that we now possess.

About one-fourth of the extant carols have musical settings, often of a cultivated polyphonic character more sophisticated than the texts. When the same piece appears in more than one manuscript, the correspondence in the music is usually close. The settings observe the distinction between burden and stanza, even when there is no likelihood that a carol was actually used in dance. Recent work by musicologists has established the carol as a musical as well as a poetic genre.

The modern usage of "carol" to mean a song in any form that is concerned with the Christmas season has evolved from the survival of those holidays, in spite of temporary Puritan disapproval, as the most loved and enjoyed of the year's Christian celebrations. In the nineteenth century many "Christmas carols," a few surviving from earlier folk songs, and others newly composed, grew to their present widespread popularity.

A typical fifteenth-century carol illustrates the metrical form and the characteristic joining of religious statement and convivial reference (Oxford, Bodleian Library, MS Eng. poet. e. 1; in Greene, *The Early English Carols,* no. 39):

(burden)

> Make we mery in this fest,
> For verbum caro factum est.

(stanzas)

> Godes Sonne, for the loue of mane
> Flesshe and blode of Mary he nam,
> As in the gospell seyth Sent Johan:
> Verbum caro factum est.

> Of joy and myrth now mowgh we syng:
> God with man is now dwellyng;
> Holy Wrytt makyth now shewyng:
> Deus homo natus est.

> God and man hath shewyd hys chyld
> That hath vs bovght fro the develys wyld;
> Hym to worshyp now be we myld;
> Congaudete m [ihi.]

> This chyldes moder, euermore
> Maydyn she was, after and befor,
> And so sayd the prophett in hys lore,
> Verbo prophesye.

BIBLIOGRAPHY

Richard Leighton Greene, ed., *A Selection of English Carols* (1962, repr. 1978), *The Early English Carols,* 2nd rev. ed. (1977), containing complete texts, without music, and "Carols," in Albert E. Hartung, ed., *A Manual of the Writings in Middle English*, VI (1980); Erik Routley, *The English Carol* (1958); John Stevens, ed., *Mediaeval Carols*, Musica Britannica no. 4, 2nd ed. (1970), contains all extant music of the carols, modernized.

RICHARD LEIGHTON GREENE

[See also **Ballata; Cantilène.**]

CARPET PAGE, a manuscript page decorated entirely with purely ornamental forms, often in geometric or interlace patterns. In a cross carpet page, the ornament frames a central cross. The carpet page was a standard feature of Hiberno-Saxon Gospelbooks, and normally introduced each of the four Gospels. The earliest example is found in an early-seventh-century Orosius manuscript written in the Irish monastery of St. Columban at Bobbio in Italy (Milan, Biblioteca Ambrosiana, MS D. 23. sup.), and most preserved carpet pages were painted by insular monks. The origins of the carpet page are, however, uncertain, for other examples are found in Syrian and Coptic books.

BIBLIOGRAPHY

J. J. G. Alexander, *Insular Manuscripts 6th to the 9th Century* (1978), 11, 28, 31.

LESLIE BRUBAKER

[See also **Gospelbook; Manuscript Illumination.**]

CARPETS. See Rugs and Carpets.

CARROCCIO, a war chariot and a symbol of the independence and military strength of an Italian town. The carroccio of Florence was well described by the fourteenth-century chronicler Giovanni Villani as "a platform on four wheels, painted crimson all over, and it carried two great crimson masts from which waved the great standard of the commune. . . . And it was drawn by a magnificent pair of oxen, covered with crimson hangings. . . . And the best and strongest foot soldiers were appointed as its special guard. . . ."

Archbishop Angilbert of Milan (824–859) is said to have designed or at least greatly enhanced the im-

Carroccio (Italian war chariot). DRAWING BY NORA JENNINGS

portance of the carroccio of Milan, the first such standard mentioned by chroniclers. It was used in the wars against Frederick Barbarossa. As Villani said, it was the rallying point for foot soldiers, whose steadfast defense of the carroccio helped the Lombard League defeat Frederick at the battle of Legnano in 1176. In 1162 the surrender of the carroccio had been a token of the submission of Milan to the emperor. A later example was the battle of Montaperti in 1260, between Siena and Florence, in which the Sienese victory was climaxed by the capture of the Florentine carroccio. By the fourteenth century, however, as armies became more professionalized, the carroccio lost its importance; Villani had to explain to his readers what it was and what it symbolized.

BIBLIOGRAPHY

Peter Munz, *Frederick Barbarossa* (1969); Ferdinand Schevill, *Siena, the History of a Medieval Commune* (1909, repr. 1964); *Villani's Chronicle*, Philip H. Wicksteed, ed., 2nd ed. rev. (1906); Pasquale Villari, *Mediaeval Italy from Charlemagne to Henry VII* (1910).

JOSEPH R. STRAYER

[See also **Angilbert of Milan; Lombard League.**]

CARTHUSIAN RITE. Because Carthusian monks lived lives of solitude and meditation, much of their devotional practice was carried out individually in their cells. But in their common liturgical services the Carthusians had their own distinctive rite. Besides records of chapter decisions, our chief sources of information are the earliest *Consuetudines* (1127), drawn up not by Bruno, the founder of the order, but by the fifth prior, Guigo; the twelfth-century statutes of Anthelm (Antelmus); the compilation of Prior Jancelin (1222); the *Statuta antiqua* (1259); and the *Statuta nova* (1368).

The rite for this monastic order, the motherhouse of which lay close to Grenoble, was almost certainly that of Lyons, the primatial see of which Grenoble was a suffragan. The rite reflects not only the Lyonese computation of Sundays in Pentecost but also the ninth-century directives of Agobard of Lyons regarding the use of scriptural compositions alone in the liturgy. Moreover, in the Divine Office the Carthusians borrowed from Benedictine usage. Like many orders founded in the eleventh and twelfth centuries, they insisted on simplicity in liturgical practice. Hence, liturgical paraphernalia were plain, with no gold and silver (except for a chalice and liturgical straw) or carpets and hangings. Processions were restricted; only one or two lights were used in the Mass; and Carthusian musical practice lacked such decorations as hymns, sequences, and proses.

BIBLIOGRAPHY

Jean Baptiste Martin, *Bibliographie liturgique de l'ordre des Chartreux* (1913); Archdale A. King, *Liturgies of the Religious Orders* (1955), 1–61; James Hogg, ed., *Analecta Cartusiana* (1970–).

ROGER E. REYNOLDS

[See also **Lyonese Rite.**]

CARTHUSIANS, the most successful and enduring manifestation of the eleventh-century movement for monastic reform that also inspired the Camaldolese and Cistercians. In 1084 St. Bruno of Cologne (*ca.* 1030–1101) withdrew with six companions to a rocky wilderness 3,250 feet up in the Dauphiné Alps, about thirty miles from Grenoble in southeastern France. On lands given by Humbert de Miribel and with the financial support of Bishop (later St.) Hugh of Grenoble, Bruno established the Chartreuse. (The word "Carthusian" derives from the Old French *chartreuse;* Latin, *cartusia;* Italian, *certosa;* English, "charterhouse.")

Bruno intended to unite in one foundation both eremitic and cenobitic forms of monastic life, following the Rule of St. Benedict; he did not propose to start a new order. The eighty chapters of the Carthusian *Consuetudines* (Customs), drawn up about 1127 by the fifth prior, Guido I (1109–1136), and combining traditional Benedictine practices with eremitical asceticism, had the following distinctive features: each monk lived in the solitude of his own cell, meeting the others in the oratory daily for Mass and the communal liturgy; permanent mortifications included a very strict diet in which meat was never allowed, the hairshirt, and total silence; in addition to preparing his own meals (except for one communal meal on Sundays), the monk executed any artistic or intellectual work within his cell and any agricultural labor in the small garden in front of the cell; all external activity, such as preaching and teaching, was forbidden; each charterhouse could house only twelve monks, plus the prior; all houses were subject to an annual visitation, and all priors met annually in general chapter at Chartreuse that maintained discipline and good observance.

The prior of Chartreuse held the office of prior general and was ultimately responsible for the government of the order. In 1133 Pope Innocent II approved the Carthusian *Consuetudines,* and the general chapter of 1141 marked the Carthusians' official beginning as an order. Additions to the *Consuetudines* made in 1259, 1368, and 1509 reduced the number of required fasts but did not alter the basic austerity of the life. The goal of sanctification through total silence and individual solitude was never changed.

Although the austerity of the Carthusian life made psychological demands that few could long tolerate, by 1200 there were thirty-six charterhouses of men and two of women in Europe; the mysticism of the fourteenth and fifteenth centuries attracted many to the Carthusian life, and the number of priories grew to 195. In addition to foundations made at Torre in Calabria (1098), which Count Roger of Sicily endowed, Mont Dieu in the diocese of Rheims, and the charterhouses established near Paris, Cologne, London, Nuremberg, Danzig, and Jülich, there were the royal or princely priories of Witham (1178–1179) and Hinton (1227) in Somerset, England, Allerheiligenthal in Mauerbach (1313), Galluzo near Florence (1342), Champmol in Burgundy (1383), and Pavia (1396).

During the Middle Ages only three events disrupted the peace of Carthusian priories. In 1132 an avalanche buried Chartreuse and forced the survivors to move lower in the valley, to the site where the Grande Chartreuse stands today. Second, in 1349 many houses suffered severe losses from the Black Death, though in the fifteenth and sixteenth centuries the order experienced a phenomenal increase in recruits. The Great Schism also split the Carthusian order, but the resignation of the two rival priors general and the election of Jean de Griffemont, prior of the Paris charterhouse, healed the division. During the Reformation many Carthusians suffered martyrdom, and in 1562 Huguenots totally destroyed the Grande Chartreuse.

Unlike other influential monastic orders, such as the Cistercians, the Carthusians had no impact on the economic development of medieval Europe. The totally contemplative life of the monks, which forbade contacts with secular society, led to the adoption of the system of *conversi*, or lay brothers, who performed major agricultural labor and handled necessary business transactions. The *Consuetudines* limited the number of lay brothers to twenty per priory. The exploitation of local resources, together with the financial assistance of wealthy benefactors, provided the necessary support for the monks' austere existence. For example, at the Grand Chartreuse, because the land was unsuited to agriculture, sheep were raised and the wool from the flocks yielded income.

The main contribution of the Carthusians to medieval society was intellectual and spiritual. Bruno of Cologne was a learned man, and his appreciation of books laid the foundation for the order's tradition of spiritual writing. In the twelfth and thirteenth centuries the copying of manuscripts occupied many monks, and some priories amassed rich libraries. In addition to the *Consuetudines*, Prior Guido I produced a life of St. Hugh of Grenoble, Prior Guido (or Guigo) II (1174–1180) composed *The Ladder of Monks*, and the prolific Denis the Carthusian (1402/1403–1471) wrote commentaries on Scripture, Boethius, and Peter Lombard, and the treatise *De contemplatione*. Perhaps the finest appreciation of Carthusian silence and solitude, *A Letter to the Brethren at Mont Dieu*, was written by the twelfth-century Cistercian William of St. Thierry. In the Middle Ages the Carthusians represented the highest monastic ideal, and they influenced such spiritual leaders as Bernard of Clairvaux, Peter the Venerable, Peter of Celle, and Geoffrey of Auxerre. With the invention of printing, the charterhouses of Cologne, Strasbourg, and Parma, among others, became printers for wide areas.

Although the Carthusians built their houses in the mountains, valleys, and villages, outside large towns, and even within town walls, everywhere a uniform architecture functioned to screen the monks from the world and to serve the specific needs of the monastery. A fortified wall usually surrounded the entire monastic compound. Within it the thirteen individual cells (miniature houses with several rooms) with small gardens encircled three sides of an open cloister; community buildings—church, chapter house, lay brothers' lodgings, kitchens, refectory, barns, stables, and guest houses—occupied the fourth side. The standard features of the Romanesque style were applied almost everywhere, changes were always discouraged, churches remained modest, and the elected poverty prevented the development of large-scale building.

The Carthusian order consistently maintained such a high level of monastic observance, such unswerving fidelity to its *Consuetudines*, that it could take legitimate pride in the now classic statement first made by Pope Alexander IV in 1257, repeated by Pius II in 1460, and reiterated by Pius XI in 1924: "The Carthusian order has never been reformed, because it has never been deformed."

BIBLIOGRAPHY

Charles Le Couteulx, *Annales ordinis cartusiensis ab anno 1084 ad 1429*, 8 vols. (1887–1891) contains the main sources of medieval Carthusian history. Texts and valuable commentary are in Bernard Bligny, *Recueil des plus anciens actes de la Grande-Chartreuse (1086–1196)* (1958). For contacts of other orders with the Carthusians and the latters' interests in books, see Giles Constable, ed., *The Letters of Peter the Venerable*, 2 vols. (1967), esp. 1:45–47, 2:112.

There is no broad and reliable history of the Carthusian Order in English. For the Grande Chartreuse and some French houses, see *La Grande Chartreuse par Un Chartreux*, 10th ed. (1963). The few English houses have received sound scholarly attention in E. Margaret Thompson, *The Carthusian Order in England* (1930), and in the sympathetic works of David Knowles: *The Monastic Order in England*, 2nd ed. (1963), 375–391, and *The Religious Orders in England*, III (1959), 222–240, which deals with the period of the dissolution of the English monasteries.

For the peculiarities of the Carthusian liturgy and its differences from the Roman rite, see Archdale A. King, "The Carthusian Rite," in *Liturgies of the Religious Orders* (1956). Wolfgang Braunfels, *Monasteries of Western*

Europe, Alastair Laing, trans. (1972), 111–124 treats Carthusian architecture.

For Carthusian spirituality, see *Guigo II: The Ladder of Monks and Twelve Meditations,* Edmund Colledge, O.S.A., and James Walsh, S.J., trans. (1981); Jean Leclercq, François Vandenbroucke, and Louis Bouyer, *The Spirituality of the Middle Ages* (1968), 150–161; and the *Dictionnaire de spiritualité,* II (1953).

BENNETT D. HILL

[See also **Bruno the Carthusian; Converso; Monasticism; Reform, Idea of.**]

CARTULARY, a copybook, occasionally in roll form, preserving copies of charters. The term comes from the medieval Latin word *c(h)artularium,* itself derived from *c(h)artula* (charter) and, in the Middle Ages, also denoting archives and formularies. Medieval as well as modern usage has sometimes applied the term to a register (*registrum* or *regestum*), but diplomatists prefer to designate as registers the books (or for Roman times and for later medieval England, the rolls) in which copies were entered by or for the party issuing the charters, and to designate as cartularies the books in which copies were entered by or for the recipient or possessor of the original charters.

The cartulary preserved a convenient record of all or some specific part of an institution's or individual's legal privileges and title deeds to lands and revenues, while saving wear and tear on the original charters. Most cartularies were compiled by ecclesiastical institutions, but seigniories, municipalities, and universities also produced them. The practice of compiling cartularies goes back at least to the ninth century and proliferated from the thirteenth. It was common also in the Byzantine world. The internal arrangement of cartularies did not follow fixed rules, but privileges tended to be arranged according to the rank of their authors and property titles tended to be arranged geographically, with chronology and the shelf numbers of the original charters also able to affect the order.

Because they were copies, charters in cartularies did not possess juridical force, though beginning in the thirteenth century they sometimes achieved this status by being certified by a notary public, and in England by the fourteenth century they were sometimes accorded evidential value when the originals were lost or destroyed and no better authenticated copies were available.

As for historical value, the compilers of cartularies normally made no attempt to imitate the exterior characteristics that are so valuable in establishing the genuineness of original charters (writing material, ink, script, and seal) and only exceptionally did they achieve a completely faithful reproduction of the internal content. Apart from making inadvertent errors, the scribes often did not hesitate to modernize spelling, grammar, and legal or dating formulas and to expand, abridge, or paraphrase the text—and sometimes they even deliberately forged it. Despite these reasons for treating cartularies with caution, there are innumerable questions on which historians would be lost without them.

BIBLIOGRAPHY

Harry Bresslau, *Handbuch der Urkundenlehre für Deutschland und Italien,* 2nd ed., I (1912, repr. 1958), 94–101; Godfrey R. C. Davis, *Medieval Cartularies of Great Britain: A Short Catalogue* (1958); Franz Dölger and Johannes Karayannopulos, *Byzantinische Urkundenlehre,* I (1968), 26; Arthur Giry, *Manuel de diplomatique* (1894, repr. 1925), 28–34; Henri Stein, *Bibliographie générale des cartulaires français ou relatifs à l'histoire de France* (1907); Georges Tessier, *La diplomatique* (1952), 23–29; David Walker, "The Organization of Material in Medieval Cartularies," in Donald A. Bullough and Robin L. Storey, eds., *The Study of Medieval Records* (1971).

JAMES J. JOHN

[See also **Charter.**]

CARVER, WILLIAM (BROMFLET), a master wood-carver active in northern England during the last quarter of the fifteenth and first quarter of the sixteenth century. Carver trained in York; by 1511 he settled in Ripon, where he was listed as a town officer (Wakeman), and headed a wood-carving workshop that mass-produced stalls, screens, and canopies for local churches.

BIBLIOGRAPHY

J. S. Purvis, "The Ripon Carvers and the Lost Choir-stalls of Bridlington Priory," in *Yorkshire Archaeological Journal,* **29** (1927–1929).

LESLIE BRUBAKER

CASBAH (Arabic: *qaṣaba*), originally, in medieval Arabic geographical terminology, the chief town of a region. In the western part of the Muslim world, it assumed the two meanings with which the term is associated in Spanish, Portuguese, and other European languages: a fortress, fortified compound, or citadel; and the most ancient part of a town. In the Iberian Peninsula qaṣaba (dialectal, qaṣba) referred primarily to a citadel, a well-fortified, semi-independent structure strategically situated and usually attached to the wall of a fortified town. A network of casbahs dotted the landscape of medieval Muslim Spain and North Africa. In case of revolt they served as a place of refuge for local governors, princes, and commanders, and in case of attack they enabled local forces to resist even after the rest of the town was overrun.

A. L. UDOVITCH

[See also **Geography and Cartography, Islamic; Urbanism, Islamic.**]

CASHEL (Irish: Caisel; from Latin: *castellum*) is the only Irish royal site that has a borrowed Latin name, a fact that, in the opinion of D. A. Binchy, is "sufficient evidence that its founders had already been in contact with Roman civilization." The traditional founder of the kingship of Cashel is Conall Corc, legendary ancestor of the Eóganacht dynasties, and an early saga tells of his "discovery" of the site. Whether or not the Eóganacht were returned emigrants from Roman Britain or late arrivals from Gaul, as some have suggested, must remain a matter for doubt. The early history of Munster, because of the lack of contemporary annals, is obscure, but the advent of the Eóganacht kingship of Cashel seems to be far later than the fifth-century date that its propagandists would have us believe, and the historical sources contain clear memories of a Munster dominated by other peoples (especially the Dáirine of Corcu Loígde).

The Eóganacht kings at Cashel did not succeed in dominating the province much before the seventh century. They encountered bitter opposition from their relatives in the west, Eóganacht Locha Léin, situated about Killarney, in the early period. In the eighth century the most powerful kings of Munster (including the famous Cathal mac Finguine, who died in 742) belonged to Eóganacht Glendamnach, yet another branch of the far-flung Eóganacht dynasty. In the second half of the ninth century, the Eóganacht of Cashel (with few exceptions) produced

most of the kings of Munster and one notable warrior, the cleric-king Feidlimid mac Crimthainn, whose ambitions in church and state extended far beyond Munster. However, they failed to concentrate royal power within narrow dynastic limits and never established a settled power base. Given the growing power of the Uí Néill to the north and the rise of Dál Cais in the west in the early tenth century, their fall was assured.

The kings of Cashel claimed to be the most Christian kings in Ireland. Four of them between 820 and 908 were clerics, and the kingship was closely linked with the dynastic church of Emly. With the fall of its dynasty, Cashel declined in political significance and its dynastic families were pushed into south Munster in the turmoil of the twelfth century. In the twelfth-century church reform it became the ecclesiastical capital of Munster and site of the metropolitan see.

BIBLIOGRAPHY

D. A. Binchy, *Celtic and Anglo-Saxon Kingship* (1970); Francis J. Byrne, *Irish Kings and High-Kings* (1973); Aubrey Gwynn, *The Twelfth-Century Reform* (1968); Donnchadh Ó Corráin, *Ireland Before the Normans* (1972).

DONNCHADH Ó CORRÁIN

[See also **Dál Cais; Eóganacht; Munster; Uí Néill.**]

CASNODYN (*ca.* 1290–1340), a Welsh poet whose poetry links him primarily with the court of Madog Fychan, steward of Tir Iarll in Glamorgan. Like other poets of his time, he traveled, exchanging poems for hospitality from Ieuan Llwyd of Gogerddan in Ceredigion and from Gwenllïant, wife of the Welsh patron Sir Gruffudd Llwyd of Gwynedd.

Casnodyn strove to protect the integrity of the Welsh bardic tradition against the growing throng of "vain poetasters" whose scatological "rubbish" was popular in the fourteenth century. He regarded praise of God and of one's patron as the only worthy expression of the poetic art.

Casnodyn's few—although quite long—surviving poems reveal his mastery of the *awdl* and *englyn* meters. His terse, closely woven lines abounding in internal rhymes and alliteration, are models from which a sophisticated system of sound correspondences, known as *cynghanedd*, evolved in Welsh poetry. And his *rhieingerdd* (maid song) to Gwenllïant compares with those of the great twelfth-century poets Gwalchmai and Cynddelw Brydydd Mawr. Casnodyn also set the fashion for descriptions piled with a mixed bag of allusions from Welsh history and legend, the classical world, Arthurian romance, and Scripture.

Casnodyn's greatest achievement is his *awdlau* addressed to the Trinity. From the bleak depths of hell's agony to the raptures of earth and heaven, this monorhyming sequence is awesome in its precise diction and vibrant imagery.

BIBLIOGRAPHY

Casnodyn's poetry is in Edward Anwyl, *The Poetry of the Gogynfeirdd from the Myvyrian Archaiology of Wales* (1909); John Gwenogvryn Evans, ed., *The Poetry in the Red Book of Hergest* (1911); and John Morris Jones, ed., *Llawysgrif Hendregadredd* (1933, repr. 1971), the Hendregadredd manuscript. There are no critical editions or English translations of his poetry. D. Myrddin Lloyd, "The Later Gogynfeirdd," in Alfred O. H. Jarman and Gwilym Rees Hughes, *A Guide to Welsh Literature*, II (1979), is the best and most accessible study.

Marilyn Kay Kenney

[See also **Welsh Literature: Poetry.**]

CASSIAN, JOHN (*ca.* 360–*ca.* 432/435), authority on monasticism. Born probably in Scythia Minor (Romania), John became a monk in Bethlehem not later than 392. He left the Holy Land with a fellow monk, Germanus, in order to experience asceticism as practiced by monks in Egypt who were strongly influenced by Origenist tradition. The oath by which the two friends had bound themselves to return quickly was honored only after seven years and considerable casuistry, a fact that earned John severe criticism from Prosper of Aquitaine in later years. Released from their oath by their Bethlehem superiors, John and Germanus returned to the Nile; by about 400 both were at Constantinople and John was ordained deacon by the patriarch, John Chrysostom. In 404 Germanus, then a priest, accompanied John to Rome with a letter in behalf of the exiled John Chrysostom from the Constantinople clergy. A priest named "Cassian" was invited to Rome from Alexandria in connection with the Antioch schism about 414–415 and he may be identical with our John Cassian, who was certainly a priest by this date. At about this time John gave institutional form to his conception of asceticism by founding two monasteries at Marseilles, Sts. Peter and Victor for men, and

St. Saviour for women, perhaps for his sister; John remained at Sts. Peter and Victor until death.

Cassian influenced the development of Western monasticism by insisting on the necessity for ascetic effort as well as grace and by providing a basis for this in speculative theology. His name is often set in somewhat exaggerated opposition to that of St. Augustine on this issue and on predestination. The Council of Orange II in 529 (its *capitula* confirmed by Pope Boniface II and thus of universal authority) consecrated a moderate position on predestination and grace. But although it is generally termed "semi-Pelagianism," the position of those who, with Cassian, opposed the partisans of Augustine (Sts. Paulinus of Nola and Prosper of Aquitaine) is susceptible of a more sympathetic interpretation than doctrinaire "Augustinians" were ready to grant. Cassian also introduced into Western monasticism the Egyptian conviction that common life in the monastery, the *coenobium,* ought ideally to prepare the beginner for the more perfect life of the hermit, but always with the support of community and superior; the pejorative "Sarabaites" is applied by John (*Inst.* 18, 17) to ascetics who acknowledge no superior. This notion is consecrated in the early-sixth-century Rule of St. Benedict and is at the heart of the foundation by Bruno the Carthusian as well as the orders that follow the Rule of St. Benedict.

In 417–418 John produced a treatise on the monastic life called *Institutiones* (Institutes), often held to deal with externals because it sets out the daily routine of the monastery. His second major work under the title of *Collationes* (Conferences), appeared in three stages: 1–10 near 420, 11–17 in 426, and 18–24 from 426 to 429. This work may not reflect literally the circumstances of composition; it is in the literary genre both of a travel account and of spiritual conferences held with sixteen Egyptian masters of the spiritual life, in company with his old friend, Germanus. One detail of John's teaching is his list of "principal vices" of which he named eight in both the *Institutiones* (5, 1) and *Collationes* (5, 2); Gregory the Great later shortened the list by collapsing vainglory and pride into one (pride) and melancholy and accidia into melancholy. He then added envy, thus inaugurating the tradition of seven "capital sins" (though Gregory still called them "principal vices"). Finally, John wrote a treatise against the Nestorians, *De incarnatione* (On the incarnation). Although he was writing in Latin for Westerners, John seems to have known Greek, at least as an adult.

BIBLIOGRAPHY

Cassian's works are to be found in *Patrologia latina,* XLIX and L (1858–1859); and in *Corpus scriptorum ecclesiasticorum latinorum,* XIII (1886) and XVII (1888); there is a Latin text with facing page French translation in *Jean Cassien: Conférences,* Eugène Pichery, ed., 3 vols. (1955–1959); *Institutions cénobitiques,* Jean-Claude Guy, ed. (1965). On his life, see Owen Chadwick, *John Cassian,* 2nd ed. (1968); Jean-Claude Guy, *Jean Cassien: Vie et doctrine spirituelle* (1961); D. J. Macqueen, "John Cassian on Grace and Free Will with Particular Reference to Institutio XII and Collatio XII," in *Recherches de théologie ancienne et medievale,* 44 (1977).

EDWARD A. SYNAN

[See also **Monasticism; Paulinus of Nola; Pelagius; Prosper of Aquitaine; Seven Deadly Sins.**]

CASSIODORUS SENATOR, FLAVIUS MAGNUS AURELIUS

CASSIODORUS SENATOR, FLAVIUS MAGNUS AURELIUS (*ca.* 490–*ca.* 583), an influential Italian politician, scholar, and educator. During the Gothic rule of Italy, he was involved in politics and held a number of official court positions. Around the age of fifty, he retired from public office and went to Constantinople to pursue an interest in religious studies. About fifteen years later he returned to Italy and took up permanent residence in the monastery of Vivarium, which he had founded sometime earlier at Scylacium (Squillace), his birthplace.

Cassiodorus was born into a family that for several generations had actively supported Italy's reigning monarchs. Not unexpectedly, he became involved in politics at an early age. At that time the Ostrogoth Theodoric had been king for at least a decade. Incapable of writing his own communiqués, Theodoric employed the literary skills of others for such tasks. As a member of an Italian senatorial family, Cassiodorus had received a traditional liberal arts education that, combined with his natural talents as a rhetor, quickly attracted attention and won him his first court position as composer of letters and public bills for the king.

During his political tenure Cassiodorus wrote several works, including *Chronica,* a chronological account of the Italian rulers up to 519, and a lost history of the Goths, in twelve books (only an abridgment by Jordanes entitled *De origine actibusque Getarum,* or *Getica,* survives). His most important work from this period of his life is the *Variae,* a work compiled shortly before he left public office.

The *Variae* (*ed.* 538) is a collection of official documents spanning Cassiodorus' years in service to the king. It includes royal edicts, proclamations, legal formulas, and individual letters that exhibit his skill as a practical rhetorician. His ability to construct routine administrative correspondence in the form of highly persuasive documents was, no doubt, a factor in maintaining the favor of the king. The *Variae* also displays certain literary characteristics typical of Cassiodorus and other medieval writers: the extensive use of rhetorical figures, lengthy digressions, and Latin etymology. Accordingly, the work provided its medieval audience not only with practical models of administrative correspondence but also with examples of artistically crafted letters and as a result was extremely popular.

Following Theodoric's death and amid the ensuing struggle between the Goths and the Byzantines for control of Italy, Cassiodorus found himself in an increasingly dangerous position politically. Consequently, about two years after compiling the *Variae,* he traveled to Constantinople, where he began his work in religious studies. Relatively little is known about his sojourn there, but he is presumed to have remained for some time, perhaps ten years or more. The subject matter of his writings from this period suggests that he may have abandoned his concern with political matters and devoted himself completely to religious scholarship.

Cassiodorus' first nonsecular work was *De anima* (*ca.* 538); his most ambitious and influential effort was *Expositio Psalmorum* (*ca.* 540–548). His avowed purpose in writing this work was to rework Augustine's sermons, *Enarrationes in Psalmos,* into a form that would be more accessible and useful to scriptural scholars; however, much of the *Expositio Psalmorum* is his original work. Specifically noteworthy is the rigid order he developed for examining each Psalm: *titulus, divisio, expositio,* and *conclusio.* That method and his approach to textual interpretation, which relied heavily upon allegory and number symbolism, were used as a model for scriptural exegesis until as late as the twelfth century.

The actual date of Cassiodorus' founding of Vivarium is unknown, but it seems likely that it was prior to his Constantinople sojourn. As early as 534 he was concerned with fostering the development of schools that taught nonsecular subjects and attempted to establish such a school in Rome. After that effort failed, he apparently decided to use his own lands at Squillace to found a theological school and scriptorium. However, it was not until after returning from Constantinople in 554 that he personally settled at Vivarium.

The most important work of Cassiodorus' monastic period is the *Institutiones* (*ca.* 562). The treatise was written as an instructional manual for the educational program of the monks at Vivarium. It is divided into two books, one for religious studies and one for secular. In Book I Cassiodorus tells how to study the Scriptures, what manuscripts can be found at Vivarium, how to copy new manuscripts, and what heretical writers should be avoided. He also explains how secular studies can be used to understand the Scriptures. In Book II Cassiodorus gives a brief, encyclopedic discussion of the seven liberal arts. As an educational manual the treatise was very influential in the following centuries. Book I proved to be a useful guide for other manuscript collections, and Book II was especially popular for its concise treatment of the seven liberal arts. Other writers, such as Isidore of Seville and Hrabanus Maurus, borrowed substantially from it.

Many of Cassiodorus' last works at Vivarium indicate his interests as a Christian educator. Concerned with protecting his monks from heretical doctrine, he carefully expurgated manuscripts to be copied or texts to be translated, such as the *Historica ecclesiastica tripartita* and the Latin translation of Josephus' *Jewish Antiquities.* For monks beginning their studies of the New Testament, he wrote an introductory text, *Complexiones in epistolis apostolorum.* And, in perhaps his final literary effort, *De orthographia,* he produced a spelling handbook for reference in manuscript copying.

The monastery at Vivarium did not survive the death of Cassiodorus. Nevertheless, much of his work did endure, and the manuscripts he had collected and had copied by the monks there were widely disseminated throughout medieval Europe.

BIBLIOGRAPHY

This article draws heavily upon the research of James Joseph O'Donnell, *Cassiodorus* (1979), the most complete study of Cassiodorus to date. Included in this study is an extensive, partially annotated bibliography.

The complete edition of Cassiodorus' works has been edited by J. Garet in *Patrologia latina,* LXIX–LXX (repr. of Venice, 1729 edition [Rouen, 1679]); critical editions of individual works have been published more recently. The *Variae* has been translated in part by Thomas Hodgkin, *The Letters of Cassiodorus* (1886). Hodgkin's work includes a long introduction on Cassiodorus, the political background of the *Variae,* and its chronology. The *Institutiones* has been translated by Leslie Webber Jones, *An Introduction to Divine and Human Readings* (1946). This translation also includes a lengthy introduction and a bibliography. For a general account of how the *Institutiones* influenced the development of medieval rhetoric, see James J. Murphy, *Rhetoric in the Middle Ages* (1974), 43–88.

Finally, much has been written on the relative importance of Cassiodorus' work at Vivarium: for example, Pierre Riché, *Education and Culture in the Barbarian West, Sixth Through Eighth Centuries,* John J. Contreni, trans. (1976), 17–189.

BETH S. BENNETT

[See also **Exegesis, Latin; Scriptorium.**]

CASTELLAN, a man who commanded a castle, either in his own right or as deputy of a superior. Because control of a castle meant control of the surrounding fortified areas, the entire district (or castellany) was often governed by the castellan and his agents, especially in regions where conditions were unsettled and where the representative of higher authority had to have military competence. Thus in southern France the *viguiers* (local administrators) were often castellans or former castellans. The same was true in the northeastern counties, where the rich and powerful towns resented any check on their virtual independence. The castellan in each town represented the authority of the king or count and was supposed to keep the town under control.

By contrast, in more peaceful areas the office of castellan was a sinecure. For example, Enguerrand de Marigny, the chief adviser of Philip the Fair during the latter part of his reign (1285–1314), was castellan of Longueville (Issoudun) in Normandy but was certainly not involved in local government. Between these extremes were castellanies given to men who performed specialized duties, such as keepers of the royal forests, who thereby gained both extra income and a local base in the area that they were policing.

The most powerful royal castellan in France in the late thirteenth and early fourteenth centuries was that of Montréal in the region of Carcassonne. He was responsible for a vast and unruly district that had long been a center of heresy, and he was directly accountable to the central government. The castellan in a peaceful area such as the Île de France was little more than a *prévôt,* a collector of small revenues and a judge in minor cases.

In general, the more important royal castellans in places such as Normandy were very much at the level of viscounts, the chief assistants of the local ruler. In peaceful areas where the castellany was almost identical with the *prévôté*, the *prévôt* was not at the level of a viscount, and there was not always a separate officer called a castellan in all these places.

Just as a viscount was not necessarily a royal or seigneurial officer, so a castellan could be simply a member of the nobility, ranking, as a baron, above an ordinary knight but below a count or duke. His title, lands, and rights were hereditary, like those of any other noble; he was not an administrator or officer of government—unless, of course, he was given a position in the service of a greater lord. Castellans would normally have a castle, which they were supposed to hold as part of their service to their lord; but some castles were neither very strong nor very well manned. These castellans, however, had extensive rights of justice in their districts, as well as knights in their service, and they were clearly superior to the holders of minor fiefs.

Castellans were numerous in France, the Low Countries, and the western parts of the empire. They were also important in the Spanish kingdoms, especially in Aragon, where their assertion of almost completely independent local power created a good deal of trouble for the king. Elsewhere the title was rare. Although there were castles throughout western Europe, and those who held them could be very independent of their overlords, these men were seldom called castellans.

England furnishes a good illustration of this situation. The keeper of the Tower of London was an important and powerful figure and, like the castellans of the Low Countries, was supposed to ensure royal control over a great city. But while the Mandevilles held the Tower for two generations, they were not sheriffs of Middlesex (the English equivalent of viscount), nor was their office hereditary. Geoffrey, the second Mandeville, was dismissed from his post in 1143, and none of his relatives succeeded him. The keepers of royal forests and sheriffs in many counties held castles that they used as their headquarters, but their power was based on their appointment as royal officials and not on their possession of a castle, which they held only at the pleasure of the king. In frontier districts, such as the north of England, Wales, and Ireland, lords of castles might have greater de facto power than the king's official representatives, but they were not called castellans of their district. In short, castellans were found for the most part in France, the Low Countries, a few border areas west of the Rhine, and Spain.

BIBLIOGRAPHY

Charles Du Fresne Du Cange, *Glossarium ad scriptores mediae et infimae Latinitatis*, 3 vols. (1678, repr. 1954–1955); Paul Guilhiermoz, *Essai sur l'origine de la noblesse en France au moyen âge* (1902); Robert Hajdu, "Castles, Castellans, and the Structure of Politics in Poitou, 1152–1271," in *Journal of Medieval History*, 4 (1978); Jan Frederik Niermeyer, *Mediae Latinitatis lexicon minus* (1976); Joseph R. Strayer, *The Reign of Philip the Fair* (1980).

JOSEPH R. STRAYER

[See also **Castles and Fortifications; Nobility, Nobles; Prévôt, Probst, Provost.**]

CASTILE. The history of Castile may be divided into four broad chronological periods. The first runs from the birth of Castile as a small county around 800 to Ferdinand I's assumption of the title of king of Castile in 1037. The second runs from 1037 to the decisive victory of the Christians over the Muslims at Las Navas de Tolosa in 1212; the third, from 1212 to the death of Alfonso XI in 1350; and the last, from the mid fourteenth century to Isabella's coronation as queen of Castile in 1474. This periodization roughly corresponds to important political, economic, and social changes in the structure of the kingdom and has been adopted, with some minor variations, by most historians of medieval Spain.

CA. 800–1037

Castile was born as a frontier outpost in the eastern part of the Asturian kingdom, its name appearing for the first time in a document dated 800. Referring loosely to a region known to the Romans as Vardulia (or Bardulia), the early Castile was, as the chronicler described it, "a small corner" in the mountains of Santander with its center at Espinosa de los Monteros and its radius extending to the area of Villarcayo and Medina de Pomar. In the late eighth and early ninth centuries fortifications and castles were built to protect the mountain passes from Muslim attacks. From them the land took its name: Castile, the land of castles.

Students of Castile have pointed to the peculiar nature of the area and the marked differences in its development from that of Asturias-León. Castile was an extension of the Asturian realm but, as Pérez de Urbel has argued, it had a personality and character of its own. Its ethnic mix of Cantabrian and Basque mountain people, the hardness and perils of the frontier life, the continuous threat of Muslim attacks,

CASTILE

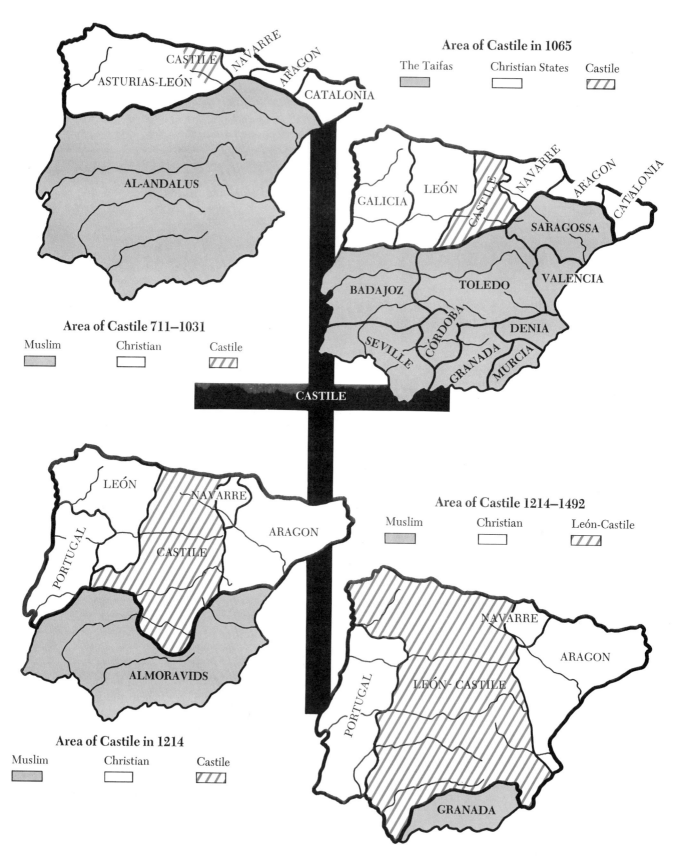

Area of Castile 711–1031

Muslim   Christian   Castile

Area of Castile in 1065

The Taifas   Christian States   Castile

ASTURIAS-LEÓN   CASTILE   NAVARRE   ARAGON   CATALONIA

AL-ANDALUS

GALICIA   LEÓN   CASTILE   NAVARRE   ARAGON   CATALONIA

SARAGOSSA

BADAJOZ   TOLEDO   VALENCIA

SEVILLE   CÓRDOBA   GRANADA   DENIA   MURCIA

CASTILE

Area of Castile in 1214

Muslim   Christian   Castile

LEÓN   NAVARRE   PORTUGAL   CASTILE   ARAGON

ALMORAVIDS

Area of Castile 1214–1492

Muslim   Christian   León-Castile

PORTUGAL   NAVARRE   LEÓN-CASTILE   ARAGON

GRANADA

126

IBERIAN PENINSULA SHOWING AREA OF CASTILE

and its remoteness from the Visigothic influences of the Asturian court at Oviedo (and later León) explained, according to Julio Valdeón Baruque, its dynamic history and independent ways.

Counts, monasteries, and free peasants were the three ingredients in the advance of the Christian frontier. In the early ninth century settlers poured down from the mountain valleys of the north into the plains of Castile. Free peasants occupied and worked the empty land on their own initiative, under that of powerful lords (counts), or, more often than not, under the auspices of newly founded monasteries. Noteworthy are the activity of the fabled abbot Vitulo, and the repopulation and granting of a charter to the settlers of Brañosera (in the present province of Palencia, 824) by Count Nuño Núñez.

127

The repopulation and the fortification of the Ebro River line survived Muslim attacks and provided a fairly effective barrier to Córdoba's incursions into the north.

The legend, accepted in varying degrees by most Castilian medievalists, of two judges who gave judgments in the new region according to local customs and their own legal tradition (*fazañas, fuero de albedrío),* marks a break with Asturian legal formulas. This may be taken as an indication of the growing autonomy of this frontier area. Differences in speech, the embryonic beginnings of the Castilian language, accentuated the break with Asturias.

By 850 Rodrigo, one of the counts ruling Castile, pushed the frontier farther south and created a new fortified line between the Ebro and the Arlanzón rivers. The resettlement of Amaya and Oca, and the Christian expansion into the Bureba Plateau and the Gap of Pancorbo, added considerable territory to the county. Rodrigo's son, Diego Rodríguez Porcelos (*ca.* 873–890) settled Burgos and Valpuesta, and made the Arlanzón River his new frontier. At the end of the ninth century the Arlanza River had been reached, and by 912 Christian fortresses rose on the banks of the Duero. Rather than wrest lands from the Muslims by force, the Castilians advanced to the south in piecemeal occupation and settlement of almost deserted lands that were weakly defended because of the internal problems plaguing Córdoba and the unattractive nature of the territory.

The Castile of the early tenth century was divided among three powerful families, each seeking to gain advantage over the others and actively courting the kings of León or intriguing against them. By 932–933 Fernán González (*d.* 970) began the task of uniting Castile under his sole rule. The hero of a thirteenth-century epic poem, and according to tradition the founder of Castile, Fernán González was a shrewd and durable ruler. His greatest accomplishment was to preserve the semi-independence and well-being of Castile at a time when Córdoba reached its political zenith. He also survived the political intrigues, enmity, and prison of the Asturian-Leonese kings and gained more than he lost in the struggle. As far south as Sepúlveda, Fernán González garrisoned his men deep into Moorish lands, a challenge to Córdoba and to the expansionist hopes of León. He united the county, made his rule hereditary, and governed not by the grace of kings in faraway León but by the grace of God and his sword. When he died in 970, his son Garcí Fernández succeeded without opposition.

The last decades of the tenth century were a time of troubles. Nothing withstood the fury unleashed by al-Mansur (*d.* 1002), the military dictator of Córdoba. Castile, although defeated, suffered less than Asturias. After the decline of centralized authority in the caliphate in 1007, Sancho García, Garcí Fernández's son, was able to intervene in Muslim affairs and to expand his territory. His premature death in 1017 and the murder of his son and heir in 1027 allowed Sancho III, king of Navarre, to claim the title of count of Castile through his wife Munia, the daughter of Sancho García. To mollify Castilian opposition, Sancho relinquished rule in the county to his second born, Ferdinand. Ferdinand's victory over the Asturian-Leonese king Vermudo III at Tamarón on 4 September 1037, and the death of Vermudo, allowed the Castilian count to assume the title of king of León, to which he added that of Castile later that year.

1037–1212

The death of Vermudo III in 1037 and the transformation of the county of Castile into a kingdom marked the beginnings of Castilian hegemony over the kingdoms of western Spain. To the west lay León, now under the kingship of Ferdinand I; to the south, the divided and frail kindgoms of the *taifas* (the small political units that resulted from the breakdown of the caliphate); and to the north, Navarre, the ancestral home of Ferdinand, ruled by his older brother García.

Ferdinand moved first against Navarre. At the Battle of Atapuerca (1054), García of Navarre died and Castile recovered borderlands formerly lost to his father, Sancho III. Of greater significance was the acquisition of the coastline between Fuenterrabía (near the present frontier of France) and Castro-Urdiales in the province of Santander. Castile thus gained access to the Bay of Biscay and eventual entry into the northern European markets. These victories in the north were quickly followed by advances in the south. The aim here was twofold. First, in the southwest, in what later would become Portugal, Ferdinand conquered Viseu in 1055 and Coimbra in 1064. Second, in the center of the peninsula he was able, by using the threat of military intervention, to extort (as Angus MacKay correctly describes it) considerable and debilitating tribute from the *taifas* of Saragossa, Toledo, Seville, and Badajoz. These tributes or *parias* financed the new Castilian monarchy while further weakening the fragmented Moorish kingdoms.

Moreover, Ferdinand followed in his father's footsteps in the "Europeanization" of the western portion of the peninsula. The rise of urban centers along the road to Compostela, with their *calles de francos,* streets inhabited by northern merchants and artisans settled in Castile under their own peculiar privileges, and the growing influence of Cluny, with its liturgy and art forms, transformed the traditional religious, artistic, and political ideas of Castile.

The reign of Ferdinand I, long and full of accomplishments, ended in 1065. In his will he dissipated his many years of toil, dividing his lands among his sons. Sancho II (1065–1072), the firstborn, received Castile and the *parias* of Saragossa. Alfonso VI (1065–1109) inherited León and the income of the *taifas* of Toledo; to the youngest, García (1065–1072), went Galicia and Portugal with the tributes of the Muslim kingdoms of Seville and Badajoz.

The years after Ferdinand's death were a replay of previous history. Sancho united the kingdoms by force while his brothers sought refuge among the Muslims. His assassination in 1072, at the siege of Zamora, allowed Alfonso VI to reclaim his former crown in León and, soon after dealing with García, to claim sole rule over Castile, León, Galicia, and Portugal. Alfonso, *rex Hispaniae,* as he entitled himself, embarked on a program of territorial expansion along all his borders. The areas of the Rioja, Álava, and Vizcaya became part of the realm, and Navarre, after the death of its king, Sancho IV, was partitioned between Castile and Aragon. In the south the siege of Toledo culminated in the conquest of the city in 1085, a momentous event in the history of the kingdom.

In many respects Alfonso VI's reign was a watershed in the history of Castile. His rule coincided with the triumph of the monastic reform movement in western Europe and the investiture controversy. Pope Gregory VII's interest in Spanish affairs and the labor of his legates intensified the bitter struggle between the partisans of the Mozarabic rite and the supporters of Roman uniformity. The issue of choosing the right liturgy was further clouded by the intrigues of the Cluniac monk Roberto, abbot of Sahagún, by the extramarital affairs of Alfonso, and by what Ramón Menéndez Pidal has described as a nationalistic reaction to papal interference. At the Council of Burgos (1080) Roberto was deposed, the king's mistress was dismissed, and the Roman liturgy became universal throughout the land.

Papal intervention had other consequences. Many Spanish historians see the reign of Alfonso VI as the beginning of the crusading ideal. What had been until then a struggle for land and tributes became, according to these historians, imbued with spiritual elements; faith became an honorable excuse for expansion. However, that faith, although deeply felt, could be quickly put aside when political reality demanded otherwise. Indeed, the new political arrangements resulting from the conquest of Toledo, an area that, unlike previous acquisitions, had a considerable Muslim population, dictated a policy of toleration. In 1085, fresh from his victory at Toledo, Alfonso VI laid claim to the rich tradition embedded there and took the title of *imperator totius Hispaniae.*

Unfortunately for Alfonso, he could savor his victory for only a short while. The kings of *taifas,* aware of his ambitions, took the drastic step, after a great deal of debate, of calling upon the Almoravids for aid. The Almoravids, an ascetic warrior group, had gained power in North Africa and now crossed the Strait of Gibraltar in force. In swift campaigns they brought the petty kingdoms of Al-Andalus under their control, and on 23 October 1086 inflicted a serious defeat upon Alfonso VI's armies at Sagrajas. The southward march of the Christians was temporarily stopped, but Toledo remained in the hands of the Castilians. After almost three decades of expansion, Alfonso was forced for the remainder of his reign to defend his new acquisitions.

One cannot leave this period without a brief mention of Rodrigo Díaz de Vivar, the Cid (*d.* 1099). The hero of a twelfth-century epic poem, Rodrigo filled the age with his heroic deeds, highlighted by his disputes with Alfonso, his subsequent exile, his exploits against Moors and Christians, his humane policies toward the Muslims, and his conquest of Valencia in 1094. Champion of the faith, shrewd opportunist, or both?—the debate has not yet come to an end.

The first years of the twelfth century were clouded by the problems of Alfonso VI's succession. His only son, Sancho, died in 1108, leaving Teresa, the king's bastard daughter, and her husband, Henry of Burgundy, free to carve out an independent Portugal and to hope for even greater gains. Alfonso's response to this quandary was to recognize his own legitimate daughter, Urraca, as his sole heir while working toward a matrimonial alliance between her and Alfonso I, king of Aragon. The wedding took place in September 1109, two months after the king's death.

If on paper the union of Urraca and Alfonso I seemed a fortunate coup, in fact it was a disaster.

The Castilian nobility and the ambitious archbishop of Compostela, Diego Gelmírez, supported the rights of Alfonso Raimúndez, son of Urraca by a previous marriage to the energetic and capable Raymond of Burgundy (d. 1107). Through the machinations of Gelmírez, the young prince was crowned king of Castile in 1111. Bourgeois rebellions in Compostela (1116–1117) and elsewhere brought to the peninsular kingdom the dreaded cry of "commune." In 1117 Urraca was beaten and stripped naked by the enraged citizens of Compostela. It was not long, however, before the lords and the Crown were once again in control.

The greatest calamity of the period was the inability of Urraca and Alfonso of Aragon to live or even to work together. For reasons that are not clear to us, they simply could not stand each other; thus, common human failings forced the union of crowns to wait a few more centuries. Not untypically, husband and wife solved their differences on the battlefield. The aggressive policies of Henry and Teresa in Portugal complete a picture of general political upheaval. The only hopeful note for Christian Spain was that the Almoravids succumbed to the sophistication of Al-Andalus, their warring zeal diluted in the pleasure gardens of Andalusia.

The death of Urraca in 1126 coincided with the coming of age of Alfonso Raimúndez, who became Alfonso VII (1126–1157). The new king led military campaigns against Portugal in 1127–1128 and against the Muslims in 1132–1133. In 1135 he was crowned at León and assumed, as his Asturian-Leonese ancestors had done, the title of emperor. Although in theory Alfonso claimed supremacy in the peninsula, the political reality was otherwise. The union of Aragon and the county of Barcelona under Ramón Berenguer IV and the rise of Portugal as an independent kingdom by 1143 denied his claims. In the south the Almohads, a new wave of ascetic warriors dedicated to a holy war, had crossed the Strait of Gibraltar from North Africa and were engaged in overthrowing the Almoravids. This opened the way for Christian advances along the frontier, highlighted by the capture of Almería in 1147, a truly international effort in which Alfonso VII and Ramón Berenguer IV were supported by crusaders from beyond the Pyrenees.

This new spirit of cooperation among the peninsular Christian kingdoms is best expressed in the Treaty of Tudellén (1151), in which both kings agreed on their future areas of expansion and on a partition of Navarre. When Alfonso VII died in 1157, his will divided his kingdoms between his two sons. The firstborn, Sancho III (1157–1158), inherited Castile and Toledo, and Ferdinand II (1157–1188) received León and Galicia. The division of Alfonso VII's lands ushered in an age described by Menéndez Pidal as that of the "five Hispanic kingdoms"—León, Castile, Navarre, Aragon-Catalonia, and Portugal—and, in the south, the growing power of the Almohads.

The death of Sancho III in 1158 left a son aged three, Alfonso VIII (1158–1214), as heir to the throne. This minority, like all the others, brought to Castile the usual sequel of baronial revolts and anarchy. The young king became the pawn and bone of contention of the two most powerful magnate families of Castile: the Castros and the Laras. Their arrogance and struggle for the tutorship of Alfonso allowed Sancho VI of Navarre to gain considerable territory on the northern frontier. Alfonso VIII's uncle, Ferdinand II of León, established a Leonese garrison in Toledo and, allied with the Castros, then became regent of Castile. While the realm suffered, its southern frontier was defended from the Almohads by the municipal militias of such cities as Ávila, Segovia, and Sepúlveda, and by the newly formed military orders. These orders became not only an instrument for the defense of the southern frontier but also the vanguard of the eventual settlement and colonization of La Mancha and Estremadura.

When Alfonso VIII assumed personal rule in 1170, he faced the tasks of recovering the lost territories and of containing the Almohad threat. A pious man, founder and patron of monasteries, the grandfather of two saints (Louis IX of France and Ferdinand III of Castile-León), he was married to Eleanor, the daughter of Henry II of England and Eleanor of Aquitaine. His wedding to an English princess brought Castile into European politics and gave his realm interests and concerns beyond the Pyrenees. By 1177 he had regained the territories lost to Navarre and more, expanding his jurisdiction to Álava and Guipúzcoa. An active repopulation effort strengthened his position on the coast of the Bay of Biscay, made more important now by the ties between England and Gascony.

In 1179 the Treaty of Cazola, between Aragon and Castile, defined new spheres of influence in the south. Although Castile received the lion's share, Alfonso relinquished the claims to primacy acquired through the Treaty of Tudellén. In the early 1180's what Ferdinand II had gained during his nephew's minority was recovered. The growth of Castilian power was, of course, not well received by the other Christian kingdoms. The years between 1190 and 1197 were a period of confusion that witnessed a series of anti-Castilian pacts (on one occasion including an alliance between León and the Almohads), frontier skirmishes, and several attempts by the pope to forge a Christian alliance against Islam.

A large North African army crossed the Strait of Gibraltar in 1195 and inflicted a serious defeat on the Castilian armies at Alarcos. The following year Castile, now under siege by Navarre, León, and Al-Andalus, resisted and prevailed. Nevertheless, the Muslim peril and the good offices of Pope Celestine III led to the marriage of Alfonso IX of León and Alfonso VIII's daughter Berenguela. The respite was only temporary, for by 1204 Pope Innocent III annulled the marriage on grounds of consanguinity. Although León and Castile continued to engage in armed conflicts for the next few years, the massing of North African troops in Marrakech and the preaching of a crusade in Spain and in southern France made the Spanish kings set their differences aside. An international army reported by contemporaries to have among its numbers as many as 70,000 knights and foot soldiers from beyond the Pyrenees, and led by all the peninsular kings with the exception of Alfonso IX of León, defeated the Almohad army at Las Navas de Tolosa on 16 July 1212. The Muslim threat to Spain had now been erased forever. Ahead lay the task of piecemeal conquest and occupation of Al-Andalus.

The economic and social structure of early Castile was essentially the same as that of Asturias-León. A rural society, Castile was socially stratified in a manner not unlike that of the rest of western medieval Europe. At the top were the king, his family, and the *ricos hombres* (rich men, magnates), who often had blood ties to the royal family. By the late eleventh century these magnates began to consolidate their holdings into large landed estates; by the twelfth century their families became established *linajes* (lineages): Lara (Núñez de Lara), Haro, Castro, and others. Below them were people of noble status dependent on birth and material possessions. The terms that had been used in Asturias-León and early Castile to describe them (*infanzones, milites*) were by the mid twelfth century replaced by *fijos dalgo (hidalgos)*, meaning "son of" someone, and *caballeros*.

As in the earlier period, the nonnoble knights (*ca-*

balleros villanos) stood between noble and nonnoble elements. Enjoying the privileges of the nobility, the *caballeros villanos* played an increasingly important role in the affairs of Castile. Peasants both free and unfree, though on the whole with greater personal freedom than their northern counterparts, constituted the bulk of the population. Of special interest are the men of *behetría*, peasants who selected their lords either from a specific family (*de linaje a linaje*) or anyone (*de mar a mar,* from sea to sea), and worked the lord's lands for a specified time or for life. Apart from these traditional categories of medieval society, there were merchants, artisans, and other city dwellers. In the twelfth century they were still few in numbers, but their economic and political influence (many of them were nonnoble knights) made them a dynamic element in the transformation of Castilian society.

Two events highlight the social and economic development of Castile in this period: the expansion south and the influx of pilgrims from beyond the Pyrenees. The conquests of Alfonso VI, above all that of Toledo, brought to Castile lands settled with substantial Muslim and Jewish populations. Unlike the previous conquests, mostly the unoccupied lands between the Duero and the Tagus rivers, Toledo, the key to the region of New Castile, was rich and well populated. Then, as later, Castile suffered what Valdeón Baruque describes as "demographic poverty." Therefore, lands on the frontier were granted to the newly formed *concejos* (city councils) of Ávila, Segovia, Sepúlveda, and other cities. These municipalities had been settled under rather magnanimous royal privileges (*fueros*) and enjoyed during this period a good deal of freedom of action. Under strong kings they served the Crown well, and in times of crisis they were the strongest bulwark of the throne. The wealth of these city councils was in livestock, and the plains of New Castile offered an ideal grazing land. Ranching, which had shared the northern plains with cereal production, was now given the leading place.

The population of Castile had been fairly homogeneous until 1085; after that date it acquired large non-Christian groups. In spite of Alfonso VI's tolerant policies, the seeds of enmity and mistrust were sown in this period, to bear fruit in the persecution of religious minorities in later years.

The second important development was the influx of foreigners, mainly French pilgrims, on their way to Santiago. Pamplona, Logroño, Burgos, León, Sahagún, Astorga, Santiago itself, and other cities and towns along the road to Compostela (the French Road) gained important foreign mercantile and artisan communities, often settled in neighborhoods of their own and protected by special royal privileges and charters.

Cities in Castile developed along two different lines. The urban centers on the pilgrimage road were dominated by merchants, their economy oriented toward trade. With a few exceptions the citizens of towns elsewhere in Castile were engaged in ranching and agricultural activities. A word of caution is necessary, however, for even important commercial cities, such as Burgos, retained throughout the Middle Ages a strong rural interest and character.

Institutionally, the kings of Castile enjoyed rights and authority seldom seen in northern Europe during the twelfth century. As leaders of the struggle against Islam, they never relinquished their regal rights and seldom allowed exemptions, immunities, or rights of justice to become hereditary. Although feudal terminology was introduced into Castile from France, vassalitic ties similar to those of northern Europe were of no great importance in the governance of the kingdom.

The Castilian Crown had a fairly solid economic foundation for its political claims. In spite of uneven cycles of development and the obvious backwardness of the realm, the monarchs could count on the income of the *parias,* the tribute exacted from the kings of the *taifas.* In addition, by the middle of the twelfth century they began to collect taxes from their own subjects. When Alfonso IX of León called the representatives of the Leonese bourgeoisie to attend a meeting of his curia at León in 1188, and obtained their consent to a subsidy, the example was not lost on his Castilian cousin.

At the opening of the thirteenth century, the Castilian kings called urban representatives to the meeting of the cortes mainly for the purpose of obtaining bourgeois consent to extraordinary new taxes and subsidies, known in the thirteenth century as *servicios.* The Castilian kings also received income from the royal domain, although there was always a tendency to squander most of it in lavish donations. Among other taxes were the *martiniega* (collected at Martinmas) and the *marzadga* (paid in March), taxes that began as rent paid in the royal domain and ended as a tax collected throughout the realm by the late twelfth century. In addition to the usual tolls on roads, taxes on trade, regalia on vacant ecclesiastical benefices, mines, and salt wells, and the *fonsadera,* a payment in lieu of military service, the Castilian Crown collected *yantar,* a form of *gîte* or purveyance.

Obviously a good number of the feudal obligations commonly found in northern Europe had become public duties in twelfth-century Castile. Nevertheless, one should not have an exaggerated view of the powers enjoyed by the rulers of Castile. The use of the title "emperor" by Alfonso VI and Alfonso VII and the final establishment of the hereditary principle are given as an example of the consolidation of kingly power in Castile. Some historians, however, have serious doubts about the real extent of royal authority in Castile. It is true that the Castilian kings had in theory acquired powers greater than those of the French and English kings; yet, either because of the many minorities and short reigns, or for reasons still to be explored, their rule was questioned again and again by members of their own family, and magnates, and, to a lesser extent, the bourgeoisie and regional movements.

As elsewhere in western Europe, the twelfth century witnessed the foundations of royal bureaucracy. Even before the twelfth century the *curia regis* in Castile began to gain in importance. Composed of members of the royal family, great magnates, bishops, royal officials, and others chosen by the king, it functioned as the Crown's consultative body, as well as ratifying royal donations and policies. It also served as a judicial body hearing appeals from lower courts: its decisions were in theory binding even on the king. Men who until the eleventh century had functioned as private administrators of the royal domain now became royal officials with public duties. Besides the court offices created during the Asturian-Leonese period, such as *alférez* (royal standard-bearer) and *camarero* (chamberlain), the royal chancery came into being in the mid twelfth century. The office of chancellor was given to the archbishop of Compostela "perpetually" (it was eventually shared with the archbishop of Toledo), with a good number of scribes and royal notaries under his orders.

In the eleventh century the *merino* emerged as a public administrator and judicial officer assigned to a specific area or region (later called the *merindad*). This position was not very different from that of bailli in thirteenth-century France. Below the *merinos* were lesser officials who fulfilled varied administrative, financial, and judicial duties. All these developments seem to indicate a sophisticated governmental machinery, yet one must also acknowledge an absence of royal archives and the presence of puzzling and awkward inefficiencies.

For the Castilian church the period marked its full entrance into the Western church. Left behind and forgotten was the Mozarabic rite. Here, as elsewhere, there were troubled relations between spiritual and temporal powers. On the issues of papal authority and regalian rights, Gregory VII and his successors perhaps did not have an easier time in Castile and Spain as a whole than they might have had in other Christian kingdoms. One can point to the recovery of Toledo with its ancient tradition, the lavish gifts and privileges bestowed by the Castilian kings on the church, the importance of the cult of St. James, the constitution of new or the restitution of old sees, and the religious aspects of the Reconquest. Further, an uncritical historian would point out that Cluniac and, by the twelfth century, Cistercian monasteries rose throughout the land. Yet, the kings of Castile also extorted from the church all the money they could and sought to advance their own political and secular interests regardless of whether they were in conflict with their professed religiosity. Moreover, the papacy had a very hard time maintaining the discipline and good behavior of the Castilian church.

Culturally, Castile, far from the centers of culture around Paris, Chartres, and Bologna, did not fully partake in the twelfth-century revival of learning. Nevertheless, Christian Castile began to emerge from a long period of artistic and literary mediocrity. Architecturally, Cluny and Romanesque ruled triumphantly along the road to Compostela. The myriad exquisite Romanesque churches and cloisters, such as those of San Domingo de Silos, Las Huelgas, Santillana del Mar, and others, pale before the magnificent accomplishment of the cathedral of St. James at Compostela and the sculptures of the Porch of Glory, perhaps the high point of Romanesque sculpture. By the late twelfth and early thirteenth centuries, the Gothic style began to appear in Castile and to challenge the Romanesque, but the great Gothic cathedrals of León and Burgos were not built until later.

Literature is treated elsewhere, and so only a short mention will suffice here. Indeed, no literary work compares with the actual formation of the language, and the language of Castile found its best expression in the epic poem *Cantar de mío Cid* (1207). Last but not least, Castile was a meeting place for three cultures: Latin, Arabic, and Jewish. The translation of many important classical works, carried out at Toledo and other Spanish cities such as Barcelona, played an important role in the scientific and philosophical achievements of the thirteenth and early fourteenth centuries.

1212–1350

The thirteenth century, which had opened with the great hopes generated by the victory at Las Navas de Tolosa, ended with Castile in the midst of serious economic, social, and political crises. In 1214 Alfonso VIII died, leaving as his heir a minor child, Henry I (1214–1217). As had been the case so many times before, the minority of the king brought aristocratic unrest. Berenguela, the king's older sister, had been named regent but could not keep control of the realm. Troubled by rebellious magnates and by the ambitions of her former husband, Alfonso IX of León, Berenguela faced an uncertain future until the accidental death of Henry opened the throne for herself—and, better yet, for her son Ferdinand.

After the queen renounced her rights to the crown in his favor, Ferdinand III (1217–1252), born of the ill-fated union of Berenguela and Alfonso IX, was acclaimed king of Castile. The new king had to deal with an invasion of his lands by the Leonese and with the long-standing aristocratic resistance. After losing a few strongholds and lands on his western frontier to his father, he sued for peace in 1218. The next six years were dedicated to the reorganization of the kingdom and to the restoration of peace. Meanwhile, Alfonso IX undertook highly successful campaigns against Cáceres (1227) and Mérida (1230), adding to his kingdom a great deal of territory in Estremadura. In this task he received the indispensable support of the military orders. In 1230, however, Alfonso IX died, leaving no clear instructions on the settlement of his inheritance, although he seemed to favor his two daughters over his only son. Ferdinand hurried to León, where through the good offices of his mother and stepmother the issue was resolved in his favor. His two sisters received large seignorial rights in Galicia, and in return recognized him as king of León. Thus, in 1230 the kingdoms of Galicia, Asturias, León, Castile, and Toledo were united under one rule, never to be divided again.

His star on the rise, Ferdinand was now free to reap the benefits of Las Navas de Tolosa. From 1230 on, one Muslim fortress after another fell or surrendered to the Christians, the highlights of the period being the taking of Córdoba, the old capital of the Umayyads, in 1236, of Murcia in 1243, of Jaén in 1246, and of Seville in 1248. A pious and capable ruler, Ferdinand died (1252) before he could deal with the problems created by his swift conquests.

The legacy of Ferdinand passed undivided to his firstborn, Alfonso X (1252–1284). This breach in the long tradition of assigning separate kingdoms to the members of the royal brood was not well received by some of the princes and by the magnates, for whom division and war meant profit. Nor did Alfonso X, also known as the Wise, show any signs of possessing political wisdom. His large grants of land in the newly conquered territories to the great magnates (ricos hombres), to the cathedral chapters, and to important monasteries of Castile indicate his desire to obtain their support or at least neutralize them in his struggle against his brother Henry.

Alfonso X faced almost insurmountable social, economic, and political crises. Some of these problems were of his own making, and others he inherited from his father. Alfonso's reign was, with the exception of his patronage of letters and his legal program, which was not accepted until a century later, a failure. After minor initial victories in the south, most of his plans collapsed. His attempts to gain political influence and lands in Navarre and Gascony came to naught. In Al-Andalus he had to deal with a serious revolt by the Mudejars (Muslims living under Christian rule) early in 1264. Although he quelled the rebellion, the subsequent expulsion of the Muslims from Christian lands had drastic consequences for the economic development of Castile.

In 1257 Alfonso was one of two men (the other was Richard of Cornwall) elected emperor of the Holy Roman Empire, a title he coveted and to which he thought he had rights through his mother, Beatrice of Swabia. For more than twenty years he pursued this chimera at great financial expense. Partly because of this, partly because of Alfonso's legal system, and partly because of the intrigues of his brother Philip, the Castilian high nobility rose in arms against the king. At Burgos in 1272, Alfonso submitted to most of the demands of the magnates. Even so, he could not prevent Philip and a number of noblemen from placing themselves at the service of the king of Granada.

Raids by Muslims and rebellious nobles in the south in the mid 1270's were further complicated by the death in 1275 of Alfonso X's heir, Ferdinand de la Cerda. When the king tried to assert the rights to the throne of his grandson Alfonso, he was opposed

by his second born, Sancho. The last years of his reign were bitter ones, spent in open conflict with Sancho. Alfonso was even forced to seek the support of the Muslims and the security of their lands. One of his wills, written in 1283, a few months before his death, reveals the anger and sadness of his later life. Alfonso willed his kingdom to his grandson and, in his absence, to the king of France. His son Sancho he cursed for all eternity.

Cursed indeed was the reign of Sancho IV (1284–1295). He came to the throne in 1284, although for all practical purposes he had been exercising regal powers in the north for a few years. His marriage to his cousin, the able and energetic María de Molina, was within the forbidden degrees of consanguinity. The reluctance of the pope to accept their union cast a shadow on the legitimacy of his line. Furthermore, during the early years of his reign, Sancho IV was under the influence and control of Lope Díaz de Haro, lord of Vizcaya, who controlled the military and financial life of Castile.

The subsequent revolt of the Castilian nobility, which now saw the spoils of the kingdom monopolized by the Haro family, and the sensible advice that Sancho received from the king of Portugal, led to the assassination of Lope Díaz. Conspiracies and revolts followed one after another, while France and Aragon used the claims of the children of Ferdinand de la Cerda for their own political ends. Except for some victories over the Muslims, especially the taking of Tarifa in 1292, Sancho had little to show but a realm divided by internal conflict and the nobility of Castile often allied to Granada against their own king.

When Sancho died in 1295, the future looked even more ominous. The heir to the crown, Ferdinand IV (1295–1312), was a minor, and Castile again sank into anarchy. The great magnate families fought each other for the regency. Several claimants sought the throne. Armies from Aragon and Portugal entered Castilian territory with the ultimate purpose of setting the son of Ferdinand de la Cerda over a dismembered kingdom. That the realm survived undivided was due to the energy and determination of the queen mother, María de Molina, who rallied the urban centers and their municipal militias to the cause of her son. The hermandades, leagues of towns, became the protectors of the boy king. Even so, Ferdinand IV could claim his throne in 1301 only after major concessions to his enemies. His troubled reign came to an end in 1312, leaving yet another child, Alfonso XI (1312–1350), just over a year old.

Thirteen more years of anarchy followed. Each noble exercised power on his own. Again the old queen mother stepped into the breach, but this time her valiant efforts were barely enough to check the rapacity of the Castilian nobility and the violent assault upon every institution of the kingdom.

This struggle lasted until Alfonso XI was declared of age in 1325. A remarkable king, one of the few truly competent rulers that Castile ever had, his reign has been ignored by historians. With determination and intelligence, the adolescent king tamed the nobility. The Infante Don Juan Manuel, chief troublemaker during Alfonso's minority, was forced to submit to the king's will; Alfonso de la Cerda relinquished his claims to the throne and paid homage to Alfonso. With an iron hand the king intervened in the affairs of the Castilian and Leonese cities and established, as early as 1345, royal control over their administration and finances. At the cortes of Alcalá de Henares in 1348, he carried out a vast and comprehensive legal reform, the *Ordenamiento de Alcalá*, which made Alfonso X's *Siete partidas* the law of the land. In the south Alfonso XI gained a major victory at Salado in 1340, captured Algeciras in 1344, and laid siege to Gibraltar in 1350. During the siege he died of the plague, the only European king to do so. His death came far too soon, with his work unfinished. He had brought peace to the land and gathered the fragments of royal authority into his hands, but his devotion to his mistress, Leonor de Guzmán, and to his five bastard children, the Trastámaras, eventually brought sorrow to the kingdom.

Ferdinand III's conquest of Córdoba in 1236 and, above all, of Seville in 1248 transformed the structure of Castilian society. With the settlement of Christians in the region of the Guadalquivir, there were no immediate technological gains in the exploitation of the land, nor was there an increase in the production of food. On the contrary, the conquest and the rebellion of the Mudejars in 1263, and their subsequent expulsion from the land, disrupted the normal pattern of irrigation, cultivation, and harvest. The economic crisis of mid-thirteenth-century Castile, which began soon after the conquest of Seville, is not well understood or studied. Yet even for contemporaries the signs were quite clear. Galloping inflation; unsuccessful efforts by Alfonso X in 1252, 1258, and 1268 to deal with inflation through price controls; sumptuary laws; petitions for remission of taxes by impoverished municipalities; demographic dislocations; the rise of anti-Semitic legislation (most of it economic in nature); famines; lawlessness in the countryside; civil war; and debasement of the coinage were some of the evils that plagued Castilian society.

Inflation, resulting from the sudden availability of new wealth from the conquest and food scarcity due to the collapse of agriculture, was a major problem until the mid fourteenth century. Although other parts of western Europe suffered only a mild inflationary rise until the late thirteenth century, in Castile prices began to rise at a fast rate as early as the 1250's. Iron, a vital export commodity, and cloth, the main import, experienced the most dramatic inflation, but less expensive cloth and other goods also increased rapidly in price. The fourteenth century did not bring any improvements. Because of the inflationary pressure, the kings of Castile had to deal with new political realities within the framework of almost impossible economic conditions.

The underdevelopment of medieval Castile should be examined briefly. As early as the twelfth century the kingdoms of Castile and León exported raw materials and imported finished goods. Fine cloth from Flanders accounted for a staggering cash outflow, and imports were not limited to luxury items but included a whole range of basic manufactured goods. Castile's main exports were iron, wool, hides and livestock (especially horses, when not banned by royal decree), grain, cordovan, wine, cumin, and almonds.

On another level, Castile almost doubled its territory as a result of the conquest of Seville without any significant increase in its population, because of the expulsion of the Moors from the cities, and eventually from the land, after 1263. What took place was a redistribution of the population of Castile. Attracted by the new lands and by the booty—houses, lands, and servants—that Ferdinand III and, above all, Alfonso X distributed to the conquering armies, a considerable number of people migrated from the northern plains to Andalusia.

Although the migration included persons from all levels of society, the magnates, the military orders, and the church received most of the newly gained territories. With them came many field hands attracted by the higher wages, the climate, and the expansion of the transhumance to the grazing lands of the south. The cereal-producing areas of the north were partially abandoned and production decreased, causing food shortages and even famines. The south was not oriented toward cereal production, but toward a wine, olive, and livestock economy. Together with the climatic changes of the early fourteenth century and the growth of wool exports and the *mesta,* the decline of northern agriculture dealt a death blow to the traditional economy of northern Castile.

An additional problem was the change in the structure of land tenure. Although large estates had been formed in northern Castile long before 1248, a good number of small, free peasants retained ownership of their lands. These independent farmers had played an important role in the Reconquest and in the development of Castilian society. The conquest of Seville marked the end of this way of life for many of them. Moreover, when they sold their lands in the north, they did not take their tenure system of free land with them.

Land in Andalusia was concentrated in the hands of a few *ricos hombres,* the military orders, and religious corporations. Moreover, Old Castile did not escape the new pattern of land tenure. The late thirteenth and early fourteenth centuries saw the formation of large estates in the north. This benefited not only the magnates but also the urban oligarchical families who acquired substantial rural estates. As a result of the acquisition of these rich new lands, there was a dramatic increase in the wealth of the magnates, of the military orders, which were controlled by magnates, and of some religious corporations, without a parallel increase of the Crown's income. This brought about a shift in the relationship between the king and the nobility.

Moreover, as a result of the conquests of Córdoba and Seville, the tribute money paid to Castile by the kings of Andalusia (the *parias*) was drastically reduced. Alfonso X's income from the tribute decreased by 58 percent from that of his father, most of the lost income finding its way to the coffers of the *ricos hombres.* The new wealth of the magnates was not used solely to the detriment of the Crown, but increased wealth could, and did, mean augmented political power. Significantly, this shift of wealth occurred at a time when Alfonso X was developing his ambitious but unsuccessful program of centralization and royal control.

The history of the century after the conquest of Seville turns, therefore, around this conflict between the Crown and the high nobility, with the nonnoble urban knights (*caballeros villanos*) as the third angle of the political triangle. Pressed by the new influence of the magnates, Alfonso took two key actions: sumptuary laws against the high nobility and the granting of tax exemption to the nonnoble knights.

In 1252 and 1258 the king imposed strict sumptuary regulations that were directed exclusively against the aristocracy. There were no attempts to enforce austerity on the kingdom as a whole; rather, the aim of Alfonso's legislation was to restrict the nobility. Other measures were needed, however, to balance their political power. In 1255 and 1256 Alfonso X granted new privileges to the nonnoble knights of most of the Castilian and Leonese cities, exempting from most taxes those citizens who owned houses within the city walls, and who also had horses fit for warfare and arms.

These and other privileges made the royal grants a turning point in the political, economic, and social history of Castile. In less than fifty years the nonnoble knights in most Castilian cities monopolized municipal offices, bought most of the land around the cities, and gained control, as they did in Burgos and Ávila, of the most important ecclesiastical benefices. In return the king hoped for, and often received, their military support against the magnates and access to the cities' fiscal resources. Moreover, as the nonnoble knights gained control of their respective cities, they came into conflict with those below them on the social scale. Pressured from below by the disfranchised petite bourgeoisie, the nonnoble knights welcomed royal interference in the affairs of the cities and, by the 1340's, the takeover of municipal administration by royal officials (the *regimiento*). For a brief period royal control of the urban centers became a reality, then the disorders of the late fourteenth century weakened royal control anew.

1350–1474

Alfonso XI's death at Gibraltar in 1350 opened the way for his son Pedro I (1350–1369), also known as the Cruel or the Just, depending on which side one chooses to believe. Alfonso, however, had given to his illegitimate children by Leonor de Guzmán such privileges and stations as to cast a permanent shadow on Pedro's authority. Henry, the firstborn and leader of the Trastámaras, was count of Trastámara and had extensive landholdings; his brother Frederick was granted the mastership of the Order of Santiago, the foremost military order in Castile. The others received lesser but nevertheless substantial grants. Pedro's reign has been seen either as one of excesses leading to his overthrow, or as one in which he paid with his life for trying to continue the policies initiated by his father. In all fairness, the enmity of his half brothers poisoned his rule. Moreover, he began his reign with Castile desolated by the plague and by a severe economic and social crisis.

Pedro I made efforts to solve some of these problems at an important meeting of the cortes in Valladolid in 1351. His economic and political program—to destroy the power of the high nobility, to make the king supreme in Castile, to make Castile supreme in Spain—was carried out with the support of the newly university-trained bourgeoisie and the Jews. The magnates, led by Juan Alfonso de Albuquerque, took a dim view of this attack against their power, and they joined the Trastámaras in opposition to the king. The bastards had ample reason to oppose Pedro. Their mother had been executed by Alfonso XI's legitimate wife, Mary of Portugal, in revenge for years of humiliation and solitude. Moreover, Pedro's behavior toward his wife, Blanche of Bourbon, whom he had abandoned for his mistress, María de Padilla, and subsequently imprisoned, led to an armed revolt in 1354.

Pedro's victory in 1356 and Henry's exile to Aragon were followed by war between Castile and Aragon and by the king's persecution and execution of his enemies. Those murdered included several of his half brothers and his wife. After years of sporadic fighting, a long civil war broke out. Henry and his ally, the king of Aragon, sought the alliance and support of Charles V of France. They also hired Bertrand du Guesclin and his mercenary companies. Pedro answered by calling for English aid. Edward of Wales, the Black Prince, entered Spain and, joining with Pedro, defeated their enemies at Nájera in 1367. Nevertheless, when the Castilian king could not fulfill his promises to the English, he was left alone, an easy target for the rebellious nobility and the French. Henry and Du Guesclin enticed Pedro to their camp at Montiel, where on 23 March 1369 Pedro was murdered by Henry.

The new king, Henry II (1369-1379), opened his reign under attack by Pedro's supporters and by a coalition of Portugal, Navarre, Aragon, and Granada. Moreover, to a large extent he owed the throne to the aid received from the nobility, and now the time to pay his debts had come. The king's huge grants to the aristocracy weakened the financial foundations of the realm and led to the formation of a powerful and extremely wealthy noble oligarchy. From this new nobility, as opposed to the old families of the Laras, Haros, and Castros, came most of the great lineages of the next three centuries. Henry, partially

through his own abilities, partially through the help of the French, survived the attacks of his external and internal enemies. In 1371 a new threat loomed on the horizon when John of Gaunt claimed the Castilian throne through his wife, Constance, Pedro I's eldest daughter. A series of Castilian victories in the English Channel, capped by that of La Rochelle in 1372, put these claims to rest for a while; they also indicated the remarkable expansion of Castile's naval power. On other fronts, marriage alliances with both Navarre and Aragon opened the possibility for peace and were the foundations of the eventual unity of Spain.

Henry's death in 1379 brought his son, John I (1379-1390), to the throne. The new king made serious efforts to check the excesses of the nobility and to centralize royal authority. His reforms of the financial and administrative bodies—the Royal Council, and audiencia, and the *hermandades*—and the prominence of the cortes were worthy accomplishments but were obscured by his failure in Portugal. At the death of Ferdinand I of Portugal (1383), John I claimed the crown through his wife, Beatriz of Portugal, but his ambitions were thwarted by the resistance of the Portuguese and their election of a new king, John of Avis. John of Gaunt's landing in Galicia and his taking of Compostela and Orense met with the solid opposition of the Castilians and led, in 1389, to a final settlement of this long-standing irritation by the projected engagement of John of Gaunt's daughter, Catherine, and Henry, the eleven-year-old heir to the throne.

A year later John I died, leaving yet another minor to inherit the crown and yet another period of anarchy for the kingdom. While the cortes and the magnates struggled for control of the regency and the nobles fought among themselves, in 1391 the social tensions and the religious and racial animosity exploded in massacres that swept Castile and all Spain. Thousands of Jews were murdered and many thousands more converted. This led eventually to the *converso* problem, which plagued Spain for centuries.

Henry III (1390-1406) reached his majority in 1393. Although handicapped by ill health, he achieved some noticeable gains. Castile began its expansion in the Atlantic with the conquest of the Canary Islands early in the fifteenth century, and the high nobility was not more troublesome during this period than had been their custom. Henry III died in 1406, having had barely enough time to carry out any of his programs. As usual, his heir was a minor, his two-year-old son, John II (1406–1454).

In the long reign of John II power was always held by people other than the king. Unlike so many previous minorities, there were no disturbances. The dual regency of Catherine of Lancaster and Ferdinand, duke of Peñafiel and brother of the late king, kept peace throughout the realm. Ferdinand, a forceful and capable statesman, prevented the nobility from making any gains. At the same time he won important victories against the kingdom of Granada, the most important that of Antequera (1410), from which he took the name Ferdinand of Antequera.

In the same year the Crown of Aragon became vacant, and after lengthy negotiations Ferdinand de Antequera was elected king of Aragon, Valencia, Catalonia, and the Mediterranean possessions of Aragon. Thus, by 1412 members of the Trastámara family ruled over the main peninsular kingdoms. Ferdinand did not lose interest in Castilian affairs, and he made sure that his children would hold unassailable powers in Castile. Two of them, Henry and Sancho, became masters of the military orders of Santiago and of Alcántara. Another, John, became duke of Peñafiel, and Alfonso eventually inherited the Aragonese crown.

After 1419 John II fell progressively under the influence of Álvaro de Luna, a grandnephew of Pope Benedict XIII and an enigmatic figure, who freed the king from his bondage to the aristocratic oligarchy. Moved certainly by personal ambition, and perhaps by the desire to serve his country, Álvaro de Luna fought for more than two decades against the nobility, the Moors of Granada, Aragon and the rebellious children of Ferdinand, and anyone who stood in the way of a centralized and strong monarchy. Although he strengthened the royal institution, Álvaro kept the king under his control. Exiled twice, he returned to the court, always with greater power, until a coalition of the high nobility and John's second queen, Isabel of Portugal, led to his execution in 1453. The king, unable to live without his master, died the following year.

The new king, Henry IV (1454–1474), a complex and tragic figure, was vilified by the supporters of his half sister Isabella, and dominated from early youth by a succession of favorites, especially the greedy John Pacheco, marquess of Villena. During the first part of his reign there is good evidence of his desire for reform, indicated by the judicious policies carried out by either the king or his advisers. Nevertheless, his war policies against Granada, a war of attrition

rather than the frontal attack desired by the aristocracy, and Henry's dependence on *conversos* and obscure nobles, led to a revolt of the magnates in 1464 and, for all practical purposes, the decline of royal influence. Henry was forced to recognize his brother Alfonso as heir to the throne over his own daughter Juana (allegedly the illegitimate daughter of Henry's favorite, Beltrán de la Cueva). When he reversed this decision, a meeting of the nobility deposed him in 1465.

After Alfonso's death in 1467, the magnates, left now without a candidate, turned to Henry's half sister, Isabella. The princess, however, was of different mettle, and she disregarded the advances of the nobility. In the pact of Los Toros de Guisando (1468), Henry recognized Isabella as his successor as long as she was willing to accept his guidance on the selection of her husband. Their peaceful relations lasted for only a short time. The next year Isabella married Ferdinand of Aragon, prince and heir of the neighboring kingdom, without her brother's consent.

When Henry recognized his daughter Juana, known in history as le Beltraneja (daughter of Beltrán), as his heir (1470), civil war broke out. After Henry's death in 1474, Isabella, with the support of the Castilian bourgeoisie and of her husband, was proclaimed queen of Castile. She tamed the unruly nobility once and for all and turned them into faithful servants of the state. Anarchy and violence were suppressed, and under the Catholic kings Castile entered the modern age.

The political developments of Castile parallel those of France and England in the late Middle Ages. Despite the political upheaval and dynastic wars, the foundations for a stable, strong, and centralized monarchy were laid down in this period. For instance, a comprehensive system of taxation was established. Most important among the taxes collected were the *servicio,* an extraordinary tax voted by the cortes during times of need that, by the fifteenth century, had become quite regular, and the *montazgo,* or *servicio y montazgo,* a tax on the transhumance. The *mesta,* in fact, became the main source of royal income after 1350. In addition, the *alcabala,* a sales tax, was turned into a permanent and generalized tax under Henry II and John I.

The decline of the cortes, which represented only the small urban oligarchies, and the reduced number of cities sending representatives to their meetings (seventeen in the late fifteenth century, down from forty-nine at the end of the fourteenth) showed the desire of the late medieval Castilian kings to rule without legislative controls or to use the cortes for their own ends. The Trastámaras, especially John I, often used the *hermandades* to keep order within the realm and the *audiencia* (a tribunal of last appeal) as a way of controlling the judicial process.

This is not to say that the period after 1350 was one of unimpeded institutional development; on the contrary, it was an age of violent passions and aristocratic unrest. Nevertheless, in the midst of magnate ascendancy the instruments of royal centralization were slowly being created. In this respect the administrative, judicial, and financial structures begun in the twelfth century came to full bloom. After the union of Castile, León, Galicia, and the other minor kingdoms, each area had its own *merino mayor*, a high official in charge of enforcing the law within each particular kingdom and responsible only to the king. Each realm was divided into smaller jurisdictions (*merindades* in Old Castile, *adelantamientos* elsewhere) under a lesser *merino*. In such frontier regions as Murcia and Álava, an *adelantado mayor*, a special royal official with extensive powers, administered each particular area.

In addition, as early as the mid thirteenth century the Castilian kings began to interfere in municipal government. This intervention reached its high point under Alfonso XI and led to the direct royal control of municipal finances. Ferdinand and Isabella carried this policy to its logical conclusion—complete and absolute subservience of the urban centers—in the late fifteenth century.

Judicially, the kings since Ferdinand III had been claiming greater jurisdiction over civil and criminal cases. This is evident in Alfonso X's *ordenamiento* of 1274, which created the *alcaldes de corte*, or *tribunal de corte*, a body of judicial officials with exclusive jurisdiction over a wide range of crimes: homicide, rape, arson, treason, robbery on the open road. Although Alfonso X met magnate opposition, the *tribunal de corte* was reshaped and, under the name of *audiencia*, became an integral part of the administration of justice under the Trastámaras.

The financial branch of government lagged far behind the rest of the administration. At the head of finances in Castile there was, in the late thirteenth and early fourteenth centuries, the *mayordomo mayor*; under him was the *almojarife mayor*, in charge of administering the royal income. The *almojarife mayor*, who was often a Jew, usually farmed the taxes. The financial administration of the kingdom was reorganized and given form only in the late fourteenth and early fifteenth centuries, as

exemplified by the slow growth in importance of the *contadores mayores* (head accountants) under John I. In 1437, during John II's reign, an independent financial branch was finally formed.

There were many important social and economic transformations during the late Middle Ages. Henry II's large grants to his supporters in the late 1360's led to the formation of a new magnate class. Large estates, which had become the norm after the conquest of Seville, were extended even more. Leonor de Albuquerque, an important magnate, could walk from the frontier with Aragon to the frontier with Portugal without stepping out of her lands. The marquess of Villena ruled over 25,000 square kilometers—and he was a newcomer, no match for older, more prestigious families.

This change in patterns of landholding coincided with a radical change in the Castilian economy. After 1350 the transhumance and the export of wool to the northern European markets (Flanders) dominated the economic life of the realm. The number of livestock rose from roughly 1,500,000 head in the early fourteenth century to 3,500,000 in the mid fifteenth. Henry IV's feeble attempts to create a textile industry enjoyed little success. Export of raw materials, mainly wool, remained the only alternative. Although the price for this underdevelopment had to be paid much later, in the late Middle Ages it brought wealth to Castile, as evidenced by the great prosperity of the fairs at Medina del Campo and elsewhere.

Socially, to the emergence of a new high nobility we must add the appearance of a large *converso* group after 1391. In a few years these "new Christians" climbed to positions of authority within the cities' administration, the royal bureaucracy, and the intelligentsia. Through marriage some even entered noble circles. After the 1440's the rivalry, and often armed conflict, between old and new Christians became a disruptive and divisive issue in Castilian life, and continued for two centuries. One of the consequences was the statutes of *limpieza de sangre* (purity or cleanliness of blood), a main motif of later Spanish history. Finally, a century and a half of growing racial and religious hatred culminated with the expulsion of the Jews from Spain (1492).

The church did not escape the troubles of the age. Facing serious economic difficulties and growing spiritual corruption, excluded from participation in the meetings of the cortes, uncertain as to its loyalties during the Great Schism, the church declined until Isabella, as she did with almost everything else, reformed its financial structure and morals with heavy-handed measures.

Culturally, the period between 1212 and 1474 saw the high point of medieval art and the appearance and acceptance of Italian Renaissance forms. The thirteenth century inherited the lyrical troubadour poetry of the twelfth, complementing it with the learned poetry of the clergy—the so-called *mester de clerecía*. Moreover, Alfonso X's patronage of the arts and scholarship led to the spread of Roman law through the legal works he commissioned. Around the king Christian, Muslim, and Jewish scholars worked together in scientific and literary pursuits.

Throughout the fourteenth century Castilian literature continued to flourish, bringing forth a first-rate writer in Juan Ruiz, the archpriest of Hita. In the fifteenth century, courtly poetry, the *cancioneros* (compilations of lyrical poetry) of Baena, and Stuñiga, and a collection of epic-lyric poems known as the *romancero* show the vitality and creativity of Castile. The century also gave birth to two poets, both of magnate families, who rate among the best in Spain: Íñigo López de Mendoza, marquess of Santillana (1398–1458), and Jorge Manrique (1440–1479). The golden age of Spanish literature, a movement that was almost exclusively Castilian, was at the end of the Middle Ages only two generations away.

BIBLIOGRAPHY

For bibliographical guides, general histories, and secondary works on early Castile, see the bibliography for Asturias-León.

General works. Antonio Benavides, ed., *Memorias de Fernando IV de Castilla*, 2 vols. (1860); Américo Castro, *The Structure of Spanish History*, Edmund L. King, trans. (1954); and *La realidad histórica de España*, 2nd ed. (1962); C. E. Dufourcq and J. Gautier-Dalché, *Histoire économique et sociale de l'Espagne chrétienne au Moyen Age* (1976); José A. García de Cortázar, *La época medieval* (1973); Luis García de Valdeavellano, *Curso de historia de las instituciones españolas* (1968); Gabriel Jackson, *The Making of Medieval Spain* (1972); Angus MacKay, *Spain in the Middle Ages* (1977); José L. Martín, *La península en la edad media* (1976); Ramón Menéndez Pidal, ed., *Historia de España*, XIV, *España cristiana* (1966), and *Los Trastámaras de Castilla y Aragón en el siglo XV* (1964); Justo Pérez de Urbel, *El condado de Castilla. Los 300 años en que se hizo Castilla*, 2nd ed., 3 vols. (1969–1970); Claudio Sánchez Albornoz y Menduina, *Spain, a Historical Enigma*, 2 vols. (1975); Julio Valdeón Baruque, *El reino de Castilla en la edad media* (1968), and with others, *Feudalismo y consolidación de los pueblos hispanicos (siglos XI-*

XV) in Manuel Tuñon de Lara, ed., *Historia de España*, IV (1980); Jaime Vicens Vives, ed., *Historia de España y América social y económica*, 2nd. ed., II and III (1971).

Monographs and articles. José Amador de los Ríos, *Historia social, política, y religiosa de los judios de España y Portugal*, 3 vols. (1876); Elías Amézaga, *Enrique Quarto* (1974); Manuel Jorge Aragoneses, *Los movimientos y luchas sociales en la baja edad media* (1949); Yitzak Baer, *A History of the Jews in Christian Spain*, 2 vols. (1961); Antonio Ballesteros y Beretta, *Alfonso X. El sabio* (1963); Anselm G. Biggs, *Diego Gelmírez, First Archbishop of Compostela* (1949); Charles J. Bishko, "The Castilian as Plainsman: The Medieval Ranching Frontier in La Mancha and Extremadura," in A. R. Lewis and T. F. McGann, eds., *The New World Looks at Its History* (1963); Isidro de las Cagigas, *Los mozárabes*, 2 vols. (1947–1948); María del Carmen Carlé, "Mercaderes en Castilla, (1252–1512)," in *Cuadernos de historia de España*, **21–22** (1954); and *Del concejo medieval castellano-leonés* (1968); Francisco Fernández y González, *Estado social y político de los mudéjares de Castilla* (1866); Mercedes Gaibrois de Ballesteros, *Historia del reinado de Sancho IV de Castilla*, 3 vols. (1922–1928); A. García y Bellido *et al.*, *Resumen histórico del urbanismo en España*, 2nd ed. (1968); J. A. García de Cortázar, *El dominio del monasterio de San Millán de la Cogolla (siglos X al XIII): Introducción a la historia rural de Castilla altomedieval* (1969); Luis García de Valdeavellano, *Orígenes de la burguesía en la España medieval* (1969); Thomas F. Glick, *Islamic and Christian Spain in the Early Middle Ages* (1979); Julio González, *Alfonso IX*, 2 vols. (1944); *El reino de Castilla en la época de Alfonso VIII*, 3 vols. (1960); and *Repoblación de Castilla la Nueva*, 2 vols. (1975); César González Minguez, *Fernando IV de Castilla (1295–1312)* (1976); Hilda Grassotti, *Las instituciones feudo-vasalláticas en León y Castilla*, 2 vols. (1969); Jocelyn N. Hillgarth, *The Spanish Kingdoms, 1250–1516*, 2 vols. (1976–1978); Ramón Menéndez Pidal, *La España del Cid*, 7th ed., 2 vols. (1969); R. B. Merriman, "The Cortes of the Spanish Kingdoms in the Later Middle Ages," in *American Historical Review*, **16** (1911); Townsend Miller, *Henry IV of Castile* (1972); Emilio Mitre Fernández, *Evolución de la nobleza en Castilla bajo Enrique III (1396–1406)* (1968); Gonzalo Moya, *Don Pedro el Cruel* (1974); Joseph F. O'Callaghan, "The Cortes and Royal Taxation During the Reign of Alfonso X of Castile," in *Traditio*, **27** (1971); Bernard F. Reilly, *The Kingdom of León-Castilla under Queen Urraca 1109–1126* (1982); Teofilo F. Ruiz, "Expansion et changement: La conquête de Seville et la société castillane (1248–1350)," in *Annales: Économies, Sociétés, Civilisations*, **3** (1979); Cayetano J. Socarrás, *Alfonso X of Castile: A Study on Imperialistic Frustration* (1976); Luis Suárez Fernández, "Evolución histórica de las Hermandades castellanas," in *Cuadernos de historia de España*, **16** (1952); *El canciller Pedro López de Ayala y su tiempo, 1332–1407* (1962); *Nobleza y monarquía: Puntos de vista sobre la historia política castellana* *del siglo XV* (1975); and *Historia del reinado de Juan I de Castilla* (1977); Julio Valdeón Baruque, *Enrique II de Castilla* (1966); "Aspectos de la crisis castellana en la primera mitad del siglo XIV," in *Hispania,* **3** (1969); and *Los conflictos sociales en el reino de Castilla en los siglos XIV y XV,* 2nd ed. (1976); Luis Vázquez de Parga, José M. Lacarra, and Juan Uria Riu, *Las peregrinaciones a Santiago de Compostela,* 3 vols. (1948–1949).

TEOFILO F. RUIZ

[See also **Alfonso X; Almoravids; Asturias-León** (718–1037); **Cid, The, History and Legend of; Converso; Córdoba; Cortes; Fuero; Hermandades; Mesta; Navarre, Kingdom of; Santiago de Compostela; Seville; Siete Partidas; Spain, Christian-Muslim Relations; Toledo.**]

CASTILIAN LANGUAGE. As the result of cultural, linguistic, and political circumstances, Castile imposed its language and institutions on most of the rest of the Iberian Peninsula after the mid fifteenth century, to the detriment of indigenous languages and dialects such as Basque, Catalan, and Galician. Thus, Castilian and Spanish are often identified as one, leading to political and ideological controversy. Under present political conditions, however, Spain is returning to its medieval linguistic pluralism.

Not unlike other western European languages, Castilian emerged from the slow development of classical Latin into Romance, but in its genesis it received words, phonemes, and syntactic construction from many other sources. The thorough romanization of Spain in the classical period still allowed some backwater rural areas, and above all the northern parts of the Iberian Peninsula (the Basque and Cantabrian regions), to retain their local speech. A few words and suffixes, mostly of Celtic origin, passed into Latin and thereafter into Romance. Moreover, Spain's Latin was modified by contact with Hellenistic civilization during the republic and early empire, and later by the numerous Greek words introduced by Christianity. This Hellenic influence on the Latin of the Iberian Peninsula and other parts of the empire was reinforced in Spain by the Byzantine occupation of the Mediterranean coast during the sixth century. Greek words and phonemes eventually passed from the Latin of the early Middle Ages to the later Romance.

Classical Latin had, of course, already begun its decline in the twilight of the empire. In Spain, as elsewhere in the Roman world, sharp distinctions arose between the Latin of the educated few and that of the masses. In a very real sense vulgar Latin, with its changes in word order and addition of local terms, was already on its way to becoming the Romance of the late medieval period. In Spain this transition was further modified by the occupation of most of the Iberian Peninsula by the Visigoths in the fifth century and by the Muslims after 711. If the Germanic impact on the evolution of Castilian was relatively small and limited to a few toponyms—Burgos being the best example—and such words as *guerra* (war), the influence of Arabic was profound and lasting. After Latin, Arabic contributed the largest number of words to the Castilian language. Arabic terms dealing with warfare, agriculture, textiles, ceramics, science, medicine, and administration became an integral part of medieval Castilian. The marked superiority of Islamic culture and political power into the early twelfth century allowed Arabic to influence the formation of Castilian, and it was not until the sixteenth and seventeenth centuries that classical Castilian, under the influence of Renaissance models and because of the relegation of Arabic speakers to the lowest segments of Spanish society, began to substitute for Arabic terms others taken from the learned Latin of the age.

In the early Middle Ages, however, when Castilian was still unborn, neither Visigoths nor Muslims were able to conquer the northern regions of Iberia. There in the mountains, and slowly moving into the plain after the eighth century, new political units were in the making. These diverse regions of Christian Spain developed their own dialects (Galician-Portuguese, Leonese, Castilian, Navarrese-Aragonese, and, in the south, the Mozarabic dialects). Although most of these dialects could be traced back to the vulgar Latin of the late Visigothic period, only Castilian proved to be innovative, flexible, and forward-looking.

The unique dynamism of Castilian emerged from political and geographical factors. Castile was among the least romanized regions in Iberia, yet its geographical location opened it to outside influences in the tenth century and later. Moreover, the inhabitants of the region, largely Basques and Cantabrians, introduced new words and linguistic patterns not found elsewhere. The Castilian dialect forged rapidly ahead while other dialects of the Iberian Peninsula evolved slowly. Through the tenth and eleventh centuries archaisms were gradually eliminated and the language gained a great deal of uniformity. The

Latin documents of the period, from simple property transactions to the *fueros,* demonstrate the radical erosion of written Latin and the appearance of words belonging fully to the vernacular. In the eleventh century the stream of pilgrims from France traveling to Compostela or even settling in Castile influenced the development of Castilian and added a large number of French and Provençal words to the language.

Coinciding with the opening of the Iberian Peninsula to northern influences, the kingdom of Castile slowly gained, from the conquest of Toledo in 1085 to that of Seville in 1248, undisputed leadership in the peninsula, and with it Castilian won the day over Leonese and Mozarabic dialects. Furthermore, medieval Castilian made an impressive literary debut around the mid twelfth century with the epic *Cantar de mío Cid,* as well as contending with Galician for primacy in lyric poetry.

In the final evolution of medieval Castilian, the reign of Alfonso X (1252–1284) marked an important watershed on two levels. First, the scientific, legal, and historical works of Alfonso and his collaborators required both new words and the rationalization and standardization of the language. The Castilian of the area of Burgos, chosen by the king for his learned works, thus became the norm for the entire realm. Second, in a move initiated in the later years of Ferdinand III and officially formalized under Alfonso X, Castilian replaced Latin as the language of the royal government. Royal charters, municipal ordinances, and all the administrative documents of the kingdom of Castile from the mid thirteenth century on were in Castilian, a veritable revolution that went a long way to making Castilian the language of the Iberian Peninsula some centuries afterward.

Castilian prose and poetry both continued to evolve through the fourteenth and fifteenth centuries under the influence of Italian Renaissance models. By the sixteenth century the political hegemony of Castile in Spain and in the Western world, as well as the remarkable growth of its language, set the stage for the transition to classical Castilian, the literary instrument of the golden age. Not surprisingly, by the late sixteenth century and afterward non-Castilian writers almost always wrote in Castilian. Thus, Castilian became the language of Spain both by the superiority of its literature and by the force of arms.

BIBLIOGRAPHY

William James Entwistle, *The Spanish Language, Together with Portuguese, Catalan, and Basque* (1936); Rafael Lapesa, *Historia de la lengua española,* 3rd ed. (1955); Ramón Menéndez Pidal, *Orígenes del español: Estado lingüístico de la península ibérica hasta el siglo XI,* 3rd ed. (1950).

TEOFILO F. RUIZ

[See also **Alfonso X; Cantar de mío Cid; Castile; Spanish Language.**]

CASTLE OF PERSEVERANCE (*ca.* 1405–1425), the earliest, most extensive, and most representative English morality play. Introduced by elaborate banns, the play follows the life of Humanum Genus from infancy through death. Accompanied by Good and Bad Angels, Humanum Genus encounters the Seven Deadly Sins, servants of The World (Mundus), The Flesh (Caro), and The Devil (Belial). When Pen-

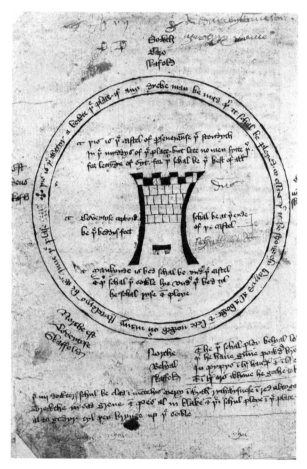

Stage plan suggesting a theater-in-the-round. From the Macro Manuscript, *ca.* 1440. THE FOLGER SHAKESPEARE LIBRARY

ance and Confession persuade him to enter the castle of the remedial virtues, the Sins attack. Covetousness entices Humanum Genus from the castle. At Death's approach he cries for mercy. His soul is finally rescued from hell after a debate by the Four Daughters of God. The source manuscript contains a uniquely informative "stage plan" suggesting a theater-in-the-round.

BIBLIOGRAPHY
Mark Eccles, ed., *The Macro Plays* (1969); David Bevington, ed., *The Macro Plays* (1972); Richard Southern, *The Medieval Theatre in the Round* (1957).

ALAN H. NELSON

[See also **Drama; Morality Play.**]

CASTLES AND FORTIFICATIONS. The art and techniques of fortification and the characteristics of castles and town walls are determined, like all constructions, by factors peculiar to individual sites (location, climate, topography, availability of raw materials) and by the social, economic, and cultural climate of the period (availability of craftsmen, types of tools, state of the building arts, social structure, and economic system). In addition, fortifications were influenced by military considerations: the methods of attack and defense in use during a specific period. To understand the combined influence of all these factors, we must first determine the functions of medieval castles and fortifications, and then consider the nature of the offensive military challenges that they faced.

The purpose of a fortification, whether a town or a castle, is to provide shelter in a commanding and centrally located position and to offer a superior fighting posture, even against a surrounding enemy. Elevation, provision for storing food, and water (if there were no wells in the castle), access for friendly forces (and denial of access to hostile ones), and protection against enemy missiles came to be the chief considerations in these most common of surviving medieval monuments.

Before the advent of modern artillery an elevated site was especially advantageous, as all missiles had to be propelled either by muscle power alone or by such power compounded through the use of wood, metal, or twisted ropes (bow, crossbow, catapult, ballista) or the use of weights and levers (mangonel, trebuchet). Situation on high ground increased the

acceleration and range of such projectiles, and hence their force of impact, while decreasing the effect of hostile engines working against the force of gravity. Therefore, medieval castles and fortifications were built as high as possible, and the building itself had to make up for the deficiencies of the site.

To describe medieval fortifications and their evolution, it is necessary to give an idea of the predecessors and prototypes of these structures. A good many of the earlier fortifications had been more or less preserved and were models for medieval builders.

The Romans had built both temporary and permanent fortifications. The temporary works were simple wooden walls and towers built on high ground, surrounded by ditches and sometimes by traps and other means designed to break up mass attacks. They also built permanent masonry forts to protect places of strategic interest, or walls for towers near the frontiers.

The Roman Empire, which enjoyed overwhelming military superiority over its neighbors, at first fortified only its frontiers, the *limes*. There are traces of these fortifications in several countries. The most spectacular is Hadrian's Wall, built between A.D. 125 and 133 across the north of England to protect the country against the raids of the Picts and the Scots. The seventy-three-mile wall, a minimum of 2.5 meters (8 feet) thick and 4 meters (12 feet) high, was built of stones and was protected by a deep ditch. There were little towers all along the wall and sixteen strong fortresses (*castella*).

Not until the end of the third century, when barbarian invasions of the empire began, was there an effort to fortify not only the frontier towns but also those of the interior. The walls built for this purpose were sometimes constructed with material taken from houses destroyed by enemy invasions or torn down to make room for the fortifications. They had rectangular towers and were protected by outlying forts.

The towers projected from the walls so that defenders could shoot from two sides at enemies who reached the foot of the wall. Since they were shooting down, the range and impact of their weapons were increased, and the towers were therefore spaced according to the minimum range of the defending weapons—the bow, sling, and javelin. By interrupting the walkway around the wall, the Roman towers made it possible to isolate a section where the enemy had gained a foothold.

In the early Middle Ages old Roman fortifications that had been repaired or reconstructed existed

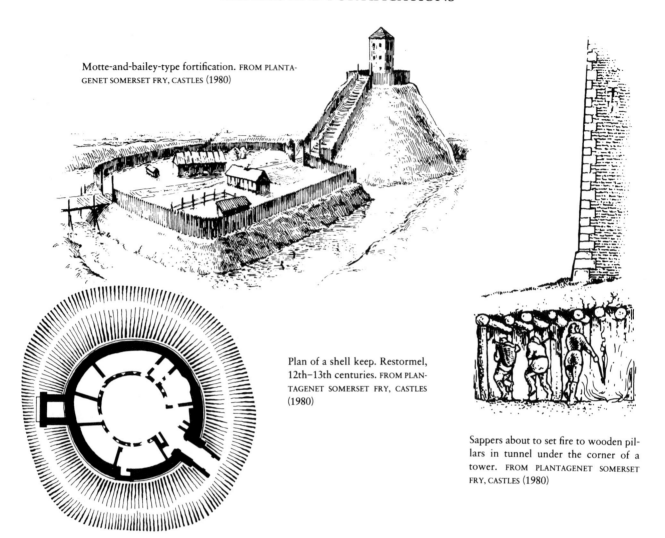

Motte-and-bailey-type fortification. FROM PLANTA-GENET SOMERSET FRY, CASTLES (1980)

Plan of a shell keep. Restormel, 12th–13th centuries. FROM PLANTAGENET SOMERSET FRY, CASTLES (1980)

Sappers about to set fire to wooden pillars in tunnel under the corner of a tower. FROM PLANTAGENET SOMERSET FRY, CASTLES (1980)

alongside constructions erected by the barbarian invaders according to their own customs. In flat country the earliest type of fortification was an earthen mound surrounded by a ditch. In order that the lower part of this kind of fortification might have a steep slope and not be too easily eroded by rain, its cohesion was increased by incorporating stones or pieces of wood and branches. This technique made it possible to have a steeper slope, a more resistant surface, and greater security against escalades. This mound, called a "motte," was usually topped by a rampart, called a "bail" or "bailey," most often of wood, where this material was available, and sometimes of hardened earth. Stone was used when the earthen mound had settled over a period of several years. Some of these castles were simply fortified houses, like the "shell keep" (French: *donjon-coquille*), a particular form common in Switzerland, northwestern France, the Netherlands, and Britain.

Shell keeps are circular or oval with beams resting on the stone surrounding wall and running to a central post, so that they can support a roof. The barbarians who invaded the Roman Empire built wooden works of these kinds. They were very like the forts built in the United States, Argentina, and Canada in the eighteenth and nineteenth centuries to defend settlers against Indian attacks.

The remains of mottes are especially numerous in France and England. Twelve French *départements* (of a total of ninety-four) show remains of more than thirty mottes each (with a maximum of seventy-seven in a single *département*). Some may date from the eighth century, but none is mentioned in documents before the eleventh century. The surrounding ditches were often 10 to 15 meters (33 to 49 feet) wide and sometimes equally deep.

The "motte and bailey" type of fortification was dominant from the end of the Empire to the twelfth

144

century. It gradually gave way to masonry constructions. Some wooden castles were large and impressive. They were erected on very large mounds, which supported several buildings, sometimes with more than one story, along with the surrounding enclosure. The wooden castle remained common throughout the early Middle Ages, when there was an abundance of timber. Often large and high, it required an enormous amount of wood. Suger of St. Denis, at the beginning of the twelfth century, reports that Milon, castellan of Chevreuse, built towers three stories high.

One advantage of a wooden castle was that it could be built rapidly. It has been calculated that a motte 30 meters (98 feet) in diameter and 12 meters (39 feet) high, surrounded by a ditch 3 to 4 meters (10 to 13 feet) deep, could be built in twenty days by a hundred men working only eight hours a day. As for the castle itself, a chronicle reports that the lord of Bourbourg, near Calais, in about 1199, built a complete fortress in a single night. It is true that he used the site of an old castle that still had its ditch and foundation, and that his carpenters had prefabricated most of the frame, but Arnold of Guînes, the adversary of the lord of Bourbourg, still had to mount a regular siege in order to take this hastily erected structure. And Louis VI had to take the castle of Hugh, lord of Le Puiset, three times in seven years (1111–1118) since the wooden castle was rebuilt each time it was destroyed by royal troops.

When William the Conqueror took England in 1066 he built many wooden castles on mottes to hold down the country as he took it over. Traces of these castles can still be seen, and some are portrayed in the Bayeux Tapestry. It is said that the castle of York was built in eight days after the Normans conquered the town.

Not until the end of the eleventh century did lords begin to build stone castles and fortifications in England and western Europe. This may be because the art of siege warfare was making progress. For example, Greek fire, an incendiary device that the West had acquired from Byzantium, began to be used frequently and wooden castles became especially vulnerable. Moreover, in France, during the twelfth and thirteenth centuries, there was a scarcity of timber, at least of timber that would make large, strong beams. Chronicles, legends, and also the sketches of the architect Villard de Honnecourt confirm this point.

There were several reasons for the shortage of wood. The growth of the population after the end of

the Norman, Muslim, and Hungarian raids in France and in Germany caused an increase in the demand for wood; and the accompanying reclamation of cultivated land that had grown back to forest also took its toll. The development of cities required constant supplies of timber for rebuilding in the wake of frequent fires, as well as for more ambitious building projects, like cathedrals. The Crusades also took their toll of timber needed to construct boats and war engines, and to build castles and churches in countries on the eastern borders of the Mediterranean, which were nearly deprived of wood. Finally, it was highly profitable to export wood to Muslim countries despite the war and the pope, who had expressly forbidden such commerce.

Even stone buildings required a great deal of wood for their construction. For example, it was necessary to cut down 3,944 oaks to build Windsor Castle in the fourteenth century. In this situation, one can understand why, after the Norman Conquest, kings of England hastened to appropriate most of the forests of their kingdom. They did so not only to ensure good hunting, and to drive out rebellious Saxons, but also to ensure the supply of materials essential for civil construction and military purposes.

Moreover, the techniques of building in stone were improving, thanks largely to advances in metallurgy. During the twelfth and thirteenth centuries the Crusades and the reconquest of much of Spain by Christians increased contacts with peoples of the Orient and stimulated arms making. A smith who could make better weapons could also make better tools. Pit saws were developed that could cut a few standard beams out of one large log instead of having to fell several smaller trees and square them approximately. In addition, the expansion of water mills made it possible to have saws that could cut stone more effectively and rapidly and with less waste than the old process of striking it with a chisel.

Thus more and more castles and town walls were built of stone. And as new and more powerful siege weapons appeared, walls had to be made higher and thicker and given foundations and shapes that made them more resistant to attack. The recommendations of Alexander of Neckham, in his treatise written at the end of the twelfth century, are pertinent:

If a castle is to be properly built, let it be surrounded with a double ditch; let its site be protected by nature, that the motte may rise from a footing on the native rock or the defect of nature be helped out by the benefit of art and the mass of the walls, built of mortar and stones, grow out or rise as a lofty work. Upon this let a bristling hedge be well set with squared pales or stakes, and thorns. Afterwards, see that the bailey is spacious; and let the wall have a foundation deep in the ground. Also let the lofty walls be buttressed with pillars placed outside and inside; and let the surface of the wall show a smoothness of mason's work as if trowelled. Let the crenellations stand in their due proportions; the brattices and turrets protect the summit of the tower; nor should hurdles be lacking, to carry stones for flinging down.

After enumerating the provisions that should be stored, Neckham adds: "Let there be also lances, catapults, bucklers, shields, arbalests, maces, and mangonels."

Despite improved building design, it became increasingly evident that the defense should not rely solely on perfecting passive resistance but should also try to mount effective counterattacks. This change in attitude affected the planning of fortifications. From the tenth- and eleventh-century emphasis on static defense a shift occurred in the thirteenth century to the more dynamic concept of the counteroffensive. Each new offensive technique (many of which derived from experience gained during the Crusades) led to further modifications in castle construction.

For example, by digging a trench, or sap, under the walls of a fortification, the attackers could cause the structure to collapse. The roof of the trench was supported by wooden pillars soaked in resin; when the sap was ready the wood was set on fire and the wall above, deprived of support, crumbled. Later, gunpowder was used in these mining operations. The defenders could counter these threats by digging countertrenches under the offensive saps, which would cause the latter to collapse.

These techniques made castles built on mottes almost useless. If a natural rock foundation could not be found, the walls had to be supported by massive blocks of masonry, sunk deep below the level of surrounding ditches that were, when possible, filled with water.

To repulse a frontal attack, the walls (whether of wood or stone) had slits, called crenels, through which the defenders could shoot while sheltered from enemy projectiles. These openings were at first merely empty spaces in the timber or masonry; later, holes were drilled in the stones to make the gap as small as possible. Moreover, because of the thickness of stone walls, niches had to be built on the inner side to allow each bowman a wide field of fire (up to sixty degrees). When a crossbow, which is held horizontally, was used, larger niches and slots were necessary.

Attackers tried to fill ditches and moats with earth, debris, or bundles of logs so that they could haul up wheeled towers provided with gangplanks or ladders to the walls. To repulse such attacks, the defense attached platforms, supported by beams attached to the wall, that projected from the ramparts. These platforms had openings through which projectiles, hot liquids, or incendiary pots could be dropped on the attackers, their machines, and the bundles of logs that they had used to fill up the moat.

These projecting platforms, called *houxds* in French, were at first temporary. Built of wood, they could be installed rapidly in case of a siege, since openings for them had already been built into the walls. Some of them during the twelfth century were built of permanent stone brackets, as at Coucy in 1140. Later they were all permanent and made of masonry, especially after the Crusades. The Christians had seen how effective such platforms were in the East, where because of the scarcity of wood, stone was used. When they were spaced out along a wall, these platforms were called *bretèches,* an old form of the adjective "British"; those that ran the full length of a wall were called machicolation (French: *machicoulis*). This word, which some have held to be of Italian origin, more likely comes from the name of the castle of Machecoul south of the river Loire, not far from Niort, which is precisely one of the towns where some of the first examples (twelfth century) of machicoulis can be found. It was not until the fourteenth century, however, that machicolation generally became part of a well-built castle, and the brackets that support the parapet and platform a prominent decorative element.

The walkways along the upper walls and platforms were sometimes protected by heavy, steeply sloping wooden roofs. But as such roofs might catch fire or be crushed by heavy projectiles the walkways were usually left uncovered. Sometimes, as at Coucy, there was a projecting cornice with a double slope, from which even very heavy projectiles would rebound and fall either behind the defenders or in the direction of the attackers.

The entrance doors to a fortress, which were also used for sorties against the enemy, were particularly vulnerable to attacks by the battering ram and its protective engine, the "cat," shielded by the skins of

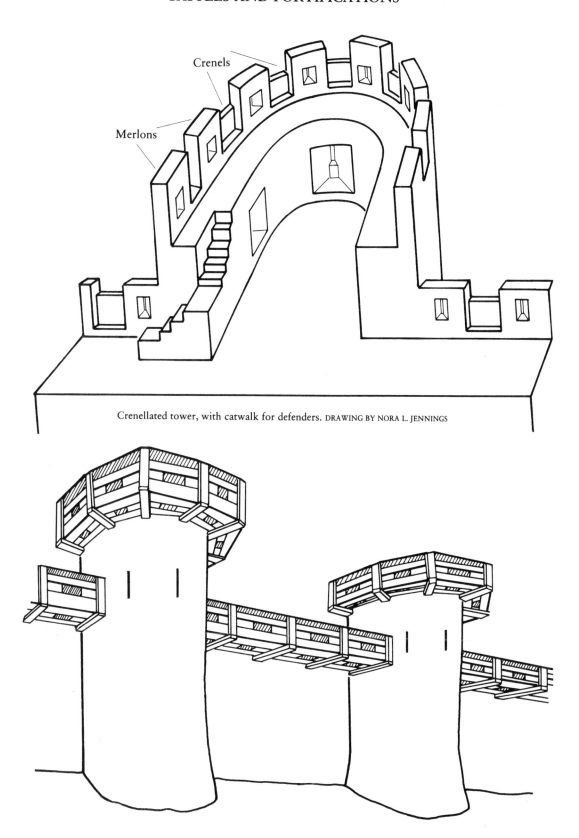

Crenels

Merlons

Crenellated tower, with catwalk for defenders. DRAWING BY NORA L. JENNINGS

Early machicolation: projecting wooden platforms. DRAWING BY NORA L. JENNINGS

freshly killed bulls. The heavy castle door was reinforced by an iron grill (portcullis) hanging from heavy chains with counterweights. To reach this door one had to cross over the moat on a drawbridge. To speed the raising of the drawbridge, there were chains at its far end that could be wound around a cylinder inside the entrance. When the drawbridge was fully raised, it came flat against the door. Sometimes the weight of the drawbridge was counterbalanced by that of the grill, which descended as the bridge was raised. A more elaborate system left the grill independent of the bridge: two bars running over an axle were attached by chains to each side of the head of the bridge and, on the other end, the bars were loaded by heavy weights, to counterbalance the weight of the bridge.

In some cases, to increase security, a narrow footbridge, balanced in the same way, by a single bar, led to a small postern near the main entrance. Thus the large bridge, which served for horsemen, carts, and troops, was seldom lowered.

The entrance, behind the gate, was often guarded by a second grill and sometimes by a second door. This made it easier to check on entrances and to avoid surprise attacks. A group of unwelcome visitors could thus be isolated and, if necessary, eliminated by the guards of the door. Sometimes, as at Pierrefonds, the far end of the main bridge rested on a high wooden ramp that could be destroyed in case of a siege, making it more difficult to reach the gate and batter it with a ram. Moreover, the entrance gates were usually flanked by towers with crenellations above, so that unwelcome approaches were hazardous. By the thirteenth century, the entrance way, flanked by its towers, was often a miniature castle itself that could resist attacks from within as well as without.

The parts of the parapet between two crenels were called merlons. To prevent the defenders from being hit sideways by the rebound of arrows or projectiles hurled by the attackers, the merlons were, during the fourteenth century, no longer built square but with oblique sides. The tops of the merlons were built with different shapes, sometimes only for decorative purposes. In England and in France they were generally square with a sloping top, but around the Mediterranean other shapes can be seen: rounded, pointed, topped by little pyramids, or split in two symmetric half-circles.

In the later Middle Ages, improved missile weapons such as the trebuchet (introduced in western Europe in 1147) and improved, rounded, aerodynamic

projectiles made it possible to hit almost the same spot repeatedly. The biggest models of such weapons could hurl missiles weighing close to 650 pounds. These continued violent blows broke down walls by dislocating the outer layer of hard stone and then the less resistant interior rubble. To resist such blows, builders during the thirteenth century reinforced the thickness of exposed walls to as much as 10 meters (33 feet) and generally stopped erecting rectangular towers with their vulnerable corner angles. Especially in northwest Europe they rounded off their buildings to make them more resistant to blows. They used circular, polygonal, almond, or spur-shaped forms to deflect the impact of the missiles. In other regions, such as southern and eastern France, Germany, Italy, and Muslim lands, the traditional rectangular towers were still being built. In regions of steep, rocky hillsides, castles could not easily be attacked by the heavy machines needed to hurl powerful projectiles. Rounded buildings being more difficult and more expensive to construct, the old rectangular form persisted in some of these regions since there was no great reason to change them.

The simplest stone castles were solitary, very solid towers. More elaborate castles comprised a large tower, called the keep, or dungeon (French: *donjon*; German: *Bergfried*), where the lord lived, and a fortified enclosure, where men-at-arms could camp and where food animals were sometimes kept and fed. In castles of the tenth and eleventh centuries the dungeon was the last line of defense if the surrounding walls were broken down. It was often detached from the rest of the fortifications.

Dungeons built at the end of the twelfth century by King Philip Augustus of France (who was attempting to conquer Normandy from Richard the Lion-hearted of England) were quite different from earlier constructions. They had thicker walls, several stories with stone ceilings, and connections with the outer walls. The dungeon was no longer the home of a feudal lord but the basic element of a purely military construction, occupied by a regular garrison and placed in strategic locations in the royal domain.

At the beginning of the thirteenth century in France the dungeons were always circular and from 25 to 40 meters (81 to 130 feet) in height (Coucy, at 54 meters or 176 feet, was exceptional). The walls, which were built with smooth surfaces and narrow joints, could be 4 to 5 meters (13 to 16 feet) thick (at Coucy 7.5 meters or 24.3 feet) and were strengthened at the base by embankments sloping outward. In France during the thirteenth century the dungeon

Battering ram with its protective engine, the cat. FROM PLANTAGENET SOMERSET FRY, CASTLES (1980)

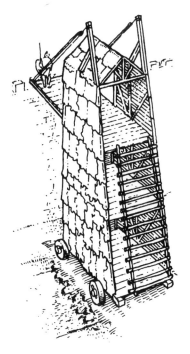

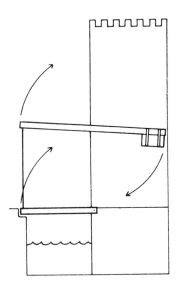

Siege tower. FROM PLANTAGENET SO-MERSET FRY, CASTLES (1980)

Early mechanism of a drawbridge and gate. FROM PLANTAGENET SOMER-SET FRY, CASTLES (1980)

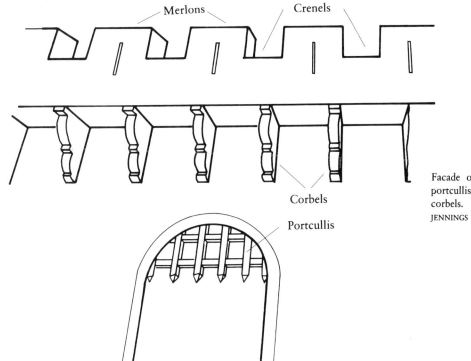

Merlons   Crenels

Corbels

Portcullis

Facade of a castle, showing the portcullis, crenels, merlons, and corbels. DRAWING BY NORA L. JENNINGS

149

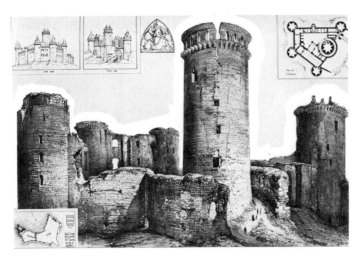

Donjon (dungeon) of Coucy Castle (at center). First half of 13th century. FROM DU SOMMERARD, LES ARTS AU MOYEN ÂGE (1838–1846)

gradually disappeared, becoming one of the towers of the encircling wall, sometimes larger than the others. At the same time, an open central court became predominant. Living quarters, administrative offices, and storerooms were placed against the surrounding outer wall. This open courtyard, 50 to 80 meters (163 to 260 feet) across (160 meters or 520 feet at Angers, only 30 to 40 meters or 98 to 130 feet in smaller castles) allowed the installation of missile weapons with indirect (curving) trajectories and also made it easier to move troops from one side of the castle to the other to meet an attack or to counter a breakthrough.

In the thirteenth century the towers of the surrounding wall could be as high as 30 meters (98 feet). They were usually spaced 15 to 25 meters (49 to 81 feet) apart with a straight section of wall between them; there were towers in each of the angles of the walls. The moats ranged from 12 to 20 meters (39 to 65 feet) wide and 8 to 10 meters (26 to 33 feet) deep and were sometimes lined with stone; some, but not all, were filled with water. The most elaborate castles had walls within walls, so that if the outer wall were broken the defenders could fall back on an inner wall.

While siege weapons were becoming more efficient and techniques of attack more sophisticated, armies (notably those of the kings of France and England and of other powerful large states) increased and became better trained. Faced by troops of professional and well-equipped soldiers, who were furnished with improved machines for throwing heavy or incendiary projectiles and assisted by

engineers and miners, the defenders had to revise their tactics. Since it was impossible to keep a permanent garrison large enough to defend the whole periphery of a castle, it became necessary to ensure maximum mobility for defenders so that they could reach threatened areas rapidly. To improve interior circulation, curtain walls connecting strongpoints had to be increased and covered galleries in the main walls had to be constructed. Moreover, the attackers' siege weapons had to be resisted, and to do this, space had to be made for batteries that could fire from inside the walls. The interior courtyard could be used for large machines, such as catapults and trebuchets. The towers could be used for lighter weapons, such as mangonels and perriers, which threw heavy darts and stones.

To keep this central area clear, all the service buildings had to be placed against the walls (which helped to reinforce them) or underground. Also, a besieged castle could be completely cut off from its supplies of food, munitions, and matériel for weapons. The defenders could not hope to hold out indefinitely unless some offensive action were taken against the besiegers. Alexander Neckham pointed out the problem:

> Should the castle be besieged, let not the defenders of our fortress be driven to surrender; let them be provided with corn and wheat, wine, hams, bacon, pickled meat, black puddings, sausages, puddings, pork, mutton, beef, lamb and various vegetables. There is need of an ever-springing well, and subtle posterne and underground ways through which help and succour may secretly be brought.

Against the besiegers, who usually had only provisional fortifications, surprise attacks could be successful. The besieged, therefore, had to be able to make sorties rapidly, as Joan of Arc did in 1429 to raise the siege of Orléans by capturing the enemy fort.

Ideas about entrances to towns and castles had to be modified. It was especially necessary to build drawbridges that could be rapidly raised. It was also important to have large open spaces behind the gates so that troops could be assembled there in secret for surprise attacks on the enemy outside.

From the thirteenth century, castles, especially those of kings and great lords, were no longer built only by local workmen and with local resources. As with the building of cathedrals, teams of specialists who were both architects and engineers went from place to place, especially in the royal domain, to di-

Campania Castle. Battipaglia, Italy, 1194–1197. ART RESOURCE

rect construction. As they became increasingly elaborate these strongholds required financial resources that only the greatest lords, and eventually the towns, could possess.

The growth in population, increased agricultural production, the cessation of hostile invasions in western Europe, and finally the Crusades had all combined with greatly increased trade to further the growth of towns. These towns enjoyed a certain autonomy, and in France their growth was favored by the king for strategic and political reasons.

Urban fortifications differed little in their general characteristics from those of castles. However, since the naturally steep elevations that were used as sites for castles were seldom available as town sites, urban fortifications depended more on the skill of the engineer and architect than on happy accidents of topography.

Just as the medieval art of fortification was reaching its zenith in the fourteenth century, gunpowder and the cannon appeared. Though progress was at first slow, within two hundred years the new technology, once fully developed, suddenly rendered the old-fashioned fortifications and medieval military architecture obsolete. This was one reason why so many medieval castles were preserved in their original state, especially in different parts of France and in Germany. But most of the old city walls in the main cities were demolished as they impeded the growth of the town. In smaller cities many have survived untouched such as Carcassonne (the most impressive of all); Aigues-Mortes, the port of embarcation for the Crusades; Avignon with the fortified

castle of the popes in the south of France; the enclosed city of Concarneau and St. Malo in Brittany; Nuremberg in Germany; the eleventh-century city walls of Avila in Spain; the island city of Dubrovnik in Yugoslavia; Suzdal in Russia with its nearby fortified monasteries; and other cities in Europe, North Africa, and the Middle East.

It took a long time for the new artillery to reach the level of precision and striking force obtained by the best machines of the old types. Joinville is the first to mention the use of gunpowder in the form of rockets, in his description of the battle of Al-Manṣūra (1250). But the idea of placing a charge of powder in a strong metal tube, open at one end to propel bullets, did not occur till the beginning of the fourteenth century. The choice of this technique meant that even until the middle of the twentieth century, the range and power of a cannon would depend directly on its size and weight.

Many problems would have to be solved before cannons would become reliable and really efficient. It took, therefore, two centuries for artillery to become the dominant arm. The first mention of an order for cannon and iron bullets comes fom Florence in 1326. The first bombards appeared during the Hundred Years War at Rouen in 1338 and at the Battle of Crécy in 1346. The campaigns of Bertrand du Guesclin at the end of the fourteenth century proved that walls strong enough to resist stone projectiles could not resist iron cannonballs. To deal with this problem, the first remedy was to thicken the walls. At Concressault (late fourteenth century) the walls were 12 and, in places, 15 meters (39 to 49 feet) thick;

Château de Pierrefonds. France, 1390–1400 (restored by Viollet-le-Duc in the 19th century). FROM SIR BANISTER FLETCHER'S A HISTORY OF ARCHITECTURE

at Ham, in the reign of Louis XI (*d.* 1483), they were 10 meters (33 feet) thick.

It soon became apparent that new types of fortification were necessary to resist firearms. Towers were then replaced by bastions, lower, wider, and covered with earth, usually with irregular or pointed exteriors instead of flat walls. Within the walls slits for archers were replaced by openings for cannons that could be moved to sweep a field of fire. Since cannonballs had a relatively long trajectory, flanking support was necessary; the foot of the walls could be defended only by enfilading fire parallel to the wall. These considerations led to a polygonal, star-shaped plan whereby each wall could be protected by its neighbor, and where slopes in front of ditches and bastions could make cannonballs lodge in great masses of earth.

The first example of this new military architecture, which marks the end of the Middle Ages, was the fortress of Salces, begun in 1497 on the border between France and Spain. With the advent of efficient cannons and gunpowder, military architecture had to advance beyond the Middle Ages.

At this time the castle lost its primarily military character and became simply a residence for the wealthy; but, even if useless in front of regular troops with artillery, it was still efficient against robbers, gangs of ruffians or deserters, and rebellious peasants, during the wars of religion and until the eighteenth century. Nevertheless, these castles were so strongly built that even during the seventeenth century, Richelieu, Louis XIV's prime minister, was compelled to pull down a great many of them in order to break once and for all the resistance of the lords against the king. But there were so many castles in France that it is still one of those countries where the greatest number of nearly untouched castles of the Middle Ages can be seen, besides the impressive remains of those which have been destroyed.

BIBLIOGRAPHY

Reginald Allen Brown, *English Castles,* rev. ed. (1962); Yves Barel, *La ville médiévale* (1975); André Chatelain, *Châteaux et guerriers de la France au Moyen Âge,* II (1961); T. K. Derry and M. G. Blakeway, *The Making of Early and Medieval Britain* (1968); Paul Deschamps, *Les châteaux des croisés en Terre-Sainte* (1936); François Gébelin, *Les châteaux en France* (1962); T. E. Lawrence, *Crusader Castles,* 2 vols. (1936); H. G. Leask, *Irish Castles and Castellated Houses* (1946): Jacques Levron, *Le château-fort et la vie au Moyen Âge* (1962); Charles Salch, J. Burnouf, and J. F. Fino, *Atlas des châteaux-forts en France* (1977);

Sidney Toy, *Castles: A Short History of Fortifications* (1939); Eugène Viollet-le-Duc, *Annals of a Fortress* (1875).

ROLAND BECHMANN

[See also **Bastide; Castellan; Catapults; Construction: Building Materials; Enguerrand VII of Coucy; Krak des Chevaliers; Machicolation; Urbanism; Warfare, Western European.**]

CASTRUM (Latin, "fortress"; in the plural [*castra*], "camp"), a Roman fortification, especially a military camp, following a regular rectangular, square, or trapezoidal plan and usually surrounded by a rampart and a wall with towers. Castra are of two main types. The quadrangular plan, used particularly for permanent forts (Ostia, Pyrgi), was divided into four roughly equal quadrants by two main streets, the north-south *cardo* and the east-west *decumanus,* leading to four major gates (Praetoria, Dextera, Sinistra, and Decumana). Headquarters (*praetoria*) were located near the center, and barracks occupied the four quadrants.

A second plan, usually rectangular, was laid out with two main streets parallel to the long sides of the castrum (Via Principalis, Via Quintana) intersected at a right angle by a wide central passage terminated by gates (Porta Praetoria, Porta Decumana) along which was the *praetorium.* Six lesser streets normally paralleled the *praetorium* road, and additional gates often led out from the Via Principalis and the Via Quintana. The regularity of the castrum plan throughout the Roman Empire allowed a soldier to feel immediately familiar with his surroundings.

In their regular layout, castra resemble some Roman towns and may have been influenced by civic architectural planning. Some provincial Greek plans (Selinus, Paestum) divided the terrain into quadrants, but, as emphasized by Polybius, the Greeks normally suited their camps to the topography and thereby eschewed regularity. Roman castra such as the one at Aosta appear fully developed at least from the time of Augustus and influenced many later town plans, especially in the provinces (Diocletian's palace complex at Split, in Yugoslavia, 300–306).

BIBLIOGRAPHY

W. R. Paton, *Polybius, the Histories,* III (1923), 328–367.

LESLIE BRUBAKER

[See also **Castles and Fortifications.**]

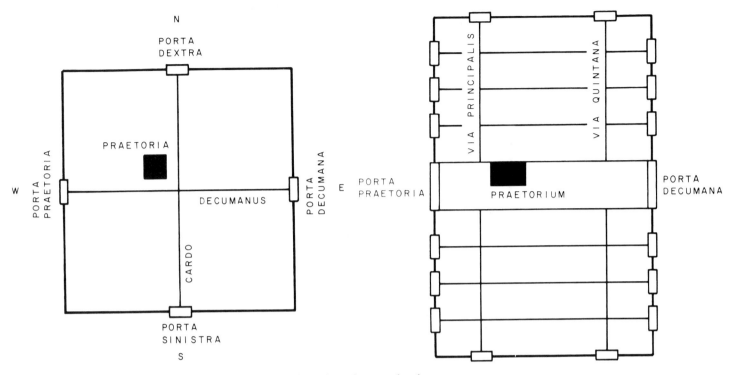

Two main types of Roman *castra:* quadrangular and rectangular plans. DRAWINGS BY NORA L. JENNINGS

CASUISTRY is a method of applying general principles of theology, law, or moral conduct to specific situations or cases *(casus).* The term is also used pejoratively to describe excessively subtle, sophistical, and intellectually dishonest approaches to moral questions. In both senses casuistry was prominent in medieval thought and literature on ethics.

Christian casuistry is as old as Christianity itself. Matthew 19:3–12, Mark 2:23–28, and Luke 6:1–11 and 20:20–40 show the use of casuistic methods in the Gospels. The Pauline Epistles also contain numerous examples of primitive Christian casuistry, derived from the methods of moral analysis practiced in the rabbinical schools.

The fathers of the early church were deeply concerned with formulating rules to enable Christians to distinguish between acceptable and unacceptable conduct. For example, St. Augustine's treatises on lying (*De mendacio* and *Contra mendacium*) discuss such questions as whether one can morally tell a lie as a joke, and whether it is permitted to use a lie as a figure of speech. Other patristic writers employed casuistry to deal with questions about the duties of Christians serving in the Roman army, the propriety of attending pagan plays, or witnessing pagan sacrifices.

During the early Middle Ages casuistic methods were applied especially to penance and confession. The penitential manuals written from the sixth century onward used casuistry to fix the gradations of sin and the corresponding penances assigned to penitents. The development of theology and canon law as academic disciplines from the twelfth century onward stimulated more systematic approaches to casuistry, not only in theoretical works used in university teaching but also in practical manuals addressed to the parish clergy. A landmark of the new genre of casuistry was the *Summa de casibus* of St. Raymond of Peñafort (written between 1224/1225 and 1226/1227; revised in 1236). The popularity and volume of casuistic writing increased markedly during the fourteenth and fifteenth centuries and, though criticized by Blaise Pascal, casuistry has remained a feature of Christian moral literature even in the twentieth century.

BIBLIOGRAPHY

For a general history of Christian penitential practice and casuistry see John T. McNeill, *A History of the Cure of Souls* (1951). On medieval casuistry and casuistic literature see Pierre Michaud-Quantin, *Sommes de casuistique et manuels de confession au moyen âge (XII–XVI siècles)*

(1962); Johannes Dietterle, "Die Summae confessorum (sive de casibus conscientiae) von ihren Anfängen an bis zu Silvester Prierias—(unter besonderer Berücksichtigung ihrer Bestimmungen über den Ablass)," in *Zeitschrift für Kirchengeschichte*, **24** (1903), **25** (1904), **26** (1905), **27** (1906), and **28** (1907); and Thomas N. Tentler, *Sin and Confession on the Eve of the Reformation* (1977).

JAMES A. BRUNDAGE

[See also **Confession; Law, Canon; Penance and Penitentials; Raymond of Peñafort.**]

CATACOMBS are subterranean cemeteries, the most famous of which are the early Christian burial complexes hewn into the soft tuffaceous stone around Rome.

HISTORICAL DEVELOPMENT

The term, now generally applied to such underground necropolises both Christian and non-Christian at Rome and elsewhere, derives from the name of the Christian cemetery *Ad Catacumbas* on the Via Appia. This cemetery was particularly well known because of its association with the tradition of the translation of the bodies of the apostles Peter and Paul and because it was the only subterranean Roman cemetery that was not deserted and forgotten in the course of the Middle Ages.

The earliest Roman catacombs, dating from

Crypt of the popes. Catacomb of Callistus, mid 3rd century. FROM LUDWIG HERTLING AND ENGLEBERT KIRSCHBAUM, THE ROMAN CATACOMBS AND THEIR MARTYRS (1956)

around A.D. 200, began as private, familial burial places that were opened to other members of the religious community and gradually, especially in the third century, became the property of the church. The greatest extension of the catacombs occurred in the fourth century, when the rapidly expanding Christian community continued to practice subterranean burial and the rapidly growing cult of martyrs drew attention to their tombs. Pope Damasus I sought out the martyrs' sepulchers and adorned them with inscriptions. Liturgical commemoration at the resting places of the saints required easier access and larger rooms, which led to physical alteration of the subterranean structures as well as to the erection of cemeterial basilicas on the surface. The desire to await the Last Judgment in proximity to the saints also produced a crowding of tombs around the martyrs' shrines.

During the first half of the fifth century new burials in the catacombs ceased, but the cemeteries continued to serve as cult centers and the goal of numerous pilgrims who came to visit the martyrs' tombs. Nevertheless, the ravages of time and invasion, combined with declining wealth and population, hampered papal attempts to maintain the physical structures and liturgical services of the cemeteries. Likewise, the increasingly common practice of placing relics in churches outside the cemeteries detracted from the catacombs' uniqueness. Following the siege of Rome in 756 by the Lombards, who wrought destruction in the cemeteries and carried off the bodies of martyrs, Pope Paul I began to bring relics into the city in large numbers. Adrian I and Leo III attempted to restore the cemeteries, but their success was limited, and beginning with Paschal I (817–824) the popes resumed the wholesale removal of the martyrs from their tombs. From the mid ninth century the catacombs, no longer used for either burial or worship, were abandoned and gradually forgotten until only the cemetery *Ad Catacumbas* remained accessible. By the end of the Middle Ages a few of the catacombs had been rediscovered, for dated graffiti record the presence of visitors beginning in the 1430's.

BIBLIOGRAPHY

Giuseppe Bovini, *Rassegna degli studi sulle catacombe e suoi cimiteri "sub divo"* (1952); Henri Leclercq, "Catacombes," in Fernand Cabrol, ed., *Dictionnaire d'archéologie chrétienne et de liturgie*, II, pt. 2 (1910); Orazio Marucchi, *Manual of Christian Archaeology* (1935); A. M.

Samson killing the Philistines with the jawbone of an ass. Fresco, Via Latina catacomb, late 4th century.
PONTIFICIO ISTITUTO DI ARCHEOLOGIA, ROME

Schneider, "Die ältesten Denkmäler der römischen Kirche," in Akademie der Wissenschaften in Göttingen, *Festschrift zur Feier des zweihundertjährigen Bestehens*, II (1951), 166–195; James Stevenson, *The Catacombs* (1978); Pasquale Testini, *Le catacombe e gli antichi cimiteri cristiani in Roma* (1966).

JOHN M. MCCULLOH

FORM AND DECORATION

Normally a shaft or stairwell led from an above-ground sanctuary down to a series of long corridors in which the individual tombs were excavated. The forms of the catacombs and the tombs vary from region to region, although corridors radiating from a central point (as at Syracuse) or laid out in a gridiron arrangement (as at Rome) were the most common plans. Tombs were dug in the floor (*formae*) or, more commonly, cut out from the walls (*loculi*). The narrow shelf tombs excavated in the walls were often cut in vertical rows, with five or six *loculi* to a row. A more elaborate type of tomb consisted of an arched niche (*arcosolium*) to contain the sarcophagus. In Rome, catacombs with several layers were customary. Small rooms (*cubicula*) were often placed at junctions in the corridors; the *cubicula* usually contained tombs and were the site of small memorial services.

Most of the preserved catacombs are in Rome, where over a half-million Christians were buried in almost a hundred miles of subterranean galleries. Many of the catacombs were decorated, usually with wall paintings. The earliest painted catacombs, such as that of Domitilla, did not include any specifically Christian subjects in their decoration and are virtually indistinguishable from pagan tomb chambers. Even in the third century, when Christian subject matter was commonly painted, the background for the religious scenes usually continued the pagan formula of light walls subdivided into sections by red lines. The scenes chosen by the early Christians to embellish their catacombs often emphasized the salvation of the Christian soul, but the range of subject matter was not limited to scenes closely tied to the funerary context or even restricted to specifically Christian iconography. The fourth-century catacomb on the Via Latina in Rome, for example, was painted with cupids and mythological figures as well as biblical scenes.

BIBLIOGRAPHY

Antonio Ferrua, *Le pitture della nuova catacomba di Via Latina* (1960); Ludwig Hertling and Englebert Kirschbaum, *The Roman Catacombs and Their Martyrs*, M. Joseph Costelloe, trans. (1956); Josef Wilpert, *Roma sotterranea* (1903).

LESLIE BRUBAKER

[See also **Death and Burial; Martyrdom; Translation of Saints.**]

CATALAN COMPANY. The Catalan-Aragonese mercenary force formed by the renegade Templar, Roger de Flor, had a widespread and generally destructive career during the fourteenth century. Its adventures began when Roger became involved in the Angevin-Aragonese struggle over Sicily, supporting Frederick II, brother of James II of Aragon, against Robert, son of Charles II of Anjou. After the success of Frederick, who with the help of the Catalan Grand Company and its effective light-armed cavalry, the *almogávares* (raiders), won the crown of Sicily in the Treaty of Caltabellotta (31 August 1302), Roger looked elsewhere for employment. He found it in Greece, where Catalans were already active as pirates and traders. Roger and his reorganized force offered to fight the Turks on behalf of the Byzantine emperor Andronikos II. What was an expedient for the emperor was a potential enterprise in the eyes of the Westerners. Frederick II and James II conceivably hoped that the Catalans could be used to conquer the Byzantine Empire in a Catholic crusade. But the Catalan Company was its own master.

The Catalans reached Constantinople in September 1303 and began to fight and plunder in Asia Minor the following spring. The progress of the Catalan Company and the ambitions (and demands for money) of Roger, who was named successively *megas dux* and caesar, as well as the dubious intentions of the company's Western patrons, alarmed Andronikos and his son Michael IX, who was probably responsible for murdering Roger in April 1305. With Roger dead, the mercenaries—far from ceasing to threaten Greece—carried out an atrocious vengeance that made their name a byword for cruelty. The company, now including Greek and Turkish contingents, overran Thrace and Macedonia, then moved through Thessaly toward Athens. From 1307 to 1309 they served the Valois under Thibaut de Chepoy (who had been sent by Charles II), ignoring Ferdinand, the infante of Majorca, who had come east to lead the company in the name of his cousin Frederick II.

In the spring of 1310 the Catalans entered the service of Walter de Brienne, claimant to the duchy of Athens and cousin of the last Burgundian duke, the late Guy II de la Roche. Walter's reluctance to pay his mercenaries, and their refusal to give up conquered territory, led to a battle in Thessaly near Halmyros, in which Walter was killed (15 March 1311). The Catalans took Thebes, their future capital, and Athens and established in Attica and Boeotia a principality of which the other major cities were Livadia (modern Lebadea), Siderocastron (modern Kastron), and Neopatras.

The Catalan Company remained legal owner of its territory even after 1312, when it subjected itself to the Catalan rulers of Sicily, to whose court appeals could be made from the court of the Catalan vicar-general. Until 1379 sentiment alone linked the settlement to Aragon, the king of which in 1314 denied to the pope that he had any authority over it. In 1312 Frederick II, at the Catalans' request, appointed his second son, Manfred, as duke of Athens. Six Catalan-Sicilian dukes were followed by two Catalan-Aragonese dukes (and assorted pretenders).

The principality was administered under the *Usatges de Barcelona* (which replaced the Assizes of Romania) by a vicar-general, who represented, and was appointed by, the duke. Under him the Catalan Company governed Athens as a corporation with Catalan officers, including a municipal council. Revenue came to the duke from feudal payments, tolls, city taxes, and royal rents and fees. The military was headed by a marshal (*mariscalcus*) appointed by the duke, but this officer was eventually eclipsed by the increasing strength of the vicar-general, who combined independent military power with political preeminence. Local administration, defense, and justice were the province of the *veguer* (vicar; the Catalan title) or *capità* (the Italian title), officers separate in origin and theory but similar in function and often identical in person. Sometimes the "captain or *veguer*" also held the post of castellan in one of the fortresses the protection of which was essential to a state surrounded by enemies.

During its seventy-five-year existence the Catalan settlement suffered not only from intermittent conflicts with the Venetians, its neighbors on Negropont (Euboea), that led to an indecisive war (1362–1365) in which the Catalans accepted Turkish assistance, but also from rivalry with Venice's Genoese competitors and from a succession marred by early deaths and factional quarrels. The settlement also had to contend with the enmity of the Avignon popes, opponents of the Catalan-Aragonese dynasty of Sicily. These popes imposed excommunication and interdict, appointed non-Catalans to ecclesiastical offices, and supported Briennist claims to the duchy. Furthermore, while suffering from Venetian impediments to its trade, from general lawlessness, and from the disaffection of the populace, the duchy lacked sufficient natural wealth and industry to give it a sound economic base. Its destruction began with the taking of Thebes by another mercenary company, that of the Navarrese John of Urtubia, in the late spring of 1379. This great blow was followed inevitably by the loss of Athens, which fell to the Florentine adventurer Nerio Acciajuoli on 2 May 1388. The Acciajuoli ruled Athens (with a Venetian interlude, 1394–1402/1403) until the Turkish conquest of the city on 4 June 1456.

The story of the Catalan Company is essentially political, consisting of a series of conflicts among leaders of several nationalities that had little effect on the culture and fortunes of the conquered peoples. On the other hand, by weakening the Byzantine Empire, by increasing hostility and hindering cooperation between Catholic Westerners and Orthodox Easterners, and by collaborating with the Turks, the Catalan Company helped to prepare the way for the expansion of Ottoman power.

BIBLIOGRAPHY

Two extensive bibliographies are in Kenneth M. Setton, *Catalan Domination of Athens, 1311–1388*, rev. ed. (1975). See vii–xi for the work done since the first (1948) edition, and 261–301. Among the primary sources noted by Setton, special mention should be made of Antonio Rubió y Lluch, *Diplomatari de l'Orient català* (1947). Secondary works include Francesco Giunta, *Aragonesi e Catalani nel Mediterraneo*, vol. 2: *La presenza Catalana nel Levante dalle origini a Giacomo II* (1959); Angeliki E. Laiou, *Constantinople and the Latins: The Foreign Policy of Andronicus II, 1282–1328* (1972), 131–199, 208–211, 220–229; and Raymond J. Loenertz, "Athènes et Néopatras: Regestes et notices pour servir à l'histoire des duchés catalans (1311–1394)," in *Archivum fratrum praedicatorum*, 25 (1955), and "Athènes et Néopatras: Regestes et documents pour servir à l'histoire ecclésiastique des duchés catalans (1311–1394)," *ibid.*, 28 (1958).

Susan M. Babbitt

[See also **Almogávares; Byzantine Empire: History (1204–1453); Frederick II of Sicily; Latin Principalities: Frankish States in Greece; Roger de Flor; Sicily, Kingdom of.**]

CATALAN LANGUAGE. Catalan is a continuation of the Latin spoken in the northeastern Iberian Peninsula and in the Roussillon on the French side of the Pyrenees. Today philologists tend to classify it as a minor Romance language (the present population that speaks it numbers around 6,000,000), but during the Middle Ages it was among the principal neo-Latin vernaculars with great cultural prestige

and high political status. In the Crown of Aragon (which comprised the principality of Catalonia and the kingdom of Aragon from 1137), Catalan was the dominant language, and it was transplanted through reconquest and resettlement to the Balearic Islands of Majorca (1229), Ibiza (1235), and Minorca (1287), and to the Valencian lands (1233–1244). It grew in importance when the Crown of Aragon became a Mediterranean power with control over Sicily, Sardinia, Corsica, the greater part of Greece, and Naples. Catalan continues to be spoken in the town of Alghero on the west coast of Sardinia, which was established in 1354 as a stronghold with settlers from the Crown of Aragon.

There are documents written entirely in Catalan dating from the first decades of the eleventh century, but the cultivation of Catalan on a meaningful scale did not begin until the last quarter of the thirteenth century. The early Catalan poets wrote in Occitan (which is often referred to as Provençal), and during the period from roughly 1160 to 1290 the Catalan contribution to the troubadour literature was very significant. Moreover, the use of that language for poetry became an established tradition after that period even though it was not adhered to in a strict sense. Ramon Lull's poetry has a general Catalan frame with a good many Occitan words and forms; this type of hybrid language with varying degrees of Occitan admixture continued until well into the fifteenth century. In the work of Ausiàs March (*ca.* 1397–1459), however, the most one can find is an occasional case ending for a needed rhyme or for archaic flavor.

Prose writing was generally done in Catalan from the outset, and the production was substantial in such varied areas as narrative genre and the philosophical, mystical, theological, sociopolitical, and encyclopedic writings of such eminent figures as Ramon Lull (*Libre de contemplació, Libre de meravelles, Libre d'Amic e Amat, Libre Blanquerna*), Arnald of Villanova (*Raonament d'Avinyó*), Francesc Eiximenis (*Lo Crestià*), Bernat Metge (*Lo somni*), and Joanot Martorell (*Tirant lo Blanch*). Also of note are the four chronicles (of James I, Bernat Desclot, Ramon Muntaner, Peter III), important juridical works (*Usatges de Barcelona, Furs de València, Costums de Tortosa*, distinguished for refined style, and the maritime law compilation *Consolat de mar*), translations of patristic literature (such as the *Legenda aurea* of Voragine), the Bible, medical and scientific treatises from Arabic or Latin, encyclopedic works (such as that of Brunetto Latini), the ancient classics, and verse and prose works of the authors of the Italian trecento (Dante, Boccaccio, Petrarch).

In Ramon Lull's works Catalan is already fully developed as a literary language with an elaborate syntax and a rich and varied lexicon. During the fourteenth century the influence of the royal chancery helped standardize the norms created by Lull, and the language was able to maintain a remarkable degree of uniformity from then on. Indeed, as one compares the language of the *Libre de contemplació* (ca. 1275) with that of *Tirant lo Blanch* (ca. 1475), the few noticeable differences consist of lexical archaisms and old verb forms (mostly of the preterit tense) in Lull's book. The royal chancery, the officials of which were normally excellent Latinists, contributed to the sophistication of Catalan syntax with salutary influences from Ciceronian writing. This is especially visible in the style of Bernat Metge, a product of the chancery, who raised Catalan prose to its ultimate perfection and elegance.

Catalan has many similarities with other Romance languages, but especially with Occitan (spoken to the north of Catalonia) and the Hispanic vernaculars (spoken to the west). Its lexicon presents greater affinity with Occitan than with the Hispanic vernaculars, and its words of Arabic origin are comparatively fewer than those of Spanish and Portuguese. Some philologists refer to Catalan as a *llengua-pont*, a bridge between the Gallo-Romance and the Ibero-Romance, and there is some justification for this once it is agreed that it has a particular character of its own and an independent status. Its phonetic solutions have developed sometimes in conjunction with both Occitan and the Hispanic group, at other times only with one of them. Its resolution of the diphthongs AU and AI as ɔ and *e* (CAUSA > resulting in Catalan *cosa* [thing]; the Latin suffix -ARIUS resulting in *-er*) were similar to those of Castilian (*cosa*, *-ero*), in contrast with those of Occitan, which kept them intact. (The symbol > means "resulting in"; < means "coming from"; and an asterisk precedes a hypothetical form.) Like Old Castilian, Catalan palatalized the *s* of the clusters -KS- and -SSI- and the geminate -NN- as ʃ and ɲ (Occitan resolved them as *is* and *n*). Catalan treatment of -LL- was reduction to *l* after a long vowel (VĪLLA > *vila*), and palatalization to λ (ĬLLA > *ella*), going halfway with Occitan, which regularly simplified the geminate, and partly with Castilian, which generally palatalized it.

Catalan coincided with Occitan in the outcome of -TĬC-, -DĬC- (VIATĬCU > *viatge* [travel], MEDĬCU > *metge* [physician]) and, like Occitan, also diphthongized the continuations of the Latin Ĕ and Ŏ before a yod (PĔCTUS > resulting first in a hypothetic **pieits* > then in *pit* [chest]; ŎCŬLU > **uoil* > *ull* [eye]; Old Occitan, *pieits*, *peits* and *uoilh*, *uolh*). More important, like Occitan and French, Catalan apocopated all its final vowels except -A, a development that resulted in a great many monosyllables ending in a consonant (*pit*, *ull*, *any* [year], *lloc* [place], *cos* [body]), giving Catalan the appearance of a Gallo-Romanic language.

From this point on, the changes affecting the consonants that remained final were often at variance with Occitan and brought about considerable differences between the two languages; they also determined to a large extent the distinct structure of Catalan as we know it today. Catalan dropped the final -*n* after a stressed vowel but not in plural forms (VĪNU > *vi* [wine]; RATĬONE > *raó* [reason]; but *vins* [wines] and *raons* [reasons]); Occitan wavered between retention and elimination. This development gave rise to a great number of words ending in a stressed vowel (*camí* [road], *veí* [neighbor], *català* [Catalan]) and led to the adoption of the abstract nouns ending with -IONE as *-ió* (*aeció*, *nació*, *noció*). The voiced prepalatal fricative ʒ, a sound of great frequency in early Catalan (being the continuation of Gᵉ, -GĬU, -JU, -DĬU), was strengthened as dʒ; later, around the third quarter of the thirteenth century, when the final voiced stops and sibilants were generally unvoiced, it became tʃ, providing Catalan with the greater number of this sound in its phonetic inventory (FŬGIT > *fuig* [he flees]; FAGEU > *faig* [beech]; MAJU > *maig* [May]; MĔDIU > *mig* [half]; RADIU > *raig* [ray]—compare Occitan, *mai* [May]; *mei* or *meg* [half], *rai* [ray]).

Both languages changed the fricative -*v* (-B-, -V-) into the semivocalic *u* (BĬBIT > *beu* [he drinks]; VĪVIT > *viu* [he lives]; NŎVEM > *nou* [nine]); but Catalan, going much further, vocalized even the fricative -ð (-D-) and also -dz (from -Cᵉˑⁱ, -TĬ-, and from the verbal ending of the second person plural -TĬS), which had merged with ð (PĔDE > *peu* [foot]; DĔCEM > *deu* [ten]; CRŬCE > Old Catalan *crou* [cross], later *creu*; PRĔTIU > *preu* [price]; CANTĀTIS > Old Catalan *cantau* [you sing], later *canteu*).

It should be noted, however, that the written language resisted adopting the -*u* ending in the verb form until quite late. With this development Catalan came to possess a large number of falling diphthongs with semivocalic *u*, a trait that gives it a distinct characteristic among kindred languages. On the other hand, Catalan checked the tendency to vocalize the internal syllable-final -*l* when the process was halfway in progress. The early texts contain many examples of forms such as *coutell* for *coltell* [knife] and *douç* for *dolç* [sweet]. A series of important words changed their original *u* to *l* through hypercorrection (*raïl* [root], from *raïu* < coming from RADĪCE; *malalt* [sick], from *malaut* < MALA HABĬTU).

Catalan had a few original phonetic solutions of its own. It palatalized all initial L-, no matter before what vowel (LŎCU > *lloc* [place]; LACU > *llac* [lake]; LĪNU > *lli* [flax]); only in the dialect of Asturias was there a similar change. More interesting was the Catalan treatment of the latin Ĕ and Ē, which, contrary to all Romance tendencies, became *e* and *ε*, respectively. This spectacular development appears to have been spearheaded by a closing of the original open *ε* (from Ĕ, AE) into *e* (except in front of -RR-, -N'R-, L, and of the δ from -D-, -Cᵉ-, -TI-) sometime during the eleventh century. In the eastern regions of Catalonia this closing caused the closed *e* (from Ē, Ĭ, OE) to shift to the center and become the neutral vowel *ə*. In that zone the language distinguished between a closed *e* (from the earlier open *ε*), an open *ε* (which was left from the original *ε* before -RR-, -N'R-, L, and δ) and the neutral *ə* (from the earlier *e*) until roughly the second half of the fourteenth century, when the neutral *ə* and the *ε* merged, thus completing the cycle from *e* to *ε*. Majorca, which received the tripartite distinction, has kept it intact in many localities. The western zone has mainly a closed *e* (from both Ĕ and Ē) and a certain number of *ε* (from Ĕ in front of -RR-, -N'R-, L, and δ).

In the fourteenth century there was yet another vocalic mutation, this time affecting the unstressed *a* and *e* that merged in the neutral *ə*. This change occurred only in the eastern zone, including the Roussillon, and in the Balearic Islands. It became, together with the difference in the outcomes of Ĕ and Ē, the major factor for the division of the Catalan language into two main zones: east Catalan (comprising today the provinces of Barcelona, Gerona, part of Tarragona, and Roussillon) and west Catalan (including the provinces of Lérida, the rest of Tar-

ragona, and Valencia). The Balearic Islands are in the east zone.

PHONETICS

In stressed position there were, as today, seven vowels: *a, ε, e, i, ɔ, o, u*. In unstressed position there were, after the merger of *a* and *e* in the fourteenth century, four vowels: *ə, o, u, i*. (The closing of the atonic *o* into *u*, which is characteristic of east Catalan, though not of Majorca, is postmedieval). The old orthography did not have different symbols for the two varieties of *e* and *o* (today the closed ones may take an acute accent while the open counterparts take the grave).

The merger of the atonic *a* and *e* in *ə* is often reflected in a graphic confusion between these letters in manuscripts dating from the end of the fourteenth century and later. In many texts one is likely to find such graphemes as *para, jutga, manjar* for *pare, jutge, menjar*, or *case, cante, gracie*, for *casa, canta, gracia*. However, the final -*e* that appears instead of -*a* in the third-person verb forms—such as *ere, estave, cante* (for *era, estava, canta*) in the texts from the western zone (for instance, in the *Homilies d'Organyà* or in the *Sermons* of St. Vincent Ferrer) is not to be attributed to the same phenomenon, for in that region the atonic *a* and *e* were not confused. The result -*e* < from the Latin verbal ending -AT was normal in the western zone.

In the consonantal system medieval Catalan differed little from the modern language. The following oppositions existed: stops—*p/b, t/d, k/g*; fricatives—*f/v, s/z, ʃ/ʒ*; affricates—*ts/dz* and *tʃ/dʒ*. There were also two laterals—*l* and *λ*; three nasals—*m, n, ɲ*; the vibrants *r* and R; and the glides *i̯* and *u̯*.

Medieval Catalan distinguished between a labiodental *v* (from V, -B-, -F-) and a bilabial *b* (from B-, -P-), as does the twentieth-century speech of Majorca, most of Valencia, and parts of Tarragona. The crystallization of the present-day system of one phoneme, *b*, with fricative and stop allophones dates from the late fifteenth century. The voiceless affricate *ts* (graphic *ç*), which developed from the initial Cᵉ or from Cᵉ and TI after a consonant, was in the process of merging with *s* during the thirteenth and fourteenth centuries. The palatal *λ* from the initial L- was normally represented by *l*, and in other positions by *ll* or *l*. It has recently been shown that the digraph *yl* (or *il* or *li*), which was used for the reflex of -LI- and -C'L-, must have represented a slightly different type of *λ* that later merged with *λ* from other sources but continued as *i* in some dialects that today say *fii* for *fill* and *ui* for *ull*.

By the thirteenth century the old orthography had developed the series of digraphs that are in use at present: *ig* for the affricate *tʃ* (*maig* [May]; *puig* [hill], from PŎDIU); *tg* before *e* and *i* and *tj* before *a*, *o*, and *u* for affricate *dʒ* (*metge* [physician]; *jutge* [judge], from JUDĬCE; *jutjar* [to judge], from JUDĬCARE); *tz* for the alveolar affricate *dz* (*tretze* [thirteen], from TREDĔCE); *ny* for the palatal nasal (*vinya* [vineyard], from VĪNEA; *plànyer* [to complain] from PLANGĔRE; *cunyat* [brother-in-law], from COGNATU); *ix* after a vowel for the pre-palatal fricative *ʃ* (*baixar* [to go down], from *BAS-SIARE; *caixa* [box], from CAPSA; *peix* [fish], from PĬSCE); and *tll* for the geminate palatal lateral λλ (*espatlla* [shoulder], from SPATŬLA). It must be noted, however, that the scribes often did not adhere to these norms and that the variant spellings, such as *peix* and *pex*, *puig* and *pug*, are frequent. Wavering was particularly common between the letters *g* and *j* for the representation of the fricative prepalatal *ʒ* (*mengar* instead of *menjar*).

The following changes took place in medieval Catalan: the diphthong *ou* became *eu* in words such as *crou* (cross) and *vou* (voice), evidently through a pressure for vocalic differentiation. In Ramon Lull *crou* and *vou* alternate with *creu* and *veu*. The final atonic -*e* (left as a supporting vowel) became *o* in a number of words through vocalic assimilation: *monge* (monk, from MONĬCU) became *monjo*; *cuire* (leather from CORIU), *cuiro*. An analogical pressure extended this formation to the final -*e* after -RR- as well: *ferro*, from *ferre* (iron, from FERRU). The same tendency was responsible for the formation of the masculine plural endings -*os* after a stressed *s*. The final -*r* was dropped before the end of the fifteenth century, except in a number of monosyllables. This development appears to have begun in plurals (-*rs*), judging by the fact that forms such as *carrés* for *carrers* and *ferrés* for *ferrers* are frequent in fourteenth-century texts. The fricative prepalatal *ʒ* was strengthened into *dʒ* in intervocalic position (*plaja* became *platja* [beach]; *correja* became *corretja* [strap]), but the phenomenon was not general.

MORPHOSYNTAX

The double case system perpetuating the Latin nominative and accusative forms (common to Old Occitan and Old French) did not survive in Catalan. In this language, as in Castilian and Portuguese, the nominative was lost in a very early period. It is true, however, that a word such as *lladre* [thief] goes back to a nominative LATRO, and a few other words are also continuations of nominative forms. In addition, a few scattered instances of nominative relics can be seen in some early texts.

The *Homilies d'Organyà* (from around the end of the twelfth century) distinguishes between *sènyer* (< SĒNIOR), *Déus* (< DĔUS) used as subject or vocative, and *senyor* (< SĒNIORE), *Déu* (< DĔUM) used as object; Ramon Lull also appears to have observed this distinction originally in these words. Some thirteenth-century texts and others of later date occasionally contain nouns and adjectives with the nominative singular ending -*s*, most likely through Occitan influence.

In the thirteenth century the plural endings were -*s* after a consonant or the final -*e*, whether the noun was masculine or feminine (*senyor, senyors; muller, mullers; mare, mares*); -*es* after a stressed -*s* (masc., *francès, franceses*); -*es* in feminine forms ending in -*a* (*terra, terres; francesa, franceses*); and -*ns* after a stressed vowel (masc., *vi, vins; català, catalans; veí, veïns*; however, analogic plurals such as *hòmens* and *àsens*, which are now dialectal, are frequent in many authors). One important development was the formation of -*os* from -*es* in masculine plurals of nouns and adjectives ending in a stressed -*s*. It first appeared in such words as *famoses* and *cosses* (plurals of *famós* and *cos*) through vocalic assimilation and, having proved useful for feminine and masculine distinctions (such as *famosos* [masc.] and *famoses* [fem.]), it was generalized to other forms as well: *francesos* (masc.) and *franceses* (fem.). The extension of this ending to plurals of nouns ending with -*ʃ* (*peix, peixos*) and with -*tʃ* is postmedieval, though some instances of *peixos* may appear in some fifteenth-century texts. The old texts often have *peis* (pronounced *peis*) for what one would expect to be as *peixs*, evidently replacing the cluster *ʃs* by *is*.

The definite articles were *lo*, *los* for the masculine, and *la*, *les* for the femine; the masculine forms were usually reduced to '*l* or *l*' and '*ls* in contact with a vowel. The modern strengthened forms *el* and *els*, which were formed from the reduced variants, are infrequent in the medieval period. Besides this set derived from ĬLLE, Old Catalan possessed another one derived from ĬPSE, written with *ç* in some early documents as *ço, ços, ça, ces* or with *s* as *so, sos, sa, ses*. It has continued in northeast Catalonia and Majorca (as *es* [masc.] sing. and pl., *sa, ses*), and must already have been of regional use in the Middle Ages.

Catalan inherited the personal pronouns as *jo, tu, ell, ella, nos, vos, ells, elles*. The strengthened *nosaltres* and *vosaltres* are quite common in Ramon Lull (a variant with *-altros* and *-atros* began to appear in the fourteenth century); *vos* continued to be used for addressing persons of respect, and *nos* was for royal use.

The possessives had two series: the stressed *meu* (from MĔUM), *teu* (from analogical *TĔUM instead of TŬUM), and *seu* (from *SEUM) had as their feminine counterparts *mia* (from MEUM), *tua* (from TŬAM), *sua* (from SŬAM)—today they are *meva, teva, seva* or the dialectal *meua, teua, seua*; the masculine *nostre* and *vostre* developed variant forms ending in -o. The third person plural was *llur* (from ILLŌRUM) for masculine and feminine. With the exception of *llur* these forms were normally used with the definite article. The unstressed series—*mon, ton, son* (masc. sing.; plurals *mos, tos, sos*), *ma, ta, sa* (fem. sing.; plurals *mes, tes, ses*)—had much greater use than at present.

The atonic pronouns were *me, te, lo, nos, vos, los*, and *les* for the direct object, with the dative forms differing only in the third persons as *li* and *lus* (today written *los*, and originally a derivative of *lur* or *lor*). They used to undergo vocalic reductions such as *'m* or *m'* in contact with a vowel, and the present-day strengthened variants *em, et, el, els* were made from such forms. Today the use of atonic pronouns after a verb is limited to affirmative command and infinitive, but in Old Catalan they could appear after a verb in any tense. The medieval syntax appears to have avoided the use of these pronouns as the first element in a sentence or a phrase. In the combinations of the direct and indirect pronouns, the order was, contrary to modern usage, the direct first and the indirect second (*ell lo nos dóna, ell lo li dóna*). Occasional examples of the present construction *l'hi* (= *lo hi*), where the adverbial *hi* was a replacement of *li*, can be seen in the fourteenth century and are quite frequent in *Tirant lo Blanch* (ca. 1475).

The relative pronouns consisted of *qui* (from QUĪ), *que* (from QUEM/QUĬD), and *qual* (from QUALIS), which was generally accompanied by the definite article. The tendency was to employ *qui* as subject pronoun and *que* as object. However, there are examples of *que* for subject in both genders; on the other hand, Bernat Metge appears to have observed a distinction between *qui* (masculine) and *que* (feminine) used as subject pronouns.

The present-day infinitive system with the endings -*ar* (*amar*), -*er* (*saber*), '-*er* (*témer*), -*re* (*perdre*), -*ure* (*beure*) was already prevalent in the thirteenth century, but the ranks of -*er* (today of limited number) included several important verbs such as *caer* (to fall), *dever* (to owe), *jaer* (to lie), and *trer* (to take out). These forms continued until well into the fifteenth century, when they passed to -*ure*. In Ramon Lull one can see beside the modern *llegir* and *fugir* the older forms *llégir* and *fúgir*, which survived only dialectally.

Originally the first person of the present indicative in the regular verbs had zero ending (*jo cant* [I sing], *jo perd* [I lose], *jo dorm* [I sleep]), though in a number of verbs, such as *parlar* and *comprar*, it was *jo parle* and *jo compre* (with the -*e* acting as a supporting vowel). By the fifteenth century the -*e* was extended, in great part, to the other verbs of the first conjugation; it is predominant in *Tirant lo Blanch* and continued in Valencia. (The first examples of the modern ending -*o* are from the sixteenth century.) The present-day forms with the velar ending -*k* (*bec* [I drink], *crec* [I believe], *moc* [I move]) originally were *beu* (from BIB[O]), *creu* (from CRED[O]); the -*k* was received from such forms as *dic* [I say] and *duc* [I carry] deriving from Latin DICO and DUCO respectively).

The second person plural forms were usually written with -*ts* (at times -*tz*) until around 1440, when the normal ending -*u̯* (from -TIS) was generalized. In the second half of the fifteenth century the first and second person plural endings, -*am* and -*au* (as in *cantam* and *cantau*) became -*em*, and -*eu* (though not in Majorca) as a result of a series of analogical influences. The inchoative verb paradigm had the following endings: first singular, -*esc*; second singular, -*eis* (= -*eixs*); third singular, -*eix*; third plural, *eixen* (now in standard Catalan first singular, -*eixo*; second singular, -*eixes*; third singular, -*eix*; third plural, -*eixen*).

The present subjunctive forms had a zero ending in the first and third persons singular of the first conjugation (first and third singular, *cant*; second singular, *cants*; first plural, *cantem*; second plural, *cantets* or *canteu*; third plural, *canten*); the paradigm of the second and third conjugations was on the basis of -A- (*perda, -es, -a, -em, -ets* or -*eu, -en; senta, -es, -a, -im, -its* or -*iu, -en*), as in Valencia today. Several verbs, among them *saber* and *caber*, had the ending -*ia* (*sàpia, càpia*) as a continuation of the Latin -ĬA(T); the -*ia*, having been extended to the first conjugation through analogy in the postmedieval period, led to the formation of the modern ending -*i*. In the *Sermons* of St. Vicent Ferrer there appear some instances of subjunctive forms in *-o-*, now common in west Catalan. The paradigm of the inchoative verbs was on the basis of *-esca-* (today *-eixi-* in standard Catalan).

The imperfect forms presented pretty well the modern system on the basis of *-ava-* in the first conjugation and *-ia-* in others. It is very likely, however, that in verbs where *-ia-* was preceded by a vowel the stress was still on the *i* (*feïa, deïa, seïa*), and not on the stem, as is the case today.

The preterit tense, which Catalan inherited in a great variety of forms, underwent a series of paradigmatic adjustments; as a result this verb form marks one of the main differences between the language of the early and late medieval texts. The regular verb paradigm of the three conjugations originally consisted of first singular, *-é* or *-í*; second singular, *-est* or *-ist*; third singular, *-à*, or *-é*, or *-í*; first plural, *-am*, *-em*, or *-im*; second plural, *-às*, *-és*, or *-ís*; third plural, *-aren*, *-eren*, or *-iren*. The irregular verbs had strong preterits of the type *dix* (from *dir* [to say]), *pres* (from *prendre* [to take]), and a group with the velar ending *-k*, including *hac* (from *haver* [to have]), *poc* (from *poder* [to be able]), *conoc* (from *conèixer* [to know]). Some had strong forms only in the first and third persons singular (first and third singular, *dix*; but second singular, *dixist*; first plural, *dixem*; second plural, *dixés*; third plural, *dixeren*), and some in first and third singular and third plural (first and third singular, *hac*; second singular, *haguest*; first plural, *haguem*; second plural, *hagués*; third plural, *hagren*).

There first arose a tendency to adjust the strong forms to the weak ones: *hac* and *hagren* were made *hagué* and *hagueren*, and *prengué* and *prengueren* replaced *pres* and *preseren*. A little later another tendency gradually extended the *-re-* of the third person plural to the second singular and first and second plural, thereby changing the paradigm to *canté, cantares, cantà, cantàrem, cantàreu, cantaren*. Besides these original forms there came into existence the periphrastic preterit formed from VADO plus the infinitive (*vaig parlar, vas parlar, va parlar,* and so on), which was fairly frequent in Ramon Muntaner's chronicle (*ca.* 1325) and by the end of the medieval period apparently replaced the original preterit forms in many parts of the country. Today the latter are heard only in parts of Valencia, and otherwise their use is literary.

The present perfect was constructed by *haver* plus the past participle in the case of transitive verbs, and by *ser* plus the past participle for intransitive and reflexive verbs. The old participles ending in *-ut* (*haüt* from *haver*, *beüt* from *beure* [to drink], *creüt* from the old *creer* [to believe]) were soon replaced by *-gut* (*hagut, begut, cregut*), while the strong participles of the type *llest* (from *llegir*) and *fuit* (from *fugir*) were regularized as *llegit* and *fugit*. The participles usually agreed in number and gender with the object, whether it preceded or followed.

The future and conditional, formed with the infinitive plus present indicative and imperfective indicative of *haver* (*cantaré* and *cantaria*) do not demonstrate any significant difference from the present system, except that the endings could be separate when the verb was used with an object pronoun.

In the imperative singular there were a few irregular forms: *ve* (go, from VADE), *fe* (make, do, from FAC), *di* (say, from DIC), *vin* (come, from VENI). Later, subjunctive forms became common in the imperative function (*digues* [say], *hages* [have]), and under their influence *fe* and *ve* were made *fes* and *ves*, while *vin* was given the ending *-e (vine)*. Some texts contain, besides *vin*, other forms with *i* (*prin* instead of *pren*). For the plural, the indicative and subjunctive forms ending in *-ts* were common (*cantats* or *cantets,* later with *-u*), but occasionally there are vestiges of the original imperative plural ending in -ĀTE, -ĒTE, and -ĪTE well into the fifteenth century (*portat, metet, dormit*).

The imperfect subjunctive of the regular verbs that were the descendants of the Latin pluperfect subjunctive ending in -'VĬSSEM had the following endings for the three conjugations: first singular, *-às*, *-és*, *-ís*; second singular, *-asses*, *-esses*, *-isses*; third singular, *-às*, *-és*, *-ís*; first plural, *-àssem*, *-éssem*, *-íssem*; second plural, *-àssets*, *-éssets*, *-íssets* (later in *-u*); third plural, *-assen*, *-essen*, *-issen* (today the first and second conjugations end in *-és*, *-éssis*, *-és*, and so on). The irregular verbs had the preterit as their basis: *hagués* (from *haver*), *pogués* (from *poder*), *volgués* (from *voler*), and so on.

Old Catalan also contained the descendants of the Latin pluperfect indicative (CANTAVĔRAM), though not in their original function. The first conjugation consisted of *cantara, cantares, cantara, cantàrem, cantàrets* (later with *-u*), *cantaren*. In the second and third conjugations the endings were on the basis of *-era-* and *-ire-*. The irregular verbs (*haver, poder, ser*) had strong forms (*hagra, pogra, fora*) in all six persons: *hagra, hagres, hagra, hagrem, hagrets* (later with *-u*), *hagren*. This verb normally expressed the meaning of conditional perfect (*pogra* being equivalent to *hauria pogut*) and was common in the apodosis of hypothetical conditional sentences. In the early period such sentences had the following structure: *si volgués, pogra fer-ho* (if he had wanted, he could have done it), with *volgues* having the original pluperfect subjunctive meaning. Later the analytical construction became common in both the protasis and apodosis: *si hagués volgut, haguera* (replacing *hagra*) *pogut fer-ho.* Today the *-ra* forms continue to be used in Valencia, but with the function of the imperfect subjunctive as in Spanish, *fora* being the only remnant in standard Catalan that is an equivalent of *seria.*

VOCABULARY

Medieval Catalan possessed a considerable number of frequently used words that later became archaic: *ahontar* (to offend), *altar* (to please), *anap* (cup), *àvol* (evil, bad), *enagar* (to incite), *estojar* (to keep), *estorçre* (to save), *gint* (gently, well), *ivàs* (fast), *lluu* (light, from LUCE), *membrar* (to remember), *nuu* (cloud), *pec* (stupid), *sútzeu* (dirty), *tost* (soon), *ujar* (to tire), and quite a good many others.

Often some old forms were replaced by their learned counterparts, especially during the period of humanism and the Renaissance: *aondar* by *abundar*, *aorar* by *adorar*, *camiar* by *canviar*, *colpa* by *culpa*, *devesir* by *dividir*, *esplegar* by *explicar*. Some words fell into disuse because of semantic concurrence: *frater* (brother) and *sor* (sister) were leveled out by *germà* and *germana; ujar* lost its vitality before *cansar* (to tire), *occir* or *aucir* (to kill) before *matar*, *maridar* (to marry) before *casar*, and *negar* (to drown) and *sutze* (dirty) lost out to *ofegar* and *brut.* It is interesting to note that in some instances the tendency has been to favor the Hispanic lexicon (*germà, cansar, matar, casar*).

Word formation through derivation was fully advanced in the language of Ramon Lull. Particularly frequent are the abstract nouns ending with *-esa* (from -ITIA) or its variant *-ea: granesa, avolesa, certesa, saviesa* (all alternating with the variant *-ea*); those ending with *-ment: acusament, ajudament, acabament, perdiment;* those ending with *-ança* or *-ença* (with learned variants ending in *-ància* or *-ència*): *acabança, dubtança, valença;* those ending in *-itat* or *-etat* (with variants ending in *-dat*): *ceguetat, altedat, sobiranitat;* those ending *-or: blancor, negror, amargor, fredor, tristor,* to which were later added nouns ending in *-aó* (from -ATIONE with partially popular treatment): *abundor, tardor;* those ending with *-ia (mestria, metgia),* and also nouns ending with *-er* indicating fruit trees (*codon-*

yer, datiler, pomer) or a trade (*hostaler, argenter, ballester*). Adjectives end in *-ós*, as in *coratjós, consirós, neguitós;* in *-ívol, -able,* or *-ible,* as in *infantívol, dubtable, creïble, volible;* in *-dor* < -TOREM, as in *faedor* (doer) or *ajudador* (helper), or in *-dor* < -TORIUM, with a passive meaning, as in *amador* (worthy of being loved) or *reprenedor* (reprehensible); and in *-al*, as in *angelical, diabolical.* The infinitives end in *-ejar*, as in *bonejar, fortejar;* in *-eir* or its variant *-ir* (evidently formed from nouns ending in *-ea* < -ITIA), as in *endureir, entristeir, enriqueir* or *enriquir.*

The learned forms or pure Latinisms were widely used by Ramon Lull. It has been observed that in his more doctrinal and philosophical works Lull showed preference for Latinisms rather than the forms of popular or semilearned origin: *abreviar* rather than *abreujar, bonitat* instead of *bonea, homicidi* instead of *homei, paupertat* instead of *pobretat, tristícia* instead of *tristea.* One century later, when the spirit of humanism was prevailing, the predilection for Latinisms reasserted itself. In Bernat Metge one finds such extreme learned forms as *inimícia, immunde, inòpia, irrepellible, incomptable,* and *diformitat.* However, the tendency was not exaggerated by the Catalan classics of the fifteenth century, the language of which usually had recourse to them in response to the requirements of theme and style.

BIBLIOGRAPHY

Antoni Badia i Margarit and Francesc de B. Moll i Casasnovas, "La llengua de Ramon Lull," in *Obres essencials* [*de Ramon Llull*], II (1960); Joan Bastardas Parera, "El catala pre-literari," in *Actes del quart colloqui internacional de llengua i literatura catalanes* (1977); Germà Colon, *El léxico catalán en la Romania* (1960); Joan Coromines, *Lleures i converses d'un filòleg* (1971), 288–384—additions to this study are in the edition of the *Vides* by Charlotte S. Maneikis-Kniazzeh and Edward J. Neugard (1977), I, 3–73; Adnan Gökçen, "The Language of *Homilies d'Organyà*," in *Catalan Studies Volume in Memory of Josephine de Boer* (1977); J. Gulsoy, "El desenvolupament de la semivocal *-w* en català," *ibid.,* 71–98; and "L'evolució de les *ee* tòniques del català," in *Mélanges de philologie et de toponymie romanes offerts à Henri Guiter* (1981); Paul Russell-Gebbett, *Mediaeval Catalan Linguistic Texts* (1965), 9–50; and "L'estructura de les oracions condicionals de realització impossible en el català medieval," in *Actes del tercer colloqui internacional de la llengua i literatura catalanes* (1976).

General works are Antoni Badia i Margarit, *Gramática histórica catalana* (1951); Joan Coromines, *Lleures i converses d'un filòleg* (1971), 246–275; Pompeyo [Pompeu] Fabra, *Gramática de la lengua catalana* (1912); Francesc de

B. Moll i Casasnovas, *Gramática histórica catalana* (1952); and Alfons Par, *Sintaxi catalana segons los escrits en prosa de Bernat Metge (1398)* (1923).

J. GULSOY

[See also **Aragon, Crown of (1137–1479); Arnald of Villanova; Lull, Ramon; Provençal Language; Provençal Literature; Spanish Language.**]

CATALAN LITERATURE

ORIGINS: WRITINGS IN LATIN AND PROVENÇAL TO 1300

After the Roman conquest a coherent subgroup of Romance dialects began to develop from the local varieties of spoken Latin in the northeastern triangle of the Iberian Peninsula, from the eastern Pyrenees (including the Roussillon) to Valencia and the Balearic Islands. The region's strong political and ecclesiastical connections with southern France, reinforced during the time of the Carolingian Spanish March and maintained throughout the feudal period of the Catalan counts of Barcelona, provided for more channels of culture, linguistic, and literary influences from beyond the Pyrenees than from the peninsula.

Catalonia's loss of territorial rights in southern France, compensated for by the union with Aragon (1137) and the reconquest of the Balearic Islands (1229–1235) and of Valencia from the Moors (1238), did not put an end to these cultural ties. Convents on both sides of the Pyrenees were the centers of early literary activity when vernacular texts were not yet written down. Sermons and political speeches in regional dialects must have been commonplace. The remaining popular devotional and religious verses, at first only orally transmitted, probably have their origins in those times (*Cant de la Sibilla*, presented at Christmas; *Epístoles farcides*, monorhyme octosyllabics enlivening liturgical readings; *virolais, goigs*, and *planys de Maria*). Traces found in the popularizing songs of the *juglaría* indicate a strong tradition of archaic songs and dances in the vernacular, with refrains *(viaderas)* that aristocratic poets judged "artless" (*Ensenyament* of Guerau de Cabrera, *ca.* 1150).

Poetry was written in Latin by monks, especially the twenty erotic songs from the convent of Ripoll, as well as hagiographic or historiographic verses (*Passio sanctae Eulaliae Barcinonensis*) and local chronicles (*Gesta comitum barcinonensium*). A monk of the eastern Pyrenees wrote the *Cançó de Santa Fe (ca.* 1070) in Provençal. The Arthurian novel *Jaufré*, a century later, may also have been composed by a Catalan author. French and Provençal literature were widely read by the higher classes in Catalonia, as evidenced in royal correspondence and inventories of libraries. These regions also produced a sizable group of lyric poets writing exclusively in Provençal, undistinguishable in language and technique from their northern models.

Twenty-five troubadours of Catalan origin contributed about two hundred surviving songs to the Provençal lyric corpus, especially between 1162 and 1213, during the reigns of the poet-kings Alphonse I (Alfons I in Catalonia; Alfons II in Aragon: 1162–1196) and Peter I (Pere I in Catalonia; Pere II in Aragon: 1196–1213). The most renowned were Berenguer de Palol, nine songs; Guillem de Cabestany; Guillem de Berguedà, about thirty poems, some about feudal disputes; and Huguet de Mataplana, poetic debates—all edited by M. de Riquer. Almost all poetic forms are represented, but in content Catalans seem to be more realistic than other poets. Under King James I the Conqueror (Jaume I in Catalonia and Aragon: 1213–1276) the court was more interested in prose chronicles but in the reign of Peter II the Great (Pere II in Catalonia; Pere III in Aragon: 1276–1285) it again became a center of troubadours (for instance, Guillem de Cervera, also called Cerverí de Girona, with over a hundred compositions, plus the moralizing *Proverbis;* and Pere Salvatge).

The Catalans also wrote Provençal grammatical and poetic treatises. Ramon Vidal de Besalú, author of several rhymed stories, compiled the *Rasós de trobar* around 1200, followed in the manuscript by a *Doctrina de compondre dictats*, in which all poetic genres are defined and exemplified. Much later, at the suggestion of the troubadour king James II (Jaume II in Catalonia and Aragon: 1291–1327; also king of Sicily: 1286–1295), the Benedictine Jofre de Foixà added to it all of his own *Regles de trobar*.

PROSE

Origins. The first written attestations of Catalan prose are the translation of the *Forum judicum* (fragment of the manuscript at Montserrat) and an adaptation of a Provençal sermonary called, from the town where the fragment was found, *Homilies d'Organyà*, both from the very end of the twelfth century. However, while the sociocultural and linguistic development of Catalonia and its recently reconquered kingdoms had attained complete self-sufficiency, original writings in Catalan remain quite rare right to the very end of the thirteenth century. The small number of translations made in the second half of that century was not sufficient to provide a basis for a supraregional written language. Catalan appears in the writings of Ramon Lull and Arnald of Villanova as a rich and fully developed language. In order to reach this level of development, preceding generations must have considered an emphasis on cultivated linguistic expression to be of much social importance.

The fourteenth century, during which the relatively small nation of Catalonia produced an amazing amount of literature, admirable even though much of it is based on foreign models, opened with the genius of the religious visionary Ramon Lull from Majorca. Lacking formal academic training, but having studied for nine years with Cistercian monks and a Muslim tutor, Lull felt no academic compulsion not to use his native tongue in order to express his philosophical or theological thoughts and flights of imagination in poetry and novels. The diffusion of his numerous works helped establish linguistic standards for a literary and scientific language. Lull's contemporary, the equally enlightened scientist Arnald of Villanova, probably from Valencia, wrote most of his multifaceted work in Latin.

Chronicles. Throughout the thirteenth century the notaries and secretaries of the royal court elaborated a standard form for writing in the vernacular. In their circles were translators of the customary legal regulations and precepts *(usatges, costums, furs)*, texts later expanded directly in Catalan, as in the case of the *Libre del Consolat del mar,* the model of maritime law for the whole Mediterranean.

The stage was now set for changing from Latin annals to Catalan chronicles, an evolution paralleled if not helped by a growing national awareness that encouraged the authors to make more personal and literary creative interventions in the writing of history. The learned writers might also have discovered, while looking for sources, the human value of the vernacular traditional epic songs. The latter were perhaps never widespread in Catalonia, and are known to us today only through prosifications in the chronicles.

The first of the four great Catalan national histories is the chronicle written by King James I the Conqueror. The king's personal intervention in its redaction (perhaps dictating it to his illegitimate son Jaume Sarroca, later bishop of Osca), is seen in the use of the first person and in the personal character and directness of many spontaneous passages. The

first part (chapters 1–327), finished by 1244, describes the defeat at Muret and, with more details, the conquests of Majorca and Valencia. At a later stage the story was brought up to date, quickly recapitulating the events of 1242–1265, then concentrating on the next ten years (James I's conquest of Murcia, his quarrels with the nobility and his own sons). In 1313 these materials were collated, divided into chapters, and translated into Latin as *Liber gestarum* by the Dominican Petrus Marsilius. Chapters 547–566, added later, carry the story up to the death of King James I in 1276.

The original Catalan materials circulated in book form as *Libre dels feyts del rey En Jacme* and are mentioned as owned by James II, who died in 1327. They were then lost, but not before 1343, when the monks of the royal convent of Poblet had a magnificent copy made, combining it with some elements of Marsilius' Latin version. The surviving version (in five manuscripts), containing highly idiosyncratic style and linguistic play on dialect forms, goes directly back to the original.

Bernat Desclot (also known as Bernat Escrivà, a royal official from 1282 to 1289) was the author of the *Libre del rei En Pere d'Aragó e dels seus antecessors passats.* Beginning with the union of Catalonia and Aragon in 1137, the somewhat disorganized and unbalanced chronicle becomes more detailed at the time of the infant Peter. Episodes of chivalric grandeur of King Peter II the Great such as the joust with Charles of Anjou at Bordeaux, and of the admiral Roger de Flor (de Llúria) are related with admiration. Bernat was present at the campaign against Philip the Bold. His accounts are objective, and the author makes frequent use of vivid dialogue and seeks literary elegance. The text became a source for later histories. (It was first edited in 1616 in a Castilian translation, and in its original in 1840 from a Parisian manuscript.) Some manuscripts transcribe at their end short anonymous chronicles of the reigns of John I (Joan I in Catalonia and Aragon: 1387–1396) and Martin I (Martí I in Catalonia and Aragon: 1396–1410).

The third and most famous of the great Catalan chronicles is the *Crònica* by Ramon Muntaner (1265–1336). In his twenties Muntaner participated in Mediterranean conquests. He served in Minorca, at Messina, and at Gallipoli, and was governor of the island of Jerba. He was a bursar for Roger de Flor and fought in thirty-two battles. As city councillor of Valencia (from 1315) he wrote a lengthy *Sermó* in alexandrines (1322), recommending the conquest of

Sardinia and Corsica (to be sung to the melody of the French epic *Gui de Nanteuil*). Three years later he started to write his memoirs as a patriotic guidebook for future kings. Using lost epics as his source, Muntaner begins with the legendary procreation of James I in 1208, then shows the "manifest destiny" of the Aragonese-Catalan dynasty through Peter II, Alphonse II (Alfons II in Catalonia; Alfons III in Aragon: 1285–1291), James II, and Alphonse III the Benign (Alfons III in Catalonia; Alfons IV in Aragon: 1328–1336) whose coronation in 1328 was presided over by Muntaner.

Containing the only Western account of the conquest of the Byzantine Empire (chapters 194–244), this firsthand, realistic personal account is of great historical importance. It is also the high point of Catalan literary prose, written in a style surpassing all other European historiography of that time. The *Crònica*'s influence on literary texts (such as *Tirant lo blanc*) is beyond doubt, and its fascination—perhaps due to the writer's search for direct contact with his audience—is still felt today. In certain manuscripts the chronicles of Desclot and Muntaner are combined; in others there are updates, such as the continuation by Admiral Galceran Marquet. Early editions appeared in 1558 and 1562; the best modern one, between 1927 and 1952.

The fourth of the great Catalan chronicles was written during the reign of Peter III the Ceremonious (Pere III in Catalonia; Pere IV in Aragon: 1336–1387), who once stated that he frequently read the *Libre dels feyts* of James II. Elaborated, with various degrees of royal intervention, by several officials of the chancellery (especially Bernat Descoll) over the period 1361–1382, with a revision (perhaps by the king himself) done before the monarch's death in 1387, the chronicle combines dry annalistic passages with more elaborate developments. The king's conceited character left its imprint on the text, as did the changing times, the decay of the old heroic chivalric ideals, and the loss of royal authority. The first edition dates from 1547, the modern one from 1941.

Of lesser importance, given its length and historical interest, is the universal history known as the *Crònica de Sant Joan de La Penya*, written in Catalan before 1366 (a possible first version in Latin is lost) and then translated into Latin and Aragonese at the request of Peter the Ceremonious.

No inspired historical writing is found after the extinction of the Catalan-Aragonese dynasty in 1410. While some writers were satisfied with simple lists of names and facts (such as the *Noticiari* by Joan

Toralles of Vic and the *Dietari* by Jaume Safont), others took to political pamphleteering (*La fi del comte d'Urgell* and Joan Francesc Boscà's *Memorial*), and still others attempted to write "world histories" (a *Flos mundi* of 1407 and the *Libre de les nobleses dels reys* by a certain Francesc, from Barcelona). The *Història* written in 1438 by Pere Tomich, concentrating on genealogies and legends, found a wide readership, especially in its expanded version, called the *Recort,* made in 1476 by Gabriel Turell. Melcior Miralles' *Dietari del capellà d'Alfons el Magnànim* disappoints by not showing any perception of the Renaissance ideals introduced by Alphonse IV the Magnanimous (Alfons IV in Catalonia; Alfons V in Aragon: 1416–1458), who conquered Naples in 1442.

Non-Catalan books of historical character known through translations—many coming from the royal chancellery of King Peter III—include Livy's *Roman History,* of which only books I to VII remain, based on Bersuire's French version (unique manuscript at the British Museum). Valerius Maximus' moralizing *Nine Books on the Romans' Famous Deeds and Sayings* was first translated by an "incompetent" anonymous into Catalan, and then by that translator's critic Antoni Canals into Valencian. This version was used as a basis for the first Castilian translation. The not infrequent distinction between "Catalan" and "Valencian" seems to have more sociopolitical than linguistic justification.

King Martin I had in his library a Catalan version of Justinus, now lost. Parts of Plutarch and Quintus Curcius were translated by Lluís de Fenollet, using Decembrio's Italian version from 1481. Josephus' *Antiquities of the Jews* was translated by a team consisting of a theologian, a lawyer, and a bookseller (1482). Important medieval Latin historical texts put into Catalan include Guido delle Colonne's *Historia destructionis Troiae,* or *Històries Trojanes* in the Catalan, very well translated by the royal notary Jaume Conesa (*ca.* 1370), and the *Speculum historiale,* abbreviated by the inquisitor Jaume Domenec (*ca.* 1380), who also translated Frontinus (manuscript lost).

Religious and devotional texts. The story of the Bible in medieval Catalonia is complicated by the use made by early translators of French and Provençal versions. In 1287 King Alphonse III ordered the lawyer Jaume de Montjuic to make a translation from the French. A reference to a Bible in Catalan given to a prince who died in 1347 provides another early date. But the surviving manuscripts, especially the ones in Paris (Bibliothèque Nationale, MSS esp. 2–4, 5486) and London (British Museum, MS Eg. 1526), that might preserve parts of those original versions have not yet been studied and edited.

Around 1400 a team headed by the Carthusian prior Bonifaci Ferrer made a very literal translation of the Vulgate, which was printed in 1478 at Valencia (only copy in the Hispanic Society in New York). The Gospels survive in another early translation. The Psalms were translated before 1313 by Romeu Sabruguera (of a somewhat later version of the Psalter only fragments remain). A versification of the Bible, perhaps done before 1243, that is preserved unpublished in the Columbine Library in Seville, is quite charming, but in general no attempts were made to improve the literary style of the prose Bible until Joan Roís de Corella's *Psalteri* (1490). Fragments of rhymed biblical stories are in the Bibliothèque Nationale, Paris (MS esp. 472). A summary of the Old Testament, the *Gènesi de Scriptura,* is a translation from the Provençal. Novelesque stories based on apocryphal materials (Nativity and Passion of Christ, the destruction of Jerusalem, vengeance of Christ, a speech against mankind by the devil's advocate) are probably translations as well. The most successful biblical commentaries were Pope Gregory I's *Moralia in Job* and commentaries on the Psalms by Nicholas of Lyra and Pope Innocent III. Gregory's *Dialogues* were translated quite early.

The life of Christ was known through extensive original works by Eiximenis and Sister Isabel de Villena (posthumous edition, 1497) and through Roís de Corella's *Cartoixà* (1495–1500), a translation of the Carthusian Ludolf of Saxony's *Vita Christi,* and an anonymous version of St. Bonaventure's *Contemplatio.* Lives of saints make up an important part of Old Catalan texts. The complete translation of Jacobus de Voragine's *Legenda aurea* (Golden legend) may date from the end of the thirteenth century; it was much expanded in a late manuscript from Vic. Rufin's *Vitae patrum* and Cassian's *Collationes* were also translated early. The *Flores sanctorum* in several medieval libraries may designate various texts and versions (one claims to be a translation from Gerson). Among the saints, Margaret, Mary of Egypt, Jerome, Honoratus of Arles, and Anthony the Abbot attracted most of the popular attention, aside from Catalonia's patron saint, George (San Jordi). Miracles of the Virgin Mary were transcribed separately or in the usual exempla collections. Among surviving verse catechisms is the *Lausor de la Divinitat* from the last decade of the fourteenth century.

There are few original Catalan treatises of the late thirteenth and fourteenth centuries on theological or dogmatic subjects. Most of the great European books were, however, rendered into Catalan at that time. Raoul de Presles's secondhand annotated French version of St. Augustine's *City of God* was translated rather too literally into Catalan, and from this text into Castilian. Gregory's forty *Homilies,* Issac's *De religione,* Humberto's *De mistica theologia,* and Hugh of St. Cher's *Speculum ecclesiae* were all available in Catalan by the end of the fourteenth century. Of mostly popular appeal are the works of Pere Pasqual from Valencia, martyred in 1300 as bishop of Jaén, of which only the Latin translation (1676) survives. His catechism was called the *Biblia parva.* Also, in order to assist in the conversion of Jews and Muslims, a translation of Peter Alfonso's *Dialogus contra Judaeos* was made. His *Disciplina clericalis* probably also circulated in Catalan. *Dels vicis e virtuts* is a translation of the *Somme le Roy* by the French confessor Laurent de Bois (eight manuscripts). The extensive *Summa collationum* (three manuscripts) of the Franciscan John of Wales, and his *Breviloquium,* were read in the original and the translation.

Sermons survive in great numbers in Catalonia. Even *artes praedicandi* were numerous, perhaps paralleling the traditional interest in political rhetoric noticeable in royal circles (for instance, the elaborate speeches to parliament). The *Contemplació de la Santa Quarentena* of Joan Eiximenis, a Franciscan from Majorca, said to be inspired by Ubertino de Casale's *Arbor vitae,* remains unpublished. The extremely popular St. Vicent Ferrer (*d.* 1419) is known to have preached, in Catalan, all over Europe; his theological articles, however, were written in Latin, and of his long but impassioned sermons there remain only about 280 summarizing transcripts taken by listeners. More influenced by the approaching Renaissance was the Dominican Antoni Canals, who lived in Valencia at the same time and was very much appreciated by the royal household. Well known for his elegant translations of short texts by the pseudo-Bernard and Hugh of St. Victor (*De arra de ànima*) and of extensive works by Valerius Maximus (with interpolations) and Seneca, and for his compilation of *Scipió e Aníbal,* based on Petrarch and Livy, Canals' most personal works are of a religious nature: *Scala de contemplació* and *Tractat de confessió.*

Mystic theology, after the towering figure of Ramon Lull, found new, original expression within the spiritualist movement and the influence of the dawning *devotio moderna*. Bonaventure's *Stimulus amoris*, Domenico Cavalca's *Specchio della croce*, and Catherine of Siena's *Dialogo della divina providenza* circulated in Catalan. Many translations, however, are now lost, and in the case of other texts that seem to be translations, the original has not yet been identified (*Floretes, Amoretes, Tractat de beatitut*, several *Contemplacions*). Bernat Oliver (*d.* 1348) wrote in Latin, but his main work was immediately put into Catalan with the title *Excitatori de la pensa a Déu*. Since Ramon Ros wrote his *Del menyspreu del món* in 1320, it cannot be related to the *Imitatio Jesucristi* attributed at the time to Gerson. The *Imitatio* was published in Catalan rhythmic prose in 1482 by Miquel Pérez. Pérez is also known for his lives of St. Catherine, of the Virgin Mary, and of St. Vicent Ferrer. Another Valencian to write saints' lives was Joan Roís de Corella, who also reacted against the misogynist literary movement and wrote on mythological themes.

Lo pecador remut (The redeemed sinner) by Felip de Malla (*d.* 1431) is an original ascetic-allegorical text that shows the literary interests of a widely traveled orator, theologian, and preacher. Humanistic ideals had less impact on the Valencian Francesc de Pertussa, author of the somewhat obtuse *Memorial de la fe cathólica* (1440). In prison for having supported Prince Charles of Viana and King Henry IV, Fra Pero Martines wrote four lengthy poems and his moving ascetic treatise *Mirall dels divinals assots* in 1463. The *Spill de la vida religiosa*, until recently attributed to the Hieronymite Miquel Comalada, a novelesque and allegorizing journey of mystical contemplation, found pan-European acceptance (published 1515; Spanish edition of 1541, *El deseoso*, was an important Erasmian pastoral work).

Practical, didactic, and philosophical prose texts. Collections of *proverbis* (famous sayings), of biblical, oriental, or (pseudo) classical origins (*Lo libre de Cató*) were as common in Catalonia as in the rest of Europe. James I wrote a *Libre de la saviesa o de doctrina*, and James II had his physician and interpreter Jafuda Bonsenyor compile the *Libre de paraules de savis e de filòsofs*, a text later plagiarized in the *Doctrina moral* (which is no longer attributed to the Majorcan Nicolau Pachs). An early translation of the pseudo-Aristotelian *Secretum secretorum* remains unpublished. Other collections of moral guidelines and rules (*castics* and *conseyls*) also seem to be translations. The apostate Franciscan Anselm Turmeda may be the author of the *Libre de tres* (lists of three

things that have something in common; compare Salomó's *Tria sunt . . .*), which surprises by its notes of satire and humor.

Among works with scientific ambitions are the astrological treatises of Dalmau Saplana and Bartomeu Tresvents, well represented in the royal library. John I was exceptionally superstitious and much disturbed by apocalyptical prophesies made by Eiximenis in his *Dotzé*. The greatest Catalan physician, Arnald of Villanova, had a predecessor in the Dominican Tederic, whose book on surgery circulated in Catalan and Castilian translations. The *Thesaurus pauperum* of Petrus Hispanus, Safid and al-Coati's ophthalmological treatise, and Guy de Chauliac's surgical manual, plus extracts from works attributed to Albertus Magnus and assembled with the title *Coses pertenents a la conservació de la vida,* all circulated in Catalan; James of Agramunt (*Regiments de preservació*), and later the Valencian Lluis d'Alcanyis, wrote on epidemics in Catalan. Manual Diez's *Menescalia* may be only a part of a more extensive veterinary manual (also in Castilian translation).

Lapidaries, bestiaries, and herbals are mostly translations. Palladius' *De agricultura*, also known as *De re rustica,* was translated twice; the 1385 version was by the royal secretary Ferrer Sayol, and the later one served as basis for the Spanish translation. Cookbooks include the *Libre de cuina de sent Soví* and the *Llibre del coch* by Master Robert. Among the medieval "encyclopedias" were translations of the *De proprietatibus rerum* of Bartholomaeus Anglicus and the *Livres dou tresor* of Brunetto Latini (a complete one by Guillem de Copons, *ca.* 1408).

Except for Lull, original philosophical treatises are rare. The book on ethics in the *Tresor* also circulated in two separate translations. Cicero's *De officiis* was poorly translated by the Franciscan Nicolau Quilis (four manuscripts), while a version of the *Paradoxa* (1444) by the Majorcan Ferran Valentí shows the humanistic training of its author. Seneca was known through a translation of Manelli's *Epistolarum Senecae expositio*, a *Sumari de Seneca* by Pere Mollà (perhaps from Valencia), and translations of the *De providentia* (by Antoni Canals), the *Moralia,* and the letters (based on a French version). A pre-1362 translation of Boethius' *De consolatione philosophiae* by the Dominican Pere Saplana, dedicated to the imprisoned prince James IV of Majorca, was later revised by Antoni de Genebreda, whose text was then put into Castilian (1488). The *Dragmaticon philosophiae* of Guillaume de Conches circulated in a Catalan version titled *Suma de filosofia* (Paris, Bibliothèque Nationale, MSS esp. 255, 473). In spite of their titles, the *Breviari d'amor* by Matfre Ermengaud, the short treatises by Albertano of Brescia, and the *Chess-book* of Jacobus de Cessolis, all translated into Catalan shortly before the end of the fourteenth century, exhibit a moralizing tone of popular philosophy.

Among books of law the *Libre del Consolat del mar,* already mentioned, is justly famous. Dating from the twelfth century, it orders and standardizes traditional maritime law, and later became fundamental for British maritime statutes. It was first printed in 1484. The *Ordinacions de la reial casa d'Aragó sobre lo regiment de tots los oficials de la sua cort,* plus a translation of parts of the Castilian *Siete partidas,* and finally the *Tractat de cavalleria de Sant Jordi* are all legal compilations written for King Peter III the Ceremonious, who was very interested in codifying court ceremony and upgrading the style and language of official oratory. Honoré Bonet's *Arbre des batailles* circulated in a translation. Of more social than literary interest are the *Lletres de batalla,* epistolary exchanges between noble knights on questions of chivalric conduct.

BELLES LETTRES

Even though the distinction between fiction and nonfiction was less sharp in the Middle Ages, some readers must have developed a feeling for literary works with an aesthetic appeal. After Lull's successful attempts at novelization in lyric prose, truly original creative literature developed in Catalonia, especially in the genre of the *noves rimades* (courtly or allegorical narratives in verse, growing out of adaptations of French lais and fabliaux and the whole cycle of the Breton-Arthurian materials).

The main classics famous in the Middle Ages were read in the Catalan-speaking kingdoms. Good translations, however, were lacking before the influence of humanism and the Renaissance, which was felt earlier in Barcelona and Valencia than in Castile. A fourteenth-century translation of Ovid, of the *Epistolae heroidum* or of the *Metamorphoses* or both, is mentioned as being in King Martin's library in 1410, and may be the one found in a Parisian manuscript. The attribution of it to Francesc de Pino or to a certain Nicolas is disputed. The version of Ovid by Francesc Alegre (1494) is preceded by an interesting prologue, and followed by a lengthy commentary based on Boccaccio's *De genealogia deorum.* Alegre also translated Bruni's account of the First

Punic War (1472), and shows Italian influence in his original *Somni* and *Raonament entre Francesc Alegre i Esperonça* (Dispute with Lady Hope). His *Passió de Jesucrist* was printed five times in the fifteenth century. It is doubtful that various anonymous works found in the Barcelona manuscript called *Jardinet d'orats* (*Amors de Neptú i Diana, Sermó d'amor, Requesta d'amor*) can be attributed to Alegre.

Seneca had an able translator in Antoni Vilaragut (*d.* 1400), but only four plays survive. Ovid's influence on Roís de Corella is obvious. Dante's *Divine Comedy* was widely admired from the early fifteenth century. Andreu Febrer finished his verse translation in 1429, acclaimed in the *Prohemio* by the marquess of Santillana. (The 1428 translator of the *Divine Comedy* into Castilian, Henry of Villena, was the son of Peter the Ceremonious; he also wrote in Catalan, but the original Catalan version of the *Doce trabajos de Hércules* is lost.) The Franciscan Joan Pasqual used the original of the *Inferno,* together with Italian commentaries, to compile his *Tractat de les penes particulars d'Infern* (1436), incorporated in his *Summa de l'altra vida.* Another imitation of the *Inferno* is *La glória d'amor* by Bernat Hug de Rocabertí.

Boccaccio was esteemed more as a medieval wise man than as a harbinger of the Renaissance. His Latin works were widely known; a translation of the *De mulieribus claris* is lost today, but was imitated by Antoni de Vallmanya in his *Sort feta en laor de les monges de Valldonzella.* Narcis Franch's pre-1397 translation of the *Corbaccio* is not very good, but the anonymous version of the *Decameron* of 1429 is excellent. The anonymous Catalan *Fiammetta* dates from 1440.

Petrarch was better known for his Latin works. Book VII of the *Africa* was ably translated by Antoni Canals as *Raonament fet entre Scipió e Aníbal.* A translation of the *De remediis utriusque fortunae* is now lost, but there survives an anthology of extracts (*Flors . . .*). The *Trionfi* were copied in Italian, but with Bernardo Lapini's commentary added in Catalan. Petrarch's *Canzoniere* did not gain much influence before the end of the fifteenth century. Jordi de Sant Jordi (*d. ca.* 1423), the best-known Petrarchist poet, will be considered apart, as will Bernat Metge, the major figure of original humanistic Catalan prose in the fourteenth century.

Apart from Bernat Metge's *Lo somni,* the genre of travel to the otherworld is represented by a *Visió de Tundal, Lo venturós pelegrí,* the *Viatge al pur-*

gatori de Sant Patrici (1397) by the Roussillonese nobleman Ramon de Perellós (no Catalan manuscript remains, only the edition of 1486), and the verse *Testament* of Bernat Serradell from Vic (before 1446).

The pearl of fifteenth-century prose is the lengthy chivalric novel *Curial e Guelfa,* by a still unknown writer active sometime between 1435 and 1462 (only one manuscript remains; there are several editions). It is less dependent on French models than the somewhat later *Història del cavaller Partinobles de Bles,* but not as historically authentic as the *Història de Jacob Xalabín* (*ca.* 1400), nor as ambitious in its originality as the lengthy *Libre del cavaller Tirant lo Blanch,* written after 1460 (for Ferdinand of Portugal, pretender to the Catalan throne) by Joanot Martorell (*d.* 1468) and published in 1490 by Martí Joan de Galba. The *Tirant,* translated into Castilian in 1511, was called, in Cervantes' *Don Quixote,* "the world's greatest book." The Italian version of 1501, now lost, influenced Ariosto, and through him Shakespeare and Spenser.

Curial and *Tirant* are, surprisingly, more realistic than the French chivalric novels. The first describes the education of a knight named Curial, a poor and timid lad patronized by a young widow whom he finally marries, after many temptations during his travels through a sophisticated world (which seems to be the one of King Peter II). Tirant, educated at the English court along the lines of the legendary Guy of Warwick, proves his worth in innumerable adventures all over the Mediterranean (for instance, at the siege of Rhodes in 1444), until his delivery of the Byzantine Empire from the Turks and his marriage to the emperor's daughter. The novel may reflect historical facts, and Tirant resembles the famous Hungarian knight John Hunyadi, who three years after the fall of Constantinople subdued the Turks at Belgrade. Catalonia, and even more so Valencia, remained a fertile ground for wandering knights throughout the fifteenth century. Even foreign squires sought adventures there, participating, often with much pomp, in the jousts, *pasos honrosos,* and other allegorical war games. The social class still living those medieval myths might have been avid readers of chivalric novels, but they did not foment any creative literary production.

POETRY AFTER 1300

The *Mirall de trobar* by the Majorcan Berenguer d'Anoya and the *Doctrinal de trobar* by Ramon de Cornet (the latter with a commentary by Joan de Castellnou, dedicated to Count Peter of Aragon) reinforced Catalonia's dependency on northern poetic models even though ever more writers had linguistic difficulties with Provençal. But the self-confident urban upper class, enriched by the mercantile expansion, could not identify with the by now anachronistic troubadour imitations in Provençal or with the simple popular religious or narrative poetry.

In the development of an autochthonous poetry, Ramon Lull is again the leading figure. A turning away from Provençal models and a growing awareness of indigenous cultural possibilities can be seen in satires like the *Disputació d'En Buc e son cavall* and in the original verse production of the misogynous Capellà de Bolquera, preserved in a poetic anthology from Ripoll transcribed in 1346. This manuscript also contains other realistic and skeptical rhymes, including a debate between a friar and a layman, a complaint of an unwilling nun, a "dance" by Pere Alamany, a Christmas song, an alba, and "The Queen of Majorca's Complaint" about her husband's absence—attributable, perhaps, to James III's second wife, Violant de Vilaragut.

However, the aristocratic circles continued to support the traditional styles, and the royal protectors and Maecenases of poets reinforced this by commissioning theoretical works. For the literary court of Peter III (1336–1387) Jaume March wrote a 6,000-word *Libre de concordances* (rhyme dictionary) in 1371, and Lluís d'Averçó, the rhetoric treatise *Torcimany* (The interpeter) and a rhyme dictionary.

At Toulouse in 1323 in the south of France, the Consistori de la Gaya Ciència was founded to revive the Provençal poetic tradition, which had fallen upon hard times under the political and religious domination of the north. Those pressures limited the range of possible topics, and most of the prize-winning entries were rather poor. Several Catalan poets participated in the yearly event, even after they had their own *jocs florals* (flower games, alluding to the prizes given). Already in 1338, before Peter III, a song festival was held in Lérida, but it was only in 1393 that King John I founded, in Barcelona, a chapter of the Toulouse Gaya Ciència. After a few years of lapses due to the city's unwillingness to finance the poetic jousts, King Martin I renewed them after 1398, using as judges the founding members Jaume March and Lluís d'Averçó. The Spanish poet Enrique de Villena, present at the 1408 festival, describes the pompous ceremonial in his *Arte de trovar.* In 1413 Ferdinand of Antequera—under the terms of the Compromise of Caspe elected successor to the heirless Martin I, over James, count of Urgell—revalidated the charter of the Consistori. Although in Toulouse the poetry competitions went on until 1484, in Catalonia the political changes led to an earlier disinterest.

Some poets, such as Lluís Icart, went on sending works to Toulouse, while others participated in privately organized poetry readings, especially in Valencia. In 1454, for instance, Pere Miquell Carbonell won the prize for the best poem in honor of St. Mary Magdalene, and in 1458 Pere Pou called upon his friends to join him in his *deseiximent* (challenge) to *Fals Amor*. In the case of only a few poems we can be sure that they were written as entries for the *gaia festa*. They are by writers already famous for other poetry collections: Gilabert de Próxita from Valencia (twenty-one poems probing the lover's morose state of mind); Andreu Febrer from Vic (eleven love songs that predate his contacts with Italy and his translation of Dante); and Guillem de Masdovelles, uncle of two other poets; with the first, Joan Berenguer, Guillem exchanged six poetic debates; the second nephew compiled the important *Cançoner de Masdovelles*. In his well-known *Prohemio* the marquess of Santillana mentions as famous the Catalan poet Pau of Bellviure, but only one complete poem of his remains.

Italian influences appear in the second half of the fourteenth century. Pere de Queralt (d. 1408) parodizes a line by Petrarch, and Melchior de Gualbes shows the conceptual influences of the *dolce stil nuovo*. Others, of more limited inspiration, followed traditional modes: Ramon Savall's lament on social decay, Arnau d'Erill's *sirventès* (satires) against his philandering nephew, Gabriel Ferruç's *Complaint* (on the death of Ferdinand of Antequera, 1416), and Fra Johan Basset's Marian lyrics. Jaume March (d. 1410) wrote symbolic and allegorical narrative poems (*Debat entre Honor et Delit*). His brother Pere (d. 1413) wrote not only a verse description of knight's armor, *Arnès del cavaller*, but also some reflective and moralizing poems. He was the father of the great Ausiàs March. Another member of the March family, Arnau, was active before 1420–1430, the years of the compilation, known today—after two former owners—as *Cançoner Vega-Aguiló*.

Fully "de-Provençalized" Catalan had become by that date the language of poetry, and it was now rather northern France that made its influence felt. Among the numerous followers of Ausiàs March, and to a lesser degree of Jordi de Sant Jordi, those considered outstanding include Lluís de Vilarrasa (five ballads), Martí Garcia (complaints about his lady's absence), Lluís de Requesens (*cobles*), Perot Joan (songs in prison), Blai Seselles (*Deseiximent d'amor*), Mossèn Avinyó (moralizing about death), Lleonard de Sors (*La nau*), Joan Moreno, and Francesc Ferrer (*Lo conhort*, the *Romanç del setge de Rodas* about the Turk's siege of Rhodes in 1444). Ferrer's *Romanç* is only one example of a briefly successful genre of verse narrations on contemporary events. Joan Fogassot used it to describe the imprisonment of Prince Charles of Viana by his own father John II (Joan II in Catalonia and Aragon: 1458–1479) in 1461, and then his liberation. The bilingual poet Pere Torroella, highly esteemed at the court of Alphonse IV the Magnanimous in Naples, was present during Prince Charles's last months, and Guillem Gibert wrote a complaint about his death.

In general, political verse was in vogue in the second half of the fifteenth century. Five poets wrote about the fall of Constantinople. An anonymous Valencian criticized Barcelona for having acclaimed as king the Castilian Henry IV, instead of the legitimate John II. It was perhaps the same Valencian who wrote two more compositions during the civil war of 1462–1472. The visit to Barcelona in 1473 of Prince Ferdinand, future king of Castile, was celebrated by an unknown poet. Valencia, which enjoyed several prosperous decades, became a center of regular literary festivals. The one in 1474 led to one of the very first books printed in Catalan, the *Trobes en laor de la Verge Maria*.

Three writers deserve special mention: Joan Roís de Corella, who corresponded with the prince of Viana and wrote an *Oració* to Mary and *Tragèdia de Caldesa* in very elaborate prose; Mossèn Bernat Fenollar (d. 1516), known for his *Scacs d'amor*, written in collaboration with other poets (with whom he also engaged in poetic debates, such as the *Procés de les olives*, 1497); and Jaume Gasull, especially fond of literary discussions among local poets, starting points for his *La brama dels llauradors* and *Lo somni de Joan Joan*.

Jaume Roig's (d. 1478) *Spill* (or *Libre de les dones*) must be mentioned under the heading of poetry because it is written in more than 8,000 couplets, four syllables to the line, a rather old-fashioned and tiring meter. It is a pessimistic satire against women in the form of a picaresque biography (not autobiography; Roig was a rich medical examiner) of a poor lad who does well and then has to suffer through a series of nightmarish marriages that make him reflect—in the company of King Solomon—on matrimony (editions in 1531, 1561, 1735).

The last poets to write in Catalan in the last decades of the fifteenth century were the army general Bernat Hug de Rocabertí (*Glòria d'amor*, a Dantesque "Hell of the Infatuated"), the Barcelona notary public Antoni Vallmanya (poems in praise of nuns), the Roussillonese squire Moner (more famous for his Spanish works), and the Barcelona city councillor Romeu Llull, who also wrote incidental rhymes in Italian and Castilian.

With the fifteenth century ends the classic period of Catalan literature, even in Valencia. Just as at its beginnings Catalan-speaking persons wrote in Provençal, now writers abandoned their native tongue in favor of Castilian. Popular poetry (the *cançoner* and *romancer*) and religious plays for Christmas, Easter, and the Assumption (*Misteri* of Elche) continued to be passed on orally throughout the next three centuries, but most attempts at higher literature were made in Spanish (or, in university circles, in Latin). This was not for linguistic or economic reasons (the total loss of political freedom came only in 1714, and of linguistic freedom in 1939), but because of the subtle social pressures of the court and the higher classes, no longer bilingual in Catalan and Aragonese but now strictly Castilian-speaking.

The imposition of foreign kings and the presence of a non-Catalan viceroyalty put an end to regional nationalism, just as humanistic and Renaissance ideals recommended the use of more universal languages. Catalan lived on in the countryside, and thus was available for readaptation by all social classes during the early nineteenth-century movement of the *renaixença*, which led to a renewed and continuing consciousness of being a separate nation in the Spanish state.

BIBLIOGRAPHY

The standard work on the history of medieval Catalan literature is Martí de Riquer, *Història de la literatura catalana*, I–III (1964, repr. 1980). Another work by Riquer is *Literatura catalana medieval* (1972). See also Rubió Balaguer, *Literatura catalana*, integrated into Guillermo Díaz-Plaja, *Historia general de las literaturas hispánicas,* I (1949), 637–746, and III (1953), 727–930; Joan Ruiz i Calonja, *Historia de la literatura catalana* (1954); Joaquim Molas and Josep Romeu, *Literatura catalana antiqua,* 4 vols. (1961–1964); Jaume Vidal Alcover, *Síntesi d'història de la literatura catalana*, III (1980), 13–232. Germá Colón, *Literatura catalana* (1975), contains about thirty removable color slides on medieval topics in special pockets in the end-pages. Medieval literature is very well represented in

Joaquim Molas and Josep Massot i Muntaner, eds., *Diccionari de la literatura catalana* (1979, reedited 1981).

Works in English are Paul Russell-Gebbet, "Medieval Catalan Literature," in his *Spain: A Companion to Spanish Studies* (1976); and Arthur Terry, *Catalan Literature* (1972), also available in an enlarged Spanish version (1976). Most of the above works contain bibliographies, which are brought up to date by announcements and reviews in *Serra d'or,* an influential cultural monthly from the monastery of Montserrat, Barcelona. Most of the reviews have been reprinted in Josep Massot, *La literatura de l'Edat Mitjana a la Renaixença* (1980). See also José Simón Díaz, *Bibliografia de la literatura hispánica* (1950–); and the bibliographic issues of *Revista de filología española, Nueva revista de filología hispánica, PMLA,* and *The Year's Work in Modern Language Studies.*

Medieval Catalan texts have been published beginning in 1847 by Próspero and Manuel Bofarull y de Palau (Colección de Documentos Inéditos del Archivo de la Corona de Aragón); between 1873 and 1905 by Marià Aguiló y Fuster and Àngel Aguiló y Miró (Biblioteca Catalana; Cançoneret); between 1908 and 1950 by Ramón Miguel y Planas (Biblioteca Catalana, 20 vols.; Històries d'Altre Temps; Textes Catalans Antichs; Bibliofilia). More recent series include the Biblioteca Catalana d'Obres Antiques, directed by Pere Bohigas, former curator of the more than 2,000 manuscripts at the Biblioteca de Catalunya in Barcelona; the Biblioteca Torres Amat, published by the Department of Catalan Philology at the University of Barcelona; the Clàssics Albatros from Valencia and the new Biblioteca Escriny de Textos Medievals Breus, directed by Jaume Riera.

The most important series is Els Nostres Clàssics, directed since 1924 by Josep M. de Casacuberta (ser. A, over 120 vols.; larger-size ser. B, 7 vols.), who also publishes the Collecció Popular Barcino. Edicions 62 publishes modernized versions of the classics in the Antologia Catalana and Les Millors Obres de la Literatura Catalana, following in the footsteps of the Editorial Selecta. Some editions are subsidized by the Foundation Vives Casajuana or appear in learned journals, such as *Anuari de l'Institut d'estudis catalans* (from its beginnings in 1907 until 1936); *Analecta sacra tarraconensia, boletín* or *Memorias de la Real Academia de buenas letras de Barcelona* (directed by Martí de Riquer); *Estudis romànics* (directed by the secretary of the Institut d'Estudis Catalans, Ramon Aramon); *Boletin de la Sociedad castellonense de cultura; Estudis franciscans; Revista valenciana de filología* (since 1951); and the newly revived *Estudis universitaris catalans.* For a survey of Old Catalan scholarship, see vol. 5 of *Estudis de llengua i literatura catalanes* (1982); and the *Repertori de catalanòfils* planned for vol. 7 of this same journal.

CURT WITTLIN

[See also **Arnald of Villanova; Chronicles; Eiximenis, Francesc; Historiography, Western European; Jordi de S.**

Jordi; Lull, Ramon; March, Ausiàs; Metge, Bernat; Peter the Ceremonious, Literary Court; Provençal Literature; Santillana, Marquess of; Translations and Translators, Western European; Troubadour, Trouvère, Trovadores; Villena, Enrique de.]

CATALAN NARRATIVE IN VERSE. Most medieval Catalan narrative was written in *noves rimades*. The Provençal *Leys d'amors* define the term *novas* (Catalan *noves*) as the name given to a poetic composition consisting of an indefinite number of couplets, normally of eight-syllable lines, without specifying its content or nature. Originally, however, the term *novas* or *noves* indicated the narrative character of a text, and *noves rimades* therefore may refer not only to a poem's stanzaic form but also to its generic nature, being then equivalent to the French *roman*.

In the late fourteenth and fifteenth centuries narrative literature was also written in *codolades*, unequal couplets consisting of one four-syllable and one eight-syllable line. The term *codolada* refers only to the poem's form. The *codolades* tend to become enjambed couplets that sound like rhythmic prose; the *noves rimades,* instead, tend to be closed couplets with clear rhyme and a reasonable degree of syntactical completeness in each line. A highly provençalized language is common to most Catalan *noves rimades* until the second quarter of the fifteenth century; the *codolades,* as a rule, are written in Catalan, though Provençal linguistic traits may be found in some of them. The *noves rimades* often reflect Provençal and French models, while the *codolades* seem to be a more autochthonous genre.

Arthurian themes, for instance, are present in Guillem de Torroella's ambitious poem *La faula* (The fable, *ca.* 1375), in the anonymous *Blandin de Cornualha,* and in the Provençal *Jaufré,* which was probably written by a Catalan. Other French influences may be felt in the three late-fourteenth-century anonymous works: *Storia de l'amat Frondino e de Brisona* (Story of the loved Frondino and Brisona), an epistolary novel in prose and *noves rimades; Frayre de Joy e Sor de Plaser* (Brother of Joy and Sister of Pleasure), which develops folkloric motifs; and *Salut d'Amor* (Greeting of Love), an allegory in letter form.

Courtly love and life seen in terms of troubadour poetry are the subject of many narrative poems, such as those written in Provençal by the Catalan Ramon

Vidal de Besalú. Some *noves rimades* within this category are only brief expositions of the lovers' feelings or descriptive vignettes of courtly scenes: the anonymous short poem *El déu d'Amor caçador* (The hunter god of Love), *Una ventura* (A happy adventure) by Vicenç Comes, and the works of Jaume (*ca.* 1335–*ca.* 1410) and Pere March (*ca.* 1338–1413), the uncle and the father of Ausiàs March. Of greater interest is the *Procés de la Senyora de Valor contra En Bertran Tudela* (Lawsuit of the Lady of Valor against Bertran Tudela, 1406), which illustrates courtly love behavior with many quotations from well-known troubadours. Its author, Francesc de la Via, also wrote an autobiographical love letter with a tenuous plot, *A Bella Venus* (To beautiful Venus, *ca.* 1420), and a satiric and amusing story in *codolades,* the *Libre de Fra Bernat* (Book of Friar Bernat, *ca.* 1435).

Lo conhort (Consolation), by Francesc Ferrer, is a complaint against love that is used as a pretext to mention several contemporary Catalan poets; and the strange poem *Vesió* (Vision, *ca.* 1382), by Bernat de So, is a complex allegory of historical and political interest.

Humorous and satiric narrative is well represented in two poems in *codolades,* the *Libre de Fra Bernat,* mentioned above, and the *Testament* (Last will, 1422–1424) of Bernat Serradell de Vic, which are colorful pictures of fifteenth-century society satirizing lecherous friars and exposing human weakness. Of similar nature and characteristics are three anonymous poems in *noves rimades* of the late fourteenth century: the *Disputació d'En Buc ab son cavall* (Debate between Buc and his horse), *El sagristà i la burgesa* (The verger and the bourgeoise), and *Planys del cavaller Mataró* (Complaint of the gentleman Mataró).

Besides two interesting texts in *noves rimades,* the *Libre de Fortuna e Prudencia* (Book of Fortune and Prudence) and *Medicina apropriada a tot mal* (Medicine good for all diseases), Bernat Metge wrote his *Sermó* in *codolades.* The *Sermó* was a pointed parody of the contemporary art of preaching, inspired by the *episcopus puerorum* sermons (sermons of the children's bishop), of which two anonymous samples, one in *noves rimades* and one in *codolades,* have survived in Catalan literature.

The masterpiece of Catalan narrative in verse is the *Spill* (The mirror), also known as *Libre de les dones* (Book of women) and *Libre de consells* (Book of good advice). Its author, Jaume Roig, was a well-known public figure in Valencia and an eminent physician who served the wife of king Alphonse V and the daughter of John II. The *Spill,* probably completed in 1459, is written in the awkward form of couplets having four-syllable lines, which Roig aptly called *noves rimades comediades* (halved noves rimades). Such short lines lead to complex syntactical structures and a monotonous rhyme that spoil the enjoyment of an otherwise remarkable text, the colorful language and intrinsic narrative values of which make it a true forerunner of the picaresque novel. The story, which is told in the first person, is misogynistic in nature and takes advantage of the protagonist's misadventures with women to present a realistic and lively tableau of fifteenth-century life.

BIBLIOGRAPHY

P. J. Bohene, *Dream and Fantasy in Early Catalan Prose* (1975); Jaime Masso Torrents, *Repertori de l'antiga literatura catalana,* I (1932); Manuel Mila y Fontanals, "Les noves rimades, la codolada," in *Obras completas,* III (1890), 361-440; Arsenio Pacheco-Ransanz, "Catalan Contribution to the Development of the Spanish Novel," in *Revista canadiense de estudios hispánicos,* 6 (1982); A. Pages, "Le fabliau en Catalogne," in *Estudis universitaris catalans,* 14 (1929); Martín de Riquer, *Història de la literatura catalan* (1964), II, 11-116, and III, 213-253; Jaime Roig, *Spill; o, Libre de consells,* Ramón Miquel y Planas, ed., 2 vols. (1929-1930).

ARSENIO PACHECO-RANSANZ

[See also **Catalan Literature.**]

CATALONIA (800-1137). Like Aragon, the eastern Pyrenees regions later known as Catalonia were first organized as a Christian frontier against the Muslims. But the Frankish activities here were more important, and their impress more lasting, than in Aragon. Charlemagne himself ordered the campaigns in which Girona and Barcelona were reconquered in 785 and 801. Moreover, the earliest counts of these districts seem to have been appointed by the Frankish king, as their successors certainly were. Whether the native populations necessarily preferred Frankish to Moorish masters was another matter. In Barcelona, as in Narbonne a generation before, the Muslim governor had found support among Christians who had prospered in the eighth century, and local coalitions of Goths and Moors troubled Frankish leaders for decades to come. On the other hand, Charlemagne's welcome of Hispano-Gothic refugees north of the Pyrenees, together with his acceptance of Visigothic law as the basis of social order, had fos-

tered sentiment favorable to Frankish rule in the diverse lands (some 40,000 square kilometers) stretching from the region of Conflent (Têt) southward to the Ebro. The Franks spoke of this region as the "March of Spain" in the ninth century.

The Frankish protectorate extended naturally from positions north of the Pyrenees. The key figure was Count William of Toulouse (*d.* 812), a cousin of Charlemagne, whose first wife was probably a Visigoth, and who retired to the monastic life in 806 (he was later canonized) after valiant campaigns against the Moors. He and his sons, in shifting and turbulent combinations, administered nine of the fourteen counties that later constituted Catalonia. But the opportunism of Bernard of Septimania (826-844) alienated his indigenous subjects as well as Charles the Bald, who found legitimist support in Sunifred of Carcassonne (844-848), who was of Visigothic descent. Conquering Cerdanya in 835 and Urgell in 838, Sunifred seems also to have checked a Muslim invasion before it reached Septimania.

These exploits, by a native equally loyal to his homeland and to the king, were not forgotten. But Sunifred fell victim, before his sons were grown, to a revolt by Bernard of Septimania's son; and the king, once having restored order (849), found it increasingly difficult to secure loyal and competent service from the Frankish counts he appointed to the Spanish March. As the Frankish kingdom reeled, it fell to the loyal house of Carcassonne to fulfill its destiny. Guifred the Hairy, Sunifred's eldest son, seems to have been invested with Urgell, Cerdanya, and Conflent as early as 870; to these were added Barcelona and Girona in 878. Guifred associated his younger brothers Miro and Radulf in the administration of Conflent and Besalú, respectively.

The Catalans of later times viewed the reign of Guifred the Hairy (870?-897) as a heroic age of national formation. He was the last count of the Spanish March to receive his commission from a Frankish king, and he supported popular initiatives in resettlement that contributed to a new sense of political and cultural identity in his lands. Guifred and his descendants were to rule Catalonia for more than 500 years.

In the 870's Guifred had encouraged colonization of the wastelands in the Lord Valley, and after 878 settlers spread into the plain of Vic and the upper Llobregat Valley. The people, coming mostly from the Pyrenees, received lands on the liberal tenure of *aprisio* (the taking of lands by freemen in fealty to the emperor and under the count's protection), the new county of Osona was organized. New parish churches were consecrated and endowed; old ones were restored. The bishopric of Vic was restored in 887. Monasteries were founded, notably S. Miquel of Cuixà in the Conflent (878) and, in the new domains, Ripoll (879) and S. Joan de les Abadesses (887). Nevertheless, the situation remained insecure. Guifred lost a battle against the Moors near Lérida in 884; he was killed resisting a Moorish invasion that reached Barcelona (897). There had been no provision for the succession, still legally at the disposition of the Frankish king.

This crisis was resolved through the resolute efforts of Guifred's sons and grandsons, in whose times the Spanish March attained a remarkable degree of political stability. The brothers of the first generation divided the counties among themselves while reserving nominal superiority to the eldest, Guifred II (897–911), who administered Barcelona, Girona, and Osona. Miro II (897–927) succeeded to Cerdanya, Conflent, and Bergueda; Sunifred II (897–948) to Urgell. Upon Guifred II's death Barcelona passed to his younger brother Sunyer (911–947), an irregular devolution for which Miro II was apparently compensated by the succession to Besalú in 913. This remarkable condominium persisted in the second generation (and in some respects much longer), although the counties soon became heritable in themselves.

Juridically nothing had changed. The embattled Guifred II thought it prudent to do homage to King Charles the Simple (899), whose protection continued to seem useful to monasteries in the Spanish March, too. As late as 986–987, following a devastating Moorish attack, appeals were directed to the king. In reality the counts had progressively assumed the Carolingian cause for their own, continuing the work of resettlement, notably in the lower Llobregat region and the Vallès, sponsoring ecclesiastical councils, and inspiring a more aggressive resistance to the Moors.

The accession of a new generation of counts was marked by political reorientation. From Cerdanya and Conflent were initiated contacts with Rome (950–951) that produced the first papal privileges of exemption for Catalonian monasteries. Simultaneously an embassy to Córdoba from Borrell II of Barcelona and Urgell (947–992) concluded a treaty with the caliph that effectively nullified the historic dependence of the March on Frankland. Improved security and confidence encouraged a precocious flowering of ecclesiastical culture. Bishops and ab-

bots, typically scions of the comital lineages, splendidly promoted and endowed their congregations. Cuixà, Vic, and Ripoll became renowned centers of letters and learning. Vic must already have had cultural contacts with Córdoba when Gerbert of Aurillac sojourned there (967–970). In the time of Oliba (b. 971), abbot of Ripoll and Cuixà (1008–1046) and bishop of Vic (1018–1046), Benedictine observance in the Pyrenees came into touch with reformed religious currents in Frankland and Italy. Lombard styling predominated in the churches dedicated at Ripoll (1032), Vic (1035), and Cuixà (1011–1047). Classical Latin, patristics, and Visigothic legal studies were revived at Ripoll.

Although the new culture was nurtured in the uplands, political and economic circumstances were raising Barcelona to predominance in the condominium. Borrell II bore the brunt of al-Manṣūr's invasion that unexpectedly broke the peace in 985. His courageous defense of Barcelona nearly coincided with the demise of the western Carolingian dynasty, which explains why in 988 he styled himself "duke and marquis by God's grace." Under Raymond Borrell, count of Barcelona and Girona (992–1017), new thrusts by al-Manṣūr and ᶜAbd al-Malik (1001–1003) were not merely parried but reversed in damaging counterattacks that culminated in a daring raid on Córdoba itself (1010). This exploit proved a turning point. Henceforth the frontier west of Llobregat was relatively secure, while the booty distributed among Christian warriors and the payments of tribute by taifa chiefs gave impetus to the economy.

The renewed raids had done little more than deflect a movement of sustained economic growth. Contacts with Moorish Spain, friendly and otherwise, resulted in exchanges of slaves, weapons, horses, and cloth. Muslim gold coins circulated around Barcelona in the 970's, and were minted there by 1018. Metallurgy developed; new markets appeared. Even more remarkable was agrarian expansion: continued resettlement, reaching to the coasts of Girona; the improvement of older peasant cultivations through better-equipped labor; the exploitation of new and marginal lands through terracing and ditching. Centered in the coastal plains and their hinterlands, the revitalized economy continued to draw people from the mountains, the primacy of which was ended.

Traditional legal and institutional structures persisted intact into the eleventh century. Ancient settlements and public (fiscal) domains adjoined new peasant settlements in the coastal and sub-Pyrenean

IBERIAN PENINSULA IN THE 11TH CENTURY

valleys. The law remained Visigothic, public, and territorial; the administration, Carolingian. Counts, viscounts, and vicars dominated their lands from well-spaced castles, and relied on the military and economic services of a mostly free population. They held public courts with the aid of judges and clerks learned in the Gothic law.

This social and institutional cohesion collapsed in the second quarter of the eleventh century. Berenguer Ramon I (1017–1035) was unable to maintain his father's momentum against the Moors, thus depriving an upwardly mobile military class of its main outlet. The castles of the aggressive lineages, manned by a new class of mounted warriors, proliferated beyond comital control. Castellans fought among themselves, ravaged peasant lands and requisitioned crops, and imposed on their tenant peasantry an array of obligations that soon hardened into banalities. The courts gave way to private settlements. Seeking to restore public order, the bishops of Elne and Vic inaugurated the Truce of God (1027, 1033) so as to curb the excesses of the new militarism. But the assault on comital prerogatives continued. The revolt of Mir Geribert, who styled himself "prince

of Olèrdola," took two decades (1040–1059) to overcome.

It was Count Ramon Berenguer I (1035–1076) who finally prevailed and established a new political order. Regaining control of the principal castles, he progressively secured the alliance or vassalage of the other counts and viscounts, as well as of other lords of castles. He insisted on the sworn fidelity even of subordinate castellans and knights, together with the right of entry to castles. But little of the old order survived. Ties of personal fidelity proliferated throughout society, replacing the weakened sanctions of the law.

The fief, having originated in the Spanish March as a form of remuneration from fiscal land, became the normal reward, and eventually the precondition, for service and fidelity. Castellans and their enfeoffed knights formed a new aristocracy, its superiority progressively defined in rites of initiation. Most fundamentally, the old free peasantry disappeared wherever castles arose—that is, almost everywhere. Because the counts and viscounts as well as the new aristocracy had violated tenant liberties for economic gain, there could be no redress for the masses, which henceforth were a subservient class. The new order was thus a feudal order dominated by the count of Barcelona. His domains were perceived by foreigners to be a land of castellans *(castlans)*, whence the new appellation "Catalonia" in the twelfth century.

About 1060 began the great age of independent Catalonia. Acting firmly as "princes of the land" to secure the new internal order, Ramon Berenguer I and his wife Almodis imposed the Peace and Truce of God as a territorial statute in 1064. They legislated so as to bring the procedures and tariffs of Visigothic law up to date. Externally, Ramon Berenguer I renewed the pressure on the *taifa* chieftains, who were again obliged to pay tribute.

Thenceforth the counts entered vigorously into affairs of the wider Mediterranean world. Ramon Berenguer II (1076–1082) married a daughter of the

Norman prince Robert Guiscard, and their son married first the Cid's daughter and later the heiress of Provence. The Gregorian reform was introduced into Catalonia in legatine councils held at Besalú (1077) and Girona (1078). Not even the domestic violence that, for the first time, marred the peace of Guifred's dynasty seriously disrupted political affairs: the matricide Peter Raymond was packed off to Spain, while Berenguer Ramon II (1082–1096), charged with the murder of his brother the count in 1082, was permitted to retain the comital title on condition of its passing ultimately to his nephew (Ramon's son) Ramon Berenguer III.

Berenguer Ramon II fought to extend Catalonian claims far to the southwest of secure frontier positions. His attempts to capture Valencia (1085, 1089) were frustrated by the Cid, and settlers were still too few to justify attacking Tortosa. But the coincidence

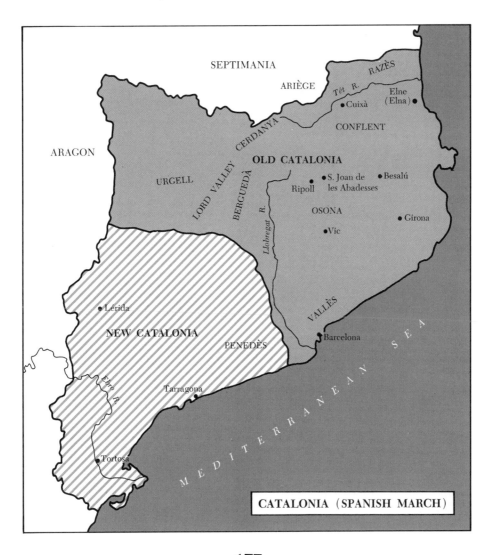

CATALONIA (SPANISH MARCH)

177

of Catalan advances in this zone with the Castilian reconquest of Toledo (1085), the primacy of which seemed to threaten Catalonian ecclesiastical autonomy, led Pope Urban II to proclaim the restoration of the archbishopric of Tarragona (1089, 1091). This was premature. Political complications, together with new invasions by the Almoravids, who devastated the Penedès and threatened Barcelona (1107, 1115), ended hopes of soon securing Tarragona and Tortosa.

Ramon Berenguer III (1086–1131) turned his attention to the possibilities of his dynastic position in Old Catalonia. In 1107 he married his child-daughter to the dotard Bernard III of Besalú on condition of succeeding to that county should Bernard die childless, a condition that was fulfilled (surely not unexpectedly) in 1111. At the death of Count Bernard William (1109–1117) without heirs, Ramon succeeded to Cerdanya, the historic dynastic homeland. These devolutions, deliberately planned, went far toward reconstituting the Guifredian patrimony. But as in the ninth century, the Pyrenees were no barrier. Having inherited the suzerainty of Carcassonne and Razès, counties acquired by his grandparents in 1067, Ramon Berenguer III secured sworn fealties from men of Carcassonne in 1107 and the homage of their count in 1112. In that year, too, Ramon married Dolça of Provence, yet another diplomatic triumph. Entitled count of Provence from 1113 and with trans-Pyrenean domains stretching from Nice to the Ariège, Ramon Berenguer III henceforth threatened the Occitanian hegemony of the count of Toulouse, with whom a treaty of partition was concluded in 1125.

Since establishing ties with Norman Sicily, the lords and merchants of Catalonia had taken to the sea. About 1100 Barcelona was a thriving place, rebuilding within its old walls, expanding in its suburbs, prospering in its trades and industries. Its shippers probably joined the Pisans and Genoese in complaining of piracy by Moors in the Balearic Islands. In 1114–1115 Ramon Berenguer III led a coalition of crusaders to seize Majorca. Although the islands were promptly recaptured by the Almoravids, the exploit was symptomatic of enlarged Catalonian designs in the Mediterranean. In 1118 began new efforts to restore Tarragona. The count commended the city and its hinterland to Bishop Olleguer of Barcelona, who was designated archbishop of Tarragona by the pope. Another decade passed, however, before resettlement began in earnest under the Norman knight Robert Bordet, to whom Olleguer ceded

his jurisdictional rights in 1129. These were trying years on the Christian frontier, for the Almoravids had cut off tributary payments from Muslim princes and otherwise discouraged campaigning. The Aragonese now seemed as threatening to Catalonian prospects as the Moors. In his last years Ramon Berenguer III worked to secure his rights—to develop mercantile tolls, to correct violators of the peace—and planned an overseas crusade.

In 1131 Ramon Berenguer IV succeeded to his father's peninsular lands and the suzerainties of Carcassonne and Razès, while Provence passed to his younger brother Berenguer Ramon (1131–1144). New Aragonese advances on Lérida and Tortosa were ended only by the death of Alphonse I the Battler in 1134. Three years later Ramon Berenguer IV was betrothed to Petronilla, the heiress of Aragon.

Catalonia was less transformed than Aragon by events of the early twelfth century. The major social and institutional changes had occurred earlier; its greatest peninsular conquests still lay ahead. While the division between Old and New Catalonia was well established by 1137, when the count of Barcelona became ruler of both Aragon and Catalonia, New Catalonia remained a deep and insecure frontier of mingled Moorish and Christian settlements. In the old counties the conditions of people remained diverse. The castellans and knights were not yet fully assimilated into the old aristocracy, which continued to command the greater fortunes. Lay estates and castles were becoming hereditary, while peasant tenants were progressively bound to their masters and the land. Unlike the Aragonese, Catalan towns possessed a rising mercantile class, but only a few places in Catalonia could yet boast charters.

Catalan government was hardly less rudimentary than the Aragonese. The counts exploited their domains through castellans and bailiffs. They relied on favored barons and clerics for counsel, and they rewarded a bellicose aristocracy in their campaigns. But the equilibrium between comital and baronial interests was balanced precariously on the prospect of continued conquests.

BIBLIOGRAPHY

Sources. Charters and memorandums are preserved in monastic and episcopal archives such as those of S. Benet de Bages or Vic; and comital (secular) archives. Monastic records are found today mostly in the Archivo de la Corona de Aragón (ACA, Barcelona), Sección Monacales; and Archivo Histórico Nacional (Madrid), Sección Clero; episcopal and capitular collections remain in the cathedral archives. A well-edited cartulary is *El "Llibre Blanch" de Santas Creus (Cartulario del siglo XII),* Federico Udina Martorell, ed. (1947). Of secular collections, the most important is that preserved in ACA, Sección Cancillería, which incorporates the comital archives of Barcelona. Three editions of fundamental importance are Pierre de Marca, *Marca hispanica* (1688), partly superseded by: *Catalunya carolíngia,* Ramón d'Abadal i de Vinyals, ed., 2 vols. in 4 (1926–1955); and *Liber feudorum maior,* Francisco Miquel Rosell, ed., 2 vols. (1945–1947), a transcription and restoration of the register of comital records preserved in ACA, Sección Cancillería. The only Christian narrative of much value is *Gesta comitum barcinonensium,* Louis Barrau-Dihigo and J. J. Massó Torrents, eds. (1925).

Secondary. Two works of fundamental importance are Ramón d'Abadal i de Vinyals, *Els primers comtes catalans,* 2nd ed. (1965); and Pierre Bonnassie, *La Catalogne du milieu du Xe à la fin du XIe siècle,* 2 vols. (1975–1976). On particular topics see Ramón d'Abadal i de Vinyals, *L'Abat Oliba, bisbe de Vic, i la seva època,* 3rd ed. (1962); A. M. Mundó, "Monastic Movements in the East Pyrenees," in Noreen Hunt, ed., *Cluniac Monasticism in the Central Middle Ages* (1971); Eduardo Junyent, *Catalunya romànica: L'arquitectura del segle XI* (1975).

THOMAS N. BISSON

[See also **Aragon, 800–1137; Charlemagne; Spain, Christian-Muslim Relations.**]

CATAPHRACTI, the heavy cavalry of the Byzantine army, probably based on Persian practices, and introduced into the Roman army in the third century A.D. Their appearance represented the first use of heavy cavalry after the infantry era of the armies of classical antiquity. The *cataphracti* were armed with bows, swords, daggers, and sometimes spears and played a particularly important role in the victories of Justinian, as the historian Procopius records. Both they and their horses were armored, the soldiers wearing a coat of mail over the whole body and a steel helmet, and the horses being protected by breast and frontal plates. They were employed in attacks in massed formation.

BIBLIOGRAPHY
Norman H. Baynes and H. St. L. B. Moss, *Byzantium: An Introduction to East Roman Civilization* (1948), 301.

LINDA ROSE

[See also **Arms and Armor; Cavalry, Byzantine.**]

CATAPULTS. Medieval artillery before the introduction of firearms can be divided into three categories of throwing engines based on the power used: tension, torsion, and gravity. Within these categories there are two subgroups relating to their ammunition: dart throwers and stone throwers *(perriers).* Medieval terminology is vague, and does not always fit the modern categorizations.

Tension propulsion was used in oversize crossbows, mounted on castle or city walls, that shot darts at besiegers, a sort of long-range sniping. Surviving specimens are from the fifteenth century; they were called arbalests (Latin: *arcus,* bow + *ballista,* throwing engine). A tension-operated stone thrower, known only from Germany, where it was called *Einarm* (one-arm), used two parallel flexible planks

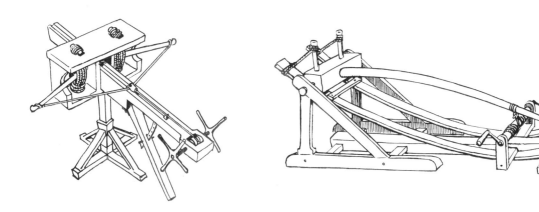

Left: ballista, springolf. Right: *Einarm.* DRAWINGS BY THE AUTHOR

as springs activating a vertically swinging arm, which could be fitted with a spoon-shaped receptacle and also with a sling, in order to throw two stones simultaneously.

Torsion engines had been used in antiquity by Greeks and Romans as ballistae and catapults. The ballista looked like a crossbow, but it was not constructed with a true bow. Instead, two short arms were stuck into two vertical bundles of rope, held under strong torsion within a stout frame. The outer ends of these arm levers were connected by a string, which could be pulled back by a claw attached to a windlass at the end of the ballista's shaft. The dart was placed in a groove on top of this shaft. Medieval versions of the ballista were the *espingale*, springald, or *Springolf* and the *Notstal* or *Selschoss* (from German: *Not*, emergency + *Gestell*, scaffold; *Seil*, rope + *Schuss*, shot).

The stone-throwing variety of torsion engine was the catapult or onager (Latin, "wild ass," because of its violent kick); its medieval version was the mangonel or *scorpion*. It consisted of a horizontal frame with an elevated crossbeam parallel to the single twisted skein of rope held by the frame. A vertically swinging arm with a spoon-shaped missile receptacle was inserted into this rope bundle; the arm was forced down by a windlass until it engaged a slip hook. When this hook was released, the arm flipped upward, to be stopped by the crossbeam, the shock aiding in flinging the projectile. Instead of stones, mangonels mounted on Byzantine or Venetian warships could hurl clay vessels filled with unquenchable Greek fire (a mixture of naphtha and phosphorus).

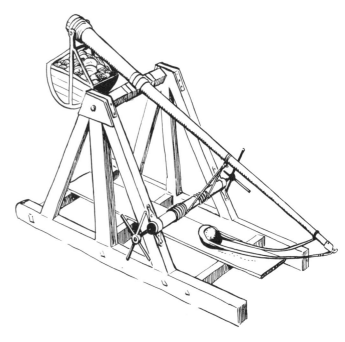

Trebuchet, *biffa*. DRAWING BY THE AUTHOR

Tension and torsion engines, however, had structural drawbacks: oversize bows were difficult to produce, wooden springs *(Einarm)* would tire, the torsion of rope skeins (ballista, mangonel) needed constant readjustment in changing weather. For this reason they were replaced by the much more easily maintained cannon, as soon as these were available in sufficient quantities.

The most widely used and truly medieval type of throwing engine was built on the gravity principle; it was called trebuchet (Latin: *trabucium*), *biffa*, or *Blide*. It had a beam with arms of unequal length balanced on a high scaffold; a heavy weight was attached to the shorter arm (the difference between trebuchet and *biffa* was that the *biffa* had the weight attached flexibly), and a hammocklike sling to the longer arm. When the long arm was pulled down by a windlass, a stone could be put into the sling, which was firmly tied to the arm with its lower strap, but only loosely held by a loop at its upper end. When the windlass was disengaged, the weighted short arm crashed downward, whipping the long arm up. The loop of the sling slipped free, letting the missile fly off at a high trajectory. Records tell of stones hundreds of pounds in weight, and even dead horses (in a kind of chemical warfare) being hurled this way.

The largest distance covered by a trebuchet throw

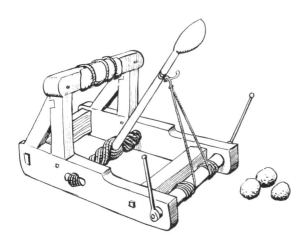

Onager, mangonel. DRAWING BY THE AUTHOR

seems to have been about 800 yards. Trebuchets were too large to be transported complete, and therefore were usually constructed on the spot from timber obtained from felled trees or demolished houses. Small trebuchets could use a crew of men jerking on ropes attached to the short arm instead of counterweights; these man-powered trebuchets could do without windlasses, because the long arm came down by itself.

The earliest trebuchet mentioned in medieval chronicles was used at the siege of Lisbon in 1147; possibly the latest (and certainly the only one in America) was constructed by Cortes for the siege of Mexico-Tenochtitlán in 1521.

BIBLIOGRAPHY

Favé (Napoleon III), *Du passé et d'avenir de l'artillerie* (1846–1871); Sir Ralph Payne-Gallwey, *The Crossbow, with a Treatise on the Ballista and the Catapult* (1903, repr. 1958); Rudolf Schneider, "Die Geschütze des Mittelalters," in *Zeitschrift für historische Waffenkunde,* 5 (1909–1911); W. Gohlke, "Das Geschützwesen des Altertums und des Mittelalters," *ibid.,* 5 (1909–1911), and 6 (1912–1914); E. W. Marsden, *Greek and Roman Artillery: Historical Development* (1969); William Reid, *Arms Through the Ages* (1976), 25–28.

HELMUT NICKEL

[See also **Bow and Arrow/Crossbow; Cannon; Greek Fire; Warfare, European.**]

CATCHWORD. See **Manuscript and Book Production.**

CATEPAN. See **Katepano.**

CATHAR LITURGY. Accounts by Catholic heresiologists (including ex-Cathars), Inquisition documents, and surviving Cathar rituals in Provençal and Latin have left us a picture of Cathar liturgical practice. Initiation as a "believer" centered on the teaching of the Our Father as in early church catechesis. Initiation (*consolamentum*) as a celibate "perfect" consisted of a homily on spiritual (not water) baptism, petition by the candidate, voting by the congregation, placing of the Gospels on the candidate's head while hands were laid on the Gospel book by

the presiding perfect (much as in Catholic episcopal consecration), and spoken prayers, especially *Pater sancte, suscipe servum tuum in tua justicia et mitte gratiam et spiritum sanctum tuum super eum* (Holy Father, receive thy servant in thy justice and send thy grace and thy Holy Spirit upon him). These originally distinct acts had been fused by the thirteenth century. For the frequent deathbed initiations, the form was simplified; it could be followed by *endura,* fasting to death.

Continuing cultic acts included perpetual recitation of the Paternoster (with the addition of "eastern" doxology and "supersubstantial bread"); adoration of the perfect by the believers and other perfects; *melioramentum,* self-abasement, probably penitential, before perfects; three annual fasts (13 November–24 December; Quinquagesima–Easter; Pentecost–29 June, the feast of Sts. Peter and Paul); and occasional cultic meals of uncertain meaning.

The development and interpretation of these rites are debated. All elements may be from Catholicism, others from a non-Christian gnosis to Christian practice. Cathar initiation was liberaton from the corruption of earth and the earthly church, and endowment with the good Spirit. It is possible that liturgical variations, such as the addition of renunciation of Catholic baptism, reflect doctrinal divergencies within Catharism, but the connection remains unclear.

BIBLIOGRAPHY

Léon Clédat, *Le Nouveau Testament, traduit au XIIIe siècle en langue provençale: Suivi d'un rituel cathare* (1887, repr. 1968); August Eduard Cunitz, *Ein katharisches Rituale* (1852); Ignaz von Döllinger, *Beiträge zur Sektengeschichte des Mittelalters,* 2 vols. (1890); Christine Thouzellier, *Rituel cathare* (1977); David H. Tripp, "Initiation Rites of the Cathari," in *Studia liturgica,* 12 (1977).

DAVID H. TRIPP

[See also **Albigensians; Bogomilism; Heresies, Western European.**]

CATHARS, the name given to a heretical sect that flourished in the twelfth and thirteenth centuries, particularly in Italy and Occitania (now southern France), with some sectaries in the Rhineland and northern France as well. The name comes from the Greek *katharos* (pure). Eckbert of Schönau used this name for them as early as 1163. By the late twelfth century they were known in France as Albigenses (from Albi) and by 1201 as *Bulgari* (from their connections with the Bogomils of Bosnia). From these names came a number of terms in the vernacular that meant "heretic," sodomite, or something else pejorative: *gazari* and *gazzerare* (Italian), *Ketzer* (German), *bougre* (French). Learned authors assimilated them to the ancient Manichaeans, to the Patarines of eleventh-century Italy, or to the biblical *publicani.* Two twelfth-century authors called them *texerant* (weavers), giving rise to a modern debate over their social origins. For later authors they were simply "the heretics." The believers called themselves "Christians" and their leaders "Cathars," "Good Men," or "Good Christians."

As with most medieval heretics, we know about the Cathars primarily through the writings of their enemies. Almost everything about them, therefore, has been an issue of scholarly dispute. Some major writings used by the Cathars or composed by them have survived, however: the *Vision of Isaiah,* a Gnostic work perhaps as old as the first century, which reached the West by way of the Bogomils by the end of the twelfth century and served as a source for Cathar mythmaking; and the *Secret Supper* or *Questions of John,* of Slavonic or Greek origin, which contained materials from early apocrypha. There are also two Cathar rituals, one in Occitan and one in Latin; fragments of a statement of faith, probably composed between 1218 and 1222; the *Book of the Two Principles,* probably written around 1240–1250 in the Lake Garda region of Italy; and a late gloss on the paternoster. This is all that has so far been found of what was once a much larger Cathar literature. After the 1240's there is, in addition, the ambiguous testimony of those heretics and suspects taken by the Inquisition, especially in southern France. Several of the Catholic writers reported from the inside. The earliest was Bonaccorso of Milan, a convert to the orthodox faith who sometime between 1176 and 1190 wrote what he knew of Cathar beliefs. The most important was Rainier Sacconi, a Cathar converted in 1245 who became a Dominican and eventually grand inquisitor of Lombardy. His *Summa on the Cathars and the Poor of Lyons* survives in fifty manuscripts—by far the most widely known tract on the subject in the Middle Ages.

Because their orthodox enemies were most interested in the Cathars' articles of faith, much of the extant polemical literature concerns their doctrines. On the Cathar side, the *Book of the Two Principles* (attributed to John of Lugio) is a scholastic treatise; it reflects a sect confronted by university-trained preachers and borrowing the weapons of its enemies to protect itself. Chroniclers and the suspects dragged before the inquisitors spoke of the way of life of the Cathar elite, the "Perfects," of the rituals they performed and the stories they told. In its earlier days, it has been argued, the Cathar religion was more a collection of myths and moral teachings than a coherent doctrine or set of doctrines. To the trained theologians, Cathar myths and teachings implied doctrinal beliefs, and polemicists had no trouble showing their contradictions and incoherence. But the nature of Cathar doctrines may not have been evident to many of the faithful who adored and protected the Good Men. For these believers and followers the stories may have served only to explain or embroider upon the rituals, the moral demands of perfection, and the way of life of the elite, which may have been the fundamental focus of their belief. Since the terms of confrontation were set by the orthodox, and almost all our evidence comes from that confrontation, it is impossible to know for certain exactly what Cathar religion was outside that context. It appears to have meant different things to different faithful at different times.

HISTORY AND BELIEFS OF THE SECT

Proto-Cathars appeared in western Europe long before the name was attached to them. Among the heretics mentioned by eleventh-century chroniclers were some whose beliefs suggest connections to the Bogomils of Byzantium and Bosnia. Such connections, and the mythic literature and rituals associated with them, were what later distinguished the Cathars from other wandering lay preachers and practitioners of voluntary poverty. These early sects are therefore part of the Cathar story, even though they did not endure.

The Bogomils, a heretical group that appeared in the Balkans early in the tenth century, shared some of their ideas with ancient dualists of Asia Minor. Unlike earlier dualists, they demanded extreme asceticism, rejected all sexuality and procreation, and did not eat meat, eggs, milk, and cheese. They rejected church buildings, the liturgy, the sacraments, the saints, normal scriptural exegesis, and the priesthood. The only prayer they accepted was the paternoster. Their induction ceremony was the laying on of hands. From the apocrypha and by a highly symbolic exegesis of the Scripture (especially the New Testament), they elaborated cosmological myths to explain the presence of evil in the world.

During the first half of the eleventh century,

chroniclers reported some similar beliefs among sectaries in the West. A group discovered at Orléans in 1022 appear to have believed in gnosis, an inner illumination conferred by the laying on of hands. They rejected material sacraments, the eating of meat, the Virgin Birth, and the Crucifixion. About the same time another group, of Italian origin, appeared at Liège. They also rejected the sacraments and the rest of the material apparatus of the church in favor of what they called "righteousness"—restraining fleshly desires, engaging in manual labor, and showing kindness to fellow believers. Righteousness took the place of baptism and the Eucharist. A third group in Piedmont rejected the priestly hierarchy, prohibited all sexual contact, and ate no meat. If humans agreed "not to experience corruption," one of them reportedly said, "they would beget without coition, like bees." Members of this sect sought to end their lives in torment, "that we may avoid eternal torments." Like the others, they rejected the Incarnation and orthodox understanding of the Trinity (which they interpreted as a symbol for the soul of man and the comprehension of divine truths).

Some elements in these beliefs—anticlericalism, rejection of the sacraments, personal illumination—were common to other religious enthusiasts in the eleventh century. Extreme asceticism, with its tendency toward dualism, had a long tradition in the West and was at that moment reinvigorated by the monastic reform movement. And any one of even the most extreme positions could have been spontaneously reinvented on the spot. But the confluence of so many Bogomillike beliefs among these sectaries (and perhaps among others) suggests that native Western tendencies were being worked upon by Greek or Balkan missionaries. After these early surfacings, however, nothing more was reported of dualists in the West for nearly a century.

When they reappeared toward the middle of the twelfth century, nothing distinguished them from other wandering preachers—orthodox or heretical—in behavior, dress, or the vehemence of their attacks on the established clergy. All these preachers attacked the worldly, wealthy, and simoniacal clergy. In this they were all children of the eleventh-century reform movement. The reemergent dualists were likewise fiercely ascetic. Commonly they demanded a simple, spiritual church. Some claimed that no sacraments were valid because the whole church had been corrupted by the world. Therefore, they said, no priest could be validly ordained.

Against the apostolic succession of the church they, like other heterodox preachers, asserted the authority of their "apostolic life." The appeal of this claim reached deeply among the laity. Not until St. Francis and St. Dominic and their followers did the church capture it for orthodoxy. Meanwhile, heretics could profit.

The first signs of Bogomil influences at work among these adepts of apostolic poverty appeared at Cologne in 1143–1144. There some sectaries called themselves the "poor of Christ." They replaced baptism with the laying on of hands, refused to drink milk or eat meat, rejected marriage, and consecrated their food with the paternoster. They claimed fellow adherents in "Greece and other lands." People called "Arians" at Toulouse in 1145, other heretics at Périgord in 1160, and those whom Eckbert called Cathars at Cologne in 1163 are among the fragmentary and disputed testimonies to the sect's spread. In 1165, at Lombers, near Albi, Cathar "Good Men" debated with orthodox preachers before an audience of bishops, the viscount of Béziers, and the countess of Toulouse. From that moment on, it is possible to tell the story of the movement's growth and fragmentation in somewhat more detail, thanks to Italian accounts of about 1214 and 1266 and writings of the Cathars themselves.

In 1167 or 1174 (the date is disputed) *papa* (priest) Niketas of the radical Bogomil church of Constantinople appeared in Italy. There he found a Cathar group led by Mark the Gravedigger, "deacon" or "bishop" of the Cathars (according to two different sources), who had been converted by a Cathar bishop from northern France. Like the group who had debated at Lombers, these Italians were moderate dualists who drew their ideas from Bulgarian sources. Niketas convinced Mark that these beliefs were wrong and converted him to the more extreme views of Dragovitsa or Dragometia (from the Slav tribe Dragoviči who settled there), north of Thessaloniki. He then consecrated Mark as bishop by the ritual laying on of hands. Then the two headed across the Alps to Occitania.

There they met a council of Cathars at St. Felix-de-Caraman (between Carcassonne and Toulouse) that included Robert of Epernon, the Cathar bishop of northern France; Sicard Cellerier, bishop of Albi; and delegates from Toulouse, Carcassonne, and (probably) Agen. (This council is known only through a seventeenth-century publication, the veracity of which has been disputed.) Niketas' success here was the same. The communities converted to the radical "order of Drogunthia" (Dragometia); bishops were elected for Toulouse, Carcassonne, and Agen; and episcopal boundaries were set. Niketas, after consecrating the bishops, returned to the East.

Both moderate and radical Cathar beliefs were based on the same assumption—the radical incompatibility of body and soul—and provided an answer to the same question: How can there be evil in a world created by a good God or good in a world that is evil? These questions they answered with elaborate genesis myths at the center of which was the figure of Satan.

Elaborating on Revelation 12:7, the early Bogomils told the story of the war of Satan with Michael, in which Satan was defeated and thrown to earth with a third of the angels and the sun, moon, and stars. According to one late story, Satan attracted the angels (all male) by introducing a woman into heaven. Having created the perishable material world, he imprisoned the angels in human bodies. According to the *Questions of John* it was only then that sexual differentiation occurred: the angels wept on discovering it. Beginning with Eckbert opponents speak of Western Cathars calling themselves fallen angels. "The flesh is born of corruption" and "the spirit is imprisoned," said the Occitan ritual. If the angel did not free itself in this life by becoming a Perfect, he was immediately imprisoned in another body when he died—either a human body or an animal. For the Cathars transmigration of souls took the place of the doctrine of purgatory. Coeternal with God and Satan, John of Lugio asserted, was Nature, from which heaven and earth were created. The good God, furthermore, had created another world like this, where the forces of the two Gods fought.

For some of the early Bogomils, Satan was an angel moved by pride to revolt; for others he was a son of God, Christ's younger brother. From this came his creative power. The radicals then took the next step and turned him into a God of equal power: the Adversary. Among the Cathars both stories appeared, the moderate first and then, after about 1180, the radical. After 1200 the Italian polemicist Salvo Burci reported beliefs in a diabolical Trinity. The stories made vivid the war between good and evil; they peopled heaven with females and males, and put arms and horses at the service of God. Meanwhile, the moderates worried about the relations between the two sons of God, Christ and Satan, and whether the latter was not in some way good. Under the influence of Aristotelian philosophy, yet other Cathars of the thirteenth century turned Satan into the ne-

cessities of nature. The pressure of the ambient orthodox culture began to break down their strict separation of good and evil.

In comparison with this elaboration of Satanic myths, Cathar speculations on God (or the good God) were indigent. Twelfth-century Cathars thought of the Trinity as three names for a single God or as a subtle allegory. By the 1230's they had been forced by orthodox polemicists to elaborate other notions, particularly of the Holy Spirit, who became the *consolator,* the heavenly guide of the Perfect. Until the thirteenth century Christ was most often not considered God. He never became the Savior. For some early Bogomils he, like Mary, was only a human creature. For others he was a sinless angel, introduced into the world through Mary's ear, his fleshly appearance a mere phantasm. Never incarnated, he did not suffer. Eleventh-century heretics in the West shared neither of these views. By the late twelfth century they appeared among the Cathars. Polemics again had forced heretical imaginations. In the thirteenth century some spoke of Christ as "incarnate angel," and accepted him even as God and man at the same time. Dualism at first made them ask whether he had therefore sinned in heaven like the other angels. But by the end of the thirteenth century the Cathars who remained seem to have adopted a Christian Christology. Most, however, continued to deny the Crucifixion. Angel, man, or God, Christ's mission on earth was that of a preacher and exemplar, sent to lead the fallen angels (the Cathars) back to heaven.

Since Satan created this world, he was the God of Genesis, and the Old Testament was his revelation. Christ, as angel, prophet, or eldest son of God, revealed the teachings of the good God. Cathar attitudes toward Moses and the patriarchs seem at first to have sprung from their demand for the "apostolic life" and its rejection of the Law. In the thirteenth century Cathars spoke of Moses as the voice of Satan and of the prophets as men through whom the devil mixed the truth (the prophecies of Christ) with his evil. Early Bogomils had proscribed the prophets entirely. Later Cathars accepted those Old Testament texts that prefigured the Gospels. For John of Lugio the prophets existed in another world, the land between this world and the heaven of the good God. To the New Testament as authority, which they used in vernacular translations for their preaching and storytelling, the Cathars added after 1190 such apocrypha as the *Questions of John* and the *Vision of Isaiah* in order to support their dualist ideas.

Moderates and radicals shared a set of rituals and moral rules. Since Satan created this world, sin was subjection to the world, a soiling of the soul by matter rather than an act of the will. The Perfect sought to liberate himself through celibacy and fasting. Free, he could see the angel in himself. Sinning, he succumbed to the devil. All sins were therefore equal. Since sexual relations continued the world of the devil, they were to be shunned, even in marriage. Children were Satan's work. Pregnant women were not admitted to the sect. When women were initiated as Perfects, they were covered with a veil to prevent physical contact with the men performing the rite. Meat could not be eaten, because the animal might have contained an imprisoned angel, a fellow soul. The prohibition of eggs, milk, and cheese (which may have been drawn from Greek Orthodox practice) was explained as avoiding the fruit of coition. Fish, they thought, were generated spontaneously by water and could therefore be consumed. From Catholic practice they borrowed the custom of three long fasts, to which they added fasts three days each week. The Perfect also refused to swear oaths or to kill, thus separating himself radically from surrounding lay society.

Admission to the state of Perfect was through the consolamentum. By the apostolic act of laying on of hands the initiate returned to his or her heavenly home and earned the right to say the Our Father. Early Cathars, in preparation for becoming Perfects, passed a long probation, including the required fasts. The consolamentum drew its powers from the perfection of the Cathar who administered it and lost its powers if the administrator ever sinned thereafter. If a Perfect lost his purity, they believed, even the souls in heaven whom he had consoled during their life on earth were immediately cast down again. This led to anxious observation of the Perfects, to frequent reconsoling (renewed administration of the consolamentum) as rumors spread, and probably to rigorous austerities. It also led to complicated schisms among the Italian Cathars (according to Catholic sources).

Niketas had apparently convinced Mark the Gravedigger that the Bulgarian tradition of consolamentum that Mark had received was defective. Mark and other Italian and Occitan Cathars were reconsoled in Niketas' tradition. Some years later Patracius of the Bulgarian Bogomils appeared in Italy to reveal that Simon, who had consoled Niketas, had been found in suspect circumstances with a woman. The consolamentum of the Lombards was once

again lost. Two parties formed, one accepting Patracius' story, the other not. When Mark died and John Judeus succeeded him, doubts were raised about Mark's death, and therefore John's consecration. The two groups eventually held a council at which Garattus was elected bishop. Before he could leave to be consoled and consecrated in Bulgaria, he was found with a woman. Soon there emerged six separate Cathar churches in Italy, each with its own tradition of consolamentum. The sources of this story of schism are all hostile to the Cathars. It is therefore hard to know how much, especially of the sexual scandals, is true. The dissensions appear to have been real, however, and were perpetuated in doctrinal differences. In contrast, the Cathars of Occitania remained united, though both radical and moderate doctrines flourished there side by side.

ORGANIZATION OF THE CATHAR CHURCH

In the thirteenth century the Cathars developed a conventional church life on the model of the surrounding Catholic organization. As bishop, Niketas had already consecrated the bishops of Italy and Occitania. In the thirteenth century Cathars produced a Latin ritual. The Perfects increasingly emphasized obedience and hierarchy, and developed a ritual to reconsole those among them who had fallen from the pure way. As the sect developed into a church, adherents began to receive the consolamentum on their deathbeds (like baptism in the early church), which was sometimes followed by the *endura* (fasting to death). Bishops and deacons claimed special importance in administering the deathbed consolamentum, excluding women from this function (their status in the sect consequently declined).

The Perfects gathered monthly for the public confession of sins, the *apparellamentum*. They formed a community "linked to each other by bonds of affection," repeating their chains of paternosters (the *dobla*), breaking bread at meals, roving black-robed from house to house to preach and to encourage adherents and sympathizers. Adherents, still sinful, could not address God as "our Father"; they therefore said no prayers. They were encouraged to act morally but were not constrained to the rigorous asceticism of the Perfects. They were obliged to greet the Perfect with *melioramentum* (called "adoration" by Catholic writers): three genuflections and "Pray God for me, a sinner, that he may make me a good Christian and lead me to a good end." To this the Perfect replied, "May God be prayed that he will make you a good Christian." Adherents might observe and share in the breaking of bread. In addition they collected funds for the Perfects, gave them refuge, and provided guides, especially when they were hounded by the Inquisition. An adherent might become a believer (the term is used by Inquisition sources). He or she "received the prayer." It is not clear if this meant a formal ceremony, moving the believer part way toward becoming a Perfect.

Bishops were at first elected by the community of the Perfects. In the thirteenth century this right was restricted to bishops alone. By 1190 lesser offices had appeared: the *filius major* and *filius minor* (greater and lesser sons), who assisted the bishop and were his presumed successors. Deacons were mentioned by 1167. They were in charge of the hospices where the Perfects gathered; they led the rituals. When in the thirteenth century the Inquisition succeeded in destroying the Cathar communities, these offices disappeared. There remained only the elder (*ancianus*) to lead whatever group survived. Offices had neither special ritual functions nor jurisdictions until the thirteenth century, when bishops reserved the consecration of bishops, and deacons the consoling of the dying.

There is no sure way to estimate the numbers who adhered to this sect. In the village of Laurac, near Carcassonne, almost all the inhabitants turned out to hear a Perfect preach around 1200; at Cambiac, near Toulouse, the priest complained that all his parishioners save four were Cathars. Various estimates have been given for the number of Perfects in early thirteenth-century Occitania: 700–800; 2,000; 1,015 "known by name." But one historian has recently concluded that no more than ten were active at any one time in the region of Albi. Rainier Sacconi estimated 4,000 Perfects in Italy in his day. Sympathizers are even more difficult to estimate. In 1209 the bishop of Béziers could name only 219, out of perhaps 10,000 inhabitants of the city. Scholarly estimates have ranged from 100,000 to 500,000, to 4,000,000 in the West about 1200. These seem grossly exaggerated.

In the early fourteenth century, only fifteen Perfects remained. Geographically, the implantation in Occitania occupied the triangle defined by Agen, the Pyrenees, and Béziers. It was especially heavy in the Lauragais between Toulouse and Carcassonne. In Italy there were Cathars in Milan, Piacenza, Cremona, Brescia, Bergamo, Vicenza, Verona, Ferrara, Rimini, Florence, and Orvieto, and along the routes between Lombardy and Occitania. There were sporadic signs of them in northeastern France, in England about 1210, and along the Rhine and Danube. In all these areas around 1200, Cathar beliefs appealed to all social classes: nobility, peasants (in Occitania), wealthy urban families (the Roaix and Maurands of Toulouse), artisans, and small traders.

PERSECUTION

As Cathar beliefs spread, the church remained unarmed. In the twelfth century it had no central agency nor special office or procedure to deal systematically with heretics. Heresy was a diocesan affair. Normally a bishop would summon suspects to respond to charges at a disciplinary synod and to purge themselves by ordeal. Sometimes an outraged mob would lynch the suspect. Others might be run out of town. Councils of Toulouse (1119), Lateran II (1139), Rheims (1157), and Tours (1163) decreed that heretics should be excommunicated, and called on secular rulers to imprison them and confiscate their property. In 1184, in his bull *Ad abolendam*, Lucius III required annual episcopal visits to those parishes where heresy was suspected. The bishops were to compel local inhabitants to testify and to require, under pain of ecclesiastical censure, that secular authorities punish those convicted. But enforcement depended on active pursuit by the local clergy and the cooperation of the laity. In Occitania and Italy there was little of either.

The response to the Cathars was therefore slow. In 1145 St. Bernard of Clairvaux joined a mission to the region of Toulouse to preach against heresy. During his brief stay he may have encountered Cathars. The next major mission did not cross Occitania until the late 1170's. It occurred in a political climate and took a form that prefigured the Albigensian Crusade of a generation later.

In the twelfth century the lands between the Pyrenees and the Alps were dominated by two political factions, one led by the counts of Toulouse-St. Gilles, the other by the counts of Barcelona (kings of Aragon after 1162). Their power depended on the shifting loyalties of the major prelates of the region (especially the archbishop of Narbonne) and of a few great families: east of the Rhône, the lords of Les Baux; west of the Rhône, the Trencavel family (viscounts of Albi, Béziers, Agde, and Nîmes, and rulers of Carcassonne), the viscounts of Narbonne, and the lords of Montpellier. In the last three decades of the century, the wars between these factions, occasionally interrupted by truces or treaties, reached a new intensity. Occitania and Provence were flooded with mercenary troops from Spain and Flanders. For popes and their legates these "bandits" became as serious a problem as heresy.

After a brief peace, war resumed in 1177, with the Trencavels and William of Montpellier supporting Alphonse II of Aragon. Raymond V of Toulouse decided to play on the danger of heresy to find allies in the north. In September he wrote to the chapter general of the Order of Cîteaux and to King Louis VII, describing the "desertion and ruin of the churches" and the spread of dualist beliefs. The cause of his own inability to act, he said, was "the corruption of the most noble of the land" and their abandonment of the faith. He asked Louis to bring an army south. Raymond thus called for the major components of the later crusade: the active intervention of the Cistercians and a Capetian army, and the direction of this attack on heresy against the Trencavels. When it finally materialized in the thirteenth century, the crusade brought down Raymond's son along with the Trencavels.

At the time the only result was a mission of Abbot Henry of Cîteaux and Peter of Pavia, the papal legate, to the Toulouse region, accompanied by an armed guard of northerners. In 1180–1181, during a tour of the area, Henry, now cardinal of Albano and papal legate, assembled a small army and laid siege to Lavaur (held by the wife of Roger Trencavel). Two notorious heretics were captured and converted. Meanwhile, the Third Lateran Council, meeting in 1179, condemned in canon 27 both the heretics and mercenaries in Occitania assimilating the latter to the former. Christian princes were summoned to "reduce them to servitude"; those who went to fight them were remitted two years of penance and given all Crusader privileges.

Aside from some local councils repeating this legislation, there was no further major action until the end of the century. By then a new generation had come to power in Catalonia, Occitania, and the papacy. Raymond V and Roger Trencavel both died in 1194, the latter leaving a minor son as heir. Peter II succeeded his father Alphonse of Aragon in 1196. And in 1198 Innocent III became pope. By 1200 Peter, Raymond VI, the archbishop of Narbonne, and Richard the Lionhearted had radically altered the traditional network of alliances in the region. Over four years they bound themselves together by marriages, joined William of Montpellier to them, and isolated the young Raymond-Roger Trencavel. One may only speculate on their motives. In the following years Raymond VI and Peter sought to shape the actions of the church to their advantage, each

presumably hoping to create a principality on the ruin of the Trencavels.

At the same time Innocent III began his campaign against the heretics. His instruments were Cistercians commissioned as papal legates: Rainier of Ponza and Brother Guy (1198–1200), Peter of Castelnau and Ralph of Fontfroide (from 1203 on), and Arnold Amalric, abbot of Cîteaux, formerly abbot of Poblet and Grandselve, who joined them in 1204. Their task was to goad the local clergy and nobility into action by deposing recalcitrant prelates, organizing the lesser nobility (against their lords if need be), and threatening the mighty with excommunication, anathema, and eventually with armed force from the north. In 1206 Diego de Azevedo, bishop of Osma, and Dominic Guzmán added a preaching mission to the church's arsenal. They urged the legates to give up their triumphal parade through the countryside and go instead "in humility, in imitation of the apostles." When Innocent supported the idea, Arnold Amalric brought twelve Cistercian abbots to preach in the towns and villages of Occitania. Their mission lasted only a year; but Dominic remained, debating the Cathars and preaching against them. In 1207 he founded a monastery for noble women at Prouille, just below the walls of the heretical stronghold of Fanjeaux.

In 1204 princes and legates began to move rapidly to secure their positions. After hearing a debate between heretics and Catholics at Carcassonne (perhaps to justify later action against Viscount Raymond-Roger), Peter II met with Raymond VI and Alfons, count of Provence, at Milhau. To secure the alliance, he celebrated his sister's marriage to Count Raymond. He then moved to seize Montpellier. Two years before, Innocent III (perhaps at Peter's urging) had refused to legitimate William VIII of Montpellier's only son, William IX, thus making his daughter Maria his heir when he died in November 1202. Peter arranged for Maria's husband to repudiate her, and in June 1204 married her himself. Aided by a municipal revolt, he took over the city. In October he sailed to Rome, where he put his lands under St. Peter's protection and recognized that he held them as fiefs of the Holy See. Was this to gain papal support for a later move against the Trencavels and the count of Toulouse? Or was it to protect himself against a possible Capetian invasion? One can only guess.

Innocent III had written to Philip Augustus earlier in 1204, asking him to invade the south or send his son to do so. Philip responded coolly that the affairs of kings were not under papal jurisdiction. Meanwhile, the papal legates were attacking the episcopate of Occitania. In 1204 they suspended the bishop of Béziers and began proceedings against the archbishop of Narbonne. In 1205 it was the turn of the bishops of Agde and Viviers, and the newly elected bishop of Toulouse. All were replaced with men favorable to the legates. Also in 1204 Peter of Castelnau supported a new alliance between Aymeric III, viscount of Narbonne, and Raymond VI, drawing the noose tighter around the Trencavel lands. But Peter soon turned against Raymond, whom he probably had never trusted, and began to organize armed leagues in the count's lands: in 1206 in Toulouse and 1207 in Provence. In 1207, while Innocent was again writing to Philip Augustus asking him to invade the south, Peter excommunicated the count. In January 1208 the two met at St. Gilles. The meeting ended in a quarrel and menacing words. The next day an unknown knight murdered the legate as he was preparing to cross the Rhône. Innocent immediately ordered his legates to preach a crusade.

THE ALBIGENSIAN CRUSADE

The Cistercians mobilized. Philip Augustus remained cool, but at last reluctantly allowed 500 knights to take the cross. Those who enlisted for forty days were granted the same indulgences as for a Palestine expedition. The army that assembled in June 1209 included the duke of Burgundy; the counts of Nevers, St. Pol, and Boulogne; the archbishops of Rouen, Rheims, and Sens; and great lords from the empire. It was "the greatest army ever assembled in Christendom," the legates gloated. With the king's refusal, Arnold Amalric took command. Raymond VI, frightened, demanded reconciliation with the church. After accepting all the charges against him and promising obedience, he was absolved, took the cross, and rushed to join the crusaders moving down the Rhône. According to a later story, he asked Raymond-Roger Trencavel to establish a joint defense, but the latter refused. The viscount, with no ally save the count of Foix, to whom he entrusted his infant son, prepared Béziers for a siege and retreated with his forces to Carcassonne.

Béziers bore the first crusader attack in July. Just as the siege was beginning, a sortie by the defenders allowed the crusaders to force a gate. The entire population was massacred. Horror spread across the land. Narbonne hastened to submit and ransom itself

to the army. So did most of the smaller towns and lords on the road to Carcassonne. For the first two weeks in August the crusaders besieged Carcassonne. On 15 August, the city suffering from lack of water, Raymond-Roger surrendered on condition that the inhabitants be spared. Those in the city were allowed to leave "bearing nothing but their sins." The viscount was imprisoned and died a few months later: murder, said some; dysentery, said others.

As the forty days necessary to gain their indulgence came to an end, the crusaders chose Simon de Montfort to remain behind as ruler of Carcassonne while they returned home to the north. Simon sought recognition of his conquest from Peter II but in vain. During the winter resistance spread; but with large loans from Raymond of Cahors, a Montpellier banker, and fresh forces from the north, he retook rebellious towns and vanquished the last Trencavel strongholds: Minerve and Termes in 1210, Cabaret and Lavaur in 1211. The lands of Roger-Raymond were subdued. Peter accepted Simon's homage as viscount of Carcassonne and Razès.

Raymond VI had left the crusading army after Carcassonne, and in a series of councils (1209–1211) he heard his excommunication renewed and confirmed. Attempts to reconcile himself with the church were in vain. In February 1211 the legates presented him with terms that were probably extreme, while the war continued inconclusively. At Pamiers (1212) Simon began to organize his conquest, imposing the customs of his native Île-de-France. The long-lasting effects of these "statutes" were felt mainly in the fiefs confiscated from rebels and granted to northern lords.

In 1212 Peter II at last decided the moment was right to intervene directly. He took Toulouse under his protection; then, after his victory over the Muslims at Las Navas de Tolosa, he wrote to Innocent III in favor of Raymond VI, complaining at length of Simon's ambition and the intransigence and political direction of the legates. He then prepared to move militarily. On 12 September 1213 his forces, allied with those of the counts of Toulouse, Foix, and Comminges, met Simon's much smaller army beneath the walls of the village of Muret, southwest of Toulouse. In one of the few pitched battles of the crusade, Simon was victorious. Peter was killed, Raymond withdrew, and the crusaders were free to subdue the region of Toulouse.

In the midst of all this, Innocent vacillated. The

new prelates of Occitania and the new legates—Peter of Benevento and Robert of Courçon—pursued their own policy. In January 1215 they recommended recognizing Simon as "sole ruler and prince" of all the lands of Raymond VI. Innocent, however, would grant only temporary custody, leaving final disposition to the Fourth Lateran Council, which he had just called. Meanwhile, Louis, the son of Philip Augustus, conducted a triumphal procession across Occitania. At the end of the year the council deprived Raymond VI of all his lands (though it did award him a pension). All the lands conquered by the crusaders were given to Simon. The marquessate of Provence, however, was to be held by the church in trust for the future Raymond VII. Raymond-Roger of Foix eventually regained his lands. The county of Comminges passed to Simon. After securing Narbonne and Toulouse, Simon de Montfort proceeded to Philip Augustus' court to do homage as count of Toulouse, duke of Narbonne, and viscount of Béziers and Carcassonne. In the vacuum left after Muret, claims to suzerainty over Occitania passed, with papal support, to the Capetians.

The war continued, however, for another thirteen years as Raymond VI and his son fought to regain their lost lands, and cities and towns revolted. In 1218, while besieging Toulouse, Simon was killed by a shot from a catapult worked by women of the city. His son Amaury was at once acclaimed successor. Despite a brief foray south by an army under Prince Louis's command, the Raymonds slowly reconquered most of their old possessions and threatened Albi and Béziers as well. By early in 1222 Amaury's fortunes had fallen so low that he offered all his father's conquests to Philip Augustus. The king turned him down. In 1224 the young Raymond Trencavel was reinstalled in Carcassonne as viscount "by the grace of God." Negotiations followed at Paris, Rome, Montpellier, and finally at Bourges, where in November 1225 Raymond VII, the count of Foix, and Raymond Trencavel were excommunicated and Louis VIII began to plan a royal conquest. After a siege of Avignon in 1226, he marched across Occitania as everyone hurried to submit. Raymond Trencavel was expelled. But Louis died on 8 November 1226, before the conquest could be consolidated.

The war had taken its toll of southern resources, however; Raymond VII, when given the chance, made peace. The Treaty of Paris (12 April 1229) brought to an end a crusade whose pretext was a battle against heresy but which had really been a war of conquest. It settled the succession of Toulouse and its county to the Capetians' benefit, and gave the marquessate of Provence to the church. Heresy was not forgotten. The treaty established a university at Toulouse to be financed by Raymond VII. The count was also required to promise his aid in tracking heretics; he was to pay a bounty for each one seized and to require an oath from all his subjects to obey the church and report heretics. In November a council at Toulouse established a systematic prosecution of heretics. Every two years, each inhabitant was to swear to support the church and to combat heresy. Laymen were forbidden to possess a Bible in any language or books of religious ritual in the vernacular. Every parish was to have a team of heretic hunters. And any lord who did not drive heretics from his land was threatened with confiscation.

THE INQUISITION AND THE DESTRUCTION OF THE CATHARS

With the war at an end, the task of combating the Cathars remained as important as ever. The crusade had sapped the political structures of Languedoc, and thus the protection or at least the toleration that Cathars had received from many of the rural nobility. The crusade had also, however, equated heresy and resistance to the northern invaders. This aided the Cathars but, at the same time, made resistance more dangerous. (It also complicates the historian's task of assessing who were really Cathars in the thirteenth century.) The confusion remained for decades to come. Cathars slowly returned to their old haunts. A Cathar council in the village of Pieusse in 1225 recreated the sect's ecclesiastical organization. Sporadic persecution occurred in Toulouse, Narbonne, and smaller towns, but some rural lords continued to protect the Good Men, who moved freely in the countryside, though with more prudence than before the war.

Innocent III, though he created precedents and legislation for combating heresy, did not alter the episcopal inquisition. Only in 1233–1234 did Gregory IX resort to special agents, first in Occitania and then elsewhere. The papal Inquisition was born. From the outset the inquisitors were usually Dominicans. Unlike the bishops, they were devoted exclusively to this task. They kept continuous records of the depositions they heard and in time developed "handbooks for heretic-hunters" summarizing the knowledge gained over years of activity. With these data and an organization that reached all over Europe, they had resources roughly comparable with those of a modern police organization; they could track suspects wherever they went and could threaten even the descendants of accused persons (who risked losing their inherited property). Any suspect could be put under oath to testify to his or her beliefs, participation in forbidden rites, and knowledge of other suspects. In 1252 Innocent IV added torture to the inquisitors' tools. Combining the roles of confessor and judge, the inquisitor was virtually unchecked except by popular wrath.

The Inquisition was first established in Valence, Montpellier, and Toulouse. It immediately met opposition from the consuls of Toulouse and Narbonne, and from mobs in those cities and at Albi. Since the penalties for heresy included confiscation of property, communities saw the Inquisition as a threat to their hard-won liberties. In 1238, for political reasons, Gregory IX suspended the Inquisition in Toulouse. Revolts during the following years, however, played directly into the hands of the inquisitors and the northerners.

In 1240 Raymond Trencavel led an invasion of refugee nobles and mercenaries across the Pyrenees from Catalonia, only to be beaten off from Carcassonne by a royal army. Reprisals against the many who supported him were immediate and completed the destruction of the local nobility. In 1242 Count Raymond VII joined an international coalition against Louis IX. The brief war that ensued prompted a group of Cathars from Montségur, near Foix, to murder several inquisitors at Avignonet. In midsummer 1243, after Raymond had thrown himself on Louis's mercy, the king's seneschal of Carcassonne besieged the Cathars' fortress. Two hundred heretics, including the hierarchy, were captured when it fell nine months later. They were questioned by the Inquisition and burned. The records served for years afterward to track down sympathizers all over the region.

Now those who had tolerated the Cathars turned against them. Raymond VII burned eighty at Agen on one day in 1249. The Inquisition could move at will. During 1245–1246 one inquisitor interrogated 5,471 witnesses in 39 villages between Toulouse and Carcassonne, condemning 207 at least—23 of them to imprisonment, the others to wearing crosses on their clothing or other penance. Hounded, the Perfects could move only in secrecy. Proselytizing became more difficult. Many emigrated to Italy. Some continued to pursue their careers despite the dangers, however: Bernard Huc and William Pagès in

the 1270's and 1280's, and the radical Peter Autier, who led a revival in the mountains around Foix in 1295–1310. They could still find the support of local castellans, such as those of Cabaret, or even of a few of the parish clergy. The career of Autier's successor, Belibasta, a Perfect who kept a concubine and sold the consolamentum, shows the degeneration of the sect in its last days. His story appears at length in the records of the Inquisition that the bishop of Pamiers conducted in 1318–1325 among the peasants of Montaillou.

In Italy, Cathars found refuge where politics—especially the fight between Emperor Frederick II and the papacy—dictated opposition to the church. The Dominican house at Orvieto was sacked in 1239, that of Parma in 1279. The inquisitor St. Peter Martyr was murdered at Milan in 1252. Other cities committed violence against imperial supporters who refused to prosecute Cathars. Nowhere, however, did Cathars become an independent political force. After the death of Frederick II and the weakening of the imperial party, they lost their patrons. The Cathar hierarchy continued unbroken in Italy into the 1280's, until one by one their protectors began to admit inquisitors within the city walls. A total of 178 Perfects were burned at Verona in 1278. A major series of trials was held at Bologna in 1291–1309. The last Cathar bishop known in the West was captured in Tuscany in 1321.

In both Occitania and Italy police measures were combined with missionary work. Dominican houses became increasingly popular as they, and the Franciscans, began to capture for orthodoxy the laity's admiration of the "apostolic life." Converted Waldensians, known as the Poor Catholics, preached against the Cathars. St. Peter Martyr established Catholic confraternities in Italy. Above all, a variety of new orthodox devotions—the Christmas crib, Franciscan emphasis on Christ's life and especially on the Crucifixion, and the mythologies of Joachim of Fiore and his followers—drew those who might have supported the Cathars into a very different kind of Christian piety.

By the second quarter of the fourteenth century, the church had destroyed Catharism in the West.

BIBLIOGRAPHY

Cathar religion. Bibliographies include C. T. Berkhout and J. B. Russell, *Medieval Heresies: A Bibliography 1960–79* (1981); Herbert Grundmann, *Bibliographie zur Ketzergeschichte des Mittelalters (1960–66)* (1967), also published in J. Le Goff, ed., *Hérésies et sociétés dans l'Europe pré-*

industrielle, (1968), 411–467; Z. Kulcsár, *Eretnekmozgal-mak a XI–XIV Században* (1964). Sources include Edina Bozóky, ed., *Le livre secret des Cathares: Interrogatio Jo-hanni* (1980), with bibliography; René Nelli, *Écritures cathares* (1968); Walter L. Wakefield and A. P. Evans, *Her-esies of the High Middle Ages* (1969). Studies include A. Borst, *Die Katharer* (1963); Jean Duvernoy, *Le religion des Cathares* (1976); and *L'histoire des cathares* (1979); Mal-colm Lambert, *Medieval Heresy* (1977), chs. 5, 8; Raoul Manselli, *L'eresia del male* (1963).

Social, political, and religious context and the Albigen-sian Crusade. Pierre Belperron, *La croisade contre les Al-bigeois et l'union du Languedoc à la France 1209–49'* (1942), for the northern French viewpoint; the journal *Ca-hiers de Fanjeaux* (1966–); Elie Griffe, *Les débuts de l'av-enture cathare en Languedoc* (1969); *Le Languedoc cathare de 1190 à 1210* (1971); *Le Languedoc cathare au temps de la Croisade* (1973); and *Le Languedoc cathare et l'inquisition* (1980), all from the Catholic viewpoint but sympathetic to Occitans; Michel Roquebert, *L'épopée cathare,* 2 vols. (1970–1977), from the Occitan-Cathar viewpoint; Jordi Ventura, *Pere el Catòlic i Simó de Mont-fort* (1960), the Catalan viewpoint; Claude de Vic and J. J. Vaissete, *Histoire générale de Languedoc,* VI (1879); and Walter L. Wakefield, *Heresy, Crusade, and Inquisition in Southern France, 1100–1250* (1974), with bibliography.

FREDRIC L. CHEYETTE

[See also **Albigensians; Bogomilism; Dominicans; Dualism; Gregory IX, Pope; Heresies, Western European; Innocent III, Pope; Inquisition; Languedoc; Philip II Augustus; Simon de Montfort; Toulouse, City and County.**]

CATHEDRA (Greek and Latin, "chair"), a bishop's throne, usually in the apse behind the high altar in the principal church of the diocese. In the Middle

Cathedra. Church of S. Michele, Monte S. Angelo, 10th century. FROM SIR BANISTER FLETCHER'S A HISTORY OF ARCHITECTURE

Ages cathedras also were sometimes placed in the chancel. Cathedras are preserved from the early Christian period on (for instance, the cathedra of Maximian, archbishop of Ravenna from 546–556, in the Museo Arcivescovile, Ravenna); they normally had high backs and solid arms, and often were richly decorated with precious metals or ivory (for in-stance, the ninth-century cathedra at St. Peter's).

LESLIE BRUBAKER

CATHEDRAL. The word "cathedral" has two con-notations, one ecclesiastical and the other, deriving from the first, architectural.

In its ecclesiastical sense the word derives from the Latin *cathedra* (chair), and possibly from the as-sumed construction *ecclesia cathedralis* (church of the chair or throne). The throne was that of the bishop, employed for ceremonial occasions and when speaking officially on church matters, whence the expression to speak ex (or in) cathedra. Thus the church of the bishop containing his cathedra was the "church cathedral," usually shortened to "cathedral" but more accurately "cathedral church."

It is widely but incorrectly believed that a medi-eval bishop owned the diocesan cathedral, but this is true only in a symbolic sense. The cathedral was controlled by a chapter (Latin: *capitulum*), an orga-nization of canon-priests who were in theory the bishop's principal diocesan administrators. From the time of St. Chrodegang of Metz's regulation of his priest-assistants into an organized body, about 755, capitular authority and prerogatives increased. Sec-ular canons were obligated to the monastic vows of chastity and obedience, but were individually and collectively permitted to own personal property. In time this property came to include the bishop's ca-thedral church, since the collective capitular income far exceeded that of the bishop.

This situation made the chapter responsible for maintenance and, when necessary, reconstruction of the cathedral. To this end most chapters maintained a special "fabric fund" (Latin: *fabrica,* work or workshop). Donations could be, and were, made *ad opus fabricae* (for the work of the fabric), although there is by no means the precise distinction many have believed between donations made *ad opus fab-ricae* and those made *ad opus ecclesiae.* A text con-cerning one or the other or both does not necessarily indicate construction in progress or about to begin.

A number of medieval building campaigns have been misdated, or even invented, by misunderstanding the significance of these expressions in medieval documents.

The successful completion of a major campaign of construction of a cathedral usually depended on cooperation between bishop and chapter. Bishops frequently took real, not merely symbolic, leads in such efforts, by donating incomes, lands, materials, and relics to the *fabrica*. The relationship between chapter and bishop has been likened to that of a modern corporation in which the chapter is the board of directors, with its provost or dean serving as chief operating officer and the bishop serving as chairman of the board. A well-documented and frequently cited example of capitular-episcopal cooperation occurred in 1195, when the chapter and bishop at Chartres agreed to devote "a not inconsiderable part" of their respective incomes for a period of three years to finance the cost of rebuilding the cathedral, badly damaged by fire in 1194.

As an architectural term "cathedral" is considerably less precise than in its ecclesiastical sense. As the most important church in a diocese, the cathedral may or may not have been its most imposing or significant monument. There is no canonically established format for a cathedral. Its form and nature varied throughout the Middle Ages, not only from one period to another, as architectural and structural patterns changed, but also simultaneously from region to region, depending on local tradition and on other considerations such as finances, materials, and the imagination and skill of architects.

Most people envision a cathedral as one of the great episcopal churches of Gothic France, whether of the twelfth century (Laon, Paris) or of the thirteenth (Amiens, Bourges, Chartres, Rheims). These differ among themselves in many ways, but the latter have certain common features: complex choir with ambulatory and radiating chapels, developed transept with aisles, long nave with aisles, twin-towered main facade with extensive sculptural program. Any imposing church with such features frequently is inaccurately referred to as a cathedral, regardless of its ecclesiastical designation. The collegial church at St. Quentin and the abbey church at St. Denis, both of which are important religious foundations and impressive churches, are often termed cathedrals although neither was an episcopal church. Conversely, former cathedrals no longer assigned bishops, such as Laon, are still commonly termed cathedrals.

The "French type" of cathedral, as exemplified by Chartres, is not an invariable standard in France, as its exact contemporary at Bourges or slightly later one at Albi prove, let alone elsewhere in Europe. English Gothic cathedrals, whether monastic (Ely, Winchester) or secular (Salisbury, York), tend to be very long, admitting of processions, but without ambulatories and radiating chapels intended principally for housing altars with relics and for accommodating pilgrims.

The contrast between the choir arrangement of French Gothic cathedrals and the simple, single-apse scheme of the early medieval period or even Italian Gothic (Orvieto) proves the changing role of bishop and chapter. In the early Christian basilica the apse was reserved for the bishop's cathedra, the focal point of the church, with the altar lower and choral activities relegated to the transept, if there was one. In the "French type" cathedral of the Gothic period, the large choir was necessary to accommodate the chapter, and the episcopal cathedra was generally set to the side of the altar. The widespread appearance of private episcopal chapels in the twelfth and thirteenth centuries indicates the extent to which cathedral churches were under capitular control, regardless of their architectural forms.

BIBLIOGRAPHY

Robert Branner, "'Fabrica,' 'Opus,' and the Dating of Mediaeval Monuments," in *Gesta,* **15,** nos. 1–2 (1976); Frank L. Cross and Elizabeth A. Livingstone, eds., *The Oxford Dictionary of the Christian Church,* 2nd ed., repr. and corr. (1977), 251–252, with extensive bibliography; Otto von Simson, *The Gothic Cathedral* (1956), 159–182.

CARL F. BARNES, Jr.

[See also **Cathedra; Chapter; Clergy; Gothic Architecture.**]

CATHERINE OF CLEVES, MASTER OF, a manuscript illuminator active around Utrecht between 1438 and 1460. He is named after a Book of Hours (Pierpont Morgan Library, MSS M. 917 and M. 945) made about 1440 for Catherine of Cleves, niece of Philip the Good. It contains numerous innovative miniatures and imaginative borders with realistically depicted still-life objects, plants, and animals.

BIBLIOGRAPHY

Robert G. Calkins, "Distribution of Labor: The Illuminators of the Hours of Catherine of Cleves and Their

Personification of Knowledge, with pupils. From the book of hours of the Master of Catherine of Cleves, *ca.* 1440. THE PIERPONT MORGAN LIBRARY, MS M. 917, p. 62

Workshop," in *Transactions of the American Philosophical Society,* 69, pt. 5 (1979); John Plummer, *The Hours of Catherine of Cleves* (1966).

ROBERT G. CALKINS

CATHOLICON. See **Katholikon.**

CATHOLICUS. See **Katholikos.**

CATO'S DISTICHS (LATIN). The *Disticha Catonis* is a collection of nearly 150 pithy phrases in verse and prose composed around the third century A.D. by an unknown author, but ascribed to Cato the

Elder. From the seventh century until the Renaissance, students memorized the Distichs as their first training in Latin. By the late Middle Ages the Distichs had been translated into most European vernaculars.

BIBLIOGRAPHY

Marcus Boas, ed., *Disticha Catonis* (1952); Wayland J. Chase, ed. and trans., *The Distichs of Cato* (1922); Martin von Schanz, *Geschichte der römischen Literatur,* III (1905), 519–520.

NATHALIE HANLET

[See also **Grammar; Latin Language; Schools, Grammar.**]

CATO'S DISTICHS (OLD FRENCH). There are seven versions in Old French of the didactic handbook ascribed to Dionysius Cato. Three are in Anglo-Norman verse and date from the twelfth century: those of Elie de Wincestre and of Everart, and an anonymous copy. The others are continental and are by Adam de Suel (thirteenth century), Jehan de Chastelet or de Paris (thirteenth century), Jean Le Fèvre (fourteenth century), and an anonymous adapter (thirteenth century), the last remaining in two fragments.

BIBLIOGRAPHY

E. P. Ruhe, *Untersuchungen zu den altfranzösischen Übersetzungen der Disticha Catonis. Beiträge zur romanischen Philologie des Mittelalters: Editionen und Abhandlungen,* II (1968), which gives details of editions.

BRIAN MERRILEES

[See also **Anglo-Norman Literature.**]

CAUCASIA, a vast geographical region including Europe and Asia on the isthmus between the Black and the Caspian seas. Caucasia is divided by the Caucasus Mountains into two subregions, North and South Caucasia, the latter often miscalled "Transcaucasia," a term valid only from a Russian point of view. North Caucasia is divided into a western sector, the basin of the Kuban River, and an eastern, the basin of the Terek. South Caucasia consists of three sections: (1) Georgia in the west, subdivided into west Georgia (successively Colchis, Lazica, Abasgia),

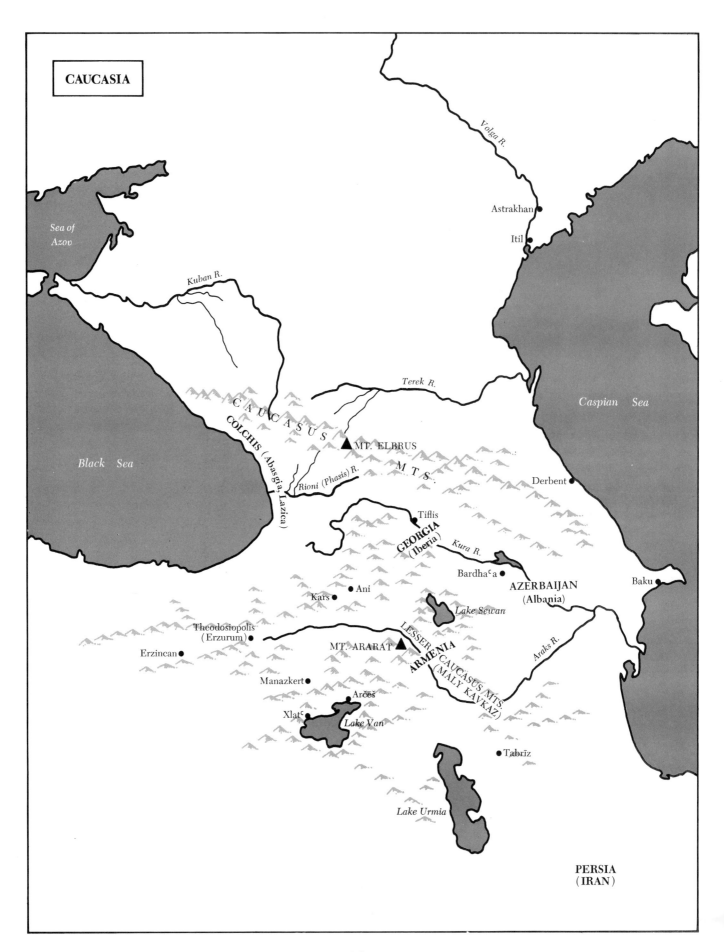

CAUCASIA

Sea of
Azov

Volga R.

Astrakhan

Itil

Kuban R.

Caspian Sea

Terek R.

C A U C A S U S

COLCHIS (Abasgia, Lazica)

Black Sea

MT. ELBRUS

M T S.

Rioni (Phasis) R.

Derbent

Tiflis

GEORGIA
(Iberia)

Kura R.

Bardhaᶜa

AZERBAIJAN
(Albania)

Baku

Ani

Kars

Lake Sevan

Theodosiopolis
(Erzurum)

Erzincan

MT. ARARAT

ARMENIA

LESSER
CAUCASUS MTS.
(MALY KAVKAZ)

Araks R.

Manazkert

Arčeš

Xlatᶜ

Lake Van

Tabrīz

Lake Urmia

PERSIA
(IRAN)

located in the basin of the Rioni (Phasis) River, and east Georgia (ancient Iberia or Kᶜartᶜli), located along the middle course of the Kura (Cyrus, Mtkvari) River; (2) Azerbaijan in the east (ancient Albania, later Arrān), the low-lying and arid Kura-Araks basin; and (3) Armenia, lying on the high southern mountainous plateau overlooking Georgia on the north and Azerbaijan to the east, and buttressed by the Lesser Caucasus (Maly Kavkaz) range.

Caucasia is remarkable for its diversity, ranging from alpine regions (which include Mt. Elbrus, the highest peak in Europe, and Mt. Ararat, the highest in the Middle East) to the semidesert steppes of Azerbaijan and the lush, humid forests of west Georgia and Talysh. Its ethnic complexity was noted as long ago as the first century. More than fifty distinct peoples inhabit Caucasia, each having its own language. The various tongues belong to the Indo-European family (Armenian, Ossetic, Kurdish), the Turkic (Azeri, Turkoman, Karachai), the Mongol (Kalmuck), or the Palaeo-Caucasian (Georgian, Circassian, Chechen), the relationships among the various Palaeo-Caucasian languages being as yet unclear. In religion the Caucasians are predominantly Christians or Muslims. The mountain tribes, however, frequently manifest only a thin veneer of Islam superimposed upon an equally thin coating of Christianity, through both of which may still be detected the remains of a highly developed paganism. The Tats are mostly Jews. The Kalmucks are largely Lamaist Buddhists. For all these differences, a communality of customs, a shared history, and a similar way of life give the area a degree of unity.

North Caucasia was dominated by the Iranian Scythians and then by the related Sarmatian tribes until about A.D. 250, after which the Sarmatian Alans controlled the area. In the seventh century the Khazars, centered at Itil, near Astrakhan at the mouth of the Volga, dominated the lesser states in northeast Caucasia, although, given the difficulty of controlling the mountain people, it seems likely that the domination of these northern borders was merely nominal. Greek colonies existed on the Black Sea coast of northwest Caucasia into the Middle Ages, and from them Greek cultural influences (and later, Christianity) penetrated the mountains. The destruction of the Khazar state in the tenth century led to a resurgence of the Alans, but their kingdom was destroyed by the Mongols, who in the thirteenth century succeeded for the first time in history in uniting North and South Caucasia under a single rule. When the Mongol empire broke into several states in the late thirteenth century, North Caucasia passed under the domination of the Golden Horde until the fifteenth century, when the native Circassian tribes gained control.

In South Caucasia the Achaemenid Empire of Iran, and then of the Seleucid successors of Alexander, prevailed until 188 B.C. Locally the state of Colchis had already emerged in Urartian times (thirteenth–seventh centuries B.C.), Armenia after the fall of Urartu, Iberia after the death of Alexander, and Albania not long after. Albania was destroyed between the eighth and tenth centuries; east and west Georgia were united in 1008; Armenia, partitioned in 387 and kingless after 428, emerged in the ninth century as several kingdoms, the last of which, Cilicia, was overrun by the Muslims in 1375.

The location of the South Caucasians upon a plateau of the highest strategic and commercial importance as a gateway to Asia has played a decisive role in their history, which has always moved on two levels: that of various East–West power struggles and that of local turbulence among succeeding conquerors and subjected peoples.

BIBLIOGRAPHY

Academy of Sciences of the USSR, Institute of Geography, *Kavkaz* (1966); Bernhard Geiger *et al., Peoples and Languages of the Caucasus* (1959); T. Halasi-Kun, "The Caucasus, An Ethno-Historical Survey," in *Studia caucasica,* **1** (1963); M. O. Kosven, *Etnografia i istoria Kavkaza* (1961).

ROBERT HEWSEN

[See also **Armenia: Geography; Azerbaijan; Georgia: Geography; Golden Horde; Mongol Empire; Russian Nomads, Invasions of.**]

CAUCASUS MOUNTAINS (Pahlavi, Kāfkōh [Kafᵓ Mountains]; Greek, Kaukasos; Armenian, Kawkaz; Arabic, al-Qaba, al-Ḳabḳ, al-Ḳabkh, al-Kabj, or Jabal al-Alsun [Mountains of Tongues]; Russian, Kavkaz), a large range of the Soviet Union extending from northwest to southeast for about 700 miles (1,127 kilometers) between the Black Sea and the Caspian and serving since antiquity as a natural frontier between Europe and Asia, between the barbarians of the steppes and the civilized lands to the south. In this high, rugged complex of parallel ridges, only one pass, the Daryal, is open year round and only the littoral pass along the Caspian shore has been a practical route of invasion. Narrow and forested in the west, the Caucasus becomes more arid toward the east. Its highest peaks are Mt. Kazbek (16,558 feet; 5,043 meters) and Mt. Elbrus (18,510 feet; 5,633 meters), the latter being the highest mountain in Europe. The chief historical interest of the range lies in its role as a barrier against the periodic raids of the northern tribes (especially the Alani and Khazars) into the Middle East and the various measures taken to keep them out.

BIBLIOGRAPHY
Academy of Sciences of the USSR, Institute of Geography, *Kavkaz* (1966); John F. Baddeley, *The Rugged Flanks of Caucasus*, 2 vols. (1940); Bernhard Geiger *et al., Peoples and Languages of the Caucasus* (1959).

ROBERT HEWSEN

[See also **Caucasia.**]

CAUDA (Latin, "tail"), a section of music without text, occurs in most thirteenth-century polyphonic conductus compositions and often repeats the music of the sections with text. Caudas usually contain internal repetition and imitative passages that are sometimes organized with strict exchange of musical motifs—*abc* combined with *bca* and *cab*. Passages sometimes occur in quite different styles, in order to introduce variety.

BIBLIOGRAPHY
Robert A. Falck, *The Notre Dame Conductus: A Study of the Repertory* (1981); Albert Seay, "An Anonymous Treatise from St. Martial," in *Annales musicologiques, moyen-âge et renaissance,* 5 (1957).

ANDREW HUGHES

[See also **Conductus.**]

CAVALCANTI, GUIDO. Few details are known about the life of this very important poet and philosopher, friend of Dante Alighieri and true founder of the *dolce stil nuovo.* He was probably born around 1250 to Cavalcante de' Cavalcanti, descendant of a powerful Florentine family belonging to the White faction of the Guelph party. Greatly damaged by the Ghibelline victory at Montaperti (1260), the family

recovered part of its power and influence after the battle of Benevento (1266).

Cavalcanti's participation in Florentine politics began early in his life, and brought him into a bitter feud with the leader of the Black faction, Corso Donati, who conspired to have him murdered on a pilgrimage to Santiago de Compostela. In 1280 Cavalcanti acted as guarantor for the Guelphs in the peace promoted by Cardinal Francesco Frangipani Malabranca (Cardinal Latino). In 1284 he was elected to the city's General Council along with the historian Dino Compagni and the rhetorician and teacher Brunetto Latini, and was reelected in 1290. The continual struggle between the Black and White factions convinced the priors of the commune, among them Dante Alighieri, to banish the leaders of both sides. Cavalcanti was sent into exile to the small border town of Sarzana on 24 June 1300. Owing to the unhealthy climate, the ban was lifted after only one month, but not in time to prevent him from contracting malaria. Cavalcanti died 27 or 28 August 1300.

"Quelli cui io chiamo primo de li miei amici" (the one I call first among my friends): with these words Dante dedicates his *Vita nuova* (3.14) to Cavalcanti, honoring him as the father of the *fedeli d'amore* (the poets of love), among whom he counted himself. Considered to be the best Italian poet before Dante, Cavalcanti established himself as the great poet-philosopher of love with the appearance of his canzone "Donna me prega." The canzone provided his contemporaries with a philosophical resolution to the poetics of love. The subsequent acknowledgment and many commentaries by writers ranging from Giovanni Boccaccio to Marsilio Ficino, from the medical-philosophical "Scriptum super cantilenam Guidonis de Cavalcantibus" by the Florentine physician Dino del Garbo to Jacques Ferrand's *Traité de la maladie de l'amour ou mélancholie erotique* (published 1610), attest to the enduring authority of the poem. "Donna me prega" thus serves as the theoretical manifesto of the *dolce stil nuovo.*

The canzone develops eight theses on love: where love resides, how it originates, on which faculties of the soul it operates, its intrinsic power, its essence, the effects it causes, why it is named love, and whether it can be seen. The hermetic language Cavalcanti uses to address the questions, together with several yet unresolved textual problems, have prompted a succession of conflicting critical theories, and have made "Donna me prega" one of the most studied poems of Italian literature.

196

Cavalcanti's theory of love has been attributed to the mysticism of the Arabian Ibn Bājja (Avempace), to the philosophy of Ibn Rushd (Averroës), to the Scholastic thought of Albertus Magnus and of St. Thomas Aquinas, or to the confluence of the aforementioned. All interpreters are otherwise in agreement when considering the love Cavalcanti describes as an overwhelming, often negative force, capable of destroying the spiritual and physical fiber of man. Love, according to the canzone, is a passion *(passio)* of the mind that resides in that part of the brain where memory also resides. Love, in fact, according to medieval philosophy, is created by the mnemonic image, the *phantasma* of the lady, perceived by the external senses and preserved in the receptacle of memory as a figure is preserved in wax. There can be no *passio*—there can be no intellection, in fact—without a mnemonic image (*Nihil potest homo intelligere sine phantasmate,* "man cannot understand anything without mnemonic images," writes St. Thomas in his *De memoria et reminiscentia commentarium,* following Aristotle's *De anima*).

The image is only a potential act of intellection. It must first be acted upon by the agent or active intellect (Aristotle's *nous poietikos*); that is, the form of the external object is within the image, and before it can become the object of thought, it must be purified of any residual materiality. This is done by the agent intellect through a process of illumination. When the image comes into contact with the agent intellect, the form within the image finds its true, innate, dynamogenic nature. This dynamogenic power is the *species intelligibilis,* located in memory. Once the agent intellect communicates the *species intelligibilis* to the possible intellect through the image, the intellect is able to understand the object of perception and to complete the act of intellection. Once the object has been perceived, once its nature has been understood, imagination *(virtus imaginativa)* presents it as something to be pursued or avoided by means of the practical intellect.

However, since the permanence of images in the faculty of imagination, and therefore in memory, is directly proportional to the level of heat and of dryness of their encephalic cavity, and since love causes a sudden increase in the internal temperature of the body, the *phantasma* of the loved one can remain firmly impressed within memory, thus never becoming *species intelligibilis.* With the power of reason obscured, the will of the lover is deceived; the object of desire, in its still material, imperfect form, is mistaken for the good, which should only be an object of contemplation. Thus the life of the lover is consumed within a never-ending pursuit of a good that is truly unattainable.

This futile grasp at vain images of good ultimately results in a melancholic delirium, convulsed by tears, sighs, tremors, and the constant fear and longing for death that characterizes Cavalcanti's poetry.

It is to this tragic concept of life, which finally denies eternal salvation to earthly love, indeed to any overwhelming passion, that we may impute the erosion in the friendship between Cavalcanti and Dante Alighieri that conceivably was expressed in the "disdain" shown by Dante toward his old friend in *Inferno* X.

BIBLIOGRAPHY

Editions and translations. Guido Cavalcanti, *Rime,* Guido Favati, ed. (1957); Gianfranco Contini, *Poeti del duecento,* I (1960); Peter Dronke, *Medieval Latin and the Rise of the European Love Lyric,* 2 vols. (1968); Ezra Pound, *Translations* (1963).

Critical studies. Guido Favati, *Inchiesta sul dolce stil nuovo* (1975); M. Marti, "Cavalcanti, Guido," in *Enciclopedia dantesca* (1970); James E. Shaw, *Guido Cavalcanti's Theory of Love: The "Canzone d'Amore" and Other Related Problems* (1949).

MASSIMO CIAVOLELLA

[See also **Courtly Love; Dante Alighieri; Florence; Italian Literature: Thirteenth-century Poetry; Philosophy/ Theology.**]

CAVALLERO ZIFAR, LIBRO DEL, Spain's oldest extant prose romance, composed about 1301, probably by Ferrán Martínez, a Toledan priest and archdeacon of Madrid. That it was one of the few medieval vernacular works to be printed (Seville, 1512) and that it influenced such major writers as Juan Ruiz, Juan Manuel, and Cervantes (who probably based Sancho Panza on Ribaldo, Zifar's peasant squire) testify to its enduring popularity. The romance has three parts: (1) the story of Zifar, his wife, and two sons, which follows the familiar Byzantine pattern of separation, adventures, and final reunion; (2) Zifar's moral and practical instruction of his sons; (3) the adventures of Roboán, the younger son. The work traces the family's progress from abject poverty to imperial status, achieved through unwavering faith in God.

Complex structural and thematic parallels bind the three sections, and the romance can be read as an elaborate Christian allegory. The basic tale is of oriental origin, and the work draws on other Eastern sources for moral teachings, exempla, other world episodes, and symbolic names. But Martínez also takes material from the Western hagiographic, epic, and chivalric traditions. In content, tone, and style *Zifar* is a fascinating tapestry incorporating strands from Muslim Arabic and Christian Latin cultures.

BIBLIOGRAPHY

James F. Burke, *History and Vision: The Figural Structure of the LCZ* (1972); Roger M. Walker, *Tradition and Technique in "El Libro del Cavallero Zifar"* (1974).

ROGER M. WALKER

[See also **Spanish Literature; Spanish Romances.**]

Christ, detail of fresco of the Last Judgment. Church of S. Cecilia, Rome, *ca.* 1290. ALINARI/EDITORIAL PHOTOCOLOR ARCHIVES

CAVALLINI, PIETRO (*fl. ca.* 1250–*ca.* 1330), Roman painter, an important but problematic figure owing to the poor preservation of his oeuvre. Cavallini's surviving works are all large-scale wall frescoes or mosaics.

He is likely the Pietro dei Cerroni, called Cavallini, who is noted in a Roman document of 1273. He is reported active between 1277 and 1290, repainting damaged frescoes for S. Paolo fuori le Mura in Rome (destroyed in a fire of 1823 but recorded in Baroque copies). About 1291 Cavallini signed the six mosaics depicting the *Life of the Virgin* that he added to a twelfth-century cycle in S. Maria in Trastevere. Of his fresco cycle for the nuns' choir of that church, only the central portion of the *Last Judgment* and the *Annunciation* have survived. Scholars most often date his frescoes for S. Cecilia in Rome in the 1290's (only the *Last Judgment* survives). An extensively restored *Christ in Glory* fresco in the apse of S. Giorgio in Velabro is dated roughly 1295. Sometime after 1302, Cavallini and his shop likely painted the lunette fresco of *Madonna and Child* and two kneeling saints with Cardinal Matteo d'Acquasparta for the cardinal's tomb in S. Maria d'Aracoeli, Rome. A document of 1308 places Cavallini in Naples, as painter to King Charles II of Anjou and his son Robert. There Cavallini is thought to have contributed to the frescoes of S. Maria Donnaregina.

Probably inspired by Roman antiquity and the increasingly human interpretation of religious imagery, Cavallini developed a clarity, cohesion, and naturalism in his work that give him an important position in the history of Italian painting. Although

he is often considered the older and influential contemporary of Giotto, who is documented in Rome in 1313, Cavallini's elusive chronology makes it difficult to speculate on the exact nature of the relationship between the two artists. Nevertheless, Cavallini's contributions and his departures from Byzantine traditions were no less revolutionary than those of his better-known contemporary.

BIBLIOGRAPHY

John White, *Art and Architecture in Italy, 1250–1400* (1966); Robert Oertel, *Early Italian Painting to 1400* (1968); Guglielmo Matthiae, *Pietro Cavallini* (1972).

ADELHEID M. GEALT

[See also **Giotto di Bondone.**]

CAVALRY, ARMENIAN. Cavalry was the principal unit of the Armenian army from antiquity, when the country was already renowned for the excellence of its horses. Just before the Christian era, King Artawazd II boasted to the Roman Mark Antony of the size and quality of his cavalry, according to the geographer Strabo (*Geography*, 11.14.9).

Under the Arsacids the right and privilege of serving in the cavalry belonged to the lesser nobility, or *azat*, who composed the bulk of the corps, although armed attendants and other mounted detachments probably swelled the noble contingents. The heavy armor of the *azat cataphracti* probably distinguished them from the inferior units. As part of his duties, each *naχarar,* or lord, was required to appear in wartime attended by his contingent of *azat* knights. According to the *Zōrnamak* (Military list), a document considered by most scholars to be apocryphal but to give a reasonably accurate if overschematized picture of the contemporary situation, the status of each lord depended on the number of knights serving under him. The greatest magnates could muster up to 10,000 men, and the entire Arsacid cavalry, including the secondary units, may have totaled 120,000 men. This cavalry was commanded by the *aspet* (master of the horse), a title hereditary in the Bagratid house (Toumanoff has questioned this assumption).

After the end of the Arsacid kingdom in A.D. 428, the Armenian cavalry continued to serve in both the Byzantine and the Sasanian armies. The Armenian historian Elišē (Book II) states that a special ceremonial existed for the reception of the Armenian cavalry at the Persian court. This contingent, the size of which was determined by census, received regular pay and probably numbered 30,000 men. This practice was continued after the Arab conquest. The Armenian historian Sebēos (chs. 35–48) says that the Armenian tribute was remitted for three years in exchange for the service of a cavalry contingent of 15,000 men, although Arabic sources do not corroborate this point. Both the census and the payments to the Armenian cavalry continued, though at times irregularly, through the Umayyad period, but they were abolished by the Abbasids in the middle of the eighth century. Thereafter, the Armenian army continued to fight primarily on horseback, and the thirteenth-century *Cilician Chronicle* attributed to Smbat Sparapet still speaks of *jiawor,* or knights (probably in the Western sense), but the formal service of the *azat* cavalry no longer seems to have existed.

BIBLIOGRAPHY

References to the *azat* cavalry are scattered throughout early Armenian historiography. See Nikolai Adonts, *Armenia in the Period of Justinian,* Nina G. Garsoïan, rev. and trans. (1970), 183–234; Cyril Toumanoff, *Studies in Christian Caucasian History* (1963), 202, 234–241, 324–325.

NINA G. GARSOÏAN

[See also **Armenia: History of; Azat; Cataphracti; Naχarar; Warfare, Byzantine.**]

CAVALRY, BYZANTINE. Cavalry were the most important Byzantine troops throughout the history of the empire. The best descriptions are found in the *History of His Own Time* of Procopius and in various tactical and strategic manuals, such as the *Strategicon* of Maurice and the *Tactica* of Leo VI. Also potentially useful as sources are manuscript illustrations of cavalry in such works as the Escorial Skylitzes, but it is unclear whether these represent Byzantine cavalry of a particular period. Archaeological survivals of Byzantine cavalry weapons have not been satisfactorily identified and analyzed.

The standard word for a cavalry soldier was *kaballarios,* and collective units were sometimes called, in the middle period, *kaballarika themata.* Although cavalry probably received cash assistance for the purchase of mounts in the early and middle sixth century, by the end of the century cavalrymen apparently bought and were responsible for the replacement of their mounts. The archery from horseback that became essential in the sixth century for fighting steppe peoples and Persians, and for defeating Germanic opponents, required extensive, difficult, and constant drill. The Byzantines probably adopted the use of the stirrup from the Avars in the sixth century.

Heavy reliance on horse created a mobile rather than a static warfare, sometimes stretching over wide areas. Cavalry were essential for opposing the overwhelmingly mounted Byzantine foes: Huns, Pechenegs, Cumans, Bulgars, Arabs, and Turks. The repeated Arab raids on Anatolia required the use of cavalry to pursue and outmaneuver, to cut off and destroy. In the middle period Byzantine cavalry were expected to appear for annual inspection of their mounts and arms at the muster *(adnoumion).* It is presumed that cavalrymen in the middle period provided for their mounts from their *stratiotika ktemata* (soldiers' properties), especially in the ninth and tenth centuries. Failure to possess a mount could result in loss of status as a soldier.

The thematic armies of the middle period were overwhelmingly mounted. A theme was normally divided into three *tourmai,* a Greek version of the very old Roman *turma* (squadron), and each *tourma* was commanded by a *tourmarch.* Each *tourma* of 6,000 soldiers was divided into three or five *droungoi* of 1,000 or more soldiers, each of which was commanded by a *droungarios.* Each *droungos* was divided into five *banda* of 200 to 400 soldiers, each commanded by a count, below whom were *kentarchs* (commanders of a hundred) and *dekarchies* of ten soldiers, each led by a *dekarch*. The precise numbers of soldiers in this theoretical schema are doubtful; the hierarchy of cavalry officers is well attested, but the accuracy of the statistics is doubtful; normal numbers were probably smaller. Pay scales varied by rank. Byzantine cavalry normally avoided the shock tactics of Western medieval cavalry, but they nevertheless represented the principal fighting strength of the empire.

BIBLIOGRAPHY

Procopius of Caesarea, [no title], Loeb Classical Library edition, H. B. Dewing, trans., 7 vols. (1953–1954); Leo VI the Wise, *Tactica,* R. Vári, ed. (1917–1921); Maurikios, *Das Strategikon,* George Dennis, ed., E. Gamillscheg, trans. (1981); English translation by George Dennis in preparation.

WALTER EMIL KAEGI, JR.

[See also **Cataphracti; Warfare, Byzantine.**]

CAVALRY, EUROPEAN. Cavalry is a branch of tactics that involves the deployment of horsemen to achieve the advantages of mobility and shock. The auxiliary functions of reconnaissance and raiding require mobility. Shock or contact cavalry fights a set battle usually in a tactical formation and in combination with foot and firepower.

TRANSITION PERIOD, CA. 100–1066

In European military history the transformation of the Roman Empire traditionally has invoked the idea of a tactical shift from the infantry of the Roman legion to the medieval mounted knight. Actually, the wider trend toward cavalry operations emerged as part of the Roman military response to a series of invasions that both required the swift action of light cavalry and also shaped the modes of fighting on horseback for mailed cavalry.

Increasing pressure on the Danubian frontier in the first century A.D. provided the Romans with the incentive for the development of heavy cavalry. Roman experimentation with new cavalry weapons and techniques is clearly depicted on Trajan's Column with the appearance for the first time of armored Roman or auxiliary horsemen. Just a few years later Hadrian established the first regular unit of auxiliary mailed cavalry. The cataphracts (*cataphracti*) were the mailed cavalry whose riders alone

were armored, while the *clibanarii* were those mailed cavalry in which both horse and rider were covered with armor. In his description of a battle in A.D. 69 between a Roman legion and a Sarmatian tribe, the Roxolani, Tacitus pointed out two weaknesses of mailed cavalry: the weight of the armor rendered an unhorsed rider defenseless, and the absence of a shield was a disadvantage in hand-to-hand combat. In battle, the mailed rider fought most frequently with a weapon resembling a long pike (*contus*), which he wielded with both hands. Fighting with the two-handed lance probably reduced effective control over the horse with the reins. The lack of stirrups obliged the rider to retain balance and control by the steady application of thigh and knee pressure. Most of the iconography shows that the rider braced himself for the shock by leaning forward.

The imperial Roman legion did not fight as an isolated infantry formation but was intended to interact with cavalry. In a treatise outlining Roman tactics against the Alans, Arrian in 134 explained that the heavy Roman infantry must maintain close order to withstand the violent shock of the enemy's cavalry attack. When the enemy retreated, the infantry opened ranks and half of the cavalry charged after them. The other half then followed more slowly in close formation to support the front-line horse should the Alans turn for a counterattack. The troops who used missiles tried to place themselves within firing range of the enemy. The combined action of infantry and cavalry was still part of late Roman tactical doctrine. Vegetius in *De re militari* required the heavy cavalry to cover the flanks of the foot, and the light horse was positioned at some distance from the combined-arms force to envelop the enemy's wings. Further enhancing the combined-arms idea, Vegetius advised a commander with cavalry deficient in numbers or training to intermingle the horsemen with light infantry who were experienced in using their small shields, swords, and javelins in this kind of service.

Until the invasions of the third century the Romans practiced a static frontier defense with legions stationed in permanent forts. The reinforcement of a frontier sector demanded the mobilization of temporary expeditionary forces, comprised of legionary detachments from other provinces. The withdrawal of these troops seriously depleted the numerical strength of their legions, exposing the frontier to attack in several places. To dispatch forces readily to any point along a threatened frontier, the third-century emperor Gallienus upgraded the status of cavalry in the Roman army, creating special cavalry detachments, or vexillations, which patrolled the area just inside the periphery. Within this combat zone these regional field reserves carried out search-and-destroy operations. These forces became the tactical cavalry units of the mobile field armies of Diocletian, the *comitatenses,* which later constituted the central field force of Constantine. According to the *Notitia dignitatum,* a list of civilian and military officials of *ca.* 408, the number of cavalry squadrons in the west was small in comparison with the east, and their distribution was uneven. More than half of the mobile squadrons had their permanent quarters in Africa and therefore were removed on the operational level from the command of the *magister equitum,* or master of the horse. The most important squadrons in relation to the emergence of shock cavalry were the armored units stationed in Gaul, the Taifal squadrons of the *comitatenses,* and the Sarmation units of the *auxilia.*

The increased emphasis on cavalry was generated within the Roman army, a view that overturns the older scholarship that the shock tactics of Germanic cavalry displaced the Roman legion at the battle of Adrianople (378). Scholarly investigation indicates that this engagement can no longer be taken to divide ancient from medieval warfare. Not the Visigoths alone, but a three-people confederation including Huns and Alans, attacked and dispersed the Roman cavalry, leaving the flanks of the legions vulnerable. The cavalry attack was made by a force just returning from a foraging expedition, indicating that the confederation did not intend to rely on cavalry as its principal striking arm against the Romans.

Among the Germanic kingdoms that succeeded the Roman Empire in the west, the Visigoths and the Lombards deployed horsemen regularly, but the Frankish army seldom used mounted warriors. Military historiography has been concerned with the extent to which the cavalry arm shaped the development of feudalism among the Franks. To explain the original feature of feudalism, the fusion of vassalage and the benefice, Heinrich Brunner suggested an expansion of cavalry, and he proposed the Muslim invasion that culminated in the battle of Poitiers (Tours) in 732 as the key event in the emergence of feudalism. He argued that Charles Martel sought to repel the Muslim advance by authorizing an increase in the numerical strength of the mounted forces in

his army. This tactical change required large estates for the maintenance of war-horses, which Charles Martel obtained by appropriating extensive tracts of church land for distribution to his military retainers.

Following to some extent in the footsteps of Brunner, Lynn White altered the discussion from the issue of numbers to that of tactical decisiveness, the critical striking force of the army. In formulating this idea, White drew inspiration from the work of Richard Lefebvre des Noëttes. This French cavalry officer brought his practical knowledge of horsemanship to an understanding of mounted shock combat, a mode of cavalry warfare that was dependent upon the combined effectiveness of the charging horse and of its technological components: the lateral support provided by the stirrup, the lance-at-rest, and the elongated shield. Departing from Brunner, White shifted the reason for Martel's tactical reforms away from the Muslim wars to technology. After tracing the westward diffusion of the stirrup, White argued that Martel or his advisers recognized the military potential of the stirrup in providing lateral stability to the rider and about 732 began to create an elite force of heavy cavalry. By offering the stirrup as the explanation for Martel's seizure of church land, White thus eliminated Brunner's causal nexus between the battle of Poitiers and church lands.

Subsequent research has undercut the entire idea of a mid-eighth or even ninth-century military revolution aimed at an expansion of cavalry, especially in three areas. First, a change in the month of mobilization: According to the continuator of Fredegar's *Chronicle,* Pepin made preparations for an Italian expedition at the end of 754 with an order for the army to assemble the following March, but subsequently changed the mobilization to May. Both Brunner and White argued that the preliminaries for this operation marked the beginning of a permanent shift in the time of mobilization from March to May to solve the problem of adequate forage for mounts. Other scholars, especially Levillain, Bullough, and Bachrach, offered a far simpler explanation for the delay, pointing out that the Alpine passes remained snowbound in March. Most of the controversy on the month of mobilization concerns the term *campus martius,* especially the passage from the *Annales Petaviani* for 755: "Tassilo came to the Field of Mars and the Field of Mars was changed to the month of May." The Field of Mars can be interpreted to mean the place of mobilization or the month of assembling the forces, more probably the former. The subsequent campaigns of the Carolingians do not indicate a regular time for mobilization.

Second, the Saxon tribute: Pepin the Short's change in the Saxon tribute of 758 from 500 cattle to 300 horses has been used as proof of a greater need for cavalry horses. This, however, does not confirm the Brunner-White thesis; Pepin accepted a tribute of 700 cattle in 748—more than a decade after Charles Martel's military revolution was supposed to have been under way. Alternatively, it could be argued that Pepin simply may have had a greater demand for cattle than for horses in 748.

Third, in describing the battle on the Dyle in 891, the *Annales Fuldenses* indicated that "the Franks were unaccustomed to fighting *pedetemptim*." This passage often has been cited as proof of a completed transformation to cavalry in Frankish armies by the end of the ninth century. The current view of the text points out the distinction between *pedetemptim* with its sense of moving forward slowly and *pedester,* denoting "on foot." The correct translation of these Latin terms changes the meaning significantly. Instead of being unused to fighting on foot, the Franks actually objected to moving forward slowly through a swamp to a fortified position of the Northmen.

The diffusion of the stirrup is replete with difficulties owing to the archaeological and iconographic evidence. The Byzantines received the stirrup probably from the Avars by the end of the sixth century, for it is mentioned as required equipment for a cavalryman in Maurice's *Strategikon.* The Avars also probably transmitted the stirrup to western Europe, possibly during Charlemagne's war with this tribe.

A systematic investigation of the artifacts was not possible until Frauke Stein's publication of an archaeological study on warrior graves. The catalog of this work identified 704 graves of fighting men in eastern Francia, ranging in date from the late seventh through the early eighth centuries. Of the 704 graves, 135 could be identified as equestrian, yet stirrups were present in only 13.

Archaeological evidence and the capitularies afford some insight into the place of cavalry in Frankish armies. Charlemagne laid down the foundations of Carolingian military organization with regulations that placed an elite force of heavy cavalry at the top of the military hierarchy. The capitularies clearly indicate that Charlemagne did not plan for the numerical superiority of cavalry but wanted to ensure the availability of horsemen. The 135 equestrian graves of the total 704 warrior burials lend support to the military regulations of the capitularies. Not a single battle or campaign provides evidence that cavalry played a tactically decisive role. In the only reported cavalry action of Charlemagne's reign, two insubordinate Frankish commanders and their mounted force prematurely charged a disciplined Saxon infantry formation and were soundly defeated.

Iconography provides evidence of the fighting style of the warriors. The earliest securely dated manuscript, the Golden Psalter of St. Gall (*ca.* 875), clearly depicts mounted warriors, not in combat but riding in full battle array, with all the components of mounted shock combat except the elongated shield. Carolingian horsemen retained the round shield. Even so, the ninth-century evidence for the lance-at-rest position is unclear. Nithard, a source roughly contemporaneous with the Golden Psalter, described an exhibition of military games near Strasbourg in 842. An examination of the text indicates that the teams did not perform their tactical maneuvers in the style of mounted shock combat; for in brandishing their lances instead of holding them in a stationary position, the participants did not employ the lance-at-rest position. Moreover, the manner of wielding the lance was inconsistent even up to the time of the Bayeux Tapestry. There were four principal ways of wielding the lance: the lance-at-rest style; throwing the lance overhead; thrusting it with an upward swing of the arm; and holding the lance with the tip pointed toward the ground, using the weapon to stab the opponent.

The component parts of medieval shock cavalry were slow in reaching completion and were not fully in place until the eve of the Crusades. The high-backed saddle, which appeared late in the eleventh century at the earliest, acted with the stirrup to stabilize the seat of the rider, preventing the impact of the lance from driving him over the rump of the horse.

Far more characteristic of the Carolingian period than shock tactics was the use of cavalry for reconnaissance and raiding. The Northmen used horses in combination with ships to increase the mobility of their raids. In the Carolingian Ostmark mounted troops were deployed largely for pillaging the territory around enemy fortifications. Shock tactics were practiced in a few set battles: Fontenoy (841), Montpensier (892), Fritzlar (906), and Lechfeld (955). The emergence of tournaments in the twelfth century provided another outlet for the use of contact cavalry. Set battles nevertheless remained infrequent; sieges were the prevailing form of warfare.

THE BIRTH OF CHIVALRY, 1066–1300

As a warrior elite, the medieval secular aristocracy of northern Europe exercised a near monopoly on the use of heavy cavalry, which they considered to be the tactically decisive arm. During the Crusades the principal striking forces were the squadrons of mailed cavalry who relied for victory on a frontal charge, a single-direction orientation that could change course only with difficulty once the charge began. The devastating impact of the successful charge against concentrated light forces was recognized by the *Tactica* of Emperor Leo VI and the *Alexiad* of Anna Komnena. Crusading knights tended to be ineffective against the light cavalry of the Muslims. These mounted archers, dispersed in small groups, always sought to envelop the flanks or rear of their enemies. Only rarely were the Franks able to deliver a decisive cavalry charge, as at Dorylaeum (1097), when the mounted Muslim archers concentrated their forces on one of the Frankish flanks and received a charge from a relief force.

Not all of western Europe adopted the shock tactics of heavy cavalry. The Magyars never developed heavy cavalry because of their constant exposure to Turkish mounted archers. In Reconquest Spain, where the rapid maneuver of a marauding band favored light cavalry, the Crusaders copied the equipment and riding techniques of the Muslims. In the style called *a la jinete,* the knight rode with short stirrups on a flat saddle and controlled the horse with a spade bit. This device exerted pressure on the palate, forcing the horse to turn far more quickly than by pulling at the sides of the mouth with a snaffle bit. Both Muslims and Christians remarked that the high cantle of the saddle used by the heavily armed knight riding *a la brida,* or with long stirrups, enabled the rider to withstand a powerful lance thrust in close combat. The Spanish also practiced the tactical maneuver of *torna-fuye,* simulated flight and counterattack, expressed by the Muslims as *karr-wa-farr.*

Modern investigation of medieval battles indicates that the knights had the discipline to fight in tactical units and were capable of executing a feigned retreat. Simulated flight is a tactical maneuver requiring a cohesion and a synchronization of forces that can be achieved only through practice in campaigns. Expert coordination is especially critical in the timing of the withdrawal, the planning of the distance to be covered, and the turning movement itself. Developed by light cavalry in the steppes of Asia and southern Russia, the tactic was transmitted to the Byzantines and the Magyars.

Historians are divided over the occurrence of a feigned retreat at the battle of Hastings (1066). On the negative side, the accounts of Hastings were written by Norman chroniclers who possibly wished to cover up an actual retreat. Moreover, once William's forces were mobilized, they had to remain ready to cross the Channel as soon as the winds changed, and would not have had an opportunity to rehearse this maneuver. In favor of feigned flight, the contemporary sources explained that it was accomplished by only part of William's forces, the Norman knights who received a direct order from the duke. At Hastings the Norman knights fought in tactical units. As contingents of the individual lords, they had had the opportunity to train together and to develop the coordination necessary to perform this maneuver successfully. The capability of Norman knights to execute this maneuver is indicated by their victory over the French at Arques in Normandy in 1053. This technique probably was borrowed from the Normans in south Italy, who used it against the Muslims at Messina (1060).

The disposition of the forces at Hastings was designed to execute a combined-arms operation with the firepower of an opening flight of arrows to soften up the enemy, followed by a heavy cavalry assault to open up breaches in the Anglo-Saxon line, and finally the exploitation of those gaps with a cavalry pursuit. At Hastings the Norman knights broke their lances on the first clash and then continued the fight with swords. Hastings had a notable impact on subsequent pitched battles, establishing a tactical doctrine that emphasized that the task of infantry, especially of the archers, was the support and protection of heavy cavalry. The interaction of heavy cavalry and mounted infantry was clearly indicated at Northallerton (1138), Tinchebray (1106), and Brémule (1119). By contrast, the battle of Thielt (1128) was exclusively a cavalry engagement; but each army was arrayed in three "battles," apparently placed one behind the other, except for one group used as a tactical reserve. This concept was also employed at the battle of Civitate (1053), a skirmish near Bourgtheroulde (1124), and at Nocera (1132).

Modern scholars have challenged the older view of medieval warfare that battles were fought as melees in which the knight's primary objective was individual prowess. Careful research into the narrative sources indicates that knights fought in disciplined formations, small tactical units called *conrois* or banners, which in turn formed larger units, *batailles* or battles, for example, the archers, infantry, and cavalry comprising separate battles at Hastings. The *conrois* was a contingent of vassals who fought as a tactical unit under their liege lord. The battle of Bouvines (1214) was once thought to have been fought in loose order, without units capable of separate maneuver. But we now know that not only did the participants fight in tactical units, they also utilized a remarkable crown formation in which a semicircular infantry force opened up and allowed the cavalry within to move out for battle, and upon their return, enclosed the horsemen to provide protection.

To keep in practice for fighting as tactical units in actual warfare, the knights refined their skills in war games called tournaments. These training exercises took the form of pitched battles arranged in advance. The knights lined up in opposing ranks; when a herald gave the signal, the two lines of heavy cavalry lowered their lances and charged at full tilt; once the lances were broken, the knights drew their swords and continued the contest, just as in real battles. Tournaments differed from regular battles in the provision of safety zones, to which incapacitated knights could retire.

In the thirteenth century the tournament began to change from its initial purpose of sharpening combat skills. The comparatively rare occurrence of set battles undermined the function of the tournament as a military exercise. There were several changes toward the amelioration of these simulated combats. The first step was the joust, a war game distinct from the tournament, in which two knights with lowered lances rode along opposite sides of a barrier, called a list, and broke lances. By the mid-thirteenth century most tournaments were preceded by a series of jousts, and in the next century were followed by hand-to-hand combats. Second, in the thirteenth and fourteenth centuries, blunted weapons with shafts deliberately constructed to be fragile were customarily used in tournaments. Finally, the development of complicated regulations and of the distinction between jousting and field armor turned these paramilitary exercises into martial sports.

DECLINE OF HEAVY CAVALRY, 1300–1500

In late medieval warfare light cavalry retained its traditional advantage of mobility in raiding expeditions. Heavy cavalry tended to operate without combined arms support when charging disciplined infantry formations skilled in the use of shock tactics and missile weapons.

Infantry developed in the least feudalized areas of Europe: the Low Countries, Scotland, and Switzerland, where cavalry operations were discouraged by the presence of mountains or lowlands that could be inundated by the opening up of sluices. The first late medieval defeats of mounted knights occurred at Courtrai (1302) and at Bannockburn (1314). In both engagements the heavy cavalry did not coordinate their attack with infantry support but charged the strong defensive positions of the Flemish and the Scots respectively, and in anticipation of a cavalry charge the defenders dug potholes camouflaged by foliage. The cavalry forces were impaled on the Flemish *godendags* and on the Scottish pikes. At Bannockburn the English archers could not be effective because they were drawn up behind the formations of knights. The entire English army had the river Bannockburn and the marshes at its back, enabling Robert Bruce to order the reserve to attack the English cavalry in the flank.

In the development of infantry shock tactics, the Swiss were most notable for their swift advance. With little or no armor, they would take the offensive in a three-column echelon, a formation that relied on mobility to protect the flanks of the advance, and took advantage of topographical features to cover the flanks of the rearward phalanxes. Their principal weapons were the pike and the halberd, an all-purpose, long-shafted ax equipped with either a concave or a convex blade and a hook to pull knights off their horses. In battle the pikemen broke the momentum of the cavalry charge, and then the halberdiers advanced to disable and kill the knights. Holding their pikes, the infantry required the discipline to stand fast and present a line of bristling spearpoints to oncoming cavalry.

War-horses likewise had to be trained to deliver the charge, but it was extremely unusual for a horse to impale itself on a pike. The length of the pike outdistanced the lance, placing the charging knight at a disadvantage. When approximately 1,600 pounds of man and horse strike a pike point with a sixteen-foot shaft at 25 to 30 miles per hour, the result is usually fatal to the horse and injurious to the rider. The momentum of the dead and the dying came into the infantry line as 1,600 pounds of dead missile. With the first wave of cavalry, the infantry probably had difficulty in retaining the integrity of their formation, but the accumulation of corpses would have reduced the shock effect of subsequent charges. The initial

Swiss victories, at Morgarten (1315) and Sempach (1386), were gained against their Habsburg overlords. As mercenaries of the French monarchy against the Burgundian dukes, the Swiss won decisive battles in combination with cavalry at Morat (1476), where cavalry provided mobility for pursuit, and at Nancy (1477), where mounted forces cut off the Burgundian retreat.

The relative length of the weapons strongly influenced the subsequent development of Swiss tactics. In the sixteenth century the Swiss pikemen confronted the short sword and the small round shield (buckler) of the Spanish infantry. The bearer of the longer weapon became helpless when his opponent closed by using the buckler to turn aside the spearpoint.

Missile weapons, especially the longbow and to some extent gunpowder technology, further reduced the effectiveness of heavy cavalry. Missiles, notably a shower of arrows from the English longbowmen, largely eliminated the shock advantage of preventing cavalry from pressing home the charge. The longbow used in the Hundred Years War originated in south Wales, where it was known in the reign of Henry II (1154–1189). After the conquest of Wales in 1284, Edward I recruited Welsh archers into the English infantry. Edward preferred the longbow to the crossbow not only because of its technical superiority (faster rate of fire and, at that time, more accurate range) but also because he could recruit large numbers of bowmen in his own country. The main disadvantage of the longbow was the training period of about six years required to achieve proficiency.

The battle of Falkirk (1298) was a demonstration of combined arms: a victory of the longbowmen and cavalry over the Scottish pikemen. The Scots were drawn up in four "schiltrons." These crown-shaped formations were supported by a reserve of armored cavalry. A forest close behind the army protected their hilltop position. Edward I used his longbowmen to thin out the ranks of the schiltrons and then committed his heavy cavalry to deliver the decisive blow. At the sight of the charging English knights, the Scottish cavalry fled, leaving their disciplined infantry unsupported to face defeat from the English combination of archers and horsemen.

In the pitched battles of the Hundred Years War, the French knights did not cover their cavalry charges with supporting infantry. As at Courtrai they trampled their own allies, the Genoese crossbowmen who were positioned in front of them. The battle of Crécy (1346) demonstrated to the English

the combined-arms strength of longbowmen and dismounted men-at-arms (armored knights who fought on foot). Edward III deployed his army in three battles of men-at-arms. On each wing and between the two battles were the archers. The meeting of the two armies was a surprise encounter. Lacking discipline, the French vanguard halted and pulled back slightly; but the subordinate French commanders, insisting on the honor of commencing battle, pushed their troops forward and opened up gaps in the front line. The Genoese crossbowmen proved ineffective, for their opening shower of bolts fell short of the mark. Moreover, the rain moistened the leather strap that draws back the bolt so that the weapons could not be fired. The cavalry charge was remarkably similar to that of Courtrai: the heavy cavalry ran down the crossbowmen and headed up a slope camouflaged with potholes but, this time, made slippery by the rain.

Most important for the subsequent fate of cavalry was the French assessment of their defeat at Crécy. Fixing special attention on the failure of the mounted charge, they decided that the cause of the English victory was their use of dismounted men-at-arms, an observation that they tried to apply at Poitiers (1356). Overlooking the stationary position of the English deployment and failing to calculate the weight of their armor, the dismounted French knights charged up a slope furrowed by narrow sunken trails, making their line of advance predictable for the archers. As at Crécy, the English were deployed in a defensive position. The French advanced, intending vainly to rely on the impact of their assault once they reached the top of the hill.

The French continued to reflect on the causes of their defeats. Honoré Bonet's *Arbre des batailles*, written between 1386 and 1389, was a practical handbook on war, not a treatise on chivalry. It advocated defensive tactics in battle and suggested that the French should make greater use of infantry. The advice was not taken. At the battle of Agincourt (1415), the French reverted to heavy cavalry, but the English archers planted stakes in the ground at an oblique angle and stood just in front of them. When the French cavalry closed, the archers stepped back, impaling the horses of the French knights.

In response to the failure of defensive armor to protect knights from the devastating effects of innovations in infantry tactics and missile weapons, full plate armor appeared after 1350, encasing both horse and rider. In shock combat the mounted knight held a shield on the left arm, reins in the left hand, and lance under the right arm. After 1420 the widespread use of the lance-rest turned the mounted knight into a living projectile. The device held the lance firm at the moment of impact and reduced the tendency of the long steel-tipped weapon to point downward and slip out of the rider's grip.

Plate armor provided maximum protection with its fluted and rippled surfaces which were designed to repel arrows and crossbow bolts. Even so, during the fifteenth century improved steel crossbows drawn by a windlass could pierce armor and surpassed the range of the longbow. After 1500 the weight of plate armor slowed the horse to a trot, mitigating the shock of the once formidable cavalry charge. The effect of heavy armor on a medieval war-horse should not be underestimated; the *destrier* more closely resembled a 1,300-pound heavy hunter than a 2,000-pound Clydesdale.

Plate armor severely restricted the freedom of movement in guiding a horse, requiring technological changes in equipment. To increase the leverage action of the bit, the cheekpieces became longer and thicker so that the rider would not have to exert so great a physical effort in controlling the horse. Also, long-necked spurs were designed to accommodate the flanchards, or horse armor, which removed the rider's foot a considerable distance from the side of the horse.

To base the history of late medieval French horse on the battles of Crécy, Poitiers, and Agincourt overlooks the contribution to the ultimate French victory over the English of mobile cavalry that engaged in unconventional war. Guerrilla operations were a countermeasure to the chief strategic feature of the war, the *chevauchée* or cavalry raid, which the English launched across France from Flanders and Gascony. Also requiring guerrilla action were bands of unemployed mercenaries, the Great Companies or *routiers,* who terrorized the French countryside. The man largely responsible for curtailing the English expeditions and the roving brigands was Bertrand du Guesclin, the high constable (commander in chief) of France, 1370–1380. Hiring *routiers,* he waged guerrilla warfare to drive the English from the country. Never engaging the enemy directly, he practiced the Fabian tactics of scorched-earth raids in the path of the English forays, harassment of enemy lines of communication, ambushes, and night attacks—all of which required mobile cavalry.

Toward the end of the Hundred Years War, from 1445 to 1448, Charles VII undertook a program of military reform. In a tactical measure, he formed combined-arms units, the *compagnies d'ordonnance,* consisting of lances. A lance included a heavily armored man-at-arms, three mounted archers, a crossbowman, a culvineer (handgunner), and a pikeman to fight on foot. Established as a year-round professional force, these units constituted the first standing army to appear in early modern Europe.

The missile weapons of gunpowder technology contributed to the demise of medieval heavy cavalry. The Hussite leader, Jan Žižka, developed the wagon fortress, a group of wagons arranged in a circle. Each vehicle was equipped with artillery to present a broadside of fire to the imperial German cavalry.

Until the later Middle Ages, there is surprisingly little information about the care and training of war-horses. The earliest treatise on equine veterinary medicine did not appear until the work of Jordanus Ruffus, who wrote before 1250 as a courtier of Emperor Frederick II. Treatises on the techniques for training war-horses to perform the complicated turning maneuvers required of mounted shock combat did not enjoy a wide circulation until the publication of Federico Grisone's *Ordini del cavalcare* in 1550, clearly the product of a long oral tradition. This genre eventually developed into manuals for training horses to execute the intricate movements of dressage.

BIBLIOGRAPHY

General works on medieval warfare. Philippe Contamine, *La guerre au moyen âge* (1980), with new directions of research and comprehensive bibliography; J. F. Verbruggen, *The Art of Warfare in Western Europe During the Middle Ages,* S. Willard and S. C. M. Southern, trans. (1976), incorporates the conclusions of recent research but without a critical apparatus; Ferdinand Lot, *L'art militaire au moyen âge et en Proche Orient,* 2 vols. (1946); Charles W. C. Oman, *The Art of Warfare in the Middle Ages,* 2 vols. (1969), partially summarized by John Beeler, *Warfare in Feudal Europe, 730–1200* (1971).

Transition period, ca. 100–ca. 1100. Paul Vigneron, *Le cheval dans l'antiquité gréco-romaine,* 2 vols. (1968), on Roman cavalry in the empire; for an analysis of the empire's earlier static defense, see Edward N. Luttwak, *The Grand Strategy of the Roman Empire* (1976); Dietrich Hoffmann, *Das spätrömische Bewegungsheer und die Notitia Dignitatum,* 2 vols. (1969), the definitive work on the development of mobile field armies under Diocletian and Constantine; Thomas S. Burns, "The Battle of Adrianople: A Reconsideration," in *Historia,* **22** (1973), and Hoffmann, *op. cit.,* 440ff. On the logistics of the invading Asian mounted forces, see Denis Sinor, "Horse and Pasture in Inner Asian History," in *Oriens extremus,* **19** (1972); and

Rudi Paul Lindner, "Nomadism, Horses and Huns," in *Past and Present*, **92** (1981). The lack of adequate pasture in Europe for large numbers of horses explains the sudden withdrawal of the Huns and the Mongol failure to penetrate Europe.

The argument for a Frankish military revolution by Charles Martel was first formulated by Heinrich Brunner, "Der Reiterdienst und die Anfänge des Lehnwesens," in *Zeitschrift der Savigny-Stiftung für Rechtsgeschichte, Germanistische Abteilung,* **8** (1887); on the battle of Poitiers (Tours), see Jean-Henri Roy and Jean Deviosse, *La bataille de Poitiers* (1966), with texts, French translations, and bibliography. On the interrelationship of technology and tactical change, see Lynn White, Jr., *Medieval Technology and Social Change* (1962); and Richard Lefebvre des Noëttes, *L'attelage; le cheval de selle à travers les âges,* 2 vols. (1931); also, J. F. Verbruggen, "L'armée et la strategie de Charlemagne," in *Karl der Grosse,* I, 3rd ed. (1967), 420–436. White's conclusions were attacked by P. Sawyer and R. Hilton, "Technical Determinism: The Stirrup and the Plough," in *Past and Present,* **24** (1963); and by D. J. A. Ogilvy, "The Stirrup and Feudalism," in *University of Colorado Studies: Series in Language and Literature,* **10** (1966). For the most extensive reevaluation of the evidence, see Bernard S. Bachrach, "Charles Martel, Mounted Shock Combat, the Stirrup, and Feudalism," in *Studies in Medieval and Renaissance History,* **7** (1970). Also, D. A. Bullogh, "*Europae Pater*: Charlemagne and his Achievement in the Light of Recent Scholarship," in *English Historical Review,* **85** (1970).

On the authenticity of Maurice's *Strategikon,* and for critical editions and secondary works on other Byzantine military treatises, see Herbert Hunger, "Kriegswissenschaft," in *Die hochsprachliche profane Literatur der Byzantiner,* II (1978), 323–338; and Alphonse Dain, "Les strategistes byzantins," in his *Travaux et mémoires,* II (1967), 317–392. For the archaeological evidence on the stirrup, see Frauke Stein, *Adelsgräber des achten Jahrhunderts in Deutschland* (1967); Wilfred A. Seaby and Paul Woodfield, "Viking Stirrups from England and Their Background," in *Medieval Archaeology,* **24** (1980).

On the Avars, see Johan Callmer, "Problems Related to a Gravefind from the Outskirts of Old Kristiana," in *Meddelanden från Lunds Universitets Historiska Museum* (1973–1974); and Josef Déer, "Karl der Grosse und der Untergang des Awarenreiches," in Wolfgang Braunfels, ed., *Karl der Grosse,* I (1965), 719–791. On the inconsistent position of holding the lance, see D. J. A. Ross, "L'originalité de 'Turoldus': le maniement de la lance," in *Cahiers de civilisation médiévale,* 6 (1963); and, on the Bayeux Tapestry, Frank Stenton, ed., *The Bayeux Tapestry* (1957). On cavalry in early medieval Germany, see Charles R. Bowlus, "Warfare and Society in the Carolingian Ostmark," in *Austrian History Yearbook,* **14** (1978); and Karl Leyser, "The Battle at the Lech, 955: A Study in Tenth-Century Warfare," in *History,* **50** (1965).

Birth of chivalry, 1066–1300. On the emergence of the medieval knight as a heavy cavalryman, see Georges Duby, *The Chivalrous Society,* Cynthia Postan, trans. (1977), esp. ch. 11. On the Crusades, see Raymond C. Smail, *Crusading Warfare, 1097–1193* (1956); John W. Nesbitt, "The Rate of March of Crusading Armies in Europe," in *Traditio,* **19** (1963); and Elena Lourie, "A Society Organized for War: Medieval Spain," in *Past and Present,* **35** (1966). See also Lynn White, Jr., "The Crusades and the Technological Thrust of the West," and V. J. Parry, "La manière de combattre" (in English), in V. J. Parry and M. E. Yapp, eds., *War, Technology, and Society in the Middle East* (1979).

On the battle of Hastings see David C. Douglas, *English Historical Documents, 1042–1189* (1953), for English translations of the sources. Also, Charles H. Lemmon, "The Campaign of 1066," in *The Norman Conquest: Its Setting and Impact,* N. T. Chevallier, ed (1966). John Beeler, *Warfare in England, 1066–1189* (1966), 16–24, considers why Harold did not oppose the deployment of the Norman army below his position. Richard Glover, "English Warfare in 1066," in *English Historical Review,* **262** (1952), gives arguments against feigned retreat. D. P. Waley, "Combined Operations in Sicily, 1060–1078," in *Papers of the British School at Rome,* **22** (1954), emphasized contact with the Normans of Apulia, Calabria, and Sicily who practiced the feigned retreat maneuver. Bernard S. Bachrach, "The Feigned Retreat of Hastings," in *Medieval Studies,* **33** (1971); David R. Cook, "The Norman Military Revolution in England," in *Proceedings of the Battle Conference on Anglo-Norman Studies,* R. Allen Brown, ed., I (1979), notes that the feigned retreat was common in Byzantine and oriental warfare.

On Anglo-Saxon military practices that relate to cavalry, see Frederick W. Brooks, *The Battle of Stamford Bridge* (1963); and N. P. Brooks, "Arms, Status, and Warfare in Late-Saxon England," in *Ethelred the Unready: Papers from the Millenary Conference,* David Hill, ed. (1978), 81–103. Nicholas Hooper, "Anglo-Saxon Warfare on the Eve of the Conquest: A Brief Survey," in *Proceedings of the Battle Conference, op. cit.,* I, examines the battle of Maldon (991) and reiterates N. P. Brooks' conclusion that the Anglo-Saxon fyrd rode to the field of battle but dismounted to fight.

On the fighting of battles in tactical units, see Verbruggen, *The Art of Warfare, op. cit.,* and especially his "La tactique militaire des armées des chevaliers," in *Revue du Nord,* **30** (1948); and "Le problème des effectifs et de la tactique à la bataille de Bouvines (1214)," *ibid.,* **31** (1949). For an exhaustive bibliography and French translations of the sources on this battle, see Georges Duby, *Le dimanche de Bouvines, 27 juillet 1214* (1973). Claude Gaier, "La cavalerie lourde en Europe occidentale du XIIe au XVIe siècle," in *Revue internationale d'histoire militaire,* **31** (1971), minimizes the role of supporting infantry in medieval battles and claims that medieval knights fought as individuals.

On tournaments, see Malcolm Vale, *War and Chivalry* (1981), for the argument that the late medieval tournament was a practice ground for war. Also, Richard W. Barber, *The Knight and Chivalry* (1970), 153–208; N. Denholm-Young, "The Tournament in the Thirteenth Century," in *Studies in Medieval History Presented to Frederick Maurice Powicke* (1948), 240–268; and K. G. Webster, "The Twelfth Century Tourney," in *Anniversary Papers by Colleagues and Pupils of George Lyman Kittredge* (1913).

Decline of heavy cavalry, 1300–1500. On the chivalric view of war, see Maurice H. Keen, *The Laws of War in the Late Middle Ages* (1965); and "Chivalry, Nobility, and the Man-at-Arms," in C. T. Allmand, ed., *War, Literature, and Politics in the Late Middle Ages* (1976), 32–45. On missile weapons, see A. T. Hatto, "Archery and Chivalry: A Noble Prejudice," in *Modern Language Review*, 35 (1940); and M. G. A. Vale, "New Techniques and Old Ideals: The Impact of Artillery on War and Chivalry at the End of the Hundred Years War," in *War, Literature, and Politics, op. cit.*, 57–72.

On the Swiss, see B. Meyer, "Die Schlacht bei Morgarten," in *Revue suisse d'histoire*, 16 (1966). On the Burgundian army, see C. Brusten, *L'armé bourguignonne de 1465 à 1468* (1953). Also, his "La fin des compagnies d'ordonnance de Charles le Téméraire," in *Cinq-centième anniversaire de la bataille de Nancy (1477): Actes du Colloque organisé par l'Institut de recherche régionale en sciences sociales, humaines et économiques de l'Université de Nancy* (1979), and "Les compagnies d'ordonnance dans l'armée bourguignonne," in *Grandson 1476, Essai d'approche pluridisciplinaire d'une action militaire du XVe siècle*, D. Reichel, ed. (1976); also his "Les campagnes liégeoises de Charles le Téméraire," in *Liège et Bourgogne, Actes du Colloque tenu à Liège les 28, 29 et 30 octobre 1968* (1972). See also G. Grosjean, "Die Murtenschlacht. Analyse eines Ereignisses," in *Actes du Ve Centenaire de la bataille de Morat* (1976).

On the use of the longbow in England before the Hundred Years War, see John E. Morris, *The Welsh Wars of Edward I* (1901). On cavalry service under Edward I, see Michael Prestwich, *War, Politics, and Finance Under Edward I* (1972), ch. 3; and Michael Powicke, "The General Obligation to Cavalry Service Under Edward I," in *Speculum*, 28 (1953).

On the Hundred Years War, the most important recent work is Philippe Contamine, *Guerre, état, et société au temps de la guerre de Cent Ans* (1971). On the role of cavalry in the set battles of this conflict, see Contamine, "Crécy (1346) et Agincourt (1415): Une comparaison," in *Divers aspects du Moyen Âge en Occident, Actes du Congrès tenu à Calais en septembre 1974* (1977), 29–44. See also Alfred H. Burne, *The Crecy War* (1955); and Herbert J. Hewitt, *The Black Prince's Expedition of 1355–1357* (1958); and his *The Organization of War Under Edward III, 1338–1362* (1966), ch. 5, on the *chevauchée* and an appendix on the transport of horses. John Keegan, *The Face of Battle* (1977), compares three battles fought in the same general area (Agincourt, Waterloo, and the Somme), emphasizing the mechanics of battle and the viewpoint of the individual fighting man.

For the development of plate armor and changes in cavalry equipment, see Vale, *War and Chivalry*, ch. 4. Also, F. Buttin, "La lance et l'arrêt de cuirasse," in *Archaeologia*, 99 (1965); and Eugene Heer, "Armes et armures au temps des guerres de Bourgogne," in *Grandson 1476, op. cit.*

On equine veterinary medicine, see Johannes Zahlten, "Die 'Hippiatria' des Jordanus Ruffus," in *Archiv für Kulturgeschichte*, 53 (1971). On the trading of war-horses, see V. Chomel, "Chevaux de bataille et roncins en Dauphiné au XIVe siècle," in *Cahiers d'histoire*, 7 (1962). Treatises on the training of war-horses are still in manuscript form or in limited printed editions; they are listed in Frederick H. Huth, *Works on Horses and Equitation* (1887).

C. M. GILLMOR

[See also **Arms and Armor; Avars; Cataphracti; France: to 987; Games and Pastimes; Hundred Years War; Normans and Normandy; Warfare.**]

CAVALRY, ISLAMIC. In legend, the Arabs were horsemen whose *khayl*, or cavalry, had conquered half the world. In fact, it seems that only an aristocratic minority was able to afford horse and armor in imitation of the Persians and Byzantines, and that the outcome of the first great battles depended essentially on infantry. Wealth from the newly conquered empire, as well as the recruitment of mounted Persian warriors, enabled this cavalry to multiply, without displacing the infantry from its central role. Horsemen engaged in preliminary skirmishing, attacked from the wings, or remained in reserve for a final charge.

At the end of the seventh century, the adoption of the stirrup gave the rider a firmer seat, to the advantage of the man in armor fighting with lance and sword, although its first use may have been as an aid to archery, in hunting as well as in war. At the same time it contributed to a rapidly growing distinction between the well-armed knights of the nobility, with their mounted escorts of clients and freedmen, and the lightly equipped horsemen who appeared on the frontiers of Islam to make their living in raids upon the infidels. With these may be classed the tribesmen, Arabs for example, or Berbers in North Africa, who acquired horses and acted either as auxiliaries or as the warriors of independent chieftains, or even as ordinary soldiers in some regular army.

In Egypt, North Africa, and Spain, the armored knight continued to form a small proportion of the army. In 880, ʿAbbās ibn Aḥmad ibn Ṭūlūn marched on Tripoli with 800 horsemen, probably his personal guard, and 5,000 camel-mounted infantry. The Fatimid knight of the tenth century wore a long-sleeved hauberk of mail, scales or quilt, and a plumed helmet of riveted plates enclosing the whole of the head apart from the face; the helmet was wrapped in a turban as a mark of rank. He carried a small, round shield and was armed with a light lance, a long straight sword, and perhaps a Scythian-type bow, which was certainly used for hunting. Ibn Ḥawqal contrasted this warrior with the cavalryman of al-Andalus, riding without stirrups, and evidently adapted to the border warfare in the north. Yet the bulk of the Fatimid cavalry was formed by Kutāma Berbers, who were too lightly equipped to match the Turkish knights whom the Fatimids encountered in Syria, and whom they were obliged to recruit to fight their battles in the Middle East. These Turks provided the kind of armored horsemen hitherto represented, perhaps, only by the princes and commanders of the Fatimid empire.

Such cavalry had been extensively used in Iraq and Iran at least since the time of the Abbasid caliph Muʿtaṣim (d. 842), providing up to half the army and constituting a formidable corps d'elite. The troopers were expensive, requiring servants to attend them, and in principle highly skilled in jousting and horse archery. Their comprehensive repertoire was only slightly modified in the course of the eleventh and twelfth centuries, first by the advent of the Turkomans, who followed the Seljuk sultans out of central Asia into the Middle East. The Turkomans formed a horde of mounted warriors whose main weapon was the bow. In the Seljuk armies they were rapidly replaced by the professional Turkish knight, but not before they had largely done away with the need for infantry on the battlefield.

The Seljuks' use of the bow meanwhile ensured that when they were confronted by the Crusaders the accent fell upon archery and not upon the development of the lance as the way to counteract the charge of the Frankish horse. The technique of fighting with the round shield and light lance was retained, while the long straight sword gave way to the scimitar, a weapon that began to spread from the East during the tenth century. The ax, mace, and

dagger were employed at close quarters. Tactics revolved around al-karr wa 'l-farr, the concerted dash forward and dash back, the charge not pressed home until the enemy was already in disarray. With the aid of the bow, this style was effective in both attack and defense, relegating infantry to an auxiliary role.

In Egypt and the Fertile Crescent, the warriors who fought in this way became generally known as mamlūks, slaves, since so many were recruited as Turkish slave boys for training and eventual manumission. By the thirteenth century they formed a military aristocracy holding fiefs of land, revenue, and government posts, and giving rise, under the pressure of the Crusades and the Mongol invasions, to the Mamluk dynasty of Egypt. The Mongols, who exploited horse archery to its fullest extent, confirmed rather than forced a change in the mamlūk style; their own armies evolved in the same way out of tribal hordes into bands of knights. Mamlūk bands owed their primary loyalty to their commander, their amīr or beg, who had often owned and trained each man; the commander in turn owed his first loyalty to the senior commander to whose troop he had himself belonged. The units thus formed might fight separately as squadrons or combine in larger divisions within a single battle line. Long trumpets, drums, tall banners, and armorial devices were employed to arrange, guide, and rally the individual and the host.

To the west of Egypt, cavalry continued in its earlier role, despite the presence of Turkish elements in North Africa in the twelfth century. The bow and the javelin remained the weapons of the infantry, which used them together with spears as the prime defense against the charge of the Christian knights of Spain. The horseman preferred light armor, round shield, spear, and straight sword, apart from an experiment by Granada in the thirteenth century with the panoply of the Castilians. In North Africa, the bulk of the cavalry was bedouin, drawn from nomadic tribes favored for their military prowess but noted for their unreliability. South of the Sahara, horses imported from North Africa helped to create a stock of mounts for a mailed cavalry in the empires of Mali, Songhai, and Kanem-Bornu, armed like the North Africans, though looking more to the Mamluks of Egypt for the inspiration of their chivalry.

BIBLIOGRAPHY

David Nicolle and Angus McBride, *The Armies of Islam, 7th–11th Centuries* (1982); Terence Wise and G. A.

Embleton, *Armies of the Crusades* (1982); S. R. Turnbull and Angus McBride, *The Mongols* (1982); Vernon J. Parry and M. E. Yapp, eds., *War, Technology and Society in the Middle East* (1975); R. C. Smail, *Crusading Warfare, 1097–1193* (1956).

MICHAEL BRETT

[See also **Mamlūk; Mamluk Dynasty; Mongol Empire: Foundations; Warfare.**]

CAXTON, WILLIAM. The details of Caxton's early life are patchy and variously interpreted. This is partly because many come from his prologues and epilogues, which adapted the information for the needs of a given book, and partly because, as a merchant, he did not belong to that section of society that is documented in detail. Today he is known because he introduced printing into England, but that event was not regarded as very important by his contemporaries. He was born between 1415 and 1424 in Kent. At about the age of fourteen he was apprenticed to an important London mercer, Robert Large. This enrollment took place by 1438, though the exact date is unknown. (His parents were clearly influential, for they apprenticed him to a man who became lord mayor in 1439.) The mercers dealt in haberdashery, cloth, and silks in England, but they were also heavily engaged in trade with the Continent. Those merchants who participated in the overseas trade were organized in a loose fraternity known as the Merchant Adventurers Company, which was dominated by the mercers at the end of the fifteenth century.

By joining Large, Caxton became a member of an influential guild; he met people who would assist him in later life; and he learned how to handle finance. After Large died in 1441, Caxton continued as an apprentice, but on becoming free he joined the overseas trade almost as a matter of course. At first he traveled between Bruges and England. He probably became resident in Bruges about 1462, when he became governor of the English Nation of Merchant Adventurers there. The election implies that he was then a successful and influential businessman, for as governor he was the spokesman for the English community and was often employed by the king on commercial and diplomatic negotiations.

The towns in the Low Countries produced manuscripts that were much sought after because of their quality. Merchant Adventurers shipped many to England; and naturally Caxton dealt in manuscripts as well as in other goods. Probably through his involvement in manuscripts he got the idea of owning a printing press. Printing with movable type was first developed in Europe by Johann Gutenberg at Mainz about 1450, and a press reached Cologne soon afterward. Printed books must have been available in Bruges by the 1460's. By becoming a printer Caxton could control both the production and the marketing of books, a fact that may have encouraged him to embark on his project. He decided to publish English translations of fashionable Burgundian prose texts. In this spirit he started to translate *Le recueil des histoires de Troye* in 1469.

In 1471 Caxton gave up the governorship and went to Cologne to acquire a press and workmen, teaming up with John Veldener, a printer there. Caxton brought in new capital that was used to finance major publications in Cologne. Caxton never became a printer as such; he was an entrepreneur who owned a press. At Cologne he finished translating *Recueil . . . Troye* and perhaps *The Game and Playe of the Chesse.* At the end of 1472 he brought Veldener back to Bruges, where he set up a press and supervised the early printing operations. Though Veldener moved to Louvain, he continued to supply Caxton with type. Caxton published *Recuyell . . . Troye,* the first book printed in English, in late 1473 (or early 1474) and *The Game . . . Chesse* on 31 March 1474. These books were intended for the English market. Caxton found it difficult to sell books in England from Bruges, so he decided to return to England; in the meantime he printed some books in French for sale on the Continent.

In 1476 Caxton moved to England, where he set up his press in the precincts of Westminster Abbey. Other shops were there, for the site is conveniently situated for the court and Parliament. In his shop Caxton also sold manuscripts and books printed on the Continent. He remained a merchant, now concentrating on books and manuscripts rather than other wares. From 1476 until his death in early 1492 he published almost 100 books, many of them his own translations from French. These include romances (*Paris and Vienne*), saints' lives (*Legenda aurea*), medieval versions of the classics (Ovid's *Metamorphoses*), and religious treatises (*The Art and Craft to Know how Well to Die*). He also published works translated by others, provided the translator was noble or the work well-known; these included works translated by Anthony Earl Rivers and the English translation of Higden's *Polychronicon* by John Trevisa. He also printed poetry by Chaucer and the English Chaucerians.

The texts Caxton chose were fashionable either because they were based on Burgundian originals or because they were in the poetic style popularized by Chaucer. He did not publish alliterative poems, which he considered somewhat archaic and provincial. It was for this reason that he modernized the language of Malory's *Morte d'Arthur*. Caxton had a monopoly of the texts he published because continental printers did not yet issue books in English and because there were few other English printers. He also printed small works, such as indulgences, to order. These provided continuous employment for his workers, for as he grew older he could not produce a sufficient supply of translated material.

The claim that Caxton slavishly printed what his patrons demanded is based on a misconception of early publishing. He chose the books to be printed, but he had to sell the finished product. To do this, he needed to persuade clients that the books were fashionable and read by the noblest in the land. Hence he dedicated his books to members of the aristocracy in order to give them respectability. In many cases the person mentioned had almost certainly not read the book. The prologues are fifteenth-century advertisements equivalent to a modern publisher's blurbs. Through his comments Caxton became the first English critic, for he was the first to explain why people should read certain texts.

Caxton allows us to see the development of fifteenth-century literary taste. Many books he published remained popular; some were used as literary sources by later authors, even though, with the spread of humanism, he came under attack for his printing of medieval versions of the classics.

After Caxton's death Wynkyn de Worde, who had been with him since Cologne, took over the business and ran it until his own death in 1535. The survival of a printing business over a sixty-year period is unique in the fifteenth century and is a testimony to Caxton's financial expertise and literary taste.

BIBLIOGRAPHY

N. F. Blake, *Caxton and His World* (1969), 224–249; *Caxton: England's First Publisher* (1976); "Eight Papers Presented to the Caxton International Congress," in *Journal of the Printing Historical Society*, 11 (1976–1977), 1– 133; Lotte Hellinga, *Caxton in Focus* (1982); George D. Painter, *William Caxton, A Quincentenary Biography of England's First Printer* (1976).

N. F. BLAKE

[See also **Manuscripts and Books; Printing, Origins of; Wynkyn de Worde.**]

CECAUMENUS. See Kekaumenos.

CECCO ANGIOLIERI, Italian poet, was born at Siena probably before 1260. His parents were members of prominent Guelph families, the Angiolieri and the Salimbeni. In 1281 he took part in the siege of Turri, and in 1288 he was sent with Sienese troops to the aid of the Florentines in their war against Arezzo. During this military campaign Cecco almost certainly met Dante Alighieri, with whom he later exchanged three sonnets. Exiled from Siena toward the end of the thirteenth century, he lived for some time in Rome. Contemporary documents show that he was tried and fined repeatedly for such civil offenses as unjustified absence during the siege of Turri, rebellion against the police, violation of the curfew, and criminal assault. His reputation was that of a dissolute and violent man, a notoriety sealed by Boccaccio in the *Decameron* (in which he recounts one of Cecco's mishaps). He died probably in 1313, the date of a document by which his five sons renounced their inheritance from him, thereby avoiding his outstanding debts.

Cecco's friendship with Dante and the wide diffusion of his poetry in a large number of important codices testify to his renown as a poet among his contemporaries. His *Canzoniere*, probably consisting of 128 sonnets, deal in large part with the tragicomic vicissitudes of his love for Becchina, a shoemaker's daughter, who at first shuns him, then gives in to his demands, and finally jilts him, deaf to his prayers, threats, and declarations of lasting love.

The salient characteristic of Cecco's sonnets, the best of which are drawn as little sketches or formulated in *contrasto* (argument), is the consummate use of the poetic language of the *dolce stil nuovo* interwoven with a carefully chosen language of vulgar origin. The effect of this ironic ornamentation, using vocabularies and imageries derived from two parallel yet quite different traditions, is a comic deformation of the traditional language of love and a verbally violent, at times bizarre, form of literary autobiography.

In Cecco's poetry nothing and no one is sacred: neither his wife, who nags him day and night, nor Becchina, who mocks his love while showing her indifference; neither his avaricious father who, although old, refuses to die and leave his inheritance to his son, nor his mother, who hates her son and would prefer him dead. In his most famous sonnet, "S'i' fosse fuoco, arderei 'l mondo" (If I were fire, I would burn up the world), all of these elements coalesce into a hyperbolic venting of the spleen. The world and all of humanity are envisioned within a final judgment by fire, wind, floods, and corporal punishment.

Yet it would not be correct to consider Cecco as a medieval *poète maudit;* his poetry, labeled by critics as comic-realistic, autobiographical and jocose, belongs to a well-established literary tradition, dating back to the medieval goliardic songs, that boasts Dante among its ranks.

BIBLIOGRAPHY

The Sonnets of a Handsome and Well-Mannered Rogue, T. C. Chubb, trans. (1970); Mario Marti, *Cultura e stile nei poeti giocosi del tempo di Dante* (1953); and *idem,* ed., *Poeti giocosi del tempo di Dante* (1956).

MASSIMO CIAVOLELLA

[See also **Dante Alighieri; Italian Literature: Lyric Poetry.**]

CEDRENUS. See **Kedrenos.**

CELESTINA, LA. The book called *La Celestina* is a prose dialogue written by two distinct authors for reading aloud (as was the custom of the time and place) to students at the University of Salamanca. It was composed in various stages between 1490 and 1502, the most crucial period in Spanish history. The description in the first act of the young gentlewoman, Melibea, was copied almost literally from that of Helen in a *Trojan Chronicle* (derived from Guido delle Colonne's *Historia destructionis Troiae*) first printed, as far as is known, in 1490. The terminal year marks the publication of the final version of *La Celestina.* Because momentous events—the dis-

covery of America, the reconquest of Granada, the expulsion of the Jews, the sudden death of the single young heir to the throne—filled men's minds during these years, little note was taken of the first private reading of the original, sixteen-act version. References to certain contemporary events and repeated quotation of a 1496 edition of Petrarch indicate that this reading took place in 1497. This early version, entitled *Comedia de Calisto y Melibea,* was later rebaptized with the name of its most diabolical and effective speaker, the go-between, Celestina.

Reticence and irony pervade the text as well as the circumstances of its creation. Neither the anonymous author of the first act nor the student who completed it and whose name, Fernando de Rojas, appears only in an acrostic, desired to call attention to himself. So it was, that in a time of immense popular enthusiasm and fanaticism, a small group of sophisticated, sardonic, and disaffected young men listened to a text that disguised its bitter satire with a veil of ostensive morality and that called into question the values of the age: love, honor, manliness, loyalty, and even faith and patriotism. In its first presentation or performance *La Celestina* was heard as a muted and semisecret voice of dissidence amid an almost unanimous chorus of national self-celebration.

However, aside from its contradictory messages ("Be virtuous and avoid the snares of courtly love" and "Do not believe anything you are told to believe") the dialogue and its speakers were so intensely fascinating as fiction that, after being first printed by Fadrique Alemán de Basiles (Friedrich Biel) in Burgos in 1499, *La Celestina* quickly became a best-seller. A century later it was considered the national masterpiece by Lope de Vega, who used its open form and its lesson in ironical ambiguity to recall his own youth in *La Dorotea,* and by Cervantes, who in *Don Quixote* further explored its crossing of points of view. And the national masterpiece it remains, second only to the novel that it made possible.

Before considering those qualities of the text which enabled that strange metamorphosis to take place, we must recall what is known about the stages of its growth. Rojas informs us in a prefatory "Letter to a Friend" that he "found" the anonymous first act and that he read and reread it with increasing delight and deepening appreciation of its significance. This assertion has been doubted (by those critics who, in the Romantic tradition, relate organic unity to single authorship) and has been endlessly discussed. Today, however, most scholars accept Rojas' account at face value. The exceptional length of the act, the tendency to explosive Rabelaisian monologue that appears only therein, and the failure to comprehend certain classical references in the act of transcription—all support separate authorship.

In any case, what Rojas read with such enthusiasm was a renovation of the traditional medieval moral dialogue of a heedlessly passionate lover (Calisto), an ostensibly reluctant beloved (Melibea), a cynical and picturesque go-between (Celestina), and corrupt servants—but with the difference that all of them are intensely alive in their speech. They hide themselves and betray themselves—and in so doing expose the society in which they live—with an oral ardor that is indeed contagious.

After reading the fragment Rojas decided to continue it through fifteen more acts and eventually to publish the whole work anonymously. Its success led to a second edition containing the explanatory letter and acrostic (1500). An amplified and revised twenty-one-act version, retitled *Tragicomedia de Calisto y Melibea*, was published in 1502. Among other modifications, it offers a new prologue mostly cribbed from Rojas' favorite treatise of moral philosophy, Petrarch's neo-Stoic *De remediis utriusque fortunae*, and the suggestion that the author of the first act might have been either of two well-known fifteenth-century poets, Juan de Mena or Rodrigo de Cota. For stylistic reasons, the second possibility has seemed far more reasonable both to Rojas' contemporaries and to recent scholars.

Why did this strangely shaped and composed work enchant in turn its student auditors at Salamanca, the Spanish reading public, and then (in translation) readers in Italy (1506), Germany (1520), France (1527), and England (before 1530)? One might point to its romantic plot, resembling that of Romeo and Juliet although more erotic; to the caustic irony of its social criticism; and to the simultaneously malign and comic fascination of the aged bawd, Celestina, one of the great characters of European literature.

Yet the most profound innovation lies in the authors' use of dialogue to explore the relationship—the continuing "process" of relationship as Rojas himself stressed—of consciousness and language. An immensely complex skein of psychic interaction between speakers and listeners is tightly woven from the very first words to the last: there are interrogatives, exclamations, insinuations, sly or rash reactions, pointed use of commonplaces and proverbs,

and innumerable forms of self-display and self-betrayal. *La Celestina* thus satisfies what a sixteenth-century commentator called our "auditory appetite," not only because of the sheer vigor of its language but also because it leads us to marvel at what we normally take for granted: the grandeur and mystery of language as a phenomenon.

Very little is known about Fernando de Rojas. He was born around 1476 in a good-sized village in New Castile called the Puebla de Montalbán, according to the acrostic. But since his father was "condemned" by the Toledo Inquisition for judaizing in 1488, he may well have been born in that city and wished to conceal his background. Like other suspect descendants of enforced converts, he may have chosen to express his bitterness and alienation in a literary and moral disguise. He attended Salamanca, where he studied civil law probably between 1494 and 1502. After graduating with the degree of *bachiller*, he returned to the Puebla, married in 1507, and moved his family to Talavera, where he practiced his profession with such distinction that he was appointed lord mayor in 1538. He died in early April 1541, having apparently never returned to literary creation.

BIBLIOGRAPHY

La Celestina, Mack Singleton, trans. (1958); Marcel Bataillon, *La célestine selon Fernando de Rojas* (1961); Stephen Gilman, *The Spain of Fernando de Rojas* (1972); Maria Rosa Lida, *La originalidad artística de "La Celestina"* (1962); Adrienne S. Mandel, *"La Celestina" Studies: A Thematic Survey and Bibliography, 1824–1970* (1971); Dorothy Severin, *Memory in "La Celestina"* (1970).

STEPHEN GILMAN

[See also **Courtly Love; Drama, Western European; Spanish Drama; Spanish Literature; Spanish Satirical Literature.**]

CELESTINE, I, POPE (*d.* 432). A native of Campania and deacon of the Roman church, Celestine was elected bishop of Rome shortly after the death on 4 September 422 of Boniface I and was consecrated on 10 September. Our knowledge of him depends on his surviving correspondence, the *Liber pontificalis,* and information from contemporaries. He strove energetically to uphold and extend the influence of his see.

Informed in 429 of the Nestorian dispute in the East, Celestine, after investigation, called a Roman synod in August 430 that condemned Nestorius. The pope demanded recantation but unfortunately entrusted execution of the sentence to Cyril of Alexandria, whose excessive zeal and questionable motivation alienated many Eastern bishops. At the Council of Ephesus (431) Celestine's legates came late but confirmed the condemnation and deposition of Nestorius already pronounced under Cyril's influence. Celestine's letter to the council and his legate Philip's statement at Ephesus constitute the most explicit claim up to that time to primacy on the part of the bishop of Rome.

Prosper of Aquitaine, a contemporary, relates in his *Chronicle* that Celestine combated Pelagianism in Britain by sending Germanus of Auxerre to preach there in 429, and that he sent a certain Palladius as first bishop to the Irish in 431. The pope's letter to the bishops of Gaul in that same year praises the teaching of the recently deceased Augustine but takes no clear position on the semi-Pelagian issue then under discussion. The attached capitula are not authentic but were added later, probably by Prosper.

In his correspondence with bishops in Illyria, Italy, and Gaul, Celestine strove to enforce discipline and orthodoxy. The African bishops, however, protested against what they regarded as his interference in their internal affairs.

BIBLIOGRAPHY

Celestine's letters are in *Patrologia latina*, L, 417–558; see also the *Supplementum*, III, 18–21; and the notice in Louis M. D. Duchesne, ed., *Liber pontificalis*, I (1886), 230–231. Studies include Trevor G. Jalland, *The Church and the Papacy* (1944), 295–300; and Hubert Jedin and John Dolan, eds., *History of the Church*, II (1980), *s.v.* Celestine.

CLAUDE J. PEIFER, O.S.B.

[See also **Councils (Ecumenical, 325–787); Germanus, St.; Nestorianism.**]

CELESTINE V, POPE (1215–1296), from 5 July to 13 December 1294, was born Peter of Morrone at Isernia and died at Castello di Fumone. He became a Benedictine in 1235 and subsequently was the hermit-founder of the Celestines, a strict eremetical order. Elected pope to end a two-year interregnum, he resigned after concluding that his age, spirituality, and asceticism ill equipped him for office. This "Great Refusal," as Dante called it, created many

problems for his successor, Boniface VIII. Clement V canonized him on 5 May 1313, but only as a private person.

BIBLIOGRAPHY

Giuseppe Celidonio, *Vita di S. Pietro del Morrone Celestino Papa V*, new ed. (1954); Dom Jean Leclercq, "La renonciation de Célestin V et l'opinion théologique en France du vivant de Boniface VIII," in *Revue d'histoire de l'Église de France*, 25 (1939).

CHARLES T. WOOD

[See also **Boniface VIII, Pope.**]

CELESTINES, an expression of the desire for monastic reform in thirteenth-century Italy, also known as the Hermits of St. Damian and as the Hermits of Morrone. Between 1227 and 1232 Peter of Isernia (later Pope Celestine V) received the habit at the Benedictine abbey of Faifoli near Benevento in southern Italy. Influenced by the austere life of St. Peter Damian, Peter withdrew into eremitical seclusion on Mount Morrone, near Sulmona in the Abruzzi region of central Italy. His piety attracted followers and in 1259 he constructed for them the church of S. Maria of Mount Morrone, later the site of the large abbey of the Holy Spirit of Maiella (or Sulmona). In 1263 Urban IV affiliated the foundation to the Benedictine order, and in 1275 Gregory X took the abbey and the fifteen houses connected with it under his protection and confirmed their possessions and privileges. Endowments had come from local magnates, especially Charles of Anjou, who promoted Peter's candidacy in the disputed papal election of 1292–1294. When Peter became pope, the congregation numbered thirty-six priories and several hundred monks.

Most of these monasteries were in central Italy, but in 1300 Philip the Fair supported a Celestine foundation at Ambert and King Charles V later made a second French foundation near Paris. These French monasteries enjoyed royal protection and such prosperity that they sent foundations to Bohemia (1368) and Barcelona (1410); but for Anglo-French hostilities, a house would have been made at Sheen in Surrey, England (1415). A reputation for religious fervor brought the Celestines considerable prestige; the order reached its peak in the fifteenth century, when it numbered about ninety monasteries, most of them reformed Benedictine houses.

The Celestine constitutions, which Peter wrote and, after he became pope, approved, reveal Cistercian and Franciscan influences. Discipline was to be maintained in all priories by an annual visit from the abbot of Holy Spirit and by an annual general chapter attended by the priors of all houses; the chapter elected the abbot general, who also governed Holy Spirit abbey, for a three-year term. Constitutional emphasis on poverty, fasting, and humility represent the desired Celestine virtues.

Although literate and a man of some organizational abilities, Peter of Isernia was not well educated, and he imbued the congregation with his own eremitical spirit. Celestine piety, however, attracted the attention of Petrarch, who mentions it in the *Solitary Life*. In the fifteenth century the French province of the congregation produced several distinguished spiritual writers. Most notable was Antoine Pocquet (*d.* 1409), whose commentaries on Cassian's *Conferences* and John Climacus' *Ladder of Paradise* were widely read. The late sixteenth century witnessed the beginning of decay.

The name Celestine is also given to a small group of Franciscan Spirituals whom Peter, as Pope Celestine V, placed under his protection.

BIBLIOGRAPHY

The earliest histories of the Celestines were written between 1303 and 1306 as hagiographic support for the canonization of Peter of Isernia. The texts of these lives, based on manuscripts in the Bibliothèque Nationale, were first published by Giuseppe Celidonio in *Analecta bollandiana*, **9–10** (1890–1891); revised texts were published *ibid.*, **16** and **18** (1897 and 1899), with a valuable discussion. These lives, together with the materials collected in Franz Xavier Seppelt, ed., *Monumenta coelestiniana* (1921), contain the known primary evidence.

Secondary literature includes Joseph Duhr, "Celestins," in *Dictionnaire de spiritualité*, II (1953); and Johannes Hollnsteiner, "Die Autobiographie Coelestins V," in *Römische Quartalschrift*, **31** (1923).

BENNETT D. HILL

[See also **Celestine V, Pope; Franciscans; Monasticism, Origins.**]

CELIBACY. The origins of clerical celibacy can best be approached by examining the rule that forbade the ordination of men who had been twice married. In the early church a general recommendation against second marriages (1 Cor. 7:39–40) was made obligatory for church leaders because of their prominence in the community (compare 1 Tim. 3:2, 12; Titus 1:6). Later this prohibition was extended to men whose wives had been married twice. A similar pattern can be discerned with regard to celibacy. A conviction that it was essential to Christianity was present in the church from the earliest times, and a few communities even attempted to impose celibacy universally at baptism. While this view was repudiated officially, its traces endured in the form of a ban on marriage after ordination for clerics in major orders: bishops, priests, and deacons. In the Greek-speaking church of the East celibacy came to be more and more expected of a bishop, a custom eventually formalized by church law; either bishops were recruited from monasteries or else the newly appointed bishop and his wife were required to separate by mutual consent.

A significant part of Christian piety was the occasional observance of sexual abstinence, even among the laity, as a help to prayer (1 Cor. 7:5). For the clergy this obligation was specified as continence before public worship, and the principle of ritual purity as found in the Old Testament and in the pagan religions of antiquity was brought to bear upon both the practice and the theory of celibacy in the Christian church.

A final influence on clerical life came from the church's position in society. When Christianity became established as the religion of the Roman Empire, its wealth and prestige grew. To prevent church property from being appropriated by the families of clerics, Justinian promulgated in 529 a law stating that no man with children or grandchildren could be ordained to the episcopate. There was also concern about the distraction from ecclesiastical duties posed by a bishop's having a family.

Other imperial laws reinforced the discipline described above, and in 691 the Trullan (or Quinisext) Synod held at Constantinople made them compulsory in the Eastern, Greek-speaking church. The wording of the canons, as well as subsequent history, indicates that they had not been, and were not to be, universally observed. Generally, however, episcopal celibacy remained the ideal and practice of the Byzantine church; the episcopacy eventually became the preserve of monks, and in reaction parish priests were selected exclusively from among married men. Some Eastern regions outside the influence of Byzantium—Persia, for example—had no special regulations governing the marital status of their clergy.

In the Latin church, continence was required of

clerics more extensively than in the East. There were the same laws against marriage after ordination and against the ordination of a man who had married more than once or had married a widow, but by 400 papal decretal and episcopal synod had imposed total sexual abstinence on all married clerics in major orders. These laws produced, in theory, a completely celibate clergy. From the mid fifth century, subdeacons were officially included, but this legislation was not universally enforced until 1207, under Innocent III. Collections of disciplinary norms, such as the one gathered by Dionysius Exiguus in the early sixth century, assured the preservation if not the observance of canons governing clerical life, and made them available to reformers of the early Middle Ages.

Married clerics were not allowed to live apart from their wives. The impracticality of this arrangement for those bound to absolute continence is indicated by the frequency and the variety of synodal canons on the matter during the fifth and sixth centuries. Under the title of *episcopa, presbytera,* or *diaconissa,* respectively, the wife of a bishop, priest, or deacon was required by some Gallican councils to have a separate chamber from her husband. Very exceptionally, different dwellings were recommended, but this was not enforced until the eleventh century. Both to avoid the excuse of ignorance and to ensure the observance of continence, a formal promise of lifelong continence *(conversio)* came to be required from the husband before ordination—and sometimes from the wife also, especially in Gaul. In the houses of married clerics other clerics were to be present to guarantee continence. Some regulations even required clerics to sleep in the bishop's bedroom or in a common dormitory. Attention was also directed to the selection and preparation of candidates for ordination.

Councils authoritatively repeated earlier legislation, but with severer penalties. These sanctions were not always retroactive, but clerics who failed to abstain from the use of marriage were at least barred from receiving any higher orders and from exercising their ministry. More commonly they were deposed and subjected to a period of public penance, particularly such as had entered into an illicit relationship with a woman. Their concubines and, at Toledo in 653 and 655, even their wives and children were reduced to the state of slavery. Major clerics who married after ordination were deposed, but their marriages were recognized as valid.

Clerical celibacy should be viewed in the context of the developing medieval attitude toward sexuality in general. The marriage act was recognized as essentially good when directed toward the generation of children, but was thought to be almost necessarily tainted by sin because of the power of concupiscence in fallen man. Married couples were often bound or encouraged to observe continence. Underlying this attitude was a primitive physiology by which it was believed, for instance, that a child conceived during the menstrual period would be deformed or diseased. Furthermore, sexual abstinence was a common form of mortification, required as a penance for certain sins, during Lent, and before communion. After any sexual action, even menstruation, childbirth, and nocturnal emission, participation in public worship was often denied or limited by regulations drawn in a complicated fashion from the theology of original sin, the principles of hygiene and ritual purity, and respect for the celibate life.

More important for understanding clerical celibacy is the influence of monasticism, which in the Latin church was closely linked with the bishop. Informal groupings of ascetics living near shrines and churches affected the ideals of the clergy and the expectations of the laity. Furthermore, the prestige of monasticism was a threat to the status of the secular clergy, and celibacy became an important safeguard of clerical power. The ordination of monks and their use as missionaries (St. Augustine of Canterbury, St. Boniface) increased monastic influence on the church and the clergy, as monastic churches spread over western Europe. Strict rules concerning clerical celibacy and continence were found in the popular penitential books propagated by the monks.

Many of the secular clergy lived a sort of monastic life in the episcopal residence, where strict celibacy was enforced. These residents were called canons, a word first so used at the Council of Clermont in 535. The desire for unity and order that characterized the Carolingian era (750–987) resulted in the first rule for canons, compiled about 755 by Chrodegang, bishop of Metz. It was largely an adaptation of the Benedictine Rule and formed the basis of the rule for canons, promulgated by Louis the Pious at Aachen in 816, that spread widely in the following centuries.

Widely flouted during the seventh and eighth centuries, and somewhat restored under Charlemagne, the ecclesiastical discipline of celibacy underwent an almost total eclipse at all levels throughout western Europe, including Rome itself, on account of the turmoil that attended the breakup of the Carolingian empire in the ninth century. Married clerics justified their state, if they thought of it at all, by the sheer numbers involved. Furthermore, important bishoprics were given as political appointments to men with little interest in celibacy. This situation was effectively countered by the Gregorian Reform which arose out of an increased awareness of earlier legislation and a movement of monastic renewal; it was effected by means of a series of synods presided over by the pope or his legate. There had been earlier attempts to restore church discipline (for example, at Pavia in 1022 where incontinent major clerics were deposed and their children made serfs of the church), but it was during the pontificate of Leo IX (1048–1054) that an effective reform began. Nevertheless, the reform rightly bears the name of Gregory VII (1073–1085) because of the vigor with which he implemented and consolidated its measures. For Gregory clerical celibacy was an essential step in freeing the church from the evils concomitant with lay control. Earlier laws regarding clerical celibacy and continence were re-enacted, but now councils and papal decrees enforced with unprecedented thoroughness the traditional observances that had fallen into disuse, often with episcopal approbation.

There was novelty, however, in the specific discipline and language employed: married clerics were required to separate from their wives, and all infringements of the rules governing celibacy, whether within or outside of marriage, were described in the same abusive terminology. A violent resistance, both theoretical and practical, was occasioned by the reform. For instance, bishops at the Synod of Paris in 1074, declared the new rulings "irrational," and assaulted and imprisoned an abbot who defended them; tracts justifying the widespread tolerant attitudes were written by Ulric, bishop of Imola, in 1060 and Norman Anonymous, ca. 1100. Ecclesiastical authorities countered by severe penalties directed toward incontinent clerics, who were excommunicated, and toward their wives and children, who were reduced to the status of slaves of the church, never to be enfranchised. Offending priests were forbidden to say Mass or perform any other functions of their state, and the people were forbidden to attend their Masses.

The Gregorian Reform was supported by the great developments in canon law beginning with Gratian's Decretum in 1142 and continuing into the fourteenth century. Clerics who married after ordination were treated with particular severity under the new laws. In 1123 the First Lateran Council pre-

scribed separation from their wives, with a suitable period of penance, for major clerics (including subdeacons) who married. At the Second Lateran Council (1139) such marriages were explicitly declared to be invalid. This legislation was confirmed by the Fourth Lateran Council of 1215 despite opinions, especially at the University of Paris, that in this matter church law should accommodate itself to the actual situation. Theologians and canonists subsequently supported the legislation by suggesting, first, that a vow of continence or celibacy was implicit in the reception of ordination and, more coherently, that the church had the right to establish by law celibacy or continence as a condition for ordination.

In the general moral decline occasioned by the Black Death, the Hundred Years War, the Great Schism, and the secular spirit of the Renaissance, some theologians and canonists continued to suggest that the Latin church should adopt the regulations of the Eastern church or that the irregularities attendant on the law were reason for altering it. The Western regulations, however, were reiterated by councils and popes. During this time the hierarchy never questioned the value of the laws of celibacy or condoned any practice that denied it in principle. But laxity in observance became so universal during the fourteenth and fifteenth centuries that the scandalous lives of even the highest church officials elicited, during the Protestant Reformation and the Catholic Counter-Reformation, still more radical attempts to solve the problems associated with clerical celibacy—Protestants by abandoning it altogether, and Catholics by adopting rigorous and more coordinated forms of priestly training and pastoral life.

BIBLIOGRAPHY

Martin Boelens, Die Klerikerehe in der Gesetzgebung der Kirche (1968), a detailed examination of legislation up to 1139 that ascribes celibacy mainly to ritual purity; C. N. L. Brooke, "Gregorian Reform in Action: Clerical Marriage in England, 1050–1200," in Cambridge Historical Journal, 12 (1956), attributes the success of the Gregorian Reform to marked increases in the number of monks and greater knowledge of earlier church legislation; Michel Dortel-Claudot, "Le prêtre et le mariage: Évolution de la législation canonique dès origines au XIIe siècle," in L'année canonique, 17 (1973), an exhaustive collection of the authoritative legislation; Ludwig Hödl, "Lex continentiae: A Study on the Problem of Celibacy," in Priesthood and Celibacy, Joseph Coppens et al., eds. (1972), traces the development of celibacy from a charisma in the church to an ecclesiastical law; John E. Lynch, "Marriage and Celibacy of the Clergy: An Historico-Canonical Synopsis," in The

Jurist, **32** (1972), an excellent overview that recognizes the variety and complexity of the law and its motivation; Edward Schillebeeckx, *Celibacy,* C. A. L. Jarrot, trans. (1968), an ingenious work that suggests that the Middle Ages moved beyond a ritual to an evangelical basis for clerical celibacy; A. M. Stickler, "The Evolution of the Discipline of Celibacy in the Western Church from the End of the Patristic Era to the Council of Trent," in *Priesthood and Celibacy,* Joseph Coppens *et al.,* eds. (1972), a masterful ordering of the synodal, canonical, theological, and penitential regulations; Johann Anton Theiner and Augustin Theiner, *Die Einführung der erzwungenen Ehelosigkeit bei den christlichen Geistlichen und ihre Folgen,* 3rd ed., 3 vols. (1891–1898), fiercely opposed to the idea of celibacy and sometimes inaccurate, but influential and noteworthy for its comprehensiveness.

DANIEL CALLAM

[See also **Clergy; Family, Western European; Gregory VII, Pope; Monasticism, Origins; Ordination; Reform, Idea of.**]

CELTIC ART. In the Middle Ages "Celtic art" is a term used chiefly to embrace the native art of the Celtic-speaking inhabitants of Britain and Ireland from the Roman withdrawal in the fifth century to the widespread establishment of the Romanesque art of western Europe in the twelfth century, although traditions of Celtic art lingered on and even regained popularity in late medieval Ireland and Scotland.

During the fifth to seventh centuries the patterns of Celtic art were largely based on the traditional abstract designs of the late Iron Age (La Tène art), with a few Roman-inspired modifications. In the seventh and eighth centuries there was a profitable encounter between Irish art and the Germanic artistic tradition, represented by Anglo-Saxon art in England, as a result of Irish missionary activities among the pagan Anglo-Saxons and the establishment of networks of monastic contacts. The resultant Hiberno-Saxon style, which also drew some of its elements from models introduced from the Mediterranean by the Anglo-Saxon (Roman) church, was the vehicle for a series of masterpieces in manuscript illumination, metalwork, and sculpture. A subsequent period of dwindling inspiration was countered in Ireland in the late eleventh and twelfth centuries as a result of the adaptation of ideas drawn from the late Viking art styles introduced into its Norse towns.

Continuity in Celtic art has always been recognized in Ireland; because it remained outside the

Elaborated initial. Cathach of St. Columba, *ca.* 600. DRAWING BY JACQUELINE AHER

Roman Empire, there was nothing to stand in the way of the transmission of the traditional motifs (spirals, scrolls, triskeles, and peltas) executed in the traditional manner (in bronze with red enamel embellishment). Roman influences can be detected only in a minor way, such as the integration of "marigold" motifs (or rosettes) into the repertoire of curvilinear patterns. Surviving examples of secular Irish ornamented metalwork of the fifth to seventh centuries are for the most part undistinguished, and the range of techniques was apparently limited to red champlevé enameling on cast and chased bronze, with the occasional use of millefiori glass set directly into the enamel.

Ecclesiastical metalwork of the same period in Ireland is seemingly unknown, but the church did not become fully established there until the sixth century, and its artistic impact, through its special requirements and patronage, was felt only with the rise of monasteries in the seventh. There are, however, simple Christian monuments of roughly dressed stone on which the incised cross motif is developed with characteristic curvilinear embellishments (for instance, at Reask, County Kerry).

Such curvilinear extensions also form ornamental additions to the major initials in Ireland's earliest surviving manuscript, a psalter known as the Cathach of St. Columba, of the late sixth or early seventh century. The Cathach displays two further ornamental features that were subsequently transferred into the manuscript art of Anglo-Saxon Northumbria, as part of the Hiberno-Saxon style: the use of red dots to outline major letters and the diminuendo motif, in which the letters gradually decrease in size from the enlarged initial to the ordinary script.

It is impossible to trace the development of early Irish manuscript art in any detail, given the very small number of surviving manuscripts; but it may be gauged in part from a few examples written at Irish monastic foundations on the Continent, most notably Bobbio in Italy (including *Codex Ambrosianus* D. 23 Sup., in which a whole page is devoted to ornament, in the form of compass-drawn rosettes within a border of twists and crosses). This early-seventh-century manuscript thus contains an important piece of evidence concerning the development of the elaborate "carpet page" (as full-page ornaments are known), which forms one of the chief glories of Insular manuscripts of which the earliest surviving example is the Book of Durrow from the 670's.

La Tène artistic traditions also survived to some extent in England and Wales, despite their having been part of the Roman Empire, for the process of Romanization had proceeded rapidly only in the peaceful and prosperous southeast and not so deeply in the military frontier zones. The "princely" stronghold of Dinas Powys, near Cardiff, has been shown by excavation to have supported, during the fifth to seventh centuries, workers in bronze and enamel who also used millefiori glass settings. The best-known products of native Celtic craftsmen during these centuries of Anglo-Saxon conquest and settlement in England are the "hanging bowls," bronze bowls with ornamented suspension mounts; these were prized by the Anglo-Saxons, for they are found among the grave goods in the burials of wealthier individuals.

Celtic hanging bowls are descended from late

Hanging bowl. Sutton Hoo royal ship burial, *ca.* 625. COURTESY OF THE TRUSTEES OF THE BRITISH MUSEUM

Roman bowls that were designed for suspension within tripods, and are thus equipped with three or four loops, each with a decorated escutcheon; further mounts could be applied to both the interior and the exterior of the bowl. The finest seventh-century examples are enameled with traditional curvilinear designs having millefiori inserts—for instance, the three bowls found in the royal ship burial at Sutton Hoo (of *ca.* 625), the finest of which is unique in having a pedestal-mounted three-dimensional fish in its interior. Knowledge of hanging bowl manufacture had certainly spread north to Pictland no later than the seventh century, the most probable date for an escutcheon mold found at Craig Phadrig, near Inverness. It probably spread to Ireland at about the same time or soon after, for despite earlier claims that all hanging bowls were made in Ireland, there is no satisfactory evidence to demonstrate their manufacture there before the eighth century, by which time the ornament of the escutcheons had been modified. These later bowls have their enamel and millefiori confined in small rectilinear compartments; the escutcheons are sometimes given new shapes, some even being anthropomorphic in form. Such bowls are not known from English contexts but have been found in ninth-century graves in Scandinavia, to which they must have been carried by the Vikings.

This development away from curvilinear champlevé patterns to rectilinear cloisonné ones in enamel and millefiori work (before the use of millefiori died out, apparently during the eighth century) must be attributed to influences from seventh-century Anglo-Saxon cloisonné jewelry, as is seen in Kentish disc brooches or the Sutton Hoo regalia. Such influences need not have been experienced directly in Ireland, for they might have been transmitted through manuscript art—the influence of such jewelry is clear in the Matthew symbol at the beginning of that saint's Gospel in the Book of Durrow. This work is generally thought to be the product of a Northumbrian scriptorium, although the Irish elements in its design and ornament continue to persuade some that it is of purely Irish workmanship.

The presence of the Celtic missionaries in Anglo-Saxon Northumbria made the circumstances ideal for the development of the Hiberno-Saxon style, for there the Irish tradition of manuscript illumination (as seen developing in the Cathach of St. Columba) was inevitably brought into contact with Anglo-Saxon artistic traditions in metalwork, including

Interlace panel. Book of Durrow, mid 7th century. DRAWING BY PETER BRIDGEWATER

stylized animal motifs (shown by the carpet page of animal interlace that forms part of the Book of Durrow).

Françoise Henry claims that the Hiberno-Saxon style developed step by step in Ireland from an initial period of direct copying of seventh-century imported Anglo-Saxon objects, although such have not been found there. It is a more economical hypothesis, as others have suggested, that this fusion of tastes and styles formed in the mixed Celtic/Anglo-Saxon milieu that existed in monastic contexts in Northumbria. From there it could have spread to western Scotland and to Ireland through networks of allegiances.

The artistic revolution apparent in the masterpieces of Irish metalwork from the eighth century, such as the Tara brooch, the Ardagh chalice, and the strainer and paten in the Derrynaflan hoard, extends not only to the adoption of a new range of motifs but also to new techniques for their execution, likewise learned from Anglo-Saxon craftsmen; the most important are filigree, chip carving, and the use of varied and elaborate settings. The new motifs (apart from the adoption of rectilinear geometric patterns that were used alongside the traditional curvilinear ones) consisted of the interlace patterns and animal ornament favored by seventh-century Anglo-Saxon artists.

Spirals, interlace, and stylized animals appear alongside each other in limited combinations in the Book of Durrow, the earliest Insular illuminated Gospel book to survive complete. By about 700, with the production of the Lindisfarne Gospels, the Hiberno-Saxon style was fully developed in Northumbria, for these motifs are totally integrated into a new and elegant whole, relying on elaborate geometric planning to crowd meticulously executed detail into carpet pages that glow with a polychromy achieved by the use of a palette vastly greater than that in the Book of Durrow, which is limited to yellow, red, and green (the colors of contemporary metalwork).

No manuscripts of the quality of the Lindisfarne Gospels are known from Ireland at this period. But this is probably an accident of survival, for Irish artists and craftsmen were certainly capable of producing the exact equivalent of the Gospels' ornament in metalwork—the penmanship translated into filigree or chip carving and the polychromy reproduced in part by a range of techniques, including the use of glass and enamel settings (as well as by the introduction of amber, which gradually came to replace them, as can be seen on the Derrynaflan chalice). The crowded surfaces, both front and back, of the so-called Tara brooch (from Bettystown, County Meath) reflect the detail of the carpet pages of the Lindisfarne Gospels; an unusual pattern of intertwined birds on the reverse of the brooch finds its closest parallel in the ornament of the arcades framing the Gospels' canon tables. Its filigree ornament is of exceptional fineness, and its quality of execution is far greater than that of Anglo-Saxon craftsmen. This is one reflection of the fact that the Irish were never satisfied by mere copying but sought instead to adapt and develop whatever took their fancy.

The Ardagh chalice is a compendium of all that is best in eighth-century Irish art. It displays a restraint in the layout of its ornament that contrasts with that of the Tara brooch, yet it makes use of the full range of metalworkers' skills at their finest. Given the similarities between elements in the design and ornament of the chalice and of the Lindisfarne Gospels (most notably of the script used for the names of the apostles incised in outline around the bowl, against a dotted background), it is not surpris-

220

ing that occasional attempts have been made to attribute it to a Northumbrian workshop. What few doubts there might have been concerning its Irish origins have now been dispelled by the discovery of the Derrynaflan hoard of ecclesiastical metalwork.

The Derrynaflan paten and ladle/strainer are of comparable quality, and of the same period, as the Ardagh chalice but include such unique designs as interlacing human figures in openwork filigree. Such a pattern can be paralleled in Ireland on a stone "trial piece" from Garryduff, County Cork, but it is best known in the Book of Kells. The Derrynaflan chalice is comparable in form with that from Ardagh (both have two handles), although its ornament suggests that it is rather later in date, from the beginning of the ninth century. The variety and design of its motifs are lively and original, but its greater use of cast ornament and exclusive use of amber for the settings reflect a trend that is evident also in secular metalwork such as early- to mid-ninth-century brooches, including those found with the Ardagh chalice.

This apparent decline should perhaps be seen in part as a reaction against the crowded and fussy surfaces with elaborate polychromy favored in the earlier eighth century, although it is inconceivable that the superlative standards of the Tara brooch and the Ardagh chalice could have been maintained indefinitely. This process of simplification seems to have commenced before the ninth-century Viking raids had begun to have any serious impact on Ireland; those raids thus can no longer be held to be exclusively responsible for this development.

During the ninth century plain silver was popular in Anglo-Saxon England (the Trewhiddle style), and there were increasing quantities of silver in circulation as a result of the raiding and trading activities of the Vikings who had established bases there. Against this background should be viewed a series of magnificent silver brooches manufactured in Ireland from the mid ninth to the mid tenth century; they demonstrate that some Irish craftsmen had by then completely discarded the eighth-century style. Most tenth-century Irish metalwork has its surfaces divided into small fields containing individual animal or interlace motifs; spiral ornament is almost nonexistent. Filigree, enamel, and chip carving are abandoned for cast and flat carved ornamentation. The overall effect is therefore simpler and bolder in appearance, if not particularly imaginative in design or detail.

The Vikings have been blamed for a decline in the art of Irish manuscript illumination, but even such a large Gospel book as that painted by Mac Regol of Birr in the early ninth century, before Viking settlement took place in Ireland, is erratic and highly individual in its ornament. The smaller pocket books that form the majority of those surviving from the eighth to the tenth centuries often display an equivalent naiveté or rustic charm. (However, elaborate decorative schemes would be out of place in books intended for private use rather than for display on the altar.)

Whatever the true nature of the Vikings' impact on Irish metalwork and manuscript illumination, it has long been noted that the same period saw the flowering of stone sculpture in the form of the "scripture cross," the fully developed Irish version of the freestanding "high cross," bearing biblical scenes in high relief. As in metalworking, the seventh and eighth centuries saw experiment by Irish stone carvers, and more elaborate treatments of standing stones and grave markers were produced. It has been suggested by some that a simple carved stone cross at Carndonagh, County Donegal, dates to the late seventh century, but there is no general agreement on such an early date for the emergence of the freestanding stone cross in Ireland—or even on the mid-eighth-century date proposed for such crosses as those at Ahenny, County Tipperary, which appear to imitate metal-covered wooden crosses in their rivet-like bosses, heavy moldings, and lightly carved abstract ornament.

In the ninth and tenth centuries, however, sculptors began to depict biblical scenes, copying continental ivories and frescoes. The distinctive ring-headed crosses became taller and their shafts were divided into panels for the display of a systematic iconography, contrasting scenes from the Old Testament with the life of Christ; the Crucifixion came to occupy one face of the head and the Last Judgment the other. The apogee of the style is generally held to have been reached in the early tenth century, when a cross like that of Muiredach at Monasterboice, County Louth, was raised—a monument of great force and originality that, with others at Kells, Clonmacnoise, and Durrow, represents a remarkable Irish contribution to the richness and variety of medieval European art.

Curiously, the impact of Viking art on Ireland was not felt to any significant extent before the late eleventh century. In metalwork datable by inscription, such major book shrines as the *Soiscél Molaise* (between 1001 and 1023) and that of the Stowe Mis-

Tara brooch, gilt silver. Bettystown, County Meath, early 8th century. NATIONAL MUSEUM OF IRELAND

Ardagh chalice, silver. Irish, early 8th century. NATIONAL MUSEUM OF IRELAND

Muiredach cross. Monasterboice, County Louth, early 10th century. COMMISSIONERS OF PUBLIC WORKS, IRELAND

Nigg stone. Class II Pictish slab, ca. 800. NATIONAL MUSEUM OF ANTIQUITIES OF SCOTLAND, EDINBURGH

sal (1045–1052) have a somewhat archaic appearance and are in the native Irish tradition; but the shrine made for the Cathach of St. Columba (1062–1098), most probably at Kells, displays a vigorous Irish version of the Scandinavian Ringerike style, matched on a bone "trial piece" from the Dublin excavations. Some of the finest masterpieces of Irish medieval metalwork were, then, produced in the late eleventh and more particularly the early twelfth century, employing Irish interpretations of the Ringerike and Urnes styles (for instance, the Cross of Cong).

Even if these styles were first developed from influences received in the Norse metropolitan centers, notably Dublin, they spread throughout the countryside; for they, or their elements, are found not only on portable metalwork objects but also on stone monuments ranging from high crosses (such as one at Kilfenora, County Clare) to the great sarcophagus at Cashel, County Tipperary, which has a composition of interlacing beasts and snakes derived from the Urnes style down one of its long sides.

Elements of these derived Urnes-style designs, together with more traditional Irish motifs, provided a distinctive aspect to Romanesque art in Ireland following its twelfth-century introduction. The Normans, however, did not invade Ireland until 1169, capturing Dublin in 1170. It was this Anglo-Norman conquest that put an end in Ireland to the original endeavors in late Celtic art.

The art of the Picts during the fifth to ninth centuries is known primarily from sculpture and to a lesser extent from metalwork, for no illuminated manuscripts survive, although it has been suggested that the Book of Kells was produced in Pictland. Class I Pictish stones are rough slabs incised with attractive but stereotyped symbols that defy detailed interpretation; some are recognizable animals (such as bull or eagle), others are objects from daily life (such as a mirror and a comb), while others are geometric shapes (such as disks and crescents, often filled in with curvilinear or fret patterns). These symbols are also found incised on a number of plain silver objects, such as the terminals of massive silver chains, or plaques (as found in the Norrie's Law hoard), which are all most probably from the sixth and seventh centuries.

Class II Pictish stones are well-shaped cross slabs, carved in relief, with the Pictish symbols generally confined to the reverse side. The crosses are filled with geometric patterns, including interlace, but on either side there may be figures, stylized animal ornament, or vine scrolls inhabited by birds and beasts drawn from Anglo-Saxon (Northumbrian) art. On the reverse there may be elaborate narrative scenes, such as the battlefield on the Aberlemno churchyard stone or the hunting scene on that from Hilton of Cadboll. The animal ornament on the Class II stones is known in metalwork on a group of silver bowls and other objects that formed part of the hoard buried about 800 on St. Ninian's Isle, Shetland.

The Class III stones of Pictland form a heterogeneous group of relief monuments, largely cross slabs, that lack the Pictish symbols (which are believed to have been abandoned following the Scottish takeover in the mid ninth century). The stones include some remarkable sculpture, such as the great sarcophagus at St. Andrews, Fife, which is a major work of European art. Some of the Class II and III slabs show a fondness for the use of prominent bosses surrounded by serpents (for instance, the Nigg stone), a motif also found on the freestanding crosses at Iona in Dalriada.

The art of the Scots of Dalriada is little known or studied with the exception of the Iona "high crosses," which, it has been suggested, may antedate the Irish series. The "high crosses" of Dalriada (which include an exceptionally fine example at Kildalton, Islay) certainly have their closest parallels in Ireland, for in form they contrast markedly with the cross slabs favored by the Picts. The Book of Kells is thought most probably to be an eighth-century product of the Iona scriptorium, although there is far from complete agreement on either its provenance or its date.

The Book of Kells is notable for the magnificence of its full-page illustrations of scenes from the life of Christ, for the intricacy and brilliant colors of its carpet pages and decorative initials, for the beauty of its script, its variety of embellished minor initials, and the vivacity of its interlinear ornaments. Its innovations in motifs include the use of human interlace, of vines and other foliate details, and of naturalistic animals (such as cats and mice). The full-page illustration of the Virgin and Child, a scene rarely depicted in late Celtic Christian art, has a parallel on St. Martin's cross at Iona. Elements of its ornament reflect Pictish influences, whereas its general style and script place it firmly in the Northumbrian tradition. The combination of art-historical and paleographical arguments suggest Iona as its likely origin, but nothing can be proved; it was presumably transferred to Kells in Ireland when Iona was largely abandoned by the monks as a consequence of the Viking raids in the early ninth century.

Portrait of Christ. Book of Kells, fol. 32v; possibly Ionian, 8th century. COURTESY OF THE BOARD OF TRINITY COLLEGE, DUBLIN

The decorated metalwork of Dalriada is little known and awaits detailed study, which will have to be based on recent finds of ornamented molds at Dunadd. Similarly, little has been established concerning the art of the north British kingdoms of Strathclyde and Rheged, in southwest Scotland, although the Mote of Mark in the latter kingdom has produced a notable group of ornamented mold fragments. It is possible that the Hunterston brooch, perhaps the earliest example of the rich filigree-ornamented brooches of the Tara type, was made around 700 in southwestern or western Scotland, drawing heavily on the expertise of an Anglo-Saxon craftsman.

It is not possible today to assess the quality of early medieval art in Wales, for there is no surviving ornamented metalwork or manuscripts to compare and contrast with those of Ireland and Scotland. The illuminated Ricemarch Psalter, dating from between 1076 and 1081, was written in Wales by a scribe called Ithael and decorated by Iewan, whose father, Sulien, was a Welsh scribe who had studied in Ire-land. Sulien clearly transmitted his training to his son, so that this psalter has decorated initials in the archaic eleventh-century Irish tradition.

Only Christian stone monuments survive in considerable number to attest to Welsh artistic endeavor in the post-Roman to pre-Norman period. These slabs and crosses do not, however, display the vigorous and imaginative qualities of the Pictish stones or Irish "high crosses," for their ornament consists largely of uninteresting geometric patterns, with only rare attempts at figural representation.

Although the Anglo-Norman invasion of Ireland did not lead to an immediate annihilation of native traditions, its ultimate effect was their extinction. But as English control waned in the later Middle Ages, a distinctive Gaelic culture arose again in Ireland. For instance, earlier manuscripts were copied for preservation, even, as in the Book of Ballymote (*ca.* 1390), down to the decorative initials of interlaced animals, imitating those of two centuries before, although they had to be simplified by artists who lacked their predecessors' training. Old shrines were restored and embellished, but generally rather crudely.

The extraordinary sophistication of the earlier medieval art of Ireland and Scotland is thus highlighted by these valiant but generally poor efforts of the Celtic revival in Ireland, and by the continued fondness for basic interlace patterns on late medieval stone monuments in the west of Scotland, where there are also freestanding crosses that hark back to older types. The international quality of the best late Celtic art in Ireland and Scotland, notably but not exclusively in the service of the church—be it in fine metalwork, illuminated manuscripts, or sculpture—represents what can truly be described as the Golden Age in Insular art.

BIBLIOGRAPHY

Ireland. P. Cone, ed., *Treasures of Irish Art 1500 B.C.– 1500 A.D.* (1977); M. and L. De Paor, *Early Christian Ireland,* rev. ed. (1978); J. A. Graham-Campbell, "The Initial Impact of the Vikings on Irish Art," in *Saga-Book of the Viking Society for Northern Research,* XX, pts. 1–2 (1978– 1979); Françoise Henry, *La sculpture irlandaise* (1932); *Irish Art in the Early Christian Period (to 800 A.D.)* (1965); *Irish Art During the Viking Invasions 800–1020 A.D.* (1967); and *Irish Art in the Romanesque Period 1020–1170 A.D.* (1969); A. Mahr and J. Raftery, eds., *Christian Art in Ancient Ireland,* 2 vols. (1932–1941); R. M. Organ, "Examination of the Ardagh Chalice—A Case History," in Museum of Fine Arts, Boston, *Applications of Science in Examination of Works of Art, Proceedings of the Seminar,*

1970 (1973); B. Ó Ríordáin, "The Derrynaflan Hoard," in *Antiquity,* **54** (1980); R. B. K. Stevenson, "The Chronology and Relationships of Some Irish and Scottish Crosses," in *Journal of the Royal Society of Antiquaries of Ireland,* 86–87 (1956–1957).

Hanging bowls. E. Fowler, "Hanging-Bowls," in J. M. Coles and D. D. A. Simpson, eds., *Studies in Ancient Europe* (1968); Françoise Henry, "Hanging Bowls," in *Journal of the Royal Society of Antiquaries of Ireland,* **66** (1936); D. Longley, *Hanging-Bowls, Penannular Brooches and the Anglo-Saxon Connexion* (1975).

Manuscript illumination. Jonathan J. G. Alexander, ed., *A History of Manuscripts Illuminated in the British Isles,* I, *Insular Manuscripts, Sixth to Ninth Century* (1978); T. J. Brown, "Northumbria and the Book of Kells," in *Anglo-Saxon England,* **1** (1972); Isabel Henderson, "Pictish Art and the Book of Kells," in Dorothy Whitelock, R. McKitterick, and D. Dumville, eds., *Ireland in Early Medieval Europe* (1982); Françoise Henry, ed., *The Book of Kells* (1974); Carl Nordenfalk, *Celtic and Anglo-Saxon Painting: Book Illumination in the British Isles 600–800* (1977). A complete facsimile of the Book of Kells is E. H. Alton, P. Meyer, eds., *Evangeliorum quattuor Codex Cenansis,* 3 vols. (1950–1951).

Picts and Scots. J. R. Allen and J. Anderson, *The Early Christian Monuments of Scotland* (1903); Isabel Henderson, *The Picts* (1967); and "Sculpture North of the Forth After the Take-over by the Scots," in J. Lang, ed., *Anglo-Saxon and Viking Age Sculpture and Its Context* (1978); Royal Commission on the Ancient and Historical Monuments of Scotland, *Argyll,* vol. IV, *Iona* (1982); A. Small, C. Thomas, and D. M. Wilson, *St. Ninian's Isle and Its Treasure,* 2 vols. (1973); R. B. K. Stevenson, "Sculpture in Scotland in the 6th–9th Centuries A.D.," in V. Milojčič, ed., *Kolloquium über spätantike und frühmittelalterliche Skulptur, Heidelberg 1970* (1971); "The Hunterston Brooch and Its Significance," in *Medieval Archaeology,* **18** (1974); and "The Earlier Metalwork of Pictland," in J. V. S. Megaw, ed., *To Illustrate the Monuments* (1976).

Wales. V. E. Nash-Williams, *The Early Christian Monuments of Wales* (1950).

JAMES A. GRAHAM-CAMPBELL

[See also **Anglo-Saxon Art; Carpet Page; Enamel; Enamel, Champlevé; Enamel, Cloisonné; Hanging Bowl; Kells, Book of; Lindisfarne Gospels; Manuscript Illumination; Metal Working; Pictish Art; Ringerike Style; Sutton Hoo; Urnes Style; Viking Art.**]

CELTIC CHURCH, a collective term to describe the medieval Christian institutions and practices of the Celtic-speaking peoples and the areas of their missionary activity. The term and concept of a Celtic church are quite recent: none of these peoples called themselves Celts, nor were they conscious of a common, unifying bond among their churches which might set them apart from the rest of Western Christendom. Some scholars, preferring to emphasize this lack of uniformity, employ the term "Celtic churches."

Geographically, the Celtic church embraced Ireland, Scotland, Wales, Cornwall, and Brittany; and for a time in the seventh and eighth centuries it also included the missionary areas of East Anglia and Northumbria in Anglo-Saxon England, and numerous monastic centers in Gaul, Italy, and Germany such as Luxeuil, Péronne, Bobbio, and St. Gall. Chronologically, the history of the Celtic church spans the period from the Christianization of Britain in the third century to the reforms of the twelfth century, which—officially, at least—removed the last traces of Celtic particularism.

ORIGINS AND DEVELOPMENT

The origins of the Celtic church go back to the Celts of Roman Britain, who accepted Christianity in the third century. Little is known about the nature or the extent of their conversion. In the fourth century the British church becomes more visible, especially to continental contemporaries. Five representatives from Britain—including three bishops—attended the Council of Arles in 314. According to St. Athanasius, the British church was represented at the Council of Sardica (about 343) and supported his position against Arianism. Another British delegation, including bishops, attended the Council of Ariminum (Rimini) in 359. The available evidence indicates that this church maintained close contacts with mainstream Western Christendom, particularly with the church of Gaul, and did not at this period show any signs of particularism.

By the fifth century the British church had grown strong enough to exert considerable influence outside its own borders. Pelagius, the protagonist in the debate on grace and free will, was British. Although he spent most of his life away from Britain—he left for Rome about 380—his doctrines enjoyed such popularity there as to require a visit by St. Germanus of Auxerre in 429 to combat them. About the same time, the British church produced two notable missionaries who worked among its neighbors to the north and east. St. Ninian established a church among the southern Picts of Galloway at Whithorn (Wigtownshire, Scotland) in the first half of the fifth century; St. Patrick, a native of southern Wales, worked as bishop in the northern part of Ireland in the fifth century. The southern and eastern parts of Ireland had already received Christianity from Britain, as suggested by a very early (fourth-century) stratum of Latin Christian loanwords in Old Irish, their content implying a primitive, pre-episcopal church, their phonology reflecting that of Latin as it was pronounced in Britain. The Brythonic names of most of the Irish saints connected with Southern Ireland during this period support the same conclusion.

Shortly after the mid fifth century the development of the British church and its missions was halted by the upheavals resulting from the Anglo-Saxon invasions. Regular, direct communication with Rome and the continental churches broke down. Internally the invasions forced the British Celts westward, leading to their consolidation in Wales, Cornwall, and Cumberland. Yet others emigrated from Cornwall and Wales to northwest Gaul, establishing there the church of Brittany. By the early sixth century the geographical extent of the Celtic church was basically defined: Wales, and Cornwall in Britain, Brittany in northwest Gaul, and Ireland.

By the second half of the sixth century Ireland had replaced Britain as the dynamic center of Celtic Christianity, and for the next two centuries would provide the major impetus for expansion. Expansion came through missions led by unusually gifted monks such as Columba and Columbanus. These men were not missionaries in the conventional, proselytizing sense; often their primary purpose in settling abroad was to mortify themselves. But once established, their foundations attracted converts.

The first missions were to Britain. St. Columba (Colum-cille) led a mission from northern Ireland to Scotland in 563, establishing a monastery on the island of Iona (off the coast of Argyll) that subsequently became the center of a vast monastic landholding (*paruchia*) embracing Irish missionary churches in western Scotland among the Irish colonists of Dál Riada and in northern Scotland among the Picts, as well as Columban foundations in Ireland at Derry, Swords, and Kells. In 634 Iona undertook a mission to Christianize Northumbria led by bishop Aidan, who established on the island of Lindisfarne the seat of both a monastery and a bishopric. Lindisfarne remained the most powerful center of religious life in Anglo-Saxon England until the Synod of Whitby in 664. Some time after 630 the Irishman Fursa founded a monastery at Cnoberesburgh (Burgh Castle) in East Anglia; a few years later, leaving his

brother Foillan in charge, he moved on to Gaul and established a mission at Lagny. He was buried at Péronne (*ca.* 650), a monastery that became the center for a flourishing Irish colony in northeastern Gaul.

But the earliest and most influential Irish missionary to continental Europe was St. Columbanus (Columban). He left Bangor (northern Ireland) about 590 and reached Burgundy, where he founded monasteries successively at Annegray, Luxeuil, and Fontaine. Columbanus finally settled at Bobbio in northern Italy, where he died in 615. More than any other Irish missionary, he stamped the mark of Celtic particularism on continental Europe. His monastery at Luxeuil with its Rule based on Irish monastic observance provided the model for religious houses in seventh-century Merovingian Gaul. In accordance with Celtic custom, he insisted on the independence of monasteries from the local bishop, thereby beginning a trend that had a lasting effect on Western Christendom. By introducing the practice of private penance and the penitential handbook, he brought about a revolution in the sacrament of penance. Finally, Columbanus initiated the public confrontation between the Celtic and the continental (especially Roman) ecclesiastical systems, which although resolved in Anglo-Saxon England at the Synod of Whitby and in Gaul—for the most part—by Carolingian ecclesiastical reforms, continued intermittently in the Celtic-speaking areas until the twelfth century, and even after.

CELTIC PARTICULARISM

The peculiarities of the Celtic church were neither as radical nor as cultivated as has been suggested by various writers from Bede (the propagandist par excellence of the Roman church in Britain) to nineteenth-century protestant apologists anxious to demonstrate the existence of a Celtic church in Great Britain and Ireland independent of Rome. At no time did any area of the Celtic church break with Rome or refuse to recognize the supremacy of the pope. Although accusations of Pelagianism were made against the Irish in the seventh century, and although those Celts who refused to accept the Roman Easter and tonsure were labeled as heretics (especially by the Anglo-Saxon church), no evidence exists of systematic, organized, doctrinal heresy at any time in any part of the medieval Celtic church.

Some of the Celtic church's most significant divergences from the rest of Western Christendom derive from its isolation, both geographical and political, the latter exacerbated by the breakdown of the

Roman Empire and the Anglo-Saxon invasions of the fifth century. Not until about 600 did normal relations with Rome resume, by which time the Celtic church was not only observing practices long abolished or gone out of use elsewhere but was even fostering reverence for their antiquity. Frequently, in the ensuing debates with advocates of the Roman church, the Celtic church's final argument was an appeal to the authority of their forefathers (seniores) and to the force of long-venerated traditions.

The shared origins of the various branches of the Celtic church and their reciprocal influence on each other reinforced this isolation. The British church, which had begun the Christianization of the other Celtic-speaking areas in the early fifth century, provided the model for the young churches. Subsequently, even during the upheavals of the Anglo-Saxon invasions, the different Celtic areas maintained closer contact with each other than with continental Europe, thus reinforcing their common practices. The church of Brittany, a colony of the Welsh and Cornish churches, had direct and permanent ties with west Britain through most of the early Middle Ages. The Welsh and Irish churches influenced each other; initially, until the sixth century, the influence came mainly from the Welsh side, thereafter from the Irish side. The Scottish monastery of Iona, which had dependent monasteries in Northumbria and Ireland, served during the seventh and eighth centuries as an entrepôt for cultural exchanges among the three areas.

Finally, the unique socioeconomic and political structure of Celtic society favored institutional particularism. This structure never exercised a dominant influence on the church in Roman Britain, where Roman secular government provided the model for ecclesiastical administration. But in those areas untouched or scarcely touched by Roman influence—particularly Ireland and Scotland—the Celtic church developed an administrative structure adapted to a society that was familial, tribal, rural, and decentralized.

Features characteristic of the Celtic church will be discussed below under five headings: Organization, Discipline, Liturgy, Spiritual life, and Intellectual life. It should be remembered, however, that practices peculiar to or characteristic of the Celtic church as outlined below were rarely in effect in all its parts at any one time; each area reflected its own degree of conservatism on any given issue or practice. Furthermore, insufficient evidence, especially in liturgical matters, prevents a full statement of these practices. The bulk of the evidence for the Celtic church comes from Irish documents and material, and it would be incorrect to assume that what obtained in the Irish church necessarily did in other Celtic areas also.

ORGANIZATION

Monasticism. The most striking feature of the institutional Celtic church was its monastic character. Every important church was monastic, run by monks and presided over by an abbot or abbess. Women such as Brigid of Kildare, Ita of Killeedy, and Hilda of Wearmouth-Jarrow played prominent roles as abbesses in Celtic monasteries. But the fact that Brigid and Hilda ruled double monasteries of men and women cannot be taken as evidence that this type of foundation was an institutional feature of Celtic monasticism. No other examples of the double monastery are known from Ireland or any other Celtic area.

Britain probably received monasticism from Gaul in the early fifth century. Subsequently it flourished in Wales and from there spread to Brittany and to Ireland, although the direct influence of Gaulish monasticism on Ireland is also likely. In Ireland by the mid sixth century the monasteries were taking over the administrative functions that elsewhere in Europe—and previously in Ireland—belonged exclusively to the diocese and its bishop. Monasticism succeeded in Celtic areas because its administrative structure allowed the local ruling families to build monasteries and churches on their own land, with their own kin as abbots, and thereby to maintain their control over family territory which in Celtic law was inalienable. Hence the custom in Ireland of referring to the abbot as the heir (Irish: comarbae) of the founder. This type of organization centering on a large monastery with its surrounding land fitted the agrarian economy and rural society of the Celtic areas much better than the diocesan church modeled on Roman administration, which required urban centers for its administration. In time some of these monasteries—Iona in Scotland, Llancarfan in Wales, Landévennec in Brittany—developed vast *paruchiae* of sister foundations ultimately owing allegiance to the founding house.

The bishop. Although the bishop in the Celtic church retained his position as the highest ecclesiastical dignitary, and administered the sacraments and spiritual duties proper to his office, he had little or no administrative jurisdiction, and was subject to the authority of the abbot.

The Culdee movement. In Ireland a reform movement of the eighth century produced a new kind of religious called the *Céle Dé* (servant, companion of God), whose aim was to combine the austere living of the anchorite with a community organization. From Ireland the *Céli Dé* (anglicized "Culdees") spread to Wales and Scotland. Although they are responsible for a considerable body of religious literature in Old Irish, little is known about their peculiar liturgical practices or their manner of living. They survived in Armagh until the sixteenth century.

DISCIPLINE

The dating of Easter. The main difference from Roman practice, and the one that brought on the Celtic churches the greatest odium and reproach, was their method for determining and observing the feast of Easter. Easter was not only the central festival of the Christian year, it also provided the basis for calculating most of the church's other festivals. Consequently, the determination of its date in any particular year was a matter of great importance. But because Christ's Passion fell on the Jewish Passover (based on lunar reckoning), the date of its commemoration could not be readily harmonized with the Julian calendar of the Christian church, which was based on solar reckoning. Various attempts were made to find a period of time when two cycles of years, as reckoned by the Jewish and the Julian calendars, would begin on the same day. In 312 Rome adopted the *supputatio romana,* an 84-year cycle, with the limits for the date of Easter fixed between the fourteenth and the twentieth day of the moon; she sporadically continued using modified versions of this cycle until 444. In 457 she adopted a 532-year cycle with limits for Easter fixed between the sixteenth and the twenty-second day of the lunar month—the *cursus paschalis* drawn up by Victorius of Aquitaine.

The British church had accepted the older *supputatio* and probably passed it on to Ireland before the arrival of St. Patrick's mission in 432. But the Victorine cycle never took hold in either Britain or Ireland, presumably because communications with Rome were cut in the mid fifth century by the Anglo-Saxon invasions. When direct communications were restored at the end of the sixth century, it became obvious that the British and Irish churches were adhering to a paschal cycle that had long since disappeared in the rest of western Europe.

The first confrontation between Celtic and Roman Easter adherents occurred in the last decade of the sixth century in Gaul, where the Irish missionary Columbanus found the Victorine cycle in full sway. He refused to abandon the 84-year cycle because, as he expressed it in a letter to Pope Gregory the Great (600), "Victorius has not been accepted by our teachers, by the former scholars of Ireland, by the mathematicians most skilled in reckoning chronology." Although Columbanus resisted the Victorine cycle, his monasteries seem to have complied with the Roman Easter soon after their founder's death in 615.

In Britain, Augustine, the head of the Roman mission sent by Pope Gregory to convert the Anglo-Saxons, confronted the Celtic bishops with their obsolete Easter cycle at a meeting held at Augustine's Oak in 603, and again in or about 605. The Celtic bishops, however, refused either to cooperate with the Roman mission in the conversion of their enemies, the Anglo-Saxons, or to conform to the Roman Easter. The Welsh church persisted in the Celtic Easter until 768, and some parts of Cornwall probably until the tenth century.

In Ireland the dating of Easter had become an issue early in the seventh century. A letter from Pope Honorius (*ca.* 625) urging the Irish church to conform to the Roman Easter brought the controversy to a head. Cummian's letter, *De controversia Paschali* (about 632), to Segene, abbot of Iona, indicates that the southern part of Ireland had accepted the Roman Easter by this time, but probably still constituted a minority. Northern Ireland came over to Roman Easter in 697, thanks mainly to the exhortations of Adamnan, abbot of Iona. Iona itself, though resisting the change until 718, had already lost the paschal controversy on two fronts: in Northumbria at the Synod of Whitby (664), and in the territory of the southern Picts, where King Nechtan IV under Anglo-Saxon influence expelled the recalcitrant monks from Iona in 716. Thus, when Bede completed his *Historia ecclesiastica gentis anglorum* in 731 he observed that only the Welsh still clung to the Celtic Easter.

Celtic tonsure. Another aspect of the conflict between the Roman and the Celtic churches concerned their different types of tonsure. Augustine and his companions, who tonsured their heads in the Roman manner, with the so-called tonsure of St. Peter—consisting of a circle of hair in the form of a crown around the shaven head—objected to the Celtic tonsure, which probably appeared as a semicircle of hair running from ear to ear above the forehead, with the hair behind allowed to grow long. The origins of this Celtic tonsure are obscure, but it may originally have served as a distinguishing mark for elite groups in Celtic society, such as the druids. Adherents of the Roman tonsure such as Aldhelm of Malmesbury and Abbot Ceolfrid of Wearmouth-Jarrow attributed this tonsure to St. Peter's rival the magician Simon Magus (Acts 8), and their own to St. Peter, apparently unaware that the latter tonsure only went back to the sixth century. Generally speaking, most areas of the Celtic church abandoned the Celtic tonsure at the same time as they accepted the Roman Easter. In Brittany, however, Matmonoc, abbot of Landévennec, admitted to Louis the Pious as late as 818 that his monastery still observed the "Irish" tonsure.

Administration of baptism. In his discussions with the Celtic bishops, Augustine insisted that they administer baptism in the Roman manner. What irregularity he had in mind is not clear—perhaps adherence to an older usage, perhaps the administration by clerics other than the bishop of the sacrament of confirmation at the end of baptism. Special or peculiar features of baptism administered by the Celtic church cannot be determined since the main source of information, the *ordo baptismi* of the Stowe Missal, bears witness to strong Roman influence.

Episcopal consecration. The Celtic church did not always conform to the canonical rule that required that at least three bishops should officiate at the consecration of a bishop. Their custom of permitting one originally grew out of the necessity imposed on early missionary bishops such as Patrick and Ninian who worked alone, but it later acquired the force of tradition. The refusal of the Roman party in Britain and of certain continental councils in the seventh and eighth centuries to accept consecration performed by Celtic bishops may have stemmed less from doubts about the ritual used than from the taint of heresy imputed to those who had refused to accept Roman Easter and tonsure. In Ireland episcopal consecration by a single bishop was current during the eleventh and twelfth centuries.

Canonical legislation. A considerable body of such legislation, enacted by synods of bishops and abbots in Ireland and Wales, has been preserved in collections of canon law made on the Continent. The best known, the *Collectio canonum hibernensis,* appeared in Gaul in the eighth century, brought thither by monks coming from Ireland. Its emphasis on certain Celtic practices—the independence of the clergy from secular control, the devotion to piety, asceticism, and fasting, the cult of relics—won it

widespread popularity in Europe. Typical of these and other Celtic canons is the effort to harmonize Mosaic traditions—such as the year of the jubilee, the obligation to pay tithes, the distinction between clean and unclean foods—with Western practices. Much of this Celtic legislation treats of secular topics and has been influenced by Celtic secular law, for example, the *Canones Wallici* (written 550–650), probably originally composed in Wales and subsequently adapted to social conditions in Brittany. The church in Brittany played a considerable role in the dissemination of these texts as evidenced by its rich manuscript tradition of Celtic canons. Although widely used in the Celtic countries and even on the Continent, none of these canons enjoyed the status and support given to continental collections such as the *Hispana* and the *Dionysiana* by continental councils and bishops.

Penitentials and private penance. Often accompanying canonical texts in the same manuscripts are the penitentials, handbooks containing schedules of penances to be imposed by the confessor on the penitent for various types of sins. These penitentials originated and developed in the Celtic church, initially, it seems, in Wales, whence the earliest penitential documents derive, such as the *Preface of Gildas on Penance,* and the decrees of the Synod of North Britain (Brevi). But these Welsh documents are not true penitentials. It was the Irish church that shaped such penitential matter into the format of a handbook containing schematized systems of penance and commutations, and in this convenient form spread its penitential practices throughout the Celtic church, Britain, and eventually western Europe. So pervasive was the influence of the penitential handbook that even Theodore of Tarsus, an avowed enemy of Celtic particularism, compiled one for the Anglo-Saxon church, which in turn propagated them on the Continent.

Hand in hand with the penitential went the Irish practice of private penance. Until the seventh century, penitential discipline in the Western church was characterized by public penance, by the exclusion of the penitent—often for long periods—from religious services. The Celtic church, however, apparently substituted for this discipline a system of private penance, imposed by a private confessor and performed privately by the penitent, usually for a limited period of time—thus enabling the penitent to receive the sacrament repeatedly—in accordance with the tariffs laid down in the penitential handbook. Most historians agree that this system of private penance had its origins in the monastic practice of receiving spiritual guidance from an older monk, as attested in Wales and Ireland, and that it passed by way of Irish missionaries such as Columbanus to the rest of Europe along with the penitential handbook.

LITURGY

The term "Celtic liturgy," first used in the nineteenth century and now generally accepted, requires clarification. The Celtic church did not possess a distinctive rite comparable to those of the Gallican, Roman, or Mozarabic liturgies. Instead it had a markedly eclectic liturgy bearing evidence of influences from the Oriental, Mozarabic, and Roman liturgies. But the dominant influence derives from the Gallican rite, reflecting both the ultimate Gallican origin of the British church and continued Gallican influence on Britain and Ireland in the fifth and sixth centuries. As a further distinction, Celtic liturgy reveals a lack of uniform practice: rituals differed from place to place, depending on the practices dictated by the closest influential monastery. Virtually all of the evidence for Celtic liturgy comes from Irish sources, which become less reliable from the mid seventh century onward as the influence of the Roman liturgy takes hold.

The Mass. For the Ordinary of the Mass the chief source of information is the early-ninth-century Stowe Missal; for the variable elements, the Bobbio Missal and some fragments. The Celtic Mass had a Gallican nucleus as demonstrated by such Gallican features as the preparation of offerings before the entry of the celebrant, the litany before the Mass, the reading of diptychs (containing the names of the dead) at the moment when the chalice is uncovered, the breaking of the Host before the *Pater,* the giving of the *Pax* (the sign of peace), and the antiphons for Communion. Statements by Gildas and Adamnan suggest that Mass was celebrated relatively infrequently by the Celtic church, only on Sundays and feast days. In the monasteries Mass was celebrated in the evening, in accordance with early Christian practice; but in the seventh century, at least at the monastery of Bangor, its celebration was moved to morning.

The divine office. Among the sources considerable variations exist concerning the number of canonical hours, either because of intrinsically different systems or because the method of dividing the hours differed from author to author. The fullest account, in the Rule of Columbanus, details a pattern of hours similar to that of the Ambrosian and Mozarabic rites. Columbanus emphasized nocturnal psalmody and the importance of the solemn vigils of Saturday and Sunday. Other features of the divine office, which also correspond to southern Gaulish and Oriental practice, are the recitation of canticles, the use of Psalm 89 at prime, and Psalms 103 and 112 at vespers. The Bangor Antiphonary (*ca.* 680–691), a collection of hymns, collects, and antiphons for use in the divine office, lists eight canonical hours: *secunda* (corresponding to prime), *tertia, sexta, nona, vespertina, initium noctis* (later replaced by compline), *nocturna* (midnight office) and *matutina* (corresponding to lauds). Neither this text nor another early-eighth-century source (an Old Irish gloss in the Vatican Library, MS Pal. lat. 68) contains any reference to the hour of compline.

The sacraments. Baptism: the principal source of information, the *ordo baptismi* of the Stowe Missal, reveals no evidence of particularism. It offers a choice of triple immersion or aspersion. It contains numerous prayers, some corresponding to those found in the Ambrosian and Gallican rites, some—presumably from after the seventh century—to the Roman rite. The *pedilavium,* the custom of washing the feet of the baptized, mentioned by Stowe, occurs also in the ancient Gallican rite.

Confirmation: Irish sources refer to this sacrament as the *consummatio*—presumably because it conferred full membership of the church—but no account of it has survived.

Eucharist: no firm evidence exists in support of the suggestion that the congregation received this sacrament under both species. A seventh-century Irish canon enjoins Communion at least at Easter. The Eucharist—carried by the priest in a small bag around his neck—was frequently administered to the sick.

Penance: the Celtic church encouraged frequent confession and the cultivation of a special relationship with the confessor, who was called in Irish the *anmchara* (soul-friend). Two surviving *ordines* for the administering of the sacrament of penance show that the Celtic rite contained the essential elements of confession, contrition, and satisfaction.

Extreme unction: three Irish manuscripts—the Books of Dimma and Mulling and the Stowe Missal—contain directions for the administration of this popular sacrament. It involved a profession of faith, unction of the body, and administration of viaticum.

Holy orders: the Celtic church—at least from the seventh century onward—recognized the seven ecclesiastical grades that obtained elsewhere in Christendom. No account of the ordination of priests has survived.

Matrimony: the evidence, both of Celtic canons and of critical outsiders, suggests that the attitude toward this sacrament and toward church regulations about impediments to its reception was generally lax in the Celtic church, no doubt reflecting the influence of native Celtic laws of marriage and divorce. No account of the sacrament has survived.

Funeral rites: fragments of a requiem mass survive in several Irish manuscripts, including the Stowe Missal and MS St. Gall 1395. Other sources, such as the penitentials and the hagiographical literature, mention elaborate funeral rites, developed perhaps in response to native funerary customs. The cononical collection, the *Hibernensis* (18.3), mentions cremation as a practice.

Exorcism, blessings, cursing: the Bangor Antiphonary contains a formula for exorcism. Formulas for the blessing of salt, water, and food (before eating) also survive. Cursing as an ecclesiastical sanction is well attested in early Irish literature, and had its own ritual involving a group of clerics who chanted psalms, struck bells, and fasted against the object of their condemnation.

SPIRITUAL LIFE

The spirit of Celtic Christianity found its most effective expression not in ritual but in the private and personal practice of the spiritual life. The following are the most striking and original manifestations of Celtic spirituality.

Private devotions. Celtic Christianity developed its own private devotions, characterized by freedom of expression and a talent for innovation. One such innovation is the *lorica,* a formulaic prayer, often written in pedantic language and couched in urgent and effusive terms, imploring protection against a list of spiritual and temporal evils. These *loricae*—usually attributed to some Celtic saint, such as Brendan or Patrick—were invested with the superstitious efficacy of magical incantations. Other forms of Celtic piety were: litanies to be recited on various occasions (collections of which are found in the Book of Cerne, the Book of Nunnaminster, and the Royal Library Prayer Book), the hymns attributed to powerful Celtic saints (found in the Irish *Liber hymnorum*), and the private recitation of the psalms, especially Psalm 118, the *Beati.*

Mortifications. Bede and certain continental writers remarked on the Irish penchant for prolonged and severe physical deprivation. A favorite practice, the *vigilia crucis* (Irish: *crossfigell*), consisted of praying for long periods with the arms extended like a cross, usually in a standing position, occasionally lying down. Constant genuflections or prostrations were another form of mortification, with as many as 300 per night attributed to holy men. A considerable number of Celtic saints are said to have practiced ascetic immersion, plunging into ice-cold water and remaining there all night. Other forms of mortification included abstaining from all food for two to four days (the *superpositio*), and flagellations.

Pilgrimage. From the late sixth century onward foreigners noted the arrival of Irish pilgrims, or *peregrini* as they were called, into Britain and Europe. They were not pilgrims in the conventional sense of travelers to the sacred places, but voluntary exiles who had vowed for love of Christ never to return to their homeland. Some were people undergoing exile as a penance for their sins. The concept of *peregrinatio pro amore Christi* may have derived from Irish secular law, which decreed banishment from the tribe as the ultimate punishment for certain heinous crimes.

Eremiticism. The practice of living the spiritual life in solitude found ready acceptance among the Celtic peoples at all periods. Some lived close to a monastery or church as anchorites; others fled to the wilderness as hermits. Particular respect was accorded to such recluses, who often acted as advisers on ecclesiastical problems.

INTELLECTUAL LIFE

In the Celtic church the monasteries constituted the main centers of ecclesiastical learning through their scriptoria and schools. Students began by learning to read and write Latin, using the Psalms as their basic text. From this they progressed to the study of the whole Bible, the basis of the monastic curriculum. The allegorical approach to Scripture, common throughout western Europe, had its place in the schools, but in Ireland at least, the rational, historical approach of Antiochan exegesis also found favor. Latin grammar, in the texts of the late Latin grammarians, especially Priscian and Donatus, was considered an essential tool for understanding Scripture; even pagan, classical authors were read for the same purpose. From these Celtic schools there emerged in the sixth century a bizarre type of Latin, Hisperic Latin, in style bombastic and enigmatical, in vocabulary replete with neologisms formed from other Latin words, from Greek and even from Hebrew.

Among the best-known products of Celtic monastic education are Gildas, Columbanus, Aldhelm, and Adamnan.

THE DECLINE OF THE CELTIC CHURCH

The imposition of continental reforms in the eleventh and twelfth centuries marks the end of Celtic particularism. In Ireland the reform, sponsored by Canterbury, was effected by Gilbert, bishop of Limerick and papal legate in Ireland, and by Malachy, archbishop of Armagh (d. 1148). In Scotland, the reforms of Queen Margaret during the second half of the eleventh century and the placing of the church under the immediate jurisdiction of the Apostolic See in the late twelfth century ensured reform. The Welsh church, after the conquest of Wales by the Anglo-Normans, came under the direct jurisdiction of Canterbury in the early twelfth century. During the eleventh century Cornwall increasingly came under the control of the Anglo-Saxon church, especially after Bishop Leofric moved his seat to Exeter about 1050. In Brittany the church was made subject to the metropolitan of Tours with the abolition of the archbishopric of Dol in 1199. Thus by the end of the twelfth century the Celtic church had relinquished its autonomy and lost most of its distinctive characteristics.

BIBLIOGRAPHY

General. Louis Gougaud, *Christianity in Celtic Lands,* Maud Joynt, trans. (1932); Nora K. Chadwick, *The Age of the Saints in the Celtic Church* (1961, repr. 1963); John T. McNeill, *The Celtic Churches: A History A.D. 200 to 1200* (1974). On the early British church, see Hugh Williams, *Christianity in Early Britain* (1912); M. W. Barley and R. P. C. Hanson, *Christianity in Britain, 300–700* (1968); and R. P. C. Hanson, *Saint Patrick: His Origins and Career* (1968), 1–71; Charles Thomas, *Christianity in Roman Britain to A.D. 500* (1981). On the medieval Welsh church, see A. W. Wade-Evans, *Welsh Christian Origins* (1934); Siân Victory, *The Celtic Church in Wales* (1977).

Brittany. Nora K. Chadwick, *Early Brittany* (1969), especially 238–291.

Scotland. William D. Simpson, *The Celtic Church in Scotland* (1935); and *Adomnan's Life of Columba,* A. O. Anderson and M. O. Anderson, eds. and trans. (1961), 18–124.

Ireland. James F. Kenney, *The Sources for the Early History of Ireland: Ecclesiastical* (1929, repr. with addenda by Ludwig Bieler, 1966); Kathleen Hughes, *The Church in Early Irish Society* (1966); and *Early Christian Ireland: Introduction to the Sources* (1972).

Irish missionary activity. Louis Gougaud, *Les saints irlandais hors d'Irlande étudiés dans le culte et dans la dévotion traditionelle* (1936).

Discipline. Bede, *Ecclesiastical History of the English People,* Bertram Colgrave and R. A. B. Mynors, eds. (1969), especially 2.2, 2.4, 3.25–26, 5.15, and 5.22 (for the Roman point of view); Paul Grosjean, "Recherches sur les débuts de la controverse paschale chez les Celtes," in *Analecta Bollandiana,* **64** (1946); Ludwig Bieler, *The Irish Penitentials* (1963), with an appendix by D. A. Binchy.

Liturgy. F. E. Warren, *The Liturgy and Ritual of the Celtic Church* (1881)—although its conclusions are dated, it contains much useful evidence; Henry Jenner, "The Celtic Rite," in *Catholic Encyclopedia,* III (1908); Louis Gougaud, "Celtiques (Liturgies)," in *Dictionnaire d'archéologie chrétienne et de liturgie,* (1924), part ii.

Spiritual life. A. B. Kuypers, *The Prayer Book of Aedeluald the Bishop, Commonly Called the Book of Cerne* (1902), with appendix containing edition of the Royal Prayer Book and liturgical note by Edmund Bishop; Kathleen Hughes, "The Changing Theory and Practice of the Irish Pilgrimage," in *Journal of Ecclesiastical History,* **11** (1960).

Monasticism. See Giles Constable, *Medieval Monasticism: A Select Bibliography* (1976), 67–68.

Intellectual life. On Latin culture see Martin R. P. McGuire and H. Dressler, *Introduction to Medieval Latin Studies: A Syllabus and Bibliographical Guide,* 2nd ed. (1977), 60–65, 100–113.

PÁDRAIG P. Ó NÉILL

[See also **Adamnan, St.; Aidan of Lindisfarne; Columba, St.; Columbanus, St.; Confession; Easter; Germanus of Auxerre, St.; Monasticism, Origins; Ninian, St.; Patrick, St.; Penance and Penitentials; Whitby, Synod of.**]

CELTIC LANGUAGES. The Celtic group of languages is part of the Indo-European family, which includes among others the Greek, Romance, Germanic, Slavic, Baltic, and Indo-Iranian languages. The earliest archaeological cultures that can be associated with speakers of Celtic languages are the Hallstatt and La Tène cultures, which extended over much of western Europe north of the Alps, and lasted from roughly the eighth century B.C. to the first century A.D. At the period of greatest expansion the Celtic peoples extended from the British Isles and Spain in the west to the Balkans and parts of present-day Turkey in the east.

All of the Celtic languages surviving into medieval times are of the so-called Insular group—the languages of the descendants of those Celts who migrated from the Continent to the British Isles. These migrations probably did not begin much earlier than the fifth century B.C. Insular Celtic consists of an Irish or Goidelic group, which evolved into Irish, Scottish Gaelic, and Manx, and a British or Brythonic group, which gave rise to Welsh, Cumbric, Cornish, and Breton. The Irish group is sometimes referred to as *q*-Celtic, and the British group as *p*-Celtic, because of the differing treatment of the Indo-European labiovelar /k^w/ (Old Irish *cethair*, Old Welsh *petguar* [four] from Indo-European *k^wetwor-* [compare Latin *quattuor*]).

The earliest physical records for the Irish group are inscriptions consisting largely of names, written in ogham, an Irish adaptation for epigraphical purposes of the Roman alphabet. These inscriptions date from the fourth to the seventh centuries, and are found in Britain as well as in Ireland. The writing of Irish in the Roman alphabet itself probably began around the end of the sixth century. The earliest datable literary composition is the *Amra Choluim Cille,* an elegy written by Dallán Forgaill shortly after the death of St. Columba (Colum-cille) in 597. The earliest extant manuscript with Irish texts is an eighth-century copy of the Pauline Epistles with glosses in Irish. In all, over 3,000 vernacular manuscripts survive, dating from the ninth century to the beginning of printing in the sixteenth.

In rounded figures, the Primitive Irish period extends from the earliest inscriptions to A.D. 600. Archaic Old Irish lasts from 600 to 700, but the language must be recovered from considerably later manuscripts. Classical Old Irish runs from 700 to 900, Middle Irish from 900 to 1250, and Early Modern Irish from 1250 to the end of the seventeenth century. From the thirteenth century to the beginning of the seventeenth century the same literary dialect was used in both Ireland and Scotland. Therefore little evidence for the development of Scottish Gaelic and Manx as separate dialects is found before 1600.

The language of the earliest Irish texts is the most archaic found in the Insular group. The verbal system is of great complexity, containing, in most tenses, an independent inflection with one set of endings, and a dependent inflection, used with prefixes or preverbs, with another set of endings (for example, *ber-id* [he carries], *ní-beir* [he does not carry]; or *do-beir* [he gives], *ní-tabair* [he does not give]). Prefixation is intensive throughout the verbal system and in word formation in general. The use of three

or even four prefixes with a single root is not uncommon. Pronouns may be infixed between preverbs and verbal roots, or suffixed to verbs, or, more commonly, to prepositions (for example. *do-m* [to me]). There are widespread phonological changes prior to the Classical Old Irish period, together with loss of final syllables and syncope of medial syllables. As a result of these changes both the vowel alternations and the palatalization, spirantization, prenasalization, and voicing of consonants play important roles in maintaining morphological and even syntactic distinctions. Moreover, consonants at the beginnings of words, under the influence of the original final sound of the preceding word, undergo the same phonological changes as medial or final consonants. Prefixed verbs are usually stressed on the second syllable. All other stress-bearing words are stressed on the first syllable.

The earliest evidence for the British group consists of names found in Latin inscriptions from the fifth to the seventh centuries, and in Latin sources composed in the sixth to eighth centuries, though generally preserved in later manuscripts. The Old Welsh period runs from the late eighth to the mid twelfth century, and the extant evidence, consisting of names, glosses, fragments, and two poems, is slight, though some legal and literary materials from this period survive in later manuscripts. Middle Welsh extends from the twelfth to the end of the fourteenth centuries, and the Early Modern Welsh period, beginning with the poetry of Dafydd ap Gwilym, runs from the end of the fourteenth to the end of the sixteenth centuries. From the period 1200–1500 only slightly more than 100 manuscripts survive.

The verbal system of Welsh and the other languages of the British group has, in contrast to Irish, only a single inflection. As in Irish, prefixation is widespread, as is the infixation and suffixation, especially to prepositions, of pronouns. The British group also undergoes parallel, but not identical, phonological changes, including the spirantization, prenasalization, and voicing of consonants, also in initial position, and the loss of final and medial syllables. Stress was originally penultimate in the British group. With the loss of final syllables, stress apparently became word-final for a short period, but reverted to the penultimate position, except in the Breton dialect of Vannes.

The Cumbric dialect of British probably survived in the north of England well into the eleventh century. A few names are found in Latin inscriptions of the fifth and sixth centuries, and three legal terms survive in an eleventh-century document. More importantly, it was probably the language of composition of the original Taliesin and Aneirin poems, now preserved only in Welsh versions.

Aside from some names in Anglo-Saxon charters and in the Domesday Book, the earliest evidence for Cornish is in manuscript glosses beginning about 1000. There is also a Latin-Cornish glossary from about 1100. The small number of Middle Cornish literary texts extant are devoted to miracle plays, and come from the fifteenth and sixteenth centuries.

Breton is in origin a purely Insular dialect, the language of the descendants of those British Celts who migrated from the Cornwall-Devon peninsula, beginning in the fifth century A.D. There are hundreds of manuscript glosses in Old Breton from the ninth century on, as well as considerable onomastic evidence in Latin charters. A small number of Middle Breton literary texts survives from the fifteenth and sixteenth centuries.

BIBLIOGRAPHY

Rachel Bromwich, *Medieval Celtic Literature: A Select Bibliography* (1974); Kenneth Hurlstone Jackson, *Historical Grammar of Irish* (in press); *Language and History in Early Britain* (1953); *A Historical Phonology of Breton* (1967).

H. ROE

[See also **Breton Literature; Irish Literature: General; Scottish Literature, Gaelic; Welsh Literature.**]

CELTIC LITERATURE. See **Irish, Scottish, Welsh Literature.**

CENNINI, CENNINO (*ca.* 1370–*ca.* 1440), Florentine painter, was born at Colle di Val d'Elsa. His *Il libro dell'arte*, written possibly around 1390 or later, is the primary source of our knowledge about painters' training, working methods, and materials during the Trecento and early Quattrocento. Probably meant to be used in the shop, this practical manual includes all aspects of the painter's craft: fresco, panels, parchment, glass and mosaics, and the painting of chests and statuary. In keeping with the tradesman's viewpoint, Cennini included many rec-

ipes for the preparation of artist's materials and their use, from charcoal to pigments, from drawing surfaces to tracing paper.

Cennini traced his artistic heritage back to Giotto through Agnolo Gaddi, with whom he studied for twelve years, to Taddeo Gaddi, Agnolo's father and pupil of Giotto. Although conscious of his illustrious heritage and of Giotto's fame, and although he argues for the right of painting to coexist with poetry and other theoretical disciplines, Cennini in his work is fundamentally practical and concerned with painters who regarded themselves as craftsmen. Written at the dawn of the Renaissance, the *Libro* reflects a basic conservatism in its advice on style, which has led most scholars to conclude that Cennini's viewpoint was essentially traditional. As a working manual, it summarizes contemporary practices used by both conservative and more independent painters.

Most scholars ascribe Cennini's book to the 1390's, while others suggest it derives from some decades later. The earliest surviving copy of the manuscript is dated 1437, but there is no proof that this is not a posthumous copy.

Although Cennini must have left behind a number of paintings, no single work is universally accepted as a product of his hand.

BIBLIOGRAPHY

Il libro dell'arte, edited and translated by Daniel V. Thompson, Jr., as *The Craftsman's Handbook* (1933, repr. 1954).

ADELHEID M. GEALT

CENTERING, a temporary timber framing or mold upon which the masonry of an arch or vault is supported during construction; the centering is removed (struck) when the keystone is in place or when the mortar has set and the arch or vault is self-supporting. A type of centering was used by Roman architects and may have been inherited by the Byzantines, although the technique seems to have died out in the early Latin West. Centering is essential for the construction of vaulted interiors, and only its reestablishment—probably around 950 in Burgundy—permitted Romanesque experiments in vaulted churches. But, although it allows the construction of complex vaults, centering raised the technical problems of either finding timber sufficiently long to span an arch or rigidly piecing together shorter lengths, and of accurately carving and fitting together a substantial wooden framework. A partial solution was found in the late Romanesque period when stone ribs, acting as a kind of permanent skeletal centering, were introduced. A rare example of medieval centering is preserved in the fourteenth-century tower at Lärbro in Gotland (Sweden).

BIBLIOGRAPHY

John Fitchen, *The Construction of Gothic Cathedrals: A Study of Medieval Vault Erection* (1961); Robert Mark, *Experiment in Gothic Structure* (1982).

LESLIE BRUBAKER

[See also **Arch; Construction: Engineering; Vault.**]

CENT NOUVELLES NOUVELLES, one of the most important prose works of the fifteenth century, consists of unsigned stories attributed to at least thirty-five different authors at the court of Philip the Good, duke of Burgundy, and even to Antoine de la Sale. These tales were most probably composed by one person, as the unity of style suggests, for the duke of Burgundy between 1456 and 1462. The tales are told with the traditional racy humor of the fabliaux, but they are not meant to be pedagogical or didactic; rather, they seek to make the reader laugh or, as Franklin Sweetser puts it, they are "a form of amusement intended to pass time pleasantly."

Even if they are not to be taken literally, as a true picture of fifteenth-century life, the tales offer a vivid gallery of contemporary portraits: cuckolds, clerics, monks, nuns, knights, peasants, bourgeois, and merchants. Although similar to Boccaccio's *Decameron,* the *Cent nouvelles nouvelles* owes little to it; it was perhaps more directly influenced by Gian Francesco Poggio Bracciolini's *Liber facetiarum,* yet retained its originality. There may not be a great deal of variety among the stories as a whole, but their tone is frequently different and a few of the stories are more realistic and coarser than others. There are also some totally nonsexual tales. All in all, the *Cent nouvelles nouvelles,* without claiming to be innovative in subject matter or style, tells amusing stories solely to please.

BIBLIOGRAPHY

An edition is Franklin P. Sweetser, *Les Cent nouvelles nouvelles* (1966). Studies include Charles Knudson, "Antoine de la Sale, le duc de Bourgogne et les *Cent nouvelles nouvelles,*" in *Romania,* 53 (1927); and L. Sozzi, "La nouvelle française au quinzième siècle," in *Cahiers de l'Association internationale des études françaises* (May 1971).

GUY MERMIER

[See also **French Literature: After 1200.**]

CENTONIZATION. "Cento" (from the Latin word for patchwork) refers to poetic and other texts of late antiquity that were composed with lines from diverse preexisting sources. Such juxtaposition created meaning that was not originally in the separate sources, and that effect often had rhetorical intent. Thus in early Christian times one recombined lines from Vergil in centos that were intended to evince the Christian thought that had lain hidden in the original poems.

Many texts of plainchants in the traditions of the medieval church are centos of lines or phrases from diverse scriptural sources. The art of juxtaposing such texts was consummated by the writers of trope texts, and there the rhetorical purpose is especially clear: Old Testament passages receive concrete Christian meaning when brought into juxtaposition with New Testament texts.

Like such texts, many chant melodies are largely composed of separately identifiable bits of traditional material, or melodic formulas. The same formulas can be found in many different chants and in different combinations. Because of this feature, Paolo Ferretti applied the "cento" label to the melodies as well, and "centonization" has come to designate the very prominent technique of chant composition with formulas in both Latin and Byzantine traditions. This definition has since been the basis for one of the main techniques for analyzing chant.

Objections have recently been raised against this general conception and methodology on several grounds. Unlike the constituent fragments of literary centos, the melodic formulas of chants were not taken from diverse originals. They are not fragments of some larger whole, nor is there a counterpart in chant of the rhetorical purpose with which such fragments were conjoined in literary centos. The melodic formulas are specific to the particular modal and liturgical categories of the chants in which they are found, and they presumably had their origins in the development of those chants.

Moreover, the conception of composition according to which the chants were pieced together like a patchwork, or mosaic, suggests a more modern situation, in which a composer, writing in advance of any performance, plans and executes a unified work; whereas virtually all the formulaic chants were the products of preliterate, oral traditions. Their formulaic aspect, under this alternate conception, represents the technique that made possible the tradition of extemporaneous, oral performance. Formulas were the signposts that constituted points of departure, goals, and markers along the singer's way. Their standardization would have been a natural consequence of the performance tradition, reinforced by the very utility of the singer's having a knowledge of formulas for use as he came to the right places in the chant.

From this point of view the centonization concept entails a fundamental misinterpretation of the nature of the chant tradition. The controversy therefore opens onto major and fundamental issues in the history of medieval music.

BIBLIOGRAPHY

Paolo Ferretti, *Estetica gregoriana; ossia, Trattato delle forme musicali del canto gregoriana*, I (1934); Helmut Hucke, "Zu einigen Problemen der Choralforschung," in *Die Musikforschung*, **11** (1958), 385–414; Leo Treitler, "'Centonate Chant,' *Übles Flickwerk* or *E pluribus unus?*" in *Journal of the American Musicological Society*, **28** (1975).

LEO TREITLER

[See also **Gregorian Chant; Music in Medieval Society.**]

CERAMICS, EUROPEAN. The Romans had developed the glazing of clay, dried "leather hard" in the oxidizing atmosphere of a kiln, by means of a glaze consisting of silica (powdered quartz) mixed with a flux and lead oxide colored by other metallic oxides. Neglected in the age of Constantine, glazing was revived in the mid ninth century at Constantinople, under the influence of Islamic glazed pottery; in the West glazing was abandoned until the Franks recaptured Narbonne from the Muslims in 759.

Unglazed gray-black sandy wares were deposited with funerary urns in Merovingian tombs. Carinated goblets copied Roman types; vases decorated with roulettes and friezes of animals characterize the Vexin burials. In eastern England and the Midlands cinerary urns with stamped and incised designs have been excavated from the sites of Saxon cremation ceremonies. In western Carolingian France terracotta was used in church architecture; and terra-cot-

Hand-made pagan Saxon cinerary urn with stamped and incised designs. Late 6th or early 7th century. UNIVERSITY MUSEUM OF ARCHEOLOGY AND ETHNOLOGY, CAMBRIDGE

St. Nicholas. Lead-glazed Byzantine tile, *ca.* 1000 A.D. WALTERS ART GALLERY, BALTIMORE

tas stamped with geometrical patterns, late antique motifs, and Christian symbols were current in Visigothic Spain.

Toward the tenth century lead glazing reached England, Friesland, and the territory north of the

Loire. The Winchester pots are rather coarse, but the bowls and spouted pitchers of Stamford (Lincolnshire) are fine examples of off-white pottery glazed in yellow, orange, and green. In northern Germany glazing helped to solidify the pots and harden their mouths. In France lead glazing was used sporadically until its expansion after 1300. Contemporary English and German aquamanilia were made for washing hands at the table.

Tiled pavements are a branch of medieval ceramics. Small lead-glazed tiles arranged like Roman mosaics covered the floor of the chevet in the abbey church of St. Denis (1144). The "rosette" in the early-thirteenth-century church at St. Pierre sur Dives alternates inlaid red clay tiles and ones coated with a slip blackened with a metallic oxide. The "rose window" of the chapter house floor at Westminster Abbey after 1255 and the pavement of the King's Chapel at Clarendon are made of inlaid tiles produced at the abbey of Chertsey in Surrey. These tiles were impressed with dies and the molds formed by the impressions were filled with pipe clay and lead glazed. The entire tile was then fired, turning the pipe clay yellow and the ground clay shades of brown and purple.

Under the Macedonian renaissance in Byzantium (867–1025) a glazed whiteware was either impressed with molding designs or painted in colors (red being stippled) within dark outlines, the whole covered with a thin transparent glaze. Some pieces were incised in sgraffito. Pottery was absent from the imperial table until the fall of the Angeloi dynasty in 1204. The upper classes used a costly earthenware decorated with gold leaf or with powdered silver or gold. Plaques executed in polychrome ware represent religious subjects and were framed in revetments, including columns. The icon of St. Theodore from Patlejna, Bulgaria, made of twenty square plaques, dates from the second third of the tenth century. The chief center of production was at Nicomedia until the Seljuk conquest (1091).

In the eleventh century a red-bodied ware with slip began to be used in Constantinople, Athens, and Corinth. Slip, a liquid mixture of fine clay coating the ware, was painted in vitreous colors under a clear glaze. In sgraffito decoration, the design scratched through the slip is delineated in the color of the body laid bare. In the medallion style the design, usually of animals, is restricted to the center; in the free style it occupies the entire piece. In the later elaborate style, which spread from Greece to the Caucasus, portions of the slip were scratched away before fir-

Plate with sgraffito decoration in the free style, drawn through white slip over a red body. Byzantine, 12th century. STAATLICHE MUSEEN, BERLIN

ing. The impoverished Palaiologoi emperors (1261–1453) used earthenware even at state banquets.

The *mezza maiolica* made at Faenza at the end of the fourteenth century adopted a sgraffito decoration on slip. Ceramics from the Maghrib, Muslim Spain, and Egypt were imported by Pisa and sold at the Viterbo fair. Frederick II installed 50,000 Muslims from Sicily in Lucera; they were displaced to Naples by Charles II of Anjou. The Muslim potters settled in south Italy and introduced the polychrome ceramic painted on tin glaze known in the Near East since the ninth century. In tin-glazed earthenware (faience), the biscuit (once-fired clay) is dipped in a potash-lead glaze opacified with tin oxide. Metallic pigments are applied on the deposit and the whole is fired at high temperature. Tin glaze gave rise to the copper green and manganese purple *maiolica arcaica* of central and northern Italy and to the protomajolica of southern Italy and Sicily, which added a cobalt blue and an antimony yellow.

The exterior walls of Italian churches exhibit an astonishing corpus of glazed bowls of Islamic origin and of their Sicilian and local imitations. In the second half of the eleventh century there appeared in the region of Lucca bowls decorated in *cuerda seca*. This technique, which developed under the Almoravids, consists of applying over a tin glaze stripes of enamels separated by lines traced in manganese under a lead glaze.

Lusterware bowls, also embedded in the walls of Italian churches, were produced by applying oxides of copper or silver over the painting of tin-glazed ceramics. Firing in a reducing atmosphere fixed them as an iridescent film. Lusterware was produced in Málaga by the mid thirteenth century and in Manises, in Valencia. Spanish makers of pavements in this technique were invited to the court of Avignon and, by the duke of Berry, to Poitiers. Plates painted in green and purple (Paterna faience) were popular in European courts in the fifteenth century.

The technique of salt-glazed stoneware, refractory clay coated with common salt and vitrified at temperatures up to 1,400°C., evolved in the Rhineland during the fourteenth century after earlier trials. In France *terres de Beauvais* (proto-stoneware) were mounted in silver for Charles VI (1399). Utilitarian vessels in blue-glazed stoneware were first made in the Beauvaisis in the fifteenth century. A Beauvais dish decorated with religious and heraldic motifs in relief is dated 1511; a similar one in the Louvre was commissioned by Louis Villiers de l'Isle-Adam, bishop of Beauvais.

BIBLIOGRAPHY

The basic bibliography is given in Robert J. Charleston, ed., *World Ceramics: An Illustrated History* (1968); and Jay D. Frierman, *Medieval Ceramics: VI to XIII Centuries* (1975). See also Elizabeth S. Ettinghausen, "Byzantine Tiles from the Basilica in the Topkapu Sarayi and Saint John of Studios," in *Cahiers archéologiques,* 7 (1954); *Medieval Pottery from Excavations: Studies Presented to G. C. Dunning* (1974), 33–65; John Nowell Linton Myres, *A Corpus of Anglo-Saxon Pottery of the Pagan Period* (1977); David Talbot Rice, "The Pottery of Byzantium and the Islamic World," in *Studies in Islamic Art and Architecture in Honor of Professor K. A. C. Creswell* (1965), 194–240; and Jane A. Wight, *Mediaeval Floor Tiles: Their Design and Distribution in Britain* (1975).

PHILIPPE VERDIER

[See also **Azulejo; Bulgarian Art and Architecture; Ceramics, Islamic; Cuerda Seca; Faience; Lusterware; Majolica; Pottery.**]

CERAMICS, ISLAMIC. The Near East was the first region to glaze pottery and to apply its technical knowledge of polychrome glazes to making large-scale wall decorations. By the advent of Islam in the seventh century, few of the traditions of Babylon (Ishtar Gate, 7 B.C.), Susa (Achaemenid Palace, fifth–

Persian bowl with Kufic inscription. Samanid period, 10th century. COURTESY OF THE FREER GALLERY OF ART, SMITHSONIAN INSTITUTION, WASHINGTON, D.C.

fourth century B.C.), and Egypt (faience pottery, *ca.* 1300 B.C.) survived. The lead-glazed wares of Egypt and Syria and the blue-green alkaline glaze wares of Persia and Mesopotamia produced during the Umayyad caliphate (661–750) were not so distinctive in shape, imaginative design, and technical control of glaze color.

When Chinese stonewares (white and green [Yüeh], and splash wares) were shipped to ninth-century Iraq, the beauty of refined and thin-bodied ceramics was revealed and challenged the Near Eastern potters to enliven their clay surfaces. While the Chinese model ("white wares" including *ch'ing-pai,* Shu-fu, and Ting wares) was characteristically plain, the Islamic craftsmen tended to see the white background as merely a support for painting in metallic oxides: blue (cobalt), green (copper), purple (manganese), and yellow (antimony). The creation of white tin-glazed earthenware imitating Chinese white wares served as a preliminary step for luster painting—the most revolutionary ceramic techniques developed by Mesopotamian potters. The secrets of how to produce luster, originally borrowed from Egyptian glassmakers, were spread throughout the Near East and Europe by potters who moved to serve new demands for luxury wares. By the tenth century, luster was being made in Fatimid Egypt; it spread to North Africa and Spain, and to Syria and Iran, in the twelfth century.

Limited numbers of Islamic ceramic pieces

Persian bowl with stripe design in blue glaze, 12th or 13th century. COURTESY OF THE KIER COLLLECTION, LONDON

it was natural to experiment with glaze types because different glazes affected the nature of the pigment color. In the twelfth century the Persians, perhaps under the influence of immigrant Egyptian potters, substituted alkaline for lead glazes and created a new range of colors; copper oxide, for instance, produces green with a lead glaze and turquoise with an alkaline one. Under alkaline glaze cobalt ran less and was more widely used. To better fit or fuse the alkaline glaze, a frit body, once produced in ancient Egypt, was "reinvented." The compositional similarities between a frit body (a composite of quartz, frit, and clay) and an alkaline glaze (powdered quartz pebbles and potash) enabled them to fuse inseparably. The frit body, somewhat akin to European soft paste, was more malleable and easier to manipulate than earthenware, thus allowing greater refinement of vessel shape and wall. This advantage was needed by the twelfth-century Persian potter who sought to counterfeit the delicacy of Chinese porcelaneous white wares. To emphasize the translucence of the Iranian materials, a shadowy ornament was lightly carved into the surface under a thick transparent glaze, or patterns were pierced through the vessel walls and filled with "windows" of molten glaze.

During the development of underglaze polychromy, which, because of the variety found in metallic ores, could involve numerous colors, there has always been a problem of reconciling the reaction of

reached Europe during the Middle Ages. The Vatican owns an Egyptian splashware vessel once used as a reliquary, and a white carved semiporcelain cup preserved for its rarity as the chalice of San Girolamo. Islamic luster-painted bowls, prized for their color and brilliant surface, were embedded in the walls of some Italian churches. However, pottery was a neglected craft in Christian Europe during the Middle Ages, and local potters were not advanced enough to respond to these objects by copying them. Not until the thirteenth century, when Italian potters began to produce painted wares, did the decorative vocabulary of Islamic ceramic decoration enter the local repertoire. Under Islamic influence from North Africa or Spain, Italian potters absorbed the techniques of tin-glazing and luster painting.

Experiments with slip painting in ninth-century Iran were an initial step toward achieving true underglaze painting that eventually had wide application. In this technique a vessel was first enveloped by a white engobe (a mixture halfway between clay and glaze) that provided a gleaming neutral surface for olive green, purplish black, or tomato-red slips (thin flowing clay). By striving for thinner and thinner slips, and testing the viscosity of their lead glazes until the pigment alone could be fixed under the glaze, the potters were limited only by their ability with the brush.

In the search for a successful underglaze formula,

Egyptian bowl with luster-painted decoration, 11th or 12th century. COURTESY OF THE KIER COLLECTION, LONDON

the ores with the glaze under the high heat of the kiln. Minai ware was the tentative solution proposed by thirteenth-century Iranian potters who laid blue, purple, and green under the glaze, followed by white, red, and brown enamels fired over the glaze at a lower temperature. Minai, along with lajvardina wares, anticipated overglaze enameling of fifteenth-century China and eighteenth-century Europe.

The final impetus for the development of polychrome underglaze painting came around 1400 with the arrival of Chinese porcelain in the Near East. This porcelain was a hard-bodied ware often decorated with bright colors and complex designs, originally made specifically to appeal to Near Eastern taste. Large quantities of Ming porcelain were amassed in Near Eastern collections, and their color scheme and formal motifs served as the dominant models for ceramic design in Iran, Syria, Egypt, and Turkey from the fifteenth century on. Gradually, as in each previous Far Eastern export wave, the Islamic craftsmen transformed and integrated this foreign inspiration. The dialogue between China and Islam on questions of technique and artistic vocabulary was one of cross-fertilization and was critical to the whole of ceramic history.

BIBLIOGRAPHY

K. A. C. Creswell, A Bibliography of the Architecture, Arts and Crafts of Islam (1961); also Supplement (1973); Alice Wilson Frothingham, Lustrewares of Spain (1951: Arthur Lane, Early Islamic Pottery: Mesopotamia, Egypt and Persia (1958); Arthur Lane, Later Islamic Pottery: Mesopotamia, Egypt and Persia (1971); O. Watson, "Persian Lustre-Painted Pottery; The Rayy and Kashan Styles," in Transactions of the Oriental Ceramic Society, 1–18 (1973–5), plates 1–16.

MARINA D. WHITMAN

[See also Lajvardina.]

CERCAMON was one of the earliest troubadours. The Old Provençal vidas report that he was a jongleur of Gascon origin and that he composed vers and pastoretas in the old fashion. No pastourelles by Cercamon survive; manuscripts preserve only seven songs that are authentically his, and an eighth bearing his name is probably apocryphal. Although it is impossible to determine the precise identity of this poet from the pseudonym Cercamon (search the world), by which he is known, allusions within his songs to specific historical persons and events help

to fix the years of his poetic activity within certain bounds. His planh (lament) on the death of William X of Aquitaine evidently dates from 1137; and a second poem, a tenso, must have been conceived at roughly the same time, for it concerns the marriage of Eleanor, daughter of William X, to the future Louis VII. Elsewhere, a probable reference to the impending Second Crusade would seem to extend his career through at least 1145. A large part of Cercamon's fame rests on the traditionally held belief contained in one of the vidas that the great Marcabru was his disciple.

BIBLIOGRAPHY

An edition is Les poésies de Cercamon, Alfred Jeanroy, ed. (1922). See also Robert Allen Taylor, La littérature occitane du moyen âge (1977), 63–64.

ELIZABETH WILSON POE

[See also **French Literature: After 1200; Marcabru; Pastourelle; Provençal Literature: To Twelfth Century; Tenso; Troubadour, Trouvère, Trovadores.**]

CHAINED BOOKS. Because of the great expense of its constituent parts and the amount of labor invested in its production, the medieval book was far more valuable than its modern counterpart. In late medieval libraries the most frequently used volumes were arranged on racks so they could be consulted easily. The books were often attached to the racks with chains to prevent displacement and removal from the library. Examples of this kind of library system can still be seen at the Hereford Cathedral Library or in the Laurentian Library, Florence.

BIBLIOGRAPHY

Fritz Milkau and George Leyh, eds., Handbuch der Bibliothekswissenschaft, III, pt. 1 (1955), 279; Burnett N. Streeter, The Chained Library (1931, repr. 1970).

MICHAEL MCCORMICK

[See also **Libraries; Manuscript and Book Production.**]

CHAIRETE, a Greek greeting, literally "Oh, joy," the first word Christ spoke after his resurrection, to Mary Magdalene and Mary, mother of James (Matthew 28:9). Representations of the Chairete showed the two Maries kneeling at Christ's feet; the two women, who were usually indistinguishable from one another, were shown either together at one side

Christ appearing to the two Maries outside the tomb. Leaf from an ivory diptych, Rome, *ca.* 400. CASTELLO SFORZESCO, CIVICHE RACCOLTE D'ARTE, MILAN

(as in the Rabula Gospels) or flanking Christ (as at St. Mark's, Venice). Latin theologians favored the version of Christ's resurrection given in the Gospel of John, where Christ's first appearance was to Mary Magdalene alone (John 20:11–18), so depictions of the Chairete, although not unknown in the West (for instance, a Carolingian ivory in the Vatican), were rare until the Trecento. In Byzantium the Chairete passage from Matthew was part of the lection on the Saturday before Easter, and representations were common in both monumental and manuscript art. Italian artists of the Trecento (such as Duccio), under Byzantine influence, also painted the Chairete.

BIBLIOGRAPHY

James Breckenridge, "Et Prima Videt: The Iconography of the Appearance of Christ to His Mother," in *Art Bulletin*, **39** (1957).

LESLIE BRUBAKER

CHALCEDON, COUNCIL OF. See **Councils, Ecumenical.**

CHALDER, a measure of capacity for dry products in England, Wales, and Scotland. In England the

standard coal chalder, first regulated in 1421, contained 32 bushels totaling 2,000 pounds (907.185 kilograms) and equal to one-twentieth keel of 20 tons. In 1676–1677 it was increased to 36 heaped bushels totaling 2,240 pounds (1,016.040 kilograms). The chalder of sea coal always varied from these standards, generally containing 48 bushels (about 21.62 hectoliters). Prior to 1695 the Newcastle coal chalder weighed 42 long hundredweight (2,133.684 kilograms); afterward it was 72 heaped bushels totaling 53 long hundredweight or 5,936 pounds (2,692.510 kilograms) and equal to one-eighth keel. The Scottish grain chalder was fixed by 1600 at 16 bolls or 140,629.44 cubic inches (23.049 hectoliters) for wheat, peas, beans, rye, and white salt, and 205,153.53 cubic inches (33.625 hectoliters) for barley, oats, and malt. In Wales and other parts of the British Isles, however, there were numerous variations for these and other products.

RONALD EDWARD ZUPKO

[See also **Weights and Measures, Western European.**]

CHALICE (from Latin *calix,* "cup"), the cup used for the eucharistic wine of the Christian Mass. Early Christian examples, known from representations in

Silver chalice with apostles. Syria, 6th century. WALTERS ART GALLERY, BALTIMORE

the catacombs, seem to have been simple, stemless bowls with handles on either side; most medieval examples are stemmed vessels, usually of precious metals elaborately decorated with gems, enamels, or incised designs.

LESLIE BRUBAKER

CHAMBERLAIN. As with most of the titles of the great officers of state, "chamberlain" has its origin in a humble set of tasks associated with a primitive level of social organization. A *camerarius (camerlengus, cambellanus)* was a household serf, domestic servant, valet, or (since the feminine form of the word had currency in the Middle Ages) lady's maid. The *camerarius* performed his menial duties in the bedroom, which was often a place to hoard treasure. From an early date, therefore, the *camerarius* of a princely household became a chamberlain in the common modern sense of the word—that is, a treasurer, a meaning attested from the time of Gregory of Tours. By extension, it was common to use *camerarius* as a synonym for any official who dealt with matters of finance, whether in a subordinate or a supervisory capacity or in the context of a monastery, a town, a cathedral, or the Roman curia.

The authority associated with the office of chamberlain varied from place to place in Europe. The chamberlain of the Roman curia, an official in existence from the time of Gregory VII, exercised supervisory control over the prebendal revenues of the cardinals. In the kingdom of Bohemia the chamberlain seems to have performed duties by the late twelfth century that have led at least one historian to refer to him as a "minister of finance." In France, on the other hand, the position of the chamberlain is not so easily described.

In the first place, the French chamberlain's administrative duties were restricted to care and supervision of objects and revenues that pertained to the personal needs of the monarch and his household. But from the late twelfth through the mid thirteenth century, when France was undergoing some of the most profound administrative changes in its history, the office of chamberlain, which might have developed into the office of treasurer, failed to do so. The reason usually invoked to explain the failure is the Crown's decision to use the Order of the Temple as its banker. The expansion of the chamberlain's duties was, therefore, arrested. By the mid thirteenth

century the position had been further diluted by the multiplication of officials who enjoyed the title but who performed the duties of financial clerks. There was a hierarchy among these clerks and some of them, such as Pierre de la Broce in the reigns of Louis IX and Philip III, exercised considerable influence. The historic office of chamberlain *du roi,* as opposed to these clerical positions, persisted as an honorific dignity.

After the suppression of the Templars in 1312, the Crown was forced to develop a sophisticated treasury within the government. The groundwork for this had already been laid by the creation of the Chambre des Comptes in the late thirteenth century, the institutional outgrowth of the auditing of royal accounts that had been going on since the twelfth century. The chamberlain *du roi* had little to do with this development, whereas the clerical chamberlains were instrumental in shaping the institution. The position of chamberlain *du roi* was suppressed in 1545.

In England, too, a striking dichotomy existed between the chamberlain as a great officer of state (the lord great chamberlain) and the chamberlains (clerks) who handled finance. In the Anglo-Saxon period no such scholarly distinction can be made. The Anglo-Saxon *camerarius* supervised public expenditures and advised his king. But the creation of the Exchequer in the twelfth century seems to have driven a wedge between the officer of state and the finances of the Crown. The Exchequer began to control finance, and although a king might often use the treasure in his personal chamber in preference to the Exchequer to pay his debts, the chamberlains who ran the chamber had nothing in common with the lord great chamberlain: they were purely clerks. By being less public and eventually less weighted by legal formality than the Exchequer, the chamber became one of the preferred instruments of royal finance, especially in times of war. The king might call upon his chamberlains to pay the expenses of war with money in the chamber (deposited there by the Exchequer).

The further history of the relations of these two institutions—chamber and Exchequer—and the emergence of a third, the wardrobe, cannot be treated here. What needs to be stated, however, is that the historic officer of the household, the lord great chamberlain, though he shared the title "chamberlain" with the clerks who monitored finances, had nothing to do with these developments. As J. H. Round put it, "In England the association of the

Chamberlain with the King's treasure is lost sight of so early that it is practically non-existent."

Indeed, the main duty of the lord great chamberlain in the Middle Ages was the ceremonial serving of water to the king at his coronation, and perhaps on the great feast days.

BIBLIOGRAPHY

Ferdinand Lot and Robert Fawtier, *Histoire des institutions françaises au moyen âge,* II (1958), 54–56; Achille Luchaire, *Manuel des institutions françaises* (1892), 523–524; Bryce Lyon, *A Constitutional and Legal History of Medieval England,* 2nd ed. (1980), 53–54, 266; Heinrich Mitteis, *Der Staat des hohen Mittelalters* (1968), 394; John Horace Round, *The King's Serjeants and Officers of State* (1911; repr. 1971), 112–140.

WILLIAM CHESTER JORDAN

[See also **Exchequer.**]

CHAMPAGNE, COUNTY. Champagne is the region of open country *(campi)* directly to the east of Paris and bounded by the Aisne, Meuse, and Yonne rivers. Lacking natural borders and a central geographical focus, it has long served as a route between the Mediterranean and the North Sea, as well as a frontier zone between France and Germany. In the twelfth century the region was forged into a cohesive principality that ranked among the most powerful and prosperous states within the kingdom of France.

EARLY HISTORY (TO 1152)

Champagne was divided between two provinces in the late Roman Empire. The northern half with the cities of Rheims and Châlons-sur-Marne lay in Belgica Secunda, a frontier province facing Germanic tribes. Rheims was the linchpin of the Roman defense system, being the pivot at which the trunk road from the Mediterranean and Lyons branched to the north and east. Troyes, Chaumont, and Langres in southern Champagne belonged to the rear-line province of Lugdunensis centered at Lyons. The Christian church, following the Roman administrative example, split Champagne between the archiepiscopal sees of Rheims and Sens.

With the collapse of Roman defenses in 406, Champagne was overrun by various tribes, which left the Franks in their wake to settle the area. Christian Romans and pagan Franks had a difficult time

of accommodation in the fifth century, but after the defeat of Attila the Hun (451) near Troyes, and the baptism of King Clovis (*ca.* 496) as an orthodox rather than Arian Christian by Remigius (St. Remi), bishop of Rheims, a rapid fusion of the two peoples followed. The division of Frankish lands at the death of Clovis in 511 placed all Champagne within the kingdom (Austrasia) of his son Clothar I.

Gregory of Tours mentions a duke of Champagne in the sixth century, but nothing is known about him or his duchy. In the late sixth or early seventh century southern Champagne became part of the duchy of Burgundy; it remained undeveloped and unimportant until the twelfth century. Northern Champagne entered the heartland of the Frankish kings, the duchy of Francia, where extensive royal fisc lands and subsidized monasteries were located, and where royal crownings and burials were celebrated. In the late ninth century, however, the Northmen reduced those flourishing lands to a war zone from which monks fled with their relics to the isolation of southern Champagne.

The legacy of Charlemagne's administrative system, whereby counts were entrusted with one or more territories *(pagi)* and prelates were granted extensive immunities, was extreme fragmentation of political authority in Champagne. In the tenth and eleventh centuries several attempts were made to regroup various counties into larger political units, although scant and uneven documentation reveals only the broad contours of those enterprises. The two most notable initiatives, by the counts of Vermandois and Blois, sought to link northern Champagne with more western counties on an east-west axis, while southern Champagne was abandoned to younger sons.

The count of Vermandois, Herbert II (900/907–943), acquired the county of Meaux by marriage and attempted to control the county of Rheims by placing his infant son on the see of Rheims (925) and seizing the episcopal temporalities. He was foiled by King Louis IV and the rival archbishop, Artaud, and his successors failed to master the emerging forces of episcopal cities, immune monasteries, and independent counties on the northern periphery of Champagne. Herbert II's youngest son, Robert, inherited Meaux (943) and secured by marriage the adjoining county of Troyes (*ca.* 950); his own son, Herbert the Younger (966–995), added Épernay and probably Châlons-sur-Marne. But the counts of Meaux-Troyes died out with Stephen (995–1019/1021), and their lands became inheritance portions

243

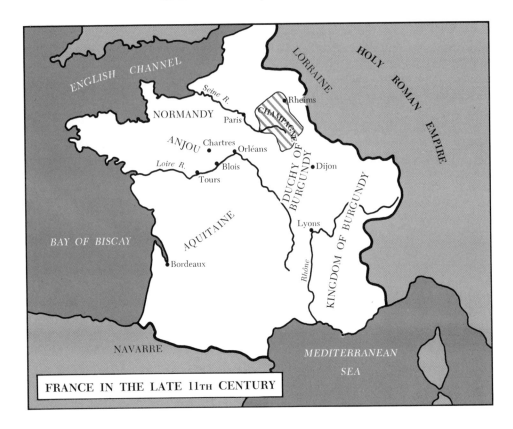

ENGLISH CHANNEL

LORRAINE

HOLY ROMAN EMPIRE

Seine R.
●Rheims

NORMANDY

Paris

CHAMPAGNE

ANJOU

Chartres
●
Orléans

Loire R.

●Blois

Tours

DUCHY OF BURGUNDY

Dijon●

BAY OF BISCAY

AQUITAINE

Lyons●

KINGDOM OF BURGUNDY

Rhône

●Bordeaux

NAVARRE

MEDITERRANEAN SEA

FRANCE IN THE LATE 11TH CENTURY

for younger sons of the counts of Blois, who were to dominate the later history of Champagne.

Count Odo II of Blois-Chartres-Tours (996–1037) nearly created a principality straddling the royal domain by acquiring almost all the lands of Champagne, including the countries of Meaux-Troyes (1021). However, in the course of the eleventh century the counts lost control of the northern episcopal cities to their prelates: Odo II sold his rights in Rheims to the archbishop (1023); and Count Thibaut I (1037–1089) was driven from Châlons-sur-Marne by its bishop and had to share Meaux with the bishop there. Thus the lands and interests of the counts became concentrated between the Marne and Yonne rivers, and the county of Troyes, with the sole remaining episcopal city from which the counts had not been displaced, emerged as the natural center of Champagne.

Count Thibaut's third son, Hugh, began the political consolidation of Champagne. Count of Troyes (1093–1125) by inheritance and master of the adjacent counties of Bar-sur-Aube and Vitry by marriage, Hugh controlled the triangular area between the espiscopal principalities of Sens, Langres, and Châlons-sur-Marne. Although a minor baron in comparison with his brother Stephen-Henry, count of Blois-Chartres-Meaux (1089–1102), Count Hugh nevertheless became the dominant political force in Champagne. After participating in the First Crusade, he actively supported the monastic reform movement of Molesme and helped to found Clairvaux (1115). His vassal Hugh of Payns founded the Knights Templar (1119), who were sponsored by Bernard of Clairvaux at the Council of Troyes (1128) and eulogized in his *In Praise of the New Knighthood*. After Count Hugh dispossessed his son on suspicion of illegitimacy, he transferred his three counties to his nephew Thibaut, count of Blois, and joined the Templars.

Thibaut II, count of Blois-Chartres-Meaux (1102–1152), realized that his lands on the Loire, encircled by powerful and aggressive neighbors (Anjou, Normandy, the royal domain), had an uncertain future. With the acquisition of Troyes, Vitry, and Bar-sur-Aube in 1125, he possessed (with Meaux) four contiguous counties in Champagne that still escaped domination by any single lord, and he turned his energies to that area. He continued Count Hugh's support of reformed monasteries, particularly of the Cistercians during their rapid expansion under Bernard of Clairvaux. It was in Thibaut's lands that Abelard found refuge and later built an oratory dedicated to the Paraclete that became a monastery under Abbess Heloise (1129). Thibaut developed close ties with King Louis VI and served as guardian to young Louis VII, whom he accompanied to Bordeaux for marriage with Eleanor of Aquitaine (1137). Later a dispute with Louis VII resulted in the invasion of Champagne by a royal army and the sack of Vitry (1142–1143). To protect his lands from seizure by the king, Thibaut established formal ties of homage with the duke of Burgundy (for the county of Troyes and other lands) and the bishop of Langres (for the county of Bar-sur-Aube). Henceforth only the county of Meaux was susceptible to direct royal confiscation.

Thibaut II initiated far-reaching economic policies in Champagne. He enticed traveling merchants from their traditional itineraries through Langres, Châlons-sur-Marne, and Rheims to new routes passing through his own lands, specifically the river routes of the Seine and Aube that led to Troyes and Bar-sur-Aube, then to Provins and Lagny. By safeguarding routes and merchants and by creating a regular cycle of fair days in his towns, he ensured that Champagne would become a distribution point for grain, wine, and salt, and later, after the fairs had become international in scope, for cloth, furs, spices, and luxury goods.

THE COUNTY (1152–1284)

When Count Henry I the Liberal (1152–1181) succeeded his father, he chose as his inheritance the lands of Champagne instead of the ancestral county of Blois, which then passed to his younger brother. The shift to Champagne, already prepared by Thibaut II, was natural for Henry, whose attachments were all in Champagne. He had acquired an excellent education there and at an early age had been associated with his father in the administration of those lands. In 1147 he accompanied Louis VII on the Second Crusade, was knighted at the request of Bernard of Clairvaux by the Byzantine emperor in Constantinople, and saw action against the Turks. Impressed by the young count's performance, the king permitted the engagement of Henry to Marie, his daughter by Eleanor of Aquitaine.

Although Henry continued to style himself count of Troyes, he was more commonly and properly known as the count of Champagne. The new principality was unusual in that the count held his lands as fiefs from an exceptional number of lords: the em-

peror (for several minor holdings), the king (for Meaux), the duke of Burgundy (for Troyes), the archbishops of Rheims (for Vitry) and Sens (for several castellanies), the bishop of Langres (for Bar-sur-Aube), and the abbot of St. Denis. For the first time these lands formed a single principality.

Within Champagne, the old counties were superseded by smaller, overlapping administrative districts of domanial and feudal lands organized around the count's towns. In his domanial lands provosts were appointed to collect rents and taxes, to select mayors of villages, and to render justice. The count's central financial bureau probably kept records of payments from each domanial district (*prévôté*), although no accounts survive from the twelfth century. The earliest known administrative register is the *Feoda Campanie* (*ca.* 1172), which lists the names of all the count's feudal tenants with the location and duration of their required castle guard. Knights who had been enfeoffed by the count or his predecessors were organized into castellanies under castellans or viscounts. In his twenty-six castellanies the count had 1,900 tenants, ranging from simple knights to great barons (such as Traînel and Joinville) and the lords of quasi-independent counties at the extremities of Champagne: Château-Porcien, Rethel, and Grandpré in the north; Brienne, Bar-sur-Seine, and Joigny in the south.

Henry I continued his father's economic policies, and from his reign Champagne experienced 150 years of sustained economic and demographic growth. Immigrants were encouraged to clear land on the count's domain and to settle in his towns, the largest urban centers in the county. Merchants from Italy and northern Europe established branch houses in the twin capitals of Troyes and Provins, whose normal populations of 15,000 and 10,000 respectively swelled during the fairs. These towns also developed local industries, particularly in cloth and leather. The count's coins, minted in Troyes and Provins, circulated throughout the county, and in the course of the thirteenth century the *provinois* came to prevail within the county and served at the fairs as an international currency. Despite its fairs, Champagne remained a principality of relatively small towns; castellany towns that served as administrative centers rarely numbered more than 2,000 persons and retained a distinctly rural flavor through the thirteenth century.

Henry I was renowned for his generosity to the church, and most of his 400 charters are grants or confirmations of gifts to religious institutions. He

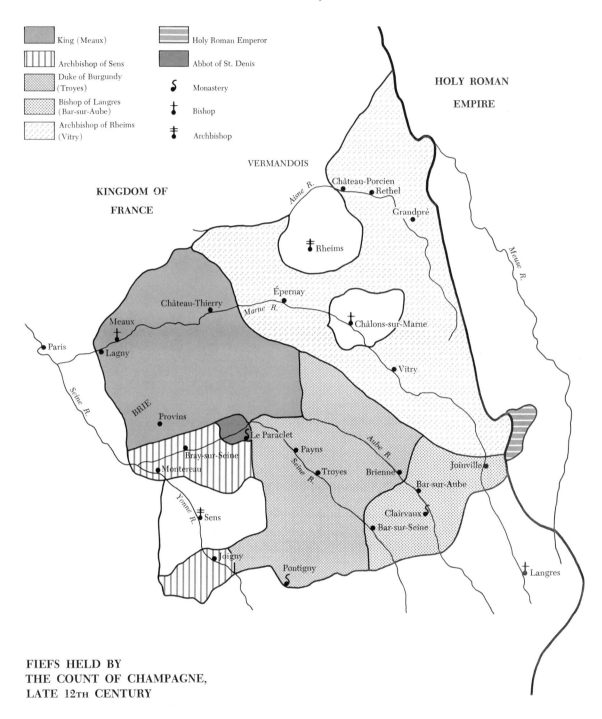

King (Meaux)

Archbishop of Sens

Duke of Burgundy (Troyes)

Bishop of Langres (Bar-sur-Aube)

Archbishop of Rheims (Vitry)

Holy Roman Emperor

Abbot of St. Denis

⌇ Monastery

☦ Bishop

☦ Archbishop

HOLY ROMAN EMPIRE

KINGDOM OF FRANCE

VERMANDOIS

Château-Porcien
Rethel
Grandpré

Rheims

Aisne R.

Meuse R.

Épernay
Château-Thierry
Marne R.
Châlons-sur-Marne

Meaux
Lagny
Paris

Vitry

Seine R.

BRIE

Provins

Le Paraclet

Bray-sur-Seine
Montereau

Payns
Seine R.
Troyes
Brienne
Aube R.
Joinville

Bar-sur-Aube

Yonne R.
Sens

Clairvaux
Bar-sur-Seine

Joigny
Pontigny

Langres

FIEFS HELD BY THE COUNT OF CHAMPAGNE, LATE 12TH CENTURY

founded several chapters of secular canons, primarily to serve his administrative needs. St. Etienne of Troyes (1157), one of the largest chapters in the kingdom, was built next to his palace to serve as his chancery and treasury. St. Quiriace of Provins performed similar functions in his second city.

Henry and his wife patronized a number of writers of various interests, such as Nicholas of Clair-

vaux (former secretary of Bernard of Clairvaux), the spiritual writer Peter of Celle, and the poets Chrétien de Troyes and Gautier d'Arras, although few of them attended the court of Champagne regularly. Henry was well read in classical and religious literature, while Marie's taste inclined to lyric poetry and romances in the current vernacular.

Henry's marriage in 1159 sealed an enduring if

not entirely harmonious alliance with the royal family. His brother Thibaut, count of Blois, married the second daughter of Louis VII and Eleanor of Aquitaine and became royal seneschal, while the king in turn married their sister Adele. Their youngest brother, William, archbishop of Rheims, acted as regent with Queen Adele in 1190 when their nephew, King Philip II, left the kingdom for the Third Crusade. In the thirteenth century the fate of Champagne on several occasions depended on the royal family.

Countess Marie acted as regent (1181–1187) for her eldest son Henry II, who ruled only briefly in his own right (1187–1190). On departing for the Third Crusade, the unmarried Henry II named his mother as regent (1190–1197) and had the Champagne barons swear to accept his younger brother Thibaut as count, in the event of his death. Henry accompanied his uncles, the counts of Blois and Sancerre, to the Holy Land and later, after the departure of Richard the Lion-hearted and Philip II, emerged as leader of the crusading forces. He was respected as much for his commitment of funds, sent regularly by his mother from Champagne, as for his military prowess. Drawn into an unsavory marriage to the queen of Jerusalem, he died in 1197 under mysterious circumstances.

Thibaut III (1197–1201) was only eighteen in 1197 but assumed control of the county after the death of Countess Marie the next year. With the enthusiastic support of the Champagne barons, in whose families crusading had become a tradition, Thibaut responded to Pope Innocent III's call to organize the Fourth Crusade. Geoffrey de Villehardouin, marshal of Champagne, supervised the logistical arrangements and helped to negotiate a treaty with the Venetians for passage to Cairo; he later wrote an account of the expedition and its diversion from crusade to outright conquest of Constantinople and Byzantine provinces. The marshal's nephew, also named Geoffrey, and William of Champlitte (descendant of Count Hugh of Troyes) led the conquest of the Morea (the Greek Peloponnese) and established a Frankish principality there (1204–1278). Thibaut III, however, died (May 1201) before the expedition left France. He had made significant territorial acquisitions to the county—the castellanies of Nogent-sur-Seine, Ste. Menehould, and Chaumont-en-Bassigny—and had initiated a policy of expansion that his widow and son continued.

Thibaut's premature death posed a delicate question of succession, for he left an infant daughter and a wife ready to deliver a second child. It was later argued that the two daughters of Henry II by his Eastern marriage had better claims to the county. Thibaut's widow, Blanche of Navarre, did homage at once to the three lords (the king, the archbishop of Rheims, and the duke of Burgundy) from whom the major part of Champagne was held in fief, and surrendered her daughter and the castles of Bray-sur-Seine and Montereau to the king. Within days she gave birth to a son, for whom she was guardian until his majority (1201–1222).

An astute and energetic regent, Countess Blanche reinforced castles and acquired or built new ones, especially in the Bassigny, where Thibaut III had recently obtained Chaumont. She generated resentment among the barons not only because she was foreign-born but also because she moved quickly and decisively to strengthen comital powers at the expense of the barons. At her order, all arrangements regarding feudal matters were put into writing and carefully preserved in a collection that would become the first systematic archives of the counts. Like Countess Marie before her, Blanche was praised by chroniclers for acting *viriliter*.

In a series of commitments King Philip II promised to protect the interests of young Thibaut IV; and at Blanche's request he took the boy's homage in 1214, although the minority would continue until 1222. A rebellion was brewing in the southeastern corner of the county as a network of families and allies rallied behind the pretensions of Erard of Brienne, lord of Ramerupt, who would marry Henry II's youngest daughter Phillipa in 1215 in order to claim the county as her inheritance. Brienne's legal challenge at the royal court of Melun (1216) was dismissed out of hand. He responded by unleashing a civil war in southern Champagne (1217–1218), but the rebellion lasted only until Blanche detached his most powerful ally, the duke of Lorraine. Brienne settled for £4,000 and an annuity of £1,200.

Contemporary chroniclers and poets painted an unflattering portrait of Thibaut IV (1222–1253). The count's unseemly haste in abandoning King Louis VIII's siege of Avignon (1226) after fulfilling the minimum forty-day feudal service was compounded by conduct suggesting a romantic attachment to the regent queen, Blanche of Castile. Delegated by recalcitrant French barons to negotiate with the queen (1227), Thibaut apparently failed to represent their position. Under Peter of Dreux and the duke of Burgundy, the French barons retaliated by invading Champagne in 1229–1230, causing much destruction

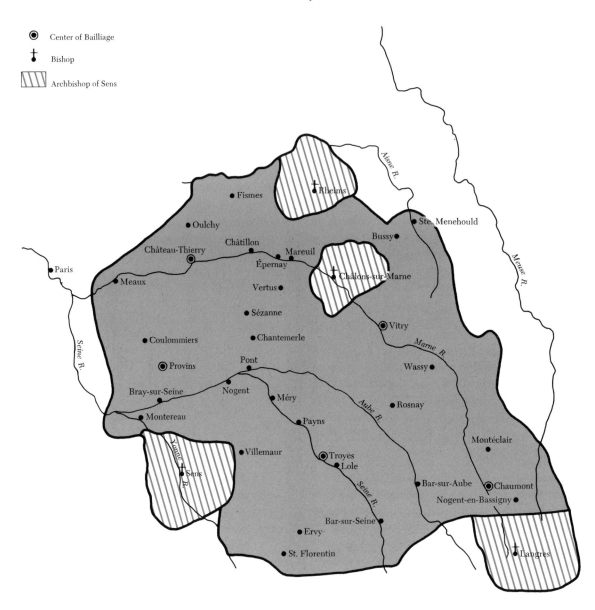

Center of Bailliage
Bishop
Archbishop of Sens

CASTELLANIES OF CHAMPAGNE,
MID 13TH CENTURY

in the area around Troyes. Only the intervention of the queen mother and young Louis IX at the head of a royal army saved Thibaut, who had already set fire to several of his own towns in a desperate scorched-earth policy.

Disaffection among the Champagne barons explains Thibaut's weak resistance. His townsmen, however, conducted a vigorous defense, in appreciation for which he granted them communal franchises in 1230–1231. Tailles and other personal taxes were commuted to self-assessed annual taxes on real property; commercial transactions were simplified and legal procedures regularized. Moreover, the townsmen were allowed to select their own mayor and town council to collect taxes and fines and to adjudicate all cases except high justice (murder, rape, larceny). Most of the Champagne castellany towns were enfranchised, including the largest population centers of Troyes, Provins, and Bar-sur-Aube. In effect the franchises created privileged areas within the county that became even more powerful magnets to immigrants, for anyone residing within the franchise for one year and one day acquired the privileges.

In 1233 the second daughter of Henry II, Alix, queen of Cyprus, arrived in France to claim the county. Thibaut bought her off for £40,000 and an annuity of £2,000; but unable to come up with ready cash, he sold his feudal rights over the ancestral lands of Blois, Sancerre, and Châteaudun to the king (1234). In the same year Thibaut inherited the kingdom of Navarre through his mother, and thereafter he and his sons spent much of their time in Navarre and traveling between their two lands.

Contemporaries knew of Thibaut IV le Chansonnier as a poet of distinction. They did not know that he was responsible for administrative reforms that made Champagne one of the best governed states of the time. Shortly after his accession, chancery record-keeping procedures at St. Etienne of Troyes were thoroughly reorganized. The archives were reclassified, and all incoming correspondence was preserved in current files. Thibaut's own acts were registered as they were issued, and all homages rendered to the count, either orally or in writing, for fiefs inherited or otherwise obtained were recorded in order of performance.

In 1234 the prospect of Thibaut's prolonged absences in Navarre compelled the reorganization of senior administrative offices. The five baillis placed in charge of fixed districts of several castellanies (bailliages) became the most important administrative officials. They handled all feudal matters directly with the feudal tenants, and they collated the financial accounts of the provosts. At the central financial bureau two receivers managed the count's revenues, while a governor acted as chief executive officer in the count's absence.

In the 1240's Thibaut became aware of the serious financial difficulties of many feudal tenants who were alienating their fiefs, especially to ecclesiastical institutions without authorization. Having recently repurchased many fiefs from his own tenants, the count became sufficiently anxious about the situation to order a countywide inquest. The chapter of St. Quiriace of Provins surveyed all thirty-four Champagne castellanies in 1249–1250 and produced one of the most detailed inventories of feudal tenants and their possessions ever attempted in medieval France. Separate lists of recent alienations (within forty years) severely compromised many ecclesiastical houses, which were dispossessed forthwith. An ec-

clesiastical council at Sens (1252) reported that the count was deaf to all pleas to return the seized properties. The number of feudal tenants had already declined sharply in the thirteenth century: between 1172 and 1250 most castellanies had lost one-third of their tenants. The impoverishment of tenants and the subsequent alienation of fiefs were due in great part to the Champagne custom of dividing inheritances equally among all children, male and female alike. Even the regular territorial epxansion of the county—by almost 20 percent since 1198—had failed to check the steady decline of feudal tenants and their military obligations.

Tenurial and familial conflicts over fiefs were often resolved by the *Jours* of Troyes, the baronial court that handled appeals from decisions of the baillis. The *Jours* probably existed from the mid thirteenth century, although its earliest known judgments date from the 1270's. Some of its decisions were later compiled in a private collection of feudal customs, the *Coutumier* (*ca.* 1290) of Champagne, which remains a valuable casebook of feudal law in the late thirteenth century.

The reigns of Thibaut V (1253–1270) and his brother Henry III (1270–1274) were peaceful. Thibaut V married King Louis IX's daughter Isabelle and often attended the king in Paris, where he maintained a residence. He died in Tunis in the company of the king on the Crusade of 1270. With Henry III the independence of the county ended. His daughter Jeanne (*b.* 1273), heir apparent after the childhood death of her brother, was affianced to a royal son in 1275. She came into full possession of the county in January 1285, several months after her marriage to the future King Philip IV, who styled himself king of Navarre and count palatine of Champagne and Brie until he assumed the throne in October 1285.

With its attachment to the crown inevitable, Champagne came under increasing royal influence. King Philip III had issued instructions to the Champagne baillis since 1280, and Philip IV staffed the *Jours* of Troyes with royal officials after 1285. Thereafter the county was administered as if it were a royal province. At the death of Queen Jeanne (2 April 1304), the future Louis X took title to Champagne although his father retained actual control. Champagne was to have passed to Louis X's daughter Jeanne when his brother Philip V became king (1316), but Jeanne was effectively dispossessed, being permitted only Navarre and a sum of money with which to purchase other lands. The last Capetian king, Charles IV, assigned most of Champagne as dower income for his wife (1325). It was probably at this time that the archives and all administrative records of Champagne were moved to the royal Chamber of Accounts in Paris; the *Jours* of Troyes had already become an appendage of the Parlement of Paris. When King John II declared in 1361 that Champagne was irrevocably attached to the crown, he was simply formalizing a state of affairs that had existed since 1285.

LATE MIDDLE AGES

Champagne suffered decline and misfortune after 1285. Its subordination to royal interests, the wars between France and England from the 1290's, and the shift of international trade from the overland to the Atlantic route all spelled disaster for the Champagne fairs and towns. Increasingly burdensome war taxes under Philip IV led to a revolt of the Champagne nobles in 1314; they joined other provincial leagues to complain about their fortunes under the royal hand, but they were not heard in Paris and royal tax collectors continued to squeeze the county.

The early stages of the Hundred Years War spared most of Champagne, but the Black Death ravaged the area in 1348. Ten years later the Jacquerie flared along the Marne and in Meaux, which was razed in retribution. As the social order unraveled, bands of brigands roamed and pillaged at will. The 1370's saw three devastating campaigns by English forces slash straight through the region from north to south. By the late fourteenth century demographic losses of 50 percent, and in some areas even 75 percent, were common. Many villages were abandoned, never to be resettled. Plague recurred through the fifteenth century, and dynastic wars between Burgundians and Orléanists prolonged the violence and hazards until the mid fifteenth century.

BIBLIOGRAPHY

Sources. There exists a huge collection of charters and cartularies, mostly unpublished, from the twelfth and thirteenth centuries; see the bibliography in Bur (cited below). The acts of the counts are imperfectly cataloged in Henri d'Arbois de Jubainville, *Histoire des ducs et des comtes de Champagne*, 6 vols. (1859–1866). Michel Bur and John F. Benton are currently editing the comital acts to 1197. The feudal, domanial, and financial registers of the counts are printed in Auguste Longnon, ed., *Documents relatifs au comté de Champagne et de Brie, 1172–1361*, 3 vols. (1901–1914); and *Rôles des fiefs du comté de Champagne sous le règne de Thibaud le Chansonnier, 1249–52* (1877). Champagne did not produce chroniclers of the counts or the county, but in the thirteenth century there appeared distinguished vernacular historians, Villehardouin and Joinville, whose works are translated in Margaret R. B. Shaw, *Chronicles of the Crusades* (1963). The feudal customary is in Paulette Portejoie, ed., *L'ancien coutumier de Champagne, XIIIᵉ siècle* (1956).

Studies. Maurice Crubellier, ed., *Histoire de la Champagne* (1975), is a general introduction. The basic work remains Arbois de Jubainville's *Histoire*, although the early period has been reworked by Michel Bur, *La formation du comté de Champagne, v. 950–v. 1150* (1977). See also John F. Benton, "The Court of Champagne as a Literary Center," in *Speculum*, 36 (1961); and "Philip the Fair and the Jours of Troyes," in *Studies in Medieval and Renaissance History*, 6 (1969); Elizabeth Chapin, *Les villes de foires de Champagne* (1937); Patrick Corbet, "Les collégiales comtales de Champagne (v. 1150–v. 1230)," in *Annales de l'Est*, 29 (1977); Theodore Evergates, *Feudal Society in the Bailliage of Troyes Under the Counts of Champagne, 1152–1284* (1975); and "A Quantitative Analysis of Fiefs in Medieval Champagne," in *Computers and the Humanities*, 9 (1975); Anne-Marie Patault, *Hommes et femmes de corps en Champagne méridionale à la fin du moyen âge* (1978); *Villages désertés et histoire économique, XIe–XVIIIe siècles* (1965), with preface by Fernand Braudel.

THEODORE EVERGATES

[See also **Chrétien de Troyes; Fairs of Champagne; Gautier d'Arras; Joinville, John of; Villehardouin, Geoffroi de.**]

CHAMPART, ROBERT. See **Robert of Jumièges.**

CHAMPION IN JUDICIAL COMBAT. In its broader sense "champion" refers to any participant in a judicial duel; in its narrower sense, which is discussed here, it means a participant who fights not in his own cause but on behalf of someone else. Such substitute combatants had a recognized role in most European legal systems. They could be used in duels settling both civil and criminal cases, though the rules for their use in the latter were much more restrictive. In civil cases it was common—indeed, at some times and in some places it was even required—that the duel occur not between the parties themselves but between witnesses, the witness on each side swearing that his principal's claim was just. The victorious champion won the case for his principal; the defeated champion not only lost his principal's case but also might be punished—by a fine, by loss of the ability to swear a valid oath in court, or even corporally (most commonly by the loss of a hand)—for his perjury in swearing to the truth of a false claim.

In criminal cases, duels were normally fought between accuser and accused, but certain obviously disadvantaged types of persons—women, children, the aged, the infirm, clerics—were usually granted the right to be represented by champions. This rule provided a dramatic situation that occurs repeatedly in literature: the inability of someone entitled or required to be represented by a champion to find one, and the consequent likelihood that that person will be unable to avenge a wrong or defend life or honor. Normally the problem is solved when a valiant champion appears by some miracle, ironic twist of fate, or other fortuitous event. If defeated in a duel stemming from a criminal charge, the champion might be punished in any of the ways indicated earlier or might even be executed. The death of a champion might also occur in the duel.

Originally champions were probably members of their principals' families; but in the later Middle Ages they did not have to be relatives, and some were professionals. Depending on the place, the period, and the type of case, the use of hired champions might be forbidden, permitted, or required. In general, in the course of time the attitude toward the use of professionals became increasingly permissive. Ecclesiastical institutions sometimes retained champions by granting them fiefs or pensions. Individuals more often hired them for particular trials; the successful champion might be rewarded with a grant of land, or a champion might be hired for a sum of money. The principal might also provide the champion's equipment and support him during a period of training. Although hired champions were subject to the same penalties for defeat as others, some men made successful careers of the profession.

Perhaps the most striking, and certainly the longest lasting, example of a champion is the Champion of England, who, at the coronation banquets of the kings and queens of England from Richard II (1377) (and perhaps earlier) through George IV (1821), ceremonially offered to fight anyone who denied the new monarch's just title to the throne.

BIBLIOGRAPHY

Cyril T. Flower, *Introduction to the Curia Regia Rolls, 1199–1230 A.D.* (1944), esp. 113–122; V. H. Galbraith, "The Death of a Champion, 1287," in R. W. Hunt, W. A. Pantin, and R. W. Southern, eds., *Studies in Medieval History Presented to Frederick Maurice Powicke* (1948), 283–295; Henry Charles Lea, *Superstition and Force* (1866), repr. as *The Duel and the Oath*, Edward Peters, ed. (1974), esp. pt. 2, ch. 7.

EMILY ZACK TABUTEAU

[See also **Chivalry; Oath; Law.**]

CHAMPLEVÉ ENAMEL. See **Enamel, Champlevé.**

CHANCEL (from Latin *cancellus*, "lattice" or "rail"), from the screen that often separated the chancel from the rest of the church. It is the area around the altar in the eastern end of a church reserved for clergy and choir, usually applied to the entire structure east of the crossing.

LESLIE BRUBAKER

CHANCEL SCREEN. See **Screen, Chancel.**

CHANCELLOR. See **Chancery.**

CHANCERY (from the Latin *cancellaria*), the office charged with preparing and dispatching the official letters and other documents issued by such public authorities as emperors, popes, and kings, and eventually by dukes, counts, seignorial lords, bishops, and cities as well. The archival function of preservation was usually also attached to the chancery.

The title *cancellarius* (chancellor) appears already in the fifth and sixth centuries for judges' assistants. The latter mediated between the judge and the parties to a case, who were separated from the judge by latticework screens *(cancelli)*. The unequivocal use of *cancellarius* for the director of the governmental secretariat seems to have originated with Charlemagne and to have spread gradually thereafter. Among many other names designating this official were *magister scrinii, primicerius notariorum, re-*

ferendarius, protonotarius, and *archicancellarius.* Since the chancellor saw all important royal documents, he was often entrusted with more substantive governmental duties. His responsibilities in the judicial, administrative, and political spheres made him at times almost a prime minister in France and in England. In such cases real control of the chancery was exercised by a vice-chancellor or another subordinate official. The title of chancellor was also applied to the *scholasticus,* originally the teacher attached to a cathedral church and then the official who, in the name of the pope, granted other teachers the license to teach and had legal jurisdiction over the members of a university community.

Governmental administrations with large volumes of official business needed to develop specialized secretariats to prepare official documents and correspondence efficiently in standardized forms. But chanceries were also needed both to make the authenticity of official documents more clearly recognizable and to render their forgery more difficult. Despite the obvious needs, the development of consistent and characteristic methods for dealing with the production and dispatch of documents was by no means everywhere uniform. As late as the twelfth century many charters issued by the kings of England had everything except their final validation prepared not by the royal chancery but by the recipient of the charter. Many lesser rulers, temporal and spiritual, had no chancery at all or at least none until the twelfth or thirteenth century.

The study of individual chanceries has become a central preoccupation of diplomatics. This discipline, first established on a solid footing by Jean Mabillon in *De re diplomatica* (1681), makes the determination of the authenticity of documents one of its primary purposes. Success in achieving this objective usually depends on the ability to show that the documents either conform or do not conform to the known practices of the chanceries from which they purport to issue.

The model, direct or indirect, for all medieval chanceries was the imperial Roman one. Its customs naturally survived under the Byzantine emperors, undergoing only the gradual changes to which any chancery would be subject during almost a millennium of existence. These practices were also taken over in varying degrees by the barbarian kingdoms that replaced the imperial authority in the West. The Ostrogoths under King Theodoric, many of whose letters are preserved in copies contained in Cassio-

dorus' *Variae,* were particularly faithful. Original documents from the chancery of the Merovingian Franks, the one barbarian kingdom established on Roman soil with a long future, begin to survive from the year 625.

But even before the barbarian kingdoms took over Roman imperial chancery ways, many of these ways had already been borrowed by the popes in the fourth century. Because the popes became directly involved in religious, and secular, matters throughout Europe and beyond, Roman practices may have exerted more influence indirectly through papal example than they had exercised directly. Eventually, of course, the papal chancery inaugurated as a result of its own needs and experiences many practices that were imitated elsewhere. The papal chancery, therefore, is preeminently worthy of study. Although no original papal document survives from before 788, many much earlier ones survive in copies.

The Carolingian dynasty began the narrow association of ecclesiastics, and particularly of bishops, with the royal or imperial chancellor's office. This association became typical of the western European monarchies until the fourteenth century or later, when laymen began to reappear in the office.

The most authoritative source material for the study of the customs of any particular chancery is furnished by the extant original documents that it issued. These not only will show whatever changes took place in the practices and formulas over the course of centuries, but may also reveal a certain variety and inconsistency in documents produced contemporaneously. The chief alternative sources are registers, formularies, chancery ordinances or guides, and cartularies. Registers contain the chancery's own copies of the documents that it has issued. For the papal chancery copies still exist of the registers of Gregory the Great, John VIII, and Gregory VII, while the original registers exist for almost all the popes beginning with Innocent III (1198–1216).

Registers for the various European royal chanceries begin to survive between the twelfth and fourteenth centuries. Those of the English kings, the first to survive, were entered on rolls. Registers do not, of course, preserve all the external features that help to characterize the products of a particular chancery, and they also omit or abbreviate some of the repeated formulas. Moreover, at least in the papal chancery, perhaps only about a tenth of the letters issued were registered. Formularies, which furnish model letters for a variety of purposes, survive from the Merovingian period onward, starting with the Formulary of Marculf from the early eighth century. Rulers or their chancellors eventually began to issue ordinances or guides for the personnel who would actually draft and copy their letters. These instructions sometimes throw light on the legal rationale for the formulas being used. Cartularies, because they consist of copies of charters, usually assembled at the behest of the recipient or beneficiary of the original charters, do not normally try to imitate the external features of a charter that help to characterize the issuing chancery, but they can offer valuable evidence about internal features.

Although one person could master all the tasks involved in the preparation of a document, the growing amount of business to be conducted generally led to an increase in personnel and a division of labor according to the separate steps involved. Some members were entrusted with drafting the text. In the papal chancery in the later Middle Ages these specialists were called *abbreviatores*.

The language of documents produced in Latin Christendom (including its Slavic and Hungarian regions) was usually Latin, though Old English was used for some pre-Conquest documents in England, and other vernacular languages began to be used in the later Middle Ages. In the Byzantine Empire, Greek began to supplant Latin in the sixth century; Arabic, Persian, Turkish, and Russian were used in other areas. If the document to be issued was in response to a petition, the petition itself would have been reformulated by a professional petition writer in the chancery in words that could serve as the basis for much of the text of the responding document.

There were many kinds of documents, differing widely in purpose and solemnity, but most of them had three main parts: an initial protocol, a body or text, and a final protocol or eschatocol. Each main part could in turn have a varying number of sections, depending on the nature and solemnity of the document of which it formed a part. The initial protocol might include an invocation, the names and titles of the author and recipient, and a greeting. The text might comprise a preamble, notification, narration, disposition, sanction, and corroboration. And the final protocol might include, along with the dating, the signatures or subscriptions of the witnesses, author, and chancery personnel. The drafter of the document could find models for the formulas used in the various sections of the document in the chancery registers, formularies, and ordinances.

At the end of the eleventh century the papal chancery under John of Gaeta began to reintroduce into the text of its letters the long-forgotten *cursus,* that is, the practice of ending clauses and sentences with certain rhythmical combinations of accented and unaccented syllables. The *cursus velox,* or rapid rhythm, the most popular of these endings in curial usage, consisted of a dactyl, a caesura, and then four syllables with a secondary accent on the first and the main accent on the third, for example, " . . . vínculum frègerámus." Although the use of the *cursus* was not limited to the papal chancery, a knowledge of it can nevertheless be helpful in unmasking forgeries of papal documents, as Pope Innocent III intimated in a decretal that he issued on this matter.

Notaries or scribes then transferred the text from the draft to the finished copy, which was normally on parchment, though papyrus continued to be used into the second half of the seventh century in the chancery of the Merovingian kings and into the mid eleventh century in the papal chancery. Paper, which was being produced in the Islamic world in the eighth century, was first used in the Byzantine imperial chancery in the second half of the eleventh century and in the Norman chancery in Sicily toward the end of that century.

A distinctive style of script was developed in many chanceries. The best known of these styles, which could help to authenticate the chanceries' products, was the Roman curial script used from the late eighth to the early twelfth centuries. It derived, as did the script of the Merovingian and Carolingian royal chanceries and that of many other documents, from the new Roman cursive script. Many later documentary scripts either were identical with the contemporary book scripts or differed from them in only a few artificial and unessential—but nevertheless very noticeable—respects. Eventually, however, most documents were written in new varieties of cursive scripts the origins of which go back only to the twelfth and thirteenth centuries. For many solemn documents the first line was written in a large grid- or trellislike script with letters elongated and otherwise distorted.

The final protocol, though it was copied mainly or entirely in the same script as the text, might involve the collaboration of other parties. This could occur if it required a personal subscription, initial, or other mark by the author, the witnesses, or higher chancery officials such as the *datarius* (who in the papal chancery became responsible for the dating) or the corrector. When a seal was used in addition to or instead of the author's signature, its custody and use were usually entrusted to the chancellor; but sometimes there was a special keeper of the seals (as in the French royal chancery under Philip II and most of his thirteenth-century successors), and in the papal chancery in the later Middle Ages the seal was in the custody of two Cistercian lay brothers called *bullatores*. Still other personnel might be entrusted with inserting the text of the document into the register.

The study of chanceries, besides answering essential questions about the authenticity of documents, can also throw light on the administrative efficiency of a governmental unit or on the degree of centralized authority that it has achieved. Because the increased efficiency made possible by a chancery may in turn increase the number of aspects of public life that a government can effectively bring under its centralized control, the study of chanceries may even be transformed from an auxiliary science into a substantive part of political history. Furthermore, seemingly innocent alterations of ancient formulas may reveal important changes either in political philosophy (for example, "king by the grace of God" instead of simply "king" in the title of a document) or in policy. A new dating formula introduced into papal documents in the late eighth century, for example, signals the subtraction of the pope's political allegiance from the emperor in Constantinople. Although the leading chanceries have been studied in great detail, the evidence they provide about life in the Middle Ages has still not been fully exploited. And for many lesser chanceries the study has hardly begun.

BIBLIOGRAPHY

Walther Björkman *et al.*, s.v. "Diplomatic," in *Encyclopaedia of Islam*, new ed., II (1965), 301–316; Harry Bresslau and Hans-Walter Klewitz, *Handbuch der Urkundenlehre für Deutschland und Italien*, 2nd ed., 2 vols. (1912–1931, repr. 1958); Christopher R. Cheney, *The Study of the Medieval Papal Chancery* (1966); Franz Dölger and Johannes Karayannopulos, *Byzantinische Urkundenlehre*, I (1968); Astrik L. Gabriel, "The Conflict Between the Chancellor and the University of Masters and Students at Paris During the Middle Ages," in *Miscellanea mediaevalia*, **10** (1976); Arthur Giry, *Manuel de diplomatique* (1894, repr. 1925); Hubert Hall, ed., *A Formula Book of English Official Historical Documents*, 2 vols. (1908–1909); Reginald L. Poole, *Lectures on the History of the Papal Chancery down to the Time of Innocent III* (1915); Michael Tangl, ed., *Die päpstlichen Kanzleiordnungen von 1200-1500* (1894, repr. 1959); Bertie Wilkinson, *The Chancery Under Edward III* (1929).

JAMES J. JOHN

[See also **Abbreviator; Alphabets; Bull, Papal; Cartulary; Charter; Diplomacy, Byzantine; Diplomacy, Islamic; Diplomacy, Western European; Paleography, Western European.**]

CHANSON. The term "chanson" poses a considerable semantic problem because it is used in so many contexts of literary scholarship and musicology, ranging from narrowly technical genre classifications to more broadly historical developments of song forms. French medieval chansons were originally any poetic forms combining words and music, including a wide range of lyric and narrative types (*chansons à danser, chansons de femme,* chansons de geste). In the twelfth and thirteenth centuries the term became more specifically limited to lyric love poems (*chansons d'amour*) of the northern trouvère poets, modeled on the canso of the southern troubadours. With technical virtuosity being a major feature of trouvère poetics, the *chanson d'amour* became a dominant form of expression, displaying an almost infinite variety of stanza patterns and rhyme schemes.

BIBLIOGRAPHY

Frederick Goldin, ed. and trans., *Lyrics of the Troubadours and Trouvères* (1973); Paul Zumthor, *Essai de poétique médiévale* (1972), 189–243.

THOMAS E. KELLY

[See also **Chansons de femme; Chansons de geste; Troubadour, Trouvère, Trovadores.**]

CHANSON D'ANTIOCHE. Lost in its original form, this poem, varying in length from 7,000 to 9,000 rhymed alexandrines, has come to us most notably through an adaptation written by Graindor de Douai around 1180. Of the original poet, only the name, Richard the Pilgrim, survives. Graindor mentions him a single time, and then merely to assure us that Richard knew the identities of the major Turkish chieftains present at the Battle of Antioch during the First Crusade. Citing this statement as well as the remarkable detail of the campaign narrative that reconstructs the Crusade from its inception with the vision of Peter the Hermit, scholars, for example, Paulin Paris, have argued that Richard personally witnessed the Crusade and recounted salient events even as they were occurring. R. F. Cook, however, has shifted interest in the text away from what he considers its dubious historical content and toward its literary form, exemplary of the Crusade Cycle, a subcategory of the chanson de geste.

Even Graindor's revision of Richard's poem retains what must have been the flavor of the original, for it is unabashedly martial, fiercely anti-Muslim, and totally unconcerned with love. Richard's *Chanson* also survives in a Provençal fragment composed sometime between 1126 and 1138 by Grégoire Béchada.

BIBLIOGRAPHY

Robert Francis Cook, *"Chanson d'Antioche," Chanson de Geste* (1980); Paul Meyer, "Fragment d'une *Chanson d'Antioche* en provençal," in *Archives de l'Orient latin,* II (1884); Paulin Paris, ed., *La chanson d'Antioche,* 2 vols. (1848); Lewis Sumberg, *La chanson d'Antioche: Étude historique et littéraire* (1968).

ELIZABETH WILSON POE

[See also **Antioch; Chansons de Geste; Crusades and Crusader States.**]

CHANSON DE LA CROISADE CONTRE LES ALBIGEOIS,

a poem in langue d'oc, offers a contemporary account of the Albigensian Crusade. It comprises 9,578 lines, grouped in monorhymed laisses, and is the work of two successive poets. The first part, approximately two-sevenths of the total text, covers the period 1209–1213. Its author identifies himself as Guilhem de Tudela, a *clercs* and an eyewitness; his sympathies lie with the Crusaders. The anonymous second part, anti-French and anticlerical in spirit, covers the period 1213–1218 and laments the destruction of Occitanian land and culture. An important source for the history of the crusade, the poem is also of high literary quality. A prose redaction dates from the turn of the fourteenth century.

BIBLIOGRAPHY

An edition of the text is *La chanson de la croisade albigeoise,* Eugène Martin-Chabot, ed. and trans., 3 vols. (1957–1961). See also Colette Bottin-Fourchotte, "L'ambi-

guïté du discours chez Guilhem de Tudela," in Jean Granarola, ed., *Hommage à Pierre Nardin* (1977), 99–110; and Jean-Marie d'Heur, "Notes sur l'histoire du manuscrit de la *Chanson de la croisade albigeoise* et sur quelques copies modernes," in *Annales du Midi,* 85 (1973).

SYLVIA HUOT

CHANSONNIER: (1) a manuscript of the Gothic period containing monophonic songs of the troubadours and trouvères; (2) a late medieval manuscript of polyphonic songs.

MONOPHONIC

The troubadours and trouvères were for the most part aristocratic poet-musicians. They usually set their melodies to verses written in one of the four basic types of poetical forms. These categories embraced: (1) the chanson de geste, laisse, *rotrouenge,* and *chanson avec refrain;* (2) the rondeau, ballade, and virelai; (3) various forms of the lai and note, or *notula;* and (4) the *vers* and various forms of the chanson. While some of these songs have been preserved without any music, about 280 troubadour and over 1,500 trouvère melodies are incorporated in the various manuscript compilations.

The music appears at the beginning of a song, with the text of the first stanza written below. The majority are notated without any rhythmic indication because—according to one school of thought—the music merely followed the rhythm of the text. Other examples, however, are transcribed in so-called mensural notation. Many of these chansonniers were illustrated, suggesting strongly that they were created for the libraries of wealthy patrons. Twenty-odd manuscripts containing these monophonic songs are preserved in libraries at Arras, London, Milan, Paris, Siena, and Vatican City.

Although the troubadours and trouvères sang their own songs on occasion, the performance of this repertory was basically left to the jongleur, an itinerant singer-instrumentalist and jack-of-all-trades entertainer. Indeed, the troubadour Guiraut Riquier himself mentioned in a letter this distinction between composers (*inventores*) and performers (*joglars*). Sometimes the songs were sung unaccompanied, while on other occasions an instrument joined in. Wace's *Roman de Brut* relates that "There were many jongleurs, / Singers and instrumentalists / At court. / You may hear chansons, rotrouenges and new melodies, / Pieces for fiddle, tuneful lais . . ." (lines 10,823ff.). A Provençal work, the *Roman de Flamenca* (*ca.* 1272–1285), in particular, reflects these practices: one jongleur played a new tune on his *vièle* (or *vielle*), another performed a chanson, a third a descort, a fourth a lai, each striving to surpass the other. Different instruments were played, and one musician sang while another accompanied him. While jongleurs had to be able to both sing and play, they did not necessarily execute these roles simultaneously: "Some gave out the word and others the tune." There is no evidence of "harmonizing" these songs; whether performed vocally or instrumentally there was only a single line of music, and any melodic instrumental accompaniment merely doubled the vocal part.

POLYPHONIC

Secular music predominated in the ars nova of the fourteenth century. The poet-musician Guillaume de Machaut, in attempting to recreate the art-world of the troubadour and trouvère, was the first to write quantities of chansons in settings of from two to four voices in ballade, virelai, and rondeau form. Only a small repertory of polyphonic songs survives from the first six or so decades of the century. Their construction is often complex, with various stylistic artifices suggesting a parallel to the elaborate rib vaulting of late medieval cathedrals such as Ely or Winchester. These chansons were sung, performed on instruments, or executed with a mixed ensemble. Whatever the medium, a contrast of sonority ("split sound") was sought by using different combinations, for example, a plucked versus a bowed instrument, or a string versus a woodwind instrument. This contrast served to bring out the essential rhythmic pattern and delineate the constantly crossing parts. The ad hoc nature of most performances, as well as the varied repertory, required a flexible ensemble, depending upon the occasion. Machaut, for example, wrote in his *Livre du voir dit* that one of his songs could be played on a variety of instruments.

A majority of the fifteenth-century chansonniers were written for court patrons and represented compilations of works by the important composers of the period. Although produced throughout Europe, their content was basically French, reflecting the predominant culture of the period with its flourishing secular poetry. Often sprinkled in was a variety of different musical forms and genres, including chansons in other vernaculars. In general, this music—three-part compositions predominated—

was stylistically simpler than before, with a growing tendency to place the melody in the top, or soprano, voice *(superius),* rather than variously in the other parts. Early anthologies of these chansons include manuscripts in the libraries of Bologna and Oxford. In his poem *Champion des dames,* Martin le Franc mentions three of these earlier composers (Cesaris, Carmen, and Tapissier), whose music "astonished" the Parisians, and then passes on to his contemporaries—Dufay and Binchois foremost—who had found "a new way" of making music: enlarging the scale at both ends; applying musica ficta, or certain chromatic notes; using rests and modulations. During the second half of the fifteenth century the so-called Franco-Flemish chanson was widely cultivated.

The evidence of fifteenth-century songbooks survives in a number of sumptuous manuscripts, often with decorated initials and miniature paintings, preserved in libraries at Dijon, Copenhagen, New Haven, Paris, Washington, and Wolfenbüttel. Some of these volumes are extremely small, meant to be held on the performer's lap. A vast output of chansons was produced by composers active at the flourishing Burgundian court, and some of the best-known chansonniers are of this provenance.

This abundance of secular music was reflected in its performance at all kinds of occasions; outdoor festivities were usually the occasion for amateur music making, both vocal and instrumental. In performance, there was more homogeneity of sound than in previous times, an attempt to blend the parts rather than set them apart. As a matter of principle, instruments (when used) were grouped into loud and soft ensembles, based upon their tonal quality. When chansons were both sung and played, one stanza would often be sung, another executed by instruments, and perhaps a third performed by a mixed group. Whatever the makeup, emphasis was usually on the highest vocal line.

BIBLIOGRAPHY

Willi Apel, *French Secular Music of the Late Fourteenth Century* (1950); Howard M. Brown, "On the Performance of Fifteenth-Century Chansons," in *Early Music,* **1** (1973); and "Instruments and Voices in the Fifteenth-Century Chanson," in John W. Grubbs, ed., *Current Thought in Musicology* (1976); T. Karp, "The Trouvère Manuscript Traditions," in *Queens College Twenty-Fifth Anniversary Festschrift* (1964); Christopher Page, "The Performance of Songs in Late Medieval France," in *Early Music,* **10** (1982); Ian Parker, "The Performance of Troubadour and Trouvère Songs," *ibid.*, 5 (1977); Hendrik J. van der Werf, *The Chansons of the Troubadours and Trouvères* (1972).

EDMUND A. BOWLES

[See also **Machaut, Guillaume de; Music, Popular; Music, Western European; Musical Performance; Troubadour, Trouvère, Trovadores.**]

CHANSONS DE FEMME, a broad label covering a variety of poetic genres in French and Provençal, including *aube, chanson d'ami, chanson de malmariée,* and *chanson de toile.* The poems are usually lyrical monologues expressing sadness or suffering in love, and are spoken through the persona of a woman. The monologue is addressed to another woman—either a friend or a mother—or, less commonly, to a lover. As a lyrical type *chansons de femme* are found in many literatures: the Spanish-Arabic *wuwashshah,* the Germanic *winileodae,* the Spanish *villancicos,* and the Portuguese *cantigas de amigo.*

BIBLIOGRAPHY

Pierre Bec, *La lyrique française au moyen âge (XIIe–XIIIe siècles),* 2 vols. (1977–1978), I, 57–68, II, 7–46; Peter Dronke, *The Medieval Lyric* (1968), 86–108; Frederick Goldin, ed. and trans., *Lyrics of the Troubadours and Trouvères* (1973), contains original texts with translations and introductions.

THOMAS E. KELLY

[See also **Cantigas de Amor, Amigo, and Escarnio; Villancicos.**]

CHANSONS DE GESTE are the Old French epics, dating from the eleventh to the fourteenth centuries, and considered to have been one of the earliest vernacular genres in France. They were composed in strophes of ten- or twelve-syllable lines to be sung or declaimed. The songs are nearly all anonymous, and the dates both of the songs themselves and of the extant manuscripts are approximate. Over a hundred texts classed as chansons de geste are extant, and they vary widely in character.

The term used today for these epics reflects medieval usage, the telling of these stories having reg-

ularly been expressed by the verb *chanter.* The characters in the stories refer, too, to the songs that will be sung about their deeds. Although only a single musical phrase associated with these texts is preserved today, it is supposed that a simple melody contributed to the strophic structure of the songs, an introductory phrase marking the opening of each strophe, another phrase accompanying the body, and a concluding phrase coming at the end of the strophe. The word *geste* (Latin: *gesta,* "deeds," from *res gesta,* "things done") is multivalent, meaning the exploits of the epic heroes, the narratives (variously chronicles, songs, or legends) relating their deeds, and subsequently both the lineage of the hero and the cycles into which the songs about the lineage were organized.

For the most part heroic narratives, the chansons de geste show some lyric characteristics in their strophic organization and use of repetition and refrain, and the later songs show many elements of romance. To a large extent the songs present themselves as histories situated primarily in France or taking France as the homeland and the French monarchy as the central power. Chief among the historical and pseudo-historical figures are Charlemagne and his weak and vacillating son Louis. Two themes in particular stand out: personal rivalries pitting the great barons against each other or against the throne, and the struggle of French Christendom against a vaguely conceived enemy called Saracens, inhabiting Spain, North Africa, and the Middle East, and conducting raids in Italy and southern France. These enemies are seen as Islamic, but they are polytheistic, worshiping a trinity composed of Mahomet, Apollin, and Tervagant.

The songs are preserved in manuscripts dating from the twelfth to the sixteenth centuries, and they range in length from less than 1,000 to over 20,000 lines. Precise figures are impossible for either the number of songs or their length because the poems are preserved in different versions of differing lengths and because branches of some stories may be considered as episodes of a single song or as separate songs. Most of the manuscripts treat the *Charroi de Nîmes* and the *Prise d'Orange* as a single poem; modern critics and editors usually take the two as separate poems. The early version of the *Chanson de Roland,* preserved in one MS and partially in a second, is roughly 4,000 lines long (editors agree on 4,002 lines in MS O, the best manuscript); the later version, amplified, rhymed, and preserved in five

257

MSS, runs to between 6,000 and 8,000 lines. The greatest number of texts are preserved in Old French, but versions of some are preserved in Old Provençal, and a number of manuscripts give texts in a hybrid of French and Italian.

The stories appear to have enjoyed considerable popularity throughout western Europe. The songs were adapted into Norse, Icelandic, Swedish, English, Welsh, Dutch, Spanish, Italian, and German during the Middle Ages. Dante listed Roland, William of Orange (Orange, located on the left bank of the Rhône, is both the seat of the epic hero William and the principality from which the House of Orange draws its name, but the epic hero should not be confused with the British king), and the grotesque giant Rainouart along with Charlemagne among the fighting saints in the fifth sphere of Heaven (*Paradiso* 43–46). Cervantes' *Don Quixote,* Ariosto's *Orlando furioso,* the Spanish *romancero,* as well as puppet plays still popular in twentieth-century Sicily and in the region of Liège in Belgium attest to the durability and adaptability of the Old French epic heroes. In France, individual songs were elaborated into cycles relating the exploits of a whole lineage; the later Middle Ages witnessed the recasting of the epic into prose versions; and the heroes endured in cheap popular romances into modern times.

During the Middle Ages, the lack of distinction drawn between epic and history resulted in the inclusion of many epic stories in works of historical intention such as Philippe Mousket's *Chronique rimée.* Thus we possess information about presumably lost chansons de geste in such foreign compilations as the Norse *Karlamagnús saga* and in would-be histories like Mousket's.

POEMS AND CYCLES

The best-known chanson de geste is the *Chanson de Roland,* preserved in two versions found in seven manuscripts and three fragments, and relating the deaths of Roland and his companion-in-arms Oliver and the annihilation of Charlemagne's rear guard in an ambush in the Pyrenees arranged through the treachery of Roland's stepfather Ganelon. The earlier, assonant, version (preserved in one manuscript and partially in a second, Franco-Italian one) is generally considered a masterpiece and the finest of the extant poems both in its portrayal of heroic purpose and in the brilliant use of the poetic resources offered by the genre. Similar in its portrayal of the hero's high purpose and glorious death in battle, the first

half of the *Chanson de Guillaume* (preserved in a single manuscript) narrates the death of Vivien refusing to withdraw as much as a foot in the face of the enemy. To some extent the poem shows artistic construction comparable to that of the *Chanson de Roland.* It also introduces comic elements in the figure of young Gui, like Vivien a nephew of William, but whose heroic ardor is somewhat tempered by the imperious demands of an adolescent appetite, and in the colorful figure of William himself. In the second half of the poem as it is preserved today, William avenges his nephew's death with the help of the comic giant Rainouart; this section of the text, different in technique from the first part and contradicting it on a number of points, is thought to have been a separate poem originally. An elaborate revised telling of the same story, preserved in thirteen manuscripts and some fragments, is known as *Aliscans,* the site of the battle in this version.

Less glorious in purpose, but quite as fiercely military as these poems, *Raoul de Cambrai,* preserved in a single manuscript, relates the devastation wrought by feudal warfare brought on by Raoul's determination to obtain and hold a fief wrongly granted to him by King Louis in compensation for a fief wrongly taken from him. The fragment known as *Gormont et Isembart* preserves what appears to be the climactic battle of the same story, in which the renegade Isembart is struck down, repents, and dies after having led Gormont's pagan army against the French in Picardy; this fragment is unique in being composed in octosyllables.

In the *Pèlerinage de Charlemagne* (also known as the *Voyage de Charlemagne à Jérusalem et à Constantinople*), Charlemagne, piqued by his wife's ill-considered remark that he is not necessarily the most glorious king in Christendom, undertakes a pilgrimage with the twelve peers. God intervenes to protect them against the immensely wealthy King Hugues of Constantinople by allowing the peers to accomplish preposterous boasts they had made when drunk.

The *Couronnement de Louis,* the *Charroi de Nîmes,* and the *Prise d'Orange* form a small cycle within the most extensively developed of the epic cycles, that of William of Orange and his family. According to Bertrand de Bar-sur-Aube at the end of the twelfth century, "There were only three epic lineages in rich France" (*N'ot que trois gestes en France la garnie*), that of the kings of France (the cycle of Charlemagne), that of Doon de Mayence (the cycle of the rebellious barons), and that of Garin de Monglane (the great-grandfather of William of

Orange). The significance of this often-quoted classification, however, is uncertain. Quite a number of poems are about Charlemagne, but they do not seem to have been assembled into cyclical manuscripts. Various songs refer to the lineage of traitors, of whom Roland's stepfather Ganelon is the most prominent, but this *geste* seems to have formed a lineage rather than a cycle. On the other hand, small cycles not named by Bertrand and possibly posterior to him have been preserved, including two cycles of poems about the First Crusade.

It appears that the cyclical tendency developed from the exploitation of successful stories or heroes. A popular hero would acquire further adventures, particularly his youthful exploits (his *Enfances*), and an epic family, particularly his ascendants, would grow around him. This process may account for the manuscripts of the poems about William's lineage. The *Chanson de Guillaume* manuscript is not cyclical: it contains no other text. *Aliscans,* on the other hand, like most of the twenty-four known poems about the family, is preserved almost solely in cyclical manuscripts. The three poems of the small cycle are not found except in cyclical manuscripts.

In the *Couronnement de Louis,* William passes his early manhood assuring the young Louis's position on the throne; in the *Charroi de Nîmes* Louis's failure to reward William's many services with a fief provokes William to capture Nîmes from the Saracens as a fief; and in the *Prise d'Orange* William completes the passage to a fully established position in society by winning a wife, the beautiful Saracen princess Orable (who takes the name Guiborc as a Christian), along with the Saracen city of Orange. The larger cycle traces William's career from his *Enfances* until he took religious orders (*Moniage Guillaume*) as well as tracing collateral and ascendant branches of the family.

Not all the songs can be attributed to cycles. Nor do all share the Carolingian setting of the greatest number of songs. The Crusade cycle poems have a roughly contemporary setting. *Florence de Rome,* set in Italy and Greece, ignores France. The *Roman d'Auberon,* prologue to *Huon de Bordeaux,* carries its characters, including one Julius Cesar, through Hungary, Austria, Italy, Arthur's Britain, and fairyland, and encounters the Holy Family during the flight into Egypt. The hagiographic element in Roland's martyrdom for the Christian cause, also found explicitly in Vivien's death, finds a prominent place in *Ami et Amile* (set in Carolingian times and featuring a *vilain* of Ganelon's lineage) and in *Florence*

de Rome, where the portrayal of saintliness in the principal characters directs the final action.

ORIGINS AND TRANSMISSION

The greatest number of songs present themselves as histories. Some even refer to their sources, written documents and eyewitness accounts, although these may be fictitious. *Raoul de Cambrai* names a certain Bertolai of Laon who witnessed the events and composed a song about them (vv. 2,442ff.). The *Chanson de Roland* refers to written documents, including the "geste," as sources of the facts related (vv. 1,684ff.; 2,095ff.; etc.).

Whether the sources are fictions or not, some of the songs portray more or less accurately identifiable historical events. Charlemagne's rear guard was indeed ambushed somewhere in the Pyrenees in August 778, although by Christian Basques (*Wascones* in Latin; they may have been Gascons, but most authorities call them Basques) rather than by Saracens; the site of the catastrophe may have been near the present-day hamlet of Roncesvalles, the Rencesvals of the poem; and a certain Hrodlandus, count of the march of Brittany, may have been among the illustrious victims. The pagan raid in *Gormont et Isembart* shows resemblances to the Viking raid of 881 on Ponthieu and defeat at Soucourt-en-Vimieu.

The nineteenth-century scholars who brought these texts to light presumed that momentous events like these led the people to create short, lyrical narrations of the events in the eighth and ninth centuries. These "cantilenas" (Latin: *cantilena,* "song") gradually coalesced, joining incidents and historical figures originally distinct. Then the songs were written down in the twelfth century, and the coalescing process continued in the creation of epic cycles.

The fact that the songs preserved in more than one manuscript show many variants from one manuscript to another, to the point that one must speak of versions of the songs (two versions of the *Chanson de Roland,* three of the small William cycle), has also suggested that the songs were composed and transmitted in some collective, oral process. The manuscripts would be transcriptions of particular performances or would have been written to help the memory of performers.

Evidence points to the existence of a class of wandering entertainers known as jongleurs (Latin: *joculatores*), a class rather ill thought of, that included the singing of stories among their skills. They entertained at fairs, in castles, anywhere that crowds might be induced to reward their performances. These people would have included in their repertories one, two, perhaps several chansons de geste. They may have memorized the songs, or they may have owned the small (no larger than 13 cm. × 20 cm., or 5.1 in. × 7.9 in.), poor-quality manuscripts of which some thirty have survived. Or, like the illiterate South Slav singers of the twentieth century, they may have acquired through practice the skill of improvising a tale in verse and may have been able to sing a great many chansons de geste simply by learning a basic plot line for each and then renewing the song, as it were, each time they fitted the plot line out with words. Variants would of course proliferate if the manuscripts derived from this kind of transmission by improvisation.

The texts themselves evoke a situation in which an audience listens to a jongleur. They abound in exhortations addressed to the audience: "Listen, and you will hear"; "Be quiet, and you will hear"; "As you will hear before nightfall"; "As you will hear if you give me enough." The particularities of versification and the repetitive nature of the diction appear to have been devices that facilitated either memorization or improvisation.

The nineteenth century appears to have seen the nearly complete absence of vernacular texts prior to the chansons de geste as a disappearance of the poetic tradition. The chansons de geste thus appeared as a primitive form, a rebirth of poetry reproducing the situation of Homeric Greece but at half the distance in time. The life of this poetry in the collective memory, primitive versification, and primitive notions of characterization and plot were signs that this poetry had been created from nothing. The rough simplicity of the texts reflected the rough simplicity of the people who created them.

Striking discrepancies between the songs and the historical events and the lack of any cantilenas preserved from the four centuries between the events and the first chansons de geste led Joseph Bédier to suggest at the beginning of the twentieth century that the poems were not created much before the earliest manuscripts that now preserve them, and he pointed to close correspondences between the songs and various sanctuaries along the pilgrimage routes in order to suggest that in the twelfth century, monasteries might have commissioned the writing of the chansons as a means of attracting pilgrims. Poetry written by individuals seemed more likely to be carefully constructed than would be the product of an anonymous and illiterate collectivity, and the *Chan-*

son de Roland in particular showed clear signs of well-balanced construction.

Scraps of evidence like the eleventh-century fashion of naming sons after the two companions Roland and Oliver do point to some sort of tradition antedating the extant poems, but the nature of that tradition and its relation to the poems we know remain matters of continuing speculation, even though Bédier's sanctuaries, like the rebirth of poetry, are no longer fashionable. And while the proliferation of variants between manuscripts could result from oral transmission, it appears quite as likely to be a manifestation of the importance of stylization in the esthetics of the genre.

ARTISTIC MERITS

Remaniement, or extensive revision, is an integral part of the chansons de geste. This floating nature of the text, also called *mouvance* in recent studies, means that any given manuscript is one of many (possible or actual) manifestations of the poem, and it constitutes a kind of reference to a tradition. The story is stylized and told by allusion as well as by straightforward statement, as if the audience is already familiar with it. The resultant simplification goes hand in hand with a high degree of repetition and can produce apparent incoherences. It has been proposed that the poems were composed from stocks of formulas (standard clauses or parts of the clause) and motifs (standard actions expressed in strings of formulas), which would have been familiar to audiences as well as to the performers. Audiences would have understood formulaic allusions. Although the mechanics of composition and audience perception were undoubtedly more complicated than a stringing together of familiar formulas, stylization gives considerable latitude in the performance (oral or written) of the poem because of its allusiveness. It may explain, too, some of the disconcerting aspects of the genre.

On the whole, the chansons de geste other than the *Chanson de Roland* are not highly thought of. Character portrayal seems simplistic, plot development jerky, diction limited, and versification monotonous. Nineteenth-century critics treated these failings in the better poems as part of the rough simplicity which they admired, and contemporary critics still have difficulty seeing these traits as other than due to the limited resources of the genre.

In some places where the nineteenth century saw inconsistencies or rough simplicity in character and plot, the twentieth century has discovered complex psychology, sophistication, or unexpected comedy. When Ganelon designates Roland for the rear guard, Roland reacts first with apparent pleasure and then with fury (vv. 740–770); it is generally accepted today that the reactions are not contradictory but complementary and reveal a complex range of strong feelings in both men. The characteristic laugh of William of Orange, expressing rage as often as amusement, adds a touch of ambiguity to his heroism. William's many hesitations when faced with danger are disconcerting in a hero but may represent a comic element in his *geste*. The repeatedly preposterous situations in which William finds himself in the *Prise d'Orange* after entering the city disguised as a Saracen bind a strong comic thread to the heroic theme.

Still, many elements of plot and character may indeed be rough simplicity. The evil brother Milon in *Florence de Rome* is given no motivation. In the *AB* version of the *Couronnement de Louis*, William promises Louis that he will always remain ready to support the crown and then suddenly remembers a fifteen-year-old vow to make a pilgrimage to Rome and departs. The abrupt appearance of the emir Baligant halfway through the *Chanson de Roland* continues to make critics wonder if he is not an interpolation into an earlier and more unified poem.

Diction and versification have also revealed sophistication in their simplicity although as yet we do not know just how to interpret it. The poems prefer coordination of clauses to subordination and the grammatical values of coordination and subordination to such lexical values as cause, consequence, or chronological succession. More and more this form of simplicity shows a relation to litotes instead of primitive linguistic resources. In the recurring dangerous situations of the *Prise d'Orange*, for example, William repeatedly expresses concern for his safety and that of his companions. On each occasion, his little nephew Gui retorts sarcastically, either declaring his intention of selling his life dearly or reminding his uncle to get on with the business of courting the beautiful Orable. Strongly marked verbal repetition underscores these recurrences as comic and highlight Gui's youthful high spirits.

Both the epic line and the epic strophe, or laisse, present a similar ambiguity. The characteristic ten- or twelve-syllable lines, with a caesura strongly marked by syntax after the fourth syllable of the ten-syllable line or the sixth syllable of the twelve-syllable line, are grouped into laisses by an approximate rhyme (closer to assonance in the earlier poems, and

to rhyme in the later ones), repeated in every line of the laisse. Depending on the song, the laisse can run from three to over three hundred lines. The repetition of the same rhyme over so many lines produces a monotony compounded by the limited range of rhymes available outside certain grammatical categories. Laisses in *-er* and *-ir* (infinitives), in *-ez* (past participle), and *-ant* (present participle) proliferate, and they show a very limited range of grammatical constructions.

A few poems seem to try to combat this monotony with affectation. In his version of *Berte aus grans piés* and in his *Buevon de Conmarchis*, Adenet le Roi alternates laisses of masculine and feminine rhymes using the same vowel. *Garin le Loherain* shows an unusually high proportion of assonances in *-i*. But it may be that the laisse is something of an organizational device like a chapter and that the "monotony" is subordinate to the way in which changes in rhyme, reinforced by concluding and introductory intonations (both in the accompanying music and in the text), break up the story line into parts.

The syntactic "monotony" of the line extends beyond the constraint of putting a limited number of grammatical categories at the rhyme. The close correspondence of syntax and meter means that most lines contain one clause per hemistich, or an auxiliary verb in the first and a main verb in the second hemistich, or a noun phrase filling one hemistich. The resulting syntactic repetitiousness appears, however, to function as a backdrop to many subtle variations. The songs derive remarkable rhythmic effects, for example, from variations in the place of the lexically heavy word in the hemistich in enumerations, and critics are beginning to discover an impressive variety of other rhythmic effects based on semantic patterns.

The *chanson de geste* has traditionally been seen as a largely pedestrian genre in which the *Chanson de Roland* stands alone as a striking epic masterpiece, accompanied perhaps by the *Chanson de Guillaume*. Recent scholarship, however, has considerably nuanced our understanding of the genre with the recognition that comedy plays an important role in the poems of the cycle of William of Orange and that repetitions are perhaps less a sign of hackneyed composition than an artistic device.

BIBLIOGRAPHY

Early studies. Gaston Paris, *Histoire poétique de Charlemagne* (1865, 2nd ed. 1905), cantilena theory; Léon Gautier, *Les épopées françaises, étude sur les origines et l'histoire de la littérature nationale,* 4 vols. plus bibliography, 2nd ed. (1865–1869, 2nd ed. 1878–1897, repr. 1966); Joseph Bédier, *Les légendes épiques: Recherches sur la formation des chansons de geste,* 4 vols. (1908–1913, 3rd ed. 1926–1929), sanctuary theory, individual poets. Bédier's approach dominated chanson de geste studies until the 1950's. For persistent dissension see Ferdinand Lot's articles, especially those collected in his *Études sur les légendes épiques* (1958).

Bibliographies and collections. The Société Rencesvals for the study of the Romance epic publishes the acts of its generally triennial international meetings, the most recent of which is *VIII Congreso de la Société Rencesvals* (1981), as well as the *Bulletin bibliographique de la Société Rencesvals* (irregular intervals since 1958). The American-Canadian branch has published a quarterly, *Olifant,* since 1973. Also see Joseph J. Duggan, *A Guide to Studies on the Chanson de Roland* (1976).

Editions and translations. There are dozens of editions and translations of the *Chanson de Roland,* fewer of the other chansons de geste. See especially Gerard J. Brault, ed. and trans., *The Song of Roland: An Analytical Edition,* 2 vols. (1978); Jeanne Wathelet-Willem, *Recherches sur la Chanson de Guillaume: Études accompagnées par une édition,* 2 vols. (1975).

The three poems of the small William cycle have been re-edited recently, two of them giving all the versions in verse: *Les rédactions en vers du Couronnement de Louis,* Yvan Lepage, ed. (1978); *Le charroi de Nîmes,* Duncan McMillan, ed. (1978); *Les rédactions en vers de la Prise d'Orange,* Claude Regnier, ed. (1966). See also Joan M. Ferrante, trans., *Guillaume d'Orange: Four Twelfth-Century Epics* (1974), including *Couronnement de Louis* and *Prise d'Orange* and extracts of *Aliscans* and the *Moniage Guillaume.*

Studies. Martín de Riquer, *Les chansons de geste françaises,* 2nd ed., French trans. by Irénée Cluzel (1957), the most recent general handbook. Appendix I gives, with facing French translation, the text of the Hague fragment, argued to show the circulation of some form of French epic as early as the late tenth century. Ramón Menéndez Pidal, *La Chanson de Roland et la tradition épique des Francs,* 2nd ed., rev. with René Louis, French trans. by Irénée-Marcel Cluzel (1960), statement of neotraditionalism, in opposition to Bédier's individualism. Argues the close connection between the historical event and the poem. Chapter X examines the eleventh-century *Nota Emilianense,* also used as evidence of a lost epic tradition preceding the extant texts. On the variations of the manuscripts, compare Cesare Segre, "Tradizione fluttuante della *Chanson de Roland?*" in *Studi medievali,* 3rd ser., **1** (1960).

Jean Rychner, *La chanson de geste, essai sur l'art épique des jongleurs* (1955), first and to date only systematic study of the formal characteristics of the genre. It needs corrections, is too dependent on the *Chanson de Ro-*

land, and argues oral transmission of the texts, but is arguably the most important book on the chansons de geste. Jean Frappier, *Les chansons de geste du cycle de Guillaume d'Orange,* 2 vols. (1955–1965); Madeleine Tyssens, *La Geste de Guillaume d'Orange dans les manuscrits cycliques* (1967), detailed study of the manuscript filiations, assumes written transmission of the texts; Robert F. Cook and Larry S. Crist, *Le deuxième cycle de la Croisade* (1972); Joseph J. Duggan, *The Song of Roland, Formulaic Style and Poetic Craft* (1973), argues that the high percentage of formulas shows the poem to have been created orally. See reviews by Edward A. Heinemann, in *Olifant,* **1** (1973); John R. Allen, in *Computers and the Humanities,* **9** (1975); John S. Miletich, in *Modern Philology,* **73** (1975); and Peter F. Dembowski, in *Romance Philology,* **31** (1978).

Some recent studies have examined closely various aspects of diction and versification: A. R. Press, "The Formula 's'en a un ris gité' in the *Charroi de Nîmes,*" in *Forum for Modern Language Studies,* **12** (1976); Edward A. Heinemann, "Sur l'art de la laisse dans le *Couronnement de Louis,*" in *Charlemagne et l'épopée romane,* II, 383–391; D. D. R. Owen, "Structural Artistry in the *Charroi de Nîmes,*" in *Forum for Modern Language Studies,* **14** (1978); Jean-Marcel Paquette, "Le texte en métamorphose: Contribution à une poétique des laisses similaires d'après six versions de la 'scène du cor' de la *Chanson de Roland,*" in *Mélanges de langue et littérature françaises du moyen-âge offerts a Pierre Jonin, Senefiance,* 7 (1979), 503–514; Barbara D. Schurfranz, "Strophic Structure Versus Alternative Divisions in the *Prise d'Orange,*" in *Romance Philology,* 33 (1979).

EDWARD A. HEINEMANN

[See also **Adenet le Roi; Ami et Amile; Assonance; Charlemagne; French Literature; Karlamagnús Saga; Laisse; Minstrels and Popular Entertainment; Roland, Song of.**]

CHANSONS DE MALMARIÉE, a lyric genre in French and Provençal poetry belonging to the larger class of *chansons de femme.* The basic theme is that of a married woman who complains in monologue form about her unhappy state or about her husband, whom she despises for various reasons and to whom she was married against her will. The wife seeks redress for her grievances from a real lover *(ami),* with whom she is already unfaithful to her husband, or else from an ideal lover she has yet to meet. In both cases thematic play arises from an unfavorable contrast between husband *(vilain:* old, mean, ugly, impotent) and lover *(courtois:* young, kind, handsome, passionate).

The *malmariée* genre encompasses a number of formal and thematic variations. Alongside the dominant monologue form, a variety of dialogue scenarios exist, such as the meeting of a *malmariée* and her *ami* to exchange thoughts on the husband, or of two unhappy wives to confide their grievances. Variant themes include the *malmarié*, with a husband expressing his grief against an unfaithful wife, and the *chanson de nonne*, in which a young nun, cloistered against her will, laments her situation and calls for her *ami* to save her.

BIBLIOGRAPHY

Pierre Bec, *La lyrique française au moyen âge (XIIe-XIIIe siècles)*, I (1977), 69–90; II (1978), 13–24; Peter Dronke, *The Medieval Lyric* (1968), 86–108; Frederick Goldin, *Lyrics of the Troubadours and Trouvères* (1973), 411–413.

THOMAS E. KELLY

[See also **Chansons de Femme; Courtly Love; French Literature; Provençal Literature; Troubadour, Trouvère, Trovadores.**]

CHANSONS DE TOILE, twenty short lyrico-narrative sewing songs from northern France (twelfth century), variously classified as *chansons de femme* or *chansons d'histoire*. The name of the genre is medieval and derives from the fact that the opening stanzas frequently present women sewing, spinning, or weaving. The songs may also have been sung by women at the spinning wheel. They tell a brief love story, usually tragic; and the stanza form is simple, built on monorhymes or single assonance with a short refrain. Seven of the songs are found inserted in romances (*Guillaume de Dole* and the *Roman de la Violette*). The others are transcribed separately in various manuscripts. Musical notation is extant for four songs: "Bele Yolanz," "Bele Doete," "Bele Oriolanz," and "En un vergier lez une fontenele."

BIBLIOGRAPHY

Pierre Bec, *La lyrique française au moyen âge (XIIe-XIIIe siècles)*, I (1977), 107–119; II (1978), 30–46; *The Penguin Book of French Verse*, Brian Woledge, ed., I (1961, repr. 1966), 83–87.

THOMAS E. KELLY

[See also **Chansons de Femme.**]

CHANT. See Ambrosian Chant; Gregorian Chant.

CHANT ROYAL, a French poetic form (fourteenth–sixteenth century) related to the ballade. It consists of five eleven-line stanzas of decasyllables followed by an envoi of five lines. The poem is constructed using five rhymes patterned [$a\ b\ a\ b\ c\ c\ d\ d$ $e\ d\ e$] in each stanza and [$d\ d\ e\ d\ e$] in the envoi. *Chants royaux* of the fourteenth century did not have a refrain, but in later centuries the last line of the initial stanza served this purpose, being repeated as the final line of each of the other four stanzas and of the envoi. A poet who followed more strict rules also developed the whole poem as a single allegory, of which he gave a full explication only in the envoi. The name *chant royal* derives from the fact that it was addressed to kings and other nobility. Many such poems were also written in honor of Prince Jesus and the Virgin Mary. The finest examples of this form were written by Eustache Deschamps, Charles of Orléans, and Clément Marot.

BIBLIOGRAPHY

Clément Marot, *Oeuvres*, Georges Guiffrey, ed. V (1969), 83–124; Paul Zumthor, *Essai de poétique médiévale* (1972), 270.

THOMAS E. KELLY

[See also **Ballade; Charles of Orléans; Deschamps, Eustace; Envoi; French Literature: After 1200.**]

CHANTRY CHAPEL. See Chapel.

CHAPEL, a part of a large church or cathedral containing a separate altar, usually dedicated to a saint different from the titular saint of the church; a shrine built to house a holy relic (the Ste. Chapelle, Paris); or a religious structure belonging to a private institution (King's College Chapel, Cambridge). In the early Christian period subsidiary chapels were rare. During the Carolingian period the growing interest in relics led to the introduction of chapels: a saint's relics were often kept in an altar that required a suitable sacred location easily accessible to pilgrims.

Carolingian chapels were usually semicircular and extended outward from the apse or eastern wall of the church (St. Philibert-de-Grandlieu). Romanesque churches of the pilgrimage type (St. Sernin, Toulouse) normally included chapels radiating from the ambulatory around the apse (apsidal chapels) and protruding from the eastern transept wall. In most Romanesque churches the apsidal chapels were separated from each other; during the Gothic period they were often merged and united into a single spatial unit with the ambulatory and apse (chevet). With the increase in the number of clergy during the late Gothic period, more chapels were needed to house enough altars for the resident clergy; these were extended from the north and south walls of the choir.

Specialized types of chapels, although known earlier, became common in the thirteenth and fourteenth centuries, especially in England. The Lady Chapel, dedicated to the Virgin, was normally a semiautonomous building attached to the eastern end of the church (Ely Cathedral). A chapel royal was a private shrine under the jurisdiction of the sovereign (Ste. Chapelle). Chantry chapels, particularly popular in England from the late thirteenth century, were founded and endowed for the celebration of daily masses for the souls of the donors: individuals, families, or guilds. A chantry chapel could be incorporated into a parish church or be built as a separate structure; it usually contained the tomb of its donor.

LESLIE BRUBAKER

CHAPLAIN. Originally a priest who had charge of a chapel, the term's meaning expanded during the Middle Ages and came to designate a broad range of hired or stipendiary clerics—distinct from those who held benefices. Chaplains served mainly as parochial assistants, as chantry priests, and as private confessors in the households of lay and ecclesiastical greats.

Their functions were most varied within the parish. Some served as priests of chapels of ease, built to accommodate those who lived great distances from the parish church. Such parochial chaplains were not to assume prerogatives of the mother church. The chaplain was to say Mass, but not baptize, marry, or bury, or to give extreme unction except in emergencies. The chaplain was paid a fixed wage and was not entitled to the income of the chapelry. In similar fashion, chapels connected to hospitals and poorhouses also hired chaplains for limited duties.

Other chaplains, of lesser status, worked directly in the parish as assistants of the rector; in this capacity they are known variously as parish priests, as curates, and as parish chaplains. They were poorly paid, often earning no more than an unskilled laborer. Similar employment also was to be found in cathedrals and monasteries. Both kinds of institution employed secular chaplains to do ecclesiastical chores and to say Mass.

In the later Middle Ages the numbers of private perpetual chantries grew and a new and extensive source of employment became available for clergy who lacked parochial benefices. Celebrating at a specific altar in a specific church, chaplains served as chantry priests—either working for a fixed sum of money established by the charter that endowed the chantry or receiving the benefits of lands and tenements. Unlike parochial and parish chaplains, they were independent of the parochial incumbent—though the terms of their employment might provide that they assist him in limited fashion. Some chaplains were organized into colleges of chantry priests. Others worked for craft and religious guilds, where their sole function was to pray for the souls of deceased members. Yet others worked as temporary cantarists—responding to the terms of wills requesting masses for short periods of time.

The salaries of perpetual cantarists serving endowed chantries were often greater than those offered in poor parishes. A rise in numbers of chantries coupled with the dearth of priests after the Black Death created an ecclesiastical labor shortage, and many chaplains abandoned their parishes to hire themselves out as chantry priests. In England the problem grew so acute that legislation intended to correct this abuse was enacted in the later fourteenth century. It not only condemned the act but limited the amount a cantarist could earn to a sum about 20 percent less than that which parish chaplains typically earned.

The final arena of employment for chaplains was the household. King, noble, and gentry each felt enlarged by the license to have a private confessor. Some such chaplains were beneficed clergy who were absentee from their livings and could be rich and considerable men themselves; others were lowly retainers, little more than another type of servant. Episcopal households also employed chaplains. These men served as aides and staffed the constantly moving chapel of the peripatetic medieval bishop.

BIBLIOGRAPHY

Margaret Bowker, *The Secular Clergy in the Diocese of Lincoln, 1495–1520* (1968); Peter Heath, *English Parish Clergy on the Eve of the Reformation* (1969); Bertha H. Putnam, "Maximum Wage-laws for Priests After the Black Death, 1348–1381," in *American Historical Review*, **21** (1915–1916); Rigaldus, *The Register of Eudes of Rouen*, S. M. Brown, trans., J. F. O'Sullivan, ed. (1964); A. Hamilton Thompson, *The English Clergy and Their Organization in the Later Middle Ages* (1947), 72–160.

ANN K. WARREN

[See also **Benefice, Ecclesiastical; Chapel; Clergy.**]

CHAPTER. This word is used in several related ecclesiastical senses. Originally the chapter was that portion of the monastic rule (or of the Scripture) read during the daily convocation of the monks of a religious house. Soon the meeting itself became known as the chapter. Finally the word was extended to the group in attendance, and the place of assemblage became known as the chapter house.

The *horarium* of the Benedictines indicates that their chapter meeting took place at about 9:00 A.M. during the winter months. At the conclusion of prime, the monks proceeded from their church to the chapter house for the day's reading. Afterward, the officiating superior commented on the passage, using the opportunity to raise issues of spiritual or disciplinary significance. Following this exhortation specific breaches of conduct were confessed, reported, recognized, and corrected. Next, announcements concerning the affairs of the community could be made and necessary business transacted. The session closed with a blessing on the day's work.

Meeting in chapter, thus, was not only a daily expression of religious communality but also a coming together of the group for the purpose of taking action in a wide variety of common concerns. The business of the chapter could be the election of a new abbot, the profession of novices, the acceptance of laypersons into confraternity, or any kind of domestic legislation such as the establishment of an anniversary or the introduction of a new liturgical rite. A matter of special importance for chapters was the acquisition or the alienation of corporate land, and charters relevant to the conveyance of land typically were witnessed by the chapter as a whole. Again, the chapter, under the presidency of the prior, could act as a regency in an interregnum. The right of monks to exert their influence in the administration of the

monastery was not always readily acknowledged, however, and the chapter meeting could become the ground where monks expressed their desire for greater participation in the life of the monastery vis-à-vis the rights and control of the abbot.

Cathedrals and collegiate churches also were served by a body known as a chapter—in this case composed of canons, both resident and nonresident. The head of the chapter was the dean, an official elected by the canons and approved by the bishop. Chapter meetings were for corporate purposes only. They were called at regular intervals for routine business; extraordinary sessions were convened as necessary. Nonresident canons rarely troubled to participate in the routine chapter.

Medieval England was unusual in having monks serve as the clerical body in many cathedrals. In ten of the seventeen dioceses of the country, the bishop's residence was in the monastery, and the cathedral church was identical with the monastery church. Nine of these English cathedral monasteries were Benedictine (Bath, Canterbury, Coventry, Durham, Ely, Norwich, Rochester, Winchester, and Worcester) and one a house of Austin canons (Carlisle). Augustinian cathedral chapters were also common on the Continent. In these houses monks met in chapter, not as members of an abbey or priory and subject to a monastic superior, but as members of a cathedral corporation and subject to the bishop.

Attempts by monastic cathedral chapters to elect their own superior were often foiled by royal pressures, especially when such an election involved the primate of England, the archbishop of Canterbury. In 1205, for example, King John forced the Canterbury chapter to renounce its candidate and choose the bishop of Norwich. In the event, Pope Innocent III quashed both elections and summoned a delegation of the chapter to Rome, thus providing for the election of Stephen Langton. More frequently the chapter was allowed to elect its prior, who served it much as would an abbot in a more traditional monastic community. Diocesan matters were left to the bishop, who also retained the right to appoint most of the officials of the cathedral. This was a right that had been won by most monastic chapters, and the loss of it caused much acrimony among cathedral monks. In such altercations as did develop between the community and its episcopal head, the prior tended to stand with his chapter against the encroachments of the secular bishop.

A cathedral or collegiate chapter could have property of its own. Income from this property was divided among the canons, not always in equal amounts. These allotments were called prebends, and a man who had the favor of king or pope could hold prebends in several churches and perform very few duties in any one of them.

The fact that a chapter held its property as a group, and not as individuals, raised a legal problem: who was the actual owner? Gradually the chapter became recognized as a corporation, a concept that influenced the early development of the law of corporations. Cathedral chapters retain certain canon law rights to this day with regard to lawmaking, property, and taxation.

BIBLIOGRAPHY

Robert L. Benson, *The Bishop-elect* (1968); Kathleen Edwards, *The English Secular Cathedrals in the Middle Ages* (1949); Philippe Guignard, *Les monuments primitifs de la règle cistercienne* (1878), 167–172; David Knowles, *The Monastic Order in England*, 2nd ed. (1963, repr. 1966) 411–417, 637; and *The Religious Orders in England,* I (1948, repr. 1974), 254–262, 275–276; Frederick Pollock and F. W. Maitland, *The History of English Law*, 2nd ed., I (1898, repr. 1968), 486–511; Alexander Hamilton Thompson, *The English Clergy and Their Organization in the Later Middle Ages* (1947, repr. 1966), 72–100.

ANN K. WARREN

[See also **Augustinian Canons; Benedictines; Canon, Cathedral; Cathedral; Clergy; Corporation; Elections, Church; Langton, Stephen; Monasticism, Origins.**]

CHAPTER HOUSE, the place in which the meetings of monastic and cathedral chapters were held. In the primitive monastery the chapter meeting convened on a portico built alongside the church building and adjoining the cloister. During the Carolingian renaissance a standard monastic layout was established that gave the chapter meeting its own building. In the classic monastic plan of the Middle Ages, the chapter house was placed just east of the cloister. Of considerable size, it was second only to the church itself in beauty and artistic detail, and also second only to the church as the chosen burial place for members of the community and for its patrons.

Most chapter houses were square or rectangular, with vaulted ceilings that repeated or reflected the architecture of the church. They were illuminated by windows along the rear wall and by arcades at the

Wells Cathedral: chapter house interior, late 13th century. PHILADELPHIA MUSEUM OF ART, PURCHASED WITH FUNDS GIVEN BY DOROTHY NORMAN

entrance end, facing the cloister. In the simplest Benedictine design the monks sat along the walls on risers of one to three steps. Cistercian chapter houses favored side aisles. In the vacant center of the room there often stood a lectern holding the necrology.

Chapter houses also were built as part of the great medieval cathedrals. Here they served as rooms of state for ruling prelates as well as the site of chapter meetings, usually of canons, but in England of monks as well. In these chambers the superior sat on a high, decorated throne with his back to the eastern wall while the monks or canons took their places on his right and left in order of seniority. The placement of the chapter house was not fixed for the secular cathedral, and it often stood alone on the north side of the cathedral.

Chapter houses of especial beauty, architectural innovation, and great size were created for English cathedrals—perhaps because of their fusion of monastic and secular functions. These chapter houses had high vaults permitting windows on all sides. Many were polygonal with diameters of up to fifty-eight feet (seventeen and a half meters) in the case of Westminster Abbey. The most famous of these buildings are the octagonal ones at Wells, Salisbury, Lichfield, York, and Westminster. The last was used as the site of the meetings of the House of Commons from the fourteenth to the sixteenth centuries.

BIBLIOGRAPHY

Wolfgang Braunfels, *Monasteries of Western Europe: The Architecture of the Orders* (1980); Lionel Butler and Chris Given-Wilson, *Medieval Monasteries of Great Britain* (1979).

ANN K. WARREN

[See also **Cathedral; Monastery.**]

CHARCOAL is a carbonized wood, obtained by slow combustion within a closed space. In proportion to weight it has a far greater heating power than wood, and therefore can be transported more economically. It burns with a more concentrated heat, and gives off little smoke and fumes. Although it has found many industrial uses in modern times, in the Middle Ages it had only two purposes: cooking, and smelting and refining iron, the latter by far the more important.

It was not until the eighteenth century that the literature on charcoal and charcoal burning became at all abundant, though the methods described can have differed very little from those used during the Middle Ages. In the fourth century B.C. Theophrastus described the making of charcoal in terms that would have been understood by Biringuccio early in the sixteenth century or Henri Duhamel de Monceau in the eighteenth. Wood was cut into short lengths and stacked in a dome-shaped heap that was then covered with clay. A hole was made near the base for introduction of the fire, and another near the top to allow the waste gases to escape. In this way the wood was partially carbonized owing to the shortage of oxygen and reduced to a brittle mass of gray or black charcoal.

Charcoal burning was carried on in most wooded areas by men who lived deep in the forest. They had a reputation for independence and lawlessness, and were in fact, if not in law, free men. A poem written in Champagne in 1517 described them as a *classe d'hommes pauvre, mal vêtue.* There is evidence that smiths and ironworkers themselves sometimes organized the burning and transport of charcoal. In 1195, for example, William de Stuteville granted a

charter to a *magistro fabro de Font[ains],* allowing him to make charcoal in the Forest of Knaresborough in Yorkshire. There are many similar cases in the English records, and the same was happening in many of the forested areas of Europe.

Needless to say, the charcoal burners wreaked havoc with the forests. Duhamel de Monceau, writing about 1760, claimed that a charcoal-burning iron furnace used the charcoal from 11,680 cords of wood a year, and that this would have required almost 500 acres of woodland. The tall furnace was not introduced until late in the fifteenth century: previously a form of hearth was used to smelt iron ore. Consumption would therefore have been at lower levels earlier in the Middle Ages. The demand for charcoal was nevertheless large, and by 1500 there was a growing scarcity of timber in areas, such as Champagne, Burgundy, and the English Weald, where ironworking was important.

Charcoal was used for domestic purposes chiefly in the cities, and its provision was a well-organized trade. It was, for example, brought to Paris by boat from the forests of Burgundy.

Charcoal burners were discriminating in their choice of wood. For most purposes they preferred hardwood, which gave a firmer charcoal and greater heat. As a general rule they cut and burned in winter, when the sap was low.

BIBLIOGRAPHY

Vanoccio Biringucci, *The Pyrotechnica,* C. S. Smith, ed. (1942); Henri Louis Duhamel de Monceau, *L'art du charbonnier* (1761); "Poème sur les forges, composé en 1517 par Nicolas Bourbon," in *Annales des Mines,* 3rd ser., vol. XII (1835), 137–148.

NORMAN J. G. POUNDS

[See also **Technology, Western European.**]

CHARDRI, an Anglo-Norman writer of the early thirteenth century, author of two saints' lives: *La vie de seint Josaphaz* (2,954 lines), a Christianized version of the story of Buddha, and *La vie des set dormanz* (1,898 lines), the story of the Seven Sleepers of Ephesus; and also of a didactic poem, *Le petit plet* (1,780 lines) or *Minor Dialogue,* all in octosyllabic rhyming couplets. The poet, whose name is possibly an anagram for Richard, is thought to have come from the west of England.

BIBLIOGRAPHY

Editions. Chardry's Josaphaz, Set Dormanz, und Petit Plet, John Koch, ed. (1879); *Le petit plet,* Brian S. Merrilees, ed. (1970); *La vie des set dormanz,* Brian S. Merrilees, ed. (1977).

BRIAN MERRILEES

[See also **Anglo-Norman Literature; Balavariani; Barlaam and Josaphat; Seven Sleepers of Ephesus.**]

CHARISTIKION, temporary grant of monastic lands and property to laymen; a Byzantine institution similar to the Western *beneficium.* The grantee *(charistikarios)* was responsible for the maintenance of the monks and the buildings, and received the revenues of the property. The *charistikion* existed before 691, when the institution, but not the term, appears in the canons of the Council in Trullo. Originally given by the church, *charistikia* were subsequently granted by the emperors and, instead of serving the interests of the monasteries, were a source of revenues for the aristocracy. *Charistikia* appear most frequently in the eleventh and twelfth centuries, and a series of church councils during this period tried to reform the abuses inherent in the system. A basic text for the institution is a treatise by the patriarch John IV of Antioch (late eleventh century), entitled *That Monasteries Should Not Be Given Over to Laymen.*

BIBLIOGRAPHY

George Ostrogorsky, *Pour l'histoire de la féodalité byzantine* (1954); F. I. Uspensky, "Mnenia i postanovlenia Konstantinopoliskikh pomestnykh Saborov, XI i XII vv. o razdachie tserkovnykh imushchestv," in *Izvestia Russkago arkheologicheskago institute v Konstantinopole,* 5 (1900); A. A. Vasiliev, "On the Question of Byzantine Feudalism," in *Byzantion,* 8 (1933).

ANGELIKI LAIOU

[See also **Benefice; Byzantine Church; Feudalism; Monasticism.**]

CHARLEMAGNE or Charles the Great was the legitimate, eldest son of King Pepin the Short and Bertrada. Following the death of his father in 768, he and his brother Carloman shared the kingdom of the Franks in a spirit of animosity until the fortuitous death of the latter in 771. From 771 until his death in 814, Charles consolidated his control over the Frankish realm, expanding its frontiers and initiating an administrative and cultural reform that became the model for subsequent generations of medieval rulers and reformers.

His conquests of the Lombard, Saxon, and Bavarian peoples and of parts of northern Spain left Charles the Great undisputed master of virtually the entire Christian West, with the exception of Britain, part of Spain, and southern Italy. The enormous booty acquired in these conquests allowed him to achieve, at least temporarily, a degree of independence from his Austrasian aristocratic supporters, and thus to institute significant administrative reforms. These included a more regularized central administration and more direct influence on local affairs through the expanded use of the written word, particularly the capitulary, and through the regular use of *missi dominici.* In part to supply adequate lay and clerical administrators, he initiated an ambitious program of educational reform and intellectual revitalization, to this end attracting to his court a considerable number of outstanding churchmen and intellectuals, including the Anglo-Saxon Alcuin, the Lombard Paul the Deacon, and the Visigoth Theodulf of Orléans.

Charles's conquest likewise led him increasingly to assume the role of ruler and spokesman for the West, a tendency encouraged by his propagandists, who presented him increasingly in imperial terms and symbolism modeled on and in competition with the Byzantine Empire. The culmination of this tendency was his acclamation as emperor at Rome on 25 December 800.

Except in his attempts to reform the national laws of his kingdoms, Charles did not attempt to use his imperial title to alter the constitutional basis for his rule. He continued to govern as king of the Franks and of the Lombards. Evidence that he viewed his new imperial title as personal is that in 806 his dispositions for his succession were arranged in the traditional Frankish manner and without mention of the imperial dignity: the empire was to be divided among his three sons. Only in 813, after the death of two sons and at the urging of his magnates, did he confer the imperial title on his son Louis.

The last years of Charles the Great's reign saw the deterioration of most aspects of his administrative, social, and religious reforms. Instead of lucrative wars of conquest, the Franks were occupied with expensive defensive operations. The Austrasian aristocracy again acquired control over the central administration, and local counts and magnates increased their power at the expense of both the emperor and the poor. By 814 corruption among administrators and the clergy seems to have been widespread.

Nevertheless, in contrast with the reigns of his son and grandsons, the age of Charles the Great quickly became idealized as a golden age of prosperity and government. This process began during the reign of his son Louis, and was continued both east and west of the Rhine by subsequent generations of Carolingians, and then by Ottonians, Salians, and Capetians.

BIBLIOGRAPHY

See the bibliography to the article "Carolingians and the Carolingian Empire." Of particular importance are the volumes edited by Wolfgang Braunfels, *Karl der Große, Lebenswerk und Nachleben,* esp. I, *Persönlichkeit und Geschichte* (1965). The best general biography of Charles in English is Donald Bullough, *The Age of Charlemagne* (1965).

PATRICK GEARY

[See also **Capitulary; Carolingians and the Carolingian Empire; France: To 987; Missi Dominici.**]

CHARLES V OF FRANCE, surnamed "the Wise," reigned as king from 1364 to 1380. Born in 1338, he was the third ruler of the Valois line, the oldest son of John II and Bona of Luxembourg. Never in good health, Charles has been depicted as frail and studious, prudent and politically adept. His favorable historical reputation owes much to the laudatory writings of Christine de Pizan, the daughter of his Italian astrologer, and to the fact that both his father and his son had conspicuously unsuccessful reigns. The early death of John II enabled Charles to benefit from developments that might have reflected favorably on his father, and Charles's early death enabled him to escape the consequences of some of his mistakes.

Charles was the first heir to the French throne to be entitled dauphin of Viennois, and his father also named him duke of Normandy. In his teens he was briefly implicated in the political conspiracies of his cousin and brother-in-law, Charles the Bad of Navarre, who was imprisoned by John II in April 1356. Five months later John was captured by the English at Poitiers, and the dauphin had to assume the leadership of a bankrupt and defeated French monarchy.

Charles acquired political maturity under very adverse circumstances. The most available advisers were officials who were under attack for financial mismanagement. The government encountered opposition from several sources: genuine reformers wanting a more efficient and less centralized government, partisans of the imprisoned king of Navarre, and those who wished to supplant the unpopular royal officials. Adding to the tension was a growing wave of resentment against the nobles. The latter, especially those of the north and the west, had been increasingly alienated from the monarchy since the early 1340's.

From the autumn of 1356 through the summer of 1358, Charles had to endure a crisis marked by hostile meetings of the Estates-General, riot and rebellion in Paris, and the antinoble uprising called the Jacquerie. It was impossible to finance an effective war effort or to raise a ransom for the king. Charles gradually managed to appropriate some of the more valuable reform proposals and to achieve a reconciliation with the disaffected nobles. The remaining opponents of the regime discredited themselves. As the internal crisis eased, the external threat reappeared, but the English invasion of 1359 became stalled after the French refused to give battle. The Treaty of Bretigny (May 1360) arranged for the ransom of John II, and Charles presided over an extraordinary financial effort to raise the first installment and secure his father's return to France. The rest of the ransom was to be raised by heavy, regular, indirect taxes (*aides*) that would give Charles valuable resources during his reign.

One major consequence of John II's capture was the brigandage by soldiers left unemployed as a result of the ensuing truces and treaty. This problem plagued the monarchy for years. Many regions and local districts took initiatives to buy off the brigands or expel them, and at the end of 1363 the Estates-General granted a direct tax (*fouage*, hearth tax), averaging three francs per household, in order to pay an army that could restore order. At this moment John II returned to England, where he died in the spring of 1364. Thus Charles V inherited a system of taxation superior to anything known in France before 1360.

He also inherited many of his father's advisers and commanders, such as Bertrand du Guesclin, whose ability to deal with the brigands caused him to rise rapidly in the new king's service. In general, however, Charles V placed greater reliance on nobles than did his father, who had aroused opposition by favoring bourgeois financiers and ennobled Parisians whom the aristocracy resented as dishonest upstarts. Charles found a highly capable governor for Languedoc in his brother, Louis of Anjou, but he had to place a tight rein on that prince's bellicose policies, foreign ambitions, and heavy fiscal exactions. Charles made a serious effort to keep up the ransom payments for his father, and his internal difficulties were reduced when du Guesclin crushed the troops of Charles the Bad at Cocherel in 1364.

After one abortive Spanish expedition, du Guesclin in 1369 helped the pro-French Henry of Trastamara seize the throne of Castile. In the same year Charles V seemed to have neutralized his difficult northern vassal, Louis II de Male, count of Flanders, by obtaining papal support for the marriage of Louis's heiress, Margaret, to Charles's brother Philip the Bold of Burgundy. In Brittany the anti-Valois duke, John IV, prevailed over the claimant to the duchy whom the French had long backed, and Charles V had to accept his homage. Once victorious, however, John IV backed away from his English alliance, while Charles V succeeded in winning over a highly influential Breton lord, Olivier de Clisson.

Charles V showed great skill in cultivating or neutralizing the dissident aristocracy, and he exploited skillfully the grievances of Gascon lords who sought his aid in resisting the fiscal demands of the English rulers of Aquitaine. Their appeal to his court led to the renewal of the Hundred Years War in 1369. The French made impressive gains, aided considerably by a Castilian naval victory over the English in 1372 and by a French policy of avoiding major engagements on land. This avoidance of pitched battles, a policy advocated by Clisson, did exact a heavy price in suffering for the French rural population. The English retained vital enclaves at Calais, Cherbourg, Brest, Bordeaux, and Bayonne.

Charles V had found it so useful to have the pope at Avignon that he reacted too eagerly in supporting the questionable election of Clement VII in 1378. He deserves considerable blame for the ensuing schism, since subsequent French governments could not undo his action. As he lay dying in 1380, Charles canceled the all-important *fouage*, a tax disliked by the nobles but necessary to maintain the army. Whether motives other than conscience induced him to take this action has been debated. Charles left behind a troubled and faction-ridden government, and a twelve-year-old heir whose subsequent men-

tal instability would be disastrous. Consequently, Charles's reign is remembered mainly for its successes.

BIBLIOGRAPHY

Raymond Cazelles, *Société politique, noblesse et couronne sous Jean le Bon et Charles V* (1982); and "Jean II le Bon: Quel homme? Quel roi?" in *Revue historique*, **232** (1974); Roland Delachenal, *Histoire de Charles V*, 5 vols. (1909–1931); Léopold Delisle, *Mandements et actes divers de Charles V (1364–1380)* (1874); John Henneman, *Royal Taxation in Fourteenth Century France: The Captivity and Ransom of John II, 1356–1370* (1976); Michael Jones, *Ducal Brittany, 1364–1399* (1970); Auguste Lefranc, *Olivier de Clisson, connétable de France* (1888); John J. N. Palmer, *England, France, and Christendom, 1377–1399* (1972).

JOHN BELL HENNEMAN

[See also **France, 1314-1494; Hundred Years War; Jacquerie; Schism, Great; Taxation, French.**]

CHARLES VII OF FRANCE, king from 1422 to 1461, was born in 1403, the last surviving son of Charles VI and Isabella of Bavaria. The derangement of Charles VI and the promiscuity of Isabella would have made it possible to challenge his legitimacy, but nobody did so in his early years and questions were raised about his paternity only when they became politically expedient. The successive deaths of his older brothers in 1415 and 1417 made Charles heir to the throne and dauphin at the moment when Henry V of England was systematically conquering northwestern France.

Resistance to the English was crippled by factional strife in France. John the Fearless, duke of Burgundy, led a powerful faction that had support from the Parisians but was out of favor with the royal government. The old anti-Burgundian party, now led by Bernard VII, count of Armagnac, had been decimated by the English at Agincourt, and soon suffered another blow when its leaders were massacred by the Burgundians at Paris in 1418. To resist the English, the French Crown made peace with the resurgent Burgundian party, but the remaining Armagnacs gathered around the dauphin Charles. When he and John met at Montereau in 1419 to negotiate, his Armagnac supporters murdered the Burgundian duke.

This assassination forced John's son, Philip the Good, into the arms of the English, and in 1420 the Treaty of Troyes was accepted by Charles VI. It disinherited the dauphin, arranged for the marriage of his sister Catherine to Henry V, and declared the English king heir to the French throne.

In 1422, the deaths of both Henry V and Charles VI made the infant son of Henry and Catherine the nominal king of both realms. Charles VII could not be crowned, because of the terms of the treaty, and above all because the English occupied Rheims. As a result, he was recognized as king of France only in some regions south of the Loire. To his English and Burgundian enemies, he was known derisively as the "king of Bourges" (his temporary capital). He has been pictured as a lethargic and indecisive prince who failed to resist the English advance led by the duke of Bedford. His fortunes changed dramatically in 1429, when a peasant girl, Joan of Arc, persuaded him that the saints had called her to break the English siege of Orléans. She led a successful relief expedition and then the remarkable march through enemy-held territory to Rheims for Charles VII's coronation. Subsequently she was captured by the Burgundians, whose English allies executed her in 1431.

Without dismissing the impact of Joan of Arc, modern scholarship has tended to redefine Charles's supposed lethargy as a struggle for political independence in a court beset by complex rivalries and factions. Lacking resources or allies, Charles VII had to maneuver skillfully to neutralize these competing interests. First, the old hard-core Armagnacs were forced from power. Then their victorious adversaries, Arthur de Richemont and Georges de La Trémoille, began a rivalry that seriously weakened the government between 1425 and 1433. The most consistent influence on Charles came from his in-laws and cousins of the house of Anjou. Richemont, a well-connected Breton noble who was constable of France, espoused a peace with Burgundy. His triumph at court in 1433 and a weakening of the Anglo-Burgundian alliance made possible the negotiations that produced the Treaty of Arras with Burgundy in 1435, the real turning point of the reign.

Once Burgundy had been won over, France quickly reversed the tide of war. Richemont took Paris in 1436, and in the same year the Estates-General finally accepted the restoration of the *aides*—general indirect taxes first instituted in 1360 but canceled in 1418. Long a vital source of royal revenue,

the *aides* had been sorely missed by the government, and the resumption of their regular collection permitted greater financial stability and a much-needed reform of the currency. In 1438 Charles felt strong enough to challenge the papacy and assert the autonomy of the French (Gallican) church in the celebrated Pragmatic Sanction of Bourges.

One major problem remained to be solved: the brigandage of unpaid soldiers. This scourge of the French countryside had first appeared in the 1350's, and it revived as a severe problem in the 1430's. In 1439 the Estates-General convened at Orléans and agreed to a *taille*, or apportioned direct tax, for the payment of troops. A similar measure in 1363 had helped to cope with the brigandage of that period, and the *taille* of 1439, which continued to be levied indefinitely, gave Charles VII additional resources for restoring order. When the English, now thoroughly on the defensive, agreed to a truce in 1444, there was danger of a vast increase in the number of unemployed troops, but Charles employed many of these potential brigands on an expedition against the Swiss, thus depleting their ranks.

Finally, in 1445, in perhaps the most important enactment of his reign, Charles VII established the *compagnies d'ordonnance,* a force of 9,000 mounted troops on regular salary that posterity would remember as the first "standing army." These companies gave unruly nobles useful employment, linked them to the fortunes of the Valois dynasty, and bolstered their esprit de corps. The new army curbed brigandage and after 1449 quickly drove the English from France, effectively ending the Hundred Years War.

By the time he was fifty, Charles VII was at last a victorious and respected king, whose reign laid the basis for the modern French state, but he never really solved the problem of defiant or nearly autonomous French princes. The man who would eventually do so, Charles's son Louis, was himself part of the problem in the 1440's. For the last fifteen years of Charles's reign, the king and his heir were estranged. Their respective councillors seem to have played an important role in prolonging the rift. The future Louis XI, for five years in exile at the court of Philip the Good of Burgundy, was overjoyed to learn of his father's death in 1461.

Charles VII was one of those French kings whose personality has been submerged beneath the spectacular exploits or foibles of those who served him. Only recently has he gained recognition for being a skillful political operator in trying circumstances.

BIBLIOGRAPHY

Gaston du Fresne de Beaucourt, *Histoire de Charles VII,* 6 vols. (1881–1891); and Malcolm G. A. Vale, *Charles VII* (1974).

JOHN BELL HENNEMAN

[See also **Burgundians; France, 1314–1494; Henry V of England; Hundred Years War; Joan of Arc; Louis XI of France; Pragmatic Sanction of Bourges; Taille, Tallage; Taxation, French.**]

CHARLES MARTEL (*ca.* 688–741) did not receive his sobriquet (meaning "the Hammer") until long after his death, but he had earned it by a long series of victories. He was a member of a great Austrasian (East Frankish) family that had long been powerful in that region. In the seventh century the old line of Merovingian kings lost all power (though they kept their titles) to the mayors of the palace, the leaders of the aristocracy. The most successful mayors in the east were Charles's ancestors; his grandfather, Pepin II of Herstal, ruled the Frankish kingdoms from 687 to 714—though he was careful to keep a Merovingian king as nominal ruler. When Pepin died in 714 his legitimate heirs were still children. Charles, the son of a concubine, took control, defeating his father's widow and her supporters. By 718 he was accepted as mayor by all the Frankish regions.

Charles did not neglect his Germanic lands (he helped St. Boniface in his efforts to convert Frisians and Saxons), but his real problem was to protect and centralize the administration of southern France. The Muslims, who had destroyed the Visigothic kingdom of Spain in 711, poured across the Pyrenees into southern France, occupying and holding most of the Mediterranean coastal area for a generation. Whether they wanted more land is uncertain, but they certainly wanted more plunder. A great raid to the north was checked by Charles Martel near Poitiers in 732. This was not as decisive a victory as is sometimes claimed; the Muslims sacked Arles and Avignon three years later and held the Narbonne region even longer, but the danger of creating a powerful Muslim state in France was averted.

Charles was a supporter of missionaries and by his lights a good Christian, but he made it clear that he controlled the Frankish church. He sought help from the Lombard king Liutprand in his wars with the Muslims, though Liutprand was often opposed

by Pope Gregory II; he named and deposed bishops and used church revenues to support his government. The pope admonished him but never broke with him; after all, Charles was the most powerful Catholic king in the West.

One final act, or rather a failure to act, was to have great future significance. When Theodoric IV, the nominal Merovingian king, died in 737, Charles—unlike all previous mayors—did not bother to replace him. Thus Charles's son Pepin the Short could later lay claim to a vacant throne and establish the Carolingian dynasty. After Charles's death his lands were divided between his sons; Carloman took the east and Pepin the west. But, once the succession was assured, Carloman became a monk, and Pepin had all of his father's lands and powers. Not surprisingly, he took the title of king in 751.

BIBLIOGRAPHY

There is no good modern biography. On the period, see especially H. M. Gwatkin and J. P. Whitney, eds., *The Cambridge Medieval History,* II (1964), chs. 4 and 5; Ferdinand Lot, *The End of the Ancient World and the Beginnings of the Middle Ages* (1931); and Henry St. Lawrence Moss, *The Birth of the Middle Ages, 395–814* (1935).

JOSEPH R. STRAYER

[See also **Boniface, St.; Carolingians and the Carolingian Empire; Islam, Conquests of; Mayor of the Palace; Merovingians; Pepin.**]

CHARLES OF ORLÉANS (*b.* Paris 24 November 1394–*d.* Amboise 4/5 January 1465), prince and poet, was the eldest surviving son of Louis, duke of Orléans (brother of King Charles VI), and Valentina Visconti (daughter of the duke of Milan). Heir to his parents' libraries, which with his own additions would provide the nucleus of the Bibliothèque Nationale, Charles lived at the center of the literary and political life of his age. He was married three times: to Isabelle of Valois, eldest child of Charles VI and widow of Richard II of England; to Bonne of Armagnac; and to Marie of Clèves, who survived him and by whom he had three children, including one son, the future King Louis XII.

After the assassination of his father in 1407 by followers of the duke of Burgundy and the death of his mother the next year, Charles became a pivotal figure in the long civil war between the Armagnac-Orléanist faction and the Burgundians, and in the renewed hostilities with England. Captured at Agincourt (1415), he spent the next twenty-five years a prisoner in England. His captivity helped to inspire the mission of Joan of Arc and her companion in arms Jean Dunois, Charles's half-brother, the Bastard of Orléans. Released in 1440, Charles sought unsuccessfully to achieve the peace for which he had promised to work. After fruitlessly pursuing his matrilineal claim to the duchy of Milan, he retired to Blois, making it a center of literary activity where François Villon, among others, flourished.

Charles himself, a poet of considerable reputation in his own day and again, after his rediscovery in the eighteenth century, in ours, has been called the last troubadour. In the present century particularly, his reputation as a poet has grown, as readers have discovered in him a sensibility quite modern, and the qualities of a symbolist poet who uses the allegorical mode of late-medieval lyric, with its personified abstractions and courtly metaphors, to give concrete, and at times ironic, expression to his self-conscious, even private, reflections on the intimate workings of heart and mind, on the psychological, emotional, and moral realities of lover, prisoner, patriot, and prince. In a fluent, pellucid, almost everyday language he presents his thoughts and feelings with directness, grace, and surface simplicity. His poems, in both French and English, are primarily rondeaux and ballades, though he also wrote other short lyrics and longer stanzaic narratives. Slightly more than half of 6,500 lines of English verse, now generally accepted as his, have analogues in his French poems, but given the difficulties with dating the various poems, the exact relations between the English and French versions are not always clear. We can, nonetheless, detect in his many lyrics, the majority of which date from the latter part of his English period and again from the time of his retirement at Blois, a progress from the conventional idealism of late medieval courtly poetry to a more realistic, even ironic, style. For some critics this development reflects the vagaries of this French prince's personal life; others would locate the origin in the poet's literary history, in his being influenced by the works of Geoffrey Chaucer.

In the case of the poet-prince of Orléans, it is extremely difficult to separate the biographical and the literary; his active involvement in the turbulent history of the fifteenth century exists in counterpoint to his contributions as poet and patron of poets. He personally embodies many of the contradictions of the waning Middle Ages.

BIBLIOGRAPHY

Editions. Pierre Champion, ed., *Poésies,* 2 vols. (1923–1927); Robert Steele and Mabel Day, eds., *The English Poems of Charles of Orleans,* 2 vols. (1941–1946); John Fox, ed., *Choix de poésies* (1973); *The Poems of Charles of Orleans,* sel. and intro. by Sally Purcell (1973).

Studies. Pierre Champion, *Vie de Charles d'Orléans (1394–1465)* (1911); Jacques Charpier, ed., *Charles d'Orléans: Un tableau synoptique de la vie et des oeuvres* (1958); John Fox, *The Lyric Poetry of Charles of Orleans* (1969); Norma L. Goodrich, *Charles, Duke of Orleans: A Literary Biography* (1963), and *Charles of Orleans: A Study of Themes in His French and in His English Poetry* (1967); Ann Tukey Harrison, *Charles d'Orléans and the Allegorical Mode* (1975); Enid McLeod, *Charles of Orleans, Prince and Poet* (1969); Daniel Poirion, *Le poète et le prince: L'évolution du lyrisme courtois de Guillaume de Machaut à Charles d'Orléans* (1965).

M. F. VAUGHAN

[See also **Agincourt, Battle of; Allegory; Burgundy; Chaucer, Geoffrey; Courtly Love; French Literature: After 1200; Hundred Years War; Joan of Arc, St.; Troubadour, Trouvère, Trovadores; Villon, François; Visconti.**]

CHARMS, OLD HIGH GERMAN. Two charms recorded in a tenth-century manuscript belonging to the library of Merseburg cathedral are commonly regarded as relics of Germanic paganism. Both employ alliteration and rhyme. One, apparently intended to effect the release of a prisoner of war, tells how three groups of women (presumably workers of magic and identified by some with the Norse Valkyries, by others with the *matronae* of Rhenish cults) held a prisoner, hindered the army, and picked at fetters. There follows the magic formula: "Leap from fetters, escape from foes." The other, more complex in form, tells how Phol and Wodan went hunting and "Balder's" horse sprained its foot. After two incantations had been performed by goddesses, Wodan charmed the horse and effected a cure. There follows the formula, presumably as uttered by the god: "Be it bone-sprain, be it blood-sprain, be it limb-sprain: bone to bone, blood to blood, limb to limbs: so be they limed together." No other German text mentions the god Balder, and possibly even here *balder* means "lord" and refers to Wodan. The word *Phol* is entirely mysterious. It may be the name of a god unattested elsewhere, or a corruption of Paulus or Apollo due to Germanic-Christian or Germanic-classical syncretism. Or it may not be a name at all, but part of an epithet for Wodan. No Germanic gods are named in other Old High German texts, except perhaps Donar, whose name may occur in a charm against epilepsy preserved in manuscripts at Paris and Munich.

All other German charms are ostensibly Christian, though perhaps adapted from pre-Christian forms. Their opening narratives recount apocryphal stories of cures worked by Christ, and the closing formula is a prayer, sometimes accompanied by a prescription for a course of action. A tenth-century manuscript now in Trier has a charm against lameness (*spurihalz* or *thaz entphangana*) in a horse. The charmer, after recounting how Christ and St. Stephen came to the city of Saloniun (Jerusalem?) and how the latter's horse became lame, goes on: "As Christ cured St. Stephen's horse of its lameness, so do I this horse with Christ's help. Pater noster." Then follows a prayer referring to the cure just recounted.

A ninth-century charm from Vienna tells, in rhyming verse, how a man leading his horse along the road met Christ. Asked why he was not riding, the man explained that his horse was lame *(errehet)*. Christ told him to take the horse aside, whisper in its ear, and tread on its right foot; then it would be cured. A Paternoster is to be said, the horse's legs and feet are to be rubbed, and a charm to be pronounced, mentioning the color of the horse and referring to the cure performed by Christ.

There are numerous charms against worms, believed to be the cause of various diseases, and against hemorrhages of different kinds. Some of the texts are corrupt and obscure.

Similar to the charms are numerous formulas for the protection of houses and livestock. A ninth-century Viennese manuscript contains a benediction for dogs, entered in the tenth century and employing alliterative phrases that may indicate early origin. It tells first how Christ was born before wolf and thief, and how St. Martin was Christ's shepherd. The dog owner beseeches these two to protect his dogs and bitches against he-wolf and she-wolf wherever they go, and to bring them home safe. A beekeeper's benediction from Lorsch exhorts the bee to obey St. Mary's command and not fly to the woods, but to sit very still and do God's will.

BIBLIOGRAPHY

Emil von Steinmeyer, *Die kleineren althochdeutschen Sprachdenkmäler* (1916, repr. 1963), 365–398; J. Knight Bostock, *A Handbook on Old High German Literature*, K. C. King and David R. McLintock, eds., 2nd ed. (1976), 26–42. On the second Merseburg charm see H. Rosenfeld, "*Phol ende Wuodan vuorun zi holza*. Baldermythe oder Fohlenzauber?" in *Beiträge zur Geschichte der deutschen Sprache und Literatur*, 95 (1973).

DAVID R. MCLINTOCK

[See also **Folklore and Magic, Western European; German Lyric.**]

CHARONTON (QUARTON), ENGUERRAND

(fl. 1444–1466), the outstanding artist of the Avignon school of painting. His two preserved documented works are a *Virgin of Mercy* (1452; Chantilly, Musée Condé) and a large, sumptuous *Coronation of the Virgin* (1454; Villeneuve-lès-Avignon, Hospice). Recently the famous *Avignon Pietà* (Paris, Louvre) has convincingly been attributed to Charonton.

BIBLIOGRAPHY

Michel Laclotte, *L'école d'Avignon; La peinture en Provence aux XIVᵉ et XVᵉ siècles* (1960); Charles Sterling, *Le "Couronnement de la Vierge" par E. Quarton* (1939), and "L'auteur de la 'Pieta' d'Avignon: Enguerrand Quarton (Charenton)," in *Bulletin de la Société nationale des antiquaires de France* (1959).

DON DENNY

CHARTER, a document recording and providing proof of a juridical act, such as a deed, contract, constitution, privilege, or mandate. The name comes from the Latin *c(h)arta* or *c(h)artula*, originally meaning a sheet of papyrus, then something written on papyrus, parchment, or paper (particularly a document, letter, or booklet). Some modern authorities would restrict the term to those medieval documents that were dispositive—that is, those which effected as well as testified to a juridical act; documents having only evidentiary value would be called notices *(notitiae)*.

Either party to a charter—the author, whose legal disposition was being recorded, or the recipient, in whose favor the charter was issued and to whom it was given to keep as proof of the juridical act—or even a third party could be responsible for composing and copying the written text, but eventually most public charters (those issued by people enjoying public trust, such as popes, emperors, and kings, and in the late Middle Ages also lesser rulers and institutions) were produced in the author's chancery.

A charter had two main parts: protocol and text. The first included at the beginning the names and titles of the author and recipient, a greeting, and possibly an invocation, and at the end (where it is sometimes called the eschatocol) it might include subscriptions of the author, witnesses, chancery officials, and scribes, along with the dating, a prayer, a seal, and other signs of validation. The text usually had a notification and exposition, and possibly a preamble preceding the disposition—the essential element—which might itself be followed by various concluding clauses.

Charters may be originals, drafts, or copies; normally only originals had legal force. Questions about the nature and genuineness of charters are dealt with in the modern science of diplomatics.

BIBLIOGRAPHY

Harry Bresslau and Hans Walter Klewitz, *Handbuch der Urkundenlehre für Deutschland und Italien*, 2nd ed., 2 vols. (1912–1931, repr. 1958); Albert Bruckner and Robert Marichal, eds., *Chartae latinae antiquiores: Facsimile-Edition of the Latin Charters Prior to the Ninth Century* (1954–); Arthur Giry, *Manuel de diplomatique* (1894); Peter H. Sawyer, *Anglo-Saxon Charters: An Annotated List and Bibliography* (1968).

JAMES J. JOHN

CHARTIER, ALAIN. Alain Chartier's life and works reflect the political and social upheaval of early-fifteenth-century France, a period marked by the Hundred Years War. Born (*ca.* 1385–1395) into a wealthy bourgeois family in Bayeux at the end of the fourteenth century, Chartier received the title *maître ès arts* from the University of Paris, was attached to the house of Yolande of Anjou, and later served as royal notary, secretary, and ambassador to the dauphin (the future Charles VII), following him into exile at Bourges in 1418. He thus allied himself politically with the dauphin's cause, which called for national unity and resistance to English domination. During his career, Chartier received a number of ecclesiastical benefices, including the canonries of Notre Dame de Paris and Tours, and the chancellorship of Bayeux. In a Latin letter of August 1429, the last official trace of him, he lauded the actions of Joan of Arc. He died at Avignon in 1430.

Chartier's patriotic feelings and moral ideas found their best expression in his prose works *Le livre de l'espérance* (often referred to as *La Consolation des Trois Vertus*), a series of political and moral lessons, and his masterpiece, *Le quadrilogue invectif* (1422), in which his oratorical style and rhythmic prose approach poetic dimensions and qualify him as "le père de l'éloquence française." In the latter work France, bemoaning her fate, confronts her children, Le Peuple, Le Chevalier, and Le Clergé, who have caused her grief by quarreling among themselves. Each attempts to justify his actions, and in the end Le Clergé calls for a halt to internecine disputes and a joining of forces against the enemy. The final passage of the work ascribes an important political role to the writer himself.

A variety of Latin works comprise part of Chartier's literary production. These include official ambassadorial speeches, political letters, invectives, and the *Dialogus familiaris*. Best known of these is the *De vita curiali*, in which the author criticizes court life and its vices. The French version, known as *Le Curial*, was apparently translated by an anonymous writer.

Chartier's poetic reputation is founded on his numerous ballades, rondeaux, and chansons composed in the French courtly tradition. A series of lengthier poetic works, such as *Le livre des quatre dames*, *La complainte*, and *Lay de paix* demonstrates an experimentation with less strictly defined lyric forms and the extended use of discourse in verse, an attempt perhaps to adapt poetry to an oratorical style.

Chartier's best-known poem and one of the most popular late medieval works, *La Belle Dame sans merci* (1424), precipitated a literary scandal and prompted a number of imitations and refutations. This debate between a suitor and his lady, who responds unfavorably to his advances, is traditional in theme and form, yet unconventional in the lady's adamant refusal, sustained by rational argumentation, to play the game of courtly love. The suitor, dominated by his emotions, futilely pleads his case, yet proves his sincerity in the end through his death. This denouement symbolizes the failure of society as much as of the lover and reflects Chartier's questioning of whether the traditional courtly ethic could be adapted to the changing society of his day.

BIBLIOGRAPHY

Les oeuvres latines d'Alain Chartier, Pascale Bourgain-Hemeryck, ed. (1977); *The Poetical Works of Alain Chartier*, J. C. Laidlaw, ed. (1974); Daniel Poirion, *Le poète et le prince: L'évolution du lyrisme courtois de Guillaume de Machaut à Charles d'Orléans* (1965); C. J. H. Walravens, *Alain Chartier: Études biographiques suivies de pièces justificatives* (1971).

CYNTHIA J. BROWN

[See also **Charles VII of France; Courtly Love; French Literature: After 1200.**]

CHARTRES CATHEDRAL. The Cathedral of Notre Dame at Chartres, approximately 90 kilometers (55 miles) southwest of Paris, is, with the cathedrals of Amiens, Bourges, Rheims, and Soissons, one of the outstanding examples of the High, or classic, phase of French Gothic. Chartres is the best known and most studied of the five because it may have been the most influential and because it preserves, more than any other Gothic building, its full original complement of sculpture and stained glass.

The Gothic cathedral of Chartres was begun after a fire on 9/10 June 1194 destroyed much of the Romanesque cathedral on the site, and was largely completed when the chapter took possession of the new choir in January 1220. This relatively brief period required for reconstruction insured stylistic unity and reflects the financial security and generosity of bishop, chapter, and city. Save for portions of the Carolingian and Romanesque crypt, the celebrated west portal *(portail royal)* and towers, and the northwest spire built after 1506 by Jean Texier (called Jean de Beauce), the entire cathedral was erected in about a quarter of a century, although seven of an intended nine spires were never built.

The designer-architect of Chartres is unknown. It has been proposed that there was no single designer-architect responsible for the building, but that the entire cathedral was designed and erected by successive crews of masons who came and went as work required and finances permitted.

The significance of Chartres in Gothic architecture is that it was one of the first High Gothic buildings of great size (the main vaults are 37 meters [121 feet] above the pavement) in which the vaulted gallery above the side aisle was eliminated, the high vaults being sustained by flying buttresses on the exterior of the building. This created the "cage" effect that characterizes the exteriors of French High Gothic buildings, and simplified the interior elevation to a large clerestory of the same width and height as the main arcade from which it is separated

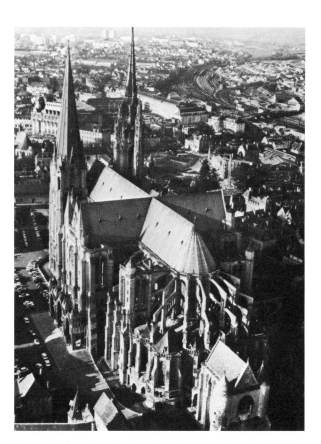

Chartres Cathedral: aerial view from the east, rebuilt 1194–1260. PHOTOGRAPH BY MONSIEUR VINCENT

by a narrow band triforium passage. This balanced scheme had substantial impact on later church design. However, both the idea of a "school of Chartres" and that of an active, conscious resistance to this design have been exaggerated. The building most influenced by Chartres was Rheims, the two cathedrals sharing a massive solidity of construction not found at Amiens or at Soissons. Bourges, begun the same year as Chartres, is different from it in design and as a spatial concept.

The sculptural programs of Chartres, dating from about 1150 to about 1250, are the most extensive of any medieval building, and exhibit the stylistic tendencies of the period as well as its significant iconographical themes. The Chartres sculptural programs, in conjunction with its extensive stained glass program, represent the full impact of a major Gothic cathedral as the *Biblia pauperorum.* The Chartres windows are of special interest because many were donated by the guilds of the city and reflect secular support of the cathedral as a major object of pilgrimage.

BIBLIOGRAPHY

Henry Adams, *Mont Saint Michel and Chartres* (1904), is the most famous general essay. The most recent are Robert Branner, *Chartres Cathedral* (1969); and George Henderson, *Chartres* (1968). Specialists should consult the numerous studies by Jan van der Meulen. The novel thesis that Chartres was built without an architect-designer is proposed by John James in *The Contractors of Chartres* (1978).

CARL F. BARNES, JR.

[See also **Gothic Architecture.**]

CHARTREUX, USE OF. See **Carthusian Rite.**

CHASOVNYA (medieval Greek: *euketērion*), a small, free-standing chapel or oratory, usually in the shape of a miniature church, but normally without an altar. Such shrines, usually containing one or more icons, are common in Eastern Orthodox lands, where they are built at sites of important events, over graves of reputed saints, and often in small cemeteries.

BIBLIOGRAPHY

The history of oratories in the Orthodox world is summarized in the article "Chasovni" in the Brockhaus-Efron *Entsiklopedichesky slovar,* XXXVIII (1903), 404–405.

GEORGE P. MAJESKA

[See also **Oratory.**]

CHASTELAINE DE VERGI, LA, a famous tragic love story repeatedly hailed as one of the gems of Old French literature. A short, dense poem of 958 octosyllabic lines composed by an unknown author between 1240 and 1288, probably in Picardy, it is one of the few tales of the period not based on legendary or Celtic material. The chastelaine has granted her favor to a young knight and has warned him not to reveal their love. When the duchess of Burgundy requires the young knight's love, he is caught between his feudal allegiance to the duke and his obligation to the chastelaine. The knight resists the duchess and privately explains his situation to his lord, but the duchess cunningly extracts the secret from her hus-

band in bed and sets out to punish the two young lovers. Through skillful innuendos the duchess drives the chastelaine to grief and a tearful death. Upon hearing this news the knight kills himself, whereupon the duke, convinced of his wife's guilt, kills her and becomes a Templar overseas.

The story reflects the traditional themes of courtly love and insists upon the importance of keeping love secret. It has affinities with Marie de France's *Lai de Lanval* and also with *Graelent, Guigemar,* and the *Lai des dous amans.* The story is also similar to that of *Pyrame et Thisbé.* Told largely in dialogue, with an exceptional economy of words, the poem employs connecting narrative only to illuminate the characters' intentions. There have been many adaptations, most notably in the *Novelle* of Matteo Bandello and the *Heptaméron* of Marie d'Angoulême (both mid sixteenth century).

BIBLIOGRAPHY

Editions. Gaston Raynand, ed., *La chastelaine de Vergi,* 4th ed. rev. by Lucien Foulet (1963); René Ernst Victor Stuip, ed., *La chastelaine de Vergi* (1970), a critical edition, includes all manuscripts from the twelfth through the fourteenth century; F. Whitehead, ed., *La chastelaine de Vergi,* 2nd ed. (1961).

Studies. Pál Lakits, *La châtelaine de Vergi et l'évolution de la nouvelle courtoisie* (1966); A. Lodge, "A New Manuscript of the *Chastelaine de Vergi,*" in *Romania,* 89 (1968); Edward B. Schlatter, *La chastelaine de Vergi* (1924); Paul Zumthor, "De la chanson au récit: *La chanson de Vergi,*" in *Vox romanica,* 27 (1968).

GUY MERMIER

[See also **Courtly Love; Marie de France.**]

CHASUBLE. See **Vestments.**

CHÂTELAIN DE COUCY. Guy de Thourotte was titular governor of Coucy castle from 1186 until his death in 1203 during the Fourth Crusade. His death and burial at sea are recorded by Villehardouin, who had become his adversary because of the châtelain's opposition to the conquest of Constantinople. A certain Jakemes, otherwise unknown, fictionalized his life in the *Roman du châtelain de Coucy et la dame de Fayel* (end of the thirteenth century). The hero, named Renaut in the romance, wins the Dame de Fayel's reluctant love by his exemplary chivalric behavior and his love songs (inserted in the narrative). Their affair is punctuated by broken promises, hesitation, illness, doubt, jealousy, betrayal, and revenge. It climaxes with the husband's tricking Renaut into setting off on a Crusade. During the expedition he dies from a poisoned arrow, but has arranged that his heart be removed from his body and returned to his Lady in a package also containing a love letter and the locks of her blond hair she had granted him as an amorous token. Fayel intercepts the missive with its damning evidence and serves the human remains to his wife for dinner. Upon learning of the deed, she falls into a mortal swoon.

Delbouille has shown that Guy de Thourotte, not Renaut (the name of two later châtelains of Coucy), was the model for the romance and the poet who inherited the legend of perfect lover. Though as many as thirty-three poems have been attributed to him, Lerond accepts only seven as sure, but admits that Guy may have composed as many as twenty-five songs. In conventional portraits he celebrates his lady, who, in contrast to the character created in the romance, is distinguished by her dark, rather than blond, hair and by quick acquiescence to her lover's wishes.

BIBLIOGRAPHY

Maurice Delbouille, ed., *Le roman du castelain de Coucy et de la dame de Fayel* (1936); Jean Frappier, *Le poésie lyrique en France aux XIIe et XIIIe siècles* (1960), 162–172, a close analysis; Alain Lerond, ed., *Chansons attribuées au Chastelain de Coucy* (1964); G. Muraille, "Le Châtelain de Coucy," in *Dictionnaire des lettres françaises: Le Moyen Age* (1964).

JOHN L. GRIGSBY

[See also **Crusades and Crusader States; French Literature.**]

CHÂTELET (or Grand Châtelet), a Parisian fortress on the right bank of the Seine, built or rebuilt in the early twelfth century by Louis VI to guard the Pont au Change leading to the Île de la Cité. From the late twelfth or early thirteenth century it housed the court and prison of the royal *prévôt* of Paris. In front of its eastern facade was the main slaughterhouse of the butchers' guild; immediately to the west of the Châtelet was the open-air morgue and the city's main fish market. The chaussée St. Lazare (now the rue St. Denis), the only street from the right bank to the Île de la Cité, went through its main gate, past

the prison and the St. Leufroy chapel (which housed the official city weight for grain and flour).

The courtroom was on the west side of the fortress. It was a single large room with two sets of benches: the "high bench," where the *prévôt* or his lieutenant sat to hear cases, and the "low bench" for the civil and criminal "auditors," whose existence was officially recognized in 1313 as judges for small claims. It was a noisy space, filled with the arguments of proctors and advocates, the cries of prisoners being sent to torture, and the jokes and songs of clerks, a place where in confusion the proctors sometimes mixed their papers with those of the judges.

The prison occupied a square tower in the northeast corner of the fortress. The higher rooms, for prisoners of quality, were open and airy; there the prisoners paid four *deniers* (or pence) a night for the bed (unless they brought one from home) and two *deniers* for the room. Food was also at the prisoner's expense. The next lower level was a single room shared by many prisoners. Below ground were the *fosse, puis, gourdaine,* and *oubliette*—dark and humid dungeons. Prisoners were dropped into the *fosse* through a trapdoor and brought out with a rope over a pulley. Even there the jailer demanded one *denier* a night for expenses.

The jurisdiction of the *Garde de la prévôté de Paris,* as he was called when the position was no longer put out at an annual lease, extended beyond Paris to a variable number of castellanies, fiefs, *prévôtés,* and ecclesiastical and rural communities in the surrounding countryside. These constituted the "*prévôté* and viscounty of Paris." Within this fluctuating field of action the *prévôt* had immediate jurisdiction over all lands not held by high-justicier lords or benefiting from some exemption, and jurisdiction on appeal from all seignorial courts and from some of the other royal *prévôtés* within the viscounty. In criminal matters, King Charles VI and his successors extended the Châtelet's jurisdiction ad hoc to other places in northern France. Out of the court's civil jurisdiction came the Custom of Paris, the most influential French regional custom of the early modern period.

The *prévôts* had all the administrative, fiscal, and military tasks of a royal bailli. With little time for the courtroom, they commissioned lieutenants to take their place or assist them. The auditors, originally deputed merely to hear witnesses, became judges and soon had their own lieutenants and clerks. (From 1325 to 1377 the auditorship was leased by the king for an annual payment.) Examiners were appointed to hear witnesses, their wages of eight *deniers* per witness within Paris paid by the parties.

The quantity of all these officials grew during the fourteenth century, as did the number of sergeants (440 at the beginning of the fifteenth century), about whom complaints were continuous. Attempts were made to fix the number of proctors appearing before the Châtelet courts, but without success. Any advocate admitted to Parlement could appear there as well. By 1320, if not before, the king had a permanent proctor and two advocates to represent him in the Châtelet. From the 1260's on, notaries, or "sworn clerks," were allowed to draw up individual private contracts, giving them the form of letters from the *prévôt* and bearing his seal. In case of dispute these were justiciable in first instance in the Châtelet. In 1302, sixty notaries practicing there took oaths to Philip IV and were installed in a large room, each with a numbered bench and a signboard over his workspace.

Few records of the medieval Châtelet courts survive: we have only one register of criminal cases (1389–1392) and fourteen registers of civil cases, some of them damaged and fragmentary (1395–1510). One can therefore only glimpse the courts at work. Criminals were charged and imprisoned only if caught in the act or accused by someone. Once caught, the accused had no rights. They were put to torture, either to force a confession or to get them to admit other crimes if they did confess. Justice, in the three years on record, was swift and harsh. Out of 127 accused in 107 cases, 98 were condemned to death, the remainder to the pillory, mutilation, or banishment, 9 of these were executed the same day and 45 more before a week had passed. Men were executed by hanging, except where the nature of the crime called for beheading or burning. Women were burned or buried alive. In this impoverished society crimes against property were feared more than crimes against persons. Of all those tried, 56 percent were convicted for theft, fraud, or possession of stolen goods. Only 13 percent of the accused thieves were able at least to save their lives, in contrast to 33 percent of those accused of other crimes. Murderers were more likely to receive royal mercy.

The civil procedure of the Châtelet, conducted in French, was formal and complex and left ample room for delays and chicanery (as it did in other courts of the era). In order to ensure that both parties could present their arguments and that the ritual of litigation was fully played, each step in the proceedings—adjournment, oral presentation of demands and responses, written presentation of the same, presentation of written "articles" (propositions of law and fact relevant to the case), oath of good faith, inquest (itself a complex procedure)—allowed defaults, exceptions, excuses, and appeals to Parlement. Sometimes the *prévôt* would consult with the Parloir aux Bourgeois (the municipal council and commercial court of the city) on points of custom, or one of the parties would demand an *enquête par turbe,* an inquest on a point of law among those in a position to know (advocates, artisans, merchants). Major procedural and substantive law was also created by the accumulation of precedents. Practitioners before the court collected these decisions in volumes often called "Style of the Châtelet." The most important of these, assembled by Jacques d'Ableiges in 1385–1389, became known as the *grand coutumier.*

BIBLIOGRAPHY

Sources. Direction des Archives de France, *Guide des recherches dans les fonds judiciaries de l'Ancien Régime* (1958), 163–220; Paris, Châtelet, *Registre criminel du Châtelet de Paris 1389–92,* H. Duplès-Agier, ed. (1861–1864); Alexandre Tuetey, ed., *Inventaire analytique des livres de couleur et des bannières du Châtelet de Paris,* 2 vols. (1899–1907); Jacques Hillairet, *Dictionnaire historique des rues de Paris* (1963), I, 330–334.

Studies. L. Batiffol, "Le Châtelet de Paris vers 1400," in *Revue historique,* 61–63 (1896–1897); L. Carolus-Barré, "L'organisation de la juridiction gracieuse à Paris: l'officialité et le Châtelet," in *Le moyen âge,* 100 (1963); J. Guerout, "La question des territoires des balliages royaux: l'exemple de la 'prévôté et vicomté' de Paris (XIIIe–XVIIIe siècles), Comité des travaux historiques et scientifiques," in *Actes du 100ᵉ Congres des sociétés savantes, Paris—1975* (1978), 7–18; J. Lavoie, "Justice, criminalité, et peine de mort en France au moyen âge," in C. Setto, ed., *Le sentiment de la mort au moyen âge* (1979), 31–55; François Olivier-Martin, *Histoire de la coutume de la prévôté et vicomté de Paris,* 2 vols. (1922–1930); Célestin Louis Tanon, *L'ordre du procès civile au XIVe siècle au Châtelet de Paris* (1886).

FREDRIC L. CHEYETTE

[See also **Law, French; Paris; Prévôt, Probst, Provost.**]

CHAUCER, GEOFFREY. According to testimony he gave in 1386, Geoffrey Chaucer was then aged "forty years and more," which implies a birthdate of

1345 or earlier: his birth may have been as early as 1340. There are few records of his personal life to balance the many of his official life, and his poetry almost entirely eschews autobiography. He was the son of John Chaucer, a prosperous wholesale wine merchant who carried on his trade at a dwelling in Thames Street in London, where Geoffrey was probably born. His mother was presumably the former Agnes de Copton who is mentioned in records dating from 1349 as John Chaucer's wife. Geoffrey was probably educated at one of the good London schools, where he could have acquired at least the beginnings of his knowledge of Ovid and of the *Aeneid,* and could have been exposed to other Latin works both classic and medieval, as well as to some science, in which he was always interested. He probably knew French from an early age, since it was the language of his father's business as well as of the court to whose service he was destined. By April 1357 he had become a member of the household of Elizabeth, countess of Ulster and the wife of Earl Lionel, second son of the reigning monarch, Edward III. It is supposed that he served as a page for the

Geoffrey Chaucer. From the Ellesmere Chaucer, *ca.* 1410. THE HENRY E. HUNTINGTON LIBRARY AND ART GALLERY, SAN MARINO, CALIFORNIA

countess, whose account book is the first historical record in which he appears.

SERVICE IN THE NORTH AND ABROAD

Since it was common for children of wealthy bourgeois families to enter the service of great households, Chaucer was only one of a number of young persons in Elizabeth's retinue, receiving training in courtly ways and probably also continuing their formal education under a tutor, performing menial and ceremonial services, and perhaps providing entertainment with songs and verse. While the countess had her principal residence at Hatfield in Yorkshire, she was a tireless traveler who never missed a state occasion, so that Chaucer may have gotten to see much of England and many of its great personages. In 1359, when King Edward crossed the Channel to enforce, once again, his claim to the French throne, Chaucer was in the invading army, probably in Earl Lionel's division. Chaucer was captured by the French, perhaps near Rheims, in late 1359 or early 1360, and on 1 March 1360 the king paid £16 (a considerable sum) for his ransom. In October the earl paid him for bearing letters from Calais to England. The Treaty of Brétigny was ratified in Calais in October, and if Chaucer's letters had to do with that, this was the first of his many diplomatic missions.

There is no record of Chaucer or his activities for the next five years. If, as some suppose, he attended the Inns of Court, it was during this period. But the rediscovery of a record in Pamplona, Spain, in which the king of Navarre grants safe conduct to Geoffrey Chaucer, "an English squire," and his three companions, makes it seem possible that he was in the service of the Prince of Wales (the Black Prince) in Aquitaine. This province had been yielded to the English by the Treaty of Brétigny, and the Prince of Wales held his court there. It has been suggested that Chaucer was passing through Navarre on a mission having to do with Peter I of Castile, whom the English were backing in his struggle to keep his crown from his French-backed brother, Henry of Trastamara.

In Aquitaine, Chaucer may have met his future wife, Philippa, daughter of Sir Paon de Roet, a knight of Hainault in the service of Edward's Queen Philippa, also of Hainault. It is as a *domicella* of Queen Philippa that Philippa Chaucer's name first appears in records. It is not known when Philippa and Geoffrey were married, but it was before 12 September 1366, when the king granted her a lifetime annuity of ten marks as a member of the queen's retinue. Marriage to one so well placed may have speeded Chaucer's preferment at court: on 20 June 1367 the king awarded a life annuity of twenty marks to his beloved *valettus* (yeoman), Geoffrey Chaucer. It may also have been through Philippa that Chaucer gained the attention of the duke of Lancaster, John of Gaunt. Philippa's sister, Katherine Swynford, became the governess of John's children and also his mistress and, in 1396, his third wife. Philippa Chaucer followed her sister into the Lancaster household sometime after the death of Queen Philippa in 1369, though perhaps not until John's marriage to Constance of Castile, daughter of Peter I, in 1371.

EARLY POEMS: THE ROMANCE OF THE ROSE

Somehow during the 1360's, despite his duties as a courtier, Chaucer managed to read voraciously, especially in French poetry, and was himself becoming a poet. Scholars assign to this period some of his ballades in the courtly French tradition, such poems as the "Complaint to His Lady" and the "Complaint to Pity." He probably wrote many more poems like these, not only at this time but during his whole career; but few of his short poems have survived. A pleasantly pious hymn to the Virgin Mary (generally called "An ABC") was, according to an old story, written at the request of Blanche of Lancaster. It is a translation of some lines of the French of Guillaume de Guilleville's *Pélerinage de la vie humaine,* a long religious allegory, interesting because it concerns a pilgrimage very different from the one Chaucer was later to invent.

Also assigned to this decade is Chaucer's translation of the *Roman de la Rose.* Only a small portion of this has survived (in three fragments), and there is doubt that he ever translated the entire French poem, which is almost 22,000 lines long. In his *Legend of Good Women* Chaucer has the God of Love reprimand his surrogate for the translation, while a ballade addressed to Chaucer by the French poet Eustache Deschamps praises him for it. Even the surviving fragment, however, appears to be only partly Chaucer's work, the first 1,705 of its 7,696 lines in octosyllabic couplets. The rest of the fragment has many non-Chaucerian usages, especially in rhyme, and seems to be the work of two different writers. Only one manuscript has survived, and without ascription; Chaucer was first named as its author in Thynne's 1532 edition of his works.

Whether or not he translated it all, Chaucer knew the *Roman* well, for his own work shows hundreds of reflections of it. The delicate courtly allegory of Guillaume de Lorris, with its psychologizing of the lover and his mistress, is a kind of fountainhead of amorous verse, as well as of the dream vision, in late medieval France and England. There is nothing in the earlier part, which is all that has survived in Chaucer's translation, to offend the God of Love; but Jean de Meun's huge continuation contains much that might offend him, for its author delights in antifeminist ideas, as, indeed, he delights in ideas of all sorts. His witty discussions of some of the dominant issues in medieval thought provided Chaucer with a kind of encyclopedia of facts and theories, philosophical, scientific, and religious. While Chaucer took much from de Lorris, including the dream vision form, one feels that the kind of poetry that characteristically presents a woman in the guise of a flower (though Chaucer himself did that once in partial jest) was not really congenial to him, as were Jean de Meun's satiric humor and delight in intellectual activity.

THE BOOK OF THE DUCHESS

Chaucer's most remarkable work during the 1360's was the *Book of the Duchess,* written in honor of John of Gaunt's first wife, Blanche of Lancaster, who had died in September 1368. Despite the absence of any record associating Chaucer or his wife with John of Gaunt before 1371, the poem suggests a certain intimacy, perhaps brought about through Katherine Swynford. The celebration of the dead lady, like the translation of the *Roman,* is written in octosyllabic couplets, and the poem demonstrates for the first time Chaucer's talent for borrowing motifs, incidents, images, and even lines, from earlier poetry—in this case mainly Froissart, Machaut, and the *Roman*—and producing from these secondhand materials something wholly new and original.

The poem also illustrates his first use of a distinctive first-person narrator that he was to develop in poem after poem. Dramatic monologue seems to have come naturally to him: he was always aware that the meaning of a narrative may acquire rich complexity by being filtered through the personality of a distinctive, often idiosyncratic, narrator. This awareness appears in many of the *Canterbury Tales,* both where the narrator is characterized in advance of his tale and where his character is allowed to define itself in the telling. Modulations in his tone, revealing implicit, perhaps subconscious attitudes, over- and underemphases, even the interstices in the narrator's own understanding of the story, may provide a meaning more interesting than what he thinks his story means. Since Chaucer was an ironist, he is apt to allow the interstices in the narrator's understanding to be very large, especially in those works like the *Book of the Duchess,* where he himself is presumably the teller.

Like the *Roman de la Rose,* the *Book of the Duchess* is a dream vision, but unlike it more than a fifth of its 1,300-odd lines are concerned with the waking narrator and his eight years' sleeplessness. This insomnia, presumably caused by frustration in love, is cured only when he learns, while reading the sad Ovidian story of Ceyx and Alcyone, of the existence of a god of sleep, Morpheus; the level of the narrator's naiveté is established by his comment that he had hitherto not heard of any god but one. A prayer to Morpheus brings sleep, from which he wakes into the May morning usual in dream visions. He joins a hunt that is just getting started, loses interest in it during a pause in the action, and while wandering down a path in the woods after a stray puppy, comes upon a knight clad in black sitting with his back to a tree. The dreamer addresses him, and although he has overheard him lament the death of his lady, he asks to learn the cause of his grief so that he might share it with him.

Responding to the dreamer's desire to be helpful, the knight describes the most attractive character of his lady White (Blanche) and tells how he fell in love with her and how she finally accepted him as her lover. The celebration of White is the major part of the poem; and whenever the knight seems about to let his grief impede his account of her, a misunderstanding or nonunderstanding comment by the dreamer forces him back on the track. The result is a kind of catharsis, through which the negative in the knight's memory—how much he had lost—is balanced by the positive—how much he had had. The dreamer offers no easy answer to the knight's loss, and at the end of the poem, still presumably ignorant of the cause of the knight's grief, he has to be told flatly that White is dead. His reply, "By God, it's a pity," is, in its very inadequacy, a brilliant recognition of the futility of condolence in a poem that has indirectly pointed out the futility of grief.

The indirection of the poem is extremely tactful. Even in his surrogate, the dreamer, Chaucer does not presume to intrude on the grief that John of Gaunt presumably felt at the death of Blanche; and the celebration of Blanche's character is dissociated from the poet by being put in the mouth of John's surro-

gate. Nor does the poem show any of the condescension that inevitably accompanies either a Christian or a philosophical consolation. Even the identification of the knight and his lady is oblique, revealed only in puns. The poem's comic moments, which some readers find offensive, are themselves tactful reminders of the pleasure that is to be found in a life that the mourner must go on living. Though the duke was not, according to history, a man of large intellect or great sensitivity, his subsequent benefactions to Geoffrey and Philippa Chaucer suggest that he approved of the poem honoring his late wife.

FURTHER TRAVELS ABROAD

Chaucer crossed the Channel in 1368, 1369, and 1370, still a member of the king's household. Edward's original grant had styled him a *valettus,* but after 1372 the records tend to refer to him as *armiger* (or *scutifer) regis,* king's esquire. The latter is a term of greater dignity, suggesting that Chaucer had won respect for his administrative (and possibly for his poetic) abilities. It is assumed that his principal value to the king was, at this time, in diplomacy: the records of the 1370's show a number of journeys overseas on royal business. The tact of the author of the *Book of the Duchess* was apparently a genuine diplomatic asset.

The first of these diplomatic journeys, and from the point of view of literary history the most important, was to Genoa and Florence in late 1372 and early 1373. The purpose of the visit to Genoa was to arrange for an English port for Genoese merchants in accordance with a commercial treaty made previously. Chaucer traveled with two Genoese who were in Edward III's service, and it is possible that he was chosen for the mission because of a knowledge of Italian. Why he went to Florence is not known. He could have met Giovanni Boccaccio on this trip, but it is unlikely that he did so; but he surely encountered Boccaccio's works, which offered him a new literary experience, very different from the French works he knew so well. On his return journey his baggage probably included manuscripts of Boccaccio's *Teseida, Filostrato, Filocolo,* and other works both Italian and Latin, though not, apparently, the *Decameron;* there is some evidence that he read the *Decameron,* but not that he possessed a copy of it.

He probably also acquired in Italy a manuscript of poetry by Italy's most famous living writer, Petrarch; and it is likely that he acquired a manuscript of Dante's *Divine Comedy.* The last two influenced

Chaucer's work in various important ways, but it was Boccaccio's Italian works that brought him the Italian Renaissance and were to make him the first English Renaissance poet a century before the English Renaissance is said to have begun. It is an odd irony that, while he mentions Dante and Petrarch several times in his works, he never mentions his greatest teacher, Boccaccio.

CONTROLLER OF THE CUSTOM

It is hard to see how Chaucer found time to digest his Italian acquisitions and even harder to see how he was so soon able to write works reflecting their influence, for the next few years are replete with records of various official duties, for which one of his rewards was the royal gift of a daily pitcher of wine. In 1374, Chaucer leased, rent-free, a house on the wall of London above the gate at Aldgate, and on 12 June he was sworn in as controller of the custom and subsidy on wool for the port of London. On the next day he was granted a life annuity of £10 by John of Gaunt in consideration of services rendered by Chaucer and his wife.

Chaucer's new position was a most important one, for the duty on the export of wool was one of the principal sources of revenue for the Crown, and the controllers at the various ports of England were the king's immediate agents. It was Chaucer's sworn duty to keep the records in his own hand, which meant daily attendance at the office on the Wool Quay. His salary was £10 a year, plus a bonus of ten marks; and this, along with the annuities he and Philippa had received from the king and the duke of Lancaster, as well as occasional other benefits, made him well-to-do. Yet by an anomaly common at the time, the two collectors of the custom, whose collections the controller recorded, were men of far greater wealth and influence than the controller.

Mercantile morality in Chaucer's England was poor at best, and men such as those who served as collectors with Chaucer were apt to use any civil office for self-enrichment. Chaucer no doubt found himself condoning if not conniving in conduct that would seem simple skulduggery to most. He was sworn by his oath of office not to accept gifts, but enormous amounts of money passed through the custom, and the Parliament of 1386, in which Chaucer sat as a member, complained that the controllers of the custom were oppressing the people with their extortions.

In any case, Chaucer carried on the job well enough so that when Edward III died in 1377, John of Gaunt and his party, who managed the realm on behalf of the boy king Richard II, reappointed Chaucer as controller. The next year Edward's grant of an annuity was confirmed by the Crown, which also commuted his earlier grant of a daily pitcher of wine into a life annuity of twenty marks. Royal favors and commissions continued during his career at the custom. In addition to receiving various wardships, forfeitures, and grants, he took part in the negotiations for a marriage between Richard and the French king's daughter Marie, who died while negotiations were still in progress. In 1378 he was sent to Italy a second time to treat with the lord of Milan, Bernabò Visconti, on a matter having to do with the war with France. These missions involved Chaucer with men of great prominence both abroad and in England.

TRANSLATION OF BOETHIUS

Despite full-time employment and journeys abroad, Chaucer still found time to increase his literary output. Though we are unable to date most of his works with any precision, it is assumed that those showing the most immediate influence of the Italians, along with others that seem immature in style or that form the basis for elements in his mature writing, belong to this period. Among the most important is his translation of Boethius' *Consolation of Philosophy,* Chaucer's longest prose work.

Chaucer probably knew the *Consolation* from his earliest years, for it was one of the best-known works of the Middle Ages. Its impact on Chaucer's thought was huge. Perhaps no other of his sources has engaged so much critical attention, since it underlies some of his greatest works. It provided him with a philosophy, ultimately optimistic, in which were contained high idealism, a strong sense of the harshness of human life combined with an appreciation for the good things that life can offer, and a kind of prescription for making the mind rise above the vagaries that fortune brings. As a supplement to Christian teaching and as a corrective to the pessimistic and anti-intellectual Christian teaching common in the period, it proved highly congenial to Chaucer; while it was written by a Christian, it eschews a Christian solution to life's ills, as Chaucer himself had done in the *Book of the Duchess* and was to do again in the Knight's Tale and elsewhere. The translation is literal down to incorporating Latin syntax even where such syntax is far removed from English, and it makes awkward reading. But Chaucer worked on it with painstaking care, using both the Latin text and a glossed French translation. Its contemporary success is suggested by its survival in eight manuscripts, as compared with three for the *Book of the Duchess* and the *House of Fame.*

HOUSE OF FAME

The latter is the most important original work that Chaucer produced during his earlier years in the custom. Like the *Book of the Duchess* and the translation of the *Roman,* it is written in octosyllabic couplets. It consists of 2,158 lines of narrative, divided into three books, the third unfinished. The proem to the first book is an encyclopedic summary of dream lore that leads to nothing but anticlimax because of the narrator's self-proclaimed inability to understand the subject. Dream visions are generally associated with May, but this one occurs on the night of 10 December. The dreamer finds himself in a temple of glass on the walls of which is depicted the action of Vergil's *Aeneid,* up through Aeneas' desertion of Dido. Having seen (or heard) Dido's lament as it appears in Ovid's *Heroides,* the dreamer leaves the temple and finds himself in a desert where the only object in view is an eagle swooping down from the sky.

Here Book I ends without having established any clear theme. Book II begins with a proem that combines passages from Boccaccio's *Teseida* and Dante's *Divine Comedy,* perhaps the first fruits of Chaucer's Italian journey, introducing a new world of poetry to supplement the old one of Vergil and Ovid. The golden eagle, borrowed from Dante, seizes the dreamer and bears him upward swooning in terror. Fear does not, however, long paralyze the dreamer's computerlike mind, which starts rehearsing examples in literature of other mortals snatched up to the heavens while still alive. The English-speaking eagle explains that he has been sent by Jupiter to reward "Geoffrey" for all the love poetry that he has written without getting any benefit from it. (The eagle's reference to the poet's spending the evenings poring over books after his day's labor of "making reckonings" is the only recognizable autobiographical reference in Chaucer's works.) Jupiter's reward is to give the poet a trip to the House of Fame, where he will learn tidings of love as a reward for his having written so assiduously if ignorantly about it.

To while away the time of the journey, the eagle treats his passenger to an explanation of how everything spoken on earth ascends to the House of Fame, and gives him a careful scientific account of the operation of sound waves. The dreamer seems not much interested in the whole experience, however,

and when offered a chance to study at first hand the constellations that he has read about, he declines: he'll trust his books. Indeed, the bookish dreamer sees his whole flight in terms of the reports he has read of such flights; and when, arriving at the House of Fame, the eagle asks him to describe the sound he hears, he does so with images borrowed from Ovid's description of the same phenomenon.

The House of Fame, where the eagle deposits the dreamer at the beginning of Book III, is a Gothic castle situated on a hill of ice, crowded with minstrels and musicians and adorned with statues of all the ancient writers whom the Middle Ages considered great. It is presided over by a goddess who disposes of suitors for her favor in a wildly whimsical way, only occasionally honoring their deserts. After a long view of her behavior, the dreamer leaves Fame's palace and is transported to the House of Rumor. In this whirling wicker structure sixty miles long the dreamer is on the verge of learning some tidings of love when the poem breaks off in midsentence.

The image that the eagle uses in describing the action of sound waves could be applied to Chaucer in this poem: that of throwing into a pond a stone that causes waves to move outward until they reach the brink. Chaucer seems to have begun with the idea of fame as something conferred by literature, as in the bad fame of an abandoned Dido; but as he ponders the topic, other possible meanings of fame began to exfoliate from the first—what the writer's writing confers on himself, oral report, rumor, and the possible truth or falsity of all of these. His imagination's pond had no brink, and we are left with a remarkable fragment from which stands out the comedy of the eagle's pedantry and of the narrator's resistance to experience as a substitute for books.

MISCELLANEOUS WRITINGS

Another work often assigned to the late 1370's is the group of exempla that were later given to the Monk in the *Canterbury Tales.* These brief biographies of famous persons inexorably demonstrate how a capitalized Fortune hurls down those who rise high on her wheel. The negative moral, to distrust Fortune, excludes even the Christian advice to trust God instead: the tone is resolutely pessimistic. The many sources include Dante and two of Boccaccio's Latin works (one of which Chaucer assigns to Petrarch). Two exempla deal with persons Chaucer knew or may have known: Peter I of Castile, father of John of Gaunt's second wife, and Bernabò Vis-

Top left: The Knight; *top middle*: The Miller; *top right*: The Wife of Bath; *bottom left*: The Clerk; *bottom middle*: The Canon's Yeoman. From the Ellesmere Chaucer MS, *ca.* 1410. THE HENRY E. HUNTINGTON LIBRARY AND ART GALLERY, SAN MARINO, CALIFORNIA

conti, with whom Chaucer dealt on his second Italian journey. He was murdered in 1385, so that Chaucer's stanza about him, bemoaning his sad but unknown fate, must have been added after the original series of exempla.

The poem may represent one of Chaucer's first extended uses of the pentameter line in which all his mature works are written. He had not yet hit upon the pentasyllabic rhymed couplet as the form that suited him best, and in the Monk's exempla he uses an eight-line stanza rhyming *a b a b b c b c.* He never employed this stanza again; but a modification of it in which the fourth *b*-rhyming line is omitted, so that the last four lines of the seven-line stanza consist of two couplets, became his favorite alternative to the rhymed couplet in narrative poetry. The earliest use in a narrative of this stanza is in the life of St. Cecilia, probably composed in the 1370's but later assigned to the Second Nun on the Canterbury pilgrimage. The technical skill of the versification of this tale, a translation from the rather drab Latin of Jacobus de Voragine's *Golden Legend,* exceeds the effectiveness of the story itself. There is one splendid prayer, based on Dante, but Chaucer did nothing to alter the arbitrarily instantaneous conversions of pagans to Christianity with no suggestion of thought on the part of the converted. The tale's artful piety is hardly a substitute for real religious awareness.

Chaucer's references in the *Legend of Good Women,* a pre-Canterbury poem, to a story he had written about Palamon and Arcite suggest that there was an earlier version of the Knight's Tale, of which they are the heroes. If so, it was probably written in this period, for it is based on Boccaccio's *Teseida* and is strongly influenced by Boethius. The abortive *Anelida and Arcite,* also influenced by the *Teseida,* was probably also a product of the period. Beginning as if it were going to be a long narrative in rhyme royal, it becomes a series of lyric lamentations before breaking off; the figure of an abandoned mistress seems both to have appealed to Chaucer and, ultimately, to have bored him. Highly Boethian short poems such as the "Former Age," "Fortune," and "Gentilesse" also probably date from this time; pleasing expressions of conventional morality, they do not show much originality. "Lack of Steadfastness," with an envoy to King Richard, complains of the sorry state of the realm and should probably be dated somewhat later, after Richard had assumed regal power and had begun to misuse it. The most Chaucerian of the moral poems, "Truth," was, ac-

cording to an old story, composed on the poet's deathbed, but the spirit is very Boethian, and the story probably reflects its inventor's recognition of how quintessentially Chaucerian is the ballade's mixture of homely imagery with high idealism, of warm humor with detached spirituality; an envoy to one Vache, a name upon which the poet puns, may have been a later addition.

CICELY CHAMPAIN'S RAPE AND THE PARLIAMENT OF FOWLS

A record from 1380 has proved most embarrassing to Chaucerians: this is a release, dated 1 May, by one Cicely Champain to Geoffrey Chaucer from all actions concerning her *raptus.* Despite efforts to interpret this otherwise, it seems to mean that Cicely is releasing Chaucer of all legal actions having to do with her rape. The incident, whatever it was, is complicated by the apparent involvement of a London cutler and an armorer. In a record dated 28 June they release Chaucer of all legal actions, and in another of the same date Cicely Champain releases them of all legal actions. On 2 July the armorer signs a recognizance that he owes Cicely £10, payable at Michaelmas. The connection of the two artisans with the matter of Chaucer and Cicely's rape seems clear, but its exact nature is not readily explicable. A further oddity is that rape was not an offense that could be settled out of court. It has been suggested that Chaucer was caught—perhaps framed—in a seduction that could be technically construed as rape.

Whatever the nature of the incident, it had no adverse effect on Chaucer's career. In 1382 he was given the additional post of collector of the petty custom, for which he was permitted to appoint a deputy. These years of full official employment were, paradoxically, extraordinarily productive ones for his poetry, for in them he completed three important works. The earliest (some would date it back to the 1370's) was the *Parliament of Fowls.* A lovely if cryptic poem in praise of love, written to celebrate St. Valentine's Day, the *Parliament* is written in rhyme royal stanzas and is some 700 lines long. The narrator begins by establishing himself as one who is as awed by love as he is ignorant of it. In search of a certain but unnamed thing he reads Macrobius' edition of Cicero's account of the dream of Scipio, of which he gives an outline. Scipio's dream is itself a dream vision, in which Scipio's ancestor, the conqueror of Carthage, takes his descendant to the skies and shows him the pettiness of earth, exhorting him to spend his life working for the common good. The narrator, though delighted by the book, does not find in it the certain thing he was looking for. He goes to sleep and dreams that the elder Scipio leads him to a wall whose gate bears a double inscription, promising any who enter the greatest happiness and the greatest misery. Scipio pushes the hesitant dreamer through the gate, where he finds himself in a lovely garden filled with allegorical figures representing aspects of sexual love. In a temple presided over by Priapus he sees Venus herself lying half-naked, and observes on the wall depictions of great lovers of literary history, most of whom came to sorry endings.

A dutiful if hardly enthusiastic tourist—though less reluctant than his counterpart in the *House of Fame*—the narrator makes a cursory inspection of the temple and then leaves, finding himself in a different garden. Here all the birds are assembled before the Goddess Nature on the annual occasion of choosing their mates. First are three male eagles who love the same female, and their courtly debate over who deserves her takes almost the whole day. The lesser birds grow impatient, and Nature suggests that each avian class (there are four) appoint a representative to help solve the eagles' dilemma. But when the representatives are unable to agree on a solution, the assembly becomes disorderly, and finally, at the female eagle's request, Nature defers the decision for another year. The rest of the birds quickly choose their mates and then sing a roundel in praise of St. Valentine that wakens the dreamer, who reaches for another book in hope some day of finding something by which he will fare the better.

The poem is a characteristic mélange of elements from Macrobius, Dante, Alan of Lille, and, most prominently, Boccaccio, so blended as to result in something wholly original. It celebrates at once love and love's frustrations. The value of love is beautifully if negatively celebrated in the narrator's lyrical yearning for that "certain thing"—that love of which he is, as usual, wholly ignorant. Similarly, the unusual sensuousness of the description of the garden of love and the temple both romanticizes love and, especially in the oppressive and enervating atmosphere of the temple, suggests the frustrating paralysis that sensuality brings. Even the contrasting noisy vitality of the assembly of birds has its own frustrations in the inability of the eagles to solve their own dilemma in love or of the rest of the birds, balked in their own amorous enterprise, to solve it

for them. Seldom has love been celebrated at once so ambiguously and so persuasively.

TROILUS AND CRISEYDE

Chaucer's greatest single poem, one of the greatest in English, is *Troilus and Criseyde,* probably completed about 1385, though it must have been in composition for a long period. It is a work in rhyme royal stanzas of some 8,000 lines, divided into five books, purporting to be a translation from the Latin of one Lollius, identified in the *House of Fame* as one of the tellers of the story of Troy. Actually, the poem is in large part a translation of Boccaccio's Italian *Filostrato,* and Lollius is a fiction arising from a misreading of a couple of lines in Horace and mischievously adopted by Chaucer to give his work "authority." Boccaccio's poem had been built upon elements drawn from Benoît de Sainte-Maure's huge *Roman de Troie,* which in turn had been built on two purported eyewitness accounts of the Trojan War ascribed to Dares of Crete and Dictys of Troy, the meager fictions that in the Middle Ages replaced the Homeric version of the war.

In Benoît's romance, and in the Latin retelling of it by Guido delle Colonne, only the end of the love affair between Troilus and Criseyde is recounted. The Trojan lady Briseida (Boccaccio's Criseida) was, at the request of her traitorous father Calchas (who had deserted Troy for the Greeks) traded for the Trojan prisoner Antenor and had to join her father in the Greek camp, where she soon forsook the Trojan prince Troilus for the Greek Diomede. Boccaccio gave the story a beginning and a middle: how Troilo fell in love with Criseida; how, with the aid of her cousin Pandaro, she and Troilo consummated their affair; and how she was sent to the Greek camp, where she became unfaithful. Chaucer used the *Filostrato* in the original and also possibly in a French translation, but he also went back to Benoît and perhaps to Guido, and also to Dares through Joseph of Exeter's Latin verse translation. Moreover, his narrative is profoundly influenced by Boethian ideas and shows some borrowing from Petrarch and Dante. And although many of Chaucer's lines are literal translations of Boccaccio's, his story emerges as something wholly original.

The poem is developed at a most leisurely pace by the narrator, who is a modified version of those of the earlier dream visions, one much preoccupied with love but with no experience in love's discipline, who, despite Criseyde's bad reputation, seems to have adopted her as a substitute for a real-life mistress. He comments long-windedly on the story's surprisingly few incidents, presents with loving care long interior monologues by the two protagonists, and relays lengthy conversations between them and the third major character, Pandarus. The latter, the most talkative of them, is promoted from Criseyde's cousin to her uncle, the go-between who literally talks the lovers into their affair.

In outline, the plot is simple. Having fallen in love with Criseyde in a temple, young Prince Troilus is paralyzed by what for him is a new emotion and retires to his bedroom. Here Pandarus finds him lamenting his fate and laboriously extracts from him the fact that he is in love and the name of his lady. Having offered to help him obtain her, Pandarus calls on Criseyde and tells her of Troilus' love for her; he extracts from her a reluctant promise to show Troilus "better cheer." Alone, Criseyde carefully considers whether to accept Troilus' suit and is the more inclined to do so when he rides by her palace returning from battle: she is greatly pleased by his person. Pandarus, using an elaborate fiction, manipulates Troilus' brother into giving a dinner party at which Criseyde will hear Troilus praised by some of Troy's most important personages. Troilus is in a bedroom in the house, feigning illness, and Pandarus manages a meeting for the couple at which Criseyde accepts Troilus' service.

But Criseyde continues to behave warily, and in order to force the issue Pandarus invites her to dine at his house, assuring her that Troilus is out of town. After dinner it begins to rain so hard that Criseyde consents to spend the night. When she is bedded, Pandarus, employing further fictions, introduces Troilus, who has been hiding in the house, to her bedroom and, when Troilus faints, to her bed. The couple's love is consummated. An indeterminate time later Calchas persuades the Greeks to ask the Trojans for Criseyde in exchange for the Trojan Antenor, and the Trojan parliament accedes to the request. Troilus, Criseyde, and Pandarus at once despair, but Pandarus arranges for the lovers to have a night together, during which Criseyde promises to return to Troy by the tenth day. The next morning she is led to the Greek camp by Diomede, who immediately begins to make love to her.

Back in the city, Pandarus and the grief-stricken Troilus agonizingly await the tenth day, but by then Criseyde has lost her resolve to return; the narrator anticipates the future by showing us her full capitulation to Diomede some time before it occurs. Troi-

lus is at last persuaded of her faithlessness when he sees on armor taken from Diomede a brooch he had given her. He tries to kill Diomede in battle but is himself killed by Achilles. His soul ascends to the eighth sphere, whence he looks down and laughs at the folly of life and love on earth. The narrator enjoins the reader not to entertain earthly loves but to love Christ, who betrays no one. The poem ends with a magnificent prayer.

The modern reader is apt to find the poem most remarkable for its characterization. Troilus is, despite the warlike reputation, an idealist with such great regard for honorable conduct that he often seems helpless, unwilling even to suggest to his mistress that he prevent her going to the Greek camp by kidnapping her: for, as he observes, the Trojan war was caused by the kidnapping of a woman. Nor will he take any action that might injure Criseyde's reputation by revealing their secret love. Even his connivance in Pandarus' deceits does not much impair one's admiration for his selfless love of his lady.

That lovely young widow seems far more sophisticated and pragmatic than her lover; but she is far harder to characterize, for she is developed with much ambiguity and, as befits a beautiful woman who is to prove faithless, with much use of paradox. She is at once timorous and self-confident, reticent and forthright, hesitant and surefooted, withdrawn yet knowingly attractive. Her motives are seldom clear, but their lack of clarity enhances her mystery. Through much of the poem she is so charming that the known ending is obliterated from the reader's mind, so that when her treachery finally occurs it can hardly be believed. The reader is thus made to share Troilus' experience, in sympathy with whom the story is primarily told. Yet from many readers Criseyde evokes as much or even more sympathy, and they find it as impossible as Troilus does to "unlove" her despite her infidelity.

Pandarus, the catalyst, is an endlessly resourceful talker, never at a loss for a proverb to support whatever course of action he is recommending to the lovers at the moment. He is witty and can appeal to Criseyde's sense of humor; he can even extract an occasional laugh from Troilus. An unsuccessful lover himself, he throws himself into the business of uniting his niece and his friend with ebullient and attractive enthusiasm. He has a fabliau hero's wildly energetic imagination in devising schemes for uniting the pair, and some of the coarse directness of one when he strips the fainting Troilus and casts him into Criseyde's bed.

But there are suggestions of depths in Pandarus that are less attractive—in his vicarious enjoyment of someone else's love affair and in the nature of his love for his niece, which at one point seems to go well beyond avuncular affection. Like our sure but suppressed knowledge of Criseyde's eventual faithlessness, our awareness of the transition of the name Pandarus to "pander" is, while dormant, not dead. Though Chaucer's narrator steadfastly fails to see the latent potentialities in Criseyde and Pandarus, Chaucer manipulates the narrative in such a way that we at once recognize them and reject them because of the affection we feel for both characters. When Criseyde's infidelity reduces her to whore and Pandarus to pimp, the narrator can only repudiate earthly love with a cry of despair. But his despair is part of Chaucer's high vision of a world whose beauty human mutability and weakness both must and cannot render valueless.

THE LEGEND OF GOOD WOMEN

Chaucer's story of an unfaithful woman seems to have drawn immediate criticism from the ladies of the court, and one of them, probably Richard's queen, Anne of Bohemia, demanded that he write a poem celebrating female fidelity. That is the situation that lies behind his next work, the *Legend of Good Women,* probably written in 1386 and the first of his poems written in pentameter couplets, the predominant form of his later work. In its prologue, the narrator speaks of his faith in the truth of old books, which he ceases to read only in May, when daisies bloom. This leads him to extravagant praise of the daisy, to which he imputes all sorts of excellent womanly qualities. He then relates how, after a day in the fields admiring the daisy, he goes to sleep and dreams he is back in the fields. There he sees approaching the God of Love with a queen dressed like a daisy, followed by a huge retinue of faithful women.

The God of Love addresses the narrator harshly as a renegade to love because of his translation of the *Roman de la Rose* and his writing of *Troilus.* The queen defends Chaucer on the grounds that he has also written poems in praise of love (she gives a useful bibliography of his works) and that he translated the *Roman* and *Troilus* in ignorance, not knowing what he was doing. The God of Love accepts her intercession, and she assigns the narrator the penance of writing a legend of faithful women and of the men who betray them. When he has finished, he is to take it to the queen (Anne). The narrator then be-

lately recognizes the daisylike queen as the very daisy he had adored in his waking guise. The God of Love identifies her as Alceste, one of the unequivocally good women in literary history; and the reader should probably recognize her as the very Queen to whom she directs him to deliver his work. Chaucer thus both pays Anne a pretty compliment and preserves his comic integrity. If a good woman is one of those things that, as the poem's prologue insists, one must take on faith from old books because they are rarely met in life, then Anne appears as perhaps the only good woman the narrator has ever met—and that was in the form, not of a woman, but of a daisy.

Chaucer completed only eight (a ninth is almost complete) of the legends, that is, saints' lives, which he derived from a number of sources but especially from Ovid's *Heroides.* His narrator's respect for old books does not invariably cure his skepticism about the goodness of the women he treats, and at times he has to alter the ingredients or emphases of the old books to make the women fit the prescription. The first legend is of Cleopatra, who becomes a good woman only by careful suppression of historical information.

The narration is so straight-faced, however, that it is by no means universally accepted that Chaucer is being less than serious. Nowhere does he walk more skillfully the fine line between pathos and comedy that Ovid had drawn so delicately. Some of the legends do seem genuinely pathetic, but there is hardly one into which is not introduced something that threatens to turn it into comedy—if only the narrator's exasperated exclamations at the monotonous regularity with which men betray women. It is hard not to feel that this mirrors Chaucer's own exasperation at being forced to work with such unpromising material. With the prologue, however, he seems to have remained pleased, for he returned to it later. In this revision the adoration of the daisy and its investiture with female qualities are greatly reduced. It is reasonable to suppose that this was accomplished after Queen Anne's death in 1394 (the reference to her is excised). Chaucer may have wished to preserve the prologue in a form that would bring no painful memories to Richard.

1385 TO 1400

During the enormous burst of literary activity in the early and mid 1380's Chaucer was living in the very center of great political and social strife, which is hardly reflected in his work though it must have affected his life. The most violent event of the time, the Peasants' Revolt of 1381, occurred while he was presumably living in London; indeed, the Essex rebels entered the city through Aldgate, over which he dwelt. The palace of his friend John of Gaunt, the Savoy, was burned to the ground; many Flemings engaged in the wool trade were slaughtered; and two of the collectors with whom he was connected were closely involved with suppressing the revolt. But Chaucer's only mention of it is a comic one, in the Nun's Priest's Tale. The power struggle involving the young King Richard, John of Gaunt, and another of the king's uncles, the duke of Gloucester, was gathering momentum in the years of *Troilus* and the *Legend,* but there is no evidence that it affected him, and in any case he survived it, unlike his old associate Nicholas Brembre and his fellow justice of the peace, Sir Simon Burley.

Chaucer was appointed justice of the peace in Kent in October 1385, and he served for that county in the "Wonderful Parliament" of 1386. He remained a justice until 1389, residing probably at Greenwich. During these years his wife disappears from the records and Chaucer seems to have been briefly out of royal favor. He was even prosecuted for debt twice in 1389. However, his period of unemployment ended on 12 July 1389, shortly after Richard had regained control of the kingdom from his uncle Gloucester: on this date Chaucer was appointed clerk of the works at Westminster, the Tower of London, and various royal estates (later also at Windsor). This was a job even more taxing than the custom had been, involving not only much accounting but also supervision, maintenance, and construction. Carrying large amounts of money, he became a natural target for highwaymen, and he was robbed three times in a four-day period in 1390, losing a total of almost £40 as well as his horse. In 1391 he was replaced in his clerkships.

By that time he may already have been appointed to his last position, substitute forester in Somersetshire, to which he was reappointed in 1399. Occasional periods of debt mark this decade, but Chaucer seems to have continued through most of it in royal favor. He may have been adversely affected by the advent of Henry IV, who, while he renewed Chaucer's annuity and his tun of wine, did not do so until some months after he ascended the throne, and not long before Chaucer died.

Much of the last decade of Chaucer's life was probably dedicated to writing, not only of the *Canterbury Tales* but also of occasional pieces and of at

least one scientific work, the *Treatise on the Astrolabe.* Based on a Latin translation of a work in Arabic, it is dedicated to his son Lewis, who may have then been a student at Oxford. Recent research strongly suggests that Chaucer had connections with Oxford and especially with Merton College, which was particularly distinguished for its astronomical studies. Chaucer had always had a strong interest in astronomy, and it may be that he had earlier been introduced to Oxford by Ralph Strode, a Merton man to whom (along with his friend and fellow poet John Gower) Chaucer dedicated *Troilus.* Another, more advanced astronomical work written about 1393, the *Equatorie of the Planetis,* has recently been tentatively ascribed to Chaucer. From this decade are also such occasional pieces as the witty envoys to Bukton and to Scogan, both of which mention Chaucer's work as a poet; his splendid parody on a courtly love lyric, "To Rosamond"; and his ballade "To His Purse," in which his purse is addressed as a fickle mistress who has left him. An envoy in the ballade is directed to Henry IV, whom he supplicates for money: his royal grants lapsed with Richard's deposition.

THE CANTERBURY TALES

Yet the major part of his time must have been spent on the *Canterbury Tales,* which he is thought to have embarked on after he left the custom and moved to Kent. Framing devices such as that used in the *Tales* were common at the time, and John Gower had probably already written the *Confessio amantis,* a collection of stories emanating, unlike Chaucer's, from a single narrator. But Boccaccio's *Ameto, Filocolo,* and *Decameron* (if Chaucer knew it) all give precedent for a number of tellers, and another Italian work by Giovanni Sercambi that Chaucer may have known presents a narrator telling stories to people traveling on horseback. Chaucer's great originality lies in the sharp characterizations he gives of the narrators in the General Prologue to the tales and in the self-characterizations many of them give in telling their stories. Moreover, the narrator of the whole pilgrimage is himself something of a fiction, and his often naive reactions to the persons he is describing complicate and enrich their portraits by enabling the reader to see two different sides of them simultaneously. At the same time his wide-eyed responses to the pilgrims help persuade the reader that Chaucer really had met rather than invented them, lending them much of the arbitrariness of real life.

The group that gathered at the Tabard Inn in

Southwark, just south of London Bridge, to begin the pilgrimage to Canterbury spans almost the whole range of English society. The Knight and his son the Squire represent the aristocracy; the Prioress, the Second Nun, the Nun's Priest, the Monk, Friar, and Parson represent the church; the Pardoner and the Summoner are ecclesiastical hangers-on; the Clerk, the Serjeant (or Man) of Law, and the Doctor of Physic represent the learned professions; the Merchant, the Wife of Bath, and the Franklin, the upper middle class; the Five Guildsmen, the Miller, the Manciple, the Shipman, and the Reeve, the lower middle class; and the Yeoman, the Cook, and the Plowman, the lower orders. The number—given by the narrator as twenty-nine—is filled out by the Host of the Tabard, who organizes the storytelling and manages it with splendidly bourgeois overconfidence. The narrator, whose status is undefined, seems to belong to the upper middle class, as Chaucer did by birth. Most of these pilgrims are described with a careful selection of details that seem sometimes exactly realistic, sometimes expressively symbolic, and not infrequently both at once.

The fifty-five fairly complete manuscripts of the *Canterbury Tales* that have survived give the stories in ten "fragments" or blocks arranged in various orders. The lack of consensus seems to reflect Chaucer's failure to determine a final order before he died or stopped work. The likely orders are now considered to be only two. The first, for which there is good manuscript evidence, is as follows: (1) General Prologue and the tales of the Knight, Miller, Reeve, and Cook (unfinished); (2) Man of Law; (3) Wife of Bath, Friar, Summoner; (4) Clerk and Merchant, which is closely connected with (5) Squire and Franklin; (6) Physician and Pardoner; (7) Shipman, Prioress, the narrator's Tale of Sir Topaze and Melibeus, Monk, Nun's Priest; (8) Second Nun and Canon's Yeoman; (9) Manciple; and (10) Parson. Largely in order to correct a geographical anomaly (a reference to Sittingbourne in (3) as if the group were approaching it before they approach Rochester in (7)—on the road to Canterbury, Rochester is nearer Southwark than Sittingbourne), some editors prefer to place (7) between (2) and (3), a satisfactory arrangement for which manuscript evidence is tenuous.

Though the Host's (and presumably Chaucer's) plan called for two stories from each pilgrim on the way to Canterbury and two on the way back, Chaucer completed only twenty-three; and one, the Canon's Yeoman's, is told by a latecomer to the group.

Yet virtually all the medieval narrative genres are represented, though often with radical modifications caused by the new dimensions that the narrators' personalities lend to their tales' implicit meanings and by the introduction of the problematical into even the simplest stories.

Pious tales and romances. Thus of the three pious tales, all of which are in rhyme royal, only the Second Nun's account of St. Cecilia is uncomplicated by attitudes or emphases unexpected in the genre, and it was composed much earlier. The Man of Law's story of Custance, victim of the machinations of two successive wicked mothers-in-law, whom God preserves from all sorts of perils and sustains through two long sea voyages in a boat alone or with her infant son, is compromised from the start by coming from the mouth of one who has been earlier described as a materialistic moneygrubber. His frequent bursts of highly emotive rhetoric have been seen by some as inadequate substitutes for genuine feeling for his endlessly passive and patient heroine. More suspect is the Prioress' delicately sentimental yet vindictively boodthirsty account of the murder by Jews of a little chorister who sings a hymn to the Virgin as he passes through the ghetto. By a miracle the Virgin enables the boy to reveal, after he is supposed dead, who his murderers are, and they are promptly and savagely executed. The narrator has described the Prioress as a charming, lovable woman but, as he fails to realize, a deplorable nun. Her version of this very popular story can be read as a commentary on her replacement of intelligent charity by unthinking sentimentality.

In the genre of romance, the Squire's Tale of the Tartar King Cambiuscan and his daughter Canace and the love-stricken female she befriends seems a straightforward attempt to produce an oriental romance, replete with magic and marvels. Yet Chaucer seems to have gotten bored with it, and has the Franklin stop the Squire from continuing what threatens to be a tale of many thousand lines. Chaucer's narrator's story of Sir Topaze is a splendid parody of all that was bad in the worst of the Middle English romances, in which the old chivalric heroes had deteriorated into bourgeois bumpkins, and the English language, imprisoned in the monotonous tail-rhyme stanza, was used without care or elegance. The Host interrupts the story as worthless, though the teller insists that it is the best rhyme he knows—a splendidly large-minded joke by the poet, who makes his surrogate the worst of a group of tellers whom Chaucer himself had created.

The Wife of Bath restructures a current Arthurian romance to serve as an exemplum of her conviction that women should have the sovereignty in marriage. To escape death for committing rape, a knight is allowed a year in which to discover what women most desire; at the end of the term an old hag gives him the correct answer, sovereignty in love. To obtain this badly needed answer, he is forced to wed her, which he does with bad grace. She poses the knight another harsh question—whether she should become beautiful and potentially unfaithful or remain ugly and faithful—but when he yields her the sovereignty by allowing *her* to decide, she rewards him by magically becoming beautiful and promising fidelity. Nothing could better illustrate the Wife of Bath's low opinion of the opposite sex than the rapist knight, or her high opinion of her own sex than the old hag who, given the sovereignty, brings him happiness.

The Franklin's and Knight's Tales also belong, if rather loosely, in the genre of romance. The former is based on a story in Boccaccio's *Filocolo* (another version appears in the *Decameron*), also modified to serve as an exemplum. In the absence of her husband a young wife rashly promises an unwanted suitor to grant him her love if he will remove from the coast the rocks that she fancies threaten her husband's return. For a thousand pounds, the lover hires a magician to make the rocks disappear for a time. When the wife learns of this, she considers suicide but instead tells her husband, who has long since returned safely home. He tells her that since "trouthe" (integrity) is the highest of principles, she must keep her word. But when she goes to meet her would-be lover, he is so moved by her grief that he forgives her the promise. The magician then forgives him his debt, and the narrator concludes by asking which of the three men was the most "free," that is, generous. The Franklin seems to intend his story to be an illustration of the Biblical verse, "And ye shall know the truth, and the truth shall make you free," and as such many readers find the story a charming one. Others, however, impressed by the earlier description of the Franklin as a materialist, although a generous one, and by the husband's readiness to sacrifice his wife's chastity, feel that the tale has an ironic dimension unperceived by the Franklin, who allows material values to supplant spiritual ones.

The Knight's Tale of Palamon and Arcite, based on Boccaccio's *Teseida* (from which Chaucer may have made an earlier version), is a romance of ideas, many of them Boethian, rather than of action. The

two young Theban knights, prisoners of war of Theseus, duke of Athens, fall in love at a distance with their captor's sister-in-law, Emily, and quarrel over who has the right to love her. After they have quarreled for a long time, both in and out of prison, Theseus arranges for them a great tournament in which to determine who shall have Emily. Arcite wins but is fatally injured when, riding about the lists in triumph, his horse rears. He dies and is given a magnificent funeral by Theseus. Some years later, Theseus summons Palamon from Thebes and marries him to Emily, and the two live happily ever after. At its simplest, the tale asks the question—which it does not try to answer—why of one of two equally deserving or undeserving young men, one ends up with his lady while the other ends up in the grave.

Throughout the poem there is given a picture of human life both dreary and predestined. Fate's agents are the planet gods Venus, Mars, and Diana, whom Palamon, Arcite, and Emily invoke and who behave like spoiled children. The description of their temples, erected by Theseus in the lists built for the tournament, presents a harsh image of the pain and suffering of human life. Palamon's prayer to Venus for Emily, and Arcite's to Mars for victory, are both granted, and the ensuing dilemma can be solved only by Saturn, most baleful of the planet gods, who arranges to have a fury cause Arcite's horse to rear. Theseus' speech in which he joins Palamon and Emily explains, in Boethian terms, the existence of a Prime Mover whose benevolent will is executed on earth by the agency of the gods but whose reasons none can know. The conclusion, that one should make a virtue of necessity, is good practical advice congenial to the Knight and Chaucer as well as Theseus, but it does not wipe out the deep pessimism of much of the poem.

Fabliaux. Five of the tales are either fabliaux or based on fabliaux. The first of them, the Miller's Tale, is the purest and best example of the genre in any language. Two young men, one an Oxford student, the other a parish priest's assistant, love Alison, the enticing young wife of an elderly jealous carpenter. One of them, Nicholas, by persuading Alison's husband that a flood is about to destroy the world, devises a fantastically complicated scheme for sleeping with her secure from her husband's discovery. Their night together is interrupted by the other clerk, Absolon, a fastidious, rather effeminate young man, who comes to the window begging for a kiss. Alison proffers her rump, which Absolon kisses. Realizing what he has done, he borrows a hot colter from an early-rising blacksmith and returns to ask another kiss. Nicholas proffers his rump this time and receives the colter. His cry for water awakens the carpenter, awaiting the flood in a trough suspended from the ceiling. Thinking the flood has come, he cuts the rope and crashes to the floor. The sheer imaginative energy, high spirits, superb characterizations, and the delicacy and candor with which the outrageous climax is handled are unmatched in the genre.

Yet the Reeve's Tale, which follows the Miller's, runs a not too distant second to it. In this tale two Cambridge students avenge themselves on a miller who has stolen some of their meal. Forced to spend the night at the mill because the miller has surreptitiously turned their horse loose, they are lodged in the same room as the miller and his wife, and their nubile daughter and infant son. One of the clerks rises in the night and joins the unresistant daughter in her bed. The other moves the cradle from the foot of the master bed to the foot of his own. When the wife returns after relieving herself, guided by the presence of the cradle, she gets into bed with the clerk, whom she mistakes for, and who behaves like, her husband. When the other clerk tries to return to his own bed, he is also misled by the cradle and gets in with the miller, to whom he boasts of having slept with his daughter. A fight ensues, the clerks beat the miller well and retrieve their stolen meal. Again, the energy is extraordinary, though the exuberance is less than in the Miller's Tale, because the Reeve is telling a tale of vengeance in order to avenge himself on the pilgrim Miller for a fancied slight. The Cook continues the series of fabliaux, but his story of a rapscallion apprentice breaks off unfinished after fifty-odd lines.

The Summoner's Tale also belongs to the genre, though it is elaborated into an exhaustive satire on friars and the pilgrim Friar in particular. A sick villager, infuriated by a friar's pompous and self-serving sermon followed by a request for money, says he has a gift hidden in the cleft of his rump which he tells the friar to grope for. When the friar gropes, the sick man breaks wind mightily. The friar hurries to the house of the lord of the village to complain; but the latter—and it now appears the friar as well—is less concerned with the disgusting nature of the gift than with the donor's seemingly impossible stipulation: that the gift be divided equally among all the members of the friar's convent. An ingenious and insulting method of dividing the gift is suggested by the lord's squire, and all, except the friar, are satis-

fied. The fabliau thus satirizes the friars both as spiritual counselors and as men of learning, since this one is unable to solve a problem in arithmetical division.

A different kind of satire informs the Shipman's Tale, a fabliau converted into a satire on a society in which all values are reduced to monetary ones. A rich merchant's wife needs a hundred francs to pay off a debt. Not wishing to ask her husband for it, she contracts with his friend, a monk, to sleep with him for that sum when her husband is away on business. The monk borrows the money from the husband and, after their night together, gives it to the wife. He later tells the husband that he has paid back to his wife the sum he borrowed. When the merchant confronts his wife with this information, she replies that she thought that the monk had made her a present of the money, and promises to pay her husband back with her body. It is believed that the story was originally written for the Wife of Bath, illustrating how a woman can use her attributes to fool her husband. Reassignment to the Shipman is arbitrary, for the teller shows little personality; nor does the story benefit from it, since the reduction of all values to monetary ones has the ice-cold impersonality of a mathematical problem working itself out.

The most original treatment of the fabliau is in the Merchant's Tale of the old lecher January, who after a lifetime of loose living as a bachelor is moved to marry by his desire for an heir and the protracted pleasure of engendering one. He chooses as bride and object of his senile lovemaking a young girl, May, with whom one of his squires promptly falls in love. May consents to repay the squire's love, but to do so becomes impossible when January, now blind and outrageously jealous, will never let her leave him. But she steals the key to his private garden and gives it to the squire, who duplicates it. One day she eggs January into taking her into the garden, into which the squire has already made his way. Protesting a hunger for pears, she climbs up on January's back into a pear tree where the squire is perched.

A royal otherworld couple, the fairies Pluto and Proserpina, see what is about to happen, and Pluto indignantly vows to give January back his sight. Proserpina in turn vows to give May a "sufficient answer." As the couple copulates in the tree, January regains his eyesight and begins to howl at what he sees. May leaps down and reproves her husband, saying that she had learned that the way to cure his blindness was to struggle with a man up in a tree. January overcomes his doubts and believes her, as

293

blind with recovered eyesight as he had always been. The telling is distinguished by the Merchant's emotional intensity. Introducing himself as the recent bridegroom of a shrew, he pours his personal bitterness into the tale, hating May for her treachery and January for his folly. Yet his bitterness and the story's high comedy do not cancel one another out, though the mixture is so rich that some readers prefer to see only the comedy, others the bitterness. Perhaps nowhere else is Chaucer's modification of a genre more radical or more effective.

Moral exempla. By far the commonest genre in the *Canterbury Tales* is the moral exemplum, to which both romance and fabliau are sometimes assimilated. The simplest of these is the Monk's outright series of world-hating biographies, written earlier and now assigned to a character whose worldliness belies the message of his stories. The Physician's Tale, of Virginius' decapitation of his daughter Virginia in order to save her from becoming the concubine of a wicked judge, fits the genre rather awkwardly, since it is hard to see what its moral is. The Physician's suggestion, that the punishment of those who connived to get possession of Virginia proves that one should avoid sin, seems so desperate that it may be seen as a reflection of the Physician's moral vacuity.

Chaucer's narrator's long prose Tale of Melibeus, which he tells after the Host has interrupted his story of Sir Topaze, is, after the Parson's Tale, the best (if least artistic) representative of a story of doctrine as opposed to one of mirth. Melibeus' wife Prudence talks her angry husband out of taking vengeance on his enemies for the injuries they have done him by a recitation of all the wise sayings advocating peace that the original author of the work, Albertanus of Brescia, with some slight help from a French translation and from Chaucer himself, could assemble.

The Manciple's Tale, remotely from Ovid, of Phoebus' punishment of his pet, a white crow with the power of speech, for informing him of his wife's infidelity, illustrates the simple principle that one should never offend anyone with one's tongue. The pragmatic counsel, as devoid of honest morality as its dishonest teller, seems a belated response on the Manciple's part to his own reproof of the drunken Cook, who would be in a position when back in London to reveal the Manciple's dishonest practices. The Friar's Tale is a moral exemplum converted into a satire on summoners. An inevitably dishonest summoner befriends a devil who carries him off to hell when the victim of his attempted extortion consigns him to the devil. The Friar's insistence that hell is the destination of all summoners brings from the pilgrim Summoner a scabrous rejoinder in the prologue to his tale.

The most curious of the exempla is the Canon's Yeoman's Tale. The Canon and his Yeoman breathlessly ride to join the pilgrims one morning; the Yeoman begins to praise his master as an alchemist, but when he encounters some skepticism from the Host, changes his approach and begins to damn the Canon for his practices. The Canon hears what he is saying and flees, and with the Host's encouragement the Yeoman launches into a discussion of alchemy. The first part is largely a listing of the terms and the materials used in alchemy, along with the description of an (inevitably) unsuccessful attempt to make a transmutation of metals. The second part is a careful description of how a fraudulent alchemist, a canon, cheats, by sleight of hand, an idle priest out of a large sum of money, showing him what appear to be three successful transmutations and then selling him the secret. The moral that alchemy and alchemists are evil is clear enough, but is perhaps somewhat weakened by the Yeoman's loving care for details of the fraud, which becomes a matter of primary interest—a wonder at how things are, that almost replaces concern with how they should be.

Rather more serious than any of these is the Clerk's Tale, a translation in rhyme royal stanzas of Petrarch's retelling in Latin of the last story in Boccaccio's *Decameron.* The story concerns the poor peasant girl Griselda, whom the local lord, the marquis Walter, takes as his wife after extracting from her a vow of perfect obedience. He tests her integrity by taking away her first-born daughter and then her second-born son, letting her believe he has had them killed. Then, claiming that his subjects are discontented at having to serve under a peasant woman, he dismisses her in order, he says, to take a new wife. She returns to her father's cottage, but Walter summons her back to prepare the palace for his wedding. Griselda obeys uncomplainingly, and he finally reveals that his supposed bride-to-be is their daughter, whom he had given to his sister along with their son to nurture; his machinations were merely tests of Griselda's ability to keep her marriage vow. She is restored to her former position, and the Clerk draws the Petrarchan moral that if a woman could be so steadfast under trials visited upon her by a mortal, we should all be steadfast in the trials visited upon us by God. But Chaucer has made Griselda rather more interesting than the Christian moral. She is not a woman of bovine patience but one who, having made an oath to love and obey Walter, does so while being fully aware of what her integrity costs in human terms. This awareness is lacking from Petrarch's version, and the result is not so much a merely patient woman, like the Man of Law's Custance, but one of magnificent constancy.

The Pardoner's Tale is divided in two parts, the first a highly emotive condemnation of gluttony, drunkenness, swearing, and dicing, and the second an exemplum illustrating the Pardoner's invariable text, "Avarice is the root of evil." Three riotous young men set out to kill Death, forget their search when a mysterious old man directs them to a hoard of gold coins, and find death in a different sense: in order to have a larger share of the treasure, two of them slay the third when he brings them food and wine that he, for the same reason, has poisoned; they drink the wine and die horribly. The story is almost unmatched for its eeriness and for the swift compulsion of its telling. It has added richness because it comes from one who boasts that, like the young men he is telling about, he is dedicated to avarice and who, like them, brings upon himself fitting retribution when his offer to the Host to sell him pardon for his sins provokes in return an insult that destroys the Pardoner's self-image.

The Nun's Priest's Tale of the rooster Chantecleer, his favorite wife Pertelote, and the fox Dan Russell, is the supreme parody of the exemplum form—and a good deal more. Chantecleer dreams of a beast that threatens him, but his wife ascribes his dream to indigestion and recommends laxatives. Ignoring both her advice and his own conviction that his dream was truly prophetic, he goes about his daily business, including making love to Pertelote. A fox duly appears and calms Chantecleer's fears by flattering him for his crowing. When Chantecleer is persuaded to close his eyes to crow the better, the fox seizes him and bears him away to the woods. All the villagers join in pursuit, and the rooster suggests to the fox that he turn and defy them. When the fox opens his mouth to do so, Chantecleer flies to safety in a tree. This barnyard event is described with splendidly elevated rhetoric and with numerous digressions on such solemn matters as God's foreknowledge and its relation to free will, the nature of woman, and the significance of dreams. Epic similes abound, and rhetoric attains its highest reaches while contemplating the rooster's tragic destiny—which anticlimactically turns out untragic. The

Nun's Priest, a teller with an elusive personality who is not described in the Prologue, concludes that his tale is a warning against negligence and trusting flattery; but his beast fable is actually a brilliant celebration of the endearing folly of barnyard fowls and of men.

A survey of the Canterbury stories themselves omits one of the poem's most important facets, its dramatic aspect, which appears in the links between the tales and in the self-revelations of several of the characters in the prologues to their tales. No matter what the nature of the stories that surround them, the links are always made lively with dramatic interplay: the drunken Miller's insistence, over the Host's objection, that he tell a tale to match the Knight's; the Reeve's anger with the Miller both before and after the Miller's Tale; the brief but bitter quarrel of the Friar and the Summoner, resulting in an exchange of slanderous stories; the introduction to the Man of Law's Tale, where the Man of Law gives a short but unflattering account of the works of someone named Chaucer; the Franklin's polite interruption of the Squire's interminable romance, the Knight's and Host's less courteous interruption of the Monk's dreary exempla, and the Host's rude interruption of Chaucer's narrator's dogtrot rhyme; the arrival of the Canon and his Yeoman, and the Canon's precipitous flight when he fears his secrets are about to be revealed; the Merchant's outrage at the Clerk's Tale of that impossibility, a constant woman; and the Cook's fall from his horse when chided by the Manciple for drunkenness.

The amazing confession of his own fraudulence in the introduction to his tale by the Pardoner, who has been described in the General Prologue as "a gelding or a mare," reveals a warped human being who at once repels and fascinates and who has provoked endless interpretation and reinterpretation from critics. In this respect he is rivaled by the Wife of Bath, whose long prologue in which she describes how she treated—and was treated by—her five husbands establishes her as one of the great comic characters of literature. A true forebear of Falstaff, she is, like him, as attractive as she is shocking. With supremely self-confident wit she at once confirms triumphantly and destroys totally the picture of womanhood handed down to Chaucer's age by centuries of teachers of antifeminism.

The Parson's Tale and the retraction. The last of the *Canterbury Tales* is the Parson's prose sermon (actually the translation from Latin or French of what had originally been two tracts) on the Seven

Deadly Sins and on repentance. It represents medieval Christian doctrine at its most illiberal, its redeeming feature being the satirical vigor with which some of the sins are treated. It may have been an earlier work of Chaucer's that he called upon as the fitting conclusion to his pilgrimage. In its short introduction the time is late afternoon, and the shadows of the pilgrims are lengthening. The Host announces that the tale-telling is almost complete—all have told except the Parson, whom he calls on to knit up the feast and make a good end. The tale is followed by a brief paragraph in which Chaucer in his own person apologizes for the wicked works he has written and retracts them: the *Book of the Duchess*, the *House of Fame*, the *Parliament of Fowls, Troilus and Criseyde*, and the *Canterbury Tales* ("those that are resonant of sin"). He exempts only his Boethius and writing of saints, homilies, morality, and devotion.

The Parson's introduction and the retraction may have been written in the last days of Chaucer's life. On 24 December 1399 he leased a house, for fifty-three years, in the garden of Westminster Abbey; he drew his annuity for the last time on 5 June 1400; and according to the inscription on his tomb (not erected until 1563) in the abbey, he died on 25 October 1400. The tone of the little introduction and of the Retraction suggests that it was Chaucer's journey, as well as the fictional pilgrimage, that was coming to an end. It is reasonable to suppose that the monks of Westminster had seen to it that, like his fiction, he would make a good end.

BIBLIOGRAPHY

The bibliography of Chaucer is so large that only book-length items can be included here. Preference is given to items that concern Chaucer's work as a whole, but important studies of individual major works are also listed. For articles and more particular studies, see the bibliographies listed below. Note also the quarterly *Chaucer Review* (1966–) and annual *Studies in the Age of Chaucer* (1979–).

Bibliographies. Eleanor P. Hammond, *Chaucer: A Bibliographical Manual* (1908); Dudley David Griffith, *Bibliography of Chaucer 1908–1953* (1955); William R. Crawford, *Bibliography of Chaucer 1954–63* (1967); Lorrayne Y. Baird, *A Bibliography of Chaucer 1964–1973* (1977); Albert C. Baugh, *Chaucer*, 2nd ed. (1977).

Biographies. Derek S. Brewer, *Chaucer*, 3rd ed. (1973), and *Chaucer and His World* (1978); *Chaucer Life-Records*, Martin M. Crow and Clair C. Olson, eds. (1966); Marchette Chute, *Geoffrey Chaucer of England* (1946); John Champlin Gardner, *The Life and Times of Chaucer* (1977).

TEXTS
Complete writings. Walter W. Skeat, ed., *The Complete Works of Geoffrey Chaucer*, 7 vols. (1894–1897); Fred N. Robinson, ed., *The Works of Geoffrey Chaucer*, 2nd ed. (1957); John H. Fisher, ed., *The Complete Poetry and Prose of Geoffrey Chaucer* (1977).

Individual works. John M. Manly and Edith Rickert, eds., *The Text of the Canterbury Tales*, 8 vols. (1940); Arthur C. Cawley, ed., *The Canterbury Tales* (1968); Robert A. Pratt, ed., *The Tales of Canterbury Complete* (1974); Robert K. Root, ed., *The Book of Troilus and Criseyde, by Geoffrey Chaucer* (1926); John Warrington, ed., *Troilus and Criseyde*, 2nd ed. (1974); Donald R. Howard and James Dean, eds., *Troilus and Criseyde* (1976); D. S. Brewer, ed., *The Parlement of Foulys* (1960); Alfred David and George B. Pace, eds., *The Minor Poems* (1982); Ronald Sutherland, ed., *The Romaunt of the Rose and Le Roman de la Rose* (1967).

MODERNIZATIONS
Complete poetry. J. S. P. Tatlock and Percy Mackaye, eds. (1912).

The Canterbury Tales. John U. Nicholson (1934); Frank E. Hill (1934, 1964); Robert M. Lumiansky (1948); Vincent F. Hopper (1948); Nevill Coghill (1951); David Wright (1964).

Troilus and Criseyde. George P. Krapp (1940); Robert M. Lumianksy (1952); Margaret Stanley-Wrench (1965).

STUDIES
General. David Aers, *Chaucer, Langland and the Creative Imagination* (1973); Paull F. Baum, *Chaucer: A Critical Appreciation* (1958); Henry Stanley Bennett, *Chaucer and the Fifteenth Century* (1947); Muriel Bowden, *A Reader's Guide to Geoffrey Chaucer* (1964); Bertrand H. Bronson, *In Search of Chaucer* (1960); Robert B. Burlin, *Chaucerian Fiction* (1977); J. D. Burnley, *Chaucer's Language and the Philosophers' Tradition* (1979); John A. Burrow, *Ricardian Poetry* (1971); Gilbert K. Chesterton, *Chaucer* (1932); Nevill Coghill, *The Poet Chaucer* (1949) and *Geoffrey Chaucer* (1956); Helen S. Corsa, *Chaucer, Poet of Mirth and Morality* (1964); Walter C. Curry, *Chaucer and the Mediaeval Sciences*, rev. ed. (1960); Alfred David, *The Strumpet Muse: Art and Morals in Chaucer's Poetry* (1976); Germaine Dempster, *Dramatic Irony in Chaucer* (1932); E. Talbot Donaldson, *Speaking of Chaucer* (1970); Peter Elbow, *Oppositions in Chaucer* (1975); Norman E. Eliason, *The Language of Chaucer's Poetry* (1972); Ralph Warren Victor Elliott, *Chaucer's English* (1974); Robert D. French, *A Chaucer Handbook*, 2nd ed. (1947); John M. Fyler, *Chaucer and Ovid* (1979); Maurice Hussey, A. C. Spearing, and James Winny, *An Introduction to Chaucer* (1965); Stanley S. Hussey, *Chaucer: An Introduction* (1971); Robert M. Jordan, *Chaucer and the Shape of Creation* (1967); Patricia M. Kean, *Chaucer and the Making of English Poetry*, 2 vols. (1972); George Lyman Kittredge, *Chaucer and His Poetry* (1915); John Lawlor, *Chaucer* (1968); John L. Lowes, *Geoffrey Chaucer and the Devel-*

opment of His Genius (1934); Kemp Malone, *Chapters on Chaucer* (1951); Charles Muscatine, *Chaucer and the French Tradition* (1957); Howard R. Patch, *On Rereading Chaucer* (1939); Robert O. Payne, *The Key of Remembrance* (1963); Raymond Preston, *Chaucer* (1952); Durant W. Robertson, Jr., *A Preface to Chaucer* (1962); Ian Robinson, *Chaucer and the English Tradition* (1972); Robert K. Root, *The Poetry of Chaucer*, 2nd ed. (1957); Thomas W. Ross, *Chaucer's Bawdy* (1972); Henry D. Sedgwick, *Dan Chaucer: An Introduction to the Poet, His Poetry and His Times* (1934); Percy V. D. Shelly, *The Living Chaucer* (1940); John Speirs, *Chaucer the Maker* (1951); John S. P. Tatlock, *The Mind and Art of Chaucer* (1950); George Guion Williams, *A New View of Chaucer* (1965).

Collections of critical essays include Derek S. Brewer, ed., *Chaucer and Chaucerians* (1966) and *Geoffrey Chaucer* (1974); John Anthony Burrow, ed., *Geoffrey Chaucer: A Critical Anthology* (1969); Arthur C. Cawley, ed., *Chaucer's Mind and Art* (1969); George D. Economou, ed., *Geoffrey Chaucer* (1975); Rossell H. Robbins, ed., *Chaucer at Albany* (1975); Donald M. Rose, ed., *New Perspectives in Chaucer Criticism* (1981); Beryl Rowland, *Companion to Chaucer Studies*, 2nd ed. (1979); Edward Vasta and Zacharias P. Thundy, eds., *Chaucerian Problems and Perspectives* (1979); Edward C. Wagenknecht, *Chaucer: Modern Essays in Criticism* (1959).

The Canterbury Tales. Muriel Bowden, *A Commentary on the General Prologue to the Canterbury Tales* (1948); William Frank Bryan and Germaine Dempster, eds., *Sources and Analogues of Chaucer's Canterbury Tales* (1941); Donald Roy Howard, *The Idea of the Canterbury Tales* (1976); Bernard Huppé, *A Reading of the Canterbury Tales* (1964); Traugott Lawler, *The One and the Many in the Canterbury Tales* (1980); William W. Lawrence, *Chaucer and the Canterbury Tales* (1950); Robert M. Lumiansky, *Of Sondry Folk: The Dramatic Principle in the Canterbury Tales* (1955); John M. Manly, *Some New Light on Chaucer* (1926); Jill Mann, *Chaucer and Medieval Estates Satire* (1973); Charles A. Owen, Jr., *Pilgrimage and Storytelling in the Canterbury Tales* (1977); Paul G. Ruggiers, *The Art of the Canterbury Tales* (1965); Trevor Whittock, *A Reading of the Canterbury Tales* (1968).

Collections of critical essays include John Julian Anderson, ed., *Chaucer: The Canterbury Tales: A Casebook* (1974); Charles A. Owen, Jr., ed., *Discussions of the Canterbury Tales* (1961); Richard J. Schoeck and Jerome Taylor, eds., *Chaucer Criticism: An Anthology*, vol. 1: *The Canterbury Tales* (1960).

Troilus and Criseyde. Ian Bishop, *Troilus and Criseyde: A Critical Study* (1981); Ida L. Gordon, *The Double Sorrow of Troilus* (1970); Thomas A. Kirby, *Chaucer's Troilus: A Study in Courtly Love* (1940); Monica E. McAlpine, *The Genre of Troilus and Criseyde* (1978); Sanford Meech, *Design in Chaucer's Troilus* (1959); Donald W. Rowe, *O Love, O Charite!: Contraries Harmonized in Chaucer's Troilus* (1976).

Collections of critical essays include Stephen A. Barney, ed., *Chaucer's "Troilus": Essays in Criticism* (1980); Mary Salu, ed., *Essays on Troilus and Criseyde* (1977); Richard J. Schoeck and Jerome Taylor, eds., *Chaucer Criticism: An Anthology*, vol. 2: *Troilus and Criseyde and the Minor Poems* (1961).

House of Fame. Jack A. W. Bennett, *Chaucer's Book of Fame* (1968); Sheila Delany, *Chaucer's House of Fame* (1972).

Parliament of Fowls. Jack A. W. Bennett, *The Parlement of Foules: An Interpretation* (1957).

Legend of Good Women. Robert W. Frank, *Chaucer and the Legend of Good Women* (1972).

Earlier poems. Wolfgang Clemen, *Chaucer's Early Poetry*, C. A. M. Sym, trans. (1963).

E. TALBOT DONALDSON

[See also **Boccaccio, Giovanni; Boethius, Anicius Manlius Severinus; Classical Literary Studies; Clergy; Exemplum; Fabliau; Jean de Meun (Meung); John of Gaunt; Middle English Literature; Petrarch (Francesco Petrarca); Pilgrimages, Western European; Romance of the Rose; Richard II of England; Troy Story; Visions, Literary Form.**]

CHELLES, JEHAN DE. See **Jean de Chelles.**

CHERUB, the highest of the nine orders of angels; described in Ezekiel 1:4–25 and 10:1–22 as beings covered with eyes, having four wings, and the heads of a man, lion, ox, and eagle (tetramorphic) who supported God. Cherubim were sometimes represented following Ezekiel's description, as on a sixth-century liturgical fan from Riha, Syria, now in Dumbarton Oaks (Washington, D.C.), but were also shown as simple angels or with six wings. The latter form was influenced by Isaiah's description of seraphim, an angelic order closely related to cherubim in function and associated with them in the liturgy.

BIBLIOGRAPHY

R. P. de Vaux, "Les chérubins et l'arche d'alliance: Les sphinx gardiens et les trônes divins dans l'ancien orient," in *Mélanges de l'Université Saint-Joseph*, 37 (1961); D. I. Pallas, "Eine Differenzierung unter den himmlischen Ordnungen (ikonographische Analyse)," in *Byzantinische Zeitschrift*, 64 (1971); R. P. Vincent, "Les cherubims," in *Revue biblique*, 35 (1926).

LESLIE BRUBAKER

[See also **Angel/Angelology.**]

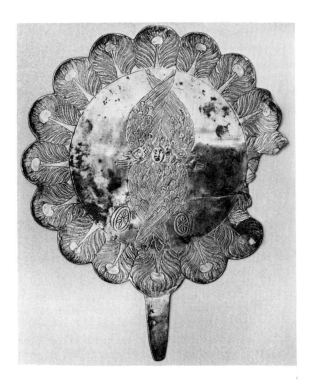

Tetramorphic cherub inscribed on a silver liturgical fan. Byzantine (discovered at Riha, Syria), *ca.* 577. COURTESY OF THE DUMBARTON OAKS COLLECTION, WASHINGTON, D.C.

Cherubim as described by the prophet Ezekiel. In English manuscript of Nicholas of Lyra, *Postilla super libros Prophetorum, ca.* 1430. BEINECKE RARE BOOK AND MANUSCRIPT LIBRARY, YALE UNIVERSITY

CHESTER PLAYS. "The Chester Plays" is a popular modern title for the version of the English Corpus Christi Play performed annually or at irregular intervals in the streets of Chester in northwest England by members of the city's craft guilds. The existence of the plays is first attested in a civic document of 1422, though the plays were obviously established before that time. The last performance was in 1575. Civic and guild records in Chester give only limited evidence for the fifteenth century, but it appears that, at that period, the plays were performed on Corpus Christi Day and were called the "Corpus Christi Play." The first sixteenth-century record (1521) indicates that the date of performance had by then been changed to Whitsun and the play was called the "Whitsun Play." By 1531–1532 that reference had become the "Whitsun Plays," possibly indicative of the fact that the plays were by then performed in three parts, on the Monday, Tuesday, and Wednesday of Whit week, an arrangement attested by later documents. The 1575 performance, however, was at Midsummer.

The manner of performance was processional, the plays being mounted on movable stages (pageant wagons), which were manhandled through the streets of Chester from one appointed station to another. The antiquarian Robert Rogers, archdeacon of Chester cathedral, has left an extended and at times puzzling account of the pageant wagon in his *Brevary of Chester History.* He also indicates a downhill route from the first station at the Abbey Gates before the clergy to the second station at the Pentice (city hall) against St. Peter's Church for the mayor and civic officials, thence circuitously to Bridge Street. The production was the occasion for large crowds, requiring barriers and scaffolds; a court case of 1568 indicates that plays were also watched from rooms adjoining stations.

Chester's cycle was an object of civic pride, and attempts to suppress it were at times resisted. It was for long erroneously held to be the earliest English cycle on the basis of traditions that assigned its authorship to the famous monk-historian Ranulf Higden and the initiation of its performance to Chester's first mayor, Sir John Arneway. These baseless traditions were incorporated into the banns in the version composed after the Reformation to proclaim a production; these "Late Banns" constitute an apology for the "popish" plays on the grounds of their antiquity and their position in Chester's history. Two mayors, John Hankey in 1572 and Sir John Savage in 1575, with the support of the majority of the corporation, ignored the evident disapproval of the archbishop of York and authorized productions of the cycle. Savage was summoned to defend his action before the Privy Council, and although he seems to have done this to their satisfaction with the aid of documentary support from his fellow aldermen, the cycle was never again performed.

It is a measure of local attachment to the cycle that the text survives in eight manuscripts, six of which are clearly later than the last performance. Three are texts of single plays: The Resurrection (Manchester Central Library, MS 822. 11C2, date uncertain); Antichrist (National Library of Wales, Peniarth MS 399, ca. 1500); and The Trial and Flagellation of Christ (1599), by George Bellin for the Coopers' Company of Chester, one of the original performing guilds, which still holds the text. The other five manuscripts are versions of the complete cycle, dated and signed: San Marino, Huntington Library, MS 2 (1591) by Edward Gregorie, self-styled scholar of the village of Bunbury in Cheshire; London, British Library, Additional MS 10305 (1592) and Harley MS 2013 (1600), both by George Bellin, clerk to the guilds of the coopers, cappers and pinners, and ironmongers, and parish clerk of Holy Trinity Church, Chester; Oxford, Bodley MS 175 (1604) by William Bedford, clerk to the Brewers' guild from 1606; and British Library Harley MS 2124 (1607) by James Miller, a minor canon of Chester cathedral, with two other scribes.

These manuscripts attest a cycle of twenty-four or (in the latest manuscript) twenty-five plays. Most plays, with the exception of the first, are written wholly or partly in an eight-line Chester stanza; $aaa^4b^3aaa^4b^3$ or $aaa^4b^3ccc^4b^3$. The cycle dramatizes the course of history from Creation to Doomsday by realizing the decisive moments of intervention by God in the manner of the English Corpus Christi Play; but it also contains a number of unique episodes—notably Abraham and Melchizedek, Balaam and Balak, Octavian and the Sibyl, the Making of the Creed, and the Prophets Before Antichrist and Coming of Antichrist. In the sixteenth century Rogers claimed that in performance Fall of Lucifer–Gifts of the Magi (plays 1–9) occupied the first day; Massacre of the Innocents–Harrowing of Hell (plays 10–17) the second day; and Resurrection–Doomsday (plays 18–24) the third day. But the version of play 5 in four manuscripts indicates a production at which the first day ended with the completion of the Old Testament material.

Influences on and sources of the cycle have been much discussed. Affinities have been noted with French drama. Close links have been found with another Chester text, the Stanzaic Life of Christ, and the episode of Abraham's Sacrifice of Isaac has un-

doubted links with the play on the same subject recorded in the Book of Brome. The play of Christ Before the Doctors is a somewhat corrupt form of the version also found in York, Wakefield, and Coventry. The text also seems to draw directly upon the Golden Legend, but much of its nonbiblical material and interpretation can be paralleled in current compendiums such as Peter Comestor's Historia scholastica. The Late Banns stress the dependence of the cycle on the Bible and the best authorities, and the cycle itself contains a number of direct biblical quotations in Latin declaimed to the audience, a substantial amount of liturgical music, and, in expositions, reference to authorities such as Jerome and Augustine.

The intelligent deployment of biblical, apocryphal, and legendary material, at times explicitly interpreted by an Expositor, produces a tight thematic and dramatic structure with a pattern of cross-reference extending over the three days of performance. The case for a single author or reviser seems strong.

BIBLIOGRAPHY

For text, see Robert M. Lumiansky and David Mills, eds., *The Chester Mystery Cycle,* vol. 1: *Text* (1974); for documentation, see Lawrence M. Clopper, ed., *Chester* (1979). The development of the cycle is discussed by Fred M. Salter, *Medieval Drama in Chester* (1955), and text, sources, development, and music, in Robert M. Lumiansky, David Mills, and Richard Rastall, *The Chester Mystery Cycle: Essays and Documents* (1983). On the structure of the cycle, see Kevin J. Harty, "The Unity and Structure of *The Chester Mystery Cycle,*" in *Mediaevalia,* 2 (1976); and Peter W. Travis, *Dramatic Design in the Chester Cycle* (1982).

DAVID MILLS

[See also Corpus Christi, Feast of; Drama, Western European; Golden Legend; Guilds and Métiers; Higden, Ranulf; Mystery Plays.]

CHESTER, TREATY OF. In 973 the West-Saxon king Edgar assembled his entire navy at Chester, and the chief kings in the British Isles gathered there to swear their alliance with and submission to him. According to the Anglo-Saxon Chronicle, six kings were present but Norman tradition counts eight. The twelfth-century chronicle of Florence of Worcester identifies them as Kenneth, king of the Scots; Malcolm, king of the Cumbrians; Maccus (or

Magnus), king of many islands; and five others, Dufnal (Dumnail), Siferth, Hywel, Jacob (Iago), and Juchil. At least six of the above fit the chronology. Kenneth II reigned from 971 to 995. Dufnal was king of Strathclyde until his pilgrimage to Rome in 975. Maccus was the son of Harold Bluetooth and is credited in the Welsh chronicles with ravishing Penmon in 971. Iago reigned in Gwynedd from 950 to 979, when his nephew Hywel ap Ieuaf, probably the aforementioned Hywel, drove him from his territory and usurped his throne.

Although the story of the ensuing pageant told in Florence, in which the kings rowed Edgar on the river Dee from the palace to the church of St. John the Baptist, may be an embellishment on the original treaty, it does illustrate Edgar's preeminence and the importance of his fleet for maintaining that power. A related tale found in the Welsh *Brenhinedd y Saesson* (Chronicle of the Saxon kings) about Edgar's forcing the Welsh kings to pay an annual tribute of 300 wolves' heads, although fabulous, also emphasizes Edgar's power on this occasion.

The treaty at Chester did not set any new precedents; Welsh kings had already submitted to King Alfred the Great in return for his protection. The alliance between Wessex and the Welsh had continued with King Hywel Dda (Hywel the Good) making submission to Athelstan. Likewise with the Scots, Athelstan's son, Edmund, had sought an alliance with Malcolm I, king of the Scots, through the lease of Strathclyde to Malcolm. These alliances were made on an individual basis and, like Edgar's at Chester, usually lasted only until the deaths of the principal parties.

BIBLIOGRAPHY
Modern English translations of the chronicles can be found in Dorothy Whitelock's editions of *The Anglo-Saxon Chronicle* (1961), D(E), 77; and *English Historical Documents*, vol. 1: *500–1042* (1979), no. 239; and in Alan O. Anderson, *Scottish Annals from English Chronicles A.D. 500 to 1286* (1908), 75–78. For the Welsh entries and their translation see Thomas Jones, ed., *Brenhinedd y Saesson, or The Kings of the Saxons* (1971); and *Brut y Tywysogyon, or The Chronicle of the Princes, Red Book of Hergest Version* (1955). Frank M. Stenton, *Anglo-Saxon England*, 3rd ed. (1971), 369–370, discusses the treaty and its implications. See also John E. Lloyd, *A History of Wales from the Earliest Times to the Edwardian Conquest*, 2nd ed. (1912, repr. 1948), 349–350.

MARILYN KAY KENNEY

[See also **Anglo-Saxons, Origins and Migrations of; Chronicles; Scotland, History of; Wales, History of.**]

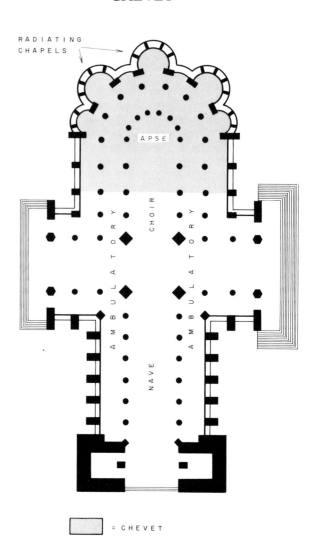

Floor plan of a cathedral showing the chevet. DRAWING BY NORA L. JENNINGS

CHEVET, the French term for the eastern end of a church composed of an apse and an ambulatory with or without radiating chapels. "Chevet" is also used to designate a specific form of the eastern end of a church in which the walls of the radiating chapels were dispensed with, thus creating a second ambulatory around the apse from which the semicircular ends of the chapels protruded. The double ambulatory was first constructed under Abbot Suger at St. Denis, near Paris, between 1140 and 1143, to facilitate the circulation of pilgrims around the apse. The fusion of apse, ambulatory, and chapels into a single spatial unit created a much lighter eastern end, and the chevet became a standard feature of High Gothic churches such as Chartres Cathedral.

BIBLIOGRAPHY

Sumner McKnight Crosby, "Crypt and Choir Plans at Saint-Denis," in *Gesta,* 5 (1966); Hans Jantzen, *High Gothic,* James Palmes, trans. (1962), 47–60.

LESLIE BRUBAKER

[See also **Ambulatory; Apse; Chapel.**]

CHILDREN'S CRUSADE. See Crusade, Children's.

CHILIASM. See Millennialism.

CHIN (Russian, "order" or "rank") refers to the fixed tiers of icons in the iconastasis. The most important tier was the Deesis *chin,* which included an icon of Christ with the Mother of God on one side and St. John the Baptist on the other. The arrangement of icons in each *chin,* and the ordering of tiers one above the other, had religious symbolism and was therefore fixed.

ANN E. FARKAS

[See also **Deesis; Iconostasis.**]

CHIP CARVING is a method of reserving a design in metal so as to keep the design flush with its frame by means of faceted, *v*-shaped grooves. It was first practiced by the provincial bronze casters of the Roman Empire. On northern German and Scandinavian fibulae it appeared before A.D. 400 with patterns of dismembered animals, monstrous drooping heads, and human masks. In the Danube basin it was restricted to abstract patterns.

BIBLIOGRAPHY

Alois Riegel, *Die spätrömische Kunstindustrie,* I (1901); Bernhard Salin, *Die altgermanische Thierornamentik* (1904, new ed. 1935).

PHILIPPE VERDIER

[See also **Metalworking.**]

CHIVALRY (French: *chevalerie;* Spanish: *caballería;* Italian: *cavalleria;* German: *Rittertum*).

Writers from the eleventh through the fifteenth century commonly spoke of chivalry, but their meaning was seldom consistent or precise. For this reason an exact yet comprehensive definition of chivalry remains elusive. It is important to recognize subtle shifts of meaning attached to chivalry in medieval and modern usage. The concept in the fifteenth century differed from that of the thirteenth, just as the thirteenth-century meaning differed from that of the eleventh. Regional usage also varied.

In origin chivalry is tied to the early history of the mounted warrior or knight (French: *chevalier;* Latin: *miles*), particularly in France in the later decades of the tenth century, when knights had become the dominant military and political figures of the countryside. The raw exercise of power by knights was possible because only they possessed the requisite military training, sufficient wealth, and the proper horse to conduct a specialized form of warfare, mounted shock combat. Social differentiation initially based on the factors of skill, means, and authority rapidly led to the development of a knightly class self-conscious of its place in the larger society, boastful of its martial behavior and values, and contemptuous of the unarmed segments of society, both peasant and clerical.

References to chivalry abound in the chronicles, vernacular literature, and other written records. In certain circumstances the term refers to a company of knights mounted for combat or to the status of being a knight, implying both a social distinction and an occupational specialization. In charters and other legal documents, references to lands held in chivalry imply a type of land tenure from which military service was owed. In some literary texts, the *Song of Roland* for example, chivalry is equated with the worthy action or behavior of a knight on the battlefield or elsewhere. From the twelfth century onward, chivalry was frequently understood to be a moral, religious, and social code of knightly conduct, variable in its particulars but generally upholding the virtues of courage, honor, and service. In a related sense, chivalry came to refer to the idealization of the life and manners of the knight in his castle and court. Although some modern commentators have sought chivalry's golden age either in the eleventh-century world of the chansons de geste, or later, in the age of courtly romance, or later still in the pageantry of the time of Froissart, such efforts have ultimately been fruitless.

Despite the divers characterizations of the nature of chivalry, the association with warfare remained fundamental throughout the medieval era. The training of a knight as a cavalryman, adept in fighting in full armor, equipped with sword, lance, and shield, and astride a specially bred war-horse, was essential for perpetuating the political and social domination of the chivalric class. The arts of war were cultivated and exalted. Above all, the medieval knight was taught to excel in feats of arms, to exhibit courage, gallantry, and loyalty, and to eschew cowardice and baseness.

The medieval knight even assumed an identification with the valor, tactics, and ideals of the ancient Romans. The well-known handbook of the ancient writer Vegetius, *De re militari,* was translated into French as *L'art de chevalerie* in the thirteenth century by Jean de Meun, better known for his extensive contribution to the *Roman de la Rose.* Later writers also drew heavily upon Vegetius. Honoré Bonet, in the late fourteenth century, in *L'arbre des batailles,* emphasized the moral significance of the laws of war that bound all who engaged in combat. In the fifteenth century Christine de Pizan interwove themes derived from Vegetius, Bonet, and Frontinus in *Livre des faits d'armes et de chevalerie.*

A related development growing out of the practice and theory of war was the introduction of heraldry and the elaborate rules perfected in the later Middle Ages for the display of coats of arms. When not on the battlefield, the chivalrous knight resided in his fortified house or castle, whose improved defenses were as much a matter of concern as the maintenance of armor and weapons. Others lived at the courts of kings, dukes, and other great lords. The skills of battle carried over into such peacetime amusements as the hunt and the tournament. The tournament, in particular, brought together military skills, battlefield virtues, moral restraint, and heraldic display.

Chivalric virtues were modified by the influence of Christianity. As early as the tenth century the church sought to refashion and civilize the brutal bloodletting of an emerging knightly class. Through the Truce of God and the Peace of God, limits were imposed upon the warmaking of armed knights, and such warriors were obliged to respect the church and its ministers, to protect the vulnerable members of society, and to serve the church in the preservation of peace.

At the same time the church, once hostile to those who shed blood, became more tolerant of war and espoused theories of the just war and of war in the defense of faith. Liturgies were introduced for the blessing of a knight's sword and somewhat later for the ceremonial bath of chivalric purification. In the second half of the eleventh century the idea of the knight of Christ *(miles Christi)* gained wide currency, especially in southern France, Spain, and Italy.

This concept of religious chivalry received its greatest elaboration in the era of the Crusades, and the Crusades themselves have been seen in part to have been chivalrous enterprises. The later Crusades of the fourteenth and fifteenth centuries also provided outlets for the exhibition of martial valor and of devotion to a religious cause. The virtues of the Christian knight consisted of fidelity, piety, and service to God. From this ethos sprang the Orders of Chivalry, the religious military orders and the later decorative orders of knighthood. But the elaboration of a Christian ideal of knightly behavior created a tension between the secular virtues of the battlefield and the Christian doctrine of devotion to God in the service of peace.

The poetry and fictional tales devoted to the theme of chivalry not only reflected contemporary values and conventions but also served to hold up idealized models of behavior. In the early French epics the hero was commonly a knight of outstanding courage, who chose death before dishonor. The interplay of literature and history is exemplified in the command of William the Conqueror, before the Battle of Hastings, to have the *Song of Roland* recited as an inspiration to his soldiers. In the twelfth and thirteenth centuries poets drawn from the ranks of knights (troubadours and minnesingers) combined in their lyric poems chivalric honor and service with a newfound respect for women. Courtly love, however it might be defined, was possible only to those who were already members of the chivalric class. New literary heroes appeared in the Arthurian romances: Lancelot, Parzival, and Tristan epitomized in their different ways the outlook and aspirations of generations of chivalric warriors.

The enduring appeal of this literary representation of the knightly world, including the theme of the knight in service to his beloved, is seen in the late medieval contributions of Chaucer in the Knight's Tale and of Malory in the *Morte d'Arthur.* The ideal of devotion to the beloved, whether in a licit or, more often, illicit relationship, created a further strain within the concept of chivalry when it competed with martial virtues and Christian piety.

The place of chivalry in the social history of medieval Europe is difficult to assess. It is still open to debate to what extent the exploits and attitudes of notable knights such as Godfrey of Bouillon, one of the leaders of the First Crusade; William Marshal, earl marshal of England at the turn of the thirteenth century; and Bertrand du Guesclin, constable of France in the fourteenth century, were reflections of existing models of behavior or set new standards for knightly conduct. Moreover, since in its origin chivalry was associated with those who bore arms, the question arises whether the ranks of knighthood were open to any who mastered the arts of the profession or were restricted to those born into knightly families.

Were chivalry and nobility competing or compatible concepts? Because regional customs differed, the answers to this question must vary. In France, for example, the ceremony of dubbing was interpreted as bestowing noble status, whereas in the Low Countries and Germany significant distinctions separated the knightly class from the higher nobility. In England relations among nobles, landowning knights, and country gentry were complex and often conflicting. The bourgeoisie, particularly in the later Middle Ages, strove to affect chivalrous attitudes. The sons of some wealthy merchants were educated at aristocratic courts, where they acquired the manners and style of the refined knight. This "democratization" of chivalry was facilitated by the production of courtesy books, guides for the behavior of a gentleman. In a loose sense, therefore, the postmedieval code of gentlemanly conduct, including the sacredness of a man's honor, respect for women, and concern for the unfortunate, derives from one aspect of the earlier ideas of chivalry.

BIBLIOGRAPHY

Larry D. Benson and John Leyerle, eds., *Chivalric Literature* (1980); Honoré Bonet, *The Tree of Battles*, G. W. Coopland, ed. and trans. (1949); Joachim Bumke, *The Concept of Knighthood in the Middle Ages*, W. T. and E. Jackson, trans. (1982); Philippe Contamine, *La guerre au moyen âge* (1980); Georges Duby, *The Chivalrous Society*, Cynthia Postan, trans. (1977), 59–80, and *The Three Orders: Feudal Society Imagined*, A. Goldhammer, trans. (1980); Arthur B. Ferguson, *The Indian Summer of English Chivalry* (1960); F. J. C. Hearnshaw, "Chivalry and Its Place in History," in Edgar Prestage, ed., *Chivalry* (1928), 1–33: Johan Huizinga, *Men and Ideas,* James S. Holmes and Hans van Marle, trans. (1959), 196–206; Maurice Keen, "Brotherhood in Arms," in *History,* n.s. **47** (1962), and "Chivalry, Nobility, and the Man-at-Arms," in C. T. Allmand, ed., *War, Literature, and Politics in the Late Middle Ages* (1976), 32–45; Raymond L. Kilgour, *The Decline of Chivalry as Shown in the French Literature of the Late Middle Ages* (1937); Ramon Lull, *The Book of the Ordre of Chyvalry, Translated and Printed by William Caxton from a French Version of Ramón Lull's "Le Libre del Ordre de Cavayleria," Together with Adam Loutfut's Scottish Transcript (Harleian MS. 6149),* A. T. P. Byles, ed. (1926); Sidney Painter, *French Chivalry: Chivalric Ideas and Practices in Mediaeval France* (1940); Christine de Pizan, *The Book of Fayttes of Armes and of Chyvalrye, Translated and Printed by William Caxton,* A. T. P. Byles, ed., 2nd ed. (1937); Flavius Vegetius Renatus, *L'art de chevalerie; traduction du De re militari de Végèce par Jean de Meun* (1897); J. F. Verbruggen, *The Art of Warfare in Western Europe During the Middle Ages,* S. Willard and S. C. M. Southern, trans. (1977).

JAMES ROSS SWEENEY

[See also **Chivalry, Orders of; Chrétien de Troyes; Christine de Pizan; Froissart, Jehan; Games and Pastimes; Jean de Meun (Meung); Peace of God, Truce of God; Roland, Song of; Wolfram von Eschenbach.**]

CHIVALRY, ORDERS OF. For the protection of Christian pilgrims in the Holy Land several groups of crusading knights organized themselves into military orders during the twelfth century. These knightly brotherhoods combined the ascetic life of Christian monks with the ideals of Christian chivalry. They took the vows of Benedictine or Augustinian monks—poverty, chastity, and obedience—and in addition vowed to help the weak and to fight the enemies of Christ.

The earliest of these orders is that of the Knights of St. John of Jerusalem, also known as the Knights Hospitalers, the Knights of Rhodes, or the Knights of Malta. They organized themselves for the protection of a pilgrims' hospital in Jerusalem, established about 1070 by benefactors from Amalfi. It had St. John the Baptist as patron saint and was part of a Benedictine monastery. However, the knights made themselves independent under Master Gerard de Martígnes and were officially recognized as a new religious order by Pope Paschal II in 1113. Under the next master, Raymond du Puy, the order became firmly organized after 1120. The Knights of St. John wore black cloaks with a white cross on the left shoulders; in battle they wore red surcoats with the white cross in front and in back. Their shields and battle flag were red with the white cross, which soon assumed a distinctive shape with eight points, commonly known as the Maltese cross.

The order was divided into three classes of members: knights, priests, and serving brothers. It became very popular and powerful through donations, building hospitals and castles in the Holy Land as well as in Europe. Its headquarters in the Holy Land, the Krak des Chevaliers, is one of the largest castles ever built. However, after the failure of the Eighth Crusade (1290–1291) and the fall of the last Christian stronghold, Acre (18 May 1291), the Knights of St. John had to withdraw to Limassol on Cyprus. Under their grand master Fulque de Villaret they conquered the island of Rhodes (1309) and were henceforth known as the Knights of Rhodes. They were particularly engaged in fighting Turkish pirates and for centuries acted as the "police of the Mediterranean." During the fifteenth century they withstood several sieges by the Turks, under grand masters Jean de Lastic (1437–1454) and Pierre d'Aubusson (1480).

When Philippe Villiers de L'Isle Adam was elected grand master in 1521, the chancellor Andreas d'Amaral betrayed the order out of jealousy and went over to the Turks. Sultan Suleiman I attacked with a fleet of 400 ships and 140,000 men, against which overwhelming force the order could muster only 600 knights and 4,500 foot soldiers. After heroic resistance the survivors made good their escape on New Year's Eve 1523 and went to Messina, Sicily. In 1530 Emperor Charles V gave Grand Master Villiers the island of Malta as a fief, on the condition that the order would deliver as an annual token of tribute one white falcon to the viceroy of Sicily (this is the story behind the "Maltese falcon"). From then on, the order was known as the Knights of Malta.

The order continued its police activity, now against the North African pirate states of Algeria, Tunisia, and Tripolitania, until 1798, when Malta was seized by Napoleon. In 1800 the island was taken by the British, who still hold it. The Order of Malta survives as a charitable organization, and since the sixteenth century there has been a Protestant branch in Germany and Sweden.

The second great order of chivalry was the Poor Knights of Christ or the Knights Templars. It was founded in 1119, when the French knights Hugh de Payens, Godeffroi de St. Omer, Rollant, Godeffroi Bisot, Paien de Montdidier, and Archembaud de St. Amand joined together as a brotherhood to defend the Holy Sepulcher, protect pilgrims, and fight the infidel. They received from King Baldwin II of Jerusalem a house on the site of the Temple of Solo-

mon and therefore were called the Knights Templars. The order was acknowledged by Pope Honorius II in 1127 and was given its constitution by St. Bernard of Clairvaux in 1128. Their distinctive dress was a white cloak with a red cross, and a white linen sword belt. Their shields were white with the red cross, but their battle flag—called Beauseant or the "piebald banner"—was black and white, supposedly to indicate that they were terrible to their enemies but kind to fellow Christians. Unfortunately, kindness toward their Christian brothers in arms was not always in the hearts of the Templars; they lived in bitter rivalry with the Hospitalers.

The Templars were originally all knights under the grand master (magister Templariorum). During the thirteenth century the order grew so rapidly—around 1260 it numbered 20,000 members and 9,000 castles, estates, and manor houses, both in the Holy Land and in Europe—that it had to be reorganized into three classes: knights, priests, and men-at-arms, like the Hospitalers. The officers were graded into grand priors, bailiffs, priors, and comturs.

Their most important grand masters were Bernard de Tremelay (d. 1153 at the siege of Ascalon), Odo de St. Amand (d. 1179), Guillaume de Beaujeu (d. 18 May 1291, at the fall of Acre), and Jacques de Molay, who in 1307, on order of Pope Clement V, relocated the order to France. Although its seal showed two knights riding double on a single horse, as an indication of its poverty-stricken beginnings, the order soon became enormously rich, not only through donations from the pious but also through active business ventures, particularly banking and money-lending.

The wealth and independence of the order had aroused much envy, especially on the part of King Philip IV, who unleashed a persecution of the Templars, accusing them of heresy, idolatry, and homosexuality. In October 1307 all Templars in France were arrested and their estates were confiscated by the Crown; the same happened in Castile and England. Over the following years there were endless trials, and many Templars were put to death. In March 1312, Clement V, who, residing in Avignon, was a pawn of the French king, abolished the order; and on 3 March 1314 the grand master de Molay was burned at the stake. With his dying breath he summoned the king before God's judgment throne within the year—and indeed King Philip died on 29 November 1314.

In other countries the Templars, now that their order had been dissolved by the pope, joined either

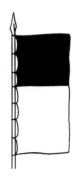

Knights Templar
(black and white)

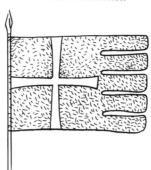

Knights of St. John
(white on red)

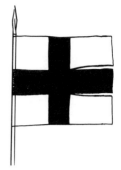

Teutonic Knights
(black on white)

Knights Templar
(red on white)

Knights of St. John
(white on black or red)

Teutonic Knights
(black on white)

Order of Christ, Portugal
(red with white center)

Knights of Alcántara, Spain (green)

Knights of Avís, Portugal (green)

Knights of Calatrava, Spain (red)

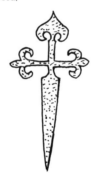

Knights of Santiago
de Compostela, Spain (red)

Knights of the Holy
Sepulcher, Jerusalem (red)

Knights of the Sword of
Cyprus

Knights of St. Anthony,
Flanders

Order of the Dragon,
Hungary

Order of the Golden
Fleece, Burgundy

Order of the White Elephant,
Denmark

Order of la Jara,
Aragon

the Hospitalers or the various national orders, which also absorbed the estates of the order.

The third of the great orders was the Teutonic Knights. It too began with a pilgrims' hospital in Jerusalem, St. Mary's of the Germans, and later (1190) with a field hospital at the siege of Acre, to which shipmasters from Lübeck donated sails to be used as tents for the wounded and sick. The hospital staff adopted the rules of the Hospitalers, and their head, Hermann (or Heinrich) Walpott (1198–1200), became the first master of this new order, which—as its name indicated—consisted of Germans (the Templars were mostly French and the Hospitalers predominantly Italian). The Teutonic Knights wore the colors of the Hospitalers reversed: white cloaks with black crosses, black crosses on their white shields and banners. Though never very numerous, the Teutonic Knights soon acquired such a reputation that in 1211 King Andrew II of Hungary asked their help; and in 1225/1226 Duke Conrad of Masovia invited their grand master, Hermann von Salza, to conquer the last remaining heathen tribes in Europe, the Prussians and the Lithuanians.

Conversion to Christianity was considered an indispensable part of the process of becoming civilized, and the Teutonic Knights went to the task with cross, sword, and a work force of settlers from Germany and Holland. Thanks to their iron discipline, organization, and devotion to duty, the wilderness of Prussia was changed into a thriving and wealthy state that was independent under the direct suzerainty of the pope, though the grand master also held the rank of a prince of the empire. Marienburg, the order's headquarters since 1309, is the largest castle in Europe.

The territory of the order extended along the Baltic coast and therefore blocked landlocked Poland's access to the sea. In 1410 the Poles and Lithuanians, with Russian and Tatar allies, defeated the order at Tannenberg, and in 1466 the order was forced to acknowledge the king of Poland as feudal overlord. The last medieval grand master was Margrave Albrecht of Brandenburg (1511–1525), who with most of his knights accepted the Reformation and became Protestant, turning the order's territory into a secular dukedom with himself as the duke. In the Catholic parts of Germany and in Austria the order continued its charitable work, though its prime fighting days were over.

Besides these three great orders there were several national military orders in countries that had long-standing conflicts with non-Christian neighbors, such as Spain and Portugal had with the Moors and Hungary with the Turks. The first of the Spanish orders was founded in 1156 by the brothers Barrientos in the border fortress San Julián del Pereiro; in 1218 the knights took up headquarters in Alcántara near Toledo and were henceforth known as the Knights of Alcántara. A second order was founded in 1158 by Abbot Ramon and the knight Diego Velásquez; they were called the Knights of Calatrava after their headquarters. In 1546 their knights were permitted to marry, and thus they became secular orders. Their emblem was a cross with fleur-de-lys terminals, green for Alcántara, red for Calatrava. The third Spanish order was that of Santiago de Compostela, founded in 1175; the Knights' badge was a red cross fleur-de-lys with a sword blade for its lower point.

The Knights of Avís in Portugal, founded in 1162, wore the same green cross as the Spanish knights of Alcántara. The Portuguese Order of Christ was established in 1318 by King Dinis as successor to the abolished Templars. Its badge was a white cross superimposed on a red cross formée.

Emperor Sigismund as king of Hungary created the Order of the Dragon for knights who vowed to fight the Turks; and the dukes of Austria had the orders of the Eagle and of St. George, directed against the heretic Hussites in Bohemia. These orders were not monastic; the Order of the Dragon even became hereditary.

Several of the minor orders were absorbed by the greater ones. After the fall of Jerusalem in 1188 the Knights of the Holy Sepulcher in Jerusalem had to join the Hospitalers; and the Brethren of the Sword in Livonia, founded in 1202, joined the Teutonic Knights in 1237.

After the loss of the Holy Land (1291), access to Jerusalem was still open to pilgrims by treaty. The king of Cyprus, as nominal king of Jerusalem, bestowed the accolade on those who made the pilgrimage to the tomb of Christ; this gave them the right to wear the cross of Jerusalem of the otherwise defunct Order of the Holy Sepulcher. Similarly he dubbed Knights of the Sword of Cyprus. Since travel was hazardous at best during the Middle Ages, such badges of knighthood testified to a considerable achievement and became status symbols without the drawback of requiring that monastic vows be taken.

One after another the monarchs of Europe followed the example of the king of Cyprus and established their own secular orders of chivalry. Membership was a signal honor and served to bind the chosen knights closer to their feudal lord in gratitude. Among the first is the English Order of the Garter, founded in 1348 by King Edward III, modeled after the legendary Knights of the Round Table, who were thought to have been the first secular order, just as the equally legendary Knights of the Holy Grail were thought to have been the first religious order. Others were the Order of the Annunziata (1360) of the dukes of Savoy, the Order of the Golden Fleece (1430) of the dukes of Burgundy, and the Lancastrian Order of Saints. To distinguish these secular orders from the religious orders, care was taken that their badges not use crosses. In fact, the names and emblems chosen, such as the French Order of the Porcupine (1394), the English Order of the Bath (1399), and the Venetian Order of the Boot, were often seemingly scurrilous, though actually fraught with deep meaning. The Golden Fleece referred not only to an untiring quest for a lofty goal but also to the Flemish wool industry that was the solid base of Burgundy's wealth. The Danish Order of the White Elephant (1462) symbolized the magnanimity of the powerful, because the elephant, as the largest of all animals, was said to be careful not to step on ants, which he blew out of his way with his trunk.

Most of the dozens of secular orders were dedicated to chivalrous conduct, the protection of the weak, and the service of ladies, but some had specific goals. The Aragonese Order of la Jara was a temperance society and had as its badge a jug holding three lilies (the flowers indicated that there was water, and not wine, in the jug); the Brandenburg Order of the Swan was dedicated to the purity of the Virgin Mary; and the Burgundian Order of St. Anthony to the maintenance of lepers' hospitals.

The custom of accepting into a prestigious order anyone who had passed a difficult test, such as the pilgrimage through enemy country to Jerusalem, and conferring the right to wear a coveted badge, led to the modern practice of awarding orders as badges of merit, though only the most exalted orders still act and exist as actual societies.

BIBLIOGRAPHY

Charles G. Addison, *The History of the Knights Templar* (1842, rev. ed. 1912); Richard W. Barber, *The Knight and Chivalry* (1970, 2nd ed. 1975), 211–290, 304–313; George F. Beltz, *Memorials of the Most Noble Order of the Garter* (1841, repr. 1973); Edgard Boutaric, *Clément V,*

Philippe le bel et les Templiers (1872); Hugh Clark, *A Concise History of Knighthood,* 2 vols. (1784); Henri Gourdon de Genouillac, *Nouveau dictionnaire des ordres de chevalerie* (1891); Henri Kervyn de Lettenhove, *La toison d'or* (1907); Edwin J. King, *The Knights Hospitallers in the Holy Land* (1931); James H. Lawrence-Archer, *The Orders of Chivalry* (1887); Georges Lizerand, ed., *Le dossier de l'affaire des Templiers* (1923); Marion Melville, *La vie des Templiers,* 2nd ed. (1974); Raymond Rudorff, *Knights and the Age of Chivalry* (1974), 117–151; Frederick C. Woodhouse, *The Military Religious Orders of the Middle Ages* (1879).

HELMUT NICKEL

[See also **Aviz, Order of; Calatrava, Order of; Knights and Knight Service.**]

CHOIR, the part of a church that contains the seats of the clergy, sometimes reserved for the seating of trained singers or for the chanting of services. During the early Christian period the clergy sat in a semicircle around the apse or in a railed-off section of the eastern end of the nave. By the Middle Ages the choir was generally established at the western end of the chancel area, between the transept crossing and the apse.

LESLIE BRUBAKER

CHORBISHOP, CHOREPISKOPOS. See **Clergy, Byzantine.**

CHOSRAU I ANŌŠARWĀN. See **Xusrō I Anōšarwān.**

CHOSRAU II PARWEZ. See **Xusrō II Abarwēz.**

CHOSROIDS (MIHRANIDS). The Chosroids (or Mihranids) were the ruling royal dynasty of Iberia (Kᶜartᶜli, that is, eastern Georgia) from the late third century to the end of the sixth century. Placed on the Iberian throne by the Persian great kings, the Chosroids were not related to the Sasanians, as they claimed, but to the Iranian Mihranids, one of the seven great houses of the empire. The first king of this line, Mirian III (Meribanes, *ca.* 282–361), known as St. Mirian for his role in the conversion of Iberia to Christianity (*ca.* 337), moved eastern Georgia away, culturally and politically, from the Persian and Zoroastrian orbit into closer contact with newly Christian Rome.

The 300 years of Chosroid rule in Iberia were marked by intense and persistent struggles between Persia and Rome over control of Caucasia. Two years after Mirian's death, the Romans were forced to cede their suzerainty over Iberia to Persia, and the Persian great kings arbitrated the selection of members of the Chosroid dynasty as rulers of Iberia. During the reign of Varaz-Bakur II (Aspacures III, 380–394), the Romans acknowledged in the Peace of Akilisene the authority of Persia over Iberia and most of Armenia. But the relationship between the Iberian kings and their Persian overlord was not consistently close. In the mid fifth century, when the Sasanian king of kings Yazdegard II (438–457) accelerated Persia's religious-political attempt to assimilate Caucasia, the young and vigorous Chosroid monarch Wakhtang I Gurgaslani (*ca.* 447–552) remained loyal to his sovereign while his neighbors, the Armenians and Albanians, rose in revolt.

Later, as the Iranophile nobility of Iberia impinged on royal power, Wakhtang joined the anti-Persian rebellion of 482–484 and gravitated toward Byzantium. Wakhtang was eventually driven from his kingdom, and his oldest son, Dach'i (522–534), adopted a pro-Persian orientation. Wakhtang's younger sons, Leo and Mithridates, remained pro-Roman, and the rivalry between the two neighboring empires tore the royal family into competing branches. In 580 the Sasanian king of kings Ohrmizd IV (579–590) responded to a request by the Iberian aristocracy, which desperately desired to be free of the crown, and abolished the Chosroid monarchy. The dynasty continued to rule as princes in Gogarene, Kakheti, and Cholarzene-Javakheti; but when the east Georgian kingdom was restored in 888, a new dynasty, the Bagratids, ascended the Iberian throne.

BIBLIOGRAPHY

William Edward David Allen, *A History of the Georgian People from the Beginning down to the Russian Conquest in the Nineteenth Century* (1932); Cyril Toumanoff, "Iberia on the Eve of Bagratid Rule: An Enquiry into the Political History of Eastern Georgia Between the VIth and the IXth Century," in *Le Muséon*, 65 (1952), and *Studies in Christian Caucasian History* (1963).

RONALD GRIGOR SUNY

[See also **Georgia: Political History; K^cart^cli; Wakhtang Gurgaslani.**]

CHRÉTIEN DE TROYES. The biography of Chrétien de Troyes can only be minimally reconstituted from the scarce data provided by his compositions. The dedication of the *Chevalier de la Charrette* to Countess Marie of Champagne suggests that he was attached as a court poet at Troyes and that he devised this particular romance for Marie subsequent to her marriage in 1164. Similarly, the dedicatory remarks contained in the *Conte du Graal* indicate that he may well have entered the service of Count Philip of Flanders (*d.* 1191) during the 1180's. Chrétien's training was that of a clerk, schooled in Latin and familiar with the seven liberal arts. At the start of his second romance, *Cligés,* Chrétien describes himself as a clerkly artisan working in the vernacular, claiming among his accomplishments the text of *Érec et Énide* as well as the translation into French of such Ovidian poems as *The Commandments of Ovid; The Art of Love; The Metamorphosis of the Hoopoe, Swallow, and Nightingale;* and *The Shoulder Bite* (probably the story of Philomela and the account of Pelops from the *Metamorphoses*). He also lists a mysterious *King Mark and the Blond Iseut*—an odd reference to the Tristan legend, which was to obsess him throughout his career.

It is generally agreed that Chrétien's extant oeuvre comprises *Érec et Énide* (*ca.* 1170), *Cligés* (*ca.* 1176), *Le Chevalier au Lion* (*Yvain*), and *Le Chevalier de la Charrette* (*Lancelot*)—worked on simultaneously from about 1177 to about 1181—and the unfinished *Conte du Graal* (*Perceval*) (before 1191). (The latter text was "continued" by various romancers. Chrétien himself entrusted the completion of *Lancelot* to a collaborator named Godefroy de Lagny.) The above dates, at best, are approximate; much controversy surrounds them.

In addition, two lyric poems are ascribed to Chrétien, whereas *Guillaume d'Angleterre,* a non-Arthurian romance with many hagiographic overtones, sometimes attributed to him, is now usually thought to be the work of another poet. Chrétien's romances are preserved in a substantial number of manuscripts—some complete, some fragmentary, but none antedating the second decade of the thirteenth century. They are composed in octosyllabic rhyming couplets, in standard literary Old French; some manuscripts, for instance Guiot, display traits of the Champagne dialect in which Chrétien may or may not have written, while others give evidence of their copyists' dialects, for example, Picard. The romances average about 7,000 lines in length, with the exception of the unfinished *Perceval,* which contains some 9,000 lines.

In *Érec* Chrétien seeks to examine and resolve the potential conflicts affecting the two partners of a married couple rather than the typical love triangle of the Tristan legend. Unlike Iseut, Énide is not sought after, not even conceptually; she is "happened upon," and Érec uses her in order to defeat a rival whom, previously, he had been unable to fight; she is a willing and docile instrument whose beauty, wisdom, and refinement are yet to be brought to light. Her perfection is revealed suddenly at Arthur's court: arrayed by Queen Guenevere in appropriate courtly attire, she receives from the king the kiss of the Custom of the White Stag. Nevertheless, she proves to be the catalyst of further adventure and, also, of proof of individual knightly value as she warns her husband against his indolence and disintegrating reputation. (Instead of performing chivalric tasks, Érec prefers to stay at home, delighting in his wife's newly discovered charms.)

The two set out on a route to the unknown, encountering envious robbers, counts who wish to take Énide away from her husband, and knights who challenge Érec's superiority. Énide disobeys Érec's injunction to keep silent and ride well ahead of him; though chastised at each instance of disobedience, she apprises him of every new danger. Her inner struggle over whether to speak or keep silent, to follow her own judgment—a judgment invariably dictated by her love and devotion—or to obey the letter of her husband's law and risk losing all, parallels Érec's struggle to prove himself as a knight willing and able to serve others, and as a husband confident in his wife's loyalty and inspired by it to choose, as well as to act, wisely. The poet's clerkly wisdom, reflected in Énide's choice to articulate the truth in a spirit of loyalty (despite risks), thus finds an answer (and support) in Érec's knightly valor, which is exercised and surpassed in degree with each new challenge.

In *Cligés,* a tour de force that is more obviously concerned with the Tristan model than was *Érec,*

Chrétien elevates the clerkly poet's role to a central, rather than a parallel, level of interest. The possibilities of comparison between the very funny *Cligés* and the tragically sad *Tristan* of Béroul, or of Thomas, are almost infinitely multilayered. One of the romance's heroines, Fénice, the empress of Constantinople, provokes many near disasters because she does not wish to appear to behave as did the lascivious Iseut, though in the end her conduct constitutes no moral improvement on that of Tristan's beloved. The manipulation of references to numerous romances is part of a major theme involving the transformation of traditional material that is a principal resource of courtly romance. The poet-narrator, in this case the Chrétien who is participating in the "translation" or transference of "culture" (*clergie* or clerkliness) from Greece to Rome to France (verses 28ff.), is the counterpart to the artisan figures of Thessala and Jehan, who invert well-known Tristan devices in order to free their master and mistress from difficulty while protecting their "innocence" and "legitimacy."

Chrétien once again investigates the theme of love and marriage in *Yvain;* he reverses, however, the proposition outlined in *Érec.* The hero decides to react before his Round Table comrades have a chance to do so, because he wishes to avenge the honor of his cousin rather than save his own reputation. The narrated history of a failed adventure prompts Yvain to fill the gap created by this failure. Yvain travels to the legendary Fountain in the forest of Brocéliande and, like his cousin before him, he pours water on the stone; this provokes a storm and the sallying forth of the lord of the nearby castle. Yvain defeats this lord—Esclados—and, after wounding him, chases him into his castle. He is hidden by Lunete, the fairylike servant of Esclados and his wife. He soon falls in love with Laudine, the grieving widow of his defeated opponent, and eventually marries her, thereby becoming the new champion of the Fountain.

Arthur and his retainers arrive and repeat once again the ritual of the Fountain and its challenge, only to have Yvain emerge victorious and reveal his double identity. Arthur's nephew, Gauvain, known as the model knight, encourages Yvain to take leave of his wife in order to participate in tourneys and the like. No Érec he, Yvain entreats his wife to grant him permission to depart; despite her forebodings she agrees, with the proviso that he return to her within exactly one year or she will forsake him. Yvain fails to keep his promise, is told by his wife's messenger that she has renounced him, goes mad, and exiles himself alone in a forest, naked and living like an animal. His basic charity persists, however, in his gentle treatment of a kind but frightened hermit. He is eventually recognized by a lady who cures him with a magic balm.

It is at this point, and after he has helped the lady who cured him, that Yvain is ready to enter on a course of service to others. He comes to the aid of the King of Beasts, a lion whose tail lies in the mouth of a serpent-dragon. The grateful animal becomes Yvain's constant companion and helpmate in combat. Yvain forges a new reputation for himself, but not under his real name: he is known as the Lion Knight. He rescues Lunete, who had once rescued him and arranged for his marriage. Lunete, in turn, once again persuades her mistress and manipulates her into a bargain to help the Lion Knight regain the favor of his lady—who is, of course, herself. The couple is reconciled, the alternate identities are fused, and the order of romance is restored.

The situation is quite different in the case of both *Lancelot* and *Perceval*. The story of the perfect knight and lover, Lancelot, as well as that of the Grail—both apparently inventions of Chrétien (at least in the Old French context)—were to have immense repercussions on medieval European literature.

Just as Yvain responded to *Érec et Énide*'s earlier exploration of marriage and knightly conduct, so *Lancelot* constitutes yet another obverse response to *Tristan*. Whereas innocence and legitimacy were preserved at all costs in *Cligés*, where the poet-narrator and his surrogates reign supreme, in the *Charrette* Lancelot and Queen Guenevere occupy a compromising position in an adulterous (and treasonous) love triangle.

In many respects Lancelot is a comic figure; his beloved mistress is haughty and less than sympathetic, even misguided, since she is the first to grant Keu (Kay) his rash boon (the consequence of which will entail her abduction to the kingdom of Gorre, whence Lancelot will have to rescue her). Furthermore, it is her rejection of the as yet unnamed knight (due to his having hesitated to get into the infamous cart), despite his superhuman efforts on her behalf, that leads to his attempted suicide—an act that, had it proved successful, would have had as consequence that Guenevere and the other captives remain in exile without a champion. It is again Guenevere, this time in conjunction with her nephew Gauvain—himself rescued by Lancelot after his failure to aid

the queen—who, believing the false letter attributed to her champion, decides to return to her husband's court, leaving Lancelot imprisoned. Neither she nor any other member of Arthur's court does anything to reciprocate Lancelot's service. On the contrary, it is other, nameless damsels who rescue, counsel, and protect Lancelot on his quest and when he is imprisoned. Served by the nameless and mysterious knight, they in turn admire and serve him, in a mutual and fruitful exchange.

Chrétien's second unfinished work is his longest and most enigmatic romance, *Le Conte du Graal*. This narrative has been termed a Bildungsroman because it recounts its protagonist's history from adolescence on, describing Perceval's education in knighthood, love, and eventually religious observance. The tone is initially comic, the narrator and reader deriving amusement from Perceval's obvious blunders in regard to proper courtly behavior, language, and attire. However, the tone and the reader's stance with respect to the protagonist eventually shift, notably at the central moment of the *Perceval* episodes when the audience waits for the youth to satisfy not only his own curiosity but also our own about the significance of the Grail procession. Suddenly the reader is made to see matters from Perceval's point of view; his education in these mysteries depends entirely on Perceval's education.

Eventually, in the last of the episodes in which Perceval figures, we and Perceval learn from a hermit—who reveals himself as the hero's uncle—that the Grail contains a single host that sustains yet another uncle, his mother's brother, at the Grail castle. Perceval, who makes his first act of confession on Good Friday in the hermit's company and receives his first Holy Communion on Easter Sunday from his uncle's hand, learns the cause of his failure to ask the necessary questions about the Lance and the Grail. His lack of charity in hurrying off on the road to his own self-gratification prevented him from dismounting and rushing to his mother's side as she fainted with grief at his departure and led to his mother's demise and to his hardening of heart and untimely silence before the Grail. Presumably an undoing of this lack of charity could lead to appropriate articulation in other circumstances that might be of benefit to others in need.

We remain in doubt as to the significance of the Bleeding Lance, however, and one wonders why Perceval failed to ask his uncle about it. Perhaps this question is meant to be resolved by Gauvain, who departs on a quest for the Lance, an instrument that apparently is fated to destroy his uncle's—Arthur's—kingdom.

All five romances constitute variations at times on one another, on the Tristan story, and on the ongoing romance tradition. Chrétien explores the relationship of clerkliness (clergie) to knightliness (chevalerie) as he also meditates on the value of the discovery of self in regard to some form of couple, to a certain community, and to a given tradition of values, whether it be that of the husband to his wife, of lover to beloved, of child to family, or of poet to literary tradition and of reader to text. Each example is entrancing, rich, and original, engendering consequences that endured, as is evidenced by the early-thirteenth-century Middle High German versions of Yvain and Erec composed by Hartmann von Aue and of the Perceval by Wolfram von Eschenbach, as well as by the numerous epigonal Old French romances like Le Bel Inconnu, Fergus, Méraugis de Portelesguer, and others that refer to Chrétien's work. The great Lancelot-Grail prose cycle and, indeed, Guillaume de Lorris' Romance of the Rose also owe much to Chrétien, whose direct and indirect influence on subsequent narrative may be traced through the fourteenth century, for example to the work of Froissart.

BIBLIOGRAPHY

Bibliographies. Douglas Kelly, Chrétien de Troyes, an Analytic Bibliography (1976), is indispensable. For work published after 1974 consult the yearly International Bibliography of the Modern Language Association.

Principal editions. Christian von Troyes Sämtliche Werke, Wendelin Foerster, ed., 4 vols. (1884–1899), copiously annotated, has been frequently revised and reissued. Der Percevalroman, not included, was edited by A. Hilka (1932, repr. 1966). For the Classiques français du Moyen Âge, Mario Roques has edited Érec et Énide (1952); Cligés (1957); Le Chevalier de la Charrette (1958); Le Chevalier au Lion (1960). Also, Le Conte du Graal, F. Lecoy, ed. (1972–1975); Le Roman de Perceval ou le Conte du Graal, William Roach, ed. (1959). Of doubtful authorship is Guillaume d'Angleterre, Maurice Wilmotte, ed. (1927). For the chansons see Hilka's Der Percevalroman, 798–803.

Translations. Of Modern French translations those based on Mario Roques's editions are the most accessible. In English see Arthurian Romances, W. W. Comfort, trans. and ed. (1914), frequently reprinted. For Perceval the best modern version is that of Lucien Foulet (1947, repr. 1970); in English see The Story of the Grail, Robert W. Linker, trans. (1952).

General studies. Jean Frappier, Chrétien de Troyes (1957, repr. 1968); Frappier has been published in English as Chrétien de Troyes: The Man and His Work, Raymond J. Cormier, trans. (1982); Alexandre Micha, La tradition manuscrite des romans de Chrétien de Troyes (1939, repr. 1966); Karl D. Uitti, Story, Myth, and Celebration in Old French Narrative Poetry, 1050–1200 (1973), 128–231; Douglas Kelly, gen. ed., The Romances of Chrétien de Troyes (1983).

Monographic studies. Jean Frappier, Chrétien de Troyes et le mythe du graal (1972); Étude sur Yvain, ou le Chevalier au lion de Chrétien de Troyes (1969), and "Pour le commentaire d'Érec et Énide: Notes de lecture," in Marche romane, 20 (1970); Michelle A. Freeman, The Poetics of Translatio Studii and Conjointure: Chrétien de Troyes's Cligés (1979); Douglas Kelly, "La forme et le sens de la quête dans l'Érec et Énide de Chrétien de Troyes," in Romania, 92 (1971), and "Sens" and "Conjointure" in the "Chevalier de la Charrette" (1966); Rupert T. Pickens, The Welsh Knight: Paradoxicality in Chrétien's Conte del Graal (1977).

MICHELLE A. FREEMAN

[See also Arthurian Literature; Courtly Love; French Literature; Holy Grail, Legend of; Tristan, Roman de.]

CHRISMON, a form of Christogram in which a monogram of Christ's initials, usually distorted, rests on a cross, a C, or a bar. "Chrismon" is also sometimes used to mean "Christogram."

BIBLIOGRAPHY

Victor Gardthausen, Das alte Monogramm (1924, repr. 1966), 150–152.

LESLIE BRUBAKER

[See also Christogram.]

CHRISTIAN OF STABLO (Christianus Druthmarus), Benedictine monk and exegete, was born in Burgundy or Aquitania in the first half of the ninth century; he died at Stablo (Stavelot), lower Lorraine (now Belgium), after 880. His major contribution was his commentary on St. Matthew (ca. 865). His work illustrates the methods of compiling scriptural expositions and of monastic teaching in the ninth century.

BIBLIOGRAPHY

Christian's works are in Patrologia latina, CVI (1864), 1259–1520. See also M. L. W. Laistner, "A Ninth-Century

Commentator on the Gospel According to Matthew," in *Harvard Theological Review*, **20** (1927).

KRISTINE T. UTTERBACK

CHRISTIAN ARCHITECTURE, EARLY. See **Early Christian and Byzantine Architecture.**

CHRISTIAN ART, EARLY. See **Early Christian Art.**

CHRISTIAN CHURCH IN PERSIA, the Aramaic-speaking Christian minority within the borders of the Sasanian Persian Empire. It was concentrated in Mesopotamia, with its principal see at Seleucia-Ctesiphon. Styling itself the "Church of the East," it was also commonly known as the Nestorian church. Because of persecution there was no Persian representation at the First Council of Nicaea and the First Council of Constantinople. But in 410 a local synod at Seleucia affirmed the canons of both councils and then began to organize the church and establish the jurisdictional primacy of the katholikos of Seleucia-Ctesiphon. By 424 the Persian church severed ties with the Byzantine church to avoid the accusation by the Sasanians that it was an alien sect with allegiance to Byzantine interests. Throughout the Sasanian period its fortunes fluctuated in accordance with the status of Persian-Byzantine relations. There was also internal pressure from the Zoroastrian priesthood, the guardians of the state religion. This situation eased somewhat in the mid fifth century, but tension continued until the overthrow of the Sasanians by the Arabs in the seventh century.

The condemnation of Nestorius in 431 marks the beginning of the Nestorianizing of the Persian church. The flight of the Nestorian theologian Narsai to Nisibis in 457 and the support he received from the Nestorian bishop of Nisibis, Bar Ṣauma, were crucial factors in the spread of Nestorianism throughout Persia. The interception by Bar Ṣauma of incriminating letters from Katholikos Babowai to Emperor Zeno which implied treasonable intent enabled Bar Ṣauma to have a pro-Nestorian katholikos placed over the church. Under his influence a Nestorian confession was adopted by the synod of Seleucia in 486. In 489 Zeno abolished the Nestorian

school of Edessa, and the faculty and students augmented the Nestorian presence at Nisibis.

Under the leadership of the reforming katholikos Mar Aba (540–552), the church recovered from the scandals and schism that marked the early sixth century. Dissident sees in Khuzistan and Fars were reconciled to the authority of the katholikos. Mar Aba helped to stop a severe persecution under Xusrō I, and in 541 founded the school of Seleucia-Ctesiphon, which eventually eclipsed the school of Nisibis. In 571 Abraham of Kashkar founded the famous monastery of Mount Īzlā, which influenced the direction taken by subsequent cenobitic foundations. The sixth century marks the beginning of Nestorian missionary expansion. The eastern coast of Arabia, Socotra, the caravan centers of Merv, Samarkand, and Herat in central Asia, Ceylon, and southern India all had Nestorian communities. This expansion was due partly to the pressure from persecutions, and even more to Syriac-speaking merchants who established themselves in the towns along the principal trade routes. By 635 Nestorian Christianity was being preached in China as the "Luminous Doctrine." In central Asia and China, Nestorians were often in competition with the Manichaeans, from whom they may have learned some of their missionary techniques. From the death of Katholikos Gregory I in 609 until 628, Xusrō II prevented the election of a katholikos. The leadership of the church fell in large part to Babai the Great. Through the landmark episcopal assembly of 612 and his own writings, he helped to commit the Persian church to the unambiguous and systematized Nestorian Christology to which it adhered throughout the medieval period. As visitor to the monasteries, Babai did much to strengthen these influential institutions. He and Mar Aba rank among the greatest leaders of their church.

The political situation changed with the destruction of the Sasanians by the Muslims in 642. The Christians were recognized as "people of protection." The dissolution of the Byzantine-Persian frontier opened western Asia and Egypt to the Nestorians, who established communities in Damascus, Alexandria, and Cyprus. From the seventh to the tenth centuries the Nestorians were left in peace, with the exception of harassment under the caliphs ᶜUmar II (717–720) and al-Mutawakkil (847–861), both the result of ultraconservative Islamic pressure. Heretical Muslims probably fared worse than the Christians.

The Abbasid caliphate (750–1055) coincided with the golden age of Nestorian Christianity. About 775 the katholikate was moved from Seleucia-Ctesiphon to Baghdad, the new capital. The katholikos gradually came to be recognized as the civil as well as ecclesiastical ruler of his own people and other Christian minorities. The Nestorians, possessors of a long scholarly tradition, were able to exercise great influence in Baghdad, especially on the arts of medicine and translation. Working at the famed Bayt al-ḥikma, founded by al-Maʾmūn in 832, Nestorian scholars translated Greek works on a wide variety of subjects into Arabic. Generations of families like the Bakhtīshū and individuals like Ḥunayn ibn Isḥāq al-ʿIbādī served as translators and hereditary court physicians.

After the Seljuk Turks took Baghdad in 1055, Persia entered a period of political anarchy and cultural decline that is reflected in the decline of the Nestorian schools and the virtual cessation of Syriac or Arabic theological writing. Great hopes were aroused when the Mongols under Hulagu Khan subjugated Persia in 1258. Earlier missionary efforts had converted whole Mongol tribes, and the leadership showed some inclination toward Christianity, if only to win Western support against the Muslims. In 1282 a Mongol monk, sent on a diplomatic mission by Kublai Khan, was consecrated katholikos as Yabhalaha III. His companion, Rabban Ṣāwmā, completed the mission, traveling as far as France to meet Edward I of England, but failed to gain Western support for a Mongol-Christian alliance. By the end of Yabhalaha's reign, Mongol vacillation had been replaced by conversion to Islam. This unsettled period saw a brief but impressive renaissance of Syriac letters.

The invasion and devastation of Mesopotamia (1392–1393) by Tamerlane, and his slaughter of Christians and destruction of their schools and monasteries, reduced the Nestorians to a handful of refugees who escaped to the mountains of Kurdistan. Almost nothing is known about them until the sixteenth century. Except for southern India, the Nestorian mission territories were de-Christianized. The see of Rome made various attempts between the thirteenth and fifteenth centuries to contact and establish communion with the Nestorians, but little was accomplished until the sixteenth century.

BIBLIOGRAPHY

For the overall context in which Persian Christianity developed, see Arthur E. Christensen, *L'Iran sous les Sassanides* (1936). J. M. Fiey covers most of the history of the Persian church to the fourteenth century in *Jalons pour une histoire de l'église en Iraq* (1970); *Chrétiens syriaques sous les Mongols (Il-Khanat de Perse, XIIIe–XXIVe s.)* (1975); and *Chrétiens syriaques sous les Abbassides surtout à Bagdad (749–1258)* (1980). Jérôme Labourt, *Le christianisme dans l'empire perse sous la dynastie sassanide (224–632)* (1904) is still an indispensable general history; see also E. Tisserant, "Nestorienne (l'église)," in *Dictionnaire de théologie catholique*, XI (1931), 157–288, 313–323. For the Nestorian missions, see François Nau, *L'expansion nestorienne en Asie* (1914). John Foster, *The Church of the T'ang Dynasty* (1939), is a good popular study.

D. W. JOHNSON

[See also **Iran: History, 650–1500; Iraq; Nestorianism.**]

CHRISTIAN HEBRAISTS. Knowledge of Hebrew by medieval Christians was first studied by the nineteenth-century French Protestant Samuel Berger. Eastern Christians, using Syriac, could easily work on Hebrew and Aramaic texts. In western Europe during the early Middle Ages, such a knowledge was exceptional. Jews who converted to Christianity used Hebrew Old Testament texts; through this channel a superficial knowledge of terms passed to Christian scholars such as Bede. The revision of the Bible by Alcuin stimulated the spread of Hebrew in the ninth century as part of the Carolingian renaissance; among the Hebraists of that period, the anonymous Pseudo-Jerome worked in the circle of Hrabanus Maurus. Small groups of Hebraists existed in the tenth and eleventh centuries in southern Italy, northern Spain, France, and Germany, learning Hebrew in order to correct exemplars of the Old Testament.

In the twelfth century contacts with Jewish scholars caused an increased interest in the language of the Bible, and its study, recommended by Abelard, became common at the school of St. Victor in Paris. The best Hebraist among the Victorines was Andrew of St. Victor. His pupil, Herbert of Bosham, added to exegesis grammatical notions acquired from Abraham ibn Ezra. Cistercian monks also studied Hebrew, stimulated by Nicholas Manjacoria's example. Scholars in England and France, such as Alexander Neckham, had a fair knowledge of Hebrew. The most valuable contribution to the study of Hebrew was made by Stephen Langton, who produced a Hebrew-Latin vocabulary of biblical terms. Hebrew was also taught at the school of translators in Toledo, but was secondary to Arabic.

Despite the development of biblical exegesis in the thirteenth century, the number of Christian-born Hebraists diminished in continental Europe, where converted Jews played the main role, using their knowledge of Hebrew mainly in polemics or apologies against their former religion. In England, Hebraists were more highly considered, supported by Robert Grosseteste, who employed William of Mara in his service. Roger Bacon, who composed a manual of Hebrew grammar, was influential in the spread of Hebrew studies. The development of the universities facilitated the establishment (primarily for missionary aims) of chairs of Hebrew in various institutions, especially by the Franciscans and Dominicans. In 1312 the Council of Vienne ordered establishment of chairs at Rome, Paris, Oxford, Salamanca, and Bologna. The best Hebraists of this period were Nicholas of Lyra at Paris and Bishop Paul of Burgos, a converted Jew.

In the late Middle Ages knowledge of Hebrew spread at the universities, at the Avignon papal court, and among humanists. Favored by Ramon Lull, Gerson, and other intellectuals, it reached its apogee with Pico della Mirandola and Johann Reuchlin.

BIBLIOGRAPHY

Aryeh Grabois, "The 'Hebraica Veritas' and Jewish-Christian Intellectual Relations in the Twelfth Century," in *Speculum*, 50 (1975); Herman Hailperin, *Rashi and the Christian Scholars* (1963); Raphael Loewe, "The Medieval Christian Hebraists of England, Herbert of Bosham and Earlier Scholars," in *Transactions of the Jewish Historical Society of England*, 17 (1953); Judah M. Rosenthal, "The Talmud on Trial; the Disputation at Paris in the Year 1240," in *Jewish Quarterly Review*, 47 (1956); Beryl Smalley, *The Study of the Bible in the Middle Ages*, 2nd ed. (1952).

ARYEH GRABOIS

[See also **Andrew of St. Victor; Bacon, Roger; Gerson, John; Grosseteste, Robert; Hebrew Language, Study of; Langton, Stephen; Lull, Ramon.**]

CHRISTIANITY, NUBIAN. Nubia is the name given to the region beginning at Syene (Aswan) on the southern border of Byzantine Egypt and stretching south along the Nile to Soba, a town on the Blue Nile just above modern Khartoum. By the sixth century, Nubia was divided into three kingdoms. Nobadia stretched from Syene to the third cataract, Makuria (Arabic: Muqarra) from the third to the sixth cataract, and Alodia (Arabic: ᶜAlwa) from there to an undetermined boundary south of Soba.

Literary and archaeological evidence for the presence of Christianity prior to the mid fifth century is ambiguous or contradictory. After the peace treaty of 453 between the Nobades and the Byzantines, some 100 years of peace ensued, a period during which there is some archaeological evidence for the presence of Christianity in Nobadia. The removal of the pagan idols from the temple at Philae about 535, which provoked no reprisals from the Nobades, may indicate a waning paganism. But no organized effort to convert the Nobades is recorded until the mission of the Monophysite bishop Julian, a protégé of Empress Theodora, which arrived at Nobadia in 542/543. According to the Monophysite historian John of Ephesus, a rival Melkite mission sponsored by Justinian was delayed at the border by the governor of the Thebaïd on Theodora's instructions. By 545 Julian had converted the Nobades and returned to Constantinople. His replacement, Longinus, was delayed by Justinian and did not arrive in Nobadia until 569. From there he was summoned by the king of Alodia to preach Christianity in that country. The kingdom of Makuria was probably converted to Melkite Christianity in 567–576. Cosmas Indicopleustes (*ca.* 547) reports that Christianity was widespread and well organized throughout Nubia. This is probably an exaggeration, as is the picture of a watertight sectarian division among the kingdoms, two Monophysite and one Melkite. The latter seems to reflect the biases of contemporary historians, and is not supported by archaeological evidence. In Lower Nubia, at least, both sects seem to have been represented. It seems unlikely that Justinian's mission was delayed indefinitely or that Julian's was so successful as to be exclusive.

After the Arab conquest of Egypt (642) and the subsequent ascendancy of Monophysitism there, Monophysitism in Nubia seized the advantage, and by 700 was adopted as the state religion without entirely displacing the Melkites. Nubia remained independent of Islamic Egypt, and in the eighth century there is still evidence of the continuing influence of Byzantine traditions in civil and ecclesiastical life.

Most documentary information about Christian Nubia after the Arab conquest of Egypt comes from Arabic sources. In recent years this has been vastly supplemented by archaeological work, much of which is still in progress. The greater amount of information relates to Lower Nubia. Virtually nothing is known about the southern kingdom, Alodia.

The richest archaeological site has been Faras (Pachoras), the metropolitan see and capital of Nobadia. Makuria and Nobadia were united around the end of the seventh century, possibly under King Merkurios, the "New Constantine." From this time until about 1193, through the examination of foundation stones, tombstones, and wall paintings inscribed in Greek or Coptic, a list of the metropolitans and kings of Lower Nubia has been reconstructed. Beginning in the eighth century, extensive church construction took place throughout Lower Nubia. Most notable are the cathedral and other churches at Faras with their extensive wall paintings reflecting the various periods in the evolution of this art. Nubian cultural and political power reached a high point in the mid tenth century. Nubian kings were recognized as the protectors of the patriarchs of Alexandria. From the middle of the eleventh century, the Melkites controlled the bishopric of Faras. Egypt's partiality to the Melkites at this time and Nubia's good relations with Egypt might explain this. The Monophysites were restored in 1058 after Patriarch Christodoulos of Alexandria visited Faras in that same year.

The Egyptians finally invaded Nubia and captured Qasr Ibrim, near Faras, in 1172. After about 1193 nothing is known about the bishopric of Faras, which seems to have declined rapidly. Subsequently the pressure of increased Arab immigration into Lower Nubia drove the Christian kings south to Dongola, where Christianity continued to survive in a weakening kingdom torn by dynastic rivalries. By the late thirteenth century the Christian kingdom was an Egyptian pawn. The last Christian king, Kudanbes, after losing and regaining his throne several times, was finally overthrown by the Muslim Kanz al-Dawla. The now uninhibited Arab immigration brought about the rapid Islamization of the country, and Christianity disappeared. Alodia seems to have survived as a Christian country until the arrival of the Fung in the early sixteenth century. Maqrizi, writing in the fourteenth century, describes the capital, Soba, as well built, spacious, and wealthy. He says that the Alodians were Monophysites who used Greek books that were translated, perhaps orally, into Nubian. But the testimony of later travelers and archaeological excavations at Soba point to a far more modest city than Maqrizi describes.

It is not clear what role the indigenous Nubian language or languages played in the life of the Christian church. Greek and Coptic are dominant among the inscriptions and other written material published so far. A small number of Nubian religious texts and some graffiti survive. Like Coptic, Nubian is written with the Greek alphabet supplemented by special signs for sounds peculiar to Nubian. Fragments of Nubian lectionaries seem to indicate that at least this part of the liturgy was available in the vernacular. The rapid decline of Christianity after the Muslim conquest may indicate a failure by the Nubian church to adapt to the culture of the common people and provide a base for itself outside the ruling classes.

BIBLIOGRAPHY

For a general overview, see P. L. Shinnie, "Christian Nubia," ch. 9 of *The Cambridge History of Africa*, II (1978); for a general treatment of the Faras excavations, with copious illustrations and a comprehensive bibliography of Christian Nubia, see Kazimierz Michałowski, *Faras, die Kathedrale aus dem Wüstenstand* (1967). The four-volume series entitled *Faras* comprises *Fouilles polonaises 1961*, Kazimierz Michałowski *et al.*, eds. (1962); *Fouilles polonaises 1961–62*, Kazimierz Michałowski *et al.*, eds. (1965); Stefan Jakobielski, *A History of the Bishopric of Pachoras on the Basis of Coptic Inscriptions* (1972), which is more extensive than the title implies; and Jadwiga Kubińska, *Inscriptions grecques chrétiennes* (1974). G. Vantini, *Oriental Sources Concerning Nubia* (1975), is a collection and translation of all the extant texts relating to Nubia from Cosmas Indicopleustes (*ca.* 547) to the Fung Chronicle (final redaction *ca.* 1870), with bibliographical notices for each selection and index of proper names.

D. W. JOHNSON

[See also **Cosmas Indicopleustes; Melkites; Monophysitism.**]

CHRISTIANS IN THE ISLAMIC WORLD. See **Abode of Islam—Abode of War; Crusades and Crusader States; Islam, Conquests of.**

CHRISTINE DE PIZAN, born in Venice in 1363 or 1364, was one of the most prolific and versatile French writers of the late Middle Ages. She provided an account of her life in the *Avision-Christine* (1405).

Her father, Thomas, was professor of astrology at the University of Bologna until 1357, after which he entered the service of the Republic of Venice. His reputation as a scholar attracted the attention of Louis I of Hungary and Charles V of France, both of whom invited him to join their courts. In 1364, Thomas went to Paris; Christine and her mother joined him there in 1368. The family enjoyed the highest favors of the Crown. In 1379 Christine married Étienne du Castel, notary and secretary to the king; they had three children.

Christine's fortunes took a turn for the worse with the death of Charles V in 1380. Her father lost his previous favor, and the family went into debt. After a long period of illness, Thomas died sometime between 1385 and 1390. Étienne du Castel died suddenly in 1389. Christine was thus widowed at the age of twenty-five; she expressed her grief in a large portion of her lyric poetry, as well as a number of her narrative works. She never remarried, professing an undying loyalty to her husband.

Christine's brothers having returned to Bologna, she was now responsible for the care of her children, her mother, and a niece. She faced a long series of lawsuits in her efforts to secure the income due her and to recover confiscated property. Christine recounts the hardships of this most difficult period in the *Avision,* and makes a plea for greater attention to the plight of widows.

Christine, who had probably received a better education than most women of her time because of the influence of her father, now turned to study as a source of comfort. She states in the *Avision* that she read ancient and modern history, science, and poetry; she finally decided to begin writing herself. Her works were highly acclaimed and brought her the favor of a number of important patrons, including the members of the royal family. She produced several codices of her collected works, beautifully made and illuminated; many of her works also appear individually. They reflect a thorough knowledge of French and Italian literature; her familiarity with Greek and Latin texts seems to have been largely through French translations.

The novelty of a woman writer about 1400 created quite a stir. Christine modestly suggests in the *Avision* that this novelty accounted for the immediate and widespread success of her works. She further states that some people refused to believe a woman capable of producing such work and accused her of perpetrating a hoax. Christine, undaunted, stood her ground. In the *Avision* she relates an incident in which a man told her that an educated woman was unattractive, since there were so few, to which she replied that an ignorant man was even less attractive, since there were so many.

Christine is perhaps best known today for her part in the *querelle* over the *Roman de la Rose,* which she initiated with her *Epistre au dieu d'amours* (1399). Christine attacked Jean de Meun for defaming women; there followed a lively debate in the form of letters exchanged between Christine and Jean de Meun's defenders, Jean de Montreuil and Gontier and Pierre Col. Christine's views were supported by the chancellor Jean Gerson, Guillaume de Tignonville, and Jean Boucicaut, marshal of France. The documents of this debate, which are included in the manuscripts of Christine's collected works, are very interesting sources for the various medieval readings of this highly influential text.

Christine's writings can be broadly categorized into works about love, religion and morality, history, and politics. Her earliest works were love poems: a collection of lyric pieces in the various *formes fixes,* often grouped in narrative sequences; love debates; and narratives with lyric interpolations. In all of these texts, Christine removes herself from the subject matter, stating repeatedly that she writes about love only for the sake of her patrons, and that she herself feels only the pain of bereavement.

The religious and didactic works, in both prose and verse, include prayers, compilations of proverbs, the *Sept psaumes allégorisés,* and meditations on human life. The major works in this category are the prose compendiums: the *Livre de prudence,* also known as *Livre de la prod'hommie de l'homme,* based largely on the pseudo-Senecan *De quatuor virtutibus;* the *Livre des trois vertus* or *Trésor de la cité des dames,* which offers moral precepts for women of all social classes; the *Livre du corps de policie,* an analogous work for men; and the *Epistre d'Othéa,* a collection of 100 exemplary figures drawn from mythology and the legends of antiquity and given allegorical interpretations.

Christine's major historical work is the verse *Livre de la mutacion de fortune* (1403), leading from the creation of the world through the histories of various ancient peoples and up to her own time. It also includes a discourse on the branches of learning and an allegorized autobiography. The prose *Livre de la cité des dames* (1405), largely inspired by Boccaccio's *De claris mulieribus,* catalogs the great women of history and their contributions to society. Christine was no less concerned with contemporary events: her works include a prose biography of Charles V, a *Ditié* celebrating the victory of Joan of Arc (1429), and several treatises on the current political turmoil, on political philosophy, and on military strategy and comportment.

The last years of Christine's life were spent in the seclusion of a convent. She died sometime after 1429, probably before 1434. The esteem in which she was held by her contemporaries is reflected in a ballad by Eustache Deschamps, who addresses her as "Muse éloquent entre les .IX., Christine." During the next 100 years, several of her prose texts were translated into English, Dutch, and Portuguese, an indication of the long-lasting and widespread admiration her works inspired.

BIBLIOGRAPHY

Modern editions and translations of the works in verse include *Ditié de Jehanne d'Arc,* Angus J. Kennedy and Kenneth Varty, eds. and trans. (1977); *Livre du chemin de long estude,* Robert Püschel, ed. (1881, repr. 1887); *Livre de la mutacion de fortune,* Suzanne Solente, ed., 4 vols. (1959–1966); *Oeuvres poétiques,* Maurice Roy, ed., 3 vols. (1886–1896).

For the prose works, see *The Book of the City of Ladies,* Earl Jeffrey Richards, trans. (1982); *Lavision-Christine,* Mary Louise Towner, ed. (1932); *Livre des fais et bonnes meurs du sage roy Charles V,* Suzanne Solente, ed., 2 vols. (1936–1941); *La Querelle de la rose: Letters and Documents,* Joseph L. Baird and John R. Kane, trans. (1978).

Studies. See Angus J. Kennedy, *Christine de Pizan: A Bibliographical Guide* (in press); Lucie Schäfer, "Die Illustrationen zu den Handschriften der Christine de Pisan," in *Marburger Jahrbuch für Kunstwissenschaft,* **10** (1937); Charity Cannon Willard, *Christine de Pizan: The First French Woman of Letters* (1982); Josette A. Wisman, "Manuscrits et éditions des oeuvres de Christine de Pisan," in *Manuscripta,* **21** (1977).

SYLVIA HUOT

[See also **Antifeminism; French Literature: After 1200; Romance of the Rose.**]

CHRISTMAS. Unlike Easter, the dating and theological significance of which were subjects that greatly exercised early Christian writers and councils, the date of Christ's birth, its theological significance, and its liturgical celebration seem to have been of little concern to the ancient church. Despite a report in the *Liber pontificalis* that Pope Telesphorus (127–136) initiated the celebration of Christmas in Rome, there is little evidence until the third cen-

tury that Christians even speculated about the exact date of Christ's birth, let alone celebrated it. According to Clement of Alexandria (*d. ca.* 215) there was some speculation about the date (17 November, 20 April, or 20 May), but in the works of Tertullian and Origen in the third century there is no mention made of a Christian feast of the Nativity. At most, there was perhaps in the ante-Nicene period in the Eastern and related Gallican churches, a feast of the Manifestation (Epiphany) of Christ on 6 January.

The fixing of 25 December as the date of Christmas made its first sure appearance in the church at Rome, where in the Philocalian Calendar of 354, whose *Depositio martyrum* (list of martyrs) goes back to 336, it is said that Christ (who is the first martyr, Apoc. 1:4) was born in Bethlehem on the VIII calends of January, that is, seven days before the first of January. But in light of the earlier variant suggestions for the date, why was 25 December chosen?

On this question there has been considerable debate. According to a minority position, this date was chosen because it fell exactly nine months after 25 March, the conception of Christ. The latter date, in turn, was the result of speculation that viewed history in perfect cycles, so that just as the world was created on 25 March (approximately the vernal equinox) and Christ died to renew the world on that date, so his conception must also have been on that day.

Against this argument it is said that the evidence on which it is based postdates the Roman statement in the *Depositio martyrum,* and is simply a Christian gloss on a date chosen for a very different reason. Rather, the argument goes, 25 December was chosen so as to compete with the pagan feastday of the *Natalis solis invicti,* or the birthday of the invincible sun. In patristic thought Christ had traditionally been associated with light or the sun, and the cult of the *Sol invictus,* sanctioned as it was by the Roman emperors since the late third century, presented a distinct threat to Christianity. Hence, to compete with this celebration the Roman church instituted a feast for the nativity of Christ, who was called the *Sol iustitiae.* This argument has further been bolstered by the observation that usually when Christians celebrated the *natalis* of a saint or martyr, it was his death or heavenly nativity, but in this case *natalis* was assigned to Christ's earthly birth, in direct competition with the pagan *natalis.* Moreover, it has been shown that the pagan celebration did indeed present a danger to Christian belief, for Pope

Leo I (440–461) chastised Christians who on Christmas celebrated the birth of the sun.

What may have been, then, a celebration originating at Rome quickly spread to other Latin-speaking churches. In North Africa, Optatus of Meleve (d. before 400) preached on the feast, emphasizing that the *Apparitio domini in carne* was in Christ's birth, the adoration of the Magi, and the massacre of the Innocents. In northern Italy, Filastrius, bishop of Brescia (*ca.* 387–391), spoke of the fast that preceded Christmas, and St. Ambrose knew the feast. From a letter of Pope Siricius (384–399) to Himerius of Tarragona it appears that the feast had spread to Spain. And in Gaul the calendar of Perpetuus, bishop of Tours (461–491), notes the vigil of Christmas.

By at least the last quarter of the fourth century Christmas had reached the churches of the East. Basil the Great, Gregory of Nyssa, and Gregory of Nazianzus all report it, and John Chrysostom noted that for the Antiochene church the date had come from Rome. The Egyptian church, under the leadership of Cyril of Alexandria, apparently accepted Christmas in part as a response to Nestorianism. But resistance to the Western custom persisted in the Armenian church, which never did accept the date, and in the Palestinian churches. In the latter, even into the late fourth century, the emphasis was on Christ's manifestation to the Magi, so Jerome reported, and a Spanish woman pilgrim, Etheria, painted a vivid picture of the liturgy on the eve of Epiphany and on the day itself. It was probably not until the late sixth or early seventh century that the almost universal custom of celebrating 25 December was fully adopted in Palestine.

As to the significance assigned to Christmas, scholars are divided on what the sermons and liturgical formulas of the ancient churches say. According to one school—which goes back even to such medieval commentators as Pseudo-Alcuin and Guillaume Durand, who cite Augustine—the day was simply a remembrance of a historical event, and it was only by the mid fifth century that the mystery of the Incarnation was celebrated, partly in reaction to Arians and Nestorians and partly to support the doctrine of the hypostatic union. Another school, however, argues that the sense of mystery and sacrament can be found even in the sermon of Optatus and in Augustine's work.

One feature of the liturgy of Christmas has caught the attention of commentators as far back as Carolingian times: the celebration of three masses in Rome, mentioned as early as Pope Gregory I (590–604). Originally there was only one mass of the day celebrated in St. Peter's basilica. But then, perhaps as early as the fifth century, a midnight mass was introduced in the basilica of S. Maria Maggiore. There is speculation that this was perhaps due to the influence of Etheria's report of the custom in Palestine, where on the eve of Epiphany there was a night service at Bethlehem (perhaps in the birth grotto). There followed a procession to the Anastasis or Church of the Resurrection in Jerusalem, where a further service was held on the day of Epiphany. This practice, according to some commentators, was adopted in the West after the doctrine of Mary as *Theotokos* (Mother of God) was proclaimed at the Council of Ephesus in 431. The old Liberian basilica, often identified with S. Maria Maggiore, was rebuilt in her honor by Pope Sixtus III (432–440). The pope celebrated a mass at midnight there (perhaps in a grotto imitating that of Bethlehem, since by the seventh century the church was called S. Maria ad Praesepe).

The third mass, another very early in the morning, also perhaps introduced under the influence of Etheria's report of the procession to a service at the Anastasis in Jerusalem, was celebrated by the pope in the Church of St. Anastasia, originally named perhaps for the church in Jerusalem (or more likely for its ancient holder of title). After the midnight mass at S. Maria Maggiore the pope went to St. Anastasia, at the foot of the Palatine Hill, perhaps to please the nearby Byzantines clustered around the imperial palace, who were devoted to St. Anastasia of Sirmium, whose cult was centered there by the sixth century. Only after celebrating this mass did the pope cross the Tiber to St. Peter's for the major mass of Christmas day. But because of the shortness of the day and the difficulty of the way—so Mabillon's *Ordo Rom.* 11 states—this mass was, at least by the twelfth century, moved back to S. Maria Maggiore, and hence closer to the papal palace of St. John Lateran, where the pope's Christmas feast lay prepared.

The idea of three masses on Christmas was widespread throughout Europe from Carolingian times with the diffusion of manuscripts of the Roman Gregorian Sacramentary, which gave texts for these three papal stational masses. Hence, it became customary for three different priests to say the masses on Christmas. But by the twelfth century one priest would say these masses.

While it was the masses that most medieval liturgical commentators and ordines emphasized, other festive elements of the day also drew their attention.

For Rome there was a double nocturnal office, and in the first, the fourth lesson was a reproach to the unbelieving Jews in a sermon of Quodvultdeus, and the response was from the famous Sybilline verses. In the offices of various churches there was much censing of altars, festive vestments, and a variety of colors used for altar cloths. Also outside Rome the *Liber generationis* from Matthew 1 was read following the ninth responsory, after which the Te Deum was sung, accompanied by bells.

Festive musical elements were also part of the ancient and medieval Christmas celebration. The use of the imperial and papal *laudes* is often cited, perhaps because of the memory of the crowning of Charlemagne on Christmas day at St. Peter's. And in many churches after mass the paraliturgical *Officia pastorum* and the dialogue "Quem vidistis pastores?" were performed, and special hymns, proses, and tropes were used. Carols and *lodi,* supposedly originating with St. Francis, were also a feature particularly of later medieval Christmas musical practice.

The modern tradition of the crèche, often said to have been originated by St. Francis, goes back perhaps to the sculptured representations of the Nativity on early Christian sarcophagi and to the grotto set up at S. Maria Maggiore, where by 1170 the relics said to have come from the crib in Bethlehem could be seen. The custom of the Christmas tree, sometimes said to have been begun by St. Boniface's hewing down of a large, sacred pagan oak in the eighth century, more likely was the product of the late medieval custom of setting up as a stage prop a tree of paradise decorated with apples and eucharistic wafers for the dramatic production of Adam and Eve, whose feast was celebrated on 24 December.

Because Christmas followed the fasting time of Advent, the day was celebrated with feasting. Among the many interesting medieval accounts of this is that of *Ordo Rom.* 11, which describes the papal procession from S. Maria Maggiore to the Lateran Palace, where a banquet was held with readings, sequences, kissing of the pope's feet, and papal gifts of wine and money.

BIBLIOGRAPHY

Bernard Botte, *Les origines de la Noël et de l'Épiphanie* (1932); H. Engberding, "Der 25. Dezember als Tag der Feier der Geburt des Herrn," in *Archiv für Liturgiewissenschaft,* **2** (1952); H. Frank, "Frühgeschichte und Ursprung des römischen Weihnachtsfestes im Lichte neuerer Forschung," *ibid.*; Joseph Lemarié, *La manifestation du Seigneur: La liturgie de Noël et de l'Épiphanie* (1957); Anselm Strittmatter, "Christmas and the Epiphany: Origins and Antecedents," in *Thought,* **17** (1942); Francis X. Weiser, *Handbook of Christian Feasts and Customs* (1958).

ROGER E. REYNOLDS

[See also **Epiphany, Feast of; Feasts and Festivals, European.**]

Silver chalice with christogram. Syria, *ca. 527–565.* COURTESY MUSEUM OF FINE ARTS, BOSTON, EDWARD J. AND MARY S. HOLMES FUND

CHRISTOGRAM, a monogram formed from the letters of Christ's name, XPICTOC, found in a variety of forms. Among the most common is the Constantinian monogram, ☧, named for the Christogram Constantine is supposed to have had blazoned on his labarum. Christograms were often flanked by an alpha and omega to signify Christ's divinity.

LESLIE BRUBAKER

[See also **Chrismon; Iconography.**]

CHRISTOLOGY. Medieval theology concerning Jesus Christ maintained the two focuses of patristic Christology: Christ's saving work through his life, death, resurrection, ascension, and sending of the Spirit, and—often derived from this—the union in Christ of the divine and the human. Modern scholars sometimes distinguish between these two focuses as Soteriology and Christology, but historically the two were so connected that they are better treated together. Expressly examined in medieval scriptural commentaries and theological treatises, these two basic themes also appeared frequently in other important doctrinal channels such as liturgy, sermons, canon law, saints' lives, popular devotions, drama, poetry, and art. These inevitably stressed the saving activity of Christ more than the subtle question of the mode of union, that is, how the human and the divine were united in him.

THE EAST

The patristic "school" of Antioch (Theodore of Mopsuestia, Nestorius, and others) had emphasized Christ's full humanity and his sharing the human condition so as to save humankind. The "school" of Alexandria (Athanasius, Cyril, and others) suspected that the Antiochene view implied a human person in Christ who would not be divine Savior, and feared that a human free will in Christ could have thwarted God the Father's plan of salvation. The Alexandrines, influenced by their Platonic tradition, began from Christ's divinity. They spoke of him as the divine Word assuming flesh, who, because he is God, "divinizes" Christians by giving them a share in divine life, especially through his eucharistic flesh and blood.

Under Cyril's influence the Council of Ephesus (431) rejected a human person in Christ united only by goodwill to the divine person of the Word; it affirmed one ontological person of the Word in Christ and so approved the title *Theotokos* (God-bearer) popularly given to his mother Mary. However, some Alexandrines, such as Eutyches, insisted that although Christ was *from* two natures, after the union he was *in* only one nature (*monē physis:* hence the label "Monophysitism"). Against them the Council of Chalcedon (451) affirmed Christ's full humanity, distinct but not separate from his full divinity, the two natures being united in his one person or hypostasis (whence the later term "hypostatic union").

The Second Council of Constantinople (553) unsuccessfully tried to reconcile the Monophysites by stressing Christ's unity, downplaying his full humanity, and condemning three Antiochene theologians ("the three chapters") posthumously. It also declared that Christians are to adore the incarnate Word of God together with his flesh, a doctrine important for later piety. Another attempt at reconciliation taught that Christ had one act of willing (*monon thelēma:* hence "Monothelitism"). The Third Council of Constantinople (681) replied that Christ had distinct divine and human wills and activities harmonized in

the one acting divine person, a harmony that would assure his sinless love and obedience all his life.

Various theologians developed the conciliar teachings. Leontius of Byzantium clarified earlier practice by his rules for predicating divine and human properties of Christ (*antidosis tōn idiomatōn:* communication of idioms or properties). Maximus the Confessor described the human nature of Christ as *enhypostaton,* that is, having its being not in and of itself but in the hypostasis of the Word; he also upheld Christ's human willing. Eulogius, patriarch of Alexandria, fought those teaching human ignorance in Christ; it then became common teaching that Christ had physical infirmities but no ignorance. John of Damascus criticized heresies and systematized patristic Christology in his *Fountain of Knowledge* (after 742), the classic exposition of Eastern dogmatics that was to influence both East and West. On christological grounds he resisted Iconoclasm, which rejected veneration of the cross and of images of Christ and of the saints. In condemning Iconoclasm, the Second Council of Nicaea (787) distinguished between *latreia* (adoration owed only to God) and *proskunēsis* of images (veneration given them insofar as they represent the persons being honored); this teaching validated art and devotion having the human Christ as object.

As for Christ's saving work, although Eastern theology and spirituality valued Christ's passion as redeeming and his death as sacrificial, it emphasized his transfiguration; his cross and harrowing of hell as victorious battle against sin, death, and the devil; and above all his resurrection and continuing lordly rule as *Pantokrator,* all these having extensive cosmic effects. This emphasis found typical expression in Byzantine liturgy, poetry, devotion, and artistic representation of Christ.

Later Eastern Christology was generally content to transmit its patristic, liturgical, and earlier theological patrimony; hence it sharply criticized the West when, from the eleventh century on, its use of dialectics and metaphysics led to increasingly complex debates about Christ and other doctrinal matters.

THE WEST

Aided by Tertullian's terminology, which was continued and developed by Hilary, Ambrose, and Augustine, the West was fairly free of christological wrangling. (It had, however, to defend Christ's divinity against Arianism, which reduced the Word or person of Christ to the level of creature.) Pope Leo

I's *Flavian Tome,* a letter to Emperor Flavian, distilled Western Christology in clear terms that aided the Council of Chalcedon's statement. Leo's homilies for liturgical feasts taught different ways of understanding Christ's saving work; they also explained the liturgical celebration as the moment (*hodie, nunc*) when Christ's past saving activity becomes present to the worshiper efficaciously *in sacramento* or *in mysterio.*

In the early sixth century Fulgentius of Ruspe wrote against Monophysitism in *De fide ad Petrum,* which later had great influence because it circulated under Augustine's name. Its plan is noteworthy in that, unlike most later treatises, it links Christ's incarnation and saving work with the study of God, one and three, prior to consideration of the creation and fall of humankind.

Boethius, in his work *Contra Eutychen et Nestorium* (also called *De una persona et duabus naturis Christi*) applied to Christ definitions of nature and person that influenced all later Western Christology. Nature he defined as "the specific difference informing anything" (*unamquamque rem informans specifica differentia,* ch. 1) and person as "an individual substance of a rational nature" (*naturae rationalis individua substantia,* ch. 3). Against Nestorianism (ch. 4) and Monophysitism (chs. 5–6), as he saw them, Boethius argued that if Christ were not one divine person in two complete but distinct natures, he could not be Savior. Boethius used the "soteriological principle" found in some of the Fathers ("only what was assumed by Christ was saved") to show the completeness of Christ's humanity, and sought to show (ch. 7) how Christ, fully human and free, was nevertheless unable to sin.

The influential writings of Gregory the Great, Isidore of Seville, and Bede summarized Western patristic teaching on Christ but added little new on the mode of union. Isidore, however, spoke of Christ's assumed humanity as *tertia persona in Trinitate* (*Sententiae,* 1.3.1), an enigmatic phrase that Abelard and Hugh of St. Cher later understood not of the Holy Spirit or some created person but as meaning "one of the three persons of the Trinity," that is, the Son. Authors in these centuries presented Christ as Savior through many themes: as Revealer of the Father and of himself, the divine Word, in ways accommodated to human beings; as Mediator between sinful humankind and the Father, and Priest offering himself in a propitiatory, reconciling sacrifice; as powerful Hero who by the instrument of his cross, his harrowing of hell, and his resurrection was glo-

rious Victor over sin, death, and the devil; as Expiator, by his loving obedience in suffering, of the penalty owed to sin; as Head of the church, his body, communicating salvation to all his members, even at the dawn of history (the theme of the "Church from Abel": *Ecclesia ab Abel*). As in the Fathers, Christ's acceptance of death was conceived as a ransom freeing humankind from slavery to sin and the devil: the devil, granted by God rights to torment and bind sinners, was said to have unjustly attacked the innocent Christ by bringing about his death, so that he was justly deprived of his hold over humankind. The literature, especially sermons, at times developed this theme in dramatic but misleading imagery, for example, by depicting Christ's divinity as a hook covered by the bait of his humanity in order to entice the devil to strike at him and thereby be captured and overcome.

Late-eighth-century Spain saw the "Adoptionism" of Elipand of Toledo and Felix of Urgel. Influenced perhaps by the Old Spanish liturgy's use of *filius adoptivus* concerning Christ, they distinguished a divine and a human sonship in Christ. In him, they maintained, there was only one person, the divine person who is natural son of God by his divine nature, whereas in his human nature he is, like others, adopted son of God by grace. Seeing "adoptive sonship" as necessarily involving a human person in Christ—and thus the "Nestorian" heresy— Popes Adrian I and Leo III as well as the Councils of Regensburg (792) and Frankfurt (794) condemned their teaching. The many theological treatises written against them included two significant ones by Alcuin.

At this time the Second Council of Nicaea's condemnation of Iconoclasm was misunderstood and attacked in the West (for example, by the *Libri Carolini*), as if the council had upheld *latreia* or absolute worship of images; in response the Western authors taught the council's actual position, the veneration of images insofar as they represent the persons being honored.

Augustine's hesitations about whether every human being could or would be saved had long troubled the West and in the ninth century led to new debates about predestination and grace. The Council of Quiercy (853) made a christological point when it declared that "God wishes all without exception to be saved" and that "there is, was, or will be no one for whom Christ did not suffer" even if some, by rejecting his offer, are in fact not saved.

The influential works of Pseudo-Dionysius the

Areopagite, written about 500 and first translated into Latin in the ninth century, present Christ as the source of all heavenly and ecclesiastical hierarchies, whom he illumines and perfects. Christ takes the entire human condition but without sin; frees Christians by the cross, Baptism, and other sacraments; and leads them in their combat. In the divine mysteries of the liturgy, especially the Eucharist, one is assimilated to Christ. The Pseudo-Dionysius' affirmation of "one theandric energy" or "activity" in Christ is not monothelite; this phrase, frequently quoted in the West, refers to the activity belonging only to Christ, who as God-man operates in two natures.

Although John Scotus Erigena says that in the Incarnation God assumed humanity to himself "in a unity of substance," he maintains the distinction of natures. Influenced by the Pseudo-Dionysius and by Maximus the Confessor's cosmic theology, he states that the Incarnation is profitable to angels, human beings, and all creation; it is the means to *theōsis,* or deification.

With Anselm and Abelard there began a reaction against overemphasis of the "rights" of the devil. Anselm influenced all subsequent Western Christology by the "necessary reasons" that he developed to show why there had to be an Incarnation (*Cur Deus homo*). Human sin infinitely violates the honor owed the all-holy God. If God's plan, to restore humankind so as to complete the heavenly city ravaged by angelic sin, is to be fulfilled, there must be adequate and therefore infinite satisfaction for this dishonor. And "if only God could do it [since it must be infinite] and only man should do it [because man sinned], it is necessary that a God-man make this satisfaction" (2.6). God's wisdom and love provides the God-man, Christ, whose free, loving, and obedient undergoing of death (and not the death itself) infinitely satisfies, merits freedom from sin, and wins the possibility of heaven for all because they are Christ's "relatives and brothers" through sharing his flesh and human nature (2.19).

Abelard rejects both the devil's rights and Anselm's necessary reasons for satisfaction or expiation. For Abelard, Christ's passion and death demonstrated God's love so intensely that one is inflamed to love in return. God's love evoking a response of love (the Holy Spirit working to effect this) justifies and frees his children, who now serve him from love rather than from fear (*Commentary on Romans,* ch. 2).

Seeing this as too subjective a view, the Council of Sens (1141) condemned Abelard as teaching that "Christ did not assume flesh in order to free us from the yoke of the devil," a judgment reflecting general concern to maintain the objectivity of Christ's saving role. Bernard of Clairvaux, for example, taught that God permitted the devil a "certain right" over humankind (*Epistles,* 190.5.14); that Christ fulfilled justice by satisfying as Head on behalf of his members (6.15), the value of this satisfaction coming not from the fact of suffering but from his love in accepting it (8.21); and that while Christ's example does indeed inspire love and humility, there is also needed "the sacrament of redemption" by which Christ endured the death he (objectively) took away (9.25). In explaining the Incarnation, Bernard lists various kinds of union and identifies the union in Christ as *dignativa* or *personalis* (*De consideratione,* 5.8.18).

Bernard dwells lovingly on the life and sufferings of the human Jesus and is a major influence in the devotion to the human Jesus that grew stronger in the twelfth century and flowered in Francis of Assisi, the Franciscan movement, popular piety, and art. Although the West paid less attention to the Resurrection than did the East, Bernard and others perceive it as the foundation of Christ's present role as King and Lord of history. Moreover, it was the risen Christ who was the object of intensified eucharistic devotion that arose in the twelfth and thirteenth centuries and found one of many expressions in the new feast of Corpus Christi.

Increased attention to Christ's humanity may have led theologians such as Hugh of St. Victor and Robert of Melun to the first of three influential opinions on the mode of union summarized by Peter Lombard in his *Sententiae* (3.5–7). Named by scholars the *assumptus homo* theory, it taught that a fully constituted man (*homo,* not only *natura humana*) was assumed by the Word of God and was the Word instantaneously before a human person could emerge. Others, seeing this as "Semi-Nestorianism," fashioned different opinions. The second opinion, named the subsistence theory, began from the divine person, simple before the union but said (using a phrase of John of Damascus) to become a "person composed" in a way from divinity and humanity and to subsist in and from two natures or three substances. Gilbert of Poitiers, whose doctrine of subject (*id quod*) and form (*id quo*) was developed from Boethius, stood behind this opinion. The third opinion, named the *habitus* theory by scholars, asserted that

Christ's body and soul were so united to the Word that the Word was not changed or "composed" in the union; rather, somewhat like our clothing ourselves in a garment (*habitus*), he clothed himself with a body and soul to make himself visible and yet not changed personally. Lombard gives a number of the patristic authorities (such as Augustine, Hilary, and Damascene) quoted by proponents of each opinion.

The second and third opinions maintained, against the first opinion, that *Christus secundum quod homo non sit aliquid,* that is, Christ as man is not something (Lombard, *Sententiae,* 3.10)—that he is not a human substance. This statement was used to deny a full or complete human substance, a human person in Christ. It did not mean that Christ was "nothing" (the so-called christological nihilism). Nevertheless, this teaching was condemned in 1170 and again in 1177 by Pope Alexander III. Since all these twelfth-century debates were complicated by Boethius' definition of person as "individual substance," theologians continued to wrestle with his definition in Christology (and in Trinitarian analyses) and, as with Alexander of Hales and Aquinas, to modify it. Because Lombard's *Sententiae* became the standard textbook in universities for centuries, the three opinions and the *non est aliquid* question became the framework for most discussions of the hypostatic union even when the opinions were no longer understood in their historical context. As for Christ's saving work, although Lombard's *Sententiae* added nothing new, his Pauline commentaries developed the theology of Christ as Head and of the unity of the church and were influential because they were frequently quoted as the *Glossa.*

The *habitus* theory, wrongly judged heretical, soon faded away. In the thirteenth century the *assumptus* theory, its difficulties more clearly discerned, yielded to various forms of the subsistence theory, which was supported by the growing influence of John of Damascus and the predominance of the Boethian and Gilbertan subject-form philosophy. Discussions of the opinions began to focus on Christ's unity, then on his unity in *esse,* which became a central issue concerning the mode of union. Here and elsewhere in Christology the entry of Aristotle's metaphysics contributed to new questions and replies.

Aquinas, while accepting the subsistence theory, profoundly modified it by his doctrine of *esse* (the act of existing) as distinct from essence or nature: the Word's one personal *esse,* in which the human na-

ture shares and is united, leaves it distinct as a nature while making it real and complete, at the same time assuring Christ's hypostatic unity within the distinction of natures.

Theologians in the twelfth and thirteenth centuries gradually came to agree that Christ had three kinds of human knowledge: acquired, infused, and the beatific vision; the last of these eliminated ignorance and assured his inability to sin but raised problems about his human freedom and how he could suffer while enjoying this vision. The grace of Christ's humanity was also perceived as threefold: the grace of union itself; the grace, virtues, and gifts of the Spirit making Christ humanly holy and eliminating disordered concupiscence (*fomes peccati*); and the grace of Headship of the Mystical Body.

Thirteenth-century theologians accepted Anselm's satisfaction theology but modified it by saying that God could have forgiven humankind without requiring adequate, complete satisfaction, and by emphasizing more than Anselm had the role of Christ as Head satisfying, meriting, and sacrificing for and with his united members. Christ's passion and death continued to dominate salvation theology, but Bonaventure's theology and spirituality included Christ's resurrection and presented the glorious stages of Christ's history, together with the earlier stages, as teaching and inspiring Christians to imitate and share them. Aquinas saw Christ's whole earthly life, death, and glory as exemplar causes of corresponding effects in Christians. He also reintegrated the long-forgotten Pauline and Eastern patristic death-and-resurrection teaching by viewing Christ's life, passion, death, and resurrection as instrumental efficient causes of salvation under God's primary efficient causality.

In the mid thirteenth century lively debate began about whether God's primary motive in the Incarnation was to share his love and evoke love, or to remit sins. Bonaventure and Thomas thought the latter opinion more probable; Albert the Great and, later, Duns Scotus opted for the former, which became the school opinion of the Franciscans, whereas Dominicans generally followed the opinion held by Aquinas and Bonaventure. The debate, frequently entitled "Would God have become incarnate if humankind had not sinned," was not hypothetical; it involved views about the central place of Christ in the actual order of creation and history.

Duns Scotus' teaching on personality as negation of dependence on another, rather than as positive entity, affects his theory of the mode of union: Christ's human nature, individuated by the perfection of "thisness" (*haecceitas*), lacked human personhood because it was actually dependent on the Word for being. Scotus also challenged the prevailing theology of salvation by his so-called "acceptance doctrine." Sin, he held, was no infinite offense; hence God's grace could help human beings satisfy for their own sins, and a very special grace could allow any one created person to satisfy for all others. Christ's merits lacked intrinsic infinity and had only extrinsic infinite value in that they had been accepted by God as infinite satisfaction for all.

Ockham's nominalism or conceptualism left him unable to grasp real distinctions among divine persons and so he could not say how only one person, the Son-Word, could become incarnate without the other two doing so. He developed in his own way Scotus' acceptance doctrine, whereas fourteenth-century Scotists such as Peter Aureoli, Durand de St. Pourçain, and Peter Paludanus (de la Palu) refused to follow Scotus on this, as of course did theologians of rival schools.

In later medieval Christology the merits of Christ and the acceptance doctrine were central issues. While others continued to oppose Scotus, his views came to be accepted in the fifteenth century by the Scotist school as well as by Gabriel Biel, who contributed important and perhaps influential developments. How much this approach influenced the Protestant Reformers is still unclear; in any case, they radically changed the issue by seeing Christ's suffering as the punishment, owed for all sin, being inflicted by God on Christ instead of on others, whereas medieval Christology had taught that Christ's loving obedience, actively accepting suffering and death, had helped to save all humankind.

Christ's death on the cross, viewed as expiatory and (in one way or another) infinitely meritorious, stood behind the theology of the Eucharist as a sacrifice atoning for the sins of the living and substituting for the unperformed penance of both the living and the dead. It also stood behind the theology of indulgences, which were seen as substitutions for due penance by one's sharing through the Mystical Body in the infinite merits of Christ, the Head. If in the later Middle Ages these doctrines fostered popular piety and devotional practices, the way lay open for the kinds of exaggerations and abuses that evoked strong protests within the church and finally led to the decisive reaction of the Reformers.

BIBLIOGRAPHY

Fulbert Cayré, *Patrologie et histoire de la théologie*, 2 vols. (1953–1955); Werner Dettloff, *Die Entwicklung der Akzeptations- und Verdienstlehre von Duns Scotus bis Luther* (1963); Alois Grillmeier, *Christ in Christian Tradition*, I, 2nd ed. (1975); *A History of Christian Doctrines*, Hubert Cunliffe-Jones, ed. (1978); John N. D. Kelly, *Early Christian Doctrines*, 5th ed. (1978); Jaroslav Pelikan, *The Christian Tradition: A History of the Development of Doctrine*, 3 vols. (1971–1978); Walter Principe, "St. Thomas on the Habitus-theory of the Incarnation," in Armand Maurer, ed., *St. Thomas Aquinas, 1274–1974: Commemorative Studies*, I (1974), 381–418; and *The Theology of the Hypostatic Union in the Early Thirteenth Century*, 4 vols. (1963–1975), esp. vol. I; Reinhold Seeberg, *Text-Book of the History of Doctrines* (1952); and *Lehrbuch der Dogmengeschichte*, 3rd ed., 4 vols. (1912–1923, repr. 1953–1954); Paul Vignaux, *Philosophy in the Middle Ages* (1959).

WALTER H. PRINCIPE

[See also **Church Fathers; Councils (Ecumenical, 325–787); Councils, Western; Monophysitism; Monothelitism; Nestorianism; Philosophy/Theology, Byzantine; Philosophy/Theology, Western European.**]

CHRISTUS, PETRUS (*d.* 1472/1473), a leading Netherlandish painter trained in the environs of Haarlem, settled in Bruges in 1444. The North Netherlandish background of his art, as well as the influence of Rogier van der Weyden, are evident in his early work (for example, *Lamentation*, Musées Royaux des Beaux Arts, Brussels, *ca.* 1445). Soon after establishing his atelier, Christus increasingly emulated the style of Jan van Eyck, as exemplified by his *Exeter Madonna* (Berlin, Museum Dahlem, *ca.* 1450) and *Madonna with Saints Francis and Jerome* (Städelsches Kunstinstitut, Frankfurt, 1457), both of which are reduced versions of van Eyck compositions. Some scholars argue that Christus was an apprentice of van Eyck, but this is not likely. His style displays the rugged realism and concern with ample spatial settings typical of the North Netherlandish masters. Several works are signed and dated between 1446 and 1457.

BIBLIOGRAPHY

Max J. Friedländer, *Early Netherlandish Painting*, I (1967), 81–91; Erwin Panofsky, *Early Netherlandish Paint-*

ing, I (1966), 309–313; Peter H. Schabacker, *Petrus Christus* (1974).

JAMES SNYDER

[See also **Flemish Painting.**]

CHRISTUS UND DIE SAMARITERIN. The manuscript of the annals of Lorsch, now in Vienna, contains thirty-one lines of Old High German rhyming verse recounting part of the conversation between Christ and the woman of Samaria (John 4:6–20). The language is apparently part Alemannic, part Frankish; the hand is tenth century. Probably composed on the Reichenau, the poem has a strophic structure similar to that of the *Georgslied* (probably also composed there) and the Latin version of Ratpert's hymn in praise of St. Gall (originally composed in German at nearby St. Gall). It employs both direct speech (not introduced by verbs of saying) and indirect speech; this style has been thought to derive from a native verse tradition going back to a period before Otfrid von Weissenburg.

BIBLIOGRAPHY

J. Knight Bostock, *A Handbook on Old High German Literature,* K. C. King and D. R. McLintock, eds., 2nd ed. (1976), 214–218; *Die deutsche Literatur des Mittelalters: Verfasserlexikon,* 2nd ed., I (1978), 1238–1241.

DAVID R. MCLINTOCK

[See also **Georgslied.**]

CHRONICLES. At the end of the medieval period three English authors made use of the prologue on the uses of history in the *Historical Library* of Diodorus Siculus. One of these was Skelton, who translated that work into English from Poggio's Latin; the second was Lord Berners, who used the prologue to introduce his translation of Froissart's *Chronicles;* the third was William Caxton, who used it in his edition of Trevisa's translation of Higden's *Polychronicon.* Caxton used a lost French version of the prologue to make his translation, which suggests that it was also appreciated in France.

Several interesting points arise from these translations. The first is the interest in history at the time,

with the evident inability of the writers to think out any uses of history for themselves. Since the medieval period had no organized philosophy of history, it had to borrow its views from the classical period. History was a topic that was beginning to need justification.

The second is that all these works are translations, though of very different works. The first is a classical historical work; the second is an account of chivalry from over 100 years earlier; and the third is a universal history that took the account of English history up to the immediate present. The taste for history was being satisfied not only by contemporary works but also by works that had become classics and inculcated a view of life that was very different from that pertaining at the time. Berners' translation contains more than a hint of the past as a golden age.

The third is that the authors are very different from the normal purveyors of history in the earlier medieval period. Skelton was a cleric, though he was not a religious; Berners was a courtier; and Caxton was a merchant and a publisher. All these works are very different from the annals and hagiography with which the medieval period opened.

The writing of history falls readily into two types that can be thought of as living and dead, respectively. The latter represents those forms of history that deal only with events in the past, with what we today would regard as the only proper concern of history. A saint's life dealing with a figure like St. George is of this type, since the writer could have no personal knowledge of the saint. Historical biographies of kings such as are found in the Renaissance, dealing with people who had died some time earlier, also belong to this category. The Icelandic family sagas also fit in this category, since they were written in the thirteenth century about people who had lived in the settlement period (from the late ninth to the tenth century).

As a general rule, however, one might say that historical writing of the medieval period did not concern itself exclusively with people from the past. The eulogizing of earlier heroes was left to the epics such as *Beowulf* and the *Chanson de Roland* or to romances such as *Havelok the Dane.* The absence of this type of historical writing in the medieval period had certain general effects. It is only if a writer can distance himself from his subject that he is able to impose a pattern on it by selecting those actions that fit in with his wider view. It is difficult for writers who deal with contemporary events to distinguish which are the significant ones. Hence, curiosity and the mere assembling of facts counted for more in the Middle Ages than any pattern of events.

The living type of historical writing embraces chronicles. Essentially they remain records of what an individual saw and heard at the time of an event; they contain all the details that the particular chronicler regarded as worth preserving. They may naturally extend into the distant past—indeed, some begin with the Creation—but their principal concern is with the present. The past provides continuity, but little focus. To this extent chronicles resemble diaries that record events day by day or year by year, and in this they betray their origins in the old annals. Naturally their writers could, and did, rearrange what they had written in the light of later events, but any rewriting hardly affected the normal approach of a contemporary annual record. The gain in immediacy is balanced by the loss of focus: many disparate facts are introduced with the sole justification that they were known to the writer. No attempt is made to relate one event to the next. Furthermore, all facts are included, whether big or little in scope, whether far or near in place or time to the writer.

This should not be taken to imply that all chronicles are similar in approach or scope. The traditional type of chronicle is that associated with monks. The Benedictines had a particular reverence for history that was not generally shared by the newer monastic orders or by the friars. In some monasteries there was a tradition of historical writing under which the chronicle was continued by another monk after the original writer had died.

Three features are important in this type of chronicle. The monks, by virtue of their residence in monasteries, lived a certain distance from the center of events, so that they had to rely on others for their information. This could lead to gaps in what they acquired and bias in how it reached them. Second, they were naturally interested in clerical matters rather than secular ones, and this could give their work a slightly unbalanced view of the world. Nevertheless, their interest in clerical affairs was often more practical than spiritual. Third, of all authors in the medieval period it is the monks who had readiest access to well-stocked libraries—well-stocked, that is, for the age. They therefore had access to works from which they could borrow material and upon which they could model their approach and style.

The tone of these works can be less personal be-cause they often represent a compilation from various sources. Monastic chronicles were frequently written in Latin, the *Grandes chroniques de France* being a noteworthy exception. The clerical chronicle is the earliest type of chronicle, and it remained important throughout the medieval period. In the later Middle Ages its importance as a source may have been less in some countries such as England and France, because other types of chronicle were also written. There are fewer chronicles of this type from the fourteenth and fifteenth centuries, perhaps because the energies of the church were diverted into different orders with other means of exhibiting their Christian commitment.

Matthew Paris of St. Albans, who wrote the *Chronica majora* in the thirteenth century, and Ranulf Higden of Chester, who wrote the *Polychronicon* in the fourteenth, are good examples of the clerical chronicler. They lived in important religious foundations with good libraries and near important urban centers. Each house must have received many important secular and religious visitors. Each chronicler is concerned with events that took place in his own lifetime, but that story is set in a historical context by describing earlier events and can be continued by others after the death of the main writer. Each is interested in making his story read well by using many of the resources of rhetoric, for medieval historians learned their trade from classical ones. Hence their narratives are full of imagined episodes in which the participants' words and reactions are largely fictitious, for they are included for rhetorical effect. The author can never have witnessed many of the scenes he describes, but verisimilitude is more important than truth. Happenings from all over Europe and the East are included in no apparent order other than the restriction of the chronological year.

Causality and connectedness are thus abandoned, for the author is not able to keep his attention on one particular theme. Furthermore, many of the names mentioned easily became corrupted because there were no means of checking who or what was being talked about. The chronicles often seem to be somewhat cavalier in the information they record. The authors have their own particular prejudices—Matthew, for instance, is very incensed by the growing power of the monarchy. They thus may interpret events in a way that shows their enemies in a bad light, and on occasion they even fabricate the material included. These prejudices can mislead modern readers who are unable to detect many new developments in medieval life and thought that go unrecorded in the chronicles because they were of no interest to the chronicler.

Not all clerical chroniclers were members of monastic orders; there is no evidence that Geoffrey of Monmouth, for example, was a monk. His *Historia regum Britanniae* covers a period of almost 2,000 years, stretching from the fall of Troy to the death of Cadwallader. It is an account of the early kings of Britain, but most of it is legendary and mythological. In Denmark, Saxo Grammaticus in his *Gesta Danorum* traced the history of the Danish kings to 1186. The earlier part of his book, which may be based on oral sources, deals with the mythological Danish kings, though the latter section is very much like other clerical chronicles.

Clearly, a chronicle that traces the history of a nation or a royal family will rely on legendary material, and in this it will differ little from the average romance. Some of this material was taken as historical—for example, the founding of Britain by Brut—but most was intended to bolster national prestige by providing the nation with a history that went back so far and to such important roots. It is difficult to distinguish the chronicles of this type from romance material. *Sir Gawain and the Green Knight* starts with the fall of Troy before passing on to Gawain and the court of King Arthur. The Arthurian stories were gathered in a collection in the French prose *Vulgate,* and this was used by Malory for his *Le morte Darthur.* Historical romances about such characters as Charlemagne are similar in tone to many early parts of chronicles. It is not easy to differentiate among the various genres.

Clerical chronicles survived longest in England and France. In England, St. Albans continued the tradition of chronicle writing into the fifteenth century. The chroniclers wrote exclusively in Latin and were generally well informed; often they adopted a rather critical stance toward royal power. Matthew Paris' work was continued intermittently at the abbey until Thomas Walsingham brought the record down to 1422, though some successors wrote a further installment down to 1440. That date marks the end of clerical chronicle writing in England.

In France the abbey of St. Denis outside Paris occupied much the same position as St. Albans in England. Historical writing began there in the twelfth century with many of the monks keeping notes or making short accounts of various events or people. These were used as the basis for chronicles and lives in Latin. From these writings there developed the *Grandes chroniques de France,* which became so influential that they acquired almost an official status in France. Some of the monks received royal pensions as state historians. Unlike the earlier lives and chronicles, the *Grandes chroniques* were written in French. They were commenced at the end of the thirteenth century by a monk called Primat, and his work was continued, in both French and Latin, into the fifteenth century by other monks. The *Grandes chroniques,* which survive in a large number of manuscripts, were printed at the end of the fifteenth century. Their popularity is attributable in large part to their use of the vernacular, and their success in manuscript numbers far outstrips that of the chronicles written at St. Albans. Even the *Grandes chroniques* declined in vigor in the fifteenth century.

The *Grandes chroniques* began its historical account with Troy, and in this way the Trojan War gained popularity in France as the background to the French nation; it was part of the story of France. The *Polychronicon,* by contrast, differed from the average clerical chronicle in that it took the whole world as its story. It did not confine itself to one country, and it was more interested in the past than in the present. Contemporary events played only a relatively small part in the original compilation. The result was that its account of the history of the world became a standard work in England and elsewhere; and it was borrowed by other chroniclers, such as Thomas Walsingham, as a narrative prelude to their own account of contemporary events. It therefore introduced a new dimension into history writing, in that clerical chronicles were not simply records of contemporary happenings; the whole of human history became their subject. The present was set in a wider context.

A new kind of chronicle that appeared in the later Middle Ages and that is particularly associated with France is the aristocratic chronicle. The *Mémoires* of Philippe de Comines and the *Chroniques* of Jehan Froissart are good examples of this type. They are not unlike political diaries in that they record what one man saw fit to record of the political events of his time. Since politics was seen in human terms rather than in the modern abstract concepts of economics and other social forces, these works depict the interaction of certain great men of the period. Usually they are written by men who had attached themselves to one or more important courts and who had linked themselves with the fortunes of a particular king or nobleman. The view of these works is more circumscribed than that of the clerical chronicles, because they record only what is of importance within very restricted geographical and social confines. Naturally they gain a certain cohesion from this restriction. Often the tone is one of narrative rather than of analysis, and that narrative is centered on the hero of the piece.

There is more than a touch of eulogy or propaganda in these works, for the author is often intent on glorifying his master and his deeds. Although Comines had served both the duke of Burgundy and the king of France, it is Louis XI who is the hero of his work. The material is selected to set him off, and no attempt is made to be comprehensive. Aristocratic chronicles are unashamedly secular and are written in the vernacular. They are often informed by the chivalric ideal of the age, though this does not necessarily cloud the authors' eyes to practical issues and their solution. Causality is not an important feature of these works except insofar as the causes of great events are personalized. They differ from the clerical chronicles in freeing themselves from the tyranny of the annual entry, though their narratives often proceed on a chronological basis. They have much in common with romances, for they set out to eulogize great heroes whose actions seem superhuman.

The story of Arthur as found in Wace may not seem very far from the deeds of contemporaries described by Enguerrand de Monstrelet. Chivalric poses and attitudes are struck, and attention is paid to what we today might consider the periphery of events—the clothes people wore, their ancestry, and their general behavior. Some aristocratic chronicles were written by the protagonists themselves. The *Conquête de Constantinople* of Geoffroi de Villehardouin describes the Fourth Crusade (1202–1204), in which he played an important part. Chronicles of this type remained popular until the end of the Middle Ages and were particularly admired by those who wanted to cut a figure in the world. They were cultivated in fifteenth-century Burgundy.

Biographies of important secular people became more popular in the Middle Ages. Henry V was the subject of many lives. At least three in prose and one in verse were written in Latin during his lifetime; and after his death one further Latin life and two English ones were composed before the end of the fifteenth century. These lives show the beginnings of Renaissance biography, though they are still largely eulogistic in tone. These early lives are not unlike the aristocratic chronicles in that they were often written by eyewitnesses, perhaps members of the court.

To some extent the Latin lives come close to being official histories of the reign, and the authors use not only their own experience but also documents available to them about the reign. One of the later lives was by Tito Livio, from Forlì. His work, written about 1437–1438, was produced at the express command of Humphrey, duke of Gloucester, who, Tito said, supplied him with much of the necessary material. Tito must have used a version of the *Brut* and other official documents, but he was writing at a time when England was debating within itself the whole question of the war in France. Clearly, a life of Henry V made a political point at that time and was, to that extent, part of the propaganda for continuing the war.

In addition to the aristocratic chronicles associated with France, the later Middle Ages witnessed the emergence of urban chronicles. These are a form of lay history. Towns are like monasteries in some ways: each is a corporation governed by various officers, it tries to preserve and extend its privileges, and so it is conscious of the need for keeping records to safeguard its interests. The major urban chronicles in England are those associated with London; few other towns produced any of significance. France also has few urban chronicles, for they flourished most where towns flourished. It is in Italy and Germany that cities became power centers and, consequently, that urban chronicles multiplied. England and France were perhaps too centralized and still too feudal to inspire many urban chronicles.

It is easy to assume that these chronicles represent the voice of the people, as against the clerical and aristocratic chronicles; but such a view should be treated with caution. The urban chronicles represent the views of the richer merchants and the civic oligarchies, though they cannot avoid reflecting to some extent the views of the whole urban population. The clerical and aristocratic chronicles hardly seem to notice the existence of ordinary people; but this is not true of the urban chronicles, which have many references to civic disturbances and celebrations, to say nothing of more petty daily events.

Urban chronicles are partly official and partly of a family nature, in that some were kept up by members of a particular family. The city governments, like monastic ones before them, found it convenient to have a record of their officers and rights as well as an account of the landmarks in their historical development. Urban chronicles usually arose through lists of city officers and notable civic events, just as monastic ones developed from simple annals. The London Chronicles arranged their annual records by the names of the city's chief officers.

Although the urban chronicles record much that is of concern only to the inhabitants of a particular city, most cities occupied key political and economic situations and thus were affected by events of a national or international scale. The attitude of English kings to France and the Hanseatic League naturally affected cross-Channel trade and, therefore, many Londoners. But the chroniclers viewed events as they affected the particular city, and so they, like monastic chroniclers before them, can be both prejudiced and selective in the material they present. Because of this the urban chronicles are often incomplete on national or international events, but in recompense they provide fuller accounts of society and the interaction among classes than other chronicles.

Although some chronicles are the work of one man, for the most part they are compilations that were constantly brought up to date by a variety of people. Even so, the entries may reflect a personal rather than a civic reaction to the events described. Insofar as these chronicles were written by lay people who had not had the same training in literary affairs as clerical authors, or who had not been exposed to the fashionable style of court as the aristocratic chroniclers, their writing often appears somewhat artless when compared with that of their more accomplished and sophisticated colleagues.

This lack of sophistication is perhaps more marked north of the Alps. There were numerous chronicles in Germany, many of which have been published in the series Chroniken der deutschen Städte. Divided as the country was into many states and often organized into leagues of cities, it is hardly surprising that each German town should have vied with the next in maintaining its chronicle. In this situation urban chronicles fulfill the same role as the more national clerical chronicles found in England and France. Even so, the Germans remembered the days of the Holy Roman Empire with nostalgia, and many urban chronicles reflect this interest. This is particularly true of the Nuremberg chronicle produced by Hartmann Schedel, which became so popular that it was put into print at the end of the fifteenth century.

The Italian urban chronicles were undoubtedly more stylistically polished than their German counterparts, for they were more imbued with classical learning. They had, however, an ambivalent attitude to the past, since some of the cities had tried to throw off the imperial yoke. One of the most impressive of these chronicles is that for Florence, which was compiled by the Villani family in the fourteenth century. Florence was a city that had international trading and political connections, and so events as far away as England could be pertinent to its well-being because of its financial investments and banking organization there. The reporting of international affairs by the Villanis is thus different in kind from the clerical chronicler's record of events in different parts of the world. The latter often had little more than mere curiosity; the former had a stake in much that took place in different countries.

In England there was an important chronicle known as the *Brut*, which is closely related to the London Chronicles. It existed in French, English, and Latin versions, though for the most part it is a lay chronicle. Immensely popular, it survives in numerous manuscripts. When printing was introduced into England, the *Brut* formed the basis of such editions as Caxton's *Chronicles of England* and his continuation (or Book VIII) of John of Trevisa's translation of Higden's *Polychronicon*.

It is not without significance, in fact, for each major European country which type of chronicle was first printed there. The views of history in the *Brut* became the most familiar in England, though not all versions reflect a uniform attitude. To some extent the Wars of the Roses in England accelerated the production of chronicles, because they were increasingly used as political documents that adopted a Yorkist or Lancastrian interpretation of the events of the immediate past. An important touchstone for many chronicles of this period is their attitude to Richard II and his deposition by Henry IV. The events of the reign, particularly those leading up to the deposition, were recorded in such a way as to throw the best possible light on one or other of these kings.

It was not possible for these chroniclers to remain aloof from the political events that racked the country. To a large extent, however, they wrote in a partisan spirit and rarely attempted to interpret the events of the past. Nevertheless, their different attitudes to past events encouraged people to realize that the past could be interpreted variously, and in this way added a further impetus to the more interpretive history that was written in the Tudor period. It is perhaps also worth noting that the *Brut* is not chivalric or aristocratic in tone. The typical chronicle in English is very different from the typical chronicle in French.

A different type of history, what some might call modern history, emerged in Italy about the fourteenth century; this arose from the growth of humanism. This new type of historical writing tried to interpret the past for particular propaganda purposes, but it also attempted to clothe its history in a correct Latin style that imitated Cicero and Livy. The author tried to distance himself from his subject, and with that there grew the concept that the past was different from the present. Chronicles had been records that flowed from one event to the next without any realization of the difference between one period and the next. Ultimately this development led to the claim that history was the purveyor of truth and hence more important than poetry or other art forms. This view was based on classical precedent and is reflected in the prologue to the *Historical Library* of Diodorus Siculus used by Skelton, Berners, and Caxton. The views expressed there—particularly the need to inculcate moral lessons through example, to inspire men to win renown, and to use eloquence to re-create reality itself—are all to some degree found in medieval chronicles.

For the Middle Ages history was a branch of rhetoric, and it was felt to be fitting that great and noble events should be presented in appropriate language. If the chroniclers apologize for their chronicles, they do so for their failures in style and not for their inability to present the truth. Chronicles are not mere records of facts; they are works of literature. They are also items of display, for to appear to be great was in many ways the same as being great. Thus, to win renown became important for many men so that their deeds could be recorded in such fitting memorials. The moral stance of the chronicles is often implicit rather than explicit, but they often show that happiness and good government spring from nobility of blood in the rulers and the assistance of God.

Finally, perhaps the most significant aspect of chronicle writing in the later Middle Ages is the large number of chronicles that were written and the survival of some of them in numerous manuscripts. History was no longer a specialized pursuit that was confined to an educated elite.

BIBLIOGRAPHY

William J. Brandt, *The Shape of Medieval History* (1966); Cyr Ulysse Chevalier, *Répertoire des sources historiques du moyen âge*, 4 vols. (1894–1907); Louisa D. Duls, *Richard II in the Early Chronicles* (1975); Ralph Flenley, *Six Town Chronicles* (1911); Antonia Gransden, *Historical Writing in England, I–II* (1974–1982); Denys Hay, *Annalists and Historians* (1977); Charles L. Kingsford, *English Historical Literature in the Fifteenth Century* (1913, repr. 1964); Ottokar Lorenz, *Deutschlands Geschichtsquellen im Mittelalter*, 3rd ed., 2 vols. (1886–1887, repr. 1966); Auguste E. Molinier, *Les sources de l'histoire de France*, 6 vols. (1901–1906); Louis J. Paetow, *A Guide to the Study of Medieval History*, rev. ed. (1931, repr. 1980); Reginald Lane Poole, *Chronicles and Annals* (1926); August Potthast, *Bibliotheca historica medii aevi*, 2nd ed., 2 vols. (1896), revised as *Repertorium fontium historiae medii aevi*, 4 vols. (1962–1976); Beryl Smalley, *Historians in the Middle Ages* (1974); Richard W. Southern, "Aspects of the European Tradition of Historical Writing," in *Transactions of the Royal Historical Society*, **20–22** (1970–1972); John Taylor, *The Use of Medieval Chronicles* (1965); James Westfall Thompson, *A History of Historical Writing*, 2 vols. (1942, repr. 1967); Thomas F. Tout, "The Study of Medieval Chronicles," in *The Collected Papers of Thomas Frederick Tout*, III (1933).

N. F. Blake

[See also **Arthurian Literature; Brut, The; Comines, Philippe de; Froissart, Jehan; Geoffrey of Monmouth; Higden, Ranulf; Historiography, Western European; Matthew Paris; Saxo Grammaticus; Villehardouin, Geoffroi de.**]

CHRONICLES, FRENCH. Vernacular chroniclers in the Middle Ages shared many presuppositions about history with the Latin chroniclers. For example, history recorded fact and not fiction; its purpose was to preserve for posterity what was worthy of record; and eyewitness testimony on a historical event was the best possible guarantee of its truth. But vernacular chronicles were intended for a lay audience that was not accustomed to distinctions between historical fact and legendary accretion. Furthermore, the literary predecessors of the early French chronicles were the chansons de geste (*Chanson de Roland, Raoul de Cambrai, Girart de Roussillon*, and many others). Such chansons were traditionally in verse, and narrative interest was an important consideration in their production.

It is not surprising, therefore, that the first vernacular chronicles used narrative conventions with which their audience was familiar. Factual and legendary material continued to be blended, and inherited verse forms were employed to new purpose.

In subject matter an impetus was provided by the Crusades, which were represented as epic in magnitude and undoubtedly worthy of being recorded by those who had participated in them. Two long poems on the Crusades attributed to Richart le Pèlerin from Arras were composed at the beginning of the twelfth century and survive in versions written by Graindor de Douai early in the thirteenth century. *Chanson d'Antioche* narrates the expedition in 1097 of Peter the Hermit and Godfrey of Bouillon's capture of Antioch; *Chanson de Jérusalem* recounts the capture of Jerusalem. Ambroise d'Évreux's *Estoire de la Guerre Sainte,* written before 1196, is an eyewitness account of the Third Crusade by a follower of Richard the Lion-hearted. The anonymous *Chétifs* relates fantastic adventures and vicissitudes of five Christians captured by the pagans at Nicaea.

Some works contained too much legendary material to be classified as anything but epics on the Crusades. In this category is the cycle comprising the *Naissance du chevalier au cygne* and the *Chevalier au cygne et enfances Godefroi,* in which Godfrey of Bouillon's fairy origins are described.

Regional loyalties and regional patronage provided another type of inspiration for the vernacular chronicle, which continued to be written in verse, in conformity with the literary tastes of its public. Geffrei Gaimar's *Estoire des Engleis* was produced in the first half of the twelfth century at the request of the wife of Robert fitz-Gislebert. It is based on the Anglo-Saxon Chronicle and begins its narration with the expedition of the Argonauts. Its obvious intent is to link contemporary Anglo-Norman nobility with the heroes of classical antiquity in a continuing historical line.

Similarly, Wace's *Roman de Rou,* written in three parts between 1160 and 1170, provides a heroic ancestry for the Anglo-Norman monarchy—this rhymed chronicle of the Norman dukes begins with Rollo and ends with the capture of Robert II in 1106. Its sources were primarily the chronicles of Dudo of St. Quentin and William of Jumièges. Wace's *Roman de Brut (ca.* 1155) loosely adapted Geoffrey of Monmouth's *Historia regum Britanniae* into Anglo-Norman. It was dedicated to Eleanor of Aquitaine.

When Benoît de Sainte-Maure replaced Wace in King Henry II's favor, he was commissioned to write the complete *Chronique des ducs de Normandie (ca.* 1170). Ironically, this vast work of more than 42,000 lines failed, as had the *Roman de Rou,* to reach the reign of the monarch then on the throne.

In the thirteenth century the production of vernacular chronicles came to rival that of chronicles in Latin. In the same century prose was established as the favorite medium for chronicles. The reason was given in the prologue of certain early translations of the *Pseudo-Turpin Chronicle:* prose was associated with truth, but rhymed tales were contrived. The vernacular *Pseudo-Turpin* translations were sponsored by such patrons as Yolande, countess of St. Pol, sister of Baldwin VIII of Flanders, and her husband, Hugh of St. Pol; the Norman Warin fitz-Gerold; and Renaud, count of Boulogne. The *Pseudo-Turpin*'s idealizations gave glorious, chivalric ancestry to the contemporary aristocracy, but prose in fact added little truth to this fantastic recreation of the Charlemagne legend.

There were prose translations of more reliable Latin histories than the mendacious Pseudo-Turpin's *Historia Karoli Magni et Rotholandi. Li fet des Romains (ca.* 1213) brings together Caesar's *Commentarii de bello gallico,* Suetonius' *Vitae Caesarum* I, Sallust's *Catilina,* and Lucan's *Bellum civile* in a vast biography of Julius Caesar. In his prologue its anonymous clerical translater advertises the didactic usefulness of Roman history. He also makes explicit comparisons between his king (Philip Augustus) and Julius Caesar, thus revealing that the translation of Roman history could have political as well as moral usefulness. *Li fet des Romains* remained the layman's source of information concerning Roman history for several centuries and was more than usually subject to the medieval chronicle's fate of being pillaged to supplement other chronicles' deficiencies.

Similarly, Jean de Thuim, who is known only through his work, compiled his *Hystoire de Julius Cesar* from Caesar's *Bellum civile* and Lucan's *Bellum civile.* His *Hystoire* was subsequently converted into rhymed alexandrines by Jacos Forest. An anonymous *Livre des estoires (ca.* 1223–1230) spans the time from the Creation to Caesar's conquest of Gaul. William of Tyre's *Historia rerum transmarinarum* was translated early in the century as the *Estoire d'outre-mer* or *Livre d'Eracles* and was several times reworked and amplified.

The abbey of St. Denis, which had already been responsible for the compilation *Abbreviatio de gestis Francorum,* treating French history from its beginnings to 1137, made a further compilation of all existing chronicles concerning the French monarchy. When in 1274 the monk Primat presented Philip III with a vernacular rendering of the corpus of material, the *Grandes chroniques de France* became an official history of the monarchy. It was later supplemented by such works as Guillaume de Nangis's *Gesta Ludovici IX* and the *Gesta Philippi III*.

St. Denis's *Historia regum Francorum* (1185–1204) provided source material for an anonymous translator at Béthune to produce his *Estoire des rois de France*. A later version, commissioned by Alphonse of Poitiers in 1260, continued as far as 1228. An anonymous writer from Béthune produced the *Estoire des rois d'Angleterre et de Normandie*, a history of the recent wars between England and France.

Two narratives, both entitled *Conquête de Constantinople*, provided laymen's accounts of the Fourth Crusade. Geoffroi de Villehardouin, marshal of Champagne, had been a leader of the expedition. As one of the French barons' six delegates, he had negotiated transport arrangements for the army with the doge of Venice. He had argued for the diversion of the Crusade from the Holy Land to Constantinople and had avoided the disintegration of the army by negotiating between the two rivals Boniface of Montferrat and Baldwin IX of Flanders. His most dangerous mission was perhaps as ambassador to Emperor Isaac II when the latter reneged on his son's commitments to the Crusaders. Villehardouin's chronicle records these and many other events from the day Fulk of Neuilly first preached the Fourth Crusade in 1198 to the death of Boniface in 1207.

The style of Villehardouin's prose is simple and sober—perhaps deceptively so. The leaders' decision to divert the Crusade was, after all, a controversial one, but Villehardouin's step-by-step narration of the Crusaders' progress suggests a logical inevitability, as if political maneuvering (between the sultan of Cairo and the Venetians, for example) had played no significant role. Villehardouin's presentation of the moral issues also is simplistic. In his re-creation of what he saw as an epic enterprise, it is the leaders who emerge as heroes. The dissidents (who wished simply to rescue the Holy Land) and the Greeks (who inhabited the Christian city of Constantinople) are vilified.

A slightly different viewpoint was put forward by Robert de Clari, whose history of "those who conquered Constantinople" reflects the bias of a "povre chevalier." He berates the improper distribution of the plunder from Constantinople, and relates anecdotal wonders from that magic and exotic city. His naive reporting of the leaders' decisions and of the army's reactions to them counterbalance Villehardouin's political selectivity. His hostility to Boniface

of Montferrat adds further information concerning the rival candidates for the position of "emperor of Romania."

In the *Récits d'un ménestrel de Reims* anecdotal chronicling prevailed. An anonymous minstrel in Rheims collected picturesque and often legendary tales from England, France, and the Holy Land from the early twelfth century on. Their historical worth is dubious at best.

In 1307 John of Joinville presented his memoir of Louis IX to the future Louis X. His "livre des saintes paroles et des bons faiz nostre roy saint Looys" is anecdotal history at its best. It had been requested by the queen in 1304, though parts of it may have been written before then. Despite its somewhat random structure it provides an excellent eyewitness account of the years that Joinville spent with Louis on the Seventh Crusade (1248–1254). Joinville had refused to join the Eighth Crusade (1270), and Louis' final expedition therefore received only brief mention ("I will recount and say nothing of the expedition he made to Tunisia, because I was not there, thanks be to God"). However, the sum of anecdotal details concerning the saint's life makes *La vie de Saint Louis* the most personally revealing of all the king's biographies.

Historical *mémoires* were also written by Philippe de Navarre, covering the years 1223–1243; and an anonymous *Vie de Guillaume le Mareschal* in octosyllabic verse was compiled in Normandy about 1226 for Count William of Pembroke (William Marshal's son). *La chronique rimée des rois de France* is a 31,000-line verse history of the French kings that begins with the fall of Troy and ends in the France of 1241.

Poetry continued to be used sporadically through the fourteenth and fifteenth centuries for historical writing—for example, by Guillaume Guiart, Geoffroi de Paris, Jean Cuvelier, Martial d'Auvergne, and Guillaume de Machaut. But the major contributions to vernacular history were in prose.

The Venetian Marco Polo dictated the first French travelogue, *Le livre de Marco Polo*, to a fellow prisoner in Genoa during his captivity there (1296–1298). His report of his travels to and from China through many hitherto unknown lands was subsequently translated into several European languages, and it remained the sole source of information on many of those lands throughout the Renaissance.

Jehan Froissart, born at Valenciennes of bourgeois parents, chronicled events in the major countries of western Europe during the first fifty years of the Hundred Years War. His work was dominated by the chivalric intention to record for posterity *les grans merveilles et les biaux faits d'armes* (the great marvels and fair feats of arms) that he had witnessed. His political loyalties fluctuated from England to France, depending on his personal circumstances. Froissart had unmatched opportunities to collect information as a result of his wide range of privileged experiences. As the protégé of Queen Philippa in England, he traveled with her entourage to Scotland, France, and Italy and visited the courts of Duke Wenceslaus of Luxembourg, Count Guy of Blois, and Gaston III of Foix. He had a parish at Mons and a canonry at Chimay.

Froissart's kaleidoscopic compilation of facts and impressions from the years between 1361 and 1400, and his extensive borrowings from Jean le Bel for the years 1327–1361, together comprised four books, of which the first was written in at least three different versions, and the second in two. Despite their neglect of certain areas (political and diplomatic history, for example), they remain a picturesque and useful source of information about aristocratic interests in the fourteenth century.

The history and artistic value of the *Chronique* of Jean le Bel (*ca.* 1290–*ca.* 1370) has been overshadowed by that of its derivative—Froissart incorporated the best of it into his first two books, with due acknowledgment. Jean's aims were, in fact, more soberly historical than Froissart's. His intention was to substitute for a mendacious poetic chronicle that was then circulating a true and factual prose account of the courts in France, England, and Flanders during the reign of his hero, Edward III of England. The resulting history was more annalistic and less partial than Froissart's, despite its pro-English inclination.

The progress of prose is obvious by the fact that Christine de Pizan employed it, despite her poetic and rhetorical skills, for her *Fais et bonnes meurs du sage roy Charles V.* Biographies abounded in the fifteenth century, many of them solicited (for Duke Louis of Bourbon, Arthur, count of Richemont, and Jean de Bueil).

Regional chroniclers, especially in Burgundy, wrote in the service of their patrons. Georges Chastellain was appointed official historiographer to the dukes of Burgundy in 1455. His *Chronique des ducs de Bourgogne*—of its six books only fragments survive—spanned the years 1419 to 1474. Olivier de la Marche succeeded Chastellain and recorded the years 1435 to 1467 in meticulous *mémoires,* for which he apologized as having a style that was neither subtle nor rhetorical.

The aims of Enguerrand de Monstrelet were slightly different. Intended as a military history, his chronicle shared Froissart's preoccupation with feats of arms as well as his tendency to partiality (this time for Burgundy). It chronicled events from 1400 to 1444 and was supplemented by the work of a somewhat pedestrian continuator, Mathieu d'Escouchy.

The most complex and "modern" of the French chroniclers was Philippe de Comines. He too had begun in the service of a Burgundian, Charles the Bold, had become Charles's *secretissimorum secretarius,* then had left him in 1472 for the court of Louis XI. After the latter's death in 1483 Comines's political machinations against the regency of Anne and Pierre de Beaujeu and against their ally René of Lorraine brought about his arrest, imprisonment, and exile. Much of the *Mémoires sur les règnes de Louis XI et de Charles VIII* was written during this period of disfavor (1489–1490) and the remainder between 1495 and 1498. The *Mémoires* had originally been requested as a source of information for a Latin biography of Louis XI that Angelo Cato, archbishop of Vienna, intended to write. But Comines's history surpassed those boundaries and, in addition to the brilliant portraits of Charles the Bold, Louis XI, and Charles VIII, it contains the political ruminations of a highly trained though poorly educated diplomat.

Samuel Kinser has called Comines's *Mémoires* an "amalgam of recollection and reflection" because they shift constantly from the narration of events to Comines's didactic philosophizing on them. It has been argued that Comines was motivated by a need to invalidate all moral assumptions by which his defection from Burgundy might be judged and found wanting. Paradoxically, his moral pessimism, and his cynical assertion that political success justified all, end with an appeal for religious conversion. Thus, despite his sophisticated analysis of cause and effect in history, Comines's interpretation of the political facts is, in the end, fatalistic. Only the fear of God could restrain princes, and *tous les maulx viennent de faulte de foy* (all evils stem from lack of faith).

BIBLIOGRAPHY
Paul Archambault, *Seven French Chroniclers* (1974); Jeanette M. A. Beer, *Villehardouin—Epic Historian* (1968); Marc Bloch, *The Historian's Craft,* Peter Putnam,

trans. (1964); Henry Chaytor, *From Script to Print* (1945); Georges Duby, *The Chivalrous Society,* Cynthia Postan, trans. (1977); Samuel Kinser, ed., *The Memoirs of Philippe de Commynes,* Isabelle Cazeaux, trans., 2 vols. (1969–1973); Donald Queller, *The Fourth Crusade* (1977); F. S. Shears, *Froissart: Chronicler and Poet* (1930).

JEANETTE M. A. BEER

[See also **Benoît de Sainte-Maure; Chansons de geste; Christine de Pizan; Comines, Philippe de; Froissart, Jehan; Gaimer, Geffrei; Joinville, John of; Marco Polo; Philippe de Navarre; Robert de Clari; Roland, Song of; Villehardouin, Geoffroi de; Wace.**]

CHRONIQUES DE LONDRES, annals of London for the period 1259–1343 in Anglo-Norman, written down in the middle of the fourteenth century and preserved in London, British Library, MS Cotton Cleopatra A VI. The commencement of each year records the names of the mayors and the sheriffs of the city.

BIBLIOGRAPHY

Croniques de London depuis l'an 44 Hen. III. jusqu'à l'an 17 Edw. III., George James Aungier, ed. (1844); *The French Chronicle of London,* Henry Thomas Riley, trans. (1863), 239–291.

BRIAN MERRILEES

[See also **Anglo-Norman Literature; London.**]

CHRYSOBULLON, or golden bull, was an imperial edict that derived its name from the gold seal with which it was closed. Representing the most solemn imperial act, it contained a picture of the emperor attached to the golden seal with silk laces. Until 1204 it was written in decorative characters. *Chrysobulla* issued by the Byzantine emperors legislated on a wide variety of subjects relating to both internal and external affairs of the empire. Among the subjects of the bulls were land grants, trading privileges extended to foreign nations, and church matters.

In addition to their use in the Byzantine Empire, *chrysobulla* were also employed in several states in western Europe. Golden bulls were issued by King András II of Hungary in 1222, at the insistence of the nobles, which attempted to limit the powers of the king; and by the Holy Roman emperor Charles

IV in 1356 to define the powers of the most important princes.

BIBLIOGRAPHY

Louis Bréhier, *Le monde byzantin,* II (1949).

LINDA ROSE

CHRYSOSTOM, JOHN, ST. See John Chrysostom, St.

CHURCH FATHERS have been variously identified by the several branches of Christendom. A composite list would include Catholics, Orthodox, Arians, Nestorians, Jacobites, and even Gnostics. This article will concentrate on Fathers recognized by the Roman and Orthodox churches. Criteria for recognition are antiquity, orthodoxy, holiness of life, and formal ecclesiastical endorsement. "Antiquity" will be taken to mean in the West the period from the Apostolic Age to the death of St. Isidore of Seville (*ca.* 636) and in the East to that of St. John of Damascus (*ca.* 750); "orthodoxy" here means adherence to a general consensus of the Eastern and Western churches. Not all Fathers are equally authoritative, and most revered are the fifteen admitted as "Doctors." Some Fathers have no memorial: Plato, Philo Judaeus, and Plotinus, whose contributions, involuntary and obliquely acknowledged, were of crucial importance.

The first postapostolic writers are attractive for their great simplicity. Their doctrine is summed up in the *Didache,* a sort of primer of the faith. But Clement of Rome, Ignatius, Polycarp, and the author of the Epistle of Barnabas survive in letters addressed to distant churches during the first two Christian centuries, stressing ethics and calling for mutual support at a time when Christians were weak, scattered, and endangered.

The Christian movement was early seen as a counterculture and Christians as social subversives. Tacitus (*Annales*) says that most Romans in Nero's time thought them guilty of *odium humani generis* ("hatred of the human race"); Minucius Felix (*Octavius*), Tertullian (*Apologeticum*), and the pagans Lucian of Samosata and Celsus record that they were suspected of child murder, cannibalism, sexual orgies, incest, atheism, and "idiocy" (indifference to politics). The conduct of certain Roman officials suggests that a decree of some sort may have been issued against them at this time. Furthermore, not only the Resurrection but the vernacular Greek of the Gospels and the claims to divinity made for an executed nationalist agitator were "to the Greeks foolishness" and to others as well.

In the second century, some Christians of intellectual stature tried to convince the emperors that Christians were good subjects and the pagan intelligentsia that they could be intellectually respectable. These apologists (Greek *apologia*, [legal] defense) included Justin Martyr, Tatian the Assyrian, Athenagoras of Athens, and Theophilus of Antioch. The emperors seem generally to have come around to the view that Christians, if perhaps simpleminded, were not dangerous, and they sanctioned "persecution" only in times of plague, famine, or military crises, when the masses were conveniently ready to blame Christian "atheism" rather than the government for loss of divine favor.

In the second century, Christianity was very nearly diverted by the Gnostic movement from its postapostolic simplicity. Christian Gnosticism offered an alternative to the Christianity of the historic church. Basically dualistic, it rejected the Jewish doctrine of Creation ("And God saw that it was good") and held the phenomenal world to be the work not of the highest godhead—nor even of a wise and loving Agent—but of an evil or ignorant inferior deity.

Gnostic teachers seem to have stimulated free thought. Sects proliferated in the largely tolerant religious climate of the classical world, but most of what we know of Gnosticism today comes from the writings of its enemies—and Irenaeus (*Adversus haereses*) and Hippolytus (*Philosophumena*) were not prepared to give the works of Basilides, Valentinus, Bardesanes, and Marcion a sympathetically symbolic interpretation in the late second and early third centuries. But these now shadowy figures were once potential "Fathers" of the church of the future, with strong appeal for many persons of culture who thought their judgment on the world of experience to be realistic and honest. The church would not compromise its claim to be the sole interpreter of Christianity and was driven to stress the unity of God, the goodness of his creation (appearances perhaps to the contrary), the historical reality of the Incarnation, and the need for a strong theological consensus to stave off what seemed like subjective chaos.

That all true Christians should see the faith in conformity with truth as defined by the church (or by one's heretical sect) became an obsession. In the early third century Tertullian inveighed against heretics, against apostates who trimmed their sails to the wind in time of persecution, and against bona fide Catholics after he himself had become a Montanist. St. Cyprian of Carthage, a strong proponent of church unity in discipline and doctrine, later expressed similar opinions in less belligerent language.

Meanwhile, the struggle for intellectual respectability continued. The Catechetical School for the systematic interpretation of Scripture was established after the middle of the second century in Alexandria, the home of Neoplatonism, which was the last great philosophical movement of classical antiquity. Clement of Alexandria, headmaster at the turn of the third century, tried to give Christianity credibility by demonstrating its resemblances to Greek philosophy. The Hebrews had been prepared for Christ's message by the Law and the Greeks by their philosophers, with Plato and the Stoics most nearly anticipating Christian teaching. In theory, philosophy's role in Christian times was neither to add to nor subtract from the deposit of faith, but to help make sense of it for educated persons. But to express one's thoughts in the intellectual idiom of an alien tradition is to risk their amendment or perversion, whether subtle or gross. Thus Clement came to accept the Platonic forms, the eternity of matter, and the creation of the Logos, propositions that the church would not endorse.

Origen, a later headmaster of the Catechetical School, prepared a brilliant composite text of the Scriptures, wrote on apologetical, polemical, dogmatic, and ascetic themes, and offered an inclusive philosophical system. But affinity with the Neoplatonists led him to insist that God the Father is unequivocally One, that the Second and Third Persons differ from him and from each other in substance, and that all created beings will eventually be redeemed (*apokatastasis*). Posterity would brand him a heretic—as indeed he was, from the standpoint of post-Nicene orthodoxy. He and Clement are not "Fathers" in good standing, but they offered an encouraging example to later theologians, like St. Gregory of Nyssa, who were more successful than they in strengthening orthodox Christian theology with borrowings from "the best secular thinking."

With Constantine's edict of toleration in 313, the church no longer needed to defend itself against external foes but could devote its energy to clarifying the meaning of the faith that all Christians supposedly shared. A golden age dawned for Christian literature. Men of cultivation and classical education had time and opportunity now to elaborate their views in theological and historical treatises and even in poetry (Prudentius).

The true nature of Christ became the absorbing question. The church in its fight against Gnosticism had committed itself uncompromisingly to the proposition that God is One, and this dogma was universally accepted by Christians. But the adherents of Arius held that only the First Person (the Father) is divine and that the Logos (the Son) and the Holy Ghost are respectively the first and second of created beings, similar to, but not identical with, the Divine (hence "*homoi*ousians," believers in like substance). But an apparent majority were committed to believing that Jesus is the Son of God, and tried to see and show how this can be reconciled with the dogma of the Oneness of God ("*homo*ousians," believers in identical substance).

Among the leaders of this majority in the fourth century were St. Athanasius, St. Basil the Great, his brother St. Gregory of Nyssa, St. Gregory of Nazianzus, St. Didymus the Blind, and the historian Eusebius. The Council of Nicaea I (325) repudiated Arius and endorsed the "Athanasian" doctrine by a majority vote espoused temporarily at least by the emperor; the Council of Constantinople I (381) disposed of various last-ditch versions of Arianism. The Council of Chalcedon (451) affirmed against Eutyches and the Monophysites that the two natures, divine and human, are united in Christ without confusion or change.

This was a great age in biblical exegesis. The "Alexandrian school" represented by St. Athanasius, St. Cyril of Alexandria, St. Didymus the Blind, and the great Cappadocians St. Basil the Great, St. Gregory of Nazianzus, and St. Gregory of Nyssa, along with the Palestinians St. Cyril of Jerusalem and Eusebius of Caesarea, located the source of knowledge not in sensation and reason but in the content of Christian faith, and employed allegorical interpretation to make Scripture come out right. The "Antiochene school" of the late fourth and early fifth centuries—St. Theodore of Mopsuestia, St. John Chrysostom, Theodoret of Cyr, and Diodorus of Tarsus—preferred a more literal historical and grammatical approach.

Meanwhile the Western church was coming to a brilliant intellectual maturity. St. Hilary of Poitiers, St. Jerome, and Rufinus sought to make the West au courant with Eastern theology; while St. Ambrose of Milan drew heavily on Origen, Hippolytus, and St.

Basil the Great for his comprehensive description of the Christian life. With St. Augustine (354–430), the West achieved speculative superiority. In addition to defending the unity of the church against the Donatist schismatics, and challenging the Manichees' reputation for intellectual honesty and moral austerity, he maintained against the Pelagians the primacy of divine grace over any human effort in the work of redemption. In his great apologetical work *De civitate Dei* he defended Christianity against the charge that it was responsible for the decline of the Roman Empire, reminding men that whether or not that or any other earthly society falls, the Christian has another home in the spiritual fastnesses of the City of God. His contemporary St. Jerome also served as a conduit for Eastern speculation and fought the Pelagians. But his great memorial is, rather, the Vulgate translation of the Bible.

Western Christians were much concerned with the institutional unity of the church in the fifth century. St. Peter Chrysologus of Ravenna bade Eutyches amend his views by submitting to the bishop of Rome, and Pope Leo the Great, who saw unity in terms of the universal primacy of Rome, would not accept the Council of Chalcedon's endorsement of a functional primacy in the east for Constantinople. By the time of the death of Pope Gregory the Great (640), the political bulwarks of the papacy had been strengthened, a *Festung christliche* against the storms ahead.

The last Latin Father, St. Isidore of Seville (560–636), a typical classicizer, touched on every branch of learning, and his *Sentences* contains classified excerpts from the works of his great predecessors. Greek interest in theological and ecclesiastical issues continued after the post-Nicene golden age, but great works of original theological speculation ceased to appear. The last father of the Greek church, St. John of Damascus (*ca.* 650–754), in the third part of his *Fountain of Wisdom,* "Accurate Exposition of the Orthodox Faith," gave the Eastern church an anthology and summary of the best theological thought of its classical period.

The fathers of the church ensured the survival of Christianity by making it intellectually respectable and politically acceptable. From the church's own perspective, their great achievements were to beat down Gnosticism, specify the true nature of Christ, strengthen the hand of the church, and confirm the Christian obsession with uniformity of belief. As regards these, the fate of Gnosticism suggests that optimism is stronger than pessimism; the doctrines of

Christ's divinity and of the mystery of the Trinity have proved to be an inspiration more often than a stumbling block; and in coming to terms with Plato and Caesar, the church gained power to discredit or suppress incongenial views, and this has made for esprit de corps if not for the rich variety of religious experience tolerated by Gnosticism or Hinduism. Christianity entered a religious milieu formed by Greek anthropomorphism, Italian animism, ancient mysteries, and imported savior gods and sacraments—a milieu given credibility by such men as Plato, Cicero, and Plutarch. Whether it really survived or whether it drew so much from this context that it lost its essential Palestinian character are questions that evoke continuing debate.

BIBLIOGRAPHY

The fundamental sources for the writings of the Church Fathers are *Patrologia latina,* 221 vols. (1844–1864) and *Patrologia graeca,* 166 vols. (1857–1866); and Edward Pusey, *et al.,* eds., *A Library of Fathers of the Holy Catholic Church, Anterior to the Division of the East and West,* 29 vols. (1838–1885). Philip Schaff, *et al.,* eds., *A Select Library of the Nicene and Post-Nicene Fathers of the Christian Church,* 14 vols. (1886–1890; repr. 1952–1956), is still of use.

See also Berthold Altaner, *Patrology,* Hilda C. Graef, trans. (1960); Otto Bardenhewer, *Patrology,* Thomas J. Shahan, trans. (1908); Hans Campenhausen, *The Fathers of the Greek Church,* Stanley Godman, trans. (1959); and *The Fathers of the Latin Church,* Manfred Hoffmann, trans. (1964); Fulbert Cayré, *Manual of Patrology and History of Theology,* H. Howitt, trans., 2 vols. (1935–1940); Johannes Quasten, *Patrology,* 2 vols. (1950); Maurice F. Wiles, *The Christian Fathers* (1966); and Harry A. Wolfson, *The Philosophy of the Church Fathers,* 2nd ed. (1964).

G. L. KEYES

[See also **Ambrose, St.; Athanasius of Alexandria, St.; Augustine of Hippo, St.; Basil the Great of Caesarea, St.; John Chrysostom, St.; Councils (Ecumenical, 325–787); Doctors of the Church; Eusebius of Caesarea; Gregory I the Great, Pope; Gregory of Nazianzus; Gregory of Nyssa, St.; Hilary of Poitiers, St.; Isidore of Seville, St.; John of Damascus, St.; Prudentius; Theodoret of Cyr.**]

CHURCH, EARLY. The establishment of the "Peace of the Church" by Emperor Constantine I and his successors can be considered the beginning of the medieval church. Previously, Christians had been considered atheists—enemies of the official Roman pagan religion—and as such had been subject to civil penalties and sporadic persecution, as well as to the general contempt of the Roman intellectual and social establishment. In the decade 311–320 a series of decrees secured the formal toleration of Christianity, replacing the burden of fear on the Christian community with the burden of wealth. The decrees permitted Christians to build and to endow their churches and, accepting them into imperial favor, made the profession of the faith an asset in a public career. Taken together, these elements augmented the size, and diluted the piety, of the church. When Emperor Theodosius I completed the process in 391–394 by outlawing paganism and declaring Christianity the official religion of the empire, the religion of the apostles began its dominance of Mediterranean society.

Constantine and his successors considered themselves leaders of the church as well as its patrons. Constantine caused the first ecumenical council to be called—at Nicaea, across the Bosporus from Constantinople—in 325. The emperor joined the discussions, manipulated the bishops, and approved doctrinal decisions, setting a precedent for imperial domination of the Christian community that endured for centuries.

The early ecumenical councils (Nicaea I, 325; Constantinople I, 381; Ephesus, 431; Chalcedon, 451) were badly needed. The rapid spread of Christianity over three centuries had created a far-flung, loosely knit community in which a broad diversity of opinions existed, often in mutual conflict. The apostles and evangelists had left the doctrines of Christianity only vaguely defined. The councils attempted to resolve the conflicts and define the doctrines.

The most important problem was the delay of the Parousia. The Christian community in the first generation following Christ believed that he would come again in glory to bring about the end of this world or age and to establish the new age, the kingdom of God. This second coming and new foundation was known as the Parousia, and it was expected daily. As generations, and then centuries, passed, Christians asked themselves why it was delayed. The usual explanation was that God needed time to prepare humanity for the second coming, just as he had needed centuries to prepare for the first. A number of corollary practical questions arose: How were Christians to live in the meanwhile? How were they to know what Christ had taught? How were they to worship? How were they to live together and in society? How did they obtain truth about God and his relationship to humankind?

The single way of knowing what Christ had taught was through tradition. Christ left no writings of any kind. His followers recounted his words and deeds to others orally. At some point, probably about twenty years after the death of Jesus, literate Christians began to put portions of the oral tradition into writing. Some of these writings are presumed lost; biblical scholars tend to believe that some of the Epistles of Paul, dating from the late 50's and the 60's, are the earliest known.

During the second and third centuries a large number of books purporting to describe the words and works of Christ appeared. The proliferation of these books raised the question of which were valid and which spurious. The first effort to establish some kind of "new testament" appears to have been made by Marcion, a Gnostic condemned by the majority of the Christian community as a heretic, in the mid second century. The church fathers were vague on the subject, sometimes referring to "our" books as distinguished from "false ones" without specifying or naming them. Shortly after 200 a consensus on most of the books was reached, but it was not until about 360 that the canon of the New Testament was finally set. Established by the consensus of the Christian bishops and church fathers, it depended in form and content on the tradition of the Christian community. The Christian community thus created the New Testament but, once created, the New Testament became the standard that the community had to follow.

The next key point was the definition of the *ekklesia*, the Christian community. A number of people called themselves Christians; did everything that anyone calling himself a Christian did or said constitute Christianity, or did any exclusionary criteria exist? One standard was consistency with the teachings of the New Testament, but the problem of defining the community preceded the fixing of the canon. Another standard was practice. By the second century the essential marks of the Christian were understood to be baptism and participation in the Eucharist, the thanksgiving service whose central event was the blessing and consuming of bread and wine believed in some way to be the body and blood of Jesus Christ.

That these sacraments were the distinguishing marks of Christians, regardless of how they might otherwise differ as to beliefs and behavior, was universally assumed, and debates on the nature and number of the sacraments did not become important until long after the age of Constantine. The eucha-ristic service also included prayers, sacred readings, the singing of psalms, and the kiss of peace expressing *agapé*, the loving concern that was the hallmark of Christian society at its best.

But Christians also disagreed and disputed with one another. Someone was needed to resolve disputes, answer questions, and preside over the sacraments. The earliest Christian communities made no distinction between laity and clergy, but as early as A.D. 100 *episkopoi* (supervisors) and *presbyteroi* (elders) were distinguished from the *laikoi* (the "people"). Soon after 100 the *episkopoi* were further distinguished from the *presbyteroi*. The Christian community in each town had its *episkopos* (now better translated in its modern sense of "bishop") and its *presbyteroi* ("priests") who obeyed the bishop. The bishops were considered the successors of the apostles. As Jesus had consecrated his apostles by laying his hands upon them and sending them out into the world to teach as he had taught, so the apostles in turn consecrated successors, and those successors further successors, down to the present.

The bishops thus stood in an unbroken line back to Christ. "Apostolic succession" gave them both organizational authority and doctrinal security, for it was believed that they were protected from egregious error by the Holy Spirit. God, having sent his Son to teach the truth, would not abandon his people thereafter, it was argued; rather, his Spirit would stay with the apostles and their successors to keep his teaching intact. In 180 Hegesippus wrote that "The unbroken chain of bishops . . . guarantees the undistorted transmission of doctrine in all churches."

By the time of Constantine, the authority of the bishops had long been established and was unquestioned. However, disagreements and disputes among the bishops had arisen; the need for a means of resolving such disputes was one of the chief reasons for summoning the ecumenical councils—councils of (theoretically) all the bishops of the church.

The ecumenical councils also had to address important unresolved theological questions, the most important of which were the nature of the Trinity, the nature of Christ, and the origin of evil. Beneath these questions lay the unspoken preliminary question of the nature of Christian theology itself. Theology, the philosophical investigation of God's nature and his relationship to humanity, consisted partly of "natural theology"—reflection on the cosmos without the aid of revelation—and partly of "revealed theology"—reflection on the content of revelation. The apostle Paul may legitimately be considered the first Christian theologian; Justin Martyr in the mid second century began a long succession of theologians. Those whom later generations accepted as orthodox are known as the "fathers of the church." Many Fathers were bishops, but the two groups were not congruent. Christian theology traditionally advanced through the double action of the reflections of the church fathers and the deliberations of the bishops in council.

The question of the Trinity was the most serious theological problem of the time of Constantine. Ancient tradition used the terms "Father," "Son," and "Holy Spirit" but left their relationship unclear. It was understood that these were not merely three names of the one God but in some way constituted different aspects of the divine nature. Christ was not only the Son of God but also in some way God himself; the church fathers of the second and third centuries did not agree how. The majority were subordinationists, holding that the Son and the Holy Spirit were truly God, yet subordinate to the Father. The Gnostics usually argued that the Son and the Holy Spirit (and other entities as well) were emanations produced by the Father. By the time of Constantine the Gnostics had been rejected as heretics, and the current was moving strongly in the direction of equality.

The question was complicated by geographical and personal rivalries. The issue came to a head in the intense personal animosity between Arius and Athanasius. Arius was an Egyptian priest who found his widest support in Syria, particularly at Antioch and at Nicomedia, whose bishop Eusebius was one of his chief proponents. Arius and Eusebius taught subordinationism. Athanasius, bishop of Alexandria from 328 to 373, attacked Arianism and defended the equality of the Three Persons.

The quarrel was felt throughout the eastern part of the church and beyond, in the theologically less sophisticated western Mediterranean. The majority of the bishops backed Athanasius. At last hostilities rose to the point that Constantine determined to put them to rest. At least one reason for his patronization of Christianity was his hope that it would become a stabilizing and unifying force in the empire, and for this he needed a united episcopate. Under his direct influence—even pressure—the Council of Nicaea condemned Arius and adopted the Athanasian position that Father, Son, and Holy Spirit were three equal Persons of the One God. The decisions of Nicaea were reiterated in 381 by the First Council of Constantinople, and the question was settled for the

majority of Christians. A sizable minority remained Arians and, because of the work of Arian missionaries, many of the "barbarian" tribes invading the Roman Empire, notably the Ostrogoths, Visigoths, Vandals, and Lombards, were Arian Christians. However, by the mid sixth century Arianism ceased to be a significant factor.

After 381 the focus of debate shifted to the corollary problem of the nature of Christ; again Antioch and Alexandria were the geographical poles of the dispute. The Christians of Alexandria—especially Cyril, patriarch about 400—tended to emphasize the divine nature of Christ. Eutyches, archimandrite of Constantinople, argued that Jesus Christ, the Second Person of the Trinity, was a wholly divine being. His human nature was merely an appearance, a medium through which he might approach and instruct humans. This "Docetism" (the idea that Christ's human body was only an appearance) had been espoused by the Gnostics, on the ground that the material universe was evil; it had been rejected by the orthodox Fathers, but suspicions of dualism remained in Christianity and now found expression in Eutychianism or Monophysitism, the doctrine of the "one nature" of Christ.

Opposition to the Monophysites centered in Antioch, especially with Nestorius, a monk of Antioch who became patriarch of Constantinople in 428, and his followers. The Nestorians argued that Jesus Christ was a composite being comprising one wholly divine person and nature and one wholly human person and nature. A variation of Nestorianism was adoptionism, the doctrine that Jesus was conceived and born as a human but that at some point in his life (usually thought to be his baptism) the Father adopted him, bestowing a second, divine personality on him.

The struggle between the Monophysites and the Nestorians became heated, even violent. The emperors, fearful of losing the united episcopate that they needed to hold the crumbling empire together, strove to end the split. At Ephesus in 431 and again at Chalcedon in 451, the bishops assembled in ecumenical council and hammered out a compromise: Jesus Christ was one united personality but with two distinct natures, the human and the divine. It was a perfect dialectical solution to the problem and one that was accepted by the majority of the church. Yet, as with the Arians, opposition persisted. The Nestorians gradually withered away—except in central Asia, where as late as the thirteenth century they maintained churches in the Mongol Empire. The

Monophysites maintained their influence in Egypt and extended that influence to Syria and Palestine. Well into the seventh century they were pressuring the emperors to dilute the Chalcedonian settlement. The disaffection of the Monophysites from the Catholic community was so great that when the Arabs invaded Syria, Palestine, and Egypt, many Monophysite communities welcomed them, contributing substantially to the Muslim triumph.

The third central question was the nature of evil. Debated by the Fathers, it never achieved definition by the bishops. The question never even received a formal name until Leibniz coined the term "theodicy," the justification of God's ways to man. God is good, God is all-powerful, but the world is full of evil. Whence does this evil come? The existence of evil seems to limit either God's goodness or his power; either he does not wish to eliminate evil, or he is unable to do so. The Gnostics, and the Manichaeans, followers of a Persian named Mani (d. ca. 275), tried to solve the problem with dualism, an option that enjoyed wide support for centuries. St. Augustine himself embraced Manichaeanism for a while in his youth, and dualism had another period of expansion during the Middle Ages, beginning with the Bogomils in tenth-century Bulgaria and spreading to western Europe with the Cathar heresy of the twelfth and thirteenth centuries.

The dualist attempt at a solution to the problem of evil postulated two deities. The creator-God of the Old Testament was really an evil deity independent (or almost so) of the ultimate, true God. The true God creates a world of spirits. Evil comes from matter, which the subordinate God creates in order to ensnare and imprison the spirits. He traps some of these spirits in human bodies. The good God of spirit then sent down the pure spirit Jesus Christ, under the appearance of a human being, to instruct us that our true nature is spiritual and that we must work to save ourselves from the slavery of matter. A philosophical variation of dualism was to posit matter itself (rather than an evil god of matter) as an eternal principle independent of deity. Dualism found some support in the apostolic view of matter and the flesh. Jesus is reputed to have taught a radical opposition between the "kingdom of God" and the "kingdom of this world" (kosmos or aion). What Jesus really meant is uncertain, but the interpretation that it was an opposition between spirit and matter is not unreasonable.

Against dualism the church fathers attempted to preserve both the goodness and the omnipotence of God, to assert the essential goodness of the material world as the creation of the one true God, and thereby to legitimize human society. But given the enormous scope of evil in this world, the orthodox approach left the question of evil unresolved. Several answers were offered. Usually the Devil was supposed to have wide power over the world and to have been granted it in order to test or to punish humanity. The original sin of men and women, represented by Adam and Eve, was blamed more directly. These and other, less dramatic explanations were used to transfer the blame for evil from God to another being or beings: God wishes only the good, but he tolerates the existence of evil in order to achieve a higher good.

The affirmation of the essential goodness of the material world and of the human body by the majority of the church fathers enabled the notion of a Christian community and society to be formed. The majority, traditional Christian position granted the seriously flawed nature of this world and its eternal and essential inferiority to the real, spiritual world of God. But it insisted, against dualism, that God had created the material world and that it must therefore have a positive purpose. Further, the fact that God was delaying the Parousia instead of installing his "kingdom" immediately indicated that he wished human beings to make something of the time and space he was allowing them. Humans therefore had to respond by organizing and maintaining the church, the Christian community, converting and transforming society so as to prepare the world for Christ's return.

By the time of Constantine the governance of the church had become formal, resting upon the apostolic succession of the bishops and their authority to lead the community. But the Trinitarian, Christological, and lesser divisions among the bishops of the first few centuries made it clear that episcopal authority in itself was not enough. The bishops could not be counted on to present the united front that the community needed in order to survive and expand, and that the emperors needed in order to cement the crumbling body politic. By the fourth century an informal means of distinguishing among bishops had already become traditional. Each bishop was a successor of the apostles, and all bishops were equal in their spiritual powers. Yet some bishops ruled in cities of surpassing importance to Christian tradition, to geopolitics, or to both. When Constantine ascended the throne, four such "patriarchal" sees were generally recognized: Jerusalem, Antioch,

Alexandria, and Rome. When Constantine rebuilt Constantinople into another seat of empire, learning, and commerce, it became the fifth great see. But, as the struggles between Antioch and Alexandria illustrate, the patriarchs could not be trusted to agree among themselves, and in any event their authority over the other bishops was ill-defined.

The fourth and fifth centuries produced three different centers of ecclesiastical authority over the bishops. The first was the emperor. The concept of the emperor as the head of the church would have astounded Ignatius of Antioch, Justin, and the other martyrs. It was not in the Christian tradition, but in the tradition of the public religion of pagan Rome, where the emperors had assumed the ancient role of high priest, *pontifex maximus*, and even claimed divinity. Constantine, keeping his bridges open to paganism as well as building new bridges to Christianity, retained his role as pagan pontifex and continued to claim divinity as a manifestation of the sun god, at the same time assuming leadership of the Christian *ekklesia*. Constantine dominated the Council of Nicaea. He thought of himself as the equal of the apostles, or as a "thirteenth apostle," arguing that his position as the lord of the world was prima facie evidence that God intended him to govern the church.

On the whole the bishops and the Christian community accepted such claims in practice. They were grateful for the emperor's shift from persecutor to patron, they were terrified of a reversion to the times of blood, and they were only too aware of their own disunity. And so the Roman Empire, which earlier church fathers had seen as the political manifestation of the kingdom of Satan, was transformed into the political manifestation of the Christian community. Constantine's Christian successors continued to assert these claims, and Theodosius' establishment of Christianity as the only legitimate religion of the empire meant that any division into "church and state" would remain unthinkable for more than a millennium. The empire and the church, the secular and ecclesiastical administrations, were two natures within one personality; the community of Christians awaiting the kingdom of God and meanwhile organizing themselves as best they could to advance the coming of that kingdom.

The second center of authority was the ecumenical council. If apostolic succession offered each bishop a certain degree of protection from error, then the bishops meeting and speaking together as one voice must enjoy even stronger protection. The canons of the ecumenical councils exercised authority second only to Scripture. The implicit limitation was that as long as the councils were under the close supervision of the emperors, they were to some extent a surrogate of imperial authority, at the same time lending that authority a Christian basis.

The third center of authority was the papacy. The growth of papal power was gradual, indeed sporadic. The only hint that the bishop of Rome exercised any wide authority in the very early church is a letter from Bishop Clement I of Rome to the Christian community at Corinth in A.D. 95, reprimanding them for their disharmony. The letter demonstrates that the see of Rome was held in respect abroad, but not that its bishop had powers beyond those of the other patriarchs. Yet Rome, the seat of empire and the site of martyrdom of the two greatest apostles, Peter and Paul, had a natural advantage. As time went on, the quantity and force of papal interventions abroad rose—for example, the intervention of popes Victor I (189–198) and Julius I (337–352) in the churches of Asia Minor. Papal theory kept pace. Damasus I (366–384) argued that "The opinion of the Roman bishop must be sought before all others." The Petrine theory, which argued that Peter was the prince of the apostles and the Roman bishop his successor, and therefore prince of the bishops, first appeared clearly in the papacies of Siricius (384–399) and Innocent I (401–417).

Conceptually, the papacy first obtained recognition of its primacy in honor throughout the church. Second, it obtained the right to judge disputes submitted to it by other dioceses. Third, it gradually obtained the right to administer the church as a whole in matters of jurisdiction and discipline. Fourth, it gradually acquired the right to define doctrine. Finally, it even claimed for a while to rule all Christian society in both spiritual and temporal matters. But these powers took centuries to develop. That papal influence was far from predominant in the first four centuries is clear from the composition of the first ecumenical councils, from which the popes were absent and in which their ideas played little or no role. Discussion at the councils was conducted in Greek, the language of the East, rather than in Latin, and the early councils were very much the show of the emperors and the patriarchs of Alexandria, Antioch, and Constantinople.

The first clear change occurred during the papacy of Leo I (440–461), at a time when the weakness of imperial power, particularly in the West, compelled the bishop of Rome to assume greater responsibility and power. The only patriarch in the Western empire, the pope became the focus of unity as the empire crumbled. In Rome and its environs, the pope was obliged to undertake many of the political, financial, diplomatic, and defense responsibilities that the imperial government found itself powerless to continue to exercise.

Leo was the first pope to exercise significant influence on an ecumenical council. The *Tome of Leo,* a set of theological position papers prepared by the papal court, was read to the Council of Chalcedon in 451 and was a basis of its Christological doctrine. Leo was the first pope to claim *plenitudo potestatis,* legal jurisdiction over the entire church. Gelasius I (492–496) advanced papal theory with his doctrine of the "two swords," but on the whole Leo's successors were unable to preserve the impetus that he had given papal power, especially when Justinian I (527–565) and his successors revived imperial power in the sixth century.

The great councils of the fourth and fifth centuries, along with the work of the church fathers in these centuries, set Christian doctrine on most major matters for centuries. Medieval theology in the West can be seen as an elaboration of the work of Chalcedon and of St. Augustine. The foundations of Christian theology were laid by such early church fathers as Justin Martyr, Tertullian, Irenaeus, Clement of Alexandria, and Origen, all of whom except Tertullian wrote in Greek. The activity of the Greek theologians continued in the fourth and fifth centuries, with Gregory of Nazianzus, Basil the Great, Gregory of Nyssa, and John Chrysostom contributing to the development of doctrine, particularly "soteriology" (salvation theory). The church agreed that Christ had saved us, opening up the road to God that original sin had blocked. But the nature of salvation remained unclear: Was Christ's saving act his incarnation, or his Passion, or both? Usually the focus was on the Passion, the suffering of Christ. But was this a sacrifice offered by the human race to God so as to reconcile itself with its angry maker, or was it a ransom paid by God to the Devil in order to redeem us, to buy us back from Satan, who after original sin had justly held us in his power? The question was debated for centuries.

The same period produced the first really great theologians in the Latin West: St. Ambrose, St. Jerome, and St. Augustine of Hippo. Augustine was the dominant theologian of his day and has had more influence on subsequent Western theology (medieval, modern Catholic, and Protestant) than any other theologian except Paul. His most influential books were *On Christian Doctrine,* the *Confessions,* and *The City of God.* Although he explored almost every aspect of theology, his most original and significant contribution was probably to the theology of grace. Plunging into the center of the eternal dispute between determinism and free will, Augustine struggled with the question throughout his life, first tending to determinism, then backing off toward giving free will a wider role. Finally, in his later years, particularly after the fall of Rome to Alaric in 410, he advanced a new determinism while nonetheless insisting on at least some element of human freedom.

For Augustine, the individual human being can do nothing to advance his own salvation; salvation is given to those who have faith, faith is generated in those on whom grace is bestowed, and God grants grace freely and gratuitously. Merit cannot obtain grace, since all merit is produced by grace. God gives grace to those whom he chooses to save, and allows the rest of humankind to pursue its own path to perdition. The problem of grace and free will is closely related to that of evil, and Christian theologians have not agreed on a coherent position on either.

The fourth through sixth centuries produced other important writers: Boethius, Cassiodorus, Gregory the Great, Dionysius the Pseudo-Areopagite, and Evagrius Ponticus. It was a period when monastic thought was coming to dominate the Christian community. St. Anthony, who withdrew into the Egyptian desert in 271, is generally regarded as the first hermit or eremitical monk; community, or cenobitic, monasticism is usually dated from St. Pachomius (*ca.* 290–346). Monasticism is basically an imitation of Christ, specifically his withdrawal into the desert; it is rooted in the deep Christian distrust of this world and worldly success. Monasticism flourished as the persecutions declined. Under the persecutions martyrdom was the arena in which the Christians most directly confronted Satan. With the end of martyrdom, it was thought that withdrawal into the desert, where demonic powers were supposed to concentrate, and the practice of an ascetic life of renunciation and prayer constituted the most effective attack on the Devil.

Monasticism was a powerful institution down to and beyond the Reformation, and from the fifth to the eleventh century it functioned as the intellectual and educational hearth of society. Yet until the eleventh century it was diverse and unorganized. One of the characteristics of cenobitic monasticism was its insistence on a life according to a strict rule *(regula)*, usually emphasizing poverty, chastity, and obedience. But the rules differed. The early Egyptian and Syrian rules and practices reported by John Cassian in his *Institutes* and *Conferences* (written 415–429) came with Cassian to Lérins in southern Gaul and thence through Ligugé and Poitiers to Ireland. St. Augustine of Hippo devised an informal rule for his own idea of an intellectually oriented community. The most important source of Western monasticism was sixth-century Italy, where St. Benedict drew up a rule largely modeled on the anonymous "Rule of the Master" *(ca.* 540), which shows Eastern influence. This rule was sometimes adopted in one form or another in Western monastic houses, but not until the ninth century was any effort made to make it standard.

The papacy of Gregory I (590–604) is a convenient border between the early church and the medieval Latin church. Gregory was a monk who fostered the monastic life; he was a pope who advanced the power of the papacy; his writings summarized and popularized the theology of earlier church fathers and councils, and addressed the practical problems of the Christian laity and clergy; he was an organizer who helped set standards for diocesan administration; and he was the first pope to take an active interest in converting the barbarian invaders of the empire, sending St. Augustine of Canterbury to open a mission to the heathen Anglo-Saxons of Kent in *ca.* 595.

BIBLIOGRAPHY

Louis Bouyer, *La vie de Saint Antoine* (1950); Peter R. L. Brown, *Augustine of Hippo* (1967); Philip Carrington, *The Early Christian Church*, 2 vols. (1957); Henry Chadwick, *The Early Church* (1967); Claude Dagens, *Saint Grégoire le Grand* (1977); Jean Daniélou and Henri Marrou, *The Christian Centuries*, I, *The First Six Hundred Years*, Vincent Cronin, trans. (1964); W. H. C. Frend, *The Rise of the Monophysite Movement* (1972); Trevor G. Jalland, *The Life and Times of St. Leo the Great* (1941); Hubert Jedin and John Dolan, eds., *History of the Church*, I (1980); John Joseph, *The Nestorians and Their Muslim Neighbors* (1961); John N. D. Kelly, *Early Christian Creeds*, 3rd ed. (1972); *Jerome: His Life, Writings, and Controversies* (1975); and *Early Christian Doctrines*, 5th ed. (1977); David Knowles, *Christian Monasticism*, (1969); Pierre de Labriolle *et al.*, *De la mort de Théodose à l'élection de Grégoire le Grand* (1937, repr. 1948); Jules Lebreton and Jacques Zeiller, *De la fin du 2ᵉ siècle à la paix constantinienne* (1948); Ramsay MacMullen, *Constantine* (1969); Karl F. Morrison, *Tradition and Authority in the Western Church 300–1140* (1969); Jean Rémy Palanque *et al.*, *De la paix constantinienne à la mort de Théodose* (1936, repr. 1950); Angelo Paredi, *Saint Ambrose, His Life and Times* (1964); Jaroslav Pelikan, *The Christian Tradition*, I–II (1971–1974); Jeffrey Richards, *Consul of God: The Life and Times of Gregory the Great* (1980); René Roques, *L'univers dionysien: Structure hiérarchique du monde selon le Pseudo-Denys* (1954); Robert V. Sellers, *The Council of Chalcedon* (1953).

JEFFREY B. RUSSELL

[See also **Adoptionism; Ambrose, St.; Apostolic Succession; Arianism; Athanasius of Alexandra, St.; Augustine of Hippo, St.; Basil the Great of Caesarea, St.; Benedict of Nursia, St.; Boethius, Anicius Manlius Severinus; Caesaropapism; Cassian, John; Cassiodorus, Flavius Magnus Aurelius; Church Fathers; Church, Latin: Organization; Clergy; Constantine I, the Great; Councils (Ecumenical, 325–787); Dionysius the Pseudo-Areopagite; Docetism; Dualism; Eutyches; Gelasius I, Pope; Gregory of Nazianzus; Gregory of Nyssa, St.; Jerome, St.; John Chrysostom, St.; Leo I, Pope; Monophysitism; Nestorianism; Papacy, Origins and Development of; Parousia.**]

CHURCH, LATIN: TO 1054. Pope Gregory I the Great (590–604) fostered the dominant institutions of Latin Christendom, the papacy and monasticism. Partly from policy, more through chance, the papacy gradually became the focus of Western religion and society. Gregory's firmly Latin and Western ideas put a marked distance between him and the contemporary Eastern church, and he was the first pope to take an active interest in spreading the Gospels to the barbarian invaders of the empire, sending St. Augustine of Canterbury to Kent in 597. A practical administrator, he helped Rome and the other episcopal sees establish closer control over their flocks and fuller independence from secular authority.

In the seventh century, secular authority still meant the Roman Empire, at least in theory. Justinian (527–565) had restored imperial authority over Italy, North Africa, and part of Spain, defeating the Ostrogoths, Visigoths, and Vandals, all of whom were Arian heretics; but the financial cost of his conquests was crippling, and his successors lost almost all of what he had gained to the heretical Lombards and the Muslim Arabs. Thus the papacy was obliged to deal with a variety of religiously hostile princes as well as with the emperors in Constantinople. Christianity's most serious, and ultimately insoluble, problem was the irruption of Islam into the Mediterranean, where it conquered the most populous Christian regions, dominated the sea, and attenuated the links between East and West, putting Christianity on the military, political, and cultural defensive.

During the seventh century the position of the papacy was desperate. The Byzantine Empire, stunned by the loss of its richest provinces to the Arabs, could offer no support to the West, where, outside of a few enclaves in Italy, it wielded no effective power. Yet the emperors clung to the shreds of their authority in Rome and used every occasion to control, even intimidate, the popes. Supporting Monothelitism (the doctrine that Christ has two natures but one will, as well as being one Person) as a compromise designed to win back the disaffected Monophysite populations of Syria and Egypt, the emperors demanded papal approval of the new theology. The emperor Constans II, having failed to induce Pope Martin I to support Monothelitism, ordered the pope arrested and humiliated and brought to Constantinople for trial. Found guilty of treason, Martin was sent off to die in exile in the Crimea in 655.

The seventh-century West could find no effective counterweight to the Byzantine Empire. For a century after King Recared (586–601) converted the Arian Visigoths to Catholicism, Spain was the most stable Christian country in the West, but in 711–713 the Arabs conquered all of Iberia except for the extreme northwestern corner. Clovis (481–511) converted the pagan Franks to Catholicism, but his Merovingian descendants had little power to control their own domains, let alone help the papacy. The Germans to the east of Frankish control were still pagans. The Lombards, who had invaded Italy in the mid sixth century, were Arians fiercely hostile to the remaining centers of Byzantine and Catholic power, including Rome. The pagan Anglo-Saxons had enslaved, driven out, or killed most of the original Christian population of Britain (though religious and social life was not so completely dislocated as was once thought). Only in the "Celtic Fringe"—Cornwall, Wales, Scotland, and Ireland—did Christianity persist and prosper. Cornwall and Wales had long been Christian, Ireland was converted in the mid fifth century, and Scotland was still pagan at the beginning of the sixth, but was converted soon after by monks from Ireland.

The Irish monastic, missionary spirit, gradually working at the westernmost edges of society, eventually called this new world in to redress the balance of the old. Irish Christianity was relatively isolated from the Continent by the intervening pagan Anglo-

Saxons, and it was characterized by a peculiar reliance on monasteries. Patrick (d. ca. 461), possibly the first missionary to Ireland, was probably a monk of Gaul, where he learned a strict monasticism derived through the writings of John Cassian from the Eastern monastic tradition. Monasteries so dominated Ireland that monks performed the duties of bishops. Irish monasticism was exceptionally ascetic and emphasized *peregrinatio*, the idea that life on earth is a brief and transitory "pilgrimage" on the way to God's eternal land. *Peregrinatio* readily became a missionary ideal of "wandering" in order to spread the Gospels.

Irish missionary monks such as St. Columba (Colum Cille), who began the evangelization of Scotland by founding a monastery at Iona in 563, and St. Columbanus (fl. ca. 600), who spent his life traveling in France, Germany, and Italy, spread both the Gospel and Celtic monastic practices as far as Austria and Switzerland. St. Aidan (the founder of the monastery at Lindisfarne around 635) and other Celtic monks began to evangelize the pagan English kingdom of Northumbria in the early seventh century, while Augustine of Canterbury was preaching Roman Christianity in Kent. The differences between the Roman and Celtic missionaries should not be overstated; but two different and sometimes competing missionary movements thrust into England from the end of the sixth century, a Roman one from the southeast and a Celtic one from the north and west. Roman Christianity won its crucial test over Celtic at the Synod of Whitby (663 or 664), when King Oswy of Northumbria chose to adopt Roman practice for his kingdom; over the following century Celtic monasteries generally yielded to Roman practice. When Spain fell to Islam, the British Isles became the most loyal and secure center of Roman Christianity.

The missionary spirit of the Irish communicated itself to the newly converted English, and in the eighth century English missionaries became the leaders of *peregrinatio*. St. Wilfrid of York, blown off course on a voyage to the Continent in 678, landed in Frisia, where he preached to the heathen without great success. St. Winfrith (ca. 680–755), whose Latin name was Boniface, went deliberately to preach to the Frisians in 716, going on to enlist the support of the Frankish leaders and of the popes. He preached to the heathen, enhanced the administrative and organizational effectiveness of the Frankish churches, and brought the Frankish and German churches into closer relationship with that of Rome.

He preached in the Rhineland, Thuringia, and Bavaria, founding churches, monasteries, schools, and dioceses, including Mainz, where he was the first archbishop. He combated ecclesiastical eccentricity and heresy; and wherever he found monasteries still tending to Celtic practices, he brought them into closer conformity with Rome. His close relations with both the Franks and the popes laid the foundations for the collaboration between these two powers that would finally provide the cement for Western society.

Just at this point, in the early eighth century, a series of exceptionally able popes responded creatively to the necessities of Byzantine weakness and the opportunities offered by Boniface and the Frankish connection. The first in this series was Gregory II (715–731). Gregory had inherited the desperate situation of the seventh century. The emperor was taxing the Roman people heavily without providing necessary services, even defense, while the Lombards were repeatedly invading the Roman and Catholic areas of central Italy. To these practical problems the emperor Leo III the Isaurian (717–741) added a doctrinal one. Leo too was a vigorous administrator, and he was determined to check the decay of his empire. Most of his reform measures did not concern the pope, but two had divisive consequences. The first was Leo's organization of the imperial administration and law so that Greek replaced Latin as the official (it had always been the cultural and commercial) language of the empire. This shift attenuated the already thin understanding between East and West, for Greek was by this time known by very few, even of the literate people of the Latin West. The second divisive measure was his series of decrees against icons (725–730).

Icons, images of God or of the saints, were widely believed to be a channel of divine grace and had long played an important role in Christian worship. Leo, probably influenced by the Umayyad caliph Yazīd I's prohibition of graven images in 723, outlawed the use of icons and ordered them destroyed. This policy of iconoclasm stirred up enormous resentment and resistance in the East, particularly in the monasteries, and in the West added a theological reason to the practical reasons for distrusting imperial authority. Gregory II denounced the decrees on icons, refused to abide by them or publish them, and stopped the payment of taxes to the empire. Leo threatened to have the pope arrested like his predecessor Martin I, but Gregory replied with scorn.

Following the example set by Gregory I, and the practice of many bishops in fragmented Western Europe, Gregory II expanded his function of *defensor civitatis* (defender of the city). Raising his own taxes, he rebuilt the walls of Rome, raised an army, fortified the harbor, and provided food and care for the population. It was Gregory II to whom Boniface first came for support for his missionary plans. Neither a seer nor a geopolitician, Gregory had no idea of the potential reward for the papacy in Boniface's plan, and he had no resources with which to support the Englishman. Nonetheless, he gave his cordial blessing and so prepared the great synthesis that was beginning to take place.

Gregory II was succeeded by Gregory III (731–741) and Zacharias (741–752), both of whom followed their predecessor's policies, resisting the Lombards and the emperor, supporting the missionaries, and developing closer relations with the Franks. Gregory III appealed for help to the Franks in 739, when the Lombards first took Ravenna, but the Franks were too busy to come. It was Zacharias and his successor Stephen II (752–757) who saw the first dramatic fruits of the tree that Gregory II and Boniface had planted.

The Merovingian kings had become more and more ineffective, and from the beginning of the eighth century their powers were increasingly usurped by a number of powerful families, one of which, later known as the Carolingian house, was to supplant them on the throne. The Carolingians had their origin in the late seventh century; by the early eighth, Pepin II of Herstal and his son Charles Martel effectively controlled the kingdom. The Carolingian Charles Martel led the Christian forces against the Muslims at the crucial Battle of Tours (or Poitiers) in 732 and supported Boniface in his missionary efforts. Charles's son Pepin III the Short decided that he wished to have the name, as well as the responsibility, of king. But to depose a king was a difficult matter, both in Germanic custom and in Christian theory. To legitimize his move, Pepin called on Pope Zacharias for help. Ferreting out a few weak historical parallels, Zacharias obliged his ally in 751 by approving the deposition of the last Merovingian ruler and the election of Pepin as king of the Franks.

The papacy soon asked a favor in return. In 751 the Lombards conquered Ravenna, the last Byzantine bastion in central Italy. The Byzantines were effectively eliminated from the Italian political equation, but now the Lombards prepared to turn their hostile attention on Rome. A few years later, with the danger from the Lombards growing continually,

Stephen II crossed the Alps to plead for help. In 754 the king and pope met at Ponthion, where Pepin acted as the pope's groom, in a symbolic gesture holding his stirrup for him when he dismounted from his horse. Pepin agreed to help Stephen, and in 755 his formidable army defeated the Lombards. The following year Pepin signed over much of central Italy to Stephen in an act known as the Donation of Pepin.

Like the symbolic stirrup, the Donation of Pepin is to be understood in the light of the dramatic forgery known as the "Donation of Constantine," a document purporting to be a gift of lands and honors to Pope Sylvester I by Constantine in the fourth century but actually emanating from the papal chancery (probably) about 750. The document was believed valid as late as the fifteenth century, and it was the basis for King Pepin's generous gestures toward Pope Stephen.

The papacy was now without ecclesiastical rival in the West. Moreover, the Arab conquests had eliminated three of the five ancient patriarchates, Antioch, Jerusalem, and Alexandria, leaving only Constantinople and Rome in Christian hands. The patriarch of Constantinople remained a formidable rival, but his power waned slowly with that of the Byzantine state. And the pope had an ideological buttress that Constantinople did not have: the Petrine theory that Peter, the chief of the apostles, had been the first bishop of Rome, so that his successors held primacy over all the bishops. In their new security, the popes did not hesitate to press their independence from the East. During the eighth century, they symbolically ceased dating their official documents by the regnal year of the Eastern emperor, first using their own, and then that of the king of the Franks. They challenged the empire in two matters of doctrine: iconoclasm and a new issue, the *Filioque.* The Nicene creed, as issued by the First Council of Constantinople in 381, had declared that the Holy Spirit "proceeded from the Father." In sixth-century Spain the custom had arisen to insert the word *Filioque* (and from the Son) into the Latin creed; the custom had passed to the Franks; and now the papacy approved it, to the disgust of the Eastern church, which argued that the Creed should not be tampered with for any reason whatever.

The alliance of pope and Franks drew closer during the reign of Pepin III's son Charles, later known as Charlemagne, who obtained joint kingship with his brother in 768 and sole kingship in 771. Charles continued his father's policy of supporting the popes and the missionaries; his own missionary policies tended to the abrupt: when he conquered the Saxons he offered them the choice of Christianity or death. At the request of Pope Adrian I he completed the subjugation of the Lombards, assuming the iron crown himself in 774. Then, in 800, a famous and dramatic event symbolized the completion of the new Western synthesis. Pope Leo III had been accused of misconduct and was physically assaulted by his enemies among the Roman nobility. He appealed to Charlemagne. The king restored the pope to power, and Leo rewarded him by crowning him emperor in St. Peter's, where the king prayed before Christmas Mass.

It is not clear what either Leo or Charlemagne intended by the act: whether Charlemagne was to be sole emperor or emperor only of the Latin West. In any event it was effective only in the West, where together the pope and the Western emperor became heads of Latin Christian society. For the church such arrangements always had both positive and negative aspects. The church could count on imperial support, but the Frankish ruler, like previous emperors East and West, decided that he himself was the head of the church.

Charlemagne took a prominent part in the iconoclastic controversy. When the Second Council of Nicaea in 787 rejected iconoclasm, thereby bringing East and West closer together again, Charlemagne and his advisers did not understand the Greek properly (or preferred to ignore the East anyway). Charlemagne's own synod at Frankfurt in 794 condemned the worship of images, modifying Nicaea II unnecessarily; for that council had affirmed only that images could be venerated, a common practice in both East and West, not that they could be worshiped. Charlemagne also used the occasion to condemn adoptionism (which was not an issue between East and West), affirming his royal right, even before assuming the imperial crown, to be the arbiter of theology and doctrine.

A further consequence of the papal-imperial alliance was that when the empire became weak, as it did during and after the reign of Charlemagne's successor Louis the Pious, the emperors ceased not only to dominate but also to protect the papacy, which found itself again at the mercy of the Roman nobility. With a few exceptions, such as Nicholas I (858–867) and Sylvester II (999–1003), the ninth and tenth centuries produced a succession of corrupt and incompetent popes, whose scandals shocked the clergy of France and Germany almost into schism. The intellectual and moral leadership of those centuries passed to the northern bishops and to the monasteries. But the northern bishops or their followers were not above creating their own forgeries. In the early ninth century a number of "false decretals," faked pronouncements of earlier popes and councils, emerged from the episcopal chanceries of northern France. Their purport was to defend episcopal power against that of king and emperor. As the papacy was weak and no threat to the bishops at this time, the anonymous authors of the decretals found it convenient to defend the power of the papacy against that of the kings. Later, the reform popes relied (innocently) on these decretals to boost their own power against both king and bishops.

The breakup of the Carolingian Empire and the degradation of the papacy led to increasing "feudalization" of the church during the ninth and tenth centuries. Not only was the papacy in the hands of the Roman nobility, but many episcopal sees and monasteries fell into the hands of barons; and even the local unit of ecclesiastical government, the parish, was often held by a secular lord. The feudal lords usually milked the parishes, dioceses, and monasteries of revenues, while appointing clergy who were corrupt, worldly, or simply uneducated.

REFORM

In such a context reform was necessary, and in fact at least three different foci of reform appeared: royal, monastic, and finally papal. The reform movements were largely pragmatic, but they also evolved an ideology of reform based on patristic thought. In the theory of reform, Christians look back to the golden age of Christ and his apostles for ideal standards. But it would not be desirable, even if it were possible, to return to the apostolic age. Since God patently is allowing considerable time to elapse between the first and second coming of Christ, he must have a purpose in doing so; he must be preparing the world to become better, more ready to receive Christ the next time. Consequently innovations can and must be made. But they must be made in conformity with the original apostolic standards. Society must be reformed, literally formed again, but the goal is not the past—not even the golden age—but something better. The theory of reform was *reformatio in melius,* reshaping the world for the better. A creative tension between conservatism and progressivism was at the heart of Christian thought.

It is impossible to say when the age of reform began, just as it is impossible to say when the age of

corruption began: both are always present in any human community. Charlemagne and his advisers were already working on reforming the church before the worst period. Charlemagne's policy was to provide for a school in every diocese to train young people studying for the priesthood; to use bishops as secular as well as ecclesiastical administrators; to send overseers to ensure that bishops and civil administrators were doing their tasks properly; and to encourage the bishops to call reform synods and to inspect their dioceses on a regular basis. His successor Louis the Pious supported the efforts of St. Benedict of Aniane to secure compliance with the Benedictine Rule throughout the empire. But most of these reforming efforts were wiped out in the ensuing decline of both ecclesiastical and civil authority.

When Otto I the Great (936–973) and his successors reestablished the empire and coherent government on German soil, the German emperors supported similar reforms and for the same combination of reasons: regard for the welfare of society and their own souls, combined with the urgent political need for a loyal and well-trained episcopate capable of preserving order. The close working relationship between secular and ecclesiastical government in the Western monarchies is illustrated in Germany by the cooperation and friendship between Otto III (983–1002) and Pope Sylvester II, in England in the joint leadership lent reform by King Edgar the Peaceable (959–975) and St. Dunstan (*d.* 988), and in France in the personal and political relationship that Louis VI (1108–1137) and Louis VII (1137–1180) shared with Abbot Suger of St. Denis. Such kings considered it their duty to advance the Christian welfare of their subjects, and they believed that their consecration as kings gave them a well-defined function in the church. That good Christian morality and good politics often shared the same social goals enabled the cooperation between kings and clergy to endure, despite many hostile clashes, through the Middle Ages.

Monastic reform also began before the age of corruption. The efforts of Boniface and his followers to bring the monasteries up to high moral standards and into closer relationship with Rome was followed by the attempt of Benedict of Aniane (at the Synod of Aachen, 817) to ensure the conformity of the Carolingian monasteries with the Rule of St. Benedict. A number of influential reform movements followed in the tenth and eleventh centuries. The first began at Cluny in 909. The abbey of Cluny first reformed itself in conformity with the Rule of St. Benedict and protected itself from lay or episcopal interference by subjecting itself to the sole authority of the pope.

The reforms at Cluny attracted widespread favorable attention and were exported to other monastic houses, and gradually Cluny had a number of "daughter houses" throughout western Europe. Under Abbot Odilo (994–1049) the number of Cluniac houses rose to over sixty; under Hugh the Great (1049–1109) to over a thousand. Odilo set up a complex, centralized organization for their administration. The abbot of Cluny retained authority over all the houses and was the only abbot in the system; each daughter house was led by a prior who was directly responsible to the abbot and who was subject to visitation by the abbot or his representatives. Cluny and its system promoted education, liturgical beauty, and moral strength. The reforms attracted the support of kings, dukes, and bishops, who bestowed gifts of gold and land, enabling a magnificent abbey in the Romanesque style to be raised. But such success meant departure from the simplicity of the Rule and a gradual loss of the original fervor of reform. Other reforms similar to, though less spectacular than, Cluny's were achieved at Brogne (from 923), Gorze (933), and Grottaferrata (*ca.* 940); by the *Regularis concordia* in England (*ca.* 970); and by Romuald (*d.* 1027) at Camaldoli.

The papal reform movement that touched the whole church in the mid eleventh century was launched by men with ties to the reform monasteries, especially Cluny. Yet the ideology of monastic reform was different from that of the papal reformers, and sometimes the two movements were in opposition. The zealous eleventh-century monastic reformer Peter Damian, for example, was a harsh critic of the reform papacy. For Damian both the royal and the papal plans to establish a Christian society badly missed the point that the kingdom of God is not of this world at all; Christians should renounce worldly wealth and power, instead of using them, and withdraw into a life of prayer. Such ideas signaled a marked change in the function of the monasteries. Before the eleventh century, in a fragmented and feudalized Europe, the monastery was the only institution regularly supplying education, medical treatment, and alms. During the eleventh century, with the growth of cities, cathedrals, and cathedral schools, Europe grew militarily and politically calmer and more secure. The monasteries lost much of their social function and returned toward their original purpose—encouraging Christians to withdraw from the world in order to prepare for the kingdom that is not of this world.

The reform popes of the mid eleventh century dispelled the decline of generations and restored the papacy to leadership in Western Christianity. The immediate background of papal reform was the reform policy of the emperor Henry III, a determined leader in the reform of the church and, like his predecessors, certain that leadership belonged in his own hands. He planned to reform the papacy and rescue it from the Roman nobility so that the popes, like the other bishops, could help him achieve both moral reform and political stability. In 1046 Henry was in Italy facing one of the numerous disputes of the Roman nobility over control of the papacy. Three popes, each supported by a group of nobles, claimed the papacy. Henry responded by deposing them all at synods in Sutri and Rome, putting in their place a German bishop, Clement II, on whom he could rely for respectability and political loyalty. Clement was succeeded by another German pope, Damasus II (1048), and then yet another, Bruno of Toul, who took the name of Leo IX (1048–1054) and who was to launch the independent reform papacy.

Leo had no intention of breaking with his imperial patron, and he followed Henry loyally. But Leo was from Lorraine, a center of monastic reform, social and intellectual change, and papalist theory. The papal court was pregnant with change owing to the existence of a large number of radical advisers whom Bruno brought down with him from the north, men such as Hugh the White, Frederick of Lorraine (later Pope Stephen IX), Humbert of Silva Candida, and Hildebrand (later Pope Gregory VII). These advisers brought with them a knowledge of canon law, something that tended to vest church leadership in the bishops and the pope in particular, not in the emperor. Canon law provided the reform papacy with precedents and with the ideology that launched it on its successful bid for independence from imperial control.

Canon law was essentially traditional, being composed of the decrees of ecumenical councils, important local synods, and popes. The first compilation had been made by Dionysius Exiguus, "Little Denis," about 500; his collection consisted of the numbered canons of each council with the addition of thirty-nine papal decretals. Spanish compilations of the seventh century organized the canons into topics, included a broader range of councils, and added an index. Charlemagne, seeing in canon law another tool with which to create order, asked Pope Adrian I for a code, and Adrian's response, the *Dionysio-Hadriana,* was adopted for the Carolingian empire in 802.

The forged decretals, notably the "Pseudo-Isidorean" collection, entered the body of canon law in the ninth century, enhancing the powers of bishops and popes. Burchard of Worms issued his *Decretum* (*ca.* 1010), a new collection based largely on the *Hadriana* but (innocently) including the false decretals and the penitentials. Burchard's *Decretum* was widely used by the papal reformers, and its emphasis on the *Hadriana* and the false decretals provided strong precedents for papal power. Key concepts of the reform papacy, notably *justitia* (justice), were drawn from canon law. The principles of law were eternal, springing from human nature (natural law) and divine will (divine law). The function of Christian society was to bring secular positive law and ecclesiastical canon law into as close a harmony with eternal law as possible. Such a congruency was a state of justice; injustice arose when human law was incongruent with eternal law. The pope was to be the judge of such congruency.

SCHISM

The greatest moments of the reform papacy were to come after the death of Leo IX in 1054; that date also marks one of the most serious events in the history of Christianity, the schism between the Western and Eastern churches. The schism had long been building. Iconoclasm, the *Filioque,* the marriage of clergy, the question of whether leavened or unleavened bread should be used in the Eucharist, the ancient rivalry of Rome and Constantinople for primacy among the bishops, jurisdictional disputes between Rome and Constantinople in the Balkans, linguistic and cultural differences, and the question of the legitimacy of the Western empire—all these and other problems added up to an estrangement that had been growing steadily since the eighth century.

In 1054 Leo IX sent a mission to Constantinople in the hope of promoting understanding and closer cooperation. But he put the mission under the charge of Humbert of Silva Candida and Frederick of Lorraine, firebrands whose purpose was to bring the erring and stubborn Greeks into line. The patriarch of Constantinople at this time was Michael Keroularios, an equally fiery and determined man who regarded the differences between the churches as error

on the part of the Latins and considered them ignorant upstarts needing correction. The emperor Constantine IX, fearing the Seljuk Turks, wished a rapprochement but was unable to quell the hostility between the two ecclesiastical leaders. The mission ended in debacle with the mutual excommunication of pope and patriarch and the narrow escape of the Latin envoys from a hostile mob.

The schism with the East was an aspect of the dark side of the papal reform movement: intolerance of dissent, an intolerance soon to be felt by heretics, Jews, and Muslims, as well as by the Eastern "schismatics." The theoretical roots of such intolerance grew out of the early church, which had a vivid sense that Christ and the Devil were locked in deadly combat in the cosmos and in human society. The church or Christian community was the mystical body of Christ. Anyone impeding the work of that body was part of the mystical body of the Devil. The potential practical consequences of this doctrine were limited as long as it was difficult to draw the boundaries of the church. But the papal reformers drew the boundaries sharply: the *ecclesia* was the *ecclesia romana,* and the mark of a true Christian was subjection to the authority of the pope. It was now possible to assign a Satanic role to all who declined to accept papal authority.

The schism of 1054 in a sense sealed the existence of Latin Christendom as an entity, and for almost five centuries Western Europe was to be dominated by a church Roman in leadership and Latin in culture.

BIBLIOGRAPHY

Émile Amann, *L'époque carolingienne* (1937); Émile Amann and Auguste Dumas, *L'église au pouvoir des laïques (888–1057)* (1940); Marshall W. Baldwin, *The Medieval Church* (1953), and *Christianity Through the Thirteenth Century* (1970); Frank Barlow, *The English Church 1000–1066: A Constitutional History* (1963); Geoffrey Barraclough, *The Medieval Papacy* (1968); Henry Bett, *Johannes Scotus Eriugena: A Study in Mediaeval Philosophy* (1925); Karl Bihlmeyer and Hermann Tüchle, *Church History,* 13th ed., I–II (1957–1959); Edward Cuthbert Butler, *Benedictine Monachism,* 2nd ed. (1924); Maïeul Cappuyns, *Jean Scot Érigène: Sa vie, son oeuvre, sa pensée* (1933); James Carney, *The Problem of Saint Patrick* (1961); Henry Chadwick, *The Early Church* (1967); Bertram Colgrave, *The Venerable Bede and His Times* (1958); Kenneth J. Conant, *Cluny* (1968); Giles Constable, *Monastic Tithes: From Their Origins to the Twelfth Century* (1964), and *Medieval Monasticism: A Select Bibliography* (1976); Claude Dagens,

Saint Grégoire le Grand: Culture et expérience chrétiennes (1977); Jean Daniélou and Henri Marrou, *The Christian Centuries: The First Six Hundred Years,* Vincent Cronin, trans. (1964); Margaret Deanesly, *The Pre-conquest Church in England* (1961); Hans-Joachim Diesner, *Isidor von Sevilla und seine Zeit* (1973), and *Isidor von Sevilla und das westgotische Spanien* (1977); Gregory Dix, *The Shape of the Liturgy* (1945), and *Jurisdiction in the Early Church* (1975); Eleanor S. Duckett, *Alcuin: Friend of Charlemagne* (1951); David L. Edwards, *Christian England: Its Story to the Reformation* (1981); Joan Evans, *Monastic Life at Cluny, 910–1157* (1931); Jacques Fontaine, *Isidore de Séville et la culture classique dans l'Espagne wisigothique,* 2 vols. (1959); Étienne Gilson, *A History of Christian Philosophy in the Middle Ages* (1955); John Godfrey, *The Church in Anglo-Saxon England* (1962); Hubert Jedin, ed., *History of the Church,* II–III (1980); Joseph A. Jungmann, *The Mass of the Roman Rite,* Francis A. Brunner, trans., 2 vols. (1951–1955), and *The Early Liturgy: To the Time of Gregory the Great,* Francis A. Brunner, trans. (1959); David Knowles, *The Monastic Order in England* (1940), and *Christian Monasticism* (1969); David Knowles and Dmitri Obolensky, *The Christian Centuries,* II (1969); Stephan Kuttner, *Harmony from Dissonance: An Interpretation of Medieval Canon Law* (1960); Pierre Champagne de Labriolle *et al., De la mort de Théodose à l'élection de Grégoire le Grand* (1937); Gerhart Ladner, *The Idea of Reform* (1959); Max L. W. Laistner, *Thought and Letters in Western Europe A.D. 500 to 900,* 2nd ed. (1957); Jean Leclercq, *The Love of Learning and the Desire for God,* Catharine Misrahi, trans. (1961); Wilhelm Levison, *The English Church and the Continent in the Eighth Century* (1946); Peter R. McKeon, *Hincmar of Laon* (1978); Rosamond McKitterick, *The Frankish Church and the Carolingian Reforms 789–895* (1977); John T. McNeill, *The Celtic Churches* (1974); Henry Mayr-Harting, *The Coming of Christianity to England* (1972); Karl Morrison, *Tradition and Authority in the Western Church 300–1140* (1969); Georg Ostrogorsky, *Studien zur Geschichte des byzantinischen Bilderstreites* (1929); Jaroslav Pelikan, *The Emergence of the Christian Tradition (100–600)* (1971), and *The Growth of Medieval Theology (600–1300)* (1978); Jeffrey Richards, *The Popes and the Papacy in the Early Middle Ages, 476–752* (1979), and *Consul of God: The Life and Times of Gregory the Great* (1980); Pierre Riché, *Education and Culture in the Barbarian West: Sixth Through Eighth Centuries,* John J. Contreni, trans. (1976); Robert Rodes, Jr., *Ecclesiastical Administration in Medieval England* (1976); Jeffrey B. Russell, *A History of Medieval Christianity: Prophecy and Order* (1968); John Joseph Ryan, *Saint Peter Damiani and His Canonical Sources* (1956); Gangolf Schrimpf, *Das Werk des Johannes Scottus Eriugena im Rahmen des Wissenschaftsverständnisses seiner Zeit* (1982); Theodor Schieffer, *Winfrid-Bonifatius* (1954); Richard W. Southern, *Western Society and the Church in the Middle Ages* (1970); Charles H. Talbot, *The Anglo-Saxon Missionaries in Germany* (1954); Walter Ullmann, *The Growth of Papal Government in the Middle Ages,* 3rd ed. (1970), and *A Short History of the Papacy in the Middle Ages* (1972); Klaus Vielhaber, *Gottschalk der Sachse* (1956).

JEFFREY B. RUSSELL

[See also **Byzantine Church; Byzantine Empire; Celtic Church; Decretals, False; Donation of Constantine; Filioque; Gregory I the Great, Pope; Holy Roman Empire; Iconoclasm; Law, Canon; Missions and Missionaries, Christian; Monasticism; Papacy, Origins and Development of; Reform, Idea of; Schisms, Eastern-Western Church.**]

CHURCH, LATIN: 1054 to 1305. Between 1054 and 1305 the Western church experienced far-reaching changes not surpassed in any comparable historical period. The church of 1305 is barely recognizable as the descendant of the mid-eleventh-century church. To be sure, there were notable continuities, guaranteed by a coherent set of fundamental beliefs, the continuing use of Latin, and a well-nurtured reverence for tradition. Yet the changes were far more striking than the continuities, and accordingly will receive a greater share of attention in this article. We need to abolish such static notions as "medieval church" or "age of faith" in order to perceive differences from one generation to the next, whether they be in institutions, matters of belief, or modes of worship. Here I will deal successively with the governance of the church, the religious orders, relations with Byzantium and Islam, intellectual life, and the laity—matters that were thoroughly intertwined and that need to be seen in the context of contemporary developments in European society. Population, stable since Carolingian times, increased threefold by the early fourteenth century. New lands were opened up, and economic activity, both urban and agricultural, became considerably more complex. Merchants emerged to take a dominant place in the new urban society, along with such new professionals as bankers, notaries, lawyers, doctors, and schoolmasters. Most pervasive of all was the greatly expanded quantity and use of money, the lifeblood of the market economy.

GOVERNANCE OF THE CHURCH

The first of a long series of reform popes, Leo IX, died in 1054. He had been chosen for the papacy and installed in it by his cousin, Emperor Henry III. Leo had brought advisers from his native Lorraine and other northern regions, in particular Humbert of Moyenmoutier, whom he named cardinal bishop of Silva Candida in 1050. He thus surrounded himself with associates free of ties to the Roman aristocracy, with the notable exception of the Roman priest and monk Hildebrand (later Pope Gregory VII), whom he placed in charge of the papal estates. On three journeys to France and Germany, Leo had conducted synod after synod in which he issued decrees against clerical concubinage and marriage and against simony. To the astonishment of many prelates, he had suspended or even deposed several intransigent bishops and abbots.

The growing incursion of the Normans into the Italian peninsula south of Rome was seen as a potential threat to papal independence, and so in 1053 Leo had led an army, provided by Henry III, against the Normans. He was captured but released shortly afterward. Just before his death he sent a delegation under Cardinal Humbert to Constantinople, to discuss with the emperor and the patriarch their shared concerns over the Normans. But where they might have united against a common enemy, they instead hammered away at their own differences of belief and practice, such as the *Filioque* clause, clerical celibacy, fasting on the sabbath, and the use of unleavened bread in Communion. Intolerance on both sides led to recriminations and ultimately to a complete, formal break, in which the cardinal excommunicated the patriarch in the name of the pope and the patriarch excommunicated the pope. (The curses then exchanged were retracted only in 1965.) Although the ideal of reuniting the churches was revived from time to time, the schism of 1054 essentially allowed the Western church to go its own way, to build up its own resources, to develop its own identity and destiny. The geopolitical entity embodied in the eleventh-century papal notion of Christendom was in reality the Western church.

After Henry III died in 1056, leaving his five-year-old son as heir, a faction of Roman nobles regained control of Rome and the papacy. The reformers, now joined by the famous hermit and writer Peter Damian, chose Nicholas II (1059–1061), whose brief pontificate was momentous. First of all, he issued a decree providing for the election of the pope by the cardinal clergy of Rome, a method that, with only slight variations, has remained in use to the present. Second, he reversed his predecessors' policies toward the Normans by making an alliance with them; the

Normans thereby became the guarantors of the new electoral system. Nicholas also decreed that no cleric could receive a church from the hands of any layman.

Hildebrand had remained influential under Nicholas and a chief adviser throughout the reign of Alexander II (1061–1073), whom he succeeded as Gregory VII. His reign (1073–1085) provided as much tension and drama, especially in the showdown with Henry IV, now of age, as any papal reign in history, although in lasting accomplishments that of Nicholas II had probably been more important. The *Dictates of the Pope* (1075), which seem to be propositions for which Gregory found support in biblical, patristic, and canonical sources, reveal his unbounded ambitions for the Roman church—for example, the propositions that the Roman pontiff alone is rightly to be called universal, that he alone can depose or reinstate bishops, that he is the only one whose feet are to be kissed by all princes, that he may depose emperors, that he may absolve subjects of unjust men from their fealty, and that the Roman church has never erred, nor ever shall err.

On a less exalted level the reform moved along: in 1074 all simoniacal priests were ordered deposed and all married priests forbidden to celebrate Mass. There were hostile reactions throughout Europe, but these decrees were repeated in 1075 along with one proclaiming the excommunication of any emperor, king, prince, or other lay power who henceforth presumed to invest anyone with a bishopric or any other ecclesiastical office. The immediate issue was the emperor's investiture of a new archbishop of Milan. Pope and emperor each claimed to depose the other during the course of 1076, but since the papacy was successful in building alliances with Henry's enemies, Henry yielded, making his famous gesture of penance at Canossa in January 1077. Still, the following years saw the creation of both an antiking and an antipope. And Henry had control of Rome in 1085 when Gregory died in Norman hands at Salerno.

Gregory had offended nearly every prince and prelate in Europe, a fact that guided his successors into more moderate modes of speech and action. The most accomplished of these was Urban II (1088–1099), a French nobleman who built himself a considerable base of support in France through his opposition to the German emperor. While Gregory's most ambitious theocratic claims were quietly dropped, the issue of investiture remained central. Agreements with the French and English kings were reached in 1107, but with the Germans only in 1122 at Worms. The emperor no longer chose bishops or invested them with ring and staff; he could be present at their election and receive homage from them for the feudal lands connected with their churches.

This rather prosaic compromise gives a pale reflection of a more substantive compromise. The theocratic monarchy or sacred kingship of Carolingian times was finished. The king was neither a priest nor a specially sacred person; in matters spiritual he was a layman. At the same time the pope had not become a theocratic monarch ruling over all Christendom, as the *Dictates of the Pope* at least hinted was Gregory's desire. The papacy, though, had gained its independence from the emperor and from the Roman nobility. The popes, moreover, had greatly expanded the range of their activity within the church itself, assembling collections of law, increasing the number of papal agents, calling synods, deposing bishops and abbots, and hearing appeals from all over. These side effects of the Gregorian reform movement lasted well beyond Gregory's time, and grew eventually into the main concern of twelfth-century popes: the building of the papal monarchy.

Urban II, a former prior of Cluny, brought extensive administrative experience to the papal throne. It was he who laid the foundations for the curia, a papal court on the model of a royal court, meaning both a court of law and the central administration as a whole. The cardinals became more of an advisory body to the pope, operating somewhat like a royal council, and they affixed their signatures to papal privileges. Urban made major innovations in the papal chapel, the writing office (later called the chancery), and the apostolic camera, the papal financial organization. The effective head of this government was the chancellor, usually a cardinal, who in several instances eventually succeeded to the papacy.

After the Concordat of Worms, Calixtus II called the First Lateran Council (1123) in Rome. It was the first ecumenical council held in the West and under the aegis of a pope. The council celebrated the settlement with the Germans as well as the papacy's success in establishing full dominion over the church. In the disputed election of 1130, victory went to a group of cardinals less interested in pushing the reform further and more interested in strengthening the papacy's position in Italy and its control over the church. Innocent II (1130–1143) was the first pope to reserve a whole class of cases, having to do with assaults on clerics, for papal dis-

pensation. He was also the first to intervene directly to secure a benefice for a particular individual. Soon the pope was claiming special rights in a particular category of benefices, those vacated by newly appointed bishops.

This gradual but unmistakable extension of papal authority had solid legal backing. Out of the relatively chaotic condition of canon law as it was in the 1050's, and after the hectic scrambles to seek justification on particular points during the investiture struggle, canon law was brought into an intellectually and functionally coherent order in Gratian's *Decretum,* completed at Bologna in about 1140. Here the rights for which earlier popes had fought were fully accepted and clearly laid out: the pope could grant and revoke privileges; the pope could interpret and even dispense with the canons of councils; the pope held supreme legislative and judicial authority within the church.

The expansion of papal government and of papal authority was not as simple a matter as a few ambitious popes trying to enhance their office. At least as much has to be credited to the thousands of individuals who sought advice, requested authoritative answers, and carried appeals to the papal curia. All governments grew in the twelfth century, but none more than that of the papacy. The bureaucracy was totally unlike anything that could have existed before, because it was staffed by university-trained lawyers. Costs of government also were increasing, and in the case of the papacy were met largely by fees. The first Cistercian pope, Eugenius III (1145–1153), had to put up with the complaints of St. Bernard of Clairvaux about the pope's apparently full-time immersion in legal affairs. Nor did Bernard and many other critics refrain from stressing the theme of avarice in and around the papal court; the anonymous, twelfth-century *Gospel According to the Mark of Silver* is the most famous of the satirical critiques on this theme.

The ascendant role of law at the curia received appropriate recognition with the accession of a noted lawyer, Alexander III (1159–1181). For the century and a half from Alexander to Boniface VIII, all the important popes were trained lawyers. With more cases coming before the pope all the time, papal decisions, conveyed in decretals, often led to modifications of the law. Hence the decretals themselves were collected and became the object of academic scrutiny. Under Alexander the day-to-day business of the pope was to sit as a judge and hear cases.

The popes of the 1140's and 1150's had faced a grave threat from a revolt by the commune of Rome, but survived with help from the Normans and then from Emperor Frederick I Barbarossa. But from 1154 to 1177, when Frederick and the papacy were engaged in a struggle for territorial power in Italy, the papacy emerged unscarred mainly as a result of the unrelenting resistance of the Lombard communes to Frederick. Then Frederick's son, Henry VI, set out on a course that seemed to realize all of the popes' nightmares. He consolidated his holdings in central Italy and conquered Sicily. He married Constance, heiress presumptive of Sicily, and when he died prematurely in 1197, his heir, Frederick II, had some kind of claim on all the territory from the North Sea to Sicily. Frederick was still a child, and at the next papal election the relatively pacific group of cardinals that had held control since the death of Alexander III was pushed aside by a more aggressive group that chose the youngest cardinal (and former law professor), Lothair of Segni, who became Innocent III (1198–1216).

Innocent saw the papacy as a supreme court of appeal for all Christendom, and he used the notion of the "fullness of power" to exercise absolute authority. His greatest challenge came from the Cathars, a dualist group regarded as heretical that since the 1160's had been growing in numbers and influence to the point where, in southern France especially, it constituted a rival church. Innocent exhorted absentee bishops to return to their flocks and sent teams of Cistercian preachers to convert Cathars to Catholic Christianity. When his legate Peter of Castelnau was assassinated in 1208, he initiated a crusade against the Cathars. At the Fourth Lateran Council in 1215, Innocent had a clear statement of orthodox faith formulated that could be used to separate the Catholics from the Cathars; he also had the Council decree that individual Christians must make a private, spoken confession to their respective parish priests once a year, in preparation for a required annual Communion at Easter time.

Whereas his predecessors had been skeptical or even hostile toward groups that were even close to the boundaries of heterodoxy, Innocent preferred to draw that boundary as precisely but as generously as possible, and then to give wide latitude to individuals and groups that displayed a new, evangelical enthusiasm. In this way he both encouraged and gained control of several groups, the most notable being the Franciscans, whom he approved perhaps by a spoken agreement in about 1210 and in writing in 1215, and

the Dominicans, whom his successor Honorius III approved in 1216.

Innocent gained far more direct control over the Papal States than his predecessors had held, especially by his levying of taxes. He lectured princes and intervened in their affairs in Germany, England, France, Aragon, Portugal, Poland, and Denmark. His interventions could all be justified on theoretical grounds, but in practical terms he had embroiled the church in political matters all over Europe and had shown a willingness to use force in support of his political objectives. These were dangerous precedents.

The volume of papal business increased in the thirteenth century. Disputed episcopal elections were of course referred to the papacy, and a growing number of situations in which the pope could intervene were enumerated, as prelude to the eventual claim by popes of the fourteenth century to the right to appoint all bishops. The canonization of saints had been reserved to the papacy from the time of Alexander III. The average number of surviving letters for each year under various popes can be taken as an index of the volume of papal business. For the time of Leo IX the figure is 35, and it did not change greatly until about 1130. The figure for the reign of Innocent II rises to 72; for Alexander III, 179; for Innocent III, 280; for Innocent IV (1243–1254), 730. By the fourteenth century the number reaches the thousands.

The reigns of Gregory IX (1227–1241) and Innocent IV were marked by such increases in business and by corresponding attempts to squeeze every bit of revenue out of the church that the well-established papal claims to supremacy would allow. Gregory instituted the Inquisition, a special tribunal directly subordinate to the pope, to deal with heretics. He also had a collection of decretals codified and added to the *Decretum* in 1234 as the *Liber Extravagantium*. But the energies of Gregory and Innocent went largely into their running conflict with Frederick II. In addition to the weapons of war, they used excommunication, interdict, and (at the First Council of Lyons in 1245) deposition. Following Frederick's death in 1250, the papacy was no less relentless in beating down his descendants and in trying to secure a friendly power in southern Italy.

The involvement in politics, the obsession with raising revenue, the ever deepening morass of judicial business, and extreme centralization all tended to erode episcopal authority and the spiritual authority of the entire hierarchy. These attitudes were forcefully expressed in reports solicited by Gregory X (1271–1276) prior to the Second Council of Lyons in 1274. Yet the papacy so monopolized power that there seemed to be no other force in the church capable of reforming it, and in the end nothing came of the council.

With the communes and the empire effectively out of the way as potential problems, the papacy had to face the national kingdoms. The most extreme expression ever given the now standard claims of the papacy was advanced by the jurist and diplomat Boniface VIII (1294–1303), but these claims sounded flat after three-quarters of a century of undistinguished fighting, politicking, tax collecting, and heretic hunting. The issues were taxation, both royal and papal, of French clerics and jurisdiction, again both royal and papal, over the secular activities of a bishop. The term "sovereignty" was not then used, but the concept we understand as underlying it was. When agents of the French king briefly held the pope prisoner at Anagni and forced his successors to pardon the assailants and to repudiate some of his more extreme statements, the grand days of the papacy were certainly numbered.

During the two and a half centuries between Leo IX, a pope who had been placed in office by the emperor, and Boniface VIII, who was humiliated by the French king, the papacy went through a series of remarkable transformations. Chief among these were the gaining of independence through election by the College of Cardinals, the codification of canon law, the building of the papal monarchy and its bureaucratic curia, and its nearly complete takeover of the administration of the Western church. Within these spheres the papacy was on the whole successful, whereas the popes' mixing in worldly affairs had largely negative results. Individual enemies were defeated, but the church was not strengthened. The papacy's control of the judicial and legislative functions gave it effective control of the church; the lack of a powerful executive, including an army and the fiscal basis to support it, rendered its involvement in European politics ultimately futile. The impact of this involvement on the spiritual life of the church cannot be calculated, but it was clearly not favorable.

THE RELIGIOUS ORDERS

While responsibilities for governing the church and for ministering to the lay faithful belonged mainly to the secular clergy, those individuals who gave up their worldly lives to devote themselves totally to religion entered what was technically called the "religious life"; they belonged to the "regular" clergy, as distinguished from the "secular," because they lived according to a rule. Between 1054 and 1305 the religious life underwent change that was as startling and comprehensive as that of the papacy itself; it exhibited inventiveness and experimentation, intellectual vitality and spiritual integrity, and intense rivalries as well.

Prior to the eleventh century the religious life consisted essentially of traditional Benedictine monasticism. Each monastery was an independent corporation, supported by gifts from the landed class and possessed of certain jurisdictional rights in its own domain. The monasteries thus fitted in not only with the basic economic structures of the period but also with the jurisdictional and political structures.

Wealthy and much concerned with liturgical opulence, the monasteries slipped quite naturally into the new money economy. With their immense domains they were among the first to turn surplus produce to a profit. The chamberlain (in charge of finances) became more important than the cellarer (in charge of provisions). Under such circumstances the claim of monastic poverty began to wear thin.

The first sustained criticism of the established monastic order originated in northern Italy at the start of the eleventh century. It came in the form of an eremitic movement that drew heavily on the examples of the Egyptian desert fathers. The major figures in this movement—Romuald of Ravenna, Peter Damian, and John Gualberti, had all had personal experience in some of the earliest of the newly activated centers of commerce as well as in some of the leading abbeys of the established monastic life, which they emphatically rejected. Toward the end of the eleventh century and the beginning of the next, a similar movement, in which the leading figures were Bernard of Tiron and Stephen of Muret, appeared in western France. These critics were judging the monks not on the monks' own terms but by new standards. Their eremitic life constituted a rejection of both the new cities and the old monasteries; it avoided the problems of the one and the compromises of the other.

Similar in inspiration to the eremitic leaders were others who, instead of establishing hermitages that evolved slowly into monasteries, passed directly to the idea of setting up monasteries as free as possible from the accumulated imperfections of the old monasticism: Bruno of Cologne, who founded the Carthusians, and Norbert of Xanten, who established the Premonstratensians.

Robert of Molesme was another such seeker after monastic perfection, familiar with the eremitic life as well. He and some of his companions moved in 1098 to the "new monastery," Cîteaux, where he was determined that they should follow the Benedictine Rule strictly. The fortunes of Cîteaux and its daughter monasteries are well known. When their greatest leader, Bernard of Clairvaux, died in 1153, the Cistercian order consisted of 343 houses, and by the end of the twelfth century the figure passed 500.

The reform of the life of canons, urged by Peter Damian and Hildebrand, and at least recommended by the Roman synod of 1059, sought in one sense to make priests live in the manner of monks. The canonical reform as it actually developed (it had started before 1059) eventually appeared in all parts of Europe, but an important distinction is to be made between those areas in which cathedral chapters were reformed and those in which, instead, new communities of regular canons were founded. The studies made so far suggest that reforms of existing communities were common in those areas where nobles lived in towns and had relatively liquid fortunes (central and northern Italy, the Alpine provinces, Provence, Aquitaine, and Spain). But in England, northern and central France, the Rhineland, and western Germany, where the nobility had an interest in retaining the landed prebends, the old canonical life changed little or not at all, and canonical reform had to enter via newly established religious communities. Those who patronized such communities were mostly people involved in commerce, industry, and finance.

The orders of mendicant friars synthesized the leading developments in the religious life of the preceding two centuries. St. Dominic was a regular canon and St. Francis was a layman. Francis, moreover, lived a quasi-eremitic existence in the early days of his movement and urged on his followers the idea of an itinerant hermitage. Both orders recognized the impelling need for preaching and the authenticating role of personal poverty in the life of the preacher.

The membership of both orders came from the dominant sectors of urban society, noble and bourgeois alike, and only rarely from the countryside. No evidence suggests that poor people joined these orders. Their leaders showed an astute understanding of urban sociology. They realized that they would find larger audiences and larger sources of material support in towns. They were aware that towns produce greater social and moral problems than the countryside. And as for a sense of obligation to rural dwellers, they were aware that cultural influences tend to work their way outward from cities into the countryside.

The changes in the religious life over the eleventh and twelfth centuries can be summarized as follows. First, the old monastic order continued to exist throughout this period, living off endowed lands. Second, the monks did not watch this proliferation of forms of religious life silently, but denounced it vigorously. Third, the secular hierarchy eventually expressed concern about this proliferation by proscribing approval of any new rules at the Fourth Lateran Council. Fourth, no religious group fostered greater enmity than the friars, bitterly denounced by the monks and also by secular clerics, especially for their incursions into the universities and into the care of souls. Fifth, the Franciscans were kept under careful control by the papacy, and when certain of their numbers felt that such control was subverting the goals of their saintly founder, they formed the faction of Franciscan Spirituals and suffered dearly for their nonconformity in the early fourteenth century. Sixth, the friars fostered the idea that lay people can lead spiritual lives as worthy as any who profess "religion" full-time and live by a rule. All those who live by the one rule of Christ, the Gospel, are truly religious; so went the argument. In such ways the monopoly on the religious life still held by the monks during the eleventh century was irreparably broken.

RELATIONS WITH BYZANTIUM AND ISLAM

During the earlier Middle Ages western Europe was, in comparison with Byzantium and Islam, something of a rural backwater, acted on by external forces rather than acting for itself. The reversal of this situation, beginning in the mid eleventh century, was essential for the subsequent development of the Western church. The Magyars and Norsemen were absorbed and converted to Christianity. When new peoples—the Seljuk Turks in the eleventh century, the Ottomans in the thirteenth—arrived at the frontiers, it was Byzantium that had to suffer the blows and act as a buffer for western Europe. Meanwhile the West regained the offensive on three fronts: Spain, the western Mediterranean, and southern Italy. The popes supported all these efforts, and Victor III (1086–1087) actually helped organize the successful Pisan-Genoese expedition against Mahdia on the coast of modern Tunisia.

This sanctioning of external aggression was the

reverse side of a policy favoring internal peace. The Peace of God, a movement that began in Aquitaine in the late tenth century, had been taken up by such strong princes as the duke of Normandy and had drawn the favorable attention of Henry III and of the reforming popes. The main idea all along was to stop fighting among Christians (meaning always Catholics, or Western Christians). Declarations of the Peace of God and Truce of God were standard parts of reforming synods as well as decrees against simony and clerical marriage.

One leading motive for travel in the eleventh century was to make a pilgrimage, a penitential journey to a holy shrine, perhaps local and obscure, perhaps faraway and famous, like Santiago de Compostela, Rome, or the Holy Land. The number of such pilgrimages to faraway places increased considerably with the improved conditions favoring western Europe in the eleventh century.

Then the Seljuk Turks, already converted to Islam, arrived. In 1071 they inflicted a crushing defeat on the Byzantine army at Manazkert in Armenia. Gregory VII hoped to organize an expedition to aid the Greeks, but the conflict with Henry IV did not permit him to carry it out. Gregory was so in need of Norman support that, instead of aiding the Greeks, he approved a Norman invasion of the Balkan peninsula. Only after Urban II had smoothed relations with the Byzantine court could talk of such an expedition resume, and by that time the Turkish incursions into the Holy Land had made the great pilgrimage all the more difficult and dangerous.

Urban skillfully interwove several papal policies at Clermont in 1095. He asserted papal leadership by calling for an armed pilgrimage to liberate the Holy Land from the Muslim infidels. Fulcher of Chartres reported the way Urban linked the Peace of God and this expedition, which was to become the First Crusade: "Let those who have been accustomed to wage private warfare against the faithful now carry on to a successful conclusion a war against infidels; let those who were for long robbers now become soldiers of Christ."

The juridical definition of the crusade came after the fact, in the twelfth century, though all the elements were present from the time of Urban. These were that the crusade be called by a pope, that it be directed against enemies of the faith, and that it be undertaken as an act of religious penitence. Moreover, the promise to go was made in the form of a religious vow; the symbol of a vow properly taken was the cross; the property of one who went re-

mained under special protection (a contribution of the Peace of God); and the participant was granted a full indulgence for his sins (a contribution of the pilgrimage).

The religious orders played their parts in sponsoring the Crusades. The Cluniacs had been among the chief propagators of the Peace of God and of the Spanish Reconquest. On his way to Clermont, Pope Urban II made an extended visit to his former abbot, Hugh of Cluny. There is no surprise in Cluny's avid support for the First Crusade. It was the same in the 1140's when the Cistercian Pope Eugenius III launched the Second Crusade, commissioned St. Bernard to preach on its behalf, and placed the growing Cistercian network at its disposal. Bernard lent his prestige and support to a group of knights who formed a military religious order, the Templars; they and the Hospitalers embodied the perfect union of the religious life with the war against Islam.

The Crusades not only constituted a full-scale war against Islam but also gave occasion for a deterioration of Greek-Latin relations to the point where, by 1204, the Fourth Crusade turned into a war against Byzantium. The passage of the Western (called "Frankish") warriors through Constantinople in 1097 caused friction, and during the passage through in the Second Crusade (1147), the French king's chaplain, Odo of Deuil, reported of the Greeks: "They were judged not to be Christians, and the Franks considered killing them a matter of no importance and hence could with the more difficulty be restrained from pillage and plundering." By the early thirteenth century no such restraint remained.

There were few exceptions to this tale of unrelieved aggression. Peter Damian expressed reservations about the church's sanctioning of force for any purpose. In the 1130's and again in the 1150's, Anselm of Havelberg, a leading spokesman for the canonical reform movement, engaged in serious theological discussions with Greek colleagues at Constantinople. And in the 1140's the abbot of Cluny, Peter the Venerable, sponsored the first Latin translation of the Koran. The First Crusade had been a great military success, and the Western church had expanded into the new Latin Kingdom of Jerusalem. The time for criticism of the crusade came only after things had started to go badly; there were isolated expressions of disillusionment in the later twelfth century, but in the thirteenth century criticism became widespread, persistent, and bitter. Two very personal approaches to the matter of Islam remained without effect, and thus stand out as oddities: one was the journey of St. Francis to Egypt to preach directly to the sultan (1219); the other was the peace treaty that Frederick II signed with the sultan (1228). Francis' initiative was greeted by silence, although in the 1270's William of Tripoli did propose the preparation of Christian missionaries trained in Arabic as a substitute for the crusade; Frederick's initiative was immediately repudiated by Pope Gregory IX.

The Eastern and Western churches were reunited under the leadership of the papacy by the conquest of Constantinople in 1204. But that reunion was never more than formal and was always dependent on the Latins' military presence. Reunion could not outlast the Latin Empire of Constantinople, which collapsed in 1261. The long-range impact of the Western adventure in Constantinople was to weaken the Byzantine Empire even more and to hasten its ultimate conquest by the Ottoman Turks.

The turning of the Fourth Crusade against schismatic Greeks instead of infidel Muslims was but one of its perversions. The crusade went into service against the Cathars, against the Hohenstaufen, and against the kingdom of Aragon. By the second half of the thirteenth century, it was a war against the pope's political enemies. The fate of the crusade was clearly linked to that of the papacy. Papal prestige benefited greatly from the early success of the crusading movement, and suffered commensurately when the overseas crusades failed so badly and the crusade in Europe displayed spiritual means directed so obviously to political ends. The lasting achievements of the crusade were most evident in Europe: in Spain, where the Reconquest was complete by 1248 except for Granada; and in eastern Europe, where German knights pushed the Slavs back from their old frontier.

INTELLECTUAL LIFE

The markedly different types of learning that prevailed at particular periods, with regard to both method and subject matter, reinforce as well as help elucidate our notion of the dynamism of the Western church. Here I will make brief reference to three central themes: monastic learning, Scholastic learning, and the role of the friars.

The kind of learning prevalent in the eleventh century was decidedly monastic: found in monasteries, dominated by monks building on traditions laid down by St. Benedict and Cassiodorus, and dedicated to the service of the monastic life. Bookish learning was pursued because it served the needs of the monastic liturgy, the needs of the missions to pagans,

and the need to preserve the sacred inheritance of Christian antiquity, including the language in which it had been passed along.

Monastic scholars learned to absorb biblical and patristic literature. They read it over and over, memorizing whole passages. They learned to revere this literature to the point that they incorporated it; its vocabulary, its imagery, became theirs. The Benedictine Rule counseled against contentiousness; and contentiousness (dialectic) is indeed missing from the formal structure of monastic education.

The monks succeeded in preserving ancient literature. They treated it and also the very books they wrote it down in as treasure. A new kind of learning was already challenging this older type in the twelfth century, when its greatest practitioner, Bernard of Clairvaux, lived and wrote. A contentious individual to be sure, Bernard knew and handled the entire Christian literary heritage more ably than any other thinker. But already in city schools in northern Italy and in France a new type of learning was coming into use, "scholastic" as opposed to monastic.

Historically it was the bishops who had responsibility for the church's teaching, but only in the eleventh century and after were the urban structures of Europe sufficiently developed to allow the regular functioning of episcopal schools, which in time, and often with papal encouragement, became universities in the thirteenth century. In these schools, students were not trained merely to reproduce the work of their predecessors, in the way that novices were supposed to perpetuate the monastic community, but to go out and do something quite different: to serve as priests (some eventually as bishops), as lawyers, as physicians, as merchants, or as government officials. They were taught not merely by elders charged with initiating their juniors but also by professional specialists, paid for their work like other urban professionals.

The method of this kind of learning was contention: the asking of questions, the posing of paradoxes, the quoting of conflicting sources and authorities, and debate. Students were trained to marshal evidence in support of theses. They had necessarily to question authorities, especially since, as Abelard demonstrated, even the most respected authorities often gave contradictory views. The attitude toward books as well as toward the authoritative authors changed; the book came to be seen as tool instead of treasure, something to be produced as rapidly and cheaply as possible for sale in university towns.

Of course there were significant continuities between monastic and Scholastic learning—for example, in the emphasis given the Bible and the church fathers. But whereas Scripture remained the object of monastic learning, the Schoolmen concentrated increasingly on a given problem, and Scripture became one adjunct to this process, useful to the extent that it could provide authoritative statements. All these developments were well under way when, toward the close of the twelfth century, the writings of Aristotle became accessible in Latin translation and greatly invigorated the search for a dialectical method and for rational explanations of natural phenomena.

The leading, though hardly exclusive, practitioners of Scholastic thought in the thirteenth-century universities were friars, who embodied a new integration of the intellectual with the religious life. The monks of the eleventh century had represented such an integration. They had a coherent intellectual program with purpose, curriculum, and methods suited to their religious life. Then, as we have seen, the religious life went off onto a series of experiments that, for all their interest and importance, were of no particular originality as far as education is concerned. The frontier in education advanced in the city schools, quite independent of the heady advances being made in the religious life. The two lines of development, religious and educational, moved along separately, converging only very briefly in the careers of certain individuals. Then in the early thirteenth century the friars reintegrated these two lines of development. The new learning, in both method and content, was put at the service of their new, urban spirituality, which was oriented toward an active apostolate to the lay faithful.

THE LAITY

In the social theory put forth by some writers in the tenth and eleventh centuries, society was made up of *oratores* (those who pray), *bellatores* (those who fight), and *laboratores* (those who work). Of interest here is the exclusive nature of the functions that defined major social divisions: monks were not supposed to fight, and knights did not work in the fields. The religious function was equally exclusive. Monks, canons, and priests did all the praying; they performed the religious function for themselves and everybody else. They were endowed, by those in the rest of society who had any surplus wealth, to serve

as vicarious holy men for the rest of society. They were the indispensable intermediaries between the natural and the supernatural, between the living and the dead. They interceded for others; they made expiatory prayers for others; they performed the liturgy. Lay people, if present at all, were spectators. The same social theory that divided social groups by function was also hierocratic: those who prayed performed the most important function in society.

One small group—anointed kings—tended to blur these distinctions, but the investiture controversy removed all ambiguity on this point. "Whoever heard of a dying person calling in a king to give the last rites?" asked Gregory VII in one of his polemical exchanges with Henry IV. In the Gregorian view, which was widely accepted, kings were henceforth relegated to the camp of the laity, and in matters spiritual all lay people were inferior to all members of the clergy. By about 1090 Bonizo of Sutri, in his *Liber de vita Christiana*, a collection of canonistic extracts with commentary, lumped together kings, nobles, merchants, and peasants in a single *ordo laicus*. The point was rubbed in during the twelfth century with the reserving of Communion in both kinds (wine as well as bread) to the clergy.

Gregorian polemics had another noteworthy, although unintended, effect in this area. By calling attention repeatedly to the sinfulness of the clergy and setting standards higher than many could meet, the papal reformers fed lay dissatisfaction with the clergy. This was dramatically clear in the Patarine affair at Milan, where the papal reformers were allied with a mostly lay movement against the clergy of that city. Similarly, the vigorous polemics among competing religious groups over the form of the religious life had the side effect of demystifying some if not all of those groups.

In the transition from monastic learning to Scholastic, education remained very much in ecclesiastical hands: first monastic, then episcopal, and then papal. One important novelty of the city schools and the universities, however, was that the education they offered was available to lay people and served some of the lay professions. The clerical monopoly on literacy and formal learning thus encountered its first challenge.

The aspirations of lay people found expression in many different ways that almost inevitably contained some element of anticlericalism. Followers of Peter of Bruys burned crosses, which they took to be a symbol of the torture and death, not the victory, of

Jesus, and they burned down churches, which they judged to be unnecessary. But such incidents stand out as spectacular exceptions. Lay enthusiasm found expression above all in the way crowds flocked to hear preachers. No longer willing to be entirely passive about religion, lay people sought avidly to hear preaching, to hear biblical stories, to hear saints' lives—and at the same time to be entertained. This was especially true in towns. Since the ordinary priest was ill prepared to preach, and the reformed religious movements of the twelfth century did not supply enough capable preachers, many unauthorized preachers stepped in to meet the popular demand. The more successful of these, such as Henry of Lausanne, combined great rhetorical skill with an appearance of apostolic poverty and humility. The story of the conversion of the wealthy Lyonnais merchant Waldes in the 1170's is instructive on this point. He was moved to change his life by hearing the account of a saint's life, and this was told not in church by a cleric but on the street corner by an entertainer. His first reaction was to go to a priest to ask what was contained in the Gospels. And once his coterie of followers took shape, they stressed preaching, by example as well as by word, in imitation of the Apostles. To this was added the use of vernacular translations of portions of the Bible.

With the appearance of the friars in the early thirteenth century, many of these earlier, unauthorized notions and practices were absorbed into orthodoxy and thus legitimized. The Dominicans were, officially, the Order of Preachers; the Franciscans engaged in preaching no less assiduously. Thus an aggressive ministry to lay people was being organized at the same time as the Fourth Lateran Council was insisting on the increased involvement of lay people in the religious life of the church. The laity were taught to memorize the Lord's Prayer and to recite it often. The Dominicans fostered the devotion known as the rosary. The feast of Corpus Christi was established in 1264 to enlist popular enthusiasm for the doctrine of the Eucharist and popular participation in eucharistic worship.

Not the least pressing problem posed for the Western church by the development of an urban society and a commercial, monetary economy was the lack of a Christian ethic properly suited to such a society and economy. Traditional Christian theology was hostile to cities, to trade, to money, to professional fees, to loans—in short, to all that was essential in the newly developing sectors of Western society. But by the thirteenth century the Schoolmen

and their scholarly heirs among the friars had produced carefully limited justifications of private property, money, commercial profits, business partnerships, and moneylending.

The status of the laity in general was being upgraded. About 1218 Jacques de Vitry observed: "Not only those who renounce the world and go into religion are *regulares*, but so are also all the faithful of Christ who serve the Lord under the Gospel's rule and live by the orders of the single greatest Abbot or Father of all." A few decades later the popular Franciscan preacher Berthold of Regensburg commented that God had sanctified marriage more than any other order in the world.

The participation of the laity in some form of the religious life went beyond these statements: lay people could, and did, belong to confraternities, starting in the thirteenth century. Some of these were established by Franciscans, some by Dominicans, some by members of the two orders working together, and still others without any friars involved. The confraternities were particularly strong in the Mediterranean countries, a fact that reflects one of their founders' motives, which was to create a defensive barrier against heresy. The members carried on their ordinary lives with their families and in their work. The typical confraternity rule called for its members to attend Mass and a sermon together on one Sunday a month, to recite the Lord's Prayer regularly, to confess their sins at least two times a year (twice the minimum required by Lateran IV), to observe some of the same fasts that the friars did, to carry out cooperative works of charity, to help support needy members of the confraternity, and to be present at the funeral of any deceased confrere. Lay people could thus remain in their secular condition and at the same time engage in regular devotions and gain some of the benefits that went with membership in a religious community.

The combined programs of Lateran IV, the early thirteenth-century popes, and the mendicant orders for a renewed ministry to the faithful were largely successful. It is important to keep in mind, however, that these programs were formulated in large measure as responses to the spread of heresy, and that they included a ruthless, systematic suppression of dissent by means of crusade and inquisition. Occasional glimpses into the lives and thought of people living in rural backwaters give some indication of the persistence of ancient pagan beliefs and practices, the limited extent of Christianization, the strength of dissent, and the limitations of the Inquisition. One such glimpse is afforded by the exceptionally well documented case of Montaillou, a village in the Pyrenees where Catharism still flourished in the early years of the fourteenth century. Another is given by the study of the cult of St. Guinefort, a greyhound venerated in the countryside near Lyons for his miraculous capacity to cure sickly children or to justify their mothers' desperate resort to infanticide. The search for further glimpses of popular religious beliefs and practices remains one of the leading challenges for historians of the Western church.

CONCLUSION

Early in 1300, pilgrims began to stream into Rome. They appealed to the pope for the traditional plenary indulgences that, as rumor had it, were always given to any Christian coming to visit the bodies of Sts. Peter and Paul in a year that was a multiple of one hundred. No one at the curia claimed to know of this tradition, but Pope Boniface and his cardinals met in council to discuss the matter and decided to grant such a special indulgence in honor of the hundredth year. They specified that pilgrims had to stay in Rome for at least fifteen days during the year and had to make a daily round of visits to the basilicas of both Peter and Paul. The pope, moreover, enjoined his successors to make the same offer every hundred years. One northern Italian cleric wrote of the huge crowds in Rome, the plentiful supplies of meat, fish, bread, and wine, and the high cost of rooms and hay. He was at S. Paolo Fuori le Mura on Christmas Eve, when in an appalling mob scene several men and women were trampled to death. But what caught his eye especially was the sight of two priests standing on either side of the main altar holding rakes, "raking in infinite money" (*rastellantes infinitam pecuniam*).

This account of the first papal Jubilee is not lacking in archaic elements: the pilgrimage itself and popular devotion to the earthly remains of saints. The rest is new: the pope sitting in council with his cardinals, the exorbitantly long period during which the faithful had to pay room and board in Rome, the traffic in indulgences, and the shower of money. We get from this an up-to-date view of the Western church on the eve of the Avignon papacy, yet it is only one view among many. The church was also found in a rich variety of types of religious life; it was present in parishes and in confraternities, on the Scandinavian and Slavic frontiers, even in Montaillou.

Overall there was far greater diversity in the church of 1305 than in that of 1054. The earlier church was solidly monastic; religion was not strictly limited to the cloister, but that is where it mainly existed. It was practiced by a very few for the many. That religion was highly formal: every act of the monastic day, even outside the sanctuary, was a ritual. Its morality was conceived in terms of actions and counteractions: things one should or should not do, and other things one had to do to atone for transgressions. The Roman papacy held an honorific headship over the Western church, but in practical terms had very little contact with, and no control over, its constituent parts; as late as the 1050's and 1060's its claim to precedence was boldly challenged by the archbishop of Milan. Priests married, held property, performed liturgical functions, but generally did not preach. Lay people, once having been converted to Christianity, received little attention but also demanded little.

Seen against that earlier church, the church of 1305 has few similarities. The dominant place of the papacy within the institution is very striking, and the conspicuous presence of the law hardly less so. The law, which served the institution so well, had also permeated the areas of religious thought and behavior, with less satisfactory results. Many people had started to experience what Marie-Dominique Chenu called "the awakening of the conscience"; they lived by a fully absorbed and fully understood ethical system that rendered obsolete (for them) the old morality of action and counteraction. The later society was far more complex than the earlier, in terms of division of labor, social and geographic mobility, cognitive development, and moral choices. The greater diversity in the church of the early fourteenth century is a reflection of this greater social complexity. Leo IX and Gregory VII could not have imagined as a unity all that Boniface VIII and Clement V had inherited and were still trying desperately to hold together.

BIBLIOGRAPHY

Robert Brentano, *Two Churches: England and Italy in the Thirteenth Century* (1968); and *Rome Before Avignon: A Social History of Thirteenth-century Rome* (1974); Marie-Dominique Chenu, *L'éveil de la conscience dans la civilisation médiévale* (1969); and *Nature, Man, and Society in the Twelfth Century: Essays on New Theological Perspectives in the Latin West*, J. Taylor and L. K. Little, trans. (1968); Jacques Le Goff, *La naissance du Purgatoire* (1981); Hubert Jedin and John Dolan, eds., *Handbook of*

Church History (1969), III and IV; Emmanuel Le Roy Ladurie, *Montaillou: The Promised Land of Error*, B. Bray, trans. (1978); Lester K. Little, *Religious Poverty and the Profit Economy in Medieval Europe* (1978); Michel Mollat, *Les pauvres au moyen âge: Étude sociale* (1978); Robert I. Moore, *The Origins of European Dissent* (1977); Alexander Murray, *Reason and Society in the Middle Ages* (1978); Peter Partner, *The Lands of St. Peter: The Papal State in the Middle Ages and the Early Renaissance* (1972); Charles M. Radding, "Evolution of Medieval Mentalities: A Cognitive, Structural Approach," in *American Historical Review*, 83 (1978); Jean-Claude Schmitt, *Le saint lévrier: Guinefort, guérisseur d'enfants depuis le XIIIᵉ siècle* (1979); Richard W. Southern, *Western Society and the Church in the Middle Ages* (1970); Brian Tierney, *Origins of Papal Infallibility, 1150–1350* (1972); Walter Ullmann, "The Papacy as an Institution of Government in the Middle Ages," in *Studies in Church History*, 2 (1965); André Vauchez, *La sainteté en Occident aux derniers siècles du Moyen Age* (1981), and *La spiritualité du moyen âge occidental* (1975); John Yunck, *The Lineage of Lady Meed* (1963).

LESTER K. LITTLE

[See also **Bernard of Clairvaux, St.; Boniface VIII, Pope; Canossa; Carthusians; Cathars; Cistercian Order; Crusades and Crusader States; Curia, Papal; Decretals; Decretum; Dictatus Papae; Dominicans; Franciscans; Gregory VII, Pope; Gregory IX, Pope; Innocent III, Pope; Investiture and Investiture Controversy; John Gualberti, St.; Law, Canon; Monasticism; Papacy; Peace of God, Truce of God; Peter Damian, St.; Premonstratensians; Reform, Idea of; Romuald of Ravenna; Scholasticism, Scholastic Method; Urban II, Pope; Waldes.**]

CHURCH, LATIN: 1305 to 1500. However one views the history of the medieval church, the opening decade of the fourteenth century constitutes something of a watershed. In the late nineteenth century it was customary to depict the church of the fourteenth and fifteenth centuries as characterized by a degree of ecclesiastical decadence, theological bankruptcy, and religious decline so grievous as finally to alienate from the traditional patterns of churchly life the most truly committed and most deeply devout. Central to that picture was the assumption that in certain critical respects the period was in sharp discontinuity with the great age of medieval religion preceding.

The French degradation of Boniface VIII at Anagni in 1303, and the subsequent removal of the papacy to Avignon, was taken as a critical turning point in the history of the medieval church, inaugurating a shameful period of "Babylonian Captivity" to the vagaries of French royal policy, laying the foundation for the Great Schism of the West, and signaling the incipient collapse of the whole structure of ecclesiastical government within which medieval Catholicism had contrived to flourish. The prolonged residence at Avignon, the emergence in the schools of the nominalist theology, the retreat from the externals of religion reflected in the mysticism of Germany, the Netherlands, and England, the onset of the Great Schism, the rise in the conciliar movement of a constitutionalist opposition to the pretensions of Rome, and the more radical undermining by such heretics as Wyclif and Hus of the hierarchical order of the church—all these and more tended to be seen as interrelated harbingers of the Protestant Reformation.

Although this interpretation survives in the current literature, few historians today subscribe to it without extensive qualification. Rather, the tendency has been to stress the continuities binding the late-medieval church to that of the centuries preceding. Historians now trace the lineage of late-medieval piety back to the great era of spiritual flowering in the late eleventh and twelfth centuries, and it is amid the turbulence churned up in that same period by the Gregorian reform that heresy is seen to have first emerged as an important element in medieval society. Similarly, it is common now to concede that the remorseless efforts of the Avignonese pontiffs to exercise the fullness of papal jurisdiction over the provincial churches of Christendom represented the culmination of a development stretching back as far as the Gregorian movement. Other late-medieval phenomena had more proximate roots, but ones still stretching well back into the thirteenth century.

It was largely by virtue of its ability to provide effective leadership for the reform and crusading movements that the papacy had risen to a position of jurisdictional supremacy in the universal church. But no one familiar with the complaints about papal centralization voiced at the First and Second Councils of Lyons (1245 and 1274) will doubt that the papacy had begun to falter in that leadership long before the Avignonese era. Again, no one familiar with the diplomatic history of the latter half of the thirteenth century and the tendency of so many popes to support Angevin ambitions and side with French interests will be disposed to regard the "Francophilia" of the Avignonese pontiffs as an unheralded novelty.

These qualifications admitted, it is proper nonetheless to insist that the opening years of the four-teenth century did indeed constitute something of a turning point in the area of churchly life that we may designate as pertaining to governance, politics, and ecclesiastical structures.

GOVERNANCE, POLITICS, AND ECCLESIASTICAL STRUCTURES

In the wake of Anagni, of the extraordinary chain of events leading up to that incident, and of Boniface VIII's death shortly thereafter, the independence of the papacy was clearly threatened by French policy and by the extremes to which Philip IV's close advisers appeared willing to go. Much, therefore, depended on the moves that Boniface's immediate successors chose to make. Those successors, however, turned out to be pliant men who preferred not to risk the type of defiance that might well have mobilized widespread support on their behalf. The pontificate of the first of them, Benedict XI, lasted only eight months. The second, Bertrand de Got, archbishop of Bordeaux, was elected in 1305.

As archbishop of Bordeaux, Clement V had been a vassal of Edward I of England (as duke of Aquitaine); but he was a subject, nevertheless, of the French king, and his pontificate was punctuated by a series of compromising concessions to French wishes. Most notorious of these were his exoneration of Philip's agents for their actions against Boniface and his scandalous suppression of the Order of Knights Templar at the Council of Vienne (1311–1312). Even more damaging was the degree to which his appointments built up French influence in the college of cardinals and the speed with which they did so. So, too, was his failure even to visit Rome: in 1309, after four years of peregrination in southern France, he took up residence at Avignon—not technically at that time in French territory but divided from it only by the Rhône River. Clement did not transfer the seat of the papal curia from Rome, and there is no reason to think that he regarded his move to Avignon as in any way permanent. It is, nonetheless, customary to date the beginning of the Avignonese papacy from that year.

The Avignonese papacy (1309–1377). The papal residence at Avignon extended through seven pontificates: those of John XXII (1316–1334), Benedict XII (1334–1342), Clement VI (1342–1352), Innocent VI (1352–1362), Urban V (1362–1370), and Gregory XI (1370–1378). As long as they had to rely on the literary sources of the day—especially the English, Italian, and German chronicles—historians continued not only to endorse the old view of the Avignonese era as one of "Babylonian Captivity" but also to depict the Avignonese popes as morally corrupt, financially extravagant, administratively tyrannical, and the principal source of the numerous evils besetting the church at large and of the disastrous schism that was to ensue in 1378.

Only with the opening of the Vatican archives in 1884 and the publication of the papal registers did a more nuanced appraisal become possible. Over the years it has been the achievement especially of Georges Mollat, Bernard Guillemain, and Yves Renouard to have modified the traditionally negative representation of the Avignonese papacy's relationship with the French monarchy, of the personal moral character of the pontiffs, and of the growing centralization and absolutism of their papal government.

On the matter of the French affiliation, the evidence now suggests that these popes—"French" admittedly to a man, but all of them from the Languedoc, an area with a distinct cultural identity—were not as abjectly submissive to French royal policy as their foreign contemporaries alleged. During most of this period the great appeal of Avignon lay less in its proximity to France than in its being safe; Rome simply was not. Only the vigorous pursuit by John XXII and by the four successors of Benedict XII of an enormously expensive (and much criticized) policy of military reconquest and pacification of the Papal States made feasible Gregory XI's eventual return to Rome.

Similarly, at least after Clement V's harassed pontificate, there was less any "servility" in the relationship of these Avignonese pontiffs with the French kings than something of a return to the older pro-Angevin and generally pro-French policy of the previous century, a revival of the sense, so painfully violated during the pontificate of Boniface VIII, that France was the papacy's natural ally. More than anything else it is this strengthened affinity that explains the partiality of these pontiffs to the French cause during the Hundred Years War as well as the fact that the financial aid that several of them extended to the French kings surpassed that granted to the rulers of other nations. It should be remembered, moreover, that the revenues the papacy drew from France far surpassed those drawn from any of the other countries of Latin Christendom.

Nevertheless, the suspicions of hostile foreign

contemporaries are easy enough to understand. During a period of intermittent Anglo-French war and of renewed papal conflict with the German emperor, the Avignonese papacy was overwhelmingly French in complexion—all seven popes, 112 of the 134 cardinals they created, and, as Guillemain's careful calculations reveal, 70 percent of the curialists whose nation of origin can be established. Those calculations reveal also the remarkable degree to which these popes preferred to confer the cardinalate or curial office on those they knew best, on churchmen from their own native regions (Quercy, Gascony, and above all Limousin), and in the cases of Clement V, John XXII, and Clement VI, on members of their own families.

Those prone to emphasize the low moral stature of the Avignonese pontiffs have made much of this nepotism, but in the cases at least of Clement V and John XXII it appears above all to have reflected their need to build a faction of supporters on whose loyalty they could truly rely. Nor, though Clement V and Clement VI were wildly extravagant, does nepotism necessarily imply an extravagant or luxurious mode of life. John XXII was a man of simple habits and unostentatious life; so too was Benedict XII. The three successors of Clement VI all lived rather frugally, and all three, like Benedict XII, were men of reforming instinct. It is in the pontificate of Clement VI alone that one can discern at the papal court truly convincing evidence of the profligacy, dissipation, and luxury that came to be associated with the Avignonese papacy *tout court.*

This being so, the explanation for the enormous amount of contemporary criticism heaped on the Avignonese papacy—from French as well as English, Italian, and German sources—must be sought elsewhere than in the overwhelmingly French complexion of that papacy or in the personal characteristics or moral stature of its incumbents. It must be sought, instead, in what these popes actually did—especially in the policies pursued by John XXII during the longest and most significant of these pontificates, and in the extension of the whole structure of administrative centralization and fiscal exploitation pursued so persistently throughout this period.

John XXII's marked capacity as an administrator has often elicited the admiration of historians. But his equally marked inflexibility and stubbornness clearly did much to diminish his effectiveness. So too did the unfortunate juxtaposition of the unwise policies he adopted toward both Louis IV the Bavarian

and the Franciscans. The death of Emperor Henry VII had been followed by a double election, with Louis and Frederick the Fair of Austria both laying claim to the title. After the battle of Mühldorf (1322), however, Louis was clearly triumphant. John's stiff-necked refusal to recognize that fact, his claim that the imperial throne was still vacant, and his subsequent decision (in the teeth of opposition within the Sacred College of Cardinals) to excommunicate Louis and to place his kingdom under interdict provoked a great deal of hostility in Germany.

At the same time his equally imperious intervention in the controversy concerning the nature and justification of the Franciscan Order's commitment to individual and collective poverty succeeded in broadening the base and deepening the bitterness of that hostility. His rejection (when applied to goods consumed by use) of the distinction between "ownership" and "simple use" did more than alienate the fanatic zealots of the Franciscan Spirituals. His condemnation as heretical of an assertion made by the general chapter of the order at Perugia in May 1322—that Christ and the apostles had owned no property either individually or collectively—split the order down the middle. In condemning the doctrine of apostolic poverty, John seemed to many to be turning his back on the New Testament itself.

The Franciscans were not reluctant to accuse him of heresy, nor did Louis hesitate, when he descended on Rome in 1328, to declare John deposed as a heretic and to sponsor an antipope. Not long after, the great Franciscan philosopher William of Ockham and the order's general, Michael of Cesena, took refuge at Louis' court, where, along with the radical Italian antipapalist Marsiglio of Padua, they mounted a formidable campaign of propaganda against pope and papacy. Their criticisms bit deepest when they focused not simply on John's alleged crimes but, rather, on the great and ever-widening gulf between the simplicity of the apostolic church, as they intuited it, and the triumphantly rationalized and increasingly bureaucratized structure of central government in the church of their own day.

To the development and articulation of that structure the Avignonese contribution was immense. The curial staff, which had numbered about 200 under Nicholas III (1277–1280) and 300 under Boniface VIII (1294–1303), grew to more than 600, a level at which it stabilized until the eighteenth century. Systematized and reorganized by John XXII, transformed by Benedict XII into a sedentary body with permanent quarters at Avignon, this enlarged curia became above all a great fiscal machine. It was designed to make up for the loss of revenues from the Papal States and to extract from the provincial churches, in the most orderly and efficient way, the vast sums of money most of these popes needed to finance their Italian wars.

The expanded curia served other ends as well, notably the vindication, at the expense of the episcopal hierarchy, of direct papal jurisdiction over those provincial churches. The exercise of jurisdiction characteristically carried its financial rewards—usually in the form of benefice taxes, and not least when it involved (as it increasingly did) the setting aside of the traditional rights of electors or patrons and the intrusion into major and minor benefices of candidates possessed, via the process known as papal provision, of legally superior title to ecclesiastical preferment. Fully elaborated by the end of the Avignonese era, this system of papal provision had come to generate benefice taxes amounting to half of the total revenues of the papacy.

Although there can be no question about the growing centralization and absolutism of papal government under the Avignonese popes, historians have come increasingly to stress the degree to which that process represented the following through of an institutional logic established by the reforming popes of the late eleventh, twelfth, and early thirteenth centuries. Likewise, the much-maligned Avignonese "fiscalism," with its intensified traffic in benefices, was a response to the characteristic failure of late-medieval peoples to accord their rulers, royal no less than papal, the type of general taxing powers they needed if they were to discharge the increasing range of governmental responsibilities expected of them. The system of papal provision presupposed the twelfth-century enshrinement in law of the early-medieval conception of the benefice along quasi-feudal lines as a material thing, an object of proprietary right rather than a focus of spiritual duty.

The system of papal provision clearly could not have been operated without widespread clerical support. If it set aside the older rights of clerical electors or patrons, many of whom had become increasingly subservient to corrupting aristocratic influences, it opened up, as university authorities quickly realized (and as reformers at the Council of Constance later conceded), opportunities for advancement to educated men whose lack of social standing would, in the view of those electors or patrons, have made

them ineligible for office. Complaints, therefore, at least in countries with which the pope's policies were not at odds, tended to come either from disgruntled patrons or from disappointed candidates for ecclesiastical preferment.

But not always. For the system of papal provision entailed its own corruptions, and in many ways did so progressively. Presupposing the material concept of the benefice, the system accordingly nourished the stubborn abuses of pluralism (accumulation of several benefices in the hands of one man) and nonresidence. Attempts were made to curb these abuses, but the wars, plagues, and deteriorating economic conditions of the fourteenth century countered such reforms. Moreover, although the system of papal provision had grown up largely in response to the need of individual petitioners, by the mid fourteenth century it had become an essential feature of the centralized administrative machinery that implemented the wishes of a monarchical papacy distinguished increasingly by the lack of institutional restraints on the exercise of its power and decreasingly (as the years of schism were to show) by any inclination to be fastidious in its fiscal manipulations when the burden of financial need became truly crushing.

All these abuses lent support to the criticisms of established ecclesiastical structures voiced so noisily by the Franciscan dissidents and by the propagandists of Philip IV and Louis the Bavarian. Nothing had come of a far-reaching program of "reform in head and members" proposed at the Council of Vienne (1311–1312) and involving the periodic assembly of general councils. In the absence of such assemblies, the sponsorship of reform and the imposition of limits on the exercise of papal power could come only from secular rulers or from the College of Cardinals. Without their complicity, however, and their ability to bend it to serve their own ends, the whole papal system could not have operated in the first place.

Thus, while not disposed to concede in principle to papal jurisdictional claims, secular rulers during the Avignonese era (notably the kings of England and France) did not refrain in practice from sharing the proceeds—tax money and ecclesiastical patronage—accruing from the implementation of that jurisdiction over the churches within their territories. Only during the latter years of the fourteenth century, under the extraordinary conditions of schism and the unprecedented degree of papal weakness generated thereby, did the strain of war, plague, and deepening economic depression induce among rulers dissatisfaction with such de facto divisions of spoils and move many of them to assert a greater measure of control over their churches.

Similarly, discontent grew among the cardinals, whose conception of ecclesiastical government was becoming increasingly oligarchic, but whose share in the spoils had grown in tandem with their deepening involvement in that government. Tensions with their papal masters undoubtedly existed, but not until 1378 did the objectives and interests of pope and cardinals truly diverge. They did so, however, under conditions of great strain in the wake of the first papal election since the return of the papacy to Rome. The outcome was the outbreak of the Great Schism. It was only in the context of that scandalously protracted rupture that cardinals, councils, and kings succeeded in coming together to cooperate, if not in effective reform of head and members, then at least in imposing their will on the rival claimants to the papal office.

The Great Schism and the conciliar movement (1378–1449). In 1377 Gregory XI finally brought the papacy back to Rome. He did so despite opposition from some of his cardinals and the threat to his life posed by the hostility of the Roman nobles. By the time of his death in March 1378, he had repented of the move and had decided to return to Avignon, where six of the twenty-two cardinals still resided and where a considerable part of the curial apparatus continued to function. After his death the Roman populace was gripped by the fear that such a move might still occur.

When the papal election took place in April, then, it did so amid considerable confusion, accompanied by rioting outside the conclave and suspicion and dissension within. Although it ended quickly with the choice of a compromise candidate, an Italian who took the title of Urban VI (1378–1389), the turbulent conditions surrounding his election and his subsequent treatment of the cardinals—violent, erratic, abusive, suggestive even of insanity, and causing them to fear for their lives—spawned apparently genuine doubts on their part about the validity of his title. By the end of September 1378, as a result, they publicly repudiated his election and went on to elect one of their number as Clement VII (1378–1394). By June of the following year, having failed in an attempt to capture Rome, Clement took up residence at Avignon. Thus began the process that was to eventuate in the crystallization of two rival "obediences," Roman and Avignonese, their territorial composition in large part predictable on the basis of the previous political and diplomatic alignments of the kings and princes of Europe.

With England and much of the empire eventually siding with Urban, and France, Castile, and Scotland with Clement, neither of the rival claimants had a decisive edge. Despite efforts to settle the issue by force (the so-called *via facti*), neither proved able to dislodge the other. As a result, the West's most serious schism endured for almost forty years. Both claimants went on to appoint new cardinals; both obdurately refused to withdraw—despite mounting pressures on behalf of this *via cessionis* by French king and German rulers alike. Loyalties hardened, and as the years passed, the rival curias sought to perpetuate their claims. At Avignon, Benedict XIII was elected in 1394 to succeed Clement VII; and at Rome, Boniface IX, Innocent VII, and Gregory XII succeeded Urban VI in 1389, 1404, and 1406, respectively. The outcome was the development within the divided church of widespread spiritual anxiety, administrative confusion, and jurisdictional conflict.

There also emerged an exceedingly grave constitutional crisis. In the conciliar movement—associated with such great theorists as John Gerson, Pierre d'Ailly, Francesco Zabarella, Nicholas of Cusa, and Panormitanus—that crisis generated a sustained attempt not only to achieve the traditional goal of reform in head and members but also to engineer a thoroughgoing "constitutionalist" revolution in the governance of the universal church.

The theory that undergirded that attempt was neither novel nor heterodox. Drawing some of its inspiration from the corporate and conciliar history of the early Christian church, but a good deal more from doctrines elaborated by the thirteenth- and fourteenth-century canonists, it combined two existing notions: the decretalist view that the fullness of jurisdictional power resided ultimately in the universal church itself and in the general council representing it, and the decretist teaching that the pope who deviated from the true faith or who was guilty of notorious crimes was liable to judgment by the church and even to deposition. Appeal was made to this theory when the prolonged obduracy of the rival popes led disgruntled cardinals from both camps to forswear allegiance to their respective masters and to summon a general council. That council met at Pisa in 1409, and after a careful legal process deposed both Gregory XII and Benedict XIII and went on to elect a new pope, Alexander V (1409–1410).

That election was unanimous, and the Roman and Avignonese pontiffs were left with drastically reduced obediences. But their survival was assured by the premature death of Alexander V and the election of John XXIII (1410–1415), a man of less than praiseworthy life who was destined to rule, not as sole pope, but as the representative of a third, or "Pisan," line of claimants. Only after his convocation, under imperial pressure, of the Council of Constance (1414–1418), the greatest ecclesiastical assembly of the Middle Ages, did it prove possible to end the schism. Moved to dramatic action by John's efforts to disrupt its activities, the council in April 1415 promulgated the decree *Haec sancta synodus,* in which it affirmed the superiority of its authority in matters pertaining to the faith, the extirpation of the schism, and the reform of the church, even to that of the pope. It followed that action by the trial and deposition of John XXIII and of Benedict XIII, by the acceptance of Gregory XII's resignation, and by the election in 1417 of a new pope whose legitimacy was not destined to be questioned. He took the name of Martin V (1417–1431), and the schism was at an end.

The conciliar movement, however, was not. Among the many important actions taken by the Council of Constance, two were destined to stimulate repeated clashes between the protagonists of the papal and of the conciliar visions of the church's constitution. The first was its condemnation of the Bohemian reformer John Hus and his execution in 1415 as a heretic. This unleashed a storm of resentment in Bohemia, culminating in a revolt against the Roman clergy who had denounced him and against Emperor Sigismund, who was felt to have betrayed him. The second fateful action was the council's passage (in the context of failure to enact a full-scale program of reform) of the decree *Frequens,* under the terms of which councils were to meet at frequent and regular intervals. In accordance with its provisions, Martin V summoned a new council to meet in 1423 at Pavia, transferred it to Siena, and in March 1424 peremptorily dissolved it before it had succeeded in addressing the task of reform. Seven years later, again in accordance with *Frequens* but this time under pressure, he convoked another council to meet at Basel, appointing Cardinal Cesarini as its president and giving him the power to dissolve it. Shortly thereafter Martin died.

The Council of Basel opened in 1431 under his successor, Eugenius IV (1431–1447), a much less capable and decisive man, who was eager to get rid of it and to pursue Martin V's plan for a council of reunion to be held on Italian soil with representatives

of the Greek Orthodox church. It was this project, along with the Hussite wars in Bohemia, that in large measure determined the fate of the Council of Basel (1431–1449). By attempting to dissolve the council prematurely in December 1431, Eugenius precipitated the crisis that led in 1432 to the assembly's reaffirmation of the Constance superiority decree *Haec sancta synodus,* and ensured that Basel's "great matter" would continue to be the constitutional question of the relationship of pope to general council. In 1433, when the council succeeded in concluding a much-acclaimed agreement with the Hussites, and with his own representative, Cardinal Cesarini, aligned on its side, Eugenius had little choice but to capitulate and formally concede that its activity had been legitimate all along.

But the council's subsequent behavior proved to be its undoing. Although the conciliarists managed to take one or two steps to promote reform of the lower clergy and discussed many more measures, the bulk of their reforming effort was devoted to the head rather than the members—largely to the curtailing of papal financial resources, the limiting of papal jurisdictional powers, and the usurpation by conciliar agencies of papal administrative functions. As a result the council began to forfeit the support of some of its most distinguished participants. When, in September 1437, Eugenius struck back and transferred the council to Ferrara (which the Greeks had accepted as the site for a council of reunion), a significant minority of the council's membership—including Cesarini, Nicholas of Cusa, and other luminaries—obeyed the decree, as well as the later order to move to Florence.

Although the Council of Florence appeared for a while to have succeeded in ending the schism between Greeks and Latins, the rump council at Basel blundered by declaring Eugenius deposed as a heretic, electing in his place Felix V (1439–1449) and thereby precipitating a new schism within the Latin church. Both events certainly worked to ensure the final victory of Eugenius IV's policy. But it was his successor, Nicholas V (1447–1455), who, when Felix resigned and Basel decreed its own dissolution, reaped in 1449 the fruits of that victory.

The papacy of the restoration and the rise of national churches (1449–1500). The conciliar movement survived as a viable theory of church government until well into the eighteenth century, powerful enough, despite Pius II's bull *Execrabilis* (1460), prohibiting appeals from pope to general council, to serve as the doctrinal underpinning for the abortive *conciliabulum* of Pisa (1511–1512) and for the later claims of the Gallicans. The conciliar movement, however, and with it the great attempt to engineer a constitutional revolution in the church, is usually regarded as having met its decisive defeat after the events of Basel-Ferrara-Florence.

The papal victory, nonetheless, was won at the price of accepting what amounted to a constitutional revolution of a different type, one that was determinative for the history of the modern papacy. Even before the outbreak of the schism some secular rulers, notably the kings of England, had begun the process of asserting their jurisdiction in an increasingly direct fashion over the provincial churches within their territorial boundaries. The schism enabled such other rulers as the kings of France and Aragon and the Visconti dukes of Milan to do likewise.

The years of schism, then, saw the definitive reversal of a tide that had been flowing since the eleventh century, when the Gregorian reformers had mounted their campaign to liberate the provincial churches from royal or imperial control. Those years marked a critical phase in the disintegration of a truly international church into a series of (de facto if not de jure) national and territorial churches dominated by kings, princes, and the rulers of such city-states as Venice and Florence.

A pattern was set that rulers were to follow throughout the century in their efforts to gain control of their churches. In the Pragmatic Sanction of Bourges (1438), Charles VII of France, taking advantage of the confusion engendered by the struggle between Eugenius IV and the Council of Basel and supported by the French clergy, gave the force of law in his kingdom to several of the council's decrees affirming conciliar supremacy, abolishing annates, restricting appeals to Rome, and limiting the papal rights of collation to benefices. The German electors did something similar in the *Acceptatio* of Mainz (1439); so, too, in the same year, did the Visconti ruler of Milan. Although the Pragmatic Sanction and like instruments were not systematically enforced, they were persistently used to blackmail the pope into conceding a more favorable share of the ecclesiastical spoils.

While Eugenius IV and the popes of the restoration era were able to recover the enjoyment of a theoretical supreme authority in the universal church, they did so at the price of damaging concessions made in order to wean kings and princes from support of the conciliar idea and from the threat of re-

form in head and members that went with it. The latter part of the fifteenth century witnessed the parceling among the secular rulers of Europe of the pope's sovereign authority over the church and of the revenues attaching thereto. The popes of the restoration era, their universal power having passed into other hands, were increasingly forced to concentrate their attention on pacifying, protecting, and exploiting their own territories in Italy. To do so, they had to involve themselves in the complex diplomacy and ever-shifting coalitions required by the need, after the Peace of Lodi (1454), to achieve a balance of power in Italy, to stave off the threat of French and Spanish intervention in the politics of the peninsula, and to diminish the impact and contain the extent of that intervention when they failed.

The success of their efforts is reflected in the gradual reconstruction of the city of Rome, the magnificence of the Renaissance papal court, the degree of general financial recovery to which this splendor gave witness, and in the fact that by the pontificate of Sixtus IV (1471–1484) the Papal States, which before the schism had contributed no more than one-fourth of the papal revenues, were now producing at least 64 percent. The price paid for that success is reflected in the questionable moral stature of some of the popes and in the almost total demise, after the pontificate of Pius II (1458–1464), of papal concern for the twin goals of reforming the church and uniting Christendom in a great crusade against the infidel—the ancient goals in pursuit of which the medieval papacy had risen to preeminence. As the almost total failure of Leo X (1513–1521) to comprehend the nature of the threat that Luther posed later made clear, the role and preoccupations of an Italian prince were not such as to promote reform-mindedness in those popes whose fate it was to cope with the rising religious expectations of the European peoples on the eve of the Reformation.

REFORM, HERESY, AND RELIGIOUS ASPIRATIONS
However ominous for the future, the ultimate failure of both the general councils and of the papal rivals to respond effectively to the widespread demand for reform in head and members should not be taken as an adequate index to the varied, fluctuating, but frequently vital realities of late-medieval religious life. In the absence of a full-scale reform of the universal church, people eventually turned their attention to the possibility of reforming particular segments of it and to more piecemeal attempts at revitalization. In the latter half of the fourteenth

century, Emperor Charles IV and Ernest of Pardubice, archbishop of Prague, had set in motion the Bohemian reform that was later linked with Czech university circles at Prague, and molded the spirituality of John Hus as well as that of other reforming leaders of more orthodox stamp.

Similar stirrings of revitalization are evidenced in the early fifteenth century by the great "revivalist" preaching missions undertaken across western Europe by St. Vincent Ferrer, St. Bernadino of Siena, and St. John of Capistrano; in mid century by the distinguished pastoral labors of St. Antoninus as bishop of Florence; and in the last decade of the century by the reforms that Girolamo Savonarola instituted at Florence during his brief period of ascendancy there, by Jean Standonck's program for reforming the secular clergy of France, and by the ultimately successful renovation of the Spanish church that the great Cardinal Jiménez de Cisneros (*d.* 1517) set in motion and that did so much to mold Counter-Reformation spirituality later on.

Nearly all of these attempts at local or regional reform reflect the degree to which the less cloistered world inhabited by the laity and secular clergy was affected by the stirrings of reform within the religious orders. It is very striking that, with the exception of the Bohemians, all the above-mentioned reformers were members of "Observant" monastic congregations. They were shaped, that is, by the "observantine" type of monastic spirit that, from the mid fourteenth century on, had led among the Franciscans, Dominicans, Augustinians, Cistercians, and (eventually) Benedictines to the purification of individual monasteries or to the creation within those orders of Observant congregations of houses committed to identifying the ideal of perfection peculiar to their order and attempting to realize that ideal by the often painful return to the precise and unqualified observance of the rule in all its original rigor.

In the conspicuous absence of the consistent central leadership that Rome alone could have provided, no one order succeeded entirely in reforming itself before the onset of the Reformation, and the Observant houses were distributed geographically in a very uneven fashion. Nevertheless, the fact that such houses came into existence witnesses to the enduring vitality of the monastic spirit. So does the foundation of new Cistercian and Carthusian houses—the latter undergoing their greatest expansion during the fourteenth and fifteenth centuries. And perhaps the same is true of the great flowering of mystical spirituality that occurred during the fourteenth century in Italy, England, the Rhineland, and the Netherlands.

Although St. Catherine of Siena became affiliated with the Dominican Third Order, she was not the product of a traditional monastic formation; nor, in England, were Julian of Norwich (author of the *Revelations of Divine Love*) and Richard Rolle, the hermit of Hampole. But the anonymous author of the *Cloud of Unknowing* was probably a solitary; and Walter Hilton, author of *The Scale of Perfection* and other mystical works, was an Augustinian canon. So too, at least for the latter part of his life, was Jan van Ruysbroeck, the greatest of the Flemish mystics; and the three great German mystics of the day—Meister Eckhardt, Johann Tauler, and Heinrich Suso—were all Dominican friars.

In their sermons and writings the three German mystics were usually discharging pastoral responsibilities toward nuns belonging to Dominican convents in the Rhineland, but it is pertinent to note that all of them, like Rolle and Ruysbroeck, were concerned to address themselves to wider audiences of clergy and laity as well. In so doing, they were responding to that deep thirst for spiritual guidance that was particularly widespread among the Beguines and Beghards of northwestern Europe, groups of religious women and men who belonged to no monastic order, lived in accordance with no official rule, took no formal vows, but, while continuing to pursue ordinary occupations, committed themselves to a community life of simplicity and celibacy. Such communities continued to proliferate into the early fourteenth century.

A similar spirit was evident in those lay confraternities that sought to carve out some sort of middle ground between the less formal modes of communal life and the traditional forms of religious life endorsed by the monastic orders. Of those groupings the most famous and influential were the Brothers and Sisters of the Common Life, who, along with the Windesheim congregation of (Observant) Augustinian canons, owed their inception during the last two decades of the fourteenth century to the work of two secular priests, Geert de Groote and Florens Radewijns. Appearing first in the region around Deventer in the eastern Netherlands, by the end of the fifteenth century houses of all three groupings—brothers, sisters, and canons—had multiplied and were found throughout the region that now forms the Netherlands and Belgium, in the Rhineland, and across a good part of western Germany.

The brothers and sisters pursued an order of life in accordance with which many of them remained lay people, working for a living, taking no permanent vows, but committing themselves nonetheless to lives of celibacy, obedience, individual poverty, and possession of goods in common. Within the framework established by that choice, however, they set out to cultivate very much the same type of meditative and intensely inward piety as that of their monastic cousins of the Windesheim congregation. To that mode of piety two of the Windesheimers, Jan Busch and Thomas à Kempis, attached the name Devotio Moderna, and in *The Imitation of Christ* the latter gave the new devotion its most notable and extraordinarily influential expression.

By using the name Devotio Moderna, the Brothers of the Common Life and Windesheimers themselves suggested that there was something new and distinctive about their spirituality. Until recently historians were prone to emphasize that element of novelty, portraying the Devotio Moderna as a harbinger of things to come—not excluding the religious individualism of the Protestant reformers. But the dominant tendency now is to acknowledge its conservatism. Rather than being concerned to reject the traditional externalities of medieval religion, the Devotionalists, through assiduous application, meditation, and the removal of worldly distractions, sought to infuse them for the individual practitioner with a rich interior significance—one hinging, characteristically, on the life and example of Christ and designed to foster a tender piety toward his humanity.

In this, as in so many of their practices, the Devotionalists looked backward to the type of piety developed and disseminated by the Cistercians and Franciscans rather than forward to sixteenth-century Protestantism. What was distinctive about their piety was the intensity and sobriety of their religious practice and their success, where so many others before them had failed, in remaining faithful to their religious ideal. That success made their example an unusually compelling one, and their influence on the religious life of northwestern Europe grew to be enormous.

While the Devotionalists, then, are certainly to be cleared of the suspicion of heterodoxy so often attached to them in the past, there were undoubtedly other late-medieval groups, devoted to the imitation of Christ and moved by the desire to live a quasi-monastic life of apostolic purity, who were led

thereby to transgress the boundaries of orthodoxy. This was true, certainly, of those Franciscan Spirituals who proved unable to accept the less rigorous interpretation of the Rule of St. Francis espoused by the majority of the order and endorsed by the papacy.

Finally nudged by John XXII into the outer darkness of heterodoxy, these Spirituals came to blend their own rigorous Franciscan teaching on apostolic poverty with apocalyptic ideas derived (with considerable distortion) from the writings of the twelfth-century Calabrian monk Joachim of Fiore. These ideas suggested that the "age of the Holy Spirit" had dawned, an age in which the "everlasting gospel" allegedly proclaimed by Joachim had superseded the traditional and familiar gospel of the Son. Thus, during the fourteenth and early fifteenth centuries at least, the Spirituals of Joachimite proclivities struggled on, distinguishing between their own "spiritual church" and the "carnal church" of Antichrist (Rome), waiting impatiently for the vindication of their doctrine of evangelical poverty and the dawning of the new and purified order of things in which they would fulfill their destiny of restoring the whole church to Christ.

Moreover, long before the emergence within the ranks of the Franciscans of the disagreements that had led to the emergence of the Spirituals, a similar impulse to preach a life of apostolic poverty and evangelical perfection had produced in the followers of Waldes of Lyons a stubborn grouping of the committed that was destined in the early years of the thirteenth century to drift (or to be nudged by unsympathetic ecclesiastical authorities) into outright heresy.

Over the following two centuries these "Waldensians" continued to increase until they constituted what was possibly the largest, and certainly the most enduring, of medieval heresies, linked across their regional subdivisions less by any shared doctrinal corpus than by a fundamental disposition common to all. Basic to that disposition was the stubborn insistence on living the life of the gospel as they themselves apprehended it: a life of rigor, simplicity, and poverty, at the heart of which lay the struggle to maintain the exacting ideal that Jesus had taught. The established church, with its hierarchy and harlotry, its qualifications and compromises, its stress on "institutional" rather than subjective holiness, had long since submerged that ideal (or so they believed) in a "Pharisaical" tradition that could no longer be regarded as fully Christian. This thinking led to their eventual rejection of the authority, priesthood, sacraments, and ritual of the Roman church, their crystallization de facto into a heterodox and missionary "counterchurch," and their survival into the modern era as an independently organized ecclesial body.

On the strength of their appeal to the peasants and artisans of the day, as well as their sheer longevity, the Waldensians contrast sharply with "the brothers and sisters of the sect of the Free Spirit and voluntary poverty" (as on one occasion they called themselves), who constituted neither organized movement nor coherent sect, whose numbers were never large, but who attained during the fourteenth and early fifteenth centuries much notoriety and a certain prominence, at least in the works of the hostile chroniclers and in the records of the Inquisition. Often depicted in the past as a movement of antinomian libertines, advocates of a mystic eroticism, of "promiscuity on principle," they have since been revealed as considerably less radical in their beliefs, committed, like the adherents of so many other late-medieval religious movements, to the pursuit, through poverty and self-abnegation, of the apostolic ideal. Their spiritual orientation, it seems, was closely related to that of the orthodox mystics of the day, but was distinguished from theirs by too unqualified an affirmation that the perfected soul might in this life be absorbed wholly into God. Hence their slide into autotheism (identification of self with God), and with it the circumvention or minimization of the sacramental mediations of the church.

Like the Joachimites, the Brothers and Sisters of the Free Spirit appear to have petered out in the latter half of the fifteenth century. Throughout the heartland of western and central Europe, that period witnessed a decline in the vigor and lasting power of heretical dissent. But the triumph of the forces of orthodoxy in those regions was shadowed by the emergence of new and powerful heterodoxies in lands on the eastern and western peripheries to which heresy had previously been foreign. And the heresies in those peripheral regions—that of the Wycliffites (Lollards) in England and of the Hussites in Bohemia, both of which endured into the age of Reformation—were linked directly (or by extension) with the teachings of a single man, in each case a theologian and a prolific author with strong academic roots and powerful political affiliations.

In the case of John Hus, theologian at the University of Prague and rector of the famous Bethlehem Chapel there, the recent tendency among historians has been to question his heterodoxy and, despite his condemnation by the Council of Constance and subsequent burning at the stake, to see him as very much a product of the indigenous (and orthodox) Czech reforming movement. He emerges as a moral zealot, whose unfortunate propensity for couching some of his perfectly orthodox positions in provocatively Wycliffite language made it possible for his conciliar judges to believe him to be a thoroughgoing Wycliffite. Having recently condemned as heretical some forty-five articles drawn from Wyclif's writings, those judges were led to see Hus as a revolutionary rather than a reformer, a subversive rather than a saint, and, acting accordingly, to make him a martyr.

About the heretical nature of many of the doctrines propounded by John Wyclif there has been no similar controversy. It is true that at the end of the fifteenth century the Lollards were fragmented, localized groups, composed largely of tradesmen and artisans, shorn of the last remnants of their academic tradition, betraying the type of variation in belief that one could expect such circumstances to produce, stressing above all moral and practical issues, and evincing a preoccupation with evangelical simplicity that suggests an affinity with the Waldensians. But as their distinctive and continuing rejection of the doctrine of transubstantiation suggests, their link with Wycliffe's more theoretical theological commitments was never entirely broken.

Although disappointment over his failure (after loyal service to the crown and years of academic prominence as an Oxford theologian) to secure appropriate ecclesiastical preferment undoubtedly fueled Wyclif's discontent with the ecclesiastical establishment and the deepening radicalism of his later years, his complex heterodox views are comprehensible only against the background of a series of commitments, philosophical as well as theological, that matured over the course of a lifetime. Central to those commitments was an ultrarealism in epistemology and metaphysics that led him to insist that whatever the human mind conceives as an entity corresponds not merely to an external reality but also to an eternal and indestructible divine archetype. This accounted for his insistence that the eucharistic bread could not be "transubstantiated" in any sense that involved its total annihilation; his tendency to view the Bible in a manner suggestive less of the Christian tradition than of Muslim attitudes toward the Koran; and his final reduction of the "true church" to the invisible, eternal, archetypal reality, the "congregation of the predestined," to which there is no guarantee that popes, bishops, or priests, simply by virtue of their office, or ordinary believers, simply by virtue of their membership, actually belong.

Condemned though such doctrines eventually were, Wyclif was by no means alone among late-medieval theologians in subscribing to predestinarian views. In that connection it must suffice to mention Duns Scotus, Thomas Bradwardine, and Gregory of Rimini. Far more characteristic of the period as a whole, however, is the stance adopted by so many theologians of the nominalist school, such as William of Ockham, Robert Holcot, Pierre d'Ailly, and Gabriel Biel. While conceding that by his absolute power God can justify men through grace alone, and predestine them to eternal happiness regardless of their deeds, they taught also that through his ineffable mercy and by his ordained power God has in fact chosen to accept men as partners in the work of their own salvation, conferring the necessary sanctifying grace on those who freely do the best they can *(faciunt quod in se est)*.

While most commentators today would reject as an inaccurate oversimplification Luther's characterization of such a theology as fundamentally Pelagian, most would concede that the theology was more in tune than its predestinarian rivals with the religious instincts of the mass of late-medieval people, uneducated as well as educated. To say that their religion was a "religion of works" is not necessarily to derogate from its quality or intensity. The "popular piety" of the day, heavily propitiatory in tone, may well have demonstrated a marked tendency to attribute a magical or quasi-magical virtue to relics, images, indulgences, and the various "bleeding hosts" so popular at that time. But even when he sought to suppress the pilgrimage to the bleeding host of Wilsnack in 1451–1452, Nicholas of Cusa himself recognized in such practices that great hunger for the divine that was so marked a feature of late-medieval life.

That hunger is also evidenced in many less questionable phenomena: the volume of legacies to ecclesiastical foundations; the willingness to undergo the discomforts of pilgrimage; the growth of an intense eucharistic piety; and the range, quality, and variety of the instrumentalities geared in some degree to the moral and religious formation of the lower clergy and laity—missionary preaching, religious theater,

vernacular bibles, spiritual biographies, manuals of catechetical instruction, "aids" written to help confessors discharge their responsibilities, the increasing attention paid to the sacrament of penance.

If the volume of legacies has encouraged the judgment that the fifteenth century was, at least in some parts of Europe, the most churchly minded as well as the most devout period of the Middle Ages, the range of instrumentalities has given rise among scholars to a dispute about the quality of late-medieval piety, about the degree to which the penitential system of the day was a source of consolation or served to make religion psychologically oppressive. Although the evidence, not surprisingly, would appear to suggest that it was both, the dispute continues. But what is not in dispute, given the mounting evidence for the vitality of late-medieval religious life, is that the wellsprings of the religiosity disseminated later by the Protestant reformers are to be sought not only in the reformers' reaction to the more obvious shortcomings of the medieval Catholic system at its weakest and most decadent, but also in the profound inadequacies they sensed in that system when they had the opportunity to encounter it even at its strongest and most pure. For that opportunity, it must now be insisted, they undoubtedly had.

BIBLIOGRAPHY

General accounts. Francis Oakley, *The Western Church in the Later Middle Ages* (1979); Francis Rapp, *L'église et la vie religieuse en Occident à la fin du moyen âge* (1971). More extensive are Étienne Delaruelle, E.-R. Labande, and Paul Ourliac, *L'église au temps du Grand Schisme et la crise conciliaire*, 2 vols. (1962–1964); Roger Aubenas and Robert Ricard, *L'église et la Renaissance (1449–1517)* (1951); and Guillaume Mollat, *Les papes d'Avignon*, 9th ed. (1949, repr. 1950), trans. by Janet Love as *The Popes at Avignon (1305–1378)* (1963). Delaruelle *et al.* and Mollat contain especially thorough bibliographies. See also the bibliographies in Hans-Georg Beck *et al.*, *From the High Middle Ages to the Eve of the Reformation*, Anselm Briggs, trans. (1970); Bernd Moeller, *Spätmittelalter*: vol. II, 4, part 1 of Kurt Schmidt and Ernst Wolf, eds., *Die Kirche in ihrer Geschichte: Ein Handbuch* (1966). Current contributions are listed regularly in *Revue d'histoire ecclésiastique* (Louvain).

Specific topics. On the Avignonese papacy see, in addition to Mollat, Geoffrey Barraclough, *Papal Provisions* (1935); Bernard Guillemain, *La cour pontificale d'Avignon: 1309–1376* (1962), and "Punti di vista sul Papato avignonese," in *Archivio storico italiano*, **111** (1953); Yves Renouard, *The Avignon Papacy: 1305–1403*, Denis Bethell, trans. (1970). On the schism, the councils, and the conciliar movement, see K. A. Fink, "Zur Beurteilung des grossen abendländischen Schismas," in *Zeitschrift für Kirchengeschichte*, 73 (1962); C. M. D. Crowder, *Unity, Heresy, and Reform: 1378–1460* (1977); A. Franzen, "The Council of Constance: Present State of the Problem," in *Concilium*, 7 (1965); Joseph Gill, *The Council of Florence* (1959); Joachim Stieber, *Pope Eugenius IV, the Council of Basel, and the Secular and Ecclesiastical Authorities in the Empire* (1978); Walter Ullmann, *Origins of the Great Schism* (1948).

For theories of papal and conciliar power, see Brian Tierney, *Foundations of the Conciliar Theory* (1955), and *Origins of Papal Infallibility* (1972); Remigius Bäumer, *Nachwirkungen des konziliaren Gedankens in der Theologie und Kanonistik des frühen 16. Jahrhunderts* (1971). On the restoration papacy see Hubert Jedin, *A History of the Council of Trent*, I, Ernest Graf, trans. (1957); Peter Partner, "The 'Budget' of the Roman Church," in Ernest F. Jacob, ed., *Italian Renaissance Studies* (1960).

On heretical movements, see Malcolm Lambert, *Medieval Heresy: Popular Movements from Bogomil to Hus* (1976); Gordon Leff, *Heresy in the Late Middle Ages: The Relation of Heterodoxy to Dissent*, 2 vols. (1967). On specific heresies, see Robert E. Lerner, *The Heresy of the Free Spirit in the Later Middle Ages* (1972); Kenneth B. McFarlane, *John Wycliffe and the Origins of English Nonconformity* (1952); Marjorie Reeves, *The Influence of Prophecy in the Later Middle Ages: A Study in Joachimism* (1969); Paul de Vooght, *L'hérésie de Jean Huss* (1960); Matthew Spinka, *John Hus: A Biography* (1968).

On monasticism, mysticism, and the Devotio Moderna, see Dom David Knowles, *The Religious Orders in England*, 3 vols. (1950–1959), and *The English Mystical Tradition* (1961); John W. O'Malley, *Giles of Viterbo on Church and Reform* (1968); Ray C. Petry, ed., *Late Medieval Mysticism* (1957); Regnerus R. Post, *The Modern Devotion: Confrontation with Reformation and Humanism* (1968). On theology and piety, Denys Hay, *The Church in Italy in the Fifteenth Century* (1977); Heiko Oberman, *The Harvest of Medieval Theology: Gabriel Biel and Late Medieval Nominalism* (1963); William A. Pantin, *The English Church in the Fourteenth Century* (1955); Thomas N. Tentler, *Sin and Confession on the Eve of the Reformation* (1977); Bernd Moeller, "Frömmigkeit in Deutschland um 1500," in *Archiv für Reformationsgeschichte*, 56 (1965); Charles Trinkaus and Heiko Oberman, eds., *The Pursuit of Holiness in Late Medieval and Renaissance Religion* (1964).

FRANCIS OAKLEY

[See also **Babylonian Captivity; Benefice, Ecclesiastical; Brethren of the Common Life; Clement V, Pope; Clement VI, Pope; Conciliar Theory; Councils, Western; Curia, Papal; Devotio Moderna; Ferrara-Florence, Council of; Franciscans; Heresies, Western European; Hus, John; Hussites; John XXII, Pope; Lollards; Mysticism, Western European; Papacy; Provisions, Ecclesiastical; Reform, Idea of; Schism, Great; Waldensians; Wyclif, John.**]

CHURCH, LATIN: ORGANIZATION. Church structure in the Middle Ages was always essentially episcopal, but considerable evolution took place during this thousand-year period. Broad generalizations are therefore of little use—as are analogies between the medieval hierarchy and the twelfth-century church. A modern Christian can ignore the territorial limits of parish and diocese, but the lives of every layman and cleric in the Middle Ages were touched by the realities of these two units. Consequently the actual development of the church's structure is made more complex by regional as well as temporal variations. The geographical differences in organization emerged from internal acts (such as the legislative decisions of episcopal synods) and external factors (such as the expropriation of church wealth by lay princes). Since the organization of secular communities was fluid and changing, ecclesiastical and secular institutions were often intermingled. The church acted on and reacted to the demands of the lay political order. Clerical organization thus was never static in either theory or practice.

By 300 the Western church was assuming a definite shape. The chief constituent was the parish (Greek: *paroikia*), or diocese (Greek: *dioikēsis*), as it was later called, which was governed by the resident bishop. These early dioceses were arranged along loose horizontal lines. The diocese was monarchical—although some were still governed by a college of clerics—and the papacy did not attempt to exert any administrative control. The bishop's authority was supreme in matters of liturgy and discipline. He was assisted by presbyters (priests), deacons, subdeacons, and minor officials (acolytes, lectors, exorcists, doorkeepers). The bishops were reminded of the unity in the church universal when they responded to imperial persecutions and pagan literary attacks, and they met in regional councils to settle questions of liturgy, clerical ordination, doctrine, and internal discipline.

After the Council of Nicaea in 325 the Western church tended to adapt itself more closely to the civil jurisdictions of the empire. The bishops defended themselves against Arian emperors, doctrinal disputes intensified, patriarchal sees competed for hegemony, and new converts in the countryside necessitated more administration. The episcopal diocese was gradually superimposed on the civil organization. The bishop was the chief pastor within the city and the areas dependent on it. His diocese was one of several within the ecclesiastical province, which was often coterminous with the civil province.

In some cases a particular diocese (later called the archdiocese) exerted administrative supervision over the other dioceses in the province. The bishop of this diocese, the metropolitan, acted as ecclesiastical superior of the entire province; the bishops of the other dioceses were his suffragans. The chaotic conditions in the West after 400 hampered the development of a systematic relationship among metropolitans, or even among dioceses within a province. Some sees acquired more prestige than others. The bishop of Rome, the leading metropolitan in the West, had summoned synods of bishops since at least the third century. The relative independence of the Western episcopate gave the Roman pontiff more freedom of action in dealing with other dioceses in the West.

Within the diocese certain clerics performed functions with geographical scope. The senior priest of the cathedral, the archpriest (later called the dean), could perform liturgical duties in the bishop's absence, and generally had some authority over the cathedral clergy. His counterpart in the rural areas was the rural archpriest, later called the rural dean. The diocese gradually became subdivided into deaneries, with an archdeacon (the bishop's "eyes") supervising them.

The coming of Germanic tribes in the fifth century had little immediate effect on ecclesiastical structure. But soon the church's outward form had changed as a result of the enlargement of the bishops' temporal responsibilities. They were landholders, judges, military advisers, and food suppliers. As a churchman the bishop was in charge of education, pastoral needs, sacraments, and discipline. Contemporary hagiography testifies to his reputation for sanctity. Despite the interference of early Merovingian kings in episcopal elections and synods, the bishops were the dominant temporal and spiritual leaders in the West.

The diocese acquired enormous landed wealth in northern Europe. Bishops were sometimes assisted by auxiliary bishops who performed pastoral functions without a clearly defined territorial jurisdiction. The coming of the barbarians gave rise to the establishment of proprietary churches which were often beyond the control of the local bishop. Lay lords treated churches and abbeys as their private property, thereby undermining the existing form of ecclesiastical organization. In many parts of Europe remnants of the proprietary system stubbornly persisted until after the thirteenth century. A parish configuration slowly emerged as converts in the rural areas increased and as new churches had to be established. Eventually a single priest presided over his own district, the parish in the modern sense.

The arrival of Celtic and Anglo-Saxon monastic missionaries on the Continent in the seventh and eighth centuries did not significantly alter the basic ecclesiastical pattern. Only in Ireland did the monastic kind of organization dominate the church structure, although elsewhere monasteries and double monasteries continued to serve neighboring villages. In England after the Synod of Whitby (664) the Roman diocesan and parish framework became standard. The minsters, missionary churches founded by kings and bishops, gradually came under the jurisdiction of the parish church.

Under the later Merovingians the episcopal structure was ineffective. Church councils ceased. Metropolitan groupings collapsed, and bishoprics lay vacant. Secular control of churches increased as papal influence beyond the Alps decreased. It was clear that the episcopal organization could not be saved from within, since it lacked political and military resources in an unstable society.

The Carolingian kings tried to restore the ancient structure of the Western church, but in the process the church was reorganized. The result was the "medieval" church, the structure of which was largely built by kings and popes, sometimes in cooperation. Influenced by the English system and the Roman canons, St. Boniface in the eighth century consecrated bishops and acted as metropolitan for several provinces. As papal legate and archbishop without see, he worked with Pepin the Short in summoning councils and enforcing their canons against heathen practices and irregular bishops.

The outcome of the Bonifatian-Frankish reforms was the creation of an imperial church under the state. The authority of Merovingian rulers over the church had been largely restricted to episcopal elections. The Carolingians extended this dominance to the church's spiritual and administrative functions. Charlemagne incorporated the church's administration into that of the Frankish realm. He freely established new bishoprics and abolished old ones in his efforts to set up an imperial administration. He assigned important spiritual duties to bishops, who were expected to induce their clergy and monks to act as pastors and men of prayer. They were also expected to assist the monarch in keeping the peace, administering justice, preparing for war, and improving the moral and intellectual life of the diocesan clergy. The monasteries were made more subject to the bishops.

Metropolitan groupings were reaffirmed. Since Charlemagne required metropolitans to be archbishops, the office of metropolitan was grafted onto archiepiscopal dignity. Previously an archbishop would have authority over metropolitans. Thus Boniface was an archbishop without a see. "Archbishop" was often a title of high dignity, yet it conferred no specific jurisdiction. The supervisory capacity of the metropolitan within his province was strengthened, and the king often employed these metropolitan-archbishops as *missi dominici* (royal agents) within the province. Nonmetropolitan archbishops continued to be created as a special dignity. But Charlemagne did not envisage the metropolitan as part of the regular system of ecclesiastical authority, though he might occasionally report to the emperor. The metropolitan's role was limited to the traditional supervisory one, with no directive authority over his clergy. Indeed, Charlemagne often made it difficult for metropolitans to exercise even these modest functions. While the boundaries of dioceses usually were clearly defined, those of the province often were not. The Carolingians rarely defended the right of these metropolitans against the pretensions of suffragan bishops or popes.

Metropolitan clusters were more closely associated with the Roman church, although the old Roman idea endured that the provincial unit was independent of the papacy. But now the metropolitan was required to obtain the archiepiscopal pallium directly from the pope within three months of his appointment or election—a custom borrowed from England. Thus the provinces became more attached to Rome. But since kings did not offer much support to their metropolitans, the effect of this innovation was to weaken archiepiscopal authority and strengthen papal power over diocesan bishops—who often appealed to the pope over the heads of assertive metropolitans.

The Carolingian church was an imperial church. No one challenged Charlemagne's right to appoint and transfer prelates, to issue capitularies on clerical duties, or to create or adjust new bishoprics and provinces. The administration of the clerical church was integrated into secular society. Carolingian manipulation of ecclesiastical organization had the indirect effect of perpetuating the idea of a unified and somewhat centralized church, and of instilling a high sense of purpose among prelates. But the primitive nature of their institutions meant that the Carolingians could not sustain effective hegemony over the church in Europe. As it happened, the episcopacy was invigorated, and the papacy became the chief beneficiary of the imperial church. Nevertheless, vestiges of the Carolingian state church continued, particularly in northern France and Ottonian-Salian Germany.

In the two centuries after Charlemagne the Western church's organization fluctuated. Germanic legal notions about proprietary churches did not disappear after 814. Under Germanic law the proprietor of a church owned the building, its landed property, and the income derived from the tithe and other sources. But Charlemagne and Louis the Pious checked the spread of proprietary churches and made them more subject to local bishops, who were to oversee the priests and preserve their income. With the collapse of the empire, lay control over rural churches increased in France, Germany, and Italy. The proprietor acquired the right to receive usufruct during a vacancy, as well as the *ius spolii*, the right to confiscate the movable property of the deceased priest. By the eleventh century the income and property of these churches were divided into myriad rights. The historical results were a Europe-wide benefice system, in which priests could be nominated by anyone (including laymen) who had rights over their church, and a large number of parishes. Many abbeys came under lay ownership.

Metropolitans in the ninth century attempted to vitalize provincial organization in the face of opposition from kings, suffragan bishops, and popes. They tried to influence the elections of their suffragans and to maintain the custom of provincial synods. The papacy, however, interpreted its granting of the pallium as a sign of superiority over the metropolitan. Besides, the pope could consecrate archbishops without making them metropolitans. The papacy came to profit from episcopal attempts—such as the use of the forged Pseudo-Isidore (False Decretals)—to declare independence from lay and metropolitan regulation.

So, too, the notion of primate bishops of super-metropolitan status never developed into a workable gradation of authority. Some kings and popes tried to elevate select bishops to this eminence, but most attempts—such as those in Gaul, Germany, and regions east of the Rhine—failed because of episcopal obstruction.

Within the diocese the bishop's position was improved with the decrease in the number of chorbishops after the ninth century. The chorbishops' duties of administration, missions, and supervision were assumed by the officials of the regular bishop, or ordinary. Many of these officials—particularly the deans—became so entrenched that they limited the bishop's authority. The diocese was carved into archdeaneries in which archdeacons served as chief judges.

The clergy nearest the bishop were also reorganized. The Council of Aachen in 817 made the canonical life binding on cathedral and collegiate churches. The Carolingians sought to transform the traditional familia (the clerics of the bishop's household who served the city churches) into a quasi-monastic community bound by vows and rule, or canon (hence the *clerici canonici*). While many cathedral and collegiate churches adopted this kind of regular life for clerics, the common property of the canons was divided into parcels of private property (called prebends). The cathedral chapters of canons were at first under the archdeacon, and later under the provost. In the chapter, offices with jurisdiction developed: dean, cantor, scholastic, penitentiary, treasurer, sacristan. The reform of the eleventh century compelled the canons to relinquish private property and adopt an Augustinian rule. In England Benedictine monks frequently acted as a chapter of cathedral canons. The Conquest introduced the secular system of prebends into many English cathedrals. Canons regular were well established in Europe by 1100.

The pre-Conquest church in England developed unevenly as reform kings and forceful bishops alternately clashed and cooperated on policies relating to parishes and monastic discipline. Often with royal support, monk-bishops such as Dunstan and Ethelwold in the tenth century utilized continental reform ideas to make changes in chapter organization and rural parishes. But in Saxon Germany strong kings subordinated monastic to episcopal jurisdiction. The Ottonian monarchs fortified the political and military authority of their bishops, thereby mixing the temporal and the spiritual within dioceses. Bishops were treated as royal administrators to offset the power of lay counts.

Insofar as the Gregorian reform of the late eleventh century determined organizational change, the most obvious effect was the increased papal control over the episcopacy. By means of a vast network of legates (papal delegates) and an expanding canon law, the popes were able to influence episcopal elections and diocesan judicial-legislative procedures. The greatly enlarged administrative and judicial operations of the Roman church resulted in increased curial activity, which in turn extended legatine ties to dioceses throughout Europe. The College of Cardinals served to make the papal curia the juridical hub of an international church. Never before had the diocesan structure appeared so well defined and free from lay interference. Cathedral chapters generally elected the bishop, though they often had to accept the nominee of a king or a great lord. The pattern of parishes within the diocese was also clarified, though many proprietary churches continued. Monastic bonds to Rome tightened as monasteries sought exemptions from local authority; Cluny looked to the papacy for guarantees of its independence from episcopal jurisdiction.

The supervisory powers of the metropolitan-archbishops were made more precise. Metropolitans summoned provincial synods, heard appeals, visited suffragans, and ensured continuity during vacancies. Their actual power over their suffragans diminished, as bishops bypassed them and appealed to Rome. The archbishops were becoming extensions of the papacy. The powers of the primates remained ambiguous because bishops saw no advantage in the existence of primatial provinces. Popes still created primatial sees—such as Lyons, Pisa, and Toledo—but their authority was largely ceremonial. The boundaries of existing provinces changed little.

Although the Gregorian popes intended to solidify the position of bishops within their sees, the authority of the bishops actually deteriorated in the late twelfth century and afterward. The torrent of appeals to Rome effectively made prelates more dependent on the Holy See. In England in particular, the importance of bishops declined as kings and popes exercised their rights of patronage over benefices. After 1200 the papacy frequently intervened in disputed episcopal elections and ecclesiastical courts. The papal-royal combination could rarely be resisted by individual bishops. Within the diocese the powerful archdeacons and cathedral chapters further eroded the bishop's authority.

England best illustrates the ambiguities of Gregorian ecclesiology. The papacy was not consistent in its support of Canterbury's claim to primatial authority over York. The struggle between Canterbury (with its eighteen dioceses including Wales) and York (with three dioceses and claims to Scotland) was conducted without much attention to papal wishes. Although the archbishop was often a papal legate, he exercised broad appellate and ordinary jurisdiction through his courts. The pope often supported the Anglo-Norman kings' rights of patronage and taxation over the English clergy.

The gradation of parish-diocese-province was complicated in England by numerous peculiars (or franchises) that often conflicted with the bishop's jurisdiction. Monasteries, royal chapels, secular colleges, and cathedral chapters—with their various kinds of endowments, estates, and jurisdictions throughout the city—possessed numerous types of privileges and exemptions. Many of the bishop's officers operated in relative independence. In his archdeaconry (there was one in each county) the archdeacon conducted his own courts. No city was without its voluntary associations, such as confraternities organized for communal prayer. Bishops in the twelfth century were, to be sure, able to check this proliferation of franchises, but in fact the monarchy profited most from the development.

The medieval church, even during its "classical age" (1140–1378), rested on a balance between two structural tendencies. Authority devolved from papacy to bishopric to parish. But there had also emerged enclaves of jurisdiction that resisted outside intrusion. The degree of integration between these two sets of organizations—the vertical and the horizontal—varied according to time and place. Within the diocese archdeacons superintended the clergy; after 1300 bishops increasingly used vicars-general to undermine archdeaconal authority. Chapters, colleges, exempt monasteries, mendicant privileges, and the papal curia compromised the normal strands of administrative authority. Jurisdiction was usually divided among several overlapping sources of legal competence.

The Gregorian reforms certainly lessened the force of local custom, yet custom remained a factor everywhere in the medieval church. The somewhat artificial distinction made between benefices with cure of souls (preaching, caring for the sick, administering sacraments) and those without cures encouraged the multiplication of the latter kind. A church organized according to strictly vertical lines of jurisdiction never developed because the hierarchical church lacked the political and military means to enforce its canonical procedures. The ecclesiastical organizations could not function freely because secular authorities intervened in them whenever they perceived political and financial advantages.

Prior to the Council of Trent, the period 1180–1300 was the time of the church's most comprehensive centralization. The Roman curia's administrative organs expanded in order to deal with the increase of business conducted there. The curia's camera managed the treasury, finance, and the Papal States. The consistory and other tribunals heard cases and appeals. Popes, curial officials, and canon lawyers often encouraged the increasing centralization of the Western church, often for reasons unrelated to pastoral considerations. The papacy's political policies—such as the attempts to curtail German imperial influence in Italy—also affected its juridical position.

This centralization is most visible in the collation of benefices. As the curia needed more revenue to handle its work load, it pressed for more control over appointments through provisions and reservations. Local prelates were usually helpless to slow the traffic in benefices because secular rulers often preferred to cooperate with the papacy as a means to reward court officials and subordinate their own clergy.

But in a broader sense papal centralization was unplanned, inefficient, and limited. The thirteenth-century papacy cannot be compared with Napoleonic government or modern corporate management. Much of the pope's authority over ecclesiastical edifices was the outcome of appeals filed at the curia. With each curial decision a precedent for further intervention in regional procedures was established. The process was largely impersonal and institutional. The undermining of prelatial authority was a result of the secular control over taxation and justice, electoral disputes, enterprising chapters and archdeacons, the rise of mendicant friars, changed economic conditions, and self-seeking papal legates and curial officials. The pontiffs never sought ordinary direction of most aspects of local ecclesiastical operations; Roman institutions and canon law were, in any case, never designed for such monumental tasks.

Thus the "structure" of the thirteenth-century church was not a self-sufficient entity separate from lay society. After 1300 ecclesiastical structures seemed even less able to adapt to changes in secular society. Contemporaries sharply criticized the church for having lost touch with its spiritual mission. Secular and ecclesiastical authorities exploited the church with little concern for pastoral needs. After 1250 there were constant complaints about the injustices resulting from conflicting jurisdictions within dioceses. The interrelationships among the basic triad (papacy, episcopacy, parish) were blurred.

This awkward juxtaposition of radical centralization and administrative disorder reached its climax during the later part of the Avignon papacy (1350–1378), at which time the centralizing drive accelerated. The papacy could create, divide, unify, and abolish dioceses unilaterally. Benedict XII regrouped monasteries according to existing provincial boundaries. Popes suppressed some religious orders (such as the Templars) and reconstituted others. They conferred university degrees, combated heresy, promoted foreign missions. Together with the College of Cardinals the pontiffs restructured the departments that dealt with juridical appeals. The camera, headed by the papally appointed *camerarius*, greatly enlarged its tax collections from the clergy and people of Europe; revenue from income taxes, provisions, annates, spoils (the right to seize the estates of prelates who died at the Curia), procurations, visitations, indulgences, Peter's Pence, subsidies, services, and sale of offices flowed into Avignon. The church's entire organization was affected by the papacy's grip on appointments to benefices, especially bishoprics and abbeys. By provisions, reservations, and expectancies this control extended to canonries, cathedral chapters, deaneries, parishes, chaplaincies, and priories.

This papal ascendancy over benefices, however, was often considered an abuse by reformers. The popes were losing some control over the College of Cardinals and the burgeoning bureaucracies. The relative passivity of most clergy and laity to this centralization continued after the accession of Clement V in 1305, perhaps because less was expected from the hierarchy in terms of spiritual leadership. As the church's organization became more funneled toward Rome, the pastoral functions of the higher clergy were subsumed into their administrative activities. The bishop thus performed his pastoral duty through hearing court cases, parish visitations, and the regulation of his clergy.

Notwithstanding these papal encroachments in benefices, the organization of the church remained the same. The major development was the further enfeebling of the bishop in his see. With the Great Schism, the failure of conciliarism, and the heightened stature of national kings, the church in the fifteenth century came under the sway of secular princes, particularly in England, France, Spain, and Germany (although the postconciliar papacy recovered some of its losses); Italian communes dominated or simply ignored their bishops, who often presided over small, impoverished dioceses. Lay powers assumed control of the church within their lands, but without important alterations in the diocesan framework. Attempts to make the hierarchical constitution of the church more democratic (conciliarism) or oligarchic (curialism) had no lasting effect on ecclesiastical government.

But even when internal conflicts and outside lay interference are taken into account, ecclesiastical structures did possess a substantial degree of administrative autonomy. What had changed between the period 1050–1300 and the period 1300–1450 was not the skeletal structure but the increased complexity of procedures within the diocese and between the diocese and Rome. Whereas in the early Middle Ages the ecclesiastical fabric had helped to shape the development of secular institutions and political units, the church of the later Middle Ages was a bewildering collage of jurisdictions. The church's administration was in danger of becoming self-perpetuating and separate from its pastoral and salvific concerns. The complicated legal apparatus of the cumbrous system vitiated attempts at reform in head and members. Late-medieval church machinery was a static fixture in the institutional makeup of Western Europe; it had little dynamic impact on cultural movements. By 1450 Christendom had long ceased to possess any kind of coherent transnational church organization that could act on the temporal order.

BIBLIOGRAPHY

Frank Barlow, *The English Church, 1000–1066* (1963), and *The English Church, 1066–1154* (1979); Geoffrey Barraclough, *Papal Provisions* (1935); Karl Bihlmeyer and Hermann Tüchle, *Church History*, I, II (1955–1963); Robert Brentano, *Two Churches: England and Italy in the Thirteenth Century* (1968); Martin Brett, *The English Church Under Henry I* (1975); Margaret Deanesly, *The Pre-Conquest Church in England* (1961); John C. Dickinson, *The Later Middle Ages* (1979), in the series An Ecclesiastical History of England; Augustin Fliche and Victor Martin, eds., *Histoire de l'église depuis les origines jusqu'à nos jours* (1934–) III–XI, and esp. XII, *Institutions ecclésiastiques*, by Gabriel Le Bras, 2 pts. (1959–1964); Hubert Jedin and John P. Dolan, eds., *Handbook of Church History*, III, IV (1969, 1980); Gabriel Le Bras, *Histoire du droit et des institutions de l'église en occident*, vol. 7: *L'âge classique, 1140–1378* (1965); Guillaume Mollat, *The Popes at Avignon 1305–1378* (1963); William A. Pantin, *The English Church in the Fourteenth Century* (1955); Robert E. Rodes, *Ecclesiastical Administration in Medieval England* (1977); U. Stutz, "The Proprietary Church," in Geoffrey Barraclough, ed., *Mediaeval Germany*, II (1961); Alexander H. Thompson, *The English Clergy and Their Organization in the Later Middle Ages* (1947).

THOMAS RENNA

[See also **Benefice, Ecclesiastical; Cardinals, College of; Clergy; Curia, Papal; Diocese; Legate, Papal; Metropolitan; Papacy; Parishes; Province, Ecclesiastical.**]

CHURCH, TYPES OF

Conch church. A plan in which semicircular niches surmounted by half-domes (conches) predominate. Plans with a regular number of conches—four (tetraconch, as at Seleucia-Pieria [Samandağ], Syria), eight (octaconch, as at Constantine's Golden Octagon, Antioch), or ten (the fourth-century St. Gereon, Cologne)—were normally centralized buildings composed of a concentric grouping of conches. The tetraconch plan was the most common and was used throughout the early Christian world (for example, S. Lorenzo, Milan; Bosra, Syria). Occasionally two of the conches were elongated to create a longitudinal axis (Resafa, Syria). The tetraconch plan does not seem to signify a particular function: the plan was used for martyria, cathedrals, and possibly palace chapels. The triconch plan with three semicircular niches was most commonly used for the eastern end of early Christian basilicas, terminating the nave. Certain triconch chancels, particularly popular in Egypt and Syria, have north and south conches that extend beyond the nave wall (Hermopolis [Al-Ashmūnein]) or the triconch enclosed within a rectangular block of masonry (Deir-el-Abiad).

Cross-domed church. A roughly square Byzantine church of which the central open space (naos) describes a cross with arms of equal or nearly equal depth. The center of the cross is surmounted by a dome on pendentives and the short crossarms by barrel vaults that spring from four massive corner piers. The cross-shaped core is enveloped on the north and south by aisles and galleries, on the west by an exonarthex with a gallery, and on the east by the apse and subsidiary chapels. All the surrounding aisles and upper-level galleries open into the adjoining arms of the central cross through arcades; the exonarthex may have either a single entrance or an arcade leading into the cross-shaped core. The earliest known example is the Koimesis Church at Nicaea (before 726), now in ruins, but the plan may have been developed under Justinian: Choricius' description of St. Sergius at Gaza seems at least to anticipate the cross-domed plan. The type persisted in Byzantium through the eleventh century and became ca-

nonical in eleventh-century Russia (Hagia Sophia, Kiev, of 1037–1046). The best example that has been preserved, though it is heavily restored, is Hagia Sophia at Thessaloniki (eighth century).

Cross-in-square (quincunx). A steep, square church of which the core is divided into nine sections. A large central square rests on four large columns or piers and is surmounted by a dome on a drum and, usually, pendentives; smaller squares, either vaulted or domed, occupy the corners, and four short, barrel-vaulted crossarms expand the main axes. Three apses normally project from the eastern end, and the remaining three sides may be enveloped by a narthex and porticoes or side chapels. The quincunx plan was used by Roman architects and is found sporadically in both Eastern and Western Christian buildings (Germigny des Prés, *ca.* 816) before the later ninth century. The earliest known Constantinopolitan example—the Nea of Basil I—was consecrated in 881, and the cross-in-square church dominated Byzantine ecclesiastical architecture of the post-Iconoclastic period (Theotokos Church at Hosios Lukas in Phocis).

Domed octagon. A Byzantine square church plan with squinches spanning the corners to create an octagon from which a dome rises (Nea Moni, Chios). The interior walls are each divided into three sections, with a wide central bay supporting part of the dome and two narrower flanking bays surmounted by squinches.

Double cathedral. An early Christian plan, used mainly in the Adriatic provinces during the fourth century, composed of two parallel basilicas joined by a transverse hall, as at Aquileia. The double cathedral may have been suggested by the local tradition of double temples in Istria and borrowed by Christian architects because the double plan accommodated certain liturgical requirements, but the precise function of the double basilica is not known.

Double-ended basilica. A basilica with an apse at each short end. Double-ended churches were built in the early Christian period but were most common during the Carolingian era. The function of the additional apse is not entirely clear. In the eighth-century rebuilding of St. Denis, near Paris, the second apse may have been meant to dignify the western entrance, since Charlemagne's father Pepin was buried there; at St. Gall, the western apse gave a feeling of enclosure to the interior that was appropriate to a monastic church. At Fulda the decision to add a western apse may have been influenced by monastic architecture or by a desire to emulate the western orientation of Old St. Peter's. Ottonian architects (as at Hildesheim) and Romanesque architects also built double-ended basilicas, apparently based on Carolingian models.

Greek cross. A plan in the form of a cross with arms of equal or nearly equal length. The center bay is often domed (Mausoleum of Galla Placidia, Ravenna; Hosios David, Thessaloniki), as are the cross-arms (Justinian's Church of the Holy Apostles, Constantinople). Although the Greek-cross plan was used throughout the medieval period, it was most common in the fifth and sixth centuries in Byzantium; the plan was also adapted for secular use (Chalke Gate, Constantinople).

Greek-cross domed octagon. A Byzantine fusion of a central domed octagon supported by *L*-shaped piers and a Greek-cross plan, enclosed in a square or rectangle. Each crossarm measures half the width of the center square, is barrel vaulted, and interrupts the surrounding belt of aisles. The eastern arm extends into an apse, which is flanked by a prothesis and a diaconicon. The aisles in the corners are usually lower than the cross and central dome (as at Daphni) but are occasionally surmounted by galleries (Katholikon, Hosios Lukas); most extant examples of the plan are in mainland Greece.

Hall church (Hallenkirche). A basilican plan in which the height of the nave(s) and aisles (if any) are approximately the same. A hall church may have two equal naves (Imbach, Austria, *ca.* 1275) or a nave and aisles of equal or nearly equal height (Spitalkirche, Landshut, 1407). Hall churches do not have clerestories but are lighted by large windows on the exterior walls. The equal height of nave and aisles produces a spacious, open interior. To heighten the effect of a unified interior, transepts are often omitted and the choir and nave are usually integrated. The roof may be either continuous or divided to reflect the longitudinal division of space on the interior; vaulting systems vary. Most hall churches were built in Germany (Bavaria), where the plan was apparently first used in the Chapel of St. Bartholomew at Paderborn (1017). The plan remained popular in Bavaria (for example, Prüll) and attained its ultimate expression under the German architect Hans von Burghausen in the Gothic period (St. Martin, Landshut). Hall churches were also built, though less frequently, outside Germany in the Gothic period (Cathedral of St. Pierre, Poitiers; Ste. Chapelle, lower chapel; Alcobaça, Spain). The hall-church plan was

also used for Lady Chapels (Salisbury, *ca.* 1225) and choirs (Schwäbisch Gmünd, *ca.* 1317).

Latin cross. A basilica with transepts resembling in plan a cross with three short arms and one long. The Latin-cross plan was particularly popular in the Romanesque and early Gothic periods and, because it was the standard form of pilgrimage churches, became widely diffused. High Gothic emphasis on unified interior space resulted in abridged transepts and elongated choirs so that cathedrals such as Chartres and Amiens, while relying on a Latin-cross plan, no longer retain the definitive form.

Pilgrimage church. A Romanesque modification of the Latin-cross plan designed to accommodate pilgrims. Pilgrimage churches were of fireproof (stone) construction. The nave was roofed with a barrel vault, often divided by transverse arches (St. Sernin, Toulouse), and was flanked by aisles and galleries covered by groin vaults. There was usually no clerestory except in the apse. The aisles and galleries continued around the transept arms and choir, creating an ambulatory around the apse to allow access to small chapels containing relics that extended from the east walls of the transept and radiated from the apse. The crossing was surmounted by a tower, and a choir was often inserted between the crossing and the apse. Important examples of pilgrimage churches are found along the four major routes leading to Santiago de Compostela: St. Martin, Tours, on the Paris–Bordeaux road (*ca.* 997–1050); St. Martial, Limoges, on the Vézelay–Périgueux route (*ca.* 1063–1095); Ste. Foi, Conques, on the Le Puy–Moissac road (*ca.* 1052); and St. Sernin, Toulouse, on the Arles–Jaca road (*ca.* 1077–1096). The architectural features of the pilgrimage churches transcended local styles and influenced numerous churches not on a pilgrimage route (St. Étienne, Nevers). The plan diffused the arrangement of an ambulatory with radiating chapels throughout the Latin West, paving the way for the Gothic chevet.

Stave church. A Scandinavian timber church, normally with a rectangular nave terminated by a smaller rectangular chancel. A wooden frame with corner posts supported walls of boards joined together by tongue-and-groove (palisade, stave) construction. The interior was sometimes divided into a nave and aisles by tall wooden posts (masts). Stave churches were usually tall buildings with steeply pitched roofs; they were often richly decorated with relief carving or elaborate shingles. Preserved examples date from the early eleventh century; a par-

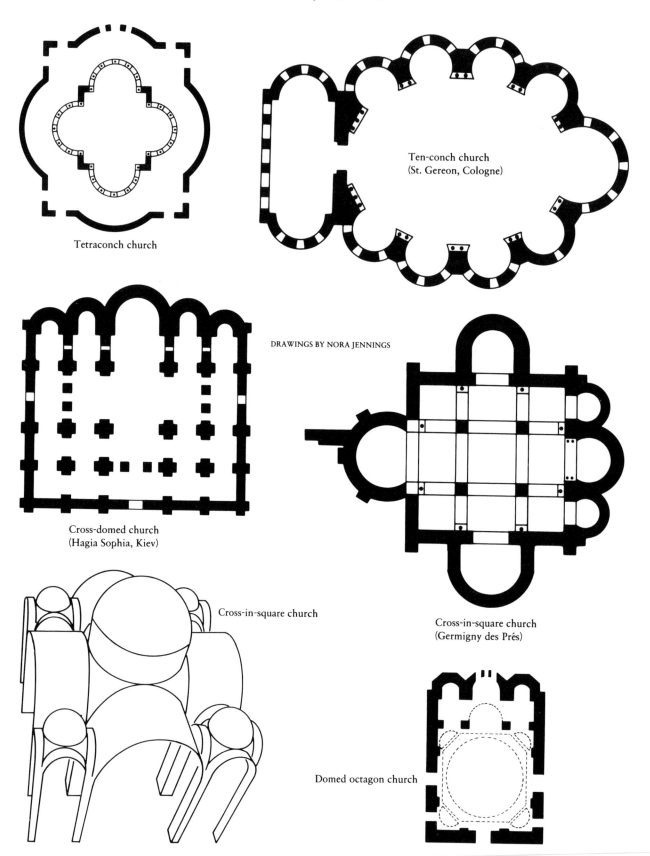

Tetraconch church

Ten-conch church
(St. Gereon, Cologne)

DRAWINGS BY NORA JENNINGS

Cross-domed church
(Hagia Sophia, Kiev)

Cross-in-square church

Cross-in-square church
(Germigny des Prés)

Domed octagon church

380

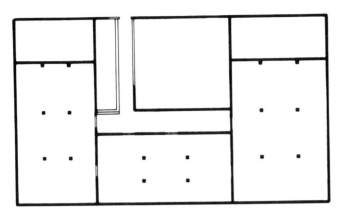

Double cathedral (Aquileia)

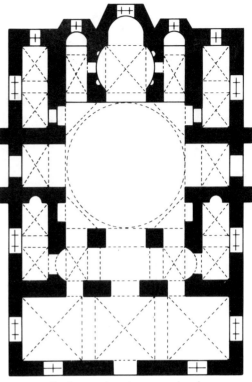

Greek cross-domed octagon church
(Daphni)

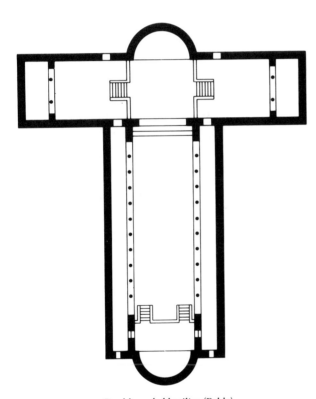

Double-ended basilica (Fulda)

Hall church

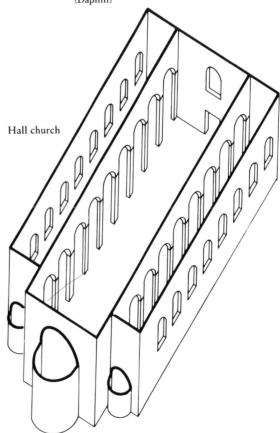

Greek cross church

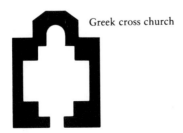

DRAWINGS BY NORA JENNINGS

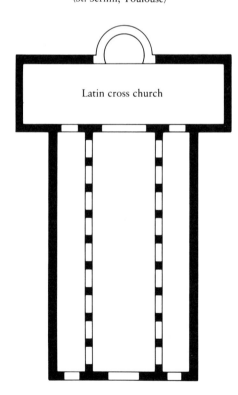

Pilgrimage church
(St. Sernin, Toulouse)

Latin cross church

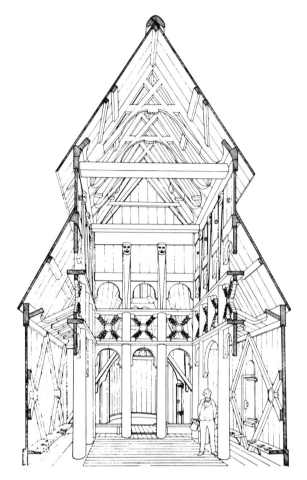

Stave church. FROM KENNETH J. CONANT, CAROLINGIAN AND ROMAN-
ESQUE ARCHITECTURE (1974)

ticularly fine stave church of about 1150 still stands
at Borgund, Norway.

BIBLIOGRAPHY

Kenneth J. Conant, *Carolingian and Romanesque Architecture, 800–1200,* rev. ed. (1974); Paul Frankl, *Gothic
Architecture,* Dieter Pevsner, trans. (1963); Richard
Krautheimer, *Early Christian and Byzantine Architecture,*
rev. ed. (1975).

LESLIE BRUBAKER

[See also **Apse; Basilica; Chancel; Chevet; Clerestory;
Cross, Forms of; Early Christian and Byzantine Architecture; Exonarthex; Gothic Architecture; Naos; Nave; Pen-
dentive; Romanesque Architecture; Squinch; Vault.**]

CHURCHING OF WOMEN. Superstitions concerning the phenomenon of birth, especially as they

pertain to the mother, were intensified in the Christian church by the adoption and ritualization of Old Testament Levitical purification regulations, first in the Eastern church and then in the West through the penitential books. Despite the clear and often repeated statement of Pope Gregory I that a woman was free to enter a church even at the hour of birth, the idea persisted that she was in some way unclean and not free to enter until some forty days after parturition. This sentiment was intensified by the ecclesiastical ritual of "churching" or the "benediction of a woman entering church after birth."

Although there are early medieval examples of benedictions of women before, during, and after childbirth, specific formulas for churching did not appear in the rituals until the eleventh century. Together with the prayers and benedictions, which contain the themes of bodily healing, thanksgiving, purification from sin, Old Testament regulations, and the example of Mary in the Temple, there was a definite ritual that, though differing from diocese to diocese, might contain the following elements. The woman, with or without child and companions, and holding a lighted candle, would wait in front of the church. A priest would meet her, and after the reading of several prayers, John 1, and psalms, and aspersion with holy water, he would lead her by the right hand into the church to one of its altars. There followed additional prayers, psalms, benedictions, aspersions, and perhaps censing of the woman.

Local variations might be added to this basic ritual, such as presentation to the priest of candles, money, or a lamb; kissing of relics or the Gospel book at the reading of John 1; reception of *pain bénit* by the woman if the churching was connected with a Mass; placing of the child on the altar or cleansing its lips and tongue with ablution wine (wine that the priest poured over his fingers after Communion) as an ersatz for communion or symbol of wisdom; and removal of the child's baptismal hood or "miter."

BIBLIOGRAPHY

Walter von Arx, "La bénédiction de la mère après la naissance: Histoire et signification," in *Concilium*, **132** (1978); Peter Browe, *Beiträge zur Sexualethik des Mittelalters* (1932); Adolf Franz, *Die kirchlichen Benediktionen im Mittelalter*, II (1909), 186–240.

ROGER E. REYNOLDS

[See also **Rituals**.]

CIBORIUM, a roof or canopy raised over an altar, usually a cupola on four columns; also, a lidded chalice made to hold the eucharistic bread.

LESLIE BRUBAKER

[See also **Baldachin**.]

CID, THE, HISTORY AND LEGEND OF

THE CID OF HISTORY

Rodrigo Díaz, Spain's national hero, is known by the Arabic honorific title Cid (*sīd, sayyid;* lord) and also by the epithet of Romance origin, Campeador (winner of battles). He was born about 1043 in the village of Vivar (or Bivar), six miles north of Burgos, the chief city of Old Castile. On the side of his father, Diego Laínez, he was descended from Laín Calvo, one of the judges who according to tradition was elected by the Castilians to govern their earldom when they rebelled against the king of León at the beginning of the tenth century. On his father's death in 1058, Rodrigo was taken to the court of Ferdinand I; there he became the ward of Prince Sancho, Ferdinand's eldest son, who knighted him in 1060.

In 1063, two years before his death, Ferdinand announced the partition of his realm. Sancho was given Castile; Alfonso inherited León; and García, the youngest, received Galicia and Portugal. Sancho was opposed to the partition because it deprived him, as the firstborn, of his rights of primogeniture. His unappeasable resentment made war between him and Alfonso inevitable after Ferdinand's death. With the decisive participation of Rodrigo, now commander in chief of the Castilian army, Sancho defeated Alfonso at Llantada (1068) and then, decisively, at Golpejera (1072). (Between these battles Sancho divided with Alfonso the kingdom of their incompetent brother, Garcia.) After the victory at Golpejera, Sancho imprisoned Alfonso briefly in the castle of Burgos and then sent him into exile to Toledo, under the custody of King Ma'mūn.

Sancho was crowned king of León on 12 January 1072, but his reign over the conquered kingdom was short-lived. Nine months later he was assassinated by a Zamoran knight, Vellido Adolpho, during his siege of Zamora, a city that Alfonso had given to his beloved sister, doña Urraca, to rule. On the liquidation of his king and lord, Rodrigo became the vassal of Alfonso.

For a time, after acceding to the throne of Castile,

Alfonso bestowed his favor on the Cid, notwithstanding his decisive role at Golpejera. The monarch's liberality was dictated by expediency. First, he put Rodrigo in his debt by making him his vassal. By thus securing the support of the Cid and his party, he solved his most pressing problem, the disaffection of Castile. Alfonso bound the Cid to him in other ways as well. In 1074 he arranged Rodrigo's marriage to his own niece, Jimena Díaz. This was a masterstroke of policy, for the marriage settlement, drawn up according to the laws of León, made her husband legally dependent on that kingdom. Although other manifestations of favor were not lacking, Alfonso was careful to deny the Cid any significant opportunity to exercise his military talents.

While Alfonso was engaged in his campaign against the kingdom of Toledo in July 1081, the Cid, without authorization from the king, took it upon himself to attack the Moors who had taken Gormaz Castle, the most important fortress on the Duero River. The king was furious and listened willingly to the Cid's enemies, who accused him of having interfered in order to betray Alfonso to the enemy. The king's baleful and unforgiving spite moved his hand to fix the royal seal that barred Rodrigo Díaz of Vivar from Castile and León.

The Campeador first offered his services to two Christian princes, Counts Berenguer II and Ramón II of Barcelona. They did not welcome him. He therefore placed himself at the disposal of al-Muqtadīr of Saragossa. Al-Muqtadīr and his heir, al-Mustaᶜīn, considered his collaboration a blessing, for Saragossa was vulnerable to the inimical surrounding powers. Over a two-year period the Cid gained victories against Saragossa's enemies, among them Berenguer, whom he took prisoner; he also defeated Sancho Ramírez of Aragon and Navarre.

In 1086 a new character, alien and formidable, made his entrance on the Peninsular stage. He was Yūsuf ibn Tāshfīn, supreme emir of the vast North African Almoravid empire. The fanatical Muslim leader invaded Spain at the desperate request of al-Muᶜtamid ibn ᶜAbbād, the ruler of Seville, who could no longer tolerate Alfonso's excessive demands. Alfonso, joined by Sancho Ramírez and knights from Italy and France, led a great army southward, encamping near Sagrajas, five miles south of Badajoz. Accustomed to man-to-man combat, in which individual valor was of paramount importance, the Christians could not cope with Yūsuf's unfamiliar coordinated group tactics, and Alfonso's army was decimated (October 1086). At this time Al-

fonso decided to restore the Cid to favor, probably because the disastrous defeat made him realize that he needed the Campeador's collaboration in the field.

The Spanish monarch was not Yūsuf's only victim. Yūsuf broke his promise to al-Muᶜtamid and other southern Muslim tributary kings, to respect their titular sovereignty, and liquidated them at intervals. By 1094 he had gained control of virtually all of southern Spain.

Having subjugated Andalusia, Yūsuf coveted above all the Valencian region, which remained in the Cid's power. In 1093 he sent his son-in-law, Abū Bakr, at the head of a huge force to rescue besieged Valencia; in 1094 he dispatched another army, under his nephew, Muḥammad ibn Tāshfīn, to take Valencia; and in January 1097, a great Almoravid force, also commanded by Muḥammad, leading a vastly superior army, finally trapped the Cid in the narrow pass of Bairén. But the Cid was victorious in each instance—the last time against great odds and in virtually impossible terrain.

More light is shed on the troubled relationship between King Alfonso and the Cid by events surrounding the vassal's second exile, which will now be viewed retrospectively. Yūsuf crossed the Strait of Gibraltar for a second time in June 1089, bent on seizing the castle of Aledo, the one remaining pocket of Christian resistance in the south. He was unable to do so because of internal dissidence and lack of support from his Andalusian allies, but he laid it under siege. Having learned that Alfonso was on the march to relieve the castle, Yūsuf withdrew to Lorca.

Before his withdrawal, Alfonso had sent the Cid an urgent message commanding him to meet him at Villena, seventy miles northeast of Aledo. The Cid left the east at once but failed to join his forces to those of Alfonso, who instead of proceeding to Villena had taken a shortcut to Molina. The Cid's enemies seized upon this contretemps to poison Alfonso's all-too-receptive ear: the Cid purposely avoided joining the expedition, they charged, expecting that without his aid the king and his army would be slaughtered. Enraged, Alfonso not only banished the Cid again but also, following a Germanic law that held the family liable in all legal matters, had the Cid's wife and their three children imprisoned.

When the Campeador returned to the Valencian region after his second exile (November 1089), he found that his position had become extremely precarious. Al-Mustaᶜīn of Saragossa, resenting the

Cid's departure from the site of their own military operations, broke off their alliance and became the ally of King Alfonso in 1090. Many Castilian knights, fearing to incur Alfonso's displeasure, deserted him. The rulers of Aragon and Lérida, always covetous of the Valencia region, had renewed their designs against it. Finally, al-Qādir, the puppet king of Valencia, confident that the new wave of Almoravids would overwhelm the Campeador, refused to pay him tribute (April 1090).

Having abandoned his own favorable position in the east to help Alfonso in the south, the Cid found himself deprived of his originally strong advantage and bereft of outside help. In this crisis he merited admiration for the valor, courage, and military skill by which he was able to extricate himself from a seemingly hopeless predicament. Undaunted by the numerically superior forces that surrounded him, he rallied his small army and set about restoring his former domination of Valencia and its environs.

While the Cid triumphed in the east, Alfonso's fortunes declined to their nadir. Heading the third Almoravid invasion, Yūsuf's first cousin Sīr (Seyr) ibn Abī Bakr rapidly conquered the entire Guadalquivir basin, captured Córdoba, and surrounded Seville. In May 1091 Alfonso sought to divert the Almoravids from Seville by leading an expedition against Granada. At this juncture Alfonso's queen, Constanza, sent a letter to the Cid begging him to go to her husband's aid. Although Liria was about to surrender to the Campeador after a seven-month siege, he did not hesitate to abandon it and met Alfonso near Granada. Prompted by his desire to ensure the king's safety, he took it upon himself—without consulting Alfonso—to advance. The Almoravids, safe within Granada, did not venture outside its walls to fight; and the Cid rejoined Alfonso only to be assailed, on grounds of lèse majesté, by an outburst of recriminations and insults. Deeply hurt, the Cid returned to the Valencian region.

Having failed to take Aledo, Yūsuf returned to the Maghrib. He commanded Muḥammad ibn Tāshfīn to dislodge the Cid from the Valencian region, where the Campeador had established the strongest possible line of defense against imminent Almoravid attack, along the Benicadell range, forty miles south of Valencia and extending twenty miles from east to west, with passes only at the ends. Al-Mustaᶜīn and Sancho Ramírez now offered to join the Cid; as the only warrior in Spain who had never been defeated, he was their sole hope against a common enemy who would give no quarter to either Moor or Christian.

Only two months later, in June 1092, Sancho Ramírez shifted his support to Alfonso, who had organized a mighty campaign to take Valencia from the Cid. Count Berenguer of Barcelona also joined Alfonso, and to cap the measure, Alfonso secured a promise of help from the two foremost maritime powers of the western Mediterranean, the republics of Genoa and Pisa. But the 400 Pisan and Genoese ships arrived late at their destination; and this delay, coupled with Alfonso's inability to continue provisioning his large forces at Yuballa (Puig), obliged him to break camp. After this fiasco Alfonso sent the Cid a conciliatory letter "pardoning" him. Rodrigo expressed his gratitude, imploring the king not to heed his bad advisers and reaffirming his loyalty.

But Alfonso's change of heart had come too late. The Cid, fully occupied in the east, could not help the king regain his ascendancy in the south. Alfonso did not give up, but his tactics against the Almoravids' new type of warfare remained ineffectual. His defeat at Jaén in 1092 was almost as disastrous as that at Sagrajas. The eclipse of the royal sun, begun in 1086, was now total. Henceforth only the vassal Rodrigo Díaz de Vivar could turn the tide.

In the late summer or early autumn of 1092 the Campeador left Valencia to eradicate pockets of resistance in Saragossa. During his absence Valencia's qadi, Ibn Yaḥḥaf, took over the city, imprisoned the Cid's vizier Ibn al-Faraj, brought about the murder of Valencia's puppet king al-Qādir, and seized his fabulous treasure.

For almost twenty months thereafter the Campeador laid siege to the city, gradually reducing Valencia to a ghoulish site of famine and death. Ibn Yaḥḥaf refused to surrender but waited for the help promised by Yūsuf and several of the latter's captains. This promise was kept in November 1093, when Abū Bakr approached the city but had to turn back, foiled by the Cid's flooding of the approaches through the destruction of causeway bridges and the release of irrigation-canal waters. These measures were providentially augmented by torrential rains.

But Abū Bakr's effort, thwarted by the Cid and literally by Heaven, instead of causing Yūsuf to waver, moved him to try again. In October 1094 he sent a huge army under the command of Muḥammad ibn Tāshfīn to take Valencia. The Cid, taking the Almoravids by surprise, defeated them at the Cuarte plain, three miles west of Valencia. Despite the Almoravids' failures, their promises to the usurping qadi continued, and he hung on until the plight of the famished population became unbearable.

Finally, on 15 June 1094, the Cid took possession of Valencia. His first order of business was to bring Ibn Yaḥḥaf to trial for perjury (the qadi had falsely sworn that he was innocent of the theft of al-Qādir's treasure) and regicide. He was convicted of both charges and executed by burning in May 1095.

During the remaining four years of his life the Cid was a severe—indeed, sometimes ruthless—but fair ruler of the city that he had conquered for Alfonso, to whom he remained loyal even though he had become a potentate in his own right. He also left his mark on Valencia as a patriot of the Reconquest, by turning the city's Great Mosque into a Christian church in 1096. Two years later it became St. Mary's Cathedral, which he also richly endowed. Also, with his endorsement, Jerome of Périgord, the battling Cluniac clergyman, was proclaimed bishop of Valencia.

In the still-turbulent military field the Campeador was victorious on three subsequent occasions. He won the battle of Bairén in January 1097 under virtually impossible conditions and, in December of that year, took Almenar after a three-month siege. In 1098 he laid siege to the fortress of Murviedro, which surrendered on 24 June. Rodrigo Díaz de Vivar, Mío Cid Campeador, "he who in a good hour was born," died a year later, on 10 July 1099.

Among his contemporaries, Christian authors naturally praise him, while the opinions of Arab historians are venomous. But if these Arab writers, Ibn Alcama and Ibn Bassām, were the first Cid-haters, they were far from the last. The Catalan Jesuit Juan Francisco Masdeu, in his *Historia crítica de España XX* (1805), called the Cid a turncoat, renegade, and mercenary enemy of his country. Basing his opinions on the anti-Cidian Arab sources and rejecting Christian ones, the influential Dutch Arabist Reinhart Dozy was instrumental in propagating the Cidophobia that permeates his *Recherches sur l'histoire politique et littéraire de l'Espagne pendant le moyen âge* (1849). Indeed, the black legend became so firmly entrenched that it has taken nothing less than Ramón Menéndez Pidal's reconstruction, *La España del Cid* (1929), to dispel it.

There is no praise as authentic as that of an enemy. Ten years after the Cid's death Ibn Bassām wrote of him: "The power of this tyrant became increasingly unbearable; its terrible weight was felt in the coastal regions and in the high plateaus, and he made tremble with fear all men, both near and far. . . . Yet this man, who was the scourge of his age was, by his unflagging and clear-sighted energy, his

virile character, and his heroism, a miracle among the great miracles of the Almighty."

THE CID OF LEGEND

The *Cantar de mío Cid,* one of the great poems of the European Middle Ages, combines fact and fiction in the story of a warrior who is invincible in battle and almost flawless in character. Composed about fifty years after his death, the story is told with great artistry by a master of the *mester de juglaría* (manner of the minstrel [oral] poets), and its extant version has endured across the centuries. The Cid's extraordinary qualities and accomplishments were also celebrated during his lifetime in shorter poems.

Given the indispensable function of jongleurs as poetic sounding-boards of collective attitudes, and as informants of notable events in an almost illiterate age, it was inevitable that such a poet would give expression to his public's admiration of its national hero. The Cid fired the popular imagination as no other medieval Spaniard was able to do. This was the result, as Peter Edward Russell says, "not only of his invincibility in the field but also of the fact that, after his career as a courtier had been ruined, he had continued to win fame, riches and rank solely by the exercise of his sword and his intelligence despite the king's disapproval and the active opposition of the great magnates."

Two systems of action, the military and the domestic, are combined in the plot. The military action consists of a series of victories won by the Campeador after his expatriation. Starting with a handful of men, but gaining ever-increasing numbers of recruits, the Cid advances deeper and deeper into Moorish territory until he conquers Valencia and defeats King Yusuf (Yúçuf; that is, Yūsuf ibn Tāshfīn) of Morocco. These military operations take place over a period of three years.

The second basic system of actions, the domestic, is a logical consequence of the military action. At the height of the Cid's success, the two infantes (heirs) of Carrion, coveting the Campeador's enormous riches, ask King Alfonso to arrange their marriage to his daughters. The king, now anxious to please his vassal, asks for his consent, which the Cid gives reluctantly because, he says, the daughters are too young and the suitors too high above them in rank. One suspects that the father really distrusts the suitors.

After two years of pampered married life in Valencia, the craven infantes one day are terrified by the Cid's escaped lion. One hides behind a bench, the other behind the beam of a wine press. Shortly thereafter, one of them, Fernando, is stricken with fear in the battle against Búcar (laisse 115). Mortified by the jibes of which they are the butt, the infantes depart for Carrión, halting along the way to give vent to their spite by beating their wives senseless at the oak grove of Corpes.

The Cid begs justice of King Alfonso, who promises reparation and convokes court at Toledo (the Toledo Cortes). Accused of infamy, the infantes are required to meet certain demands. During the ensuing heated exchanges, two messengers arrive to ask, on behalf of the princes of Navarre and Aragon, for the hands of the Cid's daughters. A judicial duel takes place in the infantes' own country. They are defeated by the Cid's champions. Then the second marriages of the Cid's daughters are celebrated. Thus the Cid becomes a kinsman of the kings of Spain.

Among the indisputable historical events in the Cantar, the most important are the Cid's exile, the king's pardon, and nearly all the raids and battles that culminate with the conquest of Valencia. The juglar, however, wrongly attributes the immediate cause of Rodrigo's exile to a false accusation concerning misappropriated tribute from the king of Seville. The embassy to Seville, the accusations of the scandalmongers, and Alfonso's giving angry credence to the accusations are all true, but they were not the immediate cause of Rodrigo's exile. The affair, however, did pave the way for the direct cause of his banishment: his unauthorized intervention at Gormaz.

One of the Cid's first victories in the poem, the taking of Alcocer, is not recorded by history, but it seems authentic because it is described at greater length and with more detail than any other warlike feat in the poem—probably because the battle takes place in the juglar's own region, the geography of which he traces with remarkable accuracy.

In contrast with the particularized account of the capture of Alcocer, the poet only enumerates in passages of rapid cinematic technique other military actions of the hero, most of which are recorded by history. According to the poem, the Cid, in his progress toward the southeast, used as a center of operations a rugged promontory (El Poyo) while he laid under tribute the whole country from Daroca to Teruel. This is substantially confirmed by an important contemporary Christian account, the Historia Roderici. The poem also mentions in passing the names of numerous towns and places taken by the Cid which correspond to fuller accounts in Arab sources.

Three of the major battles in the poem—those against Berenguer, Yūsuf, and Búcar—correspond to recorded historical events, but the juglar tells them with varying degrees of poetic license. For example, in laisse 95, he erroneously attributes the historical Cid's defeat of Yūsuf's nephew, Muḥammad ibn Tāshfīn, to Yūsuf himself, perhaps to make the Campeador's triumph (over the uncle rather than the nephew) more noteworthy. The last battle in the poem has a very tenuous connection with history. Búcar, called rey de Marruecos, is probably Abū Bakr, the historical Yūsuf's son-in-law, sent to retake Valencia. The historical Abū Bakr turned back without fighting the Cid for the reasons previously set forth. The poem's battle, depicted as a chase on horseback culminating in Rodrigo's slaying of Búcar, is therefore a striking instance of poetic license.

Finally, the fictitious elements in the poem are: (1) the trick whereby the Cid collects 300 gold and 300 silver marks from the Jewish moneylenders; (2) possibly the first marriages of the Cid's daughters; (3) the lion incident; and (4) the judicial proceedings at the Toledo court.

Being an artist, the juglar had to be selective; he also resorted to poetic license. To attain artistic unity, for example, he compressed into five years events that occurred between 1081 and 1094. Two convoluted exiles are telescoped into one with a definitive happy ending. The pardon is also made to appear irreversible so that Alfonso, who never quite ceased being envious in history, would exemplify his people's image of an ideal king. There is also a modification in the character of the hero himself. The poet idealized the protagonist by emphasizing only his unvarying benevolence and by closing his eyes to the extreme severity of which he was capable. Such idealization is, of course, to be expected in an epic poem whose hero is presented as a paragon, one whose lack of any self-destructive defect—like the wrath of Achilles or the pride of Roland—makes him the most perfect of all epic protagonists and the most successful.

In the end, the Cid's character and his military exploits are no more remarkable in the poem than they were in reality. They therefore demonstrate Aristotle's dictum from the Poetics that "there is nothing to prevent the things that really happened from being the kind of things that can happen"—that is, things as they should have been and not things as they were.

The invented parts of the Cantar are necessary to organize the plot, to establish the causal connection of incidents, to emphasize the Cid's authentic character as well as the king's changed character, and to make poetically representative of evil the character of his enemies. Rodrigo's economic ruin dictates his tricking of the moneylenders; the lion incident provides the motive for the vengeful conduct of the infantes; and nothing less than the fictitious Toledo court proceedings will suffice to exalt the true moral greatness of the hero, for on that solemn occasion the power of his word transcends the power of his sword.

In sum, in the *Cantar de mío Cid* fact and fiction are skillfully combined to form a poetic creation with a theme—the restitution of the Cid's lost honor by his own efforts—which serves as a unifying principle knitting together a system of actions whose agents are dynamic instruments in the development of that system. To a considerable extent action, character, thought, and diction reflect historical reality, especially the political and religious reality of the times; but in their poetic context these elements exert their power in the sphere of art.

Las mocedades de Rodrigo (The youthful exploits of Rodrigo), composed around 1350, provides the only extant example of the moribund, decadent phase of Castilian epic. At this stage the *juglar* strives to satisfy his public's demand for innovation by combining pseudo-historical and fictitious material. Young Rodrigo's always successful military exploits and other deeds take place not only in Spain but also beyond the Pyrenees as far away as Paris. There, Spain's enemies, in addition to the French themselves, include the German emperor and the pope.

The most decadent aspect of the *Mocedades* is the deterioration of Rodrigo's character. Even though he is not devoid of merit, his conduct is sometimes reprehensible: he is a disrespectful son, a rebellious and sometimes insolent vassal, and an inconsiderate husband. On one occasion he violates sanctuary, an offense viewed with particular horror in the Middle Ages.

Despite his defects, however, Rodrigo at one point performs a Christlike deed: he shelters a leper under his cloak. Rodrigo falls asleep, and in his dream the leper reveals himself as St. Lazarus and assures him that God will always help him. This episode is loosely based on a biblical source (Luke 3:11) and on the *Cantar de mío Cid*. In *laisse* 19, the archangel Gabriel appears to the Cid in a dream and tells him that he will fare well as long as he lives.

Another episode involves the relation of Rodrigo to his betrothed, Jimena. Rodrigo, after a quarrel between his father, Diego Laínez, and Jimena's father, Count Gómez de Gormaz, kills the latter. Jimena asks King Ferdinand for justice only, a little later, to turn around and ask to marry Rodrigo. The *juglar* tells the incident poorly and fails to exploit either the potential open clash between Rodrigo and Jimena or their individual inner conflict between love and honor.

This dramatic situation was seized upon by later perpetuators of the Cid legend. The first to do so were anonymous singers of ballads who, however, could not develop it adequately because of the concision of the ballad form. It was not until the first years of the seventeenth century that the Golden Age dramatist Guillén de Castro did justice to the complex and intense emotional situation in his *Mocedades del Cid*. Corneille's *Le Cid* (1636), one of the most influential plays in French literature, made brilliant use of this legend in depicting the inner struggle in the hearts of Ximène and Don Rodrigue.

There are some 200 Cid ballads. Some of them echo, if only faintly, the *Cantar de mío Cid*; others are the invention of a *juglar* who reflects the popular imagination; and a few derive from a lost version of the *Mocedades de Rodrigo* that has been reconstructed by means of its prosified versions in chronicles and is designated the *Gesta de las mocedades de Rodrigo*.

Among the ballads that reflect the *Cantar* the following are noteworthy: one ballad dealing with the first exile (*Primavera* 31); several concerning the Cid's pursuit of Búcar (*Primavera* 55, 56; Smith 21); two that narrate the outrage against the Cid's daughters at Corpes (*Primavera* 57, 60); and two on the judicial proceeding at the Toledo Cortes (*Primavera* 58, 59).

Of the foregoing, *Hélo, hélo por dó viene* (*Primavera* 55; Smith 21) is of special interest because it is the first of a centuries-long succession of highly fictionalized *romances* dealing with Búcar's flight from the Cid. Variants still exist in the oral tradition of the Iberian Peninsula and among the Sephardim in Morocco. *En Santa Gadea de Burgos* (Smith 21) concerns the oath that Alfonso was required to swear before the Cid, to the effect that he had had nothing to do with the murder of his brother Sancho. Menéndez Pidal believed that the oath is historical fact because self-exculpation of a crime through an oath was legally necessary in Alfonso's epoch. On the other hand, Jules Horrent considers that the *jura* (oath) cannot be historical, since there is no reference to it before the thirteenth century. My own position on the question is Pyrrhonian.

As for the ballads derived from the *Gesta de las mocedades de Rodrigo,* the best is *Cabalga Diego Laínez.* Like his counterpart in the *Mocedades de Rodrigo,* Rodrigo is a rebellious vassal here; but unlike the latter he is not awkward and ill-bred but *el soberbio castellano,* the Castilian knight of fiery temperament and aristocratic bearing, pride, and manners. The fourteenfold anaphoric enumeration of alternating and contrasting elements in the introduction of the ballad, the perfect structure, and the shocking climax that strikes like lightning all work together to produce a masterpiece.

BIBLIOGRAPHY

The Cid of history. Contemporary histories include the *Historia Roderici* (*ca.* 1110), composed by a follower of the Cid. The MS is at the Academia de la Historia, Madrid. Ramón Menéndez Pidal includes it in *España del Cid,* 7th ed., II (1969), 921–971. Ibn Alcama, *Elocuencia evidenciadora de la gran calamidad,* written sometime between 1094 and 1116; the original Arabic text is lost, but four medieval chronicles incorporate partial Spanish translations; see Menéndez Pidal, *op cit.,* II, 894–903. Ibn Bassām, *Tesoro de las excelencias de los españoles* (*ca.* 1109); the passage from vol. III describing the Cid is translated in Reinhart Dozy, *Recherches sur l'histoire politique et littéraire de l'Espagne pendant le moyen âge,* 3rd ed., II (1881), 8–28.

Modern histories include (in additon to Menéndez Pidal and Dozy, cited above) Louis Chalon, *L'histoire et l'épopée castiliane du moyen âge* (1976); G. Cirot, "Le vrai Cid," in *Bulletin hispanique,* **41** (1930); Stephen Clissold, *In Search of the Cid* (1965); Jules Horrent, *Historia y poesía en torno al "Cantar del Cid"* (1973); E. Lévi-Provençal, "Le Cid de l'histoire," in *Revue historique,* **180** (1937); Ramón Menéndez Pidal, *La España del Cid,* 7th ed., 2 vols. (1969), a monumental reconstruction of eleventh-century Spain and one of our century's foremost accomplishments in medieval scholarship; *The Cid and His Spain* (1934), an abbreviated translation of the above by Harold Sunderland; *En torno al Poema del Cid* (1963), reproducing important materials scattered among Menéndez Pidal's hundred-odd works; and *El Cid Campeador,* 6th ed. (1968); Julio Puyol, "'El Cid' de Dozy," in *Revue hispanique,* **23** (1910).

The Cid of poetry and legend. An early Latin poem is *Carmen Campidoctoris* (*ca.* 1090). The 129-line MS is at the Bibliothèque Nationale, Paris, and is reproduced by Menéndez Pidal, in *España del Cid,* 882–886.

The unique early-fourteenth-century MS of the *Cantar de mío Cid* is now in the Biblioteca Nacional, Madrid. The first sheet is lost. Therefore we do not know whether it was headed by a title. Perhaps not, if Per Abbat, the copyist, was as unmindful of the need for one as was the scribe of the mid-fourteenth-century epic that narrates the youthful exploits of Rodrigo. Modern editors therefore rightly call this later work *Las mocedades de Rodrigo.* The *juglar* of the *Mío Cid* uses both *gesta* and *cantar,* but not *poema,* in referring to his composition.

Editions of the *Poema* include Ramón Menéndez Pidal, *Cantar de mio Cid,* 3 vols., 4th ed. (1964), and *Poema de mio Cid,* 12th ed. (1968); Ian Michael, *Poema de mio Cid,* 2nd ed. (1978); Colin Smith, *Poema de mio Cid* (1972). English translations are Archer M. Huntington, *Poem of the Cid,* 3 vols. (1907–1908); W. S. Merwin, *The Poem of the Cid* (1962), verse with facing Spanish text; R. Selden Rose and L. Bacon, *The Lay of the Cid* (1919); Merriam Sherwood, *Tale of the Warrior Lord* (1930); and Lesley B. Simpson, *The Poem of the Cid* (1962), prose. Modern Spanish translations are Alfonso Reyes (1919), prose; Luis Guarner (1940), F. López Estrada (1955), M. Martínez Burgos (1955), all in octosyllables; and J. Pérez Urbel (1955), in alexandrines.

The key textual study is Franklin M. Waltman, *Concordance to "Poema de mio Cid"* (1972). For literary criticism see Dámaso Alonso, "Estilo y creación en el *Poema del Cid,*" in *Ensayos sobre poesía espanola,* 2nd ed. (1944), one of the best aesthetic evaluations; Américo Castro, "Poesía y realidad en el *Poema del Cid,*" in *Tierra firme,* **1** (1935); Edmund de Chasca, *Estructura y forma en el "Poema de mio Cid"* (1955); *El arte juglaresco en el Cantar de mio Cid,* 2nd ed. (1972); Rafael Lapesa, "La lengua de la poesía épica en los cantares de gesta y en el romancero viejo," in *De la Edad Media a nuestros días* (1967); Ramón Menéndez Pidal, "Poesía e historia en el 'Mio Cid,'" in *Nueva revista de filología hispánica,* **3** (1949); "Dos Poetas en el 'Cantar de mio Cid,'" in *Romania,* **82** (1961); "Los cantores épicos yugoslavos y los occidentales: El *Mio Cid* y dos refundidores primitivos," in *Boletín de la Real academia de buenas letras de Barcelona,* **31** (1965–1966); Aristóbulo Pardo, *Lar trayectoria de Mio Cid y la armadura del Poema* (1973); Pedro Salinas, "La vuelta al esposo: ensayo sobre la estructura y sensibilidad en el *Cantar de Mio Cid,*" in *Bulletin of Spanish Studies,* **24** (1947); Leo Spitzer, "Sobre el carácter histórico del *Cantar de Mio Cid,*" in *Nueva revista de filología hispánica,* **2** (1948); Karl Vossler, "Carta española a Hugo von Hoffmannsthal," in *Algunos carácteres de la cultura española* (1942), 11ff.

The MS of *Las mocedades de Rodrigo* (*ca.* 1350) is at the Bibliothèque Nationale, Paris, Esp. No. 12. Editions include those of A. D. Deyermond in his *Epic Poetry and the Clergy: Studies on the "Mocedades de Rodrigo"* (1968), 221–277; and Menéndez Pidal in his *Reliquias de la poesía épica española* (1951), 257–289. Among the key studies of the *Mocedades* are S. G. Armistead, "The Structure of the *Refundición de las Mocedades* de Rodrigo," in *Romance Philology,* **17** (1963–1964); A. D. Deyermond, "La decadencia de la epopeya española: *Las Mocedades de Rodrigo*," in *Anuario de estudios medievales*, **1** (1964); and *"Last Mocedades de Rodrigo, poema de Palencia,"* in *Insula*, **26** (1964).

Ballads of the Cid are collected in Juan de Escobar, ed., *Historia del muy noble y valeroso cavallero el Cid Ruy Díez de Bivar* (1611), with many subsequent editions; and F. S. R. [Federico Sainz de Robles?], ed., *Romancero del Cid* (1951), containing 152 Cid ballads. General collections that include Cid ballads are Agustín Durán, *Romancero general, o colección de romances castellanos anteriores al siglo XVIII*, 2 vols. (1849–1851, repr. 1945), with 175 Cid ballads; Antonio García Solalinde, ed., *Cien romances escogidos*, 4th ed. (1958), including ballad parodies by well-known Golden Age writers such as Quevedo and Góngora; Angel González-Palencia, *Romancero generel, 1600, 1604, 1605*, 2 vols, (1947); Ramón Menéndez Pidal, ed., *Cancionero de romances impreso en Ámberes*, 2nd ed. (1945); and *Flor nueva de romances viejos* (1943), with 31 Cid ballads. (In the *Proemio* of this latter work the usually austere savant glows with the pride of his accomplishments over a near lifetime of dedication to the *romancero*. He says: "In order to study the essence and the life of traditional poetry, I have searched for the ancient vestiges of the *Romancero* in the principal libraries of Europe, I have avidly looked for them in the living tradition, and have heard them sung in a multitude of places: from the summer pastures of Asturian vaqueros to the caves of Monte Sacro, under the sun of ballad-loving Granada; I heard them on the shores of the river Plata and at the foot of the immensity of the Andes.") Additional ballad collections are Antonio Rodríguez-Moñino, ed., *Las fuentes del Romancero general*, 12 vols. (1957), a facsimile ed. of the most important *romanceros* printed from 1589 to 1597; Luis Santullano, ed. *Romancero español*, 6th ed. (1968), with 78 Cid ballads; Christopher Colin Smith, ed., *Spanish Ballads* (1964), including 6 Cid ballads with useful commentary; Giuseppe di Stefano, ed., *El romancero* (1970), containing an excellent 74-page introduction; Ferdinand Wolf and C. Hoffman, eds., *Primavera y flor de romances* (1856), repr. by M. Menéndez y Pelayo, with additions, in his *Antología de poetas líricos castellanos*, VIII and IX (1945), including 40 Cid ballads.

On the oral tradition, see Paul Bénichou, *Creación poética en el romancero tradicional* (1968); Diego Catalán, ed., *Siete siglos de romancero* (1969); including a seventy-eight-page study of *Hélo, hélo por dó viene*, which the editor heard transmitted orally as late as 1947–1948; Ramón Menéndez Pidal, *Romancero hispánico*, 2 vols. (1953), a monumental work.

On ballad techniques, structure, and style, see the collections of Menéndez Pidal and Smith and also Edmund de Chasca, "Pluralidades anafóricas en la estructura de *Cabalga Diego Laínez, y reymen de las técnicas enumeratorias en el Romancero del Cid*," in *Revista de estudios hispánicos* (Univ. de Puerto Rico), **2** (1972); Leo Spitzer,

"Stilistisch-Syntaktisches aus den spanisch-portuguiesischen Romanzen," in *Zeitschrift für Romanische Philologie*, **35** (1911); Ruth House Webber, *Formulistic Diction in the Spanish Ballad* (1951), 175–278.

On the music of the ballads, see E. M. Torner, "Indicaciones prácticas sobre la notación musical de los romances," in *Revista de filología espanola*, **10** (1923), and "Ensayo de clasificación de las melodías de romance," in *Homenaje a Menéndez Pidal*, II (1925); John B. Trend, "The Music of the Romancero in the Sixteenth Century," in his *The Music of Spanish History* (1926).

EDMUND DE CHASCA

[See also **Almoravids; Cantar de mío Cid; Castile; Spain, Christian-Muslim Relations in; Spanish Literature** (various articles); **Valencia**.]

CILICIAN GATES (Greek: hai Pylai tes Kilikias; Latin: Ciliciae Pylae [Portae]; Turkish: Külek Boğazi; also called Syrian Gates or Bailan Pass), the main pass through the Taurus Mountains connecting Anatolia with Cilicia and Syria. Only 900 feet (274 meters) long, the pass lies at an altitude of nearly 4,000 feet (1,219 meters) about 25 miles (40 kilometers) northeast of Tarsus, and consists of a gorge 1,494 feet (455 meters) deep and 149 feet (45 meters) long through the limestone rock of the mountains. A road from Podandos (Pozanti) follows a tributary of the Cydnus River through the pass to Tarsus.

The Cilician Gates were crossed by Cyrus the Younger, Alexander the Great, and Julius Caesar. Pescennius Niger attempted to defend the pass against Septimius Severus in the third century A.D. In the medieval period the Cilician Gates were both a major point of entry for Crusaders entering Cilician Armenia by land and the logical path for invading Turkish elements as well. Thus the pass was guarded on the north by the castle of Asgouras and on the south by those of Loulon, Lambron, and Babaron (Paperon), all in the hands of Armenian feudatories.

BIBLIOGRAPHY

T. S. R. Boase, ed., *The Cilician Kingdom of Armenia* (1978).

ROBERT HEWSEN

CILICIAN KINGDOM. Referred to from the eleventh century as the Kingdom of Lesser Armenia or as Armenia Minor, it should not be confused with the late Roman province of that name. The land of Cilicia in southeast Asia Minor (Anatolia) covers an area approximately 400 kilometers in length and 48 to 80 kilometers in breadth. It is a broad plain, extending along the Mediterranean and bounded on the west by the Taurus Mountains and on the east by the Amanus (Nur) Mountains. The plain is divided into two sections. The western (lower) plain, which extends from the foothills of the Taurus to the Mediterranean, is well guarded in the north by the Cilician Gates, which command the route from the mountains to Tarsus. The eastern (upper) plain is much more vulnerable to attack from Syria, because the passes toward the Amanus Mountains are broader and less easily defended than those of the Taurus. Āyās, on the Gulf of Alexandretta (İskendarūn), was not only a principal port of the area but also a starting point for the main land routes to Tabrīz and central Asia; Tarsus was also an important port. The secondary cities of Mamistra; Sīs, which was the capital from 1162 to 1375; and Anazarba were connected to the Mediterranean by the Pyramus (Ceyhan) River.

The history of Cilician Armenia is obscure because much of the available information is vague or incomplete. Although the area had already been populated by Greeks, Arabs, Jews, and Latins, two waves of Armenian immigration from Greater (Eastern) Armenia produced an Armenian majority by the early twelfth century. Cilicia had never been part of the historical Armenian homeland, yet by the First Crusade, Armenian chieftains were in control of Melitene (Malatya), Gargar, Marᶜaš, Bira, and Edessa.

Two main feudal families emerged as the dominant forces in Cilicia: the Rubenids, who held part of the eastern plain and had their center at Anazarba and the fortress of Vahka, and the Hetᶜumids, who controlled the western plain and the strategic fortresses of Paperon and Lambron, guarding the Cilician Gates. The anti-Byzantine and aggressive expansionist policy of the Rubenids for control of the eastern plain, as opposed to the Hetᶜumids' loyal vassalage to Byzantium, brought the two houses into conflict for mastery of Cilicia. By 1198 or 1199 the Rubenid baron Leo II became sufficiently powerful to receive recognition as King Leo I from Pope Innocent III and Philip of Swabia, king of Germany, and possibly the Byzantine emperor Alexios III Angelos as well.

Leo received his crown at a time when Cilicia had become one of the most important Christian states in the Levant. The Armenians had welcomed the Crusaders as liberators from the Muslim threat, but tensions frequently arose, particularly with Cilicia's southeastern neighbor, Antioch. Leo I/II had decided, after an unsuccessful attempt to annex Antioch to Cilicia in 1193, to unite the two states through the marriage of his niece and heir presumptive, Alice, to Raymond, son of Bohemond III and heir to Antioch. But Leo's attempt to place his grandnephew on the throne of Antioch after Raymond's death was successfully opposed by Bohemond of Tripoli, Raymond's younger brother, and by the Templars, angered by Leo's earlier seizure of the Templar fortress of Baghras. The struggle lasted for nearly twenty years, with Leo finally failing to realize his ambitions.

The conflict with Antioch opened Cilicia to attack from Bohemond's Muslim allies, and both Kai-Khusraw I of Iconium and his successor inflicted defeats on Armenian forces. During the reign of Leo's successor, Hetᶜum I, the Seljuks extended their control to the Bay of Antalya, thus pushing back the western frontier of the kingdom. Hetᶜum faced an even greater threat in the growing power of the Mongols. Realizing that it would be more advantageous to come to terms with the new invaders, he traveled to the court of the Great Khan Möngke from 1253/1254 to 1256, returning with an agreement of protection for Cilicia and for all Christian churches in Mongol territories.

As a result of the Cilician-Mongol alliance, the Armenian sphere of influence in the area increased, particularly over Antioch. The situation was not to last, however, for six years after the Mongol defeat at ᶜAyn Jālūt in 1260, the Mamluks invaded Cilicia, destroying the capital of Sīs and inflicting on the kingdom a devastation from which it never recovered. Hetᶜum's son Leo II/III attempted to revive the Cilician-Mongol alliance, but Mamluk strength forced him in 1285 to agree to an annual tribute of one million dirhams and an end to the building of any new fortresses. The kingdom maintained a degree of prosperity, however, especially after the fall of Acre in 1291, which made Āyās the principal Christian port on the mainland of the Levant.

The remainder of the thirteenth century was a period of severe political instability, at a time when effective leadership was needed to deal with external affairs. Muslim persecutions began in 1304, and in 1308 Hetᶜum II and his coruler Leo III/IV were murdered with their retinues at Anazarba while vis-

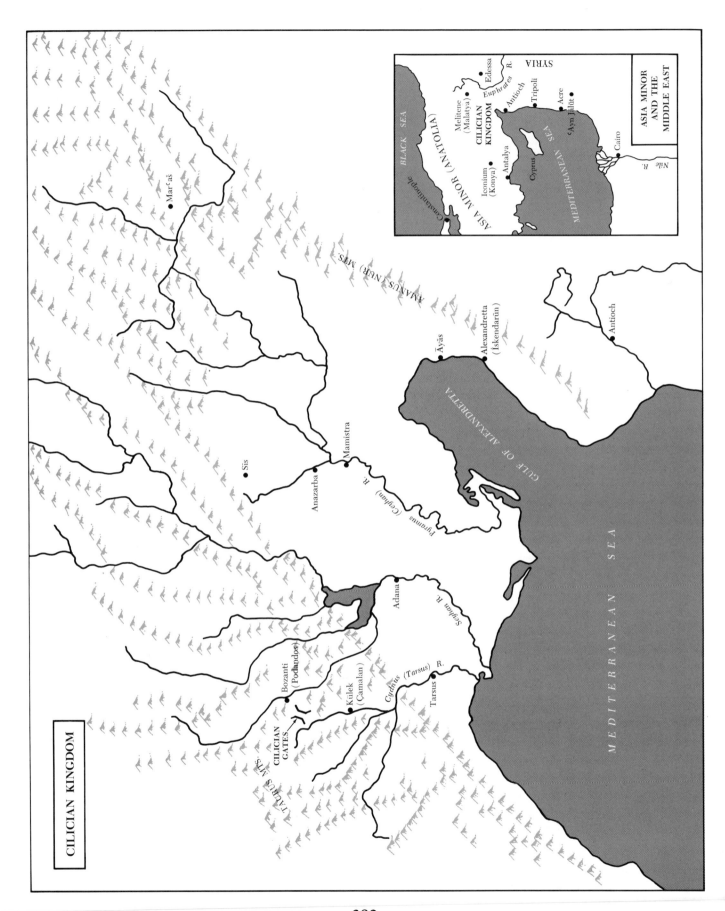

CILICIAN KINGDOM

Mar'aš

AMANUS (NUR) MTS.

Āyās

Alexandretta (İskenderûn)

Antioch

GULF OF ALEXANDRETTA

Mamistra

Sis

Anazarba

Pyramus (Ceyhan) R.

MEDITERRANEAN SEA

Adana

Sëyhan R.

Bozanti (Podandos)

Külek (Çamalan)

Cydnus (Tarsus) R.

Tarsus

CILICIAN GATES

TAURUS MTS.

BLACK SEA

Constantinople

ASIA MINOR (ANATOLIA)

Melitene (Malatya)

Edessa

Euphrates R.

SYRIA

Antioch

Tripoli

Acre

'Ayn Jālūt

CILICIAN KINGDOM

Iconium (Konya)

Antalya

Cyprus

MEDITERRANEAN SEA

Cairo

Nile R.

iting the Mongol khan. There followed another period of political instability, dynastic conflict, and assassinations.

The Mamluks, meanwhile, continued to make inroads into Cilicia, sacking Āyās in 1322 and in 1336; the port fell to the Mamluks in 1347 and was never again under Cilician control. By 1342 there was no male heir to the throne, and the crown of Cilicia passed to Guy de Lusignan through the marriage of Leo II/III's daughter Zabel (Isabel) to Amaury II of Cyprus. An active anti-Latin faction in Cilicia keenly resented Guy's ardent pro-Latin political and religious sentiments, and he and his brother Bemon were assassinated in 1344, after which the throne was seized by Constantine III/V of the Hetᶜumid line. Constantine sought the assistance of Peter I of Cyprus, who in 1360 recaptured the port of Antalya for the Armenians, thereby providing some relief for trade, which had suffered since the loss of Āyās.

The next Lusignan king, Constantine IV/VI, sought to make a treaty with the Mamluks, but the Cilician barons, fearing a surrender of the kingdom, rose up and murdered him in 1373. The following year Leo V/VI, nephew of Guy de Lusignan, was called to the throne for what was to be the kingdom's last reign. An Egyptian force sacked the city of Sīs in 1375, and Leo and his wife were taken as prisoners to Cairo. Leo was released in 1382 and spent the remainder of his life in Europe, seeking military aid for his kingdom. He died in 1393, and the title "king of Armenia" was given to the kings of Cyprus, from whom it eventually passed to the house of Savoy.

Cilicia's position made it an important center of trade in the Levant, guaranteed by treaties with Genoa, Venice, and other states from as early as 1201, granting them exemption from all duties and allowing them trading establishments at Mamistra and, for the Genoese, at Sīs and Tarsus as well. In view of Cilicia's lack of a merchant fleet, these treaties were of great economic importance to the kingdom. Among the principal exports were goatskins and goat-hair cloth, timber, wheat, and wine. The basic unit of currency in Cilicia was the *tategan*, an equivalent of the dinar coined in both gold and silver, though the bulk of Cilician coins were silver and copper.

French and Latin, as well as Armenian, were the official languages of the Cilician court, and the nomenclature as well as the nature of court offices soon became westernized: for instance, the title "con-

stable" replaced the traditional Armenian *sparapet,* and "seneschal" the Armenian *mardpet.* In law the medieval code of Mχitᶜar Goš, though translated into vernacular Armenian for use at the court, was soon replaced by the Assizes of Antioch and Assizes of Jerusalem. In fact the Assizes of Antioch have survived only in the Armenian translation made by Smbat Sparapet, brother of King Hetᶜum I.

This turning to Western feudal law was one of the most important aspects of the latinization of Armenian society in the kingdom. The traditional *naχarar* system, whereby the king was simply primus inter pares and in which feudal families held their lands of their own right and exercised a great deal of independence from the king, was now replaced with a feudal system based on land grants from the Crown and a much tighter control of the nobles by the sovereign. Knighthood, unknown to the Armenians, was introduced as early as the reign of King Leo I, and Western dress, jousting, and tilts were popular.

Such cultural changes, and especially the ongoing attempts at some agreement on union with the Roman church, led to often-strained relations with the Armenians of Greater Armenia, particularly the clergy. The seat of the Armenian *katᶜolikos* had been transferred from Zamindia, near Kars, to Hŕomkla in Cilicia in 1147, and then farther west to Sīs, the political capital of the kingdom. Although several of the kings of Cilicia were anxious to claim the title "king of all Armenians," and used it in official letters and on coins, there survive many manuscript colophons from Greater Armenia that refer only to the "king of Cilicia."

Many ruins of Cilicia have survived, particularly of castles and fortresses, which are only now being studied. The manuscript illuminations from this period of artists such as Tᶜoros Roslin (*fl.* late thirteenth century), as well as examples of silver work, indicate a high level of artistic activity in the Cilician kingdom.

BIBLIOGRAPHY

Ghevont Alishan, *Léon le Magnifique, premier roi de Sissouan ou de l'Arméno-Cilicie* (1888); and *Sissouan, ou l'Arméno-Cilicie* (1899); Thomas S. R. Boase, ed., *The Cilician Kingdom of Armenia* (1978); Claude Cahen, *La Syrie du nord à l'époque des croisades et la principauté franque d'Antioche* (1940); Gérard Dédéyan, ed., *La chronique attribuée au connétable Smbat* (1980); Sirarpie Der Nersessian, "The Kingdom of Cilician Armenia," in Kenneth M.

Setton, gen. ed., *A History of the Crusades,* II, R. L. Wolff and H. W. Hazard, eds. (1969); *Recueil des historiens des croisades: Documents arméniens,* 2 vols. (1869–1906).

ANI P. ATAMIAN

[See also **Antioch; Armenia, Geography; Armenia, Social Structure; Assizes of Jerusalem; Āyās; Edessa; Het͑um I; Het͑um II; Het͑umids; Lambron; Leo I/II of Armenia; Lusignans; Melitene; Mints and Money, Armenian; Naχarar; Rubenids; Sis; Smbat Sparapet.**]

CILICIAN-ROMAN CHURCH UNION. Attempts to unify the Armenian and Roman churches began more than a century before the formal founding of the Cilician kingdom. A letter written by Pope Gregory VII in 1080, and generally believed to be addressed to the Armenian *kat͑olikos,* Gregory II, spoke of Rome's awareness of the doctrinal and liturgical differences between the two churches and of a desire to see these differences eliminated. The next century saw the development of relations between Rome and the Armenian church based on practical considerations of mutual advantage. The period of Byzantine occupation of Cilicia and the death of the Rubenid baron Leo I in Byzantine captivity about 1140 resulted, according to Western sources, in Armenian recognition of Roman primacy and a willingness to conform to Roman liturgical practices.

Similarly, the cordial papal communications to the Armenian church hierarchy in the later twelfth century must be seen in the context of the Cilician-Byzantine-Muslim conflict—for example, Pope Lucius III's granting of the crusading indulgence to Armenians aiding the Latin armies. These cordial religious-diplomatic relations reached a high point with the coronation of King Leo I/II by Conrad of Wittelsbach, cardinal of Mainz, in 1198 or 1199, and Leo's subsequent formal recognition of the primacy of the Roman see. Relations became strained, however, in the latter part of Leo's reign because of the conflict over the succession to the principality of Antioch, a dispute that led to a diplomatic confrontation between Cilicia and Rome, and to Leo's excommunication in 1211.

It was the kings of Cilicia, rather than the *kat͑olikoi,* who controlled the course of Armenian-Roman church relations throughout the life of the kingdom. This was especially so after 1293, when the seat of the *kat͑olikos* was transferred from Hṙomkla to Sīs, the political capital of the kingdom, both to remove the see from what was now a Mamluk-held area and to keep it more easily under control of the throne. The *kat͑olikoi* were thus, if not sincerely pro-Latin, unable to oppose the usual royal policy of seeking union with Rome in return for military support in the Crusades. Standing out as a cleric of truly ecumenical spirit was Nersēs Lambronac͑i, bishop of Tarsus until 1198, who attempted a reconciliation with the Greek, as well as with the Roman, church. But the romanizing reform in liturgy and ritual that such sentiments entailed led to a serious cleavage between the Armenian clergy of Cilicia and those in Greater Armenia, who were further removed from the sphere of the Crusades and strongly opposed any alterations in the centuries-old Armenian traditions.

This opposition was led in the late thirteenth century by Step͑anos Orbelean, the metropolitan bishop of the province of Siwnik͑. The liturgical and doctrinal changes required of the Armenians by Rome in this period included the acceptance of Roman primacy and of the first four ecumenical councils; the elimination of the phrase "Who was crucified for us" in the trisagion of the Armenian Mass; the mixing of water with the wine consecrated at Mass; the making of holy chrism with oil rather than with butter; and the celebration of the Feast of the Nativity on 25 December rather than on 6 January.

The early thirteenth to the mid fourteenth century marked the height of the latinization of Cilicia in the secular as well as the religious sphere. It was in this period that the first signs of Dominican and Franciscan missionary activity appeared. Very possibly as a result of this missionary activity, there occurred, with the arrival of the Franciscan John of Montecorvino at the court of King Het͑um II in 1289, the opening of negotiations aimed specifically at the union of the Armenian and Roman churches, implying a new recognition by the papacy of the basic liturgical and doctrinal differences between them. The commencement of negotiations is supported by a letter of 1298 from Pope Boniface VIII to *Kat͑olikos* Gregory VII, mentioning the *kat͑olikos'* recognition of Roman primacy.

It was in this period as well that the Councils of Sīs (1307) and Adana (1316 or 1317) were held. At them a number of the Armenian ecclesiastical hierarchy and nobility formally agreed to conform to Latin doctrine and liturgical practice, thus arousing strong opposition among the clergy of Greater Armenia. An awareness of and attempt to mollify this opposition was shown by a letter from Pope John XXII in 1321 to the bishops of that region, urging them to support the union of the churches. The degree of communication between the Armenian church and Rome in this period is further attested to by the expanded missionary activity in Greater Armenia (almost exclusively Dominican); the granting of papal protection to a growing number of Armenian religious communities in Italy; and the granting of special indulgences to members of the Cilician royal household.

This period, however, also saw signs of an intense reaction in Cilicia to even the nominal union between the two churches. In 1222 Philip, the son of Prince Bohemond IV of Antioch, married Zabel (Isabel), the daughter of Leo I/II, and thus ascended the Armenian throne, only to be overthrown and jailed the next year because of his prounion policy. The Latin bishops of Tarsus and Mamistra were expelled from Cilicia at this time. Later in the century a dispute among the Armenian clergy over the celebration of Easter according to the Roman, as opposed to the Armenian, calendar resulted in the torture and exile of clergymen who held to the traditional Armenian date.

Beginning in the mid fourteenth century, there is evidence of strain in the Roman-Armenian negotiations, notably the growing Cilician opposition to the policies of the latinizing party and the increasing importance of the Dominicans in Roman-Armenian relations. Armenian responses to papal requests for liturgical and doctrinal reforms were not unsatisfactory to Rome, and further strain was shown later in the century by the first specific papal directives, from Pope Gregory XI, for the rebaptism of Armenian laymen and the reordination of Armenian clergymen. In 1344 the anti-Latin faction in Cilicia assassinated King Guy de Lusignan and dominated the kingdom for the next three decades. The Armenian sources for this period state that the last six *kat^co-likoi* of the Cilician period were pro-Latin and that all were poisoned. During this period Rome continued to make offers of military aid to the Cilician Kingdom, now beseiged by the Mamluks, in return for unity with the Catholic church. By 1374 the pro-Latin Armenians regained the strength to secure the throne for Leo V/VI de Lusignan, the last king of Cilicia.

The increased importance of the Dominicans from the mid fourteenth century on can be seen in the official establishment of the congregation of the Fratres Unitores in Greater Armenia in 1356 and in the call of Pope Gregory XI in 1374 for an increase in the number of missionaries to work among the Armenians. These events, together with the noticeable decrease in papal communications with the Cilician court, probably indicate that even before the fall of the kingdom in 1375, Rome had found an alternative and less "official" means of bringing Armenians into the Roman church. Actively pursuing formal church union may have seemed no longer necessary, religiously or practically. Given this view, the period of the Council of Florence-Ferrara and the proclamation of the "Bull of Union" between the Roman Catholic and Armenian churches in 1439 need not be seen as part of a direct line of negotiations between Rome and the Armenian church, particularly in view of the circuitous and indirect methods of communication between the pope and the Armenian church hierarchy, via the Genoese in Caffa, as well as the fact that the bull soon proved to be little more than a paper agreement.

BIBLIOGRAPHY

Ghevont Alishan, *Sissouan, ou l'Arméno-Cilicie* (1899); Alexandro Balgy, *Historia doctrinae catholicae inter Armenos unionisque eorum cum Romana in Concilio Florentino* (1878); Jules Gay, *Le Pape Clément VI et les affaires d'Orient (1342–1352)* (1904); Marc-Antoine van den Oudenrijn, "Les frères uniteurs de l'Arménie Orientale," in *Catholico Unio*, **19** (1951), 43–57; Pascal Tekeyan, *Controverses christologiques en Arméno-Cilicie dans la seconde moitié du XIIᵉ siècle (1165–1198)* (1939); Henri François Tournebize, *Histoire politique et religieuse d'Arménie* (1910).

ANI P. ATAMIAN

[See also Armenian Church, Doctrines and Councils; Gregory VII, Pope; John XXII, Pope; Leo I/II of Armenia; Leo V/VI of Armenia; Missions and Missionaries, Christian; Nersēs Lambronac^ci; Orbelean.]

CIMABUE, CENNI DI PEPI (*ca.* 1240–*ca.* 1302), Florentine painter and the most prominent figure of his generation according to Dante. Cimabue's fame was later eclipsed by Giotto. Despite his renown, few documents and other indicators provide the necessary guides in identifying Cimabue's surviving works, and their exact identity remains in dispute. The first surviving document places Cimabue in

Crucifixion by Cimabue. Church of S. Croce, Florence, *ca.* 1285.
ALINARI/ART RESOURCE

Rome in 1272 as a witness to an ecclesiastical matter, indicating his prominence at that time. Scholars debate the extent of Roman artists' (especially the young Pietro Cavallini's) influence on Cimabue. In 1301 Cimabue is documented working on the apse mosaic of Pisa cathedral and is mentioned in a commission for a Maestà and Crucifix for the Ospedale di S. Chiara in Pisa. In 1302 he is mentioned as a member of the Società dei Piovuti in Pisa.

None of these documents relates to a surviving work, but Cimabue's career is generally sketched out as follows. The large Crucifix panel in S. Domenico, Arezzo, is his earliest known work, dated about 1275. From about 1277 to 1280 Cimabue was likely at work on his extensive fresco contribution to the church of S. Francesco at Assisi. There he and his shop were responsible for the evangelists depicted in the vaults, scenes from the Apocalypse and a Crucifixion in the left transept, and scenes from the life of the Virgin in the apse. Images of the apostles, scenes from the lives of Peter and Paul, and a second Crucifixion were painted in the right transept of the upper church. In the lower church, Cimabue is credited with the large fresco of the Virgin and Child Enthroned with Angels and St. Francis. Painted mainly in fresco secco, the murals have suffered extensive damage with only underpainting visible in many places, leaving a ghostlike, photographic negative substitute for the original.

The Maestà of about 1280, formerly in S. Trinità and now at the Uffizi (Florence), and the overlifesized Crucifix in the S. Croce Museum (damaged in the 1966 flood and now partially restored) of about 1285 complete Cimabue's accepted oeuvre. The Louvre Maestà (formerly at S. Francesco in Pisa) and the Madonna and Child in the Church of the Servi at Bologna are generally attributed to Cimabue's shop.

Cimabue maintained the monumental feeling of Coppo di Marcovaldo's style but diminished the graphic stylizations, endowing his figures with a new delicacy of form, specificity of character, and dimensionality. Though individual, his figures exist on a profound, almost elemental plane, establishing a Florentine monumental tradition later found in the art of Giotto, Masaccio, Donatello, and Michelangelo.

BIBLIOGRAPHY

Eugenio Battisti, *Cimabue,* Robert and Catherine Enggass, trans. (1967); Alfred Nicholson, *Cimabue, a Critical Study* (1932, repr. 1972); Enio Sindona, *L'opera completa di Cimabue* (1975).

ADELHEID M. GEALT

[See also **Coppo di Marcovaldo; Giotto di Bondone.**]

CINÉAL EÓGHAIN, an Irish dynastic family reputedly descended from Eóghan, a son of Niall of the Nine Hostages. In the fifth century Cinéal Eóghain—in conjunction with two other families who also claimed descent from sons of Niall, Cinéal Conaill and Cinéal Énna—settled northwestern Ireland and appropriated the Inishowen Peninsula (County Donegal), making Aileach, a prehistoric stone fort, their seat. These three tribes were collectively called the northern Uí Néill, in contradistinction to the southern Uí Néill, those descendants of Niall occupying Meath. Over the course of the following three centuries, culminating in 789 with the Battle of Cloitech (Clady, County Tyrone), Cinéal Eóghain established dominance over its rival neighbor, Cinéal Conaill, and gained exclusive right to the kingship of the northern Uí Néill, a title that conferred the privilege of alternating with the southern Uí Néill the (largely theoretical) high kingship of Ireland.

During the same period Cinéal Eóghain expanded

eastward and southward into Derry and Tyrone. Its victory in 827 over the Airgialla, a confederation of Ulster tribes, at the Battle of Leth Cam in County Armagh assured it of eventual suzerainty over a large area of central and south Ulster covering counties Armagh, Monaghan, Louth, and Fermanagh. In keeping with its new status, Cinéal Eóghain moved the inaugural site of its kings to Tulach Óc (Tullaghoge, County Tyrone), and the place of their burial to the ecclesiastical capital of Armagh.

Cinéal Eóghain maintained its dominance in northern Ireland during the ninth and tenth centuries and successfully resisted Viking attempts to settle Ulster. Eventually, however, failure to keep pace with political changes in the rest of Ireland, especially the growth of the Viking towns as a political force, and constant rivalry with the southern Uí Néill left Cinéal Eóghain unprepared for the challenge, first, of Brian Boru's claims to the high kingship of Ireland about 1005 and, later, of Rory O Connor, king of Connaught, who effectively brought Cinéal Eóghain's power to an end in 1166. Thereafter, until the collapse of the Gaelic order in the late sixteenth century, the kingship of Cinéal Eóghain was usually held by the Ó Néills.

BIBLIOGRAPHY

Francis J. Byrne, *The Rise of the Uí Néill and the High-kingship of Ireland* (1969); and *Irish Kings and High-Kings* (1973), 114–117, 124–129, 284; Eoin MacNeill, *Celtic Ireland* (1921), 132–135; Gearóid Mac Niocaill, *Ireland Before the Vikings* (1972); Donnchadh Ó Corráin, *Ireland Before the Normans* (1972).

PADRAIG P. Ó NÉILL

[See also **Ireland, Early History; Uí Néill.**]

CINO DA PISTOIA (*ca.* 1270–1336/1337), Italian jurist and poet also known as Cino or Guittoncino Sinibuldi, was born into a powerful Pistoian family of feudal origin. His primary education was obtained under the eminent rhetorician Francesco da Colle and continued at the University of Bologna, where he obtained his degree in law probably in 1292. He then traveled to France, returning to Bologna in 1297 with a *licentia docendi*. In 1302 he was residing in Pistoia, but his familial association to the Black faction of the Guelphs resulted in his exile the following year; it was not until 1306, when the Blacks were once again in power, that he was able to return.

After having fervently embraced the cause of Emperor Henry VII on his descent into Italy, he became counselor of Ludovico of Savoy in Florence when the town was asked to open its gates to the emperor, and was later councillor to the imperial tribunal of Rome during the preparation for Henry's coronation. With the death of the emperor in 1313, Cino withdrew from political life to devote himself to his legal interests and to poetry. In 1314 he obtained his doctorate, and until his death in Pistoia, he taught law at various Italian universities (Siena, Perugia, Naples).

Cino left a considerable number of legal treatises. *Lectura in codicem* is a historical and critical commentary on the first nine books of the Justinian codex; *Additiones in codicem* comprises additional comments to the *Lectura*; *Lectura super Digesto veteri* is a collection of his university lectures. Cino was also author of a book of *Quaestiones* and a collection of his legal opinions, the *Consilia*. Cino's body of legal writings reflected the influence of the French dialectic school (especially Jacques de Révigny and Pierre de Belleperche) in his rejection of the traditional method of exegesis based on a strict gloss of the text, in favor of a method that focuses on the text interpreted in the light of its critical tradition, customs, local statutes, and the actual practice of the law. For this reason his work is considered of great importance in the study of the history of law.

Cino is now largely remembered for his poetry. In his association and friendship with Dante Alighieri, it is Dante who establishes Cino's reputation as the poet of love par excellence of the *dolce stil nuovo* movement. In *De vulgari eloquentia* Dante states that among the best Tuscan poets only he and Cino *"dulcius subtiliusque poetati vulgariter sunt"* (have written in the vulgar tongue in the sweetest and most refined manner) and, with their poetry, created an Italian vernacular. The theme of love, which dominates Cino's *canzoniere*, clearly reflects the influence of Dante and Guido Cavalcanti. Cino's discourse, however, is not concerned with the philosophical or metaphysical implications of love, as is the case with Dante or Cavalcanti. Rather, it is an intimate colloquy between the poet and his poetic "I" on the occasion of his love for the Lady Selvaggia. Unconcerned with the mystical élan of Dante and devoid of the desperate inner drama of Cavalcanti, Cino's poetry remains melodic, and as such it contributes a notable connecting link between the major poets of his era and the lyric master Petrarch.

BIBLIOGRAPHY

Gianfranco Contini, ed., *Poeti del Duecento,* II (1960), 629–690; Frederick Goldin, ed. and trans., *German and Italian Lyrics of the Middle Ages* (1973); Mario Marti, "Cino da Pistoia," in *Enciclopedia Dantesca,* II (1970); Joseph Tusiani, *The Age of Dante: An Anthology of Early Italian Poetry* (1974).

MASSIMO CIAVOLELLA

[See also **Cavalcanti, Guido; Dante Alighieri; Italian Literature: Lyric Poetry; Petrarch (Francesco Petrarca).**]

CIPRIANUS, ST. See **Cyprian, St.**

CIRCASSIANS. The Circassians are prominent in medieval Islamic history as the dominant ethnic element in the second phase of Mamluk rule over Egypt and Syria (1382–1517). Western scholars are wont to refer to this phase as the period of the Burjī Mamluks, erroneously stressing the importance of a *mamlūk* regiment that had been strong in the earlier period; but the primary Arabic sources speak only of *Dawlat al-Jarkas,* the dynasty of the Circassians, emphasizing the change that occurred in the Mamluk state when rule was assumed by persons of Circassian "race" (Arabic: *jins*). The rule by Turks during the earlier phase, *Dawlat al-Turk,* referred to as the period of the Baḥrī Mamluks by Western scholars, lasted from 1250 to 1382.

According to the Mamluk encyclopedist *al-Qalqashandī (d.* 1418), who quotes the fourteenth-century historian and geographer Abu 'l-Fidā, the land of the Circassians *(bilād al-Jarkas)* was located east of the Black Sea. "Its inhabitants lead a life of hardship, being Christians for the most part. In our day they have become the major component of the army of Egypt, since, that is, the reign of al-Ẓāhir Barqūq, for it was he who imported large numbers of them" *(Ṣubḥ,* IV, 462). Elsewhere al-Qalqashandī speaks of them as a conquered people who have had "their men killed, their women and children captured, and their slaves exported to all parts of the world" *(ibid.,* 475).

Although Mamluk historians aver that the policy of Sultan Barqūq (1382–1389, 1390–1399) was responsible for the dominance of the Circassians in the Mamluk state after 1382, they are known to have formed an important clique in the Mamluk army at a much earlier date. In fact, Circassian slaves apparently constituted the main component of the special Burjī regiment created by Sultan Qalā^ɔūn (1279–1290), which soon became a faction contesting supremacy in the state with the Baḥrī regiment, most of whose members were Qipčaq Turks. For a short time the Circassians were successful in investing one of their number, Baybars II, with the sultanate, but his reign had lasted less than a year when he was deposed in 1309. There were subsequent attempts by Circassian *mamlūk*s to regain influence in the state, most notably under Sultan Ḥajjī (1346–1347); however, after the fall of Baybars they ceased to be a significant factor until the accession of Barqūq.

The reasons behind Barqūq's decision to replace the Turks in the Mamluk armies and state with Circassians were probably two. In the first place, Barqūq was himself a Circassian, and there are ample indications in the sources that ethnic consciousness and solidarity were important in the Mamluk system, though it did not, apparently, become crucial until the *Dawlat al-Jarkas.* At any rate, the state had gone through a long period of instability following the death of the powerful sultan al-Malik al-Nāṣir (1293–1294, 1299–1309, 1310–1341), with rival Mamluk factions grouping around various of his descendants. In order to create a group whose loyalty to himself as master would be reinforced by ethnic solidarity, Barqūq began to purchase increasing numbers of fellow Circassians.

Perhaps of equal importance is the fact that the main source of slaves for replenishing the Mamluk armies during the *Dawlat al-Turk* was in deterioration. Heretofore it had been the Qipčaq Steppe, with its thriving population of Turkish nomads, that had supplied the Mamluks with the bulk of adolescent boys bought in the slave markets. But with the disintegration of the Golden Horde state in the second half of the fourteenth century and the advance of Tamerlane through western Asia, the steppe and its population fell into decline. As a result the slave merchants in the service of the Mamluks increased their activities in other areas. Thus, during the fifteenth century the Caucasus displaced the Qipčaq Steppe as a source of Mamluk manpower, and the ratio of Circassians to Turks was increased accordingly.

The Turkish *mamlūk*s did not acquiesce in the rise of the Circassians, but for the most part resistance was of little avail and served only to contribute to the instability of state and society. Beginning with Barqūq, no *mamlūk* of Turkish descent succeeded in acquiring the sultanate. Although *mamlūk*s of non-Circassian origin did accede to the throne, the Circassians maintained control of the army and state to the extent that they were referred to by contemporaries as the race par excellence (*al-jins, jins al-qawm*). Furthermore, their position in Mamluk society was consolidated by the growing practice during the fifteenth century of Mamluk officers' bringing their families from their homelands and assigning to these immigrant relatives high positions in Mamluk institutions.

It was the conviction of the Mamluk historian Ibn Taghrībirdī (*d.* 1470) that the rise of the Circassians to supremacy meant not only a transformation in the ethnic composition and character of the Mamluk state but also a turning point in its fortunes. According to him (*Al-Manhal,* fol. 397b), the affairs of the population under Mamluk rule had flourished until Barqūq came to power

and turned the administration of the kingdom inside out, a course in which he has been followed by his successors until this very day. This resulted from his preferment of his own race to the exclusion of others and his award of great fiefs and high offices to his own *mamlūk*s of his blood and in their minority. This is the greatest reason for the decline of the kingdom. What greater misfortune could there be than installing minors over their elders? Such is contrary to the practice of bygone kings, for they recognized more than one race; whenever they found nobility and courage in a person, they advanced and promoted him. No one held an office who did not deserve it.

There is little doubt that certain practices followed by Barqūq and his Circassian successors did contribute to the weakening of the Mamluk system and its decline as an imperial power in the fifteenth century. In its ideal state this system was based on a network of loyalties coupled with a straight and narrow path of training and advancement, each of which was designed to create and maintain an esprit de corps among its members. Adolescent boys were bought in the slave markets of Asia and taken to Egypt, where they were sold to or distributed among the sultan and his officers. Cut off from their families and their former religion, and completely subject to the will of their owners, the boys were given instruction in the martial arts, Islam, and Arabic. Once they had completed their education, they received their freedom along with equipment, a horse, and a land grant to sustain them. Their loyalty—indeed, their

very existence—had been directed during this apprenticeship toward the master (*ustādh*) who had bought and later freed them, and toward the companions who had undergone the same cycle of training with them (*khushdāshīya*). Those who showed merit were promoted to high rank in the army and the offices of state.

Built into the system were obvious imperfections that could, and did, promote factionalism. For example, the loyalty of the royal *mamlūk*s (those belonging to the sultan) was not automatically transferable to a new sultan, so that when a sultan died or was deposed, his successor had to buy and train new *mamlūk*s who would support him; this led to rivalry between the two groups. There was also room for strife between the royal *mamlūk*s and those belonging to emirs. Finally, even during the Turkish Dynasty there were elements of racial or ethnic friction, especially since *mamlūk*s of the same language and ethnic affiliation were at times housed in the same barracks, and therefore tended to develop and maintain their ethnic identity. In addition to a Circassian faction that was hated and feared by the Turks, we know that in the Turkish Dynasty there was also solidarity among the Mongols who had been recruited into Mamluk service as slaves, prisoners, or fugitives.

As long, however, as economic prosperity prevailed and there was a strong sultan on the throne who enjoyed the support of his officers and *mamlūk*s, and observed the guiding principles of the system, these frictions and tensions could be kept in check. Such was the case under the forceful sultans Baybars (1260–1277), Qalā'ūn, and al-Nāṣir Muḥammad. But by the time Barqūq came to the throne after a series of weak sultans, factionalism was so much out of control that he adopted his fatal expedient. There are indications that toward the end of his reign he realized that he should have tried to vary the ethnic element among his *mamlūk*s by purchasing slaves of Mongol, Turkoman, and Greek origin to offset the power of the Circassians, but this realization apparently came too late—shortly before his death—to make any difference.

As a result his son and successor Faraj (1399–1405, 1405–1412) was faced at his accession as a boy of ten with a powerful Circassian party that wished to replace him with a *mamlūk* from its own ranks. To cope with this threat Faraj and his supporters resorted to force, and the state was rocked during his reign by war between Circassians and their opponents. Faraj is credited with the extermination of hundreds of Circassians before he fell victim to his own policy and was executed by the leading Circassian emirs of Damascus. After the death of Faraj and less than a year of rule by the caliph al-Mustaᶜīn, one of the Circassians who had been purchased by Barqūq secured the throne. Al-Muʾayyad Shaykh (1412–1421), like Faraj, did not favor his fellow Circassians but instead bought and promoted Turks, presumably in an attempt to restore the ethnic balance that had prevailed before Barqūq.

Nevertheless, it is probably an indication of the extent to which the Circassians had been able to entrench themselves in the state that they were able to survive the policies of both anti-Circassian sultans and that after al-Muʾayyad Shaykh's death they were soon able to reestablish their dominance. With the exception of Khushqadam (1461–1467) and Timurbughā (1468), both of whom were Greeks, the remaining sultans were Circassians, and their supremacy remained unchallenged until the Mamluk armies were defeated by the Ottomans in Syria and Egypt in 1516 and 1517, respectively.

It should be pointed out that while historians like Ibn Taghrībirdī were undoubtedly correct in emphasizing the significance of the excessive power maintained by the Circassians during the second period of Mamluk rule, this factor cannot be regarded as the only, or even the paramount, cause of Mamluk decline. The Ottomans were able to defeat the Mamluks because the former had embraced, and the latter scorned, the use of artillery on the battlefield. Egypt and Syria suffered economic calamity during the *Dawlat al-Jarkas* not because Circassians were on the throne, but because intermittent outbreaks of plague in the fourteenth century had imposed demographic losses from which the Mamluks could not recover in time to meet the challenge of European expansion around the Red Sea. Also worthy of note is that while Ibn Taghrībirdī's analysis stresses "race," it cannot be characterized as racist because he nowhere claims the superiority of Turks to Circassians. Rather, he confines himself to denouncing the folly of showing favoritism to any one "racial" element in a system that depended on the military skill and power of its members, irrespective of their origins.

BIBLIOGRAPHY

David Ayalon, "The Circassians in the Mamluk Kingdom," in *Journal of the American Oriental Society*, **64** (1949), and *Gunpowder and Firearms in the Mamlūk Kingdom* (1956); Ibn Taghrībirdī, *Al-Manhal al-Ṣāfī*, 3 vols., Is-

tanbul Ahmet III MS 3018; William Popper, ed. and trans., *History of Egypt 1382–1469 A.D.*, 7 vols. (1954–1960); Shihāb al-Dīn al-Qalqashandī, *Ṣubḥ al-Aᶜshā*, 14 vols. (1913–1919).

DONALD P. LITTLE

[See also **Barqūq**; **Egypt, Islamic**; **Mamlūks**; **Mamluk Dynasty**; **Qalaʾun**.]

CIRCUMCISION, ISLAMIC. Although male circumcision (Arabic: *khitān*) is a universal practice in the Muslim world, and considered by Muslims everywhere as an important religious observance, it is not mentioned in the Koran. Authority for the practice is derived from a relatively small number of traditions (*ḥadīth*) handed down by the Prophet's contemporaries. Indeed, the classical legal works do not treat it as an independent subject but only incidentally under the heading of other topics. For instance, legal manuals for the use of the market inspectors included regulations for professionals who carried out circumcisions, while chapters in law books on ritual purity mention circumcision along with the other observances of "natural religion," such as cleaning the teeth, cutting the nails, and removing body hair.

The position of the law on the extent to which circumcision is prescribed varies. Most scholars hold that it is a recommended act only and that its omission is not punished in the hereafter. This view is supported by the rule that if an uncircumcised adult fears physical harm from the procedure, he is absolved from undergoing the procedure. Some scholars nonetheless regard the practice as obligatory.

Circumcision was part of the expertise of the cupper (Arabic: *hajjām*). With his instruments, the razor and scissors, he removed the foreskin to allow its retraction beyond the glans penis. Surgical texts describe the procedure in detail. The legal works, in the chapters on guarantees, discuss the extent of the cupper's liability should he err and death or harm ensue. The fines were fixed monetary rates.

The preferred time for circumcision was seven days after birth. Some scholars recommended that it be delayed beyond that date, in part to distinguish it from Jewish practice, but also to ensure that the child would be stronger and the danger reduced. However, present-day custom indicates that children may have been circumcised at any time up to thirteen years of age. The father or guardian was held responsible for seeing that the procedure was carried out. The circumcision of a boy was an occasion for processions, feasts, and other expressions of joy.

Female circumcision, mentioned less frequently but perhaps widely practiced in certain areas, was the excision of a small piece of skin at the front of the genitals, above the urethra. Contrary to the commonly held view, the procedure as described in the classical works did not interfere with sexual functioning. According to most scholars, it was a recommended observance; others held it to be "honorable" and a few, obligatory. The circumcision of girls was not accompanied by festive ceremonies.

In view of the great variety of peoples that profess Islam, it is natural that modern ethnographic studies record great differences in ritual and practice throughout the Muslim world. Presumably this was also the case during the Middle Ages. Many interpretations of the social function of circumcision have been made, including those of health, fertility, ritual purification, and rite of passage into the community.

BIBLIOGRAPHY

Christiaan Snouck Hurgronje, *Mekka in the Latter Part of the Nineteenth Century* (1931); C. M. Kieffer, "À propos de la circoncision à Caboul et dans le Logar," in *Festschrift für Wilhelm Eilers* (1967); Edward W. Lane, *The Manners and Customs of the Modern Egyptians,* 3rd ed. (repr. 1954).

JEANETTE WAKIN

CIRCUMCISION, JEWISH. The rite of circumcision (classical Hebrew: *berit* or *berit milah*) is required of Jewish males on the eighth day after birth. It is derived from the biblical source in which Abraham is commanded to *mol*, that is, remove the foreskin *(orlah)* in order to mark the covenant *(berit)* between God and himself (Gen. 17:10–14, 21:4). The obligation to perform the symbolic operation originally devolved upon the father, but by late antiquity a specialist *(mohel)* existed, who functioned legally as the father's agent. The rite was then given formal structure in specific benedictions, and the occasion was celebrated as a festive one in the home with the family.

The ceremony developed many new elaborations in the medieval period. Around the ninth century, in the Jewish communities under Islamic rule, the ceremony shifted from the home to the synagogue and usually took place immediately following the morning prayers. This transfer incorporated the event into the public liturgy by making it a communal celebration. Special Hebrew liturgical poems *(piyyutim),* the genre itself a medieval innovation, might be composed for the occasion. Now for the first time, too, the Chair of Elijah became part of the rite. The practice of placing a special chair, set aside for the prophet Elijah, near the child during the ceremony derives from the folk belief that the chair serves as a throne for the child's guardian angel, who later became identified with Elijah. He, in turn, was artificially associated with the rite of circumcision by virtue of biblical verses such as 1 Kings 19:10, where Elijah says, "for the children of Israel have forsaken thy covenant" *(beritka),* a later rationalization of the folk custom.

Another medieval innovation in the rite was the introduction of the role of assistant to the *mohel.* Known as the *sandek,* from the Late Greek word for "godfather" *(synteknos),* this honored man sat next to the Chair of Elijah and held the child on a special cushion on his knees during the procedure. The honor was shared with the *sandek's* wife, who brought the child to the synagogue entrance. The child's mother remained at home in a state of ritual impurity for four weeks following childbirth, after which time she came to the synagogue on the Sabbath. Whereas on that occasion a newborn girl was given her name, a boy received his Hebrew name at the time of his circumcision. In addition, however, boys also received a vernacular name after four weeks, and marked it in a special rite in the synagogue. The child's father was honored by being called to the Torah, and the cloth that the child had worn during circumcision—now with his name embroidered on it—was presented to the synagogue as a binder for the Torah scroll. This custom may have been linked to the reference, found in the circumcision ceremony itself, to the child's future study of Torah: for the congregation concludes the rite by saying, "As he has entered into the covenant, so may he be permitted to enter into the study of Torah, the marriage canopy, and the performance of good deeds."

BIBLIOGRAPHY

Asher Asher, *The Jewish Rite of Circumcision* (1873); Hayyim Schauss, *The Lifetime of a Jew* (1950); Solomon

Schechter, "The Child in Jewish Literature," in his *Studies in Judaism,* 1st ser. (1911).

IVAN G. MARCUS

[See also **Family and Family Law, Jewish.**]

CISTERCIAN CHANT. A cardinal principle in the organization of the first Cistercian liturgical books was authenticity, understood in terms of a return to authoritative sources. For the hymnal this meant Ambrosian texts and melodies, since the Rule of St. Benedict (prime point of reference for the Cistercian reform) equates *hymnus* with *ambrosianum* in several passages. For the Mass and Office chants, authenticity meant the repertory of texts and melodies popularly, though mistakenly, ascribed to Pope Gregory I.

The implementation of this principle of authenticity resulted, for the hymnal, in the rejection of all texts and melodies other than those of the Milanese tradition. The number of texts and hymn melodies in the primitive Cistercian hymnal was painfully small and, outside the immediate area of Milan, relatively unknown. In keeping with the Milanese practice, a single hymn, *Aeterne rerum conditor,* was chanted at vigils every day of the year. This archaic hymnal figures in Abelard's catalog of Cistercian liturgical incongruities in his *Letter 10* to Bernard of Clairvaux.

Since authenticity, in the case of Mass and Office chants, was equated with Gregorian, the first Cistercians went to Metz for their gradual and antiphonary. A major center for the diffusion of the Roman liturgy in Carolingian times, Metz was still renowned—rightly or wrongly—for the excellence of its chant tradition. In point of fact, the Metz chant of the early twelfth century had degenerated into something of a Teutonic chant dialect; and the melodies of the traditional repertory were only imperfectly transcribed by those Metz scribes responsible for the transition from notation without a staff *(campo aperto)* to notation on a staff (diastemic).

This Cistercian "return to tradition" resulted in a chant repertory the texts of which were wholly classical and virtually closed to the enrichments of the tenth and eleventh centuries. The melodies of this repertory, with its unfamiliar archaic hymn tunes and texts, and with its Metz parody of the standard chant, necessarily smacked of the bizarre to anyone accustomed to the chant styled "Gregorian." Both

within the order and outside, this peculiar chant repertory became the target of considerable comment and criticism. The demise of the last of the first-generation Cistercians cleared the way for a sweeping revision of the order's chant books.

Sometime between 1134 and 1147 a revision of the order's liturgical books was undertaken under the general aegis of St. Bernard, abbot of Clairvaux. The new chant books so effectively replaced the earlier ones that these latter survive only in occasional fragments. This systematic revision reflects two chief concerns: first, the exigencies of reason *(ratio)* as propounded by reputable music theoreticians then in vogue (Guido of Arezzo, Regino of Prüm, Aurelian of Réôme, Pseudo-Odo, John of Afflighem); second, exigencies of a pastoral nature in favor of monks living in the age of the trouvère and troubadour, monks somewhat ill at ease with the relentlessly archaic texts and peculiar melodies of the first Cistercian chant books.

The main principles of music theory operative in the revision of the Metz chant are outlined (with examples) in the anonymous treatise *Cantum quem Cisterciensis* affixed to the reformed antiphonary. The main features are as follows: (1) The principle of modal unity was applied with a view to the clarification of modal ambiguity and to the modal unification of the phrases. Application of the same principle led also to modifications in the psalmody of Mass and Office chants. (2) Melodies were restricted to the interval of a tenth. Notes exceeding this compass were either eliminated or transposed within an acceptable range. Compenetration of authentic (modes 1, 3, 5, and 7) and plagal (modes 2, 4, 6, and 8) was likewise proscribed. (3) Notation of *B*-flat was avoided to the extent possible by means of transposition to the fifth above. (4) A relatively few melodies were simplified by suppression of textual repetitions and abridgment of the longer vocalises.

Unmentioned by the author (or authors) of the treatise, but equally important, was the systematic revision of the Metz melodies with a view to conformity with the "standard" version in general use. In both antiphonary (Office) and gradual (Mass) new texts and melodies of the postclassical period were introduced, some of them composed by Cistercians. The Milanese-Cistercian hymnal was similarly revised. Melodies were reworked or even replaced by non-Milanese favorites and original tunes by Cistercian composers; and almost twenty popular standard hymns were assigned to the hours of terce and compline. This systematic revision of the archaic repertory resulted in a particular form of chant that paid tribute to traditional sources, while respecting the exigencies of contemporary music theory and the aesthetic preferences of monks of the postclassical period of chant.

Few later additions were made to this distinctive repertory, which survived relatively intact well into the seventeenth century, when the order's chant books were reedited according to the norms canonized in the lamentable Roman-rite "Medicean" chant then in vogue. In 1893 the newly formed liturgy commission of the Cistercians of the Strict Observance (Trappists) opted for a return to the twelfth-century chant still recoverable from numerous manuscripts dating from that century. The gradual (1899), antiphonary (1903), hymnal (1909), and psalter (1925), along with the order's other liturgical books, thus offer intact the substance of the repertory from the mid twelfth century.

BIBLIOGRAPHY

Francis J. Guentner, ed., *Epistola S. Bernardi De revisione cantus Cisterciensis et Tractatus ab auctore incerto Cisterciense,* Corpus scriptorum de musica, XXIV (1974); Michel Huglo, *Les tonaires: Inventaire, analyse, comparaison* (1971), 357–367; Chrysogonus Waddell, "The Origin and Early Evolution of the Early Cistercian Antiphonary," in M. Basil Pennington, ed., *The Cistercian Spirit* (1970).

CHRYSOGONUS WADDELL, O.C.S.O.

[See also **Ambrosian Chant; Bernard of Clairvaux, St.; Cistercian Order; Cistercian Rite; Organum.**]

CISTERCIAN ORDER. The eleventh century witnessed a great renewal of monasticism in western Europe. As in any age, renewal involves an examination of the basic structures of organization and patterns of life and an attempt to rebuild them according to contemporary needs. Stimulated by the desire within many monasteries for a more austere form of life, by the arrival in Italy of Greek monks from the East, and by the general impetus for reform within the church associated with Pope Gregory VII, this monastic movement stressed a return to apostolic and Eastern traditions. It was characterized by an emphasis on the strict interpretation of the Rule of St. Benedict, penance and mortification, total separation from lay society, and a more eremitic, rather than cenobitic, style of monastic life.

In 1098, wishing to institutionalize these ideals,

twenty-one monks and the abbot Robert left the rich abbey of Molesme and settled on lands given them by Raynald, viscount of Beaune, in the forest of Cîteaux, twenty kilometers south of Dijon in Burgundy. The name Cîteaux, meaning swampy land or stagnant pools, describes the site of the monastery, and the land given for it and for most early foundations from it was alodial. The first Cistercians renounced all civil possessions and manorial sources of income, such as mills, markets, fairs, and serfs; and all ecclesiastical revenues, such as tithes, rents, and advowsons. Original goals also prescribed that monasteries be established on land far from existing habitation and worked solely by the monks themselves. Early Cistercian life, while communal, was eremitic in that it sought strict separation from lay society.

By contemporary monastic standards, life at Cîteaux was severely austere. Although the original location of the New Monastery, as Cîteaux was initially called, proved so unhealthy that the site had to be changed, and while Robert and some monks returned to Molesme, the grants of Odo, duke of Burgundy, and his son Hugh allowed the community a modest prosperity from 1106 onward. Under the second abbot, St. Alberic, the monks adopted a white habit under a black scapular; hence their popular name, White Monks. In 1113, under the third abbot, the erudite Englishman Stephen Harding, Cîteaux made its first foundation at La Ferté.

The arrival in the same year of the young, well-educated, and highly charismatic Burgundian nobleman, Bernard, attracted many recruits from the lesser nobility and accelerated the movement toward expansion. New abbeys were rapidly established at Pontigny (1114), and at Clairvaux and Morimond (1115); by 1150 almost 350 monasteries scattered across Europe belonged to the Cistercian order. All were dedicated to the Virgin. An annual General Chapter, or meeting of all the abbots at Cîteaux on 14 September, held ultimate authority over all houses and legislated to maintain discipline and uniformity. An annual visitation of each monastery by the abbot of the founding house also served as a means of enforcing strict observance.

Cistercian monasteries almost invariably were situated in forests; in hilly or rocky places (such as northern England); in swampy marshes (as in the Low Countries, eastern Prussia, Silesia); or in politically contested border areas (as on the fringes of Normandy and Brittany), where the monks served as a stabilizing influence. Land grants therefore represented little or no financial loss to the noble patrons.

Through colonization and with enormous energy, the White Monks drained swamps and erected dikes and dams, cut down forests, and brought the land under cultivation. The monks acted as pioneers in undeveloped areas, and they acquired the reputation of being successful agricultural innovators. Cistercian spiritual ideals, therefore, coincided perfectly with the social and economic needs of the times.

In addition, the monks everywhere exploited local opportunities. By the end of the twelfth century, they had taken the lead from Poland to Portugal and from Scandinavia to Spain in many forms of economic enterprise: for example, in iron mining (Furness in Lancashire, Clairvaux and Igny in Champagne); in coal mining (Newbattle in Scotland, Grünhain in Bohemia); in salt mining (Wachock near Cracow in Poland, Aussee in Austria); in silver mining (Grünhain, Altzelle in Saxony); in wine making (Cîteaux in Burgundy, Eberbach and other houses in the Rhine and Moselle valleys); in sheep farming and the production of fine wools (Fountains and Rievaulx in Yorkshire, Poblet in Spain); in horse breeding (Jervaulx in Yorkshire, Otterberg in Germany); in fish hatcheries (Waldsassen in the Upper Palatinate, Tintern in the Welsh marshes); in fruit culture (Lyse, Norway's largest Cistercian abbey); and in banking for the local nobilities (Savigny in Normandy, Dore in Wales, Poblet in Spain). Many abbeys kept bees, since honey in the Middle Ages took the place of sugar; the honey was produced for sale as well as for home consumption. More important, all across Europe, wind or water mills, operated directly by the monks or leased to the peasants, proved lucrative commercial operations.

In the execution of these business activities, the Cistercians applied the system of lay brothers, which had already been adopted in some German Benedictine houses such as Hirsau. The increase in population; the availability of new lands, especially in eastern Europe; the desire to escape poverty and insecurity; and the lighter dues and services on monastic estates, in contrast to those on the lands of lay lords, attracted thousands from the peasant classes to Cistercian houses. Given a modest instruction in monastic prayer and exempt from the liturgical duties of the choir, peasants performed most of the manual labor. The White Monks utilized the conversi, as lay brothers were called, on a vast scale; and until the Black Death in the fourteenth century created a serious population shortage, Cistercian lay brothers exercised a decisive impact on the entire economy of medieval Europe.

The wealth generated by these many economic operations was applied mainly to the construction of churches and conventual buildings. In conscious reaction to the highly decorated Cluniac churches, the General Chapters required that the Cistercian style reflect a severe simplicity and a complete lack of ornamentation. Cistercian churches followed the traditional cruciform pattern with a central nave and two aisles intersected by a transept, but they adopted a rectangular apse rather than the Benedictine circular one. The bare sanctuary at the east end was used only for solemn masses. The monastic choir began in the transept and faced westward into the nave, which was often a lengthy and virtually separate church for the lay brothers, who outnumbered the choir monks at many abbeys.

Most Cistercian churches were built between 1150 and 1250. While the style varied slightly by region, most were constructed in the Burgundian "Half Gothic": basically Romanesque but with pointed arches and repeated separate bays of ribbed vaulting. The open cloister, where in good weather the monks spent a good part of each day in reading or other occupations, was the center of the monastic compound and provided direct access to the other conventual buildings: refectory, dormitory, chapter house, and fountains for washing. Because of the phenomenal costs of transportation, local materials were almost always used for building. While the site of the water supply determined the precise location of these buildings, still, the style and layout were so uniform that a monk immediately felt at home in any abbey. Although Cistercian churches lacked ornamental features, in their calm rural settings they achieved a kind of pure beauty, a rich harmony of proportions, and a quiet elegance.

Increasing prosperity also afforded the opportunity for the development of scholarship. The main elements of Cistercian piety and spirituality—absolute adherence to the Rule of St. Benedict, solitude and asceticism, silence, together with an emphasis on Christ's passion and the glories of the Virgin—were the main themes of Cistercian writing. The rural isolation of most monasteries and the anti-intellectual stance of the General Chapters worked against the growth of a tradition of learning. Abbot Stephen Harding's appreciation for beautifully illustrated manuscripts, however, and the enormous influence of the writings of Bernard of Clairvaux laid the foundations for Cistercian literary culture.

The White Monks contributed to all the major literary genres of the High Middle Ages. Writers such as Guerric of Igny, Isaac of Stella, Adam of Perseigne, and of course St. Bernard himself produced collections of sermons addressed to monastic audiences. The chroniclers of Coggeshall, Fountains, Furness, Meaux, and Waverly, among others, continued the monastic tradition of historical writing; history as a "profane subject" reached its apogee in the books of Otto of Freising, while the writings of John of Viktring are invaluable sources for German and east European history of the thirteenth and fourteenth centuries.

Among the many writers of exempla, Caesarius of the Rhineland abbey of Heisterbach made a large collection that provides useful information on contemporary monastic life and ideals. Likewise, Cistercian hagiographical works, such as the popular lives of the saints of Villers, found their way into many libraries. Second only to the writings of St. Bernard, those of the Englishman Ethelred of Rievaulx—especially his dialogue *On Spiritual Friendship,* his treatise *On the Soul,* and his many sermons—enjoyed the greatest popularity. The cartularies, or collections of charters recording gifts, provide modern students with significant social, economic, literary, and religious information; those of Savigny, Vaux-de-Cernay, and Furness are especially good examples.

In the thirteenth and fourteenth centuries opposition to formal education persisted, and the Cistercians, lacking the intellectual dynamism of the Dominicans, lost to them the ablest recruits. The General Chapter of 1184 had forbidden the study of canon law, implying that there was already an interest in such academic pursuits. With strong papal support, the English abbot of Clairvaux, Stephen of Lexington, founded the College of St. Bernard at Paris in 1245. In spite of the initial hostility of the General Chapters, the college flourished. Similar Cistercian colleges were established at the universities of Montpellier, Oxford, Bologna, and Salamanca.

In the later twelfth and throughout the thirteenth century, the "international" prestige of the order and the presence within it of able administrators led royal and papal governments to employ Cistercians in important ambassadorial, legal, crusading, and missionary positions. For example, the abbots of Ford, Buckfast, Kirkstall, Vaudey, and Wardon in England were appointed papal judges delegate. The abbots of Boxley and Robertsbridge were sent as royal legates to search for King Richard I when he was captured returning from the Third Crusade; they arranged for his ransom. Pope Innocent III appointed Luke of Sambucina to preach the Fourth Crusade and Guy of Vaux-de-Cernay as papal legate on that Crusade. Cistercians such as Arnold Amaury also played a vigorous part in the Crusade against the Albigensians. The expenses incurred by these public and secular responsibilities were borne by the monasteries. The hundreds of Cistercians promoted to episcopal office include Stephen of Alvastra, first archbishop of Uppsala (Sweden); Baldwin of Ford, archbishop of Canterbury; Henry of Clairvaux, cardinal bishop of Albano; and Peter of La Ferté, archbishop of Tarentaise. As early as 1145 a monk of Clairvaux became pope as Eugenius III.

Just as the economic dynamism and spiritual vitality of the twelfth and thirteenth centuries helped the expansion of the order, so the political, religious, and natural calamities of the fourteenth and fifteenth centuries had a disastrous effect on it. In France and England, the weaknesses of the central governments left the abbeys prey to aristocratic exploitation. The Hundred Years War isolated Cîteaux and the General Chapters from the many daughter houses, prevented the required visitations, and led to a breakdown of central authority. In central and eastern Europe, great lords claimed advocacy over the monasteries and made heavy financial demands on them. The Avignon papacy, followed by the Great Schism, damaged papal credibility and encouraged the development of national chapters, which were largely ineffective in maintaining regular monastic observance.

Everywhere as discipline weakened, decadence increased. The Black Death carried away perhaps as many as two-thirds of many monastic communities. Finally, the system of commendatory abbots, whereby the papacy exercised the right to appoint or to approve the elections of abbots in return for substantial fees, destroyed local independence and resulted in the appointment of nonresident foreigners. The debt of most houses increased and everywhere served to aggravate disorder. Such was the state of the Cistercian Order in 1500. In the seventeenth century, and again in the twentieth, it underwent a remarkable resurgence.

BIBLIOGRAPHY

The best introduction to the rich literature on the Cistercian Order is in Louis J. Lekai, *The Cistercians: Ideals and Reality* (1977), 400–441, which contains thorough, up-to-date references to sources, scholarly journals, all aspects of Cistercian art, liturgy, spirituality, and learning, economy, and customs.

For sources and reference works, Jean de la Croix Bouton and Jean-Baptiste Van Damme, eds., *Les plus anciens textes de Cîteaux* (1974) provides a complete and thoroughly annotated edition of early Cistercian documents, the most important of which have been translated with special concern for textual fidelity by Bede K. Lackner, "Early Cistercian Documents in Translation," in Lekai, *op. cit.,* 442–466.

See also Marcel Aubert, *L'architecture cistercienne en France*, 2nd ed., 2 vols. (1947); Anselme Dimier, *Recueil de plans d'églises cisterciennes* (1949); Georges Duby, *Rural Economy and Country Life in the Medieval West*, Cynthia Postan, trans. (1968), and *The Cistercians: Studies in the Geography of Medieval England and Wales* (1978); Bennett D. Hill, *English Cistercian Monasteries and Their Patrons in the Twelfth Century* (1968); Bede K. Lackner, *The Eleventh Century Background of Cîteaux* (1972); Jean Leclercq *et al., The Spirituality of the Middle Ages* (1968), 187–220; Frédéric van der Meer, *Atlas de l'Ordre cistercien* (1965); Basil Pennington, *The Cistercian Spirit* (1970); Ambrosius Schneider, *Die Cistercienser: Geschichte, Geist, Kunst* (1974); Franz Winter, *Die Cistercienser des nordöstlichen Deutschlands,* 3 vols. (1868–1871, repr. 1966).

BENNETT D. HILL

[See also **Architecture, Liturgical Aspects; Benedictine Rule; Bernard of Clairvaux, St.; Converso; Ethelred of Rievaulx, St.; Harding, Stephen, St.; Hirsau; Monasticism; Reform, Idea of; Romanesque Architecture; Savigny.**]

CISTERCIAN RITE. Central to the monastic reform inaugurated in 1098 by a group of renewal-minded monks from the abbey of Molesme was the liturgy of the new monastery. Characteristic of this liturgy was a radical return to authentic sources and a style of celebration marked by extreme simplicity and poverty. With the liturgical prescriptions of the Rule of St. Benedict serving as an absolute norm, all accretions and appendages to the Divine Office (litanies, votive offices, additional psalms) were eliminated. The calendar, essentially a simplified version of the Molesme calendar, allowed of only two ranks of celebrations for the saints: feasts with twelve lessons at the Night Office and simple commemorations appended to lauds and vespers. The organization of the sanctoral cycle in the liturgical books was based on that of ninth-century prototypes of Roman origin, while sacramentary, epistolary, and evangelary reflected similarly archaic sources. St. Benedict's equation of *ambrosianum* with *hymnus* in several passages of his Rule resulted in the adoption of a

hymnal composed exclusively of Milanese texts and melodies. The Night Office patristic lectionary drew almost exclusively from material in the standard homiliary compiled in the eighth century by Paul the Deacon and probably represents a "purged" version of the patristic lectionary then in current use at Molesme.

Apart from Sundays and a number of twelve-lesson feasts, there was only one daily conventual Mass celebrated by a priest assisted by a single server. The Mass rite, probably a simplification of Molesme practice, unfolded in a setting of great sobriety: woolen vestments of a single color, altar vessels chiefly of nonprecious materials, absence of stained glass windows and of images (apart from a wooden cross with painted corpus), and two candles.

Liturgical reforms effected toward 1147 and 1180 modified texts and melodies but served to confirm the order in its original orientation. With the waning of the Middle Ages both the spirit and the substance of the rite became progressively denatured. In 1618 the General Chapter officially adopted the Roman rite for Mass, and a similar romanization of the breviary took place in 1656.

BIBLIOGRAPHY

Columban Bock, *Les codifications du droit cistercien* (1966); J.-M. Canivez, "Le rite cistercien," in *Ephemerides liturgicae,* **63** (1949); Philippe Guignard, ed., *Les monuments primitifs de la règle cistercienne* (1878); Bede Lackner, "The Liturgy of Early Cîteaux," in *Studies in Medieval Cistercian History Presented to Jeremiah F. O'Sullivan* (1971); Archdale A. King, *Liturgies of the Religious Orders* (1955), 62–156; Chrysogonus Waddell, "The Early Cistercian Experience of Liturgy," in Basil Pennington, ed., *Rule and Life: A Symposium* (1971), 77–116.

CHRYSOGONUS WADDELL, O.C.S.O.

[See also **Benedictine Rule; Cistercian Chant; Divine Office; Paul the Deacon.**]

CITY. See Urbanism.

CIUFFAGNI, BERNARDO (1381–1457), Florentine sculptor, is first mentioned in documents as assisting Ghiberti on the second bronze doors for the baptistery at Florence in 1407. Two years later his involvement with the Duomo began, with records mentioning numerous works that no longer survive. Ciuffagni's chief surviving work is the St. Matthew (1410–1415) for the Duomo facade (now in the Museo dell'Opera del Duomo). Shortly after, he began work on a Joshua figure for the Duomo's campanile, the completion of which was given over to Nanni di Bartolo in 1421. A gifted but not brilliant sculptor, Ciuffagni worked in a style strongly influenced by Donatello.

BIBLIOGRAPHY

Luisa Becherucci and Giulia Brunetti, eds., *Il Museo dell'Opera del Duomo a Firenze*, 2 vols. (1969).

ADELHEID M. GEALT

CLANS, SCOTTISH. The word *clann* means "children," and describes a kindred or ruling group claiming descent from a single ancestor who gave them a name, and ruling a territory the inhabitants of which often claim membership in the clan. Twelfth-century texts in the *Book of Deer* (Aberdeenshire) refer to the *toiseach* (head or chief) of the clans of Morgan and Cano, which are otherwise unknown. Certain church lands were given freedom "from mormaer and toiseach"—that is, from the obligations to these men. In thirteenth-century Carrick (a Gaelic province), when the earldom passed to an heiress, the "headship of the kindred" or "clan" (*caput progeniei*) was transferred to a male cousin, thus separating aspects of landlordship (kept by the countess) from other kinship rights, notably "the leading of the men of the earldom."

In the twelfth century the western seaboard of Scotland saw the rise of a great lordship under Somerled and its partition among his sons, one of whom, Dougall, was ancestor of the MacDougall lords of Argyll; a grandson, Donald, was ancestor of the MacDonald lords of Islay and later lords of the Isles. Here the patronymic "son of Dougall," or "son of Donald" was passed to succeeding generations. When a later generation, possibly through a younger son, established its own lordship, either peaceably or by warfare, the founder's name would be similarly used—hence, for instance, the Macruaraidh lords of Garmoran, also descended from Somerled. The families of Cowal and Knapdale (MacSween, Lamont, and MacLachlan) claimed descent from the O'Neill kings of Aileach in northern Ireland (probably cor-

rectly), and hence ultimately from Niall of the Nine Hostages, but their separate names belong to historical personages of about 1200, about 1250, and about 1270, respectively. Other lines of chiefs were similarly established throughout the Middle Ages.

The territorialization of these clans could arise from conquest or from partition; little work has been done on this aspect of clan society. The chief obtained military service and, where appropriate, naval service from the peasantry—the rights of *toiseach,* and the "leading" referred to in early sources. Almost certainly tribute for land held was paid in cattle or pastoral products, notably *calpich,* the best eighth. In return the chief gave protection, possibly even weapons, and leadership, which might be in interclan warfare, the object of which was usually the seizure of cattle. The socioeconomic unit of chief, his relatives, and peasantry might be regarded as the clan, and this is the usual modern use of the term.

Because the environment was hostile to agrarian pursuits and because the Lowlands provided a ready market for cattle, there was a strong temptation to cattle raiding, which could generate feuds. By the mid fourteenth century the Highland clans were notorious for their freebooting, which could be either exacerbated or repressed by a strong over-chieftainship. Alexander, son of Robert II, as justiciar in the North organized caterans, apparently numerous small clans, in a career of pillage and extortion. The resulting feuds became so bad that an attempt was made to settle one by a combat, thirty per side, before the king at Perth in 1396. By contrast, the growth of MacDonald power as lords of the Isles in the fifteenth century imposed a balance and some restraint among the lesser clans on the western seaboard.

In those Highland areas close to Lowland influence, notably in Argyll, it is possible to find clans whose chiefs enjoyed "feudal" trappings such as stone castles and arms and armor. But Highland society as a whole was poor, and standards of living even among chiefs were simple.

BIBLIOGRAPHY

William F. Skene, *Celtic Scotland*, 3 vols. (1886–1890, repr. 1972); Ronald G. Nicholson, *Scotland, the Later Middle Ages* (1974); K. A. Steer and J. W. M. Bannerman, *Late Mediaeval Monumental Sculpture in the West Highlands* (1977).

A. A. M. DUNCAN

[See also **Scotland: History.**]

407

CLANVOWE, SIR JOHN (*ca.* 1341–1391), soldier, administrator, and diplomat at the courts of Edward III and Richard II, and also a writer of some consequence. His ancestors, who were probably Welsh, owned land in Radnorshire and Herefordshire that Clanvowe inherited. He fought in the Hundred Years War as early as 1364; he was at the skirmish at Lussac in which Sir John Chandos was killed; he was on the expedition to France of Sir Robert Knollys in 1370, and with John of Gaunt in 1373–1374 and 1378. Clanvowe entered the service of Edward III in 1373 and that of Richard II on his accession in 1377; he was a chamber knight by 1381. Between 1381 and 1385 he was largely concerned with keeping order and investigating disturbances in Wales and the Marches, and after 1385 with European diplomacy—treating for peace with France and Portugal. In 1386, like most of Richard II's "court party," Clanvowe was displaced when the government was taken over by the Lords Appellant; but when Richard II reasserted himself in 1389, Clanvowe's career resumed its former course—peace negotiations with France and Brittany in 1389 and a commission to the Marches in 1390. Later in 1390 he went on Louis of Bourbon's unsuccessful Crusade against the Moors of Tunis. He died on 17 October 1391 near Constantinople, presumably while on pilgrimage.

Clanvowe is frequently associated in the records with men who apparently formed a loose group at court: Sir William Neville, Sir William Beauchamp, Sir Lewis Clifford, Sir Richard Sturry, Sir Philip de La Vache. Most of these men were, like Clanvowe, associated with Chaucer; several were also said by contemporary chroniclers to be Lollard sympathizers.

The two pieces of writing attributable to Clanvowe differ considerably from each other, but both are important. *The Boke of Cupide* (formerly called *The Cuckoo and the Nightingale*) is the earliest English poem to take its inspiration and manner from Chaucer. It quotes the Knight's Tale (lines 1785–1786) and owes much to *The Parliament of Fowls* in terms of genre: each is a "love vision" drawing on St. Valentine's Day beliefs, and each involves a debate between birds about love. The subject of Clanvowe's poem is the irresistible but ambivalent power of love, and his main character is a first-person narrator, who describes himself as "olde and unlusty" but who nevertheless persists in hoping, against all reason, for success in love. It is a wry, self-mocking poem, which does not have the philosoph-

ical dimension of Chaucer's earlier poems, but which nevertheless catches something of his urbane, ironical manner.

The Two Ways, written in 1391, on his journey to Constantinople, is unremittingly severe. It is a religious prose treatise, one of the earliest to be written in English by a layman. Based on Matthew 7:13–14, it exhorts the reader to avoid the "broode way" that leads to hell and to take the "nargh way" that leads to heaven. Clanvowe's central recommendation—that one needs to lead a good life based on biblical teaching—is perhaps not as interesting as the incidental positions assumed in the course of the argument: though he had been a soldier, Clanvowe condemns war and the slaughter and destruction it produces; and though long a courtier, he repudiates the rich excesses of courts and their preoccupation with worldly attainment.

These attitudes were broadly shared by the Lollards, and in one passage Clanvowe takes on himself and others like him the word "loller," meaning literally "loafer" or "idler," a term often deliberately and scornfully misapplied to Lollards. But if the treatise can be said to be Lollard in sympathies, it seems that Clanvowe's Lollardry was of a nonpolemical sort, for he has nothing to say on those controversial questions of doctrine with which Wycliffe and his clerical followers were so concerned.

BIBLIOGRAPHY

The Works of Sir John Clanvowe, V. J. Scattergood, ed. (1975); G. L. Kittredge, "Chaucer and Some of his Friends," in *Modern Philology,* **1** (1903); R. H. Robbins, "The Findern Anthology," in *PMLA,* **69** (1954); Kenneth B. McFarlane, *Lancastrian Kings and Lollard Knights* (1972), 139–232.

V. J. Scattergood

[See also **Chaucer, Geoffrey; Hundred Years War; Lollards; Middle English Literature; Richard II.**]

CLARENDON, ASSIZE OF. The first innovative legislative enactment of Henry II of England, this assize was issued at a great council of archbishops, bishops, abbots, and barons held at Clarendon early in 1166. The term "assize" (Latin: *assisa*) originally meant the sitting of a court or a council. Later, as here, it came to denote the decisions taken and enactments passed at such an assembly. Consisting of twenty-two articles, this assize is the earliest official document delineating the extensive administrative changes introduced by Henry II, particularly in the area of local jurisdiction. Except for a few articles on excommunicated renegades and precautions for proper admission to religious orders, it deals with the administration of criminal justice.

Article I introduces a fundamental change in criminal legal procedure by providing for the presentment, or grand jury. Commissions of royal itinerant justices were regularly to visit the counties, and juries of twelve men of the hundred and four men of the vill would, under sworn oath, present (indict) to them and the sheriffs notorious or reputed lawbreakers. This article regularized the use of the grand jury to indict individuals, a procedure that became basic to the common law system. It indicates that under Henry II the visitations or eyres of the itinerant justices occurred annually, and that these justices had been given increased powers of criminal jurisdiction.

Article II states that persons indicted should be tried by the ordeal of cold water, a provision that had the effect of abolishing the practice of trial by compurgation at the county courts. Article XIV illustrates Henry II's distrust of the current forms of criminal trials by stipulating that individuals of notorious reputation who successfully passed the trial by ordeal still must abjure the realm as quickly as possible and return only by royal permission. Other articles improve surveillance of vagabonds and fugitives by instituting regular checks on all individuals residing in the counties. The regulations, that all qualified persons must attend the county court and serve on the presentment jury and that no feudal court could exclude the sheriff from preparing for the eyres of the itinerant justices, limited the justice dispensed at feudal courts and expanded that dispensed at royal courts while giving the sheriffs a greater role in criminal justice.

It is thought that at Clarendon, Henry II also initiated another legal procedure of exceptional importance that is not, however, included in the extant Assize of Clarendon: the assize of novel disseisin. According to this assize, no freeman was to be disseised (dispossessed) of his land unjustly and without judgment. Any person who claimed to be so dispossessed could obtain remedy by purchasing a writ of novel disseisin. In the presence of royal justices a jury was summoned and asked to state, under oath, whether the plaintiff had been disseised. If the jury gave a verdict favorable to the plaintiff, his land was to be restored.

This assize was to mold subsequent development

of civil procedure and to rechannel the direction taken by land law. The introduction of these efficient and rational legal procedures at Clarendon ensured the triumph of the common law in medieval England.

BIBLIOGRAPHY

For a translation of the Assize of Clarendon, see David C. Douglas and G. W. Greenaway, eds., *English Historical Documents,* vol. 2: *1042–1189* (1953), 408–410. For commentary, see Raoul C. van Caenegem, *Royal Writs in England from the Conquest to Glanvill* (1959); Naomi D. Hurnard, "The Jury of Presentment and the Assize of Clarendon," in *English Historical Review,* 56 (1941); and Frederick Pollock and Frederic W. Maitland, *The History of English Law Before the Time of Edward I* (1968).

BRYCE LYON

[See also **England: Norman-Angevin; Henry II of England; Law, English Common: To 1272.**]

CLARENDON, CONSTITUTIONS OF. This important document emerged from the acrimonious struggle between church and state that began in England during the reign of William II (1087–1100), intensified under Henry I (1100–1135) during his celebrated dispute with Anselm, archbishop of Canterbury, and culminated in the epic battle between Henry II (1154–1189) and his archbishop of Canterbury, Thomas Becket. Before elevation to the archbishopric in 1162, Becket had been a devoted and loyal servant of Henry II. As archbishop he immediately changed character, and became so ardent in championing church rights that Henry was led to issue the Constitutions of Clarendon during a great council held at a favorite hunting lodge in January 1164.

The purpose, evident from the principal provisions, was to define royal and church rights as they had been under Henry I. No tenant in chief or official of Henry II could be excommunicated or have his land put under interdict without royal consent. Clergy could not leave the realm without Henry's permission. Appeals to the papal court were so restricted that church disputes could go no further than the court of the archbishop of Canterbury without royal approval. Henry asserted his feudal right to enjoy the revenues from vacant church benefices, and ensured his control over elections by insisting that the electoral bodies assemble in the royal chapel and elect clerics acceptable to the king. The clerics elected had to do homage and swear fealty to the king before receiving spiritual investiture of their offices.

But the clause that most angered Becket specified that clerics accused of crime were to be turned over to a church court for trial after being interrogated by royal justices. There, in the presence of a royal justice whose purpose was to witness the proceedings, the cleric was to be tried and, if found guilty, turned over to the royal court for sentencing and punishment. This guaranteed that criminous clerics would receive their due, even hanging and mutilation. Becket immediately protested what he called "double punishment," quoting from St. Jerome that "God judges not twice for the same offense."

Henry was on firmer ground than Becket because he had consulted with expert canon lawyers. Becket's arguments were too emotional. Although for the moment Becket had to agree to the Constitutions, he soon repented his action and refused to put his seal to the document. He then inflicted penance on himself and tried unsuccessfully to flee England. Finally, in October 1164, he broke completely with Henry and fled to France, where he remained for six years. In July 1170, Henry and Becket met in Normandy and apparently reconciled their differences—but not for long. After returning to England, Becket attempted to suspend those bishops who had supported Henry, and on Christmas Day publicly castigated and excommunicated his enemies. The result is well known. Four of Henry's knights murdered Becket on 29 December as he was celebrating Mass in Canterbury Cathedral, an act that caused universal revulsion and forced Henry to retract certain provisions of the Constitutions of Clarendon. Thereafter criminous clerics arraigned in a royal court could claim benefit of clergy and be turned over to a church court for trial and sentence, a practice that remained in force in England until the nineteenth century.

BIBLIOGRAPHY

For a translation, see David C. Douglas and G. W. Greenaway, eds., *English Historical Documents*, vol. 2: *1042–1189* (1953), 718–722. For commentary, Frederic W. Maitland, "Henry II and the Criminous Clerks," in *English Historical Review*, 7 (1982); Christopher Cheney, "The Punishment of Felonious Clerks," *ibid.*, 51 (1936); David M. Knowles, *Archbishop Thomas Becket: A Character Study* (1949); Charles Duggan, "The Becket Dispute and Criminous Clerks," in *Bulletin of the Institute of Historical Research*, 35 (1962).

BRYCE LYON

[See also **Becket, Thomas, St.; England: Norman-Angevin; Henry II of England.**]

CLÁRI SAGA. See **Klári Saga.**

CLASS STRUCTURE TO 1000. See **Feudalism.**

CLASS STRUCTURE, RUSSIAN. See **Muscovy, Rise of.**

CLASS STRUCTURE, WESTERN (1000–1300)

CLASS AND CLASS FORMATION IN THE MIDDLE AGES

While social stratification certainly existed during the period 1000–1300, it is arguable whether any of the individual strata deserve to be called classes. For example, Marc Bloch refuses to call the upper stratum either a nobility or a social class before 1200; others consider it a nobility but not a class, or both a nobility and a class. Nevertheless, a careful definition may be useful for understanding certain key aspects of medieval social reality. Such a definition (which is elaborated below in the 1300–1500 article) may be stated thus: in the Middle Ages a class formed where economic position, privilege, and power came together, and only to the extent that they came together.

Such a multidimensional definition is useful because wealth, prestige, and political power all had weight in the balance that produced medieval social status and stratification—a balance very different from the modern one. Capital, for instance, had less importance in the agrarian medieval economy than it does today, and its influence was further undermined by the general economic instability and randomness that often characterized the Middle Ages. Authority over land and labor, buttressed by heritability and by legal sanctions no longer extant in modern democratic societies, had rather more importance. Legal rights and duties depended on one's legal status, with serfs barred from royal courts and clergy given their own courts. Each factor mattered, and men found themselves in similar social situations only if their wealth, power, and prestige levels happened to coincide.

Real classes that serve as the basis for social action also require a measure of class consciousness. We tend to think of society as composed of distinct horizontal strata, but medieval men had other models. No knight or merchant or cottager had ever heard of a middle class. Medieval men also had other loyalties, to land and lord and church. Peasants and burgesses were suspicious of similarly situated men from the next village or town, let alone across the kingdom.

It does not follow, however, that we should abandon all efforts to think in terms of horizontal classes. Nobles, for example, were closer to acting as a class than were peasants. Thus, a concept of class that describes a spectrum of potential degrees of class formation should produce some valuable analysis. And a concept of class that allows for a spectrum of potential degrees of class formation can also allow for different classes to be in different stages of formation throughout the period.

Western society before 1000 was marked not by a few classes and sharp class lines but rather by a variety of personal status and many small status groups, each with a place in the social order but each shading off by degrees toward the next group. The social structure allowed for so much disjunction between economic position, prestige, and power that one is not comfortable calling any of these groups a "class." Society had not jelled into an aristocracy with wealth, prestige, and power on the one hand and peasants without them on the other; no clear and conscious distinction separated aristocracy from peasantry, nor did a wide gulf exist between them. For example, France as described by Georges Duby and Constance Bouchard consisted of a nobility of Carolingian dukes and counts, small in number; assorted clerics from archbishops to doorkeepers; viscounts, castellans, nonnoble freemen with significant alodial holdings, vavasors, knights serving as armed retainers or mercenaries, free peasants, peasants at various levels of dependent tenure, shepherds, woodsmen, peddlers, servants, beggars, and so on.

One could create meaningful groups based on scales of wealth, prestige, or power; but, putting the scales together, one discovers that the rankings do not correlate. A group of prosperous men—holding, say, more than 200 acres—would have included nobles, but also many nonnobles and perhaps even a few serfs, while not including all knights. Nobility was then largely a matter of prestige stemming from blood and kinship; most nobles had extensive landholdings, but many who were not noble had equivalent landed wealth and enjoyed high status. Some occupations, such as that of cleric, carried prestige and privilege, but that group extended over an enormous range of economic levels. Knighthood offered both prestige and power, and most nobles were knights, but they shared that honored profession with many men of peasant origin with paltry resources.

The disjunction makes sense if one realizes that when early medieval men thought of the social order, they thought of families and their place in them, not of classes. Each family's particular balance of wealth, connections, privilege, occupational prestige, personal following, and officeholding gave it its rung on the social ladder. In the Middle Ages, as Paul R. Hyams has put it, men thought of society as "less a layer cake than a handicap race."

The period from 1000 to 1300 was a period of class formation, during which there emerged a larger and relatively cohesive nobility and a distinct but less united class of urban citizens. Both classes drew together men from several status groups. However, the forces of the period did not transform medieval society into a modern class society in which virtually everyone belongs to a class. They did not reduce disjunction between economic position, prestige, and power among the peasantry, and may even have increased it. Even by 1300 the agrarian population cannot have formed a class in more than a few regions. And the clerical order persisted, perhaps more influenced than before by the secular social order, but remaining as a source of prestige for men of aristocratic and humble origin alike. This structure, a class of nobles in direct relation with a fragmented peasantry, and a less fully formed class of citizens standing somewhat apart from both, would significantly mark Western Europe until the eighteenth century.

NOBLE AND PEASANT
The central class relationship of the Middle Ages was that of the nobility, who enjoyed the fruits of land, the privilege of holding it, and authority over

those who worked it, to the peasantry, who did the work, were legally inferior, and were subjected to noble authority. The factors that did most to separate nobles from peasants were the increasing cost of knighthood and two aspects of increasing political stability: castles and a central judicial system.

Between 1000 and 1300 the number of nobles in western Europe grew; persons from other status groups were becoming noble. It is not clear whether this process is best described as "upward mobility" or as the reshaping of the concept of nobility to fit more persons. But somehow, like a slow but powerful magnet, the concept of nobility increasingly pulled every principal indicator of status to it: dominance of land, knighthood, descent, political power, and legal privilege.

At the turn of the eleventh century the terms "knight" and "noble" were anything but congruent, and the division between knights and peasants was anything but sharp. The normal holding for an eleventh-century English knight was about a hide and a half (less than 200 acres). Fiefs exceeding three and a half hides were few, and 25 percent of the knights held less than three-quarters of a hide. Such holdings put the typical knight little better off than a well-to-do peasant. In fact, knights with status very close to the peasantry, or even peasant knights, seem to have been the norm in northwestern Europe. Thus contemporary sources often found it necessary to distinguish magnates, the great lords with massive holdings, from "belted knights" (men of influence, but not magnates) and "rustic" or "vavasor knights," not to mention pure mercenaries.

During the period 1000–1300, however, the cost of equipping and attending a knight skyrocketed. In the twelfth century knights came to use complete coats of mail and heavy helmets; by the thirteenth, plate armor became standard. The cost of a warhorse capable of bearing such armor rose from about £1 in the 1080's to as much as £80 in the 1280's. Such costs gradually created a line between those who could afford to equip and train themselves and those who could not. Beginning about the middle of the twelfth century mention of the "vavasor knight" virtually disappears from sources. Many such men probably turned to their land for survival and faded into the upper echelons of the peasantry. At the same time, a profession once open to many became increasingly associated with the aristocracy, since only those with holdings large enough to generate a significant surplus could afford to outfit themselves as knights and only those who received income from land without working it themselves had the time for the training and service. The greater expense of knighthood thus, in effect, marked an economic line that defined an aristocracy. Knighthood was not itself a relation to production, but it became a symbol of one.

Since the nobility began to avoid actual knight service for the crown by means of money payments in the mid twelfth century, precisely the same time that nobles began proudly asserting "knight" as a title of honor, it was not the function of knight as defender of the realm but rather its symbolic social value that really mattered. There is also little doubt that the new knightly line was more inclusive than the old nobility. Those knights with enough land, whatever their origins, came along with knighthood into the nobility.

One characteristic of greater political stability that helped to further define the nobility was the castle. As Carolingian rule staggered toward its ignominious end, the counts rapidly discovered that they could not be everywhere at once. The castle as an outpost of authority, held by a viscount or castellan of nonnoble origin supposedly dependent on the count, was one solution. Many of these holders of castles and offices quickly made themselves independent. The net effect, however, was to strengthen the nobility by enlarging it. In the eleventh century power and ambition were still enough to make a viscount or castellan an attractive marriage prospect for surplus daughters of noble families. Leopold Genicot has even found three marriages of serfs in a lord's favor to noble heiresses in eleventh-century Namurois. Apparently first the viscounts and then the castellans merged with the Carolingian nobility by intermarriage. Power became increasingly associated with nobility.

But the advent of the castle, if Karl Schmid is to be believed, may also have triggered a shift in the concepts and consciousness of kinship that eventually narrowed the door to nobility by power alone. Studies of medieval Italy and early modern Languedoc show that concepts of family, its size and shape, apparently changed in response to economic and political conditions. The castle was a focal point for this shift from one's horizontal ties to relations to one's place in a vertical line of ancestors and descendants. To Carolingian nobles "family" meant a loosely organized, more or less horizontal group of paternal and maternal kin, relatives mostly alive and working together. With the encouragement of inheritance to offices and castles, however, tenth- and

CLASS STRUCTURE, WESTERN

eleventh-century nobles began thinking of "family" as a vertical, continuing line of succession to the castle. Nobles then took surnames, "family names," often at first the name of the castle, and preserved them in the male line that held the castle.

Nobles thus developed a concept of family that separated them from peasants. Families who held castles and who could trace their vertical descent beyond their own memory were nobles. Few peasants had surnames until very late in the Middle Ages, and in some places, such as Holland, not until the eighteenth century. Like knighthood, the castle was a symbol of a larger but more sharply defined nobility.

Another characteristic of increasing political stability was centralized, territorial law. It is difficult to estimate the impact of a functioning central judicial system on a society that had barely had one. Certainly courts existed in profusion before 1000, but their jurisdiction was overwhelmingly local: hundreds, manor courts, seigneurial courts. For the latter, law was almost literally the property of the lord who held the jurisdiction. One can speak, perhaps, of county or provincial law, but not meaningfully of English or French law. Such limited jurisdictions primarily needed to know the facts of the case; the decision makers' sense of local custom and of justice served as legal principles.

The centralized systems that monarchs and princes gradually promoted from the eleventh century on, however, sought to assert the same law over widely varying populations, terrain, and conditions. In them the facts of the case were no longer enough; local circumstances had to be made to fit the developing body of recognized legal principles common throughout the jurisdiction. In other words, law became less a matter of abstract "justice" delivered by local amateurs and more a matter of fitting the local set of facts into classifications developed by legal professionals.

A judicial decision regarding succession to land could have massive economic impact, endangering aristocrats and turning relatively well-off peasants into paupers. As property and inheritance law became increasingly complex, having access to capital to finance litigation became essential merely to keep what one had, let alone acquire more. Several scholars have commented on the ever-increasing number, wealth, and status of lawyers in the later twelfth and thirteenth centuries. By the thirteenth century lawyers were as essential to noble families' survival as armed retainers had been earlier.

Legal classifications were also major determinants of personal prestige. In fact, the economic and prestige effects can scarcely be separated. By the thirteenth century English legal commentators called each type of tenure a "status" (whence "estates"). The legal categories that defined the terms for holding property also created social categories carrying prestige. One's rights as a person and one's obligations to other persons were determined by the category into which one fell. Thus, a central system that developed legal classifications and applied them over wide ranges of territory was a powerful force for welding scattered status groups into a class or for erecting prestige barriers against class formation.

Traditional scholarship has assumed that the legal status categories of the later Middle Ages were more or less static. But much of our evidence makes more sense if 1000–1300 was precisely the period during which legal nobility and legal serfdom, for example, gradually took the shape by which we know them.

In the first place, the local justice of the hundred or the manor court had very little need of such categories. Before the noun "seisin" existed—loosely, the right to possess and use a piece of land in certain ways in return for fulfilling certain obligations—all the law had was a verb, "seised" (of the land by a lord). The difference expresses the personal character of early medieval law. One did not have an abstract package of rights to land similar enough to a neighbor's package to be called by the same noun; rather, one was put on the land by a lord and had the rights in it to which he had agreed. In a very real sense the lord was the law. His court protected that seisin, and no other court could or did. Only wider-ranging systems like royal courts needed categories, devices to analogize one's tenure not only to one's neighbor's but to tenures in villages hundreds of miles away. (The systems never meshed well. A major stumbling block to interpretation of medieval legal evidence is the extent to which royal courts and customary courts simply ignored each other, going about their business on thoroughly different substantive principles.)

Further, even when a centralized system with classifications existed, the categories tended to change over time. The lawyer's job is usually to get his client into or out of some category into which the client appears to fall. And in a common-law system each judicial decision changes the contours of the category. So while in courts lawyers and judges established, defined, and altered legal categories, their efforts to draw lines reverberated up and down the social order.

Law could well have provided the crucial device by which the nobility pulled enjoyment of land, knighthood, descent, and political authority together. Legal definitions of nobility were not fully worked out until the fourteenth century or later, but since status and property law were so closely connected, the omission need not have mattered then; it matters only to modern historians in search of documentation. The crucial changes would have occurred in private grants and judicial decisions now largely lost. But since eleventh-century knighthood was not hereditary, neither, probably, were grants of land to knights in return for military service. For example, in England a grant of land by knight service by the fourteenth century had to include the formulaic phrase "and his heirs" to make the grant inheritable, though most peasant tenures were presumed hereditary without it. The addition, which became a mere formula giving the man's legal heirs no rights whatsoever, makes sense only if tenure by knight service was originally presumed to last only for the knight's lifetime.

Although centralized courts infringed on a noble's power in his jurisdiction, they also protected his inheritance in land and thus his hereditary status. In some of their earliest acts, starting in the mid twelfth century, monarchs and royal courts began intervening to make knighthood hereditary and to tie the status of landholder to the status of knight. Emperor Frederick I Barbarossa expressly excluded the sons of peasants from knighthood in 1187; James I of Aragon limited knighthood to the descendants of knights in 1234. French court decisions of the thirteenth century accomplished the same purpose. In England two of the earliest royal court interventions in customary law, the assize of mort d'ancestor and the writ of right, became available in the mid twelfth century to heirs of persons once seised of land but no longer in possession. The same courts also carefully preserved the theoretical requirement of military service in return for the seisin, creating the category of tenure by military service.

Royal interests alone cannot explain why knighthood should have remained an essential part of the terms of holding property in an age when, by mutual consent of the crown and vassals, the royal army was less and less composed of feudal hosts. The crown had some interest in the money payment of scutage in lieu of knight's service, but virtually abandoned scutage as a revenue source after 1240. Other freehold tenures that could have provided an alternative appeared in the classification scheme—for example,

sergeanty, which allowed for services other than military—but tenure by sergeanty was already dwindling in the mid thirteenth century and eventually disappeared. Making knighthood a condition for holding estates served the interests of the emerging noble class. In tenure by knight service, seisin—the bundle of rights and obligations for the holding of land—came to combine the enjoyment of land without the duty of working it, the concept of knighthood, authority over the land, and the idea of vertical descent. Since property law was the law of status, by the mid thirteenth century it wove together all the essential elements of membership in the noble class, uniting economic position, prestige, and power.

Since the new noble class had been drawn from several status groups, it retained significant stratification. Magnates stood well above knights, particularly in lands like Spain, where their role in wresting land from Muslims gave them extra wealth and power, or Germany, where after the Interregnum not the monarch but princes were the main forces for (small-scale) centralization. But wealth differences, to take the most cited example, did not mean class differences in the Middle Ages as long as members of the group stood in the same fundamental relation to production.

Thanks above all to the need of the legal system for general principles, magnates and knights shared a common relation to production, as well as a common authority over peasants and a common legal status. The magnates' great holdings were for the most part collections of small holdings. Property law thus could not protect the magnates' great holdings without protecting the knights' small ones. So there was, in the main, no special law for magnates with a different law for the rest of the nobility. Both magnates and knights held land, inherited status, and exercised authority. The trends of the period had enlarged the concept of nobility to include men who in the eleventh century might have been nonnoble knights, freeholders, officeholders, even serfs. In return, a clearer social boundary, marked by knighthood, power, descent, and law, surrounded the nobility.

The economic and legal trends of the period, however, did nothing to bring agrarian status groups together into a peasant class, and did a great deal to drive them apart. Insufficient land became one problem. Between 1000 and 1300 population expanded faster than land could be cleared to support it. Thus it became impossible to both distribute holdings equally and provide each family with enough land to feed itself. The result in most regions was a peasantry increasingly differentiated economically into relatively self-sufficient "plowmen" and laborers who worked for wages. Meanwhile, the central courts, in creating legal categories, tended to reduce the many subtle but significant variations in peasant status to a single line between serf and free. The category "serf," like "noble," also included greater numbers by 1300, a situation that also may stem neither from population increase nor mobility but rather from reshaping and extending a concept to cover more groups. But in contrast with the nobility, the economic line and the legal line did not coincide. Peasants, in short, did not share the same handicaps.

Nowhere are we more poorly informed than in trying to discern the economic position of the medieval peasantry, and the earlier the year, the poorer the information. Unquestionably agricultural production expanded between 1000 and 1300. Everywhere forests were cleared, marshes drained, and both were turned to the plow. But the simple fact of a rise in gross national product tells us nothing about individual economic conditions when population growth accompanies that rise, as it did in this period.

The period of growth was almost certainly a period of economic differentiation within the peasantry. At some point, in most villages all the land worth clearing would have been cleared. In effect, the community then had a choice of dividing the existing land into ever diminishing holdings or leaving some persons landless. Local conditions and local inheritance customs largely determined when and how that choice was made. Both Wilhelm Abel, working with German materials, and Joan Thirsk in England have suggested that the common field system emerged as a response to the effect of population pressure plus partible inheritance on the size of holdings. Farms once held as rectangular fields became splintered into strips (the strip being a convenient and visible unit for subdivision in lands using the hard-to-turn heavy plow). Once the land had been fragmented into furlongs, common planting and plowing and an agreed crop rotation became necessary.

In terms of relation to production, the line between the peasant who held a virgate or yardland, which could feed a family, and the peasant with less was the line between some economic independence and dependence on others for wage labor. Men were aware of that line; contemporary sources almost never spoke of "peasants," but increasingly they di-

vided the agrarian population into "plowmen" and "laborers." In short, the trends of the time in many regions of Europe tended to divide peasants economically—broadly, into those who could subsist on their own land and those who worked the land of others for wages.

Further opportunities existed for the few with enough land not only to subsist but also to produce a small surplus. Throughout the period the price of grain rose while wages fell. Thus, the economic distance between the peasants with a surplus and those dependent on wages could only have increased. Of course in theory serfs did not have the right to buy and sell land under the royal law as it eventually developed in most monarchies. But a principle of royal law was not necessarily a principle of the custom of the manor, and so a serf might not be disabled from such transactions by the manor court. In some regions of England, one can document thriving land markets as late as the thirteenth century.

Serfdom itself worked to differentiate the peasantry legally. In England the category "serf," embracing a large proportion of the peasantry, may only have been invented in the royal courts of the later twelfth and thirteenth centuries. Persons with the legal status of serf existed before 1000, but they seem to have constituted a much smaller proportion of the population than in 1300. Villein tenures (dependent tenures owing labor services) also existed in large numbers, but most persons holding in what would become villein tenure were legally free. The tenures themselves showed wide variation in what might be called "relative freedom"—freedom from particular labor services; freedom to give or sell, to leave, or to take to a new lord the land one worked. Until the mid twelfth century writs of naifty had been granted to great lords to help them recover any of their fugitive "men," not just peasants but also significant vassals. Only in the thirteenth century did they become the standard action to determine whether an individual had servile status. The eventual category of servile status and tenure, then, was probably created by a process of defining the category of villein tenure, making it presumptively a servile tenure, and then equating holding by villein tenure with the personal legal status of serf. The legal category introduced another dividing line that made class formation difficult for the peasantry. Serfdom, in any period for which we have documentation, never correlated with economic position. There were prosperous serfs and pauper serfs, and in many locales serfs, by the size and quality of their holdings, held distinct economic advantages over freemen. Nevertheless, a serf had a prestige handicap. As the division between plowman and laborer made it difficult for peasants to unite, so did the division between serf and free. Moreover, not all or even most plowmen were free, not all or even most laborers were serfs. Had that been true, the age might at least have seen peasant classes, formations of free plowmen and serf laborers. But since prestige lines cut across economic ones, formation of any group consistent enough to be a true class became more difficult.

CITIZENS AND CLERICS

Nobles and the various groups of the peasantry probably constituted something like 90 percent of the population of the West from 1000 to 1300. Of the remainder, two types of persons formed something more than a status group: the developing class of urban citizens and the already existing vertical order of clergy. The urban citizenry came to stand significantly apart, much less bound to the agrarian economy, feudal politics, or land law than nobility or peasantry, a crucial fact that labels like "bourgeoisie" or "middle class" tend to obscure. The clerical order, on the other hand, while remaining an important source of prestige, became less of an independent source of social status than it had been. Its structure had become something of an anomaly by about 1300, and its existence limited class formation in general but blocked class action by townsmen and peasants far more than by the nobility.

Much of the debate about the origin and development of towns has overtones of "class struggle" arguments, focusing on whether towns stemmed from a revolutionary "bourgeois" movement against the existing social and political system or developed within and from the existing system. Henri Pirenne, for example, was sure that social-outcasts-turned-merchants, such as St. Godric of Finchale, founded towns for commercial purposes; others are equally sure that bishops and princes promoted towns originally as extensions of their authority.

Both arguments seek to prove too much. Urbanization was not a revolutionary act against the medieval system; it occurred while that system was still developing. Presumably classes must form to some extent before they can struggle, but both the nobility and the urban class were still in a process of formation through much of the period. Further, some elements of the emergence of towns unquestionably came with the full cooperation and participation of the nobility. On the other hand, describing urban citizens as wholly within the medieval social system misses an important point. Economically, politically, and legally towns always stood significantly apart from the central social relation of the time, the agrarian relation of lord and peasant. Townsmen formed no "middle" class either—they did not stand between noble and peasant, but were separate from them.

Economic separation became possible with the massive expansion of trade and manufacturing in the West, beginning perhaps before 1000 and lasting at least through most of the thirteenth century. The growth of towns is an index not only of the size of that commerce but also of the extent to which men were entering it full-time. Commerce had long been practiced in the Middle Ages without permanent urban settlements. As late as the eleventh century trade in the Baltic was largely controlled by Scandinavians who were part-time peasants; in the twelfth century Germans took over, in part because they had developed towns with a resident, full-time merchant population. The increase in the number of towns in western Europe and in their populations indicates that the commercial sector of the medieval economy had expanded enough that men could support themselves primarily from trade and manufacturing. Since merchants and artisans have a fundamentally different relation to the means of production than do agrarian lords and peasants, the growth of towns also meant economic grounds for the development of a new class. It consisted of economically independent persons, working for themselves, free to accumulate and invest capital.

Most towns, especially in Italy (and to some extent Germany) also achieved a measure of political separation. Italian towns had never quite died, and a significant portion of the landed aristocracy continued to live in them. These urban knights apparently cast their lot with the growing numbers of merchants and artisans around them. After the death of Matilda of Tuscany in 1115, the emerging communes of northern Italy had no magnates to contend with. They developed their own institutions and gradually acquired powers of taxation and other jurisdictional authority from the bishop or lay lord. Thus the emerging urban class could express itself through its own governments.

Legal separation followed as town charters put the citizen outside feudal law. The town, in a sense, became its own lord, and a citizen was a member of a distinct legal community. Being a citizen was a status: neither dependent on a lord nor dominant over peasants. Property ownership and payment of taxes—in other words, economic independence—conferred citizenship. Thus economics, politics, and law all promoted the formation of a class of citizens.

Like the nobility, the citizen class drew from several status groups. The often leading role of aristocrats, lesser nobility, or ministerials, in German and Flemish as well as Italian towns, is now well established. Former freeholders and peasants of all kinds also sought their fortunes in towns, where the economy, politics, and law welded them together. The class also had some internal stratification, but no division between "patricians" or merchants or artisans was anywhere as sharp as the line between all of them, as citizens, and the dependent noncitizen wageworkers, apprentices, and servants.

What limited success of the citizen class in comparison with the nobility was not differentiation within a town's population but differences between towns. Charters and privileges went to single towns, and consciousness of a common bond normally extended only as far as town walls. In a famous passage of the *Purgatorio*, Dante has Vergil embrace a fellow Mantuan; neither would have embraced a Genoese. Where towns governed themselves, they fought each other at least as often as they combined against the nobility. Nobles, when it counted, could combine to pursue their interests on a monarchial level; with towns, even regional leagues rapidly evaporated. Citizens of a town shared independence from the agrarian economy, a degree of political autonomy, and common legal status, but only rarely did they recognize the similarity of their class situation to that of citizens of another town.

In contrast, the order of clergy bore little resemblance to a class. Classes are horizontal strata, whereas the group of clerics ran vertically, up and down the social pyramid. Clergymen shared elements of common prestige, but little else. All had the valuable privilege of being tried in church courts—which, for example, passed no death sentences—and all had, at least in theory, high social honor from their profession. But only the higher clergy had access to political power. And while a bishop or abbot with extensive landed estates might function economically as a noble, enjoying income from land without working it, the parish priest stood in essentially the same relationship to the land as an independent peasant. And clergy who lacked benefices were analogous to wageworkers, working at chantries or assisting at various parishes.

The social structure in any given historical period may include more than one system of stratification, with remnants of a system more appropriate to a previous age surviving and still conveying status within a social order increasingly based on a newer system. By 1300 the clerical order may be seen as such an anachronism. The society of about 1000 had more easily tolerated men who had very different relations to production sharing the same profession. Knighthood embraced a wide range of status groups then; by 1300 it was largely reserved for nobles. The clerical order stretched over an even wider range of groups, and thus seems more congruent with the earlier social world than with that of 1300.

In one respect the clergy and the emerging class structure moved in opposite directions from 1000 to 1300, as the Cluniac reforms stressed celibacy while aristocrats turned to a different concept of family. At the start of the period some church offices, like governmental offices, could be used as a power base for the development of a new aristocratic family. Some were even, in practice, hereditary. But after the church took a stronger stand on clerical celibacy in the eleventh century, a bishopric could no longer serve as a seat of family power like a castle or a monarchical office, passed from father to son. A policy of clerical celibacy would better have fitted a social world in which "family" meant a horizontal alliance of assorted kin. Like the church's range over relations to production, it put the clerical order ever more out of alignment with the emerging class structure. And it meant that the church, for all its prestige, gave a less firm foundation for status than did the monarchies with hereditary offices and laws that protected inheritance.

Thus there were limits on the extent to which clerical prestige could counterbalance other social handicaps. Even at the start of the period, Sylvester II did not find that becoming pope cured him of all insecurities about his humble birth. Unquestionably the church did provide an avenue of social mobility. But the social order outside the church made itself strongly felt within it. Persons of noble birth achieved high rank within the church far out of proportion to their numbers. Particular elements of the regular clergy became strongly tied to particular elements of the social structure: aristocrats virtually monopolized many monasteries and nunneries, while friars often came from citizen backgrounds. And the village priest typically had been born a villager.

Nevertheless, the existence of the clerical order

had impact on the class structure, an impact that in general worked to the advantage of the nobility. To the extent that an individual clergyman identified with the church, he did not identify with his class or stratum. And parish priests were far more likely to make such an identification than noble bishops and abbots. Clerical status set the priest not only apart from, but a bit above, peasant villagers. Similarly, the ambitious from other levels who used office in the church as a means of "rising above their station" drew on the clerical order for their status. The church thus deprived those strata of persons who might otherwise have been natural leaders. Urban clergy, for example, usually were not considered members of the citizen community. Rural clergy often worked against "class interests" by counseling deference and acceptance.

But aristocratic bishops drew their major feeling of status from their family ties, not their vocation. Thus they were far more likely to use their position on behalf of noble interests than was the parish priest to use his for peasants. The existence of the clerical order put limits on class formation generally—nothing prevented a noble bishop from using his resources primarily for the order, and to that extent his land and wealth, his prestige and his power, were outside the noble class. But it particularly retarded class formation beneath the nobility.

CONCLUSION

Since no single definition of social class has won universal agreement, we cannot expect universal agreement on whether true classes existed by 1300. But by almost any definition, classes were at least closer to existing. No one change accounts for this transformation. The economy expanded, and economic factors clearly became more important to stratification by 1300. A noble needed capital to maintain his status, a citizen needed economic independence, and those facts helped to shape their respective classes. To say that, however, is not to say that classes are determined primarily by economic factors. Increasing political stability, seen especially in the castle and centralized courts and their ramifications, accounts in large measure for the reasons why economic factors were more important. And prestige factors, particularly through the law, which not only reflected prestige but actively shaped it, made perhaps the most crucial determination of where class lines would and would not fall. Law pulled the nobility together with its rules for holding

and inheriting property while driving the wedge of serfdom into the peasantry. Urban law defined the citizenry; church courts and canon law helped ensure that the clerical order survived in the midst of emerging classes. In short, economics, power, and prestige all contributed to class formation between 1000 and 1300.

In this multidimensional process, limited but discernible class lines stretched out to draw some, but not all, of the varied status groups of early medieval society within their borders. The factors of the time welded together economic relations, power, and prestige more effectively for the nobility than for any other stratum. Urban citizens comprised a less well-formed class, standing apart from the lord-peasant relationship economically and legally, but unable effectively to unite for power beyond each town's walls. The peasantry in most locations not only stayed fragmented in status groups but became further divided economically and legally. And the vertical order of clergy stood neither entirely in nor entirely out of the emerging class structure, limiting the development of classes at each level but limiting the nobility less than others.

The changes did not create a modern class society. But they did shape a distinctive medieval class structure that, in its main features, survived well into early modern times. The next major structural transformation came in the age of the Industrial and French Revolutions. And just as the changes from 1000 to 1300 did not erase all traces of the previous social order, so echoes of the medieval system of stratification remain with us today—for example, wherever the untitled defer to men whose names signal nobility, or wherever industrial magnates have bought land and put up mansions that imitate the estates of their medieval namesakes. The class structure that developed between 1000 and 1300 may not look solid to modern eyes, but it was built to last.

BIBLIOGRAPHY

Wilhelm Abel, *Geschichte der deutschen Landwirtschaft* (1962); Constance Bouchard, "The Origins of the French Nobility: A Reassessment," in *American Historical Review,* 86 (1981); David Carpenter, "Was There a Crisis of the Knightly Class in the Thirteenth Century?" in *English Historical Review,* 95 (1980); George D. H. Cole, *Studies in Class Structure* (1955); Georges Duby, *The Three Orders: Feudal Society Imagined,* Arthur Goldhammer, trans. (1980); John B. Freed, "The Origins of the European Nobility: The Problem of the Ministerials," in *Viator,* 7 (1976); David Herlihy, Robert S. Lopez, and

Vsevolod Slessarev, eds., *Economy, Society and Government in Medieval Italy* (1969), 173–184; R. H. Hilton, ed., *Peasants, Knights and Heretics* (1976), which contains articles by Sally Harvey, R. H. Hilton, and Joan Thirsk; Paul R. Hyams, *King, Lords and Peasants in Medieval England* (1980); Jane Martindale, "The French Aristocracy in the Early Middle Ages: A Reappraisal," in *Past and Present*, 75 (1977); Stroud F. C. Milsom, *Historical Foundations of the Common Law* (1969); Michael Postan, *The Medieval Economy and Society* (1972); Timothy Reuter, ed., *The Medieval Nobility: Studies on the Ruling Class of France and Germany from the Sixth to the Twelfth Centuries* (1978), which includes articles by Leopold Genicot and Karl Schmid; Daniel Waley, *The Italian City-Republics* (1969).

RHIMAN A. ROTZ

[See also the following article, with a complete set of cross-references at the end.]

CLASS STRUCTURE, WESTERN (1300–1500). Neither historians nor sociologists agree on what they mean by "class" or "class structure," and therefore on whether the terms even apply to the Middle Ages. If the distribution of wealth, and social mobility by means of the accumulation of wealth, are seen as the determining factors, then classes did not exist before the eighteenth century. But the alternative (functionalist) model of estates or orders, which holds that social groupings are determined by the prestige given to certain occupations or to birth, is equally unsatisfactory for the Middle Ages since it fails to explain, for example, why nobles retained their place at the top of society even after the armored knight became obsolete or why some social mobility did exist, permitting wealthy townsmen to move into the nobility.

Economics, prestige, and power all helped to form late medieval social reality, and no single theory of stratification or class will suffice to cover all cases. We need to develop a concept of class that takes account of medieval reality and that could have been real to people of the time. Whether such a multidimensional, "realist" approach yields "classes" or not is moot, but at least it renders the notions of "class" and "class structure" useful for analyzing the differences between late medieval and modern society. In particular the concepts can help to explain why the catastrophes of the fourteenth and fifteenth centuries produced so little class conflict and so little change in the social order.

ECONOMIC POSITION, PRESTIGE, AND POWER

A reasonable approach to the problem of late medieval class structure would be simply to apply economic, prestige, and power concepts to various medieval groups and see what fits. And a reasonable place to start is with the oldest medieval social theory, one that today would be labeled strictly functionalist: that society was divided into the nobility who fought, the clergy who prayed, and everyone else who worked.

The noble class. Late medieval nobles were not a clearly defined wealth stratum, richer than others. H. L. Gray's estimate puts aristocrats' annual incomes in fifteenth-century England in a range from £20 to £3,230; the average income for the fifty-one barons was about thirty times the average for squires. Edouard Perroy found the incomes of nobles in one French region running from about £5 a year up to £2,400. A good many merchants and some artisans had wealth that would put them in the middle or upper middle of this range; some of them even held land. A significant number of peasant freeholders, among whom 200-acre holdings occasionally appeared, also were wealthier than some knights, and even a few serfs had larger holdings than the aristocrats on the bottom end of the scale.

But in the late Middle Ages, no class and no occupational group makes a good wealth stratum. "Merchant" spans both rich international wholesalers and small traders on the brink of starvation. Sylvia Thrupp has uncovered 245 merchant wills in London in the fourteenth and fifteenth centuries. Of them, 14 percent left over £1,000, but 11 percent were £50 or less; 69 percent fell under £400. And there were too many rich "artisans" to justify the usual assumption that they fell into a wholly different wealth stratum from merchants. A ropemaker and a pork butcher were among the wealthiest men in fourteenth-century Florence. Nor did wealth correlate clearly with specific crafts. In Überlingen in 1480, sixteen bakers were excused from taxes for lack of wealth, but eleven landed in the top tax brackets. Wealth simply did not correlate very well with occupation.

The late medieval economy was based on seeking profit through speculation rather than through control of production. Capital accumulation toward wealth was therefore a highly unstable, chancy process.

For townsmen, the road to riches was simple: buy cheap and sell dear. Unfortunately, the road could also lead to bankruptcy if one guessed wrong on price movements or which prince would repay his loans or even which ship would come in. Insurance was in its infancy in Italy and hardly used at all in the north. The steadier expectation of profits that comes from capital's control of labor and raw materials, where one can rationally estimate both costs and profit margin, was available in only a few industries. Merchants and bankers had capital, but independent artisans owned the tools and workplaces for production, and either could seek out raw materials.

The result was a race that either the tortoise or the hare could win. The craftsman, if he consistently accumulated small increments of capital by hard work and a little luck, could end up just as wealthy as many merchants and bankers. Merchants took more of a gamble, got rich faster, and could lose it all just as quickly. So in practice hardly anyone specialized very much if they could help it. Artisans tried small bets on commerce and loans in the hope of growth, and raised their bets if they won. The founder of the Fugger family fortunes was an Augsburg weaver who became a cloth merchant. Merchants, on the other hand, worried about pressing their luck and bought up landed estates, houses, or government annuities for a little security. There were late medieval exceptions, like the southern German and Flemish merchants who were developing a putting-out system, but not enough to change the overall pattern.

Nobles and peasants faced the same kind of insecurity. When eight-to-one was a good yield on one's seed, everyone who drew his principal income from agriculture needed the luck of good weather and a good harvest to acquire any surplus. One could take a gamble on more land or invest in better equipment and hope he had not stretched his resources too thinly until he started to get returns. But yields were so low that this was the tortoise route: men who avoided sticking their necks out, slowly accumulated small properties and moved up. A hare needed a stint at royal service, marriage to an heiress, a lucky inheritance—or good investments outside agriculture.

Any definition of an economic class must allow for this random nature of the medieval economy. In modern society capital's control of the means of production provides relatively stable sources of profit. Therefore occupation, wealth, and relation to production all tend to correlate with each other. In the highly unstable medieval economy, however, one would expect wide ranges of wealth differentiation within occupations. But this situation vitiates only

the current shorthand of wealth-based classes, not the whole possibility of economic classes.

If we use Karl Marx's definition of an economic class, nobles formed one. Although nobles did not constitute a wealth stratum, they shared a common relation to the means of production: they controlled land and enjoyed income from it without having to work it. Land was the principal factor of production in the agrarian economy. Nobles did not control all the land. Peasants had some—for example, about 25 percent of the arable land in Norway and almost 40 percent in the Netherlands—and the church also had large holdings. But nobles were economically independent, and others were dependent on them for a place in the economy. In Marx's terms that made nobles an economic class—in fact, the dominant class.

Nobles also held common prestige. In the social theory of the time, nobles formed an "order." Perhaps aristocratic status had originally rested in part on the nobility's function as warriors. But function alone cannot account for prestige by the late Middle Ages. The crown's cannon, infantry, and pikemen eclipsed nobles on the battlefield, yet the aristocracy held onto its prestige. That tenacity came from its successful intertwining of birth and legal privilege.

Descent can be an element of prestige, and may always have been a part of the medieval concept of nobility. But wherever nobles came from, in a process that began in the eleventh century and continued through the seventeenth, lineage increasingly superseded function as the source of noble prestige. The crown had found the feudal cavalry inadequate and had taken money instead of service, while more and more landed aristocrats found knighthood a nuisance. Thus, the new warfare at most made a quantum acceleration in an existing trend. But from the eleventh century nobles also showed greater concern with genealogy. Birth and privilege became bound together by inheritance of legal status. And that, too, accelerated in the fourteenth and fifteenth centuries, with status more clearly defined by birth than ever before. In both France and Spain, exemption from taxation became an inherited privilege that defined nobility. England, which had one hereditary rank (earl) in 1300, had five graded titles by 1500; in ascending order of prestige they were baron, viscount, earl, marquis, and duke.

Aristocrats thus came to share a distinct legal status with privileges different from either townsmen or peasants. Within the aristocracy, as title and rank appeared, magnates and lesser nobles became more carefully distinguished. This process was the logical and natural continuation of increasing emphasis on birth and legal privilege as the essential element in prestige. Armored horsemen had not totally vanished from warfare by 1500; aristocrats still appeared as officers. But now noble warriors were a result, not a cause, of other social strengths. Widespread acceptance of nobles as "natural leaders" of men—respect for lineage—plus economic position or political influence allowed nobles to retain a military role.

Nobles also held the highest prestige of any group. Nobility was ascriptive; whether by birth or dubbing, one acquired the status from those who had it, either the king or other nobles. Aristocratic status was not purely ascriptive; another requirement, even in social theories, was to "live nobly," which demanded some wealth. Of course, the same theoretical writings gave the clergy top ranking in society as a whole—but then it was the clerics who worked out the theories. Rank in the clergy itself bore a deep impress from the prestige given to nobility, and no writings ever persuaded the duke of Brunswick to defer to the curate of Kremlingen. All in all, nobles constituted a meaningful and dominant social class through common high prestige.

Nobles also had power and usually knew how to use it. Sociologists today rarely treat power as an independent variable in social stratification; "Marxists" absorb it into wealth and functionalists into prestige. But Max Weber recognized power as a separate dimension, and his concept works best for late medieval reality. Power did not automatically follow wealth even in towns. Of the twelve most active Lübeck merchants in the poundage rolls of 1368, measured by value of goods, only two ever were councillors; another two were fathers of councillors. The popes, even with all the functional prestige that theory could give them—and no small amount of wealth—were not the most powerful men in Europe and often not even the most powerful in Italy. Wealth or prestige could lead to power, of course, but the road also led the other way. Service to a magnate or monarch boosted many humble men to fortunes. Neither wealth nor birth brought Piers Gaveston the earldom of Cornwall under Edward II. The strong and clever could win knighthood—and more—on the battlefield; the first Sforza duke of Milan came out of the *condottieri*.

As with individuals, social groups with access to power had advantages in the distribution of resources over other groups. English gentlemen who wanted the opportunity to fill their coffers with

French incomes and ransoms may have helped pressure the crown into starting and continuing the Hundred Years War. To gain such advantages, of course, a group needs enough cohesion to work together for common interests. The degree to which a social group could unite for common ends over time and across distance was another factor that differentiated classes.

Nobles could exercise power in common, and precisely where it counted most, at the regional and monarchial level. They succeeded because, to use Marx's words, nobles had more class consciousness than any other group. Aristocrats had social contacts and institutions that ranged across regions and throughout monarchies. Nobles had their own house in most of the representative bodies that crystallized in the later Middle Ages. Of course, nobles also spent a great deal of energy fighting each other over family interests, but in most places enough nobles could join together to press their interests home against those of townsmen or peasants when it counted. Castilian magnates weathered the agricultural slump of the fourteenth century by investing in huge flocks of the newly bred Merino sheep, which yielded the finest wool in Europe. But they maximized their investment's potential through their influences on the crown and the judicial system, which helped the *Mesta* grazing cooperative win every legal contest with peasants over pasture and transit rights. Whether one calls aristocrats "parties" or the class with the most "class consciousness," nobles were cohesive enough to dominate other social groups.

An examination of the nobility suggests that no definition of class that draws on only one dimension of stratification will work for the late Middle Ages. As a group, nobles thus stood in a common position as independent possessors of land in an agrarian economy, held common prestige as members of a privileged order, and took common political action. But the examination also suggests a more complex definition of class: in the late Middle Ages a class formed where economic position, privilege, and power came together and to the extent that they came together. Such a definition balances economic, prestige, and power variables and is consistent with their interdependence. By that definition, nobles formed a class. Can any other social group compare with them?

The clerical order. The clergy cannot. The theory of the time gave all who pursued the occupation of priest some common prestige. Clerics also constituted a recognized legal order with common privileges. But no definition can make the clergy an economic class. A group that ran from the pope down to doorkeepers and acolytes obviously was no wealth stratum. More important, all clerics did not stand in the same relationship to the means of production. The order of clergy included vicars living off glebes, friars with vows of poverty, scholars at universities, cathedral canons, and clerks for magnates and monarchs. The variations cannot be reduced to functions of age or even rank within the clergy. Some bishoprics were dirt poor, while some parish benefices yielded substantial incomes. Bishops and abbots whose positions made them great lords had much the same economic position as nobles, enjoying the fruits of the land without laboring on it. A clergyman without a benefice, on the other hand, was for all practical purposes a wageworker, filling in for absent rectors or hiring on at a chantry.

The clergy also largely fails as a "party." The church's ties and ambitions were international. In the late medieval context, such a wide reach was not a strength but a weakness. In modern society the officers of a multinational corporation can wield great power, but only through the manipulation of fluid resources (capital) via modern communications. The church, with its wealth largely in land, could hardly threaten to disinvest and go elsewhere. And each land's clergy had internal conflicts of interests. John Ball, John Wrawe, and over a dozen other lower clergy gave the English Peasants' Rising of 1381 some of its most effective leadership, but the hierarchy backed the nobles.

Citizens of towns. The "third estate" of medieval theory, which embraced townsmen and farmers, freemen and serfs, shepherds and sailors, was clearly so amorphous that no historian or sociologist seriously tries to make it a class. Neither is there any consensus on how to tease groups out of it that would be both meaningful for the time and useful to modern analysis.

Townsmen, for example, are commonly subdivided into patrician, merchant, and artisan "classes." None of these groupings works very well. The concept of an urban "patriciate," which would take on some importance in the sixteenth and seventeenth centuries, had just gotten started in late medieval towns and has probably been greatly overemphasized. The word "patrician" was used occasionally in Tuscany and Flanders, but not until the late fifteenth century in Germany and never in England. In most

definitions an important element of any "patriciate" was political power, yet power was available only if a town had some degree of independence, and even autonomous towns differed widely in constitutions and access to town councils.

"Merchant" and "artisan" also make much less helpful groupings than they appear to at first sight. As we have seen, neither comprised a truly consistent wealth stratum. Any social line between commerce and craft cannot have cut very deeply. The later Scholastics considered the entrepreneur a type of worker: labor, as they used the term, included risking capital and organizing production. As men went back and forth from craft to commerce, so they married and formed associations with limited regard for merchant-artisan categories. Brunswick's prestigious *Lilienvente* included twenty drapers, about a dozen other merchants, and three bankers, but also a half-dozen bowlmakers, a weaver, and a butcher.

Like "patrician," any attempt to standardize a definition for merchant and artisan "classes" also must run roughshod over the enormous diversity from one town to the next. Venice or Lübeck concentrated on overseas trade, Florence banked and manufactured textiles, Bruges was a commercial entrepôt. There were local market towns, towns that sent one article into the stream of commerce but sent it all over the Continent, towns that produced for regional consumption, and bewildering mixtures of all these characteristics. The industry of Naples was government, and Rome lived off the church. Any town's history, economic role, and political status affected its social configuration.

One grouping, however, had a common meaning almost everywhere: citizens. Citizenship was admission to the legal freedom of the town, which included rights such as full enjoyment of the town's legal privileges and ownership of real property, and duties such as defense and paying taxes. The status divided urban populations economically, legally, and politically. The proportion of citizens in any town varied, from perhaps one-quarter of the families in London to half or more in many German towns. But urban citizens made up a meaningful social force in all three dimensions.

A citizen class puts artisans, merchants, and patricians in the same economic grouping, for they stood in a common relationship to medieval production: they were all economically independent but not agrarian. To become a citizen one had to meet property and stability requirements that largely excluded wageworkers and apprentices. On the whole, in the late Middle Ages craftsmen were still independent guild masters, not "workers." They and merchants both could accumulate capital. And if merchants often had more of it, still capital was not yet as important a factor in production as it would become. Machines were not so widespread that the capital that bought them could serve as a substitute for labor. Artisans and merchants both belonged to a minority group: they did not draw their principal incomes from agriculture.

Citizens also shared a common legal status that separated them from nobles, clergy, and peasants and that was ascriptive enough to be considered "prestige." Most citizens inherited that status, though one had to formalize it as an adult, usually at the same time as one married, attained economic independence, and bought property. Those who did not inherit citizenship could acquire it only from those who already had it, and the authority to make citizens usually rested with the town government.

A citizen was his own man, subject to no manor lord. Though contemporary social theory did not recognize a citizen order, the tie between legal freedom and economic independence was real and meaningful, separating burghers from the privileged aristocracy on the one hand, and from dependent peasants on the other. The town uprisings that punctuated the fourteenth and fifteenth centuries are probably the strongest proof of that. Long misinterpreted as struggles of artisans against "patricians" or merchants, on closer inspection the movements generally prove to have drawn out a cross section of the citizen population against councils that had become too high-handed. Notably in the empire, some towns developed a clique of councillors who behaved more like aristocrats, using town governments to further their ambitions for land and influence. Their decisions sparked taxpayers' revolts in which citizens expressed resentment at being treated like subjects.

Absence of legal citizenship meant economic disadvantage. Townsmen of St. Albans in Hertfordshire had never won burgess status from their monastic overlords. No matter how rich its merchants and craftsmen became, they still had to grind their wheat and full their cloth in the abbot's mills. St. Albans threw in its lot with the local peasantry in the rising of 1381. And without economic independence, a townsman could not participate fully in the citizen community. Apprentices, servants, and wageworkers attended no assemblies and guarded no towers. Ap-

parently too divided by ties to their craft or master, or by the tendency of some to drift back and forth from town to village, to form their own social group, noncitizens also played little or no role in most urban uprisings.

Citizens, however, failed to make as cohesive a "party" as nobles did. Townsmen created some institutions that exercised power, such as the autonomous city-states of Italy, Germany, and Flanders. But each town formed its own distinct community, and local particularism among towns was greater than family feuding among nobles. In Marxian terms, class consciousness had trouble carrying over town walls. The diverse nature of towns, communication difficulties, and the lack of intertown institutions all make the tension understandable. There were exceptions, such as the Hanseatic League. But on the whole while urban citizens formed an economic class with a common legal status, this social force expressed power only locally.

Peasantries. Local variation and fragmentation were even greater within the peasantry. Each rustic had his own precise combination of land, rents, duties, and labor services not quite like his neighbor's. A village was split between or among lordships almost as often as it belonged to one. In particular, the nature of the local terrain, local inheritance customs, and local lord-peasant power relationships all interreacted to affect the economic, social, and political position of peasants in a given region.

Champion country, relatively flat lands, tended toward the classic open field, tilled by the heavy plow with eight oxen. Such an environment exercised pressure to keep holdings from falling below a minimum size. So did primogeniture, if the area had it, or a strong lord who enforced differential obligations to maximize his profit. If no other opportunities existed, those without a holding had no choice but to collect around the estate as cotters or laborers; a powerful lord also could keep them there. Flatland, primogeniture, and strong manor lords all tended to produce a highly differentiated peasantry.

In such an area, peasants simply were not an economic class by any definition. Not only were they split by levels of wealth, they also were not all in the same relation to production. For example, a few had large holdings that required hired labor beyond their own families. Some had the virgate, or yardland, which sufficed to feed them and could put plow and oxteam together. A good many peasants had only their cottage, a few acres and garden, and grazing rights, which made them dependent on others for plowing and for supplementing their income with labor. Others had just their hands and feet. If use of words is any criterion, economic independence was meaningful. The word "peasant" seldom appears, but literary sources often divided rustics into plowmen and laborers.

Where serfdom still existed, villein or freeman made a crucial prestige distinction. By the late Middle Ages serfs did not constitute, and may never have been, an economic stratum. Some villeins held forty or fifty acres or more, and serfs occasionally had their own serfs. Others had little. Freemen, however, covered an even wider range. On the whole, in a given village a few freemen had large holdings, but poor smallholders and laborers were freemen as well. In some German villages serfs consistently had better tenures than freemen because with serfdom went holdings in the *Esch,* the original heart and best land of the community.

Serfdom, if enforced, did have an economic effect, since the villein faced higher rents, more irritating duties, and more obnoxious labor services than did the freeman next door. But above all, what drove thousands of peasants to spend time, energy, and funds trying to get out of serfdom was its effect on their status and power. Being a villein was demeaning. For example, by canon law serfs could not join the clergy. And only freemen had the option of evading the lord's justice by going to a royal court.

A peasantry fragmented by such economic and prestige lines was not powerless, but its power could only rarely stretch beyond the village. When the village community stood together, it could thwart the lord or his steward, notably by passive resistance and a conspiracy of silence. The "custom of the manor" also was no empty phrase; backed by the threat of collective action, it could block lords from raising rents or changing tenures for decades, even centuries. But the village community itself was led by notables who were as likely to act with the lord as against him. And while the sense of community encouraged cohesion at the village level, the same institution's suspicion of outsiders discouraged any development of common consciousness between one village and the next.

Other kinds of countryside, customs, and lordship, however, produced an agrarian population with greater similarity in economic, prestige, and power situations, and here it may be meaningful to speak of a peasant class. Hilly terrain worked with a hoe or light plow did not demand large holdings.

Where local customs dictated partible inheritance, smaller holdings divided among more holders resulted. If lordship was weak, distinctions between villein and freeman tended to disappear. Areas with forests, lakes, or seas, or with uncleared land nearby, offered opportunities to anyone dissatisfied with his lot in the village. Hills, mountains, or forests also hid the runaway from the lord. Rough country, partible inheritance, and weak lordship all tended to yield a much less differentiated peasantry.

With less of a range between large and small holdings, and less of a prestige and power gulf between serf and free, a class embracing most of the peasant population could have formed, and there is evidence that in some places it did. For example, Kentish peasants formed the core of the English rising of 1381. Kent probably had fewer serfs than any other county in England and had gavelkind, its own distinctive form of partible inheritance. The demand to abolish serfdom, and the flashes of egalitarian protest in the revolt could have reflected a peasantry that already felt a degree of equality within itself. And the one really successful national peasantry of the late Middle Ages was Sweden's. Sweden always had land, forests, and lakes in abundance; peasant inheritance apparently was partible; lordship was weak; and serfdom, which did not begin until the mid thirteenth century, was light. Throughout the period peasants held about half of the arable land. Swedish peasants had already engaged in armed resistance to nobles on a regional basis in the thirteenth century. Peasant representatives were called to the vote to choose a new king in 1319, and when the monarchs gradually worked out their parliamentary body, the Riksdag, after 1359, peasants got their own house in it.

Of all the groups, peasants were least likely to form a coherent class over any significant distance. Each area's distinctive mix of terrain, inheritance patterns, and lordship gave it a particular class structure. R. H. Hilton, drawing on sources largely from the hilly and forested English Midlands, argues strongly for a single peasant class. Georges Duby, working mostly in French champion country, finds a peasant society divided roughly into a "kulak"-type elite, plowmen, and laborers. Probably both are right. In some regions economic factors split plowman and laborer, or prestige divided serf from free, or power ranked village notables above the rest. Other regions had more unity among peasants. And each major monarchy probably contained more than one type of agrarian social formation.

In short, the term "class" can be applied to some

social groups of the late Middle Ages better than it can be to others. Nobles broadly held a common economic relationship, prestige, and power. Urban citizens made up an economic class and a legal status group but lacked the power range of nobles. Behind them on this spectrum of possible classes came not a peasantry but local and regional peasantries. Some places might have had a peasant class; others, peasant classes; and others, simply an unformed, fragmented agricultural population. The clergy as a group seem so different from nobles, citizens, and rustics that they should not come under the same label. And substantial segments of the population, like urban noncitizens or forest and hill dwellers, cannot be shaped into any class mold.

SOCIAL MOBILITY: THE WHEEL OF FORTUNE

From medieval social theories that emphasize estates or orders, functionalists have assumed that the social structure allowed for little or no mobility. Some "Marxists" conclude from evidence of wealthy men moving into the aristocracy in the fourteenth and fifteenth centuries that contemporary theory did not matter: the period had a class society, and these men showed the "rise of the middle class." Late medieval reality actually lies between these extremes. Wealthy men did move up, but their rise did not transform medieval society into a fully modern one. Medieval society allowed for social mobility and was not disrupted by it, because the concept of an order included not only men who were born into one but also men who, thanks to good fortune, "fell" into one.

The most common medieval image related to status was the wheel of fortune. Chance brought men up and took them down. It was not the absence of mobility but rather its random quality that the theories about orders were trying to express. Mobility takes a certain amount of luck in any age, but ambitious modern men can choose certain occupational tracks and have a fairly high probability of moving up. Medieval mobility seemed far less rational and more a matter of random chance, controlled by external forces. The real contrast between medieval and modern society was not that one could not move upward, but rather that one could not rationally plan for it.

A legal estate or order was not a caste, not an absolute barrier to mobility. The clergy, for example, was an estate. A cleric had his own legal status that in spite of some government inroads still sent him to church courts instead of royal or manorial ones. Yet

the clergy was fundamentally a professional group, and in theory, at least, all its members had moved into it. By canon law clergy could not pass their status on to their descendants (since they were not supposed to have descendants). Becoming noble was tougher but not impossible. English aristocratic families died out in the male line at an average rate of roughly 1 percent a year in the fourteenth and fifteenth centuries—plague or no plague—and this rate seems broadly characteristic of most countries. Yet there were as many nobles in Western Europe—perhaps more—in 1500 than in 1300. Replacements came from somewhere.

Service, war, marriage, and the church. Traditionally, new recruits came from service, war, and marriage—each something of a lottery. These traditional routes remained important throughout the late Middle Ages. The peasant could move into the lord's service, his lord could bet on a magnate, the magnate could chance the king. Enough English gentry bound themselves to magnates by formal retainer in this period that scholars speak of "bastard feudalism." Royal service in all lands was famous for its opportunities—as well as its dangers when the crown was no longer pleased. War was another means of social roulette. The Hundred Years War gave both sides a (dangerous) chance at titles, booty, and ransoms. The duke of Brittany alone ennobled about 100 commoners from 1426 to 1432, including the carpenter who designed his cannon.

Marriage provided peasants as well as aristocrats a chance to improve their economic, prestige, or power level. Nobility was selective, not exclusive. The transition from function to birth and legal privilege as the prestige element in nobility never reached the point of blocking mobility in the fourteenth and fifteenth centuries. Instead, emphasis on birth kept the aristocracy just distant enough to retain the status everyone else wanted. In the usual pattern, one first reached a certain stage of prosperity, then sought a marriage that would put one over the top. Peasants regularly managed to move into the nobility over generations this way, first piling up greater amounts of land so they could afford the lifestyle of a gentleman, and then making a good marriage or two. Some marriages provided quantum leaps: the Staffords jumped into significance on the abduction of an heiress in 1336, and the Tudors from the attraction of a royal widow for a handsome youngster. And the results of a marriage could have their lottery aspects, if certain persons happened to die. The wheel turned for the Howards, a Suffolk gentry family of no particular note, when they became dukes of Norfolk in 1483 on the strength of a marriage made over sixty years before.

For women, it usually took the death of a husband to make an independent existence possible. One cannot flatly generalize that women had the status of their husbands, because marriage could be a major device for that husband's upward mobility. The ability of women to carry their birth status with them also improved a bit in these centuries. In England at the start of the fourteenth century aristocratic heiresses took only land into their marriages, but by its end they could carry titles to their husbands as well. But single women with their own tenancies or shops were rare. Some could support themselves by spinning (hence "spinster") or brewing. Independent craftswomen also turn up in not insignificant numbers in some towns, making buttons and buttonholes in Frankfurt, for example, or weaving linen in Cologne and Paris. They also show up in the low range of tax rolls far out of proportion to their numbers, so they must have earned substantially less at these tasks than men. Also, town councils never admitted women, and apparently they did not attend citizen assemblies. But records are full of widows who ran peasant holdings or took out full citizenship (and paid taxes) to keep up a late husband's trade or shop. Traditions of jointure and dowager rights were strong, and sons could wait decades for full enjoyment of their inheritance. As a broad generalization, marriage was a woman's entry into the social structure, but if ill (or good) fortune made her a widow, she was then fully capable of carrying on her own economic and social life.

The one occupational group that offered a less random, more rational upward mobility was the clergy. Here a talented peasant's or baker's son could choose to take holy orders, acquire an education somehow, apply himself, impress his superiors, and move up in the hierarchy. But the existence of this alternative does not significantly alter the generalization for two reasons. First, such mobility was overwhelmingly individual, not familial. Only the wealthiest bishoprics provided the kind of revenues and power that could be turned toward brothers and nephews as the foundation of a new aristocratic family. Second, it cannot have happened very often, because church ranks correlated too much with status in the secular world. Nobles became bishops well out of proportion to their numbers while peasants became parish priests, and aristocrats and the wealthy deposited their surplus sons and daughters

in monasteries and nunneries to the virtual exclusion of other social types.

Not by wealth alone. The late medieval addition to these traditional patterns of mobility was the migration of some townsmen—mostly merchants, bankers, and professionals—into the aristocracy. But acquiring wealth had long been a first step upward in the traditional pattern. At most the presence of such new recruits was a recognition that there were now other forms of wealth besides land. And even that recognition must have been qualified, since some investment in land usually preceded a townsman's move into the aristocracy.

Nor did this upward movement signal a shift to a social structure wholly based on wealth. In the first place, accumulation of capital provided no more rational basis for mobility than any other kind. Success in commerce or craft came as randomly as anywhere else. Also, virtually no one moved up on wealth alone. The individual cases consistently included a component from the traditional pattern, either service, war, or marriage. Michael de la Pole, son of a merchant and banker, did indeed become earl of Suffolk in 1385. But the wealth came in part from service: his father and uncle had been merchants in a royal scheme to control the wool trade and bankers to the crown—and Michael had a long military career. Lawyers often moved into the English or French nobility, but overwhelmingly after having served as royal judges. Wealthy townsmen were ennobled in France in significant numbers, but that also served political considerations and royal needs for cash. The basic pattern was not just making money but helping the crown or magnate to make or collect money, or otherwise using one's skills to serve. Another alternative was marrying into an aristocratic house that needed its coffers restocked.

Above all, mobility of some townsmen into the aristocracy represents no "rise" of any "bourgeoisie" or "middle class." No such class existed in the late Middle Ages, not if those terms are going to retain any meaning for modern history. "Bourgeois" indeed originally meant "townsman," but as Marx used it, it meant a capitalist who used capital to control labor. In the fourteenth and fifteenth centuries both merchant and artisan were independent and self-employed, and both sold products in the market. There was no true bourgeoisie, nor could there be until the system of production shifted to industrial capitalism. Neither merchants nor artisans nor citizens as a whole make a satisfactory "middle" wealth stratum. Citizens did not stand in the middle between peasants and aristocrats. An ambitious peasant might look to a town as a place where fortune might find him, but he did not have to pass through the citizen class to get to the nobility.

And certainly if we judge upwardly mobile townsmen by their behavior, their goal was not to improve the position of any "middle class" but to get themselves into the aristocracy. As J. H. Hexter said, when the leading members of a group flee it so persistently, that hardly contributes to a sense of class solidarity. Townsmen moved into the nobility as peasants had before them, by accumulating wealth and adding service, war, or marriage. Their nobility was merely a new variation on an old theme.

The value of selective openness. In fact, the upward mobility that occurred was largely on the aristocracy's terms. Mobility was still only partly earned; as long as service, war, or marriage remained a major component, it was also partly ascriptive. And the aristocracy got about as much mobility as it wanted—or better put, about as much as it needed to survive. Such selective openness to commoners had value for the late medieval nobility. At the very least its chances for survival improved from the infusion of cash through dowries. And this openness kept the ambitious and fortunate from having to challenge the system to win recognition.

If access had totally closed, burghers or peasants might have stopped trying to cross over and worked harder at carving out a place for a burgher or peasant class. But as long as a turn of the wheel could lift one to the top, nobility exercised its power of attraction on the ambitious. Whatever it meant for the class structure in 1422, when Philip the Good made the townsman Nicolas Rolin chancellor of Burgundy, one can guess what it meant to Rolin. He made one of his sons lord of Aymeries, Autun, and Lens; another lord of Beauchamp; and the third bishop of Autun and a cardinal. The Medici may have been symbols of Florentine wealth and vitality, but Lorenzo the Magnificent married into the Roman nobility nonetheless. When the Dutch nobility overemphasized birth to the point of virtual closure from about the mid sixteenth century on, it ossified and declined, while a true bourgeoisie and peasantry slowly formed and began to challenge noble power. And Western Europe's economic organization increasingly approached industrial capitalism, capital accumulation became more stable, and wealth correlated better with occupations and places in the system of production. But in the fourteenth and fifteenth centuries, the random patterns

of mobility plus the aristocracy's relative openness combined to bolster noble resources and reduce the potential for social conflict.

CLASS FORMATION, CLASS CONFLICT, CLASS STRUCTURE

An analysis of classes and mobility patterns is most useful for explaining why things did not happen: why, after two centuries of body blows to its wealth and its position in war, the nobility survived as the dominant social group; why, in the face of economic and political confusion, the later Middle Ages saw so little class conflict.

The limits of class formation. Class lines did not harden in the Middle Ages because classes were not the sole form of social grouping. There was too much competition from other overlapping kinds of groupings—occupational, family, geographic. Not even the nobility had a monopoly on economic, prestige, or power resources at its level, since the higher clergy also enjoyed income from land without working it. Both theory and law gave churchmen considerable social honor, but the clergy included men of virtually every economic, prestige, and power level from top to bottom. To the extent that clergy thought and acted together as clergy, they belonged to no horizontal class. Clerics formed a vertical order that limited class formation.

Even modern discussions of class must consider the tensions between class loyalties, which run horizontally, and other possible ties, which run more or less vertically, reaching over differences in economic position, prestige, or power. Nationalism is perhaps the most forceful example of a modern vertical bond that competes with class. Horizontal ties were weaker and vertical loyalties much stronger in the late medieval West than in modern society. Occupation, geography, and family, for example, could all cut across potential classes and weaken them.

Yet neither was Western Europe in the fourteenth and fifteenth centuries a society without classes. In particular, the nobility deserves the label. Though not a modern industrial class, it substantially brought together economic position, prestige, and power. And the aristocracy's position as the most completely formed class of its time helps to explain how it maintained its dominance in the face of the new warfare and the agricultural depression of the fourteenth century.

In part, the nobility survived because nobles adapted economically, shedding demesne farming, increasing capital investment in mills, forges, and stock, and taking a fierce interest in management of their estates. But the depression was so severe that such measures alone cannot account for noble survival. The tenants of one lordship in Normandy paid 152 livres in 1397, 112 in 1428, 52 in 1437, and 10 in 1444.

The nobility's survival depended not on one factor but on the interrelationships of factors and on its ability to use these interrelationships as a class. With resources in all three areas, the aristocracy used its strength in one area to shore up another. The French nobility got a temporary release from taxes to lure them into fighting during the early period of the Hundred Years War; by the time its role in warfare had slipped, it had turned the exemption into a permanent legal privilege. Its English counterpart pursued the war and staved off financial disaster with the war's profits. The Danish nobility responded to depression by joining with the church to squeeze peasants off their land. Magnates utilized power to turn Castile into a sheep ranch. Nobles survived precisely because they could draw on their power or prestige to supplement falling wealth or, at another time, to use their wealth or prestige to supplement slipping power. The nobility came closest to fitting the modern concept of class as a horizontal layer across society—a layer at the top. No other group managed quite so well to overcome the late medieval tendencies that retarded class formation.

The limits of class conflict. A few historians and sociologists cherish the romantic assumption that no trace of class conflict existed in the Middle Ages. Others cast townsmen as the "enemy" of the feudal order and charge sweeping changes to conflicts between the "bourgeoisie" and other classes. Again, reality lies somewhere in between. Everyone did not docilely accept all inequalities without complaint: the fourteenth and fifteenth centuries were also the era of John Ball and John Hus and the famous couplet, "When Adam delved and Eve span / Who then was a gentleman?" But on the other hand, resentment of inequalities was not as powerful a force as it is now. Some inequalities indeed were accepted as part of the natural order of things. And class conflict is usually not very useful in explaining events. In particular, the fourteenth and fifteenth centuries should have been ripe for social transformation. The "price scissors" that characterized the agrarian depression should have shifted capital to towns by taking profit from landed aristocrats and giving it to townsmen. But none came. The nobility also sur-

vived because the structure of the time yielded just enough class formation to separate townsmen from peasants, but not enough to make either a serious threat to the nobility.

If the theory of the time had corresponded to social reality, then the "third estate" could have united to topple, or at least seriously threaten, the nobility. In fact craftsmen and merchants gave very little support to peasant unrest and vice versa. Even the seeming cooperation of London with the rebellious English peasants in 1381 apparently came when a crowd of noncitizens, against burgess objections, forced keepers to lower London Bridge and open Aldgate so the peasants could enter.

Environment alone cannot explain the failure of peasants and townsmen to collaborate, since urban life generally faded off into rural rather than sharply contrasting with it. Most town walls enclosed fields—and assorted pigs and chickens—as well as houses. But lack of citizen-peasant alliances is no surprise if one sees that each stood in a different class situation. The central class relationship was noble against peasant: enjoyer of land against laborer on it, privileged lord against those without privileges, ruler against subject. Citizens stood apart from that relationship, forming independent economic, legal, and political communities. Thus they had little common interest with peasants. Nobles directly exploited, subjected, and ruled peasants; citizens prized their independence, and nobles were not so clearly their enemy.

Yet with class lines fluid, and class consciousness weak, only rarely could either citizens or peasants take an action as a class that reached beyond the local level. Thus neither was strong enough to seriously threaten the aristocracy's place. Individual towns might fight for autonomy against a local noble, but only rarely did towns in general fight nobles in general. The "English" Peasants' Rising was actually an uprising of peasants from Essex and Kent, with few echoes in other counties. No doubt peasants performed labor services torpidly and ate all they could at the lord's noon meal. Collective village resistance limited the lord's freedom of action. That may all be "class struggle," but it hardly compares in scale with the French or Russian revolutions.

And when embryonic class conflict on a larger scale did occur, the nobles won. Local coalitions of princes easily stopped the Swabian-Rhenish League of towns at Doffingen and Worms in 1388. Noble armies dispatched the disparate groups of English peasants. An organized minority, acting in concert, will tend to dominate a disorganized majority. In the late Middle Ages only the aristocracy was organized.

The late medieval class structure fits none of the standard paradigms developed for modern society. Still there was a class structure. It consisted of a reasonably cohesive noble class at the peak of economic resources, prestige, and power, directly facing a peasantry that, depending on the region, may have formed a class, classes, or a congeries of individual village communities, and a citizen class, more consistent than the peasantry but fragmented by local particularism in comparison with the nobility, standing somewhat detached from both. This structure did not peacefully resolve all social tensions, but it did minimize the extent and duration of major class conflict. So nobles still dominated Western Europe in 1500 as they had in 1300. Like so many other late medieval institutions, the existing class structure had enough flexibility to maintain itself in spite of some new economic, social, and political conditions. Only widespread capitalist organization and industrial production, and ideologies that demanded equality at law and in politics, would be strong enough to bring it down.

BIBLIOGRAPHY

Bernard Barber and Elinor G. Barber, eds., *European Social Class: Stability and Change* (1965); Reinhard Bendix and Seymour M. Lipset, eds., *Class, Status, and Power: Social Stratification in Comparative Perspective*, 2nd ed. (1966); Thomas A. Brady, Jr., "Patricians, Nobles, Merchants: Internal Tensions and Solidarities in South German Urban Ruling Classes at the Close of the Middle Ages," in Miriam U. Chrisman and Otto Gründler, eds., *Social Groups and Religious Ideas in the Sixteenth Century* (1978), 38–45, 159–164; Aleksandr N. Čistozvonov, "Der soziale Charakter des niederländischen Bürgertums (14. bis 17. Jahrhundert)," in *Jahrbuch für Geschichte des Feudalismus*, 4 (1980); Raymond de Roover, "Labor Conditions in Florence c. 1400: Theory, Policy, and Reality," in Nicolai Rubinstein, ed., *Florentine Studies: Politics and Society in Renaissance Florence* (1968), 227–313; Georges Duby, *Rural Economy and Country Life in the Medieval West*, Cynthia Postan, trans. (1968); Edith Ennen, "Die Frau in der mittelalterlichen Stadtsgesellschaft Mitteleuropas," in *Hansische Geschichtsblätter*, 98 (1980); Leopold Genicot, "Naissance, fonction et richesse dans l'ordonnance de la société médiévale: le cas de la noblesse du Nord-Ouest du Continent," in Roland Mousnier, ed., *Problèmes de stratification sociale* (1968); H. L. Gray, "Incomes from Land in England in 1436," in *English Historical Review,* 49 (1934); Eli F. Heckscher, *An Economic History of Sweden*, Göran Ohlin, trans. (1954); Jack H. Hexter, "The Myth of the Middle Class in Tudor England," in his *Reappraisals in History* (1961), 71–116; J. R. L. Highfield, "The Catholic Kings and the Titled Nobility of Castile," in John Rigby Hale, J. R. L. Highfield, and Beryl Smalley, eds., *Europe in the Late Middle Ages* (1965), 358–385; Rodney Howard Hilton, *Bond Men Made Free: Medieval Peasant Movements and the English Rising of 1381* (1973), and *The English Peasantry in the Later Middle Ages* (1975); Cicely Howell, "Peasant Inheritance Customs in the Midlands, 1280–1700," in Jack Goody, Joan Thirsk, and E. P. Thompson, eds., *Family and Inheritance: Rural Society in Western Europe 1200–1800* (1976), 112–155; Peter Laslett, *The World We Have Lost: England Before the Industrial Age* (1965); Emmanuel le Roy Ladurie, *The Peasants of Languedoc*, John Day, trans. (1974); Robert H. Lucas, "Ennoblement in Late Medieval France," in *Mediaeval Studies*, 39 (1977); Erich Maschke, "Die Unterschichten der mittelalterlichen Städte Deutschlands," in Erich Maschke and Jürgen Sydow, eds., *Gesellschaftliche Unterschichten in den südwestdeutschen Städten* (1967), 1–74, and "Mittelschichten in deutschen Städten des Mittelalters," in Erich Maschke and Jürgen Sydow, eds., *Städtische Mittelschichten* (1972), 1–31; Kenneth B. McFarlane, *The Nobility of Later Medieval England* (1973); Michel Mollat and Philippe Wolff, *The Popular Revolutions of the Late Middle Ages*, A. L. Lyttonsells, trans. (1973); Roland Mousnier, *Social Hierarchies, 1450 to the Present*, Peter Evans, trans. (1973); Eckhard Mertens-Muller, "Bürgerlich-städtische Autonomie in der Feudalgesellschaft," in *Zeitschrift für Geschichtswissenschaft*, 29 (1981); Iris Origo, "The Domestic Enemy: The Eastern Slaves in Tuscany in the Fourteenth and Fifteenth Centuries," in *Speculum*, 30 (1955); Edouard Perroy, "Social Mobility Among the French *Noblesse* in the Later Middle Ages," in *Past and Present*, 21 (1962); Santiago Sobrequés Vidal, "La epoca del patriciado urbano" and "La epoca de los reyes católicos," in Jaime Vicens Vives, ed., *Historia social y económica de España y América*, II (1957); Sylvia L. Thrupp, *The Merchant Class of Medieval London* (1948); J. A. van Houtte, *Economische en sociale geschiedenis van der Lage Landen* (1964); Johanna Maria van Winter, *Ministerialiteit en ridderschap in Gelre en Zutphen* (1962), and "The Knightly Aristocracy of the Middle Ages as a 'Social Class,'" in Timothy Reuter, ed. and trans., *The Medieval Nobility* (1978), 313–329; Jaime Vicens Vives, *An Economic History of Spain*, Frances M. Lopez-Morillas, trans. (1969).

RHIMAN A. ROTZ

[See also **Clergy; Commune; Feudalism; Inheritance, Western European; Knights and Knight Service; Nobility, Nobles; Serfs, Serfdom, Western European; Trade, Western European; Urbanism, Western European.**]

CLASSICAL LITERARY STUDIES. The tradition of classical literary studies first took form among the Greeks of the Hellenistic period. The Romans accepted it with little change, and the Christians adapted it to their own purposes. During the Middle Ages, the tradition persisted in the Greek East and developed in the new context of Byzantine civilization; in the West it virtually disappeared, before emerging in another new context, that of Latin Christendom. It reached high points in the Carolingian Empire, in twelfth-century France, and in fourteenth- and fifteenth-century Italy.

THE GRECO-ROMAN AND CHRISTIAN BACKGROUND

Greece, from Homer through the fourth century B.C., produced an extraordinary literature in poetry and prose. However, the conquests of Alexander the Great (d. 323 B.C.) inaugurated a new period for the Greeks, and in his world society the writings of the polis or city-state were soon felt to be part of an age that was past. In this new situation classical literary studies and the education connected with them first appeared.

The center of the new studies was Alexandria under the Ptolemaic kings. Here the Hellenistic scholars worked to put into order their literary inheritance and to provide the means for preserving and understanding it. Callimachus compiled a catalog by field of all serious Greek writing. Within each field the Alexandrians selected the best authors; the Romans came to call these the "classic" authors.

For the classic authors the scholars sought first of all to secure correct texts and then to provide tools for the proper understanding of them, such as lexica, works on antiquities, and commentaries on specific works. At a later stage they developed the central discipline of "grammar." The term had a broader meaning than today, covering not only correct speaking and writing but also the careful study of the poets and prose writers.

When Rome moved into the Hellenistic world, the Romans soon encountered Alexandrian literary studies. With little hesitation they accepted the Hellenistic methods and applied them to Roman literature. By the first and second centuries of the Christian era there was a common tradition of literary studies in both the Greek and the Latin portions of the empire.

The tradition remained closely connected with the aims of the societies that employed it, and one must be careful not to place the literary studies within a modern, separate "aesthetic" area or to regard them as a form of autonomous "scholarship." In their Greek origins these studies were a part of paideia, by which the Greeks meant not only education but also its results, the achievement of man's proper end. Thus Varro and Cicero could translate paideia by *humanitas,* humanity as the highest human ideal.

Both Hellenic and Hellenistic societies thought of paideia as one of their main goals. In his famous funeral oration Pericles claimed that Athens was "the education [*paideusis*] of Hellas," and for their ecumenical society the Alexandrian scholars made the even greater claim that they had educated "not only all the Greeks but also the barbarians." Cicero, on the Roman side, expresses an equally universal claim when he speaks of the liberal arts, which "transform the childhood age into humanity."

Literary studies were, therefore, for the Greeks and Romans, integral parts of an education aimed at the highest human good. In simplest terms this appeared as a moral purpose. More generally, through their reading and study of the classics, they hoped to turn their own experience into a fully human life.

The main crisis in the ancient tradition of literary studies came with the rise and triumph of Christianity. However, with very rare exceptions the old tradition of education, including its literary studies, continued to be used by the Christians, even though there were occasional sharp attacks on it. The solution, as seen in the works of Clement of Alexandria and in Origen, was to accept the Greco-Roman tradition while redefining its place. It no longer led to the highest human ideal, and for Christians it was at best only a preliminary stage or means to salvation.

THE GREEK EAST AND BYZANTIUM

In the fourth century the leading Greek theologians confirmed and elaborated the position of Clement and Origen on the Christian use of classical literary studies. Both Basil the Great and Gregory of Nazianzus, for example, defended the traditional education as valuable preliminary study for Christians.

In the same period atticism, the doctrine that the Attic writers were the only norm for good Greek, achieved the unchallenged dominance that it retained through the end of the Byzantine Empire. Whatever its disadvantages, atticism was decisive for the continuation of classical literary studies, since it ensured that all educated Greeks would find in the classic authors a language with which they were familiar.

With the general decline of the empire after Justinian I (527–565), there was also a decline in literary studies. Education continued, but on a limited scale, and there were few new writings except in grammar, the irreducible core of the tradition. Although Leo III the Isaurian did much to restore the empire politically, the iconoclastic controversy, not finally settled until 843, delayed any literary revival.

However, the Byzantine emperors always recognized not only their primary mission to protect Greek Orthodox Christianity but also their secondary obligation toward the worldly paideia. In 863, accordingly, Emperor Bardas reorganized the university at Constantinople to take care of worldly, or external, education (in contrast with specifically Christian training). Although the university is better known for science, literary studies were of course included in the curriculum.

The ninth and tenth centuries saw a great recopying of manuscripts as the Byzantines moved from uncial to minuscule script; this was both a tribute to the vitality of literary studies and a stimulus to their continuation. Arethas, archbishop of Caesarea, commissioned many manuscripts and in some cases provided them with marginal commentaries. Otherwise we have little evidence regarding the tenth century except for the compilation of the huge dictionary and elementary encyclopedia known as *Suda*.

Progress resumed in the eleventh century, and in 1045 Constantine IX Monomachos reopened the Imperial University, which apparently had a more literary emphasis than at the time of Bardas. Michael Psellos was the dominant figure, and though his own interests were mainly in Plato and Aristotle, he had a wide acquaintance with literary texts.

It is typical of Byzantium, in contrast to the West, that literary studies were pursued in close association with philosophy and that the philosophers were read along with the other classic authors. Indeed, in Byzantium the term "philosophy" was a moving and flexible one that could refer to the writings of Plato and Aristotle, or to Christianity, or to learning in general. Partly in consequence, any serious revival of literary studies threatened the acceptance of the pagan Greek inheritance as a subordinate part of a Christian unity; there was always the danger that the ancient tradition would be reasserted as an end in itself.

Thus the success of Psellos and his associates led to a reaction from the church. The patriarchal school, directly responsible for specifically Christian education, extended its curriculum to cover all the subjects taught at the university. Further, the school introduced the important innovation that the central discipline of grammar was no longer taught primarily through the ancient authors but through new material, often written especially for that purpose. Doubtless there were educational reasons for the change, but its main purpose seems to have been to avoid the dangers that might arise from direct contact with the classic authors.

In the twelfth century, Byzantine scholarship reached new heights, notably in the work of Eustathios, archbishop of Thessaloniki. He wrote commentaries (no longer extant) on Pindar and Aristophanes; his most important surviving work is the pair of massive volumes on the *Iliad* and the *Odyssey*. Byzantine scholarship thus moved back to direct commentary on the authors with which literary studies had begun; Eustathios' work is in the best tradition of Alexandrian scholarship, and he exhibits both the virtues and the faults of his Hellenistic predecessors.

The high hopes of the twelfth century were dashed by the Latin conquest of Constantinople in 1204, with its destruction of large numbers of manuscripts and its disruption of the life of the empire. However, there was no slackening of the Byzantine commitment to classical studies even during the Latin Empire (1204–1261), and the two centuries of the restored empire saw some of the highest achievements of Byzantine scholarship. Among the leading scholars early in the period were Maximos Planudes and Demetrios Triklinios, and they had worthy successors.

There were several new general developments during the late Byzantine Empire. In the first place, demotic Greek had by then diverged so far from classic Greek that in effect the teaching of Attic Greek meant the teaching of a new language. The old grammars were not suitable for this purpose; new grammars were written, and new methods of teaching were developed. Second, Byzantine scholars during this period had more and more contacts with the Latin West, largely as a result of the negotiations for church unity. Some Latin authors were made available in translation; Maximos Planudes, for example, produced Greek versions of Augustine, Boethius, and even Ovid. Finally, it seems that during these centuries scholars moved closer than ever before in Byzantium to seeing ancient Greek civilization whole, and not simply as a subordinate part of Christianity. The new vision may have resulted in part from the gulf between demotic and Attic Greek, in part from the methods used to introduce students to a "dead" civilization that was not their own.

The new approach may be illustrated by the work of Gemisthos Plethon. He taught literary studies during his early years, and many leading figures of the fifteenth century were his pupils. His attitude toward the Hellenic past is summed up not unfairly by his opponent George Scholarios: "He did not read and study these books, first of all of the Greek poets and then of the philosophers, for the sake of their literary style, as do all Christians, but rather for the sake of associating himself with them." How far this approach could develop in Byzantium and how far it could be reconciled with Greek Orthodox civilization was never decided. The Turkish conquest of Constantinople in 1453 in effect put an end to Byzantine classical studies, though not before their main achievements and the most important Greek manuscripts had been passed on to the West, which accepted them eagerly and, indeed, had sought them out.

THE LATIN WEST THROUGH THE CAROLINGIAN PERIOD

Among the pagans the last centuries of the empire saw the consolidation and simplification of the inheritance of Latin literary studies into the form in which it would be passed on to the Middle Ages. Donatus and Priscian wrote the grammars that dominated the West for centuries; Priscian was particularly important for his inclusion of a very large number of citations from the classic authors. In the lexical and encyclopedic tradition, Nonius Marcellus in the early fourth century compiled the *De compendiosa doctrina,* an alphabetical introduction in twenty books to grammar, lexicography, and antiquities. Martianus Capella in the early fifth century wrote *De nuptiis Mercurii et Philologiae* as a summary of the seven liberal arts. There was also work in the field of commentaries, particularly on authors read in the schools; Donatus, for example, wrote on Terence and Vergil, and Servius (late fourth and early fifth century) wrote a large, standard commentary on Vergil.

Meanwhile, the Christians continued to follow the general position outlined by Clement and Origen, though in contrast to what happened in Byzantium, there was less emphasis on philosophy and less sense of a unity of the Christian and pagan components. The Latin position was formulated by St. Augustine in *De doctrina Christiana.* Classical studies were necessary and legitimate only as a means for understanding the Bible. As God told the Israelites to take for their own the gold and silver of the Egyptians, so the Christians should appropriate for themselves what is valuable in pagan learning. In Book II of his *Institutiones* Cassiodorus gave Christians a short summary, with bibliography, of the liberal arts. In his very brief treatment of grammar he relies largely on Donatus and repeats the standard definition: "Grammar is skill in speaking well collected from the illustrious poets and prose authors." Thus the Christians in the West retained a certain ambivalence toward the "Egyptian gold and silver" of classical studies, and no real unity emerged.

With the increasing decline and fragmentation of the empire, literary studies also declined, though at a different pace in different countries. Eventually the old public educational institutions disappeared completely; nothing remained except in the church, primarily in the monasteries, and there in a very rudimentary form.

After the darkest period the first revival seems to have begun in Ireland, and through the Anglo-Saxons the Irish movement came into contact with the vestiges of the ancient tradition in Gaul and Italy. Finally the various strands were brought together in the Carolingian Empire.

The details of the Irish revival are obscure, but it seems that their unique response resulted in part from their having been the first to receive the ancient literary works without any experience of the civilization that produced them. Hence they felt none of Augustine's hesitations and, with their native tradition of learning, they welcomed the new material with enthusiasm. Though their resources were very limited, they worked out methods of educating students in Latin and went on to do independent work of their own. The Irish transmitted their zeal and their methods to the Anglo-Saxons, and Roman influence also played an important role in England, particularly after the coming of Theodore of Tarsus as archbishop of Canterbury in 668.

The English developed a number of important schools, notably at York and Jarrow, where the revived studies flourished. Manuscripts were brought from the Continent, and the number of classical authors available was impressive. Bede illustrated the level of work that was now possible. It is important to note that in Bede's work the ambivalence toward classical studies had disappeared, and the new education was felt to be Christian and part of a Christian unity. The work done by Bede and such successors as Boniface was largely limited to grammar, but it was no longer backward-looking and had within it the potential for new growth.

Meanwhile, in the seventh century there had been some revival of classical studies in Italy, where it had connections with the growth of urban life and it retained some ties with the ancient tradition. Charlemagne met a number of Italian scholars on his trips to Rome, and he brought some of them, including Peter of Pisa, to his court. In 782 Charlemagne summoned Alcuin, head of the school at York, to be his cultural and religious adviser. The various revivals were thus fused in the Carolingian Empire, and there they took on a significance that would be felt throughout Europe.

Working through Alcuin, Charlemagne proceeded to institute a reform of education throughout his empire. As the head of Christian society, he saw the need for an educated clergy for religious reasons, and for his own purposes he needed educated administrators. The reform was both simple and practical; its purpose was to produce men who could read and write good Latin, and there was no interest in classical literary studies as such. As among the Anglo-Saxons, grammar remained the central discipline and the main object of new work; but it was always taught, in part at least, through citations from the ancient authors, and in time it would encourage some to study the authors directly. Charlemagne's reforms resulted in a great growth and improvement of education in the monasteries throughout his empire. There was a tremendous production of new manuscripts, and few classic authors survive who were not recopied at this time.

After Charlemagne's death, and particularly during the reign of King Charles the Bald, there was an extension of literary studies to the authors themselves. Servatus Lupus of Ferrières, an early leader, is revealed in his correspondence as eagerly searching for manuscripts through which he would be able to extend his range of reading or to improve the texts of the works that he already possessed. Lupus wrote that he was trying to go beyond the liberal arts to the authors, and that he hoped thereby to be able to write in a better style than he found in most of his contemporaries. However, Lupus criticized those who sought only elegance of style from their studies, insisting that the final goals are goodness and piety.

The new beginnings in Lupus came to fruition in the second half of the ninth century. Heiric of Auxerre, a pupil of Lupus, lectured on Persius, Juvenal, Horace, and Prudentius as well as composing commentaries on logic. Heiric's pupil, Remigius of Aux-

erre, put into writing much of what he had learned from his master. He wrote commentaries on both the *Ars minor* and the *Ars maior* of Donatus; on the grammarians Priscian, Phocas, and Eutyches; and on Martianus Capella. In addition he produced commentaries on Terence, Vergil, Persius, and Juvenal, and on Cato's Distichs. With Heiric and Remigius, Latin literary studies entered a new stage. The century-long tutelage in grammar was over, and the late Carolingians were turning, within a Christian unity, to the authors for whose sake grammar had originally been invented.

THE TWELFTH AND THIRTEENTH CENTURIES

Many of the gains of the Carolingian period were lost in the tenth and early eleventh centuries, but there was no real break in the tradition. Study of the classic authors continued, particularly in Ottonian Germany. With the general revival of culture and the standard of living throughout much of Europe in the eleventh century, literary studies also revived.

For all their continuity with Carolingian scholarship, however, these studies were now in a decidedly different situation. In the first place there was the new social context of the communes and towns, and the cathedral school had replaced the monastery school as the dominant form. Second, the movement of secularization begun by Pope Gregory VII continued, and nontheological studies moved increasingly within the quasi-autonomous realm of the world or of nature, in contrast to the "supernatural" realm of Christianity. Finally, classical literary studies were now in a far more complicated intellectual and cultural context than before. On the one hand, the vernacular literatures were growing and moving toward an equality with Latin. On the other hand, and perhaps even more important, new forms of thought were developing that would lead to Scholasticism and eventually destroy the context of the liberal arts within which grammar and literary studies had long existed.

As for the classical literary studies themselves, there was far more interest in them, notably in France and part of England, during the twelfth century than at any earlier period of the Middle Ages. The number of surviving twelfth-century manuscripts testifies to the production of new copies in large numbers. There was clearly great interest in the classics in the new cathedral schools, and elementary work in grammar led more often to an intensive reading of the authors.

The centers of literary studies were at Chartres

and at Orléans. At Chartres the classic authors were taught in close connection with the other liberal arts and with Platonist philosophy. The atmosphere was optimistic and forward-looking. Bernard of Chartres declared that the men of his time were like dwarves who, because they stood on the shoulders of giants (that is, the ancients) could see farther than the giants could. The ancients were regarded as of tremendous importance, but they did not represent any final model of perfection.

John of Salisbury has given us a good picture of the teaching methods of Bernard, whom he calls "the most perfect Platonist of the century" as well as "the most abounding fount of letters in modern times." According to John (*Metalogicon*, I, 24), in lecturing on a text, Bernard

> pointed out what was simple and set forth according to rule; he placed in the foreground the figures of grammar, the colors of the rhetoricians, and the cavils of the sophists, and how the passage with which he was concerned was related to the other disciplines.... In view of the fact that exercise both strengthens and sharpens our mind, Bernard would urge his listeners to imitate what they had read.

On the following day each student was required to recite part of what he had learned the day before. And lest the reading lose contact with its ultimate purpose, at the vesper exercise "that material was presented which would build up faith and morals, and by which those who had gathered together would be inspired to the good." Bernard's method of lecturing on the text is probably comparable to what went on elsewhere, though it appears that at Orléans the authors were read more for their writings and less in a philosophic and Christian context.

The twelfth century produced a number of commentaries, though not as many as might have been expected after the late Carolingian beginnings. Most of the school authors were glossed or commented, though the commentaries were often simply variations on ancient or early medieval works. The well-known commentary on books I–VI of the *Aeneid* by Bernard Silvester was a heavily allegorical and philosophical interpretation of the poem, and one could argue that in the twelfth century in general a tendency toward instant allegory was beginning to obscure any direct vision of the authors.

John of Salisbury is the greatest figure in classical literary studies during the twelfth century. His learning was wide, and he shows an acquaintance with far more than the usual cycle of authors. In his *Meta-logicon* John provides interesting insights into the situation in which literary studies then existed. He avowedly defends logic and does so against those who reject all disciplines. More important for our purposes, he is defending the classic authors against those who would recognize the claims only of logic and the new reason. John's own goal is to preserve literary studies within the old unity of the liberal arts, and his ideal is the union of reason and eloquence. Throughout his works John makes extensive use of his classical learning, but he does not see the classical world as a whole; what he uses of the ancient inheritance is first fragmented and then integrated into a medieval and Christian unity.

In the course of the twelfth century, the precarious balance seen in John of Salisbury tilted gradually and in various ways against the classic authors. One can see the change partly in the new grammars. Throughout the earlier period Priscian had retained supreme authority and had been the subject of innumerable commentaries. In the twelfth century Petrus Helie, a teacher of grammar at Paris about 1150, took a new step. He produced a compendium of Priscian that in general retained the theoretical portions but in large part deleted the citations from ancient authors and substituted examples from the moderns. Toward the end of the century there appeared two new grammars, the *Doctrinale puerorum* of Alexander de Villa Dei and the *Graecismus* of Evrard of Béthune. Both make few appeals to actual usage; they are concerned not with classical Latin but with the language of their own time, and their aim is to "logicize" it and make it rational. These tendencies were continued in the thirteenth century and culminated in the flowering of "speculative grammar," which claimed to be connected with no given language but to be the necessary form of all language.

The break with the tradition of classical studies may also be seen in the new educational institution, the university, that dominated the thirteenth century. Here the Aristotelian disciplines were in command. For a time grammar survived, though in the statutes of the University of Paris for 1255, only Priscian and Donatus were required, while almost all of Aristotle had to be studied. In the comparable statutes of 1366, Priscian and Donatus are replaced by the *Doctrinale* and the *Graecismus*.

The triumph of logic was put into mock-epic form by Henri d'Andell in *The Battle of the Seven Arts,* probably written in the second quarter of the thirteenth century. At the beginning of the poem:

However, logic has the students
Whereas grammar is reduced in numbers.
Grammar is much wrought up
And she has raised her banner
Outside of Orléans, in the midst of the grain fields.

There she has assembled her army,
Homer and old Claudian,
Donatus, Persius, Priscian,
These good author knights,
And those good squires who serve them.

But at the end all is lost, and logic reigns supreme:

And the authorlings fled
And deserted grammar.

Although the study and reading of the classic authors continued through the thirteenth century and into the fourteenth, the perspective through which the classics were seen had changed, and the possibility of seeing them whole seemed more remote than ever. And in the fourteenth century the evidence of the surviving manuscripts suggests that even the reading of the classics was declining.

THE FOURTEENTH AND FIFTEENTH CENTURIES IN ITALY

Classical literary studies had a new birth in Italy while they were declining in the North. This new birth, commonly called the Renaissance, does not fall strictly within the scope of the present article, and it will be sketched only in roughest outline.

Italy had remained largely separate both from the classical studies of twelfth-century France and from the Scholasticism of the thirteenth century. However, it had certain native traditions of letter writing and of speechmaking, as well as of acquaintance with the classics.

Toward the end of the thirteenth and the beginning of the fourteenth centuries, small groups at Padua and elsewhere began to display a new interest in the classic authors, particularly the poets. Petrarch knew some of these men, and during his stay at Avignon he had come into contact with the literary and philosophic movements of the North. Out of his own experience and genius he moved to a new formulation of the place and value of the "authors."

First of all, while in the North the study of the classic authors had had to retreat in the presence of the new Scholastic and Aristotelian reason and logic, Petrarch launched an attack on the Scholastic disciplines. He insisted that the wisdom by which alone man could attain to his humanity was to be found not in the disciplines but in the classic authors, both pagan and Christian. He did not try to move back to the universe of the liberal arts; rather, he placed the classic authors in what was to become the new realm of "letters." Second, Petrarch emphasized eloquence as a prime essential in all speaking and writing, insisting that the classic authors were the only guide to this eloquence, he turned completely away from the scholastic Latin that had been so powerful a tool of late medieval thought. Finally, for the first time since the decay of the ancient world, Petrarch saw the classic authors and, indeed, Roman civilization as unities in themselves; they were no longer to be broken into fragments and then integrated into a medieval unity, as they had been even by John of Salisbury.

Petrarch devoted his life, with tremendous success, to spreading this new gospel of the classic authors. He himself searched eagerly for manuscripts and spurred on others. He tried to improve the texts of the works he possessed, and from his new perspective he displayed an extraordinary philological tact and skill in his work on a number of them. Perhaps most important, in his own writings and particularly in his letters, he displayed brilliantly the eloquent wisdom of this new world of the classic authors and of those who followed in their footsteps.

In the generation after Petrarch, Colluccio Salutati (1331–1406) carried on his work from the vantage point of the chancellorship of Florence, and he began to call the new studies the *studia humanitatis*. The phrase is found in Cicero, but there it includes all of the liberal arts. In the works of Salutati and his successors it refers to the new studies connected with the classic authors. By the end of the fifteenth century the scope of the humanities had been recognized as including grammar, rhetoric, history, poetry, and some moral philosophy. After the visit of Manuel Chrysoloras to Florence from 1397 to 1400, the new studies included Greek as well as Latin authors.

In Italy the new studies were linked to, and transformed, the earlier traditions of letter writing and speechmaking. They led to the creation of new humanist schools at the secondary level, and the humanists even found a limited place in the universities. The new classes of the Italian cities seized upon them as ways through which they could express their new sense of what it meant to be fully human.

In the fifteenth century the *studia humanitatis* scored remarkable triumphs. There is the familiar story of the rediscovery of long-lost classic authors, though it must be remembered that the manuscripts found were almost always either Carolingian copies or their descendants. New accomplishments in scholarship far eclipsed those of the Middle Ages. Toward the end of the fifteenth century the new studies crossed the Alps, and Erasmus used them to create a European republic of letters. And ultimately the Renaissance tradition of literary studies led to modern classical philology and to a humanist education that was to be dominant in Europe through the end of the nineteenth century.

BIBLIOGRAPHY

General works include Robert R. Bolgar, *The Classical Heritage and Its Beneficiaries* (1954); Herbert Hunger and K. Langosch, eds., *Geschichte der Textüberlieferung der antiken und mittelalterlichen Literatur*, 2 vols. (1961–1962); Eduard Norden, *Die antike Kunstprosa*, 2 vols. (1915); Leighton D. Reynolds and Nigel G. Wilson, *Scribes and Scholars*, 2nd ed. (1974); John Edwin Sandys, *History of Classical Scholarship*, 3 vols. (1903–1908), some volumes subsequently revised.

On the Greco-Roman and Christian backgrounds, see Harald Hagendahl, *Latin Fathers and the Classics* (1958); Max Ludwig Laistner, *Christianity and Pagan Culture in the Later Roman Empire* (1951); Henri Marrou, *Histoire de l'éducation dans l'antiquité*, 6th ed. (1965), translated by George Lamb as *A History of Education in Antiquity* (1956); Arnaldo Momigliano, ed., *The Conflict Between Paganism and Christianity in the Fourth Century* (1963); Rudolf Pfeiffer, *History of Classical Scholarship* (1968).

On the Greek East and Byzantium, see Friedrich Fuchs, *Die höheren Schulen von Konstantinopel im Mittelalter* (1926); Deno J. Geanakoplos, *Byzantine East and Latin West* (1966, repr. 1976); Herbert Hunger, *Die hochsprachliche profane Literatur der Byzantiner*, 2 vols. (1978); Karl Krumbacher, *Geschichte der byzantinischen Litteratur*, 2nd ed., 2 vols. (1970); Paul Lemerle, *Le premier humanisme byzantin* (1971); Steven Runciman, *The Last Byzantine Renaissance* (1970).

General works on the Middle Ages in the West include Walter Berschin, *Greichisch-lateinisches Mittelalter* (1981); R. R. Bolgar, ed., *Classical Influences on European Culture, A.D. 500–1500* (1971); Ernst R. Curtius, *Europäische Literatur und lateinisches Mittelalter* (1948), translated by Willard R. Trask as *European Literature and the Latin Middle Ages* (1953); Günter Glauche, *Schullektüre im Mittelalter* (1970); Paul O. Kristeller, ed., *Catalogus translationum et commentariorum* (1960–); Max Manitius, *Geschichte der lateinischen Literatur des Mittelalters*, 3 vols. (1911–1931); Erwin Panofsky, *Renaissance and Renascences in Western Art* (1965).

Through the Carolingian periods, see Bernard Bischoff, ed., *Karl der Grosse. Lebenswerk und Nachleben*, vol. 2: *Das geistige Leben* (1965); M. L. W. Laistner and H. H. King, eds., *Thought and Letters in Western Europe, A.D. 500 to 900*, 2nd ed. (1966); Pierre Riché, *Éducation et culture dans l'occident barbare, vi^e–viiie siècles* (1962), translated by John J. Contreni as *Education and Culture in the Barbarian West, Sixth Through Eighth Centuries* (1976).

On the twelfth and thirteenth centuries, see Joseph de Ghellinck, *L'essor de la littérature latine au XIIe siècle* (1946); Charles Homer Haskins, *The Renaissance of the Twelfth Century* (1927); Louis J. Paetow, *The Arts Course at Medieval Universities with Special Reference to Grammar and Rhetoric* (1910, repr. 1970); Gérard Paré, Adrien Brunet, and Pierre Tremblay, *La renaissance du XIIe siècle* (1933).

On Italy in the fourteenth and fifteenth centuries, see Giuseppe Billanovich, *I primi umanisti e le tradizioni dei classici latini* (1953); August Buck and Otto Herding, eds., *Der Kommentar in der Renaissance* (1975); Eugenio Garin, *Il pensiero pedagogico dello umanesimo* (1958); Paul O. Kristeller, *Renaissance Thought*, I–II (1961–1965), and *Renaissance Thought and Its Sources*, Michael Mooney, ed. (1979); Rudolf Pfeiffer, *History of Classical Scholarship: From 1300 to 1850* (1976); Remigio Sabbadini, *Le scoperte dei cocici latini e greci ne' secoli XIV e XV*, 2 vols. (1905–1914), reprinted with the author's additions and corrections (1967); and *Storia e critica di testi latini* (1914), 2nd ed., with new indexes (1971); Berthold L. Ullman, *Studies in the Italian Renaissance*, 2nd ed., rev. and corr. (1973); Roberto Weiss, *The Renaissance Discovery of Classical Antiquity* (1969).

F. EDWARD CRANZ

[See also **Alcuin of York; Bede; Bernard of Chartres; Bernard Silvester; Boniface, St.; Cassiodorus, Flavius Magnus Aurelius; Charlemagne; Donatism; Gemisthos Plethon (Georgios); George Scholarios; Grammar; John of Salisbury; Lupus of Ferrières; Manuel Chrysoloras; Martianus Capella; Nonius; Peter of Pisa; Petrarch (Francesco Petrarca); Priscian; Psellos, Michael; Remigius of Auxerre; Translations and Translators, Byzantine; Translations and Translators, Western European; Universities; Universities, Byzantine.**]

CLAUDIUS OF TURIN (d. 827), bishop and theologian. Born near Seo de Urgel, Claudius was chaplain to Louis the Pious, who about 818 appointed him to the strategic see of Turin, where he remained until his death. Claudius composed commentaries on much of the Bible, and was a vehement opponent of the cult of images, relics, saints, and angels, and the adoration of the cross.

BIBLIOGRAPHY
Monumenta Germaniae historica, Epistolae Karolini aevi, II (1895), 586–613; *Patrologia latina*, L (1865), 893–

1208, CIV (1865), 199–250 and 615–928, and CV (1864), 457–464; Friedrich Stegmüller, *Repertorium Biblicum medii aevi*, II (1950), 1949–1975, and VIII (1976), 1948.1–1958.

MARK A. ZIER

[See also **Carolingians and the Carolingian Empire**.]

CLAUSULA (Latin: *claudere,* "to close"). The term was used in medieval grammar and rhetoric, as well as in music, in various senses, but all indicate the conclusion of a passage or section. The most important musical sense is its use as a synonym for *punctus* (point), to designate specific sections of the two-part organum settings of the *Magnus liber organi,* composed and readapted in Paris at Notre Dame and its immediate neighborhood from about 1170 to about 1225.

Notre Dame organums retained the normal plainchant of traditional choral portions of the responsorial chants for Office and Mass, but set the soloistic portions in two parts (some later settings are in three or four parts). Portions of the soloistic sections that have only one, or occasionally two or three, musical notes to each text syllable were set in "organal" style, with the upper part (or parts) organized in modal rhythmic melodic phrases set over the tenor notes, which were sustained for long but appropriate lengths. Where a text syllable was melismatic (ranging from about five to forty notes), it was set in a typical "discant" (note against note) style. These lat-

ter sections were called clausulas. The two polyphonic styles are juxtaposed in the accompanying example.

In all, there are more than 900 clausulas, either used in organums settings or collected in separate fascicles in four main repositories. The musical style ranges from simple, almost nonmodal discant settings to very elaborate tenor/*duplum* relationships, using complicated rhythmic patterns and more than one statement of the tenor. The most complex can be traced to the revisions attributed to Pérotin, dating from the late 1190's to about 1225. The clausula was the basis of the motet, which in its early development (*ca.* 1180–1225) was formed by the addition to the *duplum* of a troped Latin sacred text, thus forming a vocal line accompanied by a plainchant melisma set out in repeated rhythmic units.

BIBLIOGRAPHY

Gordon A. Anderson, "Clausulae or Transcribed-Motets in the Florence Manuscript?" in *Acta musicologica,* **42** (1970); William G. Waite, *The Rhythm of Twelfth-century Polyphony* (1954); and "The Abbreviation of the Magnus Liber," in *Journal of the American Musicological Society,* **14** (1961).

GORDON A. ANDERSON

[See also **Discantor; Melisma; Motet; Organum; Pérotin**.]

CLAVIJO. See **González de Clavijo, Ruy.**

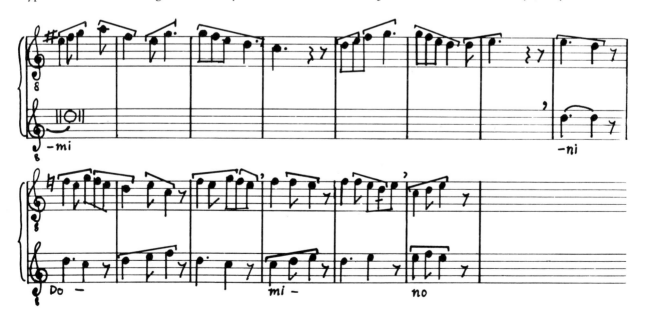

CLEF (Latin: *clavis,* key), a musical symbol chosen to indicate the letter name of the pitch that is aligned horizontally with it but not indicating the absolute pitch of the note. It was used with a stave, when that had been developed, or in musical notations having pitches aligned only by eye or by the ruling of the page. Special nonalphabetic signs were used as early as the ninth century in such musical treatises as *Musica enchiriadis.* In the eleventh century Guido d'Arezzo advocated the use of colored lines on and in the stave to serve as clefs, but also used the letter system, which quickly became the usual method. From the eleventh century the letter forms became increasingly stylized, though usually recognizable. The pitches *F* and *C* were first represented, because they stand above a semitone, which it was important to identify. The signs for *B*-flat and *B*-natural were also used. Not until the fifteenth century did the *G* clef become common. Other letters, such as *D* and *A,* appear less often. Clefs were chosen, or changed during the course of a piece, in order to keep the pitches within the stave.

BIBLIOGRAPHY

Carl Parrish, *The Notation of Medieval Music* (1957), with numerous facsimiles; J. Smits van Waesberghe, "The Musical Notation of Guido of Arezzo," in *Musica disciplina,* 5 (1951); Peter Wagner, "Aus der Frühzeit des Liniensystems," in *Archiv für Musikwissenschaft,* 8 (1926).

ANDREW HUGHES

[See also **Guido d'Arezzo; Musical Notation, Western.**]

CLEMENS SCOTUS (Clement Scottus, St. Clement of Ireland, Claudius Clemens) is not to be confused with a heretical bishop of the same name who was active in Austrasia between 743 and 747. Born in Ireland about 750, Clemens migrated to the Continent and probably resided at the Carolingian court before 796, when he succeeded Alcuin as master of the palace school. He retained that position until 826, despite opposition from Theodulf of Orléans, Einhard, and Alcuin, who objected to the influence of Irish scholars. His pupils included Modestus of Fulda and the future emperor Lothair I. To the latter Clemens dedicated his principal work, an *Ars grammatica* in three treatises: *De philosophia, De metris,* and *De barbarismo.* He is believed to have died at Würzburg while on a pilgrimage to the tomb of the Irish saint Kilian, sometime after 826.

BIBLIOGRAPHY

The *Ars grammatica* was edited by Johannes Tolkiehn in *Philologus,* Supplementband **20** (1928). Secondary literature includes James F. Kenney, *The Sources for the Early History of Ireland,* IX, *Ecclesiastical* (1929, repr. 1966), 531–549, and 522–523 and 526–527 for the heretical bishop.

WANDA CIŻEWSKI

CLEMENT V, POPE (1264–1314), was born Bertrand de Got, son of Béraud de Got, a knight who was lord of Villandraut (Gironde), Grayan, Livran, and Uzeste. After schooling with the religious of Grandmont, he studied civil and ecclesiastical law at Orléans and Bologna, then held canonries at Bordeaux, Agen, Tours, and Lyons, at Lyons serving also as vicar-general for the archbishop, his brother Béraud. In 1294 he went to England on a diplomatic mission. The following year he was consecrated bishop of Comminges and, in 1299, archbishop of Bordeaux.

Clement was elected pope in 1305 by a conclave that had sat for almost a year, but there is no foundation for the gossip recorded by Giovanni Villani that one party of deadlocked cardinals proposed three names from which the opposing party chose his. The fable reflects the opposition of "Italian" cardinals and the "French" cardinals under the influence of Philip IV the Fair, who was tenaciously carrying on his feud with the dead pope, Boniface VIII. Clement had long been on good terms with the king, who was present at his coronation on 14 November 1305 at Lyons, for disorders in Rome made it impossible for the new pope to enter the city. A month later he named nine French cardinals and one Englishman, and restored Giacomo and Pietro Colonna to the Sacred College of Cardinals, from which they had been deposed by Boniface, thus putting anti-French cardinals in a minority. He reinforced the situation when he named five more cardinals in December 1310 and nine in December 1312.

Clement convoked the Council of Vienne in 1311 and set its agenda. Deeply interested in Oriental Christendom, he was severe toward schismatics and promoted the interests of the Armenians who were in union with the Holy See. As a canonist his name is preserved by the *Constitutiones Clementinae,* legislation of the Council of Vienne that became an integral part of the canon law.

Clement's academic concerns led him to establish universities or *studia generalia,* including that at Perugia (1307); to intervene on establishing the statutes of the medical faculty at Montpellier; and to order that there be chairs of Hebrew, Syriac, and Arabic at Paris, Oxford, Bologna, and Salamanca. He confirmed Henry VII as emperor and excommunicated the Eastern emperor, Andronikos II Palaiologos, but against this show of strength must be seen his concessions to Philip: the heresy trial of Boniface reopened, the ill treatment of Boniface at Anagni pardoned, and the suppression of the Templars on evidence that Philip procured through use of torture.

Clement's ill health—perhaps cancer of the stomach or intestines—entailed long periods of isolation during which the unsupervised papal court engaged in scandalously corrupt financial practices. Enormous sums raised by bitterly resented taxation allowed Clement to lend imposing amounts to the kings of France and England, to reward his supporters, and to leave a sizable fortune in his will. He died at Roquemaure.

BIBLIOGRAPHY

Acta Clementis PP. V, Ferdinand M. Delorme and Aloysius L. Tautù, eds. (1955); *Regestrum Clementis papae V,* 9 vols. (1885–1888); and *Tables des registres de Clément V,* Yvonne Lanhers and Robert Fawtier, eds. (1948); Etienne Baluze, *Vitae paparum Avenionensium,* Guillaume Mollat, ed., I (1914).

EDWARD A. SYNAN

[See also **Boniface VIII, Pope; Philip IV the Fair.**]

CLEMENT VI, POPE (*ca.* 1291–1352), was born Pierre Roger. A monk who was a theologian and a renowned orator, he had risen to become archbishop of Rouen, chancellor to King Philip VI of France, and cardinal priest of St. Neraeus and Achilleus, before his election as pope on 7 May 1342. Both charming and generous, he wanted the papal court at Avignon to be the most splendid in Christendom. Clerics seeking posts immediately flocked to Avignon, and to satisfy them Clement declared in 1344 that the papacy had the right to dispose of every single church, dignity, office, and ecclesiastical benefice. The claim, however, provoked widespread resistance and was never actually carried out.

Clement believed in largess and in pleasing those who sought his help. The consequence was the spending of the financial surplus built up by his austere predecessor, Benedict XII. The resources were exhausted by his sumptuous court, the completion of the papal palace, the purchase of Avignon from the queen of Naples in 1348 for 80,000 florins, and the considerable loans made to the French crown and to French noblemen.

On the political front Clement tried unceasingly to mediate an end to the Hundred Years War, then in its opening stages, but he could achieve little more than periodic truces. He also formed a naval league with Venice, Cyprus, and the Knights Hospitalers to clear Turkish pirates from the eastern Mediterranean. The allied fleet achieved its goal.

Clement had less success in Italy, where he was faced with the revolt of the city of Bologna and the Papal States. Bernabò Visconti, duke of Milan, moved southward to take advantage of the turmoil. The situation discouraged the popes from returning permanently to Rome until 1377.

Despite these troubles Clement was very popular and his court was the brightest in Europe; yet he never neglected the spiritual side of his office, being ever ready to preach and to officiate at religious ceremonies. When the Black Death struck in 1348, Clement engaged doctors to care for the sick, granted extraordinary dispensations to those priests who would attend the dying, instituted stern police measures to prevent the further spread of the plague, and bought land for the prompt burial of the dead of Avignon.

Popular opinion blamed the Jews for the tragedy, and massacres soon took place. To combat this, Clement took them under his protection, granted them asylum in Avignon and the Papal States, and excommunicated anyone who sought to harm them. In Swabia a group—the flagellants—sprang up, claiming that a person who wished to escape the Black Death had to undergo a 33½-day series of floggings in order to restore his soul to its baptismal innocence. When the group multiplied and began threatening both Jews and public safety, Clement ordered their suppression.

Clement was accused by Petrarch of lascivious conduct, but little credence is now given to these charges.

BIBLIOGRAPHY

Eugène Déprez, ed., *Clément VI (1342–1352): Lettres closes, patentes et curiales se rapportant à la France,* 6 vols. (1901–1961); Eugène Déprez and Guillaume Mollat, eds., *Clément VI (1342–1352): Lettres closes, patentes et* curiales, *intéressant les pays autres que la France*, 3 pts. (1960–1961); Guillaume Mollat, *The Popes at Avignon, 1305–1378*, Janet Love, trans. (1963), 37–43; Yves Renouard, *The Avignon Papacy, 1305–1403*, Denis Bethell, trans. (1970), 42–49; John E. Wrigley, "Clement VI Before His Pontificate: The Early Life of Pierre Roger, 1290/91–1342," in *Catholic Historical Review*, 56 (1970–1971).

PAUL R. THIBAULT

[See also **Babylonian Captivity; Black Death; Flagellants.**]

CLERESTORY, a row of windows just below the roofline in the main walls of a structure. In churches the clerestory pierces the nave walls above the level of the side aisle roofs. Clerestory lighting was a standard feature of the early Christian basilica; it was sometimes abandoned in early Romanesque vaulted naves, but reappeared at Cluny and in Norman Romanesque churches and was a ubiquitous feature of Gothic architecture.

LESLIE BRUBAKER

CLERGY (from the Latin *clerus*) designates the entire body of people who, in the Christian religion, are consecrated to holy functions by an official rite; these people, who form the appointed ministers of worship, are called clerks or clerics (from the Latin *clericus*). "Clergy" or "cleric" ultimately derives from the Greek word *kleros*, signifying fate and, by extension, one's share or portion that is obtained by fate, especially inheritance or a part thereof.

At the beginning of Christianity *kleros* was applied to all Christians because they had been chosen or elected by God to participate in his inheritance. The First Letter of Peter (5:3) uses this meaning of the term (*clerus*). But very soon *clerus* and *clericus* were used in a restricted sense and designated only a segment of the Christian community: those persons entrusted to exercise the offices of worship.

It is not known when the terminology changed; but it was probably during the second century, because at the beginning of the third century the use of *clerus* or *clericus* to designate the ministers of worship, as opposed to laymen, became common. In his *Epistula ad Nepotianum*, St. Jerome sanctions the etymology of "clerk" by having it derive from the Greek *kleros*, signifying "fate" or "lot"; and Isidore

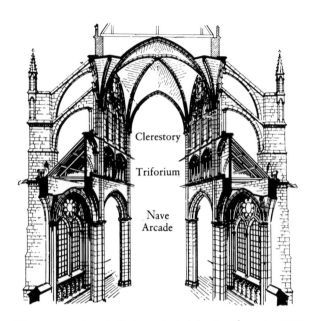

Transverse section of a Gothic cathedral showing clerestory. FROM SIR BANISTER FLETCHER'S A HISTORY OF ARCHITECTURE

of Seville returned to Jerome's explanation in his *Etymologiae* (7, 12). In the twelfth century Gratian assured the acceptance of this etymology by including Jerome's and Isidore's texts in his *Decretum* (distinctio 21, canon 1; causa 12, quaestio 1, canon 5).

ORIGINS AND DEVELOPMENT

The internal organization of the medieval clergy was the result of a slow and progressive evolution, the main lines of which must be traced.

In the apostolic age the ministers of worship consisted of two categories of persons besides apostles: the bishop priests and the deacons; the latter performed the minor functions. At the end of the first century and the beginning of the second, a unitary government of local churches began to evolve, so that from then on we find the bishop governing the local Christian community, the presbyters at his side and under his direction, and finally, as before, the deacons.

As the number of Christians increased, the liturgical service came to require a greater number of personnel to assist the bishop, the presbyters, and the deacons; the custodians of these minor functions rapidly took their place among the clergy and were considered clerks. Thus, at the beginning of the third century two minor functions appeared, those of subdeacon and lector. The subdeacon assisted the deacon, who was no longer able to perform all of his functions; the lector helped the bishop and the presbyters with the liturgical service.

Later on the minor functions were subdivided again, thereby increasing the number known to have existed at the beginning of the third century. Because these new functions developed according to the needs of various churches, their evolution was not uniform either in time or in place, and functions found in one church would not necessarily exist in others.

From the middle of the third century on, there were minor orders in both East and West, varying with churches and periods: the porter, the acolyte, the exorcist, and the psalmist (or precentor). The *Statuta ecclesiae antiqua* (*ca.* 475), probably by Gennadius of Marseilles, enumerates eight categories of clerks, indicating the rite of ordination proper to each: bishop, presbyter (priest), deacon, subdeacon, acolyte, exorcist, lector, and porter (*ostiarius*). It also mentions the psalmist; but since he does not receive ordination, properly speaking, he is technically not a clerk.

Certain minor functions mentioned in the *Statuta,* such as the exorcist, disappeared in Rome during the High Middle Ages; but the eight categories of clerks existed again at Rome in the tenth century, influenced by Gallican liturgical books. From then on, the number remained fixed at eight during the Middle Ages.

DEGREES AND HIERARCHICAL RANKS

All Christians are equal in baptism; but the organization of the church, which incorporates them through baptism, is based on the hierarchical principle. This principle regards power as deriving from above—that is, from God—and in the church creates a hierarchy of laymen subordinate to clerks and of clerks subordinate to each other.

In the ranks of clerks, the hierarchy is twofold, depending on whether it is founded on the power of order or on the power of church government, also called the power of jurisdiction. Hierarchical order comprises those who have received ordination, in the following ascending degrees: porter, lector, exorcist, acolyte, subdeacon, deacon, priest, bishop. The first four constitute the minor orders; the others, the major orders. The subdiaconate was a minor order until the middle of the fifth century, when it began to be considered a major order and celibacy was imposed on subdeacons.

The hierarchy of government also comprises various degrees. Two functions of government are of divine establishment, according to church doctrine, and thus are intangible: that of pope (papal primacy) and that of bishop. But pope and bishop can delegate part of their power to lesser clerks, thus creating other degrees in the hierarchy; since they are of human establishment, these degrees can be changed. Such is true, for example, of the functions of archdeacon, vicar-general, and parish priest.

ENTRANCE INTO THE PRIESTHOOD

During the first centuries of the Christian church, admission to the clergy was obtained by ordination to one of the liturgical functions recognized by the church. Until the end of the third century it was quite possible to accede to the priesthood or episcopate without passing through the diaconate or one of the minor orders (where they had been instituted). One became a clerk by ordination to any one of these functions.

Little by little, regulations were elaborated that required the passage through one of the minor orders—at least two, as a general rule—before entering a major order; the first elements of such regulations appeared in the fourth century. From then on, minor orders, which at their inception were supposed to answer real needs, were not considered real services; like the military and the civil service, and especially the municipal curiae, they became periods of apprenticeship and probation. Regulations concerning the passage through minor orders became more precise, eventually leading to a system regulated down to the smallest details.

From the sixth century on, the clergy constituted a real station that one entered by tonsure rather than by ordination to a liturgical function. One was part of the clergy as soon as he had been given tonsure by a competent church authority, generally the bishop.

The new manner of admission into the clergy seems to have existed at Rome in the middle of the sixth century, according to a letter of Pope Pelagius I. Throughout the Middle Ages tonsure constituted the gateway to the clergy and, at least in principle, was obligatory for those desiring access to the higher orders.

RITES OF ORDINATION

Accession to the various degrees of hierarchical orders has always been the object of liturgical ceremonial. A good description of rites of ordination from the function of porter to that of bishop is recorded in the *Statuta ecclesiae antiqua;* and a more complete compilation of the rites of ordination, including the rite of tonsure, was made at Mainz around 950. This Romano-Germanic pontifical was completed by Guillaume Durand, bishop of Mende from 1291 to 1295, and became the official pontifical of the Church of Rome (first printed in 1485). These documents enable us to obtain an idea of how one acceded to the various degrees of the clerical cursus during the Middle Ages and what significance was invested in each degree.

Tonsure. The ceremony, called *de clerico faciendo,* consists of prayers and two symbolic acts: the bishop cuts a lock of hair from the head of the candidate; the candidate recites a verse of Psalm 15(16) that recalls the Greek-derivation meaning of "inheritance" of *clericus.* Next the bishop hands the candidate a surplice, which symbolizes a clerk's vestment.

Minor orders: porter, lector, exorcist, acolyte. The ordination ceremony for each of these orders follows the same pattern, beginning with an admonition by the bishop that recalls the duties proper to each order and indicating the required qualifications. The porter's duties include ringing the bells, opening the church and the sacristy, and presenting the text to the preacher. The lector's duties are to read, to chant the lessons, and to bless the bread and the first fruits. The exorcist's duties include expelling the devil from demoniacs, dismissing those who do not take Communion, and presenting the water to the ministers at the altar. The acolyte's duties are to carry the candlesticks in the procession, to light the candles on the altar, and to bring to the altar the water and wine for the Eucharist. Next comes the essential rite: the bishop gives the candidate the object symbolizing his function. To the porter he gives the keys; to the lector, the book; to the exorcist, the collection of formulas of exorcism; to the acolyte, the candlesticks and a cruet.

The higher orders: subdeacon, deacon, priest, bishop. As in the ordination rites of the minor orders, the ceremony consists of two elements: the admonition and the rite of ordination proper. In the admonition the bishop recalls the duties proper to each order. The subdeacon prepares the water used in the Mass, assists the deacon, washes the sacred linens, and brings the chalice and the paten to the altar. The deacon has to minister at the altar, baptize, and preach. The priest offers the sacrament, blesses,

presides, and preaches. The bishop judges ecclesiastical cases, interprets church doctrine, consecrates and confers ordination, offers the sacrament, baptizes, and confirms.

In the rite proper, there is an essential difference between the subdiaconate and the three higher orders. The subdeacon's ordination is carried out in the same manner as that of the minor orders, by a prayer of benediction (*cheirothesia*) and the delivery of the objects symbolizing the function: the chalice and paten, the vestments, and the book of epistles. For the other major orders the laying on of hands (*cheirotonia*), by which the sacrament of the order is truly transmitted, intervenes.

The ordination of a deacon includes the laying on of hands by the bishop and the delivery of both the vestments and the book of Gospels. The ordination of a priest includes, besides the laying on of hands by the bishop and by all the priests present, the anointing of the candidate's hands and the delivery of the vestments and sacred vessels. A bishop's ordination, generally carried out by three bishops, consists essentially of the laying on of hands by the consecrating bishops and other bishops present; it is completed by the anointing of the candidate's head and hands with chrism and the delivery of the crozier, the episcopal ring, and the miter.

INTERSTICES

Very early, as noted above, orders leading to the priesthood or episcopate no longer constituted actual functions but were simply degrees in a cursus. From then on, it seemed normal for advancement to be progressive. This had two consequences. The first was that one could not receive a major order without passing successively through the minor ones; this resulted in the interdict called *promotio per saltum,* accession to a higher order by "skipping" an intermediate one. The second was that a candidate had to spend a certain amount of time in a lower order before acceding to a superior one. The lapse of time allowed between the two accessions was called an interstice (*interstitia*).

The rule prohibiting *promotio per saltum* was formulated in 343 by the Council of Sardica, which simply stated the principle without fixing the length of time to be spent in each order. Pope Siricius (384–399) was more precise on the subject; he asked that candidates spend two years as lector or exorcist, then five years as acolyte or subdeacon before acceding to the diaconate, with further, unspecified delays being required before accession to the priesthood and episcopate.

Circumstances subsequently compelled the popes to be less exacting about the lengths of interstices. At last only the principle was retained: progressive passage through the four minor orders could be achieved without specific interstices; in the major orders it became customary to anticipate an interval of one year between the last minor order and the subdiaconate, one year between the subdiaconate and the diaconate, and a year between diaconate and priesthood—always with the reservation that the bishop could shorten these periods if his church's needs required it.

CONDITIONS OF ADMISSION

Future clerks must present guarantees that their faith, morality, and knowledge would enable them to perform properly the functions of worship. They also must satisfy various requirements.

Masculine gender. Only men could belong to the clergy. Although deaconesses and widows did perform some minor duties, essentially of apostleship and charity, and mainly in the early church, women were never part of the clergy itself. During the Middle Ages some women, especially abbesses, assumed the rights to confess and to preach, but popes and councils reacted vigorously against such actions.

Age. Thirty was set as the minimum age for a bishop. In the early church thirty also had been the minimum for a priest, but Pope Zacharias lowered the age to twenty-five, in cases of necessity, in a decretal of 751. In the fourteenth century Clement V made twenty-five the rule for access to the priesthood. The age of access to the diaconate was set at twenty-five by various councils beginning in the sixth century. Clement V also lowered the age for deacon to twenty and the age for subdeacon to eighteen.

When the minor orders no longer entailed responsibilities but constituted only a period of passage or probation, the age requirements became less exacting. In 385 Pope Siricius had allowed a child to be ordained lector before the age of puberty. The rule that he established was confirmed by his successors and was followed throughout the Middle Ages: tonsure and minor orders could be conferred on children. Canonists of the Middle Ages specified only that to receive tonsure and accede to the minor orders, a child must be at least seven years old.

Celibacy. The law of celibacy imposed on major orders in the Latin church is formulated neither in the Scriptures nor in any text of the early church. Originally many bishops, priests, and deacons were married and were not required to renounce their rights as husbands. But celibacy was widespread very early among the clerks, and the practice became the rule about the end of the fourth century. At that time a divergence occurred between East and West that still persists.

In the East marriage was not authorized after reception of a major order, but a clerk who had married before ordination could continue his married life (although he was not allowed to remarry if widowed). Since a bishop must practice abstinence, and thus leave his wife if he was married, the practice of conferring the episcopate only on bachelors was introduced.

In the West abstinence was imposed on major orders (bishops, priests, and deacons) at the end of the fourth century, and in the mid fifth century Pope Leo the Great required it of subdeacons. Thus, in principle the Latin church conferred major orders only on bachelors or on candidates married before ordination who would renounce the married life.

It was difficult to impose the law of celibacy; popes and councils had to reaffirm it often because of the numerous abuses during the Carolingian period and later. In the eleventh century popes of the Gregorian reformation condemned the marriage of clerks and specifically insisted on observance of the law of celibacy. The Second Lateran Council (1139) declared invalid a marriage contracted by a clerk in a major order; since then, such a marriage has been forbidden in the Roman church.

Title of ordination. The purpose of ordination was originally to fill a vacant position—that is, ordination in itself (absolute ordination), without title, was not permitted. Through ordination a clerk was automatically assigned to a specific church. The councils of Nicaea (325) and of Chalcedon (451), Pope Damasus (366–384), and later the Gallic and Spanish councils insisted on the obligation of all clerks to remain assigned to their church of ordination. In this way the clerk's living was assured; the service of this church constituted his title of ordination, which in turn guaranteed him the means of a decent subsistence.

Because the law often was not observed, synods had to recall its prescriptions in the eighth and ninth centuries. From the twelfth century on, with changes occurring in the rural and commercial economies and the considerable increase in the number of clerks, the functions (benefices) were no longer numerous enough to give all candidates for orders a title of ordination founded on a function. From then on, absolute ordinations were permitted; and another title of ordination, founded on the candidate's patrimony, was finally accepted: the bishop ordered it if the candidate could show sufficient means to guarantee his subsistence. In a decretal of 1208, Innocent III officially recognized the title of patrimony as title of ordination. Both titles existed until the Council of Trent in the sixteenth century.

Disqualifications and irregularities. The candidate had to fulfill certain conditions; inability to do so made him ineligible to receive orders. Founded at first on custom, these disabilities subsequently became the object of a detailed set of regulations. In the Middle Ages canonists distinguished two types: absolute disabilities, such as not having been baptized or being a woman, which made ordination invalid; and relative disabilities, which rendered ordination illicit. Someone who had been ordained despite a relative disability was effectively ordained; but his situation was irregular and he thus was not authorized to perform the functions of the order he had received.

The relative disabilities occupied the attention of the medieval canonists. From the second half of the twelfth century they were called irregularities (*irregularitates*); the twelfth-century canonist Rufinus seems to have been the first to use the term in this context. There are two types of irregularities. Irregularities by defect (*ex defectu*) result from certain physical or mental defects, or from certain judicial situations that prevent the candidate from performing the function or from performing it with the requisite material or moral dignity. Those resulting from a serious offense committed by the candidate are called irregularities by delict (*ex delicto*).

Irregularities by defect included illegitimate birth; physical defects (the deaf, mute, blind, or deformed); mental disease; bigamy; the lack of goodness of heart (*defectus perfectae lenitatis*), as for example the judge who pronounces a death sentence or the executioner and his aides who carry it out; and lack of freedom resulting from the exercise of certain civil functions, such as prosecutor, trustee, or soldier. Irregularities by delict included voluntary homicide and abortion, self-mutilation or mutilation of others, attempted suicide, illegal reception of an order or the illegal exercise of a received order, and marriage to a person already betrothed or married.

VARIETIES OF FUNCTIONS AND TITLES

Throughout the Middle Ages the hierarchy of order consisted of eight degrees, each corresponding to a precise function and title. In the hierarchy of church government (or jurisdiction) there was a proliferation of positions following the Gregorian reform, a sort of duplication of functions that created new titles.

The pope, at the summit of this hierarchy, was surrounded by the curia. This administration consisted of the cardinals (bishops, priests, deacons) and other prelates, aided by ecclesiastical personnel with various titles: *mansionarius* (sacristan), *custodes* (guardian of martyrs' relics), *basilicarius* (man responsible for the church and its treasures, if any), *primicerius* (chancellor), *arcarius* (guardian of the sacred vessels). In the particular churches were patriarchs, primates, and metropolitans.

In the diocese, below the resident bishop were the coadjutor, the chorbishop, the auxiliary bishop, the archdeacon, the vicar-general, the official principal, and the deans. In the parish the priest was assisted by vicars. In the chapters of canons responsibilities were divided among the dean, the provost, the chancellor, the scholasticus, the precentor, the treasurer, and the cellarer, who were aided by prebendaries, chaplains, and primissaries (*primissari*).

OBLIGATIONS AND INTERDICTIONS

Clerks were generally expected to lead an honest and chaste life and to abstain from anything incompatible with the dignity of their position. They were not required to wear special dress; Pope Innocent III, in a decretal of 1201 and in the Fourth Lateran Council required only that a clerk dress appropriately. On the other hand, tonsure was obligatory.

Certain occupations and pastimes were forbidden because they were incompatible with a clerk's station: games of chance, the theater, hunting, commerce, military service, surgery, and the administration of laymen's affairs. These interdictions were the subject of papal decretals in the eleventh and twelfth centuries and of decisions of the Third (1179) and Fourth (1215) Lateran Councils.

The obligation to recite the Divine Office is based much more on custom than on law. The prayers of the daily office were originally recited communally. With the proliferation of churches and the dispersal of the clergy to the countryside, the practice of individual prayer spread. In the fourteenth century all clerks of the major orders were obliged to recite the Divine Office every day and could do so in private; only monks and canons of cathedrals and collegiate churches were obliged to pray as a group.

PRIVILEGES

In the fourth century the state conceded a special status (*lex privata*) to clerks that was justified by their station and function. That is the strictly judicial meaning of the term "privilege," and it is also the origin of the special status given to the church and its ministers. Although this status evolved over the centuries in its practical applications, its fundamental inspiration remained the same.

During the Middle Ages the special rights extended to clerks tended to protect them from attacks on the dignity of their function, to exempt them from public duties incompatible with their position, to shield them from civil justice, and to assure them a fair means of subsistence in all circumstances. These rights were expressed in four privileges, which gave rise to many quarrels with civil authority and to numerous writings.

The privilege of the canon (*privilegium canonis*) stated that any person who struck a clerk was subject to excommunication, and only the pope could give absolution for this crime. Various councils and popes had already pronounced sentences as serious as excommunication on those who attacked clerks, but these were unusual measures. The Second Lateran Council (1139) made excommunication a general measure valid in all Christendom, and this provision was the subject of canon 15 of the council.

Under privilege of the forum (*privilegium fori*) a clerk could not be summoned before a lay court of justice (*forum*), nor could he be condemned by a lay judge. From the end of the fourth century, bishops insisted on the right to judge their clerk's cases in criminal and civil matters, and opposed any attack on that right. Throughout the Middle Ages popes and councils based the privilege of the forum on both a concession by the state and on divine right.

According to the privilege of exemption or of personal immunity (*privilegium immunitatis*), clerks were exempt (*immunis*) from services and offices incompatible with their station. Since the fourth century Christian emperors had been preoccupied with sparing clerks from certain functions that were either too engrossing (the municipal magistrature,

for example) or too degrading (obligatory labor; *munera sordida*); they also relieved them of unusual fiscal expense and from the obligation of billeting troops on the march. Although the principle endured, its application varied during the Middle Ages. In the Merovingian and Carolingian periods kings called on clerks to perform many public functions because of the lack of educated people; they also asked the church, which enjoyed fiscal exemption, to make voluntary contributions to the public treasury. Under feudalism the same causes produced the same effects. Therefore medieval popes and councils were satisfied simply to affirm the principle of exemption, while authorizing numerous exemptions.

The privilege of competency (*privilegium* or *beneficium competentiae*) allowed clerks in debt to retain the sum (*competentia*) necessary for their honest keep. That is, a creditor could not obtain from a judge the clerk's entire income or property in order to satisfy his debts. The privilege did not derive from Roman law or from a papal decretal but was the result of custom and of many writings that required that a clerk must not be reduced to obtaining his living by unworthy means.

BIBLIOGRAPHY

Sources. Michel Andrieu, ed., *Le pontifical romain au moyen-âge,* 4 vols. (1938–1941); Charles Munier, ed., *Les Statuta ecclesiae antiqua* (1960); Cyrille Vogel and Reinhard Elze, eds., *Le pontifical romano-germanique du dixième siècle,* 2 vols. (1963).

Studies. F. Claeys-Bouuaert, "Clerc," in *Dictionnaire de droit canonique,* III (1942); J. E. Downs, "The Concept of Clerical Immunities," in *Canon Law Studies,* 126 (1941); Alexandre Faivre, *Naissance d'une hiérarchie: Les premières étapes du cursus clérical* (1977); Heinrich Flatten, "Klerus," in *Lexikon für Theologie und Kirche,* VI (1961); Jean Gaudemet, *L'église dans l'empire romain* (1958), 98–185, and *Le gouvernement de l'église à l'époque classique,* II (1979); Roger Gryson, *Les origines du célibat ecclésiastique du premier au septième siècle* (1970); Paul Hinschius, *System des katholischen Kirchenrechts,* I (1869, repr. 1959), 1–195; J. McBride, "Incardination and Excardination of Seculars," in *Canon Law Studies,* 145 (1941); J. McGrath, "The Privilege of the Canon," *ibid.,* 242 (1946); E. Magnin, "Immunités ecclésiastiques," in *Dictionnaire de théologie catholique,* VII (1922); René Metz, "L'accession des mineurs à la cléricature et aux bénéfices ecclésiastiques dans le droit canonique médiéval," in *Recueil de mémoires et travaux publié par la Société d'histoire du droit* (Montpellier), 9 (1974); R. Naz, "Tonsure," in *Dictionnaire de droit canonique,* VII (1965); G. Oesterlé, "Irrégularités," *ibid.,* VI (1957); Pierre de Puniet, *Le pontifical romain,* I (1930), 102–281, and II (1931), 9–62; Johannes Baptist Sägmüller, *Lehrbuch des katholischen Kirchenrechts,* 3rd ed., I (1914), 194–273; A. Villien, "For (privilège du)," in *Dictionnaire de droit canonique,* VI (1957).

RENÉ METZ

[See also **Celibacy; Clerk; Church Organization; Church, Early; Church, Latin: To 1054; Church, Latin: 1054–1305; Church, Latin: 1305–1500; Ordination.**]

CLERGY, BYZANTINE. In the Christian East ecclesiastical institutions developed in the framework of a centralized imperial system, but they were also determined by traditions going back to early Christianity and preserving the autonomy of local churches. Occasional national separatism encouraged decentralization, but the prestige of the imperial church of Constantinople was strong enough to impose a single Byzantine pattern on the entire body of "orthodox" (Melchite) Christians in the Middle East and throughout eastern Europe during the Middle Ages.

Bishops and regional primacies. In the time of Constantine, throughout the Christian East the practice of establishing a bishop in each city (the Greek *polis*) became the norm, but the ancient practice of also having bishops in villages *(chorai)* survived locally. In practice the "village bishops" *(chorepiskopoi)* were gradually deprived of their administrative and sacramental functions. *Novella* 6 of Justinian (A.D. 535) regulated the election of new bishops. It required that three candidates for a vacant episcopal see be nominated "by the clergy and the notables" of the town, and that the "best" be chosen by the metropolitan of the province. In later centuries the selection of candidates was generally made by the other bishops of the province, with the final choice still left to the metropolitan. In important sees, especially Constantinople, imperial will could also be decisive in the selection, even though canons considered the appointment of bishops by civil authorities to be "null." Before the sixth century, numerous married men were elevated to the episcopate, but Justinian required that married candidates be childless and separate from their wives at their consecration. This separation requirement was confirmed by the Quinisext Synod (or Synod in Trullo, 692). However, the synod did not mention childlessness as a prerequisite for ordination.

Since the consecration of each new bishop required the participation of several neighboring bishops (Apostolic Canon 1), and as the First Council of Nicaea in 325 adopted the principle of parallelism between the civil and the ecclesiastical administrations, the bishops of each civil "province" *(provincia;* Greek: *eparchia)* were required to meet twice a year in a council presided over by the bishop of the provincial capital *(metropolis),* who was called the metropolitan. His role in filling the empty sees was enlarged into a ministry of leadership among his fellow bishops. In the late Byzantine Empire the gradual dechristianization of Asia Minor deprived many metropolitans of their suffragans, so that the title alone remained. By special arrangement some bishops were exempt from the jurisdiction of a provincial metropolitan, and depended directly on a patriarch: they were given the title of autocephalous archbishops.

Patriarchs and patriarchates. After Constantine there appeared a strong trend toward centralization. A few major ecclesiastical centers began to exercise leadership on a scale wider than a single province. In the East the original major centers were Alexandria and Antioch, the two major cities of the Byzantine Empire. However, the bishop of the new imperial capital, Constantinople, soon competed for the first place (after the "Old Rome"), which was formally granted to him by the First Council of Constantinople in 381. The Council of Chalcedon in 451 formally acknowledged the existence of five ecclesiastical primacies, first called exarchates of dioceses and later patriarchates: Rome, Constantinople, Alexandria, Antioch, and Jerusalem. Jerusalem was added because it was a major center of pilgrimages and monastic life. In the Byzantine view the rights and privileges of these five centers were determined by purely pragmatic considerations: they were "major cities" of the empire. In the West, however, primacies were seen as originating from "Petrine" foundation. Rome was the main "apostolic" see, but Alexandria and Antioch were also considered "Petrine," because Peter preached in Antioch and sent his disciple Mark to Alexandria. These two different approaches to the origins of the patriarchates led to a direct conflict concerning the position of Constantinople as "New Rome."

Besides the primates of the five patriarchates, which eventually came to constitute a permanent pentarchy in the church, the title of patriarch was also bestowed on the heads of national churches in Georgia, Bulgaria, Serbia, and, much later, Russia.

Together with other primates situated beyond the borders of the empire, the patriarch of Georgia also carried the title of *katholikos*.

The ecumenical patriarchate. Defined by the Council of Chalcedon as enjoying privileges "equal" to those of Old Rome because it was now the residence "of the emperor and the Senate," the archbishopric of Constantinople assumed—apparently under the patriarch John the Faster (582–595)—the title of "ecumenical patriarchate." The title did not imply a usurpation of the honorary primacy of the bishop of Rome, which continued to be recognized, but rather a direct role in the life of the *oikoumene*, the ideally universal Christian empire. According to Canon 28 of Chalcedon, the territory of the patriarchate covered Asia, Pontus, and Thrace. In the eighth century Illyricum and southern Italy were added.

The patriarch governed the church with the cooperation of a permanent synod *(synodos endemousa)* of metropolitans and a numerous staff. Late Byzantine sources, such as the fourteenth-century Pseudo-Codinus, describe the forty-five principal members of the patriarchal court as divided into nine classes of five members each. In the sixth through ninth centuries the patriarchal staff was headed by the *synkellos*, a title that later became honorary. The major functions were then distributed among the *megas oikonomos* (the grand manager of all patriarchal property), the *megas sakkelarios* (in charge of all monastic establishments), the *megas skeuophylax* (in charge of all precious possessions of the church, and supervisor of lands that furnished materials used in the liturgy), and the *megas chartophylax* (chief archivist).

Lower clergy. Men married once (but not to a widow) were admitted to the orders of deacon and priest. Unmarried or widowed women could be deaconesses, who were in charge of women candidates for baptism and later (until the order disappeared in the thirteenth century) of social work. Exempt from certain taxes, the lower clergy were responsible to episcopal courts only, and their lives and obligations were strictly regulated by canon law (see especially the canons of the Synod in Trullo). Secular clergy and monasteries were subject to episcopal jurisdiction, with the exception of stavropegiac monasteries, which were responsible directly to the patriarch. In some monasteries the *hegoumenos*, or abbot, carried the title of archimandrite.

Social obligations. The constantly growing ecclesiastical properties were administered by the bishops or monastic abbots. In *Novella* 120 Justinian defined the obligations of the church in the framework of the unified Christian society. Church revenues were to be used for the upkeep of the clergy, the maintenance of churches and all objects necessary for worship, help to the sick and the poor, and redemption of war prisoners. Consequently, all charitable institutions were placed under the jurisdiction of the bishops. Furthermore, bishops and lower clergy were formally required by the Code of Justinian to supervise the moral behavior of state officials, to oppose arbitrary acts, to visit prisons, and to receive information about the functioning of courts. In some cases bishops were the formal addressees of imperial laws and responsible for their application (for instance, a law of Justinian's protecting women from being forced into dishonorable professions).

BIBLIOGRAPHY

Hans-Georg Beck, *Kirche und theologische Literatur im Byzantinischen Reich* (1959); Louis Bréhier, *Les institutions de l'empire byzantin* (1949); Demetrios J. Constantelos, *Byzantine Philanthropy and Social Welfare* (1968); Francis Dvornik, *The Idea of Apostolicity and the Legend of the Apostle Andrew in Byzantium* (1958).

JOHN MEYENDORFF

[See also **Byzantine Church; Celibacy; Councils (Ecumenical, 325–787); Justinian I, Patriarch; Province, Ecclesiastical.**]

CLERICIS LAICOS, a papal bull issued by Boniface VIII on 24 February 1296. In it, he forbade laymen to tax the clergy or the clergy to pay taxes without papal consent; either violation would incur the immediate penalty of excommunication.

In the thirteenth century taxes in any form represented something of a novelty, and it was neither clear who had the right to impose them nor who had the obligation to pay. In the mid twelfth century the canon lawyer Gratian had found the church not subject to secular taxation, a position the Fourth Lateran Council had reaffirmed in 1215; but since laymen continued to receive church subsidies, notably clerical tenths to finance crusades, confusing ambiguities inevitably arose.

Matters came to a head when, in 1294, England and France went to war, first over Gascony and then over their respective positions in Flanders. Although the French church agreed initially to a two-year subsidy, when King Philip IV the Fair sought its renewal in 1296, he met with growing resistance. The Cistercians refused absolutely and appealed to the pope, calling bishops who agreed to pay "mute dogs" and comparing the king himself with Pharaoh. Boniface responded with *Clericis laicos.*

The bull's opening lines—"Antiquity informs us that laymen have greatly oppressed the clergy, and this is clearly proved by the experiences of the present day"—were based on Gratian, and its fundamental tenets were firmly rooted in canon law. Nevertheless, *Clericis laicos* provoked vigorous opposition, largely because its hostile language and uncompromising positions seemed to suggest an author both overly insistent on his own authority and totally unaware of the extent to which the ways of the world and its governments were changing.

In France a royally convoked clerical assembly responded with the dispatch of bishops to Rome for consultations. The archbishop of Rheims feared that implementation of the bull would lead the king to withdraw all ecclesiastical protection; "this is," he lamented, "the ruin of the Church." On 17 August 1296, Philip forbade the export of gold and silver from the kingdom, thereby cutting off papal revenues, and by November he had begun a concerted propaganda campaign against the pope. In England reactions were scarcely better, for when the archbishop of Canterbury ordered *Clericis laicos* implemented (5 January 1297), Edward I responded on 30 January by outlawing the clergy, a move that denied it all legal recourse if royal officials were to be ordered to confiscate its goods in lieu of taxes.

At first Boniface stood firm, stubbornly clarifying his position with some asperity. By 1297, however, he was forced gradually to give way in the face of a mounting opposition to his pontificate that came to include not just England and France but also Sicily and members of the College of Cardinals. With the issuance of *Etsi de statu* on 31 July 1297, he can be said to have effectively abandoned the views of *Clericis laicos.*

BIBLIOGRAPHY

Thomas S. R. Boase, *Boniface VIII* (1933); Georges Digard, *Philippe le Bel et le saint-siège de 1285 à 1304,* 2 vols. (1936); Georges Digard *et al., Les registres de Boniface VIII,* 4 vols. (1904–1939), I, 584–585, no. 1567; Charles T. Wood, ed. and trans., *Philip the Fair and Boniface VIII,* 2nd ed. (1971, repr. 1976).

CHARLES T. WOOD

[See also **Boniface VIII, Pope; Edward I of England; Philip IV the Fair; Taxation, Church.**]

CLERK. The English words "clerk" and "cleric" come from the Latin *clericus,* which in turn comes from the Greek *kleros.* In the Middle Ages a clerk was a member of the clergy. He could be of any rank, but the term was most often applied to those in minor orders. In the eyes of the law any clerk, however humble, had all the privileges of the clergy, including exemption from trial by secular courts and from most forms of taxation. On the other hand, a clerk was not supposed to marry or engage in business. These rules were not strictly enforced, and there were constant complaints from government officials and urban laymen about married and trading clerks who took advantage of their immunity to make large profits or to engage in illegal activities.

There were two tests to be applied to anyone claiming benefit of clergy. One, easily passed, was tonsure (shaving the crown of the head). A French criminal in the early fourteenth century even managed to get himself tonsured while in a royal prison. The other test was the ability to read. Hence most students, and especially university students, could claim to be members of the clergy. Most, but not all of them, did eventually hold some office in the church, though students at urban grammar schools did not necessarily have an ecclesiastical career.

In the twelfth century an increase in the number of literate men coincided with the growth of political and economic institutions. All men with heavy responsibilities—kings, bishops, great lords, prominent businessmen—needed assistants to keep records, draft letters, and handle administrative details. They drew these men from the educated group of clerics—men who could read, write, and solve simple arithmetical problems. Such men, as opposed to laymen in the government (or business), were called clerks because they were members of the clergy in minor orders. To be a king's clerk, or the clerk of an archbishop or great lord, gave high status, and often high office in the church. The judges and treasurers of England and France were, for the most part, drawn from the men who were clerks, both in the medieval and in the modern sense of the word. The difference was that the medieval clerk, who might begin as a mere letter writer or accountant, could end up as an archbishop, as a chief justice, or as a minister of state. The group of clerks was the best medieval example of "the career open to the talents."

BIBLIOGRAPHY

William Searle Holdsworth, *A History of English Law* (1923), III, ch. 2; Frederick Pollock and Frederic W. Maitland, *The History of English Law*, 2nd ed. (1923), I, ch. 2; Joseph R. Strayer, *The Reign of Philip the Fair* (1980), chs. 2 and 3.

JOSEPH R. STRAYER

[See also **Class Structure; Clergy.**]

CLERMONT, COUNCIL OF. Historians agree that in 1095, in a speech at Clermont, Pope Urban II aroused a militant Christendom to recover the Holy Sepulcher—thereby initiating the Crusades that preoccupied Western society for two centuries.

The success of Urban's appeal derived from several factors. Certainly the eleventh century was more receptive to a *militia Christi* than to the old idea of athletes of Christ suffering torture. Gregory VII had urged Christian knights to help the beleaguered Byzantine Empire after the Battle of Manazkert (1071); and Urban, wishing to follow in Gregory's footsteps, was of course aware of the threat of the Seljuk Turks. In addition, rumors of Turkish atrocities stirred Christendom, and such skilled preachers as Peter the Hermit exploited the situation.

We may assume from the surviving eyewitness accounts that Urban came to Clermont with plans for a crusade. These plans must have taken months to prepare and were not based on a hasty decision at Clermont. Urban held a council at Piacenza in March 1095. A chronicler, Bernold of St. Blaise, relates that he urged Western knights to aid Emperor Alexios I in his struggle with the Turks. However, the pope did not preach a crusade but merely repeated Gregory's earlier appeal.

In the ensuing months Urban journeyed in southern France, and the enthusiastic audience that he found there may have influenced him to make his appeal at Clermont. Urban celebrated the feast of St. Gilles at the abbey named for the saint on 1 September 1095 and remained in the area for one week. Following his stay at St. Gilles, he traversed Languedoc on his way to Clermont.

Urban opened the Council of Clermont on 18 November 1095 and devoted his time to church business. The affair of King Philip I and Bertrada, wife of Fulk, count of Anjou, occupied the attention of the council, which was attended by more than 200 bishops. Urban, confronted with Philip's unwillingness to abandon Bertrada, excommunicated the king and thereby ruled out the possibility of Philip's taking the cross.

The reform legislation issued at Clermont confirmed the work of past councils and attempted to provide for more stringent enforcement. Of the thirty-two canons issued by the council, one confirmed the Truce of God, thereby making it more than a regional truce; another offered a plenary indulgence to those who would go to free God's church in Jerusalem.

On 27 November 1095 Urban addressed a crowd in the hills outside Clermont. He appealed to the pride of the Frankish people, who possessed the heritage of Charlemagne, the great warrior and enemy of Islam. Urban also stressed the brotherhood of Christianity and the obligation of Western Christians to help their Greek brothers, now beset by the Turks. The pope urged knights to abandon private warfare and to fight the infidels, pointing out the importance of the Holy Sepulcher and urging Latins to free it. Emotions of the crowd rose to fever pitch when Urban related the atrocities of the Turks and the suffering of the Christians. At the conclusion of his speech, the crowd shouted *Deus vult* (God wills it) in support of the pope's call.

At this dramatic moment Adémar, bishop of Le Puy, knelt before Urban, took the vow to go to Jerusalem, and received the papal blessing. William, bishop of Orange, and many other clergymen soon followed Adémar's example. At the opportune moment Urban continued his speech and urged volunteers to sew crosses on their garments. Soldiers of the cross now had a common symbol, a uniform identifying them as Christians marching against the infidels.

The pope warned that Crusaders who failed to fulfill their vows would be anathematized. Crusaders who died en route would receive remission of sins and would have a crown in paradise. Families and property of the Crusaders would receive papal protection. The church thereby took over secular rights and extended papal authority.

The day after his speech Urban chose "dearest brother Adémar" as vicar of the expedition and received ambassadors of Raymond IV, count of Toulouse, who pledged their master's aid. Urban set the date for departure of the Crusaders on the feast of the Assumption, 15 August 1096.

After the Council of Clermont, Urban traveled through Aquitaine, Anjou, Maine, and Gascony. On 24 May 1096 he consecrated the church of St. Sernin in Toulouse. Raymond was present, and we may assume that they discussed the forthcoming Crusade. The two met again on 6 July, when Urban dedicated the cathedral during the first session of the Council of Nîmes. On 12 July, in the presence of Urban and the council, Raymond ceded all of his rights to the abbey of St. Gilles and reaffirmed his promise to go to Jerusalem. The pope journeyed from Nîmes to St. Gilles, where he consecrated the altar of the new church. He then returned to Italy, having set the Crusades in motion.

BIBLIOGRAPHY

Fulcher of Chartres, *A History of the Expedition to Jerusalem, 1095–1125*, Harold S. Fink, ed., Frances R. Ryan, trans. (1969), gives a full account of the council, at which, presumably, Fulcher was present. See also Frederic Duncalf, "The Councils of Piacenza and Clermont," in Marshall W. Baldwin, ed., *A History of the Crusades*, I (1955); and Dana C. Munro, "The Speech of Pope Urban II at Clermont, 1095," in *American Historical Review*, 11 (1906).

JOHN H. HILL

[See also **Crusades and Crusader States: To 1192; Urban II, Pope.**]

CLETOROLOGION. See Philotheus.

CLIMATOLOGY. The distinguished French scholar Fernand Braudel, writing about early modern Europe, has questioned rhetorically why so many crucial social and economic trends have so often occurred in various places in Europe at about the same time. He concludes that "one can only imagine one single general answer to this almost complete coincidence: changes in climate."

Climatology, the study of climate and its related phenomena, has become a subject of increasing importance and concentration for medievalists, particularly for specialists in social and economic history. Braudel is by no means alone in his climatic determinism. Another French scholar, the medievalist Georges Duby, came to similar conclusions for the early medieval West; the American paleoclimatologist Ellsworth Huntington claimed that a series of central Asian dry spells led to the cyclic eruptions of Turkic and Mongol nomads east and west, and on one occasion led to the fall of the western half of the Roman Empire; and the Swedish historian Gustav Utterström attributed the general European crises of the fourteenth–fifteenth and seventeenth centuries to

colder weather. Indeed, a school of environmental determinists has evolved, stressing the autonomous effects of factors such as weather and certain exogenous infectious diseases (like bubonic plague) on the development of Western civilization.

While few authorities discount entirely the role of climate in European history, some question the extreme degree of causation championed by the environmental determinists. Among the most prominent of these skeptics is Emmanuel Le Roy Ladurie, who has demonstrated that much of the data used by paleoclimatologists is entirely local in character, sporadic in incidence, and often unreliable. He has suggested that many of the assumptions of Huntington, Utterström, and others were based on a priori arguments. For example they state that because wine was no longer produced in England in the later Middle Ages, the climate must have been colder—rather than looking for alternative, perhaps indigenous, socioeconomic changes. But irrespective of the particulars of the climatology debate, all parties to it agree on the ultimate importance of weather in shaping medieval history. European society was primarily rural, and its economic well-being hinged directly on agrarian production. Climate played a major role in grain production and animal husbandry, and therein, rather than in whether the weather triggered barbarian invasions or the discovery of America, lies the greatest importance of climatology.

One of the things Le Roy Ladurie questioned most closely was the evidence used by historical climatologists. Until the 1950's most scholars studying the history of climate, be they geographers, meteorologists, or historians, had one thing in common: they based most of their conclusions on archival research. Taken alone, these records have proved inadequate. They are too sporadic, referring only to specific, often unspectacular incidents, and rarely provide such climatological basics as accurate temperature or precipitation readings. Further, narrative information tends to be highly local in its coverage and often is highly inaccurate.

More recent researchers have expanded their efforts to include more physical and scientific evidence, specifically dendrochronology, phenology, pollen counts, carbon 14 half-life dating, and the study of glacial movements. Dendrochronology, the best-known and most widely used of these newer methods, is the study of tree rings and their growth curves. Certain species of hardwood tree have annual, concentric growth rings; by measuring each ring and its distance from and relationship to the tree's center, then correcting for age factors—trees grow most quickly in their first years—data can be taken for the weather in each given year. The data can then be plotted as growth curves, the x axis representing the sequence of years and the y axis showing the thickness of the rings.

Dendrochronology has its shortcomings. First, most European trees are not sufficiently long-lived to provide data for the Middle Ages. The only exceptions are certain hardwoods in central Germany and southern Scandinavia. The best trees for dendrochronological studies are in North America, and the most detailed studies of climate in the northern hemisphere between 500 and 1500 have been carried out for the southwestern United States. Applying such data to Europe, as some scholars have done, belies the "scientificity" of the entire dendrochronological process.

There is a second problem, even when appropriate trees can be found. In temperate zones it is virtually impossible to use tree rings to distinguish between warm and cold and wet and dry. If a tree ring from, say, Bavaria is very large, it is hard to tell whether its size is due to warm weather or wet weather, or a combination of the two, since all three conditions are conducive to growth. Alternatively, a narrow ring may represent unusual cold, dryness, or a combination of both. In extreme climates, where one of the above factors is controlled, the dendrochronological process is simplified and made more accurate. In Scandinavia, for example, where it is generally wet, a large ring usually signifies a warm year. In North Africa, where it is generally warm, a large ring signifies a wet season. But in more temperate areas of Europe, basically three-quarters of its landmass, such absolute distinctions are difficult to make. Dendrochronology is one of the best methods of investigation for the paleoclimatologist, but it is most useful when corroborated by other sources, such as the radioactivity of the half-lives of carbon or oxygen isotopes.

Phenology is a combination of scientific and archival methods. It is based on the correlation of temperature and the dates of blooming of plants and flowers, especially vines. When it is warm and sunny, harvests are early; when it is cold and damp, they are late. The recording of such harvest data was done regularly, almost religiously, in certain regions and time periods, such as seventeenth- and eighteenth-century France. Unfortunately, such regularity has not been found for any part of Europe before the mid sixteenth century. For medieval Europe there are only some isolated phenological data for late medieval France, and while unexplored Italian evidence might yield information, nothing has been discovered to date.

Two other methods of climatological research are movements of glaciers and pollen studies, coordinated with radiocarbon data. Observation of glacier movements is self-explanatory. Its major limitation is geographic. Only a few regions in Europe have glaciers, notably the Alps, parts of Scandinavia, and the North Atlantic islands, especially Greenland. Hence, even when it is available, glacial evidence presents localized results similar to those from archival records, with the same inherent shortcomings.

In many ways pollen counts corroborated by radiocarbon evidence are the most promising source of information for medieval climatology. They rely on examination of pollen breakdowns in peat bogs and the vegetable materials that have accumulated in them over the centuries. When they are done in glacial areas, such as the Tirol, data can be collected for places covered and exposed time and again, according to the glaciers' movements. Pollen investigation has the additional advantage of being geographically broad-based. Most parts of Europe have some swamp, bog, or marsh areas. Temporal pollen diagrams of selected wild and domestic plants can be made, showing detailed changes in vegetation patterns. But therein lies the weakness of pollen counts; they show plant development per se, rather than climatic changes, and do not account for possible manipulation by humans or animals. All weather data taken from pollen counts must be extrapolated.

Clearly, no single source or technique can provide definitive data on medieval climate. All the methods discussed must be combined, but even then the data are not definitive. All the information must be considered in light of its shortcomings, its inherently local quality, and the fact that by comparison to more conventional and traditional methods of historical investigation, the methods of the climatologist are somewhat haphazard.

In the Middle Ages as now, Europe was divided into three broad climatic zones: a Mediterranean zone, covering most of Iberia, southern France, Italy, and the Balkan coast, along with contiguous parts of North Africa and the Middle East; a middle, temperate zone, north of the great mountain ranges, running east from the British Isles through the Low Countries, northern and central France, Germany, and then in a narrowing strip into Russia; and a frigid northern zone, including the North Atlantic islands, Scandinavia, the eastern Baltic hinterlands, northern Russia, and the higher districts of the Alps and the Pyrenees.

All three regions have distinguishing climatic characteristics. The Mediterranean climate is the mildest of the three, and gives its region a unity that at times transcends racial, religious, and national boundaries. It is largely dictated by the Atlantic Ocean and the Sahara Desert. The Atlantic brings mist and moisture; the Sahara, dry, hot air. In winter the Atlantic predominates: from September until the middle of March, a succession of depressions drifts eastward, carrying cool winds and precipitation, the latter often heavy but usually irregular in frequency. Winter in the Mediterranean zone is usually unsettled, and in the Middle Ages a great deal of human activity ceased. Shipping, piracy, and warfare all ground to a halt. Warfare provides a fine example of climate's historical role. It became more difficult to row galleys, so navies rested and reprovisioned. Winter was a time of economic hardship, but was peaceful politically.

From mid March until September, the Sahara takes control of the Mediterranean climatic patterns. After a few short weeks of spring comes a long, hot summer. The region dries up, and parts of it become susceptible to drought. But the sea is calm and shipping resumes. Such a climate has enormous effect on the local flora and fauna. Crops are reduced to the triad of wheat, olives, and vines; and cattle can rarely be kept with any degree of success. With little fodder and limited pasture, the Mediterranean's livestock, primarily sheep and goats, are puny by north European standards. In summer the region has clear, beautiful skies but too little rain, and when precipitation does come, it often appears in the proverbial "buckets," flooding fields, ruining crops, and running off before it can be fully absorbed into the soil. Harsh southern winds from the Sahara, the infamous siroccos, come periodically and blow much of the grain crops away. All in all, climatic conditions in the Middle Ages made agriculture a risky business throughout the Mediterranean.

By contrast, Europe's temperate middle zone was well suited to agriculture and animal husbandry. Temperatures appear to have averaged about 21°C to 24°C in summer and −4°C to −1°C in winter, and in their own right rarely proved to be an obstacle to farming. As in the Mediterranean zone, the major climatic factor in the temperate region was precipitation; but just as too little was the principal problem in the south, there was often too much in the north. Parts of the temperate zone—the eastern and northern sections of the British Isles, the North Sea and Baltic Sea coasts of the Low Countries, Germany, Jutland, and Sweden—suffered from so much precipitation that they had to be drained before they could be cultivated. High levels of precipitation also fostered the dense growth of deciduous and coniferous forests, which covered perhaps 80 percent of Europe north of the Alps in A.D. 500. Cutting down these forests and developing machines that could till the damp, heavy soils beneath them proved a major problem for medieval farmers. But when the forest finally did give way to the plow, the temperate zone became one of the most fertile areas in the world.

Europe's third climatic zone was its most formidable. The northern region was covered with coniferous forest right up to the Arctic Circle, and snow lay on the ground for six to ten months each year. It has very cold, generally wet winters, and very short, rather cool summers. Fewer than five months a year have average temperatures above 10°C, and in many areas winter lows average between −28°C and −34°C. This least hospitable part of Europe was highly sensitive to any changes in climate, was the most difficult to farm, and consequently was the least populated.

Climate is a function of time, and because of this its changes can be broken into crude temporal epochs. The first such general application of climatology to medieval history concerns the fall of the western part of the Roman Empire. In the nineteenth century the Russian intellectual Peter Kropotin, fascinated by petrified vegetation on the central Asian steppes, put forth a theory that the steppes had grown progressively drier in historical times. A century later the American paleoclimatologist Ellsworth Huntington developed this idea more extensively. He claimed that the weather generally came in cyclic systems, sometimes bringing series of depressions, or lows, that moved from west to east. These depressions brought rain with them, and the greater their frequency, the more precipitation an area received. But Huntington also claimed that shifts in these cycles caused by a dominance of the Sahara rather than the Atlantic system caused a series of waves of desiccation. These dry waves became increasingly pronounced as they moved east, creating the steppes and then the deserts of central Asia.

Huntington believed that the weather cycles during the biblical and classical eras, approximately 2000 B.C. to A.D. 200, were Atlantic-dominated, providing both the Mediterranean and Asia with good weather. But from about A.D. 200 the situation changed. A new Saharan system developed, decreased the frequency of moisture cycles, and brought about a dramatic diminution of rainfall. Throughout the period of the Roman Empire, this meant a retreat of the arable; in North Africa and southern Italy, the breadbaskets of the empire, it was accompanied by an erosion of topsoil. In central Asia, which had a far more extreme climate than the Mediterranean, it meant pastoral disaster. Hence, what Huntington called "the pulse of Central Asia," the migration of the region's Turkic and Mongol peoples seeking greener pastures for their herds, began to throb. The Huns and other tribes moved east, then west, and were important catalysts in Rome's demise. So convinced of Huntington's theory were many of his contemporaries that one disciple, C. E. P. Brooks, actually turned the argument around and constructed a graph of precipitation in Asia based on the Mongol invasions.

More recently paleoclimatologists have been skeptical of Huntington's method and conclusions, and a few scholars have gone so far as to discount entirely the cyclical approach, pointing to an inherent stability in long-term temperature readings, and a striking similarity in flora and fauna throughout the historical era. But most authorities do see some merit in the approach. They distinguish several climatic cycles, beginning with a "big optimum," a period of mild weather from the end of the great Ice Age until about 1400–1300 B.C., when the Alpine glaciers began to advance once again. This advance, a second cycle, continued until about 300 B.C. and the advent of a third cycle, roughly coincident with the Roman era and lasting to A.D. 400. This third cycle was characterized by moderate temperatures and regular levels of precipitation, along with a significant retreat of the Alpine glaciers.

Further, from A.D. 350/400 there is considerable evidence that corroborates the Huntington theory. Dozens of narrative records attest to a succession of droughts in central Asia. While hundred-year measures of total rainfall from the second and the fourth centuries are about the same, those from the fourth century are less well distributed. Virtually all experts agree that the amount of arable within the empire began to shrink after 350, and in some places the land returned to its natural state. There are many possible social, economic, or political explanations for this phenomenon, and one cannot assume, as did Huntington, that climatic conditions were the sole

reason. But this shrinkage of arable, the literary evidence, and the data of glacial advance and retreat suggest that a modified version of Huntington's cyclical theory has merit, and that at the beginning of the Middle Ages Europe's climate was deteriorating.

More light is shed on this issue by carbon and oxygen isotope half-lives and by pollen studies in peat bogs from Denmark and northern Germany. While central Asia seems to have become warmer and drier, Europe from 350/400 to 750 seems to have become colder and wetter. The increased precipitation presented the greater problem. It facilitated growth of the already extensive deciduous forests, made grain growing more difficult, and restricted the types of grains that might be planted. On several estates in northern France, peasants began to divide arable into two types, warm and cold soils. Warm soils were those with light, easily drained humus; although they were comparatively easy to till, they were ultimately less productive. Cold soils were those with thick, heavy topsoils, often covered by marsh or forest. They were potentially the richest arable on the Continent, but in the first centuries of the Middle Ages could seldom be planted.

Duby has collected detailed information on the movement of Fernau Glacier in the Tirol. Carbon 14 half-life analyses of its peat bog pollens show a diminishing of vegetable materials, which further confirms the probability of inclement climatic conditions. Contemporaries, too, noticed them. Gregory of Tours, writing in the sixth century, observed: "the winters were grievous, and more severe than usual, so that streams were held in chains of frost and furnished a path for people like dry ground. Birds too were affected by the cold and hunger, and were caught in the hand without any snare when the snow was deep." Pollen diagrams charting vegetable remains from peat bogs in central Germany corroborate the evidence from France and Tirol. There was a continuous retreat of plant life from the fifth century through the eighth, and on the northern slope of the Alps there was even a retreat of the tree line.

It is important to put this climatic decline in full perspective. Le Roy Ladurie and Duby agree that the annual average diminution in temperature was at most about 1°C from the classical era. But, coupled with the increased precipitation, for which no actual data are available, it was enough to curtail certain forms of agriculture throughout the West and retard the process of clearing the forest.

The glacier and pollen evidence suggests an improvement in Europe's weather between 750/800 and 1150/1200. Paleoclimatologists have labeled this period "the early medieval warm" or, more commonly, "the little optimum," in contrast with "the big optimum" of prehistory. In the late eighth century the Alpine glaciers began to retreat. Pollen studies suggest that beech trees in forests along the Fernau Glacier and in the Ardennes Forest of northern France expanded to their A.D. 200 borders. In central Germany a number of deciduous species that apparently vanished after 200 reappeared, and cores of foraminifera lay along its North Atlantic coast. Both changes were indicative of a warming trend, which probably exceeded an average of 1°C over the average temperatures in the period 350/400 to 750. The entire era 750/800 to 1150/1200 was characterized by milder winters and generally dry summers.

The "little optimum" has been credited with facilitating a number of political, social, and economic events. Some scholars, again noting the overriding importance of agrarian activities to the medieval economy, attribute to it and a number of technological innovations the great increase of foodstuffs between the ninth and twelfth centuries. Others credit it with the era's growing sea and land travel, expanding trade and urbanization, and even the entire "commercial revolution" of the High Middle Ages. Perhaps the most important implications concern Scandinavia. From the ninth through the eleventh centuries Viking raiders pillaged, traded with, and settled much of northern and central Europe. Among the more compelling theories that explain their appearance is the warming trend of the "little optimum" in the far north. More land was cultivated in Scandinavia, population rose and pressed even on the newly expanded resources, opportunities at home diminished, and many young men went abroad to seek their fortunes.

Many of the theories connecting warmer, drier weather and greater activity, especially in Europe's central climatic zone, are at best highly tentative. But one phase of Scandinavian activity can almost certainly be attributed to the better weather. This was the settlement of the North Atlantic islands, Greenland, and perhaps even parts of the North American coast. In the far north a warming trend of even 1°C meant a great deal. Pollen analysis shows a general northward advance of cereal grains, especially in Sweden but also in Norway and Iceland. Glaciers in the North Atlantic receded toward the polar icecap, opening direct sea routes from Norway to Iceland, Iceland to Greenland, and perhaps Greenland to Labrador. Most paleoclimatologists believe that in the eleventh and twelfth centuries all the northern waters were ice-free. Whether Norsemen actually settled in Canada between the eighth and eleventh centuries remains a subject of acute historical debate; that Greenland and Iceland were colonized, permanently in the case of the latter, is not.

There was another important aspect of the "little optimum." As the weather grew warmer, it also became perceptibly drier. For Europe's northern and central zones the decrease in rainfall proved fortunate for grain growing. For the intrinsically drier Mediterranean zone it had more mixed results. Evidence from peat stratigraphy, the geological examination of peat layers, indicates that the lack of rainfall combined with warmer weather to cause more rapid evaporation of groundwater, which in turn led to a series of droughts in Castile, Aragon, and southern Italy. Sometimes the lack of precipitation had adverse effects even in the north. Excavations of the Sarthe River in north-central France suggest that it dried up at least three times during the "little optimum," becoming almost wadilike. The combination of higher temperatures, lower levels of precipitation, and rapid evaporation could disrupt planting schedules, and at times may have been responsible for drawing waves of locusts north from Africa. In 873 they were seen from Iberia to Germany; in 1195, at the very end of the "little optimum," they were as far northeast as the Carpathians. In general, then, the warmer, drier weather of the period 750 to 1150/1200 was usually, although not always, of help to farmers in the north, and somewhat problematic to those in the Mediterranean basin.

By the late twelfth century the 400 years of the "little optimum" drew to a close. From 1150/1200 it grew colder and wetter once again, a circumstance that persisted until sometime between 1300 and 1350. In many ways this era is the most difficult to research. Records are very limited, and most information comes from archival evidence, particularly concerning manorial estates in southern and central England. The best scientific data come from the Alpine glaciers Fernau, Vernagt, Aletsch, and Grindelwald. All advanced for the first time since the eighth century, the Alpine tree line retreating in their path. Radiocarbon data from Aletsch's peat bogs show that they reached a maximum retreat from 1200 to 1230. Those from Grindelwald reached their apex by 1280, and the others at some point between 1215 and 1300. Another glacier, Allalin, in the Saaser Visp Valley in Switzerland, was a major pasture area in the eleventh and twelfth centuries. Archival records from a number of livestock farmers show that the northern pastures in the valley, which had been used for hundreds of years, had to be abandoned because of the advancing glaciers, and could not be used again until after 1350.

Additional evidence of the new cold era comes from Scandinavia. As the "little optimum" had proved to be a period of expansion, so the thirteenth and fourteenth centuries were an era of contraction. Ice floes drifted far to the south, blocking traditional North Atlantic shipping lanes. The most direct westerly routes from Norway to Iceland to Greenland had to be given up, with the crucial Bergen-to-Reykjavík route thus increased by 400 miles. At certain junctures in the fourteenth century, Norwegian ships could not supply the Icelanders with foodstuffs, and the Icelanders had to reorient their trade south to the British Isles. For the Greenland settlements the new dislocations proved fatal. Many of the west coast fjords were blocked completely, part of the freeze that has recently been corroborated by research on twelfth- and thirteenth-century Alaskan glaciers. One Greenland farm after another had to be abandoned as the growing season grew shorter and shorter. A famous text describing the problem survives from a Norwegian priest, Ivar Baardson, who served as steward to Greenland's bishop of Garder from 1341 to 1364:

> From Snefelness in Iceland to Greenland, the shortest way had always been the following: two days and three nights, sailing due west. In the middle of the sea there are reefs called Gunbierneshier. That was the old route, but now the ice has come from the north, so close to the reefs that none can sail by the old route without risking his life.

The colder weather coincided with the end of European expansion in the High Middle Ages and the beginning of the crisis of the later Middle Ages. It was part of a general era of colder, wetter weather that many paleoclimatologists call the "little ice age," in which Europe's weather was as inclement as it had been during the Dark Ages, and perhaps as bad as any time period since the great Ice Age of prehistory.

There is some debate about the extent of the "little ice age." Most authorities agree that it began at some point early in the thirteenth century, and that the late sixteenth and seventeenth centuries marked its nadir, just before the modern climatic amelioration beginning in the eighteenth century. The major controversy focuses on the 200-year period from

1350 to 1550. Utterström believed that the entire period 1250–1750 was a half-millennium of poor weather, and was directly responsible for Europe's late medieval and seventeenth-century crises.

Using the archival records that Utterström researched, and then supplementing them with the newer scientific methods, Le Roy Ladurie came to different conclusions. He acknowledged a thrust of the Alpine glaciers from 1215 to 1350, but claimed that these glaciers retreated from 1350 to 1550. Good evidence from pollen analysis shows him to be correct for Aletsch and Grindelwald, and additional narrative records claim that the high pasture lands of the Saaser Visp Valley were usable once again. Le Roy Ladurie is cautious in his assessment. The fourteenth and fifteenth centuries, he argues, were not overly mild, and certainly not as balmy as the twelfth and thirteenth centuries had been.

Further, in Europe's northern climatic zone there seems to have been little respite from cold temperatures, no resumption of the thirteenth-century shipping routes, and no new settlements founded in Greenland. Even more important, while temperatures did rise slightly in the central and southern climatic zones, the high levels of precipitation persisted and may even have become worse. Archival sources show unprecedented flooding in the 1310's, 1390's, and 1430's, 1450's, and 1470's throughout western Europe. It was this continued wetness that, at least in part, prevented an agricultural resurgence and exacerbated the rural crisis that had begun around 1200/1250.

As a brief postscript to the Middle Ages, the worst, coldest, and wettest weather of the "little ice age," it is generally agreed, came late in the sixteenth century. From about 1550 all the Swiss-Austrian glaciers began a steady advance. Mine shafts throughout the northern face of the Alps and the Carpathians froze. The North Atlantic glaciers began to move south, and in central Europe the pace of *Wüstungen,* the abandoning of villages, increased at least in part because of deteriorating climatic conditions. In the Alpine village of Le Châtelard, fields were abandoned that had been used even in the thirteenth century. Obviously climate was not the sole factor in causing these conditions, but it seems to have played a crucial role.

In sum, a likely chronology of European weather from 200 to 1600 probably went as follows. From 200 to some point late in the fourth century, Europe's climate was generally good, at least when judged by agricultural standards. From 400 to 750 it grew colder and wetter. From 750 to 1150/1200 it became warmer and drier, and from 1200 to 1300/1350 it got colder and wetter once again. There is considerable debate among experts as to the state of the weather during the fourteenth and fifteenth centuries, but most agree that while temperatures moderated somewhat, the high levels of precipitation continued. Then, in the sixteenth century, climate reached a nadir, in terms of both temperature and rainfall.

It must be reemphasized that medieval Europe was an overwhelmingly rural society, dependent for the vast bulk of its wealth on the produce of the land. Because of the weather's direct influence on the agrarian economy, its importance to medieval history is paramount. A detailed assessment of the relationship of climate and farm productivity has been made by the Dutch historian B. H. Slicher van Bath. He assembled a calendar describing optimum conditions for growing wheat in the Netherlands and eastern England. During September planting the weather should be damp. From October to 20 December it should remain damp, but temperatures should not be too mild. From 21 December through the end of February, ideal conditions include generally dry weather and minimal snow, temperatures remaining above $-10°C$, and no strong winds. In March one climatic condition is essential: no frost. In April regular rains are best, with extended sunny intervals. From 1 May to 15 June temperatures should be warm but not hot, and rainfall should be regular. From 16 June to 10 July cool, cloudy weather with moderate precipitation is ideal, and from 10 July through August conditions are best when dry and warm, with no heat waves.

The English rural historian J. Z. Titow has applied similar strategy to correlating climatic conditions and grain yields from the estates of the bishop of Winchester, in south-central England. Good autumn harvests came when summers and autumns of the previous years were dry, winters were either average or severe, and springs were dry. Bad harvests came from one of two circumstances: autumn of the previous year was very wet, soaking the fields, followed by a wet winter and summer, or the previous autumn was wet, the winter average, and the summer dry. The Titow data, covering the period 1209 to 1350 and based on extensive archival research from more than 800 texts, corroborates the Le Roy Ladurie thesis that precipitation was the key element of medieval weather. Too much, especially in the central and northern zones, washed away topsoil,

killed seedlings, blanched wheat, allowed weeds to flourish, and paved the way for famine. Too little, especially in the south, meant insufficient nutriment for crops and, when coupled with strong winds, the blowing away of topsoil.

In broad terms, what was the impact of climate on medieval Europe? Can the fall of Rome and the barbarian invasions, as Huntington has suggested, be attributed in some degree to recurring dry spells in central Asia? Can the "commercial revolution" and the fruition of High medieval Europe be explained by the "little optimum," or the decline of the later Middle Ages by the onset of a new ice age? Given the paucity of proper data, it is hard to say. Many such direct correlations are simplistic and overdrawn, but often contain elements of truth. There are many contradictions in trying to explain the relationship of weather and specific events, along with their consequences. For example, the Germanic peoples of 200 B.C. allegedly left Scandinavia because of the cold. Yet the Vikings of the ninth century purportedly left because it was too warm. Historical climatologists must, above all other things, be cautious in their conclusions. They must avoid making a priori judgments and circular arguments. Archival research must be combined with newer scientific methods. But the role of climate in influencing farm techniques is assured, and for this reason alone is of major importance.

BIBLIOGRAPHY

The basic reference is Emanuel Le Roy Ladurie, *Histoire du climat*, trans. as *Times of Feast, Times of Famine* (1971), with extensive bibliography. Also see Robert I. Rotberg and Theodore K. Rabb, *Climate in History* (1981). Important articles by Le Roy Ladurie are "Histoire et climat," in *Annales: Économies, sociétés, civilisations*, **14** (1959); "Aspects historiques de la nouvelle climatologie," in *Revue historique*, **226** (1961); and "Le climat des xi et xvi siècles, séries comparées," in *Annales E.S.C.*, **20** (1965).

An alternative explanation to that of Le Roy Ladurie is in Gustav Utterström, "Climatic Fluctuations and Population Problems in Early Modern History," in *Scandinavian Economic History Review*, **3** (1955). The primary work by Ellsworth Huntington is *Civilization and Climate*, 3rd ed. (1971). See also Charles E. P. Brooks, *Climate Through the Ages*, 2nd ed. (1970).

An example of climatic history using archival evidence is J. Z. Titow, "Evidence of Weather in the Account Rolls of the Bishopric of Winchester, 1209–1350," in *Economic History Review*, 2nd ser., **12** (1959); and *Winchester Yields* (1972). For Greenland see *Meddeleser om Gronland*, XX (1899), 322. On dendrochronology see A. E. Douglass, *Cli-*

matic Cycles and Tree Growth (1971); and D. J. Shove and A. W. G. Lowther, "Tree Rings and Medieval Archaeology," in *Medieval Archaeology*, **1** (1957). On phenology see A. Angot, "Étude sur les vendages en France," in *Annales du Bureau central météorologique de France* (1883). Crucial to dating meteorological events are Charles E. Britton, ed., *A Meteorological Chronology to 1450* (1937); and Curt Weikinn, *Quellentexte zur Witterungsgeschichte Europas von der Zeitwende bis zum Jahre 1850*, 4 vols. (1958–1967).

Other important works include D. J. Shove, "Discussion: Postglacial Climate Change," in *Quarterly Journal of the Royal Meteorological Society*, **75** (1949); M. Stuiver and H. E. Suess, "On the Relationship Between Radiocarbon Dates and True Sample Ages," in *Radiocarbon*, **8** (1966). Of general use is Wilhelm Abel, *Agarkrisen und Agarkonjunktur*, 3rd ed. (1978). Works by Georges Duby are *Rural Economy and Country Life in the Medieval West*, Cynthia Postan, trans. (1968), and *The Early Growth of the European Economy*, Howard B. Clarke, trans. (1974). Works by Fernand Braudel are *The Mediterranean*, 2 vols. (1972), and *Capitalism and Material Life* (1973). See also B. H. Slicher van Bath, "Les problèmes fondamentaux de la société préindustrielle en Europe," in *A. A. G. Bijdragen*, **12** (1965).

ROBERT S. GOTTFRIED

[See also **Agriculture and Nutrition: Northern Europe** and **The Mediterranean Region**.]

CLIPEUS (CLIPEATUS), Latin term for a round shield, a shape used to frame portrait busts of honored figures from the Hellenistic period onward; hence, a medallion portrait.

LESLIE BRUBAKER

CLOCKS AND RECKONING OF TIME. Prior to the advent of the mechanical escapement clock, which first appeared in the late thirteenth or early fourteenth century, timekeeping was achieved by means of sundials and water clocks. These had evolved in a wide range of simple and complex forms in the Hellenistic and Roman cultures, and knowledge of their construction and use was transmitted to Islam, where they underwent an even greater degree of development.

The hours for Muslim prayer were determined by a sundial in the mosque; and portable examples, when correctly oriented, indicated the azimuth or di-

rection of Mecca that Muslims faced while praying. Numerous treatises on sundials were produced, of which the most comprehensive was the thirteenth-century work of Abū ʿAlī al-Ḥasan ibn Alī ibn ʿUmar al-Marrākushī of Morocco. The earliest known surviving Islamic sundial was made for the Zangid sultan of Syria in the mid twelfth century.

In the West the sundial was utilized by the Christian church primarily to establish the hours for prayer and not for telling time in the general sense of the word. One of its earliest forms was the "scratch dial," a type found in England as early as A.D. 670. In its primitive form the scratch dial consisted of a half circle having hour lines radiating from the center of the upper edge, at which point a metal gnomon was inserted. The daylight hours were divided and marked into four "tides" of approximately equal length used by the Saxons for their time division. Some of the dials were marked into six or eight parts, possibly to correspond to other systems of dividing the day; others had only one or two lines, unequally spaced, believed to indicate the times of celebration of church offices. At first these dials were literally scratched into the southern walls of churches; later they were inscribed on separate slabs of stone applied to the walls. Portable dials serving the same purpose also were used; a typical Saxon pocket dial was recovered in 1939 from a cloister of Canterbury Cathedral.

The clepsydra or water clock was used by the Greeks and Romans to regulate their law courts and their military watches, for astronomical measurement, and for the operation of automata. About 30 B.C. Vitruvius recorded a variety of sundials as well as hydraulic timepieces. Anaphoric clocks, having astrolabical dials for astronomical use, are believed to have been invented by Hipparchus about 140 B.C. Tangible evidence of the transmission of clockwork through Roman as well as Islamic sources exists in surviving fragments of two Roman anaphoric dials, one found at Grand in the Vosges and the other at Salzburg, both dated in the second century of the Christian era. In such a clock a model of the sun on a pin was plugged into one of the 360 openings drilled at equal distances around the band of the ecliptic, and could be moved each day to keep the clock current with the seasonal variation of the times of sunrise and sunset. The dial, consisting of a sheet of bronze, was powered by a float rising in a clepsydra jar and connected by a rope or chain to a counterweight. The sphere was mapped onto the plane surface by stereographic projection, and it revolved clockwise behind a fixed grid of wires marking the lines of altitude and azimuth.

Also linked to the later history of timekeeping is the invention of the gear at about the time of Archimedes, and the subsequent development of such sophisticated geared devices as the calendrical or computing machine of about 87 B.C., fragments of which were recovered off the island of Antikythera in 1900.

The Arabic texts transmitted to the West and then translated brought knowledge of Islamic forms of the sundial and the clock. Five books of the *Libros del saber de astronomía* of King Alfonso X of Castile are devoted to devices for the measurement of time. A water clock, a mercury clock, a candle clock, and two sundials are described, based on translations of Arabic treatises made about 1276 or 1277. Four of these translations were done by Isaac ben Sid, and the one on the candle clock by Samuel Ha-Levi Abulafia. The water clock was a simple, water-powered device having a float at one end of a cord and a counterweight at the other, the cord passing around an axle attached to a dial and causing it to rotate and to operate an alarm.

It is not known with certainty whether the water clock of medieval Europe was derived exclusively from Islam or also persisted from the Roman tradition of the anaphoric clock. Its purpose was not to measure the hours but to sound an alarm, and it was

in use by the twelfth century in monastic houses, and possibly earlier.

The earliest known description of the construction of a water-clock alarm is preserved in a tenth- or twelfth-century manuscript in the Benedictine monastery of Maria de Ripoll. It consisted of an axle turned by a weight hung from a rope; the weight in turn served as a flair or striker of a series of small bells hung from a rod. The device required resetting after every use.

Confirmation of the prevalence of water clocks in monastic houses is found in several of the regulations of the Cistercian Rule of the early twelfth century. Rule CXIV specified that the sacristan was to be instructed to set the "clock" and cause it to sound on winter weekdays before lauds, unless it was daylight. He was to use it to awaken himself each day before vigils and then proceed to light the dormitory of the church. Rules LXXIV and LXXXIII contain other references to the uses made of the clock as the regulator of the life of the monastic community. In the eleventh century Abbot William of Hirsau had provided his sacristan with similar instructions, and the rule of the monastery of St. Victor in Paris required that the registrar, or companion of the sacristan, adjust the clock.

A water clock figured in a fire that occurred in 1198 at the abbey of Bury St. Edmunds, as reported in the *Chronicle* of Jocelin of Brakelond. The fire originated on the wooden platform bearing the shrine of the relics of St. Edmund. Just as the clock sounded for matins, the master of the vestry arose and saw the conflagration. He gave the alarm and the monks ran for water—some to the well, and others to the clock—while the other brethren attempted to smother the flames with their cowls.

Some slate fragments recovered at Villers Abbey were found to be dated 1267 or 1268 and to be inscribed with a memorandum to the sacristan and his assistants, giving instructions for the correct setting of the clock for each day of the year, according to the varying lengths of daylight and darkness. It also noted that after the clock was set, the water supply in the reservoir was to be replenished to a prescribed level from a pot provided for the purpose, and that the same procedure was to be followed after compline, to assure the sacristan of uninterrupted sleep.

A market for water clocks existed outside the monastic houses, for by 1183 a guild of water-clock makers existed in Cologne, and by 1220 there were enough shops of water-clock makers to justify

Water clock of al-Jazarī. Arabian manuscript, 1354. COURTESY, MUSEUM OF FINE ARTS, BOSTON, GOLOUBEW COLLECTION

Monastic water clock. From a *Bible moralisée*, late 13th century.
BODLEIAN LIBRARY, OXFORD

changing the name of the street along which they were located to Urlogingasse.

One of the most important statements concerning the state of the clock in the Middle Ages occurs in manuscript copies of the lecture notes of Robertus Anglicus, used in his course of commentaries on the *Sphere* of Sacrobosco. The commentaries were compiled in 1271, when Robertus was lecturing at the University of Paris or the University of Montpellier. He wrote:

> Nor is it possible for any clock to follow the judgment of astronomy with complete accuracy. Yet clockmakers are trying to make a wheel which will make one complete revolution for every one of the equinoctial circle, but they cannot quite perfect their work. But if they could, it would be a really accurate clock and worth more than the astrolabe or other astronomical instruments for reckoning the hours, if one knew how to do this according to the method aforesaid.

Robertus went on to describe the use of the falling weight for powering a dial that would make a complete revolution between sunrise and sunset.

This statement has been taken to mean that although clockmakers were struggling to perfect a mechanical escapement clock in his time, they had not yet succeeded. It could also be interpreted to

mean that the mechanical escapement clock had already been invented but that because of an inadequate escapement and time-conversion problems, the device had not become as useful for astronomical and possible astrological purposes as Robertus would have wished. The rapid development of the art of clockmaking by the first half of the fourteenth century, as represented by the achievements of Jean Fusoris, Richard Wallingford, and Giovanni de' Dondi, would seem to confirm the latter interpretation.

The only illustration of a medieval water clock now known appears in a miniature in a French *Bible moralisée* of about 1285. The illustration and related text are concerned with the impending death of King Hezekiah and the sign given him of his assured recovery (2 Kings 20:1–11). The clockwork depicted features a large wheel segmented into fifteen parts, each having a hole, and powered by water passing at a constant rate through a series of troughs. A rope visible in the painting may have passed over a drum or axle attached to a second wheel directly behind the first that may have served as an alarm train, so that when it was released, its toothed edge struck a row of bells attached to a bar above it. The holes in the segments may have provided a means for the water to trickle from one to another, serving as a brake on the weight-driven wheel; but more likely they accommodated a movable peg that, as the wheel revolved, moved the arm or detent in such a way as to release the second toothed wheel and activate the alarm. The clock may have had some form of escapement, possibly similar to that of the astronomical clock tower of Su Sung.

The pegged dial appears to have been commonplace by 1429, when it was described thus by Alexander Carpenter in his *Destructorium viciorum*:

> As in the case of a clock, the clock-keeper places one pin [*cavillam*] in a certain wheel, and when it reaches a certain point in the clock, it immediately releases the mechanism. And then all the bells strike and the figures, in the semblance of clerks and priests, pass by chanting in procession. But how long do these things work? Assuredly until the weight reaches the ground and no longer: for after the weight has grounded, everything immediately stops.

The mention of the figures in procession is reminiscent of the automata of the clock built at Norwich Cathedral in the thirteenth century.

The monastic water clock may have been housed

in a towerlike structure such as the one illustrated in the architectural sketchbook of Villard de Honnecourt (*ca.* 1250) and described as *la maison d'une horloge*. It bears some resemblance to the drawings of the pagodalike structure housing the astronomical clock of the Chinese emperor Su Sung.

The records of English monastic houses are particularly rich with references to *horologia* in the last two decades of the thirteenth century, leading to the assumption that there was an even wider activity in the production of such devices elsewhere in Europe. The earliest record occurs in 1283, in the annals of Dunstable Priory in Bedfordshire, concerning the erection of a clock in the priory's gallery. Similar accounts are found for Exeter Cathedral in the following year; in old St. Paul's Cathedral in London in 1286; at Merton College, Oxford, about 1288; at Norwich Cathedral priory in 1290; at the Benedictine abbey in Cambridgeshire in 1291; and at Christ Church Cathedral, Canterbury, in 1292.

It has not been established whether the mechanical clock escapement originated in Europe or was transmitted from the Orient. In view of the prevalence in monastic houses in England, and presumably elsewhere in Europe, of *horologia* that admittedly consisted of alarms rather than a regulated clockwork, it is conceivable that the invention was independently made in Europe. The foliot, or balance escapement, may possibly have derived from the bell-ringing devices used in the church, such as are illustrated on the doors of Orvieto Cathedral in a panel depicting Tubal-cain, the first worker of iron and brass. The circular band on which the bells are suspended greatly resembles the balance wheel of the de' Dondi astrarium.

Another theory is that the mechanical escapement was derived from China, specifically from the astronomical clock constructed at Kaifeng by Chang Ssu-hsun for the emperor Su Sung in 979. Housed in a wooden structure three stories high was a large vertical wheel having forty-eight pivoted and counterbalanced buckets containing mercury. A heavy overload balance lever enabled the wheel, revolving a hundred times each day, to move one bucket every eighteen seconds. The Chinese divided the day into twelve, instead of twenty-four, hours. The clock was made to indicate each of the twelve Chinese hours, or every two hours of our time. The mechanism provided time announcements twice during each of the twelve time periods by means of bells, drums, and *jaquemarts* (large wooden or cast metal figures in-

stalled on the top of public clocks and operated to strike a bell on the hour). A large clockwork-driven globe in the uppermost story was marked with star positions and included an observational armillary sphere and a tellurium. (A tellurium is a hand-operated device demonstrating the annual and diurnal motion of the earth, the change of seasons, and eclipses. It is a form of planetarium relating only to the earth and the moon.) This masterwork was described in several Chinese encyclopedias and histories, and in an illustrated official report published in 1172. Other monumental timepieces were produced in China during the next several centuries, but the tradition was lost as a consequence of wars and political changes.

Historians have proposed that knowledge of the Chinese horological achievements may have been brought to Europe during the last quarter of the thirteenth century, possibly by traders, through one of the Italian ports of Amalfi, Leghorn, and Venice, and that this knowledge, which included the principle of the mechanical escapement, was first applied in Italy and transmitted from there to other parts of Europe. This theory coincides with the erection of the first public clock in Europe, in the tower of the Church of S. Eustorgio in Milan by 1309.

Other public clocks followed in short order, and those generally cited as having been mechanical instead of water clocks were erected at Milan in 1335, Modena in 1343, Padua in 1344, Monza in 1347, and Strasbourg in 1352. There is reason to believe that the earliest public clocks had no visible time indicators such as dials but were merely audible, with striking bells and possibly *jaquemarts*. By the middle of the fourteenth century, the addition of mechanical clocks with automata and *jaquemarts* to churches and other public buildings was becoming commonplace in most of Europe.

During this same period two remarkable planetary machines, for which almost complete and uncontestable documentation has survived, were produced. Following the widespread production of *horologia* in English monastic houses in the late thirteenth century, a large clock was constructed at Norwich Cathedral between 1321 and 1325. It appears to have been a mechanical clock having a large astronomical dial of iron, with models of the sun and moon, and automata in the form of a procession of monks. The construction required the services of smiths, carpenters, plasterers, masons, bell founders, wood-carvers, and gilders for three years. Consider-

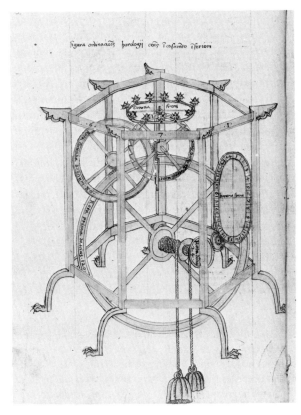

figura ordinacois horologij cois Tcafamto Tferiori

Mechanical clock. Drawn by Giovanni de' Dondi, 14th century.
BODLEIAN LIBRARY, OXFORD

able difficulty was experienced with the installation of the iron dial plate, and the material was destroyed several times until its erection was taken over by an artisan named Roger Stoke and his assistant, Laurence Stoke, who brought the project to a successful completion.

During the same period Richard of Wallingford, abbot of St. Albans, was engaged in designing and constructing a great astronomical clock or planetary machine for the abbey that had planetary trains, a tidal dial, a moon dial, and other refinements. Wallingford died before the project was completed, but it was brought to a satisfactory conclusion by Roger and Laurence Stoke within the next several years. Although no part of the clock has survived, it was described in considerable detail in the abbot's writings.

A short time later another great planetary machine was produced at Padua by Giovanni de' Dondi, physician and professor of philosophy, astrology, medicine, and logic at the university. He may have been inspired to undertake the project by the example of his father, Jacopo de' Dondi, also a physician

and lecturer in medicine, who in 1344 had designed and constructed a tower clock with astronomical dial, to be placed in the Palazzo del Capitanio in Padua, for his patron, Prince Ubertino of Carrara.

Giovanni de' Dondi began the design and construction of his planetary machine in 1348 and, building it with his own hands, completed it in 1364. He illustrated and described the work in considerable detail in a manuscript in his own hand, of which a number of versions have survived. Made in two segments upon a heptagonal framework, the upper section of the "planetarium," as de' Dondi first named it, consisted of seven large dials demonstrating, according to the Ptolemaic theory, the motions of each of the planets then known, the sun, and the moon. The lower section accommodated a series of dials, including a twenty-four-hour time dial, separate dials for the fixed and movable feasts of the church, a dial for the nodes or points of intersection of the orbit of the moon, and a dial for the times of the rising and setting of the sun. The planetarium was made of brass, probably with gears and pinions of iron, and was operated by means of a weight-driven clockwork having a curious balance-wheel escapement.

De' Dondi later improved the mechanism and renamed it "astrarium." He utilized elliptical gears to provide for the orbits of the moon and of Mercury. In his manuscript description he omitted instructions for making the clockwork, stating that it was an ordinary or "common" clock, and that if the reader was incapable of producing this part of the mechanism, he would be well advised not to attempt to make the rest of it, thus implying that the making of clocks was common knowledge.

In his manuscript description de' Dondi stated that he had undertaken the project with the intention of bringing greater appreciation to the noble study of astronomy, which had been troubled and weakened by astrological fallacies, rendering many of the earlier planetary studies useless and absurd. He therefore attempted to construct a mechanism that would demonstrate the planetary movements constantly, without the need for additional calculations. De' Dondi stated that he had been guided in the design of his project by the *Theorica planetarum* of Campanus of Novara, which had inspired it, and his astrarium may in fact be considered a mechanical equatorium having astrolabical, calendrical, and horary dials. The astrarium was seen and described by Petrarch, one of de' Dondi's intimate friends, who noted "that admirable work of the planetarium which he made, which the uneducated think is a clock. . . ."

Two decades after the astrarium had been completed, it was acquired by Duke Gian Galeazzo Visconti and installed in the library of his palace in Pavia. There it was subsequently seen and examined by Leonardo da Vinci, Donato Bramante, and Regiomontanus, among others. The astrarium remained in the possession of the Visconti and then of the Sforza families until about 1529. By then it had fallen into disrepair, and all subsequent trace of it was lost. The astrarium not only was possibly the first mechanical equatorium but also was one of the first devices to combine the tradition of the astronomical model of the universe with the recently invented mechanical clock regulated with an escapement. Both the astrarium and Wallingford's planetary clock provide tangible evidence that mechanized astronomical models developed independently of the mechanical escapement clock, from the tradition of equatoria that migrated from the Islamic world to the West.

Other innovations in telling time were introduced in the fourteenth century. In 1377 King Charles V of France owned an *orloge portative,* which indicates that the clock had been reduced from its stationary form to a portable size suitable for travel. An inventory of the king's possessions made after his death included "in the oratory, a clock in the fashion of a bell given to the king by Monseigneur de Berry; a clock of silver throughout, without iron, that had belonged to King Philip the Fair, having two counterweights of silver filled with lead; a clock of white silver, which is placed upon a pillar which he called *orlogium athos* [or *atlas* or *aethas*] weighing 3 marcs, 3 ounces, and 5 esterlins." In a manuscript owned by Marie, the king's granddaughter, is an illustration of a clock almost seventeenth-century in appearance. Completely enclosed, it is not of the open ironwork design of the type called Gothic, and has a dial indicating the twenty-four hours inscribed from one through twelve twice. Another feature is that the hours are inscribed in Arabic figures rather than Roman numerals, a very uncommon use of Arabic figures in this period (they were used almost exclusively by astronomers and mathematicians). The figures on the dials of de' Dondi's astrarium also were Arabic.

About 1430 Philip the Fair owned a spring-powered chamber clock, and such a clock is illustrated in a Burgundian painting of the same period. In 1459

King Charles VII purchased a *demi orloge doré de fin or sans contrepoix* (a small gilt clock without counterweights), a description that suggests that by this period the spring drive for clocks, which made them portable, had achieved widespread use. In this period Jean Fusoris, a talented French maker of mathematical instruments, produced an astronomical clock for the chapter at Bourges that continued to function until the nineteenth century.

The state of the art of clockmaking had some dimensions of sophistication by the third quarter of the fifteenth century, as is demonstrated in a miniature painting, probably produced between 1450 and 1488, that is part of a French translation of *The Clock of Wisdom* of Heinrich Suso, a moralized treatise written about 1327.

The description of the miniature, now in the collections of the Bibliothèque Royale at Brussels, states:

> In this illustration is shown the lady Wisdom setting and regulating a clock and an alarm that speaks through the sounds of several bells the words "God, who precedes the centuries and time, has made man in a material shape," which verse is appropriate to our Lord Jesus Christ who is the eternal wisdom and son of God the Father, who assumed human shape and was born of the Virgin Mary. And at the feet of Wisdom is the disciple contemplating the attitude of the mistress.

Featured in the right foreground is the only example known certainly to have been a medieval weight-driven alarm device. Although a weight is not shown, the device is clearly operated by means of a falling weight suspended on a rope that, as it drops, activates the wheelwork and causes the hammers to strike the bells suspended within the structure.

At the extreme left is featured a large clock having a twenty-four-hour dial twice inscribed with Roman numerals from I through XII. The details of the time and strike trains are obscured by the dial, but the latter operated a hammer that struck a bell suspended from the belfry outside the building. The clock appears to have been weight-driven, although the weights are not visible. An astrolabe is hung from the clock case; and upon a table at the right are five more instruments, all of gilt metal, that relate to the measurement of time. A horary quadrant is hung from the edge of the table, as is a shepherd's dial, a type known since the twelfth century. A portable solar dial in a carrying case, probably having a magnetic compass, is depicted at the rear of the tabletop,

Clock showing the months and phases of the moon as well as the time, with four jousting knights. Wells Cathedral, 14th century.
PHOTOGRAPH BY HERSCHEL LEVIT

while near the front is an equinoctial dial. Of particular significance is a spring-driven clock movement with fusee for equalizing the torque of the spring, an invention that until the discovery of this miniature had been attributed to the sixteenth century. In this single miniature is represented the state of the art of time-measurement devices in the third quarter of the fifteenth century. It confirms that the clock as a timekeeper had developed independently of the mechanized astronomical models, well beyond the degree previously assumed.

Deterrents to the development and production of the mechanical clock were the lack of competent artisans and the absence of a demand for timekeepers sufficient to keep them employed. The earliest records suggest that the makers of clocks emerged from other metalworking crafts, such as blacksmith, founder, locksmith, and maker of crossbows. Ubaldo of Florence, who worked as a clockmaker at Caffa (modern Feodosiya) in the Crimea in 1455, was identified as *bombardius et magister orologii comunis*, suggesting that he may have been the keeper who maintained the public clock, if not its maker.

Henricho, the keeper of the clock of the Church of S. Gottardo in Milan in 1474, was also a maker of bombards. Clockmakers were few in that period; and in the 1470's, when the marquis of Mantua searched all over Florence for a clockmaker to repair his portable clock, he sought in vain, nor could he find another clock to purchase.

Metalworkers in general were few in Europe until the sixteenth century. Those skilled in the construction of tower clocks moved from one community to another, making and repairing timepieces as the need arose, for there was generally not sufficient work to warrant a permanent establishment unless they pursued other aspects of metalworking. In the earlier periods the church was responsible for the support of many of the trades and crafts required by its installations, metalworking among them. However, the improvement of the quality of metalwork and the rapid growth of the craft by the end of the thirteenth century resulted less from the church than from military needs, such as the casting of bombards, the making of crossbows, and the replacement of chain armor by metal plate.

By 1525 the art of the clockmaker had made great strides, and skilled craftsmen began to emerge whose achievements in the production of public and domestic clocks, mechanized astronomical models, automata, and mathematical instruments reached heights of craftsmanship rarely surpassed. Notable among them is Gianello Torriano, a native of Cremona who established a shop at Milan and then went to Spain as the mechanician of Emperor Charles V.

Another was Lorenzo della Volpaia (or Golpaia or Vulparia) of Florence, who was trained as a carpenter and later became a master maker of clocks and mathematical instruments. He constructed a planetarium demonstrating the movements of the planets, the sun, and the moon, the eclipses and phases of the moon, the days of the month, and the hours of the day. Completed in 1484, and described by Angelo Poliziano, it was probably intended for the Medici family, from whom Lorenzo had received an appointment as keeper of the clock of the Palazzo Vecchio. Four years later, when the Medici were driven from Florence, he was dismissed from the position but was restored to it when his successor died several years later. The planetary machine was acquired from the leaders of the Guelph party in 1510 and installed in the Palazzo Vecchio, where it remained until the beginning of the seventeenth century. Then it was dismantled and subsequently lost. Lorenzo also produced mathematical instruments and was the founder of a dynasty of distinguished makers of clocks and instruments who continued to work in Florence until the end of the sixteenth century.

During this period the craft and art of the clockmaker flourished and was applied to other uses as well, such as the making of automata and the determination of longitude at sea. Gemma Frisius in 1530 suggested that portable clocks would serve the purpose of determining longitude at sea, a proposal that was attempted again and again during the next two centuries but that was not achieved until the second half of the eighteenth century.

BIBLIOGRAPHY

Antonio Barzon, Enrico Morpurgo, Armando Petrucci, and Giuseppe Francescato, eds., *Giovanni de' Dondi dall'orlogio, Tractatus astrarii . . .* (1960); Silvio A. Bedini and Francis R. Maddison, "Mechanical Universe: The Astrarium of Giovanni de' Dondi," in *Transactions of the American Philosophical Society*, n.s. 56 (1966); John H. Combridge, "Clocktower Millenary Reflections," in *Antiquarian Horology*, 9 (1980); C. B. Drover, "The Earliest Clock Illustration," *ibid.*, 1 (1954), "A Medieval Monastic Water-Clock," *ibid.*, "The Brussels Miniature: An Early Fusee and a Monastic Alarm," *ibid.*, 3 (1962), and "The Thirteenth-Century 'King Hezekiah' Water Clock," *ibid.*, 12 (1980); *Kritische Gesamtausgabe des Bauhüttenbuches ms. fr. 19093 der Pariser Bibliothek* (1935, 2nd ed. 1972); H. Alan Lloyd, "Giovanni de' Dondi's Horological Masterpiece, 1364," in *La Suisse horlogère*, 2 (1955); Carlo Maccagni, "The Florentine Clock- and Instrument-makers of the Della Volpaia Family," in *Der Globesfreund*, 18–20 (1969–1971); Francis Maddison, Bryan Scott, and Alan Kent, "An Early Medieval Water-Clock," in *Antiquarian Horology*, 3 (1962); Henri Michel, "Some New Documents in the History of Horology," *ibid.*

Joseph Needham, Wang Ling, and Derek J. de Solla Price, *Heavenly Clockwork: The Great Astronomical Clocks of Medieval China* (1960); J. D. North, "Monasticism and the First Mechanical Clocks," in *The Study of Time*, II (1975); Helga Pohl, *L'homme à la poursuite du temps*, Jean R. Weiland, trans. (1957); Derek J. de Solla Price, "Two Medieval Texts on Astronomical Clocks," in *Antiquarian Horology*, 1 (1956), and "On the Origin of Clockwork, Perpetual Motion Devices and the Compass," in *Contributions from the Museum of History and Technology*, U.S. National Museum Bulletin no. 218 (1959); Manuel Rico y Sinobias, *Libros del saber de astronomía del rey D. Alfonso X de Castilla*, 5 vols. (1863–1867); Paul Sheridan, "Les inscriptions sur ardoise de l'abbaye de Villiers," in *Annales de la Société d'archéologie de Bruxelles*, 9–10 (1895–1896); Eleanor P. Spencer, "L'horloge de la Sapience, Bruxelles, Bibliothèque Royale, Ms. IV.111," in *Scriptorium*, 17 (1963); Lynn Thorndike, *The Sphere of Sacrobosco and Its Commentators* (1949), 180–230; Lynn T. White, Jr., *Medieval Technology and Social Change* (1962), 119–129.

SILVIO A. BEDINI

[See also **Alfonso X; Calendars and Reckoning of Time; Clockwork, Planetary; Fusoris, Jean; Sundials; Wallingford, Richard of.**]

CLOCKWORK, PLANETARY.

The mechanical clock appeared in England toward the end of the thirteenth century and in France and Germany at the beginning of the fourteenth century. At first it was only a timepiece, driven by a falling weight and regulated by the newly invented mechanical escapement (with a verge and foliot) producing a fast but uniform rotation of the principal arbor. A gear train of toothed wheels slowed this rotation to a period of twenty-four or twelve hours, transmitting it at the same time to a rotating dial or to a rotating pointer in front of a fixed dial.

The planetary clock grew out of this device when the gear train was developed in such a way that a number of individual arbors were made to rotate with the periods of the sun, moon, and planets, taking the inequalities of these motions into account. It is not known when this first occurred, but a great clock built between 1321 and 1325 at Norwich Cathedral by Roger of Stoke had dials showing the positions of the sun and moon. This was also true of the clock designed in 1327 by Abbot Richard of Wallingford for the abbey church of St. Albans and described in his *Tractatus horologii astronomici*, the first treatise of its kind.

In 1344 Jacopo de' Dondi erected a planetary clock on the Torre dei Signori of the Palazzo del Capitanio in Padua. Between 1348 and 1364 his son Giovanni designed and made a smaller, but much more ingenious, astronomical clock called an "astrarium," and described it in his *Tractatus astrarii*. Like the Norwich and St. Albans clocks it has since disappeared, but a modern reconstruction by Bedini and Maddison (in the Smithsonian History of Technology Museum in Washington, D.C.) shows that it was a complete "mechanical universe" indicating the motions of all the heavenly bodies, each on its separate dial.

By this time the principles of a planetary clock were well established and described, and such timepieces were made in increasing numbers and complexity. About 1370 an astronomical clock that had an astrolabe dial with pointers for the sun and moon was erected in the cathedral of Strasbourg. A number of clocks showing the course of the sun and the phases of the moon were built in the last decades of the fourteenth century (Exeter and Wells cathedrals, Dover castle). The *horologium mirabile Lundense* in Lund cathedral (then in Denmark) may be from the beginning of the fifteenth century and thus contemporary with the astronomical turret clock still seen (with a few later alterations) on the Old Town Hall of Prague.

In the Renaissance, astronomical table clocks became rather common, and artisans such as John Stoeffler and Isaac Habrecht devised very ingenious models made with delicate craftsmanship. In the seventeenth and eighteenth centuries these clocks were often replaced by orreries and other planetariums without a timepiece. On the other hand, the great planetary clocks remained rare. The latest and most accomplished example is the "World Clock" of J. Olsen, in the town hall of Copenhagen (1955), designed to run without adjustment for 7,000 years.

BIBLIOGRAPHY

Antonio Barzon, Enrico Morpurgo, Armando Petrucci, and Giuseppe Francescato, *Giovanni de' Dondi dall'orologio, Tractatus astrarii . . .* (1960); Silvio A. Bedini and Francis R. Maddison, "Mechanical Universe: The Astrarium of Giovanni de' Dondi," in *Transactions of the American Philosophical Society,* n.s. 56 (1966); John D. North, ed., *Richard of Wallingford,* 3 vols. (1976); Alfred Ungerer, *Les horloges astronomiques et monumentales* (1931).

OLAF PEDERSEN

[See also **Clocks and Reckoning of Time; Wallingford, Richard of.**]

CLOISTER (from the Latin *claustrum,* "confines," in medieval monastic use), a large square or rectangular courtyard in a monastery restricted to use by monks. A cloister normally abutted the south side of a church; the three projecting sides were enclosed by galleried porches that led to the domestic parts of the monastery. The cloister kept monks and laity separated, and was used for reading, prayer, and washing. It probably developed in the late eighth century in response to the rise of Benedictine communal monasticism, which, with its stress on corporate agriculture, offered greater temptations for monks to

mingle with laity than had earlier, eremitic monastic movements.

BIBLIOGRAPHY

Walter Horn, "On the Origins of the Medieval Cloister," in *Gesta,* 12 (1973).

LESLIE BRUBAKER

[See also **Monastery.**]

CLONARD (CLUAIN-IRAIRD). According to Irish tradition, Clonard was founded about 520 by St. Finnian, shortly after his return to Ireland from Wales, where he had studied under St. David and several other prominent Welsh ecclesiastics. Historically, Clonard was an early-sixth-century monastic foundation, whose rise to preeminence and reputation for learning may have been due in part to its close connections with Wales. The traditional claim of a community of 3,000 monks is suspect, but the monastery was a large one. St. Finnian's most famous pupils, styled the Twelve Apostles of Ireland, were all prominent monastics. Since Clonard's enduring reputation encouraged later Irish hagiographers to provide their particular saints with sojourns at Clonard, the roster of those pupils is not always the same. However, it usually consists of St. Columba (Columcille) of Derry and Iona, Colum of Terryglass, Brendan of Birr, Brendan "the Navigator" of Clonfort, Cainnech (Kenneth) of Aghaboe, Ciarain (Kieran) of Clonmacnois, Ciarain (Kieran) of Saigir, Laisren (or Molaise) of Devenish, Ruadan of Lorrha, Mobi Clarainech of Glasnevin, Sinell of Cleenish, and Ninnid of Inishmacsaint.

Clonard continued to be a prominent foundation throughout the early Middle Ages, maintaining close ties with the other major Irish monastic communities of Armagh, Bangor, Clonmacnois, Duleek, and Kildare. The obituary notices of its various abbots, bishops, lectors, and *comarbai* (successors) appear frequently in the annals from the sixth to the twelfth century. In the early seventh century Clonard became involved in the controversy between the conservative and Roman factions of the Irish church over the proper observance of Easter. Bede's *History of the English Church and People* preserves a copy of a letter from Pope-elect John IV to some prominent Irish abbots, among them Colman mac Telduib, the abbot of Clonard, urging them to adopt the continental practice favored by the Roman faction. In

1111 the Synod of Rathbreasail, held during the twelfth-century reform movement, chose Clonard as the seat of the bishop of east Meath, a choice confirmed by the synod at Uisnech later that year.

Clonard's reputation did not shield it from the violence of this period. The exact number of attacks cannot be determined, since the annals do not always distinguish between deliberate and accidental fires. However, between the fire in the granary reported in 746 and the plundering of Clonard by the forces of Diarmaid Mac Muchadh of Leinster in 1170, the monastery was burned five times, "destroyed" by Norse once, and "plundered" by raiding parties, both Irish and Norse, according to the Annals of the Four Masters.

In 1144 Murtagh O'Loughlin, probably at the urging of St. Malachy of Armagh, founded a house of Augustinian canonesses of the Arroasian congregation called St. Mary's at Clonard. By 1195 St. Mary's had about thirteen dependencies, some of them double houses. At about the same time as the foundation of St. Mary's, St. Peter's Abbey of Augustinian canons regular, also Arroasian, was established at Clonard. Between 1183 and 1186 Hugh De Lacy established an Augustinian priory, St. John's, which seems to have begun with an importation of Norman monks from Dublin.

In 1200 the Norman community at Clonard was raided by the local prince, an act that may have encouraged Bishop Simon Richfort's decision to move the seat of his diocese to Trim. This transfer in 1202 took the Norman community to Trim and left Clonard to the Irish. The subsequent union of two congregations produced the single Abbey of Sts. John and Peter. The financial situation of the abbey deteriorated in the late thirteenth century and reached the point of destitution by the early fourteenth. Norman names dominate the records after 1286, but the abbey survived until 1540. In that year the English crown took the opportunity offered by the death of Abbot Gerald Walshe to dissolve the monastic communities of Clonard.

BIBLIOGRAPHY

Kathleen W. Hughes, "The Cult of St. Finnian of Clonard from the Eighth to the Eleventh Century," in *Irish Historical Studies,* 9 (1954–1955); and "The Historical Value of the Lives of St. Finnian of Clonard," in *English Historical Review,* 69 (1954); Louis Gougaud, "The Remains of Ancient Irish Monastic Libraries," in *Essays and Studies Presented to Professor Eoin MacNeill,* J. Ryan, ed. (1940), 319–334; John Ryan, *Irish Monasticism: Origins and Early Development* (1931, repr. 1972); John A. Watt, *The Church in Medieval Ireland* (1972).

DOROTHY AFRICA

[See also **Celtic Church**.]

CLOVE, a weight used in England of six and one-half, seven, or eight pounds (2.948, 3.175, or 3.629 kilograms) for cheese, wool, metals, and other agricultural and nonagricultural goods. Commonly called a half-stone, it was ultimately derived etymologically from the Latin *clavus* (nail). One of the most frequently used weights in medieval England, the clove appeared in the documents with such variant spellings as claw, clawe, clou, cloue, claue, clave, cleaue, and cleave.

RONALD EDWARD ZUPKO

CLOVIS, born about 465, was the son of Childeric I, one of the several Frankish kings who ruled in northeastern Gaul and the Rhineland. He became king on his father's death in 481 but was not in a very strong position. To the east and northeast as far as the middle Rhine were other kings who could claim descent from Merowig, the common ancestor of the line. To the south was Syagrius, officially a representative of the Roman emperor but actually an independent ruler of Romans in northern Gaul. On the middle Rhine below the Franks were the Alamanni, a pugnacious people; further south on the Rhône, the Burgundians; far to the southwest, the Visigoths. Religious differences compounded secular problems: the Franks were pagan, the Romans were Catholic, the Burgundians and Visigoths were Arians.

Clovis began by eliminating rival Frankish kings by force and, if we believe Gregory of Tours, by trickery. He then quarreled with Syagrius and defeated him in battle near Soissons (486). This victory gave Clovis control of most of northeastern Gaul and, probably, of some of the war bands who had supported Syagrius. He strengthened his position with the Romanized Gauls of the north by marrying the Burgundian princess Clotilda, who, unlike most of her family, was a Catholic.

The old quarrels with the Alamanni were sharpened by Clovis' new acquisitions, which increased the area in which the aims of the two peoples clashed. Finally, there was an all-out war in which the Alamanni were crushed at the Battle of Tolbiac (506) and Clovis was accepted as their king. There is a story that, like Constantine, Clovis had turned to the Christian God to grant him victory in a crucial battle. It is quite possible that Clovis wanted all the divine help he could get, but he was rather cautious in going all the way to baptism. As Wallace-Hadrill has pointed out, he had to weigh the doubts of his pagan Franks against the support he could get from the bishops, who were leaders of the Gallo-Romans, now his most numerous subjects.

The next campaign was against the Visigoths. They were Arians and thus offensive to a newly baptized Catholic king; they were also longtime enemies of the Franks. Franks and Visigoths had fought each other in the Loire Valley for many years; in 507 Clovis won a decisive victory at Vouillé, near Poitiers. Although this did not expel the Visigoths from Gaul (they held the southwest for many more years), it did make Clovis' kingdom overwhelmingly Gallo-Roman in population. This change reinforced the role of the church and weakened the position of the Germanic element in the Frankish kingdom. The change was marked by a shift in the king's principal place of residence, from Tournai in the semi-Germanic northeast to Tours and then to Paris. At Tours, Clovis received an honorary title from the Byzantine emperor (probably that of consul); he also gave gifts to the Church of St. Martin, who became one of the patron saints of the royal family. At Paris he favored the nearby Church of St. Denis, and on the left bank of the Seine he built the large Church of the Holy Apostles (now Ste. Geneviève), where he was buried.

All these acts conciliated the Gallo-Roman population, especially in southern regions that had found Visigothic rule quite tolerable. Clovis continued to behave like earlier Christian kings, granting land, giving gifts to churches, and encouraging the growth of monasteries. He also called a church council at Orléans just before his death in 511. Finally, again like other Christian Germanic kings, Clovis probably encouraged the composition of a law code. The earliest version of the Salian Law (the law for the Franks in his states) dates from the later years of his reign. It affected the Roman population to some extent and certainly made clearer the rules of criminal law that bound the Germans.

Clovis may have been a legislator, and if so, he was influenced by Roman precedents. He did not,

however, accept or even understand the Roman concept of the state. On his death his lands were divided among his four sons, just as if they were private property. Such divisions persisted for the next three centuries.

BIBLIOGRAPHY

The basic source is Gregory of Tours, *History of the Franks*, 2 vols., Ormonde M. Dalton, trans. and ed. (1927); John M. Wallace-Hadrill, *The Long-haired Kings* (1962), ch. 7, gives the best modern account of Clovis. See also Samuel Dill, *Roman Society in Gaul in the Merovingian Age* (1926).

JOSEPH R. STRAYER

[See also **France: To 987; Merovingians.**]

CLUNIAC RITE. The liturgical practices of Cluny during the Middle Ages are known not so much through liturgical manuscripts, such as Mass and Office books, most of which have been lost or were destroyed by pillaging Protestants in 1562, but through monastic customaries, especially those of Bernard and Ulrich of Cluny. As Benedictines, the Cluniacs followed essentially the liturgical practices set out in St. Benedict of Nursia's Rule. But during the monastic reforms of St. Benedict of Aniane in the ninth century these had been supplemented by a plethora of ritual that the Cluniacs in the tenth century and beyond enthusiastically accepted and further augmented. By the eleventh century Peter Damian commented on the heavy Cluniac liturgical load; and even the abbot of Cluny, Peter the Venerable, later lamented that the liturgy left the monks little time for other activities. As a result, the new orders of the twelfth century made determined efforts to prune what they saw as an overburdened liturgy.

The Cluniac Office was especially psalm-oriented, with the community of monks reciting, along with the 40 prescribed by St. Benedict, 215 psalms in a single day. Moreover, the whole Psalter was recited each week and the whole Bible each year. The works of the Fathers were also read extensively. The three daily masses, two in the Church of St. Mary and the *Missa maior* in the basilica, were extended by such practices as reciting from seven to eleven collects, chanting the Athanasian Creed, and censing all the altars in the basilica. Processions also occupied much time, especially the solemn processions with candles, Gospels, and liturgical paraphernalia, and Sunday processions in which various locations in the monastic complex would be asperged.

The liturgy of Holy Week and Easter was made long but dramatic with such rituals as the *mandatum*, or washing the feet of all the brothers and poor on Maundy Thursday, and the acting out of the "Diviserunt sibi vestimenta mea," or dividing-up of Christ's vestments, in the reading of the Good Friday Passion. Finally, the Cluniac liturgy was distinguished for its remembrance of the dead and its emphasis on the saints, with multiple offices of the dead and all saints each day, suffrages of saints at matins, litanies of saints before mass, and, on saints' days, the reading of extensive lives and passions during the Office and in the refectory.

BIBLIOGRAPHY

P. Schmitz, "La liturgie de Cluny," in *Spiritualità cluniacense* (1960), 83–99; André Wilmart, "Cluny (Manuscrits liturgiques de)," in *Dictionnaire d'archéologie chrétienne et de liturgie,* III (1914).

ROGER E. REYNOLDS

[See also **Benedictine Rule; Cluny, Order of; Divine Office.**]

CLUNY, ABBEY CHURCH. The Abbey Church of Sts. Peter and Paul at Cluny, in Burgundy, was the largest church in Christendom from its construction (*ca.* 1085–*ca.* 1160) until it was superseded by St. Peter's in Rome (from 1506). Known as "Cluny III" because it followed two earlier churches of the tenth century, the great church was destroyed, except for the south arm of its western transept, between 1798 and 1823. The American archaeologist Kenneth J. Conant studied Cluny from the 1920's to the 1960's and excavated the site extensively. It is largely "Conant's Cluny" that is known to specialists and to students, and there is some criticism of Conant's interpretations.

Cluny III was built under two of the order's greatest abbots, Hugh of Semur and Peter the Venerable. There is uncertainty about the actual commencement of work, but construction began before the official *fundatio* of 30 September 1088 and continued well after the dedication of the structure on 25 October 1130. A Gothic narthex was built in the thirteenth century, and construction on the west-facade towers was still going on in the 1450's.

The initial design was by Gunzo de Baume (μη-χιανίκος) and Hézelon of Liège (ἀρχιτέκτων). The scheme featured a huge archiepiscopal cross plan (more than 600 feet long), with complex radiating and projecting chapels, and a three-story interior elevation. Cluny III was the first medieval church of western Europe to employ pointed arches at large scale, possibly an Islamic influence, and to have a high vault over 100 feet above the floor.

BIBLIOGRAPHY

For general summary and bibliography see Carl F. Barnes, Jr., "Cluniac Art and Architecture," in *New Catholic Encyclopedia,* III (1967). The results of Conant's investigation are in his *Cluny: Les églises et la maison du chef d'ordre* (1968). For a different interpretation and critique, see Francis Salet's review in *Bulletin monumental,* **127** (1969); and also his "Cluny III," *ibid.,* **126** (1968).

CARL F. BARNES, JR.

[See also **Romanesque Architecture.**]

CLUNY, ORDER OF. During the tenth and eleventh centuries Cluny was a major center of monastic influence, and the Cluniac order's spectacular growth coincided with a rich period of monastic culture. Cluny offers an example of how medieval monks could remain faithful to their Benedictine ideals while attending to the spiritual needs of Christians outside the cloister.

Cluny's origins lie in Carolingian reforms. Charlemagne and Louis the Pious incorporated monks into the church's liturgical and educational life. Benedict of Aniane wanted to integrate Frankish monasteries into a uniform network founded on the Rule of St. Benedict. Through his efforts the communal praying of the divine office became more central than it had been. But the subsequent disruptions of the ninth century caused many abbeys to fall under the control of local lay magnates, often to the detriment of monastic discipline. Despite the failure of Benedict of Aniane's ambitious scheme, however, many of his ideals and customs later influenced Cluniac ways.

In 909 Duke William of Aquitaine granted a group of monks a charter to establish a monastery at Cluny in the county of Mâcon. The charter freed the abbey from all secular and ecclesiastical jurisdiction and made it the property of Sts. Peter and Paul. Although the foundation's provisions were not unusual at the time, the charter became the basis of later claims to immunity from outside authority and exemption from diocesan jurisdiction. As abbot of Cluny the duke chose Berno, already abbot of Baume, a Burgundian monastery in the tradition of Benedict of Aniane.

The order's success from 909 to 1157 can be partially explained in terms of its abbots, who proved to be exceptionally capable leaders. Berno (909–926) brought Benedictine ways to other monasteries, such as Gigny and Déols. As his successor he appointed Odo (926–944), who amplified the liturgy and insisted on a stricter adherence to the rule. Odo's writings reveal a desire to preserve and deepen the monks' commitment to contemplation. He reformed monasteries in France and Italy, reconciling feuding princes and distributing alms during the course of his travels. In his *Vita Geraldi* Odo presents an ideal of lay piety. The hero Gerald uses his sword to defend the poor and punish the insolent, while restraining those who hinder the church's attempt to check violence in the countryside.

Under Aymard (944–964) grants of land to Cluny increased substantially; he also reformed Sauxillanges in Auvergne. Majolus (964–994) introduced Cluniac customs in monasteries in Burgundy and Pavia, at times with the help of Emperor Otto I and his court. During the abbacy of St. Odilo (994–1049) Cluny's influence was extended over abbeys throughout France, Italy, and Spain, and many monasteries were annexed to Cluny in various degrees of dependency. Secular and ecclesiastical lords donated or confirmed Cluniac possessions, resulting in greatly augmented agricultural holdings. Odilo aided the peacemaking efforts of bishops and kings, and instituted a Cluniac customary and the feast of All Souls. The order's apogee was reached during the abbacy of Hugh (1049–1109), who extended the order to England and promoted new building and restorations, including a new abbey church at Cluny. Already celebrated for its manuscript illuminations and music, Cluny now came to influence architecture and sculpture as well. But Cluny's enormous prestige suffered as a result of the disputes within the order under Abbot Pons (1109–1122), who resigned in disgrace.

Cluny's last outstanding abbot, Peter the Venerable (1122–1156), began his rule by defeating Pons's bid to regain control. When contrasted with the glorious era of Hugh, the abbacy of Peter seems more of a holding action against forces that threatened Cluny's survival. Peter tried to preserve Benedictine customs, while making concessions to Cistercian simplicity, as the Cistercians had accused Cluniacs of making unwarranted additions to the Rule of St. Benedict. Following his abbacy Cluny never again held a preeminent position within monasticism. In 1100 it had been the hub of an international order; by 1300 Cluny was completely national (French). Attempts at reform were made in the fifteenth century, but by then the Cluniac abbots had become commendatory absentees, with adverse effects on monastic discipline. In the seventeenth century the order was divided into the old observance and the strict observance. Cluny was suppressed during the French Revolution.

The abbey's internal organization largely followed the Rule of St. Benedict. But gradually, especially after the abbacy of Majolus, changes in administration were made in order to accommodate the growing number of recruits (and the higher ratio of priests to laymen), the expanded ties with other monasteries, the increase of agrarian holdings, the liturgical accretions, and the abbots' extramonastic concerns. The prolonged absences of the early abbots necessitated more delegation of authority. The major prior was second only to the abbot in spiritual and temporal authority, though his term of office was usually brief. Assisting the major prior were the deans who administered the estates and the resident tenants. The claustral prior enforced the observances within the monastery. The chamberlain (after 1050) held the chief financial responsibilities. The cellarer ensured the distribution of victuals. The *opus Dei* fell to the precentor, who obtained his supplies from the sacrist. The almoner provided for the endless influx of guests. The guestmaster lodged travelers and visitors in the adjacent guesthouse, and screened visitors who sought entrance to the cloister. All the above officers had subordinates to assist them. The monastic community as a whole was divided into monks, novices, oblates, and servants. The monks themselves were either cantors, who sang, or conversi, who did not.

Cluny's peculiar structure stemmed not from its internal arrangements but from the abbey's relation to its dependent houses. Cluny had a large number (estimates run from 500 to 2,000) of subordinate priories, which in turn often had monasteries under them. The abbot of Cluny appointed all priors. All monks in the priories professed at Cluny. All Cluniac houses followed the same observances, such as the canonical hours and the calendar.

The development of monasteries around a single abbey was not unique to Cluny. In western Germany, for example, the monastery of Gorze remained true to the customs of the second Benedict. But Gorze, unlike Cluny, was not exempt from episcopal authority. The abbey of Bec stimulated reforms in Normandy and England. Bec was renowned for its distinguished scholars, while Cluny never attained a similar fame for its intellectual achievements.

Many abbeys accepted Cluniac usages without becoming priories. Some abbeys retained their abbots, while others received direction from Cluny only for a limited time. No dependency enjoyed the same exemptions as did Cluny. The connections between Cluny and its many kinds of dependencies were varied, and scholars disagree about their character. While the tendency in many monasteries after the abbacy of Majolus was clearly toward centralization around the nucleus of Cluny, the actual administrative system was loose and constantly changing. The abbot of Cluny rarely interfered in the daily operations and economy of his dependent houses; his relations with them were more often personal than institutional. The turnover of administrators was high. Competent personnel sometimes left the order for positions in the secular church or in lay government. The growing number of bureaucratic layers between the abbey of Cluny and its priories after 1050 actually inhibited the abbot's authority. Cluniac abbots were not dictatorial, preferring to allow local discretion. What Cluniac administration gained by flexibility it lost through inconsistent policies.

From its foundation Cluny enjoyed the favor of popes. In 931 John XI confirmed Cluny's liberty, a privilege renewed by Leo VII and Agapetus II. John XI also gave Cluny the right to receive monks who sought a stricter observance. Subsequent popes instructed kings and bishops of France to protect the abbey's possessions from the encroachments of lay lords. By 1032 Cluny's temporal immunity was firmly established: St. Peter and his successors were to be Cluny's sole protectors and proprietors. John XIX in 1027 made Cluny exempt from the spiritual authority of all bishops—who were forbidden to excommunicate or anathematize Cluny. Papal protection facilitated the granting of gifts to the abbey in the form of monasteries. Cluny gradually became a special possession of the popes, who saw in it the model of fidelity to the Apostolic See.

While Cluny's commitment to Gregory VII's reforms was at best incidental, Abbot Hugh often assisted Rome in diplomatic missions; Gregory VII saw in Cluny's liberty a prototype of *libertas Ro-*

mana, a papal grant of freedom from lay control that in effect made Cluny subject to the pope. Cluny, moreover, gave oblique support to the First Crusade. Cluniac abbots had worked for the Peace and the Truce of God, encouraging nobles to channel their energies toward pious ends. The notion of pilgrimage as a means of obtaining the remission of one's sins could be easily adapted to an armed pilgrimage to the Holy Land. Pope Urban II, a former Cluniac prior, confirmed the privileges granted Cluny by previous pontiffs. There is some slight, if ambiguous, evidence that at least some Cluniacs, such as those at Moissac, did recruit for the Crusade. The close relations between Cluny and Spanish rulers—King Alfonso VI in particular—probably aided in the formation of the Crusade idea. Cluny's contact with the church of Jerusalem, by way of Moissac, may have made Abbot Hugh more receptive to Urban II's summons to crusade.

This papal solicitude notwithstanding, Cluny's contribution to Gregorian reforms was largely unintended. Cluny never explicitly upheld papal claims over lay rulers or bishops. But Cluny did foster a spiritual climate that encouraged the development of a clergy dedicated to higher spiritual values, and Cluniac abbots were prominent reformers and peacemakers. Indebted to Rome's generosity, Cluniacs tended to enhance the office of Christ's vicar. While Cluny refused to take sides in the investiture controversy, the abbey's lack of opposition to papal initiatives probably helped the pope more than the emperor.

The chief characteristic of Cluniac spirituality was its openness to the world. Cluniac monks did not strive to cut themselves off from a corrupt society; rather, they saw themselvs as weak members of a weak human race. They rarely played the traditional prophetic role of castigating a wayward city of man. Cluniacs were not a righteous elite but the church's inner group, which was painfully aware of man's fallen condition. The isolated monk was never made to forget his obligations to serve those not blessed with the grace of the monastic state. The reform outlook—ever ready to express itself in works of compassion—was never far from the monk's devotions and ascetic practices. In this sense the Cluniac never left the world.

This is not to suggest that Cluniacs were social reformers. They were first of all monks. The monastery was an asylum of penance to which one came to weep for one's sins. The monk mortified his senses and prayed without ceasing. He searched for God in silence. His primary task was contemplation, itself ordained to union with God in heaven. All charitable works were extraneous to his peculiar vocation, that of the man apart who lived for God alone. His main source of inspiration was the Bible; his main source of conduct, the Rule.

Yet when this spiritual core is duly acknowledged, it must be said that the reason Cluny evolved into a social movement was that it responded to contemporary aspirations. Nonmonks looked to Cluniacs for guidance and inspiration. The Cluniac vita could be imitated in the world, at least in spirit. Cluniacs were both activators and reflectors of current trends, as can be seen in their promotion of pilgrimages and processions. Laymen sought their intercession before the king of heaven. Cluny's elaborate psalmody is testimony to its sense of participation in the rhythms of the church militant. Cluny's popularity began to wane only when Benedictine monasticism itself started to lose its influence. After 1100 other institutions provided the stability and confidence that Cluny could no longer offer.

While Cluny's itinerant abbots manifested this receptiveness to others, most Cluniac monks remained inside the cloister, oblivious to events. The attacks of the early Cistercians notwithstanding, Cluny did not undergo a moral decline after Abbot Hugh. Rather, the inherent contradiction between monastic detachment and charitable service became more apparent as Europe developed more stable institutions. Cluny's social functions were assumed by other groups, while its zeal for Benedictine discipline was seized by the new monastic orders. Cluny could not defend itself against the Cistercian charge that it had departed from the Rule, for Cluny had in fact always been receptive to a range of other influences. After 1100 Cluny's very adaptability and effectiveness had become liabilities. Peter the Venerable was dimly aware of the growing anachronism of Cluny's outstretched system. While basically conservative, Peter experimented with general chapters and eremitical alternatives.

But Cluny's historical mission was spent. Its evolution had been largely haphazard and reactive, a product of the disorders of the tenth and eleventh centuries. During that time men had found in Cluny a refreshing blend of pastoral concern and ascetic otherworldliness. They praised the monks for their sanctity and understanding. Ironically, the widespread acceptance of Cluniac values indirectly hastened its demise. Cluny found itself branded a traitor to its Benedictine ideals as well as to its dedication

to the church's common good. The Cistercians were now the new purists. The secular clergy and the mixed orders were the new reformers.

BIBLIOGRAPHY

Congrès scientifique à Cluny (1950); Giles Constable, *Cluniac Studies* (1980); Herbert Cowdrey, *The Cluniacs and the Gregorian Reform* (1970), and "Cluny and the First Crusade," in *Revue bénédictine*, **83** (1973); Joan Evans, *Monastic Life at Cluny 910–1157* (1931); Robert Heath, *Crux imperatorum philosophia: Imperial Horizons of the Cluniac Confraternitas, 964–1109* (1976); Noreen Hunt, *Cluny Under Saint Hugh, 1049–1109* (1976), and idem, ed., *Cluniac Monasticism in the Central Middle Ages* (1971); Idung of Prüfening, *Cistercians and Cluniacs: The Case for Cîteaux* (1977); David Knowles, *Cistercians and Cluniacs* (1955); Barbara Rosenwein, *Rhinoceros Bound: Cluny in the Tenth Century* (1982); T. Schieffer, "Cluny et la querelle des Investitures," in *Revue historique*, **225** (1961); Gerard Sitwell, ed. and trans., *St. Odo of Cluny* (1958); Guy de Valous, *Le monachisme clunisien dès origines au XVe siècle*, 2 vols., 2nd ed. (1970).

THOMAS RENNA

[See also **Benedict of Aniane; Benedictine Rule; Benedictines; Cistercian Order; Cluniac Rite; Hugh of Semur, St.; Monasticism; Odilo of Cluny; Odo of Cluny; Peter the Venerable; Reform, Idea of.**]

CNUT THE GREAT (995/1000–1035) was the second son of Sweyn Forkbeard, king of Denmark, and his queen Gunhild, sister of Duke (later King) Boleslav I the Brave of Poland. He took part in his father's invasion of England, and after Sweyn's death in 1014, he was elected king by the fleet. The English councillors, however, recalled Ethelred from exile in Normandy, and only after his death and that of his son Edmund Ironside (1016) was Cnut finally recognized as king of England in 1017. To secure his possession of the country, he divided it into four earldoms, of which he ruled Wessex himself and entrusted East Anglia, Mercia, and Northumbria to his leading allies. To avert a possible Norman intervention on behalf of Ethelred's children, he married the latter's widow, Emma of Normandy. Cnut's first wife was Elfgifu of Northampton, who belonged to one of the most influential Northumbrian families.

By 1018 Cnut's position was well enough established that he could disband most of his army, keeping only 40 ships and 3,000 *huscarls*, a mercenary force paid for by an annual tax. His relationship with his English subjects was settled the same year at a meeting in Oxford, where Cnut promised to rule in accordance with Edgar's laws. Basically, as a king of England, Cnut endeavored to take over the position of his predecessors and introduced few changes. This is demonstrated by his code, which is basically a restatement of the laws of Edgar and Ethelred and was drafted by Archbishop Wulfstan of York, who had also drawn up some of Ethelred's codes. Cnut, who attached much importance to the church, showed great generosity toward ecclesiastical institutions and enormous concern about the faith. There is good evidence that he was personally pious, but little doubt that his policy was dictated by considerations of political advantage.

In 1018 Cnut's elder brother Harald died without issue, and Cnut succeeded to the throne of Denmark. This did not pass unopposed and caused his first journey to Denmark in 1019; in a letter to his English subjects Cnut claims to have warded off great dangers threatening from Denmark. He later placed Denmark under the rule of earls, first Thorkel, then Ulf, and last his son Hardecnut. In 1026 Cnut faced a coalition of Scandinavian enemies, among them Ulf, and defeated them in the Battle of the Holy River. He subsequently styled himself "king of part of the Swedes," and there is convincing numismatic evidence to support this. Two years later he added Norway to his empire.

In 1027 Cnut went to Rome, partly on a pilgrimage and partly to attend the imperial coronation of the German king Conrad. He successfully negotiated concessions for English and Scandinavian travelers and traders, as well as the betrothal of his daughter Gunhild to the emperor's son Henry.

In Denmark, Cnut sought to establish practices that he had learned in England. He introduced a coinage modeled on the English system, and the Danish church came under strong English influence.

Cnut died at Shaftesbury and was buried at Winchester.

BIBLIOGRAPHY

Laurence Marcellus Larson, *Canute the Great 995 (circ.)–1035 and the Rise of Danish Imperialism During the Viking Age* (1912); Frank M. Stenton, *Anglo-Saxon England*, 3rd ed. (1971), 385–419.

NIELS LUND

[See also **Denmark; England: Anglo-Saxon; Ethelred II the Unready; Wulfstan.**]

COAL, MINING AND USE OF. Coal was little used during the Middle Ages, for both geological and socioeconomic reasons. Coal seams came to the surface of the ground and could be worked in only a few areas, and a knowledge of their true extent was not acquired until modern times. Second, the combustion of coal gives off offensive smoke and calls for specially constructed hearths and chimneys. The central fireplace of the medieval hall house was ill-suited to burning coal, and the domestic use of coal became important only after chimney stacks had come into general use. At the same time, the abundance of timber in much of Europe made it unnecessary to use the more expensive and less agreeable coal.

That the classical world knew of coal is apparent from a reference to it in Theophrastus, but it was rare in the Mediterranean region and there is no evidence that it was regularly used. The Romans used it on a very small scale in Britain, and it appears to have long been used in China when Marco Polo described it.

Coal does not appear again in the European historical record until the twelfth century, when it is mentioned by Alexander Neckham. Thereafter references to it became increasingly frequent, and by the end of the Middle Ages coal was an important though highly localized product, used in a number of industrial processes that could be carried on away from inhabited places. Among these the burning of lime and bricks was the most important, though coal came to be used by metalworkers in Liège and the Meuse Valley at a relatively early date. It was almost certainly used for heating and cooking near the pits, but general use as a household fuel did not develop until the seventeenth century.

The most important sources of coal during the Middle Ages were Britain, the southern Low Countries, and the lower Rhineland. In each the coal outcropped on the valley sides and could be transported to market by boat. Any study of the use of coal is complicated by the fact that *carbo* was used for both coal and charcoal, sometimes with the word "pit," "stone," or "sea" (only in Britain) preceding the former. It is clear, however, that in Britain the use of coal, especially for lime burning, was increasing during the thirteenth century and was widespread in the fourteenth. It was at first extracted from shallow open workings; then pits—frequently bell-shaped—were dug. There were countless complaints that these posed a danger, and in some instances they were ordered to be filled in. Coal was not obtained from below the water table, and pumps and adits for drainage appear to have been unknown except near Liège.

Little restriction appears to have been placed on coal mining. Unlike precious and some nonprecious metals, it was not subject to a regalian law by which king or prince owned subsurface rights. As a general rule coal was assimilated to building stone and sand, and its ownership was held to belong to the landowner. In 1395, for example, workmen called "mynours" were held to have "sunk pits in the King's soil . . . and thrown up and carried away . . . coals of no small value" near Newcastle. The king's rights that had been infringed were those of landowner, not those of king. Only in the Low Countries, specifically in Hainaut, was there a tendency for the prince to extend his control to coal. In Liège and throughout Germany the landholder was regarded as owner of the coal, with the right to concede permission to exploit it on payment of a royalty or rent.

In Great Britain there is evidence for the extraction of coal from most of the major coalfields by the end of the fourteenth century. Although there is no quantitative evidence, it appears that the Northumberland-Durham coalfield was by far the most important, probably because it lay close to the coast. "Sea coal" from this region was regularly used in London in the thirteenth century and was exported to the Low Countries soon afterward. The coalfields of Shropshire and the Forest of Dean were also used, perhaps because the Severn River provided a means of transportation. Other fields used regularly were those of Warwickshire, Nottinghamshire, and central Scotland.

In continental Europe the most readily accessible coalfields were those that lay along the Meuse in Hainaut and Liège, and on the Ruhr, a tributary of the Rhine. The Liège coalfield was probably the most important. It began to be worked early in the twelfth century, at Kerkrade. Mining then spread to the district of Liège and to Aachen. Near Liège medieval coal mining reached its highest level of sophistication. Not only were vertical pits sunk onto the seams, but horizontal adits were cut to drain them. The miners formed a kind of guild that settled the disputes that must have been common among them. Mining developed soon afterward to the west, at Charleroi and Mons, where coal also came to the surface and the Meuse and Sambre rivers could be used to transport it. This expansion of coal mining

in the Low Countries was not unrelated to the fact that, with the growth of population, timber had become scarce.

The Ruhr coalfield began to be worked in the thirteenth century along its southern, exposed margin, and by the fifteenth century it was sending coal via the Rhine to Cologne and the Low Countries. The Saar field and the small fields of Saxony were also exploited, and in France coal was obtained from the many small coal basins of the Central Massif. It is unlikely that coal was worked in eastern or southern Europe.

Estimates of the volume of coal extracted can be obtained only by extrapolating from the very slight documentary evidence or by projecting backward from later and better documented ages. Both methods indicate very small totals. It is unlikely that output greatly exceeded a few thousand tons a year from the best-developed fields, and production from the whole of Europe was to be measured in tens rather than in hundreds of thousands of tons.

BIBLIOGRAPHY

G. Decamps, "Mémoire historique sur l'origine et les développements de l'industrie houillère dans le bassin du couchant de Mons," in *Mémoires et publications de la Société des sciences, des arts et des lettres du Hainaut*, 4th ser., 5 (1880); Robert L. Galloway, *Annals of Coal Mining and the Coal Trade* (1896); R. Malherbe, "Historique de l'exploitation de la houille dans le pays de Liège jusqu'à nos jours," in *Mémoires de la Société libre d'émulation de Liège*, 2 (1862); John U. Nef, *The Rise of the British Coal Industry*, I (1932, repr. 1966); Louis I. Salzmann, *English Industries of the Middle Ages* (1913); Hans Spethmann, *Das Ruhrgebiet* (1933).

NORMAN J. G. POUNDS

[See also **Mining.**]

COATS OF ARMS. See **Heraldry.**

CODEX (from the Latin *caudex* or *codex*, trunk of a tree or booklet formed of wooden tablets). The codex, a revolutionary new kind of book, emerged in the first centuries of the Christian era. Previously the classical form of book had been the roll (Latin, *volumen*), in which pages were joined end to end and rolled up for storage. Not only was this system unwieldy, in that it was necessary to unroll the whole book to get to a particular passage and rolls could easily become twisted and tear, but it was wasteful, since the text was customarily copied on only one side of the writing material. In the codex or modern style of book, the sheets are folded into quires and stitched together at the center to form a series of pages. This kind of book can be opened and consulted at any point, and its pages have writing on both sides. It is also much less bulky and easier to store when closed, for its covers provide sturdy protection for the pages between them.

The inspiration for the new development seems to have come ultimately from wax tablets, which were fastened together to form a sort of booklet and served as the ancient equivalent of the modern note pad. The same structure came to be applied to parchment or papyrus sheets. With the addition of extra pages and the transcription of literary or subliterary texts, the codex was born. The poet Martial (*d. ca.* A.D. 104) mentions that his works could be purchased in this form (*Epigrams* 1.2). Because of climatic conditions, most archaelogical evidence on the early development and spread of the codex comes from papyrus discoveries in Egypt. The preeminence of Christian material among the earliest surviving codices suggests that the new religion adopted and promoted this nontraditional type of book for its writings, so that the extension of the new religion helped stimulate the spread of this new, more practical form of book. As early as the second and third centuries, the codex form began to catch on for Homer, Hesiod, and Plato. By the fifth and sixth centuries the roll was totally obsolete, except for a few particular uses in which ritualistic or legal conservatism favored the survival of the roll form.

The obvious material transformation of the book brought with it less obvious intellectual transformations. One of the most characteristic literary phenomena of late antiquity was the proliferation of technical reference manuals, the compilation of succinct encyclopedias intended for consultation rather than reading, and even the new organization of Roman legal science in "code" or codex form—for instance, the Codex Theodosianus of 438 and the Codex Justinianus of 529 and 534. This new kind of literary activity is clearly linked with the emergence of the codex.

BIBLIOGRAPHY

Colin H. Roberts, "The Codex," in *Proceedings of the British Academy,* 40 (1954); and *Manuscript, Society and Belief in Early Christian Egypt* (1979); Eric Gardiner Turner, *The Typology of the Early Codex.*

MICHAEL MCCORMICK

[See also **Codicology, Western European; Manuscripts and Books; Quire; Writing Materials.**]

CODEX AUREUS (Latin, "golden book"), a term used to describe certain opulent Gospel books in which gold was used lavishly. An example is the *codex aureus* of St. Emmeram, a Gospel made around 870 for Emperor Charles the Bald (Munich, Staatsbibliothek, codex lat. 14000).

LESLIE BRUBAKER

Page from the *Codex Aureus* of St. Emmeram written for Emperor Charles the Bald, *ca.* 870. BAYERISCHE STAATSBIBLIOTHEK, MUNICH, CLM 14000, fol. 5v

CODEX JUSTINIANUS. See **Corpus Iuris Civilis.**

CODEX THEODOSIANUS. The Eastern and Western emperors, Theodosius II and Valentinian III, issued a constitution on 26 March 429 in which they outlined a plan for an official compilation of imperial constitutions covering the reigns of all earlier emperors since Constantine (A.D. 312). Although the decree includes the names of both emperors, the initiative was Theodosius', and the work was to be completed in Constantinople. Theodosius ordered the collection to be modeled on two earlier codes, the Hermogenian and the Gregorian. The compilers were to select laws that had general force, placing them under titles that treated different topics of law.

The emperors asked that the abrogated laws of earlier emperors be included in the code and that the constitutions be arranged chronologically. The code was meant to be a repository of sources in which the history of legislative development could be seen and studied. The same constitution called for a second code that would draw on the Hermogenian, the Gregorian, and the recently completed code but would also contain the writings of the jurists on all points of law covered by the titles of the new work. In this last compilation there would be no ambiguity or error. It would be a *magisterium vitae.* Nine men were selected to write both codes.

The commission did not finish either code. On 20 December 435 another decree was promulgated, calling for yet another code. This time a commission of sixteen men was appointed. The task of the group was slightly different: they were to compile one code. The constitutions from the time of Constantine were to be placed topically under titles, but only valid imperial constitutions were to be included. The commission had the power to add necessary words, to clarify ambiguities, and to emend inconsistencies. Their editorial powers were much greater than those of the first commission, and they produced a code of laws in 438. Their rapid progress may have been the result of basing their work on the incomplete, but possibly substantial, achievement of the first commission. It is this book of laws that bears the name Codex Theodosianus.

The new code comprised sixteen books and, among other topics, covered imperial offices (book I), procedure (book II), contracts and dowries (book III), testaments (book IV), and penal law (book IX). Book XVI was particularly important, for it brought together, for the first time, imperial legislation concerning the Christian church.

We do not have a complete text of the Theodosian Code. Justinian's codification incorporated much of it into the Codex Justinianus, but Justinian also forbade the use of earlier codifications. Consequently the Theodosian Code was not used in the East after Justinian's legislation appeared. In the West a large part of the code was included in the *Lex Romana Visigothorum* (or Breviary of Alaric), issued in 506. A fairly large number of incomplete manuscripts exist, and modern editors have reconstructed, although incompletely, the text of the codex from these three sources. Books I through V in the Mommsen-Meyer edition probably contain about one-third of the original text. What little influence the Codex Theodosianus had in the West was primarily through the Breviary of Alaric.

BIBLIOGRAPHY

Gian Gualberto Archi, *Teodosio II e la sua codificazione* (1976); Theodor Mommsen and P. M. Meyer, eds., *Theodosiani libri XVI,* 2 vols. (1905); Clyde Pharr *et al.,* eds. and trans., *The Theodosian Code and Novels* (1952).

Kenneth Pennington

[See also **Breviary of Alaric; Corpus Iuris Civilis; Law, Byzantine; Theodosius II the Calligrapher.**]

CODICOLOGY, WESTERN EUROPEAN. Codicology is the study of the manuscript book as a whole. It takes into account not only the traditional subjects of manuscript study—the text, the script, the illustrations—but also the physical aspects of the book, treating the whole as one object. Codicology, according to Gerard Lieftinck, looks at manuscript books "not as little boxes for transmitting texts, nor simply as sources for preserving our knowledge of early scripts, but as objects of study for the cultural history of the Middle Ages."

This approach is older than the term itself; for example, it is apparent in the work of two pioneers in the cataloging of medieval manuscripts. Employing the techniques of codicology, Montague Rhodes James recorded such things as the material (parchment or paper), dimensions of the page, collation, number of columns and of lines, illuminations, binding, marginalia, provenance, and *secundo folio* in his catalogs of the manuscripts in Cambridge college libraries at the end of the nineteenth century. James did not coin a name for his practices but simply regarded them as a natural extension of paleography, the attitude still prevalent among British manuscript scholars. Virtually contemporary with James's Cambridge catalogs, Valentin Rose's catalogs of the Latin manuscripts in the royal library at Berlin also present quasi-codicological descriptions; like James, Rose was content to apply the techniques without giving them a name. Ludwig Traube and Klemens Löffler first used the term *Handschriftenkunde* to encompass specifically binding, material, quires, script, decoration, and text—although, in practice, the focus of *Handschriftenkunde* remained the writing.

The word "codicology" (which is by no means universally accepted) originated with French manuscript scholars centered around Charles Samaran in the 1930's. Ironically, its earliest use in print, by the Hellenist Alphonse Dain in 1949, gave a somewhat unusual definition of the term: the history of manuscripts (provenance) and of collections of manuscripts, research on an individual manuscript, problems of cataloging, collections of catalogs, and the medieval book trade. But the word *codicologie* was immediately seized upon by others, such as François Masai (1950) in Brussels and Gilbert Ouy (1961) in Paris, as the ideal French equivalent of the German *Handschriftenkunde*. Masai further expanded codicology to mean "the archaeology of the book"—that is, a special discipline that regards the handwritten book as an archaeological artifact, like a potsherd or a coin hoard, an object of research in its own right. More recently, L. M. J. Delaissé (1967) insisted—and practiced brilliantly what he preached—that a combined study of all the techniques involved in the manuscript book can reveal the methods, in various stages, by which a group of medieval craftsmen produced a book.

If codicology at its most ambitious may comprise a discipline of its own, the history of manuscript book production, its greatest utility for the greatest number of scholars—art historians, paleographers, textual critics—lies in examining the history of a given book to answer such questions as where, when, how, and why it was produced, and how it was subsequently used and altered. In this second, more practical sense, codicology is a method or technique, a "way of looking," that all branches of manuscript study should employ and that none may safely ignore. There are at least four general types of information (the number of specific ones is virtually infinite) that a codicological approach to the book may provide.

First, the physical aspects of a manuscript book may provide evidence for the date and place of origin as important and reliable as the script itself. There are certain processes virtually universal to the production of a manuscript book, and the methods of carrying them out vary from one time and/or place to another. The preparation of parchment (or the milling of paper), the arrangement of leaves in the gathering, the ruling and layout, the major and minor decoration, and the technique as well as the decoration of binding—each of these has its own history. Dating and localizing must take them into account, along with the script. Thus, for example, a French hand that writes on parchment prepared in the Italian manner very likely indicates that the writer (and not the parchment) traveled—and hence that the book is of southern origin despite its hand. Delaissé's study of sumptuously illustrated fifteenth-century books revealed that such "secondary" items as the minor decoration are in fact the only reliable elements that distinguish one atelier from another.

Second, the shape or form of a book is a reflection of the intellectual community that produced it. Changes in size, shape, layout, and binding often reveal the changing interests and uses that books served. Alternating red and blue paragraph marks in the schoolbooks of the late twelfth and early thirteenth centuries do not appear out of whimsy; they are division marks, made more prominent by their coloring. The pocket books of the thirteenth century are not curiosities but a reflection of professionalization in the disciplines of law, medicine, and parochial administration. Neil Ker's study of the manuscripts of Gregory's *Moralia* admirably demonstrates how changing demands can alter the structure of books.

Third, knowledge of the structure and layout of manuscript books is frequently a means to understanding the state of the text. Texts both ancient and medieval enjoyed a precarious existence before they were fixed in print, the ancient ones making the additional transition in format from papyrus roll to parchment codex. Books not infrequently remained unbound; they were at times copied unbound, a gathering for each scribe. Moreover, in the early modern period it was considered no great matter to dismember a codex and to exchange parts with another scholar. For instance, in the sixteenth century Pierre Daniel and Pierre Pithou occasionally traded portions of books. The opportunities for displacement or loss in such circumstances are obvious. Thus, for example, there are texts in which the lacuna is equivalent in length to the common four- or six-leaf gathering, indicating that at some point in the transmission a quire dropped out. At the beginning of the twentieth century the Oxford classicist Albert Curtis Clark effectively employed the techniques of codicology to solve mysteries in the transmission of classical texts.

Fourth, the provenance of a manuscript book often provides evidence concerning its origin and the later transmission of its text and illustrations. Although provenance has not always been included in the classic definitions of codicology, determining the medieval and early modern owners—the *Nachleben*—of a manuscript clearly constitutes a part of the book's history. At times the only clue to localizing a manuscript is the knowledge that it was owned by a particular early modern figure—for example, Robert Talbot, antiquary and prebend of Norwich Cathedral from 1547 to 1558, whose books almost certainly came from the cathedral's library; or Lord Harley, whose librarian, Humfrey Wanley, recorded in his diaries the source of each purchase, before the process of rebinding destroyed the identifying marks on flyleaves and the medieval bindings. By paying close attention to provenance, one is at the same time reassembling the medieval and early modern libraries, a not unimportant source for intellectual history and for determining the routes of cultural contact. One of the earliest to recognize the importance of grouping surviving manuscripts according to their medieval homes was Léopold Delisle in the 1860's; Bernhard Bischoff, André Vernet, and Neil Ker, among others, have continued and improved upon this tradition.

The potential importance of codicology to the study of a particular manuscript should be apparent. It follows, therefore, that every good catalog of manuscript books must employ the methods of codicology in its descriptions. Although the catalog of a collection obviously cannot be as detailed as the study in depth of a single codex, an adequate catalog description, besides identifying the texts contained, will attempt to record the following information for each book: (1) the base material (parchment or paper); (2) the layout of the manuscript and of the page, including quire structure (this will encompass any changes in the original state of the book—deletions, losses, displacement, additions), signatures and

catchwords, page size, size of written space, pricking, ruling, number of columns, number of lines per page, running headlines, early foliation; (3) the script (type of script, number of hands, location of changes in hand); (4) the artwork, including minor decoration (rubrication, decorated initials, slashed initials, paragraph marks, line fillers), major decoration (historiated initials, frames, borders), and miniatures; (5) the binding, including not only date and decoration but also the technique employed, and the remains of labels, clasps, and chains; (6) the opening words of the second folio, a common (though not universal) mark of identification recorded in medieval book lists; and (7) any marks of later use and ownership. In addition, in identifying the text(s) contained in the book, the cataloger should note the relationship of the text to the physical description (to layout, and to any changes: of hand, of decoration, of quire structure, of ruling, and so forth).

BIBLIOGRAPHY

Historiography: definitions and useful summaries. Malachi Beit-Arié, *Hebrew Codicology* (1977); T. J. Brown, "Latin Paleography Since Traube," in *Transactions of the Cambridge Bibliographical Society*, 3 (1959–1963); Alphonse Dain, *Les manuscrits* (1949); L. M. J. Delaissé, "Towards a History of the Medieval Book," in *Miscellanea André Combs*, II (1967); Albert Gruijs, "Codicology or the Archaeology of the Book? A False Dilemma," in *Quaerendo*, 2 (1972); G. I. Lieftinck, "Enige beschouwingen naar anleiding van de nieuwe editie van Thomas à Kempis," in *Tijdschrift voor Nederlandse Taal- en Letterkunde*, 76 (1958–1959); Karl Löffler, *Einführung in die Handschriftenkunde* (1929); François Masai, "Paléographie et codicologie," in *Scriptorium*, 4 (1950), and "La paléographie gréco-latine, ses tâches, ses méthodes," in *Scriptorium*, 10 (1956); Gilbert Ouy, "Les bibliothèques," in *L'histoire et ses méthodes*, Charles Samaran, ed. (1961), 1060–1108, esp. 1085–1102; Richard W. Pfaff, "M. R. James on the Cataloging of Manuscripts: A Draft Essay of 1906," in *Scriptorium*, 31 (1977); Charles Samaran, preface to *Codicologica*, I (1976), which contains several of the articles cited here; Ludwig Traube, *Vorlesungen und Abhandlungen*, I (1909).

Aspects and applications. Bernhard Bischoff, *Lorsch im Spiegel seiner Handschriften* (1974); Robert G. Calkins, "Distribution of Labor: The Illuminators of the Hours of Catherine of Cleves and Their Workshop," in *Transactions of the American Philosophical Society*, 69, pt. 5 (1979); Albert Curtis Clark, *The Descent of Manuscripts* (1918); L. M. J. Delaissé, ed., *Le manuscrit autographe de Thomas à Kempis et "L'imitation de Jésus Christ": Examen archéologique et édition diplomatique*, 2 vols. (1956);

L. M. J. Delaissé, James Marrow, and John de Wit, *The James A. de Rothschild Collection at Waddesdon Manor: Illuminated Manuscripts* (1977); Léopold Delisle, *Le cabinet des manuscrits . . .* , 3 vols. (1868–1881); Léon Gilissen, *Prolégomènes à la codicologie* (1977); Neil R. Ker, *Medieval Libraries of Great Britain*, 2nd ed. (1964), and "The English Manuscripts of the *Moralia* of Gregory the Great," in *Kunsthistorische Forschungen Otto Pächt zu seinem 70. Geburtstag*, Artur Rosenauer and Gerold Weber, eds. (1972); André Vernet, *La bibliothèque de l'abbaye de Clairvaux du XIIᵉ au XVIIIᵉ siècle*, vol. 1: *Catalogues et répertoires* (1979); Jean Vezin, "La réalisation matérielle des manuscrits latins pendant le haut Moyen Âge," in *Codicologica*, II (1978), 15–51.

R. H. ROUSE AND M. A. ROUSE

[See also **Codex; Manuscript and Book Binding; Manuscript and Book Production; Manuscript Illumination, Western European; Paleography, Western European; Paper, Introduction of; Papyrus; Parchment.**]

COENE, JAQUES, an architect, painter, and illuminator from Bruges. He was active at Paris in 1398 and the following year went to Milan to draw plans for the construction of the cathedral. In 1404 he illuminated a Bible for Philip the Bold of Burgundy. Some scholars believe Coene was the Master of the Boucicaut Hours.

BIBLIOGRAPHY
Millard Meiss, *French Painting in the Time of Jean de Berry: The Boucicaut Master* (1968), 60–62.

ROBERT G. CALKINS

[See also **Boucicaut Master.**]

COINAGE. See Mints and Money.

COLA DI RIENZO (born Niccoló, *ca.* 1313–1354), was the son of Lorenzo Gabrini, a tavern keeper in Rome. He trained as a notary and in 1343 was sent on a diplomatic mission to Pope Clement VI at Avignon by his Roman compatriots. At Avignon his literary ability gained him the friendship of the poet Petrarch and the ear of the papal court. At this period of the absence of the popes from Rome and of

weak government in the Papal States, the ruling clerks at Avignon were not unwilling to listen to advocates of the popular party in Rome, such as Cola, who protested against the disorder and tyranny of the Roman nobles. On 9 August 1344 Pope Clement VI referred to Cola di Rienzo as a papal "familiar" and instructed the senators of Rome to protect him against the unpopularity that he courted among the Roman nobles. Other minor papal privileges were given him, such as appointment as notary of the Roman city treasury.

On 20 May 1347 Cola carried out a coup d'etat in Rome that may have been prearranged with the papal government. He secured his own popular election as "tribune" to rule Rome along with the papal "vicar in spirituals." The pope accepted this arrangement and confirmed his position as joint "rector." But once in office Cola carried out a grandiloquent policy that was not at all to the liking of the pope. He energetically asserted the Roman communal rule over the Roman District, forcing the supposedly subject communes to pay salt tax and to supply soldiers. He attempted to revive single-handed the "Guelph" alliance of propapal communes of central Italy, summoning the cities of Umbria and Tuscany to send embassies and announcing a future "parliament" of communes in Rome. He attacked the nobles of the Roman District, particularly the prefect of Rome, an old enemy of papal authority, and the Colonna family.

Cola assumed a number of high-sounding titles, such as "candidate of the Holy Spirit," "tribune and liberator," and "knight of the Roman people." The clerical flavor of much of his ceremonial is noticeable, from the banners of St. Peter and St. Paul that he carried at Pentecost 1347 to the porphyry "bath of Constantine" in which he bathed (like Constantine at the instance of Sylvester I in the legend) before being knighted. He also invoked, in battle, "holy" Pope Boniface VIII. So that they should participate in the gifts of the Holy Spirit, he conferred Roman citizenship on all Italians.

Pope Clement VI took these proceedings ill and on 15 September ordered Cola's removal. The papal legate ordered to do this, Cardinal Bertrand de Déaulx, possessed no military force and was unable to carry out his instructions. Cola's regime endured for a few months more, thanks to the support of the Orsini family and of some troops of Louis I of Hungary, claimant of the Neapolitan throne. On 20 November 1347 Cola defeated Stefanuccio Colonna in a bloody battle at Porta San Lorenzo, but he was finally unseated on 15 December 1347 by a small detachment of troops belonging to a rival Neapolitan faction under Giovanni Pipino, count of Minervino. Cola went into exile in Prague and, in 1352, to Avignon to face the Inquisition. He returned as papal senator of Rome for a few months in 1354 but was murdered by the Colonna faction on 8 October.

In terms of Roman politics Cola reflected the strength of the popular faction, especially of the small landowning merchants. In terms of literature and ideas he is associated with Petrarch as an early exponent of political humanism; but he can also be attached to the tradition of medieval prophecy.

BIBLIOGRAPHY
K. Burdach and P. Piur, eds., *Briefwechsel des Cola di Rienzo*, 5 vols. (1912–1929); Eugenio Dupré-Theseider, *I papi di Avignone e la questione romana* (1939), 87ff.

PETER D. PARTNER

[See also **Clement VI, Pope; Rome.**]

COLCHIS. See **Georgia: Geography.**

COLIN MUSET. Some twenty lyrics by this mid-thirteenth-century Lorraine poet survive, several with melodies. Using great metrical inventiveness, he sings of love and of less conventional topics: the *ménestrel*'s precarious calling, the uncertain largess of patrons, the destructive side of chivalry, musical picnics on the grass, cozy fireside suppers. He prefers tournaments to battles, and creature comforts to both. A witty beggar, denouncing the stingy lord and praising the generous, he celebrates food and wine as enthusiastically as amorous play. Melancholy and bitterness mark certain poems; but typically Colin rejoices in springtime, feminine beauty, and his own heart's leap.

BIBLIOGRAPHY
M. Banitt, "Le vocabulaire de Colin Muset: Rapprochement sémantique avec celui d'un prince-poète, Thibaut de Champagne," in *Romance Philology*, 20 (1966); Joseph Bédier, ed., *Les chansons de Colin Muset*, 2nd ed. (1938).

BARBARA NELSON SARGENT-BAUR

[See also **Minstrels and Popular Entertainment.**]

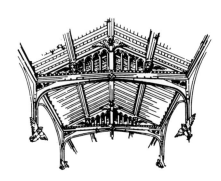

Tie-beam roof. FROM SIR BANISTER FLETCHER'S A HISTORY OF ARCHITECTURE

COLLAR BEAM, a horizontal beam or tie beam attached to two opposing common or principal rafters to provide increased resistance against sagging and wind load. The collar beam, also called span piece, top beam, or wind beam, is located about halfway between the wall plate and the ridge, and resembles the crossbar in the capital letter *A*.

CARL F. BARNES, JR.

COLLECTARIUM. From the tenth century the terms *orationale* in Italy and *collectarium, liber collectarius,* and *collectaneum* north of the Alps (the last, among the Cistercians and Premonstratensians), normally denoted the liturgical book containing the collects and capitula of the Divine Office.

The early Gelasian sacramentary contained special collects for lauds and vespers, the only hours included in the early Roman Office; and by the eighth century the Gelasians had collects for all of the canonical hours. Shortly afterward the first collectariums appeared. These were extracts from a sacramentary made especially for the Divine Office: the *orationale* copied before 807 by Pacifico of Verona from an original (*ca.* 800) of the monastery at Reichenau. As soon as the Gregorian sacramentary of Pope Adrian I was introduced in the Frankish territories, collects were extracted from it as well, not only at Reichenau but elsewhere. Thus the collectarium of Baturich, bishop of Regensburg from 817 to 848, is of the Gregorian type.

The collects thus assembled later underwent a twofold evolution. On the one hand, in the eleventh and twelfth centuries the collects, previously indicated for particular canonical hours rather than for specific days, received more precise assignments—as did the capitula. On the other hand, from the eleventh century the collects for matins and vespers were gradually replaced by the collect for the previous Sunday. Likewise, the liturgy of the Roman curia (perhaps following papal usage) had only a single collect for each liturgical day, and on this point the curial liturgy was widely imitated in the thirteenth and fourteenth centuries. This peculiarity indicates that the curia probably never used the collectarium as an independent liturgical book but, rather, sometimes used certain collects to supplement the Psalter.

The earliest collectariums contained only collects; in the ninth or tenth century the capitula of the various hours were added, with their repertoire becoming fixed during this period. The first appearance of these capitula is Salzburg, Museum Carolino-Augusteum, MS 2163, dating from the early ninth century. From the tenth century the collectarium always contains the capitula and the standard preces of the Office as well. The modern designation of the capitulary-collectarium was unknown in the Middle Ages and is irrelevant here. In the eleventh century benedictions for certain periods in the liturgical year (for ashes, palms, or candles at Candlemas) were generally added; occasionally a calendar and, in the thirteenth century, the antiphonal intonations for the presiding priest also appeared.

BIBLIOGRAPHY

Pierre-Marie Gy, "Collectaire, rituel, processional," in *Revue des sciences philosophiques et théologiques*, **44** (1960); Gérard Meersseman, E. Adda, and Jean Deshusses, *L'orazionale dell'arcidiacono Pacifico e il carpsum del cantore Stefano* (1974); Franz Unterkircher, ed., *Das Kollektar-Pontifikale des Bischofs Baturich von Regensburg (817–848)* (1962).

PIERRE-MARIE GY, O.P.

[See also **Canonical Hours; Divine Office; Sacramentary.**]

COLMAN, BISHOP OF LINDISFARNE (661?–664?), mentioned in Bede's *Ecclesiastical History* (III, 25–26; IV, 4), is not to be confused with a number of other Colmans of Irish history. Besides being bishop of Lindisfarne, he was an unsuccessful defender of the Celtic party at Whitby in 663 or 664 and founded Inishbofin and a separate settlement for his English followers at Mag Eo (Mayo).

BIBLIOGRAPHY

James F. Kenney, *The Sources for the Early History of Ireland: Ecclesiastical* (1966); Kathleen Hughes, "Evidence for Contacts Between the Churches of the Irish and English," in Peter Clemoes and Kathleen Hughes, eds., *England Before the Conquest: Studies ... Presented to Dorothy Whitelock* (1971), 49–67; Henry Mayr-Harting, *The Coming of Christianity to Anglo-Saxon England* (1972), 103–113.

MICHAEL HERREN

[See also **Whitby, Synod of.**]

COLOBIUM (COLOBION), a long tunic, usually sleeveless, worn by men. Until the ninth century the crucified Christ was normally shown in a colobium, as in the Rabula Gospels of 586.

LESLIE BRUBAKER

COLOGNE was the largest city in Germany in the Middle Ages, with an area that increased from 98.6

Crucifixion scene from the Rabula Gospels. Completed at Zagba, *ca.* 586. BIBLIOTECA MEDICEA LAURENZIANA, FLORENCE

hectares (the Roman city) to 402.6 hectares (after 1180) and a population of about 40,000 by 1300. Its favorable location, at a spot where major land routes crossed the Rhine, made it an early center of commerce. Trade in goods such as wine and metals was complemented by a diversified local industry in textiles, metal products, dressed furs, and leather goods. The diversity of its economic activity allowed Cologne to remain of central importance from the tenth century to the end of the Middle Ages.

The Roman city declined rapidly under the impact of Frankish invasions. In a distinctly nonurban age only remnants were left, in the city walls and in the ecclesiastical organization of the cathedral and the churches of the martyrs (St. Severin, St. Gereon, St. Ursula). Although Cologne may have retained a certain urban character and some merchants, it was overshadowed until the tenth century by centers in the regions of the Meuse and the Moselle.

After the Viking destruction of Cologne in 881, the first signs of the distinctively medieval city appear. It was probably under Archbishop Bruno I (953–965), brother of Emperor Otto I, that grants concerning high justice, minting, and tolls were received. This strengthening of the archbishop's lordship coincided with the interests of a new group of merchants. The Cologne *portus,* located between the Roman walls and the Rhine, was fortified down to the river around 950. A merchant guild flourished, though sure evidence of it comes only in the early twelfth century, near the end of its existence.

The first united action of the burghers against the archbishop came in 1074, when Archbishop Anno II arrogantly attempted to requisition a merchant's boat. After some initial success the revolt was crushed. In 1106 the burghers supported the beleaguered Emperor Henry IV against the revolt of his son. Henry V failed in his attempt to take the city. From this period the community of Cologne had responsibility for defense and a taxing power to support it. During most of the twelfth century there were few conflicts between the archbishop, who was often absent on imperial business, and the town. A major conflict did arise in 1180 over new urban fortifications. While Archbishop Philip of Heinsberg was absent, fighting against Henry the Lion, the burghers built a semicircular wall around Cologne. Philip demanded that his rights be respected, but he left the new fortifications intact and the burghers with the responsibility of defending them.

Meanwhile, the townspeople gained control of urban institutions. The *Burggraf* and the *Stadtvogt,*

a noble and a ministerial, respectively, were increasingly replaced by assistants recruited from among the burghers. These assistants and the urban *scabini,* who rendered judgments in the archbishop's court, controlled judicial affairs. Local matters such as property transfers were handled in each parish by organizations led by two masters with the advice of the parish guild of past masters. Two mayors for the whole town were chosen by a private organization of wealthy burghers, the *Richerzeche,* which increasingly assumed control over such economic affairs as craft regulation. By 1200 the archbishop's effective power in the city had been substantially reduced, and internal control of Cologne was in the hands of certain powerful families, the *Geschlechter.*

In the thirteenth century the archbishop exploited conflicts among the *Geschlechter* in an attempt to reestablish effective lordship in Cologne. The Great Arbitration of 1258, with Albertus Magnus as one of the arbitrators, held that all the authority within the town derived from the archbishop but also that the normal exercise of much of that authority was rightfully in the hands of urban groups. This delicate balance was later tilted toward the town, however, when the Overstolz faction defeated the Weise faction at the Ulrepforte in 1263, and the newly united *Geschlechter* derived substantial benefits from the archbishop's defeat at Worringen in 1288. By the later thirteenth century the archbishop resided in Bonn, not Cologne; and the only important rights left him in the town were those of high justice, administered by urban *scabini.* The focus of city government shifted to the town council (first mentioned in 1216).

Cologne's economic success made it a center of religious and cultural development. New orders flourished over the objections of the established clergy. Albertus Magnus organized the Dominican school in 1248; Dominicans helped to found the university in 1388. Many women were attracted to the new orders; many others, especially daughters of the *Geschlechter,* joined the less structured and more suspect Beguines. Meister Eckhart spent several years, including his last ones, in Cologne; and elements of his mystical thought were condemned there in the 1320's. The Jewish community, of great importance in the development of Cologne, was ruthlessly persecuted at various times, usually in conjunction with popular outbursts: 1096 (the First Crusade), 1146 (the Second Crusade), 1349 (the Black Death). Jews were excluded from Cologne in 1424.

The relative harmony among the members of the

ruling elite disappeared in the fourteenth century. Factional divisions among the *Geschlechter* gave merchants as well as craftsmen the opportunity to challenge and then to overthrow the *Geschlechter* rule. The weavers led a revolt in 1370 that established a mixed government based on the *Geschlechter* and the craft guilds. This attempt ended in violent failure, but in 1396 a broad-based alliance of craft guilds and merchant corporations *(Gaffeln)* overthrew the *Geschlechter* regime. They issued the *Verbundbrief,* which remained the constitutional basis for Cologne until the end of the eighteenth century. The reorganized town council was firmly controlled by the victors of 1396. The *Richerzeche* was abolished. The *scabini* still represented the *Geschlechter,* but the council chipped away at their position in the 1420's, and by 1449 anyone who had the professional qualifications could be chosen a *scabinus;* the *Geschlechter* had lost their last positions of power.

By the end of the Middle Ages, Cologne had achieved the status of a free imperial city. Internally, control of the town council was in the hands of the merchant corporations and certain important craft guilds. Economically, religiously, and culturally Cologne remained what it had been since the tenth century—a major center of European development.

BIBLIOGRAPHY

Wolfgang Herborn, *Die politische Führungsschicht der Stadt Köln im Spätmittelalter* (1977), an excellent archival study of the relation between socioeconomic and political leadership; Hermann Kellenbenz, ed., *Zwei Jahrtausende Kölner Wirtschaft,* I (1975), especially 13–193, 217–319, probably the best introductory survey; Hermann Keussen, *Topographie der Stadt Köln im Mittelalter,* 2 vols. and maps (1910), containing records of property ownership; Richard Koebner, *Die Anfänge des Gemeinwesens der Stadt Köln* (1922), still the best introduction to the formation of the community; Frederich-Wilhelm Oediger, *Das Bistum Köln von den Anfängen bis zum Ende des 12. Jahrhunderts,* 2nd ed. (1972); Paul W. Strait, *Cologne in the Twelfth Century* (1974), the only extended study in English, providing revisions of earlier work such as Koebner's.

PAUL W. STRAIT

[See also **Germany; Guilds and Métiers; Henry V of Germany; Henry the Lion; Jews in Europe, 900–1500.**]

COLOMBE, JEAN, a manuscript illuminator active at Bourges from about 1463 to about 1493. He is best known for his miniatures in the *Très riches heures* (Chantilly, Musée Condé), left incomplete by the Limbourg Brothers in 1416, which he finished for Charles I, duke of Savoy, about 1485.

BIBLIOGRAPHY

Claude Schaefer, "Les débuts de l'atelier de Jean Colombe: Jean Colombe et André Rousseau, prêtre, libraire, et 'escrivain,'" in *Gazette des beaux arts,* **90** (1977); Jean Longnon and Raymond Cazelles, eds., *Les très riches heures of Jean, Duke of Berry* (1969), 22–23 and *passim.*

ROBERT G. CALKINS

COLOMBE, MICHEL (*ca.* 1430–*ca.* 1511), a French sculptor born at Bourges. He was active at Tours from 1473. In 1474 he made a model of a tomb for Louis XI; in 1502–1507 he sculpted the tomb of Duke Francis II of Brittany and Marguerite de Foix at Nantes; and in 1508–1509 he carved the relief of St. George for the Château de Gaillon (now in the Louvre, Paris). His work is transitional between the styles of the late Gothic and early Renaissance.

BIBLIOGRAPHY

Pierre Pradel, *Michel Colombe* (1953); Theodore Müller, *Sculpture in the Netherlands, Germany, France, and Spain, 1400 to 1500* (1966), 2, 133, 139, 191, 192, 193.

ROBERT G. CALKINS

COLONIA, JUAN AND SIMON DE. See Juan and Simon de Colonia.

COLONUS, the tenant farmer of the late Roman Empire, gradually reduced to bondage by imperial policy and law. In 332 coloni, in order to be available for imperial tax assessments, were prohibited from leaving their place of birth or residence; in 371 they were exempted from tax liability but were required to remain on their tenancies and continue as productive farmers. Imperial laws of the fourth century also protected them from increases in rent and eviction by landlords, who were consequently restricted in the management and disposition of their estates. Although still legally freemen, coloni passed steadily under the de facto control of their landlords and suf-

Detail of the tomb of Francis II and Marguerite de Foix, by Michel Colombe. Nantes Cathedral, 1502–1507. PHOTO BY JEAN ROUBIER

marriage of servile tenants to women of colona status may well have accounted for the diminution of the old servile population because the status of the mother passed to her children. However, personal status did not necessarily coincide with the status of land, and coloni occupied both free and servile tenures, assuming the respective obligations. The simple division between free and service tenures was apparently transferred to the tenants themselves, for the legal documents of the ninth and tenth centuries increasingly contrast the coloni with free tenants. After the tenth century coloni are rarely mentioned, although a few individuals survived with that identity on some ecclesiastical estates until the late thirteenth century. On most estates they lost their separate identity when all tenants—whether free, dependent, or servile—were described as the *homines* (men) of a landlord.

BIBLIOGRAPHY

Emily R. Coleman, "Medieval Marriage Characteristics: A Neglected Factor in the History of Medieval Serfdom," in *Journal of Interdisciplinary History,* **2** (1971); Robert Fossier, *Histoire sociale de l'occident médiéval* (1970), 59–66; Walter Goffart, "From Roman Taxation to Medieval Seigneurie: Three Notes," in *Speculum,* **47** (1972), and *"Caput" and Colonate* (1974).

THEODORE EVERGATES

[See also **Land Tenure, Western European; Serfs and Serfdom, Western European.**]

fered a serious derogation of status by the fifth century: a law of Valentinian III classed them with tenants of servile status.

The evolution of the colonate, like that of other rural classes, is not entirely clear in the following three centuries. Brief references in several of the Germanic law codes suggest that the fate of the coloni varied in the Western kingdoms. In some areas, such as Visigothic Spain, they became indistinguishable from servile tenants, while in northern France and Germany they maintained a distinct status between freemen and slaves. Although it is impossible to measure the relative sizes of the rural classes in this period, it does seem that coloni were more numerous than the extant records indicate because they were not identified by name when grouped with all other estate tenants for local administrative purposes.

Coloni are more visible in the polyptychs and royal charters of the ninth century. No longer were they tied to the land, and on many estates they constituted the majority of the population—for instance, on the estates of St. Germain-des-Prés they represented 83 percent of all tenants (5 percent were servile tenants and 1 percent were freemen). The

COLOPHON (Greek: κολοφών, finishing touch). At the end of the transcription of a text, ancient and medieval scribes often added a note concerning the circumstances of their work. Such notes tend to identify the scribe(s), place, date, or price of the manuscript, or the client for whom it was copied. Occasionally scribes added a more personal or ribald note. They also sometimes blindly recopied older colophons, furnishing us with precious clues to lost manuscripts.

BIBLIOGRAPHY

Benedictine monks of Le Bouveret, *Colophons de manuscrits occidentaux dès origines au XVIᵉ siècle (Spicilegii Friburgensis subsidia, 2–6)* (1965–1979), is a comprehensive repertory of colophons of Western MSS. Marie Vogel and Viktor Gardthausen, *Die griechischen Schreiber des Mittelalters und der Renaissance* (1909), is the classic repertory of Greek scribes. For additional bibliography see E.

Illuminated Greek manuscript showing 16-line colophon in the right-hand column. 14th century. ROBERT GARRETT COLLECTION OF MEDIEVAL AND RENAISSANCE MANUSCRIPTS, PRINCETON UNIVERSITY LIBRARY

Gamillscheg and D. Harlfinger, "Specimin eines Repertoriums der griechischen Kopisten," in *Jahrbuch der österreichischen Byzantinistik,* 27 (1978); and C. C. Brach, "Copisti greci del Medieoevo e del Renascimento," in *Epetēris Etairēias Byzantinon Epoudon,* 42 (1975–1976).

MICHAEL MCCORMICK

[See also **Manuscript and Book Production.**]

COLORS, LITURGICAL. Liturgical usage developed in the context of biblical prescriptions for Levitical garments, as in Exodus 28, and Roman color symbolism, as in the use of purple and gold to denote imperial dignity. Very early, however, there was a concerted effort to persuade Christians to adopt such distinctive uses as the festive color of white on the death of a loved one. The early medieval fascination with color symbolism is perhaps best expressed in a little Irish tract, preserved in the *Leabhar Breac* and

Liber Flavus Fergusiorum, in which eight colors said to have been used in the ancient priestly vestments are assigned various mystical significances. Nevertheless, the great liturgical commentators of the eleventh and twelfth centuries offer no express color code.

Actual practice in the early centuries is difficult to establish because catacomb frescoes and manuscript illuminations are colored as much by artistic license as by historical verisimilitude. By the sixth century, however, there are a number of explicit indications in literary sources. For example, in the work of Gregory of Tours, perhaps in a life of Caesarius of Arles, and in the seventh-century Mass exposition incorrectly attributed to Germanus of Paris, it is said that white vestments are appropriate to Easter. Ninth- and tenth-century liturgical directories note that pope and deacons wear black on Candlemas and that all clerics wear a dark color on Good Friday.

There is more evidence from the twelfth century: black for fasts and red for Passiontide (Beroldus of Milan); white for Easter (Mabillon's *Ordo* 11); white for the St. Stephen's day procession and red for the Mass (Mabillon's *Ordo* 12). At the end of the century comes a document (in the *De sacro altaris mysterio*) by Lotario di Segni, the future Pope Innocent III. More a report on customary practice than an "official" code, this document came to enjoy great status on account of its author's prestige. Connecting the principle colors (white, red, black, and green) with Levitical tradition, and assigning mystical or biblical justification to each, Lotario offered the following catalog: white for feasts of confessors, virgins, and angels, for Christmas and the Nativity of John the Baptist, Epiphany, Candlemas, Maundy Thursday, Easter, Ascension, the feast of the dedication of a church, and All Saints; red for apostles, martyrs, feasts of the Cross (though white may also be used), Pentecost, the Feast of Sts. Peter and Paul (but white for the Conversion of Paul and the Chair of St. Peter), All Saints, and the Decollation of St. John the Baptist; black for times of sorrow and abstinence, such as Advent and the period from Septuagesima to Holy Saturday; and green for all other days.

Lotario's catalog eventually became the canon followed by later liturgical commentators, chief among whom was Gulielmus Durandus, who said that yellow could be substituted for green and gave a long list of other possible substitutions. Most of the liturgical directories for both the Roman church and other churches in the later Middle Ages that have been edited basically follow this code. Nonetheless, there are almost as many exceptions as there are local churches; and as editions and studies of later medieval liturgical books are published, the enormous variety of uses will become apparent. The most notable exceptions are listed in the standard works of Legg and Braun, cited below.

BIBLIOGRAPHY

Joseph Braun, *Die liturgische Gewandung im Occident und Orient nach Ursprung und Entwicklung, Verwendung, und Symbolik* (1907), 728–760; and *Handbuch der Paramentik* (1912), 52–58; Gulielmus Durandus, *Rationale divinorum officium* (1672), 81–83; H. Leclercq, "Couleurs liturgiques," in *Dictionnaire d'archéologie chrétienne et de liturgie*, 111, pt. 2 (1914), 2999–3004; John Wickham Legg, *Notes on the History of the Liturgical Colours* (1882); Lotario di Segni (Innocent III), *De sacro altaris mysterio*, in *Patrologia latina*, CCXVII, 799–802; Mario Righetti, *Manuale di storia liturgica*, I (1950), 495; Charles Rohault de Fleury, *La messe*, VIII (1889), 25–43; Alfred C. Rush, "The Colors of Red and Black in the Liturgy of the Dead," in *Kyriakon: Festschrift Johannes Quasten*, II (1970).

ROGER E. REYNOLDS

[See also **Durandus; Innocent III, Pope; Liturgy, Treatises on; Ordines romani; Vestments.**]

COLUMBA, ST. (*ca.* 521–*ca.* 597). Columba or Columcille (church dove), who is to be distinguished from his younger contemporary Columbanus, was one of the most influential pioneers of Irish Christianity at the beginning of the Middle Ages. The main sources for his life are Bede's *Ecclesiastical History* (III, 4 and *passim*); a Latin life by Adamnan, ninth abbot of Iona, written about 690, based partially on an earlier life by Cummine Ailbe and on oral tradition; and an obscure Irish poem, *Amra Coluim-cille*, ascribed to Dallan Forgaill, written probably in the seventh century.

Columba sprang from the cenél Conaill, a branch of the northern Uí Néill. Most of what the later sources tell us of his early life and education is dubious and occasionally contradictory. Around 563 he came with his companions to Iona (Hi), where he established a monastic church and became in effect the primate of Dál Riata. It is certain that he also founded Durrow in Ireland, and many other foundations are ascribed to him. Bede credits Columba with the conversion of the northern Picts during the reign of Brude. Adamnan's account stresses miracles, prophecies, and personal sanctity rather than missionary activity.

Clear evidence of Columba's connection to learning is sparse. The best evidence is given by the *Amra:* "He obelized glosses clearly; he secured correctness of psalms; he made known law books, books that Cassian loved." Adamnan credits him with much reading, and later tradition attributed to him the copying of the Cathach (a late-sixth-century Irish psalter). Several Latin "rhythmical" poems are assigned to him, but only the *Altus prosator* is plausibly his. Despite the inadequacy of the evidence of Columba's personal scholarly achievements, Iona was to become arguably the most important Irish center of learning in the British Isles before 800.

BIBLIOGRAPHY

Alan Orr Anderson and Marjorie O. Anderson, eds. and trans., *Adomnan's Life of Columba* (1961); D. A. Bullough, "Columba, Adomnan and the Achievement of Iona," in *Scottish Historical Review*, **43–44** (1964–1965); James Francis Kenney, *The Sources for the Early History of Ireland: Ecclesiastical* (1966), esp. 423–426; William Reeves, ed., *The Life of St. Columba* (1957).

MICHAEL HERREN

[See also **Adamnan, St.; Missions and Missionaries, Christian.**]

COLUMBANUS, ST., referred to as Columbanus and Columba by his chief biographer, is not to be confused with St. Columba of Iona or with a later Columbanus, abbot of St. Trond near Liège. He was a very influential exponent of Irish Christianity on the Continent between about 590 and 615 and was also the first Irishman writing in Latin whose works have survived in any considerable quantity. The major sources for his life are a *vita* by Jonas, a monk of Bobbio who entered Columbanus' foundation shortly after his death; Carolingian lives of St. Gall by Wettinus and Walafrid Strabo; and the genuine letters of Columbanus himself. Columbanus was apparently not known to Gregory of Tours, but is mentioned by Bede in his *Ecclesiastical History* (II, 4) and excerpts from Jonas' *vita* are employed in the so-called "Chronicle of Fredegarius" (IV, 36). Due to recent developments in the controversy over the authenticity of several poems attributed to Columbanus, the poem *Fidolio* should not be used as evidence for dating his birth.

We do not know the year of Columbanus' birth or his age when he arrived on the Continent. According to Jonas, Columbanus was born in Leinster and his early education was undertaken by a certain Sinell. Later, he studied at Comgall's foundation, Bangor. The precise nature of his studies there cannot be ascertained, but from his known genuine writings, especially the letters, one can infer that Columbanus acquired a thorough mastery of Latin prose style, a firm acquaintance with the Bible and such standard patristic authors as Jerome and Eusebius of Caesarea, and a detailed knowledge of computus as taught by the Irish of his time. There is no convincing evidence that classical authors were taught and read at Bangor or elsewhere in sixth-century Ireland.

Columbanus, with the statutory twelve companions, came to Gaul as a *peregrinus* in 590 or 591, a date established from internal evidence in his letter to the Gaulish clergy. He was given land in the Vosges by King Guntram of Burgundy. There he established in succession the monasteries of Annegray, Luxeuil, and Fontaines. These centers quickly attracted attention for the rigor of their *monastica conversatio* and gained many followers. In 603 Columbanus fell afoul of the Gaulish bishops, ostensibly over the Irish method of reckoning Easter, but other issues were doubtless involved: the refusal of Irish abbots to accept episcopal authority coupled with Columbanus' undisguised censures of the laxity of the Gaulish church. In 603 Columbanus refused to appear before the bishops at the Council of Chalon sur Saône and, perhaps in the following year, appealed to the pope for assistance in his cause. In 610 he was expelled by King Theuderic, allegedly for not approving the legitimization of his bastard sons, but Columbanus' general unpopularity with the Gaulish clergy surely contributed to the action.

However, the boat that was to take Columbanus to Ireland was forced back in a storm, and its passenger disembarked on the shores of Gaul. Columbanus was able to rejoin some of his monks in Neustria and from there went to Switzerland with his close companion Gall, with whom he later quarreled. His final years (*ca.* 612–615) were spent in Lombardy, where he established Bobbio, which became one of the greatest seats of learning of the early Middle Ages. Columbanus' last battle involved—somewhat anachronistically—the "Three Chapters" heresy; his letter to Boniface IV on that subject has survived. He died at Bobbio.

The corpus of Columbanus' genuine writings has long been a subject of dispute, and some points are still not settled. Numerous writings have been ascribed to him, including seven letters, the treatise *De saltu lunae*, seventeen sermons, a monastic rule, a penitential, and several poems, of which three are in epistolary form. Of the letters there is now general agreement that letters I–V (as printed by Walker) are genuine. The letter *De sollemnitatibus et sabbatis et neomeniis* (no. VI in Gundlach) is now judged spurious. The letter to a young man referred to as *minister* may or may not be by Columbanus. Of the seventeen sermons printed in *Patrologia latina*, at least four must be pruned, including one entitled *De octo vitiis principalibus*. The thirteen sermons given by Walker, which have a unified manuscript tradition, are possibly by Columbanus. The *De saltu lunae* belongs to the *spuria*. The penitential and the rule have a Columbanian core with later accretions.

It is the poetic output of Columbanus that has entailed the greatest controversy, specifically because of the implications for "Irish humanism" in the sixth century. Six metrical poems have at various times been ascribed to him: the epigram *In mulieres*, a *carmen navale* (hexameters), *Fidolio* (adonics), *Hunaldo* and *Ad Sethum* (hexameters), and *Monosticha* (mislabeled *Monastica*), which is also ascribed to Alcuin. A rhythmical poem, *De mundi transitu*, is also ascribed to Columbanus. No one today credits the *In mulieres* to Columbanus, but the dispute continues about the other poems. Recent work has attempted to show that the epistolary poems (*Fidolio, Hunaldo, Ad Sethum*) are not by Columbanus of Luxeuil but by a Carolingian namesake, possibly Columbanus, abbot of St. Trond. Whereas Columbanian authorship of these works has not been disproved, these poems must now be classed as *dubia*. The *Monosticha* may also have been composed at a later time, by some other Columbanus or by Alcuin. Little can be said one way or another for the authenticity of the *De mundi transitu*.

The genuine letters not only are invaluable sources for Columbanus' life and times but also reveal a Latin style of high standard: grammatical correctness, variety in vocabulary, richness of metaphor, frequent wordplay, and a capacity for long, intricate sentences employing hyperbation. Columbanus' reading embraces Finnian, Gildas, Gregory's *Pastoral Care*, and, of earlier writers, Jerome, Eusebius, Gennadius of Marseilles, and Basil (translated by Rufinus of Aquileia). Although the claims for classical reminiscences in the letters can largely be discounted, it is beyond doubt that Columbanus maintained a keen interest in reading and learning throughout his life.

BIBLIOGRAPHY

Sources. Wilhelm Gundlach, in *Monumenta Germaniae historica, Epistolae,* III (1892, repr. 1978), 154–190; G. S. M. Walker, *Sancti Columbani Opera* (1957), with facing English translation.

Studies. James Francis Kenney, *The Sources for the Early History of Ireland: Ecclesiastical* (1929, repr. 1966), 186–209; J. Laporte, "Sources de la biographie de Saint Columban," in *Mélanges Colombaniens: Actes du congrès international de Luxeuil* (1951), and "Étude d'authenticité des oeuvres attribuées à Saint Colomban," in *Revue Mabillon,* 45 (1955), 46 (1956), and 51 (1961); H. B. Clarke and Mary Brennan, eds., *Columbanus and Merovingian Monasticism* (1981).

MICHAEL HERREN

[See also **Celtic Church; Gall, St.; Missions and Missionaries, Christian.**]

COLUMN FIGURE, a human figure carved almost in the round but backed by and attached to a column, of which the figure is usually an integral part. Figures applied to columns were used to decorate church facades, especially portals, from the early twelfth century through the first half of the thirteenth, by which time the figure had been emancipated from the column. The column figure apparently originated in Italy or southern France, and spread quickly throughout western Europe; early examples appear on the west facade at St. Denis, near Paris (1137–1140), and on the west portal at Chartres (*ca.* 1145).

LESLIE BRUBAKER

COMINES (COMMYNES), PHILIPPE DE (*ca.* 1447–18 October 1511), outstanding chronicler of the fifteenth century. He began his career in the service of Charles the Bold, who became duke of Burgundy on his father's death in 1467. In August 1472 Comines left Charles and became the friend and confidant of Louis XI, who granted him attractive financial benefits and made him his chamberlain and lead-

Column figures of Old and New Testament saints. North porch of Chartres Cathedral, *ca.* 1145. PHOTO BY JEAN ROUBIER

ing minister in charge of political affairs. The first five books of his *Mémoires* concern the reigns of Louis XI and Charles VIII, and the last three books end with the coronation of Louis XII. Comines claims repeatedly that he is telling the truth about the events that he discusses, and he always states when he was not an eyewitness of the event. Comines's art may be said to be the opposite of Froissart's; it is without picturesqueness or color. In fact, the *Mémoires* have no literary pretense. They were composed originally as source material for the archbishop of Vienna, Angelo Cato, who wanted to write the history of Louis XI. Comines is more interested in what the events reveal about men than in the events themselves. Without being a great thinker, he had an original vision of the world: he believed in the importance of Providence as a power capable of controlling the equilibrium of forces in the world. Providence, according to him, could counterbalance the individual excesses of men. When describing war, Comines understates its myth and insists on its goriness and inhumanity. He also denounces the weaknesses and sins of the ruling classes and has faith only in diplomats and in secret emissaries.

BIBLIOGRAPHY

Texts. Mémoires de Philippe de Commynes, J. Calmette and G. Durville, eds., 3 vols. (1924–1925); *Mémoires sur Louis XI*, Jean Dufournet, ed. (1979).

Translations. The Memoirs of Philippe de Commynes, S. Kinsey, ed., I. Cazeaux, trans. (1973), i–xv, 369–665; *The Reign of Louis XI, 1461–1483*, Michael Jones, trans. (1972).

Studies. Jeanne Demers, *Commynes mémoraliste* (1975); Jean Dufournet, *Études sur Philippe de Commynes* (1975); Jean Liniger, *Philippe de Commynes* (1978). Also, Paul Archambault, "History as Entropy in Commynes's Mémoires," in *Symposium,* 27 (1973); Denys Hay, "History and Historians in France and England During the Fifteenth Century," in *Bulletin of the Institute of Historical Research* (London), 35 (1962); Eric de Montmollin, "Commines et le sens de l'histoire," in *Perspectives* (1949); A. Stegman, "Commynes et Machiavel," in Myron P. Gilmore, ed., *Studies on Machiavelli* (1972), 267–284.

Guy Mermier

[See also **Chronicles; Louis XI.**]

COMMANDER OF THE FAITHFUL (Arabic: *amīr al-muʾminīn*), one of the titles borne by the caliphs and later adopted by various anticaliphs to bolster their authority.

Islamic tradition makes one of the Prophet's companions the first person to bear the title, during the years when Muḥammad was establishing his authority over Arabia. Clearly, at this time it was primarily a title implying military command, and other early Muslim generals bore it—for instance, the Arab commander against the Persians at the battle of Kadisiya (635/636). It was formally adopted as a regnal title by the second caliph, ʿUmar (634–644). His predecessor, Abū Bakr (632–634) had styled himself "successor of the Messenger of God" (*khalīfat rasūl Allāh),* and ʿUmar called himself "successor of the successor of the Messenger of God," until the cumbersomeness of this title caused adoption of the simpler "commander of the faithful [or believers]," probably echoing a verse of the Koran (IV, 59/62): "Obey God and obey the Messenger and those placed in command (*ūli 'l-amr).*" It implied a more spiritual leadership over the Muslims than the earlier titles, now that the Islamic empire was beginning to comprise non-Arabs as well as Arabs, and an emphasis on military leadership in the extension of the empire through *jihād* (holy war).

Henceforth, "commander of the faithful" was a characteristically caliphal title, used by successive lines of caliphs until the extinction of the puppet Abbasid caliphs at Cairo by the Ottoman Turks in 1517. However, in 928 the Umayyad ruler of Spain ʿAbd al-Raḥmān III adopted the titles "caliph" and "commander of the faithful," in addition to "emir." This was done in rivalry to the Abbasids in distant Baghdad and as a reaction to the pretensions of his North African enemies, the extremist Shiite Fatimids, who, hostile to the powers ruling in both Córdoba and Baghdad, had assumed these titles as well as the religious one of imam.

Thus it came to be the central and eastern lands of Islam where the titles "caliph" and "commander of the faithful" were most jealously guarded by the supreme leaders of the mainstream, Sunni majority, as is pointed out by the fourteenth-century North African historian Ibn Khaldūn. The Sunni provincial dynasties that arose there on the whole respected the "caliphal fiction" that their authority was delegated by the caliphs; but this fiction was not recognized by heterodox, mainly Shiite, powers such as the radical Karmatians and Assassins, and above all not by the Fatimids, who considered themselves, rather than the Abbasids, as rightful holders of the caliphate and imamate, and consequently of the title "commander of the faithful."

Various dynasties of the Muslim West—from the Kharijite Rustamids of eastern Algeria in the ninth century to the Hafsids of Tunisia in the later Middle Ages—remote from the Near Eastern lands and regarding the Abbasids with less respect, soon arrogated caliphal titles to themselves. "Commander of the faithful" coexisted with the similar "commander of the Muslims" (*amīr al-Muslimīn),* which implied a lesser degree of independence from the caliph in the East, among, for instance, the Almoravids of Morocco and Mauretania, who in the eleventh century claimed to be restorers of Sunni orthodoxy and faithful servants of the Abbasids.

In later centuries "commander of the faithful" was used as a general regnal title by various powers claiming to be heirs of the Abbasids, and occasionally by powers on the periphery of the Islamic world, such as West Africa and western Sudan, as late as the nineteenth century, with special emphasis on the caliphal duty of acting as leader in *jihād.* The Arabic term was frequently cited in medieval Europe in such deformations as *Elmiram mommini, Miralomin,* and *Mirmumnus.*

BIBLIOGRAPHY

Thomas W. Arnold, *The Caliphate* (1924), 31–33; Max van Berchem, "Titres califiens d'Occident," in his *Opera minora,* II (1978), 787–877; Ibn Khaldūn, *The Mugaddimah,* Franz Rosenthal, trans., I (1958), 465–472; Reuben Levy, *The Social Structure of Islam* (1957), 367ff.; Émile Tyan, *Institutions du droit public musulman,* vol. 1: *Le califat* (1954), 198–199.

C. E. BOSWORTH

[See also **Caliphate.**]

COMMENDA, a partnership-like arrangement that, in medieval Mediterranean commerce, served as one of the basic legal instruments to pool capital and to bring together investors and managers. It was a commercial contract in which an investor or group of investors entrusted capital or merchandise to an agent-manager, who was to trade with it and then return it to the investor with the principal and an agreed-upon share of the profits. As a reward for his labor the agent received the remaining share of the profits. Any loss on the capital was borne by the investor, with the agent losing his expended time, effort, and anticipated profits.

The commenda contract combined the advantages of a loan with those of a regular partnership. As in a partnership, profits and risks were shared by both parties, the investor risking his capital, the agent his time and effort. However, in contrast with a partnership, in a commenda no joint capital was formed and the investor did not become liable with the agent in transactions with third parties, who were generally not aware of the investor's existence. As in a loan, the commenda entailed no liability on the part of the investor beyond the amount of his investment. When the latter was returned with a share of the profit, it corresponded functionally to the return on an interest-bearing loan.

The agent's freedom from any liability for the capital in the event of loss, and the disjunction be-

tween the investor and third parties, made this contract a particularly suitable instrument for long-distance trade. In the Italian trading cities it served as the most common instrument for overseas trade. In the unilateral commenda (in which the entire capital was contributed by the investor) the normal division of profits was three-fourths for the agent or traveling party. If the agent contributed a share of the capital (a bilateral commenda), the division of the profits was adjusted accordingly.

This contract, sometimes designated by a different name (such as *accomendatio, collegantia, societas,* or *entica*), was known and utilized from one end of the Mediterranean to the other. Its Islamic counterpart, the *qirāḍ* or *muḍāraba,* resembled the commenda in almost every detail. From the eighth century on, it was extensively used in the local and the long-distance commerce of the Islamic world and was, very likely, the origin of the European commenda.

BIBLIOGRAPHY

Robert S. Lopez and Irving W. Raymond, eds., *Medieval Trade in the Mediterranean World* (1955) 174–184; Raymond A. de Roover, "The Organization of Trade," in *Cambridge Economic History of Europe,* III (1963), esp. 46–55; A. L. Udovitch, "At the Origins of the Western *Commenda:* Islam, Israel, Byzantium?" in *Speculum,* 37 (1962), and *Partnership and Profit in Medieval Islam* (1970), 170–248.

A. L. UDOVITCH

COMMENDAM, a peculiar form of commendation that became common in the church in the fourteenth and fifteenth centuries. It had begun in the early Middle Ages as a means of safeguarding ecclesiastical properties in periods of invasion. The properties were given in trust to someone who could guard them until order was restored; meanwhile, he received the revenues. By the fourteenth century, however, grants *in commendam* were made simply to increase the revenues of churchmen (and some laymen) who enjoyed papal favor. They were no longer temporary and could last until the holder died or received a more profitable grant. Such grants were especially hard on monastic communities. They lost much of their income and received few benefits in return. The practice was curtailed in the sixteenth century.

BIBLIOGRAPHY

Jean Favier, *Les finances pontificales, 1378–1400* (1966), 295–296, 302–319; William E. Lunt, *Papal Revenues in the Middle Ages,* II (1934), 225, 232, 292–294, 347.

JOSEPH R. STRAYER

COMMENDATIO ANIMAE. See **Death and Burial, in Europe.**

COMMENDATION was a private arrangement, unrecognized at public law until the ninth century, whereby a weaker man placed himself under the protection of a stronger in return for services rendered. It grew up in a world in which the machinery of the state and of public law could no longer assure protection to the individual. None of the Germanic kingdoms newly established on the ruins of the Roman Empire could provide adequate protection for its subjects. Unable to maintain central governments of the Roman type, they suffered from civil wars and invasions, and their peoples were victims of widespread lawlessness. Everywhere the weaker sought the protection of their stronger neighbors, and the powerful sought the support of followers, in order to maintain their property, social prestige, and even their personal safety.

The result of this search for mutual protection was the rapid extension of private ties of dependence, a process whereby one man commended himself to another. Men from all classes of society commended themselves. Many small free farmers who owned their own farms lost their landownership and their personal freedom when they commended themselves. They became serfs. The stronger freemen were able to preserve their freedom, often becoming warriors in the service of their lords.

Commendation derived from both Roman and German customs. In the Roman world the ancient patron-client relationship (*clientela, patrocinium*) had never completely disappeared. Patronage had flourished especially well among the Gallo-Romans, partly because it was like the pre-Roman Celtic custom whereby local Gaulish chiefs had surrounded themselves with personal retainers, either peasants or warriors. The early medieval verb "to commend" (*se commendare*) derived from the vocabulary of the ancient Roman *patrocinium.* In the newly founded German kingdoms there still flourished the ancient

German institution that Tacitus called the comitatus: a group of warriors who had taken service of their own free will under a war chieftain. They fought with him and for him in return for food, clothing, and a share in the booty. A second German custom that promoted the development of commendation was the practice (medieval Latin: *mundiburdis,* among many other forms; modern French: *maimbour*) whereby a powerful man extended to a weaker neighbor his personal protection, or *Mund.*

Merovingian Frankish commendation (sixth and seventh centuries) is especially interesting because feudal vassalage grew out of it. The Merovingians had both servile commendation, which was for slaves and men commending themselves into serfdom in return for menial services, and free commendation, which was for men commending themselves as freemen in return for honorable services. The Merovingian commendee who expected to preserve his freedom assumed the duties of serving and respecting his dominus (lord), but with the reservation that this service and respect should be limited to what was compatible with his status as a freeman. The lord assumed the duties of protecting and maintaining his man. This mutual contract was ended by the death of either party.

Whether the Merovingian commendee preserved his freedom or not, he seems almost invariably to have taken an oath of fealty. The ritual act of submission was called homage. Although homage is first described in Frankish documents only in the second half of the eighth century, it is described in such a way as to indicate that it had undoubtedly been in use during the Merovingian period. The similarity of homage among the Franks, the Anglo-Saxons, and the Scandinavians proves its Germanic origin. Merovingian homage, both free and servile, consisted of the mixing of the hands (*immixtio manuum*). In this simple and symbolic ceremony, the man doing homage clasped his hands together, placed them between the hands of his superior, and briefly acknowledged himself to be his "man." At first the Merovingians used a variety of words to refer to the man doing homage. The word "vassal" (late Latin: *vassus;* medieval Latin: *vassallus*) was only one of them. Its root was the Celtic *gwas,* meaning servant or young boy, and for a while the Merovingian lord's vassals were his boys, his lowly servants. Such a vassal's service was menial and hence inappropriate for a freeman. But vassalage was soon used by the Merovingians for exclusively free services, primarily military; and the word "vassal" was promoted to refer to, and exclusively, a free cavalryman who was maintained as an armed retainer by a great lord.

This Merovingian military vassalage played a large role in the high politics of the seventh century. Numerous vassals commended themselves to the mayors of the palace of Neustria, Austrasia, and Burgundy in return for political offices. A mayor's vassalic officials were great lords with vassals of their own, a following that made the mayor's military and political power formidable. When the Carolingians first built up their power it was by means of their vassals. As mayors of the palace of Austrasia they received all the great lords of Austrasia into their commendation and vassalage. Mayor Pepin II, the first Carolingian to rule all of the Franks, was able to defeat the mayors of Neustria and Burgundy in 687 because he had enough land to maintain more vassals than his two rival mayors had. Vassalage was important in weakening the authority of the Merovingian local royal officials, the counts. Men escaped the tyranny of the counts by becoming the vassal of a lord who had influence in the king's palace and a private army. But the Merovingian rulers never officially recognized the commendation of military vassals as an integral part of the legal and political system of the Frankish kingdom.

When the Carolingians became rulers of the kingdom in the first half of the eighth century, they made military vassalage into a legal part of the royal state. Vassalic commendation then spread to other parts of western Europe. The Carolingian rulers of Frankland from the time of Charles Martel (716–741) built their state mainly on vassalage, rather than on public sovereignty. As a result of state encouragement, there was a sharp increase in the number and importance of vassals. Royal vassals held all the important legal and political offices in the state. They were unpaid amateurs in the work of government. The shortage of money made it impossible to use paid professional bureaucrats. These royal vassals who ran the kingdom included the counts, dukes, margraves, bishops, and abbots. They spent most of their time far away from the king and were lords of a rather widely scattered group of their own vassals. There developed a ladder of lordship and vassalage with a number of rungs. As the Carolingian empire collapsed in the course of the ninth century, lordship and vassalage, the most important elements in feudalism, became the new form of government. Feudal vassalage had emerged by a slow process of differentiation from the disparate practice of Merovingian commendation. Feudal vassalage was the highest

form of commendation ever developed. From the tenth century on, after the feudal vassal doing homage had placed his joined hands within the hands of the lord, the two men kissed each other on the mouth, symbolizing their friendship and also their social equality as the rulers of feudal society.

BIBLIOGRAPHY

Marc Bloch, *Feudal Society,* L. A. Manyon, trans. (1961); Ralph H. C. Davis, *A History of Medieval Europe* (1957); François L. Ganshof, *Feudalism,* Philip Grierson, trans., 2nd ed. (1961); and *Frankish Institutions Under Charlemagne,* Bryce Lyon and Mary Lyon, trans. (1968); Joseph R. Strayer, *Feudalism* (1965).

WILLIAM T. REEDY

[See also **Feudalism; Homage.**]

COMMENTATORS. See Postglossators.

COMMERCE. See Trade.

COMMON PLEAS, COURT OF. From the Norman conquest on, several new royal courts gradually developed out of the *curia regis,* the court that traveled with the king and met in his presence as he moved constantly around England. These new courts were in effect branches of the *curia regis.* William the Conqueror (1066–1087) began the practice of sending some members of the *curia regis* away from court for the purpose of conducting royal business locally in the king's name. In this way the *curia regis* was for the first time able to be in several places at the same time. In the reigns of Henry I (1100–1135) and Henry II (1154–1189) royal justices were increasingly sent out from the *curia regis* on eyres, journeys made by small groups of itinerant justices for the purpose of conducting locally all the royal legal and administrative work that the king wanted them to do.

It was in the reign of Henry II and probably also in the reign of Richard I (1189–1199) that the first two stationary offshoots of the *curia regis* were created. These courts came into being when certain members of the *curia regis* met in a fixed place apart from the king's traveling entourage and on a more or less full-time basis, in order to conduct certain routine procedures of royal government.

The first stationary offshoot of the *curia regis* was the court of exchequer. It was created in the reign of Henry II and met in Westminster Hall. The exchequer had existed as a semiannual audit of the royal finances ever since the 1120's. The second stationary offshoot was a central court called then the bench *(de banco)* and later, common pleas. It began as a part of the exchequer, and became a separate court either in the latter part of Henry II's reign or in the reign of Richard I. Its jurisdiction originally was virtually unlimited. It was not exclusively concerned with common pleas (civil pleas between subjects) until the reign of Edward I (1272–1307), during which it acquired its name. From the beginning the new court was the court of first instance for those litigants who did not want to wait to have their civil pleas heard until the next coming of the justices-in-eyre to their counties. The new court could hear many more common pleas than the itinerant justices could, and in the course of the thirteenth century it overtook the eyres as the normal venue for common pleas.

The early history of the court of common pleas is obscure. There is still scholarly debate over its origins. Most scholars have rejected the older view that Henry II created the court in 1178 as a brand new court. It grew out of the exchequer, but it is not certain exactly when. Clearly there was some division of labor between exchequer business and judicial business in the later years of Henry II. It is possible that the bench separated from the exchequer in the latter part of his reign, but it seems more likely that the division into two separate courts occurred in the reign of Richard I, possibly as part of the reforms enacted by Hubert Walter, archbishop of Canterbury and chief justiciar, in 1194. The new court entered its proceedings on its *curia regis* rolls, also called plea rolls. The oldest plea roll extant is from Trinity term 1194.

It is certain that two separate courts existed in the reign of John (1199–1216). King John liked the arrangement whereby in Westminster Hall the justices of the bench, who sat at one end, and the barons of the exchequer, who sat at the other end, supported and supplemented each other. The bench (also called common bench, and not to be confused with the court of king's bench) coalesced in 1209 with the court *coram rege*, the *curia regis* proper, but from 1212 on, the bench was slowly revived. Article 17 of Magna Carta (1215) provided that common pleas

(communia placita) should not follow the king as he moved about the country, but should be held at a fixed place. Thereafter that place was normally Westminster Hall. The proceedings of the thirteenth-century bench were coordinated with the proceedings of the general eyres until the effective end of the eyre system in 1294. The bench had its own chief justice by 1272.

Starting in the late fourteenth century, a rivalry grew up between the court of common pleas and the court of king's bench that lasted until 1832. By then the jurisdiction of each court was in practice much different from that of the other, and the jurisdiction of each was at last exactly defined. The court of common pleas survived the Judicature Act of 1873 as a separate division of the high court of justice, but in 1881 it was merged with the queen's bench division of the high court.

BIBLIOGRAPHY

Brian Kemp, "Exchequer and Bench in the Later Twelfth Century—Separate or Identical Tribunals?" in *English Historical Review*, 88 (1973); Doris M. Stenton, *English Justice Between the Norman Conquest and the Great Charter, 1066–1215* (1964); Ralph V. Turner, "The Origins of Common Pleas and King's Bench," in *American Journal of Legal History*, 21 (1977); Francis J. West, "The *Curia Regis* in the Late Twelfth and Early Thirteenth Centuries," in *Historical Studies (Australia and New Zealand)*, 6 (1953–1955).

WILLIAM T. REEDY

[See also **Curia, Lay; Justices, Itinerant; Justices of Common Pleas; Law, English Common.**]

COMMONPLACE BOOKS. "Commonplace" is a translation of the Latin term *locus communis*, "a theme or argument of general application," such as a statement of proverbial wisdom or an exemplary description of a person or place. A commonplace book, in this primary sense, is a book used for collecting such passages: Milton's commonplace book was organized under topics. By extension the term has been used by medievalists to refer to any manuscript collection of miscellaneous material gathered over a period by an individual for his own practical use, amusement, or interest. In this sense a commonplace book is a scrapbook filled with items of every kind: medical recipes, copies of letters, poems, tables of weights and measures, proverbs, prayers, legal formulas, and information of local or family concern.

Commonplace books first became popular in the fifteenth century, with the availability of a cheap writing material, paper; some, such as the Glastonbury Miscellany (Trinity College, Cambridge, MS 0.9.38), were originally designed as account books. The two best examples of the genre are the collection of Robert Reynes of Acle, Norfolk (Oxford, Bodleian Library, MS Tanner 407), and that of Richard Hill, a London grocer (Oxford, Balliol College, MS 354). Each commonplace book is, naturally, unique; it owes its genesis and contents to the interest of its compiler.

The literary bias of most modern editors has distorted our perception of the medieval commonplace book, which often is only incidentally "literary"; close analysis sometimes shows that a collection was made for a specific purpose, such as John Grimestone's book of preaching materials made in 1372 (Edinburgh, Advocates Library, MS 18.7.21). The value of such collections is the insight they provide into the tastes, interests, and concerns of their individual compilers.

BIBLIOGRAPHY

Cameron Louis, ed., *The Commonplace Book of Robert Reynes of Acle* (1980), esp. 99–103.

A. G. RIGG

[See also **Anthologies**.]

COMMUNE. For the purpose of simple definition it may be said that a medieval commune was a self-governing town that obtained this status from the territorial ruler either through collective negotiation by the townsmen or through a foundation charter. In cases in which peaceful bargaining did not result in the desired liberties, the townsmen frequently swore an oath of mutual aid in the common cause and inaugurated a revolutionary movement to resist oppression and to win self-government. Communes are first recorded during the late eleventh and early twelfth centuries, becoming thereafter a widespread phenomenon.

The English and French word "commune" appears in the records in various Latin forms. Frequently used was the classical Latin *communio*, which means an association or mutual participation. In other cases the classical Latin *commune*, meaning a people with interests in common, was employed. More often the Low Latin *communia* appears, the

form from which the Romance *commune* was derived. Occasionally one finds the words *communa* and *communitas*. When self-government was won by means of insurrection, the annalists and chroniclers were wont to refer to the commune established as a *coniuratio* or *conspiratio*. As the various vernaculars gradually replaced Latin, words such as the Italian *campagna* were substituted for *communia*. In any event it should not be assumed that all medieval towns become communes; many did not. Just as the Latin *civitas* may signify any sort of city or town, so it is with the vernacular words "borough," *ville, Stadt,* and *città*.

EARLY URBAN PRIVILEGES

Throughout the Roman Empire there had been self-governing *civitates*, but during the serious social, economic, and political deterioration of the third and fourth centuries the emperors were forced to intervene in municipal affairs and to assume management of local administration and finance. When the imperial government in the West collapsed during the fourth and fifth centuries, the faltering towns were left to their own devices. Despite political anarchy, subjugation to German leaders, and primitive economic conditions, some towns in Italy, Spain, and southern France managed to survive as urban entities, but on so elemental a level as to preclude the necessity or possibility of local self-government. Local rule came to be the responsibility of officials of the new German rulers. To the north, economic, social, and political conditions became so desperate in the early Middle Ages as to force the virtual disappearance of urban life. With little trade or industry, a middle class of merchants and artisans disappeared—and with it its traditional abode, the town. Into the late tenth century most of medieval Europe was predominantly agrarian, organized on and sustained by the seignorial system that exploited the land and by the feudal system that provided a rudimentary military and political organization. During this period there are few references to towns and none to self-governing urban communities.

With the upturn of European political and economic fortunes in the late tenth century, trade revived, goods were fabricated, and merchants and craftsmen reappeared. Again there existed a bourgeoisie, which congregated at strategically located points to engage in mercantile and industrial activities. At these points town life revived or developed for the first time. Walls were constructed for protection. During the urban revival the towns were under the direct rule of kings, of secular feudal lords such as counts and dukes, and of archbishops, bishops, and abbots. On their behalf officers such as castellans, provosts, and sheriffs supervised all the necessary military, political, fiscal, and judicial functions.

By the early eleventh century the townsmen were beginning to demand and to obtain recognition of various economic, legal, and social privileges that were essential for their urban and mercantile way of life. Basically what they sought was a privileged status that would liberate them from the exactions and customs of seignorialism and feudalism. With their new occupations they could not continue to live under the traditional restrictions of the peasants in the countryside. They had to be free and mobile, to live under conditions favorable to their professions. The initial stage, therefore, in the movement toward self-government was the acquisition of what may be called elementary bourgeois liberties.

First, the urban inhabitants sought and secured the guarantee of personal freedom—that is, the right to come and go as they pleased, to engage in the kinds of economic activity that suited them, to marry, and to give their children in marriage without the necessity of some lord's costly permission. Second, they required free tenure for their goods and lands, which meant the liberty to alienate or bequeath them when and as they wished, liability for only a fixed cash rent for their houses and lands, and emancipation from all customary seignorial exactions and services such as mainmort, taille, and corvée. Ordinarily the townsmen also achieved limitations on other lordly powers, such as the military levy and rights of purveyance, hospitality, and credit. To ensure freedom from the seignorial court, they obtained the privilege of having their legal disputes litigated in a town court, the law and procedure of which were developed to meet the legal needs of the new merchant class. Fines and penalties were limited to fit the gravity of the offense. The inhabitants of most towns were excused from paying local indirect taxes. Ordinarily they received a monopoly over local trade and industry, or at least a favored position vis-à-vis merchants and craftsmen from other towns. Often the merchants were also guaranteed the right of trading freely throughout the territory of the ruling prince. Such, then, were the fundamental privileges that were essential for mercantile and craft occupations and that differentiated the bourgeois from the peasantry and feudal aristocracy. Towns became islands of freedom and privilege surrounded by the unfree countryside. Peasants escaped to these communities in search of freedom and new occupations. It was not long before it became necessary to grant a peasant his freedom if he remained undetected in a town for a year and a day, a custom that gave rise to the German phrase *Stadtluft macht frei.*

In the older and well-established towns these elementary bourgeois liberties were generally acquired bit by bit, informally, and by oral promise of the ruler. For example, a town such as Cologne never received a single charter guaranteeing these liberties, though subsequently, sometimes as long as a century after their acquisition, a document listing them would be drawn up. For specific knowledge of these privileges one must turn to the charters that were granted to the new towns (*villes neuves*) established by rulers during the eleventh and twelfth centuries. Almost always these charters were modeled on the privileges enjoyed by the established towns.

Well-known examples of such charters are that granted by Louis VI of France early in the twelfth century to Lorris; those to Verneuil in Normandy and to Newcastle upon Tyne in England, granted by Henry I of England in the early twelfth century; that to Freiburg-im-Breisgau, granted by Duke Conrad of Zähringen in 1120; that to Montauban in the Midi, granted by the count of Toulouse in 1144; and that to Beaumont-en-Argonne, granted by the archbishop of Rheims in 1182. These charters served as models for charters granted to other *villes neuves.* Except for that of Beaumont-en-Argonne, none of these charters guaranteed other than social, economic, and legal privileges. Politically, town government remained in the hands of princely officials who continued to collect taxes, preside over the courts, and supervise local administration.

Having obtained these privileges, it was only natural that the townsmen should desire to secure some participation in local government. The local officials of the territorial rulers, generally from the feudal or clerical class, either did not understand bourgeois needs and aspirations or were unsympathetic to them. No wonder that friction was common between the townsmen and the castellans and provosts, whose headquarters were usually castles or fortresses within or near the towns. The townsmen did not aspire to independence from princely rule but only to removal of these feudal enclaves and to control local government. It was reasonable that they should consider themselves more capable than outsiders of levying and collecting taxes, holding town courts, and acting as town administrators. As subjects of the territorial ruler they were, however, prepared to pay him taxes, to obey his laws, and to render necessary political and military services.

THE MEANING OF COMMUNE

Historians have long debated over how urban self-government was achieved, and they have differed over whether only communes were self-governing. French historians have generally explained the development of the commune as a part of French feudal history, as an institution encouraged for military and political reasons by the French and English kings. According to them, the kings desired to incorporate the growing urban centers into the feudal system so as to obtain military and political service. The kings regarded a fortified town as much like a feudal castle, and they demanded military service from the inhabitants just as they did from their feudal vassals. The communal oath sworn by the townsmen was, in reality, not an oath of association but one of vassalage producing a feudal tie to the royal overlord and obligations to him.

Such an interpretation portrays the commune as being incorporated into the feudal system. According to Achille Luchaire, who popularized this view, the commune was a kind of collective seigniory bound by all the obligations of vassalage. It took a veritable oath of fidelity and homage, was liable for the customary three feudal aids, rendered military service through its militia, constituted a feudal fortress, and exercised its feudal rights locally just as a vassal would by levying taxes and administering justice. Such authority was symbolized by possession of a seal for authenticating communal acts and by the town belfry. However attractive this theory may be, it is supported by little evidence and ignores the fact that towns were by their nature nonfeudal and one of the prime causes of the decline of the feudal system.

Another explanation insists that no true commune existed where there was no sworn oath taken by the townsmen. A self-governing town was a commune only when such an oath had been sworn. In France self-governing towns where this oath had not been sworn were simply known as *bonnes villes*. Yet another explanation states that the commune derived from the ecclesiastical Peace of God that developed as a concept and movement in the late tenth century. The peace movement was based on oath-bound associations and, cognizant that peace was a prime ingredient of urban life and prosperity, urban communities borrowed the idea of sworn associations and adapted it to their own ends, ensuring that all townsmen swore an oath of peace that was obligatory for all to maintain. Once this had been done, the town was known as a commune.

THE FIRST FRENCH COMMUNES

Turning from theory to pertinent evidence, it is obvious that during the eleventh century, when communes are first heard of, they appeared as the result of opposition to feudal and church lords and of a collective movement to secure local political franchises. When such a movement failed to secure its objectives peacefully it often became revolutionary in order to end repression by the territorial ruler. The townsmen swore a solemn oath of mutual aid in the common cause, obedience to designated leaders, and vengeance against all enemies. Sometimes the revolts succeeded, and sometimes they did not. In the former case concessions won were generally written down and formally granted in a charter by the ruler. The charter became a kind of constitution for the autonomous government of the town.

During the twelfth century "commune" acquired the meaning that has subsequently been associated with it—that is, a self-governing town. In this connection it is essential to understand that scores of towns secured self-government by means of peaceful negotiation with rulers who granted charters. Often there were no sworn associations, but through liberality, indifference, or weakness of rulers self-government was secured. Eventually rulers voluntarily granted charters to towns that converted them into communes. In such cases it was not unusual for the townsmen to pay a sum of money to the ruler in exchange for the charter. Communal privileges were often granted by rulers to stimulate urban growth and economic prosperity.

By the late twelfth century it is evident that many towns, however they became autonomous, were known as communes. It is also clear that some towns, which had been known as communes since the late eleventh and early twelfth centuries and which had become communes by virtue of a collective sworn oath and by force, enjoyed less political authority than other towns that had never borne the name "commune." It must be concluded that there were a number of avenues to municipal freedom, that there were differences in the amount of political authority exercised, and that although numerous self-governing towns were known as communes, many were not.

The oldest and best-known example of a revolutionary commune in northern Europe is that of Cambrai in northeastern France. Under the political authority of its bishop, whose overlord in the tenth and eleventh centuries was the German emperor, Cambrai by the late tenth century had a faubourg of merchants at the foot of the bishop's fortress. About 1070 a stone wall had been constructed around the faubourg from which the insurrections of the next years were to come. Unhappy living under the authority of the bishop and his castellan, the townsmen secretly prepared to revolt against Bishop Gerard II when, in 1077, he was preparing to travel to Germany to receive investiture of his office from the emperor. Just after his departure the townsmen, including the poor, artisans, and weavers, revolted under the leadership of the principal merchants, swore a commune, and took possession of Cambrai. On the return of the bishop, the insurrection was subdued. Later, however, another conspiracy was successful, resulting in a communal charter that remained in force until quashed in 1106, when the German emperor intervened in support of the bishop. It was some time before Cambrai secured permanent recognition as a self-governing town.

In would appear that the commune of Cambrai served as an example for other towns in the region. In most cases these towns were controlled by bishops bitterly opposed to the extension of political privileges to their urban subjects. This meant that the townsmen, after having sworn the commune, had to revolt to obtain concessions. About 1080 a commune was established at St. Quentin, about 1099 at Beauvais, in 1108–1109 at Noyon, in 1113 at Amiens, and in 1115 at Laon. Though prejudiced against the townsmen of Laon, Abbot Guibert of Nogent, a contemporary of the disturbances, has provided one of the finest accounts of the bloody uprising against the hated bishop and of the royal intervention by Louis VI. The charters of privileges won by some of these communes served as models for charters granted to other towns, many of which secured political privileges by peaceful negotiation. The charter of Beauvais served as a model for that granted to Soissons, which became the model for still other charters. By the time of Louis VI the French kings had become powerful enough to intervene in these struggles, and they often supported the urban aspirations for self-government in order to achieve their objective of expanding royal authority at the expense of local feudal and ecclesiastical power.

The communal charter granted to Beauvais was issued by Louis VI in order to terminate the conflict between the bishop and the bourgeois. According to this charter, all inhabitants of the town, on whatever land they resided, were, under penalty of property and body, to swear the commune, agreeing to assist each other in all legal ways and to obey the decisions of constituted authorities. The peers (administrators) of the commune had to swear an oath not to exile or harm any inhabitant through love or hate, but to render just judgments. When any man who had sworn the commune suffered an injury, the culprit was, if possible, to be tried by the peers. Should the culprit take refuge outside Beauvais with a protector, the commune should attempt to obtain satisfaction from the latter. Should such an attempt fail, all men of the commune then had to join in securing revenge on the body and property of the accused or of his protector. Merchants coming to Beauvais from elsewhere were similarly protected. It was stipulated that enemies of the commune were to be excluded and that any person dealing with them was to be punished. Other provisions dealt with the collection of debts, protection of the citizens' food, regulation of the mills, and restriction of transport services for the bishop.

Beauvais is an excellent example of a self-governing town based on a revolutionary government. The principal concern of the sworn association was to secure the lives and property of the members. Officals were elected, courts were established, and legal procedures were agreed upon. If the bishop did not fulfill the provisions of the charter, the townsmen were able to negotiate with him; if this failed, they could resort to force, a procedure common in feudal society. The fact that the French king had intervened on the side of the citizens of Beauvais definitely strengthened their position vis-à-vis the bishop, who, along with the lords of the region, lost most of his seignorial rights in Beauvais.

In this connection it should be noted that when the charter of Beauvais became the model for that issued to Soissons, provisions were added so as to preserve various seignorial rights over certain inhabitants of Soissons. In the case of Laon an *institutio pacis* proclaimed in 1128 stipulated that the town was to be recognized as an asylum of peace and security for all persons, free or unfree, except for serfs of local lords and churchmen. Other provisions served to restrict urban authority, the result being a commune with less political power than Beauvais.

In their early period of development communes enjoyed different levels of political authority. The situation of each could, however, change. Depending on such considerations as their size, economic power, and relations with the territorial ruler, communes acquired more power or lost it. In general those towns situated in regions with ineffective political authority, such as northern Italy and Rhenish Germany, won extensive power. In France and England, where kingship was more effective, the political authority of the towns was restricted.

During this period communal privileges developed in other regions of France where there had been economic and urban development. In Normandy, Rouen had acquired elementary bourgeois privileges during the reign of Henry I of England, who was also duke of Normandy. In fact, it may well have obtained some political concessions from him. By the reign of his grandson Henry II (1154–1189), Rouen achieved the authority enjoyed by the well-established communes. To the south, in the Midi, achievement of political liberties was peaceful and was accompanied by few sworn associations. The leading towns of Gascony, Languedoc, and Provence secured self-government during the first half of the twelfth century, seldom finding it necessary to resort to force.

COMMUNES IN THE LOW COUNTRIES AND
GERMANY

To the northeast, in the neighboring county of Flanders, where economic revival had come early and the leading towns had developed by the late tenth century, some of them may well have obtained political and legal concessions before the twelfth century. We have definite evidence that by the early part of that century the large towns had full-fledged political authority. The assassination of Count Charles the Good in 1127 provided the occasion for the townsmen to bargain for political concessions guaranteed by charter. Because Charles had no heirs, a number of contenders, among them William Clito of Normandy, William of Ypres, and Thierry of Alsace, claimed the countship. In the war that ensued, William Clito first prevailed but was ultimately defeated and lost the countship to Thierry of Alsace. During the troubled events, which are graphically described in a chronicle by a well-placed witness, the notary Galbert of Bruges, the towns pledged their support to the contender who promised the most generous privileges.

The charter granted by William Clito to St. Omer in 1127 is one of the earliest of such charters to have survived in the original. It may well have served as a model for the charters obtained by the other Flemish towns. It recognized St. Omer as a distinct legal territory, provided for a special law to be enforced in a court composed of citizens of St. Omer, and granted full communal autonomy. During the same period Bruges, Ghent, and Ypres received similar charters. Subsequently, during the countships of Thierry and his son Philip, which extended to the end of the century, many Flemish towns became self-governing. Regarding urban development as a source of comital revenue, the counts followed an enlightened policy toward the towns, usually according privileges to them by peaceful negotiation or on their own initiative.

Because of slower economic development in the duchy of Brabant, the bishopric of Liège, and the counties of Holland and Hainaut, communal status came to towns later; but by the thirteenth century towns such as Brussels, Louvain, Liège, and Utrecht had secured advanced political rights. Along the Rhine, where economic revival and urban development had come early, political power came sooner to towns, but usually without severing the political authority of the overlords as quickly or completely. Here, political and religious disputes associated with the investiture controversy enabled the towns to bargain for concessions in return for their support. In 1074 the merchants of Cologne rose against the archbishop, who escaped the enraged crowd only just in time. This revolt was cruelly suppressed, but in 1106 another rising drove out a successor, who was forced to reside outside Cologne. At this point the townsmen established political institutions compatible with their urban existence and extended the town fortifications. In 1112 a *coniuratio pro libertate* brought more concessions, resulting in the inauguration of *magistri civium,* based on a parochial organization, which assumed responsibility for various administrative and judicial functions.

Later, during the reign of Emperor Frederick Barbarossa (1152–1190), Cologne received its own seal, one of the oldest city seals of Germany. Meanwhile, the authority of the local officials of the archbishop declined. In 1149 and 1178 Cologne concluded treaties with Trier and Verdun, acting almost as an independent state. Little by little, bourgeois control was established. In the following century a true urban constitution with a *Bürgermeister* and a council came into existence. All these concessions came without the issuance of a charter. It was a matter of bargaining and of oral agreements. About all that the archbishop retained was a remnant of political authority. After 1288 he was politically impotent.

In Mainz the townsmen were rewarded with concessions because of their intercession with Emperor Henry V in 1115 on behalf of their archbishop, who had been imprisoned. After his release the archbishop granted the city freedom from alien laws and dues. Such was the beginning of self-government for Mainz, which continued to receive more concessions during the remainder of the century. Other German towns were slower to achieve self-government. Speier and Worms, for example, only gained exemption from seignorial obligations under Frederick Barbarossa, with self-government coming considerably later. A twelfth-century custumal of Strasbourg shows the bishop in control of urban administration, appointing all the local officials. Only the merchant class, through a special concession, enjoyed some elementary liberties; the rest of the population did not. During the thirteenth century this distinction was blotted out, with the result that all inhabitants came to enjoy bourgeois status. Before the end of the century Strasbourg was governed by twelve elected consuls. The Strasbourg pattern was repeated by many other German towns, old and newly established. Needless to say, self-government came later to those towns located to the east of the Rhine, many of which had been founded outright by German kings and lords only during the twelfth and thirteenth centuries.

THE ENGLISH COMMUNES

In England self-government came more slowly to boroughs (towns) than it did on the Continent. This may be because during the tenth and eleventh centuries, England's economic development lagged. Some of the leading boroughs, such as London, Lincoln, and York, secured elementary bourgeois privileges in the late tenth and eleventh centuries. After the Norman Conquest in 1066 urban development quickened among the older boroughs, and the Norman kings, particularly Henry I, founded a considerable number of *villes neuves,* such as Newcastle upon Tyne, a policy imitated by the greater barons throughout England. Particularly notable were the earls of Chester, Shrewsbury, and Gloucester, and the bishop of Durham. Under the Angevin kings this development continued but the Norman and An-

gevin kings were clearly less sympathetic to urban self-government.

London may well have obtained some communal privileges prior to Henry I, but it was not until 1129 or 1130 that it received a formal charter guaranteeing certain rights. Until Henry I's reign the sheriffs of London, who exercised local political authority on behalf of the kings, came from the feudal aristocracy and were appointed by the kings. After 1100, though still royal appointees, the sheriffs were selected from Londoners. Henry I's charter provided for the election of the sheriff by the burgesses of London, who appear to have been the first in England to have had an elected magistracy. Although the matter is uncertain in the charter, it seems logical to assume that the burgesses also acquired the right to elect the aldermen, the members of the borough council. Such was definitely the case later with boroughs that acquired self-governing status. Beyond this right London was permitted to collect and pay into the treasury all incomes and revenues due the king (the so-called farm). Moreover, it was to be free from arbitrary taxation and empowered to levy voluntary aids (extraordinary levies) whenever it was agreed that the king should receive them. It was at such times that the elected sheriff and aldermen negotiated with royal officials on the appropriateness and the amount of such a tax. Furthermore, trials of burgesses were restricted to the borough court, which was to be presided over by an elected judge and, apparently, was composed of aldermen; even royal cases were to be heard by this court.

During the civil war (1135–1154) between Matilda and Stephen, London did not fare well. Having obtained as complete self-government as that enjoyed by the leading towns on the Continent, London suffered from the feudal reaction under Stephen. Despite London's support of Stephen, he deprived it of the liberties in Henry I's charter, even appointing the feudatory Geoffrey de Mandeville as sheriff. It was at this point that a commune was formed by the burgesses to maintain and to recover their liberties. In this the commune was unsuccessful, because upon his triumph in 1154, Henry II punished London for having driven his mother, Matilda, from its walls by refusing to restore its liberties. In the case of Rouen, which had been loyal to Matilda, he confirmed its commune. All that Henry did in a charter of 1154 was to confirm London's elementary bourgeois privileges; until his death London was governed by royal sheriffs, burdened with a heavy farm, and subjected to severe, extraordinary taxes.

Soon after Richard I's accession in 1189, the Londoners organized a commune in an attempt to regain their status of 1130. Taking advantage of Richard's absence on the Third Crusade and of dissension among those left in charge of the government, London managed in 1190 to regain the right of electing its own sheriff and of rendering its farm direct to the treasury. As the dispute between Richard's brother John and William Longchamp grew more severe, London moved to better its position. In 1191 its inhabitants swore a commune and forced from John recognition as a self-governing municipality. By 1193 London had a constitution and elected a mayor and a council of aldermen. When Richard returned in 1194, he confirmed the liberties of London and reduced its farm in return for payment to him of 1,500 marks. The first charter of communal liberties did not come, however, until 1199, when, after his accession, John granted one in return for 3,000 marks. Subsequently there was popular agitation over the manner in which the mayor and aldermen managed municipal affairs, but after the outbreak of disturbances in 1201 and 1206, this governing body became firmly entrenched. The only other change in the London constitution occurred just prior to Magna Carta. Courting the loyalty of the Londoners against the barons, John permitted them the right to discard the rule of life tenure for the mayoralty and to elect a mayor annually. By 1215, then, London had become a self-governing municipality with rights guaranteed by royal charter.

After London the clearest evidence on borough government in this period comes from Northampton and Ipswich. Though not until 1215 can one safely say that Northampton had received John's permission to elect a mayor and a council of twelve, there is strong presumption that it exercised this right as early as 1200; in that year John granted Northampton a charter that served as the model for that given to Ipswich in the same year, definitely granting it the right to elect its magistracy. Other boroughs receiving self-government modeled on the Northampton charter were Gloucester, Lincoln, and Shrewsbury.

COMMUNES IN ITALY

In the Mediterranean area, although there were comparable stages of communal development, there were also striking differences. Because of its excep-

tional maritime position at the head of the Adriatic Sea, Venice had never been a part of the seignorial or feudal system, and never had to resort to negotiation or uprising to obtain political power. Almost from the outset of its existence Venice behaved like a sovereign power. Long before the twelfth century considerable political power was wielded by an official known as the doge, one who has aptly been described as a kind of "city king." The doge's authority began to be shared during the twelfth century by the leading patrician families, whose power and position derived from success in commerce and finance. Members of these families formed the Council of the Wise (Sapientes), with which the doge consulted on important political, financial, and military matters. As for the mass of the inhabitants, their only role in the government was to assemble in a large group known as a *placitum*, in order to declare their assent to whatever the doge and Council of the Wise had decided. When Venice joined the Italian town league against Frederick Barbarossa in 1164, it became necessary to broaden consultation so as to provide for increased pecuniary exactions needed to finance resistance against Frederick. The doge and Council of the Wise drew on eight tribunician patricians from families that had controlled the various islands around Venice. On such occasions the Council of the Wise became the Great Council. Eventually forty patrician electors chosen by four patrician honorable men (*probi homines*) elected the doge.

The kind of political power that developed at Venice was unique. Elsewhere communal development was different, especially in northern Italy, where there were numerous cases of sworn communes. In 1057 Milan, the principal town of Lombardy, was in revolt against its archbishop. The so-called Pataria, a movement of the Patarines for radical church reform, amounted to a *coniuratio* that lasted for more than twenty years. The strife resulted in the expulsion of the archbishop and the formation of a commune based on various religious factions, each composed of a different social class. There emerged a strange alliance of reformers—noble houses calling for clerical celibacy and an end to simony, and the poor of Milan, the Patarines ("rag pickers"). The noble captain and leader Erlembald urged the Milanese to seize political autonomy. Associated with him was a kind of council of thirty. By 1097 consuls are first mentioned, an indication that they were the elected rulers of the commune. In contrast to the towns of northern Europe, the political authority of Milan extended over a considerable territory beyond the walls, a territory made up of districts known as *contadi* and headed by landed aristocrats. In the case of Milan these lords were elected consuls and shared authority with the consuls from within the walls, some of whom came from families less elevated socially and economically.

Because of the internecine strife characteristic of medieval Italian urban life, it is often impossible to ascertain what groups or alliances of people triggered the movements for political power, a situation complicated by the struggle between the popes and emperors, during which the towns took sides either because they were forced to or because they hoped to profit politically from their support. But it is clear that these movements for civic liberty cut across class lines, depended more on religious sentiment and affiliation, and embraced both urban and rural territory. At Lucca the people, assisted both by the clergy and by some nobles, rose in 1080 against a reform bishop and Countess Matilda, and elected consuls for the governance of the town. In 1081 Emperor Henry IV agreed to appoint no marquis of Tuscany without the assent of twelve Pisans elected in the *commune colloquium*. By 1084 Pisa elected its consuls, and certainly functioned as a commune from this time on. All over northern Italy communes developed early in the twelfth century at towns that in the eleventh century had only semiautonomy or elementary bourgeois privileges. Councils are mentioned at Asti in 1093, at Genoa in 1099, at Pavia in 1105, at Brescia in 1127, and at Bologna in 1123. To the south in Tuscany, Arezzo had consuls by 1098, Siena by 1125, and Florence by 1138.

In the rest of Italy the development was not very different except in southern Italy and Sicily, where the strong Norman rulers denied those conditions conducive to urban revolt and freedom. In these Norman lands communal development was more like that in Normandy and England. From Italy the system of the consulate spread to the towns of Provence. Early in the twelfth century Marseilles had consuls; soon they were also at Arles and Nîmes.

RURAL COMMUNES

Communal privileges have usually been associated with urban centers, but it must be recognized that hundreds of smaller communities, many of which remained agrarian villages throughout the Middle Ages, acquired self-government or a degree of it. This was especially true of many agrarian *villes neuves*. Such communes have been called *communes rurales* by French historians. A famous example is Beaumont-en-Argonne, the charter of which served as a model for more than 500 granted in Champagne, Burgundy, and Luxembourg. Other rural communes, many of them bastides, were clustered in southwestern France. Still others developed in maritime Flanders, northern Germany, and mountainous regions.

COMMUNAL GOVERNMENT

Historians have devoted much research to the motive forces of communal government without coming to a consensus. Obviously the groups and classes associated with the drive for political authority varied from region to region. In the Mediterranean area, where the aristocracy lived in both the country and the towns, nobles were generally involved in communal movements. This was less true in the German lands, where the *ministeriales,* the seignorial and feudal officials of the great lords, commonly dissociated themselves from their traditional ties and functions, joined the inhabitants of the towns in the movements for self-government, and became members of the new urban governments. In the Low Countries, France, and England the motive force was almost always provided by the bourgeois inhabitants of the towns; the feudal aristocracy and the higher clergy generally opposed urban self-government and seldom joined movements to obtain it.

Throughout Europe it is obvious, however, that the leading and most notable citizens of the towns led the negotiations and struggles. This does not mean that the lesser classes did not participate in the uprisings, but that the notable citizens inevitably were the leaders and the ones who assumed political authority once it had been won. It is simply a matter of determining who the notable men were. In Italy the notable men came from within and outside the towns. Known as the *boni homines,* they were the greater and lesser lords, the principal merchants, and sometimes the jurists. Often having advised the bishop and his court or the secular prince and his council, such men assumed direction of the *commune colloquium*. As the need for a more definite executive grew, a commission of *boni homines* was appointed for special business. The next step was the appointment or election of these men as consuls to govern the town. Twelve such men represented Siena in business at Rome in 1124, and by the next year were consuls.

North of the Alps the leading merchants assumed leadership in securing the elementary bourgeois privileges. It was only natural that they should remain the leaders in the movements for self-government. With their experience in trade, industry, and finance, such men were eminently qualified for such a role. By the late eleventh and twelfth centuries merchants had begun to organize economic and social associations known as guilds merchant, with the objective of regulating local trade and prices, securing economic privileges outside the towns, and, by pooling their resources, gaining advantageous situations for buying and selling. Invariably members of the guilds merchant were those who negotiated with the lords of the towns. It follows, therefore, that the guild merchant was the logical organization through which to work to obtain communal government. It was only natural that, after the establishment of self-government, the principal members of the guilds merchant became the officials and members of the governing councils.

One of the best examples of how this worked is the town of St. Omer. The oldest extant guild ordinances of northern Europe come from St. Omer and indicate that a guild merchant had been organized there sometime before 1050. By their membership the merchants secured increased protection and improved opportunities for profit. Regular meetings were held under elected officers in the guildhall—some for business and others for conviviality. Formal wine drinkings were obligatory and paid for by special dues. Whatever funds were left over were to be devoted to charity or to improve the streets and walls of the town. It should be noted that in St. Omer's communal charter of 1127, the same intimate connection between guild and municipality is emphasized. The charter granted the comital mint to the burghers for the benefit of their guild. Other of its provisions granted freedom from certain tolls to members of the guild, indicating how an association, orginally private and voluntary, tended to become an official body.

Throughout northern Europe such guilds merchant provided the leadership, experience, and machinery for communal movements and then provided the officials of the new urban governments. Until the towns had the resources or were forced to provide more space for their municipal governments, the meetings of the councils and courts were held at the guildhalls. Only later were the functions of government and justice transferred to the town halls with their soaring towers symbolizing civic independence. In the great communes of northern Italy, Rhenish Germany, and the Low Countries the

majestic palazzo, *Rathaus,* and hôtel de ville were to the civic life what the cathedrals were to the spiritual. In the halls where the council meetings were held, painted or sculpted scenes depicted communal heroes and famous events. The guild and town halls were portrayed on the communal seals. In the twelfth and thirteenth centuries each commune had a strong civic spirit and pride, a kind of urban patriotism.

It would be erroneous to state that the humbler classes, composed of lesser merchants, craftsmen, and various laborers, never participated in communal government, because during the fourteenth and fifteenth centuries they did in some of the communes of northern Italy and Flanders. Almost invariably, however, such participation came only after bloody urban struggles, and seldom lasted for long. During the Middle Ages communal governments were controlled by the wealthy and powerful citizens, those referred to as the *probi* or *boni homines.* Urban government was patrician and oligarchic or, as often in Italy, despotic.

The most informative description of how communal government was organized, of its close relation with the guild merchant, and of its exclusive, oligarchic nature is provided by a document setting forth the proceedings in Ipswich immediately following receipt of John's charter dated 25 May 1200. The burgesses assembled in a churchyard and chose two good men as bailiffs or reeves. They then elected four coroners to keep the pleas of the crown, two of them being the bailiffs. At the same meeting it was agreed that twelve good men should be elected to a town council, which should be charged with the governance. The burgesses assembled for this election the following Sunday. The bailiffs and coroners selected from each parish four good men, who then selected the councilmen and included among them the bailiffs and coroners. This done, the twelve councilmen had the burgesses swear that they would obey their new governing body. Other meetings were subsequently convened for the selection of more officers.

To collect taxes and pay the borough farm, four leading citizens were chosen to assist the bailiffs. Two beadles, also men of means, were appointed to make attachments and distresses and to carry out commands of the council. When later it was decided to have a common seal for the borough, it, along with the charter, was turned over to the custody of the two bailiffs and one coroner. One of the council was chosen alderman of the guild merchant with four other councilmen as his associates; they were to administer the guild affairs. They then proclaimed to all people of Ipswich that they should appear before them on an appointed day to enroll in the guild and to pay their fees.

This graphic account shows that the government established was in the hands of a group that wielded judicial, executive, and financial powers. The oligarchic nature of the government is patent; a limited group of influential men held all the offices and were selected by a limited number of the leading citizens. The majority of the burgesses merely approved previous actions by this oligarchy. Eight of the twelve councilmen held fourteen offices in the borough and guild. In effect, the borough or communal government was the equivalent of the guild merchant; both were governed by the same officers, all leading merchants of the guild. There is no better example of the oligarchic complexion of medieval town government or of the dynamic role of the guild merchant in securing and controlling urban self-government. What occurred at Ipswich may be taken as quite typical of the development of communal government throughout medieval Europe. There were, of course, variations in the classes of people who took the lead in attaining self-government and who exercised the authority achieved.

In England borough government was characterized by a town council composed of councilmen or aldermen and headed by a kind of president or presiding officer known as the mayor, who came to exercise a variety of executive functions. The mayor of London had an important position not only in local history but in that of the realm during the fourteenth and fifteenth centuries. In northern France the councils were composed of members called *jurés*, men sworn to carry out the decisions of the commune. They were headed by a *maire*. In Flanders and some of the other Low Country states, the councilmen were called *échevins* (Latin: *scabini*; Flemish: *schepenen*) and the councils *échevinages*, names taken over from preexisting institutions when local administrative districts including the towns were under the political and legal power of boards of officials wielding authority on behalf of the territorial ruler, a system that dated back to the Carolingian period. French communes adjacent to Flanders also styled their council members *échevins*. In Germany the council was known as a *Rat*, the councillors as *Ratsherrn*, and the head as a *Bürgermeister*. In Italy and southern France the council bore the name of

consulate and its members that of consuls. The head of the council in Italy frequently was styled a *podesta*.

Inasmuch as a commune was recognized as a distinct legal and political entity, these organs of government were to guarantee that the political, legal, and economic objectives of the commune were fulfilled. The council therefore occupied itself with a variety of business. It served as a court hearing all cases under its jurisdiction; while so engaged, its members were judges. It had charge of finance, commerce, and industry. It supervised public works, organized the provisioning of the town, planned for and controlled the militia as well as the urban defenses, established schools and hospitals, and provided for the care of the poor, aged, and sick. It also levied direct and indirect taxes and passed municipal legislation.

POLITICAL AUTONOMY OF COMMUNES

The political autonomy of communes varied enormously from region to region. In England and France, where central government was strong and effective, the towns with self-government never got more than that. They always recognized royal authority and had to abide by the laws of the realm, pay royal taxes, and provide military service. Occasionally by acting collectively the towns became effective pressure groups, winning concessions from the kings. Examples of such action in England are well known. The voice of the English boroughs was much more effective than that of the French towns because by the fourteenth century the boroughs were regularly represented in Parliament, with the result that, through their representative burgesses, they gave consent to taxation, passed laws, presented petitions, and had some influence in the affairs of the realm.

In France self-governing towns never had such influence. An assembly of the realm such as developed in England never emerged in France. Early in the fourteenth century the three estates of the realm were assembled for a few meetings with the king but thereafter, seldom. Consequently, the towns had few opportunities to be represented at this level or to cooperate with each other so as to exert pressure on the royal government. Moreover, in contrast with England, towns in France seldom had effective relations with the first and second estates, a situation that reduced their political effectiveness and isolated them. Unlike most other communes on the Continent, which retained their local political authority to the end of the medieval period and, in some cases, acquired more, the French communes did not.

The early fourteenth century was a period of disintegration for the communes, spelling the end of many. Usually inability to manage their finances explains the malaise. Often the patrician class mismanaged the finances or engaged in corrupt practices for its own benefit. Exacerbating this trouble were the exorbitant demands for royal taxes. Unable to manage their finances or to pay the royal taxes, the governments of many communes were dismantled and placed under the authority of royal officials such as the *prévots*. In 1320, for example, the commune of Senlis, having become bankrupt, was abolished by decree of the *parlement*. A few years later a large majority of the citizens of Provins voted that they wished to be "outside the government of mayors and *échevins* and to be governed by the king alone." In France, therefore, the kings reestablished direct rule over many of their towns, which thus ceased to be communes.

In the Low Countries the communes increased their power to such an extent that in Flanders the counts almost lost control over the great ones during the fourteenth century. While Louis de Nevers was count (1322–1346), Ghent, Bruges, and Ypres virtually controlled Flanders. In the early 1340's, under the leadership of Jacob van Artevelde, Ghent did. Only in the fifteenth century were the Burgundian dukes able to impose their authority over these communes. The deterioration of royal authority and the rise of particularism in thirteenth- and fourteenth-century Germany nourished the rise of many de facto autonomous, miniature urban states known as the free cities. A similar development of much greater magnitude occurred in Italy. Such communes as Milan, Venice, Genoa, Pisa, Florence, Siena, Lucca, and Pavia were independent city-states in the fourteenth and fifteenth centuries. The history of these centuries is one of incessant war and diplomacy to gain political power and territory. The political, economic, and military stress during this period largely explains the civil unrest and war within these communes and the rise to power of the despots. The communes of late medieval Italy thus resemble the Greek city-states of the fifth and fourth centuries B.C.

BIBLIOGRAPHY

The medieval commune has been the subject of extensive research, most of which is, unfortunately, limited to regions or states. Only a few works discuss the commune as a European phenomenon. Henri Pirenne, *Les villes de moyen âge* (1927), provides such a synthesis but is in need of revision; see Frank D. Halsey, trans., *Medieval Cities* (1925, rev. ed. 1956). Edith Ennen, *Die europäische Stadt des Mittelalters* (1972), available in English as *The Medieval Town* (1979), has a very useful bibliography but is disorganized and in some cases unclear. More limited but interesting is Jean Lestocquoy, *Les villes de Flandre et d'Italie sous le gouvernement des patriciens (XIᵉ–XVᵉ siècles)* (1952).

A few of the most helpful regional studies are the following. England: Mary McKisack, *The Parliamentary Representation of the English Boroughs During the Middle Ages* (1932); Susan Reynolds, *An Introduction to the History of English Medieval Towns* (1977); Carl Stephenson, *Borough and Town, a Study of Urban Origins in England* (1933); James Tait, *The Medieval English Borough* (1936). France: Achille Luchaire, *Les communes françaises à l'époque des Capétiens directs* (1890); Charles Petit-Dutaillis, *Les communes françaises* (1947), trans. as *The French Commune in the Middle Ages* (1978); Albert Vermeesch, *Essai sur les origines et la signification de la commune dans le Nord de la France (XIᵉ–XIIᵉ siècles)* (1966). Low Countries: Henri Pirenne, *Belgian Democracy: Its Early History* (1915), and *Les villes et les institutions urbaines*, 2 vols. (1939). German: (in addition to Ennen) Carl Haase, ed., *Die Stadt des Mittelalters*, vol. 2: *Recht und Verfassung* (1972). Italy: Gerhard Dilcher, *Die Entstehung der lombardischen Stadtkommune* (1967); Gina Fasoli, *Dalla civitas al commune nell'Italia settentrionale* (1969); Gina Fasoli and F. Bocchi, *La città medievale italiana* (1973); C. W. Previté-Orton, "The Italian Cities till *c.* 1200," in *The Cambridge Medieval History*, V (1929), ch. 5; E. Sestan, "La città comunale italiana dei secoli XI–XIII nelle sue note caratteristiche rispetto al movimento comunale europeo," in International Committee of Historical Sciences, *Miscellanea historiae ecclesiasticae* (1960).

In addition to extensive bibliographies in the books of Ennen and Petit-Dutaillis, see International Commission for Urban History, *Guide international pour l'histoire urbaine*, I (1969); Philippe Dollinger, P. Wolff, and S. Guenée, *Bibliographie d'histoire des villes de France* (1967); and Erich Keyser, ed., *Bibliographie zur Stadtgeschichte Deutschlands* (1969).

BRYCE LYON

[See also **Bastide; Castellan; Cologne; Consuls, Consulate; Échevin; Fairs; Feudalism; German Towns; Guilds and Métiers; Italy, Rise of Towns in; London; Mainmort; Markets, European; Mayor; Milan; Ministerials; Urbanism, Western European; Venice.**]

COMMUNION. See Eucharist.

COMMUNION CHANT. A chant of the Proper of the Mass, sung during or after the distribution of consecrated bread and wine. In the early church, both Eastern and Western, it was the custom to sing a psalm at Communion. Often this was Psalm 33, which contains the verse "Gustate et videte, quoniam suavis est Dominus" (Taste and see how sweet is the Lord). In Western liturgical manuscripts of the ninth century and later, the texts of Communion chants are drawn most often from either the book of Psalms or the New Testament. In the latter instance the chant text is an excerpt from the same passage as that which served as the Gospel lesson of the day. In some manuscripts the Communion chants have verses, which were chanted to formulas resembling psalm tones, making it possible to prolong the chant until all present had received Communion.

The melodies of the Communion antiphons are neumatic in style—that is, in general, for many syllables there are a few notes; for some, only one; and in rare instances there may be a chain of notes (a melisma). There are some 150 Communion chants in the classic repertory; all of the ecclesiastical modes are represented in them, though not equally: the first mode is the most popular, and the second and third are relatively little used. Disagreements among the manuscripts concerning the mode of a particular chant are more frequent with respect to Communion chants than other chants of the Mass. Various reasons have been given for this; it is evident in some cases that the original melody for the chant, created at a time when neither musical notation nor the system of the ecclesiastical modes had been developed, was based on a system of intervals for which later theorists were unable to formulate an explanation. The procedures devised to "correct" such melodies in various manuscripts in some instances expose (to a modern trained eye) rather than remove the irregularities and lead to varying modal assignments.

For certain Communion chants on Gospel texts several melodies have been preserved; these are substitutes for earlier antiphons on psalm texts. The reason for disagreement concerning these melodies is thought to lie in the relative recency of their composition. Both in the length and structure of its text and in the character of its music, one Communion chant may differ greatly from another. An orderly system is sometimes evident in the choice of texts; for example, those for the weekdays of Lent were drawn from Psalms 1–26, in order; but no counterpart to this in the music has been identified.

BIBLIOGRAPHY

"Communion," in *New Grove Dictionary of Music and Musicians,* IV (1980); Josef A. Jungmann, *The Mass of the Roman Rite,* Francis A. Brunner, trans., II (1955), 391–400.

RUTH STEINER

COMMUNION UNDER BOTH KINDS for the laity was an integral part of the Hussite revolution of fifteenth-century Bohemia. Friends of John Hus introduced the practice of offering the communicating faithful both bread and wine in certain Prague churches in the fall of 1414 while he was at the Council of Constance, answering charges of heresy. This ritual innovation was in open opposition to the church's mode, in which only the bread was dispensed, and did nothing to ease the lot of Hus at the council, which in July 1415 had him burned at the stake.

Throughout its history the church had accepted a variety of modes of communion. In the third century small children, and later the ill, who might have difficulty swallowing the bread, were sometimes given only wine. Frequently the clergy also dipped the bread in the wine (intinction) and offered wine-soaked bread when the sacrament was brought to the homes of invalids. This was done to avoid dangers of spilling the consecrated wine in transport.

The twelfth century saw a growing reverence for the Eucharist as well as increasing theological speculation as to the nature of Christ's presence in the elements. At the same time the church became increasingly concerned that the unlettered faithful would allow a drop of the consecrated wine, the Savior's blood, to fall to the floor. Theologians placed greater stress on the idea that the full Godhead—Father, Son, and Holy Spirit—was present in the bread alone and in the wine alone. Some, such as Cardinal Robert Pullan (*d.* 1146), concluded that there was therefore no real need for the believer to participate in both kinds. The implications of this teaching slowly led to a withdrawal of the chalice from the laity, so that by the late thirteenth century communion in one kind was common. There were, however, no official papal decrees defining the eucharistic mode until the fifteenth century.

The Bohemian reformers, led by Jakoubek of Stříbro, adopted communion under both kinds as part of an attempt to imitate apostolic practices in church life. Two fourteenth-century developments influenced the Hussites. Matthew of Janov, a reform preacher active in the 1370's and 1380's, placed stress on frequent communion as an aid to heightened piety, and the Englishman John Wyclif emphasized the separation between the two elements in the Eucharist—that is, the wine alone as the blood and the bread alone as the body. In an environment filled with Janov's and Wyclif's influence, Jakoubek in 1414 had what he called a revelation: that communion under both kinds was the New Testament mode and ought to be the normal practice. His innovation elicited the official condemnation of the Council of Constance on 15 June 1415.

In the ensuing debates that culminated in 1433–1436, the church repeated its position, developed in the twelfth century, that since Christ is wholly present in each of the two species, the person who receives only the bread also partakes of the blood. Furthermore, it argued that Christ had addressed his instructions to the disciples, who prefigured the priestly estate, not to the whole church.

The Hussites defended their position by appealing to Christ's instructions. He had told his disciples to take and eat the bread, his body, and to drink the wine, his blood (Matthew 26:26–28; Mark 14:22–24), and in John 6:53 he had stated that eating his flesh and drinking his blood were prerequisites for eternal life. The Hussites also strongly objected to the clergy's claim to represent Christ's disciples. According to Jakoubek, the "whole future church militant," including the laity, followed in place of the disciples. The Hussites' ideal of a regenerated church was one in which all believers, priestly and lay, followed Christ's commands and imitated his virtues. In giving the chalice to the laity, the Hussites consolidated the intellectual and theological development according to which they sought to follow New Testament models.

The chalice soon became a political and religious symbol for the Hussites. By 10 March 1417 the University of Prague, the official spokesman for the Hussites who had withdrawn from the Roman hierarchy, declared itself in favor of communion under both kinds. At the same time, the archbishop of Prague, in ferreting out unorthodox priests, ordered that anyone dispensing communion under both kinds should be expelled from his parish. After 1420 the Four Articles of Prague were the minimal program on which the various parties in the Hussite revolution, from radicals to conservatives, could agree.

The first article stated: "We stand for the ministry of the body and blood of the Lord to the laity in both kinds." The chalice also became the symbol on the flag under which the Hussites fought and dominated most of central Europe from 1420 to 1434. John Žižka, the military hero of the revolution, named one of his castles Kalich (the chalice).

At the Council of Basel in 1433, the first item of substance on the agenda was communion under both kinds. It was defended by John Rokycana, archbishop-elect of the Hussite church. He repeated the main Hussite argument that communion under one kind was a recent introduction contrary to the practice of the New Testament church. Under strong pressure from Emperor Sigismund, the council reluctantly recognized communion under both kinds. Because he wanted to assume the Czech throne, Sigismund compelled the representatives of the council to declare, on 5 July 1436, from the town square of Jihlava in Moravia, that the church would tolerate communion under both kinds and would ordain and accept the Hussite clergy as legitimate. The practice of communion under both kinds survived the repudiation by Pope Pius II of the 1436 agreement in 1462. However, Czech Hussites and Protestants lost their right to communion under both kinds after the Habsburgs defeated the Bohemian Estates in 1620, giving the Catholic Counter-Reformation free rein to impose the Roman faith as the only legal one in Bohemia.

BIBLIOGRAPHY

J. A. Barton, "The Lord's Supper in the Old Unity," in *Proceedings of the Conference of Spiritual Descendants of John Hus* (1938); William R. Cook, "The Eucharist in Hussite Theology," in *Archiv für Reformationsgeschichte*, **66** (1975); Frederick G. Heymann, *John Žižka and the Hussite Revolution* (1955, repr. 1969); Howard Kaminsky, *A History of the Hussite Revolution* (1967); John M. Klassen, *The Nobility and the Making of the Hussite Revolution* (1978); Enrico C. S. Molnár, "The Restoration of Holy Communion in Both Kinds," in *Anglican Theological Review*, **36** (1954); Otakar Odložilík, *The Hussite King* (1965).

JOHN M. KLASSEN

[See also **Councils, Western (1311–1445); Eucharist; Hussites; Wyclif, John.**]

COMMYNES, PHILIPPE DE. See Comines, Philippe de.

COMNENI. See **Komnenoi.**

COMPASS, MAGNETIC. The magnetic compass has been known and used in the Western world since the late twelfth century. It is believed to have been invented in the Mediterranean region, probably at the Italian port of Amalfi, which was engaged in shipping magnetic ores from the mines of Elba. It seems to have been first used for direction finding at sea and later adapted for use on land.

The compass was first mentioned by the English scholar Alexander Neckham. "They also have a needle placed upon . . . a dart," he wrote in his work *De naturis rerum* (1187), probably after having seen the device on shipboard when returning to England from France, "and it is turned and whirled round till the point of the needle looks north-east. And so the sailors know which way to steer when the Cynosura is hidden by clouds." In another work, *De utensilibus,* Neckham noted that after the needle had been placed upon a magnetic stone, it turned in a circular fashion and came to rest pointing in the northern sector. "Sailors do this," he stated, "because when they are crossing the sea they lose the advantage of the bright Sun during cloudy weather in the day, which hides the Sun, or when the world is wrapped in darkness at night, so that they do not know in which direction the ship's prow points."

Other early references include those of Hugues de Berzé (1204) and Guiot of Provins, who wrote in his *La Bible Guyot (ca.* 1206):

> By the virtue of the magnetic-stone they [sailors] practice an art which cannot lie. Taking this ugly dark stone, to which iron will attach itself of its own accord, they find the right point on which they touch it with a needle. Then they lay the needle in a straw and simply place it in water, where the straw makes it float. The point then turns exactly to the star. There is never any doubt about it, it will never deceive. When the sea is dark and misty, so that neither star nor moon can be seen, they put a light beside the needle, and then they know their way.

In 1269 Petrus Peregrinus de Maricourt (also known as Pierre Pelerin) published *Epistola de magnete,* in which he described an early form of the magnetic compass. It had pivots placed above and below a vertical arbor for the needle, the arbor having a transverse arm of nonmagnetic metal such as brass or silver placed at right angles to the needle and pointing east-west when the needle pointed north-south. A sighting rule and transparent cover were provided, and the compass box was graduated in the degrees of arc.

From these sources it is apparent that the first knowledge of the compass came from France. The compass needle was magnetized by rubbing it with a piece of lodestone before floating it, or afterward by bringing the lodestone near it. The form of the earliest lodestones is not known, and it was not until the sixteenth century that armed lodestones, capped with pole pieces, came into being.

The only development of the compass made in the next three centuries was the addition of a graduated compass card or "fly." At first two needles were used; these were subsequently replaced with a single piece of soft iron wire bent into a lozenge shape and attached to the reverse side of the compass card by means of paper strips glued to the card. The card was suspended on a brass pivot attached to the center of the compass box, which generally was in the form of a wooden bowl. Often the bottom of the compass was removable for retouching the wire with a lodestone as required. The top of the box was covered with a glass pane sealed to protect the card from rain and seawater. Gimbals enabling the compass box to be kept level at all times were introduced in the sixteenth century.

The addition of a compass card bearing the rose of the winds is attributed to Flavio di Gioia of Amalfi about 1302. Before the addition of the compass card, medieval compasses generally had a meridian line and the four cardinal points marked on the base of the compass box. The *stella maris,* which became the standard form of decoration of the compass rose, first appeared in an illustration of a poem by either Gregorio or Leonardo Dati in the late fourteenth century.

Early compass cards were divided into equal sectors of eight, sixteen, or thirty-two points, with the north point originally identified by a special device such as a dart, trident, triangle, or star. The fleur-de-lis became the common symbol for the north point from about 1500. The east point was originally indicated with a cross to signify the direction of the Holy Land, while the remaining six points were indicated by the first letters of the Frankish or Italian names for the appropriate winds. The rhumbs were customarily painted in black, though blue and gold were sometimes used in alternating order. A wind rose of twelve winds was known to have been used by the Greeks in antiquity, and by about the fourteenth century one of sixteen points was in use among Frankish navigators; later a transition to a wind rose of eight points with subdivisions into sixteen and thirty-two points occurred.

The application of the wind rose to the marine compass had an important effect on sea travel because it enabled the mariner to know the direction of his course and to delineate with greater accuracy the coastal outlines of routes traveled. It led directly to the development of loxodromic sailing charts for use in the Mediterranean by the early fourteenth century. Direct routes were indicated by the directions of the winds, the lines emanating from a center that formed the *rosa ventorum* (rose of the winds). The charts had no fixed points, and the radius for the lines had no fixed length. The loxodromic charts and the thirty-two-point wind rose may have evolved at about the same time and been used in conjuction with each other.

As sea travel increased during the period of discovery, it was noted that the compass needle did not point to true north, but at an angle that was later described at its "magnetic variation." By the second half of the fourteenth century, European compass makers had become aware of this variation, and thereafter frequently mounted the needle on a graduated card so that it pointed to the angle of variation, though the upper surface was marked with the fleur-de-lis at magnetic north.

The declination of the compass is claimed to have been known to the Chinese long before the magnetic compass was applied to use at sea. In Europe credit is traditionally given to Christopher Columbus for having discovered the variation of the compass from one location to another, as reported by Las Casas in his journal of Columbus' first voyage. Another claim is made for Sebastian Cabot, who, after his voyage to Labrador in 1497–1498, is supposed to have reported that the compass varied in many places and was not regulated by distance from a particular meridian; but modern scholars dispute the claim. Recent studies indicate that mariners had some awareness of magnetic variation for several centuries before Columbus or Cabot.

A significant improvement was made in the magnetic compass at the beginning of the sixteenth century with the addition of a graduated brass rim to the edge of the compass box; an alidade or sight rule was added so that it turned on the rim to form the azimuth compass. A wire or thread was attached to the

top of the alidade and stretched to the center of the rule. A slit through the center of the upright stylus enabled the sun to cast a shadow of the wire or string on the graduated scale to render a precise magnetic bearing of the sun. When the latitude, declination, and altitude of the sun, and the time of observation, were known, the true azimuth of the sun could be calculated. A form of the azimuth compass had been described by Peregrinus, though in the thirteenth century it was apparently used only on land. The first description of the azimuth compass after Peregrinus was in a work by João de Lisboa published in 1514.

BIBLIOGRAPHY

Francis R. Maddison, *Medieval Scientific Instruments and the Development of Navigational Instruments in the XVth and XVIth Centuries* (1969); W. E. May, "Alexander Neckham and the Pivoted Compass Needle," in *Journal of the Institute of Navigation*, 8 (1955); Petrus Peregrinus, *Epistle ... Concerning the Magnet*, Silvanus P. Thompson, ed. (1902); E. G. R. Taylor, "Early Charts and the Origin of the Compass Rose," in *Journal of the Institute of Navigation*, 4 (1951), and "The South Pointing Needle," in *Imago mundi*, 8 (1951); Silvanus P. Thompson, "The Rose of the Winds: The Origin and Development of the Compass Card," in *Proceedings of the British Academy*, 6 (1913–1914).

SILVIO A. BEDINI

[See also **Navigation, Southern Mediterranean; Navigation, Western European.**]

COMPLAINTE. Arising from early medieval Latin laments and the Provençal *planh*, the French *complainte* appeared in vernacular literature by the thirteenth century and had become a distinct class of poetry by the fifteenth century. Often composed in octosyllabic couplets, the *complainte* never truly acquired a specified structure, but was typified by a plaintive character resulting from regret, desire, separation, or death.

The subject of the earlier death lament, probably the most important kind of *complainte*, was typically a great noble, as in Rutebeuf's *complainte* on Thibaut V de Navarre, but this broadened to encompass female aristocrats (Isabelle de Bourbon in Pierre Michault's lament) and artists (Georges Chastellain in Jean Robertet's *complainte*). The length of the *plainte funèbre* also grew from about 200 verses, as in the anonymous thirteenth-century pieces of Louis

VIII and Louis IX, to over 700 verses, as typified in Simon Greban's fifteenth-century *complainte* on Charles VIII.

BIBLIOGRAPHY

Daniel Poirion, *Le poète et le prince: L'évolution du lyrisme courtois de Guillaume de Machaut à Charles d'Orléans* (1965), 399–426; Claude Thiry, *La plainte funèbre* (1978); Jean Lemaire de Belges, *La plainte du désiré*, Dora Yabsley, ed. (1932), 25–47.

CYNTHIA J. BROWN

[See also **French Literature**.]

COMPOSTELA. See **Santiago de Compostela**.

COMPURGATION, also known in England as wager of law, was a Germanic form of judicial proof, found most often in Anglo-Saxon and Lombard law, in which oaths were used to establish the truth or falsity of an accusation. These oaths differed from those of later law that attest to the veracity of evidence, for the oath helper, or compurgator, often had no direct knowledge of the facts and did not offer evidence to be assessed by a judge or jury. Instead, the idea was that the oaths invoked the judgment of God, who would permit the compurgators to complete them successfully only if justice were on their side. Compurgation, therefore, is best understood as a variety of ordeal.

Since the oaths, not being evidence, did not require skilled assessment, there usually were only two legal issues the courts had to consider. The first of these was how large an oath was to be required—that is, how many oath helpers would be demanded and how complex a verbal formula they would have to swear. These factors in general were determined by the seriousness of the charge and the reputation of the defendant. Thus, a defendant who had previously been accused of a misdeed might be required to meet a more exacting standard of proof. The usual method of making an oath more difficult was to demand that the defendant bring more oath helpers; since the "size" of the oath was stated as a sum that had to be made up by the wergilds of the compurgators, however, this demand could also be fulfilled by bringing oath helpers of a higher rank, and one

Anglo-Saxon document reveals that an accused sold his land to a neighbor to obtain that man's high wergild as part of the oath on his behalf. The second means of making an oath more difficult was to have the compurgators recite a more complicated verbal formula. A slight mistake in wording could ruin the oath and lose the case, and in the twelfth century there were some oaths of such difficulty that litigants would prefer battle to the necessity of swearing them.

It was believed that oaths were easy to make, and consequently a second area of law was deciding which party would be permitted to swear. Usually the right to make an oath was given to the accused, who would swear to his innocence or to deny the accusation. This practice struck Otto I as inequitable, because in Italy it gave men the chance to forge charters to pieces of property and then perjure themselves by an oath that the charter was authentic. Otto therefore permitted the other side to choose between oath and battle as a means of proof. In England one also finds that frequently accused men were sometimes barred from the oath and compelled to make another kind of proof.

Trust in compurgation as a means of proof was eroded by the shift in attitudes that led to the abolition of the ordeal in the early thirteenth century. In English law, for example, the Constitutions of Clarendon of 1164 eliminated compurgation as a proof against certain serious accusations. Merchant law was slower to change even though in English royal courts judges, by the end of the thirteenth century, preferred to obtain the opinion of a jury rather than to rely on the oaths of swearers. In London, for example, compurgation was still a common form of proof in the thirteenth century, even against charges of felony, and jury trial became the rule only in the fourteenth century.

In common law there were two areas in which compurgation remained possible: the actions of debt and of detinue, both old actions that had taken shape before the turn against divine judgments was complete and that therefore, from the very beginning, had permitted compurgation. The common law would enforce the payment of a debt in a variety of cases: a loan of money, services rendered, and sales were among the earliest admitted causes of a debt. But when it came to a question of evidence, of proving that the debt existed, defendants were commonly permitted to wage their law to acquit themselves, even though it might have been possible to find a jury conversant with the facts. The plaintiff could bar a wager of law by showing a "specialty," a sealed document attesting to the existence of the debt, but other proofs were not generally admitted, at least in the thirteenth century, and many defendants must have escaped their debts by perjuring themselves.

The possibility of wager of law, by rendering the action of debt ineffective, encouraged the growth in the later Middle Ages of actions on the case that followed the more modern procedure and did not permit wager of law under any circumstances. It was not, however, until the early seventeenth century that wager of law ceased to be an important factor in the considerations of common-law lawyers.

The situation was similar for the action of detinue, to retrieve a chattel, which permitted wager in some cases and came to be replaced by trover, another form of action on the case. In both these cases the desire of lawyers and judges to replace the manifest inequities produced by wager of law was clearly a key motivation in extending the domain of the action on the case at the expense of older actions that had their origins in a time when compurgation was still intellectually respectable.

BIBLIOGRAPHY

The Lombard Laws, Katherine Fischer Drew, trans. (1973); Frederick Pollock and Frederic W. Maitland, The History of English Law Before the Time of Edward I, 2nd ed., 2 vols. (1968).

CHARLES RADDING

[See also **Clarendon, Constitutions of; Law, Early German; Law, English Common; Oath; Ordeals; Trespass; Wergild.**]

COMPUTUS, the art of reckoning time or a book containing knowledge of this art (narrowing the word's original meaning of an enumeration, computation, or account). Its chief purpose was to determine the date of Easter, an aim accomplished through an intricate coordination of lunar and solar cycles with the cycle of the days of the week. Computistical books were often accompanied by Easter tables and a perpetual calendar. Computus became a required part of the medieval school curriculum in the Carolingian period. Noteworthy computists were Dionysius Exiguus, Bede, John of Holywood (Johannes de Sacrobosco), Roger Bacon, and Regiomontanus.

BIBLIOGRAPHY

Alfred Cordoliani, "Les traités de comput du haut moyen âge (526–1003)," in Bulletin Du Cange, 17 (1943), and "Comput, chronologie, calendriers," in L'histoire et ses méthodes, Charles Samaran, ed. (1961); Reginald Lane Poole, Medieval Reckonings of Time (1918).

JAMES J. JOHN

[See also **Calendars and Reckoning of Time.**]

COMTESSA DE DIA. Four impassioned love songs (cansos) are attributed to this Provençal trobairitz, but next to nothing is known about her identity. She seems to have lived and composed in the late twelfth or early thirteenth century, near the small town of Die in the Drôme Valley of southern France. Her thirteenth-century vida contributes further mystification rather than clarification to her biography. It states simply that she was the wife of Guilhem de Peitieus and that she fell in love with Raimbaut d'Aurenga, but these men have been impossible to identify with any certainty; they do not, in any case, represent the famous troubadours of the same names. An early hypothesis, since discredited, gave her the name of Beatritz, which has remained attached to her person with great tenacity in popular tradition, without any historical justification.

For other reasons the Countess has been referred to as the "Sappho of the Rhône," an appellation that has at least some poetic justification; her poems contain some of the same fervor, sensuality, and fiery passion that characterize Sappho's lyrics. She sings, at times plaintively, at times aggressively, of the attachment she feels for her handsome, esteemed lover, who seems to have answered her entreaties with arrogance, hurtful accusations, or worst of all, cool aloofness. She attacks ferociously the envious slanderers (lauzengiers) at court, who are trying to drive the lovers apart through lies and deceit. In Estat ai en greu cossirier she reveals with unabashed simplicity her yearning to hold her beloved knight naked in her arms "in place of her husband."

But the Countess has more to offer than the dramatically re-created outpourings of a passionate heart. The themes and images that she employs belong to the highly developed traditions of the courtly lyric, as embodied in the poems of such illustrious predecessors as Jaufré Rudel and Bernart de Ventadorn. The qualities that she praises in her beloved are those that characterize the ideal poet-lover in the classical presentations of *fin'amors*. The qualities that she points out in herself to persuade her lover to consider her worthy of his full attention are likewise those of the ritualized *domna* of the male troubadour tradition. Even the existence of the amorous code of ethics that declared perfect love to be inevitable between two such perfect people is assumed from the preexistent pattern. She refers to Ovidian themes and figures, and to standard contemporary literature in the same manner as the classical troubadours.

The Countess' style is elegant in its simplicity, a perfect example of the *trobar leu* style, which sought to be directly accessible to all listeners; and yet there is refinement as well, such as may be found in her tastefully delicate use of challenging derivative rhymes, interior rhymes, and alliterations in order to create musically harmonious, limpid songs of lasting appeal.

BIBLIOGRAPHY

Gabrielle Kussler-Ratyé, "Les chanson de la comtesse Béatrix de Dia," in *Archivum romanicum*, **1** (1917); Martín de Riquer, *Los trovadores*, II (1975), 791–802; James J. Wilhelm, *Seven Troubadours* (1970), 133–141.

ROBERT TAYLOR

[See also **Courtly Love; Provençal Literature: After the Twelfth Century; Troubadour, Trouvère, Trovadores.**]

CONCEPTUALISM is a philosophical theory stating that universals are mental or mind-dependent. It therefore represents an alternative solution to realism, according to which universals are nonmental or mind-independent, being either transcendent in relation to spatiotemporal objects (Platonism) or immanent in those objects (Aristotelianism).

In the Middle Ages conceptualism is associated primarily with William of Ockham. However, since he employs the term *nomen mentale* to signify such a universal concept (*Quodlibeta septem*, IV, q. 19), his theory has alternatively been called nominalism.

It is sometimes argued that Peter Abelard anticipated conceptualism. This seems unlikely, since his solution to the problem of universals was grammatical rather than conceptual in character.

BIBLIOGRAPHY

Relevant selections from Ockham are translated in Richard McKeon, *Selections from Medieval Philosophers*,

II (1930), 351–421; and *Ockham: Philosophical Writings*, Philotheus Bochner, trans. (1957). See also Ernest A. Moody, *The Logic of William of Ockham* (1935, repr. 1965), 66–117; and Philotheus Böhner, "The Realistic Conceptualism of William Ockham," in *Traditio*, **4** (1946).

STEPHEN GERSH

[See also **Nominalism; Ockham, William of; Realism; Universals.**]

CONCILIAR THEORY, a term often used interchangeably with conciliarism, is a doctrine concerning the nature of the church's unity and the locus of the supreme jurisdictional authority within it. Although some of its roots are engaged in scriptural soil and in the corporate and conciliar history of the early Christian church, it did not grow to maturity until the thirteenth and fourteenth centuries, flowering in the years after the beginning of the Great Schism in 1378 and winning widespread acceptance in the ensuing "conciliar epoch" dominated by the general councils of Pisa (1409), Constance (1414–1418), Pavia-Siena (1423–1424), and Basel-Ferrara-Florence (1431–1449). After the dissolution of Basel it continued to enjoy enough support to remain a viable ecclesiological option into the sixteenth century, lingering on in Gallican circles into the nineteenth. Given what appeared to be the coup de grace by the First Vatican Council's solemn definitions of papal primacy and infallibility (*Pastor aeternus*, 1870), it has recently become once more a focus of attention in Roman Catholic theological circles and, in the wake of the Second Vatican Council, has revealed unambiguous signs of renewed vitality.

THE NATURE OF CONCILIAR THEORY

Of the four marks of the church designated in the Nicene Creed—one, holy, catholic, apostolic—it was the mark of holiness that lay at the heart of some of the earliest ecclesiological controversies. It was the mark of unity, however, that gave rise to the most thoroughgoing later medieval debate concerning the nature of the church. For some, the key to that unity was the firm subordination of all the members of the Christian community to a single papal head. For others, that key lay in the corporate association of those members.

Committed to the belief that the papal headship of the church was indeed of divine foundation, but moved also by the scriptural vision of the Christian community as forming a single body with Christ, the proponents of conciliar theory sought to harmonize those two convictions. They did so by arguing that side by side with the institution of papal monarchy, it was necessary to give the church's corporate dimension more prominent and regular institutional expression, most notably by the assembly of general councils representing the entire community of the faithful.

In so doing, they advanced a complex of ideas susceptible to many more variations than used commonly to be assumed—too many, certainly, and too elusive to trap within the simple formula of the superiority of council to pope. Nevertheless, it is possible to discern within conciliar theory—at least as it emerged during the Great Schism and the conciliar epoch, its "classical age" of greatest prominence—three broad strands, distinct in their origins and in their subsequent careers, but woven momentarily and fatefully into a meaningful and historic pattern.

The first and most prominent of these three strands is the demand for reform of the church "in head and members" and the belief that this reform could best be achieved and consolidated through the periodic assembly of general councils. Though lacking in the *Epistola concordiae* (1380) of Conrad of Gelnhausen, this strand was present in the thinking of most of the other leading conciliarists of the late fourteenth and early fifteenth centuries: Henry of Langenstein, Pierre d'Ailly, John Gerson, Dietrich of Niem, Francesco Zabarella, John of Ragusa, Andrew of Escobar, John of Segovia, Nicholas of Cusa, and Nicholaus de Tudeschis ("Panormitanus"). Although it received official conciliar ratification in the important decree *Frequens,* promulgated at the Council of Constance in 1417 and closely associated in the minds of its framers with the superiority decree *Haec sancta synodus* (1415), sometimes known as *Sacrosancta,* it did not necessarily involve any assertion of the superiority of council to pope.

Given the fact that reform was most persistently conceived as reform of the Roman curia and the restriction of its authority over the universal church, the second strand in the conciliar thinking of the classical era was a less prominent one. For it sought to give institutional expression to the church's corporate nature by envisaging its constitution in quasi-oligarchic terms, its government ordinarily in the hands of the curia and the pope being limited in the exercise of his power by that of the cardinals, with whose "advice, consent, direction, and remembrance" he had to rule. In 1378 the dissident cardi-

nals were moved by this point of view when they rejected the demand for a general council and took it upon themselves to pass judgment on the validity of Urban VI's election, thereby precipitating the Great Schism. Those who were not members of the Sacred College, and who were already convinced that a general council alone was the proper forum for deciding so important a question, were understandably unimpressed, and one would look in vain for any trace of sympathy with such oligarchic ambitions in the *Epistola concordiae* of Conrad of Gelnhausen or the *Epistola concilii pacis* (1381) of Henry of Langenstein.

As time passed, however, and as the immediate circumstances surrounding the beginning of the Great Schism receded, it became possible for conciliar theorists to attempt to harmonize what had previously seemed dissonant and to envisage a constitutional role in the governance of the universal church for the College of Cardinals as well as the general council. Thus, in describing the church as a "polity" or "mixed government," John Gerson referred to the College of Cardinals as "imitating" the aristocratic power, but he did not develop the idea. In the era of Pisa and Constance it was, instead, his former teacher, Pierre d'Ailly, and the distinguished canonist Francesco Zabarella who did so; while in that of Basel, Nicholas of Cusa and Denys Rijkel (the Carthusian) did likewise. Cusa and Denys were indebted for their ideas on this matter to the views of Pierre d'Ailly, but it was Zabarella who, in his *Tractatus de schismate,* gave this quasi-oligarchic strand its most forceful and classic expression.

Although the pope is said to possess the plenitude of power, he argued, that does not mean that he alone can do everything. The expression "apostolic see" does not refer simply to the pope but to the pope and cardinals, who together form a single body of which the pope is the head and the cardinals are the members. Hence, if under the deplorable circumstances of schism the pope were to refuse to summon a general council, that right would devolve upon the cardinals. Similarly, under any circumstances, "without the cardinals the pope cannot establish a general law concerning the whole Church" *(Tractatus de schismate);* nor, without consulting them, can he take action in matters of importance. On the other hand, if circumstances warrant it, the cardinals can exert their authority to the extent of withdrawing allegiance from the pope. And during a vacancy or even a "quasi-vacancy" (which occurs when the pope cannot effectively rule the church), they succeed to the full power of the Apostolic See. For, after all, they represent the universal church and can act in its place.

This last sentiment was not uncommon at the time and helps explain how a thinker like Zabarella, though he stressed the supreme authority of the general council in the church, could align himself also with the quasi-oligarchic curialist position that others saw as being in tension with conciliarist views. For it reflects the fact that if Zabarella (and, less clearly, d'Ailly) saw the (local) Roman church or Apostolic See as itself a corporate body composed of popes and cardinals—with all that this may have implied constitutionally—they also saw it as the head, in turn, of a greater corporate body, the universal church, from which it derived its authority and the well-being of which it existed to promote. By so doing, of course, they were affirming the third and most fundamental strand in the conciliarist position, a strand that, to avoid confusion, will be referred to henceforth as "the strict conciliar theory."

Whatever its subsequent encapsulations might suggest, this strict conciliar theory possessed no monolithic unity. Even if one restricts oneself firmly to the classical age of Constance and Basel (thereby avoiding the problems posed by the atypical views espoused earlier by Marsiglius of Padua and William of Ockham), one finds that the conciliar theory took a variety of forms. Common to all of them, however, were the beliefs that the pope, however divinely instituted his office, was not an absolute ruler or incapable of doctrinal error but in some sense a constitutional ruler, and therefore susceptible to correction; that he possessed a merely ministerial authority delegated to him by the community of the faithful for the good of the whole church, which itself possessed the gift of indefectibility; that that community had not exhausted its inherent authority in the mere act of electing its ruler but had retained instead whatever residual power was necessary to preserve the truths of the Christian faith and to prevent its own subversion or destruction; that it could exercise that power through its representatives assembled in a general council, could do so in certain critical cases even against the wishes of the pope, and, in such cases, could proceed, if need be, to judge, chastise, and even depose him.

Around this shared pattern of belief the various conciliar thinkers wove theories of differing dimensions and textures. The differences involved reflect the various temperaments of their authors, the several callings—theologian, curial official, canon law-

yer—that had helped to shape them, and the individual capacities (cardinals; bishops; representatives of princes, kings, councils, universities, and religious orders) in which they were serving when they made their particular conciliarist pronouncements. They also reflect the political and diplomatic, as well as strictly ecclesiastical, circumstances under which they wrote: the confused year or two immediately following the outbreak of schism, when a conciliar judgment on the disputed election was the main desideratum; the vigorous decade of Pisa and Constance, when energies were focused and hope ran high; the tense years from 1431 to 1436, when the Council of Basel was bringing Pope Eugenius IV to heel and Nicholas of Cusa was finishing *De concordantia catholica;* the bitter decade after 1439, when such leading conciliarists as Panormitanus, John of Ragusa, and John of Segovia were pushed into the role of diplomats or public relations men, struggling against skillful papal propaganda to win from the German princes and emperor a recognition of Basel's continuing legitimacy, of its deposition of Eugenius IV, and of its election of Felix V.

The impact of such factors is easy to illustrate. Thus, modern commentators on Panormitanus have rightly stressed the difficulty of extracting a fully consistent viewpoint from his multiple statements of pro-conciliar advocacy. What he had to say depended very much on the party he was representing in his official capacity. Again, the theologians were in general more prone than the lawyers to ground their conciliar theories not only in Scripture, church history, ecclesiastical custom, or canon laws, but also (and more fundamentally) in the mandates of natural law. Similarly, whereas the conciliar theorists of Constance (notably Dietrich of Niem, John Gerson, and Pierre d'Ailly), in describing the universal church as a mystical body *(corpus mysticum ecclesiae),* used that term as a synonym for "moral and collective body" *(corpus morale et politicum)* and certainly regarded constitutionalist arguments drawn from secular political practice as applicable to the church and vice versa, some of the conciliarists at the time of Basel (John of Segovia and, to a lesser degree, Panormitanus and Andrew of Escobar) adopted a more cautious approach.

In so doing, they were in some measure moved by the urgent need to respond to the ideological counterattack launched by the papalist propagandists in an attempt to rally the secular rulers of Europe to the Eugenian banner. In pressing that attack, the papalists had repeatedly returned to the charge that the "democratic" ideas of the conciliarists posed a dire threat to every form of monarchical authority, secular no less than papal. In response, John of Segovia argued that the papalists' parallels between ecclesiastical conciliarism and secular constitutionalism were improper. Such parallels between church and polity were to be admitted as valid only insofar as the church was regarded as a *corpus politicum*, the governance of which, like the governance of any kingdom, God assists by a "general" rather than a "special" influence. But it was precisely to the church as a *corpus mysticum* guided by the Holy Spirit, as a unique community in which Christ rules by a special and not merely a general influence, that the arguments for the superiority of council to pope pertained (*Deutsche Reichstagsakten*, XV, 682–683). Their relevance, then, to the mundane realm of secular principalities and powers was understandably remote.

Variations such as these make it well-nigh impossible, without coercing the texts, to move beyond the general description of the central pattern of conciliarist belief already given and closer to an account truly faithful to the views of the full range of conciliar theorists. What is possible, however—and, given the influence and prestige they enjoyed at Constance and in later years, highly desirable—is a closer analysis of the views advanced by Pierre d'Ailly, John Gerson, and Francesco Zabarella. They were the leading exponents of the strict conciliar theory at Constance; their views were moderate ones widely shared by the council fathers and clearly reflected in the famous superiority decree *Haec sancta synodus* (April 1415). Those views are not identical. Although Gerson had been a student of d'Ailly's, differences of nuance distinguish their theories; and Zabarella, writing a canonistic treatise with a very specific objective, does not range as widely as either of them. What is explicit in their works is sometimes only implicit in his. Nonetheless, it is possible, without misrepresentation, to align for purposes of examination the fundamental conciliar commitments of the three men.

Their basic assumption, shared with their papalist opponents, is that of the divine institution of all ecclesiastical power. This power they divide, again like the papalists and in accordance with established canonistic practice, into a sacramental power or power of order (*potestas ordinis*), which all priests and bishops possess in virtue of having received the sacrament of holy orders, and a power of ecclesiastical jurisdiction (*potestas jurisdictionis*). They have very

little to say about the former. The pope, after all, does not base his preeminence in the church on his possession of priestly orders. The papacy is not a distinct sacerdotal order, nor does the pope possess the *potestas ordinis* in any degree higher than the other bishops. His claims to invulnerability rest instead upon the nature of his jurisdictional power and, above all, on his power of jurisdiction in the public sphere (*potestas jurisdictionis in foro exteriori*)— the coercive, truly governmental power that pertains not to any merely voluntary society but to the public authority, and that medieval canonists (unlike some of their modern counterparts) took to include the teaching power (*magisterium*).

It is this type of jurisdictional power that these conciliar theorists had in mind when they asserted the superiority of council to pope. For not even the highest papalist would deny that the pope was subject to ecclesiastical jurisdiction in the internal or penitential forum (*potestas jurisdictionis in foro interiori*). And not even the most radical conciliarist would claim that the general council as such was endowed with the power of order. Therefore, upon an analysis of this jurisdictional or governmental power and of the precise manner in which it was distributed throughout the ranks of the faithful these men bent their efforts.

The claims of the high papalists notwithstanding, these conciliarists denied that Christ gave the power of jurisdiction to Peter alone and not to all the apostles, and that the jurisdiction of inferior prelates must be derived, therefore, from the pope and not directly from God. Against those claims, accordingly, they also denied that the fullness of jurisdictional power (*plenitudo potestatis*) can reside in the pope alone. They did not wish thereby to deny the divine origin of the papal primacy; nor did they wish the council to encroach more than necessary upon the day-to-day working of the papal monarchy. But while the office itself is of divine institution, its bestowal upon a particular individual is the work of men. And when the cardinals elect a pope, they do so not in their own right but as representatives of the community of the faithful. For the final authority of the universal church, like that of other, more restricted congregations, resides in the whole body of its corporate membership.

It would be improper to regard that final corporate authority as being exhausted by the mere act of electing a head. Even after a papal election the fullness of power still resides, in some sense, in the church as well as in the pope. In what precise sense, the formulations of these men do not succeed in conveying with any great degree of clarity, though, given the frequent references to the normal procedures followed in the ecclesiastical corporations of the day, they may well have been clearer to contemporaries than to us. Thus, as Zabarella puts it, in a succinct version later echoed by Panormitanus and Andrew of Escobar, the plenitude of power is fundamentally in the whole church as in a corporate body and derivatively in the pope as the "principal minister" of that corporation (*Tractatus de schismate*). Or, in Gerson's more complex formulations, the plenitude of power is in the whole church and the council representing it, as in the goal to which it is ordained, as in the medium through which power is conferred on individual officeholders, and as in the means by which the use of that power is regulated.

Thus, although the fullness of power may be ascribed to the pope by virtue of his normal exercise of it and his superiority to any other single ecclesiastic, he is not superior to the universal church or to the general council representing it, and he must exercise that power for the good of the whole church. It follows that the council, like any other corporation in relation to its head, has the right to set limits to his exercise of the *plenitudo potestatis* in order to prevent his abusing it to the destruction of the church (*De ecclesiastica potestate, Opera omnia*, du Pin, ed., II, 243).

These conciliar theorists conceived of that right as capable of exercise both under emergency conditions and on a more continuing basis. The emergency situation most readily envisaged (though by no means the only one) is that which occurs when the pope lapses into heresy or, by being the occasion of schism, endangers the faith of the whole church. Under such conditions the church, which, unlike the pope, possesses the gift of doctrinal inerrancy, also possesses the power to prevent its own ruin. Infallibility is not necessarily to be ascribed to the doctrinal decisions of a general council (to d'Ailly that ascription was no more than a matter of pious belief). But, in the determination of orthodoxy and even acting alone, the council possesses an authority superior to that of the pope and can therefore stand in judgment over him, correct him, and even, if need be, depose him.

Concerning the exercise of this inherent ecclesiastical authority under nonemergency conditions, these conciliar theorists are not as precise. All three being advocates of the second strand in conciliar thinking, they regarded the College of Cardinals as sharing with the pope in the exercise of the reduced plenitude of power they allotted to him and as functioning, therefore, as a continuously operating institutional restraint on the abuse of that power. But beyond that, by virtue of their adherence to the strict conciliar theory, they also envisaged some sort of continuing role for the general council in matters concerning the faith and also, it seems, in decisions affecting the general state or well-being of the church. After all, "what touches all by all must be approved"—or, as d'Ailly reformulated that old maxim drawn from the Roman law—"at least by many and by the more notable ones."

THE MATTER OF ORIGINS

Such, then, was the complex of ideas that encouraged the cardinals of both obediences, despite the condemnations of their respective pontiffs, to the fateful step of convoking the Council of Pisa in 1409. Such was the pattern of thinking that found clear expression also in the Constance decrees *Haec sancta synodus* and *Frequens*, emboldened that council to take the drastic steps necessary to end the schism, and fueled the efforts of the council fathers at Basel, no less than at Pavia-Siena or Constance, to pursue the elusive goal of conciliar reform in head and members. If, in analyzing the nature of that pattern of thinking, it was necessary to distinguish the three main strands that determined its conformation, similarly, in investigating its origins, it will be helpful to address each of those strands in turn.

For a correct understanding of the strict conciliar theory and its development, a considerable importance attaches to this matter of origins. As early as 1378, in the wake of the disputed election of Urban VI and of his Avignonese rival, voices were raised suggesting that there must be recourse to a general council for a judgment between the claims of the rival pontiffs. But it was not until the appearance in May 1380 of Conrad of Gelnhausen's *Epistola concordiae* that the schism generated its first coherent statement of the strict conciliar theory.

The early historians of conciliarism—such as August Kneer and Franz Bliemetzrieder—were by and large content to regard the views expressed in Conrad's tract primarily as a response to the grievous difficulties occasioned by the schism. Later historians, however, pushed back beyond the immediate context in which Conrad of Gelnhausen and Henry of Langenstein had framed their views, and claimed to have found an earlier source for conciliar theory in the great efflorescence of publicistic literature occasioned in the first half of the fourteenth century by the bitter clashes between Pope Boniface VIII and Philip IV of France and between Pope John XXII and King Louis of Bavaria. And not altogether without reason. In particular, following in this the views of the fifteenth-century papalist Johannes de Turrecremata, they claimed to have found that source in the works of two imperialist publicists, William of Ockham and Marsilius of Padua, and the implications of this attribution should not escape us.

In the last great medieval dispute between the supreme spiritual and temporal authorities in Latin Christendom, these men had sided with the temporal, and neither were to be in good standing with Roman Catholic theologians of the modern era. If the strict conciliar theory was indeed rooted in their thinking, then a considerable cogency attaches to the ultramontane claim that what the conciliar theorists were involved in was nothing less than an attempt to foist upon the church an unorthodox ecclesiology of revolutionary vintage. As far as Ockham is concerned, however, if the later conciliar theorists drew their central ideas from him, they must have done so at the price of distorting and simplifying them. For if one cuts through the convoluted antipapalisms of his *Dialogus* and other publicistic writings, it is difficult to extract from them any fully developed theory of the prerogatives of the general council, let alone any clear endorsement of the strict conciliar theory as it was formulated by the conciliarists of the classical era.

Borrow from Ockham those conciliarists frequently did, but in a highly selective and piecemeal fashion and largely with the object of cashing in on his effective critique of the traditional papalist ecclesiology. And if Ockham was something less than a conciliarist, Marsilius was something more. Like Ockham, and like the later conciliar theorists whose orthodoxy has not been impugned, he argued that the church is to be defined not as a clerical body alone but as "the whole body of the faithful who believe in and invoke the name of Christ" (*Defensor pacis*, II, ii, 3). But, unlike Ockham and those others, Marsilius concludes from this that, faith being a voluntary thing, the congregation of the faithful must lack the type of coerced unity that is proper to truly political bodies. His church, then, is nothing more than a spiritual congregation. It is a community of believers welded by the faith they share and the sac-

raments in which they participate. This being so, there is no room in that church for the exercise by its ministers of any coercive jurisdictional power, any *potestas jurisdictionis in foro exteriori*. Indeed, the traditional division of ecclesiastical authority into power of order and power of jurisdiction cannot really be sanctioned, for the latter is the prerogative of the temporal authority alone.

Marsilius was not disposed to question that the priesthood is divinely established. What had no divine basis for him was the presence of inequalities within its ranks. The church can have no real head but Christ, its founder. The great hierarchical structure of bishops, archbishops, and pope is not of divine provenance; it is simply a human contrivance, explicable only in terms of administrative convenience and justifiable only to the extent that it is grounded in the consent of the faithful. And that consent is to be expressed by direct election of priests, bishops, and "head bishop." It is to be expressed also by the general council—an elective body composed of laity as well as clergy, the supreme prerogative of which, as the body representative of the faithful, is to express itself on matters of faith with that infallibility which Christ promised neither to Peter or his supposed successors, nor to the apostles or their clerical successors, but to the universal church.

The radical nature of this ecclesiology is clear. If it is the source to which the strict conciliar theory is to be traced, then that theory does indeed represent a revolutionary deviation from the line of thinking about the nature of the church characteristic of the Middle Ages. It is clear, however, that its premises are much more extreme than those of the later conciliar theorists. When one examines their writings, signs of Marsilian influence are not very much in evidence. Dietrich of Niem and Nicholas of Cusa both drew some material from the *Defensor pacis*, and parallelisms have been seen in the conciliarist formulations of John of Segovia. But the presence even of piecemeal borrowings in the works of most of the conciliarists of the era of Constance and Basel is hard to detect. It would seem that the radicalism of the Marsilian ecclesiology was simply too much for them to accept, and as a result his more extreme views failed to enter the mainstream of conciliar theory.

That this should have been so is not, it turns out, too difficult to explain. If the tide of scholarship on conciliar matters that has been flowing since World

War II has made it clear that the strict conciliar theory of the classical age was an essentially moderate doctrine of ecclesiastical constitutionalism, it has also established the fact that it possessed unimpeachably orthodox foundations in the traditional respectabilities of the pre-Marsilian era. Over the years, scholars working their way through the conciliarist tracts, or through the works of such forerunners as William of Ockham, more than once had occasion to note the frequency with which the commentaries of the earlier canon lawyers were cited in those tracts. It is only since World War II, with the growth of interest in the history of medieval canon law, that the importance of those citations has become clear and the profound indebtedness of the conciliar theorists to the teaching of the canon lawyers has been realized.

Thus, in the 1950's, building on the arguments and suggestions of earlier scholars (notable among them Walter Ullmann of the University of Cambridge), Brian Tierney of Cornell University made a powerful and highly influential case for believing that the strict conciliar theory, far from being a reaction to canonistic views or an importation onto ecclesial soil of secular constitutionalist notions, was in fact the logical outgrowth of certain elements of canonist thought itself. The first of those elements derives from the commentaries on the *Decretum* of Gratian in the twelfth and early thirteenth centuries and, above all, on the case of the heretical pope. The "decretists," or commentators on the *Decretum*, denied both to the pope himself and to the (local) Roman church of pope and cardinals the prerogative of doctrinal inerrancy that they willingly accorded to the universal church. On the basis of this stand, some of them (most notably Joannes Teutonicus [*d.* 1245/1246], author of the influential *Glossa ordinaria* or standard commentary on the *Decretum*) concluded that the general council must be "above the pope" in matters of faith.

Their language was not always lacking in ambiguity, and by so concluding they probably meant no more than to affirm that on such matters the decisions of pope and council acting together, as they normally would, were superior to the decisions of the pope acting alone. But what if a pope lapsed into heresy? In what was to become a much-glossed text (dist. 40, ch. 6), Gratian had repeated in the *Decretum* the ancient legal maxim "the pope can be judged by no one." He had also included, however, the qualification appended in the eleventh century to that maxim: "unless he is caught deviating from the

faith." But if the pope is accused of heresy (or, for that matter, of any notorious crime tantamount to heresy), by whom is he to be judged? There was no single decretist theory on this point, and many important canonistic texts still await scholarly assessment. It is possible, however, to discern two principal schools of thought.

According to one, the principal spokesman for which was Huguccio (Hugh of Pisa; *d.* 1210), a pope who lapsed into heresy ceased ipso facto to be pope. If he contumaciously persisted in his heresy, recourse to a judicial superior might be necessary in order to make it clear that he was, in fact, guilty of heresy and in order to have a declaratory sentence of deposition proclaimed. The judicial superior envisaged, however, might be the College of Cardinals and not the general council. According to the other school, a heretical pope did not cease ipso facto to be pope; he had to be subjected to trial, judgment, and deposition. The body possessing the requisite superior authority enabling it to stand in judgment was the general council, since, even acting in opposition to the pope, it possessed a superior jurisdiction in matters pertaining to the faith. The chief advocate of this point of view was Alanus Anglicus (*fl. ca.* 1216). On this crucial point the teaching of the *Glossa ordinaria* is ambiguous, but many came to understand it as backing the latter school of thought; and in the glosses of the late thirteenth and fourteenth centuries, that latter school prevailed.

It is in the combination of this second decretist theory of papal liability with another element of canonistic thinking that we find the foundations of the strict conciliar theory. That other element stems from the corporatist thinking of some of the "decretalists," the commentators on the *Decretales* of Gregory IX. Applying the Roman law of corporations first to the individual churches of Christendom and to the (local) Roman church, and later to the universal church itself, they came to stress, in opposition to the high papalists, that the key to that church's unity lay in the corporate association of its members. Those members, they argued, were capable of exercising their corporate authority even apart from their papal head. For if the members of the church had, through the agency of the cardinals, endowed the pope with authority, it remained their prerogative, should he fall into doctrinal error or abuse his authority in a manner detrimental to the well-being of the whole church, to withdraw that authority.

It took the trying circumstances of schism to

elicit the classic structure of the strict conciliar theory that Conrad of Gelnhausen, Pierre d'Ailly, John Gerson, Dietrich of Niem, and Francesco Zabarella erected on the canonistic foundations described above. By the start of the fourteenth century, however, in the context of the struggle between Boniface VIII and Philip IV of France, John of Paris had produced in his *Tractatus de potestate regia et papali* (1302) a succinct but precociously complete formulation of that same theory. In the same tract, moreover, he argues that although a general council would be "more appropriate" for the task, the College of Cardinals possesses the power to depose a pope, "for it would seem that the body whose consent, in place of the whole Church, makes a pope, might conversely unmake him" (cap. 24). And, in so doing, he reveals the presence in his thinking of that second, quasi-oligarchic strand that Gerson, d'Ailly, Cusa, Denys the Carthusian, and above all Zabarella combined so effectively with the strict conciliar theory.

Like the strict conciliar theory, this quasi-oligarchic vision of the ecclesiastical constitution was rooted in canonistic soil. The reforming and centralizing drive of the great popes of the twelfth and thirteenth centuries had redounded to the benefit of their most intimate advisers and collaborators, whose involvement in the government of the church had been deepening ever since the election of the pope had become their prerogative in the eleventh century. Around this de facto share in government there developed curialist claims of a quasi-constitutional nature that received what appears to have been their first theoretical formulation in an anonymous commentary on Gratian's *Decretum* written early in the thirteenth century. This formulation was given more explicit expression by the canonists Hostiensis (d. 1271) and Johannes Monachus (d. 1313), who maintained that the cardinals shared with the pope in the exercise of the *plenitudo potestatis*.

All of these men took as their premise the notion that as "part of the pope's body" the cardinals constituted, under him, a corporate body in the technical legal sense. Thus, the same rules of corporation law that governed a bishop in relation to his cathedral chapter were seen to govern the pope in relation to his cardinals, those successors to the "Sacred College or Senate of the Apostles." And it was questionable whether the corporate head (in this instance the pope) could legitimately act on matters touching the "state" or well-being of the corporate whole without the consent of its members.

Whether Hostiensis intended to ascribe to the cardinals a strictly "constitutionalist," as opposed to a merely "consultative," role, scholars have failed to agree. But it is clear that he believed they should have a vital and intimate role in the decision-making process, and it was easy enough for the later conciliarists to build upon such beliefs and to look to the Sacred College for the imposition of some continuously operating restraints on the pope. Those who did so, however, constituted a distinct minority among the advocates of the strict conciliar theory. They were far outnumbered by those thinkers who combined with their advocacy of that theory the first of the strands that made up the pattern of conciliar thinking in the classical era: the demand for reform of the church in head and members and the conviction that such a reform could best be achieved through the periodic assembly of general councils.

The origins of this first strand long predated the schism. Directed especially at the papal centralization of authority in Rome and the affiliated systems of papal taxation and provision to benefices, the call for reform in head and members had emanated from the provincial churches and had been bruited in 1245 and 1276 at the First and Second Councils of Lyons. Not until the opening years of the fourteenth century, however, did it begin to achieve so widespread a credibility and to assume so hostile a tone as to call into question the position of jurisdictional supremacy that the papacy had come to occupy in the universal church. The papacy had attained that position by virtue of the effective leadership that the popes of the late eleventh and twelfth centuries had given to both the reforming and the crusading movements. But by the beginning of the fourteenth century it had long since ceased to be able to give that type of leadership. The clamor of criticism that William Lemaire, bishop of Angers, and Guillaume Durand, the Younger, bishop of Mende, raised at the Council of Vienne (1311–1312) constituted something more than a mere straw in the wind.

Concerned in *De modo generalis concilii celebrandi* ... (1311) to vindicate the rights of the provincial churches against curial encroachment, Durand took pains in acknowledging the divine foundation of papal authority to affirm the similarly divine foundation of the church's episcopal organization. If it was the responsibility of the Roman church, as "head and mother of all the churches," to give a lead in reform that the others would follow (*De modo*, pars III, rub. l; fol. 173r), it was also its duty to respect the rights of local churches and to restrain within the narrowest of bounds those damaging privileges and exemptions from the jurisdiction of the ordinary that were undermining the authority of the bishops within their dioceses.

In so arguing, Durand clearly felt that he was simply demanding of the pope that he too observe the church's ancient law. He may also have felt, though mistakenly, that he was doing no more than that when he went on to assert that, since "what touches all by all should be approved," a general council should be assembled "whenever a new law was to be established or anything was to be ordained concerning matters that affect the common state of the church" (De modo, pars II, rub. xli; fol. 165v). But even he must have realized that he was introducing something of a novelty when he went on to urge that general councils should be assembled regularly at ten-year intervals.

We would be ill-advised to take for granted this association of the demand for reform in head and members with the call to establish the general council as a regularly functioning constitutional mechanism within the structure of church government. The reforming agitation at Vienne came to nothing. The half century and more that followed went without benefit of council and witnessed the energetic extension and consolidation of the pope's fiscal prerogatives and jurisdictional powers. Still less should we take for granted the further combination of those two notions with the claims advanced on behalf of the council's authority by those who subscribed to the strict conciliar theory. Of that theory there is nothing in Durand's tract—no more, indeed, than there is about reform in John of Paris' Tractatus de potestate regia et papali.

It was only with the onset of the Great Schism in 1378 that an effective cry was raised once more for the assembly of a general council and, with it, for a renewed attempt at churchwide reform. Only the stubborn persistence of the schism, moreover, persuaded many among the tentative supporters of the via concilii to become truly committed advocates of the strict conciliar theory. For endorsement of the view that the general council was the proper court of judgment concerning the disputed papal election did not necessarily mean commitment to any fully fledged version of the strict conciliar theory or to the alliance of that theory with the call for a reform in head and members. Pierre d'Ailly's cautious advocacy of the via concilii in his Epistola diaboli Leviathan (1381) is simply that. Similarly, in his Epistola

concilii pacis (1381) Henry of Langenstein made no more of the conciliarist superiority principle than was strictly necessary to meet the objections of those who claimed that the general council did not possess the requisite authority to decide a disputed papal election.

Only in the opening years of the fifteenth century, in a climate of mounting impatience and growing disillusionment with the intentions of the rival pontiffs, do we encounter the thoroughgoing combination of the strict conciliar theory with the call for a churchwide reform in head and members that would (among other things) erect permanent constitutional barriers to the pope's abuse of his jurisdictional power. Thus, in his Tractatus de materia concilii generalis (1402–1403), Pierre d'Ailly sketched out a whole plan of reform that he later presented to the Council of Constance. Similarly, in his De modis uniendi et reformandi ecclesiae (1410), Dietrich of Niem assumed that reunion and reform of the church went hand in hand and that a council was necessary to achieve both. Both of these tracts contain clear affirmations of the strict conciliar theory, and the combination of that theory with the call for reform was to become something of a cliché among the fathers of Constance, Pavia-Siena, and Basel.

THE CAREER OF CONCILIAR THEORY

It was once common to suppose that conciliar theory lapsed swiftly into desuetude during the age of papal restoration subsequent to the dissolution of the Council of Basel. That supposition was in no small degree conditioned by the demise of Gallicanism after the First Vatican Council and the more or less ultramontane reading subsequently given to the history of the late-medieval and early-modern papacy. Much emphasis was placed on Laetentur coeli, the decree of union with the Greeks promulgated in 1439 by the Council of Ferrara-Florence, which concluded with the definition of the Roman primacy that was to be the model for the First Vatican Council's comparable definition. Great stress was also placed on Pius II's bull Execrabilis (1460), which condemned as "erroneous and abominable" appeals from existing papal policies to the judgment of a future general council, and on the bull Pastor aeternus, promulgated in 1516 at the Fifth Lateran Council, which stated that popes, having authority over all councils, had the right to convoke, transfer, and dissolve them. Thus, if Execrabilis was seen as the definitive condemnation of the appeal from papal to conciliar authority, *Pastor aeternus* was seen as nothing less than the definitive condemnation of the conciliar theory itself.

Recognition of the rich complexities of fifteenth-century ecclesiastical history, however, calls such emphases into question. Eugenius IV's promulgation at Florence of *Laetentur coeli* did not prevent his own deposition at Basel a couple of months later. Nor, for the better part of a decade, did it discourage some of the most powerful European princes from steering a course of studied neutrality between pope and council. In its own day *Execrabilis* was regarded not as a binding dogmatic judgment but as the understandable reaction of one particular faction. Within a year of having issued it, Pius II was obliged to renew its prohibition of appeals from pope to council; and in 1483 and 1509, respectively, Sixtus IV and Julius II were forced to do likewise.

Indeed, had the practice of making such appeals not persisted, leading in 1511 to the assembly on conciliarist principles of a dissident antipapal *conciliabulum* at Pisa, it is hard to imagine Julius II's having overcome his own distaste for general councils and having summoned the Fifth Lateran Council. And if some of the fathers assembled at that council felt unable to accord any validity to the provisions of the Constance superiority decree *Haec sancta synodus,* few of them seem to have been willing to say as much. About conciliar theory *Pastor aeternus* says very little—and then only indirectly. It is concerned with the conciliar question only at one remove. It addresses itself explicitly to no more than the papal right of convoking, transferring, and dissolving councils. It does not spurn the superiority decrees of Basel, nor is there any mention of Constance or any rejection of *Haec sancta*. Not, it should be noted, because such a move would have been regarded as redundant at the time, for Ferdinand of Spain, in his instructions to his representatives at the council, specifically suggested the need for a formal repudiation of *Haec sancta,* a repudiation that never occurred.

That this should have been so reflects, among other things, the tenacity of conciliar theory, which survived as a viable ecclesiological option well into the sixteenth century and as something more than a theological museum piece long after that. Even among the supporters of the restored papacy the lingering impact of conciliarist principles was strong enough to generate debilitating tensions that were partly constitutional in nature, and their papalism

was often more qualified than the slogans under which they served. As a result, the ecclesiological picture that emerges is a complex and sometimes a rather confusing one. The complexities involved, however, correspond in no small degree to the complexities of conciliar thinking itself, and the confusion can in some measure be diminished if one distinguishes once more the three strands that were woven together in the conciliar thinking of the classical age. For those strands, just as they had been distinct in their origins, were distinct in their subsequent careers.

Under the stresses and strains of the latter years of Basel and immediately afterward, the intricate complex of ideas that had made up the fabric of conciliar thought began to unravel. The first strand to detach itself was the quasi-oligarchic view that had ascribed to the cardinals of the Roman curia an enhanced constitutional role in the structure of ecclesiastical government. While, in his *De auctoritate summi pontificis et generalis concilii,* a conciliarist sympathizer like Denys the Carthusian could indicate his adherence to Pierre d'Ailly's views on the subject, he was something of an exception. If those views were indeed handed on to future generations, it was to generations of curialists rather than conciliarists. And they were handed on not by such later advocates of the strict conciliar theory as Jacques Almain (d. 1515) or John Major (d. 1550), who drew so much else from d'Ailly's writings, but by such curialists and high papalists as Domenico de' Domenichi (*fl. ca.* 1460) and John of Turrecremata (d. 1468). Much of the discussion of the cardinalate in Turrecremata's great *Summa de ecclesia* (*ca.* 1453) is taken verbatim (though without acknowledgment) from d'Ailly's *Tractatus de ecclesiastica potestate.*

The advocacy of such views by the dean of papalists himself was an event of some importance, for the latter half of the fifteenth century witnessed a sharpening of the tensions that for a century and a half had plagued the relationship between pope and cardinals. In the ensuing struggle the efforts of the cardinals to advance their own position met with little success. The electoral capitulations that they imposed on one pope-elect after another have been described as little more than rear-guard actions. But they do reflect the fact that the old curialist oligarchic tradition found its home in the late fifteenth century where it had found it before—not among the advocates of the strict conciliar theory but in the Roman curia. And that fact is underlined, too, by the tendency, widespread even among those who rejected the strict conciliar theory, to ascribe to the cardinals the right to convoke a general council in cases of emergency, even against the expressed wish of the pope.

In their electoral capitulations the cardinals were accustomed to including, along with private demands for guarantees of the privileges of their state, public acknowledgments of the persistent demand for reform in head and members and of the continuing belief that this could best be achieved through the periodic assembly of general councils. During the classical era this first and most prominent strand in conciliarist thinking had had little to do with the quasi-oligarchic view, and its alliance with the strict conciliar theory was very much the product of the extraordinary circumstances of the Great Schism. By the mid fifteenth century, as the desertion of Basel by such distinguished conciliarists as Cardinal Giuliano Cesarini and Nicholas of Cusa illustrates so dramatically, that alliance was crumbling.

As late as the early sixteenth century, the curialist lawyer Giovanni Gozzadini (d. 1517) could still combine in his De electione romani pontificis clear advocacy of the strict conciliar theory and the traditional commitment to reform in head and members. By that time, however, such a combination had become something of an exception. In the years after Basel, those who believed that it would take a general council to achieve the necessary reform churchwide had begun increasingly to recoil from any unambiguous endorsement of the strict conciliar theory. Thus, when Louis XII of France was able in 1511 to secure the assembly on conciliarist principles of the conciliabulum of Pisa, those who defended it most vigorously had little to say about reform; while the majority of those churchmen most interested in reform held aloof and chose to align themselves instead with the rival assembly that Julius II convoked at the Lateran.

That they did so did not necessarily mean that they found it impossible to ascribe any validity to the Constance superiority decrees. Julius II could indicate his own belief that, under the changed circumstances of the day, the provisions of Frequens were no longer applicable. But in his instructions to the Spanish envoys to the Fifth Lateran Council, Ferdinand of Spain could still demand (and not without reference to Frequens) that general councils be held every ten or fifteen years. And that demand was made again in the Libellus ad Leonem X, the great

program of reform that the Camaldolese monks Tommaso Giustiniani and Vincenzo Quirini presented to the pope. They stated quite explicitly that they regarded it as vital to the recovery and maintenance of the church's health that general councils be held every five years.

While precise attitudes toward Haec sancta synodus are somewhat harder to determine, it is well to remember that Turrecremata, his general ecclesiology notwithstanding, certainly admitted in his influential Summa de ecclesia that the council had some role to play in the dismissal of an erroneous pope. Quirini, in his Tractatus super concilium generale (ca. 1511), and Tommaso de Vio, Cardinal Cajetan, the most formidable adversary of the Pisan conciliarists, in his De comparatione auctoritatis papae et concilii (1511), did likewise. Similar hesitancies characterize the ecclesiologies of other churchmen in the era of papal restoration whom we are otherwise tempted to classify unambiguously as high papalists.

The position of their conciliarist opponents betrayed no comparable hesitancies or qualifications. Despite the ultimate failure of Basel to sustain its case against Eugenius IV, the clerical leadership in the Holy Roman Empire continued to adhere with considerable tenacity to conciliarist principles. The same cannot be said of Italy; yet that country, even in the sixteenth century, produced some very important restatements of the strict conciliar theory—notably the Consilium . . . de auctoritate papae et concilii of Philippus Decius (Philippe de Dexio), the Apologia sacri Pisani concilii moderni of Zacharia Ferreri, the Synodia . . . de conciliis of Matthias Ugonius, and the De electione romani pontificis of Giovanni Gozzadini. In Scotland there was a similarly continuous conciliarist tradition, and it is now clear that Thomas Livingstone (d. 1460) and John Ireland (d. 1496) must be added to the list of those who espoused the strict conciliar theory. And in France, where that theory enjoyed a vigorous and continuing public life, the theologians of the University of Paris defended it as a traditional teaching going back to the days of Constance.

It was from France, then, as well as from Scotland and Italy, that the strict conciliar theory drew its "silver age" apologists when the assembly of the conciliabulum of Pisa called forth a flurry of papalist attacks on it. Notable among those apologists were Jacques Almain and his former teacher, the Scotsman John Major. In their works—especially Almain's *Tractatus de auctoritate ecclesiae et conciliorum generalium* (1512) and Major's *Disputatio de auctoritate concilii supra pontificem maximum* (1518)—no endorsement of the quasi-oligarchic strand of conciliar thinking is to be found, and scarcely a mention of reform. Those omissions apart, however, what is most strikingly revealed by a comparison of those works with the conciliarist literature of the classical era is the element of continuity.

In recent years it has sometimes been claimed that if the papalism of the supporters of the Fifth Lateran Council was very much a "qualified" one, so, too, was the position of their conciliarist adversaries, amounting to little more than an endorsement of the decretist teaching on the case of the heretical pope. But what in fact we see in these tracts of Almain and Major—rigorously shaped, surrounded by many of the old arguments, and buttressed by the addition of some new ones—is the strict conciliar theory itself, bearing the imprint of its decretalist as well as its decretist sources, and in very much the same form as it had taken in the works of Pierre d'Ailly and John Gerson, their Parisian forebears. Almain's and Major's tracts belong to the mainstream of conciliar thinking, and it is their particular historical value to signal the fact that that stream was flowing strong on the very eve of the Reformation.

THE LEGACY OF CONCILIAR THEORY

In the wake of the Reformation and the vigorous reassertion of reforming leadership by the papacy of the Counter-Reformation era, the conciliarist hope for a constitutionalist revolution in the church was pushed to one side. The continuing advocacy of conciliarist principles by Gallican writers (and later by the Febronians in Germany) served only to nudge those principles further and further into the shadows of heterodoxy. And there can be no doubt that the alleged heterodoxy of the conciliarist position has left a profound mark on the manner in which conciliar theory has been understood and its history written, down to the present day. In few areas of historical scholarship has the intrusion of extrahistorical (that is, theological and canonistic) considerations been more pronounced.

Nonetheless, the degree to which the strict conciliar theory lived on in the writings of the theological Gallicans is both noteworthy and important. Edmond Richer, syndic of the Sorbonne, published in 1606 a very influential edition of the works of Gerson (including conciliar tracts by John of Paris,

d'Ailly, Major, and Almain) and, in 1611, his famous and controversial *Libellus de ecclesiastica et politica potestate*, which relied very heavily on the conciliarist views of Gerson, d'Ailly, Major, and Almain. Later in the century Jacques Bossuet, bishop of Meaux and architect of the Declaration of the Gallican clergy (1682), proclaimed his own adherence to the strict conciliar theory (the Declaration, after all, had endorsed *Haec sancta*) and supported his stand by citing the views of the same four men. At the start of the next century the example of Richer and Bossuet was followed by Louis Ellies du Pin, who not only included numerous tracts by d'Ailly, Major, Almain, and other conciliarists in his 1706 edition of Gerson's complete works, but also claimed in 1707 that the University of Paris had always held "as a fundamental point of its ecclesiastical discipline that the council is above the pope" (*Traité de la puissance ecclésiastique et temporelle*).

The significance of the degree to which the conciliarist views of the Parisian divines from John of Paris to Jacques Almain were kept before the eyes of the public extends beyond the immediate context of Gallican ecclesiology, and even the larger world of Roman Catholic theology, to touch the ideological controversies of Protestant Europe and the development of the constitutionalist strand in early-modern political thought. Otto von Gierke, and after him John Neville Figgis, argued that this was the case. And while it would be easy to exaggerate the importance of the influence that such conciliar theorists as Gerson, d'Ailly, Major, and Almain exerted on sixteenth- and seventeenth-century resistance theories, it would equally be improper to pass over that influence in silence.

Presumably the assembly of the *conciliabulum* of Pisa in 1511 and the renewed circulation of conciliarist literature occasioned thereby explain the ease with which, later in the century, constitutionalists and the advocates of active resistance against tyrants made use of the strict conciliar theory in their own discussions of secular politics. In five important works, three of which exerted an immense influence on the political thinking of seventeenth-century England, there is clear evidence of dependence on conciliar political ideas. *Du droit des magistrats* (1574) of Theodore Beza, if brief on the matter, is quite explicit. Lengthy appeals to conciliar theory and practice are to be found in the *Shorte Treatise of Politicke Power* written in 1556 by John Ponet, exiled Anglican bishop of Winchester; in the *De jure regni apud Scotos* (1579) of George Buchanan, the Scottish humanist who, in his earlier Catholic days, had adhered to the conciliar position; in the anonymous *Discours politique des diverses puissances* (1574); and in the most famous of all Huguenot resistance tracts, the *Vindiciae contra tyrannos* (1579).

Even if the Parliamentary opponents of royal absolutism in seventeenth-century England had not had direct access to the conciliarist literature (and we know that they did), the works of Ponet and Buchanan, and the *Vindiciae contra tyrannos*, all of them in circulation during the Civil War era, would have been enough to alert them to the relevance of the strict conciliar theory to their cause. Certainly, during the early years of the first Civil War, when the opponents of Charles I still pursued the moderate goal of lawful resistance, some of them chose to cite the conciliarists and to invoke the conciliar analogy in much the same way as their sixteenth-century predecessors. And the efforts of some of their royalist adversaries were deflected into attempts to best those "Sorbonnist" arguments. For if, as the author of the *Vindiciae* said (in the words of the English translation printed, significantly enough, in 1642 and 1689):

> according to the opinions of most of the learned, by decrees of Councils, and by custom of like occasions, it plainly appears that the Council may depose a Pope, who notwithstanding vaunts himself to be the King of Kings, and as much in Dignity above the Emperour, as the Sun is above the Moon . . . [then] . . . who will make any doubt or question that the general Assembly of the Estates of any Kingdom, who are the representative body thereof, may not only degrade and disthronize a tyrant, but also disthronize and depose a King, whose weakness or folly is hurtful or pernicious to the State.

BIBLIOGRAPHY

Bibliographies. The best point of departure is the select bibliography in C. M. D. Crowder, ed., *Unity, Heresy and Reform, 1378-1460* (1977), 190-205. More extensive bibliographical data are in Étienne Delaruelle, Edmond-René Labande, and Paul Ourliac, *L'église au temps du grand schisme et de la crise conciliaire*, 2 vols. (1962-1964); and Hans-Georg Beck *et al.*, *From the High Middle Ages to the Eve of the Reformation*, Anselm Briggs, trans. (1970). For the more recent literature see Remigius Bäumer, ed., *Die Entwicklung des Konziliarismus* (1976), 3-56; Giuseppe Alberigo, "Il movimento conciliare (XIV-XV sec.) nella ricerca storica recente," in *Studi medievali*, 3rd ser., **19** (1978); Joachim W. Stieber, *Pope Eugenius IV, the Council of Basel, and the Secular and Ecclesiastical Authorities in the Empire* (1978), app. D, 378-404.

Selected primary sources. For the proto-conciliarist writings of Guillaume Durand, John of Paris, Marsilius of Padua, and William of Ockham, see *Tractatus Guilielmi Durand Speculatoris de modo generalis concilii celebrandi*, in *Tractatus illustrium jurisconsultorum*, XIII; *Tractatus de potestate regia et papali*, in Fritz Bleienstein, ed., *Johannes Quidort von Paris: Über königliche und päpstliche Gewalt* (1969); Charles W. Previté-Orton, ed., *The Defensor Pacis of Marsilius of Padua* (1928); for Ockham's *Dialogus*, Goldast, *Monarchia*, II, 392-917 (see below).

The bulk of the conciliarist treatises of Henry of Langenstein, Pierre d'Ailly, John Gerson, Andrew of Escobar, Matthias Doering, Gregor Heimburg, Philippus Decius, Zacharia Ferrari, John Major, and Jacques Almain are in the following collections: Heinrich Finke, ed., *Acta concilii Constanciensis*, 4 vols. (1896-1928); John Gerson, *Opera omnia*, Louis Ellies du Pin, ed., 5 vols. (1706); and his *Oeuvres complètes*, Palémon Glorieux, ed., 10 vols. (1960-1973); Melchior Goldast, ed., *Monarchia S. Romani Imperii*, 3 vols. (1611-1614); Edmond Martène and Ursin Durand, *Veterum scriptorum et monumentorum historicum, dogmaticorum moralium amplissima collectio*, 9 vols. (1724-1733); Hermann von der Hardt, *Magnum oecumenicum Constantiense concilium*, 6 vols. (1697-1700).

Conrad of Gelnhausen's *Epistola concordie* is printed in Franz Bliemetzrieder, *Literarischer Polemik zur Beginn des grossen abendländischen Schismas* (1910); Pierre d'Ailly's *Tractatus de materia concilii generalis*, in Francis Oakley, ed., *The Political Thought of Pierre d'Ailly* (1964); Dietrich of Niem's *De modis uniendi et reformandi ecclesiam in concilio universali*, in Hermann Heimpel, ed., *Dietrich von Niem* (1932); Francesco Zabarella, *De ejus temporis schismate tractatus* (1609); Nicholas of Cusa's *De concordantia catholica*, in *Nicolai de Cusa Opera omnia*, Gerhard Kallen, ed., XIV (1963); John of Segovia's speech of 28 March 1441, before the Congress of Mainz, in H. Weigel *et al.*, eds., *Deutsche Reichstagsakten*, 1st ser., XV (1914), and his later, expanded version of that discourse, the *Amplificatio disputacionis*, in F. Palacky *et al.*, eds., *Monumenta conciliorum generalium saeculi decimi quinti*, III; Denys the Carthusian, *De auctoritate summi pontificis et generalis concilii*, in *D. Dionysii Cartusiani Opera omnia*, XXXVI (1908); Matthias Ugonius, *Synodia Ugonia episcopi Phamagustani de conciliis* (1532); Giovanni Gozzadini, *De electione romani pontificis*, remains unprinted—Biblioteca Apostolica Vaticana, Cod. Vat. lat. 4144, fols. 1r-307r.

For English translations of the treatises of John of Paris and Marsilius of Padua, see John of Paris, *On Royal and Papal Power*, John A. Watt, trans. (1971); and Alan Gewirth, *Marsilius of Padua: The Defender of Peace*, II (1956). There are English translations of extracts from the conciliarist writings of Henry of Langenstein, Pierre d'Ailly, John Gerson, Dietrich of Niem, and John of Ragusa in Crowder, *Unity, Heresy and Reform*; and Matthew Spinka, *Advocates of Reform* (1958).

Selected secondary accounts. On the origins of conciliar theory, see Brian Tierney, *Foundations of the Conciliar Theory* (1955), and "Pope and Council: Some New Decretist Texts," in *Medieval Studies,* **19** (1957). For recent studies of the leading conciliar theorists, see (for Dietrich of Niem) Ernest F. Jacob, *Essays in the Conciliar Epoch,* 3rd ed. (1963), 24–63; (for Zabarella) Walter Ullmann, *The Origins of the Great Schism* (1948), 191–231; John B. Morrall, *Gerson and the Great Schism* (1960); Posthumus Meyjes, *Jean Gerson, zijn kerkpolitick en ecclesiologie* (1963); Louis Pascoe, *Jean Gerson, Principles of Church Reform* (1973); Paul E. Sigmund, *Nicholas of Cusa and Medieval Political Thought* (1963); Morimichi Watanabe, *The Political Ideas of Nicholas of Cusa with Special Reference to his De Concordantia Catholica* (1963); Francis Oakley, *The Political Thought of Pierre d'Ailly, op. cit.;* (for John of Segovia) Antony J. Black, *Monarchy and Community* (1970).

There is a sizable body of literature focused on the decree *Haec sancta synodus,* most of which is summarized, criticized, or commented on in Francis Oakley, *Council over Pope? Towards a Provisional Ecclesiology* (1969), 105–141; and Paul de Vooght, "Les controverses sur les pouvoirs du concile et l'autorité du pape au Concile de Constance," in *Revue théologique de Louvain,* **1** (1970). There is an extension and updating of some of these comments and criticisms in Francis Oakley, "The 'New Conciliarism' and Its Implications," in *Journal of Ecumenical Studies,* **8** (1971), on which see Brian Tierney, "'Divided Sovereignty' at Constance," in *Annuarium historiae conciliorum,* **7** (1975). Decent synoptic overviews are in Hans Schneider, *Der Konziliarismus als Problem der neueren katholischen Theologie* (1976).

For the later career of conciliar theory, Francis Oakley, "Almain the Major: Conciliar Theory on the Eve of the Reformation," in *American Historical Review,* **70** (1965), and "Conciliarism at the Fifth Lateran Council?" in *Church History,* **41** (1972). For the role of conciliar theory in the history of political thought, see Otto von Gierke, *Political Theories of the Middle Ages,* F. W. Maitland, trans. (1900, repr. 1958); John Neville Figgis, *Studies of Political Thought from Gerson to Grotius* (1907, repr. 1976); Francis Oakley, "Figgis, Constance, and the Divines of Paris," in *American Historical Review,* **75** (1969); Quentin Skinner, *The Foundations of Modern Political Thought,* II (1978); Francis Oakley, "Natural Law, the *Corpus Mysticum,* and Consent in Conciliar Thought," in *Speculum,* **56** (1981).

FRANCIS OAKLEY

[See also **Ailly, Pierre d'; Cardinals, College of; Councils, Western (1311–1445); Curia, Papal; Decretists; Durand, Guillaume; Gerson, John; Hostiensis; John of Paris; Marsilius (Marsiglio) of Padua; Nicholas of Cusa; Ockham,** William of; Panormitanus; Papacy, Origins and Development of; Reform, Idea of; Schism, Great.]

CONCLAVE, PAPAL. Before the fourteenth century papal elections frequently caused difficulties. The electoral decree issued by Nicholas II in 1059 had solved some, but not all, of the problems. There was further discussion and some action in the next two centuries, but only when Boniface VIII in 1298 incorporated into his *Liber sextus* the decree *Ubi periculum,* issued by Gregory X at or shortly after the Second Council of Lyons in 1274 (Sext. 1.6.3) was a procedure introduced into canon law to secure secret, free, and indisputable papal elections. Although the decree could not remove all difficulties, only once (in 1378) did a schism originate from uncertainty about the validity of the electoral process.

The system that produced the conclave procedure originated largely by accident. *Ubi periculum* was to some extent a codification and legitimization of methods similar to those used at the election of Gregory X in 1271, ending a three-year interregnum. Those methods themselves had reflected the vicissitudes of contemporary Italian politics. But there were precedents of the procedure adopted in 1271, whereby the inhabitants of Viterbo, exasperated at the failure of the cardinals to elect, had incarcerated them and forced them by a series of deprivations to make an election. The notion of employing the conclave itself as a means of forcing the divided and irreconcilable cardinals to produce a pope is to be found in canonistic compilations from the late twelfth and early thirteenth centuries.

The word "conclave" is Latin in origin, signifying a room that can be locked. The first accepted conclave affecting the papacy occurred following the death of Gregory IX in 1241, when Matteo Orsini, anxious to dominate the papacy, imprisoned the electing cardinals at Rome under exceptionally brutal conditions and refused to liberate them until an acceptable pope was chosen. In the event, the election (of Celestine IV) proved worthless, as he died less than a month later, and thereafter the papacy was vacant for two years.

The procedure to be used at a papal election was set out in considerable detail in *Ubi periculum.* After the pope's death, a period of ten days was allowed to summon absent cardinals. The cardinals, with strictly limited households, were then to be confined within the palace in which the pope had died or, if he died in the country, within the city of the territory in which he died, provided it was not under interdict or in rebellion against the papacy. Virtually cut off from the outside world, except for the receipt of food, and living in common, the cardinals were to begin the elective process. If no choice was made within three days, their rations were to be reduced; if after a further five days there had still been no election, their diet was to be restricted to bread, wine, and water. During the vacancy all the cardinals' income from the papal camera was cut off, and the governmental machinery of the church was suspended (with a few exceptions). The decree also made provision for those cardinals who fell ill during the conclave and for the admission of cardinals who arrived late. Sick cardinals who left the conclave, but recovered before an election, could reenter to participate in the choice. Further provisions dealt with external security and with the responsibilities of papal officials.

Ubi periculum scarcely survived the death of its proclaimer. Its provisions aroused hostility among the cardinals, and the decree was suspended in 1276 by Adrian V and again by John XXI. It was reintroduced by Celestine V in 1294 and formally incorporated into the lawbooks of the church by his successor. Though still opposed by several cardinals, and often challenged during conclaves, it remained in force, subject to occasional modifications. Thus in 1311, Clement V in the decree *Ne Romani* legislated to confirm the voting rights of excommunicate cardinals, and made other minor changes (Clem. 1.3.2); while in the decree *Licet in consuetudine* in 1351, Clement VI eased the regulations for the accommodation and feeding of the cardinals during the conclave.

The mere statement of a procedure did not guarantee that it would be effective. The college of cardinals was itself a victim of tensions, which were reflected in the conclaves, especially the rivalries between groups from different nations. In the fifteenth century, particularly important was the reflection of international rivalry between the French and the Spaniards, and between both these groups and the Italians. Nor was the conclave free from external influences. When the schism of 1378 broke out, part of the justification produced by the opponents of Urban VI for their actions in electing a rival pontiff was the mob outside, which had demanded a Roman or Italian pope under threat of massacring the car-

dinals. The mob had eventually broken in, forcing the cardinals to flee. More subtle pressure might be applied by kings and princes acting through their agents within the conclave. The negotiations between individual cardinals hankering after the papal throne also affected the electoral process.

Because of all this, papal elections did not always follow the smooth procedure that *Ubi periculum* had laid down. Vacancies of several months—even years—still occurred, as in 1314–1316 when the first conclave broke up without an election. Moreover, the decrees could not hope to cover all circumstances. When the time came to settle the Great Schism in 1417, the reliability of the cardinals was questioned, but there was a need to ensure that the pope who was elected would be universally acceptable. To this end, the conclave was widened beyond the cardinals to include representatives of the various "nations" assembled at the Council of Constance, who were given votes in the election that produced Martin V. At the Council of Basel, following the deposition of Eugenius IV, and with only one cardinal adhering to the conciliarists, a totally novel procedure had to be devised for the election of Felix V in 1439.

Ubi periculum and its amendments undoubtedly helped stabilize the procedure for the transfer of supreme authority, but it did not smooth out all the difficulties. The aspirations of the Roman nobility and others to dominate the papacy shifted from external influence on the election to securing agents within the conclave. Moreover, the formalization of the cardinals' role within the transfer of power allowed them to formulate their own ideas on the government of the church, and to attempt to control the programs of the papal candidates.

Despite the ban on electoral pacts in *Ubi periculum*, the cardinals sought to oblige the papal candidates to accept policy statements, known as electoral capitulations. Indications of attempts to make such agreements survive from as early as 1294, but the first formal agreement drawn up within a conclave seems to have been composed prior to the election of Innocent VI in 1352. Such electoral pacts were common thereafter, detailing changes to be made within the church and in effect stipulating the price a candidate was prepared to pay for his election. During the schism of 1378–1418 the validity of these agreements was much debated, since those drawn up at the elections of the rivals Benedict XIII (1394) and Gregory XII (1406) bound the pontiffs to work to unify the church. No pope ever acknowledged the validity of these compacts, arguing that an agreement made as cardinal—even if backed up by an oath—could not bind a pope.

The conclave system certainly stabilized the succession procedure for the papacy in the fourteenth and fifteenth centuries. On the other hand, it also undoubtedly encouraged the process whereby, at the end of the Middle Ages, the office of pope was little more than the perquisite of one or another of the major Italian families and the object of political machinations among the great Catholic powers.

BIBLIOGRAPHY

The two papal decreees, *Ubi periculum* and *Ne Romani*, are printed in Emil A. Friedberg, ed., *Corpus juris canonici*, II (1881, repr. 1959), 946–949 and 1135–1136. An English translation of the former is in Henry J. Schroeder, ed., *Disciplinary Decrees of the General Councils: Text, Translations, and Commentary* (1937), 371–375. See also Thomas van Cleve, *The Emperor Frederick II of Hohenstaufen* (1972), 456–459; Ludovico Gatto, *Il pontificato di Gregorio X, 1271–1276* (1959), 11–27, 157–161; Walter Ullmann, "The Legal Validity of the Papal Electoral Pacts," in his *The Papacy and Political Ideas in the Middle Ages* (1976); Karl Wenck, "Das erste Konklave der Papstgeschichte: Rom, August bis Oktober, 1241," in *Quellen und Forschungen aus italienischen Archiven und Bibliotheken*, 18 (1926).

R. N. SWANSON

[See also **Cardinals, College of; Councils, Western (1311–1445); Papacy, Origins and Development of; Rome; Schism, Great.**]

CONCORDAT. Etymologically, a concordat is simply an agreement, an amicable settlement of differences. Its restricted meaning as some sort of treaty between the church (specifically represented by the papacy) and the state concerning the administration of a national church is essentially postmedieval. Nevertheless, agreements formalizing such a modus vivendi, sometimes no better than a conspiracy between pope and secular ruler for the exploitation of the local church to their mutual advantage, were drawn up in the Middle Ages, some of which are traditionally called concordats. Chief among these are the Concordat of Worms (1122), those of the Council of Constance (1417), and various agreements between papacy and princes made during the fifteenth century. Other, less formal agreements are often brought into this group, such as the settlement after the Becket crisis in England (1176) and the Anglo-papal agreements of 1375, 1392, and 1398, which were chiefly concerned with taxes and papal provisions. The agreements between popes and emperors of the ninth through eleventh centuries are also sometimes called concordats, but this is possibly overstretching the definition.

The legal validity and enforceability of concordats were uncertain. On the papal side any concessions might be viewed as voluntary, temporary restrictions on papal prerogatives, to be recovered later: they were not renunciations of authority but privileges of exemption—dispensations—from the full exercise of that authority. From the secular standpoint, however, there was a more direct intention: the concordats represented a formal definition and restriction of papal authority, preventing papal intervention in areas of ecclesiastical administration that the secular power considered properly its own in practice, if not in theory. Moreover, such treaties were seen as a means of extending royal or princely power over the local church, even in alliance with the papacy. To this extent they perhaps reflect political rather than ecclesiological sensibilities.

Medieval concordats cannot be viewed simply as straightforward treaties. That of Worms, traditionally seen as ending the struggles of the investiture controversy, is drawn up in bilateral contractual terms, but others are less clear-cut. The concordats offered to the nations at the Council of Constance were not between pope and princes, but between pope and local churches, making reformist statements as a continuation of the work begun at the council. These concordats were framed as papal grants of privileges to the particular churches, with no corresponding statements from the churches concerned. They were also intended to be short-term measures. Other concordats, such as that with Portugal in 1289, or Naples in 1451, reflected papal approval of local agreements made between kings and bishops.

During the fifteenth century the concordats with the princes might be unilateral papal grants, as was the Concordat of Vienna of 1448, or more complex in format, as was the Franco-papal agreement of 1472. On the papal side the latter took the form of a bull and accompanying letter stating the restrictions of papal powers within France, often in vague terms and very much as privileges and concessions. On the French side the concordat gained its force not by papal but by royal authority, as set out in an ordinance. The wording of this ordinance differed slightly but materially from the papal version, thus laying the basis for future discord. In this instance, moreover, the dependence on royal authority for enforcement was made evident when Louis XI died in 1483. There was a marked reaction against what many considered the too extensive application of papal authority conceded in the concordat, which thereafter became a dead letter, pending further agreement.

The difficulties of actually implementing any concordat were apparent in other instances, and all concordats reflected some sort of compromise. Those issued at Constance were mainly short-term provisions but, even so, seem to have had little success. Their failure reflected the inability of the late-medieval church to reform itself voluntarily. Later concordats resulted from direct negotiations between popes and princes, and were often motivated by political considerations. Even the Constance pope, Martin V, had to offer negotiated concordats to the rulers of France and Castile, though these were framed very much in terms of the "national" agreements. The Concordat of Vienna reflected the need for Nicholas V to reach an agreement with the secular authorities within the empire to secure his recognition as pope in opposition to Felix V and his adherents at the Council of Basel. His concessions to the princes to secure that recognition formed the basis for the administration of the German Catholic church in succeeding centuries and established princely control over the local ecclesiastical structures.

Not every country needed to have its relations with the papacy defined so precisely; the making of a concordat was often only the formalization of a compromise solution to a conflict over jurisdiction. In the fifteenth century England made no formal concordats other than the Constance agreement; the Spanish kingdoms likewise generally regulated their churches in an informal manner. Against such informality the popes, despite their attempts, proved powerless. Insofar as there was no specific statement of opposition to papal authority, there was no need for a formal compromise. The German and French concordats of 1448 and 1472 (and also, to some extent, the Breton-papal Concordat of Redon of 1441) were formulated in response to such statements of opposition: the Acceptation of Mainz (1440) and the Pragmatic Sanction of Bourges (1438). Against the "national churches" established by these declarations, the papacy felt obliged to act to restore its claims to universal ecclesiastical jurisdiction. On the papal side

these concordats could thus be viewed as the halfway stage toward a restoration of the full plenitude of power, though that full restoration was never achieved.

The topics covered in concordats varied greatly. Generally they concentrated on the role of the secular power in local ecclesiastical administration, and its relations with the central organs of the church at Rome: matters of appointments to benefices (especially bishoprics and other high offices that traditionally provided leading figures in medieval secular administration); the church's jurisdiction over clerics and cases involving "spiritual" matters (particularly those that might be tried at Rome); and papal taxation of local churches. Other subjects were occasionally included, as in the post-Constance concordats, which contained clauses concerning the composition of the cardinalate, and provisions for the employment of graduates in the church, as part of the general program of reform.

Generally speaking, the medieval concordats, interpreted as agreements concerning the local administration of the church, reflect the gradual decline of papal administrative authority over the universal church and the fragmentation of the catholicity of that church into a number of "national" segments. These still looked to Rome for their theology and spiritual direction but sought to liberate themselves from the papacy's administrative clutches. The concordats also represent the consummation of royal authority over the local churches, in which the papacy became an accomplice because agreement was to its advantage as much as to that of the prince. Thus, the concordats between popes and princes during the medieval period can be seen as a gradual erosion of "imperialist" papalism, thereby giving grudging papal approbation to the claims to local ecclesiastical jurisdiction inherent in royal claims, made since the thirteenth century, to be "emperors" within their own kingdoms.

BIBLIOGRAPHY

The standard collection of medieval concordats is Angelo Mercati, ed., *Raccolta di concordati su materie ecclesiastiche tra la Santa Sede e le autorità civili,* vol. 1: *1098–1914,* new ed. (1954), 1–233.

The following are more specifically concerned with concordats: Clemens Bauer, "Studien zur spanischen Konkordatsgeschichte des späten Mittelalters: Das spanische Konkordat von 1482," in *Spanische Forschungen der Görresgesellschaft, erste Reihe,* **11** (1950); Bernhard Hübler, *Die Constanzer Reformation und die Concordate von 1418* (1867); Ernest F. Jacob, "A Note on the English Concordat of 1418," in John A. Watt, John B. Morrall, and Francis X. Martin, eds., *Medieval Studies Presented to Aubrey Gwynn, S.J.* (1971); Paul Ourliac, "The Concordat of 1472: An Essay on the Relations Between Louis XI and Sixtus IV," in Peter S. Lewis, ed., *The Recovery of France in the Fifteenth Century* (1971); Joachim W. Steiber, *Pope Eugenius IV, the Council of Basel, and the Secular and Ecclesiastical Authorities in the Empire* (1978), 313–321; John A. F. Thompson, *Popes and Princes, 1417–1517* (1980).

R. N. SWANSON

[See also **Pragmatic Sanction of Bourges; Taxation, Church; Worms, Concordat of.**]

CONCUBINAGE, ISLAMIC. The English word "concubinage," derived from the Latin *concubinare* (to lie together), commonly designates in Western societies a type of informal but semipermanent sexual relationship between a man and a woman that is by definition outside of the established laws of marriage and inheritance. Such a relationship, depending on the specific cultural context, may or may not be socially acceptable but is always legally inconsequential, for the children produced in concubinage are necessarily illegitimate.

The institution in medieval Muslim society that we term "concubinage" bears very little relation to the Western phenomenon described above. Islamic concubinage was a clearly defined legal institution that served a vitally important social function: the production of free, legitimate offspring; furthermore, it was an integral part of the greater institution of slavery. While not all female slaves were necessarily concubines, all concubines were by definition slaves. This fact distinguishes Islamic concubinage from concubinage in the West, which usually signified a relationship between a man of higher social status and a woman of lower social status but did not necessarily imply a relationship between a master and his female slave.

The Koran grants the free Muslim rights of sexual access to as many as four legally contracted wives and to an unlimited number of his female slaves. A sexual relationship with any woman who does not fall into the category of wife or slave is adultery (*zinā*) and in many cases is punishable by death. Moreover, a man may have sexual relations only with a female slave in his personal possession; he does not, for example, have sexual rights over a slave belonging to his wife.

The concubine, then, as defined within an Islamic context, is a woman of servile status who performs sexual services for the man who owns her. The sexual exploitation of female slaves is a common feature of all slaveholding societies whether or not it is openly condoned by law or custom. Islamic society proved no exception: the Koran, the *sunna*, and the highly developed legal system of Islam gave a formal sanction to what was in any case an undeniable aspect of slavery.

Slave women fulfilled a variety of functions within the Muslim household, and the wealthier the household the more likely there was to be a high degree of specialization among them. While not all female slaves were concubines, the very language of Islamic jurisprudence makes it clear that the primary service of the female slave, as opposed to that of the male slave, was considered to be sexual in character. Some medieval jurists maintained, for example, that the discovery of such faults as offensive breath, body odor, or a propensity for fornication in a recently purchased slave provided grounds for the purchaser to annul the sale in the case of a female slave but not in the case of a male slave. The explanation given for this distinction is that there are different reasons for buying a slave: one buys a female slave because one desires sexual intercourse (*istifrāsh*) and the production of children (*talab al-wuld*), whereas one purchases a male slave only for service (*istikhdām*). Another example of the Islamic legal conception of the female slave as primarily fulfilling a sexual role is the verbal statement "Your sexual organ is free" (*farjuki hurrun*), which served as a valid formula for manumission of a female slave but not of a male slave.

The Arabic terminology of slavery—a complex subject in itself—contains certain words that refer specifically to concubines: *surrīya*, from the root *s-r-r*, denoting pleasure; *hazīya* (favorite); and *mawtū*a, from the verb *watiʾa*, meaning to have sexual intercourse with a woman. A woman described by any of these terms was specifically a concubine, a female slave whose primary function within the household was to provide sexual services for her master, and who had probably been purchased at a higher price than a female slave destined simply for domestic labor. However, even the term *jarīya* (plural: *jawārī*), meaning young girl, which in and of itself had no sexual connotation but was merely a common term for a female slave regardless of her function, often was used in reference to concubines. A whole corpus of medieval Arabic literature exists that describes the amorous attractions of *jawārī* who are obviously concubines. Thus even though there existed a specific terminology in Arabic for concubines, any female slave, no matter what term was used to describe her, was, by virtue of her servile status, at the sexual disposal of her master and thus a potential concubine.

There were only a few conditions recognized by Islamic law that limited the master's sexual rights over his female slaves: (1) consanguinity within a prohibited degree; (2) the woman's professing a pagan religion; and (3) the master's cohabiting with two sisters at the same time. These restrictions applied to marriage as well as to concubinage. Islamic law, however, accepted one other barrier to sexual relations with a female slave: her entrance into a legally contracted marriage with her master's permission. The recognition of the validity of slave marriages—provided that the master give his consent—is one of the distinctive features of Islamic slavery. The master who allows his female slave to marry (and he may, if he wishes, marry her off against her will) knowingly relinquishes his sexual rights over her. The married female slave ceases to be a potential concubine.

Whereas the concubine was by definition a slave, her child by her master was not. This is the fundamental difference between the role of the female slave in Islamic society and her role in most Western slaveholding societies. Roman law set down the harsh principle that the child of a slave mother followed her into slavery *(partus ventrum sequitur)* regardless of the father's status—a principle upheld by subsequent slaveholding societies in the West, including those in the New World. Islamic law, however, maintained that the child of a slave woman by her master was born into freedom. Thus the female slave became something more than a mere object for her master's sexual gratification: she was a potential childbearer for her master and, by extension, for her master's kinship group.

The free status of a concubine's child in medieval Muslim society rested technically on the father's acknowledgment of his paternity. However, the nature of the Islamic laws of paternity and the social circumstances of concubinage were such that it was practically impossible for a master to deny a child born to one of his female slaves. If it could be proved that he had never had sexual relations with her, or if the slave in question was already married, the child followed its mother's status (as in Roman law); like its mother it was a chattel of its master. However, historical evidence indicates that denial of paternity

in the case of children born to concubines was not common. Medieval Muslim society placed a high social premium on children—particularly male children. Thus concubinage, in a society where polygamy was common, became a widespread and accepted institution for the production of offspring, a supplement and possibly an alternative to the institution of marriage in regard to this vital social function.

The child of a concubine by her master was thus a free, legitimate heir of the father with legal and social status equal to that of any of the father's children by his wives. A certain prejudice against the children of concubines probably did exist in the first century of Islam—a vestige of pre-Islamic Arab attitudes concerning the necessity of "pure" Arab lineage on the part of the mother as well as the father of a child. The Abbasid revolution (750), however, seems to have effected or simply confirmed a major change in social attitudes by shifting the emphasis in terms of status and lineage onto the father. Indeed, from Abbasid times on, a significant majority of the members of the ruling elite were the children of slave concubines and free fathers. It seems clear that during the greater part of the Middle Ages, there existed no obvious distinction in most Muslim households between the children of concubines and the children of legally contracted wives.

A concubine who bore her master a child—even if the child was stillborn or died shortly after birth—achieved the legal status of *umm al-walad* (mother of the child) and could no longer be sold, pawned, or given away. All her subsequent children were considered to be free. Furthermore, most jurists agreed that the *umm al-walad* was automatically freed on her master's death. In every other respect, she was still a slave; her body and her labor remained at her master's disposal. She did not have the right of *ḥa-ḍāna* (maternal custody) over her free child; that right or obligation devolved on the father's female relatives. The status of the *umm al-walad*, however, was undoubtedly higher than that of the ordinary female slave within the household. Surviving medieval documents of *waqf*, or endowments, often contain bequests on the part of a master to his *mustawladāt* (another common term for concubine mothers of free children), and the use of the word ᶜ*atīqa* (freedwoman) in reference to these women indicates that it was not uncommon for a master to manumit his *mustawladāt* during his own lifetime.

The concubine who belonged to a man in the

upper echelons of society and who was thus the potential mother of a powerful heir could herself acquire wealth and influence. Perhaps the best-known example of a concubine's rise to power is that of Shajar al-Durr, the slave of al-Ṣāliḥ Najm al-Dīn ᶜAyyūb. Shajar al-Durr actually ruled Egypt briefly following the assassination in 1250 of Tūrān Shāh and was a major figure in the events leading to the establishment of the Mamluk sultanate. Few concubines had careers as dramatic as that of Shajar al-Durr, but medieval Islamic history contains several examples of slave mothers who exercised considerable influence behind the scenes through the persons of their children or the fathers of their children.

Despite the importance of concubinage as a social institution, and despite the potential power and influence of individual concubines, concubinage never replaced marriage in medieval Muslim society. There may have existed circumstances under which it was less expensive and complicated for a man to buy a female slave than to enter into a legally contracted marriage. Concubinage could serve as an alternative to marriage in regard to the production of offspring and, insofar as it fulfilled this function, seems to have been a common supplement to marriage. The great Mamluk historian Yūsuf Ibn Taghrī Birdī, for example, was one of ten siblings who were the children of nine different women—eight concubines and one legal wife. Only two of these children were full siblings (ashiqqāʾ), and only one of them, a girl, was the child of the free wife. All of these children—or at least the six who lived to an age of some maturity—occupied positions of high social status in terms of their education, marriages, economic level, and, in the case of the males, their military-political rank.

Marriage, however, unlike concubinage, remained a legal contract that governed mutual obligations and rights on the part of both husband and wife; it also often constituted a social and in some cases political alliance between two families. A wife had well-defined rights related to her own and her family's property, to her custody of her own children up to a certain age, and to her husband's marital obligations toward her. A concubine was a childbearer only, a slave completely subject to her master's authority. The significance of her role as a childbearer, however, gave the Islamic concubine, the unfree mother of the free, the special status that distinguishes her from concubines and slave women in most non-Muslim societies.

BIBLIOGRAPHY

The best discussion of the early development of concubinage in Islamic law is Joseph Schacht, "Umm al-Walad," in *Encyclopaedia of Islam*, 1st ed.; this should be supplemented by the discussion of female slaves in Robert Brunschvig, "ᶜAbd," *ibid.*, 2nd ed.

S. E. MARMON

[See also **Family, Islamic; Harem; Inheritance, Islamic; Slavery in the Islamic World; Sunna.**]

CONCUBINAGE, WESTERN. Concubinage is a stable but not indissoluble sexual liaison between a man and woman. While it does not necessarily require that they live together under the same roof or exclude other relationships, exclusive cohabitation as part of one household is the form that the institution has normally taken in the West. Distinguished both from marriage and from prostitution or fornication, concubinage enjoyed a peculiar status and entailed peculiar consequences throughout the Middle Ages.

The institution was largely inherited from the Roman world. The Germanic tribes seem to have ascribed no special status to semipermanent, nonmarital unions. The law of imperial Rome, however, treated concubinage as a special and permissible form of union, one that in itself carried little or no social stigma. Unlike full marriage, concubinage was subject to few restrictive formalities in its formation, and it was generally contracted with a person of lower social status. But the movement of law during the late ancient period was in the direction of its approximation to marriage. It was early established, for instance, that some of the laws barring marriages between close relatives also applied to concubinage. Public opinion, and perhaps even imperial legislation, denied the right of a married man to retain a concubine. He might choose either concubinage or marriage, but not both, and the differences between them narrowed.

The introduction of Christianity made little initial difference to the legal institution of concubinage, although the Christian emperors carried the process of approximation to marriage further, most notably by creating a presumption that all unions between persons free to marry were to be considered marriages unless the parties formally declared that they had intended only to enter into concubinage. The

Christian church took an oscillating position toward an institution that it could neither wholly eliminate nor wholeheartedly approve.

On the one hand, the principle of monogamy and the desire to encourage the institution of marriage led some churchmen to treat all concubinage as almost equivalent to true marriage. The Council of Toledo (A.D. 400), for example, expressly permitted Christians to retain concubines without ecclesiastical censure, on condition that they not be married to someone else at the same time. On the other hand, the same doctrines regarding marriage led other churchmen to condemn concubinage root and branch. St. Augustine, who had dismissed his concubine on his conversion to Christianity, denounced concubinage in strident tones: "It has never been lawful [for Christians] to hold concubines, and it never will be lawful." Pope Leo I embraced the same position, approving a man's decision to repudiate his concubine in favor of marriage. Probably the majority of influential churchmen during the early Middle Ages took this sterner view, although it was tempered by occasional expression of the older and more lenient view and by the weakness of the church's hold on actual practice of the laity.

The next important step in the history of concubinage was taken in the twelfth century by Gratian, the systematic compiler of the canon law. He was confronted by contradictory texts, some apparently allowing, others clearly reproving, concubinage. Gratian's solution was to interpret all texts that permitted concubinage as referring to valid marriages contracted privately by words of present consent but without the formalities (such as endowment and banns) prescribed by law. This solution, which was adopted throughout the Western church, allowed the ambivalence of the ecclesiastical attitude toward concubinage to continue in a slightly altered form.

Since the medieval church held that private contracts of marriage, entered into without ecclesiastical ceremony, were nevertheless full and valid marriages, the church could not treat them as nullities nor regard the partners as rightless or their offspring as wholly illegitimate. Thus, for example, the children of concubinage were entitled under the canon law to inherit their mother's goods—and even their father's in the absence of children of a legitimate marriage. But on the other hand, the church held that where no express contract of marriage existed— that is, where no valid though private contract could be proved—none would be presumed, and the resulting union would not be entitled to any separate

status or to full protection of the law. Thus, some writers insisted that concubinage was no more than an aggravated kind of fornication.

In sum, the church indirectly encouraged concubinage by the principle that no public ceremony was necessary for marriage, while at the same time it discouraged concubinage by refusing to treat it as a distinct legal category. It was, perhaps, an indecisive position, one that was compatible with "laxist" practices on the part of many men and women. It was only with the Council of Trent in the sixteenth century that the Roman Catholic church felt able to deny Communion to those who lived in concubinage.

The actual extent of concubinage during the Middle Ages is difficult to estimate. Evidence is scarce, but there is some. For instance, the thirteenth-century English treatise *De legibus* attributed to Henry Bracton speaks of a "legitimate concubine" (*concubina legitima*), surely tribute to the continued recognition by educated men of an intermediate state between full marriage and repeated fornication. There also exist fair numbers of records of prosecutions undertaken in church courts against couples who had lived together for several years, brought to force the offending couples either to marry or to separate. They are another sign of the persistence of the habit of entering stable unions without undertaking all the obligations of canonical marriage.

The prevalence of clerical concubinage is equally difficult to assess, though equally demonstrable in its existence. Certainly, stable relationships between clerics and women persisted after the Gregorian reforms had deprived such unions of respectability. But there is no statistical evidence to measure its extent, and the Protestant reformers perhaps exaggerated its persistence because of its usefulness as an argument in favor of legalizing marriage for the church's ministers.

BIBLIOGRAPHY
Gian Luigi Barna, "Un contratto di concubinato in Corsica nel XIIIᵉ secolo," in *Rivista di storia del diritto italiano*, 22 (1949); James A. Brundage, "Concubinage and Marriage in Medieval Canon Law," in *Journal of Medieval History*, 1 (1975); Adhemar Esmein, *Le mariage en droit canonique*, 2nd ed., II (1935), 104–117; E. Jombart, "Concubinage," in *Dictionnaire de droit canonique*, III (1942).

R. H. HELMHOLZ

[See also **Family, Western European, Legal Aspects of; Law, Canon: To Gratian; Law, Canon: After Gratian.**]

CONDOTTIERI. The condottieri were mercenary captains in Renaissance Italy, prominent from the fourteenth to the sixteenth century. In a strict sense a condottiere was a commander of a company of cavalry and/or infantry, whose services he offered to a prince, a state, or another captain in exchange for payment. He was so called because he held a contract *(condotta)* that regulated the duration and the nature of his obligations.

Nonetheless, condottieri often enjoyed considerable independence. The fourteenth century, for example, was the age of the Great Companies, or Companies of Adventure, led by such figures as Sir John Hawkwood, Werner von Ürslingen, Monreale d'Albano, and Alberico da Barbiano. These warring bands, active in central and northern Italy, easily changed their allegiances and caught the attention of contemporaries by their ability to profit from plunder and to extract financial and political concessions from the states they threatened. Moreover, throughout the Renaissance there were condottieri who were princes. In the early fifteenth century Pandolfo Malatesta, the lord of Brescia, served as a commander for Venice, and in 1450 Francesco Sforza used his military power to capture the duchy of Milan.

The role of condottieri, who were generally nobles from leading military families, became increasingly decisive in the fourteenth century, as citizen militias proved less adequate. The expansionist policies of several of the states, the growing complexity and regularity of warfare, the intensification of the social costs that participation in the militias imposed, and social tensions within the states made professional soldiers desirable. Nonetheless, throughout the fourteenth century citizen militias, professional soldiers, and Great Companies endured an uneasy coexistence.

It was not until late in the century that more regularized contracts became common. The various states sought to develop systems in which the activities of the captains could be closely monitored and their loyalty ensured. Thus, civilian overseers were established, the duration of the *condotta* was lengthened, and the condottieri were often granted honors: palaces, citizenship, even lordships. Despite considerable geographic diversity, the overall movement in the fifteenth century was toward standing armies, permanent rather than occasional military forces.

Several humanists of the early fifteenth century viewed the condottieri with disdain, believing that they undermined the civic virtues intrinsic to the citizen militias; Machiavelli, writing after the invasions of Italy in the late fifteenth and the early sixteenth centuries, blamed them for the ease with which foreign powers managed to subjugate many of the Italian states. To a large degree such views mistook symptoms for causes, and they doubtless exaggerated the deficiencies of the system and the perfidiousness of its leaders. Muzio Attendolo Sforza and Braccio da Montone, rival captains of the early fifteenth century, developed highly disciplined forces; and their strategies and tactics, stressing cautious use of their soldiers and mobility of attack, were among the most modern in Europe. Many captains, such as Gentile da Leonessa, who faithfully served Venice, remained loyal to the states on behalf of which they fought.

BIBLIOGRAPHY

Charles C. Bayley, *War and Society in Renaissance Florence* (1961); Michael Mallett, *Mercenaries and Their Masters* (1974); Daniel P. Waley, "The Army of the Florentine Republic from the Twelfth to the Fourteenth Century," in Nicolai Rubinstein, ed., *Florentine Studies* (1968).

JOHN MARTIN

[See also **Italy in the Fourteenth and Fifteenth Centuries; Warfare, European.**]

CONDUCTUS. A genre of musical composition, usually polyphonic, that is distinguished from much other medieval polyphony by the absence in the vast majority of a preexistent cantus firmus. It is characterized further by its note-against-note musical setting, which again distinguishes it from the other principal medieval style, in which faster-moving voices are set above a slow-moving tenor voice. The word is usually applied to the large repertory of conducti from the Notre Dame school, though it is also found in earlier polyphonic manuscripts, such as the Codex Calixtinus, and is currently applied more loosely to almost any medieval polyphony that fits the above description.

As a musical term the word is first encountered in rubrics used, beginning in the twelfth century, to identify musical pieces as processionals, or that introduce a reading or some other liturgical action, or, in the miracle plays, that accompany some dramatic action. Two samples from the thirteenth-century manuscript Egerton 2615 (British Museum) may stand for many others of a similar type from both the twelfth and thirteenth centuries. The formula *Conductus ante evangelium* (fol. 49) introduces a biblical lesson, and a rubric in the *Play of Daniel* neatly combines the accompanying and processional meanings of the word: *Conductus Danielis venientis ad Regem* (fol. 99). "Conductus" as used in this sense never achieved a fixed meaning or liturgical placement, however, and even in the twelfth century it began to be used in a much less specific sense for virtually any kind of newly composed Latin song, polyphonic or monophonic, the text of which was religious or at least serious in content.

As such, "conductus" entered the vocabulary of formal music theory in the thirteenth century as part of the new terminology of musical genera associated with the polyphonic repertory of the Notre Dame school. One theorist, known to music historians only as Anonymous IV, specifically identifies these genera with the various divisions of what he calls the *Magnus liber organi de gradali et antifonario,* going so far as to name specific conducti, all of which are found in the principal surviving sources for the Notre Dame repertory.

The repertory of polyphonic and monophonic Notre Dame conducti is large by any standard and is certainly the largest of freely composed polyphony prior to the fourteenth century. Although its boundaries are difficult to define precisely, not quite 400 pieces may be considered as belonging to it. While most of the pieces probably originated in the cathedral of Notre Dame or the immediate vicinity, fewer than 10 percent can be traced definitely to Paris. A few pieces can be traced to other French cities and to places outside France, notably England and Spain. Datable events referred to in the poems suggest that the repertory was created during the period from about 1170 to 1240. The repertory is overwhelmingly anonymous, but a small number of poems are attributed to Philip the Chancellor of Paris and Walter of Châtillon, and Anonymous IV attributes the music of three conducti to Magister Perotinus (Pérotin).

While virtually all of the texts are religious or devotional, it is not possible to determine a specific liturgical function for the repertory. Indeed, it is clear that the older meaning discussed above had been all but forgotten by the time the repertory came into existence. Some tendencies may be noted, however. The most striking is the association of a number of pieces with the *Benedicamus domino*. Not only are there three conductus-style settings of the formula (that is, without a plainchant tenor or organal treat-

ment), but there are also a dozen pieces to which the formula is appended. These pieces must be considered *Benedicamus domino* tropes and were often written so that the formula fitted the prevailing rhyme and rhythmic scheme. One piece, for instance, concludes " . . . regni carentis termino, Benedicamus domino." The existence of independent settings, and settings that appear with more than one piece, suggests that many other conducti could be converted to *Benedicamus domino* tropes. The three-voice conductus "O felix bituria" (Falck cat. no. 232), for instance, concludes with one such independent setting but disguises the borrowing by omitting the text: "Tibi preces inclite, pro me funde christo, ut sub recto tramite, cursu curram isto (Benedicamus domino)."

This last example introduces another important type within the repertory, the "political" or topical conductus. "O felix bituria" was written on the death of Guillaume, archbishop of Bourges, in 1209. There are about twenty pieces in the repertory that commemorate the coronations of French and English kings, or the deaths of lesser nobles and ecclesiastics. Other prominent types include pieces for Advent (about 15 percent of the repertory) and the Pascal season (about 11 percent), Marian poems (10 percent), and a large number of the sermonizing *admonitio* type (about 20 percent). Contrary to the general style of the prevailing rhymed, rhythmic poems are a handful of settings in *discantus* style of prose texts such as "Ave Maria" and "Pater noster." In addition, a number of conducti are contrafacta based on contemporary vernacular songs, or they "borrow" clausula sections from Notre Dame organa.

Anonymous IV mentions two subclasses of conductus based on their musical style: with and without caudae, or melismatic embellishments inserted at the beginning, interspersed throughout, or most typically, placed at the ends of pieces. There are many simple, syllabic settings without caudae in the repertory; but the most characteristic, and musically most interesting, of the Notre Dame conducti are those that are melismatic. All of the large pieces for major feasts, as well as the "topical" pieces, are richly embellished. Other pieces use short, quite perfunctory texts as a vehicle for the most exuberant kind of polyphonic composition, which surpasses the contemporary polyphonic genres of motet and organum in complexity and inventiveness.

In the later thirteenth century the word "conductus" continued to be used in an ever widening variety of contexts, until it was virtually synonymous with "song," and was applied to vernacular texts and even to dance songs. By the fourteenth century it had passed almost entirely out of the vocabulary of musical terminology but was still used in Germany well into the fifteenth century to identify religious songs with Latin texts.

BIBLIOGRAPHY

Robert Falck, *The Notre Dame Conductus* (1981); F. Reckow, "Conductus," in Hans Eggebrecht, ed., *Handwörterbuch der musikalischen Terminologie* (1973).

ROBERT FALCK

[See also **Anonymous IV; Benedicamus Domino; Notre Dame School; Pérotin; Walter of Châtillon.**]

CONFESSION, the revelation of sins to another in order to receive God's forgiveness, counts among the most complex of Christian ritual actions, a complexity reflected in its changing shape and place in medieval life. In early Christian public penance (before 500) "confession" referred primarily to the public acknowledgment of charges laid against the sinner (Latin usage) or to the performance of prescribed penitential works (*exomologesis* in Greek usage). By 1500, in both the Latin West and Byzantine-Slavic East, confession *(confessio/exagoreusis)* denoted the entire complex of acts constituting the now more privately celebrated sacrament of penance: revelation of sins to the priest, assignment and performance of penances, and sacerdotal reconciliation or "absolution."

In the late sixth century the monastic penitential institutions of Celtic Christianity came to Europe with Irish missionaries. Unlike early Christian penance these Celtic forms allowed the repeated reconciliation of the same sinner in a more private fashion involving only priest and penitent. Penitents were not yet anonymous, however, and much greater stress was laid on the act of confession itself. Those elements of early Christian penance that had in practice made the rite pastorally relevant only to the dying, the very devout, or the very notorious (public reconciliation, lifelong disabilities for penitents, access to penance only once in a lifetime) were thus overcome.

Despite some opposition from local councils and bishops, the new rite, together with the penitential handbooks for confessors that accompanied it, spread throughout Western Christendom, finally gaining acceptance at Rome in the eleventh century. By the twelfth century the ordinary experience of ecclesiastical penance had everywhere been recast in the form of "confession." In 1215 the Fourth Lateran Council required in effect that all Christians make a yearly confession to their parish priest. This prescription, together with the almost simultaneous extension of jurisdiction over confessions to the new mendicant orders (1221), made confession a fundamental element in the popular piety of the medieval West.

Development in the Christian East was similar but less dramatic. The spread of the monastic custom of confession to the laity was gradual, largely unopposed, and more or less complete by the eleventh century. Prescriptions of early Christian penance remained anachronistically in Eastern canon law, and Eastern Christians always preferred monastic to secular clergy as confessors. But by the twelfth century, little distinguished the place that confession held in the lives of lay Christians in East and West.

Ordinary Christians have never found confession easy, and the practice of medieval Christians was more flexible than canon law might suggest. Into the ninth century most Eastern and Western Christians confessed, if at all, only on their deathbeds. From the mid eighth century, however, confession as the ordinary preparation (and later prerequisite) for Holy Communion began to take root among the laity. This led in the West to the expectation of thrice-yearly or at least yearly confession for all, and in the East to an association of confession with the four fasts of the ecclesiastical calendar. Although in both East and West most Christians probably received Communion during the Easter season, not all of these would have confessed their sins beforehand. Even in the West after 1215, annual confession was still not a universal practice. The means used to try to make Western Christians comply with their duty of annual confession included parish registers of penitents, Communion tickets, denial of Christian burial, and stricter canonical protection of secrecy (the "seal" of confession). More successful was pastoral encouragement of confession as the proper preparation for the significant moments of ordinary life (marriage, childbirth, pilgrimage) and as a condition for receiving indulgences. From the fifteenth century especially, the pastoral approach resulted in the wider and more frequent practice of confession among ordinary Christians.

Confessions were usually heard during Lent at priests' houses or in parish churches, either before the altar (Latin ritual) or before the icon of Christ on the iconostasis (Byzantine ritual). Fixed places for confession appeared first in Western churches at Pisa in the fourteenth century, but the anonymity of the later form of the confessional was not part of the medieval experience of confession. Penitential manuals enjoined confessors to receive penitents affably but discreetly, and it was common for penitents to offer alms to the confessor.

The rite began with certain prayers recited by the priest. Originally both priest and penitent stood for these prayers and the subsequent confession of sins; kneeling came later. The confession itself ordinarily took the form of a lengthy interrogation by the priest, who used questions found in his penitential book. After the interrogation priest and penitent sat for the assigning of a penance; the penitent then stood or knelt, and the confessor, standing, recited prayers of absolution over him while laying hands on the penitent's head or placing his stole (symbol of the power of the keys) either in the penitent's right hand (Latin ritual) or upon his neck (Byzantine ritual). In the West many of these gestures disappeared after the fourteenth century through fear of scandal (particularly in the case of women penitents) or due to the spread of the confessional with its attendant anonymity.

Theological understanding of confession developed greatly from 500 to 1500. In early Christian penance the revelation of sins served primarily to begin the process of reconciliation that remained the theological center of the rite. As new forms of penance emerged, the focus of theological reflection shifted to the act of confession itself. Theologians began to consider the element of shame (erubescentia) inseparable from confession, as constituting the penitential act par excellence and thus containing in itself power to secure forgiveness. This new emphasis on the inner dispositions of the penitent led to the rich medieval exploration of the nature and kinds of interior repentance (contrition/attrition) but left unexplained the theological meaning of the priest's traditional role in securing forgiveness. The problem was all the greater insofar as "private" confession had now obscured the older form and experience of penance as reconciliation with the community of the church. Medieval theologians listed confession among the seven sacraments and after 1200 were much concerned to explain the nature and meaning of the absolution uttered by the priest after the penitent's confession. In this matter, as in the whole area of sacramental theology, Eastern Christian thought moved principally by way of reaction to developments in the Latin West.

BIBLIOGRAPHY

The best bibliographical guide is Herbert Vorgrimler, Busse und Krankensalbung (1978), 69–159, to which should be added Allen J. Frantzen, "The Significance of the Frankish Penitentials," in Journal of Ecclesiastical History, 30 (1979); Pierre-Marie Gy, "Le précepte de la confession annuelle et la nécessité de la confession," in Revue des sciences philosophique et theologiques, 63 (1979); and Lee W. Patterson, "Chaucerian Confession: Penitential Literature and the Pardoner," in Medievalia et humanistica, n.s. 7 (1976). For the neglected Eastern Christian experience of confession, see Vorgrimler, op. cit., 70, 86–89; Robert Barringer, "The Pseudo-Amphilochian Life of St. Basil: Ecclesiastical Penance and Byzantine Hagiography," in Theologia (Athens), 51 (1980); and Georgy P. Fedotov, The Russian Religious Mind, I (1960) 236–244.

ROBERT BARRINGER

[See also Church, Latin: 1054–1305; Councils, Western (869–1179) and (1215–1274); Missions and Missionaries, Christian; Penance and Penitentials.]

CONFESSOR, ROYAL. From the time of Constantine, Christian emperors visited holy bishops and monks to receive spiritual counsel. During the sixth and seventh centuries the Celtic institution of the king's monastic "soul-friend" (anmchara), a spiritual guide and confessor, may also have passed to the Continent with the new Irish penitential practices, but evidence that European rulers had their own personal confessors appears first among the eighth-century Franks. These earliest royal confessors were prominent bishops and abbots but were not yet resident at court. The first Byzantine emperor attested as having a spiritual father and confessor (patēr pneumatikos) was Leo VI (886–912), but the older pattern of consulting abbots and hieromonks outside the court continued longer among Byzantine and Slavic rulers than in the West. There the king's confessor was already a familiar member of the royal household by the thirteenth century and remained so throughout the medieval period.

The choice of a royal confessor was governed by traditional dynastic or family loyalties toward particular religious orders (commonly the Dominicans but also Carmelites, Augustinians, and others) and also by the personal wishes of the monarch. A change of confessor or of order might reflect wider shifts in royal policy, but confessors normally represented an element of continuity at court. Thus it sometimes happened that the same confessor served both father and son, as the Carmelite Stephen Patrington with Henry IV and Henry V of England.

Within the royal household the confessor's duties differed from those of chaplain or almoner. He lodged in the palace, usually with a companion from his order, and attended the king constantly in case there was need to hear his confession and grant absolution. More pious or demanding rulers might require the services of more than one confessor. Living and travel expenses were charged against the royal treasury, and confessors frequently helped with administration of the royal household, especially in adjudicating internal disputes. After leaving office they normally continued to enjoy the king's patronage.

The confessor's intimate relationship to the royal conscience led to his employment in wider spheres of public business. William of Paris, confessor to the children of Philip the Fair and later to the king, served also as general inquisitor in France from 1303. The dual role illustrates both his influence with the king and his usefulness as an instrument of Philip's policy in the suppression of the Knights Templar.

As a member of the king's personal council the confessor was often used as a personal royal ambassador or legate, and from the thirteenth century an informal diplomatic network of Dominican royal confessors existed linking courts as widely separated as those of England, Hungary, Spain, and Sweden. Confessors also served as trusted agents in domestic matters ranging from the collection of tithes to the handling of political negotiations involving the king's interests. Confessors ranked after cardinals and bishops at court, but their position and political experience might bring them a cardinal's hat and usually made them candidates for advancement to bishoprics or to higher administrative positions within their own orders. In some cases, like those of Geoffrey of Beaulieu for Louis IX of France or Conrad of Marburg for Elizabeth of Hungary, the confessor's unique familiarity with court life has provided invaluable historical materials for the biographies of their royal penitents.

BIBLIOGRAPHY

William Hinnebusch, *The Early English Friars Preachers* (1951), 460–472; Bede Jarrett, *The English Dominicans* (1921), 106–128; John C. Parsons, *The Court and Household of Eleanor of Castile in 1290* (1977). For an individual biography see Paul Braun, *Der Beichtvater der heiligen Elizabeth und deutsche Inquisitor Konrad von Marburg* (1909); and for evidence of Eastern practice, Patricia Karlin-Hayter, ed., *Vita Euthymii Patriarchae CP.* (1970).

ROBERT BARRINGER

[See also **Dominicans**.]

CONFESSOR: SAINT. Basically a confessor is one who has clearly manifested his faith in Christ and has remained true to it in spite of difficulties and danger. The early church made no distinction between confessor and martyr; but after Christianity became the official religion of the empire, it was no longer dangerous to profess it and martyrdom became rare except among missionaries. The problem then, especially for the rich and powerful, was to lead a truly Christian life in the midst of a very worldly society. St. Edward the Confessor, the last Anglo-Saxon king of England (except for the ephemeral reign of Harold), was a good example of those who were given the title of confessor. He was pious, ascetic, and devoted to the church, and he founded Westminster Abbey and worked miracles after his death.

JOSEPH R. STRAYER

CONFIRMATION is defined by the Decree for the Armenians (1439) as a sacrament of which the matter is chrism, made with oil and balsam blessed by a bishop, and the form is "I sign you with the sign of the cross, and I confirm you with the chrism of salvation, in the name of the Father and of the Son and of the Holy Spirit." The ordinary minister is the bishop, and the effect of the sacrament is that the Holy Spirit is given, as he was to the apostles on Pentecost.

The noun *confirmatio* as a name for a liturgical rite is used in canon 2 of the First Council of Orange (441). Its original meaning was apparently the completion of the sacrament, and it was used to describe the final rite of Christian initiation, the sealing or *consignatio*, the signing of the forehead of the newly baptized with chrism. In the Roman rite this was done only by the bishop and associated with the laying on of hands. The term is also used for the reception of Communion from the chalice, which completes the sacrament of the Eucharist (according to the Gregorian Sacramentary). It is not used for the chrismation in the Byzantine rite, which remained an integral part of the baptismal liturgy.

In the classical Roman sacramentaries of the eighth century, *consignatio* was an integral part of baptism, although it was administered separately when the bishop was not present at the baptism, as was the case with increasing frequency, particularly in the large dioceses of northern Europe.

Confirmation as a separate rite administered by a bishop was introduced, along with the Roman liturgy, into the Carolingian empire at the end of the eighth century. Its theology was developed by Alcuin and Hrabanus Maurus, apparently because the Gallican clergy was unfamiliar with it and did not understand its meaning. Alcuin said it strengthened the receivers so that they could preach to others the gift received in baptism. Hrabanus Maurus identified confirmation with the Pentecostal gift of the apostles.

A Pentecost sermon preached about 460 described confirmation as bestowing an increase *(augmentum)* of grace and strengthening recipients for combat *(ad pugnam)*. The False Decretals attributed the view to Pope Urban I and Pope Miltiades. It passed from the False Decretals to Gratian, to Peter Lombard, and to Aquinas. Lost in the transmittal was the provision that baptism and confirmation could be separated only by the death of the recipient.

Until the thirteenth century it was expected that confirmation, if not a part of baptism, would be supplied as speedily as possible. Bishops were expected to travel around their dioceses to confirm, though this frequently did not happen, and confirmation was often administered from the saddle when (and if) the faithful encountered the bishop. By the fourteenth century seven had become the proper age for confirmation, and by 1500 its administration to infants was unusual.

BIBLIOGRAPHY

John D. C. Fisher, *Christian Initiation: Baptism in the Medieval West* (1965); John D. C. Fisher and E. J. Yarnhold, S.J., "The West from about A.D. 500 to the Reformation," in Cheslyn Jones *et al., The Study of Liturgy* (1978), 110–117; Austin P. Milner, *Theology of Confirmation* (1972); Leonel L. Mitchell, *Baptismal Anointing* (1978).

LEONEL L. MITCHELL

[See also **Baptism; Pentecost.**]

CONFRÉRIE was the group within a trade guild that had charge of religious and cultural activities; the latter might include poetic contests and dramatic representations. The *confrérie* of the Paris goldsmiths' guild, for example, produced miracle plays in the fourteenth century. There were also purely literary and dramatic *confréries,* such as the Confrérie de la Passion, which produced the Passion play in Paris during the fifteenth century.

BIBLIOGRAPHY

Graham Runnalls, "Mediaeval Trade Guilds and the *Miracles de Nostre Dame par personnages,*" in *Medium aevum,* 39 (1970).

ALAN E. KNIGHT

[See also **Drama, Liturgical; Guilds and Métiers.**]

CONGÉ, a poetic leave-taking practiced in northern France in the thirteenth century. In 1202 Jean Bodel, preparing to embark on the Fourth Crusade, contracted leprosy and had to retire to a leper colony. His *congé* is a moving farewell to his friends in Arras. The poem combines pathos with humor and introduces a personal element into the conventional poetic themes of the period. Seventy years later Baude Fastoul, also of Arras, wrote a *congé* in similar circumstances. A third, more satirical *congé* was composed by Adam de la Halle when he left Arras to study in Paris. The three poems are written in stanzas of twelve lines, and range in length from thirteen to forty-eight stanzas. The genre is related to the poetic testament practiced by such later writers as François Villon.

BIBLIOGRAPHY

Pierre Ruelle, *Les congés d'Arras* (1965).

ALAN E. KNIGHT

[See also **Adam de la Halle; Bodel, Jean.**]

CONGÉ D'ÉLIRE (license to elect). France avoided most of the troubles of the investiture controversy of the eleventh and twelfth centuries. The Capetian kings had no wish to quarrel with the church, which had usually supported them, and the reforming popes had enough enemies without adding the kings of France to the list. Thus, while direct appointment of bishops by the king was abandoned, thus satisfying a basic demand of the reformers, in practice the king had great and often decisive influence over the election of bishops. The right of the cathedral chapters to elect their bishops was not denied, but the right to hold an election was controlled by the king. Until the king gave permission (*congé d'élire*), no election could take place.

Delay was profitable for the king and harmful to the cathedral clergy, for the king also had the right of regalia. Since all the income-producing holdings of a bishop had been granted to him (at least in theory) by one of the king's predecessors, they reverted to the king when there was no bishop to enjoy them. Thus, prolonging a vacancy by refusing license to elect increased the king's income, and often decreased the value of the episcopal estates because royal administrators, anxious for quick profits, would cut down timber, empty fishponds, oppress tenant farmers, and fail to repair mills or bridges. When, after some delay, the license to elect was accompanied by a request to choose someone favored by the king, the electors usually took the hint.

The king, however, did not always have a candidate. There were free elections and elections in which the pope, or a great noble, had more influence than the king. On the whole, however, the combination of the *congé d'élire* and the right of regalia gave the king enough control that the French episcopate usually supported him and seldom interfered with his policies.

BIBLIOGRAPHY

Robert Fawtier, *The Capetian Kings of France* (1960), 72–75, gives a good description of the process of choosing a bishop in France. The basic study is Pierre Imbart de la Tour, *Les élections épiscopales dans l'église de France* (1890), esp. 438–447.

JOSEPH R. STRAYER

[See also **Investiture and Investiture Controversy; Regalia.**]

CONNACHT. The Connachta are named for Conn Cétchathach, legendary ancestor of the Uí Néill, and in the genealogical schema of the eighth century the leading Connacht dynasties—Uí Briúin, Uí Fiachrach, and Uí Ailella—are represented as the descendants of three brothers of Niall, ancestors of *na teóra Connachta* (the three Connachts). The historical reality, so far as it can be reconstructed, was oth-

erwise and more complex. Tírechán, writing toward the end of the seventh century, gives considerable detail on the Uí Fiachrach but has only one brief reference to the Uí Briúin. He makes no mention of an overkingship of the province.

Uí Fiachrach, the earlier dominant dynasty, was divided into two segments: Uí Fiachrach Muaide in the north of the province, the fertile basin of the Moy, and Uí Fiachrach Aidni in the south, where its overlordship apparently extended to the Shannon. The power of Uí Fiachrach Aidni began to decline in the late seventh century. The last king of Connacht of Uí Fiachrach Muaide died in 773.

The Uí Briúin, who were to displace Uí Fiachrach, rose to power in central Connacht and based themselves about Mag nAí on the plains of Roscommon. Much of the surviving historical record has been refashioned to show that the Uí Briúin were of the same stock as the Uí Fiachrach and in ancient times ruled as kings of Connacht. The record of the first two Uí Briúin kings who are said to have been kings of Connacht—Ragallach (or Rogallach) mac Uatach (*d.* 649) and Cenn Fáelad mac Colgan (*d.* 682)—has certainly been touched up in the interest of Uí Briúin. Uí Briúin began to divide into three branches—Uí Briúin Aí, Uí Briúin Seóla, and Uí Briúin Bréifne—and in the eighth century a dynastic segment of Uí Briúin Aí, Síl Muiredaig, emerged as the dominant group.

By about 800 Síl Muiredaig had excluded the other dynastic families of Connacht from the overkingship of the province, and held it as its exclusive possession until 956. From Síl Muiredaig sprang the O'Connor kings of Connacht, who made themselves masters of the province and of most of Ireland in the twelfth century. Uí Briúin Seóla occupied Galway to the east of Lough Corrib and were successful contenders for the kingship of Connacht in the eleventh century, but subsequently declined to the status of local lords. Uí Briúin Bréifne carved out a new kingdom for itself in the northeast, in Cavan and Leitrim, where it drove a strategic wedge between the northern and southern branches of the Uí Néill. In the late tenth and eleventh centuries they were powerful enough to contest the kingship of Connacht, but never with great success. By the twelfth century they had become the dependent nobility of the O'Connor kings of Connacht.

In a sense early-medieval Connacht was a palimpsest of new arrivals and old survivals. Archaic peoples—Domnainn, Partraige, Sogain, Corco Trí, and others—survived longest here as petty kingdoms that were gradually overlaid by the expanding branches of the Uí Fiachrach and Uí Briúin. In the east of the province lay the large subkingdom of Uí Maine, whose rulers claimed no relationship with the kings of Connacht and who lorded it over many subject peoples of obscure origins. Uí Maine was among the most powerful kingdoms in Connacht in the seventh and eighth centuries.

Despite its relative poverty and remoteness, Connacht enjoyed great political power in the first half of the twelfth century, largely due to the military successes of the great Tairdelbach O'Connor. He divided Munster, carved up the kingdom of Meath, and waged a fifty-year struggle to make himself king of Ireland. His son, Rory, had effectively achieved that ambition on the eve of the Norman invasion.

BIBLIOGRAPHY

M. V. Duignan, "The Kingdom of Bréifne," in *Journal of the Royal Society of Antiquaries of Ireland*, 65 (1935); John V. Kelleher, "Uí Maine in the Annals and Genealogies to 1225," in *Celtica*, 9 (1971); John Ryan, *Toirdelbach O Conchubair* (1966); Paul Walsh, "The Christian Kings of Connacht," in *Journal of the Galway Historical and Archaeological Society*, 17 (1937).

DONNCHADH Ó CORRÁIN

[See also **Ireland, Early History.**]

CONON DE BÉTHUNE. The trouvère Conon de Béthune—variously identified in manuscripts as Guesnes, Quenes, or Cunes—was born in the mid twelfth century, the son of Robert V of Béthune; he appears in documents from 1180 on. References in one of his songs indicate that he sang at the court of France before the queen Alix of Champagne, and Marie of Champagne, daughter of Louis VII and Eleanor of Aquitaine. He participated in the Third Crusade and played a major role in the Fourth, during which he was prized for his skills as an orator. The chronicler Villehardouin praised his wisdom and eloquence. A relative of Baldwin IX of Flanders, first Latin emperor of Constantinople, Conon was involved in governing the empire, and was appointed regent after the death of Empress Yolande in 1219. He died soon after, in December 1219 or 1220.

Fourteen songs have been attributed to Conon in various manuscripts, of which the editor Axel Wallensköld accepts ten as authentic. All are preserved with melodies. Two are *chansons de croisade* dating from the Third Crusade. These express the poet's grief at leaving his lady, his dedication to the cause, and his rage over the abuse of a tax originally meant to finance the crusade.

The remaining songs depict various facets of the love experience, covering a range of emotional situations. In some Conon portrays himself as a traditional *fins amans* too shy to declare himself to his lady, whom he exalts for her beauty and virtue. In others he speaks bitterly of his lady's betrayal and withdraws his love from her; in one he announces that he has found a new love. His one song in dialogue form presents the scenario of a lady who decides to grant her favors to a knight who has long served her without reward, only to be told that she is past her prime and no longer desirable.

Conon several times refers to his skill and reputation as a singer, acknowledging a certain "maistre d'Oisi" (Huon III d'Oisi, châtelain de Cambrai) as his teacher. In one song he complains that the queen of France and her son criticized his Artesian dialect, which he defends as a legitimate manner of speaking (or singing) resulting naturally from his background. In another he defends himself against charges of defaming women, pointing out that he sang of one woman only and that her behavior warranted harsh comment. Conon presents his songs not as generalizations but as records of unique personal experience, just as their language derives from his upbringing and need not conform to "standard" French.

The sincerity of the song and its direct grounding in experience is, of course, a convention of trouvère lyric; it would be misleading to take Conon's songs as autobiographical in the modern sense. His personal stamp lies, rather, in the polished style, in the polemical force of the crusade poems, and in the vigor with which his personae are created.

BIBLIOGRAPHY

Chansons de Conon de Béthune, Axel Wallensköld, ed. (1921); *Trouvères-Melodien*, I, Hendrik van der Werf, ed. (1977); Roger Dragonetti, *La technique poétique des trouvères dans la chanson courtoise* (1960).

SYLVIA HUOT

[See also **Baldwin I of the Latin Empire; Courtly Love; Crusades and Crusader States: To 1187; Crusades and Crusader States: Fourth; Latin Empire of Constantinople; Troubadour, Trouvère, Trovadores.**]

CONRAD OF MEGENBERG (*ca.* 1309–1374), born at Mäbenberg (near Nuremberg). He studied at the University of Paris and then was professor there until 1342, and he was canon of Regensburg from 1348 until his death. He was also a prolific writer in both German and Latin. Conrad's *Buch der Natur*, a natural history based on the work of Thomas of Cantimpré, was very popular; his *Deutsche Sphaera* (a translation of John of Holywood's *Sphaera mundi*) was less appreciated. He also wrote political and religious tracts. One of his most interesting works, the *Oeconomica*, was known only in fragments until a complete text was published by Thomas Kaepeli in 1950. This book deals with the proper organization and management of the household, of the imperial court, and of the church, beginning with universities (a remarkably good description of the process of gaining a master's degree at Paris is included) and ending with the papacy.

Conrad's thought is not always consistent. In an earlier treatise, arguing against William of Ockham, he says that a pope accused of heresy by the cardinals may be deposed by a council, and a council may ask the aid of the emperor in enforcing its decision. This is not his position in the *Oeconomica*. He also tended in his early work to give the emperor more independence from papal authority than he did later. Nevertheless, while Conrad tended to magnify papal authority in his later writings, he always thought of the empire as a viable and necessary political organization.

BIBLIOGRAPHY

August Pelzer and Thomas Kaepeli, "Conrad de Megenberg," in *Revue d'histoire ecclésiastique*, 45 (1950), includes some bibliographical information. See also Michael Wilks, *The Problem of Sovereignty in the Later Middle Ages* (1963), 333–345, 419, 544. Older but still useful is Helmut Ibach, *Leben und Schriften des Konrad von Megenberg* (1938).

JOSEPH R. STRAYER

[See also **Conciliar Theory; John of Holywood.**]

CONRAD, PRIOR. As prior of Canterbury cathedral (1108/1109–1126), Conrad completed the choir begun about 1100. (It was mostly destroyed in 1174.) The richness of its decoration awed William of Malmesbury and prompted Eadmer to call it

"Conrad's glorious choir." Having served also as Henry I's confessor, Conrad passed his last weeks as abbot of St. Benet of Hulme.

BIBLIOGRAPHY

David Knowles, ed., *The Heads of Religious Houses: England and Wales 940–1216* (1972), 33, 68; Robert Willis, *The Architectural History of Canterbury Cathedral* (1845), 17, 41–42.

STEPHEN GARDNER

[See also **Canterbury Cathedral.**]

CONSANGUINITY is the kinship relation created by the existence of close blood ties. It is defined by descent from a common ancestor, called the stock, and the degree of consanguinity depends on the number of steps needed to reach the stock. Lineal consanguinity exists between two persons related by direct line of descent, as a father and son or a grandmother and grandson. Collateral consanguinity exists between persons who share a common ancestor but are not descended one from the other, as first cousins or an uncle and his niece. It is important to remember that the relationship depends on blood ties rather than legitimate marriage; consanguinity exists between father and son even though the son is born out of wedlock. The same is true in collateral lines.

The importance of consanguinity in medieval Europe is attested by the wholesale survival, in manuscript and printed treatises, of examples of the *arbor consanguinitatis*, a chart used in computing degrees of consanguinity. They took the form of either a tree or a man, each branch or human limb representing persons within a kinship structure. One could thus easily compute the degree of consanguinity between two people by starting from the branch or limb representing each and counting upward to the common stock. If this required two steps for each, then the persons were related in the second degree of consanguinity (under the Roman and canon law systems) or in the fourth degree (under the Germanic way of counting).

Such computation was important during the Middle Ages in two principal areas: determining the inheritance of property between generations, and regulating the choice of a marriage partner. The first was necessary because property almost always passed along lines of consanguinity. Not only did the social strength of family ties work toward that end, but in many places positive rules of law required it. In England and in parts of France and Germany, for example, much land could not be left directly by will; it could only descend to the person or persons determined by lines of consanguinity. Elsewhere, the possibility of intestacy further increased the necessity for accurate determination of consanguinity, because intricate legal questions could arise when a property owner died without surviving children.

A wide variety of local custom determined precisely which relative would acquire such property by succession; consanguinity merely set the outside boundaries. Although generalization is therefore difficult, two tendencies were widespread. First, lineal descendants, no matter how distant, normally inherited, to the exclusion of collateral heirs. Second, male kin excluded female. Inheritance limited to one person, however, as in the English primogeniture, cannot be called the dominant practice.

Consanguinity played a complex and disputed role in regulating the choice of one's spouse. Both Mosaic and Roman law contained prohibitions against marriage between persons related by consanguinity, but the Christian church early opted for more stringent rules. As in several areas of moral thought, the church fathers reacted strongly against what they regarded as Roman laxity, taking an extreme opposing position. Only St. Augustine provided an appealing rationale for the church's rules: that they promoted charity among all Christians by encouraging marriage outside local and tribal communities (Gratian, *Decretum*, 35.1.1). Although there was not uniformity in formulation of the early rules, the most frequently mentioned forbade marriage between blood kin, defined as those capable of acquiring property under the Roman law of inheritance. That meant all those who could trace a common ancestor by counting back six or even seven steps. This was the strictest rule, and it was certainly not everywhere enforced. However, it dominated church teaching until the Fourth Lateran Council in 1215. Citing the needs of changing times and the precedent of the New Testament, the council reduced the prohibited degrees to four, thus barring marriages between persons with the same great great grandfather but permitting marriages between those related more distantly (see *Decretales Gregorii IX*, 4.14.8).

Even this reduced level of prohibition made many marriages unlawful, and one can only conclude that

it often complicated the process of finding a lawful spouse in areas where population was small and mobility limited. At least for the upper classes the rules were tempered in practice by the papal power of dispensation. The Roman curia exercised a discretionary right to permit marriages between persons related in any but the closest degrees of consanguinity. It also seems that among the common people, ignorance of the extent of kinship ties provided a mitigating factor in a society without written records of birth or family.

The rules may have been less restrictive than they might seem. It has often been suggested that medieval men and women cynically made use of the consanguinity prohibitions to free themselves from irksome bonds of matrimony. However, except for certain causes célèbres, the evidence fails to show that the consanguinity prohibitions provided the medieval equivalent of the easy modern divorce.

BIBLIOGRAPHY

Adhémar Esmein, *Le mariage en droit canonique*, 2nd ed., I (1929), 371–393; R. H. Helmholz, *Marriage Litigation in Medieval England* (1974); Francis X. Wahl, *The Matrimonial Impediments of Consanguinity and Affinity* (1934).

R. H. HELMHOLZ

[See also **Family, Western European; Inheritance, Western European.**]

CONSECRATION OF CEMETERIES. In the early Middle Ages the sanctity of burial grounds was already a well-established tradition. However, the first explicit mention of their consecration or benediction is in Gregory of Tours's *Liber in gloria confessorum* (*ca.* 587). He relates that the nuns of Poitiers considered the burial of their founder, Queen Radegunda, unthinkable without a blessing of the sepulcher. Urged by the crowd, Gregory himself took the place of the absent local bishop and performed the blessing.

The earliest extant directives for the conduct of the ceremony of consecration date from the tenth century. The Pontifical of Egbert of York (Paris, Bibliothèque Nationale, MS lat. 10575), the Pontifical of St. German's in Cornwall (Rouen, Bibliothèque Municipale, MS A27), and the Pontifical of Archbishop Robert (Rouen, Bibliothèque Municipale, MS Y7) describe a ceremony in which the bishop asperges the cemetery, then reads five prayers, one while standing at each point of the compass and one at the center of the cemetery. A Mass of consecration concludes the ordo. An abbreviated version is found in the tenth-century Roman-German Pontifical. The manuscripts of the twelfth-century Roman Pontifical include copies of both the complete and the abbreviated texts.

The Roman Pontifical of Guillaume Durand contains an elaborate ordo for the consecration of a cemetery. The prayers are those found in the tenth-century pontificals. The rubrics are akin in structure to the earlier examples but more explicit in detail. The need for consecration is discussed. Some jurists, according to Durand, argue that the blessing of the exterior of the church during its dedication suffices for consecrating the cemetery. He notes, however, that churches and cemeteries are not always contiguous, nor is every church consecrated.

The ceremony commences with an episcopal homily on the sanctity and liberty of cemeteries. Then the bishop recites a prayer before a cross set in the center of the cemetery. A litany is sung, water is blessed, and the cemetery is asperged. Prayers are read at five crosses, the largest in the center of the cemetery and the remaining four on the eastern, western, southern, and northern boundaries. At each station the bishop censes the cross and places three lit candles on it. The ordo concludes with a preface to be read in the cemetery and a Mass text to be said in the church.

Durand also describes the ceremony for the reconciliation of a cemetery. He relates in the *Rationale divinorum officiorum* that cemeteries need to be reconsecrated when a neighboring church has been desecrated or when the cemetery itself has been profaned by a violent deed or the burial of an excommunicate or pagan. The principal element of the ordo is an aspersion of the entire cemetery, especially the desecrated spot. Durand's texts formed the basis for the normative later editions of the Roman Pontifical.

The medieval texts for the consecration of cemeteries reveal few substantial variants. The homogeneity and continuity of the tradition are notable in contrast to the fluidity characteristic of many medieval liturgical practices.

BIBLIOGRAPHY

Michel Andrieu, *Le pontifical romain au moyen-âge*, 4 vols. (1938–1941), I, 285–288; II, 440–441, 443–445; III, 504–518; Edmond Martène, *De antiquis ecclesiae ritibus libri tres*, 2nd ed., 4 vols. (1736–1738), II, lib. 2, cap. 20, 822–828; cf. Aimé-Georges Martimort, *La documentation liturgique de Dom Edmond Martène* (1978), 405–406; Cornelius M. Power, *The Blessing of Cemeteries* (1943); Cyrille Vogel and Reinhard Elze, eds., *Le pontifical romano-germanique du dixième siècle*, 3 vols. (1963–1972), I, 192–194.

R. F. GYUG

[See also **Death and Burial, in Europe; Durand, Guillaume.**]

CONSECRATION OF CHURCH OFFICERS. See **Ordination.**

CONSECRATION, ROYAL. See **Kingship (Coronation) Rituals of.**

CONSISTORIUM. The Roman emperors, from Augustine onward, sat regularly with an advisory committee known as the *consilium principis*. Diocletian, however, required members to stand *(consistere)* in his presence. The imperial cabinet was henceforth called the *consistorium* (consistory), a term later used by the church for the pope together with his cardinals.

BIBLIOGRAPHY

Arnold H. M. Jones, *The Later Roman Empire (284–602): A Social, Economic, and Administrative Survey,* I (1964), 333–341; Walter Ullmann, *A Short History of the Papacy in the Middle Ages* (1972), 232, 246–249.

G. W. BOWERSOCK

[See also **Papacy, Origins and Development of; Roman Empire, Late.**]

CONSONANCE/DISSONANCE, the most central of all musical concepts, was the constant preoccupation of medieval theorists, both practical and speculative. The pair of opposites now most commonly expressed by the words "consonance" and "dissonance" was perhaps more frequently expressed in the Middle Ages by *concordantia/discordantia* or *symphonia/diaphonia,* and even exceptionally by *consonantia/inconsonantia.*

Throughout the Middle Ages the core of the theory of consonance/dissonance remained those intervals formed by superparticular ratios of the numbers through four. These were normally called *symphoniae* until the thirteenth century and *concordantiae (consonantiae) perfectae* afterward. Thus the unison (1:1), octave (2:1), fifth (3:2), and fourth (4:3) are the backbone of the system, and the latter two intervals still retain the qualification "perfect" in the language of music theory. Except in discussions of polyphonic music, the other intervals are not normally subject to any systematic treatment prior to the thirteenth century. For instance Hucbald of St. Amand, in his *De harmonica institutione* (*ca.* 880), demonstrates all of the melodic intervals before singling out as consonances the four intervals named above; all other intervals become dissonances by inference. Guido of Arezzo in his *Micrologus* (*ca.* 1020–1030) admits the major second, the major and minor third, and the fourth in organum, excluding, among other intervals, the fifth. These intervals are considered consonant not because Guido's concept of consonance is radically different from that of his predecessors and followers, but because the second and the third occur naturally in contemporary organum when the accompanying voice departs from or returns to a unison with the cantus firmus on its way to or from a perfect fourth.

It was evidently this concern for the structuring of the phrase in polyphony that led to a more refined classification of intervals that departs from rigid adherence to the superparticular ratios. In the Milan organum treatise, also known as *Ad organum faciendum* (*ca.* 1100), for instance, unison and octave are the preferred intervals at the beginning and end of the phrase, with fourths and fifths preferred in the middle. In related treatises, such as the Berlin treatise (twelfth century), the third is admitted as well, particularly preceding the unison at the end of a phrase.

The most fully developed system of classification, that (*ca.* 1240) of Johannes de Garlandia (also called John of Garland), seems to be a natural outgrowth of this rather more casual system. Garlandia proposes a sixfold classification embracing all the intervals, in a system unparalleled in complexity before or since. Garlandia first divides the *consonantiae* into *concordantiae* and *discordantiae,* which he further subdivides into *perfectae, imperfectae,* and *mediae:*

	consonantiae
concordantiae	*discordantiae*
perfectae (unison, octave)	*perfectae* (minor second, tritone, major seventh)
mediae (fourth, fifth)	*mediae* (major second, minor sixth)
imperfectae (major and minor thirds)	*imperfectae* (major sixth, minor seventh)

It is noteworthy that the fourth and the fifth have dropped to the second rank among the consonances and that the thirds are not considered dissonant. Perhaps the "intermediate" position of the fourth and fifth is a heritage of their intermediate position in the phrase according to the doctrine of the Milan treatise. The relatively high ranking of the thirds may be a heritage of the earliest doctrine of organum, as exemplified by Guido of Arezzo.

Though modeled on Garlandia directly or indirectly, all later classifications of consonance and dissonance are simpler and confined to perfect and imperfect consonances. Unisons, octaves, and fifths constitute the former category; thirds (later sixths), the latter. All other intervals, including the perfect fourth, have been lumped together as dissonant since the fourteenth century, a categorization that remained unchanged through the nineteenth century.

BIBLIOGRAPHY

Warren Babb and Claude V. Palisca, *Hucbald, Guido, and John on Music: Three Medieval Treatises* (1978); Hans Heinrich Eggebrecht and Frieder Zaminer, *Ad organum faciendum: Lehrschriften der Mehrstimmigkeit in nachguidonischer Zeit* (1970); Erich Reimer, ed., *Johannes de Garlandia: De mensurabili musica,* 2 vols. (1972).

ROBERT FALCK

[See also **Guido of Arezzo; Hucbald of St. Amand; Musical Treastises; Organum.**]

CONSTABLE, LOCAL. Although the title "constable" might denote major authority in the central military or administrative work of the king's government, in the localities of medieval England the office was usually humble. Three local government officials bore the title. The most exalted was the constable of some royal castle with authority (sometimes not well defined) in the surrounding area to allow him to provision his garrison and maintain the fortress. Often he combined this castle charge with another office, perhaps that of sheriff; in any case he would cooperate closely with the sheriff, though he was named directly by the crown. More numerous were the constables of the hundred and of the township.

The hundred constables seem to have originated in a defense scheme hastily put into effect in 1205, when a French invasion was thought imminent. This clearly military function lasted throughout the medieval life of the office. The hundred constable was the captain of the *posse,* the legitimate armed force, of the hundred. The defense he was to supervise, however, could be focused on internal as well as external enemies, and the office was involved in the complex development that produced the keepers, and later the justices, of the peace. Only gradually did the emerging justices of the peace shed their early military functions and acquire considerable administrative and judicial power. In the late thirteenth and early fourteenth centuries, the constables of the hundred received and recorded indictments as the crown struggled to find suitable institutions and officers to deal with the problem of public order. More regularly these constables held inquests concerning the public-order provisions of the Statute of Winchester (1285), which required local men to possess weapons according to their status and to clear from public highways the cover useful for robbers and assailants.

The township constables merged police and military functions on an even more local level. Depending on its size, each township chose one, two, or three constables annually. Their duties included making arrests when the hue and cry was raised, arresting those who carried arms at fairs and markets—an offense specified by the Statute of Northampton (1332)—and even arresting the suspicious characters "commonly called roberdesmen and drawlatches" (in the language of the Statute of Winchester). In general they might be expected to carry out orders from the sheriff, guarding persons or property involved in legal process; they might, for example, supervise the watch set when a fugitive entered a sanctuary. But their freedom of action was considerable, and they took many steps without specific shrieval order.

BIBLIOGRAPHY

John G. Bellamy, *Crime and Public Order in England in the Later Middle Ages* (1973); Helen Cam, *The Hundred and the Hundred Rolls* (1930); and "Shire Officials: Coro-ners, Constables, and Bailiffs," in James F. Willard, William A. Morris, and William H. Dunham, Jr., eds., *The English Government at Work,* III, *Local Administration and Justice* (1950); Alan Harding, "The Origins and Early History of the Keeper of the Peace," in *Transactions of the Royal Historical Society,* 5th ser., **10** (1960).

RICHARD W. KAEUPER

[See also **Hundred (Land Division); Justices of the Peace; Law, English Common; Sheriff.**]

CONSTABLE OF THE REALM. Constables were high officials in princely households. The etymology of the word (from *comes stabuli,* count of the stable) gives a hint of the original service performed by the constable and of the preeminent service to which he aspired in the Middle Ages: supervision of the army or command of a military force or castle. Only in France, however, and not until the late Middle Ages, is it permissible to speak of the constable of the king as the official head of the royal army.

The dignity of constable existed in the retinues of royal houses and of great feudal houses, among which were those of the Norman dukes and the counts of Toulouse. The dignity was often hereditary (England, Normandy, Toulouse; and in the comparable papal office, *praefectus stabuli*), but in the most important example, France, this was never so. While military responsibilities were common to constables whenever and wherever the office appeared in the Middle Ages—from Visigothic Spain to the Kingdom of Naples—some judicial competence, more or less limited, and certain ceremonial duties usually fell to them as well. In England, where the office was never very powerful, the incumbent of the constableship presided in the "court of chivalry," the jurisdiction of which touched primarily military crimes and military precedence and prestige. Like many courts in England, this one tended to augment its jurisdiction, to the injury of the common law, until the sixteenth century.

In France the office of constable went back to the Carolingian period, the concept apparently having been borrowed from existing organization in the Byzantine Empire. Although in France the constable had much greater authority in military matters than did the marshals, he remained subordinate to the seneschal in the chain of command as long as the latter official existed—that is, through the twelfth century. The constable subscribed to important royal diplomas, exercised jurisdiction of a quasi-military sort, and as time went on, governed regions that were giving particular trouble to the crown. In the fourteenth century the office reached its formal apex with the supreme command of the army being vested in it. For reasons connected with disputes over the competence of its court and for reasons of changing military organization, the dignity lost some of its importance and luster in the early modern period. It was suppressed in 1627.

The word "constable" in modern parlance carries with it the medieval legacy of the constable as an official who uses force to reestablish peace. It was already being used in this sense in English in the fourteenth century. The judicial authority of the medieval constable as a military officer also has modern resonances in courts-martial with their peculiar procedures.

BIBLIOGRAPHY

Achille Luchaire, *Manuel des institutions françaises* (1892), 526–527; C. T. Onions, *Oxford Dictionary of English Etymology* (1966), *s.v.* "Constable"; Horace Round, *The King's Serjeants and Officers of the State* (1911, repr. 1971), 76–81.

WILLIAM CHESTER JORDAN

[See also **Marshal.**]

CONSTANCE, COUNCIL OF. See **Councils, Western (1311–1445).**

CONSTANS II, EMPEROR. Constans II, grandson of Heraklios I and son of Constantine III, was born in 630 and became sole Byzantine emperor late in 641, after an uprising removed Heraklios' second wife, Martina, and her young son Heraklonas from power. Because of his youth a regency, the senate, and the army exercised effective authority early in his reign. The sources for his reign are sparse and inadequate.

In addition to the grave crisis of the imperial succession and the crisis of authority, the Byzantine Empire was threatened by possible destruction through Slavic raids and penetration from the north and Arab invasions from the south and east. In the reign of Constans II, Byzantium began to adjust to the hard reality of its territorial diminution in the Balkans and, especially, in Asia. Egypt and Cyrenaica irrevocably fell to the Arabs at the beginning of Constans' reign, and it became apparent that Syria and Mesopotamia could not be recovered. Devastating Arab raids began into Byzantine Armenia and Asia Minor.

Extensive fortification of towns and strategic points in Asia Minor appears to have begun in his reign. Various military units were dispersed and stationed in Asia Minor in a manner that ultimately resulted in the emergence of the Byzantine themes of Asia. Constans proved to be a vigorous soldier-emperor who personally led troops against Slavs in the Balkans, though he narrowly avoided death in the naval battle and defeat at Phoenix in Lycia (655) at the hands of the Umayyad fleet.

Constans II unsuccessfully followed his dynasty's Monothelite christological policies. In 648 he sought to suppress further discussion and debate of Christology by issuing the edict *Typus*. He zealously prosecuted, exiled, and imprisoned such religious opponents as St. Maximus the Confessor, and he arrested, accused, and then exiled Pope Martin I to the Crimea in 653. His persecution of Chalcedonians failed to halt dissent, and he left a bitterly divided church at his death.

Constans' execution of his brother Theodosius in 659 aroused great criticism. Because of opposition at Constantinople and a desire to reassert control in the empire's central Mediterranean territories, Constans traveled to Thessaloniki and Athens, reimposing Byzantine authority in the countryside, which had been lost to the Slavs. Accompanied by some of his most loyal soldiers, he crossed to Italy in 662 and inconclusively fought the Lombards in 663. He was the first Byzantine emperor since Theodosius I to visit Rome, and the last for more than half a millennium. After unsuccessful efforts in Italy, Constans crossed to Sicily, where he was assassinated at Syracuse in the summer of 668, while Armenian conspirators unsuccessfully tried to establish a new emperor. His son Constantine IV, his coemperor since 654, together with Constantine's brothers and coemperors Heraklios and Tiberius, managed to succeed Constans at Constantinople.

BIBLIOGRAPHY

Andreas Stratos, *Byzantium in the Seventh Century,* Marc Ogilvie, trans., 5 vols. (1968–1980).

WALTER EMIL KAEGI, JR.

[See also **Byzantine Empire: History (330–1025)**; **Constantine IV**; **Maximus the Confessor, St.**; **Monothelitism**; **Themes.**]

CONSTANTINE. See **Cyril and Methodios, Sts.**

CONSTANTINE I, THE GREAT (*ca.* 280–337), was born in the Balkan provincial center of Naissus (modern Niš), the son of the future tetrarch Constantius Chlorus and Helena. He was not included in the Diocletianic plans for the succession, but when his father died at York in 306 Constantine was hailed by the troops as emperor. There followed a long struggle among the former tetrarchs and their successors for control of the empire. From his base in Gaul, Constantine either defeated or outlasted his rivals until, by 324, he was master of the undivided Roman Empire. Decisive events in that struggle were Constantine's victory over Maxentius at the Battle of the Milvian Bridge (312) and his war with Licinius in the East (324).

Like all other contemporary political figures, Constantine was concerned with religion, both because it might aid him in his dealings with his subjects and because he clearly felt in need of divine support. Thus, at an early stage Constantine apparently identified with Apollo; later, when he was allied to the family of the tetrarch Maximianus, Constantine worshiped Hercules; and later still he favored Sol Invictus.

From an early date Constantine appears to have been tolerant toward Christianity, but as he marched from Gaul into Italy to engage Maxentius in 312, he seems to have made some greater commitment to the Christian God. According to the *Vita Constantini* the emperor saw a vision of a cross in the sky with the words "conquer with this," thus inducing him to inscribe a sign on his soldiers' shields. The facts behind this episode are hopelessly confused by developing Christian tradition; but it is clear that, while Constantine obviously did not understand all the ramifications of his action, he did feel that he had entered into a kind of contractual relationship with the Christian God. Much of the next twenty-five years was devoted to the elaboration and fulfillment of that relationship.

Constantine had probably already decreed the toleration of Christianity before the Battle of the Milvian Bridge, but he soon began to favor it more actively, first by contributing money for the construction of churches, especially in the Holy Land. This activity and a growing awareness of his special place within the Christian community brought the emperor face to face with the issue of heresy and schism. Already in 312 Constantine was made aware of the Donatist controversy, and he soon undertook to help adjudicate the difficulty.

Slightly later Constantine intervened in the Arian controversy, and it was he who summoned and presided over the First Ecumenical Council at Nicaea (325). The extent and nature of the emperor's role at that council is debatable, but we know that he did agree to the triumph of the extreme anti-Arians and to the acceptance of the homoousion as the test of orthodoxy. For the rest of his life, however, Constantine questioned the decisions of Nicaea; and after the execution of both his wife and son (326) he came closer and closer to the Arian position. Although he never formally reversed the theology of Nicaea, he was baptized on his deathbed by the Arian bishop Eusebius of Nicomedia. Nevertheless, Constantine can be described as the first Christian emperor. By the end of his reign Christianity was well on its way to becoming the official religion of the empire.

In administrative and military matters, Constantine completed the reforms begun by Diocletian. He developed large-scale mobile field armies (*comitatenses*) and completed the separation of the civil and military branches of government. Unlike Diocletian, Constantine favored the senatorial order, which again became the governing class of the empire. Constantine regularized and structured the imperial court (comitatus) and the heads of its various bureaus, and he established a sound gold coin, the solidus, struck at seventy-two to the pound, which was to remain the basic unit of international exchange for over 700 years. Finally, in 330 Constantine presided at the dedication of his new imperial capital of Constantinople, a city that endured as a center of Byzantine civilization and Eastern Christian culture for 1,100 years.

BIBLIOGRAPHY

Eusebius, *Vita Constantini*, Friedhelm Winkelmann, ed. (1975); Timothy D. Barnes, *Constantine and Eusebius* (1981); Norman H. Baynes, *Constantine the Great and the Christian Church* (1930, repr. 1972); Arnold H. M. Jones, *Constantine and the Conversion of Europe* (1949).

TIMOTHY E. GREGORY

[See also **Arianism; Church, Early; Constantinople; Councils (Ecumenical, 325–787); Donation of Constantine; Donatism; Nicaea, Councils of; Roman Empire, Late.**]

CONSTANTINE IV, energetic Byzantine emperor (668–685) who, at the Third Council of Constantinople, initiated and enforced the restoration of Chalcedonianism and thereby abandoned his Heraklid dynastic policy of Monothelitism. He successfully directed the defense of Constantinople during the Arab siege and blockade of 674–678. Despite reversals at the hands of the Bulgars, he left a strengthened and stabilized empire to his son, Justinian II.

BIBLIOGRAPHY

Ralf-Johannes Lilie, *Die byzantinische Reaktion auf die Ausbreitung der Araber* (1976); Andreas Stratos, *Byzantium in the Seventh Century*, Marc Ogilvie, trans., 5 vols. (1968–1980), esp. vol. IV (1980).

WALTER EMIL KAEGI, JR.

[See also **Byzantine Empire: History (330–1025); Councils (Ecumenical, 325–787); Monothelitism.**]

CONSTANTINE V (718–775), Byzantine emperor, was the only son of Leo III and renowned as a military leader and iconoclast theologian. His reign (741–775) is characterized by two developments: the decisive check on Arab and Bulgar invasions of Byzantium, which permitted a gradual stabilization and strengthening of imperial administration through the theme system; and the final and decisive loss of central Italy, with the fall of Ravenna to the Lombards (751) and the shift in papal policy to a Frankish alliance. Both developments were extremely significant for the history of Byzantium and Europe respectively.

But the most striking aspect of Constantine's reign was his iconoclast policy. For under his authority 338 bishops of the Eastern church met in 754 at the Hiereia palace near Constantinople to impose the doctrine of iconoclasm throughout the Christian world. They composed a definition *(Horos)* denouncing the veneration of icons as idolatry and compiled a florilegium listing biblical and patristic prohibitions of religious images. This gathering claimed to constitute the seventh ecumenical council but was not recognized as such. Its canons were never implemented in areas beyond Byzantine political control, and its work was undone by the Second Council of Nicaea (787).

Constantine V played a central role both in the doctrinal pronouncements of 754, as author of two *Peuseis* (inquiries), and in the following persecution of image worshipers (Iconophiles) and replacement of religious images by secular subjects (as in the Church of the Virgin at Blachernae, Constantinople). This iconoclast activity was limited and had few lasting effects, despite several martyrdoms and the destruction of some monasteries, manuscripts, icons, and other ecclesiastical decoration, particularly by overzealous administrators like the provincial governor Michael Lachanodrakon.

Thus Constantine V's iconoclasm proved ephemeral in contrast to his military and administrative successes, which laid the basis for the subsequent political and cultural revival of Byzantium.

BIBLIOGRAPHY

Paul J. Alexander, "Church Councils and Patristic Authority: The Iconoclastic Councils of Hiereia (754) and St. Sophia (815)," in *Harvard Studies in Classical Philology,* 63 (1958); Stephen Gero, *Byzantine Iconoclasm During the Reign of Constantine V* (1977); Georg Ostrogorsky, *Studien zur Geschichte des byzantinischen Bilderstreites* (1929, repr. 1964), 7–45.

JUDITH HERRIN

[See also **Byzantine Empire: History (330–1025); Hiereia, Council of; Iconoclasm, Christian.**]

CONSTANTINE VII PORPHYROGENITOS (905–959), Byzantine emperor, was the illegitimate son of Leo VI and his mistress Zoë Karbonopsina (or Karbonopsis). Born in Constantinople, he was crowned coemperor on Whitsunday probably of 908 (15 May). He remained under the sway of his uncle Alexander (912–913); of the regency council presided over by the patriarch Nikolaos Mystikos (913–914); of his mother, Zoë (914–918); and of Romanos Lekapenos, who married his daughter Helena to Constantine in May 919. He was proclaimed coemperor on 17 December 920; but not until after Romanos' sons had been dethroned in 945 did Constantine come to power, reigning until his death, in Constantinople.

Constantine supported and was endorsed by the military aristocracy. According to the *Theophanes continuatus* he was surrounded by nobles *(eugeneis)* whom he endowed with titles and gifts, and from whose ranks he chose his bodyguards. This proaristocratic policy was inconsistent, however, and Skylitzes later affirmed that Constantine had appointed functionaries without regard to nobility of birth. In his legislation Constantine proposed a complete rupture with his predecessor's policy. Calling Romanos' officials venal, negligent, and unwarlike, he condemned his policy on taxation and, according to *Theophanes continuatus,* sent pious and honest people to alleviate the burden of taxes that had been levied on the poor by his father-in-law. However, in fact, Constantine did not abandon the basic principle of the previous legislation. A law of March 947 ordered the immediate restitution of all peasant lands acquired by the *dunatoi* since the beginning of Constantine's sole rule two years earlier. In another, undated Novel, Constantine declared that allotments from which *stratiotai* derived their livelihood should not have been sold. Romanos restricted the alienation of peasants' lands to *dunatoi* and urged the *dunatoi* to return allotments that had been sold by peasants under duress.

Certain nuances distinguish Constantine's agrarian legislation from that of Romanos. Constantine dealt extensively with the restitution of alienated peasant holdings. If the peasant possessed a medium-sized holding he was obliged to return within three years the price he had received for it. If the buyer was one of the smaller *archontes* (landlords) or was a poor monastery, he would get not only the price delivered but also a refund on the planting of vineyards, building of water mills, and so on. Constantine's Novel, now lost, extended the obligation to restore the price received to the very poorest peasants.

Constantine had no significant success in external affairs. The Byzantines captured Germanicea (Maraṣ) in Asia Minor in 949, and in 952 they crossed the Euphrates; but they were subsequently defeated by Sayf al-Dawla, and their great expedition against the corsairs of Crete in 949 was a failure. Constantine did manage to maintain peace along the empire's northern border, and in the autumn of 955 or 957 the Russian princess Olga visited Constantinople.

Constantine's major contribution to education was in the realm of encyclopedism. After the cultural gap of the eighth century, Byzantium had been attempting to establish a uniform civilization based on the perfunctory revival of the ancient heritage. All preserved knowledge had to be systematized, and the genre of the encyclopedia became especially popular.

With the help of a group of scholars, Constantine established an encyclopedia comprising fifty-three sections, most of which have been lost; surviving sections contain excerpts from such writers as Priscus, Petros Patrikios, Menander Protector, and Dio Cassius. Constantine also encouraged the compilation of collections of excerpts on military tactics, agriculture, medicine, and horse doctoring. He may also have assembled excerpts on "the history of animals"; and other tenth-century encyclopedic works and compilations, such as Metaphrastes' collection of saints' lives, could have been produced by Constantine's contemporaries.

Constantine encouraged historical writing, the goal of which was to praise his grandfather Basil I, the founder of the so-called Macedonian dynasty, and accordingly to present Basil's predecessors as vile and inept. This goal was achieved by the anonymous author of the *Imperial Histories,* ascribed to a certain (Joseph?) Genesios. A collection conventionally called *Theophanes continuatus,* in which the book on Basil was written around 950, either by Constantine himself or under his careful supervision, is the first surviving example of Byzantine secular biography. A treatise on statecraft addressed to "my son Romanos" *(On the Administration of the Empire)* and written in 948–952, a description of the provinces *(On the Themes)* written in 934–944, and a manual of court ritual *(On the Ceremonies)* are preserved under Constantine's name but were his work only in part. They include observations essential for managing both the empire's internal administrative structure and its foreign relations, excerpts from archives, and reminiscenses of classical reading that sometimes have no relation to the ostensible subject. The main thesis of these treatises is the eternity of the Roman-Byzantine empire, the structure of which reflects the heavenly order. Several speeches, letters, and specimens of liturgical poetry also belong to Constantine's literary heritage.

BIBLIOGRAPHY

Sources. De administrando imperio, Gyula Moravcsik, ed., R. J. H. Jenkins, trans., 2 vols. (1962–1967); De caerimoniis, Johann Jakob Reiske, ed., 2 vols. (1829–1830); De caerimoniis, Albert Vogt, ed. (1935–1940), incomplete; De thematibus, Agostino Pertusi, ed. (1952).

Studies. Arnold Toynbee, *Constantine Porphyrogenitus and His World* (1973); see also P. Grierson and R. J. H. Jenkins, "The Date of Constantine VII's Coronation," in *Byzantion,* **32** (1962); Herbert Hunger, *Die hochsprachliche profane Literatur der Byzantiner,* I (1978), 360–367; Paul Lemerle, *Le premier humanisme byzantin* (1971);

Gyula Moravcsik, *Byzantinoturcica*, 2nd ed., I (1958), 356–390.

ALEXANDER P. KAZHDAN

[See also **Byzantine Empire; Dunatoi; Genesios, Joseph; Law, Byzantine; Menander Protector; Nikolaos Mystikos, Patriarch; Olga/Helen; Romanos I Lekapenos; Soldiers' Portion; Theophanes Continuatus.**]

CONSTANTINE IX MONOMACHOS became Byzantine emperor (1042–1055) by marrying the Empress Zoë, daughter of Constantine VIII. He was a patron of scholarship but neglected the army and system of taxation and began the ultimately disastrous process of debasing the coinage. During his reign the schism between the Byzantine and Western churches became final (1054).

BIBLIOGRAPHY

Gustave Schlumberger, *L'épopée byzantine*, III (1905), 385–748, is the most extensive treatment. See also George Ostrogorsky, *History of the Byzantine State*, rev. ed. (1969), 326–337, with bibliography, p. 320.

WARREN T. TREADGOLD

[See also **Byzantine Empire: History (1025–1204); Schism, Eastern-Western Church.**]

CONSTANTINE XI PALAIOLOGOS (1405–1453), Byzantine emperor, was the fourth son of Manuel II and Helena Dragaš (thus his nickname "Dragases"). He completed the Greek reconquest of the Morea, where he ruled as Despot. Having succeeded his brother, John VIII, as the last emperor in 1448, he died bravely when the Turks stormed Constantinople.

BIBLIOGRAPHY

Čedomilj Mijatović, *Constantine, the Last Emperor of the Greeks* (1892); Edwin Pears, *The Destruction of the Greek Empire and the Story of the Capture of Constantinople by the Turks* (1903); Steven Runciman, *The Fall of Constantinople, 1453* (1965).

JOHN W. BARKER

[See also **Byzantine Empire: History (1204–1453).**]

CONSTANTINE THE AFRICAN (*d. ca.* 1087), a Muslim converted to Christianity, was the foremost medical writer of the West in the eleventh century. According to the Salernitan physician Magister Mathaeus F. (Ferrarius) (twelfth century or early thirteenth century), he was a medically knowledgeable merchant who visited Salerno between 1052 and 1077; having learned that the medical center had few Latin books on medicine, he studied medicine in Africa for three years before returning to Salerno.

Our principal source for his life and works is Peter the Deacon of Monte Cassino, who devoted chapter 23 of his *Liber illustrium virorum archisterii Casinensis* (*ca.* 1133) and chapter 35 of Book III of the *Chronica monasterii Casinensis* to Constantine. Peter maintains that Constantine spent thirty-nine years studying the liberal arts and medicine in "Babilonia" (Cairo) and traveling widely in India and Ethiopia. While in Salerno, he was held in high regard by Duke Robert Guiscard and Archbishop Alfanus of Salerno, who recommended him to his friend, Abbot Desiderius of Monte Cassino (1058–1087).

Desiderius received Constantine as a monk and enthusiastically backed his project of translating from Arabic into Latin a large body of medical literature, the Arab and Jewish authors of which had in turn derived their works from Greek sources. He accomplished this in barely ten years.

His main work, the *Pantegni* in ten books, is a free translation of the *Kitāb al-mālikī* by ᶜAli ibn al-ᶜAbbas and is dedicated to Desiderius. At least twenty-five other treatises are known. His writings played a crucial part in introducing to Europe the achievements of ancient Greek and medieval Arab medicine, and they influenced the teaching and study of this discipline for 500 years.

BIBLIOGRAPHY

A critical edition of the chapter in the *Liber* of Peter the Deacon is in Herbert Bloch, *Monte Cassino in the Middle Ages*, I (1983), 98–110, 127–134. See also Marie-Thérèse d'Alverny, "Translations and Translators," in Robert L. Benson and Giles Constable, eds., *Renaissance and Renewal in the Twelfth Century* (1982), 421–462; Paul O. Kristeller, *Studies in Renaissance Thought and Letters* (1956), 494–551; Heinrich Schipperges, "Die frühen Übersetzer der arabischen Medizin in chronologischer Sicht," in *Sudhoffs Archiv*, 39 (1955); Lynn Thorndike, *A History of Magic and Experimental Science*, I (1923), 742–759.

HERBERT BLOCH

[See also **Alphanus of Salerno; Desiderius of Monte Cassino; Medicine, History of; Medicine, Schools of; Peter the Deacon.**]

CONSTANTINE (KOSTANDIN) THE ARMENIAN, a thirteenth-century illuminator in one of Cilicia's important scriptoria. He was a principal painter from about 1263 to 1270 for John, bishop of Molevon and abbot of Grner; he is recorded working for John's father as early as 1237. One of Constantine's signed works is a 1263 Gospel book now in Washington, D.C. (Freer Gallery of Art, MS 56.11).

BIBLIOGRAPHY

Sirarpie Der Nersessian, *Armenian Manuscripts in the Freer Gallery of Art* (1963), 55–72.

LESLIE BRUBAKER

[See also **Armenian Art.**]

CONSTANTINOPLE. The Byzantines referred to the capital of their empire as either "Byzantium," recalling the earlier city on that site; or Constantinople, "the City of Constantine," after its founder, around whom hagiographic memories had rapidly clustered; or "New Rome" (often simply "Rome"), to underscore the Roman legitimacy transferred to it. The praise lavished on Constantinople—"queen of cities" (because it was unquestionably a capital and an uncommonly large center of population), "protected by God" (as a sign of devotion to orthodoxy), "fair city," "New Athens" (because it was the heir of the masterpieces and values of Greco-Roman civilization that are largely known to us through its transmission)—clearly demonstrates the exceptional political, economic, and cultural importance of this mighty center of the Christian East throughout the Middle Ages.

THE FOUNDATION OF THE CITY

The roots of the city chosen by Constantine in 324 to become the second center of the Roman Empire go back to the mythological tradition of Byzas, son of a local nymph, who married the daughter of the king of Thrace and founded Byzantium with her.

The Bosporus shores had been settled at the beginning of the second millennium B.C., and the site had been occupied later by Phoenician merchants replaced *ca.* 658 B.C. by a Megaran colony. The oracle of Apollo had supposedly advised the new colonists to settle "opposite the city of the blind" (Chalcedon), the founders of which had chosen the less desirable Asiatic shore of the Bosporus rather than the European side.

The site of Constantinople was an exceptional one, with its natural harbor (the Golden Horn), its acropolis (the present Topkapi), its key position athwart all land routes between Europe and Asia, and its control of the straits linking the Mediterranean and the Black Sea. Because of its strategic and commercial importance Byzantium played its part in the leading events of Greek history, and it held the position of a free city (*civitas libera*) under Roman dominion until A.D. 196. Septimius Severus punished the city's resistance to his rule by razing its walls and reducing its status to that of a country village. But Byzantium soon acquired the status of a Roman colony and the dynastic name of "Antoniana." The first elements of its monumental decoration—the restoration of the pagan temples, the Baths of Zeuxippos, and the unfinished Hippodrome—date from this period.

In a sense Constantine merely revived and developed the plan of Severus. After reuniting the entire empire, he decided to found a new capital bearing his name, but neither the date nor the motivation is certain. Various stories attest to the miraculous designation of the site of Byzantium. These legendary tales set the character of the new capital: oriental—it marks a return to the origins of Rome (the Troy of the Aeneid); Roman—it is set as a bulwark on the edge of the empire; Christian—it is built in consequence of a divine command. The subsequent steps of the foundation can be traced from literary and numismatic evidence. On 8 November 324 Constantinople received during a ritual consecration, still marked by strong pagan overtones, both its official name and its mystical one, Anthusa (the Flourishing One), and its new urban boundaries. Construction moved swiftly, and the dedication of the city, commemorated every year as its birthdate, took place on 11 May 330 with a double ceremony in the Forum and the Hippodrome. The essential building activity continued until at least 335–336 with a haste that impaired its soundness.

Whatever may have urged Constantine in this

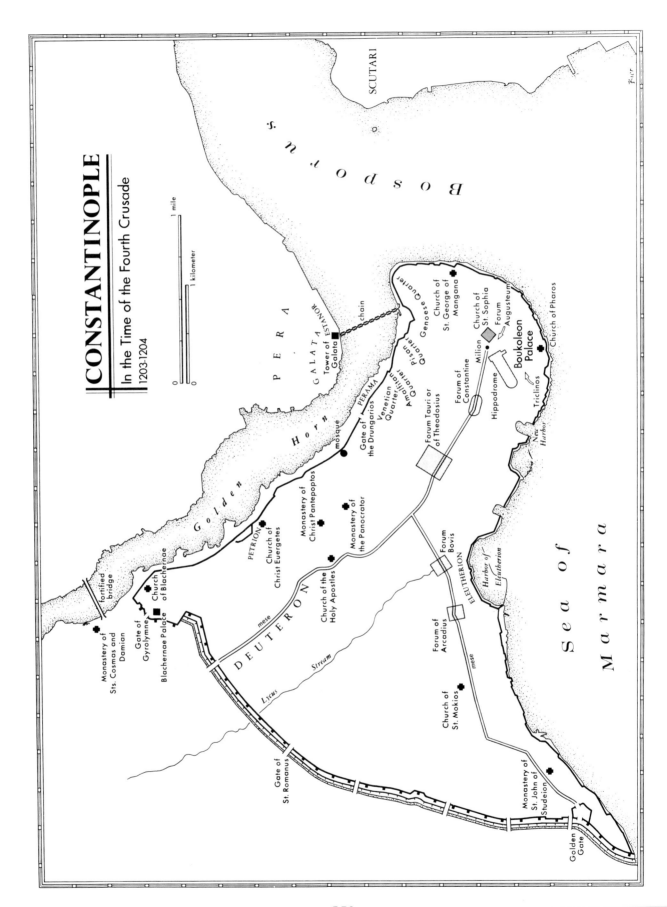

CONSTANTINOPLE

In the Time of the Fourth Crusade
1203-1204

1 mile

1 kilometer

SCUTARI

B o s p o r u s

PERA

GALATA

Tower of Galata

ESTANOR

chain

Golden   Horn

mosque

PERAMA

Gate of the Drungarios

Pisan Quarter

Amalfitan Quarter

Venetian Quarter

Genoese Quarter

Church of St. George of Mangana

Milion

Church of St. Sophia

Forum Augusteum

Boukoleon Palace

Church of Pharos

Forum of Constantine

Hippodrome

New Triclinos

Harbor

Forum Tauri or of Theodosius

PETRION

Church of Christ Euergetes

Monastery of Christ Pantepoptos

Monastery of the Panocrator

fortified bridge

Monastery of Sts. Cosmas and Damian

Gate of Gyrolymne

Blachernae Palace

Church of Blachernae

DEUTERON

mese

Lycus

Stream

Church of the Holy Apostles

Forum Bovis

ELEUTHERION

Harbor of Eleutherion

Forum of Arcadius

mese

Sea of Marmara

Gate of St. Romanus

Church of St. Mokios

Monastery of St. John of Studeion

Golden Gate

550

foundation—the desire to strengthen the threatened oriental and Danubian frontiers, the eastward shift of the demographic and economic center of the empire, the rejection of Rome for political or even religious reasons—his intentions are beyond question. He was creating a dynastic capital, the twin, if not yet the replacement, of Rome. One century later the historian Socrates Scholasticus speaks of a law, engraved in 330 on a stele placed in the Strategion, whereby Constantine granted to his new foundation the official name "Second Rome" and rights equal to those of the "First." The empire now had two "queen cities."

To be sure, it is an exaggeration to gather so many important and progressive changes under a single date. In 330 Constantinople still lacked many of its distinguishing monuments. To Constantine should be attributed the main thoroughfares and porticoes (among them the Mesē), the Forum Constantini and the Augusteion, the church of Hagia Irene, the church-mausoleum of the Holy Apostles, where the emperors were buried, and the first palace complex. Constantius (337–361) built the first Hagia Sophia and several baths; Valens (364–378) gave the city its water supply (aqueducts and cisterns); Theodosius I and his successors (379–450) erected the squares along the Mesē (Forum Tauri, Forum Bovis, Xerolophos) and the aristocratic palaces scattered throughout the city.

Constantinople did not have the dimensions of a great city until the building of the Theodosian walls (412–413). Nor did it achieve its sovereignty over the empire before the development of its senate with the creation of a senatorial class, the establishment of an urban prefecture, and the raising of its episcopal see to the rank of a patriarchate (451). In short, nearly a century and a half was needed before the institutional parity, the demographic growth, and most of all the *partitio imperii* that led to the *translatio imperii* made Constantinople the new Roman capital in the East after the eclipse of the older Rome. At Constantine's death in 337 many of his contemporaries still wondered whether his foundation would survive him, since it depended so much on the imperial will. But, faithful to the ideal that created it, the city was to survive for more than a millennium (330–1453).

THE POSITION OF THE CITY IN THE EMPIRE

During the long period bridging the transition from antiquity to modern times, the role and aspect of Constantinople altered in a constantly perturbed world.

From its foundation, a demographic gamble without precedent made a city of some 20,000 inhabitants the only major urban center of the Near East before the rise of Baghdad, and the equal of Rome. Constantine tripled the area of ancient Byzantium, projecting a population of 150,000 to 200,000. The Theodosian walls increased its area from 700 to 1,400 hectares and gave the city the dimensions it has kept to the present and the possibility of sheltering up to a million inhabitants. The figure 400,000 to 500,000 is generally accepted for the period when the emigration that emptied the countryside and provincial cities for the benefit of an overpopulated capital was dramatically condemned (539). The resultant shift in balance of the entire Roman Orient focused politics and economics on Constantinople, which thus drained the empire of its gold through taxation and of men through its attraction. Between the fourth and the sixth centuries the institutions of the capital were established, its imperial ideology set, and its Christian setting laid out. This was also the period of the great heresies that divided the population and of the murderous riots of the Hippodrome. The architectural and artistic "golden age" of Justinian I (527–565) marked the end of an era amid a series of natural catastrophes (earthquake, endemic plague from 542) that led contemporaries to expect the imminent end of the world.

Constantinople was firmly rooted in its role of great cosmopolitan capital when it was called on to face the major crises of its history in the seventh through ninth centuries. In 626 the Persians, Avars, and Slavs besieged Constantinople; the entire empire was overrun, and the city attributed its salvation to the intervention of the Virgin. Next came the Arab blockade of 674–678, the siege of 717–718, and finally the terrifying appearance of the Russians in 860. Protected by its walls, the city survived, but the world had changed around it: the eastern provinces were abandoned to Islam, the Balkans were with difficulty brought back under imperial control. These waves of invasions and conquests transformed a Mediterranean empire into a continental empire with Asia Minor as its essential element, reorganized militarily for the defense of the frontiers, and agitated by the religious iconoclastic crisis (especially violent in the capital) that was the cultural reaction to these alterations. In this context the population of Constantinople collapsed dramatically in the seventh and eighth centuries (the great plague of 746–747 adding its effect to the external threats), then rose in the ninth. The city clearly emerged as a capital with a stature exceeding that of a shrunken and deurbanized empire.

The life of Constantinople is better known to us under the Macedonian dynasty (867–1056) through an extensive and diversified literature (official treatises, saints' lives, letters, and the like). Except for the threat of Symeon of Bulgaria (913–927), the city was secure from military attacks and formed a brilliant exception in an empire with a fiscal and military organization still based on the peasantry. The palace was more than ever the center of all ceremonies and of political decisions. Great monasteries such as the Myrelaion were founded. The free play of the Roman legal rights of succession constantly subdivided real estate holdings and contributed to the extreme complexity of the urban layout. Constantinople was the first and almost the only city to benefit from the continuous economic growth lasting to the middle of the eleventh century, when it was cut short by the Seljuk invasions and the resultant collapse of the currency. Consequently the city acquired a middle class composed of officials and merchants, and displayed the political turmoil characteristic of the eleventh century. This led to the struggle between the landed military aristocracy firmly based in Asia Minor and the "civilian party" of the capital, a struggle that marked the divorce of Constantinople from the empire.

War returned to the foreground under the Komnenoi and the Angeloi, both against the Turks, who penetrated into the heart of Asia Minor, and against the Petchenegs and Cumans, who threatened Constantinople in 1090–1091. New ethnic groups (Armenians, Syrians), Norman mercenaries, and Italian merchants appeared in the capital, which maintained its prestige and was renewed by various foundations. The relations on the arrival of the Westerners during the First Crusade (1096–1097) show the fascination exercised by the gold, the relics, and the luxury of Constantinople within the setting of the mobilization of Christendom against the infidel. Taken in 1204 by the diversion of the Fourth Crusade at the instigation of the Venetians, the city was systematically looted. The fifty-seven years of the Latin Empire created there, with Baldwin of Flanders as its first emperor and Thomas Morosini as patriarch, were a long agony, but the break caused by its presence was sufficient to effect a fundamental transformation of the city, in which thirty churches and convents had been occupied by the Latin clergy abhorred by the "Greek" population.

In 1261 Michael VIII Palaiologos reconquered a partially ruined and depopulated capital in which the influence of the Genoese, Venetians, and Pisans grew unceasingly and which had become far too large for the modest Balkan state that Byzantium had become. In this period Constantinople presented a striking contrast between its brilliant intellectual and artistic life, as well as the new buildings exemplifying the renaissance of religious and aristocratic art, and the desolate scene it displayed to the "travelers to the Levant": central monuments and colonnades in ruin, a population reduced to 50,000–75,000 inhabitants scattered in neighborhoods that had become isolated villages. Only a few monasteries and Hagia Sophia, the dome of which was repaired in 1346 and 1353, survived. The Ottomans were at the gates from the time of Bāyāzid I (1394). The long-delayed final assault came on 29 May 1453, when Mehmed II hurled a sizable army against some 9,000 defenders and with modern artillery breached the walls that had withstood so many sieges.

THE IMPERIAL CITY

Constantinople was an imperial city from many points of view: because it was born from the will of an emperor, because it contained the Great Palace, because it was the arbiter of the competitions for the empire and of political life. Under the tetrarchy that Constantine brought to an end, the itinerant emperors had established multiple residential cities throughout their territories. Constantinople halted this scattering. It was the city from which the emperor watched over the world and that he left only when the military situation required it. Some moralists complained of this, and opposed the model of the emperor locked within his capital and palace to that of an emperor visiting his provinces and defending the frontiers. But over the centuries the emperor was truly emperor only in Constantinople, and "whoever held Constantinople held the empire."

For this reason the "Great" or "Sacred Palace" took on a particular form and function. Covering more than 10,000 square meters, it was a city within the city, having its own walls, gates, and harbors, its somewhat anarchic accumulation of rooms, official halls, galleries, baths, libraries, and sanctuaries (of which only a few substructures have been found, together with the so-called House of Justinian and a fine mosaic of the sixth century). This architecture, known primarily from texts such as the *Book of Ceremonies*, developed and was renewed generation after generation. After Constantine, who built the Daphne, the Chalke, and the Magnaura, Justinian rebuilt part of the structure destroyed by the fire of 532. Justin II (565–578) erected the Chrysotriklinos, the sumptuous throne room in the shape of a domed octagon. Theophilos (829–842) conceived a new palace architecture imitating that of Baghdad. Basil I (867–886) built within the palace the Nea, the first church with the plan of an inscribed Greek cross.

The palace achieved its greatest splendor in the tenth century. It was out of fashion by the end of the eleventh, and mere ruins when Buondelmonti visited it in 1422. The cause of this disaffection is to be found in the evolution of the imperial institution. Constantine IX Monomachos undertook to establish himself in the new palace of the Magnaura. Alexios Komnenos and his successors, as well as the later Palaiologoi, chose the Palace of the Blachernae at the northernmost edge of the city, near the renowned sanctuary of the Virgin. In addition a number of suburban residences on the European (Hebdomon) or Asiatic shores (Bryas, Hieria) were reserved for summer visits or used to mark the sites of pilgrimages and processions. For these processions itineraries followed by the emperor and his court were laid out within the city, and the representatives of the demes received them at certain "stations." The Great Palace, moreover, had direct access to the Hippodrome and the Great Church (Hagia Sophia), and this architectural linkage, intended to free the emperor from the danger of an often seditious crowd, projected onto the urban plan the special relationships between the emperor and the patriarch who crowned him and the people who acclaimed his legitimacy or, when necessary, challenged it.

On a more general plane the palace, since the time of Justinian, had become the center of the imperial cult and the institution that gradually absorbed all others and transformed the very foundations of the state. In it officials became courtiers, ancient Roman offices gradually turned into court dignities, imperial offices replaced the great administrative services. As Emperor Leo VI wrote at the end of the ninth century, in this new politeia all power emanated from the emperor, and the "imperial providence," which reflected that of God on earth, watched over all. Consequently Byzantine "nobility" became feudalized comparatively late. The creation of a senate equivalent to that of Rome gave rise to a relatively open senatorial class entered through offices as well as through grant of dignities. Until the eleventh century at least, even after the senate had lost all political function, the aristocracy did not become a closed hereditary caste, and it remained closely tied

to the capital. It was effectively controlled by the emperor through the grant of hierarchical titles, through rigorous rules of precedence, and through a system of annual remunerations (roga) or gifts that made it dependent on him.

THE URBAN ADMINISTRATION AND THE DEMES

Following the pattern of Rome, Constantinople was removed from all provincial linkage and administered from 359 by an eparch, or urban prefect. This high civilian official was named for a limited time by the emperor, whom he represented and whom he eventually replaced within the city. At first the president of the senate and a member ex officio of the imperial consistory, he ranked in the lists of precedence in the ninth and tenth centuries immediately after the strategoi and at the head of the judges. His office declined in the twelfth century and especially after 1204.

Various legal codifications give an idea of the breadth of functions attributed to the prefect. To him were addressed laws on buildings and public works, on the status of senators, on the university and libraries, on wills and the protection of orphans, on prostitution, on food distributions to civilians (annona), on the control of foreigners; but the mainstay of his political power derived from his role in the maintenance of order, in certain legal cases under his jurisdiction, in the difficult supply of food for the urban population, and in the supervision of professional guilds. From this point of view he may be compared with the muḥtasib of Muslim cities: his seal guaranteed the accuracy of weights and measures, and it was required for the exportation of certain goods.

The prefect was assisted in all these duties by an office and a number of services. In the fifth century each of the fourteen regions of the city (the same number as at Rome) had its curator, its vicomagistri (responsible for individual wards or districts), and its fire department. In the ninth and tenth centuries each of these regions had a judge fulfilling the duties of a police chief. The supervision of the streets, which were lit through the night, the repression of night crimes in a city considered quite unsafe, and the control of a transient or vagrant population were all within the purview of the prefect of the watch, and subsequently of the urban praetor.

In the absence of any archaeological evidence, the regulations addressed to the prefect are the only source on the urban development of Constantinople between the fourth and the sixth centuries. The supportive measures of the early emperors reveal their concern to create a population for a city having walls that preceded both houses and inhabitants: the fiscal exemptions to architects and masons; the free bread for new houses; the obligation laid on great landlords to build in the capital; the construction, perhaps by Constantine himself, of houses for the senators who had followed him to the East. These policies created a characteristic urban layout. Low aristocratic houses were surrounded by tall rental buildings, by artisan workshops (ergasteria), or by service structures such as baths. In this way they became the centers of highly individualized districts that for centuries bore the names of their owners and founders (Kyros, Anthemios). Regulations attempted to set the distance between buildings, to forbid balconies crossing narrow lanes, and to prevent the extensive use of wood in construction. But the overrun of public space by temporary structures was widely tolerated, so that wooden stalls turned the porticoed streets into bazaars. An unregulated, spontaneous, medieval, and oriental urbanism triumphed outside the monumental center of the city.

The city administration also concerned itself with horse races and the activities of the demes, which for several centuries were a characteristic part of Constantinopolitan life. One of the first acts of the founding emperor had been to grant to the population of his capital a free distribution of bread and to complete the Great Hippodrome begun by Septimius Severus on the model of the Circus Maximus—bread and circuses. In this vast enclosure of some 450 meters, the setting of which, with its obelisks and statues, was the most famous in the city, the chariots of the four "colors" or factions competed before the emperor and the people. These factions were associations responsible for organizing the games, maintaining stud farms, hiring the coachmen who were the great "stars" of the capital, as well as various employees and singers. These races were not mere sports events and distractions; they derived from the ritual of agricultural renewal and had turned into the ceremonial acclamation of, or opposition to, the imperial authority. Thus the factions or "demes" of the Greens and the Blues played a "political" role throughout the city: their representatives could recruit their own militia, and their partisans often clashed in riots.

Some modern historians wondered whether this opposition reflected a social, professional, or even religious polarization, as well as a division by districts. The Greens, for instance, were reported to have been

particularly drawn from the ship caulkers and dock workers with Monophysite leanings who worked the Golden Horn. It is said in the sources that, from Theodosius II (408) to Heraklios (610), the emperors "chose a color" at their accession, thus provoking political disturbances that could become violent or even turn to revolution when the two factions joined forces against the emperor, as was the case in the Nika riots of 532 and the revolt of 602 against Maurice. This overwhelming power of the Hippodrome factions, branded as "democracy," lasted for only a short time. During the ninth and tenth centuries the demes appear only as tame ceremonial bodies, the heads of which (demarchs or democrats) took their place in the court hierarchy.

INDUSTRY AND COMMERCE

The tenth-century Book of the Eparch, which regulated the activity of the city guilds, gives some idea of their organization. At the head of the twenty-one corporations listed (this document is probably incomplete) was the guild of twenty-four notaries (tabularioi) of Constantinople, trained in a special professional school. We are thus reminded that this was a society based on Roman law, where wills, sales, and contracts were sanctioned by actual deeds. Goldsmiths were strictly controlled in order to obviate possible fraud, and gold and silver were consequently worked under official supervision in workshops grouped along the Mese. The chapters dealing with the silk industry reveal a high degree of specialization, indicating both a high level of technology and the wish of the emperor to control and limit production to such a degree that silk was turned into a secondary currency. The corporations concerned with the food supply were strictly regulated in order to avoid all forms of speculation, cornering of the market, or sudden price fluctuations that might result in popular discontent and riots. The weight of a loaf of bread, which had a constant price, was set by the prefect's office according to the price of wheat.

From the descriptions given of them, the guilds seem to have been less associations for professional interest than a framework imposed by the state, according to the Roman tradition, to control the economic life, to halt free trading, and to segregate the various specialties in the districts or streets where they were grouped (perfume vendors between the Milion and the Chalke; candlemakers near Hagia Sophia). Foreigners coming to Constantinople fell under the jurisdiction of the prefect's deputy. They were forbidden to export gold or certain types of silk. Syrian merchants were required to lodge in a particular inn where they might not sojourn more than three months and where the appropriate corporation negotiated the purchase of their entire stock. Even the manner in which the Bulgars might exchange their flax and honey for silk was determined.

Such regulations obviously limited initiative, even if customary cheating is taken into account. Consequently the merchant-artisan, who usually rented his shop, remained a minor figure in the tenth century. Constantinopolitan sales contracts dated 959 show the obligations that weighed upon him: taxes owed to the state or, by devolution, to a monastic foundation, and a rent of some 6 percent on the price of the shop, to be paid to the owner.

Commerce met with unfavorable prejudices. Aristocratic or monastic wealth was invested, without risk or excessive gain, in real estate and did not venture into large-scale trading. At the most we can detect a slight change in this regard in the mid eleventh century, with the return of peace and the renewal of Mediterranean exchanges. "Men from the professions" exceptionally entered the senate at that time. But this significant evolution came to an end.

Nevertheless, Constantinople remained the irreplaceable crossroad between East and West, North and South—a commerce that from the time of Justinian assured the state of the sizable revenue of the Abydos customs but that was increasingly left to foreign middlemen: Bulgars, Russians after the treaty of 944, Armenians, Arabs, and especially Italians. From the end of the tenth century, and especially after the accession of the Komnenoi, imperial policy deliberately sacrificed the economic interests of the city and of the empire to its military and diplomatic advantages. In 1082 a chrysobull of Alexios I granted the Venetians an exemption of all taxes on their merchants (thus favoring them over the Byzantines themselves) as well as the concession of shops and a wharf at Constantinople in exchange for the support of their fleet and a vague recognition of imperial suzerainty. The same privileges were subsequently granted to Venice's rivals, especially Genoa and Pisa. Each of them received a district along the Golden Horn or in Pera/Galata where it settled its traders, built its own churches, and set up a community enjoying a special status and jurisdiction.

This progressive colonization gradually altered both the appearance of Constantinople and its economic bases. This transformation did not go unopposed: in 1171 Manuel Komnenos had some 10,000 Venetians arrested; in 1182 the population of the capital massacred the Latins and looted their settlements. The Westerners never ceased to tighten their hold in order to protect their compatriots and strengthen their power, and the Crusades gave them the opportunity to seize the city itself in 1204. Even after its reconquest by Michael VIII, the capital continued to depend on them for its trade and maritime protection.

THE CHRISTIAN CITY

From the fifth century the foundation of Constantinople was explained as the result of Constantine's wish to create a Christian capital as against pagan Rome. To be sure, this was merely a pious legend, but the city soon became the symbol of faith and orthodoxy. Its Christian personality emerged from the great heresies that enthralled its population (Arianism, Nestorianism, and Monophysitism in the fourth to sixth centuries, iconoclasm in the eighth and ninth), and its appearance was marked by the multiplicity of churches that renewed both aesthetics and building techniques. Outstanding among these was Justinian's Hagia Sophia, replacing the earlier basilica burned in 532. It was an extraordinary building from every point of view, because of its enormous proportions (71 × 77 meters, or 78 × 84 yards), because of its plan and the balance of its cupola conceived by the scientists Anthemios of Tralles and Isidore of Miletos, because of its powerful clergy, which numbered as many as 600 members, because of the legend that made it the equal of the Temple of Solomon. The Great Church, the seat of the patriarchate, the site of the most solemn ceremonies, the goal of long pilgrimages, marked the living center of Oriental Christianity.

The position of Constantinople within the universal church was clarified slowly and in a climate of controversy. The third canon of the First Council of Constantinople (381) had proclaimed that "the bishop of Constantinople shall have the precedence in honor after the see of Rome, since this city is the New Rome." This second place was confirmed by the Council of Chalcedon in 451 "because the city which is honored by the presence of the emperor and of the senate and which enjoys privileges equal to those of Rome must have a greatness equal to it in ecclesiastical affairs as well."

These canons created the patriarchate of Constantinople (part of which were the dioceses of Thrace, Asia, and Pontus) through an accommodation of the ecclesiastical hierarchy to the contemporary political reality, without taking any account of seniority or apostolicity. Under Justinian the opinion prevailed that the church was a "pentarchy" in which Constantinople owed its eminent position, second only to Rome, to the fact that it was the only political center in the Roman world and that it was the home of a "permanent synod." The situation changed after the Arab conquest engulfed the patriarchates of Antioch, Jerusalem, and Alexandria. Left face to face, Rome and Constantinople clashed over numerous jurisdictional, liturgical, and doctrinal questions. Patriarch Photios (858–867, 877–886) provoked a conflict that led to an open breach under Patriarch Michael Keroularios (1054), but the real "schism" should be sought in the climate of hatred that followed the sack of the city in 1204. Supported by the legendary tradition of its foundation by the apostle Andrew, Constantinople ruled over the whole of the Christian East and was the image of Orthodoxy.

According to the definition of the *Epanagogue* given at the end of the iconoclastic crisis, the ecumenical patriarch was the second personage within the realm; the defense of the faith and the care of souls were in his keeping. From this point of view even the emperor was subject to him. At Hagia Sophia he headed a hierarchy parallel to that of the Imperial Palace, and directed a powerful administration and a chancellery the acts of which reflected every aspect of social and religious life. His judicial authority grew constantly. But it was above all the enormous wealth of the Great Church that explained its expanding role in the life of Constantinople. Through testamentary donations, exemptions, and fiscal devolutions it had become the greatest landlord of the capital with the one stipulation of taking over the charitable functions of the state. In fact, it dominated the economic life of the city.

Popular piety took other forms. Within the city walls it multiplied small martyria, private sanctuaries, and monastic groups lying outside of any regulations. The disorders caused by these monks, on the fringe of the ecclesiastical hierarchy or directed against it, were one of the characteristics of the daily life of Constantinople. As the scourges of heresy they roamed the streets in moments of crisis or mobilized public opinion against the attempts at union with the Latins in 1274 and 1439. As "fools for Christ" they indulged in provocations or prophesied the end of the world. Over the centuries Constantinople acquired numerous relics and miraculous icons brought back from the Holy Land and other *loca*

sancta of the East: the wood of the Cross, the nails of the Passion, the trumpets of Jericho, the lip of Jacob's well, the Virgin Hodegetria, and other icons from Edessa, Beirut, and elsewhere. This precious symbolic wealth made it a New Jerusalem rather than a New Rome. It was in any case a city "protected by God" or, even more, by the Theotokos, whose cult (especially in the sanctuary of the Blachernae, where her veil was kept), iconographic representations, and liturgical invocations (the Akathistos hymn) reflected the deep devotion of the entire city.

EDUCATION AND CULTURAL LIFE

Constantinople has transmitted the culture of antiquity, which it had kept alive through its educational system and successfully integrated into the new forms of a Christian civilization. As early as 357 a large scriptorium copied the works of ancient writers and an imperial library preserved them. In 425 Theodosius II founded a university that first rivaled, then replaced, those of Athens, Beirut, and Alexandria. This inheritance and tradition nourished a renaissance in the period following the crises of the seventh and eighth centuries. The monastery of Studios became the main center for copyists, who developed there such new writing techniques as the shift from uncial to minuscule script. Great scholars, such as John the Grammarian, Leo the Mathematician, Photios, and Arethas enhanced the reputation of Constantinople in the eyes of the caliphs of Baghdad.

"Middle" schooling was carried on in secular private schools, which grew more numerous in the eleventh century but eventually passed under the control of the patriarch. In them the future officials or dignitaries of church and state were trained in the classical disciplines of the trivium and the quadrivium. University tradition was reborn in the School of the Magnaura with its chairs of philosophy, grammar, geometry, and astronomy, and it developed thereafter to support the great encyclopedic projects of Constantine VII Porphyrogenitos (913–959). Innovations followed with the foundation around 1045 of a school of law entrusted to John Xiphilinos as *nomophylax,* and of the new title "consul of philosophers" to cover the multifaceted teaching of Michael Psellos. In the Palaiologan period the intellectual life of the capital was still marked by its antiquarian tastes and extreme learning (Theodore Metochites, Nikephoros Gregoras), and by its openness to Iranian or Arab influence in the exact sciences, such as astronomy—characteristics that helped prepare the way for the Italian Renaissance.

BIBLIOGRAPHY

Sources. *The Book of the Eparch* (1970); Constantine Porphyrogenitos, *De cerimoniis aulae byzantinae*, I–II (1829–1830); *Le livre des cérémonies* (incomplete), I–II (1935–1939).

Secondary literature. Paul Alexander, "The Strength of Empire and Capital as Seen through Byzantine Eyes," in *Speculum*, 37 (1962); Hans-Georg Beck , "Konstantinopel, zur Sozialgeschichte einer frühmittelalterlichen Hauptstadt," in *Byzantinische Zeitschrift*, 28 (1965); and "Senat und Volk von Konstantinopel, Probleme der byzantinischen Verfassungsgeschichte," in *Sitzungsberichte der Bayerischen Akademie der Wissenschaften, philologische-historische Klasse* (1966); Alan Cameron, *Circus Factions; Blues and Greens at Rome and Byzantium* (1976); G. de Costa-Louillet, "Saints de Constantinople aux VIIIe, IXe et Xe siècles," in *Byzantion*, 24 (1954); Gilbert Dagron, *Naissance d'une capitale, Constantinople et ses institutions de 330 à 451* (1974); Glanville Downey, *Constantinople in the Age of Justinian* (1960); Jean Ebersolt, *Constantinople byzantine et les voyageurs du Levant* (1918); Rodolphe Guilland, *Études de topographie de Constantinople byzantine*, I–II (1967); David Jacoby, "La population de Constantinople à l'époque byzantine: Un problème de démographie urbaine," in *Byzantion*, 31 (1961); Raymond Janin, *Constantinople byzantine, développement urbain et répertoire topographique*, 2nd ed. (1964), and *La géographie ecclésiastique de l'Empire byzantin*, 2nd ed., I, *Le siège de Constantinople et le patriarcat oecuménique*, and III, *Les églises et les monastères* (1969); Paul Lemerle, *Le premier humanisme byzantin (notes et remarques sur enseignement et culture à Byzance des origines au Xe siècle)* (1971); Cyril Mango, "Constantinopolitana," in *Jahrbuch des Deutschen archäologischen Instituts*, 80 (1965); Thomas F. Mathews, *The Early Churches of Constantinople: Architecture and Liturgy* (1971); J. R. Melville, *The Siege of Constantinople 1453: Seven Contemporary Accounts* (1972); Wolfgang Müller-Wiener, *Bildlexikon zur Topographie Istanbuls* (1977); Steven Runciman, *The Fall of Constantinople 1453* (1965); Ihor Ševčenko, "Constantinople Viewed from the Eastern Provinces in the Middle Byzantine Period," in *Harvard Ukrainian Studies*, 3–4 (1979–1980); Philip Sherrard, *Constantinople, Iconography of a Sacred City* (1965); Paul Speck, *Die kaiserliche Universität von Konstantinopel* (1974); Speros Vryonis, "Byzantine Δημοκρατία and the Guilds in the Eleventh Century," in *Dumbarton Oaks Papers*, 17 (1963).

GILBERT DAGRON

[See also **Byzantine Art, 843–1453; Byzantine Church; Byzantine Empire: History; Constantine I, the Great; Demes; Eparch; Hagia Sophia (Constantinople); Latin Empire of Constantinople; Roman Empire, Late; Trade, Byzantine; Trade, European.**]

CONSTANTINOPLE, COUNCILS OF. See **Councils.**

CONSTANTINOPLE, HISTOIRE DE LA CONQUÊTE DE. See **Villehardouin, Geoffroi de.**

CONSTANTINOPLE, LATIN EMPIRE OF. See **Latin Empire of Constantinople.**

CONSTITUTIO DE FEUDIS (ordinance on fiefs), a document promulgated by Emperor Conrad II on 28 May 1037, at the height of his conflict with Archbishop Aribert II of Milan. Aribert had blocked the lay magnates' offer of the Italian crown to the son of Duke William V of Aquitaine in 1024 and had helped to secure Burgundy for the empire in 1034, but fear of the archbishop's power caused Conrad in the mid 1030's to abandon his predecessors' traditional alliance with the Italian episcopate. The emperor obtained the support of the lay magnates and intervened in the troubled affairs of Milan.

The *capitanei* or *milites maiores*, the tenants-in-chief of the church who exercised quasi-comital authority, possessed their fiefs by hereditary tenure; but the subvassals, the *valvassores*, *milites minores*, or *milites secundi*, as they were variously described, did not. When Aribert confiscated the property of one of the *valvassores* in 1035, they rebelled and were expelled from Milan, after which they defeated the archiepiscopal forces at Campo Malo. Both sides appealed to Conrad. Aribert refused to submit to the emperor's judgment in Pavia at the beginning of 1037 and was imprisoned, but escaped two months later and returned to Milan. Conrad besieged the city and, after an indecisive battle on 19 May, issued the imperial diploma before lifting the siege.

Conrad wished, as the constitution states, to reconcile the lay feudatories and to attach them to the crown. He recognized the right of the *valvassores* to inherit their fiefs in the male line, ruled that any vassal could be deprived of his fiefs only by the judgment of his peers in accordance with the law, prohibited a lord from alienating a fief without his vassals' consent, promised to demand no more than the customary *fodrum* (the requisitioning of supplies for the imperial army), and established procedures for appeals. The great vassals were permitted to appeal directly to the emperor, the lesser vassals to the judgment of the great lords or an imperial *missus* (envoy). The vassal was allowed to retain possession of the fief, even if the decision had gone against him, until the appeal was decided. The constitution applied to the vassals of any lord, lay or clerical.

Henry III reversed his father's policy and was soon reconciled with Aribert and the other Italian bishops, but the constitution is nevertheless important. The *valvassores* were transformed into small landed proprietors and played a leading role in the formation of the Italian commune. The issuance of the diploma was part of Conrad II's general policy of turning to the lower strata of society for support against his powerful vassals. He had allied with the Swabian counts and lords against his stepson, Duke Ernest of Swabia. More important, Conrad promoted the development of a royal domain in Germany garrisoned by servile retainers, the precursors and ancestors of the ministerials, the functional equivalents of the *valvassores*. The broader implications of Conrad's policy are what make the *Constitutio de feudis* truly significant.

BIBLIOGRAPHY

Hans Anton, "Bonifaz von Canossa, Markgraf von Tuszien, und die Italienpolitik der frühen Salier," in *Historische Zeitschrift,* **214** (1972); H. E. J. Cowdrey, "Archbishop Aribert II of Milan," in *History,* n. s. **51** (1966); Boyd H. Hill, Jr., *Medieval Monarchy in Action* (1972), 70–84, 205–207; Heinrich Mitteis, *Lehnrecht und Staatsgewalt* (1958), 398–402.

JOHN B. FREED

[See also **Feudalism; Germany: 843–1137; Law, German: After the Carolingians.**]

CONSTRUCTION: BUILDING MATERIALS. Wood is easy to work with and its shaping is possible with only a few tools. Therefore it is the chief construction material in areas where it is reasonably abundant. Such was the case in western, central, and northern Europe during the Middle Ages. For most Mediterranean peoples, by contrast, very little wood was available and so, from ancient times, they used stone and brick and rammed earth, with as little wood as possible.

WOOD

The vast majority of buildings in western Europe, whether houses, castles, or religious edifices, were of wood. Very few of these structures have survived. Most of them were destroyed, replaced by stone buildings, or completely rebuilt in later periods. For this reason, and because of a bias toward prestigious buildings, archaeologists have not studied, until recently, the humble rural dwellings that were the homes of the great majority of the population. These dwellings evolved from the primitive huts built of interwoven branches, the most common type of construction in the early Middle Ages being a framework of wooden poles leaning toward each other in a v-shaped pattern. These main rafters were tied together in pairs at the top, and rested directly on the ground supporting the roof and enclosing the living space. Usually a ridgepole bound these simple trusses together at the top and sometimes they were bound at their low end by a wall plate.

At each end of the building stability was assured by slanting poles pushing against the last truss. This framework thus formed a roof with four pitches or, sometimes, with roughly rounded ends. Inside, there were often horizontal beams crossing overhead that bound the rafters together in pairs and kept them from spreading. These trusses, usually spaced 2½ to 4 meters (8 feet to 11½ feet) apart, supported horizontal parallel beams (purlins) that bore the weight of the roof through smaller rafters that ran from the ridgepole down to the wall plate.

Another similar type of construction used no main rafters but rather regularly spaced rafters with a smaller cross section placed close together (60 to 90 centimeters or 2 to 3 feet apart). These rafters formed light trusses on which the weight of the roof covering (battens or branches) was distributed.

The first style required beams of large cross sections for the main parts of the frame, but made it much easier to install doors and windows or chimney stacks in the roof. The second style, which builders of the Gothic period often adopted, was used wherever heavy timber was lacking.

In order to enlarge the amount of habitable space without increasing the amount of building material used and also to gain better protection from the wind and the cold, men in the early Middle Ages sometimes created half-buried dwellings. A pit, a meter or so deep, was excavated under the whole surface of the roof, thus creating extra habitable room. This type of house was very common in many rural areas during the early Middle Ages, but it disappeared almost entirely after 1000, except in some places (France, England, and Ireland, among others) where it was still used for temporary shelters for herdsmen or for buildings where a constant, cool, and damp atmosphere was essential for activities such as weaving or cheese-making.

Later, when upright sides were built of masonry, rammed earth, or wood supporting a roof, it became necessary to connect the bases of the trusses from wall to wall by pieces of wood. These tie beams, when they were very close together or reinforced by intervening joists, often supported an upper floor that could be used for storage. Sometimes the tie beams supported an upright beam, the king post, to which the main rafters were attached at their peak. The tie beams could also be attached to other vertical or slanting pieces of timber that helped to keep the structure rigid and to relieve some of the stress on the main rafters.

Walls at each end of the building could be built up to the level of the ridgepole, thus forming a gable, which could be used to build an outlet for smoke

Timber built church. St. Andrew's, Greensted, England, ca. 1000.
PHOTO BY JEAN ROUBIER

from the fireplace. In this case the stiffening and bracing of the frame were assured by crosspieces, either oblique or in the form of a St. Andrews cross, which prevented the roof from being deformed longitudinally and made the gables able to resist wind pressure.

When the roof was made of thatch, it was easy to make it round or four-pitched. When the roofing was composed of small, usually rectangular units, such as terra-cotta tiles, slate, wooden shingles, or roofing stones, a gabled roof was easier to construct. The roof could either end on a projecting gable or go beyond the top of the gable wall, thus sheltering the wall.

The long house (which in rural areas generally sheltered both animals and humans) was characteristic of poor regions where the peasants grew grain and raised only a few animals. This type of house still exists in Brittany and in the French mountains. Thatched roofing was the most common type in western Europe during the Middle Ages. It was plentiful because grain was the basic element in the diet and thatching could easily be repaired and replaced by the peasants themselves.

The walls supporting the frame of a house were often made of wood, or of wooden posts with lighter material between them such as planks, bricks, rubble, broken pottery or tiles, rammed earth, wattle, plaster, or lath, all covered with mortar or plaster. The simplest form was the palisade wall, vertical posts made of whole or split logs. These posts, in the most primitive constructions, were driven into the ground beside one another. Gaps between the posts were filled with dirt or moss. Later, builders realized that it was preferable to place the bases of the posts on rails or wall plates in order to avoid rotting, since moisture can more easily rise vertically along wood fibers than horizontally. Later, palisade walls were made of posts connected by a tongue from one fitting into a groove in its neighbor.

One of the oldest wooden structures that can still be found in something close to its original form is the eleventh-century church at Greensted, near Ongar, not far from London. Its type of construction—split logs placed side by side vertically and locked in place into a wall plate by means of a mortise-and-tenon system—is like that of many houses whose remains have been found by archaeologists. The church was originally roofed with thatch.

Another construction style was to pile up the logs horizontally. They were held together at each end by an interlocking system and were roughly squared only on two sides. One can find many examples of this type of building in northern and eastern regions and in mountainous parts of Europe Many have been repaired since the Middle Ages but some have remained untouched. An eleventh-century house at Charavines in the French Alps is partly of this type. This kind of building required trees with long, straight trunks and wood that is not too heavy, such as pine and related woods. It also consumed hundreds of trees to build one house and could be used only where timber of the right species was abundant. However, such buildings, because wood provides good thermal insulation and because they could be quickly heated, were very suitable for cold climates.

Little by little from the tenth to the thirteenth century more economical and better designed structures appeared, using different materials in a wooden framework. This development was possible because the techniques of building in wood had been perfected, especially the mortise-and-tenon system for putting together walls and frames. One no longer built only with an ax; advances in metallurgy in the twelfth and thirteenth centuries provided new tools for builders. Augers, files, wood chisels, adzes, planes, and saws appeared in the lumber yards. The use of specialized tools permitted more elaborate structures with new forms.

The use of wooden wall structures developed especially in towns. They made it easy to build a house of several stories, which was essential in the limited space available within town walls. In the fourteenth century many houses had two or three stories. In the fifteenth century a house in the Rue St. Martin, Paris, is said to have had seven stories. This technique of using wooden walls lent itself especially to the construction of overhangs, which provided extra space above the streets. These projections also gave some protection against bad weather to the lower floors, where the stores and booths of the artisans were located. Wooden structures in the facades had different designs in different regions with various numbers of slanting or curved pieces, crossbars, and more or less closely spaced struts.

Throughout western Europe from the twelfth century on, the amount of building in stone or masonry gradually increased for various reasons. First of all, urban fires were common. The city of Rouen, for example, burned down six times between 1200 and 1225, and a great fire destroyed almost the entire city of London in 1136. Therefore the authorities tried to eliminate combustible building materials as far as possible. The Assizes of Building (1189) illustrates this point:

> In ancient times the greater part of the city was built of wood, and the houses covered with straw and thatch and the like forms of roofing; so that when any house has caught fire most of the City was burnt in that same fire, as happened in the first year of the reign of King Stephen.... Afterwards, many citizens, to avoid such risks as far as they could, built on their sites a stone house roofed with thick tiles.

Elsewhere it was ordained that dividing walls must be built of stone to prevent fires from spreading from house to house. Wood, however, could be used for facades.

There were other reasons for building more and more often in stone rather than in wood. For one thing, it became increasingly difficult to acquire timber for construction. Wood was the basic material for all kinds of construction as well as the only fuel. From the eleventh century on, the population of western Europe had been growing as a result of greater security and an increase in agricultural production. The invasions of the ninth and tenth centuries had ended. The Vikings had settled in France in 911; the Hungarians were pushed back from western Europe in 955; the Muslims were driven from their last stronghold in southern France in 978. The founding of the Truce of God, which forbade fighting on certain days; the establishment of the Peace of God, which attempted to protect the poor, the weak, and the clergy; and the stabilization of the feudal system all combined to improve living conditions in the countryside. Moreover, a somewhat warmer climate allowed agricultural production to increase. There was a corresponding increase in European population, from 40 million to 70 million inhabitants between 1000 and 1300. This increase meant that more wood was consumed for domestic purposes and for such growing industries as metallurgy, brick, tile, and pottery making, glassworks, lime kilns, and salt works.

At the same time more forest land was cleared in order to establish new agricultural settlements, further reducing the production of wood. In many regions it was common practice to clear a forest, cultivate it for some time, then allow it to revert to forest for twenty or thirty years, too short a period for trees to reach their full size. Most settlements became permanent and, all over western Europe, the forests were replaced by fields. Between the eighth and the fourteenth centuries, forests were reduced by nearly 50 percent. This trend was stopped only by the Hundred Years War and by the Black Death, which in the middle of the fourteenth century killed about one-third of the population. Finally, more and more wood was needed for military purposes (which always had priority) and for shipbuilding.

During the thirteenth century, chronicles and legends both record that large logs were becoming scarce, and the sketches by the architect Villard de Honnecourt confirm the worries of his contemporaries on this point. Villard suggests several devices for saving wood or for using pieces of wood that would normally be too short or too small in diameter.

Progress in the metallurgy of weapons during the crusades induced the development of iron tools and the new tools facilitated the exploitation of forests and the cutting of wood. Saws and more efficient steel tools also made it easier to cut and shape soft and semisoft stone.

By the late twelfth and early thirteenth centuries the development of saws, especially of water-powered saws, made longitudinal sawing easier, eliminating the necessity to shape each piece of construction timber from a log of about the same diameter. Much larger (and therefore older) trees could now be used to supply pieces of lumber of the same width for rafters, planks, and cross pieces. Trees did not have to be harvested any longer in their early stages of growth, and forests could have been used in a more sensible and productive way. A fully grown forest yields 50 percent more wood than an immature one. Nevertheless, till the end of the fifteenth century carpenters still very seldom used longitudinally sawed beams or rafters.

MASONRY

The Mediterranean lands, especially Italy, Provence, Languedoc, and Spain, had lost most of their forested regions except in mountainous areas. Masonry construction was in any case better suited to climatic conditions in these regions for, in sunny countries, buildings need to have greater resistance to changes in temperature and fewer openings.

Massive stone or rammed earth with very thick walls keeps the coolness of the night during the day. Wooden buildings, since they provide good insulation and have light walls, are quickly heated even when not heated all the time. Of course, if the house is permanently heated in the winter, it can be advantageous to have thick, massive walls. But in a cold

Masons building an octagonal tower. In the distance is a thatched shed for the masons. THE BRITISH MUSEUM, Add. MS 35313, fol. 34

climate fuel would become very expensive. In western Europe with its temperate climate, for people working outside all day long (95 percent of the people were cultivators) heating the house when nobody was inside was not only unneccessarily expensive in fuel, but it was also dangerous to keep untended open fires. In very cold climates in which permanent heating was unavoidable in winter, people used stoves made of pottery or brick that were less dangerous and burned wood less quickly. Hence, apart from the abundance of wood or stone, weather conditions and heating requirements actually favored wooden structures in the cooler climates and stone in the warmer Mediterranean regions.

Around the Mediterranean, wood, which often had to be imported, was used chiefly for frameworks, beams, and lintels. The walls were made of stone, brick, or rammed earth. This last material, dug from the site itself, and sometimes mixed with straw, and formed into pisé, was by no means reserved for humble dwellings and in fact it is still used today in several parts of France.

Transport was one of the most difficult jobs in building with stone. It was very expensive to haul stone by land. Wagons could only carry a few stones, roads were bad, highwaymen were common, and tolls were numerous. Transport by water was easier and less expensive, although on the rivers there were also tolls. A boat could carry many more stones and more safely than a wagon, and could even deliver them overseas.

One of the factors that favored the development of Gothic architecture in the Paris basin, northern France, the Low Countries, Germany, and England was the existence of navigable rivers close to beds of good stone. In some cases channels were specially dug from the sea or the nearest river to the site of the building. But, when necessary, stone was also transported over long distances.

After the Norman Conquest, many English castles and churches were built of stone shipped from France across the Channel. Caen stone was used for Battle Abbey at Hastings, and for the castles of Rochester and Winchester as well as for the Tower of London. Stone came from Rouen for the building of Westminster Abbey and from Marquise (near Calais) for the cathedral at Canterbury.

Shaping stones at the quarry facilitated transport by drastically reducing their weight. Stones used in Gothic buildings were often fully shaped at the quarry using wooden models sent by the designers. A considerable amount of finished stone was brought in 1253 from the quarries of Oxford and Reigate to Westminster. For repair of the castle of Rochester in 1367, large quantities of finished stone were prepared at Boughton. In the fifteenth century the quarries of Kent provided finished stone for the building of the bridge at Rochester and of Eton College.

In many cases the same hewers or stone cutters who later fitted the stones into the buildings were sent to the quarries to shape the stones themselves. In 1277 several masons with their assistants were sent to the quarry to cut a thousand stones for the building of the Vale Royal Abbey. Certain kinds of hard stone are easier to cut when they have just been extracted. Stones could also be shaped at the quarry in a sheltered workshop in the winter when bad weather interrupted work on the building.

However, to make prefabrication of stone possible, there had to be standardization. Gothic archi-

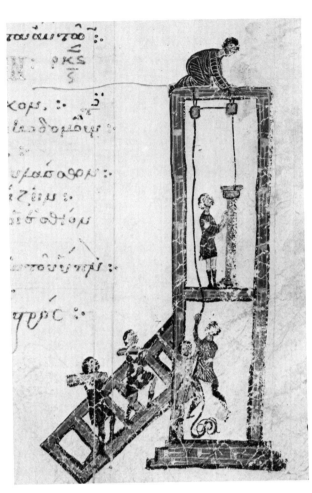

Masons at work. Byzantine psalter, 1066. THE BRITISH MUSEUM, Add. MS 19352, fol. 30

tects perfected the techniques that made it possible to preshape stone for the construction of vaults. Vaults were not a new technique in western Europe. Even in rural buildings in all areas where masonry construction was traditional for dwellings such as southern France and Italy, the ground floor and the basement were often vaulted. In small buildings the vaults seldom exceeded 3½ meters (11½ feet) in width. The ceilings were not high, and thick walls—even those above ground level—were usually strong enough to withstand the thrust of the vault without buttresses.

The barrel vault, which has only one curve, is the easiest to construct. But it is difficult to open windows in a barrel vault and its thrust must be withstood all along the side walls. Therefore it was used mainly underground. The need for space and light and the advantage of concentrating the thrust on four points led builders to develop the groin vault, formed by the intersection of two barrel vaults. This made it possible to have vertical walls, or passages, on each of the four sides. This type of vault was traditional in Italy, the Alps, the Massif Central, and southern France, and was frequently used in Romanesque architecture.

Such vaults were difficult to construct with pre-shaped stone. The arris formed by the intersection of two cylinders having circular sections are ellipses with constantly varying curvature. The stones that form these ellipses are difficult to design if they are precut, especially since each stone in each semicircle is different. Builders of this period, who had only a rudimentary knowledge of geometry, solved this problem by forming the vaults from an agglomeration of small chips covered with plaster. In such vaults the arris were soft, not very accurately shaped, and almost nonexistent at the apex of the curve. Some Romanesque builders (such as those of the church of Notre-Dame-la-Grande at Poitiers) had the idea of making the arris stand out by marking them with bands of paint that contrasted with the color of the vault. The great idea of Gothic builders was to emphasize the arris by making them project from the vault as ribs.

The Gothic builders gradually discovered the advantages of the ribs, especially for the groin vault. First of all, although the ribs did not carry the weight of the vault (as is often believed), the building of the ribs was a very important stage of construction. They were put in place before the rest of the vaulting on light trusses and they formed a precise guide for framing and building the vault. The rest of the vaulting could, then, be built on a light framing supported by the main trusses of the ribs.

After the mortar had hardened between the stones, the vault could support itself, and the trusses for the ribs and the framing under the vault could be removed for another bay. For builders who had very elementary notions of geometry, ribs made possible the use of vaults for virtually all parts of a building: circular galleries with polygonal bays, stairways with supporting vaults divided by ribs, rooms of any shape.

With the rib system, two types of stone were used and differently skilled masons worked them. The stones for the ribs and molding were cut along regular curves and carefully fitted into place by skilled masons, while the vaults between were filled with pieces of varying or uniform dimensions or with bricks by less skilled workmen or assistants.

In their efforts to simplify and standardize, Gothic builders almost always planned the intersection of their vaults (marked by ribs called ogives) as semicircles. For the side arches (which by rigorous geometrical construction should have been ellipses) they adopted the pointed arch, formed by two symmetrical partial arches. The pointed or "broken" arch had been used by the Armenians, the Romans, and the Arabs. Its main advantages are ease of planning, a lateral thrust less than that of a full arch of the same width, and the ability to build successive arches of different widths while keeping the height of the arch constant. Gothic builders used this construction systematically and made the most of the possibilities it afforded for standardizing the curved pieces that formed the arch. It also became a decorative motif.

Increased use of stone in buildings did not mean that wood was no longer used, but Gothic construction in wood, at least in France, had special characteristics. During the twelfth and thirteenth centuries the technique of rafters worked into trusses was almost the only one used. It allowed the use of narrower pieces of wood than trusses with purlins, and so was more suitable for the wood supply of that period. It also made construction easier for such high buildings as the French cathedrals because the pieces of timber were lighter and helped to distribute the weight of the roof on the walls. In England, thinly populated, rich in forests, and near Scandinavian timber supplies, builders still constructed massive wooden frames with very elaborate plans.

Until the eleventh and twelfth centuries, the roofs of nonecclesiastical buildings were generally of thatch; up to the eleventh century many churches had the same covering. But little by little, tiles, which had long been used in the Mediterranean countries, began to be used along with slate or, for the very wealthy, lead.

By the eleventh and twelfth centuries, flat tiles were used in Burgundy, Nivernais, and Champagne, then in eastern France and in Germany, replacing wooden shingles. Increased use of tiles was aided by the establishment of rules governing their size and characteristics. Centuries after their size and characteristics had been fixed, the tiles made in Champagne were still called "tiles of Count Henry," the ruler who standardized their manufacture.

For housing, especially in the cities, building in

stone was influenced by the earlier tradition of building in wood. As soon as glass began to replace wooden shutters or oiled cloth as a window covering, timber framing made it possible to create glass facades with very little solid material.

In the towns, confined by their city walls, most houses had to be built on deep, narrow lots (a type inherited from the rural past) and could receive light only through openings on the street and on the courtyard, the ends of the narrow corridor that was the core of most urban housing. As in the Gothic churches, the walls of which contained much glass, the builders of urban houses and stone castles sought to lessen the amount of blank wall space and to let in more light and solar heat.

BIBLIOGRAPHY

Roland Bechmann, *Les racines des cathédrales* (1981); Marjorie M. Boyer, *Medieval French Bridges* (1976); Jean Chapelet and Robert Fossier, *Le village et la maison au moyen âge* (1980); Thomas K. Derry and M. G. Blakeway, *The Making of Britain,* I (1968); Jean Gimpel, *Les bâtisseurs de cathédrales* (1958); John Harvey, *The Medieval Architect* (1972); Douglas Knoop and P. G. Jones, *The Medieval Mason,* 3rd ed. (1967); Louis F. Salzman, *Building in England down to 1540* (1967, repr. 1979); Villard de Honnecourt, *Sketch Book,* commented on by J. B. A. Lassus (1858, repr. 1976); Eugène Emmanuel Viollet-le-Duc, *Dictionnaire raisonné de l'architecture française du XIe au XVIe siècle,* 10 vols. (1858–1868).

Roland Bechmann

[See also **Arch; Architect, Status of; Construction: Engineering; Gothic Architecture; Masons and Builders; Vault.**]

CONSTRUCTION: ENGINEERING. The major buildings that survive from the Middle Ages, mostly large churches and some castles, display skills of construction in masonry and timber that were passed down to succeeding generations of professional builders. From examining the buildings we know that in the eleventh century these skills began to be more finely honed. By the end of the following century the improved state of the art allowed construction of what is still considered to be the triumph of masonry building: the Gothic cathedral. The principal structural features of these spacious, lightweight, and tall building forms are pointed ribbed vaults supported at regular intervals by extensions of the piers

of the nave arcade. The pier extensions, in turn, are supported laterally at the level of the clerestory by flying buttresses that lead to the pier buttresses (the towerlike structures along the church perimeter). Intervening load-bearing walls were not required, and so they were largely supplanted by window openings, effectively creating a giant stone skeleton.

The evolution over a relatively short period of the new structural systems that led to this development can be illustrated by a comparison of three major buildings whose construction dates span the epoch: Ste. Foy at Conques, a rural pilgrimage church begun around 1050 and largely completed in the first quarter of the twelfth century; the early Gothic cathedral of Laon, begun around 1160 and completed by about 1215; and the High Gothic cathedral of Rheims, begun in 1211 and remaining in various phases of construction for some eighty years.

Notwithstanding the considerable height of Ste. Foy—21 meters (69 feet) to the keystones of its barrel

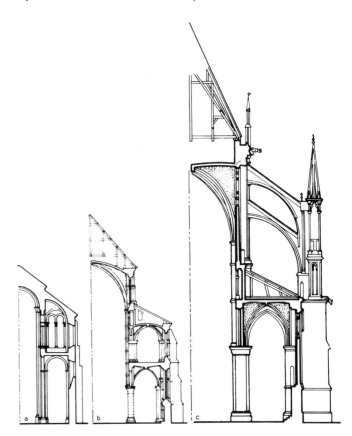

Comparative cross-sections through the nave: (a) Conques, Ste. Foy, begun *ca.* 1050; (b) Laon Cathedral, begun *ca.* 1160; (c) Rheims Cathedral, begun 1211. REPRODUCED FROM ROBERT MARK, EXPERIMENTS IN GOTHIC STRUCTURE, PUBLISHED BY MIT PRESS © 1982

vaults—and the fairly wide openings along the arcade, its interior presents an almost tunnellike quality (the barrel vault, a structure originally designed to be placed upon a continuous, solid supporting wall, adds to this effect) compared with the light, open stone frame of the considerably taller (38 meters, 124 feet) Rheims Cathedral or even with Laon Cathedral, which is not significantly higher than Ste. Foy (24 meters, 79 feet). The cross section of Ste. Foy reveals that the vertical weight and the outward thrust from the vaulting are carried by the heavy piers, which in turn are laterally braced at the point of vault attachment by transverse (diaphragm) walls above the side aisle galleries. Light enters the upper region of the church through small window openings in the perimeter wall, so that the central aisle is only indirectly lighted.

At Laon a four-story interior elevation adding a raised clerestory and a triforium passage replaces the two-story elevation of Ste. Foy. Transverse walls abutted against the blind triforium story are placed above the side aisle galleries to provide lateral support to the raised wall. And the clerestory, together with the use of pointed, ribbed quadripartite vaulting, creates an entirely different quality of interior space and illumination.

At Rheims the lofty clerestory wall with stained glass in enlarged openings provides a display of light and daring structure. In addition to having to resist the outward thrust of the vaulting, the clerestory walls were now subject to great wind forces, as were the high wooden roofs resting upon them. As these buildings grew larger, the design problems were exacerbated by the great costs of obtaining and transporting vast amounts of stone, often from distant quarries, and of shaping and setting the stones into place. Still another design restraint was imposed by the need to reduce the weight of the superstructure in order to relieve foundation loadings, and hence to reduce building settlements.

It was the combination of all these factors that led to the invention of the exposed flying buttress above the side aisle roof, and the consequent redefining of the style of Gothic churches. The first true flying buttresses were used to provide stability to the extremely tall clerestory of the nave of Notre Dame in Paris (*ca.* 1180). By the turn of the twelfth century, at the even taller cathedrals of Chartres and Bourges, flying buttresses permitted the clerestory wall to be reduced to a stone frame enclosing large areas of glass. This technical achievement is all the more awesome when we realize that it came about centuries before the development of the analytical scientific methods of structural design that are used today to predict structural behavior.

Contemporaneous records of medieval design and construction techniques are practically nonexistent; our knowledge is based almost entirely on details that have come to light in modern restorations. Yet we do have access to one important technical sketchbook preserved from the thirteenth century, and we can also extrapolate certain information from fifteenth-century Gothic design booklets. Villard de Honnecourt's thirteenth-century sketchbook contains plans and views of major buildings of his time along with a number of sketches and some slight text dealing with such topics as the setting out and the cutting of stone, timber roof and floor details, machines (including a water-powered sawmill and a jackscrew), and applied geometry. But Villard provides no clues about the construction sequence or what is probably the most crucial aspect of masonry construction, the extensive timber centering that provides support for both workmen and stonework during the course of the building's erection.

In a number of instances historians have been able to determine how the construction of particular buildings was ordered. Some were built by raising the superstructure of one bay at a time, while others were constructed in essentially horizontal "layers." We also know that the high timber roof across the main arcade was generally placed prior to the erection of the high vaults, so that the roof framing could be employed as part of a lifting system to raise the materials needed for vault construction.

There is no reference in Villard—or, for that matter, in any of the later notebooks prior to the end of the fifteenth century—to any rules that might ensure sound structure. Rather, design techniques seem to have been almost wholly concerned with inscribing geometric figures—circles, squares, triangles, and octagons—to construct the configurations of architectural elements. This type of constructive geometry, rather than any form of mathematical computation, seems to have been all-important—the more so, as there is good reason to believe that the medieval builder was unfamiliar even with simple multiplication. Villard demonstrates the extensive use of this geometry in such matters as shaping a keystone of an arch or in employing similar triangles to measure the height of a great tower from observations taken on the ground. A number of medieval tracing

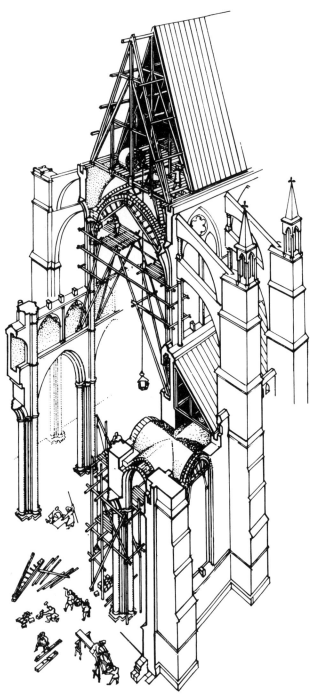

Gothic constructional technique. REPRODUCED FROM JAMES H. AC-LAND, MEDIEVAL STRUCTURE: THE GOTHIC VAULT, BY PERMISSION OF UNIVERSITY OF TORONTO PRESS, © UNIVERSITY OF TORONTO PRESS 1972

floors have been discovered, for example, on lead or stone surfaces over side-aisle roofs, where geometric constructions were carried out at full scale. But models and drawings used for design have survived only from the late Middle Ages.

To ensure stability—that is, the resistance of a building form against overturning or rotating to destruction under the action of gravity forces—the medieval master could have taken advantage of the fact that a small-scale model constructed similarly to the full-scale prototype would provide this information. Such a model, however, could not have been used to predict a building's overall structural performance because, as the scale of any structure is enlarged, its volume—and therefore its weight—increases by the cube of its length while the cross-sectional areas of its constituent elements increase only by the square. Hence, the larger structure is subjected to greater stresses from deadweight loadings in direct proportion to scale; for example, a structure of the same material and ten times the scale of the model will experience from its own weight ten times as much stress. It does not appear likely, moreover, that any small-scale technical modeling was performed. Nevertheless, building at full scale without modeling data was not so perilous as it might seem, since the facts of structural behavior, even if not fully grasped by the medieval builders, mitigated some of the problems of new, larger-scale design.

In the first place, the form and the method of construction of each new building retained many elements from earlier designs. By the twelfth century, building crews consisted of relatively well-paid, highly skilled teams of masons and carpenters and their supporting staffs, including the apprentices who maintained the continuity of these skills. The building organization that allowed apprentices to rise through the ranks and even to become master builder-designers ensured familiarity with earlier buildings. Indeed, the design progression illustrated by the building sections shown in the first illustration makes it clear that High Gothic architecture did not come into being "overnight." In effect, an earlier building often acted as an approximate "model" confirming the stability of the new, larger building.

The second mitigating factor derives from the high compressive, or crushing, strength of masonry. Granite, limestone, and sandstone were commonly used in medieval masonry construction. However, because of its general availability, good endurance, and relatively easy workability, limestone was most often used for load-bearing walls and piers. The compressive strength of limestone is quite variable. It is sensitive to such factors as the orientation of the applied force with respect to the inclination of the stone in its natural bed, in situ. Still, in almost all instances the range of tensile strengths—failure caused by stresses tending to pull the stones apart—is an order of magnitude less than the compression strengths, but the latter in turn are an order of magnitude greater than the tensile strengths of the mortar used as grout between the imperfectly finished surfaces of the ashlar. Hence, the strength of the masonry in compression rarely governs structural failure. Gross stability considerations and the absence or presence of tension within the weak mortar between the stones usually determine whether a masonry building is sound. These criteria also influence the choice of modern technical approaches used to analyze medieval structure. A particularly fruitful approach is mainly concerned with locating and assessing possible regions of tension in small-scale models that can then be scaled to predict tension within the mortar of the full-scale building.

Modeling of the long vessels of medieval cathedrals is facilitated by their repeating, modular bay design. The buildings can be considered to be supported by a series of parallel, transverse planar frames consisting of the principal load-bearing structural elements: piers, buttresses, lateral walls, and ribbed vaults. The ends of the linear vessel are usually of three-dimensional form, but because of the greater stiffness and strength of this type of structure, they are rarely subjected to the problems found in the more open, straight bay sections.

Structural forces within the masonry frame are also assumed to be distributed as they would be in an equivalent frame constructed from a perfectly elastic, homogeneous material. For this simplification to be applied to masonry, it must be assumed that the entire frame is undergoing compressive action—that is, that all the individual stones are pressed against adjacent stones by compressive forces within the interior of the structure. This assumption coincides with criteria for successful medieval masonry performance because of the extremely low tensile strength of medieval mortar. Hence, structural continuity cannot be maintained if any substantial amount of tensile stress is present. Studies of medieval buildings confirm that compressive stresses prevail and that there are usually only a few highly localized regions of tension.

A final assumption inherent in this type of analysis is that gravity begins to act only after the construction of the building is completed. This is not far from reality with respect to the vaulting and the flying buttresses. These were usually assembled on rigid centering and hence were not subject to deadweight loadings until their completion, when the

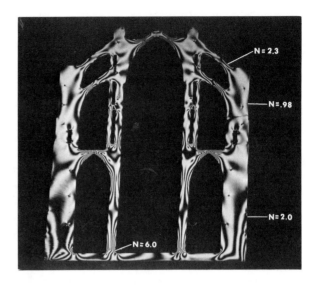

Photoelastic interference pattern in Amiens Nave section under simulated wind loading. The numbers give interference orders that relate to the intensity of internal forces in the structure. PHOTOGRAPH BY THE AUTHOR

centering was removed. At the other end of the time scale, deadweight loadings over the centuries can cause some unrecoverable plastic flow of the masonry. Nevertheless, if the basic support and form of a structure remain unchanged with time, the distribution of internal forces will be little altered from the initial elastic distribution indicated by the model.

The model may be a mathematical description of the building form set out in an electronic computer, or a physical model. A convenient approach to the latter is photoelastic modeling. With this technique epoxy models are loaded with arrays of weights representing the distributions of wind and deadweight forces acting on the building. The model is then viewed through polarizing filters; and the interference pattern, interpreted with calibration and scaling theory, can predict the force distributions in the full-scale structure.

Model studies of a series of medieval buildings have begun to provide new insights about medieval structural design. A study of the buttressing system of the nave of Amiens Cathedral revealed that the pinnacle placed atop the outer edges of the pier buttresses helped to maintain integrity of the buttress by overcoming local tension caused by the combination of deadweight and wind loadings: the weight of the pinnacle engenders compression in the pier buttress that cancels the tension. The pinnacle acts as a prestressing element. This finding is startling because the technical function of the pinnacle is masked by its overpowering decorative role and because gross stability considerations would have placed the pinnacle on the inside rather than the outside edge of the pier buttress.

How, then, can the sophistication of the placement of the Amiens pinnacles to prestress the outside edge of the pier buttress be explained? Examination of the model leads us to speculate that the medieval builder had available a parallel experimental method that embraced the full-scale building. Tensile cracking caused either by high winds or by the removal of temporary construction supports could have been observed in the newly set, weak lime mortar between the stones during the relatively long periods of construction. Successive modifications made to the structure to prevent mortar cracking could then have been the source of structural innovation, with the Amiens pinnacled pier buttress as an outstanding example.

A less sanguine view of the state of medieval design art emerged from a study of the influence of the choir of Bourges Cathedral on subsequent building. The Bourges choir, constructed contemporaneously with Chartres and of similar overall vessel dimensions, is a much simpler, lighter, and more daring structure than Chartres. But in spite of the technical superiority of Bourges to Chartres—or to any contemporary building—the form of its structure was not prescribed for any other major High Gothic church. Indeed, the original design was altered when the Bourges nave addition was begun by another master, a decade after the completion of the choir. In this instance, High Gothic builders did not appear to fully understand the principles and consequences of construction with flying buttresses. Even the original master's immediate successors at Bourges timidly altered his design of the bay section with no important structural gain, while others who followed his spatial program for the interior elevations of a number of important churches ignored the technical innovations of his work. Because the problems addressed by the experiment at Bourges were not well understood, the technical beauty of its solution appears to have been generally unappreciated.

However, it should not be inferred from this conclusion that builders did not continue to experiment with structure in later designs. That they did can be demonstrated by the great variation in the structural systems employed. This variation can be illustrated by examining the ratio of height to width (the "slenderness ratio") of a critical structural member from

Interior view of the nave. Cathedral of Palma, Majorca, begun mid 13th century. PHOTOGRAPH BY THE AUTHOR

a number of major cathedrals, namely, the main arcade pier supporting the clerestory wall. The table (facing page) reveals that the contemporary designs of Chartres and Bourges show as great a difference in the slenderness ratios of their piers as they do in almost every other element, and adds further credence to the observation that the designer of the Bourges choir was far more daring than the designer of Chartres. Through Rheims, Amiens, Cologne, and Beauvais, the most important High Gothic cathedrals following Chartres, there is a gradual increase in pier-slenderness ratio, a parameter not directly related to vault height (which ranges from 38 meters at Rheims to 48 meters at Beauvais) or to any other obvious vessel dimension.

At the giant cathedral of Palma on the island of Majorca the pier-slenderness ratio increases by almost 50 percent over any used previously, and the technical and visual difference is even more dramatic than the numbers convey. The piers of the earlier buildings are surrounded by attached shafts that were not accounted for in the table but that make the piers look much heavier and in fact do lend them considerable reinforcement. Palma's lithe masonry

Gothic Cathedral Pier Dimensions (in meters) and
Slenderness Ratios

Building Site	Height	Width	Slenderness Ratio
Chartres (nave)	8.0	1.6	5.0
Bourges (choir)	14.9	1.6	9.3
Rheims (nave)	9.6	1.6	6.0
Amiens (nave)	12.5	1.5	8.3
Cologne (choir)	11.9	1.3	9.2
Beauvais (choir)	14.6	1.5	9.7
Palma (nave)	22.0	1.6	13.8

Height is distance from top of base to bottom of capital—that is, straight section length of load-bearing, coursed construction.

Width is diameter for round piers and distance between flats for hexagonal piers.

piers have no attached shafts, and the result, striking even to a modern eye accustomed to thin reinforced concrete construction, must have appeared miraculous in the Middle Ages. Model testing of Palma has revealed that the designer accomplished an almost perfect (and almost miraculous) balancing of loadings applied to the great piers so that they do not bend from off-center forces.

The spirit of experimentation as exemplified at Palma seems to have largely disappeared with the end of the medieval era. One suggested reason for its loss is the intrinsic power of the new publications of the Renaissance. The writing down of design rules and the publication of drawings of existing buildings might have tended to codify design. Furthermore, once certain building types were established and rules for their construction accepted, there was little reason to modify them. This situation prevailed until the pressing needs of nineteenth-century industrial development and its introduction of new construction materials brought the more common use of scientific methods into structural design. After the fourteenth century, experimentation with building structure still took place, but it became rare and was usually confined to unusual structures for which there were no written rules.

BIBLIOGRAPHY

François Bucher, "Medieval Architectural Design Methods, 800–1500," in *Gesta,* **11** (1972); John Fitchen, *The Construction of Gothic Cathedrals* (1961); Jacques Heyman, "On the Rubber Vaults of the Middle Ages and Other Matters," in *Gazette des beaux-arts,* **71** (1968); John James, *The Contractors of Chartres,* II (1981); Douglas

Knoop and G. P. Jones, *The Medieval Mason,* 3rd ed. (1967); Robert Mark, "Structural Experimentation in Gothic Architecture," in *American Scientist,* 66 (1978); and *Experiments in Gothic Structure* (1982); Lon R. Shelby, *Gothic Design Techniques* (1977); Lon R. Shelby and Robert Mark, "Late Gothic Structural Design in the 'Instructions' of Lorenz Lechler," in *Architectura,* 9 (1979); Whitney S. Stoddard, *Monastery and Cathedral in France* (1966); William Taylor and Robert Mark, "The Technology of Transition: Sexpartite to Quadripartite Vaulting in High Gothic Architecture," in *Art Bulletin,* 64 (1982); Eugène-Emmanuel Viollet-le-Duc, "Construction," in *Dictionnaire raisonné de l'architecture française du XIe au XVIe siècle,* IV (n.d. [1859]), translated by George M. Huss as *Rational Building* (1895); Robert Willis, "On the Construction of the Vaults of the Middle Ages," in *Transactions of the Royal Institute of British Architects,* 1 (1842); and *Facsimile of the Sketch-Book of Wilars de Honecort* (1859).

ROBERT MARK

[See also **Amiens Cathedral; Chartres Cathedral; Construction: Building Materials; Gothic Architecture; Notre Dame de Paris (Cathedral); Rheims Cathedral; Vault; Villard de Honnecourt.**]

CONSULATE OF THE SEA. Laws and customs regulating maritime affairs in the Mediterranean seaports were codified in the later Middle Ages in several collections. The most famous is the *Llibre del consolat de mar,* compiled for the court of Barcelona around 1370.

At the beginning of the Middle Ages the maritime law generally accepted in the eastern Mediterranean was a combination of Byzantine and early Western customs and rules called the *Nomos Rodion nautikos* (Rhodian sea law). Developed piecemeal between the eighth and tenth centuries, the Rhodian Law laid the foundation for the medieval laws of navigation and commerce, particularly the principles of contribution for jettison and wreckage at sea. In the thirteenth century the Assizes of Jerusalem contained elements of Germanic law in maritime rules for the kingdoms of Jerusalem and Cyprus.

The oldest maritime legislation as such appeared in 1075 at Pisa, in a redaction of rules to settle disputes in seaports as far north as Marseilles. Pisa became a principal source of maritime law when a court called the *consulatus maris* (consulate of the sea) was established there between 1188 and 1201. Subsequently consulates of the sea were established in the principal ports of Italy, Sicily, southern France, and Spain to regulate the commercial affairs of seafarers by reference to unwritten customs, called *mercadanzias*. Maritime judges were known as consuls. In Genoa as early as 1154 traces of a primitive maritime law can be found; in 1206 there was a consulate of the sea, and in 1306 a written edition of maritime law. Under Doge Pietro Ziani (1205–1299) Venice set up a consulate of the sea with written statutes contained in the *Capitulare nauticum,* published in 1229 and 1255. These statutes were translated into Italian and published as part of the civil statutes of Venice in 1477.

Zara (Zadar), Spoleto, Cataro, Lesina (Hvar), Curzola (Korčula), and Melita (Sardinia) enacted maritime rules at the beginning of the fourteenth century. The laws of Trani date from the twelfth and thirteenth centuries, and were published in five editions at Fermo between 1509 and 1691 as *Ordinamenta et consuetudo maris edita per consules civitatis Tranis.* In Messina a maritime consulate dates to 1129; maritime legislation was enacted in Sicily between 1298 and 1300, and in Naples six collections of texts were prepared between 1239 and 1519.

The port cities of the North Sea and the Baltic—Schleswig, Riga, Wisby (Visby), Hamburg, Lübeck, and other cities of the Hanseatic League—adopted some of these laws as early as the tenth century. In the thirteenth and fourteenth centuries maritime laws, called *Waterrecht,* were published by the Hanseatic League. These laws are usually referred to as the Laws of Wisby. In the thirteenth century the French Laws of Oléron were promulgated by Louis IX. The English Black Book of the Admiralty dates from the thirteenth century.

The most famous of the consulates of the sea, at Valencia and Barcelona, trace their laws either to the thirteenth-century *Consuetudines et usus maris,* found in the episcopal archives of Vich, or to the maritime laws of Amalfi, which they were using certainly before the fourteenth century. Ordinances of Ramon Berenguer IV (1131–1162), the *Costums de la mar* of Valencia (1283–1343), and the *Costum de Tortosa* (before 1272) are the earlier, preconsular written sources of Spanish maritime law. All of these elements found their way into the earliest manuscript redaction of the *Llibre del consolat de mar,* after an earlier redaction, *Capitols del consolat de mar* (1343–1345), was made for the consulate of the sea in Palma, Majorca. The jurisprudence of the consulate of Barcelona spread to influence the development of maritime law in the entire Mediterranean world.

The classic edition of the Book of the Consulate of the Sea was compiled by Francis Celelles at Barcelona in 1494. It was quickly translated from the original Catalan into Castilian, French, and Italian as the authoritative source of maritime law. German and Dutch translations followed.

The manuscript consists of three separate codifications of statutes. Part I contains forty-three articles governing procedures used in the consular courts. Part II, articles 44–297, is a collection of the ancient customs of the sea. Part III, articles 298–334, contains rules relating to armed ships engaging in privateering and armed naval expeditions. An addendum comprises maritime ordinances of the kings of Aragon and of the city of Barcelona.

BIBLIOGRAPHY

Antonio de Capmany, ed., *Libro del consulado del mar,* with "Estudio preliminar" by José María Font Rius (1965); Luigi Genuardi, ed., *Il libro dei capitoli della corte del consolato di mare di Messina* (1924); Stanley S. Jados, trans., *Consulate of the Sea and Related Documents* (1975); Reginald G. Marsden, *Select Pleas in the Court of Admiralty,* 2 vols. (1892–1897); Travers Twiss, ed., *The Black Book of the Admiralty,* 4 vols. (1871–1876).

WILLIAM W. BASSETT

[See also **Admiralty, Court of.**]

CONSULS, CONSULATE. Consuls were officials who formed the supreme governing body of a town in northern Italy, southern France, and parts of Germany during the High Middle Ages. Although the name "consuls" was an echo of Roman times, such bodies of bourgeois were a completely medieval phenomenon quite like the *échevins,* aldermen, or lawmen who served in a similar capacity in urban centers in other parts of Europe.

Consuls seem to have appeared initially in Italy, where the first reference to them is at Pisa in 1081. By 1100 they were found in a number of other northern Italian towns, and by 1160 they reigned supreme in most urban centers north of Rome. In southern France they are first documented about 1130. For three decades thereafter they seem to have been concentrated in towns of Provence and Languedoc near the lower Rhône Valley. Only later, between 1190 and 1220, did they spread to new urban centers throughout the entire Midi south of Poitou and Burgundy.

Although consulates ceased to expand and to appear in new towns in Italy (and by 1220 in France), the institution had sufficient vitality to cross the Alps and reach cities in parts of Switzerland and Germany during the late twelfth century and to expand into parts of Gascony and just north of Lyons in the late thirteenth and early fourteenth centuries. Such later extensions, however, were short-lived and relatively unimportant.

There may have been some connection between the Italian consulates and the French. The fact that many Italian merchants arrived as traders in French communities could account for the appearance of consulates there. Also, there was a close connection between the spread of Roman law throughout the Midi and the appearance of consuls in its cities. The use of the Latin word *consul* seems to emphasize this connection.

It seems more probable, though, that both the spread of consulates and the geographical limits of this spread were more related to the political and socioeconomic factors that these two parts of Europe had in common than to some kind of automatic diffusion process. In both areas the appearance of consulates seems to coincide with the rise of new urban centers at a time when there was no effective central governing authority other than the resident bishops. In both regions they also first appeared during struggles between strong outside parties: the papacy and the empire in Italy, the house of Barcelona and the house of Toulouse in southern France, and later the northern French and the southern French during the Albigensian Crusade. And in towns of both areas one finds an unusual mixture of nobles, merchants, and artisans who furnished these communities with a special kind of leadership. All of this explains why, with a few exceptions, the Iberian Peninsula never developed consulates in its towns. Despite a similar mixture of noble and nonnoble, royal authority was too pervasive; there were too few seigneurial bishops; and there was insufficient internal conflict to provide a fertile soil for consular government.

The great age of Italian consulates was between 1150 and 1250, during the reigns of emperors Frederick I Barbarossa, Henry VI, and Frederick II, when consuls led their towns into combinations such as the Lombard League, thus winning considerable independence for themselves and their surrounding districts (*contados*). After this period, and in some cases even earlier, they tended to lose authority within their own towns to other forces. Sometimes this was due to a rise of one-man rule, legal or illegal in nature, and exercised by an outside noble or a specially chosen *podestà* (mayor). Or it came about because consulates found themselves unable to control competing internal organizations, such as associations of nobles with their fortified towers, or broad *populari* groups representing the mass of population and led by specially chosen captains. All of these factors so undermined consular authority almost everywhere in Italy that by 1300 consulates disappeared and were replaced by various forms of one-man rule or *signoria*.

In France consulates were never able to exercise comparable authority except briefly, at the time of the Albigensian Crusade, in Toulouse, Montpellier, and Marseilles. By 1231 this flurry of consular independence had been ended by Raymond VII of Toulouse and James I of Aragon in the first two cities, and some years later by Charles of Anjou in Marseilles.

Consulates continued in the Midi, though they had to share their urban authority with the great princes of the region and to turn to them for help in suppressing the popular elements in their communities that, as in Italy, were eager to seize power. By 1300 they still survived in France, but as an increasingly less important element in a realm that was steadily coming under the control of the centralized royal bureaucracy.

BIBLIOGRAPHY

France. André Gouron, "Diffusion des consulats méridionaux et expansion du droit romain aux XII⁰ et XIII⁰ siècles," in *Bibliothèque de l'École des chartes*, **121** (1963); John Mundy, *Liberty and Political Power in Toulouse, 1050–1230* (1954); Pierre Timbal, "Les villes de consulat dans le Midi méditerranéen au moyen âge," in *Recueils de la Société Jean Bodin*, **6** (1955).

Germany. Philippe Dollinger, "Les villes allemandes au Moyen Age," ibid.

Italy. Paolo Brezzi, *I comuni medioevali nella storia d'Italia* (1959); Philip J. Jones, "Communes and Despots: The City-State in Late Medieval Italy," in *Transactions of the Royal Historical Society*, 5th ser., **15** (1965); Daniel Waley, *The Italian City-Republics* (1969).

Spain. José María Font Rius, *Orígenes del régimen municipal de Cataluña* (1946).

ARCHIBALD R. LEWIS

[See also **Aldermen; Commune; Échevin; Italy, Rise of Towns in; Podestà; Urbanism, Western European.**]

CONTE DEL LELLO ORLANDI

CONTE DEL LELLO ORLANDI, Italian sculptor and metalsmith, was active in the first half of the Trecento. In 1335/1336 he signed a grate for the transept of S. Croce in Florence and in 1337–1338 he and his son Giacomo executed and signed the wrought-iron nave screen for the Duomo in Orvieto. His signature is found on a wrought-iron screen door of the Capella di Piazza in the Siena Duomo. He also signed a similar screen for the Chiesa del Loretino in San Miniato al Tedesco.

BIBLIOGRAPHY

Ulrich Thieme and Felix Becker, *Allgemeines Lexikon der bildenden Künstler,* VII (1912); John White, *Art and Architecture in Italy, 1250–1400* (1966), 299–300, 328.

ADELHEID M. GEALT

[See also **Metalworking.**]

CONTRACEPTION, EUROPEAN

MEANS

Root potions believed to prevent conception were known to the peoples of the Roman Empire and to the Celts and Germans who came to inhabit Europe. The eleventh-century *Canon of Medicine* of Ibn Sīnā contained most of the contraceptive pharmacopeia of the ancient world, ranging from spermicides for men to potions for women, and failed only in not discriminating the proved from the plausible. Translated into Latin in the twelfth century, used as the standard textbook to teach medicine in Europe, and uncensored, Ibn Sīnā was the basis for popular herbals naming plants with contraceptive properties and for other medical works alluding to contraception, such as John of Gaddesden's *Rosa anglica.* The Bible itself, in the story of Onan (Gen. 38:8–10), provided information on coitus interruptus. Anal and oral intercourse, as the penitentials indicate, were known. Sexual intercourse without conception was, in short, possible in a variety of effective and ineffective ways.

MOTIVES

Economic motive existed in the desire of the rich to restrict their heirs and of the needy not to increase their burdens: Burchard of Worms speaks of "a poor little woman" preventing conception because of "the difficulty of feeding" (*Decretum,* 19). Therapeutic reason existed if a woman's health could not stand another pregnancy (see Peter the Chanter, *Summa de sacramentis,* III², 463). Sexual motive existed in the desire to conceal adultery or fornication, and prostitutes had professional reason to avoid conception. Religious motive existed among the Cathars, who regarded procreation as the devil's work. Hostile magic also employed sterilizing potions, called *maleficia* (Regino of Prüm, *De ecclesiasticis disciplinis,* 89).

PRACTICE

Action branded as sinful in Europe and naturally secret, never studied by surveys or documented by public records, practice must be a matter of inference. In both Islam and Christendom the combination of occasionally effective means and often powerful motives makes it certain that contraception was sometimes practiced; it is probable, however, that Ibn Sīnā's remedies were more often tried in Damascus than in Paris. European secular law does not focus on contraception as a problem. Chaucer is exceptional among secular authors in referring to a woman "drynkynge venenouse herbes thrugh which she may not conceyve" (Parson's Tale, "De ira," lines 579–580). Chaucer's source, however, is theological, and it is European theologians who show the greatest interest in such acts. To a substantial extent their interest is inherited—that is, they work with a concept found in their tradition; to a lesser degree they appear to be responding to actual contraceptive practice.

Unnatural intercourse, a notion often including coitus interruptus as well as anal and oral intercourse, was treated as a serious sin not only by the standard theologians but also, sometimes, in vulgarizations for the laity such as *Jacob's Well* (*ca.* 1425) and in preaching such as that of St. Bernardino of Siena. St. Catherine of Siena's somber vision of those now in hell "who sinned in the married state" reflects the conviction that in such an urban center as Siena deliberately nongenerative marital intercourse was not infrequent. In the Cathar-infiltrated culture of Montaillou, evidence of practice—whether magical or effective—has been found by E. Leroy Ladurie. Contraception, one may conclude, was known and practiced throughout the Middle Ages, not everywhere, not by everyone, and not with assured effectiveness, but locally, occasionally, and with varied success.

THEOLOGICAL AND CANONICAL TREATMENT

For medieval Judaism the Babylonian Talmud permitted contraception in a few therapeutic cases while generally teaching that Onan's act was unnatural (*Yevamot* 34b). The Koran took no position on contraception, and Islam did not reject the means developed by Arabic medicine. Christianity, both Byzantine and Western, condemned contraception.

Christian condemnation had been formed in part as a defense of human life (it was difficult to distinguish contraceptives from abortifacients; a sharp line between semen and early embryo had not been drawn biologically); in part as a defense of marriage and procreation (denied as values by Gnostics and Manichaeans); in part as a defense of the dignity of woman and the integrity of marriage (challenged by contraceptive sexual exploitation, by prostitution and adultery). The crystallized Christian position was transmitted to the Middle Ages by the Vulgate, in which Genesis 38:10 described Onan's destruction by God for his "detestable deed" and Galatians 5:20 repudiated *veneficia* (bad medicine), including abortifacients and contraceptives. The condemnation was also found in the teaching of the church fathers, both East (St. John Chrysostom) and West (St. Jerome). In the West St. Augustine's anti-Manichaean polemic against contraception and his anti-Pelagian assertion of procreation as the justifying purpose of marital intercourse were of especial importance.

Caesarius of Arles and Martin of Braga both denounced contraception. The penitentials of the eighth century and the ninth-century diocesan legislation of Theodulf of Orléans condemned it. The twelfth century inherited a tradition of abhorrence and, against the threat of a rising Cathar movement perceived as the reenactment of the Manichaeans, Augustine's major text against contraception was installed in the canon law (*Concordia discordantium canonum* 2.32.2.7, the canon *Aliquando*) and in the standard theological textbook (Peter Lombard, *Sententiae*, 4.31.3).

The canon law of the thirteenth century completed this condemnation with *Si aliquis* (*Decretales* of Gregory IX, 5.12.5), treating the employment of contraceptive potions as homicide, and with *Si conditiones* (4.5.3) treating as null a marriage in which the couple agreed to avoid having children. Major canonists and theologians of the later Middle Ages—Hostiensis, Albertus Magnus, John Gerson, St. Antoninus—expounded the evil of contraception in the context formed by scriptural, patristic, and canonical rejection. The analysis of Thomas Aquinas is typical: natural coitus was instituted by God; man should not alter it; if he does so, he injures the social good of the species, and he injures God, the ordainer of nature (*Summa theologica*, 2–2.154.12).

The condemnation of contraception coexisted with other concepts and values pointing in a different direction. Christian theology was not unreservedly philoprogenitive. Fornication was objected to because it would produce children without homes; the value of procreating children was not disjoined from their education (Aquinas, *On 1 Corinthians 7:1*). Implicitly, in both these positions quality was rated higher than quantity of offspring; a tension was set up between the procreation of many children and the education of fewer children. Further, following the teaching of 1 Corinthians 7, some theologians affirmed the value of marital intercourse apart from procreation; Albertus Magnus suggested a sacramental value in marital intercourse, and the Franciscan Richard Middleton saw no sin in seeking moderate delight therein.

Although Chaucer's Cenobia, who would not have intercourse with her husband during pregnancy (the Monk's Tale), is more typical of the dominant theology, plainly a minority position was tenable. In the fifteenth century strong voices defended the married "who mutually love each other because of the mutual pleasure they have in the marital act" (Denis the Carthusian, *De laudabili vita coniugatorum*, 8) and even intercourse for "pleasure" (Martin Le Maistre, *Quaestiones morales*, 2, 51v). These strands of medieval scholastic teaching—the importance of the education of children, the value of marital intercourse in itself—were elements from which, at a later time, a different judgment on contraception could arise.

BIBLIOGRAPHY

Individual medieval authors do not treat contraception at length but refer to it occasionally and in passing. Further documentation is in John T. Noonan, Jr., *Contraception: A History of Its Treatment by the Catholic Theologians and Canonists* (1965). See also Pedro Abellán, *El fin y la significación sacramental del matrimonio desde S. Anselmo hasta Guillermo de Auxerre* (1939); Leopold Brandl, *Die Sexualethik des heiligen Albertus Magnus* (1955); Louis Flandrin, *L'église et le contrôle des naissances* (1970); E. Leroy Ladurie, *Montaillou, village occitan* (1975), 247–248; Dominikus Lindner, *Der Usus matrimonii* (1929).

JOHN T. NOONAN, JR.

[See also **Family, Western European; Sīnā, Ibn.**]

573

CONTRACEPTION, ISLAMIC. Medieval Arabic sources show that birth control was sanctioned by Islamic law and opinion, that relatively effective methods were available, and that Muslims recommended contraception for social, economic, medical, and personal reasons. Islamic jurisprudence, scientific medicine, belles lettres *(adab),* and materia medica each dealt with birth control in a way that reflected its own preoccupations. Jurisprudence and popular literature were generally directed toward male practice; medicine and materia medica, toward female.

Muslim jurists dealt principally with coitus interruptus, historically the most common method. From the tenth to the nineteenth century, there was a remarkable consensus among jurists of all historical schools that coitus interruptus was licit with a free woman—provided she gave her permission. Women were considered to have rights (to children and complete sexual fulfillment) that withdrawal was judged to diminish. The jurists were not concerned with female contraceptives as a legal problem, and occasional references to them were primarily a reflection of social practice. Jurisprudence was distinguished by its concentration on coitus interruptus, and equally by its disregard of potions and magic. It contains the best evidence anywhere for male involvement in premodern birth control.

Arabic medical writers devoted special chapters to contraception and abortion, always paying attention to birth control as a normal part of the physician's art. The primary Arabic medical text is al-Rāzī's *al-Ḥāwī,* or *Liber continens,* which contains all of Greek and Arabic medical knowledge of birth control, from which later physicians depart only rarely. The dominant technique in the *Ḥāwī,* and in Arabic medicine in general, was a female method involving a suppository or tampon, which functioned by impeding the entrance of sperm into the cervical os, plugging the vagina, or changing the alkaline or acid condition of the vagina and uterus.

Ibn Sīnā's *al-Qānūn,* or *Canon,* is a document of the medieval culture of Europe as well as of the Middle East. The Latin version contains Ibn Sīnā's birth control material and shows no sign of censorship. But when Europeans wrote about contraception, they invariably used the circumlocution "poisons of sterility," that is, herbal potions. Ibn Sīnā provided twenty specific contraceptives, mostly intravaginal suppositories and tampons, and only one potion. The European writers who used Ibn Sīnā were unwilling to pass on his specific prescriptions, and

when they said that the *Canon* had a chapter on "poisons of sterility," they suppressed Ibn Sīnā's techniques quite effectively.

Arabic medicine paid equal attention to abortion and used the same reasons to justify both contraception and abortion. All the indications were purely medical—religious permission of contraception had left the physicians free to mention only the reasons proper to their profession. They advanced two principal reasons: contraception or abortion were indicated when the woman was young (fifteen or under), or when a disease or abnormality of the uterus was suspected.

Although medieval physicians paid extraordinary attention to birth control, the most significant method was coitus interruptus; and it was Islamic jurisprudence, not medicine, that contained detailed information on this technique. Dealing as they did with the practical consequences of contraception (for example, the problem of unwanted children), jurists knew as much about it as did the physicians. Islamic jurisprudence is not only our primary guide to religious and social attitudes but also an indispensable source for the premodern means of control.

The difference between man and the other animals is that only man practices contraception. Al-Jāḥiẓ made this distinction in his *Book of Animals,* a ninth-century classic of Arabic literature, and *adab* continued its interest in contraception as in the works of Ibn Qutayba, al-Raghib al-Iṣfahānī, and al-Nuwayrī. Erotica was that branch of *adab* which concentrated on sexuality and usually gave birth control a separate chapter of its own.

Many prescriptions in erotica and *adab* reflected a separate popular tradition. Erotica-*adab* recognized female contraceptives, but this male-oriented literature rather emphasized contraceptive ointments to cover the penis (53 percent of all references). The pronounced fascination with this technique, which could not possibly have been as effective as withdrawal, perhaps reflects the old search for a more agreeable male contraceptive.

Materia medica also drew on the popular, nonscientific tradition, and many magical or fantastic recipes were the rejects of scientific medicine. The physicians had selected their own prescriptions from the mixed mass of materia medica on the basis of a clear preference for direct physical or chemical means of control. Out of fifty contraceptives in the *Ḥāwī* only one was magical, and al-Rāzī reported it as hearsay. The most significant characteristic of materia medica is that, except for one drug (wood tar), it recognized only female contraceptives. This nearly exclusive emphasis on female contraceptives makes one wonder whether most persons requiring this service were women.

The Koran, unlike the Bible, did not mention contraception and therefore never figured directly in the Islamic legal discussion. The sayings of the Prophet, mostly permissive, were not decisive by themselves. It seems that Muslim jurists simply used the *ḥadīth* (the recognized reports of the Prophet's words and actions) together with the available biological knowledge to reach an agreement that contraception was licit.

The Muslims knew that Judaism prohibited coitus interruptus. They believed that the Jewish prohibition rested on the erroneous assumption that coitus interruptus was foolproof: "Coitus interruptus does not stop pregnancy altogether as abstention would, but it is effective in reducing it" (Ibn Qayyim). Even with the most careful use of medieval contraceptive techniques, unwanted pregnancies occurred frequently. To the Muslims this gap between intention and achievement left ample room for God's will to operate. In one representative *ḥadīth*, asked about coitus interruptus, the Prophet answered, "Do as you please, whatever God has willed will happen, and not all semen result in children." The possibility of failure was thus essential to the argument for permission.

The most thorough statement of the Islamic position was made by al-Ghazālī, whose cardinal argument was the lawfulness of the act of withdrawal itself. According to him, in the process of conception the two male and female emissions were analogous to the two elements "offer" and "acceptance" that constitute a legal contract in Islamic law. Someone who submits an offer and then withdraws it before acceptance is not guilty of any violation, for a contract does not exist until it is accepted. On the basis of this argument all methods of contraception that stopped the semen from reaching the uterus could be permitted.

Ghazālī's emphasis on the equal contribution of both parents to the formation of the fetus pervaded all Islamic thought, and the remarkable consensus that contraception was licit is difficult to understand completely without it. Ghazālī called the male semen "nothing" unless it united with the female semen and "settled" in the womb. Qurṭubī in his commentary on the Koran did not mince words: "the semen is nothing definite, and it is of no consequence if a woman gets rid of it before it settles in the womb."

In Islamic thought no special sanctity was attached to the semen as such, and some orthodox jurists were able to permit even masturbation.

Attitudes toward abortion depended even more directly on ideas regarding the stages of fetal development. The fundamental question for the religious law was: at what point of development is the fetus a human being? The Muslims believed that point to be the end of the fourth month of pregnancy, when the fetus was ensouled, and many jurists permitted abortion until that stage.

Medieval Muslims advanced various explicit reasons for birth control: to avoid the material hardships of a large number of dependents; to safeguard property; to guarantee the education of a child; to protect a woman from the dangers of childbirth, especially if she was young or sickly, or simply to preserve her health and beauty; to avoid fathering children who will be born slaves; to protect a nursing infant from the ill effects of a new pregnancy; and, most generally, from fear of "bad times."

Without statistical data, it is difficult to gauge the impact of birth control as a factor in demographic change; no doubt mortality was more important in determining population size in the medieval Middle East. But even if birth control had a very small impact, it deserves special attention because it was the most directly volitional factor. Observations that birth control was a proper reaction to the perilously shifting conditions of life reveal a temperament that must have affected behavior in other areas of social and economic life.

BIBLIOGRAPHY

A comprehensive account is B. F. Musallam, *Sex and Society in Islam: Birth Control Before the Nineteenth Century* (1983).

B. F. MUSALLAM

[See also **Arabic Literature; Family, Islamic; Medicine, History of; Sīnā, Ibn; Rāzī, al-**.]

CONTRAFACTUM, in the vocabulary of the musicologist, means the substitution of one text for another while retaining the same, or nearly the same, music. As such, it is most often applied to the very common practice of composing new poems to existent melodies in the repertories of vernacular song in the twelfth and thirteenth centuries. The practice was equally common in the repertory of plainchant, however, where the texts of newer feasts were routinely adapted to older melodies. Many sequence and hymn melodies were likewise reused many times in the Middle Ages and beyond. Text substitution was also practiced in medieval polyphony, though it was perhaps less common. A number of thirteenth century motets, for instance, are preserved with both Latin and Old French texts, and some polyphonic conducti are transmitted with different texts.

Although it goes beyond the boundaries of contrafactum proper, it should be noted that the constant reuse of older sacred melodies was so fundamental to both the technique and the spirit of medieval polyphony that it was not really a special usage. Contrafactum must be viewed within the larger context of medieval music, in which originality often meant less than reference to established authority.

The word "contrafactum" was not part of the classical language but did appear, normally in the verb form *contrafacere,* in medieval texts to mean imitation in general, often with the negative connotation of counterfeit, its nearest English cognate. The earliest use of the term "contrafactum" in a musical context is in a fifteenth-century German manuscript, where it refers to the "conversion" of secular verses to devotional purposes. This has led some scholars, particularly in Germany, to restrict the term to such secular-to-sacred conversions.

It is unclear whether this fifteenth-century German rubric may be understood as referring to the music at all, and thus the modern term must be considered a neologism. As such, it has been used in a variety of ways. Beyond the secular-to-sacred meaning, there is no general agreement about when a contrafactum becomes a free adaptation, or when conscious adaptation becomes coincidental similarity. Strict contrafactum would be the deliberate imitation of an existent poem, as in Gautier de Coincy's "Amours dont sui espris," which uses the melody and the first line of Blondel de Nesle's "Amours dont sui espris." More common is the contrafactum that employs an older melody but has a text that leaves room for doubt about the intentions of its author. In such cases we cannot know whether a contrafactum is a conscious and deliberate imitation or simply casual reuse of a well-known melody or common melodic type.

A potentially valuable source of information about medieval music lies in the discovery of textual contrafacta. The scarcity of authentic melodies for the German *Minnesang* has led some scholars to supply melodies from trouvère or troubadour songs when the German poems match the poems of those songs in form, rhyme scheme, and, sometimes, content. Such methods must be used with great care, however, since songs with totally different melodies may employ identical rhyme and metric schemes. Beyond this, the discovery of musical contrafacta may provide important information about dating, chronology, and the interrelationship of otherwise separate repertories.

A number of melodies enjoyed great popularity in the Middle Ages. The melody to Blondel's "Amours dont sui espris," for instance, was used for three Latin conducti, two of them set to music contrapuntally. The eleventh-century sequence "Laetabundus exsultet fidelis chorus" inspired countless sacred and secular contrafacta and freer adapatations, both in Latin and in the vernacular languages. The melody of Bernart de Ventadorn's spring song "Can vei la lauzeta mover" was used for new songs in Latin, German, and French. While "contrafactum" in this sense is not medieval, the phenomenon that it describes is one of the most characteristic features of medieval music. Since the practice was so common and natural a feature of medieval music, it is not surprising that it required no special term and no justification or theoretical discussion.

BIBLIOGRAPHY

Ursula Aarburg, "Melodien zum frühen deutschen Minnesang," in Hans Fromm, ed., *Der deutsche Minnesang* (1961); Robert Falck, "Contrafactum," in *Handwörterbuch der musikalischen Terminologie* (1971), and "Parody and Contrafactum: A Terminological Clarification," in *Musical Quarterly,* 65 (1979); Friedrich Gennrich, *Die Kontrafaktur im Liedschaffen des Mittelalters* (1965).

ROBERT FALCK

[See also **Gregorian Chant; Music, Western European.**]

CONTRATENOR, in its English usage, is the name given to a high and distinctive range of the male voice, the use of which was revived in the twentieth century by such singers as Alfred Deller. This range, though almost certainly used in the Middle Ages, was not referred to by the Latin word. It literally means "against the tenor." "Tenor" and "contratenor" were not, as they are now, specific ranges of the voice, but referred to particular melodic lines of a piece and the function they played in its melodic, harmonic, and rhythmic structure. The contratenor evolved in fourteenth-century French polyphonic music and spread to English music in the later part of the century. Unlike other melodic parts, which were usually added above the tenor, it occupied the same range as the tenor.

There were two kinds of contratenor. The first appears mostly in secular part music of the period. Here the voice is not essential to the structure of the music: the tenor and the upper part(s) with the text form a piece of music that is correct and complete in the "grammatical" sense. To this texture the contratenor adds notes above or below the tenor, to fill out the harmonies, and supplies rhythmic movement where the other voices have none. Both its melodic and its rhythmic shape are determined in advance by the other parts, and thus are different in style: the melody is characterized by large leaps, often straddling the tenor; the rhythm is erratic, moving where necessary. An important consequence of the distinctive melodic style is the "octave-leap cadence." Because of the unwieldy melodic and rhythmic characteristics and the lack of text, some scholars assert that the line would have been played on an instrument rather than sung; others maintain that special singers performed such parts.

In the fifteenth century the range of the line was expanded, and eventually the notes above the tenor and those below it were divided between two parts. The upper of these was called the high contratenor (*contratenor altus*) and the other the low contratenor (*contratenor bassus*). The origin of the modern voice names is clear. Because the contratenor was not an essential part of the composition, it could be left out in performance, or alternative contratenor parts for the same piece could be provided, sometimes by later composers.

The second kind of contratenor was used mostly in motets of the fourteenth and early fifteenth centuries. Its range is the same as that of the tenor, but it has melodic and rhythmic features similar to those of the tenor: the two parts cross freely, but in this style the tenor and contratenor seem to have been thought of as a unit, perhaps composed before the upper parts and providing a harmonic foundation above which they could be added. The contratenor, for example, sings notes that are grammatically essential.

Both kinds of contratenor reflect a trend away from composition in which melodies are added to each other and toward one in which a consideration of chords was becoming more important.

BIBLIOGRAPHY

Anonymous XI, "Ars contratenoris," in Edmond de Coussemaker, ed., *Scriptorum de musica medii aevi*, III (1869, repr. 1963); Kurt Gudewill, "Contratenor," in *Die Musik in Geschichte und Gegenwart*, II (1952); K. von Fischer, "Les compositions à trois voix chez les compositeurs du trecento," in *L'ars nova italiana del trecento*, I, Bianca Becherini, ed. (1962); Andrew Hughes, "Some Notes on the Early Fifteenth-century Contratenor," in *Music and Letters*, 50 (1969).

ANDREW HUGHES

[See also **Ars Nova; Cadence; Tenor** .]

CONVENT. See **Monastery.**

CONVERSO, Spanish term for a convert, forced or otherwise, from Judaism to Christianity; the term was used almost exclusively to refer to converted Jews (and their descendants). Although such conversions occurred in medieval Spain long before the establishment of the Inquisition, the converso problem acquired a unique historical importance in the Spanish kingdoms as the history of these converted Jews became intertwined with the work of the reinvigorated Spanish Inquisition in the late 1400's and afterward.

Although there had been Jewish conversions to Christianity in late Roman and early Visigothic Spain, after Recared I, king of the Visigoths (586–601), turned from Arianism to the Roman confession, a good number of Jews converted, many of them under duress. After the Muslim conquest of Spain in 711, the Jews knew a period of relative respite from persecution, and this did not change radically when a large number of them came under Christian rule after the Castilian conquest of Toledo in 1085. Nevertheless, by the late thirteenth century deteriorating economic conditions, a widespread rise in anti-Semitic sentiments, and the impact of failed Messianic expectations among the Jews led to some significant conversions. Notable among them was that of Abner of Burgos, who under the name of Alfonso of Valladolid wrote a polemical tract (*The Wars of the Lord*) against his former coreligionists.

In 1391 and in the early fifteenth century violent persecutions took place throughout the Spanish lands, and thousands of Jews converted, often out of fear. In the next two centuries these recent converts gained an important foothold among the ruling oligarchies of Castile, connected themselves with most of the prominent noble families of Spain, and enjoyed a significant share of ecclesiastical benefices. Their social, political, and economic prominence soon brought them into open conflict with the "Old Christians." It also led the Inquisition to look more closely into their activities and to cast doubt on the sincerity of their faith. Racial hatred, social hostility, and fear of the conversos' prominence, as well as the conversos' desire to prove the truth of their conversion may both have been among the causes leading to the expulsion of the remaining Jews from Spain in 1492. The history of that nation for two centuries afterward continued to be marred by this conflict between "Old" and "New" Christians, by societal suspicion of conversos, and by the enactment of statutes of cleanliness of blood aimed at the exclusion of conversos from the profitable ranks of the military orders.

BIBLIOGRAPHY

Henry Kamen, *The Spanish Inquisition* (1965); Antonio Domínquez Ortiz, *Los conversos de orígen judío después de la expulsión* (1957).

TEOFILO F. RUIZ

[See also **Anti-Semitism; Inquisition; Jews in Christian Spain; New Christians**.]

CONVOCATIONS OF CANTERBURY AND YORK.

The convocations of Canterbury and York are the provincial synods of the church in England, held in accordance with the series of canons governing such bodies, beginning with those of the Council of Nicaea (325). The separation of the two provinces in England was slow to establish itself, and was affected by the many changes of kingdoms and political boundaries before 1066. After the Norman Conquest the provincial boundaries became clearer and the organization of the church more fully developed. It is unlikely that the law requiring provincial synods to meet twice a year was observed in England any more than it was on the Continent, but such councils were held from time to time during the eleventh and twelfth centuries.

From early in the reign of Henry III the meeting of provincial synods became more frequent in England as elsewhere, under the impetus provided by the Fourth Lateran Council (1215). The Council of Lambeth held by Archbishop of Canterbury Stephen Langton at Oxford in 1222 marked a significant stage in the legislation of the English church; it is with the canons of this council that most medieval collections of the English provincial canons begin.

The same period saw the beginning of a long struggle by the clergy against attempts on the part of both the papacy and the crown to tax them. The bishops were unwilling or unable to commit the rest of the clergy in this matter, and this led the archbishop of Canterbury to summon a number of assemblies, distinct from the provincial synods, for the purpose of obtaining consent to taxation. These assemblies included representatives of the cathedrals, religious houses, and the lower clergy. The reign of Edward I (1272–1307) was a time of especially sharp conflict, which continued in the earlier years of his successor, Edward II. During the first decade of the reign of Edward III (1327–1377), a working arrangement seems to have been reached, by which the archbishop, on receiving a request from the king, would summon a representative clerical assembly, which usually granted a tax on clerical revenues.

The canon law concerning provincial synods makes clear that these are primarily synods of bishops, and that in the synod it is the bishops alone who are the legislators and the judges. The canon law also provides that the chapters of the cathedrals should be given the opportunity to attend, and at most English provincial synods there was a rather miscellaneous attendance of deans, archdeacons, abbots, priors, and other clerical administrators. Eventually the summoning of the taxing assemblies began to influence the composition of the provincial synods. The bishops remained the only essential members, serving as both judges and legislators, but the attendance of other members of the clergy gradually became formalized along lines similar to the taxing assemblies. A climax of this development was reached in 1342 when Archbishop John Stratford sent out a citation for a provincial synod or council to meet at St. Paul's Cathedral, London, on 14 October, and a few days after the issue of that citation sent another summoning a taxing assembly to meet at St. Paul's on 9 October. The same persons were summoned in each citation, but whereas attendance of the lower clergy was optional for the provincial synod, it was compulsory for the taxing assembly. During the remainder of the century a gradual fusion of the two bodies took place, and by the time of Archbishop Henry Chichele (1414–1443) it was complete.

The provincial synod is generally referred to in the medieval English documents as *concilium provinciale*. The taxing assembly was most usually called *convocatio*. That is the title that came to prevail, but the body known by the end of the Middle Ages as "convocation" clearly has a double root. It is really the ancient provincial synod, its membership greatly expanded and formalized by its fusion with a body that came into being for the purpose of obtaining clerical consent to taxation. Once the fusion of the two had taken place, the lower clergy's right of giving or withholding consent began to extend to other business besides taxation. It is this characteristic above all that distinguishes the English provincial synods from those of other parts of the Western church.

The development of the provincial synod is most fully documented for the province of Canterbury, and it is the legislation of that province that forms the bulk of the legislation of the medieval English church. There was a parallel development in the province of York. That province, though geographically large, contained only three dioceses, compared with Canterbury's eighteen. Moreover, there was constant rivalry between the archbishop of York and his powerful and prestigious suffragan, the bishop of Durham. The diocese of Carlisle was small by comparison, much liable to depredations by the Scots, and its bishops frequently resided outside the province. At York, therefore, the personal attendance of the bishops was not frequent, and the convocation was often presided over by the archbishop's vicar-general. It was summoned for taxation purposes at roughly the same time as the Convocation of Canterbury, and there is less evidence of conflict.

From the fourteenth century the composition of the two convocations was approximately the same. The bishops of the province were required to attend or to send representatives. The deans of cathedral chapters and priors of cathedral monasteries were summoned along with the archdeacons and the majority of abbots or priors of religious houses, excluding the mendicant orders. Each cathedral chapter was to be represented by one proctor, and the clergy of each diocese by two. In the province of Canterbury the archbishop addressed his citation to the bishop of London, as dean of the province; the latter was responsible for transmitting it to the other bishops, who had to see that it was executed in their respective dioceses and to send in, or present in person at a meeting of the convocation, a list of those who had been cited and those elected. In the province of York the archbishop's citation went directly to the other bishops. In the dioceses there were often local conventions governing the election of proctors. For example, in dioceses with two archdeaconries one proctor was chosen for each archdeaconry. The clergy were summoned to various centers for the election, and the surviving evidence suggests that the persons elected were often diocesan officials.

The Canterbury convocation came more and more to function like Parliament, in two houses. The lower house consisted principally of the cathedral clergy, the archdeacons, and the elected proctors. They chose a spokesman, called prolocutor, who presided over their separate deliberations and reported their decisions to the archbishop and bishops in the upper house. The terms "upper" and "lower" appear to derive from the place in which the convocation usually met, the two-story chapter house of old St. Paul's Cathedral. The full synod met on the main floor, and the clergy withdrew to the lower floor, or undercroft, for their separate meetings. By contrast, the smaller York convocation seems normally to have met as one body in the chapter house at York.

In addition to legislating and taxing, the convocation acted as a court. In the first half of the fifteenth century the Canterbury convocation was the scene of several heresy trials, mostly connected with Lollardy.

The records of the sessions of convocation are chiefly found in the registers of the archbishops, but sometimes the episcopal registers and the letter books of monastic houses contain records of the summoning, the appointment of proctors, the tax granted and arrangements for collecting it, and constitutions made in the convocations.

BIBLIOGRAPHY

Eric Kemp, *Counsel and Consent* (1961); Frederick M. Powicke and Christopher R. Cheney, eds., *Councils and Synods*, II (1964); Dorothy B. Weske, *Convocation of the Clergy* (1937); David Wilkins, *Concilia magnae Britanniae et Hiberniae*, 4 vols. (1737).

ERIC KEMP

[See also **Church, Latin: Organization; Taxation, Church.**]

CONWAY, PEACE OF. The treaty called the Peace of Conway was drawn up on 9 November 1277 to end the war waged by Edward I of England against Llywelyn ap Gruffydd, prince of Wales. Under the terms, Llywelyn lost the four cantrefs of Per-feddwlad granted him by Henry III in the Treaty of Montgomery (1267) and all land acquired through conquest. He kept only Anglesey and the area above the Conway River, for which an annual rent of 1,000 marks was exacted and with the proviso that the land would revert to the crown if he died without heirs.

Of the five minor vassals Llywelyn was still allowed until his death, the two grandsons of Owain Brogyntyn of Dyffryn Edeirnion in Meirionnydd—Dafydd ap Gruffydd and Elise ab Iorwerth—were allies of the king. The remaining three were Owain Bleddyn's two sons, also from Edeirnion, and Rhys Fychan ap Rhys ap Maelgwn, who had lost his land in Ceredigion and had settled in Meirionnydd.

Llywelyn also agreed to make peace with his three brothers Owain Goch, Rhodri, and Dafydd and to free Owain ap Guffydd ap Gwenwynwyn, Rhys ap Gruffydd, Madog ab Einion, and Owain Brogyntyn's grandsons. Llywelyn settled Owain Goch in the Lleyn peninsula and paid Rhodri the balance owing from a 1,000-marks quitclaim promised him in 1272. Dafydd received reparation directly from Edward in the form of lands outside Gwynedd-Rhufoniog, Dyffryn Clwyd, and the lordship of Hope—and the hand of Elizabeth, daughter of the earl of Derby and widow of William Marshal of Norfolk. On Dafydd's death his land would also revert to the crown.

The treaty further stipulated that all disputes within the march of Wales would be settled by marcher law, while those within Wales would be subject to Welsh law.

As compensation for war damages Llywelyn was fined 50,000 pounds sterling. Both the fine and the 1,000 marks of annual tribute for his domains, however, were remitted by Edward after Llywelyn submitted in person to the king at Rhuddlan on the following day.

BIBLIOGRAPHY

The Latin text of the Peace of Conway is in *Littere Wallie*, John Goronwy Edwards, ed. (1940), 116–122. For English itemization and in-depth analysis of the Peace see Frederick Maurice Powicke, *King Henry III and the Lord Edward*, II (1947), 648–662. His entire chapter 15, 618–685, is excellent for understanding the treaty's background and aftermath. See too John E. Lloyd, *A History of Wales from the Earliest Times to the Edwardian Conquest*, II (1911), 746, 759–770.

MARILYN KAY KENNEY

[See also **Llywelyn ap Gruffydd; Wales, Later History.**]

COOK (COKE), HUMPHREY (*d.* 1531), English master carpenter active in Oxfordshire in the first third of the sixteenth century. Cook worked with the master masons William Vertue and Henry Redman; as the King's Chief Carpenter he roofed the Hall of Corpus Christi College, Oxford, in 1516 in the finest tradition of timber design. Among other works by Cook still preserved in the Oxford area is the roof at Christ Church College.

LESLIE BRUBAKER

COOKERY, EUROPEAN. Medieval European food was not coarse and crude, nor was it gorged by gluttons. Great varieties of food and drink were available in western Europe from the twelfth through the sixteenth centuries. Local harvests, meats, fish, and fowl, as well as imported spices, sauces, and wines were obtainable, augmenting domestic produce and appealing to commoner and nobleman alike. In fourteenth-century London, for instance, it was possible to purchase fifty-six types of French wine as well as thirty varieties of Italian, Spanish, and Canarian. The quality and price of all beverages and foods were carefully controlled by civil laws that were enforced in courts such as the assize of bread and the assize of ale.

Artistically prepared food was served with ceremony, satisfying political as well as social purpose. A royal entertainment, a guild festival, or a town holiday feast followed a pattern as elaborate as tradition, wealth, or whimsy allowed.

Ecclesiastical feasts often rivaled the secular in splendor. However, Christian concern for the spirituality of eating—ranging from the bread and wine of the Eucharist to moral disquisitions on gluttony as deadly sin—made the culinary calendar an alternation between feast and fast. Certain sects such as the Albigensians completely abjured meat. Some monastic communities were vegetarian, while others alternated flesh with vegetable diets, usually allowing their members to accept food gifts called pittances for holidays of particular sanctity. Since most Christians avoided meat at least one day a week (or as many as four), the required or desired abstinence inspired vegetarian variations on many dishes, substituting cheese, nuts, or grains for proscribed ingredients. Humorous clerical discourses distinguished animals classifiable as fish from prohibited mammals

Banquet. Woodcut from *Der Schatzbehalter*, Nuremberg, 1491.
THE METROPOLITAN MUSEUM OF ART, ROGERS FUND, 1919 (19.49.4)

raised on a dais; all others were arranged in descending social rank at long tables called sideboards. A fanfare announced the surveyor's presentation of the salt, an elaborately embellished salt cellar, signifying social place of the most noble—who thus sat "above the salt." The pantler, the officer in charge of bread, then cut the upper crust from a round, fragrant loaf, perhaps spiced and colored green with parsley, gold with saffron, or red with rose petal. It was presented to honor a guest (hence the term "upper crust"). The remaining loaves were carved into platters called trenchers. Absorbing juices and sauces during the meal, these slices were also eaten at the end of the feast, or saved to be toasted and floated the next day in breakfast wine, or given to the dogs or to the poor begging alms at the gate.

The butler or cupbearer then performed the credence test of the wine for purity and safety, by tasting it or utilizing a stone such as the bezoar, which changed color in the presence of poison. Next, the laverer poured warm herbed water from an animal-shaped pitcher called an aquamanile on the hands of each feaster. Hygiene as well as etiquette demanded laving: food was eaten with the fingers, and dining forks were disdained as foppish until the early sixteenth century. Elegant gestures intimated education and refinement. A specific finger and the thumb were used for a particular class of foods: forefinger for fish, middle finger for flesh, fourth for fowl, and the fifth was reserved, extended, for spices.

After grace, a fanfare signaled service of the first course. Small portions artfully alternated tastes, textures, colors, and fragrances. Pork, beef, and mutton dishes were no less common than ox, boar, beaver, and bear. Whale, seal, and porpoise were classified as fish and prepared accordingly. In addition to chicken, duck, and goose, more exotic birds such as curlew, lark, heron, and peacock were bountiful. Definitive demonstration of such variety is observable in various household account books, market laws, cookery texts, medical nutritional treatises, popular health handbooks, herbals, and commercial account books. A fourteenth-century Florentine document, for example, lists 288 "spices."

Fresh fruits and vegetables were served in season and preserved for winter, and were celebrated not only for their taste but also for their alleged salutary effect on mental hygiene. A celibate feaster, for example, delighting in rare roast beef wrapped in saffron-and-apple pastry (believed to be erotically stimulating) might subsequently quench his amorous ardor with a sensually cooling salad of lettuce tossed

and birds; the beaver, which culminates in an edible tail, was considered fish.

Medicine imposed important strictures on what should be eaten or avoided for good hygiene and how it should best be served for proper digestion. Diet, believed to help or hinder health, was not only used as therapy for disease but also was adjuvant to medication and surgery. Foods of love, sensual stimulants and depressants, were thought to regulate sexuality, as requisite to mental health as to spiritual well-being. Menus of medieval feasts were often guided as much by physicians and philosophers as by cooks and personal taste.

While details varied according to time, place, and purpose of celebration, a typical feast began with music, with the surveyor of ceremonies directing musicians to play until all guests were seated. The most honored guest was seated at the high table

Kitchen. Woodcut from Diederich's *Deutsches Leben I*, 1507. THE METROPOLITAN MUSEUM OF ART, ROGERS FUND

with golden pastry and topped with green marzipan leaves. Appraylere, seemingly an elaborate jewel-encrusted water pitcher, was a meatloaf sculpture, as was urcheon, made to look like a hedgehog—complete with pointed, almond quills. Peacock well roasted with cumin was served strutted and refeathered so as to look alive, its beak and claws gilded; cotton and camphor ignited in its mouth made it appear to breathe fire. Four-and-twenty-blackbird pie, safe for the tethered birds inserted after baking, was cut to cheers and fanfares, liberating the birds to fly around the hall.

Subtleties were sculpted from marzipan, painted pastry, or spun sugar and represented allegorical, historical, or contemporary subjects. They were displayed to great admiration and were eaten by the end of the meal. Those who could not afford their expense made edible table sculptures called entremets. Their purpose, like that of the popular allemaine, a cool soup or pudding presented in a huge tureen with a submerged juggler ready to leap out, was to delight by surprise.

Certain foods were generally served for their symbolic appeal at calendar feasts, such as heart-shaped love cakes on St. Valentine's Day or gingerbread Yule dolls at Christmas. Wedding feasts had requisite foods such as herbed eggs, spiced capon, and pomegranate wine, contrived to stimulate the couple's erotic desires. Funeral banquets also suited food to mood while satisfying guests' culinary requirements. The funeral banquet on 4 December 1424 for Nicholas Bibbesworth, bishop of Bath and Wells, offered capon, pork chop, swan, heron, woodcock, pheasant, lark, plover, snipe, and puff pastry to the secular mourners. But for the bishop's ecclesiastical colleagues there was herring, salmon, pike, perch, bream, minnow, crab, haddock, sole, and eel.

Since every food or drink was considered to have physiological effects, diet for general hygiene was augmented during illness by nutritional therapy. Food adjuncts to medication and surgery were thought to alleviate symptoms and prepare the body for incision or cauterization, and to promote the healing of wounds. Some chronic diseases were believed best managed by diet. Maimonides' *Treatise on Asthma* (1199), for example, recommended remarkably detailed menus, lists of encouraged or forbidden foods, cooking instructions, beneficial cuts of meat such as the fat-free foreparts, recipes for chicken soup, postprandial nut combinations, and honey wines to clear the bronchi and alveoli.

with chicory and rue. The effects of fruits considered to be aphrodisiac—fig, pomegranate, and pear— could be counteracted by capers, considered sexually depressant, cooked in light hemlock wine.

The modern misconception that fruits and vegetables were unfamiliar in the Middle Ages derives from a misreading of the medieval documents. Certain foods were forbidden not arbitrarily but for specific reasons. Asthmatics were enjoined to avoid foods that produced "cold and moist" phlegm, such as squash and melons. Fried and heavily spiced fruits and vegetables were prohibited for ca er patients, just as other nutrients were encourag for their therapeutic effect. Moreover, certain fruits were recommended as digestives and were routinely served at the end of meals.

Some foods were served not only as sustenance but also as entertainment and were crafted to present a deceiving appearance. Pommes dorées, simulating golden apples, were made of chopped veal wrapped

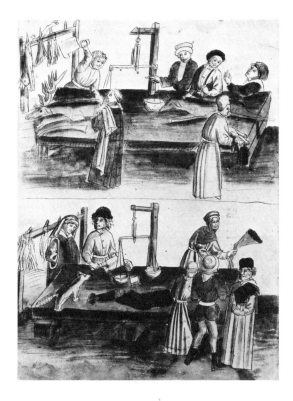

Butchers; scene from market life. From Ulrich von Richenthal, *Beschreibung des Constanzer Conziliums*, Germany, 1450–1470. NEW YORK PUBLIC LIBRARY, SPENCER COLLECTION

house, pantry, larder, brew house, and vinting chamber. Yet even a modest country house generally possessed a full complement of butchering tools, cooking utensils, and baking implements.

Transferring well-cooked, sauced, and decorated foods from kitchen to banquet table required a formidable number of servitors. Each of them had an identifying instrument of his craft, as well as special responsibilities in the theater of feasting. Smaller townhouses compressed several tasks into a single servant's job. In a great manor house the menu was directed and food was prepared by the chief cook. The surveyor directed banquet ceremony, while the steward supervised the service of food. The cupbearer performed the credence test; the saucer prepared gravies and sauces; the butler directed service and the spicing of wine; and the pantler guarded the bread. The warner prepared subtleties (also called warners), calling attention to the introduction of each new course. The carver created individual portions of large roasts with elegant genuflexions and multiple knives. The sewer arranged dishes after they reached the table, while the almoner collected food gifts and leftovers for the poor. Other servants included marshals, squires, ushers, and sergeants at arms.

Medieval cookery, often mistakenly characterized either as gluttonous crudity or uninventive dullness, clearly was a creative exercise of the consuming passions.

BIBLIOGRAPHY

Madeleine Pelner Cosman, *Fabulous Feasts: Medieval Cookery and Ceremony* (1976, repr. 1978), with bibliography of 300 manuscripts and 700 secondary sources, and "A Feast for Aesculapius," in *Annual Review of Nutrition*, 3 (1983); Bridget Henisch, *Fast and Feast: Food in Medieval Society* (1976). Accessible original sources in modern print or facsimile include Thomas Austin, ed., *Two Fifteenth-century Cookery-books* (1888); Frederick J. Furnivall, *Early English Meals and Manners* (1868, repr. 1969), which includes Wynkyn de Worde's *Boke of Kervynge*; Bartolomeo Platina, *De honesta voluptate* (1475), in Elizabeth B. Andrews' trans. as *On Honest Indulgence and Good Health* (1967); Richard Warner, *Antiquitates culinariae* (1791, repr. 1982).

MADELEINE PELNER COSMAN

[See also **Agriculture and Nutrition; Bread; Brewing; Dietary Laws, Jewish; Fasting, Christian; Feasts and Festivals, European; Food Trades; Herbals; Herbs; Sumptuary Laws; Wine and Winemaking.**]

Added to the requirements of health and ceremony were two significant contributors to medieval menus: sumptuary legislation and astrological consideration. Who could eat what—and when—was sometimes determined less by season or availability than by law. Sumptuary rules relegated certain foods to particular social classes, even specifying anatomical parts of the same animal as proper for one group but not another. Goose neck and wing were treats for the nobles; daintees, the testicles of deer, were reserved for the highest-born hunters; whale liver, said to smell like violets, was suitable for dukes and kings. Those violating such strictures risked reprimand, fines, or jail.

The highly complicated cookery of the Middle Ages was prepared in kitchens that varied in size and complexity according to the wealth and status of the household. The duke of Berry, for example, had a special kitchen house for almost every one of his castles and, on certain estates, a bake house, smoke-

COOKERY, ISLAMIC

COOKERY, ISLAMIC. The study of medieval Islamic cookery is just beginning. Few texts have been published, translated, or even examined. Almost nothing has been done to make the written recipes intelligible or to analyze the customary practices and discover the rules implicit in them. Regional differences abounded in the vast domain of Islam, and ingredients must often be inferred by reference to the region of the manuscript. The surviving cookbooks reflect almost exclusively the princely cuisine of the courts and castles. Only from literary and historical texts can we get an idea of the nutritional habits and dietary staples of the other classes, and these sources reveal very little of the mode of preparation.

The basic ingredients were wheat and barley in various forms, rice in varying degrees of prevalence, many vegetables and fruits depending on the region, chicken and lamb, fish in the maritime regions, dairy products (mainly melted butter), and honey. The range of beverages was extremely limited because of the Koranic prohibition of fermented liquors, even if this rule was often loosely interpreted. The Muslims had to restrict themselves to water and to varied fruit juices and syrups. The main sweetener was honey, sugar being a luxury item.

Food preparation relied on the usual methods: direct flame (spit or grill), oven, or heating in setting containers. Meats were most often boiled before being cooked or roasted.

Within the various regional traditions some localities were distinguished for their specialties, which often bore their name. Refinement, which increased with wealth, consisted in following different culinary traditions, even those of countries outside the world of Islam. Pre-Islamic traditions were also followed, mainly those emanating from the prestigious royal tradition of Iran. Some recipes demanded long and arduous preparation together with the use of rare and precious ingredients. Multiple and varied spices were added.

Muslim cuisine enjoyed great prestige in Europe toward the end of the Middle Ages. Arabic works on nutrition, containing many concise recipes, were widely circulated. Some dishes were borrowed intact with their original names; other recipes simply exerted a general influence.

Gastronomy was an esteemed art at the Abbasid court. Numerous poems were devoted to the description and praise of various dishes, and gastronomical poetic competitions were even held in the midst of feasts. A rich culinary literature was already reported in the eighth century, and a list of prominent ninth-and tenth-century treatises has been preserved. The works themselves have been lost, but later books preserve and embellish many of their elements. After the thirteenth century less elaborate works predominate.

BIBLIOGRAPHY

Few of the surviving manuscripts have been edited or analyzed. S. Toimikutsa (Helsinki) is preparing an edition and translation of the tenth-century *Kitāb aṭ-ṭabīḥ wa-iṣlaḥ al-agdiya al-maʾkūlāt* (Book of the cooking and correct preparation of edible foods) of Abū Muḥammad al-Muẓaffar ibn Naṣr ibn as-Sayyār al-Warrāq. From the thirteenth-century *Kitāb al-aṭʿima al-muʿtāda* (Book of customary dishes) comes the *Kitāb aṭ-ṭabīḥ* (Cookbook) of Muḥammad ibn al-Ḥasan al-Kātib al-Bagdādī (d. 1239) published in 1934 with translation by Arthur J. Arberry. The *Kitāb al-Wuṣla ilā l'ḥabib* (Book of the bond with the friend, also thirteenth century) has been analyzed by Maxime Rodinson and is to be translated by Charles Perry.

See also A. J. Arberry, "A Baghdad Cookery-Book," in *Islamic Culture,* **13** (1939); Ambrosio Huici Miranda, *La cocina hispano-magrebí en la época almohade según un manuscrito anónimo* (1965), and *Traduccion española de un manuscrito anónimo del siglo XIII sobre la cocina hispano-magribí* (1966); Maxime Rodinson, "Recherches sur les documents arabes relatifs à la cuisine," in *Revue des études islamiques,* **17** (1949), and "Les influences de la civilisation musulmane sur la civilisation européenne médiévale: L'alimentation," in *Convegno internazionale Oriente e Occidente nel Medioevo: Filosofia e scienze* (1971), 479–499.

MAXIME RODINSON

[See also **Agriculture and Nutrition; Beverages, Islamic; Dietary Laws, Islamic; Fasting, Islamic; Feasts and Festivals, Islamic; Sumptuary Laws, Islamic.**]

COPLA

COPLA (Spanish, "stanza"); the plural *(coplas)* denotes a poem in uniform stanzas having limitations in rhyme patterning. Virtually the only medium, other than song, for fifteenth-century learned poetry, *coplas* were prominent in epic, lyric, and dramatic poetry, and in the verse essay. Examples include the *Coplas de Mingo Revulgo* and works by Juan de Mena, Jorge Manrique, and Juan del Encina.

The *copla de arte mayor* normally consists of eight *versos de arte mayor,* in which the basic twelve-syllable pattern of each verse is varied according to a complex rhythmic formula. The *copla de arte menor* has eight to twelve octosyllables. With the addition of semidependent half-lines, and sometimes of additional rhymes, it becomes the *copla de pie quebrado* (broken-foot *copla*). The *copla real* is a ten-line *copla de arte menor* rhyming like a pair of quintets, each on two rhymes in restricted order.

BIBLIOGRAPHY

Juan del Encina, *Cancionero de Juan del Encina … 1496*, facs. ed. (1928), fol. 5, chs. 7 and 9, a late medieval major poet's description of the *copla's* metric forms; Pierre Le Gentil, *La poésie lyrique espagnole et portugaise à la fin du moyen âge*, II (1953), 32–109, 184, treats primarily forms and contains bibliographic notes; Jacqueline Steunou and Lothar Knapp, *Bibliografía de los cancioneros castellanos del siglo XV y repertorio de sus géneros poéticos*, 3 vols. (1975–), computer-generated classified lists of keys to form, content, and other items of information on individual poems of fifteenth-century collections of Castilian poetry.

DOROTHY CLOTELLE CLARKE

[See also **Spanish Versification and Prosody.**]

COPPO DI MARCOVALDO, Florentine painter, active 1260–1274. Coppo's earliest known signed and dated work is the *Madonna and Child* (1261) for S. Maria dei Servi, Siena, which he perhaps painted as a Sienese prisoner of war. Other extant works include the *Madonna and Child Enthroned* for S. Maria dei Servi, Orvieto (now in the Museo Nazionale, Perugia) and the *Crucifix* (*ca.* 1260, now in the Museo Civico, San Gimignano). A damaged *Crucifix* is all that survives from a major commission of 1274 for a series of panels for the Duomo at Pistoia. A *Madonna and Child* in S. Maria Maggiore and the mosaic of Christ in the Baptistery at Florence have been attributed to Coppo.

Using Romanesque and Italo-Byzantine styles, Coppo forged images of powerful monumentality and forceful emotion. His crisp, vigorous line defines forms at once schematic and organic, and endows his images with a spontaneity and immediacy that led the way to the later developments of Cimabue, Duccio, and Giotto.

BIBLIOGRAPHY

Gertrude Coor-Achenbach, "A Visual Basis for the Documents Relating to Coppo di Marcovaldo and His Son Salerno," in *Art Bulletin*, 28 (1946); Edward Garrison, *Italian Romanesque Panel Painting* (1949); Robert Oertel, *Early Italian Painting to 1400* (1968).

ADELHEID M. GEALT

COPTIC ART. Coptic art is frequently discussed in terms of the superimposing of influences, notably the Greek tradition of Hellenistic Alexandria and, later, that of Islam, onto a local folk art that retained its roots in ancient Egyptian art. A wide interpretation to the limits of Coptic art was adumbrated by Josef Strzygowski in 1904, in a work that focused on the minor arts. Largely in reaction to the stimulus of the major European exhibitions of Coptic art in the early 1960's, scholars have since attempted to define more closely both the relationship and the distinction between Coptic art and Greco-Roman traditions of late antique art in Egypt. Convenient though somewhat arbitrary divisions have been suggested between the forerunners of Coptic art: "proto-Coptic" art of the early third to the early fifth century; Coptic art proper from the late fifth to the late seventh century; and finally the period after the Arab conquest, from the eighth to the twelfth century.

Such definitions are in practice bedeviled by the problem of dating numerous important objects of Coptic art. Many surviving examples were retrieved at a time when accurate stratigraphic archaeological techniques were in their infancy. Consequently the provenance and date of many pieces now scattered among various collections, and on occasion their very legitimacy, remain at issue. The present article attempts to discuss representative examples of art produced by the Copts in various media before the Mamluk period, with emphasis on dated material. Of the monumental and applied arts, the major areas of architecture, sculpture, textiles, manuscripts, and painting are selected for study.

ARCHITECTURE

Typical Egyptian building techniques, such as construction in mud brick, were adapted by the Copts to building with a specifically Christian function, especially the monasteries, of which Apa Apollo at Bawit, founded in the late fourth century, is a prominent example. In the same way, Coptic towns and other settlements had their roots in predecessors of the Greco-Roman period. The Coptic town of Djime (anc. Thebes), for instance, was built over the late Roman settlement, near the site of the ancient temple at Medinet Habu.

Coptic religious architecture employs predominantly the basilica in a variety of forms. One of the most important early sites is that of Abu Mina in the Maryut Desert southwest of Alexandria, known to have enjoyed imperial patronage and comparable to fourth- and fifth-century imperial foundations in

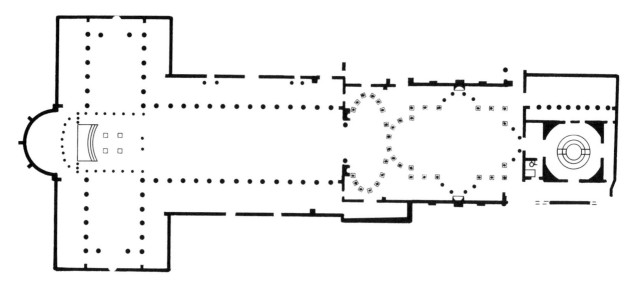

Plan of Church of St. Menas, Abu Mina, 5th century. DRAWING BY NORA JENNINGS

Constantinople in aspects of its architectural layout and sculptural decoration. A cult grew up at the shrine of St. Menas, possibly a local figure, and between the late fourth century and the early sixth century the site grew from a simple chapel into a large complex comprising three main elements, mostly built of sandstone.

The foundation of the crypt basilica over the tomb itself, of uncertain date, is flanked on the east by a large basilica with a transept measuring 66.5 meters in length and 51.5 meters in width, and on the west by an octagonal baptistery; these were probably begun by Patriarch Theophilus under Emperor Arcadius at the beginning of the fifth century. Other buildings followed the growth of the site as a pilgrimage center. A bath complex was constructed, including thermae with a trefoil apse plan, previously known from Greco-Roman catacombs in Alexandria. Later building phases, notably under Emperor Zeno during the last quarter of the fifth century and in Anastasius' reign in the early sixth, expanded and modified the basilica, especially with the addition of two side aisles and the tomb church. Following the decline of the site, the tomb church was rebuilt on a reduced scale shortly before the mid ninth century, and the large basilica was abandoned.

The church of El-Ashmunein (Hermopolis), apparently constructed between 430 and 440, combines the transept and double aisles of the large basilica with the trefoil plan of the bath at Abu Mina in a basilica with a triconch chancel. The triconch chancel appears in other fifth- and sixth-century basilicas in Egypt—for instance, the church of Deir el-Abiad (the White Monastery) at Sohag, thought to have been founded by the great Coptic theologian Shenute in 440. It is also a feature of the nearby church of Deir el-Ahmar (the Red Monastery), the basilica of Dendera, and the church of St. Simeon's monastery (also known as Deir Anba Hadra) at Aswan (late tenth or eleventh century). It is likely that the plan is related to other early Christian examples in North Africa and southern Italy.

Other monastery churches of the fifth and sixth centuries developed the plan of a basilica with either a semicircular or a square apse, flanked by side chambers. Instances are the principal church of the monastery of Jeremiah at Saqqara, both churches at Djime (Medinet Habu), churches at Ostracina and at Deir Abu Hennis, and the urban churches of Old Cairo such as Abu Sarga (St. Sergius). These churches were vaulted with timber or stone, and their decoration of sculptural friezes and capitals frequently survives. Such basilica forms have sometimes been compared to Syrian and Mesopotamian church plans, while other scholars, especially Badawy, argue an indigenous development.

Reduced political and economic circumstances after the seventh century and the ensuing replacement of timber and stone with brick for building purposes affected both church plans and the restoration of existing buildings. The longitudinal orientation of the basilica plan gave way to a less unified

586

plan, comprising chapels, choir, and nave in transverse sections. Thus the chancel or *haikal* became emphasized at the expense of other parts of the church plan, with a row of brick-domed chapels divided from the rectangular areas of the choir and nave to the west by a brick screen. This plan became widely adopted: at Deir el-Shuhada at Esna in the eighth century and at Deir Anba Bishoi, among churches of the Wadi Natrun monasteries, in the ninth century, and at Deir el Muharraq in the tenth century. Older churches restored at this time, such as Deir es-Salib at Naqada, show the addition of transverse walls in accordance with the transverse emphasis. Eventually the easily constructed brick cupola absorbed the entire church design, so that the later Coptic churches of rural Upper Egypt and the Wadi Natrun monasteries have rows of cupolas divided on a grid system by wooden screens between columns.

SCULPTURE AND CARVING

Coptic sculpture and carving include works of widely different scale and materials, among them statuary, architectural friezes, pediments and capitals, funerary stelae and reliefs, woodwork, and small-scale plaques and objects in ivory and bone. The latter include caskets, pyxides, and objects of daily use, such as combs and furniture. During the fourth and fifth centuries pagan mythological scenes continued to be represented along with Christian iconography and ornamental geometric and foliage motifs. An allegorical justification was found for some pagan motifs, and the Virgo Lactans image is clearly derived from Hellenistic and Roman representations of Isis suckling Horus-Harpocrates.

Discussion of Coptic sculpture has largely centered on stylistic considerations, since few pieces can be dated by any other criteria. The overall picture that emerges is of a tendency away from Hellenism and toward an increasingly abstract, two-dimensional style. This is not a gradual process that can be neatly documented; rather, it is punctuated, or interrupted, by revivals of Hellenism inspired particularly from Constantinople. The problem is posed of the role of Alexandria in the preservation of Hellenism in sculpture, as in other art forms. The breadth of external contacts during late antiquity has been acknowledged in discussion of the sources of Coptic sculpture, and its dependence on the art of the eastern Roman provinces, especially the sculpture of Baalbek, Palmyra, and Khirbet el-Tannur in Trans-

Sculpted niche from Bawit. MUSÉE DU LOUVRE, PARIS

jordan, has been cited. Additional Greco-Roman centers along the Nile in Upper Egypt and the Faiyūm are now recognized, along with Alexandria, as contributing to the survival of Hellenism.

During the tetrarchic and early Constantinian period, official imperial commissions of sarcophagi and portrait sculpture, of which the figures of the tetrarchs now at St. Mark's in Venice are but one example, were likely to have been executed in Alexandrian workshops. Porphyry, from which they were carved, was quarried near Coptos (Qift) until the mid fourth century. Attempts have been made to stress the continuing importance of Alexandria on the basis of numbers of ivory and bone carvings found in or near the city, many of which have also, paradoxically, been cited to illustrate the decline of Hellenistic style.

Sculpture of the fourth and fifth centuries demonstrates both the continuation of classical precepts and the emergence of an identifiable Coptic style. A relief now in the Greco-Roman Museum in Alexandria shows St. Menas in the praying position between the two camels—a reference to the legend surrounding his burial—as he is frequently depicted on ampullae. From the monastery of St. Thecla at Ennaton (or Hennaton), west of Alexandria, this relief is probably a copy of one from Abu Mina and contemporary with the basilica of Arcadius (early fifth century). It has been suggested that this relief reflects aspects of Theodosian work from Constantinople, a supposition supported by the abundance of acanthus capitals on the site of Abu Mina.

The beginning of a stylistic progression away

587

from Hellenism is evident in the sculpture of Oxyrhynchos in Middle Egypt during the fourth century. The modeled style of several carved stone niches and reliefs of mythological scenes looks toward the "soft" style produced at Ahnās (Heracleopolis Magna) at the end of the century. A niche enclosing the figure of Aphrodite posed in a conch shell, now in the Coptic Museum in Cairo, is an example of this phase at Ahnās, where the continued appearance of a wide variety of mythological scenes, possibly sepulchral in origin, mostly outnumbers the production of sculpture with specifically Christian iconography. U. Monneret de Villard contrasted this style with a "hard," more abstract style that emerged in the mid fifth century. Confirmation of the evolution of this characteristically Coptic style has been sought by Ernst Kitzinger in the style of the similarly abstract acanthus capitals from Ahnās, which can be compared with more accurately documented capitals from Constantinople and Palestine.

It is from the later Ahnās style that subsequent sculpture at the major monastic sites of Bawit (El Bawiti) and Saqqara is derived. Here the emphasis shifts from figural sculpture to geometric and floral architectural sculpture of friezes and niches. An ornamental pediment from Bawit, probably of the sixth century, shows a shell niche as in the Ahnās piece, but has no figure and is banded with spiky acanthus leaves and volutes, with two crosses in circles between the tripartite pointed molding above. The sharp, crisp, abstract quality of the Bawit piece demonstrates a recognizable break with Hellenistic traditions.

Sculpture from other monastic sites fits less comfortably into this sequence. Sculptural friezes from the church of Deir el-Abiad at Sohag appear to be a collection of reused pieces from elsewhere rather than a homogeneous group. They have been compared with work from the church at Dendera, perhaps of the late fifth century, and thus were conceivably put into position in the church some time after its foundation.

Concurrent with these stylistic developments prior to the Islamic invasions were revivals of classicism, attributable to direct influence from Constantinople. Many of the capitals from Bawit and Saqqara compare with some from El-Ashmunein and Alexandria, and are related to Justinianic work at Ravenna and Constantinople. This points to a resurgence of influence from the Byzantine capital during the sixth century, and perhaps also a century later. Another instance of this direct influence is found in the decoration of a pilaster from the south church at Bawit, now in the Louvre, with foliage ornament comparable to carving on the throne of Maximian at Ravenna, now generally accepted as Justinianic work. Kitzinger has proposed a similarity between the figure style of the archangel surmounting the pilaster and the ivory of the archangel Michael in the British Museum.

Subsequently the suggested dating of several other pieces of Coptic carving, once frequently placed in the late fourth or fifth century, has been adjusted in accordance with the early-sixth-century dating of the pilaster. Among these are foliate wooden panels from the door of the Church of Sitt Barbara in Old Cairo, the Antinoë comb, and the wooden lintel from the church of al-Mo^callaqa, the last two carved with New Testament scenes. (All are now in the Coptic Museum in Cairo.)

Torp has proposed a comparable further revival in the Heraklian period, in the last years before the Islamic invasions. This is argued on the basis of the association of the ivory reliefs now decorating the pulpit of Henry II at Aachen and more usually dated to the sixth century with, on the one hand, Heraklian silverware and, on the other, the Hellenistic style of the wall paintings of chapel 17 at Bawit. Such dating accords with the recent later dating of several Coptic textiles.

Despite the disruption caused by the invasions, Coptic art persisted under Islam in sculpture as in other branches. Beckwith attributes the very stylized limestone relief depicting Christ's entry into Jerusalem from Deir el-Abiad (now in the Staatliche Museen, Berlin) to the seventh or early eighth century through comparison with textiles with Kufic inscriptions. Dated ninth- or tenth-century miniatures in Coptic manuscripts provide a basis for the dating of other Coptic works, such as the ivory statue of the Virgin and Child enthroned between angels (now in the Walters Art Gallery in Baltimore). The carving of funerary stelae and bone and ivory objects also continued throughout this period. Coptic woodwork of the tenth to thirteenth centuries, found on screens and doors, reflects strongly the influence of contemporary Islamic art. A panel of the Nativity from the Church of Abu Sarga in Old Cairo, for instance, merges Coptic figure style with ornamental motifs previously found in Islamic stucco work.

TEXTILES

The tradition of textile manufacture in Egypt, established in the Ptolemaic and Roman periods,

Textile roundel illustrating scenes from the life of Joseph. Egyptian, 8th century. THE METROPOLITAN MUSEUM OF ART, GIFT OF MR. AND MRS. CHARLES K. WILKINSON (63.178.2)

formed the basis for Coptic textile production, in organization as well as in techniques. Most commonly produced were tunics of undyed linen onto which decorative woolen panels were worked, either in horizontal or vertical bands (clavi) or in square or circular patches over the shoulders and knees. Examples of these garments can be seen in Coptic wall paintings, as at Bawit. Silk was also manufactured and, more rarely, pure woolen materials. Three general divisions have been suggested for linen and wool manufacture. The earliest textiles are of fine tabby weaves, with designs formed by the insertion of colored threads. During the fourth through seventh centuries the tapestry weave was developed. In it the design is surrounded by an area of plain tapestry backed by tabby weave. After the seventh century the entire textile is tapestry. Embroidered textiles, usually of flat stitching, became more common only after this date.

Textiles have been preserved in burial grounds in the sand. The principal finds have been made at Akhmīm in Upper Egypt; at various sites near Antinoë, in the Faiyūm; at the monastic sites of Bawit and Saqqara; at bishoprics such as Asyut; and at Alexandria. It is assumed that most textiles were of local manufacture, though some may have been brought from other towns. Museum collections of textiles in Europe, North America, and Japan consist largely of finds made during excavations in the late nineteenth and early twentieth centuries, before modern archaeological retrieval methods were developed, or of acquisitions from the art market. This has presented serious problems for scholarship, both in discerning the precise origin and date of individual pieces and in the establishment of any chronological sequence of the development of textile production.

Early research proposed a distinction between the styles of Akhmīm and Antinoë, an assumption that ignored several nuances and overlappings and initiated a tenacious tradition of very early dating for textiles. In the 1930's R. Pfister attempted to differentiate between local and imported textiles, which also were later found to overlap. Subsequent work by P. M. Du Bourguet and John N. Beckwith has encouraged a redating of textiles, assigning more to after the Islamic invasions, often on the basis of comparison with Umayyad or Byzantine art. In pointing out the discrepancies of dating between the Essen and Paris catalogs of the Coptic art exhibition of the early 1960's, M. H. Torp noted that this adjustment is contingent on the recognition of revivals of Hellenism in Coptic art, as opposed to a simple continuous decline.

Textiles of the earliest period (proto-Coptic), either polychrome or purple, preserve strongly Hellenistic stylistic features. A woolen tapestry panel in the British Museum, woven into a tabby background, shows erotes in a boat, surrounded by a stylized leaf frame with four medallions enclosing masks. The subject conforms to late antique Nilotic scenes, and the rounded figure style has been compared with mosaics and tomb paintings of the fourth century. Pagan iconography is continued into the Coptic period proper, as the tapestry hanging of Hestia Polyolbos in the Dumbarton Oaks collection demonstrates. The goddess of the hearth is shown seated in the center, flanked by putti who present disks naming her virtues, with personifications (one of light) standing on either side. The lunette shape of the piece and the frontal pose of the haloed goddess reflect monumental prototypes, particularly of the Justinianic period and of wall paintings at Bawit, and it is thus considered to date from the late sixth century.

Similar criteria led Kitzinger to his dating of the Horse and Lion woolen tapestry, also at Dumbarton Oaks, including the association of addorsed animal heads with Justinianic capitals. His conclusion that the piece is a sixth-century interpretation of a Sasanian design is challenged by Beckwith, who argues for an early Islamic date, at a time when Persian and Hellenistic traditions were fused.

Other decorative motifs are common after the Arab conquest, including those of the "Antinoë rinceaux" group of silks worked in red and buff, and the motif of the Tree of Life with addorsed birds in roundels of silk and tapestry in linen and wool. Such roundels employ a variety of colors, including green, dark blue, buff, and a dull red produced from lac instead of the earlier vegetable madder. Scenes are varied. Pagan scenes figuring Dionysus, Ariadne, Pan, satyrs, and maenads, as well as animals in combat and hunting scenes, appear.

Other scenes have recognizable Christian connotations. An instance is the woolen tapestry roundel in the Metropolitan Museum of Art, New York. One of a few such surviving, it illustrates nine scenes of the life of Joseph, starting in the center and moving counterclockwise around the main field, and is brightly colored in tan and green on a red background. The piece, with others similar to it, has been dated between the sixth and eighth centuries. Gary Vikan has suggested a manuscript source for its iconography, on the basis of iconographic comparisons with the Joseph scenes from the Cotton Genesis and related cycles of the same recension, which Weitzmann was the first to propose to be of Alexandrian origin. Silk roundels in the Vatican represent the Annunciation and Nativity; and many more, illustrating a wide range of subjects, have been attributed to Alexandria during the eighth and ninth centuries, though the Zachariou group, so called after their Greek and Coptic inscriptions, are said to have been found at Akhmīm and could date as late as the tenth century. Figural textiles of the same date bear inscriptions that they were made at Faiyūm. The tendency toward abstraction, of both figural and ornamental forms, intensifies until the late Fatimid and early Ayyubid periods, in the twelfth century.

ILLUSTRATED MANUSCRIPTS

The major collections of Coptic manuscripts are housed in the Vatican libraries, the British Library, the Pierpont Morgan Library in New York, and in collections in Cairo, Leiden, Oxford, and Naples. The majority were brought from Egyptian monasteries by European travelers between the seventeenth and nineteenth centuries. Most were originally from the monastic libraries of Deir el-Abiad and St. Michael in the Faiyūm, where the southern, Sahidic dialect of the Coptic language was in use, and from Abu Makar in the Wadi Natrun, whence northern,

Bohairic books were taken. These manuscripts comprise theological and liturgical works, acts of the martyrs, and lives of the saints. They sometimes retain their original bindings of tooled leather.

Especially characteristic of the decoration of Coptic manuscripts is the variety of ornamental motifs of foliage and leaves, often with birds and animals, in bold reds, browns, greens, and yellows, which appear as paragraph marks or marginal ornaments. Interlace crosses are also common at the beginnings of books, sometimes including busts of Christ and the evangelists. In a celebrated early instance, the Glazier Codex (Pierpont Morgan Library, Glazier Coll. G.67), a pharaonic ankh appears at the end of the manuscript, with affronted birds and peacocks, as representative of Christ's life on earth. Dating to about 400, the manuscript contains part of the text of the Acts of the Apostles in an archaic Coptic dialect. Its interlace cross has raised the question of Coptic art as a source for Hiberno-Saxon illumination.

In his study of about forty illuminated Coptic manuscripts, Jules Leroy proposed the date of about 1000 as the dividing line between general categories of earlier and later surviving manuscripts. The earlier ones can be subdivided into those of 500–800 and those of 800–1000.

Many of the illustrations of Coptic manuscripts of the seventh and eighth centuries are outlined frontal figures of saints, evangelists, angels, and the Virgin and Child that are comparable to wall paintings of the same period, such as those at Bawit and Saqqara. A drawing suggested as dating from this period and as representing Job and his family, found at the end of a manuscript of the Book of Job (Naples, Biblioteca Nazionale, MS 487) from Deir el-Abiad, is exceptional in both its antique style and its Old Testament iconography.

New Testament scenes are not common at this time. Only some fragments of a manuscript (London, British Library, MS Or. 3367) from Akhmīm, probably of the ninth or tenth century, attest to the illustration of a marginal Gospel cycle. Other manuscripts of the period continue the linear style of earlier illumination, an instance being the Virgo Lactans with St. John (British Library, MS Or. 6782) of 989–990, perhaps from Deir el-Abiad, which shows the figures facing front with very stylized drapery etched in narrow, parallel lines. A similar drafting line is used to depict the equestrian saints Theodore and Mercurius (Biblioteca Apostolica Vaticana, MS Copto 66). A different trend is visible in

Ankh cross. Manuscript of the Acts of the Apostles, *ca.* 400. THE PIERPONT MORGAN LIBRARY G 67, fol. 215

illuminations of the period that display external influences, from Byzantium in particular. A portrait, perhaps of Paul and Timothy, in an Arabic manuscript of the Epistles of St. Paul dated to 892 (Leningrad, Public Library, N.F. 327) shows modeling derived from Byzantine painting, while the Byzantine Hodegetria type of Virgin and Child is added to a Pentateuch manuscript (Biblioteca Apostolica Vaticana, MS Copto 1).

From the early eleventh century, Arabic became more prominent in Coptic church practice. Manuscripts are frequently bilingual, with the Coptic and Arabic texts in parallel columns, often on paper rather than on parchment. Their decoration demonstrates an associated shift toward contemporary Islamic art, as well as an emphasis on New Testament iconography under the influence of strengthened contacts with other Oriental Christian, especially Syrian and Armenian, churches. Evangelist portraits ultimately derived from Greek manuscripts appear in Bodleian Library, MS Hunt. 17 of 1173 and Biblioteca Apostolica Vaticana, MS Copto 9 of 1204–1205, the latter also containing an ornamental frontispiece of crosses comparable with Koranic decoration. The extensive cycle of Gospel scenes of

Bibliothèque Nationale, MS Copte 13, made at Damietta in 1179–1180, combines the influence of earlier Greek and Syriac cycles with contemporary secular Islamic painting in its lively narrative style. The Copto-Arabic New Testament manuscript produced at Cairo in 1249–1250 (Paris, Institut Catholique Copte-Arabe 1/Cairo, Coptic Museum Bibl. 94) shows the convergence of these external influences in the mid thirteenth century.

The vitality of Coptic manuscript illumination did not survive the end of the thirteenth century. Perhaps owing to the Mamluk repression of non-Muslim populations, later Coptic manuscript painting, like other arts, tended to become introverted and derivative of its own tradition.

PAINTING

Among the antecedents of Coptic painting are the Faiyūm portraits and the decoration of the imperial chamber at Luxor, which provide instances of private, funerary, and public monumental patronage. Much of the earliest surviving Coptic wall painting is funerary and is datable to the fourth through sixth centuries. Paintings with allegorical biblical subjects survive in circumstances similar to those of early

Christ before Pilate. Damietta, 1179–1180. BIBLIOTHÈQUE NATIONALE, MS Copte 13, fol. 82v

Christian Rome. Among the earliest are those of the funerary chapels of Bagawat in the Kharga oasis of the Libyan desert, which have greatly deteriorated since they were first photographed in the early twentieth century.

The paintings of two of the chapels are of particular interest. The "Mausoleum of the Exodus" (Fakhry no. 30) is constructed on a square plan (about five meters on a side) surmounted by a cupola, and is painted in a rough, naive style. A straggling vine occupies the upper part, its trunk issuing from near the center of the south arch and its grapes pecked by birds. Narrative scenes proceed in two registers around the base of the cupola. The Exodus is illustrated counterclockwise, with biblical and martyrdom scenes below, between Old Testament scenes above the four main arches. Many of the figures are labeled in Greek or Coptic. Below, the walls are painted with geometric panels in red, green, and yellow separated by mock painted Corinthian capitals and completed by a socle beneath. While some details are open to interpretation, the program as a whole undoubtedly represents symbols of salvation found elsewhere in early Christian art. It may be dated between the Constantinian period and the mid fifth century, a terminus that is supported by inscriptions in other mausoleums at Bagawat. The cupola of chapel 80 is decorated with a similar vine above, and allegorical figures of Peace, Righteousness, and Prayer in a rather more Hellenistic style.

Further funerary paintings of the fifth and sixth centuries, known from copies, once existed in and around Alexandria. Examples are the praying figure at Abū Girga and the christological cycle at Karmuz. A mural painting found in an arcosolium at Antinoë, now also destroyed, showed the deceased Theodosia

in the praying position between St. Kallouthos (Colluthius) and St. Mary.

Monastic sites provide much of the evidence of Coptic painting. The fifth-century underground church at Deir Abu Hennis is unusual in its depiction of christological scenes, though such iconography reappears at Bawit during the sixth to eighth centuries. Parts of the monastery of Apa Apollo at Bawit were excavated during the early twentieth century, and many of the buildings were found to have painted decoration, including the north and south churches and the structures termed "chapels" by Clédat. In the "chapels" decoration extended to niches and elaborate geometric and floral dadoes. Figural scenes included Old Testament iconography, especially the life of David, New Testament scenes, figures of monks and saints, and allegories and virtues. Pictures of animals, birds, and hunting scenes were also common.

Various depictions of Christ Pantokrator and the Virgin occupied the most prominent niches. A niche painting in two registers from chapel 6 is one of several instances of the illustration of Christ in Majesty above, holding the Gospel with his other hand raised in blessing, flanked by the four apocalyptic beasts of Ezekiel's vision. On either side are the sun and moon and an angel, and below, the enthroned Virgin and Child with the apostles. The frontality of the figures, their linear style, their staring eyes, and the bright red, yellow, black, green, and blue epitomize the features associated with Coptic art. Ihm has discussed Bawit niche paintings with the Ascension/Theophany theme, while Grabar has stressed the emphasis on the Theophany in this combination of elements. Torp proposed that the function of such "chapels" here and at other monastic sites was memorial, with the cells or habitation of the monks in the upper story.

Other monastic painting, particularly of the monastery of Apa Jeremiah at Saqqara, is comparable with that of Bawit, with further variations on the iconography of Christ in Majesty and the Virgin and Child enthroned. Old Testament scenes also appear, such as the Hebrews in the furnace, which is the subject of a sixth-century mural painting from Wadi Sarga (now in the British Museum). Panel paintings of the sixth and seventh centuries found at Bawit are closely related to the frontally painted mural icons of monks and saints at Bawit and Saqqara. One of these depicts Christ and St. Menas, both haloed. Christ holds a jeweled Gospel book in one hand and places his other arm on the saint's shoulder. A Bawit

Christ and St. Menas; painted panel from Abu Mina. MUSÉE DU LOUVRE, PARIS

panel now in Berlin shows Apa Abraham in a very linear, abstract form.

The tradition of this early Coptic painting continues beyond the twelfth century in an apse painting of Christ in Majesty between two angels in the Church of St. Simeon, Aswan, while others of this later period reflect the influence of Armenian and Syrian artists. The decoration of the church of Deir el-Abiad, where Armenian inscriptions with Coptic are found, includes in the southern apse a painted veiled cross in a mandorla supported by angels. The activity of Syrians, also documented by inscriptions, is evident in the decoration of the Church of el-Adra at Deir es-Suriani in the Wadi Natrūn, where paintings of the Annunciation, Nativity, Dormition, and Ascension can be dated to the early thirteenth century.

BIBLIOGRAPHY

Bibliographies. Extensive bibliographies on Coptic art and archaeology are included in the following publications: Alexander Badawy, *Coptic Art and Archaeology* (1978); Winifred Kammerer, *A Coptic Bibliography,* compiled with the collaboration of E. M. Husserl and L. A. Shier (1950); M. Krause, "Ägypten," in *Reallexikon zur Byzantinischen Kunst,* Klaus Wessel, ed., I (1966); Jean Simon, "Bibliographie copte," annually in *Orientalia* (Rome), since 1949; and Klaus Wessel, *Koptische Kunst* (1963), trans. by Jean Carroll and Sheila Hatton as *Coptic Art* (1965).

Studies. J. Beckwith, "Coptic Textiles," in *Ciba Review,* **12,** no. 133 (1949); Jean Clédat, *Le monastère et la nécropole de Baouît,* 2 vols. (1904–1906); Pierre M. Du Bourguet, *Musée Nationale du Louvre, Catalogue des étoffes Coptes,* I (1964); André Grabar, "Deux monuments chrétiens d'Égypte," and Hjalmar Torp, "Byzance et la sculpture copte du VIᵉ siècle à Baouit et Sakkara," in André Grabar *et al., Synthronon* (1968); Christa Ihm, *Die Programme der christlichen Apsismalerei vom vierten Jahrhundert bis zur Mitte des achten Jahrhunderts* (1960); Ernst Kitzinger, "Notes on Early Coptic Sculpture," in *Archaeologia,* **87** (1937), and "The Horse and Lion Tapestry at Dumbarton Oaks," in *Dumbarton Oaks Papers,* **3** (1946); Jules Leroy, *Les manuscrits coptes et coptes-arabes illustrés* (1974), *Les peintures des couvents du désert d'Esna* (1975), and *Les peintures des couvents du Ouadi Natroun* (1982); Ugo Monneret de Villard, *La scultura ad Ahnâ* (1923); R. Pfister, "Teinture et alchimie dans l'Orient hellenistique," in *Seminarium Kondakovianum,* **7** (1935); Hjalmar Torp, "Leda Christiana: The Problem of the Interpretation of Coptic Sculpture with Mythological Motifs," in *Acta ad archaeologiam et artium historiam pertinentia,* **4** (1969); Gary Vikan, "Joseph Iconography on Coptic Textiles," in *Gesta,* **18** (1979); C. C. Walters, *Monastic Archaeology in Egypt* (1974); Kurt Weitzmann, ed., *Age of Spirituality* (1979).

LUCY-ANNE HUNT

[See also **Copts and Coptic Church; Early Christian Art; Egypt, Late Empire; Egypt, Islamic.**]

COPTS AND COPTIC CHURCH. The Coptic church (as distinct from the relatively modern Coptic rite of the Roman Catholic church in Egypt) traces its descent from the ancient Egyptians. Indeed the term "Copt" (Arabic: *qibṭ*) is derived from the Greek *aigyptios,* a corruption of the hieroglyphic *Het-Ka-Ptah,* which signified the house of the temple of the spirit of Ptah in Memphis. After the introduction of Christianity into Egypt by St. Mark, traditionally regarded as first patriarch of the Coptic church, the Copts played a significant role in early Christianity. Today there are approximately seven million Copts in Egypt and a gradually increasing number in other countries.

Their most important contributions emerged from the Catechetical School of Alexandria. From the time of its first president, Pantaenus (*d. ca.* 190), this school became a bulwark of theological and biblical studies. Famous among its subsequent leaders are Clement of Alexandria and Origen, the latter of pure Coptic stock. Many of the church fathers from both Rome and Byzantium received their education at this school—Cyril, Athanasius, Gregory of Nazianzus, Basil, Jerome, and Rufinus. The definitive text of the Greek Bible was established here, amid a vast crop of exegetical literature. And it was in this, the chief arena for the free discussion of Christian doctrines, that the stage was set for the ecumenical movement and the formalization of canonical beliefs and traditions.

Chief among the disputes addressed by the councils of Constantinople (381) and Ephesus (431) were the heresies of Eutychianism, which denuded Christ of his humanity, and Nestorianism, which repudiated the unity of Christ's divinity and humanity by denying that Mary was really the Mother of God (*Theotokos*). A second council at Ephesus (449), under the leadership of the Coptic patriarch Dioscorus I, adopted the credal formula of Cyril I of Alexandria and deposed Nestorius, which led to the schism of the East Syrians. However, Dioscorus, described by the Copts as a "pillar of the faith," was said to have defied Pope Leo I and was therefore stigmatized by the Roman and Byzantine bishops, who, resentful of Alexandrian leadership, united to secure his deposition at Chalcedon in 451. Dioscorus was never branded a heretic, but the second Council of Ephesus was rejected as a "Robber Council" (*Latrocinium*).

The action was the parting of the ways for the Coptic church and the rest of Christendom. Once described as "pharaohs of the church," the Copts were now condemned as Monophysites, that is, as followers of the Eutychian heresy that Christ's sole nature was divine and that his humanity was only an apparent manifestation. The accusation of Monophysitism, however, was rejected by the Copts, who maintained the doctrine of the divinity and humanity of Jesus, but insisted on their perfect unity. In a sense, both churches were very much alike in this respect; but politics seems to have dictated a somewhat duophysitic outlook on the part of the Western churches, in order to give them reason to humiliate their Eastern adversary.

The Copts were not alone in their rejection of Chalcedonianism; they have been followed to this day by the Ethiopians, the Armenians, and the West Syrian Jacobites. But for their independence, the Copts suffered a wave of Byzantine persecutions (451–640), which led to the rise of Coptic nationalism identified with the church. Consequently, two lines of succession to St. Mark emerged: the Melkite,

following Constantinople in Chalcedonian orthodoxy, and the native "Monophysite" majority, under the leadership of a persecuted, fugitive patriarch. To achieve their aim by force, the Byzantine emperors even vested the Melkite patriarchs as prefects for Egypt and as generals, thus enabling them to use secular force to curb popular religious upheavals. This sordid regime persisted, with disastrous results, until the Arab conquest of 640.

The new chapter in Coptic church history began well with the religious freedom that ᶜAmr ibn al-ᶜĀṣ extended to the Coptic patriarch Benjamin I (632–662). The Copts were retained in the administration of the country, but their relation with their new masters rested on their collection of the *jizya,* a special levy on nonadherents of Islam, and the *kharāj,* or general taxation. The governors of the caliphal province thus came to seek self-enrichment at the expense of the population during their short tenure of office. Their extortions increased in bulk with the passing of centuries, while agriculture declined as a result of neglect of the irrigation system and the low Nile floods. Progressive Islamization ensued as the poor farmers sought to escape the *jizya* by joining the religion of their masters, whereas those capable of meeting that impost survived in their native church. The Bashmouric Rebellion of 829–830 in the lower Nile Delta, probably the last serious Coptic uprising against a worsening situation, was quelled by the Abbasid caliph al-Maʾmūn.

Ultimately the Copts and their church received some relief from the heavy-handed financial pressures of the caliphs' viceroys when the country regained local independence under the dynasties of the Tulunids (868–905) and the Ikhshidids (939–969). The greatest tolerance toward the Copts was reached under the Shiite Fatimid caliphate (969–1171), if we except the reign of al-Ḥākim (996–1020), the unbalanced ruler who ended up by persecuting Copts, Jews, and Muslims alike. The succession of the Ayyubid (1169–1250) and Mamluk (1250–1517) sultanates proved to be an age of repression, intensified by the crusades and a declining economy. The Mamluk period was perhaps the blackest in medieval Egypt, owing to the intermittent mob uproar against Copts who became enriched in public service on account of their natural ability to handle the finances of the country and their intensive training in accounting. Consequently, the sultans responded by dismissing all of them from the administration and confiscating their possessions. The net result was confusion in the government machinery, and the sultans were constrained to reinstate the Copts in office. This policy endured until the downfall of the Mamluks in 1517, when Egypt fell under the Turkish yoke.

Although it lost its position of leadership in the fifth century, the Coptic church has made enduring contributions to Christian civilization, most notably through the institution of monasticism, destined to become the unique custodian of learning during the Dark Ages of the West. The Coptic cenobitic communities that multiplied on the fringe of the desert became the wonder of Christian antiquity.

The first stage in the development of monasticism is associated with St. Anthony of Egypt (*ca.* 250–356), a Coptic Christian who crossed into the desert near Herakleopolis in Middle Egypt at the age of twenty to lead a solitary life. His sanctity attracted numerous followers who practiced the Antonian way of life based on solitude, poverty, and the principle of torturing the body to save the soul. In a second phase, which may be termed "collective eremitism," the solitaries congregated in separate caves around that of the saint for guidance and self-defense.

Eventually, under St. Pachomius (*ca.* 290–346), a third phase ensued. A converted legionary and an educated man, Pachomius initiated his new rule by prescribing communal life in a cenobium (monastery), where, although self-mortification was replaced by manual labor and intellectual pursuits, the principles of celibate chastity, poverty, and obedience were preserved. Under the Pachomian system monasteries multiplied and were organized into national groups in order to accommodate the monks of many nations who came to live with the desert fathers.

Among the illustrious figures who were edified in Coptic convents and became themselves apostles of Coptic monasticism in their native countries were St. Jerome, who translated the Rule of St. Pachomius from Greek into Latin, and whose version must have been utilized later by St. Benedict in the composition of his own Rule; St. John Chrysostom; Rufinus; St. Basil, the founder of a Byzantine or Greek monastic order on the Pachomian model; John Cassian, father of monasticism in Gaul; Palladius, who compiled the lives of the desert fathers in his works entitled the *Lausiac History,* or *Paradise of the Fathers;* St. Augen, or Eugenius of Clysma, father of Syrian monasticism; and many others.

A by-product of Coptic monasticism was its mis-sionary endeavor. In Africa the greatest success came in Abyssinia, where Frumentius baptized King Ēzānā (Aezianus) around the middle of the fourth century, thus establishing Christianity as the state religion. By the sixth century, Coptic Christianity had penetrated deep into the Sudan. It is even said that the Nubian kings pleaded with the Coptic church to send emissaries to preach the gospel beyond Syene (Aswan). In Europe, members of the Theban legion, martyred near Zurich, provide the most famous example of Coptic religious heroism. Coptic missionaries touched Britain long before Augustine, and seven Coptic monks are known to have been buried at "Disert Uldith" (in County Donegal, Northern Ireland), before the coming of St. Patrick.

BIBLIOGRAPHY

Aziz S. Atiya, *The Copts and Christian Civilization* (1979), and *History of Eastern Christianity,* rev. ed. (1980); Edith L. Butcher, *The Story of the Church of Egypt,* 2 vols. (1897); Alfred J. Butler, *The Ancient Coptic Churches of Egypt,* 2 vols. (1884); *Coptic Egypt,* W. L. Westermann *et al.,* eds. (1944); *The Egyptian or Coptic Church,* Oswald Burmester, ed. (1967); Edward R. Hardy, *Christian Egypt; Church and People* (1952); Iris H. El-Masry, *The Story of the Copts* (1978); William H. MacKean, *Christian Monasticism in Egypt to the Close of the Fourth Century* (1920); Otto Meinardus, *Monks and Monasteries of the Egyptian Desert* (1961), and *Christian Egypt, Ancient and Modern,* 2nd ed. (1977); William H. Worrell, *A Short Account of the Copts* (1945).

AZIZ S. ATIYA

[See also **Alexandria; Alexandrian Rite; Church Fathers; Councils (Ecumenical, 325–787); Cyril of Alexandria, St.; Egypt; Melkites; Missions and Missionaries, Christian; Monasticism, Origins; Monophysites.**]

COPULA, from the Latin word for a binding agent or the resulting union of parts, had a number of grammatical, rhetorical, and liturgical meanings in the Middle Ages—for example, the combination of two different poetical feet; the grammatical connection between subject and predicate; the linking of sound to semantic content. In poetry *copula* (Provençal: *cobla*) denoted the joining of verses into a strophe or part of a strophe. In music theory *copula* and *copulatio* are frequently used for the combining of tones into an interval (usually consonant) or a melody, as well as the combining of voices in polyphony. In the late Middle Ages *copula* repeatedly stood for the binding of several notes into a ligature.

In the theory of polyphony around and after 1100 (the Milan and Montpellier organum treatises), *copula* usually refers to the final consonance (unison, octave) of a section in two voices; *copulatio*, to the way it is reached—that is, the step from the penultimate to the final interval. The final consonance could also be ornamented melismatically in the *vox organalis* that was added to the preexisting chant. It is perhaps from this context that *copula* was transferred in the thirteenth century to short, rhythmically free transitional and concluding passages in the three- and four-voiced chant settings of the Notre Dame school (*copula non ligata*).

The term *copula* was also used by Johannes de Garlandia (also known as John of Garland) around 1240 and by others for a type of two-voiced composition in the Notre Dame repertoire that stands "between discant and organum." It shares with discant the strict modal rhythm of the upper voice and, with organum, the sustained tone of the tenor. However, here the word probably refers to the relatively "symmetrical" construction out of parts that are of equal length and are rhythmically and melodically analogous following the model of a poetic strophe.

During the thirteenth century, as a result of the Notre Dame composers' further experience with polyphonic composition, the character of copula as described by the theorists (strict proportional rhythm, complementary parts) was increasingly realized in discant and organum sections. The original, typical differences between the traditional types of composition were leveled off in the direction of a (perhaps monotonous) homogeneity. Eventually, therefore, individual sections came to be consciously performed "irregularly" in order to provide new variety: tempo and rhythm were varied, and modes were interchanged.

Similar "deviations" are included under the designation *copula* in the late thirteenth century. The meaning of this designation had obviously changed: no longer a special type of composition, *copula* instead applies to all those sections that—as a result of irregular performance—could not be designated as pure discant or pure organum. Copula now assumed, in a new sense, a position "between discant and organum."

BIBLIOGRAPHY

Fritz Reckow, *Der Musiktraktat des Anonymus 4* (1967), and *Die Copula* (1972); Erich Reimer, ed., *Johannes de Garlandia: De mensurabili musica*, 2 vols. (1972); William G. Waite, "Discantus, Copula, Organum," in *Journal of the American Musicological Society*, 5 (1952); Jeremy Yudkin, "The *Copula* According to Johannes de Garlandia," in *Musica disciplina*, 34 (1980).

FRITZ RECKOW

[See also **Franco of Cologne; John of Garland; Musical Treatises; Notre Dame School; Organum.**]

COPYHOLD. "A thorough history of copyhold would occupy a very important position in the social and legal history of England." This claim by Theodore Plucknett for the importance of copyhold could be made because an account of the evolution and nature of this tenure stands at the center of a great transformation that took place in late medieval English serfdom, or villeinage, and in the structure of the manor.

If the manorial economy (with its characteristic division of land into the lord's demesne, worked by unfree labor or by hired labor, and dependent peasant tenancies) showed at all times a great deal of regional variation, it also followed a cycle of several discernible phases operating over the centuries. For most of the twelfth century there was a movement away from demesne farming and from serfdom, that is, away from direct exploitation by the lords using unfree labor. In the thirteenth century this movement was slowed or even reversed in what is sometimes called a manorial reaction. Then, especially from the mid fourteenth century, the movement away from demesne farming and serfdom gathered force and brought an end to the manor and villeinage; landlords were transformed from seigneurs with a mass of unfree tenants into rentiers collecting rents from free tenants who held their land by what was frequently termed copyhold.

The last stage in this process has elicited much historical debate. An old view, no longer given credence, posited massive landlord efforts to revive serfdom, in the process provoking the Peasants' Revolt of 1381. In fact the condition of most villagers seems to have improved in the generation before the Peasants' Revolt, mainly because after the Black Death there were fewer villagers and their wages rose in consequence. A lord had to give his agricultural tenants acceptable terms or they might seek better ones from another landlord. Increasingly, the conditions of tenancy were copied out explicitly on the roll of the manorial court, and the tenure took the name of copyhold.

Thus, changes long in process proceeded apace in the fifteenth century. Enterprising peasants could put together a patchwork of scattered pieces of land held at favorable terms and could come up in the world; some even employed laborers to work all of their holdings. At the same time more substantial men became involved in leasing customary or villein holdings as they acquired parcels of land in a fluid market. Given these changes in the nature of rural tenancies, the law (which had previously declared that the freehold in a villein's land was in the lord, not the villein himself, and that the common law thus did not apply to his tenure), began to provide some protection to the manorial tenant.

Early in the fifteenth century the courts of equity (council and chancery) upheld the customary terms of manorial tenures, and in the late fifteenth century even the common law took steps; common-law courts began to protect copyhold tenure by entertaining trespass actions brought by copyhold tenants against their lords. In time the legal protection given copyhold tenure was nearly as strong as that given freehold; the copy of the conditions of tenure in the manorial court roll was considered as the tenant's title deed. Villeinage was never abolished in medieval or Tudor England, but as the evolution of copyhold reveals, "in general rural serfdom had gone out of the land and was all but forgotten by the time Queen Elizabeth ascended the throne" (M. M. Postan).

BIBLIOGRAPHY

Charles M. Gray, *Copyhold, Equity, and the Common Law* (1963); Theodore F. T. Plucknett, *A Concise History of the Common Law*, 5th ed. (1956); Michael M. Postan, *The Medieval Economy and Society; An Economic History of Britain, 1100–1500* (1972).

RICHARD W. KAEUPER

[See also **Land Tenure, Western European; Law, English Common; Serfs and Serfdom, Western European.**]

CORBEL, a block, usually of stone, that projects from a wall to support a beam or other horizontal piece. Ornamental corbels were also used as decoration, particularly in the Romanesque period.

LESLIE BRUBAKER

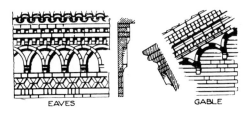

Corbel tables. FROM SIR BANISTER FLETCHER'S A HISTORY OF ARCHITECTURE

CORBEL TABLE, a row of corbels just below the eaves, often used as decoration in Norman Romanesque architecture, as on the facade at Jumièges cathedral (1037–1066).

LESLIE BRUBAKER

CÓRDOBA. This city—whose originally Iberian name is preserved in Latin Corduba, Visigothic Kordhoba, Arabic Qurṭuba—was a Phoenician foundation, then becoming the Carthaginian Baetis, identified by some with the biblical Tarshish. Situated in southern Spain (Andalusia), on the northern bank of the Guadalquivir River (*al-wādī al-kabīr*, "the great river"), it is to this day the capital of the province of Córdoba. It was taken by the Roman general Marcellus in 152 B.C. and was quickly colonized by Roman citizens; as Colonia Patricia it became the capital of Hispania Ulterior. Under Augustus, when Córdoba was one of the four judicial centers of Baetica province, were built the great sixteen-arch bridge (which still survives, though with Moorish alterations) and the road that bisects the city on a north-south axis. The two Senecas, Lucan, Hadrian, and Trajan were all natives of Córdoba; so too was Bishop Hosius (*ca.* 255–*ca.* 358), a leading opponent of Arianism and president of the first Nicene Council. In imperial times, then, Córdoba was a commercial and cultural center of some importance. It was devastated by the Vandals in the early fifth century, and much of this prosperity disappeared. In the following century it was a center of the revolt against the Gothic ruler Agila, whose reign, from 549 to 554, was a prelude to brief Byzantine hegemony; and it was also the center of the religious struggles between Arians and Catholics around 570. Then in 571 Córdoba fell to Leovigild, king of the Visigoths.

Its pre-Islamic history alone suggests that Córdoba owed its political importance to its favorable setting, and its subsequent history confirms this claim. To north and south the broad, flat plain of Córdoba is bordered by mountain ranges, and the serpentine course of the Guadalquivir, which in antiquity was navigable all the way to the city, makes the approaches of Córdoba still more readily defensible. Its agricultural hinterland produced wheat, olives, and wine in abundance, with lead and other mines nearby.

The capture of the city in 711 by Mughīth al-Rūmī, a manumitted slave, at the head of an Arab and Berber Muslim army, began a new chapter in its history. The lenient treatment accorded to the Christians on this occasion augured well for the future. That future was assured when between 716 and 719 al-Ḥurr ibn ᶜAbd al-Raḥmān al-Thaqafī, the third of twenty-three Umayyad governors of Andalusia (their tenure of office averaged less than two years apiece), transferred the seat of government from Seville to Córdoba. Andalusia was racked by tribal rivalries that the Arabs had imported from the Hejaz, and this disunity was very soon to have portentous consequences.

The wholesale massacre of the Syrian Umayyad house by the Abbasids of Baghdad in 750 had failed to extirpate that family entirely, and a sole surviving Umayyad prince, ᶜAbd al-Raḥmān ibn Muᶜāwiya, managed after many adventures to reach Spain. Taking advantage of the endemic tribal disputes there, he overthrew Yūsuf al-Fihrī, the last governor of Andalusia but the longest in office, in 756 and made Córdoba the capital of his new emirate. In addition to founding the Alcazar on the ruins of the Visigothic palace and the Great Mosque on those of a Roman temple and Christian church, like the Damascus jāmiᶜ, in 766 he extended the city ramparts (themselves of Roman foundation), which eventually comprised 132 towers and 13 gates; enlarged the Roman bridge; improved and fortified the city's aqueduct; and replaced the Visigothic administrative building by his own dār al-imārah. Two miles outside the city he built himself a country villa—named Munyat al-Ruṣāfa after his caliphal grandfather's favorite Syrian town—the garden of which was stocked with Syrian plants, including a palm tree to which he wrote a nostalgic ode. Later Umayyad rulers built similar pleasure cities.

While ᶜAbd al-Raḥmān followed Visigothic precedent in the division of Spain into provinces, he made Córdoba the administrative, political, military, religious, and cultural capital. Here too was the seat of the qāḍī al-quḍāt, the supreme judge of Muslim Spain. It was not long, however, before the internal tensions of the Muslim state exploded in Córdoba. The southern suburb (rabaḍ) of the city—the ancient Secunda (Shaqunda)—had been settled by Christian converts to Islam, the so-called muwalladūn, who were treated as inferior by the Arabs despite Koranic injunctions. The pleasure-loving al-Ḥakam I (796–822) and his bodyguard—so foreign that they knew no Arabic—became the targets for several violent revolts from 805 to 814 in which Berber theologians played a leading part. This resulted in the total demolition of the quarter in 818—it subsequently became a necropolis—and the deportation of its people to Morocco and Egypt.

Relations with the Christians were also strained at times. As a certain Alvaro remarked around 850, his coreligionists preferred Muslim to Christian writings, "building up great libraries of them at enormous cost ... hardly one can write a passable Latin letter to a friend, but innumerable are those who can express themselves in Arabic and can compose poetry in that language with greater art than the Arabs themselves." A reaction was inevitable. Inflamed by an ascetic priest named Eulogius, Christians began to court the death penalty by reviling Islam in public. ᶜAbd al-Raḥmān II thereupon induced the reluctant Spanish bishops to convene a council, which in 852 condemned these fanatics and repudiated their claims to perform miracles or to be true martyrs. The movement ended with the execution of Eulogius himself in 859; it had claimed forty-four martyrs.

The ninth century as a whole saw a steady decline in the power of the Umayyad emirate, with the secession of most of the areas conquered by ᶜAbd al-Raḥmān I. Muwalladūn, Mozarabs (Arabized Christians), and Berbers were prominent in these revolts, which resulted in the emirate contracting to the immediate neighborhood of Córdoba itself by 912. Nevertheless, the ninth century also laid the foundations for Córdoba's golden age. A disciple of Mālik ibn Anas established the Maliki legal rite, which henceforth dominated Andalusia, and he exerted much influence on ᶜAbd al-Raḥmān II. So too, in lighter vein, did the celebrated Ziryāb, a singer from Baghdad who became the arbiter of fashion in Córdoba, dictating modes of dress, dining, and speech.

The long reign (912–961) of ᶜAbd al-Raḥmān III witnessed the apogee of Córdoba. Under this energetic and dazzlingly successful monarch, who took the symbolic title of caliph in 929, the territorial expansion and cultural achievement of Spanish Islam reached its zenith. For Arab chroniclers, Córdoba was "the bride of al-Andalus," and even the contemporary Saxon nun Hrotsvitha called it "the ornament of the world." Seven centuries later the Maghrebi historian al-Maqqarī could write of this period: "in four things Córdoba surpasses the capitals of the world. Among them are the bridge over the river and the mosque. These are the first two; the third is Madīnat al-Zahrāᵓ; but the greatest of all things is knowledge—and that is the fourth."

The city—clean, well paved and lighted, abundantly supplied with running water—was huge. Its three sectors comprised an upper town and a lower town (Ajerquia) on the right bank of the river, enclosed by a single wall of Roman foundation but divided by a further wall, and also the area south of the river. The upper and lower towns expanded laterally to reach their eastern and western termini at Madīnat al-Ẓāhira and Madīnat al-Zahrāᵓ, respectively. Al-Maqqarī's oft-quoted figures on the buildings of Córdoba at this time are apt to mislead by their apparent precision, especially as modern demographic studies suggest that they exaggerate tenfold. Nevertheless, they clearly establish the image of Córdoba that lingered in the Islamic world: 1,600 mosques; 900 public baths; 213,077 homes for ordinary people; 60,300 mansions for notables, officials, and military commanders; and 80,455 shops. These buildings, we are invited to believe, were scattered throughout a conurbation measuring up to twenty-four by six miles and containing a million people.

Caliphal Córdoba was above all an intellectual center. Education was a priority. Al-Ḥakam II built 27 free schools and had a library of 400,000 volumes, of which the catalog alone ran to 44 registers of 50 leaves apiece. He was not alone. According to the chronicler Ibn Saᶜīd, "Córdoba held more books than any other city of al-Andalus . . . collections were regarded as symbols of status and social leadership." The contemporary monastery of St. Gall, by contrast, had one of northern Europe's major libraries with perhaps 400 to 600 books. The use of paper instead of vellum in Andalusia contributed to this astonishing disparity, as did the Islamic schools employing scores of female copyists; such schools were the medieval equivalent of publishing houses. Nor was this exceptional. The poet Ibn Hazm wrote "women taught me the Koran, they recited to me

much poetry, they trained me in calligraphy." Córdoba now disputed with Baghdad the intellectual leadership of the Islamic world. Its scholars continued the work of the bayt al-ḥikmā, the Abbasid translation institute, and thereby brought Greek and oriental learning to the West, a practice continued under Christian rule in a similar institution in Toledo. Major contributions were made in music, philology, geography, alchemy, chemistry, medicine, surgery, astronomy, philosophy, botany, and mathematics.

Even so, a sternly orthodox government curbed free speculation, especially in Muᶜtazilite and Sufi studies, occasionally burning books on "logic, astronomy, and other sciences cultivated by the Greeks" and banishing those who worked in such fields. Appropriately enough, the expertise of Córdoban scholars in tafsīr and fiqh was renowned, for Córdoba was conservative even to its calligraphy, and its Great Mosque contained the very arm of the Prophet and the Koran of ᶜUthmān. The arts and crafts flourished. The city boasted some 13,000 weavers, and its woolens, silks, and brocades were famous. So too was its craftsmanship in embossed goat leather, memorialized in the English words "cordovan" and "cordwainer." Gold and silver filigree, often inlaid in the manner of Damascus, was a speciality; indeed, Córdoban gold and silver were acceptable currency in northern Europe. Jewelry and ivory carving were widely exported and the process of manufacturing crystal was discovered here. The Christian Reconquest depressed most of these industries.

The role of non-Muslims in this cultural flowering was crucial, especially as Arabs, Christians, and Jews alike were bilingual in Arabic and the local Hispano-Roman dialect. Córdoban poets like Ibn Hazm developed forms unknown to the Muslim East which according to some scholars strongly influenced the poetry of the troubadours, while other Christians served as administrators, financiers, physicians, artists, and master craftsmen. The Christians were at first allowed to retain their churches, schools, and libraries. But the increasing pressure of the Reconquest eroded Muslim tolerance, so that under the later Umayyads Latin was banned and Christian children had to attend Arabic schools. The Mozarabic community had its own cadi, presumably administering Visigothic law, and was organized under its comes, the community spokesman in dealings with the government. In 970 the comes was

Mu-ᶜāwiya ibn Lope, while the bishop of Córdoba was ᶜĪsā ibn Manṣūr, and the foremost Christian, whom ᶜAbd al-Raḥmān III sent as ambassador to Germany, was Rabiᶜ ibn Zaid. Such names speak for themselves.

But Córdoba was also the center of a brilliant Jewish culture epitomized by Ḥisdai ibn Shaprut, a physician and diplomat serving ᶜAbd al-Raḥmān III, who attracted numerous Jewish scholars, poets, and philosophers to the city. Talmudic studies, too, revived under Rabbi Moses ibn Ḥanokh. For all its multiracial quality, however, its society was still rigidly stratifed in a descending hierarchy of Arabs; *muwalladūn;* Mozarabs; Christians, Jews, and Berbers; and finally the slaves on whom the entire economy depended.

The golden prime of Córdoba was encapsulated in Madīnat al-Zahrāᵓ, a palace city six miles northwest of Córdoba that was named after the favorite wife of ᶜAbd al-Raḥmān III and founded in 936. Its open-plan palaces, 4,313 marble columns, quicksilver ponds, translucent alabaster windows, bejeweled doors, marble Roman Venus, spacious gardens, and matchless views were justly celebrated. But excavations suggest that the sources exaggerate in stating that a court of 25,000 lived and worked here. Later in the century the usurper Abū ᶜĀmir al-Manṣūr built a similar city, Madīnat al-Ẓāhira, east of Córdoba; this, like Madīnat al-Zahrāᵓ, was destroyed during the sack of Córdoba in the Berber revolt of 1013. The simultaneous and still enigmatic decline of the Amirid family and the Umayyad dynasty had precipitated this disaster. The court mercenaries, mainly Ṣaqāliba (literally "Slavs" but in fact mainly Italians), the populace of Córdoba, and the Berbers all had their candidates for the caliphate, and the brief reign of Hishām III (1029–1031) failed to wrest order from chaos. With his death the Umayyad caliphate was extinguished and by degrees Muslim Spain broke into a mosaic of at least twenty-three separate principalities, the *taifas.*

Córdoba now became a republic under the presidency of three successive nobles of the Jahwarid family, but in 1070 it passed to the Abbadids of Seville and thence to the Almoravids in 1091. They in turn yielded Córdoba to the even more repressive and puritanical Almohad regime in 1172. These turbulent 150 years, dominated by party strife and the growing momentum of the Christian Reconquest, robbed Córdoba of its military and political importance but nevertheless produced some of her greatest

scholars, such as the philosopher and physician Ibn Rushd (Averroës). Although the Almohads forcibly converted the Jews and thereby eradicated the Córdoban Jewish community for a time, that community had shortly before included the greatest of Spanish Jews, Moses Maimonides, rabbi, physician to Saladin, philosopher, and diplomat.

When the last Almohad caliph died in 1223, Córdoba fell victim to party strife once more and was taken by Ferdinand III of León and Castile in 1236. The Muslims never controlled it again; indeed, Córdoba now served as the principal military base in the war against Granada. Many Castilian noble and military families settled there and it became an episcopal see. But its prosperity declined, partly because its all-important textile industry was cut from its source of raw material—the silk farms of Granada. A new Alcazar was built by Alphonse XI of Castile in 1328, and various churches followed. Even so, the Christians did not at once eradicate the traces of Córdoba's Muslim past, contenting themselves with turning the Great Mosque into a church and building chapels within it.

Atypically enough, the Jewish community for a time fared better than it had done under recent Muslim rule, but in 1250 a papal directive was aimed at their new synagogue because of the richness and splendor of the building, and in 1254 Alphonse X introduced new restrictions. The surviving medieval synagogue was built in 1315 by Isaac Moḥeb ibn Ephraim in Mudejar style and bears inscriptions from the Psalms. Córdoban Jewry specialized in making and marketing textiles; its wealth may be gauged from the annual tax of 38,000 maravedis it paid in 1294, a tax psychologically compounded by a symbolic payment of 30 denarii demanded by the church. Most of the community was massacred in the riots of 1391, and like the rest of the city it suffered grievously from the plague in this period. Right up to 1400 Córdoban Jews spoke Arabic. Forcible conversions were the rule in the fifteenth century, and even after all Jews had been ordered out of Andalusia in 1483, the poor remnant in Córdoba still had to pay two years later a special levy for the war against Granada, which was prosecuted from their city. The main Jewish quarter was situated near the Alcazar in the southwest of the city, and a further quarter seems to have been sited in the north, near the Jewish Gate (Bāb al-Yahūd), which stood until 1903. Today the medieval Judería comprises some 100 small informal patios strung out along minor streets and fronted on three sides by double-storied courtyard houses, whitewashed, balconied, and festooned with flowers.

ROBERT HILLENBRAND

[See also Andalusia; Eulogius of Córdoba; Hazm, Ibn; Islam, Conquests of; Jews in Muslim Spain; Maimonides, Moses; Mozarabic Art; Mozarabic Literature; Rushd, Ibn; Spain, Christian-Muslim Relations in; Spain, Moorish Kingdoms of; Umayyads.]

CÓRDOBA, PEDRO DE. See **Pedro de Córdoba.**

CORIPPUS (*fl.* sixth century), poet and historian. Flavius Cresconius Corippus composed the *Libyan Wars* at Carthage in 548. Later, at the imperial court in Constantinople, he wrote *In Praise of Justin II* (*ca.* 567). Corippus was steeped in the traditions of classical and Christian Latin poetry. His works also provide a wealth of historical detail on North Africa and Constantinople.

BIBLIOGRAPHY

Editions of Corippus' works are *Iohannidos seu de bellis Libycis libri 8*, James Diggle and F. R. D. Goodyear, eds. (1970); *In laudem Iustini Augusti minoris libri 4*, Averil Cameron, ed. and trans. (1976). See also L. Krestan and K. Winkler, "Corippus," in *Reallexikon für Antike und Christentum*, III (1957).

MARK A. ZIER

[See also **Historiography, Western European.**]

CORMAC MAC AIRT. Cormac son of Art son of Conn is a prestige ancestor of the Uí Néill kings of Tara. He is the ideal king of Irish tradition, and his life and reign are abundantly celebrated in medieval Irish literature. Cormac's reign is generally assigned to the third century A.D., but the earlier tradition would seem to be that he belonged to the fourth century. In either case, he is well beyond the reach of contemporary documentation in Ireland, so that the question of his historicity must be left open. In the literature, Cormac is the exemplar of *fír flathemon* (the truth [and justice] of a ruler), the quality that

secures fertility, peace, and justice in the kingdom. The legends about him embody and express in narrative form the political ideology of medieval Ireland and tell us something of the political claims of the Uí Néill.

Cormac's life, as recounted in Irish texts from the eighth century on, is depicted in terms of the "heroic biography"; this is a sequence of episodes of the type traditionally associated with heroes in Ireland and elsewhere. Thus, we are told of the extraordinary circumstances surrounding his birth, of how he won the hand of the goddess Ethne, of his perilous journey to the Otherworld, and so on. His accession to the kingship of Tara was achieved by peaceful means: he delivered a true judgment that showed him to be possessed of *fír flathemon* and was thus deemed worthy to be invested with the kingship. Cormac is presented in the tradition as a great builder at Tara, as an innovator, and as a lawgiver, and his reign is portrayed as a golden age of peace and plenty in which Ireland took on the character of the Otherworld.

BIBLIOGRAPHY

Tomás Ó Cathasaigh, *The Heroic Biography of Cormac mac Airt* (1977); Máirín O Daly, *Cath Maige Mucrama* (1975).

TOMÁS Ó CATHASAIGH

[See also **Ireland, Early History; Uí Néill.**]

CORMAC MAC CUILENNÁIN (*d.* 908), bishop of Cashel and, from 902, king of Munster. His combining of the two positions reflects the growing secularization of the Irish church from the ninth century on and the active role of its members in politics. Cormac's origins are obscure; the pedigree given to him in the genealogies, though suspect, does at least show that he did not belong to the inner dynastic circles of the Eóganacht Chaisil, who usually provided candidates for the Munster kingship. He may have been a compromise choice, or perhaps even a puppet advanced by the rival Uí Néill tribes of northern and central Ireland who actively discouraged the emergence of a strong, unified dynasty in Munster.

Once king of Munster, Cormac's main concern was to secure the overlordship of Osraige (Ossory) and Leinster, the territories to the east and north of

Munster, as a first step toward halting and overcoming the growing power of the Uí Néill. In 907 Cormac defeated Flann Sinna mac Máel Sechnaill, king of Tara and of the southern Uí Néill, in a battle at Mag Léna (near Durrow, County Offaly); later that year he crossed into Connacht and took hostages there. But in 908, while advancing through Leinster, Cormac suffered defeat and death at the Battle of Belach Mugna (Ballaghmoone, County Kildare), fighting against Flann and his allies from Leinster and Connacht.

Both as a man of action and as a clerical scholar, Cormac exercises a remarkable influence on subsequent Irish literary traditions. Numerous poems, many of them elaborating aspects of his political career, were fathered on or written about him. Virtually all of these attributions to Cormac must be rejected; many are products of later Munster propagandists. Cormac's rule, a versified monastic rule, moderate—by Irish standards—in tone and precept, has traditionally been ascribed to Cormac; certainly the linguistic evidence, which points to a date of the late ninth century, supports the attribution. Most scholars agree that Cormac is the author of *Sanas Cormaic,* a glossary of Irish words difficult and obsolete in his time, which are explained by reference to false Latin etymologies. Despite its pseudo-learning, this glossary provides valuable information about Irish mythology and legends as they were understood in the early tenth century, and it cites sources now lost; it also attests to ecclesiastical interest in native Irish secular literature. Another work, the lost manuscript referred to in late medieval Irish works as the "Psalter of Cashel," has also been claimed for Cormac. This manuscript—apparently still in existence in 1453, when portions of it were copied into the Oxford, Bodleian Library, MS Laud Misc. 610—contained, *inter alia,* the *Sanas Cormaic,* an earlier Munster version of the "Book of Rights" (a statement of the tributes due to and the gifts given by the king of Munster), and synthetic genealogies of Ireland. A genealogy found in the Oxford, Bodleian Library, MS Rawlinson B 502 (early twelfth century), purporting to come from the "Psalter of Cashel," has an introduction in Latin that may also be the work of Cormac.

BIBLIOGRAPHY

For brief historical discussions of Cormac's role in the dynastic struggles between Munster and the Uí Néill, see Francis J. Byrne, *Irish Kings and High-kings* (1973), pas-

sim; John V. Kelleher, "The Rise of the Dál Cais," in Etienne Rynne, ed., *North Munster Studies* (1967), 230–242, esp. 235–236; and Donnchadh Ó Corráin, *Ireland Before the Normans* (1972), 111–113. For the poems attributed to Cormac see Richard I. Best, *Bibliography of Irish Philology and of Printed Irish Literature* (1913), and *Bibliography of Irish Philology and Manuscript Literature: Publications 1913–1941* (1942).

PADRAIG P. Ó NÉILL

[See also **Ireland, Early History; Uí Néill.**]

CORMONT, REGNAULT DE. See **Regnault de Cormont.**

CORMONT, THOMAS DE. See **Thomas de Cormont.**

CORONA VAULT. See **Vault.**

CORONATION, PAPAL. Since the end of the thirteenth century, the term "coronation" has designated all liturgical acts by which a newly elected pope was invested in office; previously, various customs and terminology were usual. For this reason, each historical period must be treated separately.

Late antiquity. With the establishment of the monarchic episcopate in Rome at the end of the second century, it became necessary to regulate the bishop's ordination. For the initial period, the *Apostolic Tradition* of Hippolytus of Rome and the letters of Cyprian of Carthage are by far the most informative sources. These texts indicate that the bishop was elected by the faithful—laymen as well as clerics—on Sundays, when the congregation gathered to celebrate the Eucharist. Divine inspiration was sometimes invoked, as Eusebius' embellished report on the election of Fabian in 236 shows. The candidate was consecrated by the laying on of hands of several bishops from around Rome, at which time the consecrators implored God's protection for the new bishop. Where the election and consecration were held is uncertain because no bishop's church yet existed in Rome.

With the construction of the Basilica Sancti Salvatoris, or Basilica Constantiniana, at the Lateran by Emperor Constantine, the ordination ceremonies were concentrated more and more heavily at this church. They took place there exclusively from around 400, except when schism necessitated the use of other churces, such as St. Peter's. By this time, election and consecration had become two separate events. The election was conducted as soon as possible after the death of the last pope. The clergy and people of Rome acted as electors, but the leading clerics—presbyters and deacons—as well as the members of the senatorial upper class were the determining factor. In the case of contested elections, the city prefect, as representative of the emperor, or the emperor himself intervened. From the end of the fifth century, it was generally the Ostrogothic king who intervened. The archdeacon of that time or another member of the diaconate was usually elected. The consecration took place then, as before, on a Sunday. The most important consecrator was the bishop of Ostia; two other bishops from the Roman church province assisted him. The fundamental act of consecration was still the laying on of hands. Furthermore, an evangelistary was laid on his head, and perhaps a pallium would be handed to him as a sign of his new rank. Then he probably sat on the throne of the Lateran Basilica while the clergy paid him homage. Whether the newly elected pope solemnly took possession of the bishop's palace and then proceeded to St. Peter's to show himself as the successor and vicar of Peter, cannot be determined with certainty.

Byzantine period. Once Rome became part of the Byzantine Empire, the newly elected pope had to be endorsed by the emperor or by the exarch of Ravenna before he could be consecrated. Consequently, the importance of the election increased and the significance of the consecration diminished. Gregory the Great already took steps to secure the leadership of his diocese before he was consecrated in 590. The election probably took place in the Lateran Basilica or in the church to which the candidate had belonged. The leaders of the Byzantine militia and the Roman army, in addition to the higher clerics, now counted among the electors. After the election, the new pope received the homage of his electors while seated on the apse throne of the Lateran Basilica. He then took possession of the Lateran Palace, where he held a ceremonial banquet. Afterward he was acclaimed by the populace. Contrary to older custom, his consecration took place in St. Peter's, where it is

held to the present day. Before the Gloria of the consecration mass, the bishops of Albano, Porto, and Ostia recited the consecration prayers and held an evangelistary over his head. Then the archdeacon probably handed him the pallium. Besides, he was again paid homage, either before or after the Gloria. The ceremonies in St. Peter's were intended to show the new pope as the leader of all Christianity, while those in the Lateran symbolized his taking charge of the Roman diocese. As a result of the increasing universal importance of the papacy, the liturgy in St. Peter's slowly displaced that in the Lateran.

Carolingian period. With the beginning of the pope's secular rule in the eighth century, the significance of the Lateran Palace, to which had been attributed imperial status in the *Constitutum Constantini,* rose. For that reason, occupation *(possesso)* of the palace stood in the center of the election procedures while the Lateran Basilica was disregarded. After the election—where, is uncertain—of a new pope, who ordinarily was a cardinal priest or cardinal deacon, the candidate was ceremoniously visited and led to the Lateran Palace. There—perhaps in Leo III's Triclinium—he received the papal vestments and was seated on a throne, where his feet were kissed by the leading clerics and laymen as a sign of homage. He then received from them an oath of allegiance.

The consecration in St. Peter's followed on a Sunday or a feast day, after the emperor's representatives had sanctioned the election (required since 824). As in the previous period, the cardinal bishops of Albano, Porto, and Ostia pronounced the three prayers of consecration and an evangelistary was held over the pope's head. The archdeacon then attached the pallium to his chasuble and escorted him to the apse throne, built by Gregory the Great, which was considered as the throne of Peter. There the pope was kissed again and intoned the Gloria. After the mass, the pope changed garments and went to the steps of the church, where he was met with acclamation. There a crown *(phrygium, regnum,* later tiara) supposedly donated by Constantine was placed on his head. From this time, the coronation, originally only one of the symbols of the pope's secular rule, increased in importance. With the crown on his head, the pope then rode back to the Lateran Palace.

Period of the German emperors. Tenth-century sources are relatively sparse, and much of our limited knowledge is indirect. Two changes must be considered. From the time of Marinus I (882–884), but especially under emperors Otto III and Henry III, bishops of dioceses other than Rome, who no longer required consecration because of their previous office, came increasingly to be elected popes, contrary to prevailing law. On the other hand, beginning with Otto I's appointment of Pope Leo VIII in 963, the German rulers invested more and more popes with their office. Both changes caused a transformation in the procedure for elevation to the papacy. It is noteworthy that the Lateran Palace is not mentioned with reference to papal elections even though its importance for the papacy had increased, especially in the tenth century. On the contrary, all important ceremonies were concentrated in St. Peter's.

If the pope was elected by the Roman clergy and populace, the heads of Roman society, as before, went to his residence and acclaimed him; if installed by the German ruler he received the tokens of his status from him. In addition to the traditional pallium, the *ferula* (a jeweled staff with a cross) and, in the eleventh century, a purple pluvial were presented to him. If the pope was not already a bishop, he was consecrated as usual in St. Peter's before the Gloria; if he had already been bishop, he was only blessed there by the same three cardinal bishops.

His ceremonious enthronement by bishops in St. Peter's was now, according to the German model and with allusion to older legal theories, the decisive act. From 955 the taking of a new name was incorporated in this ritual. Hence the term *inthronizatio* designated all proceedings as well as succession to the papal office. The sources do not mention a subsequent coronation procession.

Nicholas II to Alexander III (1059–1159). With the papal election decree of 1059, the right to elect a pope became increasingly restricted to the cardinals, even though members of the Roman clergy and populace were, in practice, often instrumental in the election. The lawful pope was now whomever the majority or a smaller, but "sounder part" (*sanior pars*) of the cardinals had elected. Furthermore, because the German emperor's right of investiture was being challenged due to political circumstances, and because many elections took place outside of Rome, the installation procedures, which could take place only in Rome, were often conducted afterward—if at all. As a result, the enthronement proceedings became subordinate to the enmantling with the purple pluvial, as well as to the presentation of the pallium and the consecration or benediction. However, if the pope was elected in Rome, his taking possession of the Lateran became central.

1179 to 1303. As a result of previous turmoil, above all the schism of 1159, Alexander III had the fathers of the Third Lateran Council pass a resolution in 1179 that the lawful pope was the one whom two-thirds of the cardinals had elected. Since then the papal election has remained the most important, often the only, constitutive act for elevation to the papacy. For that reason the post-election rite increasingly lost all legal significance, though the liturgical ceremony became all the more elaborate.

If the pope was elected in Rome, the traditional ceremonies took place, but with their former order reversed. After being consecrated or blessed, as well as presented with the pallium in St. Peter's, he was then enthroned in the apse throne. Following the mass, he was crowned with the tiara on the steps of St. Peter's. A solemn procession along the edge of populated sections into the Lateran Basilica and Palace concluded the ceremonies. The precedents for the procession changed somewhat in 1198 with the coronation of Innocent III. Until then the palace clergy stood next to the pope; now the cardinals and foreign prelates occupied that place. With this change, it became obvious that the pope was less the bishop of Rome than the leader of the universal church. Furthermore, because most popes had already been bishops and the benediction did not constitute a sacramental act, the coronation received increasing emphasis and was used as an expression of all ceremonial acts from the end of the thirteenth century on.

The late Middle Ages. This trend grew stronger during the fourteenth century. The enthronement was totally omitted during the Avignon period; and because the Avignon practices survived at the papal court even after the end of the Great Schism, the enthronement played hardly any role even in Rome. The enmantling was likewise forgotten. For that reason and because of the diminished significance of the benediction, the coronation—now with triple diadems—and procession became stronger in ceremonial importance. An innovation from Avignon was that, in an attempt to retain the customs of the solemn papal mass, a ceremonial cleric burned oakum three times during the procession to the main altar and before the benediction. Furthermore, the cleric reminded the pope of the transitory nature of his high position by means of the cry, "Holy Father, thus the glory of the world passes away" (*Pater sancte, sic transit gloria mundi*).

From the end of the fifteenth century, the coronation in front of St. Peter's had become so important, and taking possession of the Lateran so secondary, that the latter act could take place several days after the coronation, as in the case of Julius II (1503). For the later Middle Ages it is debated whether the new pope had to wait until he had been crowned before performing certain functions such as granting consistorial prebends to bishops or abbots or offering solemn masses.

BIBLIOGRAPHY

Robert L. Benson, *The Bishop Elect* (1968); Francesco Cancellieri, *Storia de' solenni possessi de' Sommi Pontefici* (1802); Eduard Eichmann, *Weihe und Krönung des Papstes im Mittelalter* (1951); Carl Gerold Fürst, "Statim ordinetur episcopus," in *Ex aequo et bono: Willibald M. Plöchl zum 70. Geburtstag* (1977), 45–65; Nikolaus Gussone, *Thron und Inthronisation des Papstes von den Anfängen bis zum 12. Jahrhundert* (1978); Hans Walter Klewitz, "Die Krönung des Papstes," in *Zeitschrift für Rechtsgeschichte, Kanonistische Abeteilung*, 30 (1941); Bernhard Schimmelpfennig, "Die in St. Peter verehrte Cathedra Petri," in *Quellen und Forschungen aus italienischen Archiven und Bibliotheken*, 53 (1973), and "Die Krönung des Papstes im Mittelalter," *ibid.*, 54 (1974); Franz Wasner, "De consecratione, inthronizatione, coronatione Summi Pontificis," in *Apollinaris*, 8 (1935).

BERNHARD SCHIMMELPFENNIG

[See also **Conclave, Papal; Lateran; Papacy, Origins and Development of; Rome; St. Peter's Church, Rome.**]

CORONATION RITUALS. See **Kingship (Coronation), Rituals of.**

CORONER. In the twelfth and thirteenth centuries the English monarchy broke up the concentration of powers that had been held by the sheriffs of counties, by establishing new local officers to take over various duties. One of the new officers was the coroner. The position was created in 1194 and modified in the decades just after, to emerge in the 1220's in what proved to be its permanent form. In each county there were commonly two or four coroners for the county itself, and others for boroughs and franchises. They were elected in the county or borough courts or appointed by lords of franchises. Their work, which was "to keep the pleas of the crown," entailed several responsibilities in the detection and prosecution of crime.

Every sudden or suspicious death had to be investigated by a coroner. With a jury (but no professional medical help) he viewed the body, inquired, and concluded as best he could whether it was natural death, misadventure, homicide, or suicide. As the case required, he attached finders, neighbors, and eyewitnesses; took indictments of homicide from his jury; ordered the arrest of the indicted; and secured property that might fall to the crown. The case would be finally reviewed, and indictments tried, by royal justices; the coroner prepared it for their consideration.

A second duty was to record "appeals," charges of felony prosecuted by individuals. Jurisdiction over appeals belonged to royal justices, who were not always present in the county, but every appeal had to be moved in strict form immediately upon discovery of the offense. So the coroner "kept" the appeal, first by making an exact record of it when it was raised, and then by seeing to the arrest or attachment of the accused. Some of the appeals that he kept were those of approvers, accused felons who confessed and appealed their accomplices to save their own lives.

Third, coroners dealt with felons who took sanctuary in church to escape arrest. Their privilege was to confess before the coroner and abjure, swearing to leave England forever. The coroner assigned a port of exit, saw the man off, and secured his property.

Finally, it was the coroner's duty to record in the county court the process of exaction and outlawry against felons and others who had absconded.

Other, miscellaneous tasks were given by command of the chancery or royal justices. Thus coroners were often directed to join the sheriff in making special investigations or to substitute for him in executing legal process where the sheriff was personally disqualified—for instance, as if he should be party to a case.

During the thirteenth century the office of coroner spread to Wales, Ireland, and Scotland. In Scotland, however, it was rather different. Scottish coroners were appointed by the crown or the justices in ayre. Like their English counterparts, they held postmortem inquests, but otherwise their principal duty was to arrest persons indicted in the ayres.

BIBLIOGRAPHY

Roy F. Hunnisett, *The Medieval Coroner* (1961), is a thorough study of the office in England. For its introduction into Glamorgan, see Michael Altschul, *A Baronial*

Family in Medieval England: The Clares, 1217–1314 (1965), 264; for Ireland, see Annette J. Otway-Ruthven, *A History of Medieval Ireland* (1968), 179–180; for Scotland, see *Acts of the Parliament of Scotland*, I (1844), 737–739; James MacKinnon, *The Constitutional History of Scotland* (1924), 128, 139; Thomas Murray (of Glendook), *The Laws and Acts of Parliament ... of Scotland* (1681), "Abridgement," *s.v.* "Crowner," and Archibald A. M. Duncan, *Scotland: The Making of the Kingdom* (1975), 496.

DONALD W. SUTHERLAND

[See also **Law, English Common.**]

CORPORATION. Medieval society embraced a mass of vital, burgeoning corporate institutions. These extended from lowly monasteries, manorial courts, and trade guilds to their universal counterparts, the *communitas regni* (community of the kingdom) and *communitas ecclesiae* (community of the church). During the twelfth and thirteenth centuries canonists and lay jurists adapted Roman legal principles to the needs and expedients of these ecclesiastical and secular groups to produce the foundations in legal theory of the modern corporation. The development of the theory of the corporation as a distinct legal institution spans an era beginning with the use of Justinian's *Corpus iuris civilis* to protect and define church institutions and culminating in an essential configuration of the legal structure of the corporate body in the well-known doctrine of the *Commentarius super libros quinque decretalium* of Pope Innocent IV (1243–1254): "As in the case of a university, a college is fictionalized as if it were a single person, so also a university, a cathedral chapter, a nation or a similar type of entity, are really not names of persons, but rather terms of law." (c. *Praesentium 57, X, de testibus et attestationibus*, II, 20). By the early fourteenth century Marsiglio of Padua could confidently assert a widespread belief in the fundamental right of any civil or ecclesiastical community to enact laws to regulate its activities, and to appoint a chief officer to administer these laws.

While the outline of the legal structure of a corporate entity can be found in numerous provisions in the *Corpus iuris canonici* concerning the right of church institutions to receive and administer property, the transformation of the Roman legal precedent into an identifiable concept of the corporation is more clearly attributable to the commentators on the canons, the decretists and the decretalists. The canon law counted as ecclesiastical corporations, among others, the Roman church itself, dioceses, parishes, the goods of the church (*fabrica*), the episcopal patrimony (*mensa*), prebends, cathedral chapters, universities, religious orders, monasteries, and charitable foundations. In England the crown was regarded in the common law as a corporation sole certainly from the duchy of Lancaster case decided in 1562. Earlier, village charters and bylaws, the gradual extension of rights and privileges to trade and merchant guilds, the societies of lawyers that developed into the Inns of Court, and the formation of alms and mutual benefit societies all attest to the existence of a variety of corporate entities in civil life.

The common features of the corporation that medieval jurists derived from Roman law and their own creative wisdom include the idea of a multitude forming one man; a group of persons united for a common purpose, a *universitas bonorum aut personarum* as a single person with rights and duties at law; its internal rules and actions seen as the expression of the overriding will of a corporate personality; the determination of laws by majority decision; the *pars maior* or *sanior* (the greater or wiser part); and the notion of continuing existence of the collective whole beyond the lives of its members.

Corporate entities were known in Roman law from the earliest times, notably the *populus Romanus*, municipalities (*municipia* or *civitates*), and private organizations such as trade guilds, burial societies, and the like. But the Romans had no theory of collective personality as such. Roman lawyers may have said that entities today regarded as juristic persons had *corpus* (body), but there is no evidence that they conceived of the personality of the corporation as somehow distinct from its members, as in English law, or as distinct from its administrators, as in the German *Stiftung*. Although they could own property, manumit slaves, receive under a will, and even, in the time of Hadrian, receive trusts (*fideicommissa*), towns and colonies were still mostly in the hands of magistrates and public functionaries—and thus not totally in the domain of private law, where a corporate theory might have acquired more cogency. Private associations (*sodalites, collegia, societates*), trade associations, burial clubs, and business associations had freedom of formation in the Roman Republic as long as they were not contrary to the public order. They could own property, be the beneficiaries of obligations, and litigate in private law through *actores*.

In the later empire there was a steady proliferation of guilds of merchants, such as *dendrophori* (wood carriers) and *centonarii* (ragpickers), having the rights in private law of *collegia*. Religious and benevolent societies, churches, and *piae causae* grew rapidly with the advent of Christianity, particularly after the grant to churches by Constantine of the rights of heirship and reception of legacies. Yet even with the growth of benefactions, such as orphanages, hospitals, and geriatric homes, the right of the local bishop to supervise the administration of their goods may have precluded the need for a theory of personality as such. Thus, the seeds of development were scattered through Roman law in provisions for many different kinds of entities bearing rights and duties in private law. The theory of the corporation, as such, however, would await the revival of Roman law and its fertilization by medieval canonistic jurisprudence.

The antecedents in canon law for the attribution of juristic personality to ecclesiastical communities date to the constitution of bishops as trustees of property in their own dioceses. These canons, implying the right of the diocese to own property, can be found clearly in the Synod of Gangra (324), canons 7 and 8, the Council of Antioch (341), canons 24 and 25, and the Council of Chalcedon (451), canon 25. From here on, the influence of the church on Roman law was clear. The law provided for the appointment by the bishop of the administrators of orphanages and charitable homes; and Justinian's *Novellae* declared that the representatives of the bishop were bound to render account to him. Under the Code of Justinian, the bishop was authorized to appoint defenders of ecclesiastical property and to act as judge in lawsuits in which ecclesiastical property was involved. The whole field of charitable bequests was entrusted to the bishop's court to such an extent that any contrary provision of the donor was null. Such ample authority leads to the conclusion that both the diocese and a variety of benevolent institutions under the authority of the bishop were considered distinct corporate entities.

Following Roman jurisprudence and the practice of ecclesiastics, the English kings conferred corporate charters first on municipalities, towns, and boroughs, and second on trade guilds. The charters spelled out a corporate role for the officers, the mayors and councillors, similar to that given clerics in the canon law. The Weavers Guild was incorporated by the time of Henry III's reign (1216–1272), the Goldsmiths in 1327, Mercers in 1393, Haberdashers in 1407, the Fishmongers in 1433, Vintners in 1437, and the Merchant Taylors in 1466. These were fol-

lowed by the great international trading companies of the sixteenth century.

The terms "corporation" and "body corporate" first appeared in public documents during the reign of Henry IV (1399–1413), although the idea, borrowed perhaps from canon law, appears earlier in Bracton (*d.* 1268): "In colleges and chapters [common medieval corporate bodies] the same body always remains, although each member dies one after the other and others are put in their places, just as one may speak of a herd of sheep as always the same, although all the sheep die in succession" (*De legibus et consuetudinibus Angliae* f. 374b [ed. Thorne, IV, 175]). The way had been paved by the concept of the church and its subdivisions and the practices of ecclesiastics within their own domains. This chronological advantage of the church in the creation of corporations was long maintained in the right conceded the church by common law jurists to establish its own corporations independent of the state. It was from the example of incorporated monasteries that English common law first applied the principle of incorporation to mayors and communities (though in England a "head" was regarded as fundamental, so that the legal person was not the town of Norwich but the mayor, sheriff, and commonalty of Norwich). It is thus from usages of the religious orders, most probably, that the Roman law principle of agency, *quod omnes tangit, ab omnibus approbari debet* (what touches all should be approved by all), evolved into a principle of corporate representation.

BIBLIOGRAPHY

W. O. Ault, "Village By-Laws by Common Consent," in *Speculum*, 29 (1954); Brendan F. Brown, *The Canonical Juristic Personality* (1927); Patrick W. Duff, *Personality in Roman Private Law* (1938, repr. 1971); Herbert F. Jolowicz, *Roman Foundations of Modern Law* (1957, repr. 1978); Ernst H. Kantorowicz, *The King's Two Bodies* (1957, repr. 1981); A. Marongui, "The Theory of Democracy and Consent in the Fourteenth Century," in Fredric L. Cheyette, ed., *Lordship and Community in Medieval Europe* (1968 repr. 1975); Pierre Michaud-Quantin, "Collectivités médiévales et institutions antiques," in Paul Wilpert, ed., *Miscellanea Medievalia*, I (1962), 239–252; Ricardo Orestano, *Il problema delle persone giuridiche in diritto romano* (1968); Gaines Post, *Studies in Medieval Legal Thought, Public Law, and the State, 1100–1322* (1964).

WILLIAM W. BASSETT

[See also **Charter; Corpus Iuris Civilis; Decretists; Guilds and Métiers; Law, Canon; Law, Civil; Law Codes: 1000–**

1500; Law, English Common; Urbanism, Western European.]

CORPUS CHRISTI, FEAST OF. The feast of Corpus Christi (the body of Christ) was a distinctively medieval development in Christian piety and practice regarding the Eucharist. Twelfth-century theology had emphasized the real, substantial presence of Christ in the bread and wine of the sacrament, even apart from the activities of the Mass. At the time the doctrine of transubstantiation was definitively formulated at the Fourth Lateran Council (1215), a young Augustinian nun named Juliana of Liège experienced several visions of a full moon with one dark spot. She understood the moon to represent the church, and the darkened area to indicate the absence of a separate feast in honor of the Eucharist. Some colleagues and superiors, including the archdeacon of Liège, Jacques Pantaléon, supported her in advocating a new festival. In 1246 Robert de Torote, bishop of Liège, officially established the feast throughout his diocese on the first Thursday after the octave of Pentecost. Archdeacon Jacques later became Pope Urban IV, and in 1264 he formally extended his hometown feast to the whole Roman Catholic church (*Transiturus de hoc mundo,* issued at Orvieto).

Of course the original institution of the Eucharist at the Last Supper was already observed on Maundy Thursday. But Pope Urban noted that on that day the church was fully occupied with reconciling penitents, consecrating the holy oil, washing feet, and the severely somber remembrance of Christ's passion. Another context was needed, he wrote, to rejoice appropriately over the gift of the sacrament. Despite this decree it was only through the efforts of popes Clement V and John XXII fifty years later that the church at large observed this occasion, known then as the feast of the Eucharist.

Devotion to the reserved elements of the sacrament had previously included a few moments of ceremonial procession on Palm Sunday and Maundy Thursday. But starting in Cologne around 1275, the procession of the "body of Christ" became an occasion for the whole community to proceed triumphantly throughout the town and even into the countryside. By 1350 the custom of a full procession was widespread and threatened to overshadow the Mass itself. By the fifteenth century special vessels made for this annual procession replaced the ciboria and reliquaries previously borrowed from other contexts. Late medieval piety and society attached great importance to the feast of Corpus Christi, especially the procession. It was often accompanied by great displays of flowers and occasionally by reports of miracles. In Germany the procession often included four stations with prayers for good weather.

The texts of the day's office and Mass have a complicated history going back to Juliana. Thomas Aquinas is often credited with writing this service, especially the hymns *Lauda Sion* and *Pange lingua,* but it seems that other authors were also involved. Liturgical dramas staged on that day evolved into great pageants covering the history of the world from creation to Last Judgment, as seen in the English Corpus Christi plays of York and Chester.

BIBLIOGRAPHY

Verdel A. Kolve, *The Play Called Corpus Christi* (1966).

PAUL ROREM

[See also **Chester Plays; Eucharist; Feasts and Festivals, European.**]

CORPUS IURIS CIVILIS. The *Corpus iuris civilis* (Collection of Civil Law) is the collective name given to the legislation of Emperor Justinian (527–565). Early in his reign Justinian ordered a commission of ten men, under John of Cappadocia, to codify Roman imperial constitutions from the second century to his own time, drawing on three earlier collections of imperial decrees: the *Codex Gregorianus,* the *Codex Hermogenianus,* and the *Codex Theodosianus.* The commission produced a *Codex (Code)* that was published in 529. This work has not survived, for it was replaced by a revised text five years later.

In 530 Justinian decided to create a new commission under Tribonian, the quaestor of the Sacred Palace. This commission, which included professors from Constantinople and Beirut, the two principal centers for the study of law in the Eastern Empire, was charged with producing a volume that contained the writings of the ancient jurisconsults who had interpreted the law, and with eliminating everything that was superfluous, contradictory, and outdated. The resulting work, finished in 533, was called the *Digest* (or *Pandects*) and covered all aspects of legal thought from property law to marriage, as found in the legal works of the great jurists of the past.

Justinian also commissioned an introductory legal textbook, issued in 533 as the *Institutiones (Institutes)*, and a revised version of the 529 codex in 534. In his constitutions *Omnem* and *Tanta*, which he issued with the *Digest*, Justinian forbade commentaries on the *Digest* and gave detailed instructions how these new books should be used in the schools and how they should be copied. He also ordered that only these books could be used "where laws were necessary." Justinian's legislation from 534 until his death was gathered together in three unofficial collections that have survived as the *Novellae* (new laws, or Novels).

The immediate influence of Justinian's *Corpus iuris* was limited. The use of Latin in the *Code* and the *Digest* rendered them inaccessible to much of Greek-speaking Constantinople and the Eastern Empire, whereas the Latin half of the empire, where the codification could have been used, was severed almost completely from the eastern half by the end of the sixth century. The *Digest* left almost no trace in any legal collection and was practically forgotten during the seventh through tenth centuries. The *Code*, however, was important as a source of law. Epitomes of the *Code* were made, its titles excerpted, the last three books left off, and the Greek constitutions eliminated. These shortened versions circulated fairly widely.

In the eleventh century the growth of cities and the rise of trade created a need for a more sophisticated legal system. The European kingdoms also began to establish central royal courts, for which primitive Germanic customary law proved inadequate. Those who studied Roman law discovered a systematic set of rules and coherent doctrines that offered solutions to complex problems involving contracts, loans, possessory rights, testaments, and rules of evidence.

We know little of how the *Corpus iuris* was rediscovered, particularly the *Digest*, which was essential to the understanding of Roman legal thought. Manuscripts containing the *Digest* were rare. Only one complete manuscript survives from before the twelfth century, the *Codex Florentinus* (formerly *Pisanus*) of *ca.* 600. This was not the direct source of the vulgate text *(littera Bononiensis);* but a corrected copy of a manuscript perhaps related to *Florentinus* provided lawyers with their first copies of the *Digest*.

The format of the collection in the Middle Ages was different from Justinian's codification. Because of the small number of manuscripts, the *Digest* was not recovered in one piece, and the early glossators (as the teachers of the law were called) divided it into three sections: *Digestum vetus, Infortiatum,* and *Digestum novum.* The *Code* remained in two parts, the first nine books in one volume, and the last three *(Tres libri Codicis)* in another. The medieval manuscripts that contain the *Tres libri* often include the *Institutes*, the *Authenticum* (a collection containing the *Novellae),* the *Feudorum liber,* and the *Longobardorum leges;* the early printed editions of the *Corpus iuris* maintained the arrangement found in most manuscripts. There were a few manuscripts, however, that contained the entire *Corpus iuris* in one volume; only six of these survive.

When Bologna emerged as a center for legal studies, the first teachers were Pepo and Irnerius (late eleventh century). Irnerius was probably the first to teach the *Digest,* and for this reason is often called the father of Roman law in the West. These two figures were succeeded by the "four doctors" of the twelfth century: Bulgarus, Hugo, Jacobus, and Martinus. They in turn were succeeded by Placentinus, Azo, and Accursius. The last *(d. ca.* 1263) wrote glosses to the entire *Corpus iuris* and rearranged and glossed the *Feudorum liber.* His glosses became the standard gloss *(Glossa ordinaria)* of the schools and were copied into all the manuscripts of the *Corpus iuris* and printed in the early editions.

The impact of Roman law, as transmitted by Justinian's *Corpus iuris civilis,* on European legal systems was profound. Concepts and doctrines of Roman law were received into secular, customary law throughout Europe. During the twelfth century judges in Italy, France, Germany, and England often had some training in Roman law and applied this knowledge to legal problems. Roman law served as a source from which the defects and lacunae of customary law could be remedied. It also formed the intellectual skeleton of canon law. The canonists quickly applied Roman principles to problems in the ecclesiastical courts, and Roman legal doctrines became an intrinsic part of canonistic thought. Soon a student of canon law had to study Roman law in order to understand much of the church's legal system. This first "reception" of Roman law was responsible in large part for the rapid evolution and development of canon law in the twelfth century.

Perhaps the greatest contribution of Roman law in the twelfth century was the influence it had on procedure. In no one place is court procedure set out clearly in the *Corpus iuris,* and from the early twelfth century lawyers began to write tracts that brought together the scattered texts touching on procedure in the *Code* and the *Digest*. By the early thirteenth century the lawyers had a clear understanding of Roman procedure and the rules of evidence. Consequently, when Pope Innocent III outlawed the participation of priests in ordeals at the Fourth Lateran Council (1215), he did so because ecclesiastical courts had already adopted many of the elements of Roman procedure. With ordeals no longer possible, secular courts all over Europe were forced to develop new methods of proof, and they often used Roman law principles to define proper courtroom practice.

Roman law continued to flourish as the learned law of Europe (along with canon law) for the rest of the Middle Ages. By the fourteenth century a law student would normally study both Justinian's *Corpus iuris civilis* in its medieval garb and canon law while at the university. The doctrines of Roman law continued to shape and influence legal thought and practice of western Europe until well into the nineteenth century.

BIBLIOGRAPHY

Sources. The standard edition is Theodor Mommsen, P. Krüger, R. Schöll, and W. Kroll, *Corpus iuris civilis* (1872–1895, many reprints). This is based on separate editions of the *Digest* (Mommsen, 1870) and the *Code* (Krüger, 1875–1877), each containing detailed critical apparatus. The vulgate text of the *Corpus iuris* used during the Middle Ages has not been edited in modern times, and the best editions remain those printed in the sixteenth century. For manuscripts of Roman law in various European archives, see Gero Dolezalek, *Verzeichnis der Handschriften zum römischen Recht bis 1600,* 4 vols. (1972).

Studies. Hermann Kantorowicz and W. W. Buckland, *Studies in the Glossators of the Roman Law* (1938); Leopold Wenger, *Die Quellen des römischen Rechts* (1953); Pierre Legendre, *La pénétration du droit romain dans le droit canonique classique de Gratien à Innocent IV* (1964); Paul Vinogradoff, *Roman Law in Medieval Europe,* P. Stein, ed. (1968); H. F. Jolowicz, *Historical Introduction to the Study of Roman Law,* 3rd ed., Barry Nicholas, ed. (1972), 478–515; Peter Weimar, "Die legistische Literatur der Glossatorenzeit," and Knut Norr, "Die Literatur zum gemeinen Zivilprozess," in *Handbuch der Quellen und Literatur der neueren europäischen Privatrechtsgeschichte,* vol. 1: *Mittelalter (1100–1500),* Helmut Coing, ed. (1973), 129–260, 383–397; Walter Ullmann, *Law and Politics in the Middle Ages* (1975), 51–116.

KENNETH PENNINGTON

[See also **Azo; Bologna, University of; Bulgarus; Codex Theodosianus; Irnerius; Justinian I; Law, Byzantine; Law,** Canon: **After Gratian; Law, Civil; Law, Schools of; Martinus Gosia; Placentinus.**]

CORTES. The development of parliamentary institutions was a common phenomenon throughout western Europe from the thirteenth century on. In the Iberian Peninsula the cortes emerged in Castile-León, Portugal, Aragon, and Catalonia by the middle or close of the century. In each state the king traditionally consulted on matters of great significance with the nobles and bishops of his curia. As towns grew in importance as centers of administration, trade, and industry, and as sources of military forces, their representatives were also summoned to counsel the king. With that the *curia regis* was transformed into the cortes. "Cortes" is the plural of *corte,* the Spanish vernacular term for the king's court. The use of the plural emphasized both the size and the importance of the assembly. The cortes came to be seen as an assembly of estates—prelates, nobles, and townsmen—who, together with the king, formed the body politic.

Representatives of towns were summoned to the curia as early as 1188 by Alphonse IX of León. A parallel development took place in Castile, and after the union of the two kingdoms in 1230, joint assemblies such as that held in 1250 by Ferdinand III became common. Occasionally, during the minority of Ferdinand IV (1295–1312), the regents found it easier to summon separate cortes for León and Castile, but in 1301 they bowed to the demand that only joint cortes should be convened thereafter. Alphonse XI (1312–1350) tended to divide the cortes, even holding partial assemblies of towns in order to weaken that body. The earliest recorded cortes attended by Portuguese bishops, nobles, and townsmen took place in 1254. In the Crown of Aragon separate parliaments were convened for Aragon, Catalonia, and Valencia, though from time to time general assemblies of all the king's dominions were held, as in 1214, 1287, and 1362. Possibly the first meeting of the *generalis curia* or *corts* (Catalan usage) took place in Catalonia in 1225. In Aragon this occurred in 1227, and in Valencia in 1283. The first cortes of Navarre may have taken place in 1253.

The ecclesiastical estate included archbishops, bishops, abbots, canons of cathedral chapters, and masters of the military orders. The lower clergy were usually not summoned. Individual summonses were sent to the prelates, but cathedral chapters were represented by procurators. The noble estate consisted of magnates summoned individually, *infanzones,* and knights, who probably received a general summons. Cities and towns directly dependent on the crown were ordered to send procurators (usually two) with full powers to consent to whatever was decided in the cortes and to bind their constituents by their actions. The towns paid their procurators a per diem rate, and the king guaranteed their security and arranged lodgings for them.

The prerogative of summoning the cortes belonged exclusively to the king, or in case of a minority, to the regents. The king's presence was essential to the legality of the cortes. Members of his family and the officers of his court also attended. Letters of summons indicated the purpose, the place, and the date of the meeting. The Castilian cortes of 1313 asked that sessions be held every two years, but Alphonse XI, once he attained his majority, tended to convoke the cortes at irregular intervals. Peter III of Aragon pledged in 1283 to convene the Catalan *corts* every year, but James II declared in 1301 that the *corts* would meet every three years. Peter III in 1283 and Alphonse III in 1287, in response to the demands of the Aragonese Union (of nobles, knights, and towns), promised to summon the cortes annually, but James II stated in 1307 that he would do so every two years.

Pledges of this sort were never observed absolutely, but on the whole the cortes in each of the peninsular kingdoms met with reasonable regularity, often as frequently as every two to four years. Sessions usually lasted for a few weeks or a month, and were held in centrally located towns such as Burgos, Valladolid, Saragossa, Lérida, Barcelona, Lisbon, and Coimbra. Royal palaces and cathedral and monastic cloisters often served as assembly halls.

Once the cortes gathered, the king, in his opening discourse, set forth the reasons for convocation and probably asked for a subsidy. Each estate replied, if only to ask permission to deliberate on his proposals. There is little information concerning the procedures followed as the estates debated separately, but they usually prepared petitions to present to the king and agreed on a tax levy. The Catalans consistently reserved the grant of a subsidy until they had received the king's response to their demands for redress of grievances. Once the subsidy was voted and the petitions approved, the session was closed. Texts containing the record of the actions taken in the cortes were given to the participants.

The cortes played a role in matters relating to the succession, legislation, taxation, and other aspects of foreign and domestic policy. Peter III described the competence of the cortes when he declared in 1283 that the Catalan estates should meet annually to consider "the good estate and reformation" of the realm. On his accession the king of Aragon convoked the cortes of each of his realms to swear to uphold the laws. Assemblies of estates helped to resolve the succession crisis of 1410–1412, and the Portuguese estates elected a king (John I) in 1385. The Castilian cortes not only recognized the heir to the throne but also took a decisive part in establishing regencies during several royal minorities.

Peter III in 1283 defined the legislative functions of the Catalan *corts* when he declared that "no general constitution or statute" should be enacted without the consent of the estates. The fifteenth-century jurist Jaume Callis restated this and also declared, "Whatever is enacted by the *corts* . . . cannot be revoked except by a general assembly." The parliaments of Valencia and Aragon participated in legislation mainly by exercising the right of petition, but James I thought it important to promulgate the Code of Huesca, a code of Aragonese law, in the cortes of 1247. Alphonse III in 1289 affirmed that the king alone could not abrogate any of the enactments of the cortes in any of his realms.

The Castilian cortes submitted petitions to the crown that, on being drawn up as ordinances and approved by the king, had the full force of law. Alphonse XI in 1348 promulgated the *Ordenamiento de Alcalá,* an extensive law code prepared by his jurists, in the cortes. The principle that the laws enacted in the cortes could be abrogated only by the cortes was stated in 1305, 1313, 1379, and 1387. The Portuguese king often ignored or infringed upon the petitions presented by the cortes, provoking the protests of that body in 1451 and 1455. Little is known of the legislative role of the Navarrese cortes, but in 1330 the king and cortes appointed a commission to revise the laws. Charles III stated in 1418 that he was promulgating the *Fuero general* with the consent of the cortes.

Taxation was perhaps the most important function of the cortes. Since ordinary revenues no longer sufficed to meet the increasing needs of the crown, the king had to ask consent for extraordinary taxes. The nobles and clergy usually were exempt, so the burden fell chiefly on the townsmen. In León (1202), Aragon (1236), and Portugal (1254) the kings bargained with the cortes, promising not to debase the coinage for seven years, provided they were allowed to collect a regular tax. Other taxes were levied on hearths, livestock, and imports and exports. The Catalan *corts* affirmed that the subsidy was granted of their own generosity, not as an obligation, and without prejudice to their liberties. The Castilian cortes several times in the fourteenth century insisted on the king's duty to obtain consent, and in 1391 and 1393 asked the regents not to "levy any tribute other than that granted by the cortes."

Taxes usually were voted for a fixed term of a year or two, but there were exceptions. Also, the money was granted for specific purposes. The Castilian cortes in 1407, for example, asked the regents not to expend the money on anything other than the war against the Moors. The cortes tried to prevent abuses in collection by insisting that only townsmen be employed as tax collectors, to the exclusion of nobles, clerics, Jews, and Muslims. The Castilian cortes obtained an accounting of royal revenues before approving a subsidy on several occasions in the fourteenth century. Complaints of abuses by collectors prompted the cortes of 1386 to appoint officials to receive and disburse the tax money, but this important step toward controlling royal finance was never developed beyond this point. John II (1406–1454) and Henry IV (1454–1474) were not overly concerned with seeking consent to taxes or using the money only for the purpose for which it was granted.

The appointment of commissions by the Catalan *corts* in the late thirteenth and fourteenth centuries to supervise the collection of taxes eventually gave birth to the *Generalitat*. A permanent deputation of the *corts*, with a fixed residence in Barcelona, this body championed Catalan liberty during the reign of John II (1458–1479). Agencies with similar responsibilities for the collection and disbursement of taxes were established in Aragon in 1412, Valencia in 1419, and Navarre in 1501.

From its inception until the close of the Middle Ages, the cortes enjoyed a vigorous growth and development. It served as a forum in which the estates could express their views on a wide range of public issues, and insist on the observance of the laws. The cortes was a major element in the medieval legacy, but the civil wars of the late fifteenth century, and the thrust toward absolutism in the sixteenth, greatly lessened its influence.

BIBLIOGRAPHY

Cortes de los antiguos reinos de Aragón y de Valencia y principado de Cataluña, 25 vols. (1896–1919); *Cortes de los antiguos reinos de León y de Castilla*, 5 vols. (1861–1903); Luis González Antón, *Las uniones aragonesas y las cortes del reino, 1282–1301*, 2 vols. (1975); and *Las cortes de Aragón* (1978); Joseph F. O'Callaghan, "The Beginnings of the Cortes of León-Castile," in *American Historical Review*, 74 (1969); and "The Cortes and Royal Taxation During the Reign of Alfonso X of Castile," in *Traditio*, 27 (1971); Wladimir Piskorski, *Las cortes de Castilla en el período de tránsito de la edad media a la moderna, 1188–1520*, Claudio Sánchez Albornoz, trans. (1930), repr. with "Estudio sobre las cortes medievales castellano-leonesas en la historiografía reciente," by Julio Valdeón (1977); Evelyn S. Procter, "The Development of the Catalan Corts in the Thirteenth Century," in *Estudis universitaris catalans*, 22 (1936); and *Curia and Cortes in León and Castile, 1072–1295* (1980).

JOSEPH F. O'CALLAGHAN

[See also **Aragon, Crown of (1137–1479); Castile; Law, Spanish.**]

CORVÉE. Everywhere and in all times obligations have been laid upon people to contribute their labor and services for the achievement of certain tasks without—token benevolences aside—direct remuneration. The species of such obligations range from slave labor, as practiced in many Nazi factories during World War II, to voluntary labor, as in the American barn raisings of the nineteenth century. The nature of the tasks performed has also varied: from small and localized to large-scale and supraregional; from agricultural to industrial; from needing long, almost indefinite commitment to needing short-term or intermittent participation; from private to public. Finally, the force that could legitimately be employed to encourage participation has run between two poles, the one being corporal, extensive, virtually unlimited (as in chain gangs, slave galleys, and labor camps); the other being psycho-cultural, such as shunning, a device used by some sects to chastise those who fail to perform requisite religious works. Neither impressment nor conscription can properly be included in the foregoing description because, despite the high level of coercion and the inadequacy of traditional military pay schemes, both were supposed to eventuate in a paid labor force.

At its most general, corvée (a French word from the Latin *corrogare*, to requisition) pertains to a great part of the phenomenon described above. Only the truly voluntary or the truly slavish can be excluded. It is right, therefore, to speak of corvées or corvée systems (statute labor) having existed in ancient Rome (the *operae* of various legal distinctions), in imperial Japan (the *yō*), in modern Egypt (Nile canal cleaning), and in seventeenth- and eighteenth-century France (road work).

But in stricter usage corvée applies to the unpaid agricultural labor, limited in duration, required of medieval European rustics on the estates (demesnes) of those on whom they were dependent. The character of the dependency is frequently termed servile. That is, it was serfs who owed the corvée to those who owned their bodies. But this frequent statement is not accurate. Free (nonservile) people could, and often did, owe corvées because of regional customs to that effect. Liability to corvée was not itself necessary or sufficient to establish a person's servility, though in lawyers' writings of the time one senses that it was one of the signs that raised, particularly in the presence of other signs (such as formariage and mainmortability), the presumption of servility.

To discuss the tasks accomplished by corvées would be to write a labor taxonomy of medieval agriculture in Europe, though plowing and harvesting predominated. Three interrelated points do need to be made beyond this general observation. First, corvées tended to be tied to the cyclic rhythm of the agricultural year—planting, harvest, vintage. But, of course, the work that was needed on a lord's property at these times was also needed on the rustics' own plots. Consequently, corvées seem to have contributed profoundly to a resentment of the landlord class. Second, although corvées were not remunerated, there were incidental benevolences. These were well regulated by custom and may be interpreted as a form of cultural exchange of labor from the dependents for an abundance of drink and food, often consumed on the spot, from the landlord. The significance of this fact needs further investigation, given the results of recent work on gift giving between masters and slaves in plantation economies and on the early Middle Ages as a gift economy.

Third, many historians believe that corvées were inefficient by standards current in the Middle Ages, the resentment of the laborers being one factor in their analysis. This may be so. What is certain is that there are identifiable secular trends in the imposition and enforcement of corvées, with commutation (money payments) increasingly substituting for them by the later Middle Ages. By the sixteenth century, corvée, in the strictly agricultural meaning I have given it, was largely moribund.

One additional connotation of "corvée" needs to be mentioned, its application to forced requisition of military equipment. Cartage, the suzerain's right to demand wagons for transport of supplies, is the most important example. And, like all corvées, it was frequently an object of resentment.

BIBLIOGRAPHY

Marc Bloch, *French Rural History,* Janet Sondheimer, trans. (1966); Jerome Blum, *The End of the Old Order in Rural Europe* (1978); Georges Duby, "Medieval Agriculture, 900–1500," in *The Fontana Economic History of Europe: The Middle Ages,* Carlo M. Cipolla, ed. (1972), 175–220; Robert Fossier, *La terre et les hommes en Picardie,* 2 vols. (1968); *Histoire de la France rurale,* I, Georges Duby, ed. (1975); Paul Hyams, *King, Lords and Peasants in Medieval England* (1980); Achille Luchaire, *Manuel des institutions françaises: Période des Capétiens directs* (1892), 346–351, and, more generally, 293–351; Anne-Marie Patault, *Hommes et femmes de corps en Champagne méridionale à la fin du moyen-âge* (1978); J. Ambrose Raftis, *Warboys: Two Hundred Years in the Life of a Mediaeval English Village* (1974); Gérard Sivery, *Structures agraires et vie rurale dans le Hainault à la fin du moyen-âge,* 2 vols. (1977–1979).

WILLIAM CHESTER JORDAN

[See also **Serf, Serfdom: Western European.**]

COSMAS INDICOPLEUSTES, an Egyptian probably born in Alexandria, was a sixth-century merchant whose many travels to the East make him a valuable source on a number of areas. His *Christian Topography* attempts to show that the principles of physical geography are in harmony with the Scriptures. It includes accounts of his travels to Ethiopia and possibly to Ceylon and India, information on commercial relations with China and India, and descriptions of the animals of Africa and India. He discusses and evaluates his sources, and includes illustrations. A Nestorian, he became a monk in later life.

BIBLIOGRAPHY

The Greek text of the *Christian Topography* is in *Patrologia graeca,* CLXXXVIII (1864), cols. 51–476; see also Eric O. Winstedt, ed., *The Christian Topography of Cosmas Indicopleustes* (1909).

LINDA ROSE

[See also **Byzantine Literature.**]

COSMAS OF PRAGUE (*ca.* 1045–1125) was born into the minor Czech nobility, entered the clerical life at a young age, and became secretary to Bishop Gebhard of Prague. From 1075 to 1081 he studied grammar and dialectic at Liège. He was ordained in 1099, and became canon and dean of St. Vitus Cathedral chapter in Prague. His principal work is the *Chronica Boemorum,* a history in three books of Bohemia from its beginnings to 1125. He died in Prague.

BIBLIOGRAPHY

Cosmae Pragensis chronica Boemorum, Bertold Bretholtz, ed., in *Monumenta Germaniae historica, Scriptores rerum Germanicorum,* n.s. II (1923); Francis Dvornik, *The Making of Central and Eastern Europe* (1949), 75–81; Ludvik Nemec, "The New Historical Portrait of St. Adalbert," in *Polish Review,* 7, no. 2 (1962).

WANDA CIŻEWSKI

[See also **Bohemia-Moravia.**]

COSMATI WORK is the generic name for decorative work of marble inlaid in geometrical patterns with colored stone or glass that was used on walls, floors, and church furniture from about 1100 to 1300, especially in Italy. The term is derived from Cosma (Cosmas, Cosmatus), a popular name among the Roman marble workers who initiated this style, and particularly the Cosmatus who signed the portal at S. Tomaso in Formis, in Rome.

BIBLIOGRAPHY

Dorothy F. Glass, *Studies on Cosmatesque Pavements* (1980); Edward Hutton, *The Cosmati, the Roman Marble Workers of the XIIth and XIIIth Centuries* (1950).

LESLIE BRUBAKER

COSMETICS. See **Beauty Aids, Cosmetics.**

COSTUME, BYZANTINE. The basic Byzantine garment was a belted tunic, or chiton. Women's tunics were long, worn with a looser outer tunic and a headcloth covering the hair and—in public—the face. The man's tunic was knee-length for the soldier and worker, long for the bureaucrat and courtier,

and worn over narrow trousers. A cloak fastened on one shoulder served as a coat. This basic repertoire was then modified to signal specialized social roles—emperor and empress, courtier, clergyman, monk or nun—and it is above all the specialized costumes that have shaped our image of Byzantine dress.

This is especially true of Byzantine imperial garb, known from the descriptions of Constantine VII Porphyrogenitos (tenth century) and Pseudo-Kodinos (fourteenth century), and from images in art and on coins. The emperor had three official costumes. His war garb, rarely worn in Constantinople, consisted of short tunic, purple boots and cloak, golden breastplate and diademed helmet, and sword, spear, and shield. His military dress uniform, far more frequently seen and standard for religious ceremonies,

Ivory relief of Emperor Constantine VII Porphyrogenitos. *ca.* 945. MUSEUM OF FINE ARTS, MOSCOW (VICTORIA AND ALBERT MUSEUM, LONDON)

Arab and Greek rulers exchange emissaries. Byzantine miniature. BIBLIOTECA NACIONALE, MADRID, MS VITR. 26-2, fol. 75v

included purple slippers, long, tight-sleeved silk tunic or *scaramangion,* and the enveloping general's cloak, or chlamys—a deep arc of gold and/or purple cloth fastened with a fibula on the right shoulder, leaving the right arm free but falling to ankle length over the rest of the body. Most distinctive of all was the triumphal garb: a gold *scaramangion,* a short-sleeved, gold or purple outer tunic or *dibitision,* purple boots, and the uniquely Byzantine *loros*—a long strip of cloth heavily studded with gems, enamels, and pearls that was draped around the upper body so that one end hung to the hem in front and the other end was caught up from behind and thrown over the left arm. Chlamys and *loros* were worn with the stemma, or crested crown of gold plaques enameled with figures; a cluster of pearls, called *pendilia,* hung to shoulder length from each side. From the twelfth century on, the emperors wore the kamelaukion, or closed crown, when they wore the *loros;* from the later thirteenth century on, the *dibitision* was replaced by a black, long-sleeved tunic or sakkos.

The empress, too, had both civilian and triumphal costumes, which were very similar in form to the emperor's. Her *loros,* however, was often modified so that the portion drawn around from the rear formed a smooth, shieldlike triangle of cloth tucked into the belt in front and tapering to the right ankle. Her crown, of jeweled or enameled plaques, often comprised several tiers. The imperial bodyguard wore the *loros,* too; hence it became standard for depictions of archangels, the heavenly bodyguard, as well. Courtiers wore the chlamys or, in the Palaiologan period (1261–1453), a long tunic and an ever more extravagant turban. Women of the court wore loose outer tunics with long, open sleeves, ornate belts and jewelry, and a domed headdress. Court fabric was silk, not thinly draped but firm and rich with heavily embroidered cuffs and hems, generalizing the body's shape.

Priests' garments, known from Theodore Balsamon of Antioch (late twelfth century) and from depictions in art, consisted essentially of the long, straight-sleeved tunic or sticharion, the looser phelonion or sakkos, and the insignia of office. The sticharion initially had embroidery on the sleeves; by the eleventh century, however, this had passed to richly worked detachable cuffs called epimanikia. The phelonion was a circular garment with a central hole for the head. During the eleventh century, the patriarch's phelonion came to be studded with crosses, and this cross-studded phelonion, or *polystaurion,* by the fourteenth century had become the distinctive garb of metropolitans. The patriarch, meanwhile, came to wear the sakkos instead, a broad tunic with wide sleeves sewn like a poncho from a single piece of gorgeously embroidered cloth. Under the front of his phelonion hung the priest's stole, or *epitrachelion,* its two ends sewn together to form a

615

single, rich panel. Over the phelonion (later the *polystaurion*), the bishop wore an omophorion, a long scarf with crosses at the ends, on the shoulders, and at the neck. From the late twelfth century onward, bishops also wore a stylized handkerchief, or epigonation, a rectangle of stiffened cloth suspended by a string from the belt to hang at knee level below the hem of the *polystaurion*. Throughout the Byzantine Empire, all priests were bareheaded. Monks, by contrast, wore a shirt, a cotton coat, and the heavy, hooded black mandyas, or tunic-shaped monastic habit. Nuns wore a similar black habit, and a black, wimplelike headcloth.

BIBLIOGRAPHY

Sources. Constantine VII Porphyrogenitos, *De administrando imperii*, Gyula Moravcsik, ed., Romilly Jenkins, trans. (1967); Pseudo-Kodinos, *Traité des offices*, Jean Verpaux, trans. (1966).

Studies. Andras Alföldi, *Insignien und Tracht der römischen Kaiser* (1935), 1–171; Pauline Johnstone, *The Byzantine Tradition in Church Embroidery* (1967), 12–19; Iohannis Spatharakis, *The Portrait in Byzantine Illuminated Manuscripts* (1976); Klaus Wessel, Elisabeth Piltz, and Corina Nicolescu, "Insignien," in Klauss Wessel, ed., *Reallexikon zur byzantinischen Kunst*, III (1978), 369–498.

ANNEMARIE WEYL CARR

[See also **Byzantine Empire: Bureaucracy; Byzantine Church; Textiles.**]

COSTUME, ISLAMIC. Medieval Islamic costume developed from a gradual, long-term fusion of three different styles of dress, those of pre-Islamic Arabia, the Hellenistic Mediterranean, and Irano-Turkic central Asia. To some extent the fusion had already begun when Islam was born in seventh-century Arabia.

The general term for clothing throughout the medieval Muslim world was *libās*. The medieval lexicographers defined the word as "that which conceals or covers the pudenda," citing the Koran (sura 7:26): "O Children of Adam! We have revealed unto you clothing to conceal your shame, and finery too, but the garment of piety is best." This attitude toward clothing was in complete keeping with Judeo-Christian tradition. Only secondarily was clothing for adornment or protection against the elements.

Despite changes in fashion over time and regional stylistic differences, the basic outlines of the Islamic vestment system remained remarkably constant

throughout the Middle Ages. The norm was several layers of clothing. A person might wear many garments or only one, depending on a variety of factors including weather, occasion, and economic means. The basic articles of clothing consisted of an undergarment (originally a loincloth [*izār* or *ḥakw*], but later replaced by a variety of pantaloons [*sirwāl*]), a body shirt (*qamīṣ*), a tunic (*thawb*), and an overgarment such as a mantle (*ridā*), coat (*qabāʾ*), or wrap (*burd*). In addition to these were shoes (*khuff*) or sandals (*naʿl*) and one or more head coverings. Already in Muḥammad's time the ancient Near Eastern practice of covering the head out of modesty and respect was the norm for both sexes. The *ʿimāma*, or turban, had been worn since pre-Islamic times. By the High Middle Ages it had become a composite headdress consisting of one or two caps and a winding cloth, and by the late Middle Ages "the badge of Islam" (*sīmā al-Islām*). Women, of course, wore veils.

The austerity of the early Muslim community did not encourage luxury of any kind. The Koran promises the righteous garments of silk in Paradise, but Muḥammad felt that such clothes were inappropriate in this life for men, though not for women. With the development of the Islamic empire, however, and with the rise of a leisured class, luxury garments were adopted by men as well. This was given religious justification by the fabrication of traditions ascribed to Muḥammad expressing the permissibility of silks and brocades. The Umayyad caliph Sulaymān (715–717) and his retinue wore only clothes of *washī* (variegated silk). Walīd II (743–744) is reported to have worn special white caliphal garments. The Abbasid caliphs, who supplanted the Umayyads, chose black for their robes of office.

Two of the most significant phenomena of Islamic costume history originated in the Umayyad period, namely, the laws requiring distinguishing clothing for the non-Muslim subject population and the production of regal embroidered fabrics for clothing. According to the laws of differentiation, or *ghiyār*, non-Muslims were forbidden to wear Arab-style headgear, military dress, and certain robes. Christians, though not Jews and Zoroastrians, had to wear a distinguishing outer belt, or *zunnār* (related to the Greek *zonarion*). By the reign of Hārūn al-Rashīd (786–809), these rules were well refined and ascribed back to ʿUmar.

The production of costly embroidered fabrics, or *ṭirāz*, in palace factories also began in Umayyad times and became a standard feature of Islamic cul-

Two men obtaining clay for medical use. Manuscript attributed to ᶜAbdallah ibn al-Fadl, Iraq (Mesopotamia), 1224, Baghdad School. COURTESY OF THE FREER GALLERY OF ART, SMITHSONIAN INSTITUTION, WASHINGTON, D.C.

Two doctors preparing a medicine. Page from a *Materia medica* by Dioscorides, attributed to ᶜAbdallah ibn al-Fadl, Iraq (Mesopotamia), 1224, Baghdad School. THE ST. LOUIS ART MUSEUM, PURCHASE

Garden scene. Persian painting, Timurid period, *ca.* 1470–1480. THE METROPOLITAN MUSEUM OF ART, THE CORA TIMKEN BURNETT COLLECTION OF PERSIAN MINIATURES AND OTHER PERSIAN ART OBJECTS, BEQUEST OF CORA TIMKEN BURNETT, 1957 (57.51.24)

ture. *Ṭirāz* garments were bestowed as tokens of royal favor and were among the standard gifts brought by diplomatic embassies to other rulers as part of foreign policy. The most common *ṭirāz* garment was the *khilᶜa*, or robe of honor. It usually bore an embroidered or woven inscription with the name of the ruler or vizier, the place of production, date, and, most frequently, pious formulas. Imitations of the royal *ṭirāz* were made in private ateliers for the *haute bourgeoisie*, who copied the practice of bestowing robes of honor on friends and relations.

Muslim society became highly fashion-minded in ninth- and tenth-century Baghdad under the cultural leadership of the Persian secretarial class. Al-Washshāᵓ (*d*. 936) devoted several chapters of his *On Elegance and Elegant People* to the subject of proper dress. Persian cultural influences became more pronounced under the Abbasids and a number of Persian garments came into fashion. Among these were the *qalansuwa ṭawīla*, a tall conical hat, and the caftan, a fine robe with long sleeves that buttons down the front. Fine garments were brought to Baghdad from all over the world. From India came the *fūṭa*, a long piece of sarilike cloth that served as loincloth, apron, and shawl. From China came the *mimṭara*, or oilcloth raincloak. Fine garments in ninth-century Iraq cost from five to thirty dinars, and throughout the Middle Ages clothing was generally expensive compared with the other necessities of life.

No dynasty was more clothes-conscious than the Fatimids (909–1171), whose pomp and ceremony exceeded anything known in Baghdad. Every functionary from the caliph down to mere clerks was supplied by an official bureau with a ceremonial costume (*badla mawkibiyya*) for public occasions.

The feudal Turkish dynasties that controlled one part or another of the Middle East from the late eleventh to the early sixteenth century introduced many central Asian styles, particularly in military and ceremonial dress. These, however, were the distinguishing uniforms of the military elite. The dress of the native Arab population was little affected at first. Throughout much of this period the typical outer garment for the ruling class was one of a variety of coats (*aqbiya*). The Seljuks and Ayyubids preferred the so-called Turkish coats, the hem of which crossed the chest in a diagonal from right to left. The Mamluks wore Tatar coats with the hem crossing the opposite way. The sleeves of the coats were frequently indicative of rank and social status. The

longer and more ample the sleeves, the higher the standing of the wearer. The normal headgear was a stiff cap with a triangular front, which was sometimes trimmed with fur (*sharbūsh*). The *qabāᵓ* and *sharbūsh* were the distinctive uniform of a Muslim knight, so much so in fact that even a crusader was prepared to wear them as a gesture of friendship for Saladin. Eventually some of the garments that were at first restricted to the military elite were adopted by the native bourgeoisie, for example, the *bughlu-ṭāq* and the *sallāriyya*, two popular short-sleeved coats.

The Ottoman conquest of the Arab East in the sixteenth century marked a continuation rather than an abrupt change in the costume history of the Islamic world.

BIBLIOGRAPHY

Reinhart Dozy, *Dictionnaire détaillé des noms des vêtements chez les Arabes* (1845); Reuben Levy, "Notes on Costumes from Arabic Sources," in *Journal of the Royal Asiatic Society* (1935); Leo A. Mayer, *Mamluk Costume* (1952); Adam Mez, *The Renaissance of Islam*, Salahuddin Khuda Bakhsh and D. S. Margoliouth, trans. (1937); R. B. Serjeant, *Islamic Textiles: Material for a History up to the Mongol Conquest* (1972); Yedida K. Stillman, "The Importance of the Cairo Geniza Manuscripts for the History of Medieval Female Attire," in *International Journal of Middle East Studies*, 7 (1976), and *Palestinian Costume and Jewelry* (1979).

YEDIDA K. STILLMAN

[See also **Khilᶜa; Sumptuary Laws, Islamic; Textiles, Islamic.**]

COSTUME, JEWISH. Little is known about Jewish attire during the early Middle Ages in either the Sasanian and Byzantine East or the Latin West. It may be assumed, however, that Jewish dress did not differ greatly from that of the societies in which they lived.

The Babylonian Talmud (Tractate Shabbat 120a), which was redacted during the fifth century, lists eighteen essential garments worn by Jews (though pairs are counted as two items). A slightly different list appears in the earlier Jerusalem Talmud (16:15). Most of these garments were standard items in the late Greco-Roman and Iranian wardrobes: various layers of tunics (the *ūnqelay*, *qolobūs*, and *savrīqīn*, whose Greek equivalents are the *anacholos*, *kolbion*, and *subrichion*), shirts (*ḥālūg*), mantles (*miqtorīn*, *birōs*, and *isṭōla*; Latin: *amictorium*, *birrus*, and *stola*), and a variety of head- and footgear. In those

Interior of a synagogue in the 15th century. The congregation is shown wearing cloaks with ṣīṣīt hanging from the undergarments. VATICAN LIBRARY, MS ROSSIANO 555, 12v

areas within the Iranian political and cultural sphere, trousers and leggings (impīlāyōt, afrīqīn, and pimalniya; Latin: impilia, bracae, and feminalia) were also worn.

Although early medieval Jewish costume was probably very similar to that of the Jews' Gentile neighbors, there were some details or markings that were specifically Jewish. One such detail was the "show fringe" (ṣīṣīt) on the four corners of mens' garments in accordance with the injunction found in Num. 15:37–39ff. The ṣīṣīt were attached to the corners of such popular cloaks as the appiliyōn (Latin: pallium) and the istōla. These large outer cloaks eventually became reduced in size to the tallith, the prayer shawl worn by Jewish men at morning prayers. That these cloaks were distinguished only by their ṣīṣīt is clear from the talmudic prohibition against selling a cloak to a pagan prior to removal of the show fringe (BT Tractate Menaḥot 43a). Sometime during the Middle Ages the ṣīṣīt ceased to be worn on the outer garment, but were transferred to an undershirt called ṭallīt qāṭān. Another detail of difference was in occasional ornamentation of a specifically Jewish character. For example, a woolen tapestry roundel from sixth-century Egypt, which was used to decorate a tunic and is identical with

thousands of Coptic ones, has two small Hebrew letters worked into the design marking it as Jewish. Yet another detail in which Jewish dress might differ from Gentile was the absence of fabrics combining linen and wool (shaᶜaṭnez), a mixture forbidden by the Mosaic code (Deut. 22:11).

In the earliest Middle Ages, the custom of covering the head was limited mainly to scholars and men of distinction (BT Tractates Pesahim 11b; Shabbat 118b; and elsewhere). It still had not become a universal practice for Jewish men even when praying. The Talmud states that it was optional and dependent on local custom whether or not a man covered his head (BT Tractate Nedarim 30b). By contrast, married Jewish women all wore veils as a sign of modesty. In fact, appearing in public without a head covering was considered grounds for divorce without return of dowry (Mishna Ketubbot 7:6).

When the Muslims conquered the Middle East, North Africa, and Spain, the Jews—like other members of the local populations—did not dress in the Arab fashion. As a security measure the conquerors banned their non-Muslim subjects from dressing like them. Under the laws of differentiation (ghiyār) stipulated in the so-called Pact of ᶜUmar, Jews, Christians, and Zoroastrians were specifically forbidden to wear the Arab headgear (most notably the ᶜimāma, or turban), Arab military dress, and the robe known as the qabāᵓ, a coat of Persian origin. By the ninth century, however, an ecumenical Islamicate style of dress had developed. The Abbasid caliph al-Mutawakkil issued an edict in 849 ordering all non-Muslim men to wear honey-colored mantles, known as ṭayālisa, and all non-Muslim women to wear uzur (enveloping body wraps) of a similar hue. Those non-Muslim males who wore the popular Persian pointed cap known as the qalansuwa had to affix distinguishing buttons to it on front and back. While those who wore turbans, which had previously been forbidden altogether, had to dye them like their mantles. It is clear that only color and added outer marks distinguished non-Muslim from Muslim attire. Discriminatory laws regarding dress were reiterated and enforced only sporadically until the thirteenth century.

Among the rare representations that may depict Jews from the early Islamic centuries are some Chinese ceramic figurines from T'ang Dynasty tombs (618–907) situated close to K'aifeng, which had a well-known Jewish community. The figurines thought to be Jewish are of bearded, Levantine merchants and peddlars dressed in a Persian knee-length

619

Pedlar in Persian hat and caftan. Pottery tomb figure, T'ang dynasty, China, *ca.* 618–907. COURTESY OF FRANK CARO

qabāʾ of the type still worn in Khorāsān, cinched at the waist with a large sash (Persian: *kamarband*). On each figure's head is a pointed *qalansuwa.*

The most important source for Jewish attire in the medieval Muslim world is the Cairo Genizah. Trousseau lists from the Fatimid, Ayyubid, and to a lesser extent, Mamluk periods offer a wealth of detail on the dress of Jewish women in medieval Egypt. Information for male costume comes from commercial documents, but is not nearly as extensive or detailed. The Genizah documents show that the Jewish bourgeoisie imitated the modes and mores of the rul-

ing class. Jewish merchants bestowed robes of honor (*khilaᶜ*) and garments with embroidered inscriptions on relatives and friends. The Jewish upper class wore all the precious fabrics known to us from descriptions of Islamic court ceremonies. There was an enormous variety of garments. The Genizah trousseaux mention almost seventy items for women alone. The single most important group was headgear and veils, making up more than half the names of garments in the trousseau lists.

From the mid thirteenth century on, Jewish costume in the Muslim world became more distinctive with strict imposition of *ghiyār* laws by intolerant regimes that also sought to humble the unbelievers in accordance with the koranic injunction (sura 9:29).

In Christendom between the sixth and twelfth centuries there was probably little noticeable difference between Jewish dress and that of their Gentile neighbors. Due to the greater economic prosperity of the Jews as a group, however, a greater proportion of them were able to wear fine garments. Pope Nicholas I (858–867) threatened to exclude Arsenius, bishop of Orta, from the Palatine procession if the latter wore fur garments in the Jewish fashion (*judaicae peluciae*). In a letter entitled *De insolentia Judaeorum* addressed to Louis the Pious in 826 by Agobard of Lyons, the anti-Semitic archbishop decries Jews flaunting the elegant garments that their womenfolk received from court ladies.

The most distinctively Jewish garment of the later Middle Ages was the pointed hat (*pileus cornutus* or *Judenhut*), which came in several varieties. These hats first appear in illustrations from the eleventh century and may originally have been a voluntary Jewish fashion that only later became a required badge. The *Judenhut* was worn by Jewish men throughout Europe, surviving in some places into the fifteenth century.

The watershed in European Jewish costume history occurred with the Fourth Lateran Council in 1215, which decreed that Jews and Saracens "of both sexes in every Christian province and at all times shall be distinguished . . . by the character of their dress" (canon 68). The ordinance was carried out with regional variations. In France, Jews had to wear a circular badge (*rota*) on their outer clothes. In England, the badge was of yellow taffeta cut to resemble the Tablets of the Law (*tabula*). In Germany, the *Judenhut* usually served as a badge, though in some places the *rota* was also required. Special

620

COSTUME, WESTERN EUROPEAN

English Jew wearing a robe with Jewish badge and hood. Drawing, 1275. THE BRITISH LIBRARY, COTTONIAN MS NERO DII

Adolf Rosenzweig, *Kleidung und Schmuck im biblischen und talmudischen Schrifttum* (1905); Alfred Rubens, *A History of Jewish Costume* (1967); Yedida K. Stillman, "Female Attire in Medieval Egypt" (diss., Univ. of Pennsylvania, 1972); "The Wardrobe of a Jewish Bride in Medieval Egypt" in Issachar Ben-Ami and D. Noy, eds., *Studies in Marriage Customs* (1974), 297–304, and "The Importance of the Cairo Geniza Manuscripts for the History of Medieval Female Attire," in *International Journal of Middle East Studies*, 7 (1976); R. Straus, "The Jewish Hat as an Aspect of Social History," in *Jewish Social Studies*, 4 (1942).

YEDIDA K. STILLMAN

[See also, **Anti-Semitism; Cairo Genizah; Jews** (various articles); **Sumptuary Laws.**]

COSTUME, WESTERN EUROPEAN. Magnificence was not simply a feminine prerogative in western European costume. Men as well as women were accustomed to clothes of velvet, brocade, silk, and fine wool in lustrous colors emblazoned or decorated with embroidery, feathers, furs, jewels, pendants, daggings, and tippets, and topped by flamboyant hats. While wealthier people enjoyed much of such finery, and the most noble might indulge in it all, even townsmen and country folk had, in addition to their functional work clothes, which were not necessarily drab or ill-fitting, holiday costumes that by custom or by imitation were as artful as wealth or law allowed.

Clothes were social signatures. At a glance clothing informed an observer of the wearer's class, religion, particular craft or profession (and rank within it), geographic locale, and thanks to coats of arms and heraldic devices, the ancestral heritage of self or employer. Those in service in a rich household wore the symbolic colors and design of its livery. Craftsmen wore their guild's uniform for ceremonial occasions and sometimes on the job. A physician's or surgeon's customary gown was flowing, floor-length, and red, with a medical astrolabe pendant from a belt. Jews often were required to wear a conical hat, the Jew's hat or *Judenhut,* and a circular gold pin or badge, the *rouelle* or *rota.*

Within such restraints of fashion, individual taste revealed character. Clothing predilections, even of literary characters, defined their temperaments, as Chaucer's Canterbury guildsmen suggest; the swag-

hoods or cowls sometimes replaced the hat. Attempts to enforce the wearing of badges in Christian Spain were not successful until the fourteenth century, when the position of the Jews there declined dramatically.

Jewish communal ordinances (*takkanot*) issued from the thirteenth century on reinforced the separation of Jewish from Gentile dress styles. In general Jewish costume remained conservative. In Germany, for example, medieval costumes among Jews persisted well into the Renaissance.

Courtiers with roses. Wool tapestry, Franco-Flemish, *ca.* 1435–1440. THE METROPOLITAN MUSEUM OF ART, ROGERS FUND, 1909 (09.137.2)

gering newly wealthy weaver, tailor, and upholsterer and their pushy, preening wives dress with garish ostentation to appear "royal." Since both ecclesiastical and secular clothes asserted social rank, hypocrites could resort to disguise and sartorial deception. Fashion's social effects were amusingly evoked in Menachem ben Judah da Lozano's sixteenth-century Hebrew lyric: "If you can wear the latest styles of clothes with grace and class / You will surely win respectful smiles although you are a perfect ass."

Three types of law governed fashion. Sumptuary legislation attempted to regulate personal extravagance, mandating who might wear what and when. Civil mercantile edicts controlled importation and exportation, quality, price, and availability of fabrics as well as finished goods and ornaments. Ecclesiastical laws established standards for Christian religious garments; for secular avoidance by simple dress of the deadly sins of avarice and envy; and for identifying by costume the non-Christians such as Jews and Muslims. Costumery law reached its greatest frequency and complexity in the fourteenth century.

So did sartorial splendor. While dress varied markedly according to century, country, and class, and might change dramatically in a particular year because of a royal marriage or an entertainment introducing a foreign style, nevertheless generalizations are reasonable. Clothing style in western Europe of the tenth through thirteenth centuries was comparatively restrained, and surprisingly consistent from country to country. In the fourteenth and fifteenth centuries fashion floresced with multiple delicate and hardy stylistic blooms, flashing and fading, or surviving and thriving after transplantation from one country to another. There were many stimuli for this notable flourishing of clothes styles, in which men's coat hems rose from ankle to hipbone and women's necklines plunged to deep décolletage.

Fine fabrics were increasingly available because of routine international commerce. A psychological hedonism pervaded actions of workers, tradesmen, and noblemen who survived the Black Death. Technological refinements affected fashions, such as elastic, form-fitting fine wools for stockings and tights, making the doublet with hose attractive. Rigid body armor replaced flexible chain mail, requiring for men tight-fitting underclothing, the shape of which generalized to peacetime wear. Fashions of individual arbiters of taste, such as the Burgundian princes, were socially pervasive: townsmen imitated courtiers. Clemency of climate in northern Europe, such as the absence of winter frosts for several successive years in the fifteenth century, permitted a costume more abbreviated and eccentrically sculptural, such as the heroic-shouldered, cinch-waisted, pubis-grazing pourpoint, rather than warm and practical clothing. Leisure also encouraged excess, permitting cobblers' flights from utility such as the poulaines, shoes with long, thin toe points sometimes requiring gold chains to suspend them from the wearer's shins or thighs lest they trip him.

In the fourteenth and fifteenth centuries the international style was emended by local variation. Mindful of the caveat that fashion rules were often proved by their exceptions, it is nevertheless possible to review specific articles of clothing as typical of their times.

Hats were preeminent social signifiers, worn everywhere, indoors and out, by everyone of every age. Variations on a simple skull-fitting hat with a chin strap, the coif, were worn daily by men, women, and children and as a nightcap to protect ears and head from cottage cold or castle drafts, and to prevent tangles in long hair, periodically in and out of fash-

Head of a woman from a tomb sculpture. She is wearing a stiffened linen cap and barbette, with a veil. France, possibly late 13th to 14th centuries. INDIANA UNIVERSITY ART MUSEUM, STAFFORD GIFT

ion for both men and women. Also frequent were soft berets and long or short stocking caps.

From the tenth through fourteenth centuries, such simple, functional outdoor headgear as coif, beret, a close-fitting, helmetlike cap with a pointed top called the Phrygian cap, and a simple veil or kerchief for women called a coverchief or headrail were all indicators of secular craft or class, depending on the fabrics of which they were made; the colors; and ornaments such as jewels, furs, feathers, brims, and thin pendants, topped and lined with contrasting colors, called liripipes. However, in the fourteenth and fifteenth centuries these styles became undercaps for more elaborate, several-layer hats, the multivalencia, the most popular of which were hoods, chaperons, and hennins.

Hoods were common toppers worn by men and women not only for function. Of course, farmers used hoods for protection against sun, rain, cold, or snow; miners wore hoods to keep off tunnel dust and debris, as at Kutna Hora in the fifteenth century; and lepers' hoods warned the unwary of their approach, signaled by costume as well as by sound of clapper or bell. Hoods otherwise were fashionable articles worn separately or attached to capes or cloaks. Who wore which hood shape, color, lining, fur, embroidery, or inscription was determined by custom and mandated by sumptuary law. When prostitutes arrogated "noble" hoods in London of 1351, thereby deceiving people about their true rank, the law insisted that whores be prohibited from wearing cloaks lined with ermine, miniver, squirrel, brown rabbit, or hare, or to have hoods with fur trim, lest they be mistaken for good women. Violators would forfeit their hoods or vestments, or their freedom by imprisonment.

Chaperons, elaborated turbans for men, consisted of three parts: a coif or skullcap had set on it a firm, doughnut-shaped circlet or roundlet with very long liripipes that wound round it, clasped with a decorative brooch or jewel. Equaling the chaperon's popularity for men was the women's hennin, both styles probably derived from the courts of Burgundy. The hennin was a tall, conical hat of velvet, brocade, silk, or other fine fabric set atop a skullcap or coif to anchor it to the head. Hiding all or most of the hair, the hennin usually had a long, diaphanous veil suspended from its peak, reaching down to shoulders or ankles, or a wire frame floating veils front and back. Given to a beloved as a love token, the veil was worn on his armored helmet and called a lambrequin.

Some hennins had transparent, stiffened forehead veils. Some peaks rose four feet high; others were jauntily cropped and cylindrical; others bifurcated to produce two peaks. Two-horned hennins were called *atours*. A variation in the Low Countries consisted of a wire, horsehair, or stiff buckram armature over which gracefully draped transparent fabric made a "butterfly" headdress.

Women's horned headdresses were not popular in Italy, where hair itself formed a crown. Horns of hair or other elaborate braided and teased hairstyles were adorned by interlaced strands of precious ribbon and jeweled cords, or covered by delicate frets (corded hairnets), *crespines* (more elaborate nets encrusted with jewels and pearls), and *tressours* (the most bejeweled reticulated hair covers). Women outside Italy wore these as well, sometimes under other hats or hoods.

Women's headdresses emphasized height of forehead. The effect was helped cosmetically by tweezing and shaving; a tall expanse of skin, brow to hairline, was considered the sign of keen intelligence and moral probity; therefore Chaucer's Prioress proudly vaunted her hand-span-high forehead. A wimple, a wide, straight or pleated horizontal fabric band worn high on the head, accentuated a beautiful forehead. Worn lower, it demurely covered it. A wimple connected to a wide, ear-covering chin strap was the barbette. A chaplet, worn by men or women, was a narrow fabric band worn at the hairline or across the forehead and around the head, often ornamented with jewels, sequins, or flowers. A wider one was called a fillet.

Three hats for men typify medieval symbolic millinery: the Jew's hat, the bishop's miter, and the jester's cap. Ecclesiastical or civil laws required Jews in particular areas to wear a conical cap, often yellow; this identifier was so frequent that Jews themselves, in their manuscript art, such as the illuminated Haggadoth, used the *Judenhut* as an attribute differentiating them from gentiles. This pointed or horned hat may have been derived from the concept of "the horned Moses"; St. Jerome's fourth-century mistranslation of the Hebrew word for Moses' "radiance" (after receiving God's law) into the Latin expression for horns affected art and iconography ever after. Mosaic "horns" also influenced the "double-horned" shape of the Christian bishop's miter. A bishop's investiture promise to teach "the two horns of faith," the Old Testament and the New, was symbolized by his miter. Bishop Guillaume Durand of Mende said in 1292 that "the miter was the helmet

of defense and salvation against opponents of truth, just as God adorned Moses with resplendent horns of His brightness and truth."

The fool's cap consisted of a single "horn" or several floppy, pendant peaks terminated with bells, pompoms, bangles, or tippets. The hat plus the fool's bauble, a rattle, doll, or puppet similarly capped, and his variegated motley costume protected the court entertainer, who among the flatterers and office seekers was employed to tell the truth.

Fashions for men and women resembled each other until the fourteenth century. Earlier long, ankle- or floor-length garments worn by both sexes often were elegant, banded by brocade, embroidery, and fur at neckline, cuff, and hem, and worn loose or belted at waistline or hip. Two basic types persisted through most of western Europe during the eleventh through thirteenth centuries: the tunic and the cotehardie. The basic boat-necked tunic usually was covered by a hooded supertunic or cape, hip-length to floor-length. Women's tunic sleeves ranged from slender and fitted, shoulder to wrist, to wide bell and bag sleeves with pendulous cuffs. By 1200 in England such cuffs swept the floor, requiring their knotting for practical mobility.

Simplicity of style in men's and women's tunics was balanced by extravagance of fabric: damask, the richly woven and figured silk from Damascus; velvet; baldekin, an expensive silk woven with gold from Baghdad; samite and sendal, pure silks interwoven with precious metal threads and finely embroidered; glistening cloths of gold and silver; fine resilient wools such as sharlach or scarlet, which was so popular dyed rich red that the cloth's name was transferred to the color.

The cotehardie, similarly made from a wide range of cloth, was a long, thigh-length high-necked garment with an adjustable drawstring at the neck, usually with slender sleeves, and loosely circled by a belt. An overcloak or cape was clasped with an agrafe or brooch. Over it women, particularly in Germany, wore the sleeveless overdress called the suckenie, and in France and England the cotelette, split to the hip at the sides, closed to the floor, the borders of the deep armholes accentuated by braid, fur, or contrasting fine cloth.

Two constants of fashion were parti-colored fabrics and elaborate sleeves. *Mi-parti* was the lengthwise use of contrasting fabric, neck to hem, such as a tunic half gold and half green, or half red and half white, for symbolic, heraldic, or whimsical purpose. This was popular in both men's and women's wear from the twelfth to the sixteenth century. Stockings, tights, or leggings similarly were divided, one color on the left leg, another on the right. As the length of men's garments ascended to the thigh, then the pelvis, the *mi-parti* leg divisions became more extravagant, with one leg in striped fabric and the other dotted, or one patterned and the other plain.

Sleeve length, shape, and linings changed from the eleventh century on, from short to long, from sheath-shaped to funnels, bags, and caverns. Some sleeves were frilled, shirred, pleated, and laced; others were slashed and pierced to allow undersleeves to show. Cuffs were furred, braided, fringed, scalloped, belled, and dagged, and hung with lappets and liripipes from shoulders, elbows, or wrists. Usually sleeves were separable from their garments for style or color changes, and for easy laundering. A love sleeve, given as a token of affection to a man or woman, would be worn over or above the recipient's own sleeve—thus "wearing the heart on the sleeve."

The fourteenth and fifteenth centuries' sexual differentiation in costume accentuated anatomy. Over kirtle robes women wore surcoats tightly fitting the breasts, the collars or closures plunging to the level of wide belts at the waistline. The neckline revealed an interior border of the underrobe and an expanse of neck and chest requiring elaborate pendant jewelry and lacy collars called reticules. The surcoat was bordered at wrist and skirt hem with fur, embroidery, braiding, or jewels, and belted with a fabric or metal girdle often elaborated with enamel, inlay, or cloisonné. From this belt hung any of several ornaments: an *aumônière,* a purse originally shaped like an alms bag; a key hook, later called a *clavendier;* a ring for keys and knife, called a chatelaine; a *feral* or pouch bag; an etui, a fitted case for necessaries such as scissors, file, knife, and tweezers, most often made of tooled and worked leather, cuir-bouilli; or a tassel tipped with a jewel; or a pomander, an apple-shaped, sectioned container for spice, perfume, and cosmetics; or a memento mori, a carved boxwood skull or skeleton, reminder of the vanity of fashion and life's brevity.

Menswear was astonishingly sculptural. Both men and women originally wore the houppelande, thought to have been brought from the East by crusaders, a long, full robe with padded shoulders, generally belted at the waist or, if at the hips, by a *demiceint.* Sleeves were huge, funnel- or bag-shaped, fur-lined or fur-bordered. In the fourteenth century the men's houppelande might be floor-length; or it might reach ankle, calf, or crotch. Worn with tights,

Extreme form of poulaine or crakow. From *Chronique d'Angleterre,* Flemish, 15th century. THE BRITISH LIBRARY, MS ROYAL 14.E.IV

ankle or high boots, its requisite underpinnings were well-turned legs and finely shaped buttocks. A specifically male garment was the pourpoint, which, particularly in Franco-Flemish circles, exaggerated male triangularity. Padding, quilting, and tufting of *mahoître* shoulders overlaid upon horsehair shoulder struts called bombasts accentuated a narrow waistline cinched tightly by a selfsame or jeweled belt. From it might hang any of the practical adornments women might also wear, with addition of a *gibecière* pouch and a dagger. The pourpoint, worn as short as the thigh or just below the waist, was balanced below by the extravagantly long pointed *poulaines.*

Poulaines, also called crakows, thought to have been influenced by Polish fashion, were soft leather shoes, low-heeled and, as the German name *schnabelschuhe* suggests, long-snouted. The points often required ornamental thongs or chains to draw them to the leg, or even the waistline, for safety. Other footgear antedating the fourteenth century yet persisting through the fifteenth included boots of all heights, from below the ankle to the thigh, often laced or buttoned on the side. Sandals with foot or ankle straps were popular among all social classes, as were flat leather shoes with an instep strap, the upper toe portion pierced with cutouts emulating the shape of a stained glass rose window. Other footgear consisted of simple flat heels and soles sewn onto stockings or leggings, prototypes of modern slipper socks. Over these, wooden clogs or pattens with a high heel or platform were worn in rough or wet weather.

The more impractical these shoes, garments, and hats, the more leisured their wearers. Laborers and craftsmen throughout Europe wore costumes with a form that closely followed function. Silver miners crawling through tunnels and shafts wore knee-padded leggings beneath their leprechaunic hooded cloaks. Mountain shepherds wore climbing boots beneath their hooded tunics. Farmers wore long shirts covering *chausses,* a pair of stockings with breeches, which ultimately became leggings with a drawstring at the waist, and low boots. Farm women covered their skirts with aprons useful for carrying gathered produce. Craftsmen and tradesmen wore comfortable, loose-fitting jacketlike doublets over hose, or poncholike tabards protected, when necessary, by aprons and decorated according to personal predilection or craft necessity. The less physical labor required for work, the more adorned the body with attractive frippery.

Children's wear imitated adults'. The more functional the parent's costume, so the child's. The newborn and infants were wrapped in swaddling bands, long strips of soft fabric binding the child upright to assure good posture and bone growth, and safe transport.

Fashion, though Folly's child and guide of fools (as George Crabbe said), ruled even the wisest.

BIBLIOGRAPHY

Costume histories with good medieval sections are Nancy Bradfield, *Historical Costumes of England* (1970); Millia Davenport, *The Book of Costume* (1948); Carl Köhler and Emma von Sichart, *A History of Costume* (1928; 1963); Cesare Vecellio, *Habiti antichi e moderni* (1590; 1598), published as *Costumes anciens et modernes* (1859), the illustrations only as *Vecellio's Renaissance Costume Book* (1977); Doreen Yarwood, *European Costume* (1975).

Dependable studies solely on medieval fashion are Iris Brooke, *English Costume of the Later Middle Ages* (1935, repr. 1977) and *English Costume of the Early Middle Ages* (1936, repr. 1977); C. Willett Cunnington and Phillis Cunnington, *Handbook of English Medieval Costume* (1952); Dorothy Hartley, *Medieval Costume and Life* (1931); H. W. Lonsdale, *Illustrations of Medieval Costume* (1874); Alga Šroňková, *Gothic Woman's Fashion* (1954).

On costume law, symbol, and social status, see Frances E. Baldwin, *Sumptuary Legislation and Personal Regulation in England* (1926, repr. 1978); Phillis Cunnington, *Costume for Births, Marriages, and Deaths* (1972, repr.

1978); Phillis Cunnington and Catherine Lucas, *Costume of Household Servants* (1974), and *Charity Costumes* (1978); Elizabeth Ewing, *History of Children's Costume* (1977); Ruth Mellinkoff, *The Horned Moses in Medieval Art and Thought* (1970); Alfred Rubens, *A History of Jewish Costume* (1967).

MADELEINE PELNER COSMAN

[See also **Beauty Aids, Cosmetics; Furs, Fur Trade; Hose; Ornement des Dames; Shoes and Shoemakers; Sumptuary Laws; Textiles; Vestments.**]

COTTON, JOHN. See **John of Afflighem.**

COTTON, a textile plant introduced into Europe by the Moors (Arabic: *quṭun*), probably from Egypt, as early as the ninth century. Cotton never became a major component of the medieval European textile industries and was always considered a luxury textile, rivaling the finest linen in price and desirability.

Cotton is a monsoon crop, requiring three to four inches of rainfall each month for the growth of harvest-quality bolls, and a climate providing six to seven months of uninterrupted warmth. Outside of Egypt, which had the requisite climate and made up for the lack of rainfall by the ineluctable flooding of the Nile, no area of the medieval world north of 35° north latitude provided these basic requirements.

Sicily, southern Italy, the valley of the Po, and southern Spain offered adequate conditions of warmth but lacked the requisite rainfall, as well as Egypt's blessing of a natural, predictable, annual flooding. Hence, cotton production in southern Europe had to await large-scale artificial irrigation projects for its beginnings.

Irrigation projects on a large enough scale to make cotton production a profitable venture required long-term planning, careful execution, some knowledge of hydraulic engineering, political stability, a degree of economic self-consciousness, and considerable capital outlay. Such conditions, natural and human, were first conjoined in the Arab colonies of Spain and, to a lesser degree, in Sicily; and the earliest evidence of cotton cultivation is found in Spain, especially in the provinces of Saragossa, Andalusia, Murcia, and Valencia. Cotton production in southern Italy predates that in the north, as a glance at the political and cultural history of the country will suggest. Irrigation projects in northern Italy, dating from the Peace of Constance (1183) and later, were followed within half a century by the beginnings of cotton production in the area.

BIBLIOGRAPHY

Georges Duby, *Rural Economy and Country Life in the Medieval West,* Cynthia Postan, trans. (1968); James W. Thompson, *Economic and Social History of the Middle Ages,* 2 vols. (1928, repr. 1959).

MICHAEL J. HODDER

[See also **Textiles**.]

COUCY, CHÂTELAIN DE. See **Châtelain de Coucy.**

COUCY, ENGUERRAND DE. See **Enguerrand VII of Coucy.**

COUCY, ROBERT DE. See **Robert de Coucy.**

COUNCILS, ARMENIAN. See **Armenian Church, Doctrines and Councils.**

COUNCILS (ECUMENICAL, 325–787). Regular or extraordinary gatherings *(synodoi)* of bishops, who were seen as persons responsible for the maintenance of doctrinal orthodoxy and proper discipline, were the norm in Christianity on a regional level by the third century. Such meetings were also necessary to fulfill the requirement that new bishops be ordained by several of their peers. With the new relationships established between the church and the Roman state under Emperor Constantine (324–337), the need arose for ecclesiastical pronouncements and decisions that could be included in the state legislation and determine the policies of the empire. Since the empire was, in practice, identified with the "universe," the councils representing the episcopate of the empire were labeled "universal" or "ecumenical"

(oikomene ge, inhabited earth). Such councils were always convoked by the emperor, whose confirmation made their decrees obligatory throughout the empire.

The Orthodox church of Byzantium and of later centuries recognized seven councils as authentically "ecumenical." They all met in the period between the peace of Constantine and the end of iconoclasm in the ninth century. The schism between East and West ended the possibility of joint councils, although a series of councils of the Latin church was later recognized as ecumenical in the West. This article will treat the first seven ecumenical councils.

THE FIRST COUNCIL OF NICAEA (325)

The documents of the period do not conclusively indicate who initiated the idea of the first "ecumenical" council. We know, however, that the bishops of the empire received a respectful letter of invitation from the emperor, who also provided them, as means of transportation to Nicaea, with the *cursus publicus,* normally used by government officials.

There are no minutes or other official records of the assembly. Various authors give different figures of attendance, ranging between 200 and 300. However, the later tradition adopted the symbolic figure of "319 fathers" (compare Gen. 14:14). With the exception of no more than six or seven bishops coming from the Latin West, all the members were Easterners. The first session, held on 20 May 325 at an imperial residence, was attended by Constantine, who, while not yet a Christian himself, was accompanied by Christian members of his court.

The two major topics on the agenda were the teaching of the Alexandrian theologian Arius and the date of Easter.

The condemnation of Arius, who considered the Son of God incarnate to be a creature, and not God coeternal with the Father, does not seem to have taken much time. The bishops rapidly accepted the view of Bishop Alexander of Alexandria and his deacon, Athanasius, in affirming the divinity of the Son. They also adopted the idea of a common creed that would formalize the unity of faith in the entire church: before Nicaea a variety of baptismal creeds were in use throughout the local churches. Using the Creed of Caesarea in Palestine as a basis, the council drafted a text that included the key word "consubstantial" *(homoousios),* affirming that the Son is of the same divine substance (ousia) as the Father. The word, which reflected a terminology more akin to Latin thought than to Greek theology, may have

COUNCILS (ECUMENICAL, 325–787)

been suggested by Bishop Hosius of Córdoba, who acted as Constantine's adviser.

The date of Easter was defined in accordance with the Alexandrian computation: it was to be celebrated on the Sunday after the full moon following the vernal equinox. The definition had an obvious importance for the imperial government, since Easter was to become a state holiday. Some communities of Syria and Asia Minor that celebrated Christian Easter together with the Jewish Passover, on the fourteenth day of the Jewish month of Nisan, opposed the decision. They were known as Quartodecimans.

The council also approved a number of rules (or canons) referring to discipline and administration. Particularly important were canons 4–6, which, with only a few exceptions, endorsed a system of ecclesiastical administration matching the administrative divisions of the empire: in each civil *provincia* the affairs of the church were to be administered by a synod of bishops headed by the metropolitan, the bishop of the provincial capital.

Thus, aside from condemning Arianism, the council responded positively to the pragmatic and centralizing requirements of the newly established alliance between church and state.

THE FIRST COUNCIL OF CONSTANTINOPLE (381)

The condemnation of Arius at Nicaea did not end the theological debates concerning the Christian doctrine of the Trinity. It seems that most of the bishops accepted the term "consubstantial," used in the Nicene Creed, without considering the implications. In the later reign of Constantine, Arius was readmitted into the church. Furthermore, most of the Eastern bishops, while rejecting the Arian view that the Son of God was a "creature," were unhappy with the Nicene formula, which appeared to them as "modalistic" (or Sabellian); if God was "one essence," were not the three persons—the Father, the Son, and the Spirit—nothing but "modes" of a single reality?

In the East the lonely defender of the Nicene faith was Athanasius, bishop of Alexandria (328–373). Sharp controversies, numerous councils, and direct imperial interventions marked the history of the debates. Athanasius went into exile five times. Under Emperor Constantius II (337–361), the Nicenes were persecuted even in the West, where the use of "consubstantial" had previously been well accepted.

In the latter part of the fourth century, the crisis

was overcome through the efforts of the Cappadocian fathers, particularly St. Basil the Great of Caesarea (*d.* 379). They sided with Nicene orthodoxy, and rejected modalism by affirming the real existence of the three Persons or *hypostaseis* in God. This made Nicaea acceptable to the vast majority of Easterners.

Emperor Theodosius I (379–395) supported the Cappadocian position. In May 381 he convoked a general council at Constantinople that reaffirmed the Nicene faith while also condemning modalism. Other heretical movements, including those denying the divinity of the Holy Spirit (*pneumatomachoi*), were also rejected.

The council was an exclusively Eastern assembly of about 150 bishops. Neither Alexandria nor Rome was formally represented because the doctrine of the "three hypostases" remained suspicious to the leaders of those churches. Only at the Council of Chalcedon (451) did the assembly of 381 find universal acceptance. It was then also that the text known as the Creed of Nicaea-Constantinople was post factum attributed to it.

The Council of 381 also settled the internal affairs of the important churches of Constantinople and Antioch, where personal conflicts, provoked by the fierce debates of the Arian crisis, had disrupted unity. Furthermore, it affirmed the preeminence of Constantinople, as "New Rome," over Alexandria and gave it the second place of honor, among the major sees, after "Old Rome."

THE COUNCIL OF EPHESUS (431)

The triumph of Nicene orthodoxy and the recognition of the divinity of Jesus Christ did not fully solve the issue of his full identity: if he is fully God, how is his humanity, so well described in the Gospels, related to the Divinity? Debates on this issue determined the agenda of the following councils and eventually led to permanent schisms in Eastern Christendom.

Following the theological traditions of his native Antioch, Nestorius, archbishop of Constantinople (428–431), delivered sermons insisting on the reality and the distinctiveness of humanity in Jesus. While fully recognizing him as Son of God existing eternally, he found it impossible to call Mary anything but "mother of the man" Jesus or "Mother of Christ" (*Christotokos*). The teaching of Nestorius appeared to undermine the unity of Christ's person; his logic seemed to imply that there were actually "two sons," the divine Son of God dwelling in—but not personally identical with—the human son of Mary. His use of the Greek term *prosopon* to designate the one person of Christ was not entirely convincing to his critics, because this term (just like the Latin *persona*) could also mean "appearance" or "mask."

Major opposition to Nestorius came from the archbishop of Alexandria, Cyril, whose fiery letters and ultimatums convinced Emperor Theodosius II (408-450) of the need for a new ecumenical council, which was summoned for Pentecost, 7 June 431, at Ephesus. Since the arrival of some delegates was delayed, the first session took place on 22 June, but even on that date the delegates from Antioch, from whom Nestorius could expect support, had not arrived. Refusing further delays and rejecting the formal protests of the imperial commissioner, Candidianus, Cyril presided over an assembly of about 150 bishops, which deposed Nestorius. Arriving two days later, the Antiochenes discovered that the issue was decided in their absence, and formed another conciliar assembly. The two groups anathematized each other.

The rather scandalous results of the events of 431 were resolved in 433, when an exchange of letters between Cyril and John of Antioch confirmed the main positions of the Cyrillian majority at Ephesus: the unity of Christ's personal identity was accepted by the affirmation that Mary should be properly designated as "Mother of God" (*Theotokos*). The Antiochenes dropped their support of Nestorius. However, the exchange of letters between Cyril and John also avoided the use of the more extreme Cyrillian formulations, such as the expression "one nature incarnate of God the Word."

THE COUNCIL OF CHALCEDON (451)

Following the victory of Alexandrian theology at Ephesus, some ardent and unenlightened disciples of Cyril began to oppose both the substance and the letter of the moderate compromise of 433. Most prominent among them was Eutyches, archimandrite of Constantinople: his teaching insisted so much on the divinity of Jesus that he refused to admit in him a humanity "consubstantial to us." In the teaching of Eutyches, humanity seemed absorbed by divinity. A local synod in August 448, presided over by Flavian of Constantinople, deposed Eutyches and condemned his "Monophysitism" (the doctrine of "one nature" in Christ). This sentence received an author-

itative confirmation from Pope Leo I, who wrote his "Tome to Flavian" on this occasion.

However, Eutyches was able to rally the support of Dioscoros of Alexandria, nephew and successor of Cyril. Emperor Theodosius II thought it proper to extend to Dioscoros the patronage he had earlier given to his uncle. In August 449, under the presidency of Dioscoros, a second council of Ephesus—also known as the Robber Synod—restored Eutyches, deposed Flavian of Constantinople, Domnes of Antioch, and Juvenal of Jerusalem, and assured a brief triumph of Monophysitism.

The death of Theodosius II and the enthronement of Marcian (450-457) completely reversed the situation. The new government accepted the appeals of those, including particularly Pope Leo, who were demanding a new council. Attended by more than 500 bishops representing all regions of the empire, including Rome, the Council of Chalcedon (451), held in a suburb of Constantinople, was the largest and the longest deliberative assembly of the church until that time. It deposed Dioscoros and canceled all the sentences pronounced by the Robber Synod.

Most of the fathers of Chalcedon were in total agreement with the Christology of Cyril, but they were appalled by the Monophysitism of Eutyches and the brutal behavior of Dioscoros in 449 against respected leaders of the church. They also listened to the balanced arguments of Pope Leo, formulated in the "Tome to Flavian," and to some objections of the Antiochenes. The result was the carefully phrased Chalcedonian definition, which was produced after lengthy discussion and several revisions. While affirming the Cyrillian term *Theotokos*, it also acknowledged Christ "in two natures," with "the characteristic property of each nature being preserved, and concurring into one person and one hypostasis." The mystery of the two natures of Christ is emphasized in the four negations that describe the union: "without confusion, without change, without division, without separation."

Unfortunately, the careful wording of the definition did not satisfy the supporters of Dioscoros, who thought of themselves as true disciples of Cyril. The council had defined the union of divinity and humanity of Christ as a "hypostatic" union and not as a "natural" one, but without formally indicating that the hypostasis of union was the preexisting hypostasis of the Logos, second person of the Trinity, as strict Cyrillian Christology would require. Most of Egypt and large sections of Syria rejected Chalcedon, as did the more distant national churches of Armenia and Ethiopia.

Among the canonical decisions of the council the most prominent was a further strengthening of the powers of Constantinople. Its bishops received the right to hear appeals from regional metropolitans (canons 9 and 17), to consecrate metropolitans in the three civilian dioceses of Pontus, Asia, and Thrace, and to send bishops into missionary ("barbarian") areas. As in 381 these privileges were defined as equal to those of "Old Rome." Furthermore, the prestige of both "Romes" was interpreted in political categories, as determined by the presence "of the emperor and the Senate" (canon 28). This interpretation, which anticipates the schism between East and West, was strenuously opposed by Pope Leo, who defined his own powers in terms of apostolic succession from Peter.

THE SECOND COUNCIL OF CONSTANTINOPLE (553)

The schism of the Monophysites, which since 451 had involved the majority of the non-Greek-speaking population of the Eastern Empire, was a permanent challenge to the unity of Christendom. The successive Byzantine rulers attempted to heal the schism, which had acquired ethnic, cultural, and political dimensions. Under Emperor Justinian I (527–565) these attempts resulted in a fifth ecumenical council.

Since the main objection of the Monophysites to the Council of Chalcedon was that it abandoned the Christology of Cyril of Alexandria, Justinian and his advisers undertook to demonstrate that Christian orthodoxy was represented by both Cyril and Chalcedon, even if there were differences in Christological formulations. Convoked on 5 May 553 at the church of St. Sophia, the council was attended by 145 bishops. In order to restore the authority of Chalcedon in the mind of the Monophysites, it proceeded with the condemnation of the "Three Chapters": the writings of the Antiochene theologian Theodore of Mopsuestia, teacher of Nestorius; the anti-Cyrillian writings of Theodoret of Cyr; and a letter of Ibas of Edessa. Theodore, Theodoret, and Ibas were personalities of the preceding century whose anti-Cyrillian positions were used by the Monophysites as a proof of the "Nestorian" character of the Council of Chalcedon, which both Theodoret and Ibas had attended.

Pope Vigilius, present in Constantinople, was afraid that these condemnations were harmful to the authority of Chalcedon, and refused to take part.

Nevertheless, he accepted the decisions in December 553. The council also endorsed previous decrees condemning Origen and some of his extreme disciples.

The decisions of 553 did not resolve the schism; the Monophysites, strongly entrenched in their positions and resenting imperial pressures, maintained their hostility to the Council of Chalcedon.

THE THIRD COUNCIL OF CONSTANTINOPLE (680)

The debates on the identity of Christ saw a new development under the reign of Heraklios (610–641), when Patriarch Sergios of Constantinople (610–638) wrote the *Ekthesis,* a statement endorsing the Chalcedonian doctrine of the two natures but affirming that the unique hypostasis of Christ had only one will. This position, known as Monothelitism, had received written approval of Pope Honorius and was instrumental in achieving local unions with the Monophysites in Armenia and Egypt. In 648 Emperor Constans II (641–668), facing opposition, published the *Typos,* an edict forbidding discussions on the wills of Christ, but in fact allowing for a development of Monothelitism.

The new doctrine was opposed by Patriarch Sophronius of Jerusalem and, particularly, by the great Byzantine theologian St. Maximus the Confessor. Pope Martin I condemned it also (649). Both Maximus and Martin were arrested, tortured, and exiled by Constans II.

The reign of Constantine IV (668–685) saw a reversal of official religious policy. On 7 November 680 the sixth ecumenical council, meeting in the imperial palace of the Trullon at Constantinople, condemned Monothelitism and its supporters, including Pope Honorius and the earlier patriarchs of Constantinople. According to the conciliar decree, the doctrine of "one will" in Christ reduced his humanity to a mere abstraction: Jesus could be genuinely a man only with a distinctly human will, or "energy," that freely followed his divine will.

In 691–692, under Emperor Justinian II, another council met at the Trullon and published a corpus of disciplinary canons that served as the basis for later developments of Byzantine canon law. Since neither the fifth nor the sixth council published any disciplinary rules, the council of 692 was known as the Synod in Trullo or *Trullanum* or *Quinisext* (Greek, *Penthekte*), since it was considered a complement to the work of those councils. In Byzantine collections the canons of 692 were frequently listed as canons of the "Sixth Council."

COUNCILS (ECUMENICAL, 325–787)

THE SECOND COUNCIL OF NICAEA (787)

Assembled on 24 September 787 by Empress Irene, the seventh ecumenical council was called to solve the crisis of iconoclasm. Initiated by Emperor Leo III (717–741) and pursued by his son Constantine V (741–775), the iconoclastic movement had been sanctioned by a "pseudo council" in 754. It opposed the veneration of religious images or icons. Probably under the influence of Islam and of some spiritualistic trends proper to Hellenism, the iconoclasts affirmed the impossibility of representing God in any form and rejected the images of saints as a form of idolatry. The veneration of images was defended by orthodox theologians—John of Damascus and, later, Theodore of Studios and Patriarch Nikephoros—who insisted on the Christian doctrine of the Incarnation: God became man and, therefore, became visible and depictable in the person of Jesus Christ. The debate thus involved the christological issues of the relationship between divinity and humanity of Christ that had been debated in previous centuries.

The Council of 787 condemned iconoclasm; proclaimed the legitimacy of depicting the person (or hypostasis) of Christ, the incarnate Son of God, and the saints; and distinguished between the legitimate "veneration" (proskynesis) of images and "worship" (latreia), which belongs to God alone and would be a form of idolatry if addressed to icons. A new wave of iconoclasm led to a temporary rejection of the Second Council of Nicaea, but the veneration of images was at last fully reinstated in 843.

The council of 787 issued twenty-two canons referring primarily to clerical and monastic discipline, and condemning the interference of civil authorities in episcopal elections.

BIBLIOGRAPHY

The most complete edition of the acts of the ecumenical councils remains J. D. Mansi, ed., *Sacrorum conciliorum nova et amplissima collectio*, 31 vols. (1759–1798). For Ephesus, Chalcedon, and Constantinople I, see *Acta conciliorum oecumenicorum*, E. Schwartz, ed. (1914–). See also *Conciliorum oecumenicorum decreta*, J. Alberigo *et al.*, eds., 3rd ed. (1973). For a general history see C. J. von Hefele and Henri Leclercq, *Histoire des conciles*, 10 vols. in 19 (1907–1938).

JOHN MEYENDORFF

[See also **Arianism; Athanasius of Alexandria, St.; Basil the Great of Caesarea, St.; Church, Latin; Constantine I, the Great; Cyril of Alexandria, St.; Ekthesis; Eutyches; Iconoclasm, Christian; Leo I, Emperor; Monophysitism; Mono-**

COUNCILS, BYZANTINE (859–1368)

thelitism; Nestorianism; Nicaea, Council of; Sergios, Patriarch; Theodoret of Cyr.]

COUNCILS, BYZANTINE (859–1368). The barbarian invasions in the West, the Monophysite schism in the East, and, in the seventh century, the conquests of Islam resulted in the growth of the role of Constantinople as the major center of Orthodox (Chalcedonian) Christianity in the East. Its de facto supremacy in theological and ecclesiastical affairs extended to the West with the reconquest of Italy by Emperor Justinian (527–565). Thus the ecumenical councils of 553, 680, and 787, which involved the participation of the pope, are frequently designated as Byzantine councils.

Following the end of iconoclasm in Byzantium (843), the archbishop of Constantinople, whose ecclesiastical jurisdiction expanded to newly converted areas of eastern Europe (the Balkans, Russia, the Caucasus), normally administered his vast patriarchate in cooperation with a permanent council or synod (synodos endemousa), composed of neighboring or visiting bishops. When extraordinary situations or doctrinal conflicts demanded, a larger council was convoked and often presided over by the emperor. Its decrees were normally published in the form of a special tomos (definition), and sometimes enshrined in the *Synodikon of Orthodoxy*, a solemn text read on the first Sunday of Lent and containing the periodically updated doctrinal teachings of the church.

In the ninth and tenth centuries such councils were attended by papal legates, but after the Gregorian reform in the West, the schism became final, and the councils in Byzantium were composed of representatives from the Orthodox East only.

The larger councils held in Constantinople played particularly important roles in the historical, doctrinal, and disciplinary development of the Eastern church.

The Council of 859–861 is known in Byzantine canonical collections as the first–second (protodeutera). The reason for this unusual appellation is that two separate assemblies met in August 859 and in the spring of 861, to confirm the patriarchal election of Photios (Christmas 858), which was challenged by the Ignatian opposition. The council of 859 issued a routine condemnation of the Ignatians, whereas the council of 861 gave an opportunity to the papal le-

631

gates, who presided at the meeting, to issue against Ignatios a judgment on appeal, in conformity with the canons of Sardica (343). Since the two assemblies dealt with essentially the same issue, they were procedurally considered as a single first–second council. The seventeen disciplinary canons issued on that occasion concern primarily episcopal authority over monastic communities.

At the Fourth Council of Constantinople (869–870), Photios was formally deposed and Ignatios reinstated as patriarch. The legates of Pope Adrian II played a decisive role at the assembly, which was, after the Gregorian reforms, added to the list of "ecumenical" councils recognized by the Western church. Its acts are only partially preserved. They condemn the participation of civil rulers in ecclesiastical assemblies (but still recognize the role of the emperor in convoking ecumenical councils) and reaffirm the moral authority of the Roman pope.

The Great Council of Union, held at St. Sophia, Constantinople, in 879–880, reinstated Photios and formally canceled the decisions of 869–870. Attended by the legates of Pope John VIII, this council was convoked as "ecumenical" and was recognized as such in Latin canonical collections until the eleventh century, as well as by some Greek authorities of the late-Byzantine period. It put an end to the conflict between Byzantium and Rome connected with the elevation of Photios to the patriarchate and the activities of Frankish missionaries in Bulgaria. While recognizing the "privileges" of "Old Rome," it defined in terms of equality the canonical and judicial authority of the pope and of the patriarch of Constantinople. It also condemned "unauthentic and falsified expressions" added to the Nicene-Constantinopolitan Creed, clearly meaning the Latin addition of Filioque, which was accepted in Frankish lands (but still at that time rejected in Rome).

The Council of July 920 terminated the controversy that had arisen from the fourth marriage of Emperor Leo VI. The number of marriages that could be blessed by the church was formally restricted to three; the penitential discipline applied for second and third marriages was defined. Fourth marriages were declared illegitimate in a special "Tome of Union."

Councils met in 1082, 1117, 1156–1157, and 1166–1167 to solve doctrinal disputes involving the philosopher John Italos, Bishop Eustratios of Nicaea, the theologian Soterichos Panteugenos, and the right interpretation of John 14:28 ("The Father is greater than I").

The Council of 1285, under Patriarch Gregory of Cyprus, rejected the ecclesiastical union concluded at Lyons (1274) by representatives of Emperor Michael VIII Palaiologos. The council criticized in detail the Latin doctrine of the Filioque, but recognized that there is an "eternal manifestation" of the Spirit through the Son, whereas earlier Byzantine anti-Latin polemics rejected any "procession" of the Holy Spirit from the Son, except "in time."

The Council of 1341 condemned the attacks of Barlaam of Calabria against the spirituality of the hesychasts and sanctioned the anti-barlaamite position of Gregory Palamas.

The Council of 1347 condemned the anti-Palamite theologian Gregory Akindynos and gave a new endorsement to the theology of Gregory Palamas.

The Council of 1351 gave the most solemn and detailed approval to the theological positions of Gregory Palamas concerning the uncreated energies of God, distinct from the divine essence, and to his defense of the doctrine of deification of man in Christ.

At the Council of 1368 Patriarch Philotheos proceeded with the excommunication of Prochoros Kydones, an Athonite monk who, with his brother Demetrios, had undertaken the translation into Greek of the works of Thomas Aquinas and had become a convinced Thomist. This council also canonized Gregory Palamas as a saint.

BIBLIOGRAPHY

Hans-Georg Beck, *Kirche und theologische Literatur im byzantinischen Reich* (1959); *Les régestes du patriarchat de Constantinople*, V. Grumel, ed., 4 vols. (1932–1971), nos. 925–927, 1003, 1038, 1041, 1060, 1062, 1065, 1075; J. D. Mansi, ed., *Sacrorum conciliorum nova et amplissima collectio*, XVI, 1–208, 300–413, and XVII, 365–525; John Meyendorff, "Le tome synodal de 1347," in *Vizantoloski Institut, Sbornik radova*, 8 (1963); and *Byzantine Theology: Historical Trends and Doctrinal Themes*, 2nd ed. with revisions (1983); *Patrologia graeca*, CXLII (1865), 233–246, and CLI (1965), 696–764; Georgios Rallès and M. Potles, *Syntagma kanonon*, I (1852), 647–704, and V (1855), 4–10.

JOHN MEYENDORFF

[See also **Byzantine Church; Filioque; Ignatios, Patriarch; John Italos; Leo VI the Wise, Emperor; Photios; Synodikon of Orthodoxy.**]

COUNCILS, WESTERN (869–1179). The history of the Latin Church from the ninth to the fourteenth centuries is marked by councils of various types: the great royal-imperial assemblies of the Carolingian age, the general councils convened under papal presidency from the eleventh century on, provincial gatherings directed by a papal legate or the metropolitan of a province, and diocesan synods at which the clergy of a diocese assembled under the leadership of a local bishop. (Although modern parlance distinguishes between "council" and "synod," usually employing the latter for diocesan assemblies, the medieval sources are not at all consistent in using the words *concilium* and *synodus,* and they often are synonymous. Those terms will be considered here as synonyms.)

This article will treat only councils that are termed "universal" or "general"—also words that were used synonymously in the Middle Ages—and it must be stressed at the outset that for the period under discussion, this designation often has been misunderstood. The Roman Catholic church today counts twenty-one ecumenical or universal councils, from the First Council of Nicaea of 325 through the Second Vatican Council of 1962-1965. This enumeration rests on tradition, and not on any conciliar or papal definition stipulating the number of such councils. At different times in the church's history different gatherings have been granted universal status, and the present numbering (excluding, of course, the two Vatican councils) emerged only in the sixteenth century.

The Fourth Council of Constantinople (869-870) is more closely related to the great councils of earlier centuries than to the papal general councils convened in the West in the High Middle Ages. The synod met in the East, under imperial auspices, and the Latin church was represented only by a small papal delegation. The principal issue treated—the condemnation of Patriarch Photios—was an Eastern question, but the consent of the West to the proceedings, in the form of papal approbation, was crucial for the synod. Although the Greek church, in light of the subsequent history of the Photian affair, rejected the council of 869-870, in the Latin church from the eleventh century it was ranked with the seven earlier ecumenical councils (Nicaea I to Nicaea II, 787) as the eighth universal synod. The Roman cardinal and canonist Deusdedit, writing *ca.* 1086, was one of the first Western authorities to speak of "eight universal synods."

Deusdedit's statement goes even further, not only noting eight *universales sinodi* but also pointing out that these gatherings have been celebrated with

papal authority. The Latin church, working under the initiatives of the eleventh-century ecclesiastical reform, was in the process of evolving a new synodal conception, the papal general council. The notion that for a council to be accorded that status the decisive factor was papal approbation has roots extending back into the patristic period. The idea was developed in the ninth century in the hands of the Pseudo-Isidorian forgers and in the pronouncements of Pope Nicholas I, and found expression in the eleventh century in letters of Pope Leo IX—and, perhaps most widely known to modern investigators, in the sixteenth item of Pope Gregory VII's *Dictatus papae,* which stated that no general council is possible without papal command.

What these and similar statements meant was not that the pope reserved to himself the right to convoke great synods representative of all of Christendom. Not even Nicaea I or the Council of Chalcedon (451) was universal in the sense of attendance. What the eleventh-century reformers were asserting was the right of the bishop of Rome to confirm that the decisions of a conciliar gathering are in harmony with the teachings of the universal church. The pope was, in the minds of those reformers, the touchstone of ecumenicity. Only the approbation of the Roman see could give a council the certainty of being consistent with the true traditions of the universal church. This principle having been stated, the possibilities of general councils became numerous. Even provincial synods could be elevated to that rank if they met under the presidency of representatives of the Roman church, for in that case a papal legate could guarantee that the synod's decisions were consistent with the teachings of the church universal. By the second half of the twelfth century, canonical commentaries would state that a council is general if it is celebrated by the pope or by a legate exercising papal authority.

None of the papal reforming councils of the eleventh century is cataloged among those twenty-one councils that the Roman church today counts as ecumenical. That status is, however, granted to three twelfth-century synods—those convened at the Lateran in 1123, 1139, and 1179. But to sketch the history of the general councils of the early High Middle Ages only in terms of these synods is to impose an anachronistic criterion. Between the middle of the eleventh century and 1179, many important councils were convened directly under papal auspices or by papal legates, and any treatment of the "general councils" of that age must consider those assemblies and not merely the gatherings of 1123, 1139, and 1179.

The first papal council of the eleventh-century reforming period for which an extensive record survives is the synod convened by Pope Leo IX at Rheims in October 1049. This was not Leo's first council, but it is the first for which detailed information is available. The circumstances surrounding the event are noteworthy. While touring France and Germany, Leo had been invited by Abbot Herimar of the venerable monastery of St. Rémi at Rheims to preside at ceremonies for the translation of the relics of St. Rémi (Remigius) and the dedication of a new abbey church. Despite opposition from King Henry I of France, Leo took advantage of this solemn occasion to convene a synod at the monastery. A detailed account of these events was written at Herimar's urging about a decade after the council by a monk of St. Rémi named Anselm. That narrative was meant to extol the power of St. Rémi and to glorify his monastery, but it also offers a detailed picture of the synod, showing Leo presiding over a group of clerics assembled before St. Rémi's relics, which the pontiff had ordered placed on the main altar, in full view of the gathering.

Anselm's report provides an opportunity both to observe the liturgical procedures of a papal synod and to see, in one case, how the medieval papacy began to work out in practice claims of sovereignty over the church. The number of participants was small—Anselm noted only twenty bishops and about forty abbots as present—and Leo was decidedly in control of the proceedings. The assembled clergymen were asked to confess whether or not they were simoniacs; the recalcitrant were condemned, and in some cases commanded to appear later in Rome for further hearings. Although there is no unambiguous condemnation of clerical incontinence at Rheims— this was done at Leo's council convened at Mainz two weeks later—the offensive against simony that was to characterize much of the eleventh- and twelfth-century papal reform is strikingly visible. The decrees from the council at St. Rémi seem not to have circulated as widely as similar texts from later eleventh-century papal synods, but the elaborate description of the gathering preserved by Anselm should be studied for details about how a papal synod operated in the middle of the eleventh century.

Between the 1049 Council of Rheims and the Lateran Council of 1123—which is ranked as the ninth ecumenical council of the Roman Catholic church—

several dozen important synods met under the presidency of the bishop of Rome. It is impossible here to note all or even most of those councils, but a few must receive attention. In April 1059 Pope Nicholas II convened a synod at the Lateran that is remarkable not only for its widely circulated decrees about reform—condemnation of simony (canon 9); a stipulation of continence for clergymen at the rank of the subdiaconate and above (canon 3); condemnation of lay involvement in clerical promotion (in all probability, however, no specific censure of lay investiture) (canon 6)—but also for the famous regulation about the process of selecting a pope.

On the death of the bishop of Rome, the prime responsibility for choosing a successor was to rest with the cardinal bishops, who were to consult the other cardinal clergy, the remaining clerics of the Roman church and the Roman people being then asked to consent to whomever was chosen. Although the process of deliberation is not specified in detail, the election was in the hands of the cardinal clergy of the Roman church, the cardinal bishops playing the leading role. The decree notes that the person chosen should be from the clergy attached to the local Roman church, but if a suitable man cannot be found there, a candidate from another church can be elected. The text concludes with an exceedingly ambiguous concession that promises to respect the "honor" and "reverence" due to the young King Henry IV of Germany, a concession that has been the subject of much scholarly speculation. Although the decree does not stipulate any quantitative procedure for the election of a new pope, the location of that process unambiguously under the control of the cardinals marks this regulation as the basis of the method still used for choosing the Roman pontiff. The council of 1059 also marked the first appearance in a Roman synod of Berengar of Tours. That assembly brought humiliation to Berengar, for he was forced to recite a eucharistic profession drafted by Cardinal Humbert of Silva Candida that stressed the physical presence of Christ's body and blood in the sacrament. Much more would be heard from this scholar from the Loire Valley in the years to come.

The councils of Pope Gregory VII (1073–1085) are perhaps most famous for the first specific condemnation of lay investiture, a decree that in all likelihood was formulated initially at the Roman synod convened in February 1075, and repeated at later assemblies. No synopsis can do justice to the variety of conciliar rulings that emerged from Gregory's synods and were addressed to particular aspects of the reforming themes of purity and liberty for the church, and the leadership of the Roman see over all of Christendom. Scholars of Gregory's reign are fortunate in that his papal register contains a number of lengthy conciliar texts, including materials relating to the important synod of February 1079. At this council Berengar of Tours made his second, and final, appearance before a Roman council. As in 1059 he was forced to abjure his views on the Eucharist, and the 1079 formula is noteworthy for the initial appearance in a profession from a papal synod of the word *substantialiter* to characterize the process of change that occurs in the sacrament, after sacerdotal consecration, from bread and wine to Christ's body and blood.

The end of Gregory VII's pontificate brought the papal reform party to the edge of great disaster. Isolated in southern Italy, where Gregory had fled in 1084 after the Normans had rescued him from virtual imprisonment in Rome, his followers were forced to contend both with the pressures brought on the program of reform by Gregory's political policies and with the necessity of combating the schismatic Guibert of Ravenna, who had been installed by Henry IV as Pope Clement III. That the heirs of Gregory VII were successful in reasserting their leadership throughout Latin Christendom was due to a great extent to Pope Urban II (1088–1099).

Urban held a number of synods during his eleven-year pontificate, but the most important were those in March and November 1095, at Piacenza and at Clermont. Piacenza served both a propagandistic and a pastoral function. No area had been devastated more by the papal schism and the concomitant military campaigns of the 1080's and the 1090's than northern Italy. Lombardy thus was an appropriate area in which to hold a large synod that would demonstrate the extent of Urban's support and legislate on issues relating to reform and to conditions resulting from the Clementine schism. The decrees of Piacenza contain condemnations of simony and clerical incontinence, and a series of detailed regulations about the legality of orders received from simoniacs and schismatics.

Although the last issue was urgent, Urban II had deferred consideration of it at the synod of Melfi in 1089, preferring to await a larger forum, which the Council of Piacenza provided. The Piacenzan canons about orders, landmarks in the history of canon law, were inserted into many canonical collections of the time, and eventually made their way into Gratian's *Decretum*. Piacenza is also significant in crusading history, for it seems that ambassadors from the Byzantine emperor Alexios I Komnenos were permitted to deliver an appeal at the synod for Western troops to help Byzantium battle the Turks.

The Council of Clermont was the first papal synod held outside Italy since Leo IX's councils at Rheims and Mainz in 1049. The convocation of this assembly too often has been seen in terms only of the preaching of the First Crusade, but the council ought to be viewed within the framework of the effort of Urban II both to enhance his cause and, in general, to further the efforts of the Gregorian program. One tradition of the canons of Clermont notes that the synod confirmed all of Urban's earlier conciliar legislation. The records of the council survive in confusing form, and the topics found in the various series of canons cover a wide range of issues, from such great reform matters as condemnations of simony, stipulations of clerical celibacy, and strongly worded prohibitions against lay investiture, to such questions of pastoral concern as a statement, in one version of the decrees, commanding that laymen can wed only three times.

The First Crusade was, of course, not neglected, but it is imperative to see it as one of the many subjects of the assembly's legislation, and not as the council's sole or even most important consideration. Regulations were enacted defining the indulgence applicable to those who undertook the venture, and stipulating that during their absence the property of participants should remain under the Peace of God. It also is possible—the evidence is unclear—that at Clermont decisions were made about the composition and leadership of the armies of the First Crusade, and about the retention of captured territory and the disposition of churches in such territory. But what is clear is that by means of the Council of Clermont—a synod attended by a throng of clerics from many sections of Latin Christendom—Urban II was able to disseminate throughout Europe clear evidence of a reinvigorated Gregorian papacy laboring to take charge both of reform and of the day-to-day operation of church affairs.

The councils of Urban's successor, Paschal II (1099–1118), are in the process of being studied in detail. Sixteen papal councils are known from that pontificate, but attention most often has been devoted to the dramatic events and the concomitant synods of 1111–1112. Paschal, taken captive by Emperor Henry V, conceded to Henry the right of investiture and then, under great pressure from many quarters, quickly renounced that concession. Paschal's reign thus marked a turning point in the investiture conflict, and prepared the ground for the formal solution to that question that was to be worked out between the church and the German realm in the pontificate of Calixtus II (1119–1124). This was the case not only because of the impact of the dramatic confrontation between pope and emperor, but also because of new ideas about the nature of churchmen's duties and of compromise solutions inaugurated during the time of Paschal II for the investiture issue in England and France. Following the brief reign of Paschal's immediate successor, Gelasius II (1118–1119), the true heir to those debates and compromises was Archbishop Guy of Vienne, one of Paschal's most vigorous critics in 1111–1112, who assumed the papal throne as Calixtus II.

Calixtus convened three synods: at Toulouse in July 1119, at Rheims in October 1119, and at the Lateran in March 1123. This last council is considered the ninth ecumenical council in the Roman Catholic tradition, yet the gathering ought not to be viewed apart from the series of papal synods stretching back to the time of popes Leo IX and Nicholas II. That the 1123 Lateran assembly was remembered in a grander way can, at least in part, be attributed to factors such as its convocation in Rome—although there is nothing unusual about this location in the eleventh or twelfth century—its size, and preeminently the fact that with its ratification of the terms of the Concordat of Worms on the issue of investiture, the compromise worked out in the previous year between Calixtus and Henry V, the council readily appears as the ecclesiastical termination of the investiture dispute.

The Council of Rheims is worth a few words, for an eyewitness account of this assembly survives, written by a cleric named Hesso. As with the report from Anselm of St. Rémi, composed six decades earlier and describing Leo IX's council at St. Rémi in Rheims, Hesso's narrative offers a wealth of information about how Calixtus' synod conducted its business, and about the negotiations that the pope was simultaneously conducting with Henry V, in an attempt to end the investiture conflict. These diplomatic initiatives in 1119 failed, and the papal-imperial dispute over investiture continued for many months, but the importance of the 1119 synod at Rheims should nonetheless be stressed. Although the canons promulgated there repeat statements about the long-standing issues of the Gregorian reform, thanks to Hesso's account and another detailed description of the assembly given by the Norman his-

torian Ordericus Vitalis, more is known about what occurred at that gathering than about any other papal synod since Pope Leo IX's assembly at Rheims seventy years earlier.

Less is known about the operations of the Lateran Synod of 1123 than is known about the Council of Rheims. The decrees from both of these assemblies occur frequently in twelfth-century canon law manuscripts, though only texts from the Lateran Council made their way into Gratian's *Decretum.* The canons of the 1123 synod have been characterized, not inaccurately, by Msgr. Philip Hughes as "a curiously mixed collection," with both general matters and questions such as considerations about revenues of local churches treated in the same series of legislation.

The Lateran I texts offer few surprises, and include familiar condemnations of simony, lay interference in ecclesiastical affairs, and clerical incontinence. The provisions from the time of Urban II and the Council of Clermont about the indulgence for crusaders and the protection of their goods are repeated, and the promotions made by the antipope Gregory VIII—the papal rival of Calixtus—are censured. Although the Lateran Synod of 1123, with its ratification of the Concordat of Worms on lay investiture, marks a turning point in the direction of ecclesiastical reform, scholars should be wary when according this assembly special treatment apart from the dozens of other papal councils held during the eleventh and twelfth centuries.

Following the Lateran Council of 1123, no important papal councils were called until 1130. But less than a decade after the First Lateran Council, a dual election following the death of Pope Honorius II in 1130 produced a schism in the Roman church between Pope Innocent II and the antipope Anacletus II. Several well-documented synods were convened as a result, especially by Innocent II, who was often in residence away from Rome during the first half of the decade. Innocent convened councils at Clermont in 1130, at Rheims in 1131 (perhaps also at Liège in that same year), at Piacenza in 1132, at Pisa in 1135, and at the Lateran in 1139. This last council is ranked as the tenth ecumenical council in the Roman Catholic church, but the comments just made about the Lateran Council of 1123 are applicable to it as well. The influence of the 1139 synod, even though a number of its decrees are in the *Decretum* of Gratian, seems to have been less than that of the Lateran synod convened by Calixtus. Its claim to a listing among the ecumenical synods no doubt arises from its convocation at Rome, plus the fact that it can be viewed as defining the end of the Innocentian-Anacletian schism, thus achieving status as a landmark, similar to the perceived relationship of the 1123 Lateran Council to the investiture dispute.

The canons of the synods of Innocent II reveal nearly a verbatim repetition. Beginning in 1130 at Clermont, and continuing to 1139, a single canonical program was promulgated and repromulgated, allowance being made for some discrepancy in the number of canons at each synod, a fact perhaps related to the state of surviving documentation rather than to the synods themselves. By the time of Pope Calixtus II, the decrees promulgated in papal councils were primarily versions of regulations that had grown venerable in the service of the eleventh- and twelfth-century reform movement. Occasionally it would be noted (for instance, at Urban II's Council of Clermont) that a synod actually repromulgated the legislation from earlier councils. Only from Innocent II's synods, however, does a set of texts survive that was copied from council to council, with only minor variations and omissions that could well be due to the form in which the canons survive rather than to the provisions set forth in the councils.

Many of these regulations were, of course, not new. Condemnations of simony and clerical incontinence recurred, as did prohibitions against lay involvement in ecclesiastical appointments and affirmations of the Peace and Truce of God. Beyond these well-known matters a prohibition against monks and regular canons forsaking their religious vocations to study either medicine or Roman law was issued at all of Innocent's councils for which decrees have survived; the Council of Pisa held in 1135 promulgated a condemnation of slave trade; several of Innocent's synods issued condemnations of tournaments and of Anacletus II and his supporters; and the 1139 gathering promulgated a condemnation of the use of crossbows against Christians and "catholics" (that last word meaning, no doubt, nonschismatics).

The 1139 Lateran Council coincided with the completion of the *Decretum* of Gratian, which generally is dated about 1140/1141. The second quarter of the twelfth century was a transitional period in the Latin church between the so-called *ius antiquum* and the *ius novum*, a transition that is defined by the appearance of Gratian's work and the use made of it, especially in the schools. But beyond the value of Gratian's *Decretum* as a textbook for the study of law, it was through this work in particular that canons from many earlier synods were transmitted to the High Middle Ages and beyond. The *Decretum* contains canons from councils of Nicholas II, Alexander II, and Gregory VII, plus significant sequences of decrees from Urban II's synods, especially the councils of Piacenza and Clermont, from the 1123 Lateran Council of Calixtus II, and from the Lateran Council of 1139 under Innocent II. (The transmission of conciliar canons through Gratian, is, however, not without problems for modern scholars.)

Following the Second Lateran Council of 1139, papal councils seem to have been dormant for more than two decades, aside from the councils of Pope Eugenius III in 1148. The question of the frequency of papal councils in this period probably should be seen as a by-product of the increasingly centralized papal bureaucracy in the twelfth century. The age of the *ius novum*, symbolized by the appearance of Gratian's *Decretum*, marks the beginning of an age when the Roman pontiffs, invigorated by the gains in papal prerogatives made during the earlier reform struggles, were becoming in fact as well as in theory the prime legal arbiters of Latin Christendom. The dispatch of papal decretal letters and the increased use of papal legates and judges delegate meant that affairs that earlier would have been brought before synods now could be settled differently. Other forms of papal administration were replacing the assemblies of popes, bishops, and abbots.

But crises still demanded the conciliar forum. After the death of Pope Adrian IV in 1159, a papal schism erupted between Pope Alexander III and the antipope supported by Frederick I Barbarossa, Victor IV. As had been true thirty years earlier, this schism produced several councils called by both pope and antipope. The most important of these was held at Tours by Alexander III and his supporters in 1163. That synod was a show of strength by the Alexandrians in the face of the challenge by Victor and Frederick to Alexander's legitimacy as Roman pontiff. Tours was a substantial gathering of more than 100 bishops, mainly from England and France, but with significant delegations from Spain.

In addition to the normal synodal business of hearing and judging disputes, Tours promulgated a set of canons concerning usury, heresy in southern France, appointments to ecclesiastical benefices, the issue of professed religious' studying medicine and civil law, and condemnation of the Victorines and their supporters—but excluding a sentence of excommunication against Emperor Frederick. The bulk of these decrees was received into various collections of canon law assembled between the reign of Alexander III and the early thirteenth century. Eventually nearly all of the regulations from Tours were incorporated into the canonical *Quinque compilationes antiquae,* and then into the great papal compilation of law made under Gregory IX and promulgated in 1234, The *Liber extravagantium decretalium,* or *Decretales.*

The papal schism that began in 1159 continued between Alexander III and a series of successors to Victor IV—Paschal III, Calixtus III, and Innocent III—until 1180. With the reconciliation between Alexander and Frederick at Venice in July 1177, however, the schism essentially was liquidated. In the aftermath of the peace, and with a view toward addressing disciplinary and institutional problems in the church, Alexander convoked a great council at the Lateran in March 1179. This assembly ranks as the eleventh ecumenical council in the Roman Catholic church, but like the Lateran synods of 1123 and 1139, its elevation to such eminence is a post-twelfth-century matter, and the comments made about Lateran I and Lateran II are applicable to it.

Lateran III is, in part, remembered as an ecumenical council because it came at the end of the protracted struggle between Alexander and Frederick. There is no question, however, that the synod of 1179 was the grandest council that the Latin church had yet seen. The council sat for only three days but was very carefully planned and administered, despite some protests against the inherent legalism that some churchmen saw usurping the true function of Christian ministry (see the remarks in the council attributed to John of Salisbury, recorded by Peter the Chanter).

There survives from the 1179 synod a sermon prepared for delivery at the opening of the council. Dom Germain Morin, the discoverer and editor of this text, attributed the homily to Rufinus, bishop of Assisi and renowned commentator on Gratian's *Decretum.* The sermon is an exaltation of the Roman church and an exhortation of the council fathers for reform of the church through canonical norms. It is difficult to offer a synopsis of the canons promulgated by the assembly. The decrees are long and rich in detail, truly products of the age of the *ius novum.*

The first decree takes up the question of papal election. This issue had not been treated in council since Nicholas II's council of 1059, and Lateran III, clearly with an eye on the events of 1159, stipulated

that a two-thirds majority of the cardinals was necessary to select a pope. The complications of the schisms of 1130 and of 1159 would have been easier to unravel had such a rule been in effect, and it is surprising that the 1139 Lateran Council produced no modification of Nicholas II's canon.

The synod in 1179 went on to condemn the schismatics and the Cathar heretics, offering an indulgence to those who would take up arms against the latter. The synod also dealt in its decrees with several measures aimed at reforming aspects of church life, such as promotions to benefices—no one under the age of thirty should be promoted to the episcopate—clerical conduct, the process of appeal of ecclesiastical judgments, and regulations concerning the use of secular tribunals by clerics.

Furthermore, Lateran III enacted legislation requiring each cathedral church to assign a benefice to a *magister* who was to instruct, free of charge, both the clergy of that church and indigent students, presumably in theology and the liberal arts. Lateran III also renewed Innocent II's condemnation of tournaments, which had been repeated by Pope Eugenius III in his council held at Rheims in 1148, and enacted a series of regulations defining relations between Christians and Jews.

In the critical edition of the canons from the Third Lateran Council, the decrees are presented as twenty-nine canons, and cover fourteen pages. Those texts are filled with detailed information about Alexander III's vision of how the church should be structured. As with the canons from Alexander's Council of Tours, the 1179 texts were taken up into many collections of canon law in the late twelfth and early thirteenth centuries, eventually finding their way into the *Decretales* of Pope Gregory IX. In the 130 years from 1049 to 1179, the papal conciliar operations of Latin Christendom had evolved from the small gathering around the relics of St. Rémi under Leo IX, to the great juridical assembly at the Lateran that, among other things, was a celebration of the triumph of the Roman church, "which alone has the prerogative and power to convoke a universal council, to formulate new canons, and to erase the old," as the opening sermon of that gathering declared.

BIBLIOGRAPHY

A scholarly journal devoted to councils is *Annuarium historiae conciliorum (AHC)*, published twice yearly and containing bibliographies.

The principal collection of the primary sources for medieval papal synods is J. D. Mansi, ed., *Sacrorum conciliorum nova et amplissima collectio*, 31 vols. (1759–1798), but it must be used with caution. Philipp Jaffé, *Regesta pontificum Romanorum*, 2 vols. (1885–1888), is necessary for papal councils down to 1198. For the council at Constantinople of 869–870 and the twelfth-century Lateran councils, the texts of the canons in *Conciliorum oecumenicorum decreta*, J. Alberigo *et al.*, eds., 3rd ed. (1973), supersede those in Mansi. For several eleventh- and twelfth-century papal synods new editions were prepared by Ludwig Weiland, *Monumenta Germaniae historica, Leges*, IV, 1 (1893). The standard narrative history is C. J. von Hefele and Henri Leclercq, *Histoire des conciles* (1907–1952), but for the so-called ecumenical councils of the Roman Catholic church, see the series in progress entitled Histoire des conciles oecumeniques, edited by Gervais Dumeige, S.J. See also Philip Hughes, *The Church in Crisis: A History of the General Councils, 325–1870* (1964), 117. Much useful general information is in Georgine Tangl, *Die Teilnehmer an den allgemeinen Konzilien des Mittelalters* (1922).

For the development of the notion of general councils in the High Middle Ages, and the relation of that concept to the ecumenical councils of the Roman church, see Horst Fuhrmann, "Das ökumenische Konzil und seine historischen Grundlagen," in *Geschichte in Wissenschaft und Unterricht*, 12 (1961), which in places corrects the work of A. Hauck, "Die Rezeption und Umbildung der allgemeinen Synode im Mittelalter," in *Historische Vierteljahrschrift*, 10 (1907); Further information is available in Remigius Bäumer, "Die Zahl der allgemeinen Konzilien in der Sicht von Theologen des 15. und 16. Jahrhunderts," in *AHC*, 1 (1969).

The following works are relevant for individual papal councils of the period 869–1179 (the councils listed chronologically): C. Leonardi, "Das achte ökumenische Konzil," in *AHC*, 10 (1978), and V. Peri, "Postilla sul concilio ecumenico ottavo," *ibid.*; Uta-Renate Blumenthal, "Ein neuer Text für das Reimser Konzil Leos IX. (1049)?" in *Deutsches Archiv*, 32 (1976); H.-G. Krause, *Das Papstwahldekret von 1059 und seine Rolle im Investiturstreit* (1960); G. Miccoli, "Il problema delle ordinazioni simoniache e le sinodi Lateranensi del 1060 e 1061," in *Studi gregoriani*, 5 (1956); John Gilchrist, "The Reception of Pope Gregory VII into the Canon Law (1073–1141)," in *Zeitschrift der Savigny-Stiftung für Rechtsgeschichte, Kanonistische Abteilung*, 69 (1973); Robert Somerville, *The Councils of Urban II*, I, *Decreta Claramontensia* (1972); and "The Council of Clermont and the First Crusade," in *Studia Gratiana*, 20 (1976); Uta-Renate Blumenthal, *The Early Councils of Pope Paschal II, 1100–1110* (1978); Robert Somerville, "The Councils of Pope Calixtus II: Reims 1119," in *Proceedings of the Fifth International Congress of Medieval Canon Law (Salamanca, 21–25 September 1976)* (1980); Stephen Kuttner, "Brief Notes," in *Traditio*, 24 (1968), for the problems of conciliar texts in Gratians' *Decretum*;

Robert Somerville, "The Canons of Reims (1131)," in *Bulletin of Medieval Canon Law*, 5 (1975); D. Girgensohn, "Das Pisaner Konzil von 1135 in der Überlieferunge des Pisaner Konzils von 1409," in *Festschrift für Hermann Heimpel*, II (1972); Nikolaus M. Häring, "Notes on the Council and the Consistory of Reims (1148)," in *Medieval Studies*, 28 (1966), and "Die spanischen Teilnehmer am Konzil von Reims im März 1148," *ibid.*, 32 (1970); Robert Somerville, *Pope Alexander III and the Council of Tours (1163)* (1977); C. R. Cheney, "The Numbering of the Lateran Councils in 1179 and 1215," in R. C. Cheney, ed., *Medieval Texts and Studies* (1973); Dom Germain Morin, "Le discours d'ouverture du Concile général de Latran (1179) et l'oeuvre littéraire de maitre Rufin, évêque d'Assise," in *Atti della Pontificia accademia romana di archeologia*, 3rd ser., *Memorie*, 2 (1928).

ROBERT SOMERVILLE

[See also **Alexander II, Pope; Alexander III, Pope; Berengar of Tours; Celibacy; Church, Latin; Decretum; Deusdedit, Cardinal; Frederick I Barbarossa; Gregory VII, Pope; Gregory IX, Pope; Humbert of Silva Candida, Cardinal; Investiture and Investiture Controversy; Leo IX, Pope; Paschal II, Pope; Simony; Urban II, Pope; Worms, Concordat of.**]

COUNCILS, WESTERN (1215–1274). A major but unrealized objective since the beginning of the pontificate of Innocent III (1198–1216), a general council was formally announced in the bull *Vineam domini Sabaoth* on 19 April 1213. Representatives of both the clergy and the laity from the Eastern and Western churches were summoned to meet in the Lateran basilica in November 1215 to discuss the recovery of the Holy Land and the reform of the entire church. The intervening two and a half years were to be devoted to vigorous promotion of the Fifth Crusade, announced by the pope on 5 May 1213, and to ascertaining the problems with which the council must deal.

The meticulous preparation by the curia was reflected in the attendance of 412 prelates, many from the farthest corners of Christendom—Ireland, Scotland, Poland, Lithuania, Estonia, and Hungary—and more than 800 abbots, priors, chapter representatives, and lay dignitaries, *confirming* in fact those theories of primacy that had been developing for centuries and that Innocent III utilized with consummate skill. Noticeably absent, however, were envoys of the Greek church, undoubtedly due to the Latin conquest of Constantinople in 1204; in a figurative sense only, the Eastern church was represented by the Latin patriarch of Constantinople, the primate of the Maronites, and proxies from the Crusader states.

The first of three solemn sessions commenced at dawn on 11 November 1215 as Innocent celebrated Mass. Following a sermon on the text "Desiderio desideravi hoc Pascha manducare vobiscum ante patiar," in which the pontiff presented the dual themes of the council, an appeal for aid to the Holy Land was made by the patriarch of Jerusalem, and the bishop of Agde reported on efforts to combat the spread of Catharism in southern France.

The second session (20 November) was devoted to the question of the Holy Roman Empire, eventually degenerating into a contest of insults exchanged between the envoys of Frederick II and Otto IV, and ending without a final decision.

Before and between the solemn assemblies numerous other deliberations were held, and decisions were reached on issues pending before the curia. Disputed elections at York and Constantinople were resolved. The election of the bishop of Passau and the establishment of a new bishopric of Chiemsee by the archbishop of Salzburg were confirmed. The proposal to erect a bishopric in Vienna was also discussed, as was the years-old request by the king of Bohemia to have Prague elevated to metropolitan status. The primatial claims of Toledo against the opposition of Braga, Santiago de Compostela, Tarragona, and Narbonne were taken up, but an equitable solution remained to be found. A jurisdictional dispute between Magdeburg and Gnesen (modern Gniezno) over the see of Kamin was discussed, and a curial proposal that the central machinery of papal administration be supported in future by a tax on the clergy was rejected.

Of major consequence was the case involving Count Raymond VI of Toulouse, who came to the council with his wife and son, hoping to secure a reversal of a previous papal grant of wardship over conquered Toulouse lands to Simon de Montfort. In spite of their pleas the pope was reluctantly swayed to accept judgment against them. Also demanding lengthy attention were the prior actions of Pandulf, the papal legate in England: declaring Magna Carta invalid, suspending the archbishop of Canterbury, Stephen Langton, and excommunicating the rebellious barons.

In the concluding session of the council (30 November) Innocent publicly pronounced sentence on Count Raymond VI, avoiding the direct charge of heresy but declaring him somehow *culpabilis* for the

Albigensian threat to the church and therefore deprived of his lands. The solemn conciliar excommunication of the English barons was also delivered, followed by the council's decision to ratify the election and coronation of Frederick II by the German princes. Otto IV's plea for absolution from the ban of excommunication was ignored altogether.

The question of the crusade was again taken up, with the proclamation of a general peace for four years and the prohibition of tournaments for three years. All crusade provisions from the first and third sessions were later drawn together and published on 14 December 1215 as the constitution *Ad liberandum.*

The most enduring action by the council was the adoption of two dogmatic constitutions and sixty-eight disciplinary decrees. The first constitution, *Firmiter credimus,* was a solemn profession of faith touching on the orthodox teachings of the Trinity, the Incarnation, baptism, penance, and matrimony, and giving canonical sanction to the term *transubstantiatio* in the doctrine of the Eucharist. It was essentially a condemnation of the doctrines of the Cathars and, to a lesser extent, the Waldensians. The second constitution was a rejection of the ideas of Joachim of Fiore on the Trinity and of the pantheistic heresy of Amalric of Bène.

The unifying theme of the reform legislation was the care of souls. Stress was placed on the responsibility of prelates for holding regular synods, implementing the Inquisition for the suppression of heretics and their protectors, preaching, conducting visitations of nonexempt religious houses, the education of priests, and the conferring of benefices. Episcopal election procedures were clarified, enlarging the role of the cathedral clergy. Previous injunctions against clerical abuses such as drunkenness, secular pursuits, and concubinage were renewed.

Affecting laymen were the decrees reducing the restrictions on consanguinity and affinity, prohibiting clandestine marriages, and introducing the practice of banns. Yearly confession and the receipt of the Eucharist at least at Easter were made obligatory. Priests were forbidden to be present at ordeals, ecclesiastical and secular courts were more clearly distinguished, and a warning was given against encroachment on secular prerogatives by the clergy. The right of towns to tax the clergy was made contingent on papal approval.

All other monastic orders were required to follow the pattern of the Cistercian general chapter, a prohibition was placed on the founding of any new orders, and nonexempt religious were brought under tighter control of the diocesan bishops.

The final canons imposed clothing restrictions on the Jews, curtailed their movements during Holy Week, and limited intercourse between Christians and Jews, decrees that reflected the feelings of an age of crusades and religious uncertainty.

The Fourth Lateran Council marks the high point in medieval legislation and is generally considered the most important Western council before Trent. Although Innocent III died soon after its conclusion, his canons were incorporated into the *Compilatio quarta* and later passed, with few exceptions, into the *Decretales* of 1234.

For almost three decades following Lateran IV, the Roman pontiffs sparred with Frederick II over his promise to undertake a crusade and his intentions in Italy. In 1241 the emperor exacerbated relations by capturing more than 100 prelates who were en route to a Roman council and by seizing papal territory and forcing Pope Innocent IV to seek refuge at Lyons. To deal with the renewed imperial threat, and to consider matters of ecclesiastical reform, a new crusade, aid to Constantinople, and measures against the Mongols, Innocent IV convoked a general council for Lyons in June 1245.

The emperor was called upon to appear personally to answer charges of heresy, and as late as 6 May 1245 the pope was prepared to reconcile. But Frederick's further hostility shattered that hope and, when the council commenced, a major issue was to be his condemnation.

Attendance from lands ruled by Frederick was sparse. Thus, Innocent IV addressed a predominantly Spanish, French, and English assembly of 140 bishops, plus abbots, generals of the new orders, and deputies of invited chapters, cities, and provinces on the "five wounds" of the church at the first general session, 28 June 1245.

At the urging of Frederick II's envoy, Thaddeus of Suëssa, that no one should be condemned for heresy without being heard, the second session (5 July) was adjourned for twelve days to allow the emperor time to appear. He had no intention of doing so, however, and when the deadline had passed, the third session of the council (17 July) approved a bull of deposition, charging him with perjury, breach of peace, sacrilege in imprisoning the prelates, and heresy. Against the appeal of Thaddeus to a future pope and a general council, Innocent argued that the emperor's actions had prevented many of those who had been invited from attending, and that the coun-

cil was both general and legitimate. The council then declared the Hohenstaufen ruler deposed as emperor, king of Germany, and king of Sicily; stripped of all honors and dignities; and no longer entitled to loyalty from his subjects. The prince-electors were instructed to choose a successor to the German throne, while the disposition of Sicily was claimed by the pope as suzerain.

The council also adopted twenty-two constitutions touching on defensive measures against the Mongol peril, taxes on the clergy to aid the Latin Empire, judicial reform, limitations on the powers of judges delegate, and responsible stewardship of church property. Drawing on the provisions of Lateran IV, an effort was made to aid the Holy Land, but specific plans for a new crusade were not presented.

The matter of the Holy Land could still evoke enthusiasm when, on 13 April 1272, Pope Gregory X summoned a general council for 1274 at Lyons. Like Innocent III he also entertained hope for a union with the Greek church and ecclesiastical reform. Although the Latin Empire had fallen, threats to restore it by Charles of Anjou, the king of Sicily, made the Greek emperor Michael VIII Palaiologos amicable to union with Rome as a means of preserving his throne.

That reform of the church was a pressing need is revealed in extant testimonials that Gregory requested as an aid to curial preparations. Most of the formulating of reform measures was done by the pope himself, aided by his trusted collaborators, the Dominican cardinal Peter of Tarentaise and the Franciscan cardinal Bonaventure. The presentation and discussion of the legislation were done piecemeal at the various sessions of the council, but the formal set of decrees was not published until 1 November. Among them were new prohibitions against the establishment of new religious orders, temporarily restricting those (such as the Carmelites and the Augustinian Hermits) that had been founded or confirmed since 1215; exempt, however, were the Dominicans and Franciscans, whose service to the church was readily apparent. Excessively long vacancies, especially those of benefices connected with the care of souls, were to be stopped, and only worthy candidates were to be appointed to them. Pluralism, or the accumulation of multiple prebends to which the care of souls was appended, was curtailed, and the obligation of residency was reinforced.

Of lasting significance was the constitution *Ubi periculum,* which Gregory enacted over the opposition of some of the cardinals. Having been elected after a vacancy of almost three years, the pontiff declared that within ten days of the pope's death, the cardinals must assemble at the place of death to choose a successor, remaining together and cut off from contact with the outside world. If after three days they had not reached a decision, their ration of food was to be reduced daily until a pope was elected. Although this decree was annulled by Gregory's successors, it was restored by Celestine V (1294), was included in the *Liber sextus* of Boniface VIII, and thence made its way into the *Codex iuris canonici*. Though frequently revised, it is still in force.

The question of the crusade and union with the Greeks had to await the arrival of the Byzantine delegation, which was detained by shipwreck until 24 June. They carried a letter from Emperor Michael, expressing his desire for union with Rome and purporting to represent the views of hundreds of prelates within his church. Through the diplomatic efforts of Bonaventure and others, that union was formally effected at the fourth session (6 July) with the solemn oath taken in the name of the emperor by the imperial plenipotentiary, George Akropolites, to abjure the schism, profess the true, holy, and orthodox (that is, Catholic) faith, and to recognize the primacy of the Roman church. No opposition was raised to the *Filioque*, purgatory, or the seven sacraments, but Palaiologos had urged in his letter that the Greek church be permitted to retain its own rites. Given time, he believed, the aversion felt by his people and clergy toward Rome could be overcome.

Assured of Greek support, Gregory addressed the matter of the crusade, imposing a tithe on all ecclesiastical incomes for a six-year period and drawing on other provisions of 1215 and 1245. More detailed plans were not revealed and, as in 1245, no date of departure was set.

On 4 July the pope received sixteen envoys from the Mongol khan of Persia, asking for help in a common front against the Mamluks of Egypt. The establishment of friendly relations facilitated the later spread of the Christian faith into east Asia by such missionaries as John of Monte Corvino, who arrived in Peking (Khanbalik) in 1294.

In his closing address Gregory charged the bishops to pay greater attention to their pastoral obligations, reforming themselves first, then their clergy, and ultimately the entire church. The early death of the pontiff prevented his seeing the impact of his efforts. The crusade lost its driving impulse; union

with the Greeks proved unpopular in the East, and on the death of Emperor Michael (1282) it quickly dissolved. Gregory's decrees alone survived, becoming part of the *Codex iuris canonici* and affecting church law to the present day.

BIBLIOGRAPHY

Lateran IV. U. Berlière, "Innocent III et la réorganisation des monastères bénédictins," in *Revue bénédictin*, **32** (1920); Peter Browe, *Die häufige Kommunion im Mittelalter* (1938); Jean Dauvillier, *Le mariage dans le droit classique de l'église depuis le Décret de Gratien (1140) à la mort de Clement V (1314)* (1933); Raymonde Foreville, *Latran I, II, III, et Latran IV* (1965); Marion Gibbs and J. Lang, *Bishops and Reform, 1215–1272* (1934); Solomon Grayzell, *The Church and the Jews in the XIIIth Century* (1933); Stephan Kuttner and A. García y García, eds., "A New Eyewitness Account of the Fourth Lateran Council," in *Traditio*, **20** (1964); T. P. McLaughlin, "The Teaching of the Canonists on Usury," in *Mediaeval Studies*, **1** (1939) and **2** (1940).

Lyons I. August Folz, *Kaiser Friedrich II. und papst Innocenz IV.* (1905); James M. Powell, "Frederick II and the Church: A Revisionist View," in *Catholic Historical Review*, **48** (1962–1963).

Lyons II. Deno J. Geanakoplos, *Emperor Michael Palaeologus and the West, 1258–1282* (1959), 258–304; Stephan Kuttner, "Conciliar Law in the Making: The Lyonese Constitutions (1274) of Gregory X," in *Miscellanea Pio Paschini*, II (1949).

Also see Henry J. Schroeder, ed., *Disciplinary Decrees of the General Councils*, (1937), 236–364.

PAUL B. PIXTON

[See also **Amalric of Bène; Church, Latin; Frederick II of Sicily; Innocent III, Pope; Innocent IV, Pope; Jews and the Catholic Church; Joachim of Fiore; Michael VIII Palaiologos.**]

COUNCILS, WESTERN (1311–1449). In the long history of the general councils of the Latin church, the years from the beginning of the Great Schism in 1378 to the dissolution of the Council of Basel in 1449 possess an obvious unity. Punctuated by the councils of Pisa (1409), Constance (1414–1418), Pavia-Siena (1423–1424), Basel (1431–1449), and Ferrara-Florence (1438–1449), and dominated by the great constitutional question of the relative authority of pope and council, these years together form the era of conciliarism.

The fourteenth and fifteenth centuries, however, constitute in themselves no comparably intelligible unit. The Council of Vienne (1311–1312), the only general council to assemble in the fourteenth century, has sometimes been seen as belonging essentially to an earlier era, as the last in the great series of reform councils reaching back at least to the Third Lateran Council (1179), witnessing powerfully to the leadership of the papacy in the work of reform and the crusade against the Saracens, and looking forward to the general councils of the modern era: Trent, Vatican I, and Vatican II. All of these assemblies were called into being by papal initiative, shaped by papal concerns, and responsive, though in differing measure, to papal control. Nonetheless, if the shape taken, on the one hand, by the great papal councils of the twelfth and thirteenth centuries and, on the other, by the modern councils is to be understood as constituting something of a conciliar norm, then Vienne was already in significant ways an exception to that norm. It can more fittingly be addressed as a prologue to the era of conciliarism. Similarly, though the Fifth Lateran Council (1512–1517) met after the turn of the century and reflected in its organization and procedure a self-conscious attempt to return to the conciliar norm, that very attempt was conditioned by the need to respond to the *conciliabulum* of Pisa (1511–1512), itself an effort to revive the type of council characteristic of the era of conciliarism. The Fifth Lateran Council can properly be treated, therefore, as an epilogue to the general councils of that era, without which no account of those councils would be truly complete.

THE COUNCIL OF VIENNE (1311–1312) AND THE CRISIS OF PAPAL MONARCHY

About the actual proceedings of the Council of Vienne our knowledge, because of the state of the sources, is regrettably uneven and insecure. About its general context we are much better informed. Three major developments set that context: the senescence of the crusading movement, the emergence of clerical discontent with the price being paid for the mounting centralization of ecclesiastical administration in Rome, and the breakdown of the special relationship with the Capetian kings of France, which, since the early twelfth century, had helped the papacy through some of the more desperate moments in its history. It was by virtue of vigorous leadership exerted both as sponsor of the crusading movement and as initiator and implementer of ecclesiastical reform that the papacy from the time of Gregory VII on had risen to greater and greater eminence. Accordingly, when it began to show signs of faltering

in its leadership, it was threatened with a fall from that high estate.

Falter of course it did, especially in the decades immediately prior to Vienne. Throughout the Middle Ages, and with melancholy insistence, successive popes had appealed to the princes of Christendom to unite in a crusade against the Muslims. By the late thirteenth century, however, such appeals had come to have the ring of a debased coinage. When Acre fell to the Muslims in 1291 and the crusader states ceased shortly thereafter to exist, the popes proved unable to do anything about it. The stage was set for the transition from the crusading to the missionary impulse so evident at Vienne and also for the destruction of the Crusading Order of Knights Templar, the primary achievement of that council.

A similar faltering is evident also in papal leadership of ecclesiastical reform. Prior to the Second Council of Lyons (1274) Gregory X had requested that memoranda be submitted detailing the state of affairs in the church and recommending appropriate reforms. Prior to Vienne, Clement V did likewise. But surviving memoranda—notably that of Humbert of Romans, former master general of the Dominicans—suggest that the papacy, with its centralizing encroachment on the traditional pattern of episcopal government and its lavish heaping of privileges on the mendicant orders, was itself coming to be seen as part of the problem. For well over a century the clergy of the local churches had by and large welcomed the extension of papal control into the provinces, and by their own petitions and appeals had done much to stimulate and accelerate the process. And they did not necessarily cease to do so now. But from the closing decades of the thirteenth century evidence of clerical opposition to papal policy begins to increase—evidence of bodies of clergy so disgruntled as to be willing, in moments of critical tension, to side with their rulers against the pope or, at least, to acquiesce in policies directed by their rulers against the pope.

The pontificate of Boniface VIII (1294–1303) and that pope's disastrous clash with Philip IV of France marked such a moment of critical tension. His two unfortunate successors, Benedict XI (1303–1304) and Clement V (1305–1314), both pliant men who preferred not to risk the type of defiance that might have mobilized support on their behalf across Europe, were forced to scramble amid the wreckage of Boniface's hierocratic ambitions in order to stave off the French king's demands for the posthumous judgment and condemnation of that pope and for the assembly of a general council to achieve that end. Those demands were almost certainly intended as a diplomatic weapon designed to render the pope amenable to making concessions on other fronts and were, in fact, eventually dropped.

But they were dropped only after Clement had absolved Guillaume de Nogaret, Boniface's chief assailant, and canceled in the official register the bulls that that pope had hurled against France—and only after he had also agreed, at a meeting with Philip IV at Poitiers in June–July 1308, to convoke a council at Vienne on 1 October 1310, there to bring to a conclusion the process of investigation that Philip had launched against the Order of Knights Templar. Indicative of the degree of leverage the French king had been able to exert on Clement is his apparent influence on the composition of the forthcoming council's membership. In an abrogation of custom, not all bishops were summoned to the council, but only those whose names appeared on a list of 231 previously discussed, it would seem, with Philip. Little more than half of the bishops in question attended; with proxies, cardinals, abbots, and priors, however, the overall attendance came to about 300.

Originally established to protect pilgrims visiting the Holy Land, the Templars had found themselves deprived of their raison d'être by the loss of the crusader states, and because of their deep involvement in finance, they were cruelly exposed to the greed and jealousy of those rulers who coveted their riches and resented their independence. Though much remains uncertain about the whole sorry affair, it was probably the wealth of the order that brought about its downfall. It had long had detractors, and there may well have been some moral laxity in its ranks. But the failure of the authorities in countries other than France, despite the use of torture, to elicit the type of confessions wrung by royal officials from the unfortunate French Templars suggests the order's innocence. Nonetheless, once Clement's will to resist had been broken at Poitiers, the Council of Vienne convoked, and the Templars cited to appear before it, the fate of the order appears to have been sealed. A general papal commission and a series of episcopal commissions were appointed to gather incriminating evidence to be presented at the council. The French king was permitted a say in the composition of those commissions, and when further confessions proved hard to elicit, Clement first extended the use of torture and then postponed the opening of the council for a full year until the autumn of 1311.

When the Council of Vienne did meet on 16 October for the first of its three sessions, the general distaste for the whole affair was reflected in the poor attendance of bishops from countries other than France. When the conciliar commission charged with the task of examining the record and the summaries of evidence indicated that it wished to give the Templars their day in court and a chance to defend themselves before the council, the pope, succumbing once more to French pressure, abandoned the judicial process. Instead, two days after Philip IV's arrival at Vienne, Clement suppressed the order by direct administrative fiat, and that suppression was proclaimed in the bull *Vox in excelso* at the council's second public session (3 April 1312). On 2 May the council ordered the transfer of Templar property in most parts of Europe to the Knights Hospitalers. In subsequent years, however, during the slow implementation of that order, it seems probable that the bulk of Templar property in France found its way into royal hands.

In his bull of convocation and in his opening discourse, Clement V had assigned three tasks to the council: the settlement of the affair of the Templars, the recovery of the Holy Land, and the reform of the church. But at the opening session it was the question of the Templars that was given unambiguous priority, and it is not clear that the expressed concern with a crusade amounted to anything more than window dressing. Nothing much—apart from public pronouncements of Philip IV's willingness to go on crusade—was done about the fate of the Holy Land. Of more enduring significance was the decree *Inter sollicitudines,* passed at the prompting of Ramon Lull and with the stated object of aiding the church's missionary endeavors. It prescribed the creation at the papal court and at the universities of Paris, Oxford, Bologna, and Salamanca of chairs for the teaching of Hebrew, Arabic, and Chaldean. Although lack of teachers was to hinder its implementation, the decree was not without influence in subsequent centuries. When Cardinal Ximénez de Cisneros made provision two centuries later for the teaching of the oriental languages at his new University of Alcalá, it was not without reference to *Inter sollicitudines.*

Also of more enduring significance, though it failed ultimately to reconcile the warring parties, was the council's attempt to mediate in practical terms the rancorous dispute that had divided the Franciscan friars into a rigorous, "Spiritual" minority and a less rigorous "Conventual" majority whom the minority accused of having abandoned the original commitment to the ideal of individual and collective poverty that St. Francis had prescribed in imitation of the life of Christ and the apostles. That prescription had long since given rise to difficulties of interpretation, and new strains had arisen concerning the via media charted by popes Gregory IX (1227–1241), Innocent IV (1243–1254), and Nicholas III (1277–1280). An investigation by a conciliar commission led now to an attempt to respond in some measure to the complaints of both sides. As a result, in the decree *Exivi de paradiso*, while steering clear of the dogmatic question of Christ's own poverty and, in effect, reaffirming the modus vivendi hammered out by the popes of the previous century, the council did so in such a way as to respond in practical terms at least to the more rigorous Spiritual interpretation of the rule.

Along with such bulls and decrees the council was responsible for a series of enactments, some of which—for example, two decrees proscribing errors attributed to some of the communities of Beghards and Beguines—were concerned with matters doctrinal. Most of those enactments, however, can loosely be classified as pertaining to the third of the goals that Clement V had assigned to the council, that of church reform. Given the loss of much of the official documentation pertaining to the council, the fact that few of these decrees were ready for promulgation at its last general session, and that all were to owe their official status to John XXII (who, by publishing them in revised form, was ultimately responsible for their inclusion as "the Clementines" in the *Corpus juris canonici*), some irreducible uncertainties attach to their history and to the exact role of the Council of Vienne in their formation.

Concerned largely with the encroachment of the temporal authorities on the rights, liberties, and properties of the clergy and with the confusion in diocesan government spawned by the multiplication of papal exemptions granted to the mendicant orders, to cathedral chapters, and to individual monasteries, the enactments clearly stemmed from the lists of grievances that Clement's command had elicited from the bishops. And while they reflected the efforts of the conciliar reform commission that he had appointed to draw some general conclusions from the mass of material submitted and to recommend an appropriate legislative response, that response fell far short of the sweeping demands for re-

form "in head as well as members" that the bishops William Lemaire of Angers and Guillaume Durand of Mende had submitted.

In his *Tractatus de modo concilio celebrandi*, and as part of his attempt to restore and defend the integrity of episcopal authority, Durand had urged that general councils be regularly assembled at ten-year intervals. But the half century and more subsequent to the dissolution of Vienne on 6 May 1312 saw the assembly of no new general councils. Instead, it was to witness at the hands of the Avignonese pontiffs (notably John XXII) the energetic consolidation and extension of the pope's fiscal prerogatives and jurisdictional powers. Only after the return of the papacy to Rome and the onset of the Great Schism in 1378 was an effective cry raised once more for the assembly of a general council and, with it, for a renewed attack on the problems of churchwide reform. Even then, it was another forty years before a council assembled, and quite a good many more before a significant start could be made on the task of reform.

THE COUNCILS OF PISA (1409) AND CONSTANCE (1414–1418) AND THE STRUGGLE FOR CHURCH UNITY

The schism that broke out in 1378 was more serious than any of its predecessors. Since neither of the rival claimants—Urban VI (1378–1389) at Rome and Clement VII (1378–1394) at Avignon—proved able to displace the other or to win the allegiance of all the Christian nations, most of the kings and princes of Europe fell into alignment with one of the two rival "obediences" that emerged. Despite the efforts of churchmen and temporal rulers to end it, the schism endured for almost forty years. Both claimants went on to appoint whole new cardinals; both obdurately refused to withdraw either individually or concurrently. Loyalties quickly hardened, and as the years went by, their rival curias strove to perpetuate their claims. Benedict XIII was elected in 1394 to succeed Clement VII at Avignon, and Boniface IX, Innocent VII, and Gregory XII, in 1389, 1404, and 1406, respectively, to succeed Urban VI at Rome. The outcome was the development within the church of widespread administrative disorder and of a debilitating degree of uncertainty well caught by the action of Peter Tenorio, archbishop of Toledo, who, Martin de Alpartils reports in his *Chronica actitatorum*, substituted in the canon of the Mass for the name of the pope the words *pro illo qui est verus papa* (for him who is the true pope; Ehrle, p. 519).

More pertinent to the histories of Pisa and Constance, the outcome was also the emergence within the church of a grave constitutional crisis.

Initial efforts by the rival pontiffs to settle the issue by force of arms (the *via facti*) having proved abortive, hope centered first on the possibility of some successful arbitration between them, and still more on the possibility of assembling a general council representing the entire church to render a judgment on the validity of the contested elections. This latter view, aired originally by the Italian cardinals in the wake of Urban's election, was given forceful expression at Avignon by St. Vincent Ferrer and at Paris in 1379–1381 by the German theologians Conrad of Gelnhausen and Henry of Langenstein, as well as by their younger French colleague Pierre d'Ailly. The "conciliar movement," then, was something of a reality from the beginning of the schism, although the pressure that the French king successfully exerted on the University of Paris in order to align it with Clement quickly led to the proscription of such views there.

Time, however, was to lead to their reconsideration. Members of the two obediences came gradually to regard both claimants as sharing the responsibility for protracting the schism. Support shifted, accordingly, to what was known as the *via cessionis,* a plan that envisaged the renunciation of their claims by the rival pontiffs and the subsequent combination of the two colleges of cardinals to elect a new and universally accepted pope. It was the failure of that approach that led in 1408 to the revival of the idea of a general council. This became a feasible alternative when the collapse of a final round of negotiations between the Roman and Avignonese popes led disgruntled cardinals from both camps to forswear allegiance to their respective pontiffs. Gathering at Leghorn and addressing themselves to the bishops and secular rulers of both obediences, the cardinals assumed the prerogative of convoking a general council of the whole church to meet in Italy, and followed up their summons with diplomatic missions. When that bold action began to draw widespread support, the rival pontiffs, Gregory XII and Benedict XIII, in desperation assembled their own councils at Cividale del Friuli and Perpignan, respectively. Neither of those councils, however, was well attended; neither, certainly, could boast of the impressively ecumenical character of the general council that opened at Pisa on 25 March 1409.

The divisions in the church notwithstanding, Pisa was better attended than the Council of Vienne had been. It was not in vain that the cardinals had sent out their diplomatic missions; the Council of Pisa enjoyed the support of the greater part of Christendom. At its peak those attending included four patriarchs; twenty-four cardinals; more than eighty archbishops and bishops (with more than another hundred represented by proxies); more than a hundred abbots (nearly double that number sent their proxies); the generals of the leading orders; some seven hundred theologians and canonists; and representatives of thirteen universities, of numerous cathedral chapters, and of most European princes (notable exceptions being the German king, Rupert, and the kings of the Iberian Peninsula). The French sent the single largest delegation, and its leader, Simon of Cramaud, patriarch of Alexandria, was the council's leading personality.

Although the opening ceremonies of 25 March 1409 were the traditional ones, the unusual circumstances surrounding the council's convocation entailed some departures from the conciliar norm—notably the fact that until the election of the new pope the college of cardinals as a corporate body was deemed to be discharging the office of president. Different, too, was the manner in which the preparatory work for the council's twenty-two sessions was accomplished. While the cardinals worked together as a college, the other members gathered in five "nations": English, French, German, Italian, and Provençal. Different, also, was the fact that practically the entire effort of the council, both in its preparatory meetings and in its public assemblies, was devoted to a careful legal process directed against the two popes. While a reform committee was indeed appointed, it discharged no function; at the council's closing session on 7 August 1409, the newly elected pope (Alexander V) announced that the matter of reform was to be addressed at a council to be held in 1412.

Having repeatedly summoned the rival pontiffs to appear, having reacted to their failure to do so by declaring them contumacious, and having approved the appointment of an investigating committee, the council at its eighth session responded to earlier challenges to its legitimacy by declaring itself to have been legally and legitimately assembled, in virtue of its summons by the united cardinals; to be "a general council, representative of the whole, universal and Catholic church, duly, fitly, and reasonably established and met together"; and to be possessed of the necessary jurisdictional power to stand in judgment over Benedict and Gregory. In the sessions that followed, it acted on that claim, hearing multiple witnesses, receiving and examining documentary evidence, and on 5 June at its fifteenth session, declaring the two popes deposed as "notorious schismatics," "nourishers" of schism, "notorious heretics," "incorrigible, contumacious, and impenitent."

The fact that the signatures of no fewer than 213 council fathers (24 of them cardinals) appear in this sentence confirms the sense that in proceeding thus the Council of Pisa was not acting in wholly revolutionary fashion. Instead, it was following the generally accepted canonistic teaching of the day that a pope who deviated from the true faith, or who was obdurately guilty of notorious crimes scandalizing the church—and tantamount, therefore, to heresy—was liable to judgment by the church and even to deposition. It was also following a widespread and well-established canonistic opinion to the effect that although in such a process the cardinals had certain powers of initiative, the body competent to proceed to judgment was the general council. Certainly the greater part of Christendom seems to have regarded its action as valid—and also the subsequent and unanimous election by the united cardinals from both obediences of a new pope, Peter of Candia, the Franciscan cardinal of Milan, who assumed the name Alexander V (1409-1410).

The Roman and Avignonese pontiffs were left with drastically reduced obediences, and their survival may well have been assured only by the death of Alexander V in 1410 and the succession of John XXIII (1410-1415)—by the most favorable of estimates a man of unpraiseworthy life and a less than fitting candidate for the high office into which he was thrust. But survive they did, even though John XXIII was able to establish himself at Rome. As a result, what emerged from Pisa was the addition of a third line of papal pretenders and of a third obedience—clearly an intolerable situation, which, in the view especially of Sigismund, the new emperor-elect, called for no less radical a solution than the withdrawal (or removal) of all three claimants.

John XXIII did appoint several cardinals of genuine reforming commitments, notably the Italian canonist Francesco Zabarella, the French theologian Pierre d'Ailly, and his compatriot, the canonist Guillaume Fillastre. He also honored the wishes expressed at Pisa for the assembly of another council by summoning such a body to meet at Rome in April 1412. But he adjourned that gathering in March 1413, after it had met only once in solemn session and had done nothing more than condemn as heret-

ical a series of propositions attributed to the Oxford theologian John Wyclif. Reform was clearly not the highest of John XXIII's priorities. Nonetheless, the growing threat that Ladislas of Naples posed to Rome obliged John XXIII to turn for protection to Sigismund, whose commitment to the cause of reform was a firm one and who did not hesitate to apply the appropriate pressure in order to bring about the assembly of yet another council. On 3 December 1413, therefore, though with extreme reluctance, John XXIII issued a bull convoking a general council to meet at Constance in November 1414.

When John XXIII solemnly opened that council on 5 November, the attendance was slight. But with the arrival on Christmas Eve of Emperor Sigismund, who was to play so prominent a role in the conciliar proceedings, attendance began to increase, and it was eventually to include an unusually strong representation of the laity (noblemen predominantly) and of the theologians and canonists of the great universities. At the peak of conciliar activity several thousand visitors—participants, their retinues, and sundry hangers-on—were crammed into the city, and the Council of Constance was undoubtedly the greatest ecclesiastical assembly of the Middle Ages. Further, given the presence of the imperial chancery and the extraordinarily large body of delegates representing kings, princes, and autonomous cities, it can with some cogency be claimed to have been the greatest of all medieval representative assemblies.

It was also the general council destined to last longer than all previous councils, which had usually succeeded in completing their tasks within a matter of months rather than years. Its duration reflects the complexity of the tasks confronting it. These, as contemporaries readily acknowledged, were three in number: the restoration of church unity; disputed matters of faith; the reformation of the church in head and members. All three matters were continuously before the council—in its commissions and committees, if not necessarily in its solemn assemblies. The two last, however, cannot vie in importance with the first: the successful termination of the schism and the election of a pope whose validity was acceptable to the whole church. It is this last task, therefore, that must be addressed first.

For John XXIII, whose enthusiasms were scarcely engaged in the conciliar enterprise, Constance was to be regarded as no more than a continuation of the Council of Pisa. With the support of the multitudinous Italian bishops, many of them dependent very directly on his favor, he hoped to dissolve it after having secured another condemnation of his rivals and renewed confirmation of his own papal title. Such hopes were dashed, however, during the first months of 1415. At the initiative especially of d'Ailly and Fillastre, the northern Europeans insisted that voting be by conciliar nation, each voting by head in its individual meetings, where much of the council's policy was to be formed and where the influence of kings and princes was to be strongly felt, but each, regardless of the number of its members, casting a single vote in the general assemblies of the council. At first there were four such nations: French, Italian, German, and English. From July 1415 on, however, the college of cardinals, as a corporate body comparable with the nations, was permitted to cast a single vote in the council's general sessions. And after autumn 1416, the erstwhile supporters of Benedict XIII in Aragon and Castile came to constitute a fifth, Spanish nation.

The adoption of this mode of organization neutralized the numerical preponderance of the Italian bishops and freed the council to address on its own terms the problem of the schism. Without questioning the legitimacy of the Council of Pisa or of John XXIII's election, it quickly concluded that the only real hope for success lay in securing the resignation of that pope and of his two rivals, already deposed at Pisa. Eager to bring pressure to bear on the pope in order to secure his cooperation, members of the assembly began to focus on the alleged notorieties of his life. In return, discouraged by the defection of the Italian nation (which had aligned itself with the rest) and intimidated by threats that his alleged misdeeds warranted a public investigation, John XXIII played desperately for time. He did so by letting it be known at the second general session on 2 March 1415 that at the appropriate moment he would be willing to resign. At the same time, or so it seems, he planned in secret to flee the council and thereby disrupt its activities.

His plan very nearly succeeded. His flight to Schaffhausen on 20 March caused great alarm and confusion among the council fathers, the more so in that a significant segment of the curia joined him there. In the absence of the pope who had convoked it and the validity of whose title the majority recognized, the assembly might well have disintegrated had not Sigismund moved decisively to bolster its confidence and had not John Gerson, chancellor of the University of Paris and a widely respected Scholastic of moderate leanings, rallied it on 23 March with the sermon *Ambulate dum lucem habetis.* In

that sermon he affirmed the belief central to conciliar theory (and already widespread among the fathers of the council) that "the church, as the general council representing it, is a model or example so directed by the Holy Spirit and influenced by Christ that everyone of whatever rank, even the papal, is obliged to listen to and obey it."

As it became clear that John was unlikely to return and was probably going back on his pledge to resign, the sentiments of the fathers became aligned increasingly with Gerson's conciliarist stance, and their determination to proceed accordingly hardened. As a result, at the fifth general session on 6 April 1415, the council formally promulgated the decree *Haec sancta synodus* on the superiority of council to pope, the crucial section of which reads as follows:

> This sacred council of Constance ... declares, in the first place, that it forms a general council, legitimately assembled in the Holy Spirit and representing the Catholic Church Militant, that it has its power immediately from Christ, and that all men, of every rank and position, including even the pope himself, are bound to obey it in those matters that pertain to the faith, the extirpation of the said schism, and to the reformation of the said Church in head and members. It declares also that anyone, of any rank, condition or office—even the papal—who shall contumaciously refuse to obey the mandates, statutes, decrees or instructions made by this holy synod or by any other lawfully assembled general council on the matters aforesaid or on things pertaining to them, shall, unless he recovers his senses, be subjected to fitting penance and punished as is appropriate. (Alberigo, p. 385)

Among modern Roman Catholic theologians this decree has continued to be a controversial one, but there can be little doubt that the subsequent activity of Constance, and much of that of Basel, were grounded in the claims it advanced.

Events now moved quite rapidly. A mission under the leadership of Cardinal Fillastre having secured John XXIII's return in custody, a formal (if hasty) legal process was instituted against him. On 29 May, at the twelfth solemn session of the council, he was declared deposed—not, it should be noted, because the council questioned the legitimacy of his title, but because it had tried him and found him guilty of simony, perjury, and other scandalous misconduct. That sentence he accepted.

Less than two months later Gregory XII, the Roman pontiff already deposed at Pisa, made it clear that he was willing to resign if he was permitted to convoke the council, thus legitimating it in his own eyes and in those of his followers. By so doing he could also claim to have received from the council at least tacit confirmation of the legitimacy of the Roman line of popes. The council fathers were not unaware of this possibility, but their overriding goal was unity and they were even less disposed to make a fuss about a formality, which very few of them took seriously, than they had been the previous year, when they had treated the ambassadors of both Gregory XII and Benedict XIII as official papal delegates rather than merely as individual members of the faithful. And that was despite the fact that the council fathers endorsed the sentences of Pisa and accorded the title of legitimate pope to John XXIII.

On 4 July 1415, at the fourteenth solemn session, Cardinal John Dominici read the bull of convocation, whereupon Gregory's resignation was announced and accepted. Benedict XIII, whose belief in the legitimacy of his title had always been stronger, proved to be more stubborn. Although Sigismund's negotiation of the Treaty of Narbonne finally deprived Benedict of the support of the Spanish kingdoms in December 1415, until his death in 1423 he persisted in his claim to be true pope. By then, however, events had long since passed him by. On 26 July 1417, at the thirty-seventh solemn session, after a lengthy legal process and after the members of his obedience had declared their adherence to the council, he was deposed.

Less than a year later, after a protracted wrangle shaped in part by the shifting diplomatic alignments of France, Germany, and England and focused on the issue of what should take precedence, reform or the election of a new pope, a compromise was struck. An enlarged body of electors, including representatives from each conciliar nation as well as the cardinals from all three of the former obediences, went into conclave to choose a new pope. Within three days they succeeded in doing so. With the election on 11 November of Odo Colonna, a cardinal of the Roman obedience who had adhered to the Council of Pisa and who took the name of Martin V (1417–1431), the schism was at an end. The church had at last an unquestionably legitimate pope, and the council now passed under his direction.

By that time it had already disposed of those major issues pertaining to matters of faith that had come before it. Left pending were such subordinate issues as the attacks of the Dominican Matthew Grabow on the Brethren of the Common Life and the Polish demand for the condemnation of the argu-

ments advanced by another Dominican, John of Falkenberg, on behalf of tyrannicide. These issues were destined to receive no final disposition before the council was dissolved. The matter of tyrannicide, however, had already been the object of close scrutiny. Its advocacy (or apparent advocacy) by the French Franciscan Jean Petit (Joannes Parvus) had succeeded most in exercising the passions of the council fathers and dividing them. The divisions were partly the result of disagreements concerning what exactly it was that Jean Petit had maintained in his attempt to defend the Burgundian assassination of Louis of Orléans, brother of the French king, Charles VI, and partly the outcome of the shifting balance between Orléanist and Anglo-Burgundian influence at Paris and (therefore) at Constance. On 6 July 1415, shortly after the deposition of John XXIII and during its fifteenth session, the council did condemn tyrannicide.

But the theses proscribed were not explicitly attributed to Jean Petit; his Burgundian supporters struggled hard to prevent their being associated with his name; and the debate was to rage intermittently and indecisively until the end of the council.

Greater unanimity marked the disposition, in July 1415, of the most important matter of faith to come before the council. With the condemnation as a heretic of the Bohemian reformer John Hus, and his immediate execution, the fathers at Constance sought to put a stop once and for all to the spread of the unquestionably heretical views spawned by the English heresiarch John Wyclif, condemned in 1412 and again in May 1415, at the council's eighth session. The storm of resentment aroused in Bohemia by the burning of Hus and (in 1416) of his fellow reformer and friend, Jerome of Prague, swiftly made it clear that such hopes were illusory. As a result the Hussite problem was to be one of the major issues confronting the Council of Basel.

That his own beliefs should have come to be so closely associated in the minds of the council fathers with those of Wyclif speaks directly to the tragedy of Hus's life. If it has properly been claimed (by Johann Loserth) that Wyclif was "the man for whose doctrine Hus went to the stake," modern scholarship would suggest that he did so improperly. Despite the ambivalence of his doctrinal formulations, his commitment appears to have been fundamentally moral rather than metaphysical; he was very much the product of a long-established and perfectly orthodox indigenous reform movement in Bohemia. Although by the vigor of his preaching at Prague he had risen to symbolic leadership of that reform movement and of the circle of Czech theologians sympathetic to Wycliffite views, Hus was by no means the most radical of the Bohemian reformers. It was in an attempt to break the impasse that had developed between Rome and the Bohemian reform movement that he set out to plead the reform's cause before the council. He went to Constance hoping for exoneration, and it was in the expectation of such an outcome that Emperor Sigismund had issued him the safe conduct that proved in the end to be worthless.

Zabarella, Gerson, and d'Ailly, who dominated the commission that condemned Hus, were by no means fanatics. But they clearly found it impossible to believe that he was not a more thoroughgoing Wycliffite than he would have them believe. Under interrogation he alternated disconcertingly between submissiveness and defiance. This, coupled with his lack of clarity and candor in responding to some of the erroneous articles attributed to him, made it difficult for them to penetrate the confusing screen of rumor, falsehood, charge, and countercharge that the rivalry at Prague between Czech and German masters had helped to erect. That screen had come to blur the outlines of a religious commitment that was certainly not Wycliffite, that was traditionally orthodox in intent, and that was within a hair's breadth of being orthodox in fact. As a result of that difficulty, and given his obdurate refusal to endorse even a moderate formula of abjuration, Hus was condemned to die. A council that, within a few months, had witnessed so many moments of high drama, witnessed now its moment of tragedy.

No comparable drama attended the council's efforts to accomplish the third of the tasks confronting it, one with which Hus, ironically enough, would have been in the deepest sympathy. Blueprints for reform were readily at hand in such tracts of the period as Pierre d'Ailly's *Tractatus de materia concilii generalis* or the anonymous *Capitula agendorum* emanating from Parisian reform circles. But the obstacles in the way of implementing such reform plans became clear in the spring and summer of 1417, when the council fathers bogged down in a wrangle about their future priorities. From one point of view, the first priority had to be the energetic prosecution of reform (with which numerous committees and two successive reform commissions had busied themselves since 1415) and the enactment, prior to the election of a new pope, of legislation designed to eliminate abuses at the curia and to limit the papal exercise of fiscal and jurisdictional power

over the provincial churches. The ranks of the reformers, however, were split by the organization of the council into nations, which exposed them to national pressures in a highly concentrated form. And, of the temporal rulers, only the emperor Sigismund, who had to cope with the Hussite problem, appears to have felt that he had a practical stake in reform.

Ranged on the other side were the rulers of France and (eventually) of England, who had succeeded in coming to more or less favorable terms with the papal system of taxation and preferment, and who, though they might later want to tilt the system still further in their own favor, clearly felt they had nothing to gain and much to lose by destroying it. Hence they decided to support those at the council (including the cardinals, the Castilians, and most of the Italians) whose first priority was to proceed to the election of a new pope.

The outcome was an English-sponsored compromise whereby in October 1417, at its thirty-ninth session and before the papal election, the council promulgated the five reform decrees to which all the conciliar nations had already given their approval. Of those decrees *Frequens,* which legislated the assembly of future councils at stated and regular intervals, was clearly the most important. The others enacted provisions for the avoidance of future schisms, required in the future a profession of faith from every newly elected pope, forbade "except for great and reasonable cause" the translation from church to church of higher prelates, and decreed the abolition of "spoils" and procurations. In accord with the terms of the compromise, it was also decreed that the pope who was to be elected "must reform the church in [its] head and the Roman curia" before the dissolution of the council. Action was called for on a list of eighteen items ranging from simony, dispensations, and indulgences, to annates, reservations, and collations, to the composition of the college of cardinals.

While this represented a promising start on the work of reform, it turned out to be no more than a start. Subsequent negotiations between the newly elected Martin V, a newly appointed reform commission (the council's third), and the several conciliar nations (whose concerns differed widely) produced general agreement on only a handful of not very sweeping decrees concerning simony, dispensations, exemptions, and the like. These were promulgated on 21 March 1418, at the council's forty-third session. At that session were read also the concordats that Martin V had negotiated separately with the five nations. These concordats amounted, in effect, to a division of ecclesiastical spoils between pope and nation, the variations among them reflecting differences in the balance of power between the pope and the rulers concerned, and all of them (with the exception of the English) to be valid for no more than five years.

While Constance, then, had accomplished the first of its three tasks—that of restoring unity to the church—and had acted decisively (if not conclusively) on the second—that concerning disputed matters of faith—most of the work of reform would have to await the assembly of another council. And before dissolving the Council of Constance on 22 April 1418, Martin V proclaimed that, in accordance with the provisions of *Frequens,* the next council would assemble in five years and would do so at Pavia.

THE COUNCILS OF PAVIA-SIENA (1423–1424), BASEL (1431–1449), FERRARA-FLORENCE (1438–1447), AND THE STRUGGLE FOR REFORM

The Great Schism had been ended only because the fathers assembled at Constance had formally endorsed the conciliarist claim that the general council was the legitimate repository of supreme power in the church on certain critical issues, had been able and willing to enforce that claim, and, in the decree *Frequens,* had been careful to set up constitutional machinery to impede any reversion to papal absolutism.

This machinery was to prove less effective than the council fathers had hoped, but not as ineffective as Martin V may have wished, for he sympathized neither with conciliar reform nor with the conciliarist sentiments that tended to go with it. But even had he been a convinced reformer, the enormous difficulties confronting him—the political and fiscal fragility of his position, the political alignments in Italy, and the expenses associated with attendance at another assembly (especially on top of the crushing costs incurred at Constance)—militated against the success of a reform council.

Because of the depredations of the condottiere Braccio da Montone in central Italy, Martin was unable to enter Rome until 28 September 1420. And because of his indigence he was forced, when the time limit ran out on several of the concordats negotiated at Constance, to go back to the earlier arrangements governing reservations and provisions. Moreover, though he struggled hard to reestablish order in the operations of the curia, sponsoring administrative

reforms to that end, he hoped to restore the papacy to the position it had occupied before the disastrous years of schism.

The pressure of public opinion within the church obliged Martin V to assemble the Council of Pavia in 1423 and later, after the lapse of the seven years stipulated by *Frequens,* to summon the next council to meet at Basel. But he never went to the Council of Pavia, which was sparsely attended; transferred it to Siena; and then, perhaps frightened by the threat of collusion between the conciliarist faction and his enemy, the king of Aragon, hastily dissolved it. He did so before it had really succeeded in getting its teeth into the task of reform—and did so, it should be added, without any prior consultation with the council fathers.

When Martin V died on 20 February 1431, he left behind a reorganized curia in control of the resources of a pacified papal state (this latter no mean achievement), but he also bequeathed to his successor some very severe problems. The college of cardinals was experiencing a reaction to his authoritarian administration, and when the Council of Basel opened on 23 July 1431, it did so burdened by an enormous freight of reforming expectations. It was all the heavier because demands for reform were included in the electoral capitulations drawn up by the cardinals after Martin's death and imposed on his successor. The council was also burdened by having as that successor Eugenius IV, who shared all of Martin V's hostility to conciliar reform but none of the judgment and ability that had enabled the latter to cope with it.

Reform, then, was the overriding concern. But the course of the council was to be shaped (and distorted) by four other factors—two of them internal, two external. The internal factors were its novel organization and the growing prominence in its deliberations of the great constitutional question of the relationship of papal to conciliar authority; the external factors were the Hussite wars and the quest for reunion with the Greek Orthodox church.

It was at the suggestion of the Dominican theologian John of Ragusa that the council abandoned the organization by nations that had prevailed at Constance. Instead, at its second solemn session, 15 February 1432, it chose to organize itself into four deputations or commissions, each representative of all the nations and ecclesiastical ranks, and concerned, respectively, with matters of faith, with reform, with the task of engineering reunion with the Greeks, and with "common matters" (including the administration of the council and increasingly, as time went on, that of the church at large). These deputations acted as preparatory legislative committees, with the agreement of three of the four being required for approval of a matter by the general congregation, and with subsequent approval and publication at a solemn session being the practice where major items were concerned.

Each member of the council was individually incorporated, taking an oath to obey conciliar decisions; the members from the several nations and the various ecclesiastical ranks were spread equally among the four deputations; and at the solemn sessions all voted individually and with an equal voice. Among the members, as a result, an atmosphere of greater equality than at previous councils prevailed. The members of the ecclesiastical hierarchy found it much harder to dominate their clerical subordinates, and in the absence of the national structure, secular rulers lacked the leverage possessed at Constance to marshal support for their own policies among the delegates from their territories. At Basel, accordingly, the lower clergy in general and the university masters in particular came to play a much more influential role and one less subject to hierarchical guidance or (at least at first) to princely manipulation.

Hence, or so it may be surmised, the sweeping nature of the reforms that issued from the deputation on reform and that were approved, most of them after extensive deliberation and most during the first four years of the council's life. They concerned, among other things, the makeup of the college of cardinals, the procedures governing papal elections, and the need to restrict in favor of the ordinary courts the jurisdiction of the courts at Rome. Most striking were the decrees on elections and on annates promulgated, respectively, at the twelfth solemn session on 13 July 1433 and at the twenty-fourth solemn session on 9 June 1435. These prohibited, except in cases of manifestly unusual circumstance, all general and special reservations to bishoprics and abbacies, and, without any exception whatsoever, all payments connected with the filling of benefices.

Such reforming decrees reflected not only the unfulfilled aspirations of successive reform commissions at Constance but also the persistent concerns of reformers all the way back to Guillaume Durand at the Council of Vienne and beyond. That they should have included the renewal of the Constance decrees *Haec sancta synodus* and *Frequens,* and the stern reaffirmation of the constitutionalist vision embodied in those decrees, reflected also the response of the council fathers to the ill-judged hostility that Eugenius IV betrayed toward the council. That hostility was to distort the course of Basel, leading to bitter disagreement, schism, the blunting of the drive toward reform, and a lengthy conflict of principle concerning the ultimate locus of supreme authority in the church. That conflict was ultimately to be settled less by ecclesiological argument or the force of theological persuasion than by general exhaustion, skillful papal diplomacy, and the power of the temporal princes of Europe.

It was unquestionably Eugenius who precipitated the crisis. Because he was opposed to the council from the start, and because Martin V had reached an agreement with the Greeks to hold a council of reunion on Italian soil, Eugenius was not eager to prolong the life of the Basel assembly. Misled, perhaps, by the initially poor attendance at the council and in the teeth of opposition from some of his cardinals, he ordered the dissolution of Basel and the convocation of another council at Bologna. On 18 December 1431 he published in consistory a bull to that effect. In so doing, Eugenius misjudged the mood both of the council fathers and of the cardinals, of whom fifteen (out of twenty-one) chose to side with Basel. He also misjudged the priorities of Cardinal Giuliano Cesarini, the legate whom he (and Martin V before him) had appointed to preside over Basel.

The effect of the treatment of Hus and Jerome of Prague at Constance had been to stimulate a revolt of Hussite sympathizers against the Romanists who had denounced the martyr and against Emperor Sigismund who, they felt, had betrayed him. In the wake of a crusade against the Hussites that had met, in August 1431, with disastrous defeat, Cesarini had committed the Council of Basel to vital negotiations with the moderate wing of the victorious party. Those negotiations he now saw threatened by the papal bull of dissolution. When it arrived, therefore, he joined the council fathers in refusing to obey the pope. Deadlock ensued, and as support for the pope dwindled and as men of the stature of Cesarini and Nicholas of Cusa rallied to the side of the council, that body was understandably led to reaffirm conciliarist principles and to act in terms of them.

The beginning of negotiations between Hussites and council in 1433 and the prospect of an agreement's being concluded between them (eventually promulgated in 1436 as the *Compactata* of Prague and ratified by Basel in 1437) helped bring the pope to heel. The prospect of that settlement was greeted with great relief in Germany and eastern Europe, enhancing the council's prestige and making the pope's opposition to its activities well-nigh indefensible. On 15 December 1433, therefore, he capitulated. In the bull *Dudum sacrum* Eugenius declared his earlier dissolution of the council invalid and agreed that the council's activity had been valid all along.

Eugenius' subsequent behavior, however, made it clear that what had been achieved was a truce rather than a final settlement. Being unable to prevent the passage of reforms that would limit him in the exercise of his power, he contrived to disregard them in practice. So much so, that in January 1436 the council found it necessary formally to enjoin him to respect its decrees on reservations and annates, and in March of the same year to issue a more precisely worded version of its 1431 decree on reservations. Similarly, although it was the council that had taken the initiative in the negotiations with the Greeks, and although the bulk of its membership insisted that the council of reunion should be held at Basel (or at least outside Italy), Eugenius held out for the transfer of the assembly to Italian soil. As early as 1435 Ambrogio Traversari, the Camaldolese superior general and one of the pope's representatives at Basel, had argued that Eugenius would do well to transfer the council to Italy, to limit voting membership there to the bishops (the Italians thus predominating), and to get that reconstituted council to abrogate *Haec sancta* and *Frequens*.

In 1437 Eugenius adopted this course of action. By that time the council fathers at Basel had begun to forfeit some of their credibility because of their internal disagreements, their one-sided interpretation of reform in head and members to mean reform in head alone, and their arrogation to themselves of some of the functions that had belonged traditionally to the Roman curia. When, on 7 May 1437, at the twenty-fifth solemn assembly, the majority of the fathers once more rejected the pope's demand that the council remove itself to an Italian city, Eugenius quickly sided with the dissenting decree of the minority, later declaring that minority to be the assembly's *sanior pars*. On 18 September, in the bull *Doctoris gentium*, he formally transferred the council to Ferrara. And in January 1439, probably for financial reasons but allegedly because of the threat of plague, the assembly was transferred once more, this time to Florence.

Although most of the Italians and such luminaries as Cesarini and Nicholas of Cusa obeyed the pope's bull and aligned themselves with the Council of Ferrara-Florence, the majority remained at Basel and the papal assembly was not well attended. Charles VII of France forbade his clergy to attend it, and while the English and Burgundian rulers moved to recognize it, England sent no delegation. Apart from three Burgundian bishops, the only non-Italian bishops present were officials from the papal curia. Because of this it has been said that the reunion agreement reached with the Greek representatives on 6 July 1439 (embodying agreement on controverted doctrinal issues pertaining to purgatory, the Eucharist, the papal primacy, and the presence of the *Filioque* clause in the Latin versions of the Nicene Creed, and proclaimed in the decree *Laetentur coeli*) was fundamentally an agreement between Eugenius and the Byzantine emperor, as well as small coteries of dependent clerics on both sides. The speed with which it was rejected by the clergy and people of the Eastern Empire suggests the accuracy of that appraisal. The most significant feature of *Laetentur coeli* may well have been the fact that it contained the first conciliar definition of the Roman primacy, declaring the pope to be the successor of Peter, true vicar of Christ, head of the whole church. This definition Hubert Jedin has described as "the Magna Carta of the papal restoration," and in 1870 it was to serve as the basis for the First Vatican Council's solemn definition of the primacy.

The Council of Ferrara-Florence achieved little else. In September 1439 Eugenius secured from it an endorsement of his bull *Moyses vir Dei*, proscribing as heretical and schismatic Basel's recent declaration that the superiority of council to pope was, as defined in *Haec sancta synodus*, an undeniable article of the Catholic faith. But he appears to have had little further use for the council. In 1443 he transferred it to Rome. Thereafter it rapidly faded from view, and no date is recorded for its termination.

Meanwhile, the rump council at Basel had not only proclaimed the superiority of council to pope to be an article of faith, but had also embarked on a formal process leading first to Eugenius' citation to appear before the assembly, then to his suspension from office, and finally (25 June 1439) to his deposition as a schismatic, a heretic, and one incapable of administering the papal office. It then proceeded to elect in his place Duke Amadeus VIII of Savoy, who took the name Felix V (1439–1449). But it was a blunder on the part of the council thus to have precipitated a new schism within the Latin church, especially when the rival assembly of Ferrara-Florence had apparently succeeded, only a few months before, in ending the ancient schism between the Greeks and Latins. The attitude of the secular powers proved to be revealing. Although, on the one hand, the duke of Burgundy and the Angevins were the only secular rulers to send official delegations to Ferrara-Florence, on the other hand, Felix V was able to secure recognition from only a very restricted area. The general tone was set by the declared neutrality of France and the empire, which was to endure for the better part of a decade.

The precise nature of that neutrality is worthy of note. While it reflected an unwillingness to recognize the deposition of Eugenius IV, which would have made the breach between pope and council irreparable, it did not signify any rejection of conciliar reform or of the conciliarist constitutionalist vision. Under the terms of the Pragmatic Sanction of Bourges (1438) and the *Acceptatio* of Mainz (1439), the bulk of the reforms legislated at Basel between 1436 and 1438 were put into force, at least on a spasmodic basis. And those terms included the reaffirmation of the principles laid down at Constance in *Haec sancta synodus* and *Frequens*.

The new posture of neutrality, then, involved a drawn-out attempt to mediate the dispute between Eugenius and Basel on a basis much closer to the conciliarist position of Basel than to that of the pope. It was only when Basel refused to respond to mediation even on terms so favorable, and when Felix V failed to enlarge the area of his support, that Eugenius IV's skillful diplomacy and his willingness to make exceedingly generous practical concessions in return for princely support began to have the desired effect. The critical shift occurred when Emperor Frederick III broke ranks with the electors and initiated the move to recognize Eugenius IV without insisting on extensive preconditions. He did so in February 1447; that same month Eugenius IV died. Under his successor, Nicholas V (1447–1455), the general mood became a good deal less charged. On 7 April 1449, with France following the example of Germany in renouncing its neutrality and rallying to the Roman pope, Felix V resigned. On 25 April the Council of Basel, transferred earlier to Lausanne and having been permitted the formality of electing Nicholas V, decreed its own dissolution.

EPILOGUE: THE CONCILIABULUM OF PISA (1511–1512), THE FIFTH LATERAN COUNCIL (1512–1517), AND THE FAILURE OF REFORM

The councils of Constance and Basel inevitably had effects that reached far beyond the purview of the business with which they were officially concerned. It could scarcely have been otherwise. Much lengthier in their deliberations than their predecessors, these assemblies acted as magnets drawing from all over Europe delegations of the most varied composition. At Constance both the papal and the imperial chanceries were in residence, and with them a host of officials concerned with nonconciliar as well as conciliar matters. These officials included such distinguished humanists as Pier Paolo Vergerio, Leonardo Bruni, and Gian Francesco Poggio Bracciolini, who scoured the libraries of the neighboring monasteries in search of better manuscripts of the known classics and any manuscripts of those hitherto unknown. Similarly, the time spent at Florence by so many Byzantine men of letters had the effect of deepening their knowledge of the Western intellectual and technological achievement (we have the explicit witness of Cardinal Bessarion to that), and also of stimulating in Italy an already growing interest in the language and literature of the Greeks.

The presence of so much of their leadership at Constance enabled the Franciscans, Cistercians, and Benedictines to hold, outside the official conciliar proceedings, meetings that came close to being chapters-general of the orders and to promote internal disciplinary reform of the "Observant" type.

But while the efforts of Pisa and Constance led to an end of the schism, and while Basel-Ferrara-Florence succeeded in negotiating a settlement with the Hussites and a temporary end to the ancient schism between Greeks and Latins, the vision of reform in head and members that had beckoned the reforming imagination since the time of Vienne and beyond still remained, when Basel dissolved itself in 1449, by and large a dream. It was one, however, that lingered to trouble the ecclesiastical slumbers of the age of papal restoration that ensued. Indeed, it is only the benefit of historical hindsight that permits one to think of the conciliar movement as having ended with Basel.

At the time the outcome was by no means clear. The hope for conciliar reform certainly endured, and north of the Alps the sentiment of the clerical leadership (especially that of the regular clergy) and of the bulk of the secular rulers remained overwhelmingly conciliarist. An exaggerated importance has been accorded to Pius II's bull *Execrabilis* (1460), prohibiting "the execrable abuse" of appealing to a general council. In its own day it was regarded as no binding judgment, but simply as the understandable reaction of a single faction. The half century and more between the ending of Basel and the onset of the Reformation was punctuated by appeals from the judgment of the pope to that of a general council. And despite the understandable proclivity of their princely rivals to use such appeals as diplomatic sticks with which to beat the popes, the canonists defended the procedure, and against it not only Pius II (1458–1464) but also Sixtus IV (1471–1484) and Julius II (1503–1513) railed in vain.

The persistence of such appeals led in 1511 to the convocation by the cardinals of the opposition, and with the support of the French king, of the would-be general council that has gone down in history as the *conciliabulum* of Pisa (1511–1512). Although that assembly turned out to be a small and entirely French affair, it did serve to evoke some ringing affirmations of conciliarist principles. The cardinals in convoking it had appealed to the provisions of *Frequens,* and the council itself reissued the Constance decree *Haec sancta synodus.* And while Julius II succeeded in taking the wind out of its sails by himself convoking the Fifth Lateran Council (1512–1517), it is not correct to claim, as has often been done, that that council, in its decree *Pastor aeternus,* promulgated any formal condemnation of conciliar theory.

Taken together, however, what the histories of these two councils do reveal is the growing separation in the half century after Basel of the strict conciliar theory, with its constitutionalist insistence on the jurisdictional superiority of council to pope, and the more widespread belief that the desired reform in head and members could be achieved only through the agency of the general council. What they reveal, too, is the degree to which that belief was a misguided one—at least under the conditions prevailing in the era prior to the crisis of the Protestant Reformation. There is little or no mention of reform in the writings of the conciliarist defenders of the *conciliabulum* of Pisa. And even though reformers of the stature of the Camaldolese monks Tommaso Giustiniani and Vincenzo Quirini, or of the Augustinian vicar-general Giles of Viterbo, aligned themselves with the papal assembly, the actual reforming achievement of the Fifth Lateran Council was negligible.

A year after the dissolution of the Fifth Lateran Council in 1517, Luther could appeal from the judgment of the pope to that of a general council, and anxious talk of the need to assemble a council of reform "in German lands" was to punctuate the religious discussions of the next two decades and more. But conditions had changed, and men at the time re-

alized that such talk had taken a tone different from that of earlier years. It is not simply historical hindsight, then, that emboldens one to claim that with the passing of the *conciliabulum* of Pisa and of the Fifth Lateran Council, the conciliar epoch, however generously defined, had drawn unquestionably to a close.

BIBLIOGRAPHY

Bibliographies. Extensive bibliographic data are in the "orientations bibliographiques" in vols. VIII–X of Gervais Dumeige, S.J., ed., Histoire des conciles oecuméniques: Joseph Lecler, *Vienne* (1964), 203–208; Joseph Gill, *Constance et Bâle-Florence* (1965), 388–395; Olivier de la Brosse *et al., Latran V et Trente* (1975), 471–473. See also Hans-Georg Beck *et al., From the High Middle Ages to the Eve of the Reformation,* Anselm Briggs, trans. (1980); Guillaume Mollat, *The Popes at Avignon, 1305–1378,* Janet Love, trans. (1963); Étienne Delaruelle, Edmonde-René Labande, and Paul Ourliac, *L'église au temps du grand schisme et de la crise conciliaire,* 2 vols. (1962–1964); Roger Aubenas and Robert Ricard, *L'église et la Renaissance (1449–1517)* (1951).

Valuable discussions of the primary sources for Vienne, Pisa, Constance, Pavia-Siena, Basel, and Ferrara-Florence, and of the questions surrounding them, are in Ewald Müller, *Das Konzil von Vienne 1311–1312* (1934); Heinrich Finke, ed., *Acta concilii Constanciensis,* IV (1928), i-cxi; K. A. Fink, "Zu den Quellen für die Geschichte des Konstanzer Konzils," in A. Franzen and W. Müller, eds., *Das Konzil von Konstanz* (1964); Walter Brandmüller, *Das Konzil von Pavia-Siena, 1423–1424,* 2 vols. (1968–1974), esp. II, 1–18; A. J. Meijknecht, "Le Concile de Bâle, aperçu général sur ses sources," in *Revue d'histoire ecclésiastique,* 65 (1970); Joachim W. Stieber, *Pope Eugenius IV, the Council of Basel, and the Secular and Ecclesiastical Authorities in the Empire* (1978), app. D., 378–385; Joseph Gill, *The Council of Florence* (1959), and *Personalities at the Council of Florence* (1964), 125–177.

For the rich collection of manuscripts in the Vatican Archives concerning the origins of the Great Schism and the competing views that form the background to Pisa and Constance, see M. Seidlmayer, "Die spanischen 'Libri de schismate' des Vatikanischen Archivs," in *Gesammelte Aufsätze zur Kulturgeschichte Spaniens,* 8 (1940).

For secondary studies on Pisa, Constance, Basel, and Ferrara-Florence, reasonably up-to-date select bibliographical listings and commentary are in E. F. Jacob, "Reflections Upon the Study of the General Councils in the Fifteenth Century," in Ecclesiastical History Society, *Studies in Church History,* I (1964); A. Franzen, "The Council of Constance: Present State of the Problem," in *Concilium,* 7 (1965); C. M. D. Crowder, ed., *Unity, Heresy, and Reform, 1378–1460* (1977), 190–205; Stieber, *op. cit.,* app. D., 385–404; Giuseppe Alberigo, "Il movimento conciliare (XIV–

XV sec.) nella ricerca storica recente," in *Studi medievali,* 3rd ser., **19,** no. 2 (1978).

Annual listings of new works pertaining to the councils are in *Annuarium historiae conciliorum, Archivum historiae pontificiae,* and the comprehensive classified bibliographies in *Revue d'histoire ecclésiastique.*

Selected primary sources. A useful (if uneven) selection from the decrees of the councils from Vienne to Lateran V is in Giuseppe Alberigo *et al.,* eds., *Conciliorum oecumenicorum decreta* (1962), 309–631. For Pisa, Constance, Basel-Ferrara-Florence, and Lateran V, the following collections are rich in pertinent documentary materials: J. D. Mansi, ed., *Sacrorum conciliorum nova et amplissima collectio,* XXVII–XXXI (1759–1798); *Acta primi concilii Pisani celebrati ad tollendum schisma A.D. 1409 ad concilii Senensis 1423 . . . Item constitutiones factae in diversis sessionibus sacri concilii Pisani II 1511* (1612); J. Vincke, "Acta concilii Pisani," in *Römische Quartalschrift für Christliche Altertumskunde und Kirchengeschichte,* **46** (1938–1941); Finke, ed., *op. cit.;* Hermann von der Hardt, *Magnum oecumenicum Constantiense concilium,* 7 vols. (1697–1742); Franz Ehrle, ed., *Martin de Alpartils Chronica actitatorum temporibus domini Benedicti XIII* (1906); Ulrich Richental, *Das Konzil du Konstanz MCDXIV-MCDXVIII, Kommentar und Text,* 2 vols. (1964).

John Gerson, *Oeuvres complètes,* Palémon Glorieux, ed., 10 vols. (1960–), *Opera omnia,* Louis Ellies du Pin, ed., 5 vols. (1706), the latter containing tracts by the other leading conciliarists from Henry of Langenstein to Jacques Almain; František Palacky *et al.,* eds., *Monumenta conciliorum generalium seculi decimi quinti,* 4 vols. (1857–1935); Aeneas Sylvius Piccolomini, *De gestis concilii Basiliensis commentariorum libri II,* Denys Hay and W. K. Smith, eds. and trans. (1967); Johannes Haller *et al.,* eds., *Concilium Basiliense,* 8 vols. (1896–1936); Historical Commission of the Bayerische Akademie der Wissenschaften, *Deutsche Reichstagsakten (Ältere Reihe),* 17 vols. (1867–1957), see X–XVII, covering 1431–1445; Joseph Gill *et al.,* eds., *Concilium Florentinum: Documenta et Scriptores,* 8 vols. (1940–1964); G. Baronius, O. Raynaldus, and J. Laderchius, eds., *Annales ecclesiastici,* 37 vols. (1864–1883), see XXX and XXXI for Lateran V.

There are useful English translations of extracts from the pertinent sources in Crowder, ed., *op. cit.;* Matthew Spinka, *Advocates of Reform* (1958), and *John Hus at the Council of Constance* (1965); John H. Mundy and Kennerly M. Woody, eds., *The Council of Constance,* Louise R. Loomis, trans. (1961), which contains extracts from Richental's chronicle, Fillastre's diary, and Cerretano's journal.

Selected secondary accounts. There are good introductions to the history and significance of the councils in Hubert Jedin, *A History of the Council of Trent,* Ernest Graf, trans., I (1957), 1–165; and Hubert Jedin and John P. Dolan, *Handbook of Church History,* IV, chs. 37, 46, 48, 49, 50, and 57 (all by K. A. Fink). Much fuller accounts are

C. J. von Hefele, *Histoire des conciles d'après les documents originaux,* Henri Leclercq, trans. and ed., 11 vols. (1907–1952), VI–VIII; and Lecler, *op. cit.;* Gill, *Constance et Bâle-Florence;* De la Brosse *et al., op. cit.*

Among the studies of particular councils, aspects of conciliar activities, or matters related thereto, see Müller, *op. cit.;* Mollat, *op. cit.;* Michael Seidlmayer, *Die Anfänge des grossen abendländischen Schismas* (1940); Walter Ullmann, *Origins of the Great Schism* (1948); Olderico Přerovský, *L'elezione di Urbano VI e l'insorgere dello scisma d'Occidente* (1960); Louis Salembier, *Le grand schisme d'Occident* (1900); Noël Valois, *La France et le grand schisme d'Occident,* 4 vols. (1896–1902), and *La crise religieuse du XVᵉ siècle,* 2 vols. (1909); Delaruelle, Labande, and Ourliac, *op. cit.;* Victor Martin, *Les origines du Gallicanisme,* 2 vols. (1939); Stieber, *op. cit.;* Gill, *The Council of Florence;* Augustin Renaudet, *Préréforme et humanisme à Paris pendant les premières guerres d'Italie,* 2nd ed. (1953).

Nearly all the extensive recent literature focused on the Constance decree *Haec sancta synodus* and its subsequent career is summarized, criticized, or commented on in Francis Oakley, *Council over Pope?* (1969); Paul de Vooght, "Les controverses sur les pouvoirs du concile et l'autorité du pape au concile de Constance," in *Revue théologique de Louvain,* **1** (1970); Hans Schneider, *Der Konziliarismus als Problem der neuren katholischen Theologie* (1976).

FRANCIS OAKLEY

[See also **Ailly, Pierre d'; Alexander V; Charles VII of France; Church, Latin: 1305 to 1500; Clement V, Pope; Conciliar Theory; Durand, Guillaume; Franciscans; Henry of Langenstein; Hus, John; John XXII, Pope; Military Orders; Nicholas of Cusa; Philip IV the Fair; Pragmatic Sanction of Bourges; Reform, Idea of; Schism, Great; Wyclif, John; Zabarella, Francesco.**]

COUNT. See **County.**

COUNTERPOINT (Latin: *contrapunctus,* from *contra punctum,* against note), a method of combining two or more musical lines according to a specific set of musical principles. The theory of counterpoint was an outgrowth of the earlier discant theory, which provided rules for the addition of a second musical line to a preexistent melody. The word *contrapunctus* replaced *discantus* as the standard term for this compositional procedure at some point in the fourteenth century, though the word must have been in use before that time. The Provençal forms *contraponchamens* and *contrapointamens* appear among other musical terms in the *Tesaur* of Pierre de Corbiac (*ca.* 1250). One fourteenth-century theorist ascribes its origin to Boethius. Throughout the fourteenth and fifteenth centuries the terms discant and counterpoint were used rather loosely in referring to the newly created voice part and to the entire two-voice musical work, as well as to the compositional technique.

The manner of constructing a new voice part was based on two factors: the types of vertical sonorities it created with the original melody (the tenor), and the sequential order of those sonorities within the composition. According to the theory of discant, the sequence of intervals in a musical composition was governed by a hierarchy of acceptable sounds, which were assigned to one of three categories. The perfect consonances consisted of the unison, octave, fifth, and fourth. The imperfect consonances included the major and minor thirds, the major sixth, and (later) the minor sixth. All other intervals were classified as dissonances. The successful creation of a two-voice composition required that these interval types be mixed according to certain guidelines. The discant should begin and close with a perfect consonance. Throughout a composition consonances might alternate with dissonances, but the former should always fall at the beginning of the perfection, or mensural unit (Franco of Cologne's *in principiis perfectionis* rule).

Thirteenth-century discant theory was meant to embrace two compositional styles, the melismatic (organum) and the note-against-note (discantus). It was the latter that eventually came to be called counterpoint (*punctus contra punctum*). Despite its origins in the note-against-note discant style described by Franco and his contemporaries, early counterpoint was distinguished from discant by a complete avoidance of dissonant intervals. The earlier system, which had provided for the alternation of consonant and dissonant intervals, had by the early fourteenth century evolved into a theory based on the succession of intervals that were all concordant to varying degrees. At the same time, the status of certain intervals shifted: the fourth was reclassified as a dissonance, while by 1350 the minor sixth had been added to the category of imperfect consonances. The transition to a theory concerned with the succession of consonant intervals reflected a broader stylistic trend away from the thirteenth-century system of modal rhythm and notation in which only the beginning of the modal unit required a consonance. The establishment of mensural notation at

the end of the thirteenth century made every note a significant and independent musical entity.

The most important structural components of the new counterpoint were the interval sequences of major sixth–octave, major third–fifth, and minor third–unison. These sequences were considered ideal in that they all involved stepwise motion in each of the two voice parts, contrary motion between the parts, and a change of quality from imperfect to perfect consonance. This theoretical norm was often interrupted, for the sake of musical interest, by a succession of parallel imperfect consonances. Sequences of parallel perfect intervals were considered unacceptable, more on subjective than purely theoretical grounds.

The theory of counterpoint was intended to apply solely to two-voice note-against-note composition. Soon after its initial appearance in medieval theoretical literature, however, the term came to be applied even to cases in which several notes were set against one, a situation that prompted a critical response from several theorists. The anonymous compiler of the *Ars contrapunctus secundum Philippum de Vitriaco* (fourteenth century) distinguishes between true note-against-note *contrapunctus* and the more florid *cantus fractibilis*. Prosdocimus de Beldemandis (1412) reiterated the fact that the setting of several notes against one did not represent true *contrapunctus* in the strict sense. Other liberties taken with the system involved the introduction of dissonances into a *cantus fractibilis*. The use of dissonant intervals was allowed by Petrus Frater Dictus Palma Ociosa (*ca.* 1336), Antonius de Leno (*ca.* 1400), and Goscalcus (1375), who pointed out that the creation of absolute counterpoint consisting entirely of consonant intervals was "difficult and irksome," if not impossible.

Rules for the composition of three-voice works were first elaborated systematically in treatises of the fifteenth century. In the case of a three-voice work, the composition was treated as two two-part counterpoints. Each of the added voices (discant and contratenor) was to be consonant with the tenor. The most significant fifteenth-century work on counterpoint is the *Liber de arte contrapuncti* (1477) of Johannes Tinctoris, which includes descriptions of both *contrapunctus simplex* (note against note) and *contrapunctus diminutus* or *floridus* (several notes against one). In addition, he distinguishes between counterpoint that is improvised (*super librum cantare*) and that which is written (*res facta*), the latter involving a more controlled use of dissonance. According to Tinctoris, the treatment of dissonant intervals in written *contrapunctus diminutus* should be based on rhythmic and melodic position. Note values that may receive dissonances vary depending on the mensuration of the composition. Tinctoris suggests the use of suspensions as a means of introducing dissonances into the musical texture, though contemporary composers treat these suspensions more freely than the theorist recommends.

Theorists immediately after Tinctoris, such as Adam of Fulda, attempted primarily to clarify certain details of the existing system. The works of Vicentino and Zarlino in the mid sixteenth century represent the eventual synthesis of traditional contrapuntal theory and contemporary compositional practices in a comprehensive system.

BIBLIOGRAPHY

Richard Crocker, "Discant, Counterpoint, and Harmony," in *Journal of the American Musicological Society,* **15** (1962); Sylvia W. Kenney, "'English Discant' and Discant in England," in *Musical Quarterly,* **45** (1959); Claude V. Palisca, "Kontrapunkt," in *Die Musik in Geschichte und Gegenwart,* VII (1958); Klaus-Jürgen Sachs, *Der Contrapunctus im 14. and 15. Jahrhundert: Untersuchungen zur Terminus, zur Lehre, und zu den Quellen* (1974).

MICHAEL P. LONG

[See also **Contratenor; Discant; Franco of Cologne; Harmony; Music, Western European; Musical Notation, Modal; Musical Treatises; Tenor.**]

COUNTY. The term "count" (Latin: *comes;* German: *Graf*) originally designated a companion and, in the early Middle Ages, the companion of a prince in particular. The term always retained this descriptive sense, but from the time of the early Germanic kingdoms it was also used to designate local agents of public power exercising their authority (at least in theory) as royal representatives. The district over which their authority extended, the county (*comitatus*), was, within the limits of the empire, the successor of the administrative unit, the *civitas.* In Germania and in Anglo-Saxon England, where *civitates* had never existed or had been eliminated, counties corresponded to old, apparently tribal units that were called respectively *Gaue* and *shires.* Throughout Europe, the physical boundaries of counties maintained remarkable consistency from late antiquity during the Middle Ages.

In Merovingian Gaul, counts were subordinate to dukes (*duces*), who controlled large and at times autonomous regions. Under the Carolingians the title of duke, except as a temporary military command entrusted to a count, disappeared, and counts became the main officers of royal regional administration. While certain members of the royal household were designated *comites* without any reference to a county, Carolingian counts were generally members of important aristocratic families entrusted with responsibility for one or occasionally more of the approximately 250–350 counties into which the empire was divided.

These counts were responsible for the maintenance of public peace, the conduct of military affairs, and, most important, for the administration of justice within their county. In this they were assisted by a small group of agents and vassals. Given the size of his staff, the count could administer the county only with the assistance of the local notables. Particularly in the administration of justice, the persons who made up the count's court (*boni homines* or *scabini*) appear to have been leading figures of the county who cooperated with the count in the same way that, at a higher level, the imperial aristocracy and the Carolingian monarch cooperated as partners in governance.

Carolingian counts were often called on to serve the ruler in a variety of missions and hence were often away from their counties. Moreover, in theory, and at least under the early Carolingians in fact, counts could be removed from their counties or transferred elsewhere in the empire. Increasingly, however, in the tenth century the king lost control of his counts who turned their counties into hereditary properties and appropriated the royal ban as their own. Simultaneously, the same process of decentralization, particularly through the growth of smaller lordships, deprived the counts themselves of much of their traditional power in their counties. Only gradually in the twelfth century did European counts begin to reconstruct vassalic ties of dependence and to establish a new form of feudal control over their counties.

The most successful counts, such as those of Flanders, Champagne, and Toulouse, added many counties to their original holdings and built up real principalities. Some small counties remained virtually independent, especially when they could play off one powerful neighbor against another.

In France the king gradually gained control of the counts and, through war and marriages, annexed the larger counties; they were careful, however, to preserve local laws and institutions. In England the earls (who were called counts by the French) were prevented from establishing independent principalities by the Norman Conquest and by the strength of the kings of the twelfth and thirteenth centuries. In Germany the frontier counts (margraves) built up real principalities, such as Brandenburg. The others were virtually independent, though they often found it expedient to ally themselves with more powerful neighbors. And almost everywhere in western Europe the county remained a basic unit of local government, no matter who controlled it.

BIBLIOGRAPHY

Karl Brunner, "Der fränkische Fürstentitel im neunten und zehnten Jahrhundert," in *Mitteilungen des Instituts für österreichische Geschichtsforschung,* Ergänzungsband **24** (1973), esp. 192–207; Jan Dhondt, *Études sur la naissance des principautés territoriales en France, IXe–Xe siècle* (1948); Georges Duby, *La société aux XIe et XIIe siècles dans la région mâconnaise,* 2nd ed. (1971), 89–108, 401–437, and *Hommes et structures du moyen âge* (1973), 7–60; François L. Ganshof, *The Carolingians and the Frankish Monarchy,* Janet Sondheimer, trans. (1971), 86–110; Charles E. Odegaard, *Vassi and Fideles in the Carolingian Empire* (1945), esp. the bibliography for "Feudalism"; Karl Ferdinand Werner, "Untersuchungen zur Frühzeit des französischen Fürstentums, 9. bis 10. Jahrhundert," in *Die Welt als Geschichte,* **18–20** (1958–1960).

PATRICK GEARY

COURSON (COURÇON), ROBERT OF (*ca.* 1160–1219), theologian and cardinal, was born in England. He studied under Peter the Chanter and, while teaching theology in Paris, acted as papal judge delegate in a number of important cases (1200–1222). Innocent III raised him to the cardinalate in 1212 and appointed him legate to France the following year. Recalled to Rome at the start of the Fourth Lateran Council (1215), he remained at the curia until 1218, when he joined the Fifth Crusade as official preacher. He died in Egypt during the siege of Damietta.

Robert was the author of an important *Summa,* known by its incipit "Tota celestis philosophia," that is moral and practical in emphasis. A zealous reformer, as legate he promulgated the landmark decrees for the masters and students of Paris that prescribed the curriculum and recognized the corporate structure of the nascent university (August 1215).

BIBLIOGRAPHY

The Paris statutes can be found (in English) in Lynn Thorndike, *University Records and Life in the Middle Ages* (1944, repr. 1971), 27–30. See also M. Dickson and C. Dickson, "Le cardinal Robert de Courson. Sa vie," in *Archives d'histoire doctrinale et littéraire du moyen âge,* **9** (1934), the standard work; and V. L. Kennedy, "The Contents of Courson's *Summa,*" in *Mediaeval Studies,* **9** (1947).

S. C. FERRUOLO

[See also **Paris, University of.**]

COURT LEET. Even in as centralized a feudal state as medieval England, the administration of justice necessarily involved considerable overlap of royal and private jurisdiction, particularly at the lowest rung on the ladder of courts. As a fusion of the seigneurial jurisdiction of the manor and the royal jurisdiction of the hundred (a subdivision of the county), the court leet illustrates this overlap especially well.

From time immemorial lords must have exercised what was in effect police-court jurisdiction over their dependents and settled their minor disputes. When a system of local royal courts at the county and hundred levels was established over most of England by the descendants of King Alfred, the hundredal jurisdiction, as Alan Harding put it, "seems more likely to have been an expansion and definition of the peace-keeping functions of the lord than the annexation by him of the 'public' jurisdiction of an ancient folk court." Another increase of this jurisdiction came in the twelfth century with the legal innovations of Henry II, which included the jury of presentment.

Feudal lords grasped eagerly at this new procedure. In theory, twice a year the sheriff visited each hundred of his shire on his circuit or tourn (in imitation of the itinerant justices who visited the shires); he received jury presentment of offenses both against the king's peace and against private persons; and he took a view of frankpledge—that is, he checked the mutual suretyship groups of about ten men (called tithings) into which most of the adult male population was divided for purposes of maintaining public order. After Magna Carta the sheriff no longer "held" the serious charges, called crown pleas, but merely "kept" them—that is he received accusations but did not try them; he bound over the accused; and he kept appropriate records for the itinerant justices who actually tried the cases. Minor charges—petty theft, violations of the assize of bread and beer, obstruction of roads, diversion of watercourses, false raising of the hue and cry, minor bloodshed, and the like—he continued to settle on the spot by imposing fines.

Increasingly in practice, much of this jurisdiction was in the hands of local feudal lords rather than the sheriff. The simplest explanation of the court leet is that it was a private jurisdiction taking over that of the sheriff on his tourn, meeting at the same time and asking for accusations about the same set of offenses. The court leet was probably the most common franchise in medieval England and became the standard form of seigneurial justice for centuries. To the lord who enjoyed the franchise it brought additional profit, from the fines imposed on the guilty, and also additional power, from supervising the frankpledge system, settling the disputes, and punishing the minor offenses of all men in the region, bond or free. This legitimation and buttressing of the power inherent in every lord of a manor may have been more prized than the profit from court fines.

As the king's lawyers elaborated their theory of a royal source for all jurisdiction, they pressed for acknowledgment of the derived, delegated nature of all franchisal justice. But even after the quo warranto inquests of Edward I, the court leet remained with its jurisdiction, though perhaps the jurisdiction was now more standardized throughout the realm. Late medieval lords continued to exercise leet jurisdiction not only over entire vills and hundreds (which the crown accepted) but also over groups of men who were their tenants on scattered pieces of land not making up any public administrative unit (which the crown unwillingly accepted). But the court leet may have survived longest not in the countryside but in boroughs, where view of frankpledge and police court jurisdiction, either for the entire town or for each of its separate wards, was likewise a replacement for the sheriff's tourn.

BIBLIOGRAPHY

Helen M. Cam, *The Hundred and the Hundred Rolls* (1930, repr. 1960); and "The Evolution of the Mediaeval English Franchise," in *Speculum,* 32 (1957); Alan Harding, *The Law Courts of Medieval England* (1973); William A. Morris, *The Frankpledge System* (1910); Frederick Pollock and Frederic W. Maitland, *The History of English Law Before the Time of Edward I,* 2nd ed. (1968).

RICHARD W. KAEUPER

[See also **Edward I of England; Henry II of England; Hundred (Land Division); Jury; Sheriff.**]

COURTESY BOOKS were the how-to manuals of the Middle Ages, the medieval equivalent of today's books on how to succeed in business, in various professions, in marriage, in relationships with the opposite sex, and in one's personal life. They set forth a code of conduct or etiquette that was considered suitable for a particular group of persons that was identified by age, sex, occupation, and social class. During the late Middle Ages many of these works were written for pages, squires, knights, gentlemen, household officials, and ladies. They were popular from the twelfth century through the Renaissance. The earliest ones appeared in Provence, where the aristocratic code of courtesy first flourished; later ones are found in northern France, Italy, Spain, Germany, and England. Wherever the aristocratic code of chivalry and courtesy traveled, the courtesy book appeared.

Households of the nobility and ecclesiastical officials were the training schools for the aristocracy. Within those schools courtesy books were the textbooks. They set forth the information one had to know and the manners one had to practice to be an accepted member of upper-class society. We often find a frank acknowledgment of opportunistic motives. Author and audience were interested in the doctrine that was calculated to assure success in the social world.

The simplest type of courtesy book is the treatise for the page, which focuses on rules of etiquette. It tells the young boys who served as pages how to behave in the dining hall as servant or guest, describes the proper demeanor to be observed with social superiors, and sets forth rules of personal cleanliness. A great deal of attention is given to table manners. There is an amusing contrast between the elaborate rules of etiquette and the admonitions given to the young men, some of whom apparently needed very elementary instruction: they are cautioned not to dip their meat into the saltcellar, not to lick crumbs out of dishes, not to wipe their noses on the tablecloth, and not to pick their teeth with their knives.

Courtesy books written in English did not appear until the fifteenth century, since earlier works written in England were composed in Latin or Anglo-Norman, the languages of the aristocracy. Among the Latin works is the twelfth-century treatise known as the *Liber Urbani,* written by Daniel Churche for Henry II. The *Liber Faceti,* written during the thirteenth century, served as a basis for parts of the English *Boke of Curtasye* and is claimed as a source by the author of the *Babees Book,* both written during the fifteenth century.

Among the Anglo-Norman works, *Urbain le courtois* was the most popular. It survives in several versions in manuscripts ranging from the thirteenth to the fifteenth century. It advises the young boy on how to behave with his parents, in church, in school, with his social superiors, with women, and in the dining hall. The *Bon enfant* provides similar information. *Edward* has a strong clerical flavor and emphasizes moral behavior and serving God. The *Apprise* and the *Petit traitise* focus mainly on table manners.

The English works are similar in subject matter and style. Verse is used as a mnemonic device, the rhymed couplet being the most common form. The *Babees Book,* a fifteenth-century translation from the Latin, deals almost entirely with table manners. The *Boke of Curtasye,* also written during the fifteenth century, is a longer work in three parts: part I deals with table manners; part II concerns behavior at church, in school, with parents, and with friends, and provides general moral maxims; and part III discusses the duties of household officials. *Urbanitatis,* although typical of its kind, has a special historic interest because this work, or one like it, was used at the court of Edward IV. It emphasizes how to greet and speak to others, appearance, cleanliness, table manners, dignity, poise, discretion, and, most important, how to ingratiate oneself with influential lords. John Lydgate's *Stans puer ad mensam* deals mainly with behavior while serving or eating in the dining hall.

The ideal of the page is presented in greatest detail in the *Book of Curtesye* or *Lytel John,* printed around 1477 by William Caxton. The author provides the usual precepts concerning appearance and gives a great deal of attention to demeanor. The boy is told to practice good table manners, to walk with dignity, not to throw sticks or stones at animals or wrestle with dogs, to greet people with courtesy, to perform the proper rituals in church, to behave cour-

teously toward women, and to follow the commands of his master. The author warns against uncultivated pastimes and recommends the activities of playing the harp or lute, singing, and dancing. He particularly endorses the reading of literature and enthusiastically praises the works of Chaucer, Gower, Hoccleve, and Lydgate. Literature is presented as a suitable subject for polite conversation. Instead of simply providing a list of "do nots," the author draws a satirical portrait of Reckless Ruskyn, an ill-mannered gallant and servant whom he compares to the foppish Absolon in Chaucer's Miller's Tale.

The largest number of courtesy books were addressed to pages because these young boys, in the early stages of their apprenticeship, needed the most instruction. However, we also find works written for other household officials. Part III of the *Book of Curtesye* deals with the duties of the porter, the marshal of the hall, the groom, the butler, the usher, the steward, the surveyor, the comptroller, the clerk of the kitchen, the chancellor, the treasurer, the receiver of rents, the avener (the keeper of the stables), the baker, the huntsman, the water bearer, the panter (the head of the pantry), the almoner, the sewer (the server and taster of dishes), and the chandler. *A General Rule to Teche Every Man That Is Willyng for to Lerne to Serve a Lorde or Mayster in Every Thyng to his Pleasure* deals mainly with the responsibilities of a marshal and briefly mentions the duties of carvers and other servers. John Russell, usher to Humphrey, duke of Gloucester, wrote a treatise in verse on household management that was based on his personal experience. His *Boke of Nurture* (before 1447) is a detailed manual for the valet, butler, footman, carver, taster, dinner arranger, sewer, and usher or marshal of a nobleman of the fifteenth century. Wynkyn de Worde's *Boke of Kervinge* (1513) is identical with many parts of Russell's book. Either he abstracted Russell's work in prose, or both authors used a common source.

A more personal form of the courtesy book appears in the treatise of instruction from parent to child. Although there is some material dealing with etiquette, these works focus on moral advice that will lead to success in the secular world. Some were written by a known parent—even by a famous historical figure; Louis IX of France wrote letters of instruction for his son and daughters. Some were written anonymously. In these cases it is possible that the writer was merely adopting the form of a parental address.

Treatises for sons give a great deal of attention to the boy's behavior in the public sphere and in his future career. Christine de Pizan's *Enseignemens à son filz Jean de Castel* is particularly interesting because it is the only parental address by a known woman to her son (sons usually were advised by fathers or male figures). Christine offers prudent moral advice about how to live honestly in the various professions that Jean might choose and in his personal life. Although she focuses on moral instruction, there is some advice on table manners, social behavior, and demeanor. Her feminism emerges in her criticism of Ovid, the *Roman de la rose,* and antifeminist literature. She tells Jean not to believe the lies about women found in those works; he should let his wife be the mistress of the house, not a servant, and should respect her.

Peter Idley's *Instructions to His Son* contains the views of a typical fifteenth-century English gentleman. Idley was a knight of Oxfordshire who was active in the local government. Part I is a courtesy book offering advice regarding dress, manners, behavior, morality, and public and private policy. He tells his son to love and dread God and the king (his reference to the king reflects the emerging nationalism of the fifteenth century), to respect his superiors, to honor his father and mother, to choose his company carefully, and to get a good education. Idley particularly recommends studying the law. The boy should be prudent, moderate, mild in temper, patient, and charitable. He should choose his counselors carefully, be kind and fair to servants, and treat his wife well. He should not overvalue the riches of the world. This religious sentiment is a suitable prelude to part II, a treatise of religious instruction based on Robert Mannyng's *Handlyng Synne.*

Much of the same advice appears in *How the Wise Man Taught His Son,* an anonymous English work written in the fifteenth century. The author offers advice regarding religion, morality, and worldly prudence. He tells his son to pray to God the first thing every morning; to be discreet in speech; to keep busy; and to avoid the tavern, gambling, and lechery. Unlike Idley, he does not approve of serving in the government, believing that a government official will unavoidably displease or injure his neighbors, become dishonest, or fail to do his job.

Der Winsbeke is a book of instruction by a thirteenth-century German knight for his son. He advises him not to contradict people, to be merciful and pity the unfortunate, to speak courteously to ladies, to be steady of spirit, to be prudent in speech,

to serve his friends, and always to display his good breeding.

A considerable number of works were written by parents for their daughters. Such treatises focus on behavior within the private sphere and on the girl's future role as a wife and mother. One of the most popular was the *Livre du chevalier de La Tour-Landry.* It was composed between 1371 and 1372 by Geoffroy de La Tour-Landry, a knight banneret of Maine-et-Loire, for his three young daughters. It was translated into German as *Der Ritter vom Turn* by Marquard vom Stein for his two daughters, and this version was first published at Basel in 1493. It was translated twice into English during the fifteenth century, once by an anonymous translator during the reign of Henry VI, and once by William Caxton in 1484.

The knight uses a large number of exempla to illustrate his points. His ideal women are the Virgin Mary and biblical heroines such as Sarah and Rebecca, rather than heroines from romance. He also refers to a number of virtuous women of his own time. Although the lady's rank is acknowledged in regard to behavior at social gatherings, it is not considered at all in regard to her relationship with her husband. She is dealt with simply as a wife who must please her husband and be totally obedient to him, even when he is unjust or violent. The knight places a great deal of emphasis on piety: women should frequently go to church, pray, give alms, and fast. Restraint is recommended in regard to eating, drinking, and sexual behavior. There is a great deal of emphasis on the importance of chastity, the foundation of a woman's honor, and the need to preserve one's reputation. A lady's demeanor should be dignified, sober, and modest. She should be courteous to members of all social classes and should not be bold. She should not be jealous, even if her husband gives her cause. Envy, anger, pride, gluttony, and all of the other sins are to be avoided. The knight is particularly harsh in criticizing women who spend a great deal of time and money on their clothes and appearance. He approves of teaching women how to read, but the only works they should read are the Bible, the church fathers, and moral treatises.

An anonymous English work known as *The Good Wife Taught Her Daughter* contains a middle-class mother's advice to her daughter. The earliest surviving manuscript dates from about 1350. Some of the admonitions reveal the relative freedom enjoyed by middle-class women. They were allowed to go to town on their own, to attend public spectacles, and to refresh themselves at taverns. The mother does not forbid her daughter to drink but tells her to do so moderately. The ideal of behavior is one of Christian morality and bourgeois prudence. The mother advises her daughter to attend church regularly, and to pay tithes and give alms willingly. The moral virtues that are stressed are piety, humility, obedience, temperance, and prudence. Meekness and obedience are particularly emphasized in regard to her relationship with her husband. Her speech should be mild and gentle, and she should not talk too much or gossip with friends or relatives. She should walk and move in a sober, dignified manner. Her clothes should be plain and suitable for housework during the week; good clothing should be saved for Sunday and for church. She should be a thrifty housewife and should manage her servants well. She should provide well for her children but should not spoil them—and should use the rod when they misbehave.

A similar social ideal appears in a number of other Middle English courtesy books for women. *The Good Wyfe Wold a Pylgremage* is shorter than *The Good Wife Taught Her Daughter* but is similar in form, content, and setting. *The Thewis* [customs] *of Gud Women* is similar in content but not in form. The introduction states that the precepts are those of a "gud wyf," but the treatise is not in the form of a parental address. Both of these works survive in manuscripts of the fifteenth century.

A number of treatises from parent to daughter survive in other languages. In German there is *Die Winsbekin,* a thirteenth-century poem addressed by a mother to her daughter. It is found in the same manuscript as *Der Winsbeke,* but it is not known whether they are by the same author. The mother states that she learned the precepts she is teaching her daughter at court. She advises her to have a certain distance in her manner yet to be courteous and modest. She should be timid and moderate, and should have control of her feelings. She should beware of deceitful men and should not get involved in passionate love.

In the *Dodici avvertimenti che deve dare la madre alla figliuola quando la manda a marito,* a fourteenth-century Italian work addressed by a mother to her daughter, there is less attention given to love than in *Die Winsbekin* and more to the practical matter of how to get along with a husband. The twelve precepts are avoid anything that might annoy your husband; see that he is served the dishes that please him; be sure not to wake him when he is

asleep; be faithful and honest; don't be too curious about his affairs, but keep his secrets when he confides in you; be good to his family and friends; don't do anything important without his advice; don't make unreasonable demands; be fresh, clean, and attractive at all times, but dress modestly; don't be too familiar with servants; don't desire to go out too often; and don't do anything to arouse jealousy.

The *Castigas y doctrinas que un sabio dava a sus hijas* is a fifteenth-century Spanish work addressed by a father to his daughters. From the comments made in the work, the family appears to have belonged to the middle class. The father advises his daughters to love God above all things, to treat other people as they wish to be treated themselves, to be obedient to their husbands, to be chaste, to be modest in dress and appearance, not to go out frequently to games, jousts, and bullfights, not to speak to strange men, to be moderate in eating and drinking, to be prudent and thrifty, to maintain peace in their households, to be fair to servants, and not to be jealous.

Le ménagier de Paris was written between 1392 and 1394 by an elderly middle-class husband for his fifteen-year-old wife. In the first part, which contains religious and moral instruction, the *ménagier* advises his wife to love God and serve him, to conduct herself with dignity, to be chaste, to be humble and obedient, to love her husband and care for his health, to be discreet in speech, and to dress modestly and neatly. The second part contains practical information on caring for household, gardening, managing servants, marketing, and preparing dinners. The third part is a treatise on hunting with the hawk, a sport that was popular with the upper middle class as well as the aristocracy.

Since the above works are addressed to a daughter or wife, we are not surprised to find them focused on the family; however, the same social ideal is found in the more general courtesy books for women. No matter what the lady's rank, she is always dealt with primarily as a wife and mother. The authors consider her life to be mainly within the private sphere and see that as the one in which she belongs. Although girls served in noble households, there is very little literature addressed to them in that capacity—in contrast with the many books for the page. The *Ensenhamen de la donzela* by En Amanieu de Sescas, an Aragonese writer of the thirteenth century, is the only work addressed exclusively to the lady-in-waiting. He instructs her to get up early every morning and to wash and dress with care. She should go to help her mistress with her toilette, and then she may go down into the hall and politely greet everyone in the household. She should walk, sing, and dance gracefully and should never amuse herself in a vulgar way. She should have good table manners and should know the rules of etiquette. She should know how to converse with men and may even flirt, but she should not become involved in a dishonorable relationship.

Garin lo Brun wrote an *Ensenhamen* for the noble lady in the second half of the twelfth century. (*Ensenhamen* means "instruction" and is the Provençal equivalent for the French *enseignement*.) She is advised to be fresh, clean, and attractive and to wear flattering clothes. She should walk slowly and ride gracefully. She should receive people courteously and should suit her mood to that of her company, being gay with those who are happy and serious with those who are in a somber mood. She should be charming to her male guests and should know how to turn down a proposition gracefully. She should receive troubadours and minstrels with a hospitable welcome, should listen to their poems and learn the lines that please her, and should honor them with gifts (there was obviously some self-interest involved in this last instruction).

Similar works for the noble lady appeared in northern France a bit later. Robert of Blois wrote the *Chastoiement des dames* in the thirteenth century. He addressed his work to the married noblewoman, advising her to observe moderation in all things. She should walk and speak with dignity, and should be courteous and pleasant. Her dress should be neat and attractive but modest. She should not be too familiar with any man except her husband; only he should embrace her.

Francesco da Barberino's *Reggimento e costumi di donna*, written between 1307 and 1315, is a detailed treatise addressed to women of all social classes. Barberino was a lawyer and public official in Florence. His categorization is based mainly on marital status; he deals with women as young girls, young women at the age to be married, spinsters, married women, and widows. He states that young girls should be carefully guarded. They should be modest in dress, appearance, and behavior and should not speak too much. They should sing and dance gracefully, and should have good table manners. An ideal of modesty, chastity, and courtesy is set forth for women at every stage of their life. Barberino adapts the ideal for women of different social classes, allowing for more freedom where necessary.

He addresses princesses, noblewomen, ladies, daughters of professional men, middle-class women, and women employed in such occupations as hairdressers, bakers, weavers, vendors, innkeepers, and servants.

Christine de Pizan's *Livre des trois vertus,* written about 1405, is one of the most detailed and interesting courtesy books for women. Although we have anonymous works by mothers to daughters, Christine's work is the only one written for women by a known woman author. The treatise is divided into three parts: book I is addressed to princesses and is actually a mirror for the princess; book II is addressed to ladies-in-waiting and ladies living on their estates; and book III concerns middle-class women and the wives of laborers. Christine advises the princess on how to fulfill her public and private responsibilities. She should be pious, merciful, just, charitable, and courteous and should not become spoiled or lazy because of her privileged position. She should get up early every day, hear Mass, and attend to her public duties, which might include receiving ambassadors, hearing complaints and petitions of the people, and sitting in on meetings of the council. One of her most important functions is to maintain peace between her husband and his barons. She should set a good example and maintain a respectable household. Much attention is given to her role as a wife and mother. She should be obedient and humble to her husband, should look after his health, and should supervise the education of her children.

Christine discusses the many responsibilities of the lady of the manor, whose husband often left her to manage the estate on her own. She must supervise both the internal and the external economy of her household; for this she needs a knowledge of accounting, agriculture, and marketing. She must know how to perform the many chores within the household so that she can supervise her servants properly. Christine advises middle-class women and the wives of laborers on how to help their husbands in their occupations while running their households. She provides advice for widows who are left on their own to pursue legal battles, look after their property, and bring up their children. Here she speaks from personal experience, for at twenty-five she became a widow with three children to support. The *Livre des trois vertus* provides the most complete picture of the busy, active lives of medieval women.

A number of courtesy books deal with the honorable life in general and are addressed to both men and women. The earliest surviving Provençal *Ensen-*

hamen, written by Arnaut de Mareuil in the twelfth century, falls into this category. He states that those who wish to live the courteous life must fear and honor God. They must observe the actions and behavior of others and imitate the good. Knowledge, wisdom, liberality, and power bestow worth upon people. Men are honored for being good warriors, good table companions, good servants, stylish dressers, and pleasing courtiers. Women are valued for their beauty, pleasing manners, wisdom, and fair speech. Sordello, a thirteenth-century Italian troubadour, sets forth advice on how to lead an honorable life in his *Ensenhamen d'onor.*

Der Wälsche Gast, a long didactic poem on the moral and intellectual life of men and women, was written in German by Thomasin von Zerklaere, an Italian by birth, about 1215. He advises people to avoid laziness, be steadfast, and lead productive lives. They should observe the rules of courtesy at all times. He provides instructions regarding how to greet people; how to speak properly; how to walk, ride, and dress; how to behave at the table; and how to treat a husband or wife. Rules of chastity and fidelity are provided for both sexes. Thomasin treats men and women with greater equality than most authors.

An elaborate treatise on the etiquette of dining, entitled *De quinquagenta curialitatibus ad mensam,* was written by Bonvicino da Riva, a friar and professor of rhetoric at Milan, about 1290. He provides rules regarding washing, taking one's proper place, sitting, speaking at the table, eating, drinking, handling utensils, serving guests, and personal cleanliness. The material is similar to that in the treatises for pages, but the work was meant for adults.

A large number of courtesy books were written only for men. When we compare them with the works written for women, we find that more attention is given to the rank and public role of men. For women their most important roles were as wives and mothers, regardless of their rank. For men their roles as husbands and fathers were treated as secondary to their positions as squires, knights, princes, and governors. The works are addressed to men of the upper class.

Arnaut Guilhem de Marsan wrote an *Ensenhamen* in the late twelfth century that was meant to instruct a noble youth in courtly life. He places the work within a narrative setting. The poet meets a handsome but despondent young man who cannot please his lady, and agrees to instruct him. He tells him stories of lovers of the past, including Paris, Tristan, Aeneas, and Arthur. This is followed by more typical courtesy book material: rules regarding personal cleanliness, dress, demeanor, the treatment of guests, behavior at court, the choice of a horse and weapons, and behavior in war and at tournaments.

En Amanieu de Sescas wrote an *Ensenhamen* for the instruction of a squire. He also uses a narrative setting. He portrays himself as being with a group of squires at a social gathering, where he is asked for instruction. He advises the squire to be generous, truthful, bold, and well-spoken. His dress should be neat, handsome, and suitable to his rank. He should be gay, clever, and learned. He should be a true, discreet lover of his lady and ready to obey her will. He should serve a worthy lord who loves honor and fame, and should be loyal to his lord as a soldier and counselor in war and peace. De Sescas' *Ensenhamen* was imitated in a poem, written in 1326 by Lunel de Monteg, that discusses the squire's dress, appearance, manners, moral qualities, and service to his lord.

Robert of Blois's *Enseignement des princes,* written during the thirteenth century, began as a didactic passage in the romance of *Beaudous* and was abstracted as a separate treatise in later manuscripts. In spite of the title, it is not a mirror for the prince but a treatise of chivalric deportment. Beaudous, the son of Gawain, is instructed by his mother in the ways of true knighthood before he sets out for court. She advises him to attend church, honor God, give gifts generously on the day of knighting, avoid envy, and speak well of women. There follows an account of the investiture and its symbolism in terms of chivalric virtue.

A long allegorical work on etiquette and morality entitled *Documenti d'amore* was composed by Francesco da Barberino between 1309 and 1313. The work is divided into twelve parts, each dictated by Love to one of his female attendants: Docility, Industry, Constancy, Discretion, Patience, Hope, Prudence, Glory, Justice, Innocence, Gratitude, and Eternity. Each part contains *documenti* (precepts) relating to the attribute represented by the allegorical figure; rules regarding etiquette, for example, appear mainly under Docility. They concern how to associate with people of different ranks, how to be pleasing and courteous, and how to conduct oneself at the table.

Christine de Pizan's *Epître d'Othea à Hector,* composed about 1400, is a moral and social code for the knight and gentleman in the form of an elaborate allegory. The work is divided into 100 three-part sections. The first part is a text in octosyllabic verse, which represents the letter of Othea (Athena), the Greek goddess of wisdom, to Hector of Troy, her protégé. The texts provide moral precepts or rules of behavior through allusions to mythology, romance, and ancient history. They are followed by two prose commentaries, a gloss consisting of the story announced in the text together with a moral lesson for the knight, and an allegory that gives the story a spiritual interpretation and deduces a lesson for the Christian. Christine emphasizes virtues such as prudence, fortitude, justice, liberality, courtesy, temperance, magnanimity, eloquence, and grace. The *Othea* was translated by Stephen Scrope for Sir John Fastolf about 1440, and again in the late fifteenth or early sixteenth century, possibly by Anthony Babington.

The book of chivalry can be considered a special variety of the courtesy book. It contains a great deal of esoteric lore about knighthood that has little to do with the real social world, but it also provides practical information regarding the appearance and virtues suitable for the knight, material typical of the courtesy books. One of the earliest works in this genre is the *Ordene de chevalerie,* written during the early thirteenth century. It concerns the supposed knighting of Saladin by Hughes de Tabarie. Within this narrative framework are a discussion of the symbolism of the knight's clothing and equipment, and instructions on behavior suitable for a knight. A knight should never be guilty of false judgment, should be temperate in eating and drinking, should aid women, and should defend the church.

In the fourteenth-century *Livre de chevalerie* Geoffrey of Charni discusses the symbolism of the knight's equipment as well as the ways of the true knight. The knight should not waste time but should always seek deeds of honor. He should not give much thought to eating, drinking, and gambling but should spend his time jousting, dancing, singing, and conversing in the company of ladies. He should be humble, gentle, and merciful to friends but proud and unyielding to enemies, as well as brave, prudent, and courteous. He should maintain a clear conscience and should fight only for worthy causes.

One of the most popular works in this genre was the *Libre del orde de cavayleria,* written about 1276 in Catalan by Ramon Lull, a courtier who became a mystic and missionary. The work was translated into French prose during the fourteenth century as the *Livre de l'ordre de chevalerie.* This version was translated in 1456 by Sir Gilbert Hay, a Scottish knight, as the *Buke of Knychthede* and, in 1484, by William Caxton as the *Book of the Ordre of Chyvalry.*

Chapter 1 establishes a narrative framework. A young squire sets out on a journey to his king's court to be made a knight, falls asleep on his horse, and gets lost in a forest. Waking by a fountain, he encounters an old hermit-knight, who gives him a book containing the rules of chivalry; the body of the treatise purports to be this book. In the following seven chapters Lull discusses the origin of chivalry; the responsibilities of the knight, which are to defend the church, punish unbelievers and criminals, govern his land, maintain justice, support his feudal lord, hunt and exercise himself in arms, protect the people, and cultivate the virtues; the examination of the squire; the knighting ceremony; the symbolism of the knight's equipment; the customs of a knight, including virtues to be practiced and vices to be avoided; and the honor due to a knight.

The treatise on knighthood contains a great deal of esoteric lore not related to the real world. Yet part of being a medieval knight or gentleman was being interested in chivalry and having a knowledge of chivalric customs. In fact, many of the rules found within the courtesy books were not at all practical. Rules of etiquette became highly elaborated and artificial in the late Middle Ages. One of their purposes was to mark aristocrats as a separate class and to make them seem like special creatures who deserved their position of power. Anyone who wished to associate with the aristocracy had to learn the rules of the game—hence, the popularity of the courtesy books and the emphasis placed on manners in courtly training.

BIBLIOGRAPHY

Sources. Carl Appel, ed., "L'*Enseignement* de Garin lo Brun," in *Revue des langues romanes,* **33** (1889); Francesco da Barberino, *Del reggimento e costumi di donna,* Carlo Baudi di Vesme, ed. (1875); Robert of Blois, *Robert von Blois sämmtliche Werke,* Jacob Ulrich, ed., 3 vols. (1889–1895); Frederick J. Furnivall, ed., *Early English Meals and Manners* (1868); *Caxton's Book of Curtesye* (1868), and A *Booke of Precedence* (1869); Pietro Gori, ed., *I dodici avvertimenti che deve dare la madre alla figliuola quando la manda a marito* (1885); Roy Temple House, ed., *L'ordene de chevalerie* (1918); Peter Idley, *Peter Idley's Instructions to His Son,* Charlotte D'Evelyn, ed. (1935); Hermann Knust, ed., "Castigos y doctrinas que un sabio dava a sus hijas," in *Dos obras didácticas y dos leyendas, saca-*

das de manuscritos de la Biblioteca del Escorial (1878); Geoffroy de La Tour-Landry, *The Book of the Knight of the Tower,* M. Y. Offord, ed. (1971); Albert Leitzmann, ed., *König Tirol, Winsbeke und Winsbekin* (1888); Ramon Lull, *The Book of the Ordre of Chyualry,* Alfred T. P. Byles, ed. (1926); Tauno F. Mustanoja, ed., *The Good Wife Taught Her Daughter; The Good Wyfe Wold a Pylgremage; The Thewis of Gud Women* (1948); H. Rosamond Parsons, "Anglo-Norman Books of Courtesy and Nurture," in *PMLA,* **44** (1929); Jérome F. Pichon, ed., *Le ménagier de Paris,* 2 vols. (1846); Christine de Pizan, *The Epistle of Othea,* Curt F. Bühler, ed. (1970); Eileen E. Power, ed. and trans., *The Goodman of Paris* (1928).

Studies. Diane Bornstein, *Mirrors of Courtesy* (1975), and *The Lady in the Tower* (1983); A. T. P. Byles, "Medieval Courtesy Books and the Prose Romances of Chivalry," in Edgar Prestage, ed., *Chivalry* (1928); Alice A. Hentsch, *De la littérature didactique du moyen âge s'adressant spécialement aux femmes* (1903); Mathilde Laigle, *Le livre de trois vertus de Christine de Pisan et son milieu historique et littéraire* (1912); John E. Mason, *Gentlefolk in the Making* (1935); Fred B. Millett, *English Courtesy Literature Before 1557* (1919); Eugene Oswald, "Early German Courtesy Books," in F. J. Furnivall, ed., *A Booke of Precedence,* Early English Texts Society, E.S., VIII (1869); William M. Rossetti, "Italian Courtesy Books," *ibid.*

DIANE BORNSTEIN

[See also **Caxton, William; Chivalry; Christine de Pizan; Lull, Ramon; Thomasin von Zerklaere; Wynkyn de Worde.**]

COURTLY LOVE

INTRODUCTION

Courtly love is the name given to a conception of love elaborated in the courts of southern France at the end of the eleventh century. Since its introduction into the vocabulary of criticism by Gaston Paris in 1883, the term has been subjected to a variety of uses and definitions, and has even been dismissed as a fiction of nineteenth-century scholarship. It has been interpreted as a cover for adultery, a cult of chastity, a game, a poetic convention, a collective fantasy, and a universal phenomenon. It has been argued that it was an importation from Muslim Spain, a product of sociological factors, a consequence of the interaction of Christianity and a pre-Christian matriarchal culture, a vehicle for Cathar doctrines, an ideology influenced by Neoplatonism, a secular

A lady crowning her lover. Ivory mirror case, French, 14th century. VICTORIA AND ALBERT MUSEUM

response to Marianism, a misreading of the ironies of Ovid's *Ars amatoria,* and a tradition evolving out of folk ritual.

In view of the present uneasiness about the use of the term "courtly love," three points should be made. First, medieval love poets did write within a literary tradition inspired by a particular ideal of "true love": Provençal poets spoke of *verai' amors, bon'amors,* and *fin'amors,* words that find their counterparts in other Romance languages. Second, the use of the adjective "courtly" establishes a link between Provençal poetry of the early twelfth century, northern French romances of the late twelfth century, German minnesinger poems and romances of the thirteenth century, Galician-Portuguese lyrics of the same period, Italian literature of the early fourteenth century, English literature of the late fourteenth century, and Catalan and Castilian literature of the fifteenth century. Third, most critics since the sixteenth century have shared the conviction that modern European poetry begins in twelfth-century Provence and that the troubadour concept of love is utterly different from that which was current in antiquity.

In essence, courtly love was an experience of contradiction founded on the precarious coexistence of

667

erotic desire and spiritual aspiration; "a love," according to F. X. Newman, "at once illicit and morally elevating, passionate and self-disciplined, humiliating and exalting, human and transcendent." These paradoxes, and the social and literary conventions that embodied them, provided the aristocracy with an outlet for fantasy, tempered the arrogance of men trained as warriors, and inculcated ideals of courtesy and courtship whose civilizing influence has only recently begun to wane.

BIBLIOGRAPHY

Francis X. Newman, ed., *The Meaning of Courtly Love* (1968), vii; Gaston Paris, "Études sur les romans de la Table Ronde: Lancelot du Lac, II: *Le conte de la charrette*," in *Romania,* **12** (1883). (For a comprehensive bibliography, see the second part of this article.)

ROGER BOASE

ITS NATURE AND SETTING

The term "courtly love" *(amour courtois)* was first popularized in 1883 by Gaston Paris in his article on Chrétien de Troyes's *Lancelot,* or *The Knight of the Cart,* in *Romania.* Paris characterized *amour courtois* as a relationship that was a kind of idolatry and ennobling discipline. According to Paris, the lover accepted the sovereignty of his mistress and humbly attempted to render himself worthy of her by acting bravely and honorably in society and by performing whatever daring or ignominious deeds she might command. Although the lover did not always attain or even seek sexual satisfaction, his love was not Platonic since it was based on sexual attraction.

At first, Paris's use of the term and his definition of it were so widely accepted that the concept of courtly love became a commonplace of medieval criticism. An influential discussion of it appeared in C. S. Lewis' *The Allegory of Love* (1936), which describes courtly love as "love of a highly specialized sort, whose characteristics may be enumerated as Humility, Courtesy, Adultery, and the Religion of Love" (p. 2). Later, reacting against excessive theorizing, a number of scholars, including D. W. Robertson, Jr., and E. Talbot Donaldson, criticized the use of the term "courtly love" as a modern invention with little corroboration in medieval texts.

The term "courtly love" (as *cortez amors*) appears only once in extant Provençal poetry, in a late-twelfth-century lyric by Peire d'Alvernhe. Nevertheless, the closely related term *fin'amor* (fine love) appears frequently in Provençal, French, and other Romance languages and is translated in the German lyrics as *hohe Minne.* Terms referring to courtliness and love are commonly associated in medieval texts in Provençal, French, Italian, German, and Middle English from the earliest vernacular poets through the fifteenth century, so there is considerable medieval precedent for the use of the term "courtly love." Rather than coining a neologism, Paris was in fact rediscovering or popularizing the term "courtly love." It continues to be of value, both because it has become the traditional name for a particular conception of love and because it focuses on the courtliness that was its essence.

First developed in the castles of Provence, courtly love flourished within an aristocratic milieu and expressed the ideals and values of an aristocratic class. Some of the troubadours, like Duke William IX of Aquitaine, were powerful lords; others were humble knights or minstrels turned poets who depended on the generosity of wealthy patrons for their living. The model for their ideal lady was the wife of their employer. The woman addressed in troubadour lyrics is always married. At first glance, this looks like open adultery, but in fact the poems were a kind of game, and the courtship engaged in by the troubadours was a coquetry of class and a bid for patronage under the guise of sexual flirtation. The lady of the castle was rich and powerful. If her husband was away on military escapades or on crusade, she was his replacement; and even when he was at home, it was often she who dominated the household and made cultural decisions.

The poets adopted the terminology of feudalism, declaring themselves the vassal and servant of the lady and addressing her as *midons.* Linguistically, this word is odd since *mi* is a shortened form of the feminine possessive *mia* (my), whereas *dons* derives from *dominus* (lord) and is clearly masculine. The word served as a *senhal* or code name so that the poet did not have to reveal the lady's name. It was a clever form of flattery, since several women could identify with the code name. While making the lady the object of his secret passion, he gave her an aggrandized self-image by addressing her as his lord.

Playing the role of the lover, the poet gave voice to the aspirations of the courtly class. Love made him noble, for only the noble in spirit could engage in courtly love. This new kind of love incorporated the concept that nobility was based on character and actions rather than on wealth and rank; in so doing, it appealed to the poor but aspiring knights. It also celebrated woman as an ennobling spiritual and moral force, thus expressing a new feminism that contradicted both the antifeminism of the ecclesiastical establishment and the sexual attitudes endorsed by the church. Rather than criticize romantic and sexual love as sinful, the troubadours praised it as the highest good, a force that enabled the individual to realize his greatest potential.

Love inspired the lover to be temperate because he did not desire other women, and to be courteous, generous, and brave in order to win a good reputation and impress his lady. It thus acted as a refining, socializing force. Although courtly love was mainly an aesthetic and erotic ideal, it acted as a moral force, ennobling those who followed it.

One of the points of controversy about courtly love is the extent to which the love celebrated by the troubadours was sexual. The troubadours often speak of the physical beauty of their lady and of the feelings of desire it inspires in them, so that emotion referred to is not Platonic. What remains unclear is what the practitioner of *fin'amor* was supposed to do with those feelings—sublimate them toward higher ends and live in a perpetual state of desire, or seek physical consummation. Scholars have answered this question in contradictory ways. Some have seen *fin'amor* as purely spiritual. Denis de Rougement claimed that the troubadours were influenced by mystical, dualistic Cathar doctrines that rejected the flesh and elevated the soul. When the troubadours were singing to their lady, they may have been secretly addressing the soul, the anima, the spiritual element in man, which was envisioned by the Cathars as feminine. This controversial view has not achieved wide acceptance.

Edmund Reiss claims that *fin'amor* was a spiritual love that had much in common with Christian love, or *caritas*. According to this view, the opposition set up by the early-twelfth-century troubadour Marcabru between *fin'amor* (spiritual love) and *fals'amor* (false love or sexual passion) was the norm. When a poet such as Bernart de Ventadorn described human sexual desire as the spiritual ideal represented by *fin'amor*, he was being ironic and was describing something inadequate as though it were entirely adequate.

On the other hand, many scholars see Marcabru's treatment of *fin'amor* as an uncourtly exception to the dominant line of troubadour poetry, which idealized human sexual love. Moshé Lazar claims that *fin'amor*, a conception of love common to all the troubadours, was adulterous sexual love having physical possession of the lady as its desired end,

whereas *amour courtois,* a conception of love found in the northern French romances, was a noble affection compatible with conjugal love and capable of suggesting Christian mystical love. This was just what earlier scholars had found *fin'amor* to be, a view reaffirmed by Charles Camproux in his study of *Le joy d'amor des troubadours.*

Many scholars identify *fin'amor* as the pure love described by Andreas Capellanus in *De amore libri tres* (Three books about love), also known as *De arte honeste amandi* (The art of loving honorably). Andreas states that "it is the pure love which binds together the hearts of two lovers with every feeling of delight. This kind consists in the contemplation of the mind and the affection of the heart; it goes as far as the kiss and the embrace and the modest contact with the nude lover, omitting the final solace, for that is not permitted to those who wish to love purely. . . . That is called mixed love which gets its effect from every delight of the flesh and culminates in the final act of Venus." Andreas praises pure love and criticizes mixed love. However, since his work was written rather late (1184) and at the court of Marie of Champagne, we cannot take it as a reliable guide to the attitudes of the troubadours.

When we examine the actual poems of the troubadours, we find a wide range of attitudes, even in the work of the same poet. Duke William IX of Aquitaine can be bawdy and satirical or courtly and idealistic, and sometimes plays one role against the other. Bernart de Ventadorn always plays the role of the courtly lover, but he is sometimes comic and sometimes serious. Some of the poems are very physical and sensual, with the poet imagining himself embracing the nude body of his lady, whereas others are highly spiritual, verging on Platonic love.

IN LITERATURE

Courtly love appears in the works of most major medieval authors, including Chaucer, Gower, Dante, Marie de France, Chrétien de Troyes, Gottfried von Strassburg, and Malory. As celebrated in poetry and prose, it was not an established doctrine, a rigid system of rules of behavior, but a mode of thought expressed in literary conventions that can be traced through a great deal of medieval literature from the twelfth century onward. The same conventions are used to describe various kinds of love: adulterous love, love between two unmarried people, conjugal love, sexual passion, and even spiritual love. Courtly love means different things in the works of different poets and in different genres and periods. One can make generalizations about particular genres, but ultimately the best method for dealing with literary works that use the conventions of courtly love is to examine each work in its own terms.

The lyric. Courtly love first appears as a literary convention in the Provençal lyric, in which many of the themes that appear in later literature are developed. The lover declares himself the servant of his lady, calling her *midons* and borrowing words and images from feudal and religious contexts: he is the vassal and she the lord, he is the pilgrim and she the saint. His worship is carried out through the songs that celebrate his love and praise his lady. Usually he plays the role of the humble, obedient lover, but sometimes he complains about being rejected or unrewarded and threatens to abandon his service. Love is often described as an illness: the lover suffers from the fever of love, grows thin, pale, and trembles in the sight of his lady. Love is associated with the spring; when the lover is happy, he is in tune with the season, and when he is despondent, the season contrasts with his mood. Some poems are highly spiritual; the poet seems to be worshiping an ideal, incarnated in a woman. The continual striving to be worthy of that ideal is what ennobles the lover. In these poems, courtly love is close to Platonic love. Other poems are frankly sensual; the poet imagines the naked body of his lady and wishes he were lying next to her.

There were a number of women troubadours, called *trobairitz,* and their attitudes differed significantly from those of the men. This difference can be explained partially by their social position. The male troubadours were often professional poets seeking patronage, whereas the *trobairitz* were aristocratic women writing for personal rather than professional reasons. This allowed them to use their poems as vehicles of self-expression. Sometimes they adopted the same poses as the men, such as that of the humble lover; but more often they broke out of the conventional roles to speak in clear, natural voices. Their language is direct, unambiguous, and personal, with an intimate tone that is usually lacking in works by the male troubadours. There is less striving for cleverness and sophistication, more concentration on emotion and experience. The *trobairitz* write of love, but they often abandon the conventional courtly formulas. They do not play the formal, distant *midons,* nor do they place their lovers in that role. They express anger, frustration, impatience, resentment, eagerness, humor, and sexual passion. In their poems, we get beyond the artificial conventions

of courtly love and hear real women addressing real men.

Romance. In the romance, the love affair has to be placed within a narrative context, and its social consequences have to be dealt with. If one or both of the lovers are married, the poet has to either get rid of the mates or deal with an adulterous relationship and the problems it causes. If the lovers are not married, the poet has to show how they are able to overcome the obstacles to their love. Both types of plots, particularly the second, were to have a long history in the novel, the modern descendant of the romance. Other conventions of courtly love were also developed in the romance and later adopted in the novel. The lovers usually fall in love at first sight. As in the lyric, their love is described as an illness and suffering. They engage in long monologues in which they analyze their feelings and express their fear that their love is not reciprocated. The service that the lyric lover performs by composing and singing his poetry is transformed into physical service, chivalric activity on the battlefield or at the tournament. The narrative poet often deals with conflicts the knight faces between loyalty to his lady and to his feudal lord, or between his lady and his devotion to chivalry.

Allegory. In the allegory, courtly love becomes much more of a codified system. The feelings, attitudes, and qualities associated with love are turned into personified abstractions which play the role of characters in a symbolic narrative illustrating the psychology of love. The first part of *The Romance of the Rose* provides a good example. The poet falls asleep and dreams that he comes to a large, fair garden. Knocking on the gate, he is let in by a beautiful young woman named Idleness. Her companions are Mirth, Gladness, Courtesy, Sweet Looks, Beauty, Wealth, Generosity, Openness, and Youth, all qualities associated with or conducive to love. Within the garden the poet meets the God of Love, who gives him the rules of love: be courteous and avoid villainy; be discreet and do not gossip; be reasonable, companionable, and moderate; avoid ribaldry and vulgar language; take pains to serve, honor, and champion ladies; avoid pride; dress well and be well groomed; be cheerful; display your skills and abilities; cultivate the arts of singing, dancing, and playing musical instruments; be generous. These rules show the importance of the association between courtliness and love and the later tendency to elaborate courtly love into a system.

Andreas Capellanus. The codification of courtly

love is exemplified in the *ars amandi* (art of love), the medieval adaptations of Ovid's *Ars amatoria* (Art of love). The most important one, from the point of view of both its popularity during the Middle Ages and its influence on later scholarship, is the work mentioned above by Andreas Capellanus.

The popularity of Andreas' work is shown by the number of surviving manuscripts and by translations into the vernaculars. Twelve complete manuscripts survive (twice as many as we have of Chrétien de Troyes's *Chevalier de la charrette*) besides several that contain extracts. Two French translations were made in the thirteenth century, one in verse and one in prose; two Italian translations in the fourteenth century; and two German translations in the fifteenth century. An early printed edition was published at Strasbourg in 1473 or 1474. Albertano da Brescia quotes from Andreas' work in his *De dilectione Dei et proximi* (1238) and in his *De arte loquendi et tacendi* (1245). By 1277, it was so widely known that Bishop Étienne Tempier of Paris felt obliged to condemn some of its errors.

Book I of Andreas' work on the nature of love and Book II on how love may be retained, are based on Ovid's *Art of Love;* Book III, on the rejection of love, is based on Ovid's *Remedies of Love.* The work is not a translation but a free adaptation of Ovid's ideas to a medieval setting. There was a time when it was read as a serious codification of the doctrine of courtly love. Later scholars, however, have tended to see Andreas' treatise as comic and satirical, especially in view of his emphasis on playful dialogue as opposed to outright seduction.

Andreas' tendency to codify courtly love can be seen in his presentation of two versions of the rules of love. The first is set forth by the King of Love: be generous; be chaste; do not try to break up someone else's love affair; do not choose someone as a lover whom you would not marry; be truthful; be discreet in discussing your love affair; be obedient to the commands of ladies; be modest in making love; speak no evil; do not discuss other people's love affairs; be polite and courteous; in making love, do not go beyond the desires of your lover (1.6.5). As in *The Romance of the Rose*, these rules show the importance of the association between courtliness and love.

The second set of rules, also said to be written by the King of Love, purports to be a document that a knight was given at the court of King Arthur. This narrative framework shows the reputation that the Arthurian court had achieved as a center for courtliness and the practice of courtly love. These rules involve such observations as that marriage is no real excuse for not loving; no one should be deprived of love without good reason; a true lover desires no other than his beloved; love fades when it ceases to be secret; difficulty of attainment makes love more precious; a new love puts an old one to flight; good character alone makes a man worthy of love; jealousy increases love; the true lover eats and sleeps little; the lover is constantly possessed by the thought of his beloved; and that nothing forbids one woman being loved by two men or one man by two women.

Courtly love is much more of a rigid system of rules of behavior in Andreas than it is in most literary works. Nevertheless, in their entirety, his rules are useful since they incorporate most of the conventions of courtly love. An important exception is that in later works courtly love was considered compatible with marriage.

LATIN AND MOORISH INFLUENCES

Andreas' list of the rules of love shows the strong influence of Ovid, not only on his own work but on the entire concept of courtly love. Ovid, a skilled poet of love, parodied the technical treatises of his day in *The Art of Love,* which tells how to engage in a love affair. *The Remedies of Love* tells those who are anxious to terminate a love affair how to fall out of love. In these works Ovid is actually discussing the art of seduction rather than romantic love. For him, love is frankly sensual and extramarital. He states that husbands and wives cannot love each other. Trouble arises if a woman's husband finds out about her love affair, so it is important to keep it secret. Ovid describes love as an art that has its rules. He also describes it as a kind of warfare, with every lover a soldier in Cupid's army.

Many of the conventions of courtly love can be traced to Ovid, but Ovid's comic, satirical spirit has little in common with the elevated, refined spirit of courtly love. A source that has been proposed for this difference in tone is the Arabic poetry of Muslim Spain. There were periods in Spain, particularly during the eleventh century, when the Muslims and Christians lived side by side and benefited from each other's culture. A group of wandering poets came into existence who passed from court to court and sometimes visited the courts of neighboring Christian countries. The situation closely resembled the one that developed a century later in southern France. Contacts between these Spanish poets and the troubadours of southern France were frequent.

The Spanish poets used metrical forms and themes that were similar to the ones later used by the troubadours, and an influence seems possible, particularly since Mozarabic poetry provides many of the motifs that cannot be traced to Ovid.

In Mozarabic poetry, we find two different attitudes toward love: a sensual tradition, which may have been influenced by Ovid, and a spiritual tradition, which seems to be based on the work of Plato as it had come down through the commentary of Arabic scholars. The *Tawq al-ḥamāma* (The dove's neck ring), written about 1022 by the Andalusian Ibn Ḥazm, illustrates the spiritual tradition. Ibn Ḥazm defines love as a reunion of parts of souls which were separated in the creation. Its usual cause is an outwardly beautiful form, for the soul is beautiful and desires anything beautiful and inclines toward perfect images. True love does not ignore the physical aspect, but the union of souls is a thousand times finer in its effects than that of bodies. True love is not forbidden by religious law, and it makes the lover better in many ways, for he tries with all his power to show his good qualities and make himself desirable. Whether the beloved is of high or low rank, the lover is always abject before her. If she is not favorable to him or if circumstances prevent the union, the man tries to be content and hopes for more favors later.

IN SOCIETY

A continuing point of controversy about courtly love is whether it was purely a literary convention or had a place in real life. Historical records provide little help. In examining law codes, court cases, chronicles, and other historical documents of the court of Champagne, John Benton has found no evidence for the practice of courtly love. This is to be expected, however: while adultery and illegitimate births might have been documented, the manner in which a flirtation or an affair was carried on was not. Various genres of nonfictional secular literature, such as the *ars amandi* and the courtesy books, provide some insight into such matters.

Most scholars who deal with courtly love admit the importance of Andreas Capellanus' *De amore libri tres* as a codification of the behavior involved, whether literary or real, satirical or serious. At first glance, Andreas seems to be offering directions for committing adultery, as was Ovid in *The Art of Love*. The love he describes encompasses the desire for sexual possession. He states that married people cannot truly love each other and that marriage is no

excuse for not loving someone else. Yet the bulk of his treatise is devoted not to strategies of seduction, but to playful dialogues between men and women. The men make romantic, exaggerated statements, while the women offer playful but realistic replies. Not one case of seduction actually occurs. The main aim seems to be to keep the conversation going rather than to get into bed. Although the ostensible aim of the conversation is to seduce the women, both men and women seem to be enjoying the conversation in its own right. It is all like an amusing game of flirtation.

The same emphasis is found in other adaptations of Ovid's *Art of Love,* such as the *Cour d'amour,* Jacques d'Amiens's *Art d'amor,* and the anonymous *Clef d'amors,* all written during the thirteenth century. Statements in favor of adultery are modeled directly on Ovid and cannot be taken seriously. When the authors speak in their own voices, what they actually advocate and describe is nothing more than flirtation.

A similar attitude is found in the courtesy books that approve of courtly love. Works such as Garin lo Brun's *Ensenhamen* (treatise of instruction, twelfth century), Matfre Ermengaud's *Breviari d'amor* (thirteenth century), Sordello's *Ensenhamen d'onor* (thirteenth century), and Amanieu de Sescas's *Ensenhamen de la donzela* (thirteenth century) give detailed instructions on how to entertain and flirt with men but do not condone adultery. Ermengaud and de Sescas specifically tell women how to turn down propositions graciously.

Even the courtesy books that disapprove of courtly love, such as *The Book of the Knight of the Tower* (1371–1372) and Christine de Pizan's *Book of the Three Virtues* (*ca.* 1405) bear witness to its existence in the real world. Christine's discussions suggest that the conventions of courtly love were used to justify and carry on illicit love affairs. Of course, such affairs were condemned. The punishment for women who committed adultery was severe during the Middle Ages, although the transgressions of men were viewed more lightly. What was accepted was a courtly game of coquetry. The code of courtly love set forth the rules of the game, defining the roles of the players and providing a source for "lines" that could be delivered sincerely or insincerely. The main goal of the game was not physical seduction but verbal flirtation in a play world where the players could demonstrate their courtly and rhetorical skills.

The role of courtly love in the real world involves the related issue of the existence of "courts of love."

These are mentioned by Andreas and by various troubadours and trouvères. Nineteenth-century scholars tended to take medieval poets literally, neglecting their propensity to develop formalized word games. Victor Balaguer stated that the most celebrated, accomplished, and beautiful ladies, to the number of ten, twelve, forty, and even seventy, formed tribunals of judgment, deliberating and passing sentence according to the usages of love. John J. Parry adopted a similar view. He describes the court of love established by Eleanor of Aquitaine at Poitiers and speculates that Marie de Champagne revived her mother's social experiment when her husband died in 1181, thus creating the literary center for which Andreas wrote his treatise. Amy Kelly also used Andreas' treatise as evidence for courts of love, "to which lovers brought their complaints for the judgment of the ladies" (p. 164).

Such fanciful historiography was bound to provoke a reaction, which occurred in 1961 with John Benton's article on "The Court of Champagne as a Literary Center." Benton denied "that Marie's court was a center for 'courtly love' as either a social or a literary phenomenon. 'Courtly love' was sufficiently revolutionary to attract attention if it were advocated in any serious fashion. If Chrétien de Troyes and Andreas truly and seriously reflect Marie's beliefs, then it must have been common knowledge that she was openly subversive of the position upheld by the men of her day. Yet none of the abundant letters, chronicles, laudatory songs, and pious dedications suggests that Marie or her court was in any way unusual or unorthodox" (p. 590).

Nevertheless, we have the undeniable reference to courts of love and the unorthodox doctrines of courtly love in Andreas and in the poems of the troubadours. Once again, one way to reconcile these references with the laws and religion of the time is to recognize the play elements in courtly love. Word games dealing with love, such as debates on *demandes d'amor* (questions of love), were played at social gatherings. The courts of love seem to have been literary salons where people read poems and romances, debated questions of love, and played word games of flirtation.

CONCLUSION

A phenomenon produced by the interaction of Latin and Moorish elements with the social conditions of Provence, courtly love existed mainly in a play world; the courts of love and the code of courtly love can best be understood as social and literary

games. Nevertheless, the phenomenon of courtly love exerted a significant social and literary influence that persists to this day. One of its main tenets was that love could exist only between people who were free to choose their mates. In a society of arranged marriages based on property, this was a revolutionary idea, yet by the sixteenth century it began to be accepted as the basis for marriage. This social development was influenced by the conventions of courtly love, with their emphasis on free choice. In a world rife with antifeminism, it set forth the idea of woman as an elevating, ennobling force. The chivalric attitudes of the modern gentleman go back to those of the medieval knight. In the literary realm, many of the conventions of romantic love—love at first sight, secret love, the suffering of the lover, love as an illness or fever, the opposition between lovers and society—were adopted from courtly love to lead a long life in lyric poetry, the novel, and the drama. Courtly love thus had a lasting influence on the concept of romantic love in Western life and literature.

BIBLIOGRAPHY

Sources. Amanieu de Sescas, "L'ensenhamen de la donzela," in Karl Bartsch, ed., *Provenzalisches Lesebuch* (1855); Andreas Capellanus, *The Art of Courtly Love,* John J. Parry, trans. (1941, repr. 1969); Meg Bogin, trans., *The Woman Troubadours* (1976); William Caxton, *The Book of the Knight of the Tower,* M. Y. Offord, ed. (1971); *La clef d'amors,* A. Doutrepont, ed. (1890); L. Constans, ed., "La cour d'amour," in *Revue des langues romances,* 3rd ser., 6 (1881); Matfré Ermengaud, *Le breviari d'amor de Matfré Ermengaude,* Peter T. Ricketts, ed. (1976); Garin lo Brun, "L'enseignement de Garin lo Brun," Carl Appel, ed., in *Revue des langues romance,* 33 (1889); Guillaume de Lorris and Jean de Meun, *The Romance of the Rose,* Charles Dahlberg, trans. (1971); Abu Muḥammad Ali Ibn Ḥazm, *A Book Containing the Risala Known as The Dove's Neck Ring,* A. R. Nykl, ed. (1931); Jacques d'Amiens, *L'art d'amors und Li Remedes d'amors,* G. Körting, ed. (1868); Ovid, *The Art of Love,* Rolfe Humphries, trans. (1957); Christine de Pizan, *The Book of the City of Ladies,* Earl Jeffrey Richards, trans. (1982); Sordello, *Le poesie inedite di Sordello,* Giuseppe Palazzi, ed. (1887).

Studies. Victor Balaguer, *Historia politica y literaria de los trovadores,* 6 vols. (1878–1879); John F. Benton, "The Court of Champagne as a Literary Center," in *Speculum,* 36 (1961); and "The Evidence for Andreas Capellanus Reexamined Again," in *Studies in Philology,* 59 (1962); Reto R. Bezzola, *Les origines et la formation de la littérature courtoise en Occident (500–1200),* 3 pts. (1944–1963); Roger Boase, *The Origin and Meaning of Courtly Love* (1977); Diane Bornstein, *The Lady in the Tower* (1983);

Betsy Bowden, "The Art of Courtly Copulation," in *Medievalia et humanistica*, n.s. 9 (1979); Charles Camproux, *Le joy d'amor des troubadours* (1965); Alexander J. Denomy, "An Inquiry into the Origins of Courtly Love," in *Medieval Studies*, 6 (1944); *The Heresy of Courtly Love* (1947); "Courtly Love and Courtliness," in *Speculum*, 28 (1953); and "Concerning the Accessibility of Arabic Influences to the Earliest Provençal Troubadours," in *Medieval Studies*, 15 (1953); E. Talbot Donaldson, "The Myth of Courtly Love," in his *Speaking of Chaucer* (1970); Peter Dronke, *Medieval Latin and the Rise of European Love-lyric*, 2 vols. (1965–1966); Joan M. Ferrante, "Cortes'Amor in Medieval Texts," in *Speculum*, 55 (1980); Joan M. Ferrante, George Economou, *et al.*, eds. *In Pursuit of Perfection* (1975); Jean Frappier, *Amour Courtois et Table Ronde* (1973); Paul Imbs, "De la fin'amor," in *Cahiers de civilisation médiévale*, 12 (1969); W. T. H. Jackson, "The *De amore* of Andreas Capellanus and the Practice of Love at Court," in *Romanic Review*, 49 (1958); Amy Kelly, "Eleanor of Aquitaine and her Courts of Love," in *Speculum*, 12 (1937); and *Eleanor of Aquitaine and the Four Kings* (1952); Douglas Kelly, "Courtly Love in Perspective: The Hierarchy of Love in Andreas Capellanus," in *Traditio*, 24 (1968), and *Medieval Imagination: Rhetoric and the Poetry of Courtly Love* (1978); Henry A. Kelly, *Love and Marriage in the Age of Chaucer* (1975); Jacques Lafitte-Houssat, *Troubadours et cours d'amour* (1950); John Lawlor, ed., *Patterns of Love and Courtesy* (1966); Moshé Lazar, *Amour courtois et "fin'amors" dans le littérature du XIIᵉ siècle* (1964); C. S. Lewis, *The Allegory of Love* (1936); June Hall Martin McCash, "Marie de Champagne and Eleanor of Aquitaine: A Relationship Re-examined," in *Speculum*, 54 (1979); Stephen Manning, "Game and Earnest in the Middle English and Provençal Love Lyrics," in *Comparative Literature*, 18 (1966); Robert P. Miller, "The Wounded Heart: Courtly Love and the Medieval Antifeminist Tradition," in *Women's Studies*, 2 (1974); Herbert Moller, "The Social Causation of the Courtly Love Complex," in *Comparative Studies in Society and History*, 1 (1958), and "The Meaning of Courtly Love," in *Journal of American Folklore*, 73 (1960); John C. Moore, *Love in Twelfth-Century France* (1972); René Nelli, *L'érotique des troubadours* (1963); Francis X. Newman, ed., *The Meaning of Courtly Love* (1968); Alois R. Nykl, *Hispano-Arabic Poetry and Its Relations with the Old Provençal Troubadours* (1946); Douglas D. R. Owen, *Noble Lovers* (1975); Gaston Paris, "Études sur les romans de la Table Ronde: Lancelot du Lac, II: *Le conte de la charrette*," in *Romania*, 12 (1883); Alan R. Press, "The Adulterous Nature of Fin'Amors," in *Forum for Modern Language Studies*, 6 (1970); Edmund Reiss, "Fin'amors: Its History and Meaning in Medieval Literature," in *Journal of Medieval and Renaissance Studies*, 8 (1979); D. W. Robertson, Jr., "The Subject of the *De amore* of Andreas Capellanus," in *Modern Philology*, 50 (1952–1953), and "Some Medieval Doctrines of Love," in *A Preface to Chaucer* (1962); Denis de Rougement, *Love in the Western World*, M. Belgion, trans. (1956); John F. Rowbotham, *The Troubadours and Courts of Love* (1895); L. T. Topsfield, *Troubadours and Love* (1975); Francis Lee Utley, "Must We Abandon the Concept of Courtly Love?" in *Medievalia et humanistica*, n.s. 3 (1972); Maurice Valency, *In Praise of Love* (1958); Charity C. Willard, "Christine de Pizan's *Cent ballades d'amant et de dame:* Criticism of Courtly Love," in *Court and Poet*, Glyn S. Burgess, ed. (1981).

DIANE BORNSTEIN

[See also **Capellanus, Andreas; Champagne, County; Chaucer, Geoffrey; Chrétien de Troyes; Courtesy Books; Dante Alighieri; Ermengaud, Matfre; Family, Western European; French Literature; Gottfried von Strassburg; Gower, John; Ḥazm, Ibn; Hispano-Arabic Language and Literature; Malory, Sir Thomas; Marcabru; Marie de Champagne; Middle High German Literature; Ovid in the Middle Ages; Provençal Literature; Romance of the Rose; Troubadour, Trouvère, Trovadores.**]

COURTOIS D'ARRAS, a northern French dramatization of the parable of the Prodigal Son by an unknown author of the late twelfth or early thirteenth century. Set in Arras, the play enlarges on the Biblical story by adding a lively tavern scene representing the Prodigal's life of debauchery before his repentance. Such realism made the play's moral more forceful for the original audience.

BIBLIOGRAPHY

Richard Axton and John Stevens, trans., *Medieval French Plays* (1971), 137–164; Edmond Faral, ed., *Courtois d'Arras*, 2nd ed., rev. (1922); Grace Frank, *The Medieval French Drama*, 2nd ed. (1960), 217–221.

ALAN E. KNIGHT

[See also **Drama, French.**]

COUTUMES DE BEAUVAISIS. In 1283 Philippe de Rémi, sire of Beaumanoir, completed his record of the customs and practices of the people of Beauvais as he perceived them. The seventy chapters treat duties of public officials, trial procedures, regulations for road maintenance, weights and measures, the protection of churches, and criminal and civil codes. He recognized four authorities: the county of Clermont's judicial precedents, jurisprudence in neighboring castellanies, custom, and common law in France (the Roman code).

BIBLIOGRAPHY

R. Howard Bloch, *Medieval French Literature and Law* (1977), often interprets the *Coutumes* in his literary analyses; Amédée Salmon, ed., *Coutumes de Beauvoisis,* 2 vols. (1899–1900, repr. 1970), the standard edition; Rhéa Tchacos, "Personnalité et oeuvres de Philippe de Beaumanoir" (diss., University of Paris-III, 1975).

JOHN L. GRIGSBY

[See also **Beaumanoir, Philippe de; Law, French: In North.**]

CREDO. See **Creeds, Liturgical Use of.**

CREEDS, LITURGICAL USE OF. In the centuries when the Christian liturgy was assuming its earliest shape, it turned for inspiration to contemporary statements of faith. Creeds were well suited to public worship, for they were among the most versatile of religious texts. They defined Christian belief and provided safeguards against heresy. But they were at the same time prayers—whether individual or communal—that served to acknowledge, petition, and give thanks to the Lord. Their functions, then, were multiple: for those who listened to them, creeds supplied instruction and edification; for those who pronounced them, they signified the establishment of a bond with the deity. During the Middle Ages creeds came to be used primarily in the liturgies of baptism and the Holy Eucharist.

The baptismal liturgy is the oldest for which there is evidence of the use of creeds. In the early church, candidates for baptism were required to confess their personal belief in the presence of the congregation. It is difficult to know precisely what words were spoken, or in what fashion they were delivered, since the history of the liturgy in the first three centuries of the Christian era is obscure. By the fourth century, however, the ceremonies that made up the rites of initiation had begun to take on a discernible form. Despite many local variations in composition and performance, these initiatory rites displayed some common features. There were two moments in the ritual when candidates for baptism were expected to make a profession of faith.

One such moment occurred originally in the catechumenate, the period of preparation leading up to baptism. The ritual of the tradition and reddition of the creed emerged in the third century, with Rome probably taking the lead in its development. In the rite technically known as the *traditio symboli,* the bishop formally "delivered" or "handed over" the creed to the more advanced catechumens. The creed was regarded as a secret formula that was to be memorized by the faithful rather than written down. The catechumens, who had not previously heard it, were required to learn the text and to recite it prior to their initiation. With the *redditio symboli* they "rendered" or "gave back" the creed to the bishop.

The time for the tradition varied, but it generally took place on a Sunday in the middle of Lent. The reddition seems to have occurred more than once in some churches, especially in the East. But in most rites (the Gallican was an exception), provision was made for a particularly solemn reddition on the day of baptism. The ritual as practiced in the fourth century is described by Egeria, St. Hilary of Poitiers, and St. Augustine.

The ceremony of baptism itself gave a second opportunity for the recitation of a creed. Here the candidate did not recite a declaratory creed, but answered a series of questions. *The Apostolic Tradition* of Hippolytus (*ca.* 217), which may represent Roman usage at the beginning of the third century, directed that the candidate be immersed in water three times, in conjunction with the naming of the three persons of the Trinity. The profession of faith took the form of question and answer: "Do you believe in God the Father almighty?" "I believe." Following this exchange, the candidate was plunged into the water, and the process was repeated for the Son and the Holy Spirit.

In the Eastern churches the Nicene-Constantinopolitan Creed became the standard baptismal text. It was probably used in Constantinople and the surrounding region from early times, and by 451 was established as the official baptismal creed of the Constantinopolitan church. Theodore Lector reported that it was pronounced at public worship on Good Friday while the bishop catechized the candidates for baptism. From the capital city the use of the Nicene-Constantinopolitan Creed spread throughout the East, supplanting other baptismal symbols. It attained a virtual monopoly of baptism in the sixth century that, with very few exceptions (such as the Jacobite church of Syria, and the Nestorian, Armenian, and Abyssinian churches), it has enjoyed ever since.

The development of creedal formulas in the Western church was more complex. The type of triple interrogation described by Hippolytus (and based on the baptismal command of Matthew 28:19) was sometimes elaborated into a rudimentary creed. This Old Roman Creed, with texts available in Greek and Latin, became the baptismal formula of the Roman church.

At some time in the sixth century, the Old Roman Creed was replaced by the Nicene-Constantinopolitan. Both the Gelasian Sacramentary and the *Ordo romanus* VII observed that the creed handed out at the tradition and, presumably, rendered back at the reddition was the Nicene-Constantinopolitan. Again, it was recited in either Greek or Latin, depending on the language normally spoken by the candidates or their sponsors. The interrogations addressed to the candidates at the moment of baptism continued to be the traditional ones, similar in form and content to the Old Roman Creed.

The entry of the Nicene-Constantinopolitan Creed into the Roman baptismal liturgy was surprising, for it had originally been viewed with disfavor in the West. It owed its adoption, perhaps, to the deference paid by the Roman church to the Byzantine in the period following Justinian's reconquest of Italy. Perhaps, too, it seemed to provide a more compelling defense against the renewed threat of the Arian heresy. In any case, the Nicene-Constantinopolitan Creed was employed as the declaratory formula of the Roman church until at least the early ninth century. In 810 Pope Leo III suggested that it fulfilled a catechetical role in baptism.

North of the Alps the Apostles' Creed, an elaborated form of the Old Roman Creed, came to be used with increasing frequency. In an effort to establish a uniform liturgy throughout his empire, Charlemagne recommended that it be adopted as the official baptismal text. The custom was carried to Rome, and there too the Apostles' Creed displaced the Nicene-Constantinopolitan. The transformation of the Roman baptismal rite probably occurred in the late tenth or early eleventh century, when Rome was in general under the liturgical influence of the German church. From the twelfth century on, certainly, the Apostles' Creed was regarded as authoritative. Today it is the sole baptismal confession of the Western church, and is also used in the ordination of priests.

Creeds found a second major application in the liturgy of the Eucharist. During the Middle Ages—first in the East, and then in the West—the Nicene-Constantinopolitan Creed entered the Mass. This was a significant development, because the Mass had not originally contained a formal confession of faith. The initial appearances of the creed were connected with the problem of heresy.

In 511, according to Theodore Lector, Patriarch Timothy of Constantinople ordered the recitation of the creed at every service. Timothy, who held Monophysite views, apparently wished to make a demonstration of the correctness of his belief. Perhaps the creed had appeared in the eucharistic liturgy even earlier. An anonymous interpolation in the history of Theodore credits Peter the Fuller, Monophysite bishop of Antioch (476–488), with the innovation. For the Monophysites the renewed emphasis given to the creed of Nicaea-Constantinople signified an attack on the Definition of Chalcedon, to which they were strongly opposed.

Although the practice had originated among Monophysite heretics, it spread rapidly throughout the East. By 518 the recitation of the Nicene-Constantinopolitan Creed was considered customary in Constantinople. Its use was further regularized by an ordinance issued by Emperor Justin II in 568.

The creed entered the eucharistic liturgies of all the Eastern churches. Its position in the various rites is after the Prayer of the Faithful and the Great Entrance, either before or after the Kiss of Peace. The creed is, as a rule, recited by the people or by a representative of the people, rather than by the priest. It is spoken, not sung.

The inclusion of the creed in the Western liturgies was prompted by the struggle against heresy. When, in 589, King Reccared and the Visigoths renounced Arianism, they made their profession of faith in the creed of Nicaea-Constantinople. The Third Council of Toledo directed that this creed be recited by the congregation at all masses in Spain and Gaul, "according to the usage of the Eastern churches." It was to be said just before the Lord's Prayer—an unusual position, in which it served to strengthen the faith of the people before Communion.

In Ireland the creed moved to the place it now holds in the Mass. The Stowe Missal, written early in the ninth century, prescribed the singing of the creed after the Gospel. From Ireland the custom spread to the north of England, where its appearance was recorded by Alcuin.

On the advice of Alcuin, Charlemagne introduced

the chanting of the creed after the Gospel into services in his palace chapel at Aachen. The Carolingian text (which forms the basis for the modern version) was a new translation from the Greek promulgated by Paulinus of Aquileia at the synod of Cividale del Fruili in 797. The reason for the liturgical innovation seems to have been an outbreak of adoptionism in Spain in the last decades of the eighth century. Paulinus believed that the Nicene-Constantinopolitan Creed was an effective rebuttal of the christological error, and Alcuin shared his views. Walafrid Strabo later observed that it was after the deposition of the Spanish adoptionist bishop Felix of Urgel in 798 that the repetition of the creed became "more widespread and frequent" in Frankish lands.

Although Pope Leo III gave permission for the chanting of the creed in the Frankish rite, he objected to the inclusion of the *Filioque.* In Rome the creed did not enter the Mass until 1014. Emperor Henry II, in the city for his coronation, expressed surprise at its absence. The Roman clerics explained that their church "had never been tainted with any dregs of heresy," and that frequent profession of the creed was therefore unnecessary. At the emperor's insistence, however, Pope Benedict VIII consented to have the Nicene-Constantinopolitan Creed sung at the Eucharist, and the Roman usage was brought into conformity with the rest of Christendom. It was probably at the same time that the *Filioque* was admitted to the Roman creedal formula.

The use of the creed was at first restricted to Sundays and the feasts expressly mentioned in the symbol. Later medieval commentators multiplied the occasions for chanting the creed, for they believed that it enhanced the solemnity of worship. In this way creeds came to be seen not only as formulas of religious belief but also as valued elements in the communal life of the Christian church.

BIBLIOGRAPHY

Frank E. Brightman, ed., *Liturgies Eastern and Western,* I, *Eastern Liturgies* (1896, repr. 1965), 162, 226, 383; Bernard Capelle, "Alcuin et l'histoire du symbole de la messe," in *Recherches de théologie ancienne et médiévale,* 6 (1934), and "L'introduction du symbole à la messe," in *Mélanges Joseph de Ghellinck,* II (1951); Gregory Dix, *The Shape of the Liturgy,* 2nd ed. (1945, repr. 1970), 485–488; John D. C. Fisher, *Christian Initiation: Baptism in the Medieval West* (1965), 9–11; Cheslyn Jones, Geoffrey Wainwright, and Edward Yarnold, eds., *The Study of Liturgy* (1978), 95–117; Joseph A. Jungmann, *The Mass of the Roman Rite,* Francis A. Brunner, trans.) (1961), I, 569–584; J. N. D. Kelly, *Early Christian Creeds,* 3rd ed. (1972), 32–36, 344–367, 420–434; Theodor Klauser, "Die liturgischen Austauschbeziehungen zwischen der römischen und der fränkisch-deutschen Kirche vom achten bis zum elften Jahrhundert," in his *Gesammelte Arbeiten zur Liturgiegeschichte, Kirchengeschichte, und christlichen Archäologie* (1974).

BERNICE M. KACZYNSKI

[See also **Baptism; Byzantine Church; Eucharist; Filioque; Nicaea, Council of.**]

CRESCAS, ḤASDAI (*ca.* 1340–1412), one of Spanish Jewry's most active and able defenders and advocates, in a period beset by persecution and apostasy. As court-appointed intermediary to the Jewish community of Aragon, Crescas used his political influence to attempt to reconstruct Jewish life there in the 1390's. As a rabbinical authority, he wrote (in Catalan) two polemical works in defense of the Jewish faith.

Blaming Jewish philosophy in its prevailing Maimonidean garb for the defection of Jewish intellectuals from the faith and people of Israel, Crescas undertook, in a Hebrew work called *Or Adonai* (Light of the Lord), a thoroughgoing critique of the Aristotelian principles on which this philosophy was based. The work is a brilliant attack, influenced in part by contemporary scholastic thought, on such formerly sacrosanct Aristotelian principles as the finitude of the world and the impossibility of an infinite magnitude, causal series, and a vacuum. As opposed to the concept of a deity who in some irreducible sense is part of an intelligible and necessarily impersonal natural universe, Crescas affirms the concept of a God of love who impresses his design upon a naturally indifferent world.

BIBLIOGRAPHY

Crescas' polemical work, *Refutation of the Principles of the Christians,* written in Catalan, exists only in Joseph ben Shem Tov's Hebrew translation, Ephraim Dernard, ed., *Bitul ᶜikare ha-Notsrim* (1904). Parts of *Or Adonai* are translated in Harry Wolfson, *Crescas' Critique of Aristotle* (1929, repr. 1971). More recent scholarship includes Shlomo Pines, *Scholasticism After Thomas Aquinas and the Teaching of Ḥasdai Crescas and His Predecessors* (1967); Seymour Feldman, "The Theory of Eternal Creation in Hasdai Crescas and His Predecessors," in *Viator,* **11** (1980).

ALFRED L. IVRY

[See also **Aristotle in the Middle Ages; Jews in Christian Spain; Maimonides, Moses; Scholasticism.**]

CRETE. Situated in the eastern Mediterranean, where it lies at the southern edge of the Aegean Sea, Crete is the fourth largest island in the Mediterranean after Sicily, Sardinia, and Cyprus. For a thousand years the seat of the Minoan civilization, an important ancient culture that flourished from the middle of the third millennium B.C., Crete, a long, narrow island with four main groups of mountain ranges, possesses great natural wealth. Because it has a considerable water supply, unlike Greece, the cultivation of vines and olives formed the basis for its prosperity.

As part of the Roman and, later, the Byzantine empires, Crete was subject to attack from various enemies. In the third century A.D. it was attacked by the Goths and in 623 by the Slavs, many of whom had settled in Greece by that time. In the 730's religious jurisdiction over Crete was transferred from Rome to Constantinople, thus tying it more closely to the East. The Arabs began their attacks on Crete in the second half of the seventh century, but it remained in Byzantine hands.

In the early ninth century the fate of Crete became linked indirectly with events in Spain. In 805 a series of revolts in Córdoba against the Umayyad caliph of Spain began, culminating in 814 in the destruction of the suburb of Córdoba where the rebels lived and in their expulsion from Spain. A large group of them fled to Egypt, where they took the city of Alexandria, but conflict with the Egyptian authorities resulted in an agreement that they would seek their fortunes elsewhere. In 826 or 827 these Muslims had sent an expedition against Crete, taking many prisoners and a great deal of booty, and in 827 or 828 they returned, attacking Crete with forty vessels. There was no apparent resistance, suggesting that the inhabitants may have been chafing under Byzantine rule. The Arabs took control of the entire island and built a fortress surrounded by a moat or *khandaq,* giving the island its later name of Candia.

The Byzantine emperor Michael II sent a series of expeditions to reconquer Crete, but these were largely unsuccessful. We do, however, have evidence, on a ninth-century seal of an archon of Crete, that there may have been a brief recapture by Theoktistos, the logothete of the Drome and an important

member of the council of regency under Theodora. But for well over 100 years the Arabs controlled Crete, which became a center of piracy in the eastern Mediterranean, continually harassing the Byzantine fleet. In 949 the Byzantines mounted another unsuccessful expedition, but finally in 961 a large expedition under Nikephoros Phokas succeeded in retaking Crete. It remained a Byzantine possession until the Fourth Crusade (1204), when it passed first to Boniface of Montferrat and then to Venice, which bought it from him. Crete remained under Venetian rule until its conquest by the Ottomans in 1669.

BIBLIOGRAPHY

Archibald R. Lewis, *Naval Power and Trade in the Mediterranean: A. D. 500 to 1100* (1951, repr. 1970).

LINDA ROSE

[See also **Boniface of Montferrat; Byzantine Empire: History (330–1025).**]

CRIMEA, KHANATE OF. The khanate of Crimea was founded between 1426 and 1430 by Haji Giray, son of Ghiyasseddin, a descendant of Genghis Khan. The Girays ruled over the Crimean peninsula and the vast steppe territory lying north of the Black Sea between the Dnieper and the Don until 1783, when the khanate was annexed by the Russians.

Three major problems dominated the political history of the khanate. The first problem was the suzerainty of the Golden Horde. In the period 1430–1502 the khanate had to defend itself against its suzerains, the khans of the Golden Horde; their successors, the rulers of the Great Horde; and the Italian colonies of Caffa (Feodosiya) and Tana. In the struggle Haji Giray entered into alliances with the Ottoman Turks and, between 1430 and 1466, with his Christian neighbor Poland-Lithuania. Mengli Giray (1467–1514), his son and successor, was forced into a similar alliance with Muscovy, with the help of which the struggle came to an end following the destruction of Saray.

The second problem was the Ottoman suzerainty. In 1475 the Turks conquered the Genoese colonies of Crimea and later extended their domination over the entire south coast of Crimea. In 1538 they occupied the Bujak, and in 1582 their Crimean possessions became an *eyalet* administered from Kefe (formerly Caffa) by an Ottoman *beylerbey* protected by strong Turkish garrisons in Kefe, Azak, Kil-Burun, Özü, Cherzeti (Kerch), Yeni-Kale, Taman, and Temrük. The khanate had been gradually turned into a de facto Ottoman protectorate.

The election of the khans by the Tatar nobility was, from the reign of Mengli Giray, subject to the confirmation *(tesdik)* of the Ottoman sultan. Under Selim I (1467–1520) the sultan-caliph became the spiritual head of the khanate, and his name was mentioned at Friday prayers in the Crimean mosques. Ottoman control over the Girays was reinforced in the sixteenth century by the *rehinlik,* a practice that consisted of keeping the heirs presumptive of the ruling Tatar princes as hostages at the court of the padishah in Constantinople.

The khans preserved their authority in internal and economic matters, but after the expedition against Moldavia in 1538, the Tatar troops were regularly called on to assist Ottoman armies in their campaigns. During the seventeenth and eighteenth centuries Tatar cavalry took part in almost all the Turkish expeditions into Europe—against the Austrian Empire, Poland, and Russia—as well as against the Iranians in the Caucasus and in Mesopotamia.

The Ottoman protectorate that limited Tatar sovereignty was not accepted without resistance. In the sixteenth century Giray II "Semiz" (the Fat) refused to join the Turkish army in the Caucasus, and instead attacked the Ottoman fortress of Kefe. He was defeated and killed in 1584. In the seventeenth century several khans rebelled against the Ottomans and concluded an alliance with the Zaporog Cossacks, the most dangerous enemies of the Turks in the Black Sea area: Muḥammad Giray III (1623–1625) was killed in a battle against the Turks, Inayet Giray (1635–1637) was exectued at Constantinople, Muḥammad Giray IV (1641–1644, 1654–1666) was left destitute by the Turks, and Islam Giray III supported Bohdan Hmelnitski.

It was only in the eighteenth century that the khanate, its power weakened and territory reduced by the Russian advance, finally became a real protectorate of the Ottoman Empire. One final and unsuccessful effort was made by the last great Tatar ruler, Khan Krim Giray (1758–1764, 1768–1769), to stop the decay of the khanate by reorganizing its administration and economy. The khan also tried to establish direct diplomatic contacts with France and Prussia.

The third problem was the relations of the Crimean khanate with Russia. These relations were

dominated by competition for the control of the two main trade roads of medieval eastern Europe, the "fur route" and the "silk route." The first, connecting western Siberia to the Crimea, was under the control of three Tatar khanates: Sibir, Kazan, and the Crimea. The khanate of Astrakhan controlled the "silk and spices road" connecting Turkistan to the Ottoman possessions on the Black Sea. The conflict between Crimea and Moscow began in 1515 with a major Crimean offensive. Khan Muḥammad Giray I (1514–1523) succeeded for a short time in installing his candidates on the thrones of Kazan and Astrakhan and in reunifying around the Crimea the entire *Ulus* of Batu. The Russian counteroffensive began in 1540; the Kazan and Astrakhan khanates were destroyed in 1552 and 1556, respectively, and their territories annexed by Moscow.

An almost uninterrupted Crimean offensive against Moscow occurred in the second half of the sixteenth century, with the objective of reestablishing the Kazan and Astrakhan khanates. Major Tatar raids were launched in 1571, 1572, 1573, 1576, 1580, 1587, and 1591. The great expedition of 1571, led by Khan Devlet Giray, burned Moscow in 1572. The last important raid, commanded by Khan Gazi Giray II ("Bora") in 1591, resulted in a severe defeat south of Moscow, and in 1592 the khanate officially waived its claim to Kazan and Astrakhan. The eighty-year conflict aimed at the reunification of the Western Mongol Empire, the *Ulus* of Batu, ended in Russian victory.

During the seventeenth and eighteenth centuries the Crimean Tatars led several plundering raids against Russia's borderlands and the Ukraine. The last great expedition, directed by Khan Krim Giray against Ukraine, took place in 1768–1769, but its objectives were economic rather than political. The death of Krim Giray in 1769 marked the beginning of the end of the khanate. Occupied and ruined by the Russian army in 1771, it was granted the status of an independent state by the treaty of Küchük-Kaynarji in 1774. In February 1783, it was incorporated into Russia.

Politically the Crimean khanate remained to the end an anachronistic survival of the Mongol Empire. The supreme power was divided among three institutions: The Ottoman sultan-caliph, suzerain of the khan and head of the religious hierarchy of the khanate; the khan, obligatorily a member of the Giray dynasty, and his two deputies, the *kalgha* and the *nureddin,* also members of the Giray family; and the chiefs of the noble clans of Mongol origin, four of whom, the *karacha,* were particularly notable: Shirin, Argyn, Baryn, and Kipchak. At the end of the sixteenth century, two other clans were added: the Mangyt, of Nogay origin, and the Sejeut.

The chiefs of the clans elected the khan, and his election was "confirmed" by the Ottoman sultan. No khan could rule without the agreement of the clans. The attempts of some khans, in particular of Saadet Giray (1524–1532) and Sahib Giray (1532–1551), to oppose to the clans' authority a regular administration modeled on the Ottoman *Kapi-Kulu* system met with failure.

BIBLIOGRAPHY
Alexandre Bennigsen, Pertev N. Boratav, Dilek Desaive, and Chantal Lemercier-Quelquejay, *Le khanat de Crimée dans les archives du Musée du Palais de Topkapı* (1978); Alan W. Fisher, *The Crimean Tatars* (1978); Halim Giray, *Gülbün-ü Khanan Yahud QırımTarikhi* (1911); H. Inalcık, "Yeni vesikalara gore Kırım Hanlığının Osmanli tabıtigınagirmesi ve ahitname meselesi," in *Belleten,* 8 (1944); Akdes N. Kurat, ed., *Topkapi Sarayi Müzesi Arşivindeki Altin Ordu, Kirim ve Türkistan Hanlarina ait Yarlik ve bitikler* (1940); Bronovius (Broniewski) Marcin, *Russia seu Moscovia i temque Tartaria* (1595, repr. 1630); *Sbornik Imperatorskogo Russkogo-Istoricheskogo Obshchestva: Pamiatniki diplomatitcheskih snoshenii Moskovskogo Gosudarstva s Krymskoiu i Nogaiskoiu Ordami i s Turtsiei,* pt. I, vol. 4 (1474–1505), pt. II, vol. 95 (1508–1521).

ALEXANDRE BENNIGSEN

[See also **Caffa; Golden Horde; Mongol Empire: Foundations; Ottomans.**]